20 BEST PLAYS

OF THE MODERN AMERICAN THEATRE

TWENTY BEST PLAYS

Of The Modern American Theatre

Edited with an introduction by
John Gassner

CROWN PUBLISHERS, INC.
New York

First Printing, October, 1939
Second Printing, December, 1939
Third Printing, January, 1940
Fourth Printing, March, 1940
Fifth Printing, January, 1941
Sixth Printing, November, 1941
Seventh Printing, March, 1943
Eighth Printing, October, 1943
Ninth Printing, June, 1944
Tenth Printing, May, 1945
Eleventh Printing, November, 1945
Twelfth Printing, July, 1946
Thirteenth Printing, June, 1947
Fourteenth Printing, March, 1948
Fifteenth Printing, January, 1949
Sixteenth Printing, May, 1950
Seventeenth Printing, August, 1952
Eighteenth Printing, January, 1955
Nineteenth Printing, April, 1957
Twentieth Printing, September, 1959

PRINTED IN THE UNITED STATES OF AMERICA
AMERICAN BOOK—STRATFORD PRESS, INC., NEW YORK

CONTENTS

Introduction

AN AMERICAN DECADE

By JOHN GASSNER

It is no secret that America has the youngest national drama of any importance in the world. Although it has been officially in existence since 1787 when an American play on an American subject, Royall Tyler's *The Contrast,* appeared on the local stage, a century had to elapse before the country could boast a playwright of some importance in James A. Herne. Another quarter of a century had to be consumed in tentative efforts to hammer out some heavy artillery that might vie with European achievements, and even then it was impossible to mention such worthies as Fitch, Moody, Thomas and Walter in the same breath with their contemporaries across the Atlantic. Something momentous, it is true, occurred in 1915 when the Washington Square Players (later The Theatre Guild), the Provincetown Players, and the Neighborhood Playhouse arose almost simultaneously. But even then one would have had to be unusually optimistic to conclude that America was on the threshold of an important dramatic period. Moreover, our entry into the World War soon reduced the activities of the nascent organizations, and it was only four or five years later that their playwrights developed their molars.

In 1920, however, American drama attained maturity. On February second appeared Eugene O'Neill's *Beyond the Horizon,* and this event was followed a month later by this dramatist's first version of *Anna Christie* and, eight months later, by *Emperor Jones.* Within three years, moreover, O'Neill was no longer a lone figure: Maxwell Anderson, George Kelly, Elmer Rice, George S. Kaufman, Marc Connelly, Sidney Howard, John Howard Lawson, and Philip Barry were joining him in the theatre, bringing intelligence and observation to bear upon the American scene. A little later arrived those talented recruits Robert Sherwood, Paul Green, and S. N. Behrman, as well as a host of better than average privates.

The years 1920-1929 comprised a period of unparalleled expansion in the economic and social life of the nation. Our pioneering days were now definitely a thing of the past, and the surplus of our energies flowed into the arts. We adopted the best that we could find in European culture without allowing it to stifle native growths. We emancipated ourselves from provincialism and from the gaunt hand of fanatical puritanism, although we allowed it to keep a tight finger on our liquor supply. We began to explore human nature with the lantern of philosophy and the scalpel of modern surgery. The lantern revealed the richness of our resources, dreams, and strivings; the scalpel probed our intestinal tumors of complacency, intolerance, and acquisitiveness. In short, we achieved a criticism of life without which the drama is nothing but evanescent showmanship.

Then on October 29, 1929, amidst a flurry of ticker-tape and a rain of suicides from office windows, the bubble of our financial structure burst with a deafening explosion. Its fragments littered the landscape of the richest country in the world with apple-stands and bread lines. Unwilling to admit defeat, the country fed on windy promises, elected a new administration, and tried to coast along with the aid of relief and federal employment projects. At this writing, a decade is coming to an end without our having repaired the damage to our economic life.

That the theatre should have been severely affected was inevitable. Inflated real estate values on Broadway were deflated; business men who financed commercial productions or supported experimental enterprises retrenched; productions diminished in number, actors became a drug on the market, and the theatre's clientele became smaller as incomes diminished. Playwrights, directors and the better known actors found themselves frequently constrained to transfer their allegiance to the films. All told, the theatre of the thirties was a diminished quantity.

A literal application of economics to the stage could only lead to the conclusion that the American drama was coming to an untimely end. But man is not the passive creature of dollars or even of history; it is, after all, he who *makes* history, and the same exercise of will enables him to rise above defeat. How long he can remain in the slough of a depressed economy without losing his spirit or his sanity or both, it is of course impossible to tell with any precision. It is easier to record the past than to chart the future. But it is with the past that we are concerned here, a past which moreover provides a link with the immediate future—and that is about as far as most of us dare to look. The fact is that the thirties in America witnessed a period of drama equal in quality to the work of the preceding decade. The period has been rightly described by the sagacious critic John Mason Brown as "these full lean years."

2

In the physical theatre—if such a human phenomenon as the theatre may be called physical!—there were notable developments. It is true that the Provincetown Players and the Neighborhood Playhouse had disappeared some years before the stock-market crash; that the Civic Repertory Company came to an end; that the "Little Theatres" which had once dotted the country died or hibernated by the dozens, until in 1932 they omitted their national tournament for the first time since its inception in 1923; that the "road" back of cosmopolitan New York was almost closed for a time to the wagon-cars of Thespis. But there was at least one survivor from the wreckage, and the fertilizing time-spirit soon gave birth to a succession of younger enterprises that kept the drama not only distinctly alive, but also literally kicking.

The survivor, The Theatre Guild, which had shared honors with the Provincetown in the first decade, held its own—albeit sometimes precariously—by virtue of accumulated resources and the ability of its older playwrights. Amid many unwise choices—as is the way of the theatre—it managed to reveal such honorable native plays, in addition to imports, as *Hotel Universe, Elizabeth, the Queen, Green Grow the Lilacs, Mourning Becomes Electra, Reunion in Vienna, American Dream, Biography, Both Your Houses, Ah, Wilderness, Mary of Scotland, They Shall Not Die, Valley Forge, Rain from Heaven, Porgy and Bess, End of Summer,* and *The Philadelphia Story.* The Guild was, moreover, instrumental in founding the American Theatre Society which possesses a substantial subscription audience in a number of cities. Its efforts, combined with the successful tours of its Lunts, Katherine Cornell, Helen Hayes and others, helped considerably to reopen traffic on the road.

New sources of energy, moreover, were quickly forthcoming in response to new promptings. First to emerge was a group of actors and young directors who had been associated with The Theatre Guild for some time. They had tried their wings as early as the winter of 1928 when they worked on Waldo Frank's *New*

Year's Eve and Padraic Colum's *Balloon* for experimental purposes. They became inspired with the ideal of a collective theatre that would perfect ensemble playing and would give itself wholly to the badly shattered world beyond the footlights. They began to hold meetings between November, 1930, and May, 1931, and started rehearsals at Brookfield Center, Connecticut, in June. The play was Paul Green's memorable *House of Connelly,* which they presented a few months later under the auspices of the parent organization. Acting independently thereafter, this company, now known as The Group Theatre, produced the first full-length treatment of the depression, the Siftons' *1931.* This availed them little, nor did its successor Maxwell Anderson's *Night Over Taos.* But in the fall of 1932 John Howard Lawson's *Success Story* was almost faithful to its title. Then Sidney Kingsley's Pulitzer Prize hospital play, *Men in White,* produced in association with a commercial management, added strength to the Group's moorings at the same time that it revealed the potency of planned production by a permanent company.

A crisis impended when the next two productions met with disaster, for it is not usually given to young theatres to weather the Broadway climate. But at this point life came out of the Group's own body, and the company gave birth to a bouncing baby playwright who grew up almost instantaneously and made himself the foremost new dramatist of the thirties. Clifford Odets had worked with the Group as an actor and had shared its aims as a member of the collective from the beginning. He was ideally suited to the theatre he had helped to create along with its more expert actors and its directors, Cheryl Crawford, Harold Clurman, and Lee Strasberg. He found, in turn, that this theatre was suited to his particular style of dramaturgy. The association has continued without interruption, and to it we owe the plays—*Waiting for Lefty, Till the Day I Die, Awake and Sing, Paradise Lost, Golden Boy,* and *Rocket to the Moon*— which, regardless of their limitations, have given the drama of the thirties much of its claim to vitality. The Group, moreover, owes to Clifford Odets much of its present stability. It nearly foundered in 1937 in consequence of four financial failures when *Golden Boy* gave this intrepid company its deserved security under the present management of its able director, Mr. Harold Clurman. Then, profiting by this change in its fortunes, the Group gave another new writer, Irwin Shaw, his first Broadway success with *The Gentle People,* and brought William Saroyan into the theatre with the boldly experimental *My Heart's in the Highlands.*

In the theatre, however, no one works alone. The parturition that brought forth Clifford Odets and Irwin Shaw was a joint delivery. The partner was the New Theatre League, with its increasingly successful organ the New Theatre magazine, itself a joint product of the depression and of earlier attempts to create a working-class theatre. In the benign twenties only a small minority had felt the need for such a forum. After October, 1929, the necessary stimulus was only too abundantly present in unemployed millions, depressed wages, embattled labor unions, darkened theatres, and hungering actors. At first, small radical groups created "agit-prop" ("agitation" and "propaganda") plays. By 1933, however, this movement, known as the League of Workers Theatres, had been penetrated by more expert and less militant members, and the millenium of a social upheaval became a receding expectation.

Recognizing the fact that it was now an association of theatre people united only by an aversion to fascism, by sympathy with the underdog, or simply by a desire to create a vital stage, the movement renamed itself the New Theatre

League. Its productions, mostly one-acters, grew in number until these filled at least a portion of the gap left by the moribund state of the country's Little Theatres. In accordance with the new policy, New Theatre magazine announced an annual award for the best short play of "social significance", promising to produce it at benefit nights with the assistance of sympathetic acting groups.

Clifford Odets, who had been unable to dispose of his full-length script *Awake and Sing*, saw the announcement, locked himself in a hotel room for three days, and turned the scales with his one-acter *Waiting for Lefty*, a kaleidoscopic picture of American life caught within the frame of a taxicab strike. After its premiere by Group Theatre actors, it was produced throughout the country, as well as abroad, winning acclaim from many who were far more impressed with the young author's pungent talent than with his social philosophy. The Group discovered it had an exceptional playwright in its midst, and Odets became its mainstay. This event, little short of momentous, occurred in January, 1935.

Other contests and New Theatre nights followed, one of them in January, 1936 bringing to light Paul Green's notable and provocative chain-gang one-acter *Hymn to the Rising Sun*, which linked a leading figure of the twenties with a movement that was peculiarly a product of the new decade. Then came Irwin Shaw's expressionistic long one-acter *Bury the Dead*, in which the victims of a new war, refusing to be buried, return to wrest a richer life from the world. Thus another powerful playwright was added to the lists. He has not operated long enough to realize himself completely. But, after one slip, *Siege*, he carved out the richly humorous parable of the revolt of the meek against the bullies of the world, *The Gentle People*. It was warmly received in New York despite a mixed press, and it is currently captivating the British people, who have grown restive under too much international hijacking.

In 1937, the New Theatre League began to suffer a recession, but retained sufficient vitality to discover at least one other playwright, Marc Blitzstein.

During this period, the social movement also managed to create a forum for full-length plays, The Theatre Union. For several seasons it became a haven for socially conscious playwrights and provided a popular-priced theatre. Except for a brief foray into the Middle West, it confined its activities to New York; it suffered from sectarian management; and it closed its doors, after some uneven productions, when John Howard Lawson's stirring but special strike drama *Marching Song* ended its run in the spring of 1937.

But this theatre was not padlocked before it had produced an exciting drama of racial conflict in the South, *Stevedore;* a touching picture of the mining regions in Albert Maltz's *Black Pit;* and Albert Bein's vivid epic of harassed Southern mountaineers in the grip of the industrial system, *Let Freedom Ring*. The Theatre Union's example, moreover, inspired the creation of Labor Stage, owned and operated by the progressive International Ladies Garment Workers Union in New York. This organization is still presenting, contrary to expectations, the freshest and most entertaining musical revue of the thirties, *Pins and Needles*.

Still more characteristic of the era was the Federal Theatre, a unit of the Works Progress Administration with which the government strove to stem the tide of unemployment. Started in 1935 under the direction of Miss Hallie Flanagan of Vassar College, and ended with one blow of the congressional axe in the summer of 1939, the project had a chequered career partly perhaps owing to the uneven quality of its personnel, but largely to red tape and continual reorganization. Nevertheless, its services as the first national low-priced theatre in America cannot be discounted; it went far toward filling gaps in the "road" and toward acclimatizing hitherto lethargic citizens to the stage.

It attempted to create a poetic theatre, and succeeded in giving an inkling of its potentialities in this sadly prosaic age with T. S. Eliot's *Murder in the Cathedral.* The Negro Theatre branch introduced a vigorous note with its Haitian version of *Macbeth* and with William Du Bois' *Haiti.* The Children's Theatre showed what could be done in the direction of fostering a feeling for the stage among America's younger millions with *Pinocchio,* as well as with sundry less publicized ventures. Other affiliates sponsored democratic drama with the country-wide production of *It Can't Happen Here,* a much needed warning against fascism in a troubled age. Finally, the subsidized theatre created America's most original contribution to the world's drama, the Living Newspapers—dramatizations of vital facts concerning the problems of agriculture, labor, utilities, venereal disease, and housing. "As American as Walt Disney, the *March of Time* and the *Congressional Record*," the new form created purposeful native *commedia dell' arte* in *Power* and in the more sombre *One-third of a Nation.* Drama of the people and for the people, the Living Newspaper does not appear to advantage on the printed page except for the most imaginative reader. But without regard for literary permanence it tended to enrich the theatre honorably, stirringly, and entertainingly. The absence of the Federal Theatre will, we fear, be deeply felt in the imminent forties.

Not the least of its gifts to the stage, however, was the directorial genius of Orson Welles, which was instrumental in forming another remarkable, if temporarily stalemated, theatrical enterprise. After providing highly original revivals for the Federal Theatre culminating in Marlowe's *Dr. Faustus,* Orson Welles and his partner, John Houseman, created the Mercury Theatre that gave memorable modern productions of *Julius Caesar* and Dekker's *Shoemakers' Holiday.* These respectively illuminated the tragedy of liberalism in an era of dictatorship and demagoguery and glorified the homely democratic spirit. Although primarily a revival theatre, the Mercury moreover brought forth that scintillating sublimation of "agit-pop" in operatic or oratorio form, *The Cradle Will Rock,* memorable equally for its dramatic style and its engaging sceneryless production.

A rich and fruitful life was assured by these various enterprises, though not exactly in proportion to their interest in the reformation of American society or the defence of what was best in it. Nor were the theatre's resources monopolized by the institutional stage. Commercial enterprise had been elevated appreciably in the twenties, and the next decade did not fall below that level. As usual, the ordinary producer promoted the amenities for the greater glory of the box-office, and this, too, was to the good since the playgoer is entitled to relaxation. To provide it is also an art, as well as a function, of the eternal theatre. Moreover, a number of producers did not fail to honor their profession with work of rare distinction. It was Guthrie McClintic who produced the poetic dramas *Winterset* and *High Tor,* Jed Harris *Our Town,* Sam Harris *Of Mice and Men.* Finally, in the fall of 1938 came an association of five older dramatists, The Playwrights' Theatre, devoted to no program other than personal interest and yet achieving thus far one season of uncommon lustre. This group was completely free from concessions to commerce whether its plays were successful as was eminently the case with *Abe Lincoln in Illinois* and *No Time for Comedy* or unsuccessful in the instance of Elmer Rice's *American Landscape.* The chronicle of "these full lean years" is that of a theatre venturesome, spirited, and resourceful despite economic chaos within and beyond its boundaries.

To insist upon this fact is important because it is a tribute to our general resilience, as well as to the particular resilience of the theatre. It is only too easy to lose one's patience with that madcap institution, and he is a poor friend indeed who does not at some time or other pelt it with epithets born of mingled vexation and devotion. But one does not expect perfection from anything so human and therefore so fallible as the stage. All one requires of it is protoplasmic activity, and in this respect the theatre reacted better than prophets of disaster could have predicted. It even displayed that index of vitality "trial and error" or "experiment" in stagecraft. Fantasy found abundant scope in the production of *High Tor*. The only approximation of the famous but ambiguous "Stanislavsky system" in this country came from the Group Theatre. A new technique was evolved by the "Living Newspaper." The "learning play" combination of dramatic and lecture methods was imported on two occasions by the Theatre Union and the Group Theatre, and was modified in the Group's production of *Johnny Johnson*. Largely sceneryless, stylized treatment was accorded to *Our Town* and *The Cradle Will Rock*. Even *surréalisme* was pressed into service, in the Group's staging of *My Heart's in the Highlands*. And these methods, it is important to note, were employed not by long-haired esthetes but by toughminded organizations addressing the plebes in the name of collective welfare, as well as by a hardboiled producer whose business it is to make the theatre *pay*.

Athens crowned the theatre with glory while fighting for its existence against a host of enemies. Germany advanced stagecraft by leaps and bounds at a time when it suffered the miseries of inflation and national humiliation. America, struggling through a decade of economic distress, likewise affirmed the strength of the human spirit that often proves so painfully blind and bestial under the whiplash of accumulated errors. The approaching decade may confront us with an ominous question mark, and our hearts may falter at the prospect. But it is something to be able to say that we held our own as long as we could, and that as yet we are undefeated and have no intention of surrendering. And, be it known, as this anthology seeks to show, we laughed, too. Moreover, ours was free and hearty laughter.

3

By their fruit ye shall know them. But in the theatre the only fruit that can be packed away and retained is its literary crop—its drama. The most conclusive proof the period's vitality is the quality of its plays, and this anthology collects some of them.

Naturally they fall into two broad groups—serious and light. But this classification tells us nothing about their nature. They were the product of different minds and temperaments, different outlooks and allegiances, different conditioning. For convenience a more definite line may be drawn between those writers who passed their novitiate in the twenties and those who grew to maturity in the next decade. It is not a hard and fast line; for some of the latter wrote farces with as much insouciance as older practitioners, while some of the older dramatists stood on common ground with the younger revolutionists or sociologists. Moreover, neither the young nor the old remained fixed in their respective grooves. Still there were differences.

Generally, the serious dramatists of the previous decade were variously liberal in politics but remained chiefly interested in individual psychology and in personal matters. Thus Eugene O'Neill, their master, continued to work in the spirit of the twenties. His masterpiece, *Mourning Becomes Electra*, was a psychological tragedy of passion, fixations, and complexes; its point of reference with respect to American society was the narrow puritanism and acquisitiveness which his contemporaries had deplored in many a debunking biography or history. *Days Without End* continued this author's concern with problems of faith and dual personality. His sole departure from his norm was an unexpected tribute to normality in *Ah, Wilderness,* a comedy of rare humor and geniality. True, however, to his introspective, Freudian approach, he suggested that radicalism in the young was only a passing phase of the libido. The point was made without malice and with a good deal of tolerance which enhanced the understanding and amiability of the play. But to apply it to the rampant sons of the thirties would have been incongruous in view of the fact that their particular distemper was caused by unemployment and want.

Maxwell Anderson oscillated between the past and the present. He seemed, in fact, to be definitely committed to romanticism with his successes *Elizabeth, the Queen* and *Mary of Scotland.* Although there were contemporary implications in *Night Over Taos, The Wingless Victory, High Tor, The Masque of Kings,* and *Knickerbocker Holiday,* the romantic afflatus was more or less present in all these plays. In addition, he was concerned with a stylistic problem of great importance—how to create poetic drama in a prosaic age. Since it is comparatively easy to write poetic plays when the subject is set in the past, he proceeded cautiously at first with Elizabethan tragedies, *Elizabeth, the Queen* and *Mary of Scotland.* Tactfully he moved closer to our own time and place with *Valley Forge.* Then with one bold leap he applied poetry to a contemporary background of gangsters, East Siders and the Sacco and Vanzetti case in *Winterset.* Fantasy in *High Tor* enabled him to make the same application to a tale about land speculators and a plucky lad who refused to be devoured by the leviathan of our industrial civilization. Musical comedy in *Knickerbocker Holiday* gave him an opportunity to indulge his lyric gift with a travesty on old Peter Stuyvesant, for whom the name of Franklin D. Roosevelt could be substituted by those who were so minded.

The desire to create drama of absolute beauty nevertheless shared interest in Mr. Anderson's mind with a keen awareness of contemporary realities. As a former journalist, he was not inclined to forget them. In 1933 he castigated Congress with the prose satire of *Both Your Houses. Night Over Taos* more than hinted that the old order must make room for the new. *Valley Forge* was a reminder that the tree of Liberty is a precious plant nourished by the blood and dreams of the American people. *Winterset,* pointing to an old sore in the American body, was a scathing attack on the perversion of justice by class prejudice; *High Tor* excoriated business ethics; *The Masque of Kings* stressed the futility of revolutions which right one wrong with another and substitute new tyrants for old. *Knickerbocker Holiday* satirized dictatorial ambitions, honored the chronic rebelliousness of the American people, and paid the institution of democracy the left-handed compliment that the tyranny of the majority was less efficient and therefore more tolerable than the rule of a single individual.

No one represented the old-fashioned, but by no means extinct liberal position more consistently than Maxwell Anderson. On the one hand, he spoke up eloquently against social corruption, but on the other hand, he maintained a consistent distrust of government interference and an antipathy to revolutionary action. This he did in defiance of all who favored either the destruction of the *status quo* or the partial socialization of America by reform. If he became a source of irritation to some, he nevertheless represented one segment of opinion. Moreover, his great talent as a showman and dramatist must

xiii

remain unquestioned. Whatever flaws one will find in his dramatic logic or in his poetic style, he is the master of the period. He is variously derivative, wordy, sentimental, circuitious and tangential. But at his best he is imaginative, fiery, humane, and noble. Or so he was, in the main, in the thirties.

His peers in the serious vein were generally less successful, but almost equally enterprising. Sidney Howard turned out a charming adaptation from the French in *The Late Christopher Bean,* and a creative dramatization of a Sinclair Lewis novel, *Dodsworth.* He remained a man of the twenties: *Dodsworth* was at most a common sense reaction to the adulation of European manners and the passion for self-expression that prevailed in that decade; *Alien Corn* was one of those studies of personal frustration which were dear to it. He came closer to the thirties with his *Yellow Jack,* a drama which moved away from personal complications, honoring the services of science to society in the battle against yellow fever in Cuba. It was a noble and spirited work, and it belonged to the bolder experiments by virtue of its shifting scenes unified by the omission of intermissions. In *The Ghost of Yankee Doodle* this playwright turned to a theme still closer to the problems of the thirties. The war-making of magnates of the press and the dilemma of liberals who are torn between pacifism and profits concerned him here. But the play lacked elevation and excitement, as is often the way of considered and reasoned documents in the theatre. In the main, Sidney Howard failed to catch fire from the period. Nevertheless, he helped to keep the drama intelligent and expert.

Paul Green, Pulitzer Prize winner of 1927, tried to fuse music, symbolism, and drama in several unsuccessful experiments which did not reach Broadway. But he mastered the full-length realistic drama in *The House of Connelly.* This sensitive character play acquired additional interest from its social picture of the decay of the Southern aristocracy and the advent of a more vigorous order. The chain-gang system of the South fired him to write one of the finest American one-acters in *Hymn to the Rising Sun,* a tragedy that wrests poetry from what is sordid and properly colloquial in his material; it is a vivid telescoping of brutal social fact and human psychology. Finally, he topped his efforts to create imaginative drama with *Johnny Johnson,* supported by the notable music of the German refugee Kurt Weill. Moreover, this was no mere exercise in expressionism but a bitter and poignant tragi-comedy of a good man in a vile world, of a homespun lover of peace in the midst of sadists, madmen, and fools.

More definitely irate and embattled were Elmer Rice and John Howard Lawson, who joined hands with the younger rebels. The former poured vitriol, in *The Left Bank,* on the affectations of bohemian artists who coddle their souls in Paris. He followed this with an excellent character play, *Counsellor-at-Law.* By 1933, however, he had worked up a blinding indignation at the state of the nation, and his *We, the People* became a kaleidoscopic and overcrowded indictment. An exposé of fascist justice (*Judgment Day*), a comparison between American and Soviet viewpoints favorable to the latter ·(*Between Two Worlds*), and a call for a socially responsible liberalism, with American ancestors rising from the grave to instruct the age (*American Landscape*), completed his contribution to the thirties. He was poorly rewarded for his social dramas and their artistry left much to be desired; they were more honorable than satisfying. Intellectually even more inclined to the "left", John Howard Lawson deplored the corruption of character by the profit motive in his generally effective *Success Story.* He decried the waste of American life in his gangster and show-girl melodrama *The Pure in Heart,* and juxtaposed a rich woman and revolutionary lover in *Gentlefolk.* Then realizing that the last two unsuccessful efforts were muddled, and fired by the cause of the working-class, he wrote the panoramic strike play *Marching Song,* too hortatory but poetic and exciting.

4

The twenties had revealed several extremely competent writers of comedy. They continued to function variously, some of them turning to serious drama, others intensifying their interest in ideas or problems, still others remaining content to be merely clever and entertaining. Among the latter, that expert team Mr. and Mrs. Spewack continued to be sharp and ingenious in *Clear All Wires,* as well as in the delightful musical comedy *Leave It to Me.* They achieved a native farce of rare vigor and bite in *Boy Meets Girl* by falling back upon one of the staples of American humor—Hollywood.

Philip Barry, an old friend of the amenities in the twenties, wavered. His temperament deepened, and he produced the psychoanalytical fantasy *Hotel Universe,* an original study of bedevilled members of the upper-class and of the intelligentsia. This was at the beginning of the decade. At its end he added another testament to the serious side of his nature in *Here Come the Clowns.* This was an allegory of the search for the justice of God and of the unequal conflict between love and hatred in the contemporary world. Both works were distinctly flawed; both added considerable nobility and aspiration to the theatre. He also tapped a serious vein in *Tomorrow and Tomorrow,* but with no marked reference to the world beyond the household of a childless couple. His other more moralistic efforts, however, failed, and their author returned to the comic spirit. Without being noticeably ebullient in *The Animal Kingdom,* produced in 1932, he had nevertheless extracted humor out of a predatory wife and an intelligent mistress. In *The Philadelphia Story,* seven years later, Mr. Barry moved into the mansions of our plutocracy to combine an entertaining analysis of a proud girl with a playful plea for tolerance for "the rich and mighty." His contribution to the problems that troubled his contemporaries was the "liberal" point that the upper brackets, as well as the radical movement, did not necessarily teem with ogres.

S. N. Behrman never wavered; his province had been high comedy, and high comedy it continued to be. Less of a master of plot than Philip Barry, he is inimitable in his mastery of dialogue and in his illumination of different viewpoints. And since ideas and viewpoints clashed audibly in the period, he made the time-spirit his own. From the mild flare-up of a wealthy man who marries out of his class in *Brief Moment,* Mr. Behrman moved on to a succession of controversial comedies. In the love story of *Biography* he maintained an understanding balance between the volatile temperament that is merely amused at self-seeking or toryism and the acerb spirit of a young man who, having suffered from the world's injustice, cannot give quarter. Moving closer to tragedy in *Rain from Heaven,* Mr. Behrman showed the world of the artist and thinker crashing about his ears in the hailstorm of fascism and antisemitism. Recovering his spirits, this inquiring playwright then investigated the failure of wealth and the rebellion of the younger generation in the generally blithe *End of Summer.* Then, after his polished adaption of a French comedy *Amphitryon 38,* he wrote an unintegrated defense of liberalism in *Wine of Choice.* He closed with an amusing triangle woven around a writer of comedies who makes a *gauche* attempt to grapple with social realities foreign to his nature. This last-mentioned work, *No Time for Comedy,* is still running. Sometimes inconsistent, nearly always between two stools as is the case when men consider ideas dispassionately, and generally also more conversational than dramatic, this brilliant author nevertheless was responsible for much of the intelligence and scintillation of the decade's theatre.

The rest of the comic tribe followed individual inclinations. The veteran Rachel Crothers continued to display character and domestic situations with shrewd humor. Without any marked concern for problems now that feminism was an issue of the past, Miss Crothers in *As Husbands Go, When Ladies Meet,* and *Susan and God* kept her weather-eye on the miniature tempests of middle-class women. Marc Connelly, whose comic bent had been charitable and flavorsome, found glorious material in Roark Bradford's *Ol' Man Adam an' his Chillun,* a collection of negro biblical tales. The result was the most lovable play of the thirties *Green Pastures.* Historically never remote, the play was close to the human heart, and the trials it recounted are eternally relevant.

His erstwhile collaborator, the fertile George S. Kaufman continued, with the aid of various collaborators, to reveal the multiple facets of his temperament. Above all, he remained a showman. But the stresses of the period met with a continual response from his nimble spirit, playful on the boards and unencumbered by profundity. While the Hoover administration was waning during 1930-1932 amid clouds of disapproval, Mr. Kaufman (with Morrie Ryskind) delivered himself of that brilliant musical travesty *Of Thee I Sing,* and its less successful sequel *Let 'Em Eat Cake* had reference to the economic upheaval. Both did much to lift musical comedy from the saccharine in which it was usually imbedded. Without benefit of an orchestra, *First Lady* satirized Washington society; and another musical comedy, *I'd Rather Be Right,* dealt ambidextrously with the aims and measures of the New Deal. Turning to the arts, Mr. Kaufman, with Moss Hart, waxed lugubrious (and somewhat autobiographical) in *Merrily We Roll Along* over a writer's loss of his ideals. Then, with Miss Edna Ferber, he described the struggles of the valiant young people who try to remain loyal to the theatre despite its neglect of them in *Stage Door.* This play was not devoid of sentimentality despite its humor, but it touched a raw wound in view of the theatre's doldrums.

Soon Mr. Kaufman hastened to pour balm on all wounds with the madcap, philosophical plea to let life slide in *You Can't Take It With You.* Although strictly considered, most Americans could not afford that luxury, this was an amiable prescription. Coupled with a disarming tolerance, it promoted good feeling and hilarity in the theatre. But this playwright's final contribution noticed that a state of bliss was growing precarious in an era of unsolved problems. His most recent play, *The American Way,* challenged the visible threat of fascism with a glowing chronicle of "the American Way." With a showman's partiality for theatrical effects, he oversimplified matters, sentimentalized, and came perilously close to chauvinism. But there was never any doubt about his intentions, and the total effect was inspiriting.

Most remarkable, however, was the evolution of the youngest of the "old men". After two sentimental melodramas of no great moment—*Waterloo Bridge* and *This is New York*—it seemed as if Robert Sherwood's forte was comedy. He had first attracted attention with his historical comedy *The Road to Rome* in 1927, and his first success in the thirties was the Austrian triangle *Reunion in Vienna.* But it was apparent that his historical bent was considerable and that it was neither antiquarian nor dilettante. He was much concerned with the passing of systems, the death of societies; like John Webster during the twilight of the English renaissance, Sherwood saw the skull beneath the skin. *Reunion in Vienna,* in addition to being excellent comedy when a psychoanalyst was caught in his own cerebral coils, was a vivid picture of the decayed and exiled Hapsburg aristocracy. This was followed by a static eulogy on the dying civilization of Athens, *Acropolis,* which was professionally produced only in London. For all its shortcomings, it was a searching work, and it was not difficult to discover in it an eloquent lament for the passing of European civilization. Then came *The Petrified Forest,* an attempt, as he declared, "to show the passing of an epoch in the terms of melodrama and assembled characters" in an American locale. Its suicidal intellectual clearly symbolized the defeat of spirit by matter, of culture by brute force. The playwright was not, however, happy in his choice of a hero, and his elegiac mood was somewhat maudlin, so that only the melodrama *per se* was completely realized.

Finally, he struck home with *Idiot's Delight,* a satiric and mournful evocation of the madness of war and chauvinism which engulfs even the most intelligent members of society. Once again he showed civilization going to pot in a welter of wasted or corrupted lives. And again the author's past welled up to dilute the force of his meaning and enhance his showmanship; this time it was his tried talent for comedy that brought debit and credit to his pacifist play in the form of savory chorus girl episodes. "The trouble with me," he has said, perhaps with his tongue in his cheek, "is that I start off with a big message and end with nothing but good entertainment." For his final contribution to the thirties, however, Mr. Sherwood needed no such apology. His current *Abe Lincoln in Illinois* has succeeded without concessions to the public. Moreover, he has at least temporarily shed his negativism. His biographical drama is a noble, if at first leisurely and unexciting, affirmation of American ideals through the one national hero who best embodied them both as a political figure and a man.

5

After this chronicle, it might seem that the new blood of the thirties could not have boiled more perceptibly than that which had started flowing in the twenties. And a glance at comedy might confirm the assumption. The most incisive high comedy by the new generation, Clare Boothe's *The Women,* differed at most from the satires of the elders only in its more abundant use of acid. No American writer has ever arranged such an exhibit of parasitism as Miss Boothe's gallery of idle, backbiting and unscrupulous women. If one did not know something about this author's background, one might accuse her of being a "bolshie" and of boring from within. Yet there is no fear of this. She is or seems oblivious of the fact that her only good woman is also useless (and for the most part without the excuse of being interesting). Moreover, the amenities are restored by a happy conclusion. Mark Reed's *Yes, My Darling Daughter* pokes gentle fun at the ex-radicals of Greenwich Village days and generously allows their children a taste of their parents' liberty. But respectability is hardly stormed by this genial comedy, the author's first major contribution to the theatre although he has been writing since 1919—which perhaps entitles him to be listed with the youngsters.

Finally, not even a microscope could reveal any cleavage between that excellent farce of the thirties *Three Men on a Horse* and older products. It consists of those ever-fresh but hardly novel ingredients of American low comedy: salty colloquialism, an amusingly realized background which alternates between the suburbs and a racetrack den, a lovable nitwit, and a series of fortuitous circumstances. The formula also applies, with various modifications, to such other expertly contrived farces of the decade as *Room Service, Brother Rat,* and *Personal Appearance.*

Nor is there anything topical in the content of that two-thirds excellent drama *Our Town* by Thornton Wilder, who as a dramatist (but not as a novelist) belongs to the thirties. This cross-section of small-town life in America is an affirmation of the simple humanity that seeks to round its cycle of life, love, and death quietly. *Our Town* belongs to the classic tradition by its "above-the-battle" viewpoint. If its flavor is wholly and great-heartedly American, if its nostalgic recollection of vanished tranquility (only a partial reality, as Mr. Wilder knows) has contemporary implications, its prime interest is the most universal of universals "Life". Something to the same effect also appears in the most charming fantasy of recent years *On Borrowed Time,* in which Death reaps his harvest with a gentleness that is rapidly becoming anomalous. These plays did not grapple with the age. Their authors were eager only to make breathing in it more tolerable.

Still, as the first portion of this essay suggested, many of the new playwrights were burning with indignation at the state of the world or were at least sensible of much social injustice and ferment. Even so genial a comedy as Arthur Kober's *Having Wonderful Time* injected into its summer camp antics the ache of the younger generation, deprived of its claim to happiness but struggling for it with pathetic intensity. Less successful plays traced the ravages of the depression with varying seriousness, ranging from tearfully comic imbroglios of *The Three-Cornered Moon* to the tragedy of wasted youth in *Class of 29* and the angry melodrama of the Siftons' *1931*. These works, deficient in the polish that their authors could not, and would not, supply, told a darker and more immediate tale than the survivors of the twenties cared to put on the stage. Depression plays were indeed legion, when one-acters and unproduced scripts are added to the list. Nor were they confined to the doldrums of youth; a jeremiad like *But for the Grace of God* distributed suffering impartially between parent and children.

Tobacco Road is the classic of this school. No other play of the period conveyed such misery, such degradation, and such hopelessness as Jack Kirkland's dramatization of Erskine Caldwell's inferno of "white trash" life in the South. Fortunately its earthiness produced a naturalistic comedy which could make its gravest implications acceptable as theatre. Historians might be tempted to consider it the corner-stone of the decade's drama on the strength of its long run. It has held the stage since December, 1933, and has been held up as a case-history by nearly every reformer. To suggest that the Rip Van Winkle story of a shiftless farmer and the salacious details stressed by the production have attracted more customers than the social message detracts only slightly from the significance of *Tobacco Road*. Only a sensational play could have made Erskine Caldwell's original material so palatable to the nation.

It is one of several realistic expositions which commanded attention and comment. Such an exposé, in a sense, is that excellent dramatization John Steinbeck's *Of Mice and Men,* which brought the itinerant worker into the limelight. Few plays have conveyed so much pathos as this tragedy of homeless men holding fast to each other and dreaming of a place of their own. Unlike *Tobacco Road,* moreover, Steinbeck's humane treatment of the theme lifts one from the depths; the characters have an inarticulate nobility and the light of common things shines in them. Moreover, as is generally the case with work of singular merit, its poetry of the soul relates it to the efforts of other times and places. There are touches of Gorky in Steinbeck's play, and the material recalls O'Neill's sea-pieces in which wandering men also seek a haven. Despite some contrived melodrama in the murder of a somewhat Hollywoodish "vamp" by a half-wit, and despite the lack of tragic stature in the latter, *Of Mice and Men* was one of the most moving plays of the period.

Exposition was indeed the forte of the younger men, another striking example being Sidney Kingsley's *Dead End,* a pungent drama of slum life. This author's critical viewpoint had been subordinated in *Men in White* to a love story between an interne and a girl. Although a love story between an unemployed architect and a kept woman also played a part—and a distracting one—in *Dead End,* the emphasis rested on a group of children who, but for the grace of God, would grow up into gangsters like the killer who is tracked down on its waterfront. Rounding out the picture, Mr. Kingsley indicated a sharp cleavage between poor and rich in this land of plenty by setting the fire-trap tenements flush against a swanky East River residence. There is war between its residents and the denizens of the slums, and the "dead end" of the street might easily suggest both the trapped lives of its children and the unneccessary impasse of American society. Although somewhat contrived and sentimentally resolved, *Dead End* lived richly in its young ragamuffins while casting the shadow of larger matters upon their pier.

Here, moreover, we find the three main pillars of the younger militant drama—exposition of social evil, economic determinism, and stress upon the struggle of the classes. It is significant that Mr. Kingsley topped *Dead End* with a vitriolic assault, in *Ten Million Ghosts,* on the munitions makers who promote wars for profit but escape its ravages. This unwieldly protest is closely related to the propagandist plays of the radical movement. It is noteworthy that the Theatre Union had raised its curtain two years earlier on a similar play, *Peace on Earth* by Albert Maltz and George Sklar.

Symptomatic was the work of Lillian Hellman. *The Children's Hour* might be classed with the psychological dramas of the twenties. It explored abnormality in a maladjusted child and a homosexually inclined teacher. Yet the play did not confine itself to purely clinical details; Miss Hellman suggested a powerful antagonist in the well-to-do community that accepted a child's testimony and persecuted her victims. This intensely tragic drama, replete with well-drawn characters, was however only the beginning of Miss Hellman's invasion of the social scene. It was followed by the short-lived strike play *Days to Come,* poorly focussed and overcrowded but permeated with her talent for incisive characterization. Finally came *The Little Foxes,* a trenchant account of the making of some American fortunes, the rise of industrialism in the South, and the triumph of the predatory dog-eat-dog dispensation. Miss Hellman's ability to combine intense indignation with a sharp analysis of social fact and of individual character was one of the major accomplishments of the period. Only a slight halting in her third acts, a penchant for inconsequential conversions incompletely rooted in the logic of the play, weakened this author's work.

The writers we have considered above were either more or less associated with the so-called left-wing movement in the theatre or they shared its outlook. But one must know its most active proponents to understand its intellectual basis. The playwrights of the Theatre Union, George Sklar, Albert Maltz, Paul Peters, Victor Wolfson, Michael Blankfort, and Albert Bein, along with the new Theatre League discoveries, Clifford Odets and Irwin Shaw, started with a fixed philosophy. Whether or not they adhered to the party programs of Communism or Socialism, they recognized the Marxist principle that modern society is divided between two camps—capital and labor. In the world-wide depression, the rearming of the nations, and fascism they discerned the writhings of the dying monster, Capitalism. In the strikes that flared up throughout the nation they saw dress rehearsals for revolution. In racial conflicts they found machiavellian machinations by a frightened master-class. In the plight of the middle-class they located a major symptom of the era of the social wars—namely, the proletarianization of the small business man. Had not Marx predicted that the time would come when there would be only workers and monopolistic capitalists in the world, and that the preponderance of the former would create a socialist society!

Indisputably these younger men were firebrands, and their work suffered from violence and one-sidedness. But out of their fire (and smoke) sometimes came theatrical excitement, a commodity that the stage can rarely afford to neglect. *Stevedore* was a gripping purposeful melodrama; John Wexley's *They Shall not Die* made stirring drama out of the Scottsboro Case; Odets' *Waiting for Lefty* assembled a multitude of complaints into a sweeping call for revolutionary action so striking that the play became a *tour de force*. Moreover, these apostolic youngsters knew how to enrich the stage with vivid pictures of proletarian and lower middle-class life in generally overlooked locales from the South to the Bronx. This trenchant kind of realism had not been seen to much advantage in the theatre since *Street Scene* and O'Neill's early works. A good example was Albert Maltz's harrowing description of life among the miners in *Black Pit*. Still another concomitant of such writing was flavorsome dialogue, for which the stage is ever grateful without respect to creed or party-line; it appeared in *Stevedore*, *Black Pit* and *Let Freedom Ring*, and it became memorable in the work of Clifford Odets.

Imagination also flourished, along with striking dramatic methods. *Waiting for Lefty* employed the expressionistic device of flash-backs, each realistic in content and background but imaginatively projected. Finally, fantasy prevailed in Irwin Shaw's *Bury the Dead;* the dead returned to life on a future battlefield to signify the common man's refusal to be twice-buried by poverty and war. Although Irwin Shaw's long one-acter was somewhat wordy and disjointed, it proved that a socially minded playwright did not have to keep his nose to the grindstone of literal realism in order to convey his meaning or purpose. And soon there arose two other playwrights, Marc Blitzstein and Archibald MacLeish, one an embattled musician and the other a sympathetic poet, to confirm the point.

Marc Blitztein turned out a rebellious opus compounded of satire, indignation, and challenge, *The Cradle Will Rock*. All the depreciated stock-in-trade of "agit-prop" was here converted into a pungent and original short opera. Its telescoped scenes must have struck many of us as a welcome relief from at least some of the aerated caterwaulings of the Metropolitan Opera House's repertoire. But even more important was the work of Archibald MacLeish, a notable poet and a man of noble convictions. His *Fall of the City* was significant not only because it was a brilliantly imaginative treatment of fascism or because its poetry was superior to any that had been written for the American stage. (If it was equalled and here and there even surpassed by T. S. Eliot's *Murder in the Cathedral,* one must still give the palm to Mr. MacLeish. Mr. Eliot's contribution mixed prose and verse, reached its highest dramatic moment in the concluding prose section, and treated the medieval matter of St. Becket's martyrdoom which belongs to an older poetic tradition.) For the future, the greatest significance of *The Fall of the City* lies in the fact that with it a real poet and an intelligent dramatist invaded the broadcasting studios.

Radio drama had been beneath contempt when suddenly the air vibrated with the fresh and incisive lines of this parable of the masses, here seen submitting to a Leader who is nothing but a piece of empty armor. This was the poet's second play, the first—*Panic,* a tragedy of the stock-market crash—having been written for the stage, where it was somewhat ill at ease. Having found his metier in radio drama, this poet also wrote *Air Raid.* This piece sounded a gripping protest against the massacre of unarmed civilians by those who "make war on life itself". Thanks largely to Archibald MacLeish the air-waves are no longer completely monopolized by Pollyanna and her laxative-sponsored cousins.

Finally, "honey" began to come from the "strong" when the lions of the left stopped pawing the ground and roaring. Irwin Shaw's whimsical *The Gentle People* was quiescent by comparison with his *Bury the Dead.* Although his viewpoint was unaltered, and he still defended the common man and proclaimed his revolt, the treatment was leisurely, unhortatory, and oblique. It is unfair to call Odets' later plays a departure from his earliest work *Awake and Sing,* a poignant and dissolving picture of the poor to which the revolutionary ending was a mere appendage and a not very convincing one. But his later work differed materially from the "direct action" of *Waiting for Lefty.* After a semi-symbolic picture of the destruction of middle-class security in *Paradise Lost,* he wrote his best constructed and least rampant play, *Golden Boy.*

Superficially, this saga of a violinist turned prize-fighter might have come from the Beverly Hills studios. Its background was reminiscent of many a flicker, as was perhaps the rather arbitrary transformation of a violinist into a bruiser. But Odets aimed at something higher. Taking a theme from popular life as ready material for critical interpretation, he dramatized the waste inherent in contemporary life. His Joe Bonaparte may never have become a Heifetz, but he was at least a sensitive and moderately gifted lad. Fear of poverty and obscurity, coupled with the extravagant desires fostered by our high-pressure civilization, made him seek a field for easy success. Then the machinations of a prize-fight promoter, himself a victim of economic pressure, snared him to his doom. The "honey" came from Odets' touching picture of the lad's father, from his understanding of the boy, and from his humane evaluation of the prize-fight addicts. Odets' comet dipped somewhat in his next play *Rocket to the Moon,* the story of a love-harassed and work-driven dentist and his variously capsized neighbors. But here again there was more sweetness than thunder, and once more characterization supplanted direct preachment.

The short cycle of the years closed with the young militants located somewhere in the vicinity of their elders. Simultaneously, the latter moved forward a little in the direction of the "social" school with such work as *Abe Lincoln in Illinois* and *The American Way.* They were intrenching democracy against the assault of social misery and fascism. Thus the progress of America's dramatists brought the two generations together more than might have been expected. And between them they brought the contracted theatre of the decade to fruition. The waste, the stumbling, and the lagging of the theatre notwithstanding, the record of the drama was distinctly honorable.

———————

This collection of twenty plays is an obviously incomplete harvest. To have included more than a portion of the crop would have required a book twice as large and expensive. Moreover, the copyright situation is always an impediment to anthologists, and anyone familiar with our recent drama will know that this problem has been only partially surmounted here. Upon being approached by the publisher to edit and introduce this volume, the present writer had more qualms than he should perhaps confess in public.

Fortunately, however, it has been possible to represent the four main currents of our recent drama. Here are the exaltations and the relaxations of both the survivors from the twenties and the newcomers of the thirties. Five serious plays (*Winterset, High Tor, Idiot's Delight, Johnny Johnson,* and *Green Pastures*) and five comedies (*You Can't Take It With You, End of Summer, The Animal Kingdom, Boy Meets Girl,* with *Stage Door* as a final olio to remind us of some of the ardors and endurances of the theatre) represent the veterans. Three comedies (*The Women, Yes, My Darling Daughter,* and *Three Men on a Horse*) and seven weighty contributions (*The Children's Hour, Tobacco Road, Of Mice and Men, Dead End, Golden Boy, Bury the Dead,* and *The Fall of the City*) testify to the proficiency of the recruits. Regret is in order for our inability to include *Mourning Becomes Electra* because of its length, *Our Town* and two or three of last season's items because they were unavailable, and a few other items for related reasons. But there is, I trust, ample compensation in our ability to present *Winterset, High Tor, Idiot's Delight, The Green Pastures, Of Mice and Men, The Children's Hour, The Fall of the City,* and other notable contributions to the contemporary stage. For this much the editor is grateful. Perhaps the reader will be too.

Winterset

BY MAXWELL ANDERSON

CHARACTERS

TROCK	CARR
SHADOW	HERMAN
GARTH	LUCIA
MIRIAMNE	PINY
ESDRAS	A SAILOR
THE HOBO	STREET URCHIN
FIRST GIRL	POLICEMAN
SECOND GIRL	RADICAL
JUDGE GAUNT	SERGEANT
MIO	

Non-speaking

URCHINS	TWO MEN IN BLUE SERGE

WINTERSET

ACT ONE

SCENE I

SCENE: *The scene is the bank of a river under a bridgehead. A gigantic span starts from the rear of the stage and appears to lift over the heads of the audience and out to the left. At the right rear is a wall of solid supporting masonry. To the left an apartment building abuts against the bridge and forms the left wall of the stage with a dark basement window and a door in the brick wall. To the right, and in the foreground, an outcropping of original rock makes a barricade behind which one may enter through a cleft. To the rear, against the masonry, two sheds have been built by waifs and strays for shelter. The river bank, in the foreground, is black rock worn smooth by years of trampling. There is room for exit and entrance to the left around the apartment house, also around the rock to the right. A single street lamp is seen at the left—and a glimmer of apartment lights in the background beyond. It is an early, dark December morning.*

Two Young Men in Serge lean against the masonry, matching bills. Trock Estrella and Shadow come in from the left.

TROCK. Go back and watch the car. (*The TWO YOUNG MEN go out.* TROCK *walks to the corner and looks toward the city.*)
You roost of punks and gulls! Sleep it off,
whatever you had last night, get down in warm,
one big ham-fat against another—sleep,
cling, sleep and rot! Rot out your pasty guts
with diddling, you had no brain to begin.
  If you had
there'd be no need for us to sleep on iron
who had too much brains for you.

SHADOW. Now look, Trock, look,
what would the warden say to talk like that?

TROCK. May they die as I die!
By God, what life they've left me
they shall keep me well! I'll have that out of them—
these pismires that walk like men!

SHADOW. Because, look, chief,
it's all against science and penology
for you to get out and begin to cuss that way
before your prison vittles are out of you.
  Hell,
you're supposed to leave the pen full of high thought,
kind of noble-like, loving toward all mankind,
ready to kiss their feet—or whatever parts
they stick out toward you. Look at me!

TROCK. I see you.
And even you may not live as long as you think.

You think too many things are funny. Well, laugh.
But it's not so funny.

SHADOW. Come on, Trock, you know me.
Anything you say goes, but give me leave
to kid a little.

TROCK. Then laugh at somebody else!
It's a lot safer! They've soaked me once too often
in that vat of poisoned hell they keep up-state
to soak men in, and I'm rotten inside, I'm all
one liquid puke inside where I had lungs
once, like yourself! And now they want to get me
and stir me in again—and that'd kill me—
and that's fine for them. But before that happens to me
a lot of these healthy boys'll know what it's like
when you try to breathe and have no place to put air—
they'll learn it from me!

SHADOW. They've got nothing on you, chief.

TROCK. I don't know yet. That's what I'm here to find out.
If they've got what they might have
it's not a year this time—
no, nor ten. It's screwed down under a lid.—
I can die quick enough, without help.

SHADOW. You're the skinny kind
that lives forever.

2

TROCK. He gave me a half a year,
the doc at the gate.

SHADOW. Jesus.

TROCK. Six months I get,
and the rest's dirt, six feet. (LUCIA, *the street-piano man, comes in right from behind the rock and goes to the shed where he keeps his piano.* PINY, *the apple woman, follows and stands in the entrance.* LUCIA *speaks to Estrella, who still stands facing Shadow.*)

LUCIA. Morning. (TROCK *and* SHADOW *go out round the apartment house without speaking.*)

PINY. Now what would you call them?

LUCIA. Maybe someting da river washed up.

PINY. Nothing ever washed him—that black one.

LUCIA. Maybe not, maybe so. More like his pa and ma raise-a heem in da cellar .(*He wheels out the piano.*)

PINY. He certainly gave me a turn. (*She lays a hand on the rock.*)

LUCIA. You don' live-a right, ol' gal. Take heem easy. Look on da bright-a side. Never say-a die. Me, every day in every way I getta be da regular heller. (*He starts out.*)

CURTAIN

SCENE II

SCENE: *A cellar apartment under the apartment building, floored with cement and roofed with huge boa constrictor pipes that run slantwise from left to right, dwarfing the room. An outside door opens to the left and a door at the right rear leads to the interior of the place. A low squat window to the left. A table at the rear and a few chairs and books make up the furniture.* GARTH, *son of* ESDRAS, *sits alone, holding a violin upside down to inspect a crack at its base. He lays the bow on the floor and runs his fingers over the joint.* MIRIAMNE *enters from the rear, a girl of fifteen.* GARTH *looks up, then down again.*

MIRIAMNE. Garth—

GARTH. The glue lets go. It's the steam, I
    guess.
It splits the hair on your head.

MIRIAMNE. It can't be mended?

GARTH. I can't mend it.
No doubt there are fellows somewhere
who'd mend it for a dollar—and glad to
    do it.
That is if I had a dollar.—Got a dollar?
No, I thought not.

MIRIAMNE. Garth, you've sat at home here
three days now. You haven't gone out at all.
Something frightens you.

GARTH. Yes?

MIRIAMNE. And father's frightened.
He reads without knowing where. When a
    shadow falls
across the page he waits for a blow to follow
after the shadow. Then in a little while
he puts his book down softly and goes out
to see who passed.

GARTH. A bill collector, maybe.
We haven't paid the rent.

MIRIAMNE. No.

GARTH. You're a bright girl, sis.—
You see too much. You run along and cook.
Why don't you go to school?

MIRIAMNE. I don't like school.
They whisper behind my back.

GARTH. Yes? About what?

MIRIAMNE. What did the lawyer mean
that wrote to you?

GARTH (*rising*). What lawyer?

MIRIAMNE. I found a letter
on the floor of your room. He said, "Don't
    get me wrong,
but stay in out of the rain the next few days,
just for instance."

GARTH. I thought I burned that letter.

MIRIAMNE. Afterward you did. And then
    what was printed
about the Estrella gang—you hid it from me,

you and father. What is it—about this murder—?

GARTH. Will you shut up, you fool!

MIRIAMNE. But if you know
why don't you tell them, Garth?
If it's true—what they say—
you knew all the time Romagna wasn't
guilty,
and could have said so—

GARTH. Everybody knew
Romagna wasn't guilty! But they weren't
listening
to evidence in his favor. They didn't want it.
They don't want it now.

MIRIAMNE. But was that why
they never called on you?—

GARTH. So far as I know
they never'd heard of me—and I can assure
you
I knew nothing about it—

MIRIAMNE. But something's wrong—
and it worries father—

GARTH. What could be wrong?

MIRIAMNE. I don't know. (*A pause.*)

GARTH. And I don't know. You're a good
kid, Miriamne,
but you see too many movies. I wasn't
mixed up
in any murder, and I don't mean to be.
If I had a dollar to get my fiddle fixed
and another to hire a hall, by God I'd fiddle
some of the prodigies back into Sunday
School
where they belong, but I won't get either,
and so
I sit here and bite my nails—but if you
hoped
I had some criminal romantic past
you'll have to look again!

MIRIAMNE. Oh, Garth, forgive me—
But I want you to be so far above such
things
nothing could frighten you. When you seem
to shrink
and be afraid, and you're the brother I
love,
I want to run there and cry, if there's any
question
they care to ask, you'll be quick and glad
to answer,
for there's nothing to conceal!

GARTH. And that's all true—

MIRIAMNE. But then I remember—
how you dim the lights—
and we go early to bed—and speak in
whispers—
and I could think there's a death somewhere
behind us—
an evil death—

GARTH (*hearing a step*). Now for God's
sake, be quiet! (ESDRAS, *an old rabbi with
a kindly face, enters from the outside. He
is hurried and troubled.*)

ESDRAS. I wish to speak alone with someone
here
if I may have this room. Miriamne—

MIRIAMNE (*turning to go*). Yes, father.
(*The outer door is suddenly thrown open.*
TROCK *appears.*)

TROCK (*after a pause*). You'll excuse me
for not knocking. (SHADOW *follows* TROCK
in.)
Sometimes it's best to come in quiet. Sometimes
it's a good way to go out. Garth's home,
I see.
He might not have been here if I made a
point
of knocking at doors.

GARTH. How are you, Trock?

TROCK. I guess
you can see how I am.
(*To* MIRIAMNE). Stay here. Stay where you
are.
We'd like to make your acquaintance.
—If you want the facts
I'm no better than usual, thanks. Not
enough sun,
my physician tells me. Too much close confinement.
A lack of exercise and an overplus
of beans in the diet. You've done well, no
doubt?

GARTH. I don't know what makes you think
so.

TROCK. Who's the family?

GARTH. My father and my sister.

TROCK. Happy to meet you.
Step inside a minute. The boy and I
have something to talk about.

ESDRAS. No, no—he's said nothing—
nothing, sir, nothing!

TROCK. When I say go out, you go—

ESDRAS (*pointing to the door*). Miriamne—

GARTH. Go on out, both of you!

ESDRAS. Oh, sir—I'm old—
old and unhappy—

GARTH. Go on! (MIRIAMNE *and* ESDRAS *go inside.*)

TROCK. And if you listen
I'll riddle that door! (SHADOW *shuts the door behind them and stands against it.*)
I just got out, you see,
and I pay my first call on you.

GARTH. Maybe you think
I'm not in the same jam you are.

TROCK. That's what I do think.
Who started looking this up?

GARTH. I wish I knew,
and I wish he was in hell! Some damned professor
with nothing else to do. If you saw his stuff
you know as much as I do.

TROCK. It wasn't you
turning state's evidence?

GARTH. Hell, Trock, use your brain!
The case was closed. They burned Romagna for it
and that finished it. Why should I look for trouble
and maybe get burned myself?

TROCK. Boy, I don't know,
but I just thought I'd find out.

GARTH. I'm going straight, Trock.
I can play this thing, and I'm trying to make a living.
I haven't talked and nobody's talked to me.
Christ—it's the last thing I'd want!

TROCK. Your old man knows.

GARTH. That's where I got the money that last time
when you needed it. He had a little saved up,
but I had to tell him to get it. He's as safe
as Shadow there.

TROCK (*looking at Shadow*). There could be people safer
than that son-of-a-bitch.

SHADOW. Who?

TROCK. You'd be safer dead
along with some other gorillas.

SHADOW. It's beginning to look
as if you'd feel safer with everybody dead,
the whole god-damn world.

TROCK. I would. These Jesus-bitten
professors! Looking up their half-ass cases!
We've got enough without that.

GARTH. There's no evidence
to reopen the thing.

TROCK. And suppose they called on you
and asked you to testify?

GARTH. Why then I'd tell 'em
that all I know is what I read in the papers.
And I'd stick to that.

TROCK. How much does your sister know?

GARTH. I'm honest with you, Trock. She read my name
in the professor's pamphlet, and she was scared
the way anybody would be. She got nothing
from me, and anyway she's go to the chair
herself before she'd send me there.

TROCK. Like hell.

GARTH. Besides, who wants to go to trial again
except the radicals?—You and I won't spill
and unless we did there's nothing to take to court
as far as I know. Let the radicals go on howling
about getting a dirty deal. They always howl
and nobody gives a damn. This professor's red—
everybody knows it.

TROCK. You're forgetting the judge.
Where's the damn judge?

GARTH. What judge?

TROCK. Read the morning papers.
It says Judge Gaunt's gone off his nuts. He's got

that damn trial on his mind, and been going
round
proving to everybody he was right all the
time
and the radicals were guilty—stopping
people
in the street to prove it—and now he's nuts
entirely
and nobody knows where he is.

GARTH. Why don't they know?

TROCK. Because he's on the loose somewhere!
They've got the police of three cities looking
for him.

GARTH. Judge Gaunt?

TROCK. Yes. Judge Gaunt.

SHADOW. Why should that worry you?
He's crazy, ain't he? And even if he wasn't
he's arguing on your side. You're jittery,
chief.
God, all the judges are looney. You've got
the jitters,
and you'll damn well give yourself away
some time
peeing yourself in public. (TROCK *half turns
toward* SHADOW *in anger.*)
Don't jump the gun now,
I've got pockets in my clothes, too. (*His
hand is in his coat pocket.*)

TROCK. All right. Take it easy. (*He takes
his hand from his pocket, and* SHADOW *does
the same.*) (*To* GARTH)
Maybe you're lying to me and maybe you're
not.
Stay at home a few days.

GARTH. Sure thing. Why not?

TROCK. And when I say stay at home I
mean stay home.
If I have to go looking for you you'll stay
a long time
wherever I find you. (*To* SHADOW)
Come on. We'll get out of here. (*To* GARTH)
Be seeing you. (SHADOW *and* TROCK *go out.
After a pause* GARTH *walks over to his chair
and picks up the violin. Then he puts it
down and goes to the inside door, which he
opens.*)

GARTH. He's gone. (MIRIAMNE *enters,* ESDRAS
behind her.)

MIRIAMNE (*going up to* GARTH.) Let's not
stay here. (*She puts her hands on his
arms.*)

I thought he'd come for something—horrible.
Is he coming back?

GARTH. I don't know.

MIRIAMNE. Who is he, Garth?

GARTH. He'd kill me if I told you who he is,
that is, if he knew.

MIRIAMNE. Then don't say it—

GARTH. Yes, and I'll say it! I was with a
gang one time
that robbed a pay roll. I saw murder done,
and Trock Estrella did it. If that got out
I'd go to the chair and so would he—that's
why
he was here today—

MIRIAMNE. But that's not true—

ESDRAS. He says it
to frighten you, child.

GARTH. Oh, no I don't! I say it
because I've held it in too long! I'm damned
if I sit here forever, and look at the door,
waiting for Trock with his sub-machine gun,
waiting
for police with a warrant!—I say I'm damned, and I am,
no matter what I do! These piddling scales
on a violin—first position, third, fifth,
arpeggios in E—and what I'm thinking
is Romagna dead for the murder—dead
while I sat here
dying inside—dead for the thing Trock did
while I looked on—and I could have saved
him, yes—
but I sat here and let him die instead of me
because I wanted to live! Well, it's no life,
and it doesn't matter who I tell, because
I mean to get it over!

MIRIAMNE. Garth, it's not true!

GARTH. I'd take some scum down with me
if I died—
that'd be one good deed—

ESDRAS. Son, son, you're mad—
someone will hear—

GARTH. Then let them hear! I've lived
with ghosts too long, and lied too long.
God damn you
if you keep me from the truth!—(*He turns
away.*)

Oh, God damn the world!
I don't want to die! (*He throws himself
down.*)

ESDRAS. I should have known.
I thought you hard and sullen,
Garth, my son. And you were a child, and
   hurt
with a wound that might be healed.
—All men have crimes,
and most of them are hidden, and many
   are heavy
as yours must be to you. (GARTH *sobs.*)
They walk the streets
to buy and sell, but a spreading crimson
   stain
tinges the inner vestments, touches flesh,
and burns the quick. You're not alone.

GARTH. I'm alone
in this.

ESDRAS. Yes, if you hold with the world that
   only
those who die suddenly should be revenged.
But those whose hearts are cancered, drop
   by drop
in small ways, little by little, till they've
   borne
all they can bear, and die—these deaths will
   go
unpunished now as always. When we're
   young
we have faith in what is seen, but when
   we're old
we know that what is seen is traced in air
and built on water. There's no guilt under
   heaven,
just as there's no heaven, till men believe it—
no earth, till men have seen it, and have a
   word
to say this is the earth.

GARTH. Well, I say there's an earth,
and I say I'm guilty on it, guilty as hell.

ESDRAS. Yet till it's known you bear no guilt
   at all—
unless you wish. The days go by like film,
like a long written scroll, a figured veil
unrolling out of darkness into fire
and utterly consumed. And on this veil,
running in sounds and symbols of men's
   minds

reflected back, life flickers and is shadow
going toward flame. Only what men can see
exists in that shadow. Why must you rise
   and cry out:
That was I, there in the ravelled tapestry,
there, in that pistol flash, when the man was
   killed.
I was there, and was one, and am bloodstained!
Let the wind
and fire take that hour to ashes out of time
and out of mind! This thing that men call
   justice,
this blind snake that strikes men down in
   the dark,
mindless with fury, keep your hand back
   from it,
pass by in silence—let it be forgotten, forgotten!—
Oh, my son, my son—have pity!

MIRIAMNE. But if it was true
and someone died—then it was more than
   shadow—
and it doesn't blow away—

GARTH. Well, it was true.

ESDRAS. Say it if you must. If you have heart
   to die,
say it, and let them take what's left—there
   was little
to keep, even before—

GARTH. Oh, I'm a coward—
I always was. I'll be quiet and live. I'll live
even if I have to crawl. I know. (*He gets
up and goes into the inner room.*)

MIRIAMNE. Is it better
to tell a lie and live?

ESDRAS. Yes, child. It's better.

MIRIAMNE. But if I had to do it—
I think I'd die.

ESDRAS. Yes, child. Because you're young.

MIRIAMNE. Is that the only reason?

ESDRAS. The only reason.

CURTAIN

SCENE III

SCENE: *Under the bridge, evening of the same day. When the curtain rises* MIRIAMNE *is sitting alone on the ledge at the rear of the apartment house. A spray of light fall on her from a street lamp above. She shivers a little in her thin coat, but sits still as if heedless of the weather. Through the rocks on the other side a* TRAMP *comes down to the river bank, hunting a place to sleep. He goes softly to the apple-woman's hut and looks in, then turns away, evidently not daring to preempt it. He looks at* MIRIAMNE *doubtfully. The door of the street-piano man is shut. The vagabond passes it and picks carefully among some rags and shavings to the right.* MIRIAMNE *looks up and sees him but makes no sign. She looks down again, and the man curls himself up in a makeshift bed in the corner, pulling a piece of sacking over his shoulders.* TWO GIRLS *come in from round the apartment house.*

FIRST GIRL. Honest, I never heard of anything so romantic. Because you never liked him.

SECOND GIRL. I certainly never did.

FIRST GIRL. You've got to tell me how it happened. You've got to.

SECOND GIRL. I couldn't. As long as I live I couldn't. Honest, it was terrible. It was terrible.

FIRST GIRL. What was so terrible?

SECOND GIRL. The way it happened.

FIRST GIRL. Oh, please—not to a soul, never.

SECOND GIRL. Well, you know how I hated him because he had such a big mouth. So he reached over and grabbed me, and I began all falling to pieces inside, the way you do—and I said, "Oh no you don't, mister," and started screaming and kicked a hole through the windshield and lost a shoe, and he let go and was cursing and growling because he borrowed the car and didn't have money to pay for the windshield, and he started to cry, and I got so sorry for him I let him, and now he wants to marry me.

FIRST GIRL. Honest, I never heard of anything so romantic! (*She sees the sleeping Tramp.*) My God, what you won't see! (*They give the Tramp a wide berth, and go out right. The* TRAMP *sits up looking about him.* JUDGE GAUNT, *an elderly, quiet man, well dressed but in clothes that have seen some weather, comes in uncertainly from the left. He holds a small clipping in his hand and goes up to the* HOBO.)

GAUNT (*tentatively*). Your pardon, sir. Your

pardon, but perhaps you can tell me the name of this street.

HOBO. Huh?

GAUNT. The name of this street?

HOBO. This ain't no street.

GAUNT. There, where the street lamps are.

HOBO. That's the alley.

GAUNT. Thank you. It has a name, no doubt?

HOBO. That's the alley.

GAUNT. I see. I won't trouble you. You wonder why I ask, I daresay.—I'm a stranger.—Why do you look at me? (*He steps back.*) I—I'm not the man you think. You've mistaken me, sir.

HOBO. Huh?

JUDGE. Perhaps misled by a resemblance. But you're mistaken—I had an errand in this city. It's only by accident that I'm here—

HOBO (*muttering*). You go to hell.

JUDGE (*going nearer to him, bending over him*). Yet why should I deceive you? Before God, I held the proofs in my hands. I hold them still. I tell you the defense was cunning beyond belief, and unscrupulous in its use of propaganda—they gagged at nothing—not even—(*He rises.*) No, no—I'm sorry—this will hardly interest you. I'm sorry. I have an errand. (*He looks toward the street.* ESDRAS *enters from the basement and goes to* MIRIAMNE. *The* JUDGE *steps back into the shadows.*)

ESDRAS. Come in, my daughter. You'll be cold here.

MIRIAMNE. After a while.

ESDRAS. You'll be cold. There's a storm coming.

MIRIAMNE. I didn't want him to see me crying. That was all.

ESDRAS. I know.

MIRIAMNE. I'll come soon. (ESDRAS *turns reluctantly and goes out the way he came.* MIRIAMNE *rises to go, pausing to dry her eyes.* MIO *and* CARR, *road boys of seventeen or so, come round the apartment house. The* JUDGE *has disappeared.*)

CARR. Thought you said you were never coming east again.

MIO. Yeah, but—I heard something changed my mind.

CARR. Same old business?

MIO. Yes. Just as soon not talk about it.

CARR. Where did you go from Portland?

MIO. Fishing—I went fishing. God's truth.

CARR. Right after I left?

MIO. Fell in with a fisherman's family on the coast and went after the beautiful mackerel fish that swim in the beautiful sea. Family of Greeks—Aristides Marinos was his lovely name. He sang while he fished. Made the pea-green Pacific ring with his bastard Greek chanties. Then I went to Hollywood High School for a while.

CARR. I'll bet that's a seat of learning.

MIO. It's the hind end of all wisdom. They kicked me out after a time.

CARR. For cause?

MIO. Because I had no permanent address, you see. That means nobody's paying school taxes for you, so out you go. (*To* MIRIAMNE.) What's the matter, kid?

MIRIAMNE. Nothing. (*She looks up at him, and they pause for a moment.*) Nothing.

MIO. I'm sorry.

MIRIAMNE. It's all right. (*She withdraws her eyes from his and goes out past him. He turns and looks after her.*)

CARR. Control your chivalry.

MIO. A pretty kid.

CARR. A baby.

MIO. Wait for me.

CARR. Be a long wait? (MIO *steps swiftly out after* MIRIAMNE, *then returns.*) Yeah?

MIO. She's gone.

CARR. Think of that.

MIO. No, but I mean—vanished. Presto—into nothing—prodigioso.

CARR. Damn good thing, if you ask me. The homely ones are bad enough, but the lookers are fatal.

MIO. You exaggerate, Carr.

CARR. I doubt it.

MIO. Well, let her go. This river bank's loaded with typhus rats, too. Might as well die one death as another.

CARR. They say chronic alcoholism is nice but expensive. You can always starve to death.

MIO. Not always. I tried it. After the second day I walked thirty miles to Niagara Falls and made a tour of the plant to get the sample of shredded wheat biscuit on the way out.

CARR. Last time I saw you you couldn't think of anything you wanted to do except curse God and pass out. Still feeling low?

MIO. Not much different. (*He turns away, then comes back.*) Talk about the lost generation, I'm the only one fits that title. When the State executes your father and your mother dies of grief, and you know damn well he was innocent, and the authorities of your home town politely inform you they'd consider it a favor if you lived somewhere else—that cuts you off from the world—with a meat-axe.

CARR. They asked you to move?

MIO. It came to that.

CARR. God, that was white of them.

MIO. It probably gave them a headache just to see me after all that agitation. They knew as well as I did my father never staged a hold-up. Anyway, I've got a new interest in life now.

CARR. Yes—I saw her.

MIO. I don't mean the skirt.—No, I got wind of something, out west, some college professor investigating the trial and turning up new evidence. Couldn't find anything he'd written out there, so I beat it east and arrived on this blessed island just in time to find the bums holing up in the public library for the winter. I know now what the unemployed have been doing since the depression started. They've been catching up on their reading in the main reference room. Man, what a stench! Maybe I stank, too, but a hobo has the stench of ten because his shoes are poor.

CARR. Tennyson.

MIO. Right. Jeez, I'm glad we met up again! Never knew anybody else that could track me through the driven snow of Victorian literature.

CARR. Now you're cribbing from some half-forgotten criticism of Ben Jonson's Roman plagiarisms.

MIO. Where did you get your education, sap?

CARR. Not in the public library, sap. My father kept a news-stand.

MIO. Well, you're right again. (*There is a faint rumble of thunder.*) What's that? Winter thunder?

CARR. Or Mister God, beating on His little tocsin. Maybe announcing the advent of a new social order.

MIO. Or maybe it's going to rain coffee and doughnuts.

CARR. Or maybe it's going to rain.

MIO. Seems more likely. (*Lowering his voice.*) Anyhow, I found Professor Hobhouse's discussion of the Romagna case. I think he has something. It occurred to me I might follow it up by doing a little sleuthing on my own account.

CARR. Yes?

MIO. I have done a little. And it leads me to somewhere in that tenement house that backs up against the bridge. That's how I happen to be here.

CARR. They'll never let you get anywhere with it, Mio. I told you that before.

MIO. I know you did.

CARR. The State can't afford to admit it was wrong, you see. Not when there's been that much of a row kicked up over it. So for all practical purposes the State was right and your father robbed the pay roll.

MIO. There's still such a thing as evidence.

CARR. It's something you can buy. In fact, at the moment I don't think of anything you can't buy, including life, honor, virtue, glory, public office, conjugal affection and all kinds of justice, from the traffic court to the immortal nine. Go out and make yourself a pot of money and you can buy all the justice you want. Convictions obtained, convictions averted. Lowest rates in years.

MIO. I know all that.

CARR. Sure.

MIO. This thing didn't happen to you.
They've left you your name
and whatever place you can take. For my heritage
they've left me one thing only, and that's to be
my father's voice crying up out of the earth
and quicklime where they stuck him. Electrocution
doesn't kill, you know. They eviscerate them
with a turn of the knife in the dissecting room.
The blood spurts out. The man was alive. Then into
the lime pit, leave no trace. Make it short shrift
and chemical dissolution. That's what they thought
of the man that was my father. Then my mother—
I tell you these county burials are swift
and cheap and run for profit! Out of the house
and into the ground, you wife of a dead dog. Wait,
here's some Romagna spawn left.
Something crawls here—
something they called a son. Why couldn't he die
along with his mother? Well, ease him out of town,
ease him out, boys, and see you're not too gentle.
He might come back. And, by their own living Jesus,

I will go back, and hang the carrion
around their necks that made it!
Maybe I can sleep then.
Or even live.

CARR. You have to try it?

MIO. Yes.
Yes. It won't let me alone. I've tried to live
and forget it—but I was birthmarked with
    hot iron
into the entrails. I've got to find out who
    did it
and make them see it till it scalds their eyes
and make them admit it till their tongues
    are blistered
with saying how black they lied! (HERMAN,
a gawky shoe salesman, enters from the left.)

HERMAN. Hello. Did you see a couple of girls
go this way?

CARR. Couple of girls? Did we see a couple
of girls?

MIO. No.

CARR. No. No girls. (HERMAN *hesitates, then
goes out right.* LUCIA *comes in from the
left, trundling his piano.* PINY *follows him,
weeping.*)

PINY. They've got no right to do it—

LUCIA. All right, hell what, no matter, I
got to put him away, I got to put him away,
that's what the hell! (TWO STREET URCHINS
follow him in.)

PINY. They want everybody on the relief
rolls and nobody making a living?

LUCIA. The cops, they do what the big boss
says. The big boss, that's the mayor, he says
he heard it once too often, the sextette—

PINY. They want graft, that's all. It's a new
way to get graft—

LUCIA. Oh, no, no, no! He's a good man,
the mayor. He's just don't care for music,
that's all.

PINY. Why shouldn't you make a living on
the street? The National Biscuit Company
ropes off Eighth Avenue—and does the
mayor do anything? No, the police hit you
over the head if you try to go through!

LUCIA. You got the big dough, you get the
pull, fine. No big dough, no pull, what the
hell, get off the city property! Tomorrow I

start cooking chestnuts . . . (*He strokes
the piano fondly. The* TWO GIRLS *and* HER-
MAN *comes back from the right.*) She's a
good little machine, this baby. Cost plenty—
and two new records I only played twice.
See, this one. (*He starts turning the crank,
talking while he plays.*) Two weeks since
they play this one in a picture house. (A
SAILOR *wanders in from the left. One of
the* STREET URCHINS *begins suddenly to
dance a wild rumba, the others watch.*)
Good boy—see, it's a lulu—it itches in the
feet! (HERMAN, *standing with his girl, tosses
the boy a penny. He bows and goes on dancing; the other* URCHIN *joins him. The* SAILOR
tosses a coin.)

SAILOR. Go it, Cuba! Go it! (LUCIA *turns the
crank, beaming.*)

SECOND GIRL. Oh, Herman! (*She throws her
arms round* HERMAN *and they dance.*)

FIRST URCHIN. Hey, pipe the professionals!

FIRST GIRL. Do your glide, Shirley! Do your
glide!

LUCIA. Maybe we can't play in front, maybe
we can play behind! (*The* HOBO *gets up from
his nest and comes over to watch. A* YOUNG
RADICAL *wanders in.*) Maybe you don't
know, folks! Tonight we play good-bye to
the piano! Good-bye forever! No more
piano on the streets! No more music! No
more money for the music-man! Last time,
folks! Good-bye to the piano—good-bye
forever! (MIRIAMNE *comes out the rear
door of the apartment and stands watching. The* SAILOR *goes over to the* FIRST GIRL
and they dance together.) Maybe you don't
know, folks! Tomorrow will be sad as
hell, tonight we dance! Tomorrow no more
Verdi, no more rumba, no more good time!
Tonight we play good-bye to the piano,
good-bye forever! (*The* RADICAL *edges up
to* MIRIAMNE, *and asks her to dance. She
shakes her head and he goes to* PINY, *who
dances with him. The* HOBO *begins to do
a few lonely curvets on the side above.*)
Hoy! Hoy! Pick 'em up and take 'em
around! Use the head, use the feet! Last
time forever! (*He begins to sing to the air.*)

MIO. Wait for me, will you?

CARR. Now's your chance. (MIO *goes over to
MIRIAMNE and holds out a hand, smiling.
She stands for a moment uncertain, then*

dances with him. ESDRAS *comes out to watch.* JUDGE GAUNT *comes in from the left. There is a rumble of thunder.*)

LUCIA. Hoy! Hoy! Maybe it rains tonight, maybe it snows tomorrow! Tonight we dance good-bye. (*He sings the air lustily. A* POLICEMAN *comes in from the left and looks on. Two or three* PEDESTRIANS *follow him.*)

POLICEMAN. Hey you! (LUCIA *goes on singing.*)Hey, you!

LUCIA (*still playing*). What you want?

POLICEMAN. Sign off!

LUCIA. What you mean? I get off the street!

POLICEMAN. Sign off!

LUCIA (*still playing*). What you mean? (*The* POLICEMAN *walks over to him.* LUCIA *stops playing and the* DANCERS *pause.*)

POLICEMAN. Cut it.

LUCIA. Is this a street?

POLICEMAN. I say cut it out. (*The* HOBO *goes back to his nest and sits in it, watching.*)

LUCIA. It's the last time. We dance good-bye to the piano.

POLICEMAN. You'll dance good-bye to something else if I catch you cranking that thing again.

LUCIA. All right.

PINY. I'll bet you don't say that to the National Biscuit Company!

POLICEMAN. Lady, you've been selling apples on my beat for some time now, and I said nothing about it—

PINY. Selling apples is allowed—

POLICEMAN. You watch yourself—(*He takes a short walk around the place and comes upon the* HOBO.) What are you doing here? (*The* HOBO *opens his mouth, points to it, and shakes his head.*) Oh, you are, are you? (*He comes back to* LUCIA.) So you trundle your so-called musical instrument to wherever you keep it, and don't let me hear it again. (*The* RADICAL *leaps on the base of the rock at right. The* FIRST GIRL *turns away from the* SAILOR *toward the* SECOND GIRL *and* HERMAN.)

SAILOR. Hey, captain, what's the matter with the music?

POLICEMAN. Not a thing, admiral.

SAILOR. Well, we had a little party going here—

POLICEMAN. I'll say you did.

SECOND GIRL. Please, officer, we want to dance.

POLICEMAN. Go ahead. Dance.

SECOND GIRL. But we want music!

POLICEMAN (*turning to go*). Sorry. Can't help you.

RADICAL. And there you see it, the perfect example of capitalistic oppression! In a land where music should be free as air and the arts should be encouraged, a uniformed minion of the rich, a guardian myrmidon of the Park Avenue pleasure hunters, steps in and puts a limit on the innocent enjoyments of the poor! We don't go to theatres! Why not? We can't afford it! We don't go to night clubs, where women dance naked and the music drips from saxophones and leaks out of Rudy Vallee—we can't afford that either!—But we might at least dance on the river bank to the strains of a barrel organ—! (GARTH *comes out of the apartment and listens.*)

POLICEMAN. It's against the law!

RADICAL. What law? I challenge you to tell me what law of God or man—what ordinance—is violated by this spontaneous diversion? None! I say none! An official whim of the masters who should be our servants!—

POLICEMAN. Get down! Get down and shut up!

RADICAL. By what law, by what ordinance do you order me to be quiet?

POLICEMAN. Speaking without a flag. You know it.

RADICAL (*pulling out a small American flag*). There's my flag! There's the flag of this United States which used to guarantee the rights of man—the rights of man now violated by every third statute of the commonweal—

POLICEMAN. Don't try to pull tricks on me! I've seen you before! You're not making any speech, and you're climbing down—

JUDGE GAUNT (*who has come quietly forward*). One moment, officer. There is some difference of opinion even on the bench as to the elasticity of police power when applied in minor emergencies to preserve civil order. But the weight of authority would certainly favor the defendant in any equable court, and he would be upheld in his demand to be heard.

POLICEMAN. Who are you?

JUDGE GAUNT. Sir, I am not accustomed to answer that question.

POLICEMAN. I don't know you.

GAUNT. I am a judge of some standing, not in your city, but in another with similar statutes. You are aware, of course, that the bill of rights is not to be set aside lightly by the officers of any municipality—

POLICEMAN (*looking over GAUNT's somewhat bedraggled costume*). Maybe they understand you better in the town you come from, but I don't get your drift.— (*To the* RADICAL.) I don't want any trouble, but if you ask for it you'll get plenty. Get down!

RADICAL. I'm not asking for trouble, but I'm staying right here. (*The* POLICEMAN *moves toward him.*)

GAUNT (*taking the policeman's arm, but shaken off roughly*). I ask this for yourself, truly, not for the dignity of the law nor the maintenance of precedent. Be gentle with them when their threats are childish—be tolerant while you can—for your harsh word will return on you in the night—return in a storm of cries!—(*He takes the* POLICEMAN's *arm again.*) Whatever they may have said or done, let them disperse in peace! It is better that they go softly, lest when they are dead you see their eyes pleading, and their outstretched hands touch you, fingering cold on your heart!—I have been harsher than you. I have sent men down that long corridor into blinding light and blind darkness! (*He suddenly draws himself erect and speaks defiantly.*) And it was well that I did so! I have been an upright judge! They are all liars! Liars!

POLICEMAN (*shaking* GAUNT *off so that he falls*). Why, you fool, you're crazy!

GAUNT. Yes, and there are liars on the force! They came to me with their shifty lies! (*He catches at the* POLICEMAN, *who pushes him away with his foot.*)

POLICEMAN. You think I've got nothing better to do than listen to a crazy fool?

FIRST GIRL. Shame, shame!

POLICEMAN. What have I got to be ashamed of? And what's going on here, anyway? Where in hell did you all come from?

RADICAL. Tread on him! That's right! Tread down the poor and the innocent! (*There is a protesting murmur in the crowd.*)

SAILOR (*moving in a little*). Say, big boy, you don't have to step on the guy.

POLICEMAN (*facing them, stepping back*). What's the matter with you? I haven't stepped on anybody!

MIO (*at the right, across from the* POLICEMAN). Listen now, fellows, give the badge a chance.
He's doing his job, what he gets paid to do,
the same as any of you. They're all picked men,
these metropolitan police, hand picked
for loyalty and a fine up-standing pair
of shoulders on their legs—it's not so easy
to represent the law. Think what he does
for all of us, stamping out crime!
Do you want to be robbed and murdered in your beds?

SAILOR. What's eating you?

RADICAL. He must be a capitalist.

MIO. They pluck them fresh
from Ireland, and a paucity of headpiece
is a prime prerequisite. You from Ireland, buddy?

POLICEMAN (*surly*). Where are you from?

MIO. Buddy, I tell you flat
I wish I was from Ireland, and could boast
some Tammany connections. There's only one drawback
about working on the force. It infects the brain,
it eats the cerebrum. There've been cases known,

fine specimens of manhood, too, where
    autopsies,
conducted in approved scientific fashion,
revealed conditions quite incredible
in policemen's upper layers. In some, a trace,
in others, when they've swung a stick too
    long,
there was nothing there!—but nothing! Oh,
    my friends,
this fine athletic figure of a man
that stands so grim before us, what will
    they find
when they saw his skull for the last in-
    spection?
I fear me a little puffball dust will blow
    away
rejoining earth, our mother—and this same
    dust,
this smoke, this ash on the wind, will re-
    present
all he had left to think with!

THE HOBO. Hooray! (*The* POLICEMAN *turns
on his heels and looks hard at the* HOBO, *who
slinks away.*)

POLICEMAN. Oh, yeah?

MIO. My theme
gives ears to the deaf and voice to the dumb!
    But now
forgive me if I say you were most unkind
in troubling the officer. He's a simple man
of simple tastes, and easily confused
when faced with complex issues. He may
    reflect
on returning home, that is, so far as he
is capable of reflection, and conclude
that he was kidded out of his uniform pants,
and in his fury when this dawns on him
may smack his wife down!

POLICEMAN. That'll be about enough from
you, too, professor!

MIO. May I say that I think you have
managed this whole situation rather badly,
from the beginning?—

POLICEMAN. You may not! (TROCK *slips in
from the background. The* TWO YOUNG MEN
IN SERGE *come with him.*)

MIO. Oh, but your pardon, sir! It's apparent
to the least competent among us that you
should have gone about your task more
subtly—the glove of velvet, the hand of iron,
and all that sort of thing—

POLICEMAN. Shut that hole in your face!

MIO. Sir, for that remark I shall be satisfied
with nothing less than an unconditional
apology! I have an old score to settle with
policemen, brother, because they're fools
and fat-heads, and you're one of the most
fatuous fat-heads that ever walked his feet
flat collecting graft! Tell that to your
sergeant back in the booby-hatch.

POLICEMAN. Oh, you want an apology, do
you? You'll get an apology out of the other
side of your mouth! (*He steps toward* MIO.
CARR *suddenly stands in his path.*) Get out
of my way! (*He pauses and looks round
him; the crowd looks less and less friendly.
He lays a hand on his gun and backs to a
position where there is nobody behind him.*)
Get out of here, all of you! Get out! What
are you trying to do—start a riot?

MIO. There now, that's better! That's in the
best police tradition. Incite a riot yourself
and then accuse the crowd.

POLICEMAN. It won't be pleasant if I decide
to let somebody have it! Get out! (*The onlookers begin to melt away. The* SAILOR *goes
out left with the* GIRLS *and* HERMAN. CARR
and MIO *go out right,* CARR *whistling "The
Star Spangled Banner." The* HOBO *follows
them. The* RADICAL *walks past with his head
in the air.* PINY *and* LUCIA *leave the piano
where it stands and slip away to the left. At
the end the* POLICEMAN *is left standing in the
center, the* JUDGE *near him.* ESDRAS *stands in
the doorway.* MIRIAMNE *is left sitting half
in shadow unseen by* ESDRAS.)

JUDGE GAUNT (*to the* POLICEMAN). Yes, but
should a man die, should it be necessary that
one man die for the good of many, make not
yourself the instrument of death, lest you
sleep to wake sobbing! Nay, it avails nothing
that you are the law—this delicate ganglion
that is the brain, it will not bear these
things—! (*The* POLICEMAN *gives the* JUDGE
*the once-over, shrugs, decides to leave him
there and starts out left.* GARTH *goes to his
father—a fine sleet begins to fall through the
street lights.* TROCK *is still visible.*)

GARTH. Get him in here, quick.

ESDRAS. Who, son?

GARTH. The Judge, damn him!

ESDRAS. Is it Judge Gaunt?

GARTH. Who did you think it was? He's crazy as a bedbug and telling the world. Get him inside! (*He looks round.*)

ESDRAS (*going up to* GAUNT). Will you come in, sir?

GAUNT. You will understand, sir. We old men know how softly we must proceed with these things.

ESDRAS. Yes, surely, sir.

GAUNT. It was always my practice—always. They will tell you that of me where I am known. Yet even I am not free of regret— even I. Would you believe it?

ESDRAS. I believe we are none of us free of regret.

GAUNT. None of us? I would it were true. I would I thought it were true.

ESDRAS. Shall we go in, sir? This is sleet that's falling.

GAUNT. Yes. Let us go in. (ESDRAS *and* GARTH *enter the basement and shut the door.* TROCK *goes out with his men. After a pause* MIO *comes back from the right, alone. He stands at a little distance from* MIRIAMNE.)

MIO. Looks like rain. (*She is silent.*)
You live around here? (*She nods gravely.*)
I guess
you thought I meant it—about waiting here
    to meet me. (*She nods again.*)
I'd forgotten about it till I got that winter
across the face. You'd better go inside.
I'm not your kind. I'm nobody's kind but
    my own.
I'm waiting for this to blow over. (*She rises.*)
I lied. I meant it—
I meant it when I said it—but there's too
    much black
whirling inside me—for any girl to know.
So go on in. You're somebody's angel child
and they're waiting for you.

MIRIAMNE. Yes. I'll go. (*She turns.*)

MIO. And tell them
when you get inside where it's warm,
and you love each other,
and mother comes to kiss her darling, tell
    them
to hang on to it while they can, believe while
    they can
it's a warm safe world, and Jesus finds his
    lambs

and carries them in his bosom.—I've seen
    some lambs
that Jesus missed. If they ever want the truth
tell them that nothing's guaranteed in this
    climate
except it gets cold in winter, nor on this
    earth
except you die sometime. (*He turns away.*)

MIRIAMNE. I have no mother.
And my people are Jews.

MIO. Then you know something about it.

MIRIAMNE. Yes.

MIO. Do you have enough to eat?

MIRIAMNE. Not always.

MIO. What do you believe in?

MIRIAMNE. Nothing.

MIO. Why?

MIRIAMNE. How can one?

MIO. It's easy if you're a fool. You see the
    words
in books. Honor, it says there, chivalry, free-
    dom,
heroism, enduring love—and these
are words on paper. It's something to have
    them there.
You'll get them nowhere else.

MIRIAMNE. What hurts you?

MIO. Just that.
You'll get them nowhere else.

MIRIAMNE. Why should you want them?

MIO. I'm alone, that's why. You see those
    lights,
along the river, cutting across the rain—?
those are the hearths of Brooklyn, and up
    this way
the love-nests of Manhattan—they turn their
    points
like knives against me—outcast of the world,
snake in the streets.—I don't want a hand-
    out.
I sleep and eat.

MIRIAMNE. Do you want me to go with
you?

MIO. Where?

MIRIAMNE. Where you go. (*A pause. He
goes nearer to her.*)

MIO. Why, you god-damned little fool—
what made you say that?

MIRIAMNE. I don't know.

MIO. If you have a home
stay in it. I ask for nothing. I've schooled
  myself
to ask for nothing, and take what I can get,
and get along. If I fell for you, that's my
  look-out,
and I'll starve it down.

MIRIAMNE. Wherever you go, I'd go.

MIO. What do you know about loving?
How could you know?
Have you ever had a man?

MIRIAMNE (after a slight pause). No. But I
  know.
Tell me your name.

MIO. Mio. What's yours?

MIRIAMNE. Miriamne.

MIO. There's no such name.

MIRIAMNE. But there's no such name as Mio!
M.I.O. It's no name.

MIO. It's for Bartolomeo.

MIRIAMNE. My mother's name was Miriam,
so they called me Miriamne.

MIO. Meaning little Miriam?

MIRIAMNE. Yes.

MIO. So now little Miriamne will go in
and take up quietly where she dropped them
  all
her small housewifely cares.—When I first
  saw you,
not a half-hour ago, I heard myself saying,
this is the face that launches ships for me—
and if I owned a dream—yes, half a dream—
we'd share it. But I have no dream. This
  earth
came tumbling down from chaos, fire and
  rock,
and bred up worms, blind worms that sting
  each other
here in the dark. These blind worms of the
  earth
took out my father—and killed him, and set
  a sign
on me—the heir of the serpent—and he was
  a man
such as men might be if the gods were
  men—

but they killed him—
as they'll kill all others like him
till the sun cools down to the stabler mole-
  cules,
yes, till men spin their tent-worm webs to
  the stars
and what they think is done, even in the
  thinking,
and they are the gods, and immortal, and
  constellations
turn from them all like mill wheels—still
  as they are
they will be, worms and blind. Enduring
  love,
oh gods and worms, what mockery!—And
  yet
I have blood enough in my veins. It goes
  like music,
singing, because you're here. My body turns
as if you were the sun, and warm. This men
  called love
in happier times, before the Freudians
  taught us
to blame it on the glands. Only go in
before you breathe too much of my atmosphere
and catch death from me.

MIRIAMNE. I will take my hands
and weave them to a little house, and there
you shall keep a dream—

MIO. God knows I could use a dream
and even a house.

MIRIAMNE. You're laughing at me, Mio!

MIO. The worms are laughing.
I tell you there's death about me
and you're a child! And I'm alone and
  half mad
with hate and longing. I shall let you love
  me
and love you in return, and then, why then
God knows what happens!

MIRIAMNE. Something most unpleasant?

MIO. Love in a box car—love among the
  children.
I've seen to much of it. Are we to live
in this same house you make with your two
  hands
mystically, out of air?

MIRIAMNE. No roof, no mortgage!
Well, I shall marry a banker out in Flatbush,
it gives hot bread in the morning! Oh, Mio,
  Mio,
in all the unwanted places and waste lands

that roll up into the darkness out of sun
and into sun out of darkness, there should
  be one empty
for you and me.

MIO. No.

MIRIAMNE. Then go now and leave me.
I'm only a girl you saw in the tenements,
and there's been nothing said.

MIO. Miriamne. (*She takes a step toward
him.*)

MIRIAMNE. Yes. (*He kisses her lips lightly.*)

MIO. Why, girl, the transfiguration on the
  mount
was nothing to your face. It lights from
  within—
a white chalice holding fire, a flower in
  flame,
this is your face.

MIRIAMNE. And you shall drink the flame
and never lessen it. And round your head
the aureole shall burn that burns there now,
forever. This I can give you. And so forever
the Freudians are wrong.

MIO. They're well-forgotten
at any rate.

MIRIAMNE. Why did you speak to me
when you first saw me?

MIO. I knew then.

MIRIAMNE. And I came back
because I must see you again. And we
  danced together
and my heart hurt me. Never, never, never,
though they should bind me down and tear
  out my eyes,
would I ever hurt you now. Take me with
  you, Mio,
let them look for us, whoever there is to
  look,
but we'll be away. (MIO *turns away toward
the tenement.*)

MIO. When I was four years old
we climbed through an iron gate, my mother
  and I,
to see my father in prison. He stood in the
  death-cell
and put his hand through the bars and said,
  My Mio,
I have only this to leave you, that I love you,
and will love you after I die. Love me then,
  Mio,

when this hard thing comes on you, that you
  must live
a man despised for your father. That night
  the guards,
walking in flood-lights brighter than high
  noon,
led him between them with his trousers slit
and a shaven head for the cathodes. This
  sleet and rain
that I feel cold here on my face and hands
will find him under thirteen years of clay
in prison ground. Lie still and rest, my
  father,
for I have not forgotten. When I forget
may I lie blind as you. No other love,
time passing, nor the spaced light-years of
  suns
shall blur your voice, or tempt me from the
  path
that clears your name—
till I have these rats in my grip
or sleep deep where you sleep. (*To* MIR-
IAMNE.)
I have no house,
nor home, nor love of life, nor fear of death,
nor care for what I eat, or who I sleep with,
or what color of calcimine the Government
will wash itself this year or next to lure
the sheep and feed the wolves. Love somewhere else,
and get your children in some other image
more acceptable to the State! This face of
  mine
is stamped for sewage! (*She steps back, sur-
mising.*)

MIRIAMNE. Mio—

MIO. My road is cut
in rock, and leads to one end. If I hurt you,
  I'm sorry.
One gets over hurts.

MIRIAMNE. What was his name—
your father's name?

MIO. Bartolomeo Romagna.
I'm not ashamed of it.

MIRIAMNE. Why are you here?

MIO. For the reason
I've never had a home. Because I'm a cry
out of a shallow grave, and all roads are
  mine
that might revenge him!

MIRIAMNE. But Mio—why here—why here?

MIO. I can't tell you that.

MIRIAMNE. No—but—there's someone
lives here—lives not far—and you mean to
see him—
you mean to ask him—(*She pauses.*)

MIO. Who told you that?

MIRIAMNE. His name
is Garth—Garth Esdras—

MIO (*after a pause, coming nearer*). Who are
you then? You seem
to know a good deal about me.—Were you
sent
to say this?

MIRIAMNE. You said there was death about
you! Yes,
but nearer than you think! Let it be as
it is—
let it all be as it is, never see this place
nor think of it—forget the streets you came
when you're away and safe! Go before
you're seen
or spoken to!

MIO. Will you tell me why?

MIRIAMNE. As I love you
I can't tell you—and I can never see you—

MIO. I walk where I please—

MIRIAMNE. Do you think it's easy for me
to send you away? (*She steps back as if to
go.*)

MIO. Where will I find you then
if I should want to see you?

MIRIAMNE. Never—I tell you
I'd bring you death! Even now. Listen!

(SHADOW *and* TROCK *enter between the
bridge and the tenement house.* MIRIAMNE
pulls MIO *back into the shadow of the rock
to avoid being seen.*)

TROCK. Why, fine.

SHADOW. You watch it now—just for the
record, Trock—
you're going to thank me for staying away
from it
and keeping you out. I've seen men get that
way,
thinking they had to plug a couple of guys
and then a few more to cover it up, and then
maybe a dozen more. You can't own all
and territory adjacent, and you can't
slough all the witnesses, because every man
you put away has friends—

TROCK. I said all right.
I said fine.

SHADOW. They're going to find this judge,
and if they find him dead it's just too bad,
and I don't want to know anything about
it—
and you don't either.

TROCK. You all through?

SHADOW. Why sure.

TROCK. All right.
We're through, too, you know.

SHADOW. Yeah? (*He becomes wary.*)

TROCK. Yeah, we're through.

SHADOW. I've heard that said before, and
afterwards
somebody died. (TROCK *is silent.*)
Is that what you mean?

TROCK. You can go.
I don't want to see you.

SHADOW. Sure, I'll go.
Maybe you won't mind if I just find out
what you've got on you. Before I turn my
back
I'd like to know. (*Silently and expertly he
touches* TROCK's *pockets, extracting a gun.*)
Not that I'd distrust you,
but you know how it is. (*He pockets the
gun.*)
So long, Trock.

TROCK. So long.

SHADOW. I won't talk.
You can be sure of that.

TROCK. I know you won't.

(SHADOW *turns and goes out right, past the
rock and along the bank. As he goes the
TWO YOUNG MEN IN BLUE SERGE enter from
the left and walk slowly after* SHADOW. *They
look toward* TROCK *as they enter and he
motions with his thumb in the direction
taken by* SHADOW. *They follow* SHADOW *out
without haste.* TROCK *watches them disappear, then slips out the way he came.* MIO
comes a step forward, looking after the TWO
MEN. *Two or three shots are heard, then
silence.* MIO *starts to run after* SHADOW.)

MIRIAMNE. Mio!

MIO. What do you know about this?

MIRIAMNE. The other way,
Mio—quick! (CARR *slips in from the right,
in haste.*)

CARR. Look, somebody's just been shot.
He fell in the river. The guys that did the
shooting
ran up the bank.

MIO. Come on.

(MIO *and* CARR *run out right.* MIRIAMNE
*watches uncertainly, then slowly turns and
walks to the rear door of the tenement. She
stands there a moment, looking after* MIO,
then goes in, closing the door. CARR *and* MIO
return.)

CARR. There's a rip tide past the point. You'd
never find him.

MIO. No.

CARR. You know a man ought to carry insurance living around here.—God, it's easy,
putting a fellow away. I never saw it done
before.

MIO (*looking at the place where* MIRIAMNE
stood). They have it all worked out.

CARR. What are you doing now?

MIO. I have a little business to transact in this
neighborhood.

CARR. You'd better forget it.

MIO. No.

CARR. Need any help?

MIO. Well, if I did I'd ask you first. But I
don't see how it would do any good. So
you keep out of it and take care of yourself.

CARR. So long, then.

MIO. So long, Carr.

CARR (*looking down-stream*). He was drifting face up. Must he halfway to the island
the way the tide runs. (*He shivers.*) Good,
it's cold here. Well—

(*He goes out to the left.* MIO *sits on the edge
of the rock.* LUCIA *comes stealthily back from
between the bridge and the tenement, goes
to the street-piano and wheels it away.* PINY
comes in. They take a look at MIO, *but say
nothing.* LUCIA *goes into his shelter and*
PINY *into hers.* MIO *rises, looks up at the
tenement, and goes out to the left.*)

CURTAIN

ACT TWO

SCENE: *The basement as in Scene 2 of Act One. The same evening.* ESDRAS *sits at the
table reading,* MIRIAMNE *is seated at the left, listening and intent. The door of the inner
room is half open and* GARTH'S *violin is heard. He is playing the theme from the third
movement of Beethoven's Archduke Trio.* ESDRAS *looks up.*

ESDRAS. I remember when I came to the end
of all the Talmud said, and the commen-
taries,
then I was fifty years old—and it was time
to ask what I had learned. I asked this
question
and gave myself the answer. In all the Talmud
there was nothing to find but the names of
things,
set down that we might call them by those
names
and walk without fear among things known.
Since then
I have had twenty years to read on and on
and end with Ecclesiastes. Names of names,
evanid days, evanid nights and days

and words that shift their meaning. Space
is time,
that which was is now—the men of tomorrow
live, and this is their yesterday. All things
that were and are and will be, have their
being
then and now and to come. If this means
little
when you are young, remember it. It will
return
to mean more when you are old.

MIRIAMNE. I'm sorry—I
was listening for something.

ESDRAS. It doesn't matter.
It's a useless wisdom. It's all I have,

but useless. It may be there is no time,
but we grow old. Do you know his name?

MIRIAMNE. Whose name?

ESDRAS. Why, when we're young and listen
for a step
the step should have a name—(MIRIAMNE,
not hearing, rises and goes to the window.
GARTH *enters from within, carrying his
violin and carefully closing the door.*)

GARTH (*as* ESDRAS *looks at him*). Asleep.

ESDRAS. He may
sleep on through the whole night—then in
the morning
we can let them know.

GARTH. We'd be wiser to say nothing—
let him find his own way back.

ESDRAS. How did he come here?

GARTH. He's not too crazy for that. If he
wakes again
we'll keep him quiet and shift him off tomorrow.
Somebody'd pick him up.

ESDRAS. How have I come
to this sunken end of a street, at a life's
end—?

GARTH. It was cheaper here—not to be
transcendental—
So—we say nothing—?

ESDRAS. Nothing.

MIRIAMNE. Garth, there's no place
in this whole city—not one—
where you wouldn't be safer
than here—tonight—or tomorrow.

GARTH (*bitterly*). Well, that may be.
What of it?

MIRIAMNE. If you slipped away and took
a place somewhere where Trock couldn't
find you—

GARTH. Yes—
using what for money? and why do you
think
I've sat here so far—because I love my home
so much? No, but if I stepped round the
corner
it'd be my last corner and my last step.

MIRIAMNE. And yet—
if you're here—they'll find you here—
Trock will come again—
and there's worse to follow—

GARTH. Do you want to get me killed?

MIRIAMNE. No.

GARTH. There's no way out of it. We'll wait
and take what they send us.

ESDRAS. Hush! You'll wake him.

GARTH. I've done it.
I hear him stirring now. (*They wait quietly.*
JUDGE GAUNT *opens the door and enters.*)

GAUNT (*in the doorway*). I beg your
pardon—
no, no, be seated—keep your place—I've
made
your evening difficult enough, I fear;
and I must thank you doubly for your kindness,
for I've been ill—I know it.

ESDRAS. You're better, sir?

GAUNT. Quite recovered, thank you. Able,
I hope,
to manage nicely now. You'll be rewarded
for your hospitality—though at this moment
(*He smiles*)
I'm low in funds. (*He inspects his billfold.*)
Sir, my embarrassment
is great indeed—and more than monetary,
for I must own my recollection's vague
of how I came here—how we came together—
and what we may have said. My name is
Gaunt,
Judge Gaunt, a name long known in the
criminal courts,
and not unhonored there.

ESDRAS. My name is Esdras—
and this is Garth, my son. And Miriamne,
the daughter of my old age.

GAUNT. I'm glad to meet you.
Esdras. Garth Esdras. (*He passes a hand
over his eyes.*)
It's not a usual name.
Of late it's been connected with a case—
a case I knew. But this is hardly the man.
Though it's not a usual name. (*They are
silent.*)
Sir, how I came here,
as I have said, I don't well know. Such
things
are sometimes not quite accident.

ESDRAS. We found you
outside our door and brought you in.

GAUNT. The brain
can be overworked, and weary, even when
   the man
would swear to his good health. Sir, on my
   word
I don't know why I came here, nor how,
   nor when,
nor what would explain it. Shall we say the
   machine
begins to wear? I felt no twinge of it.—
You will imagine how much more than
   galling
I feel it, to ask my way home—and where
   I am—
but I do ask you that.

ESDRAS. This is New York City—
or part of it.

GAUNT. Not the best part, I presume? (*He
smiles grimly.*)
No, not the best.

ESDRAS. Not typical, no.

GAUNT. And you—(*To* GARTH.)
you are Garth Esdras?

GARTH. That's my name.

GAUNT. Well, sir, (*to* ESDRAS)
I shall lie under the deepest obligation
if you will set an old man on his path,
for I lack the homing instinct, if the truth
were known. North, east and south mean
   nothing to me
here in this room.

ESDRAS. I can put you in your way.

GARTH. Only you'd be wiser to wait a while—
if I'm any judge.—

GAUNT. It happens I'm the judge—(*with
stiff humor*)
in more ways than one. You'll forgive me
   if I say
I find this place and my predicament
somewhat distasteful. (*He looks round
him.*)

GARTH. I don't doubt you do;
but you're better off here.

GAUNT. Nor will you find it wise
to cross my word as lightly as you seem
inclined to do. You've seen me ill and
   shaken—
and you presume on that.

GARTH. Have it your way.

GAUNT. Doubtless what information is required
we'll find nearby.

ESDRAS. Yes, sir—the terminal,—
if you could walk so far.

GAUNT. I've done some walking—
to look at my shoes. (*He looks down, then
puts out a hand to steady himself.*)
That—that was why I came—
never mind—it was there—and it's gone.
(*To* GARTH.)
Professor Hobhouse—
that's the name—he wrote some trash about
   you
and printed it in a broadside.
—Since I'm here I can tell you
it's a pure fabrication—lacking facts
and legal import. Senseless and impudent,
written with bias—with malicious intent
to undermine the public confidence
in justice and the courts. I knew it then—
all he brings out about this testimony
you might have given. It's true I could have
   called you,
but the case was clear—Romagna was
   known guilty,
and there was nothing to add. If I've en-
   dured
some hours of torture over their attacks
upon my probity—and in this torture
have wandered from my place, wandered
   perhaps
in mind and body—and found my way to
   face you—
why, yes, it is so—I know it—I beg of you
say nothing. It's not easy to give up
a fair name after a full half century
of service to a state. It may well rock
the surest reason. Therefore I ask of you
say nothing of this visit.

GARTH. I'll say nothing.

ESDRAS. Nor any of us.

GAUNT. Why, no—for you'd lose, too.
You'd have nothing to gain.

ESDRAS. Indeed we know it.

GAUNT. I'll remember you kindly. When I've
   returned,
there may be some mystery made of where
   I was—
we'll leave it a mystery?

GARTH. Anything you say.

GAUNT. Why, now I go with much more
    peace of mind—
if I can call you friends.

ESDRAS. We shall be grateful
for silence on your part, Your Honor.

GAUNT. Sir—
if there were any just end to be served
by speaking out, I'd speak! There is none.
    No—
bear that in mind!

ESDRAS. We will, Your Honor.

GAUNT. Then—
I'm in some haste. If you can be my guide,
we'll set out now.

ESDRAS. Yes, surely. (*There is a knock at
the door. The four look at each other with
some apprehension.* MIRIAMNE *rises.*) I'll
answer it.

MIRIAMNE. Yes. (*She goes into the inner
room and closes the door.* ESDRAS *goes to the
outer door. The knock is repeated. He opens
the door.* MIO *is there.*)

ESDRAS. Yes, sir.

MIO. May I come in?

ESDRAS. Will you state your business, sir?
It's late—and I'm not at liberty—

MIO. Why, I might say
that I was trying to earn my tuition fees
by peddling magazines. I could say that,
or collecting old newspapers—paying cash—
highest rates—no questions asked—(*He
looks round sharply.*)

GARTH. We've nothing to sell.
What do you want?

MIO. Your pardon, gentlemen.
My business is not of an ordinary kind,
and I felt the need of this slight introduction
while I might get my bearings. Your name is
    Esdras,
or they told me so outside.

GARTH. What do you want?

MIO. Is that the name?

GARTH. Yes.

MIO. I'll be quick and brief.
I'm the son of a man who died many years
    ago
for a pay roll robbery in New England.
    You

should be Garth Esdras, by what I've heard.
    You have
some knowledge of the crime, if one can
    believe
what he reads in the public prints, and it
    might be
that your testimony, if given, would clear
    my father
of any share in the murder. You may not
    care
whether he was guilty or not. You may not
    know.
But I do care—and care deeply, and I've
    come
to ask you face to face.

GARTH. To ask me what?

MIO. What do you know of it?

ESDRAS. This man Romagna,
did he have a son?

MIO. Yes, sir, this man Romagna,
as you choose to call him, had a son, and I
am that son, and proud.

ESDRAS. Forgive me.

MIO. Had you known him,
and heard him speak, you'd know why I'm
    proud, and why
he was no malefactor.

ESDRAS. I quite believe you.
If my son can help he will. But at this
    moment,
as I told you—could you, I wonder, come
    tomorrow,
at your own hour?

MIO. Yes.

ESDRAS. By coincidence
we too of late have had this thing in mind—
there have been comments printed, and
    much discussion
which we could hardly avoid.

MIO. Could you tell me then
in a word?—What you know—
is it for him or against him?—
that's all I need.

ESDRAS. My son knows nothing.

GARTH. No.
The picture-papers lash themselves to a fury
over any rumor—make them up when
    they're short
of bedroom slops.—This is what happened. I
had known a few members of a gang one
    time

up there—and after the murder they picked
  me up
because I looked like someone that was seen
in what they called the murder car. They
  held me
a little while, but they couldn't identify me
for the most excellent reason I wasn't there
when the thing occurred. A dozen years
  later now
a professor comes across this, and sees red
and asks why I wasn't called on as a witness
and yips so loud they syndicate his picture
in all the rotos. That's all I know about it.
I wish I could tell you more.

ESDRAS. Let me say too
that I have read some words your father said,
and you were a son fortunate in your father,
whatever the verdict of the world.

MIO. There are few
who think so, but it's true, and I thank you.
  Then—
that's the whole story?

GARTH. All I know of it.

MIO. They cover their tracks well, the inner
  ring
that distributes murder. I came three thousand miles
to this dead end.

ESDRAS. If he was innocent
and you know him so, believe it, and let
  the others
believe as they like.

MIO. Will you tell me how a man's
to live, and face his life, if he can't believe
that truth's like a fire,
and will burn through and be seen
though it takes all the years there are?
While I stand up and have breath in my
  lungs
I shall be one flame of that fire;
it's all the life I have.

ESDRAS. Then you must live so.
One must live as he can.

MIO. It's the only way
of life my father left me.

ESDRAS. Yes? Yet it's true.
the ground we walk on is impacted down
and hard with blood and bones of those who
  died
unjustly. There's not one title to land or life,
even your own, but was built on rape and
  murder,

back a few years. It would take a fire indeed
to burn out all this error.

MIO. Then let it burn down,
all of it!

ESDRAS. We ask a great deal of the world
at first—then less—and then less.
We ask for truth
and justice. But this truth's a thing unknown
in the lightest, smallest matter—and as for
  justice,
who has once seen it done? You loved your
  father,
and I could have loved him, for every word
  he spoke
in his trial was sweet and tolerant, but the
  weight
of what men are and have, rests heavy on
the graves of those who lost. They'll not
  rise again,
and their causes lie there with them.

GAUNT. If you mean to say
that Bartolomeo Romagna was innocent,
you are wrong. He was guilty.
There may have been injustice
from time to time, by regrettable chance, in
  our courts,
but not in that case, I assure you.

MIO. Oh, you assure me!
You lie in your scrag teeth, whoever you
  are!
My father was murdered!

GAUNT. Romagna was found guilty
by all due process of law, and given his
  chance
to prove his innocence.

MIO. What chance? When a court
panders to mob hysterics, and the jury
comes in loaded to soak an anarchist
and a foreigner, it may be due process of law
but it's also murder!

GAUNT. He should have thought of that
before he spilled blood.

MIO. He?

GAUNT. Sir, I know too well
that he was guilty.

MIO. Who are you? How do you know?
I've searched the records through, the trial
  and what
came after, and in all that million words
I found not one unbiased argument
to fix the crime on him.

GAUNT. And you yourself,
were you unprejudiced?

MIO. Who are you?

ESDRAS. Sir,
this gentleman is here, as you are here,
to ask my son, as you have asked, what
  ground
there might be for this talk of new evidence
in your father's case. We gave him the same
  answer
we've given you.

MIO. I'm sorry. I'd supposed
his cause forgotten except by myself. There's
  still
a defense committee then?

GAUNT. There may be. I
am not connected with it.

ESDRAS. He is my guest,
and asks to remain unknown.

MIO (after a pause, looking at GAUNT). The
  judge at the trial
was younger, but he had your face. Can it be
that you're the man?—Yes—Yes.—The jury
  charge—
I sat there as a child and heard your voice,
and watched that Brahminical mouth. I
  knew even then
you meant no good to him. And now you're
  here
to winnow out truth and justice—the
  fountain-head
of the lies that slew him! Are you Judge
  Gaunt?

GAUNT. I am.

MIO. Then tell me what damnation to what
  inferno
would fit the toad that sat in robes and lied
when he gave the charge, and knew he lied!
  Judge that,
and then go to your place in that hell!

GAUNT. I know and have known
what bitterness can rise against a court
when it must say, putting aside all weakness,
that a man's to die. I can forgive you that,
for you are your father's son, and you think
  of him
as a son thinks of his father. Certain laws
seem cruel in their operation; it's necessary
that we be cruel to uphold them. This
  cruelty
is kindness to those I serve.

MIO. I don't doubt that.
I know who it is you serve.

GAUNT. Would I have chosen
to rack myself with other men's despairs,
stop my ears, harden my heart, and listen
  only
to the voice of law and light, if I had hoped
some private gain for serving? In all my
  years
on the bench of a long-established commonwealth
not once has my decision been in question
save in this case. Not once before or since.
For hope of heaven or place on earth, or
  power
or gold, no man has had my voice, nor will
while I still keep the trust that laid on me
to sentence and define.

MIO. Then why are you here?

GAUNT. My record's clean. I've kept it so.
  But suppose
with the best intent, among the myriad
  tongues
that come to testify, I had missed my way
and followed a perjured tale to a lethal end
till a man was forsworn to death? Could
  I rest or sleep
while there was doubt of this,
even while there was question in a layman's
  mind?
For always, night and day,
there lies on my brain like a weight, the
  admonition:
see truly, let nothing sway you; among all
  functions
there's but one godlike, to judge. Then see
  to it
you judge as a god would judge, with clarity,
with truth, with what mercy is found con-
  sonant
with order and law. Without law men are
  beasts,
and it's a judge's task to lift and hold them
above themselves. Let a judge be once
  mistaken
or step aside for a friend, and a gap is made
in the dykes that hold back anarchy and
  chaos,
and leave men bond but free.

MIO. Then the gap's been made,
and you made it.

GAUNT. I feared that too. May you be a judge
sometime, and know in what fear,

through what nights long
in fear, I scanned and verified and compared
the transcripts of the trial.

MIO. Without prejudice,
no doubt. It was never in your mind to prove
that you'd been right.

GAUNT. And conscious of that, too—
that that might be my purpose—watchful
of that,
and jealous as his own lawyer of the rights
that should hedge the defendant!
And still I found no error,
shook not one staple of the bolts that linked
the door to the deed! Still following on
from step to step, I watched all modern
comment,
and saw it centered finally on one fact—
Garth Esdras was not called. This is Garth
Esdras,
and you have heard him. Would his deposi-
tion
have justified a new trial?

MIO. No. It would not.

GAUNT. And there I come, myself. If the man
were still
in his cell, and waiting, I'd have no faint
excuse
for another hearing.

MIO. I've told you that I read
the trial from beginning to end. Every word
you spoke
was balanced carefully to keep the letter
of the law and still convict—convict, by
Christ,
if it tore the seven veils! You stand here now
running cascades of casuistry, to prove
to yourself and me that no judge of rank
and breeding
could burn a man out of hate! But that's
what you did
under all your varnish!

GAUNT. I've sought for evidence,
and you have sought. Have you found it?
Can you cite
one fresh word in defence?

MIO. The trial itself
was shot full of legerdemain, prearranged
to lead
the jury astray—

GAUNT. Could you prove that?

MIO. Yes!

GAUNT. And if
the jury were led astray, remember it's
the jury, by our Anglo-Saxon custom,
that finds for guilt or innocence. The judge
is powerless in that matter.

MIO. Not you! Your charge
misled the jury more than the evidence,
accepted every biased meaning, distilled
the poison for them!

GAUNT. But if that were so
I'd be the first, I swear it, to step down
among all men, and hold out both my hands
for manacles—yes, publish it in the streets,
that all I've held most sacred was defiled
by my own act. A judge's brain becomes
a delicate instrument to weigh men's lives
for good and ill—too delicate to bear
much tampering. If he should push aside
the weights and throw the beam, and say,
this once
the man is guilty, and I will have it so
though his mouth cry out from the ground,
and all the world
revoke my word, he'd have a short way to go
to madness. I think you'd find him in the
squares,
stopping the passers-by with arguments,—
see, I was right, the man was guilty there—
this was brought in against him, this— and
this—
and I was left no choice! It's no light thing
when a long life's been dedicated to one end
to wrench the mind awry!

MIO. By your own thesis
you should be mad, and no doubt you are.

GAUNT. But my madness
is only this—that I would fain look back
on a life well spent—without one stain—
one breath
of stain to flaw the glass—not in men's
minds
nor in my own. I take my God as witness
I meant to earn that clearness, and believe
that I have earned it. Yet my name is
clouded
with the blackest, fiercest scandal of our age
that's touched a judge. What I can do to
wipe
that smutch from my fame I will. I think
you know
how deeply I've been hated, for no cause
that I can find there. Can it not be—and I
ask this
quite honestly—that the great injustice lies

on your side and not mine? Time and time
again
men have come before me perfect in their
lives,
loved by all who knew them, loved at home,
gentle, not vicious, yet caught so ripe red-
handed
in some dark violence there was no denying
where the onus lay.

MIO. That was not so with my father!

GAUNT. And yet it seemed so to me. To other
men
who sat in judgment on him. Can you be
sure—
I ask this in humility—that you,
who were touched closest by the tragedy,
may not have lost perspective—may have
brooded
day and night on one theme—till your eyes
are tranced
and show you one side only?

MIO. I see well enough.

GAUNT. And would that not be part of the
malady—
to look quite steadily at the drift of things
but see there what you wish—not what is
there—
not what another man to whom the story
was fresh would say is there?

MIO. You think I'm crazy.
Is that what you meant to say?

GAUNT. I've seen it happen
with the best and wisest men. I but ask the
question.
I can't speak for you. Is it not true wherever
you walk, through the little town where
you knew him well,
or flying from it, inland or by the sea,
still walking at your side, and sleeping only
when you too sleep, a shadow not your own
follows, pleading and holding out its hands
to be delivered from shame?

MIO. How you know that
by God I don't know.

GAUNT. Because one spectre haunted you and
me—
and haunts you still, but for me it's laid to
rest
now that my mind is satisfied. He died
justly and not by error. (A pause.)

MIO (stepping forward). Do you care to
know

you've come so near to death it's miracle
that pulse still beats in your splotchy throat?
Do you know
there's murder in me?

GAUNT. There was murder in your sire,
and it's to be expected! I say he died
justly, and he deserved it!

MIO. Yes, you'd like too well
to have me kill you! That would prove your
case
and clear your name, and dip my father's
name
in stench forever! You'll not get that from
me!
Go home and die in bed, get it under cover,
your lux-et-lex putrefaction of the right
thing,
you man that walks like a god!

GAUNT. Have I made you angry
by coming too near the truth?

MIO. This sets him up,
this venomous slug, this sets him up in a
gown,
deciding who's to walk above the earth
and who's to lie beneath! And giving
reasons!
The cobra giving reasons; I'm a god,
by Buddha, holy and worshipful my fang,
and can I sink it in! (He pauses, turns as if
to go, then sits.)
This is no good.
This won't help much. (The JUDGE and
ESDRAS look at each other.)

GAUNT. We should be going.

ESDRAS. Yes. (They prepare to go.)
I'll lend you my coat.

GAUNT (looking at it with distaste). No,
keep it. A little rain
shouldn't matter to me.

ESDRAS. It freezes as it falls,
and you've a long way to go.

GAUNT. I'll manage, thank you. (GAUNT and
ESDRAS go out, ESDRAS obsequious, closing the
door.)

GARTH (looking at MIO's back). Well?

MIO (not moving). Let me sit here a
moment.

(GARTH shrugs his shoulders and goes toward
the inner door. MIRIAMNE opens it and comes
out. GARTH looks at her, then at MIO, then

lays his fingers on his lips. She nods. GARTH
goes out. MIRIAMNE *sits and watches* MIO.
After a little he turns and sees her.)

MIO. How did you come here?

MIRIAMNE. I live here.

MIO. Here?

MIRIAMNE. My name is Esdras. Garth
is my brother. The walls are thin.
I heard what was said.

MIO (*stirring wearily*). I'm going. This is
no place for me.

MIRIAMNE. What place
would be better?

MIO. None. Only it's better to go.
Just to go. (*She comes over to him, puts her
arm round him and kisses his forehead.*)

MIRIAMNE. Mio.

MIO. What do you want?
Your kisses burn me—and your arms. Don't
offer
what I'm never to have! I can have nothing.
They say
they'll cross the void sometime to the other
planets
and men will breathe in that air.
Well, I could breathe there,
but not here now. Not on this ball of mud.
I don't want it.

MIRIAMNE. They can take away so little
with all their words. For you're a king
among them.
I heard you, and loved your voice.

MIO. I thought I'd fallen
so low there was no further, and now a pit
opens beneath. It was bad enough that he
should have died innocent, but if he were
guilty—
then what's my life—what have I left to
do—?
The son of a felon—and what they spat on
me
was earned—and I'm drenched with the
stuff.
Here on my hands
and cheeks, their spittle hanging! I liked
my hands
because they were like his. I tell you I've
lived
by his innocence, lived to see it flash
and blind them all—

MIRIAMNE. Never believe them, Mio,
never. (*She looks toward the inner door.*)

MIO. But it was truth I wanted, truth—
not the lies you'd tell yourself, or tell a
woman,
or a woman tells you! The judge with his
cobra mouth
may have spat truth—and I may be mad!
For me—
your hands are too clean to touch me. I'm
to have
the scraps from hotel kitchens—and instead
of love
those mottled bodies that hitch themselves
through alleys
to sell for dimes or nickels. Go, keep yourself chaste
for the baker bridegroom—baker and son
of a baker,
let him get his baker's dozen on you!

MIRIAMNE. No—
say once you love me—say it once; I'll never
ask to hear it twice, nor for any kindness,
and you shall take all I have! (GARTH *opens
the inner door and comes out.*)

GARTH. I interrupt
a love scene, I believe. We can do without
your adolescent mawkishness. (*To* MIRI-
AMNE)
You're a child.
You'll both remember that.

MIRIAMNE. I've said nothing to harm you—
and will say nothing.

GARTH. You're my sister, though,
and I take a certain interest in you. Where
have you two met?

MIRIAMNE. We danced together.

GARTH. Then
the dance is over, I think.

MIRIAMNE. I've always loved you
and tried to help you, Garth. And you've
been kind.
Don't spoil it now.

GARTH. Spoil it how?

MIRIAMNE. Because I love him.
I didn't know it would happen. We danced
together.
And the world's all changed. I see through
a mist,
and our father, too. If you brought this to
nothing
I'd want to die.

GARTH (*to* MIO). You'd better go.

MIO. Yes, I know. (*He rises. There is a trembling knock at the door.* MIRIAMNE *goes to it. The* HOBO *is there shivering.*)

HOBO. Miss, could I sleep under the pipes tonight, miss?
Could I, please?

MIRIAMNE. I think—not tonight.

HOBO. There won't be any more nights—
if I don't get warm, miss.

MIRIAMNE. Come in. (*The* HOBO *comes in, looks round deprecatingly, then goes to a corner beneath a huge heating pipe, which he crawls under as if he's been there before.*)

HOBO. Yes, miss, thank you.

GARTH. Must we put up with that?

MIRIAMNE. Father let him sleep there—
last winter.

GARTH. Yes, God, yes.

MIO. Well, good night.

MIRIAMNE. Where will you go?

MIO. Yes, where? As if it mattered.

GARTH. Oh, sleep here, too.
We'll have a row of you under the pipes.

MIO. No, thanks.

MIRIAMNE. Mio, I've saved a little money.
It's only
some pennies, but you must take it. (*She shakes some coins out of a box into her hand.*)

MIO. No, thanks.

MIRIAMNE. And I love you.
You've never said you love me.

MIO. Why wouldn't I love you
when you're clean and sweet,
and I've seen nothing sweet or clean
this last ten years? I love you. I leave you that
for what good it may do you. It's none to me.

MIRIAMNE. Then kiss me.

MIO (*looking at* GARTH). With that scowling over us? No.
When it rains, some spring

on the planet Mercury, where the spring comes often,
I'll meet you there, let's say. We'll wait for that.
It may be some time till then.
(*The outside door opens and* ESDRAS *enters with* JUDGE GAUNT, *then, after a slight interval,* TROCK *follows.* TROCK *surveys the interior and its occupants one by one, carefully.*)

TROCK. I wouldn't want to cause you inconvenience,
any of you, and especially the Judge.
I think you know that. You've all got things to do—
trains to catch, and so on. But trains can wait.
Hell, nearly anything can wait, you'll find,
only I can't. I'm the only one that can't
because I've got no time. Who's all this here?
Who's that? (*He points to the* HOBO.)

ESDRAS. He's a poor half-wit, sir,
that sometimes sleeps there.

TROCK. Come out. I say come out,
whoever you are. (*The* HOBO *stirs and looks up.*)
Yes, I mean you. Come out. (*The* HOBO *emerges.*)
What's your name?

HOBO. They mostly call me Oke.

TROCK. What do you know?

HOBO. No, sir.

TROCK. Where are you from?

HOBO. I got a piece of bread. (*He brings it out, trembling.*)

TROCK. Get back in there! (*The* HOBO *crawls back into his corner.*)
Maybe you want to know why I'm doing this.
Well, I've been robbed, that's why—
robbed five or six times;
the police can't find a thing—so I'm out for myself—
if you want to know. (*To* MIO.)
Who are you?

MIO. Oh, I'm a half-wit,
came in here by mistake. The difference is
I've got no piece of bread.

TROCK. What's your name?

MIO. My name?
Theophrastus Such. That's respectable.
You'll find it all the way from here to the coast
on the best police blotters.
Only the truth is we're a little touched in the head,
Oke and me. You'd better ask somebody else.

TROCK. Who is he?

ESDRAS. His name's Romagna. He's the son.

TROCK. Then what's he doing here? You said you were on the level.

GARTH. He just walked in. On account of the stuff in the papers. We didn't ask him.

TROCK. God, we are a gathering. Now if we had Shadow we'd be all here, huh? Only I guess we won't see Shadow. No, that's too much to ask.

MIO. Who's Shadow?

TROCK. Now you're putting questions. Shadow was just nobody, you see. He blew away. It might happen to anybody. (*He looks at* GARTH.) Yes, anyone at all.

MIO. Why do you keep your hand in your pocket, friend?

TROCK. Because I'm cold, punk. Because I've been outside and it's cold as the tomb of Christ. (*To* GARTH.) Listen, there's a car waiting up at the street to take the Judge home. We'll take him to the car.

GARTH. That's not necessary.

ESDRAS. No.

TROCK. I say it is, see? You wouldn't want to let the Judge walk, would you? The Judge is going to ride where he's going, with a couple of chauffeurs, and everything done in style. Don't you worry about the Judge. He'll be taken care of. For good.

GARTH. I want no hand in it.

TROCK. Anything happens to me happens to you too, musician.

GARTH. I know that.

TROCK. Keep your mouth out of it then. And you'd better keep the punk here to-night, just for luck. (*He turns toward the door. There is a brilliant lightning flash through the windows, followed slowly by dying thunder.* TROCK *opens the door. The rain begins to pour in sheets.*) Jesus, somebody tipped it over again! (*A cough racks him.*) Wait till it's over. It takes ten days off me every time I step into it. (*He closes the door.*) Sit down and wait. (*Lightning flashes again. The thunder is fainter.* ESDRAS, GARTH *and the* JUDGE *sit down.*)

GAUNT. We were born too early. Even you who are young
are not of the elect. In a hundred years
man will put his finger on life itself, and then
he will live as long as he likes. For you and me
we shall die soon—one day, one year more or less,
when or where, it's no matter. It's what we call
an indeterminate sentence. I'm hungry.
(GARTH *looks at* MIRIAMNE.)

MIRIAMNE. There was nothing left tonight.

HOBO. I've got a piece of bread. (*He breaks his bread in two and hands half to the* JUDGE.)

GAUNT. I thank you, sir. (*He eats.*)
This is not good bread. (*He rises.*)
Sir, I am used
to other company. Not better, perhaps, but their clothes
were different. These are what it's the fashion to call
the underprivileged.

TROCK. Oh, hell! (*He turn toward the door.*)

MIO (*to* TROCK). It would seem that you and the Judge know each other. (TROCK *faces him.*)

TROCK. I've been around.

MIO. Maybe you've met before.

TROCK. Maybe we have.

MIO. Will you tell me where?

TROCK. How long do you want to live?

MIO. How long? Oh, I've got big ideas about that.

TROCK. I thought so. Well, so far I've got nothing against you but your name, see? You keep it that way. (*He opens the door. The rain still falls in torrents. He closes the door. As he turns from it, it opens again, and* SHADOW, *white, bloodstained and dripping, stands in the doorway.* GARTH *rises.* TROCK *turns.*)

GAUNT (*to the* HOBO). Yet if one were careful of his health, ate sparingly, drank not at all, used himself wisely, it might be that even an old man could live to touch immortality. They may come on the secret sooner than we dare hope. You see? It does no harm to try.

TROCK (*backing away from* SHADOW). By God, he's out of his grave!

SHADOW (*leaning against the doorway, holding a gun in his hands*). Keep your hands where they belong, Trock.
You know me.

TROCK. Don't! Don't! I had nothing to do with it! (*He backs to the opposite wall.*)

SHADOW. You said the doctor gave you six months to live—
well, I don't give you that much. That's what you had,
six months, and so you start bumping off your friends
to make sure of your damn six months. I got it from you.
I know where I got it.
Because I wouldn't give it to the Judge.
So he wouldn't talk.

TROCK. Honest to God—

SHADOW. What God?
The one that let you put three holes in me when I was your friend? Well, He let me get up again
and walk till I could find you. That's as far as I get,
but I got there, by God! And I can hear you even if I can't see! (*He takes a staggering step forward.*)
A man needs blood
to keep going.—I got this far.—And now I can't see!
It runs out too fast—too fast—
when you've got three slugs
clean through you.
Show me where he is, you fools! He's here!
I got here! (*He drops the gun.*)

Help me! Help me! Oh, God! Oh, God! I'm going to die! Where does a man lie down?
I want to lie down!

(MIRIAMNE *starts toward* SHADOW. GARTH *and* ESDRAS *help him into the next room,* MIRIAMNE *following.* TROCK *squats in his corner, breathing hard, looking at the door.* MIO *stands, watching* TROCK. GARTH *returns, wiping his hand with a handkerchief.* MIO *picks up and pockets the gun.* MIRIAMNE *comes back and leans against the door jamb.*)

GAUNT. You will hear it said that an old man makes a good judge, being calm, clear-eyed, without passion. But this is not true. Only the young love truth and justice. The old are savage, wary, violent, swayed by maniac desires, cynical of friendship or love, open to bribery and the temptations of lust, corrupt and dastardly to the heart. I know these old men. What have they left to believe, what have they left to lose? Whorers of daughters, lickers of girls' shoes, contrivers of nastiness in the night, purveyors of perversion, worshippers of possession! Death is the only radical. He comes late, but he comes at last to put away the old men and give the young their places. It was time. (*He leers.*) Here's one I heard yesterday:
  Marmaduke behind the barn
    got his sister in a fix;
  he says damn instead of darn;
    ain't he cute? He's only six!

THE HOBO. He, he, he!

GAUNT. And the hoot-owl hoots all night,
    and the cuckoo cooks all day,
  and what with a minimum grace of God
    we pass the time away.

THE HOBO. He, he, he—I got ya! (*He makes a sign with his thumb.*)

GAUNT (*sings*). And he led her all around
    and he laid her on the ground
  and he ruffled up the feathers of her
    cuckoo's nest!

HOBO. Ho, ho, ho!

GAUNT. I am not taken with the way you laugh. You should cultivate restraint. (ESDRAS *reënters.*)

TROCK. Shut the door.

ESDRAS. He won't come back again.

TROCK. I want the door shut! He was dead, I tell you! (ESDRAS *closes the door.*) And Romagna was dead, too, once! Can't they keep a man under ground?

MIO. No. No more! They don't stay under ground any more, and they don't stay under water! Why did you have him killed?

TROCK. Stay away from me! I know you!

MIO. Who am I, then?

TROCK. I know you, damn you! Your name's Romagna!

MIO. Yes! And Romagna was dead, too, and Shadow was dead, but the time's come when you can't keep them down, these dead men! They won't stay down! They come in with their heads shot off and their entrails dragging! Hundreds of them! One by one— all you ever had killed! Watch the door! See!—It moves!

TROCK (*looking, fascinated, at the door*). Let me out of here! (*He tries to rise.*)

MIO (*the gun in his hand*). Oh, no! You'll sit there and wait for them! One by one they'll come through that door, pulling their heads out of the gunny-sacks where you tied them—glauming over you with their rotten hands! They'll see without eyes and crawl over you—Shadow and the paymaster and all the rest of them—putrescent bones without eyes! Now! Look! Look! For I'm first among them!

TROCK. I've done for better men than you! And I'll do for you!

GAUNT (*rapping on the table*). Order, gentlemen, order! The witness will remember that a certain decorum is essential in the court-room!

MIO. By God, he'll answer me!

GAUNT (*thundering*). Silence! Silence! Let me remind you of courtesy toward the witness! What case is this you try?

MIO. The case of the state against Bartolomeo Romagna for the murder of the paymaster!

GAUNT. Sir, that was disposed of long ago!

MIO. Never disposed of, never, not while I live!

GAUNT. Then we'll have done with it now! I deny the appeal! I have denied the appeal before and I do so again!

HOBO. He, he!—He thinks he's in the moving pictures! (*A flash of lightning.*)

GAUNT. Who set that flash! Bailiff, clear the court! This is not Flemington, gentlemen! We are not conducting this case to make a journalistic holiday! (*The thunder rumbles faintly.* GARTH *opens the outside door and faces a solid wall of rain.*) Stop that man! He's one of the defendants! (GARTH *closes the door.*)

MIO. Then put him on the stand!

GARTH. What do you think you're doing?

MIO. Have you any objection?

GAUNT. The objection is not sustained. We will hear the new evidence. Call your witness.

MIO. Garth Esdras!

GAUNT. He will take the stand!

GARTH. If you want me to say what I said before, I'll say it!

MIO. Call Trock Estrella then!

GAUNT. Trock Estrella to the stand!

TROCK. No, by God!

MIO. Call Shadow, then! He'll talk! You thought he was dead, but he'll get up again and talk!

TROCK (*screaming*). What do you want of me?

MIO. You killed the paymaster! You!

TROCK. You lie! It was Shadow killed him!

MIO. And now I know! Now I know!

GAUNT. Again I remind you of courtesy toward the witness!

MIO. I know them now!
Let me remind you of courtesy toward the dead!
He says that Shadow killed him! If Shadow were here
he'd say it was Trock! There were three men involved
in the new version of the crime for which my father died! Shadow and Trock Estrella

as principals in the murder—Garth as witness!—
Why are they here together?—and you—the Judge—
why are you here? Why, because you were all afraid
and you drew together out of that fear to arrange
a story you could tell! And Trock killed Shadow
and meant to kill the Judge out of that same fear—
to keep them quiet! This is the thing I've hunted
over the earth to find out, and I'd be blind
indeed if I missed it now! (*To* GAUNT.)
You heard what he said:
It was Shadow killed him! Now let the night conspire
with the sperm of hell! It's plain beyond denial
even to this fox of justice—and all his words
are curses on the wind! You lied! You lied!
You knew this too!

GAUNT (*low*). Let me go. Let me go!

MIO. Then why
did you let my father die?

GAUNT. Suppose it known,
but there are things a judge must not believe
though they should head and fester underneath
and press in on his brain. Justice once rendered
in a clear burst of anger, righteously,
upon a very common laborer,
confessed an anarchist, the verdict found
and the precise machinery of law
invoked to know him guilty—think what furor
would rock the state if the court then flatly said;
all this was lies—must be reversed? It's better,
as any judge can tell you, in such cases,
holding the common good to be worth more
than small injustice, to let the record stand,
let one man die. For justice, in the main,
is governed by opinion. Communities
will have what they will have, and it's quite as well,
after all, to be rid of anarchists. Our rights
as citizens can be maintained as rights
only while we are held to be the peers

of those who live about us. A vendor of fish
is not protected as a man might be
who kept a market. I own I've sometimes wished
this was not so, but it is. The man you defend
was unfortunate—and his misfortune bore
almost as heavily on me.—I'm broken—
broken across. You're much too young to know
how bitter it is when a worn connection chars
and you can't remember—can't remember.
(*He steps forward.*)
You
will not repeat this? It will go no further?

MIO. No.
No further than the moon takes the tides—no further
than the news went when he died—
when you found him guilty
and they flashed that round the earth. Wherever men
still breathe and think, and know what's done to them
by the powers above, they'll know. That's all I ask.
That'll be enough. (TROCK *has risen and looks darkly at* MIO.)

GAUNT. Thank you. For I've said some things
a judge should never say.

TROCK. Go right on talking.
Both of you. It won't get far, I guess.

MIO. Oh, you'll see to that?

TROCK. I'll see to it. Me and some others.
Maybe I lost my grip there just for a minute.
That's all right.

MIO. Then see to it! Let it rain!
What can you do to me now when the night's on fire
with this thing I know? Now I could almost wish
there was a god somewhere—I could almost think
there was a god—and he somehow brought me here
and set you down before me here in the rain
where I could wring this out of you! For it's said,
and I've heard it, and I'm free! He was as I thought him,
true and noble and upright, even when he went

to a death contrived because he was as he
  was
and not your kind! Let it rain! Let the night
  speak fire
and the city go out with the tide, for he was
  a man
and I know you now, and I have my day!
(*There is a heavy knock at the outside door.*
MIRIAMNE *opens it, at a glance from* GARTH.
The POLICEMAN *is there in oilskins.*)

POLICEMAN. Evening. (*He steps in, followed
by a* SERGEANT, *similarly dressed.*) We're
  looking for someone
might be here. Seen an old man around
acting a little off? (*To* ESDRAS.)
You know the one
I mean. You saw him out there. Jeez! You've
  got
a funny crowd here! (*He looks round. The*
HOBO *shrinks into his corner.*)
That's the one I saw.
What do you think?

SERGEANT. That's him. You mean to say
you didn't know him by this pictures? (*He
goes to* GAUNT.)
Come on, old man.
You're going home.

GAUNT. Yes, sir. I've lost my way.
I think I've lost my way.

SERGEANT. I'll say you have.
About three hundred miles. Now don't you
  worry.
We'll get you back.

GAUNT. I'm a person of some rank
in my own city.

SERGEANT. We know that. One look at you
and we'd know that.

GAUNT. Yes, sir.

POLICEMAN. If it isn't Trock!
Trock Estrella. How are you, Trock?

TROCK. Pretty good,
Thanks.

POLICEMAN. Got out yesterday again, I hear?

TROCK. That's right.

SERGEANT. Hi'ye, Trock?

TROCK. O.K.

SERGEANT. You know we got orders
to watch you pretty close. Be good now,
  baby.

or back you go. Don't try to pull anything,
not in my district.

TROCK. No, sir.

SERGEANT. No bumping off.
If you want my advice quit carrying a gun.
Try earning your living for once.

TROCK. Yeah.

SERGEANT. That's an idea.
Because if we find any stiffs on the river
  bank
we'll know who to look for.

MIO. Then look in the other room!
I accuse that man of murder! Trock Estrella!
He's a murderer!

POLICEMAN. Hello. I remember you.

SERGEANT. Well, what murder?

MIO. It was Trock Estrella
that robbed the pay roll thirteen years ago
and did the killing my father died for!
  You know
the Romagna case! Romagna was innocent,
and Trock Estrella guilty!

SERGEANT (*disgusted*). Oh, what the hell!
That's old stuff—the Romagna case.

POLICEMAN. Hey, Sarge! (*The* SERGEANT *and*
POLICEMAN *come closer together.*)
The boy's a professional kidder. He took me
  over
about half an hour ago. He kids the police
and then ducks out!

SERGEANT. Oh, yeah?

MIO. I'm not kidding now.
You'll find a dead man there in the next
  room
and Estrella killed him!

SERGEANT. Thirteen years ago?
And nobody smelled him yet?

MIO (*pointing*). I accuse this man
of two murders! He killed the paymaster
  long ago
and had Shadow killed tonight. Look, look
  for yourself!
He's there all right!

POLICEMAN. Look boy. You stood out there
and put the booby sign on the dumb police
because they're fresh out of Ireland. Don't
  try it twice.

SERGEANT (*to* GARTH). Any corpses here?

GARTH. Not that I know of.

SERGEANT. I thought so. (MIO *looks at* MIRIAMNE.*)*

(*To* MIO.)
Think up a better one.

MIO. Have I got to drag him
out here where you can see him? (*He goes
toward the inner door.*)
Can't you scent a murder
when it's under your nose? Look in!

MIRIAMNE. No, no—there's no one—there's
no one there!

SERGEANT (*looking at* MIRIAMNE). Take a
look inside.

POLICEMAN. Yes, sir. (*He goes into the inside
room. The* SERGEANT *goes up to the door.
The* POLICEMAN *returns.*)
He's kidding, Sarge. If there's a cadaver
in here I don't see it.

MIO. You're blind then! (*He goes into the
room, the* SERGEANT *following him.*)

SERGEANT. What do you mean? (*He comes
out,* MIO *following him.*)
When you make a charge of murder it's
better to have
the corpus delicti, son. You're the kind puts
in
fire alarms to see the engine!

MIO. By God, he was there!
He went in there to die.

SERGEANT. I'll bet he did.
And I'm Haile Selassie's aunt! What's your
name?

MIO. Romagna. (*To* GARTH).
What have you done with him?

GARTH. I don't know what you mean.

SERGEANT (*to* GARTH). What's he talking
about?

GARTH. I wish I could tell you.
I don't know.

SERGEANT. He must have seen something.

POLICEMAN. He's got
the Romagna case on the brain. You watch
yourself,
chump, or you'll get run in.

MIO. Then they're in it together!
All of them! (*To* MIRIAMNE.)
Yes, and you!

GARTH. He's nuts, I say.

MIRIAMNE (*gently*). You have dreamed
something—isn't it true?
You've dreamed—
But truly, there was no one—(MIO *looks at
her comprehendingly.*)

MIO. You want me to say it. (*He pauses.*)
Yes, by God, I was dreaming.

SERGEANT (*to* POLICEMAN). I guess you're
right.
We'd better be going. Haven't you got a
coat?

GAUNT. No, sir.

SERGEANT. I guess I'll have to lend you mine.
(*He puts his oilskins on* GAUNT.)
Come on, now. It's getting late. (GAUNT, *the*
POLICEMAN *and the* SERGEANT *go out.*)

TROCK. They're welcome to him.
His fuse is damp. Where is that walking
fool
with the three slugs in him?

ESDRAS. He fell in the hall beyond
and we left him there.

TROCK. That's lucky for some of us. Is he
out this time
or is he still butting around?

ESDRAS. He's dead.

TROCK. That's perfect. (*To* MIO.)
Don't try using your firearms, amigo baby,
the Sarge is outside. (*He turns to go.*)
Better ship that carrion
back in the river! The one that walks when
he's dead;
maybe he'll walk the distance for you.

GARTH. Coming back?

TROCK. Well, if I come back,
you'll see me. If I don't, you won't. Let the
punk
go far as he likes. Turn him loose and let
him go.
And may you all rot in hell. (*He pulls his
coat around him and goes to the left.* MIR-
IAMNE *climbs up to look out a window.*)

MIRIAMNE. He's climbing up to the street, along the bridgehead. (*She turns.*) Quick, Mio! It's safe now! Quick!

GARTH. Let him do as he likes.

MIRIAMNE. What do you mean? Garth! He means to kill him! You know that!

GARTH. I've no doubt Master Romagna can run his own campaign.

MIRIAMNE. But he'll be killed!

MIO. Why did you lie about Shadow? (*There is a pause.* GARTH *shrugs, walks across the room, and sits.*) You were one of the gang!

GARTH. I can take a death if I have to! Go tell your story, only watch your step, for I warn you, Trock's out gunning and you may not walk very far. Oh, I could defend it but it's hardly worth while. If they get Trock they get me too. Go tell them. You owe me nothing.

ESDRAS. This Trock you saw, no one defends him. He's earned his death so often there's nobody to regret it. But his crime, his same crime that has dogged you, dogged us down from what little we had, to live here among the drains, where the waterbugs break out like a scrofula on what we eat—and if there's lower to go we'll go there when you've told your story. And more that I haven't heart to speak—

MIO (*to* GARTH). My father died in your place. And you could have saved him! You were one of the gang!

GARTH. Why, there you are. You certainly owe me nothing.

MIRIAMNE (*moaning*). I want to die. I want to go away.

MIO. Yes, and you lied! And trapped me into it!

MIRIAMNE. But Mio, he's my brother. I couldn't give them my brother.

MIO. No. You couldn't. You were quite right. The gods were damned ironic tonight, and they've worked it out.

ESDRAS. What will be changed if it comes to trial again? More blood poured out to a mythical justice, but your father lying still where he lies now.

MIO. The bright, ironical gods! What fun they have in heaven! When a man prays hard for any gift, they give it, and then one more to boot that makes it useless. (*To* MIR-IAMNE.) You might have picked some other stranger to dance with!

MIRIAMNE. I know.

MIO. Or chosen some other evening to sit outside in the rain. But no, it had to be this. All my life long I've wanted only one thing, to say to the world and prove it: the man you killed was clean and true and full of love as the twelve-year-old that stood and taught in the temple. I can say that now and give my proofs—and now you stick a girl's face between me and the rites I've sworn the dead shall have of me! You ask too much! Your brother can take his chance! He was ready enough to let an innocent man take certainty for him to pay for the years he's had. That parts us, then, but we're parted anyway, by the same dark wind that blew us together. I shall say what I have to say. (*He steps back.*) And I'm not welcome here.

MIRIAMNE. But don't go now! You've stayed too long! He'll be waiting!

MIO. Well, is this any safer? Let the winds blow, the four winds of the world, and take us to the four winds.

(*The three are silent before him. He turns and goes out.*)

CURTAIN

ACT THREE

SCENE: *The river bank outside the tenement, a little before the close of the previous act. The rain still falls through the street lamps. The* TWO NATTY YOUNG MEN IN SERGE AND GRAY *are leaning against the masonry in a ray of light, concentrating on a game of chance. Each holds in his hand a packet of ten or fifteen crisp bills. They compare the numbers on the top notes and immediately a bill changes hands. This goes on with varying fortune until the tide begins to run toward the* FIRST GUNMAN, *who has accumulated nearly the whole supply. They play on in complete silence, evidently not wishing to make any noise. Occasionally they raise their heads slightly to look carefully about. Luck begins to favor the* SECOND GUNMAN, *and the notes come his way. Neither evinces the slightest interest in how the game goes. They merely play on, bored, half-absorbed. There is a slight noise at the tenement door. They put the bills away and watch.* TROCK *comes out, pulls the door shut and comes over to them. He says a few words too low to be heard, and without changing expression the* YOUNG MEN *saunter toward the right.* TROCK *goes out to the left, and the* SECOND PLAYER, *catching that out of the corner of his eye, lingers in a glimmer of light to go on with the game. The* FIRST, *with an eye on the tenement door, begins to play without ado, and the bills again shift back and forth, then concentrate in the hands of the* FIRST GUNMAN. *The* SECOND *shrugs his shoulders, searches his pockets, finds one bill, and playing with it begins to win heavily. They hear the door opening, and putting the notes away, slip out in front of the rock.* MIO *emerges, closes the door, looks round him and walks to the left. Near the corner of the tenement he pauses, reaches out his hand to try the rain, looks up toward the street, and stands uncertainly a moment. He returns and leans against the tenement wall.* MIRIAMNE *comes out.* MIO *continues to look off into space as if unaware of her. She looks away.*

MIO. This rather takes one off his high horse.—What I mean, tough weather for a hegira. You see, this is my sleeping suit, and if I get it wet—basta!

MIRIAMNE. If you could only hide here.

MIO. Hide?

MIRIAMNE. Lucia would take you in. The street-piano man.

MIO. At the moment I'm afflicted with claustrophobia. I prefer to die in the open, seeking air.

MIRIAMNE. But you could stay there till daylight.

MIO. You're concerned about me.

MIRIAMNE. Shall I ask him?

MIO. No. On the other hand there's a certain reason in your concern. I looked up the street and our old friend Trock hunches patiently under the warehouse eaves.

MIRIAMNE. I was sure of that.

MIO. And here I am, a young man on a cold night, waiting the end of the rain.

Being read my lesson by a boy, a blind boy— you know the one I mean. Knee-deep in the salt-marsh, Miriam, bitten from within, fought.

MIRIAMNE. Wouldn't it be better if you came back in the house?

MIO. You forget my claustrophobia.

MIRIAMNE. Let me walk with you, then. Please. If I stay beside you he wouldn't dare.

MIO. And then again he might.—We don't speak the same language, Miriamne.

MIRIAMNE. I betrayed you. Forgive me.

MIO. I wish I knew this region. There's probably a path along the bank.

MIRIAMNE. Yes. Shadow went that way.

MIO. That's true, too. So here I am, a young man on a wet night, and blind in my weather eye. Stay and talk to me.

MIRIAMNE. If it happens—it's my fault.

MIO. Not at all, sweet. You warned me to keep away. But I would have it. Now I have to find a way out. It's like a chess game.

If you think long enough there's always a way out.—For one or the other.—I wonder why white always wins and black always loses in the problems. White to move and mate in three moves. But what if white were to lose—ah, what then? Why, in that case, obviously black would be white and white would be black.—As it often it.—As we often are.—Might makes white. Losers turn black. Do you think I'd have time to draw a gun?

MIRIAMNE. No.

MIO. I'm a fair shot. Also I'm fair game. (*The door of the tenement opens and* GARTH *comes out to look about quickly. Seeing only* MIO *and* MIRIAMNE *he goes in and comes out again almost immediately carrying one end of a door on which a body lies covered with a cloth. The* HOBO *carries the other end. They go out to the right with their burden.*) This is the burial of Shadow, then; feet first he dips, and leaves the haunts of men. Let us make mourn for Shadow, wetly lying, in elegiac stanzas and sweet crying. Be gentle with him, little cold waves and fishes; nibble him not, respect his skin and tissues—

MIRIAMNE. Must you say such things?

MIO. My dear, some requiem is fitting over the dead, even for Shadow. But the last rhyme was bad. Whittle him not, respect his dying wishes. That's better. And then to conclude: His aromatic virtues, slowly rising will circumnamb the isle, beyond disguising. He clung to life beyond the wont of men. Time and his silence drink us all. Amen. How I hate these identicals. The French allow them, but the French have no principles anyway. You know, Miriamne, there's really nothing mysterious about human life. It's purely mechanical, like an electric appliance. Stop the engine that runs the generator and the current's broken. When we think the brain gives off a small electric discharge—quite measurable, and constant within limits. But that's not what makes your hair stand up when frightened.

MIRIAMNE. I think it's a mystery.

MIO. Human life? We'll have to wear veils if we're to keep it a mystery much longer.

Now if Shadow and I were made up into sausages we'd probably make very good sausages.

MIRIAMNE. Don't—

MIO. I'm sorry. I speak from a high place, far off, long ago, looking down. The cortège returns. (GARTH *and the* HOBO *return, carrying the door, the cloth lying loosely over it.*) I hoped you placed an obol in his mouth to pay the ferry-man? Even among the Greeks a little money was prerequisite to Elysium. (GARTH *and the* HOBO *go inside, silent.*) No? It's grim to think of Shadow lingering among lesser shades on the hither side. For lack of a small gratuity. (ESDRAS *comes out the open door and closes it behind him.*)

ESDRAS. You must wait here, Mio, or go inside. I know you don't trust me, and I haven't earned your trust. You're young enough to seek truth— and there is no truth; and I know that— but I shall call the police and see that you get safely off.

MIO. It's a little late for that.

ESDRAS. I shall try.

MIO. And your terms? For I daresay you make terms?

ESDRAS. No.

MIO. Then let me remind you what will happen. The police will ask some questions. When they're answered they'll ask more, and before they're done with it your son will be implicated.

ESDRAS. Must he be?

MIO. I shall not keep quiet. (*A pause.*)

ESDRAS. Still, I'll go.

MIO. I don't ask help, remember. I make no truce. He's not on my conscience, and I'm not on yours.

ESDRAS. But you could make it easier, so easily. He's my only son. Let him live.

MIO. His chance of survival's
better than mine, I'd say.

ESDRAS. I'll go.

MIO. I don't urge it.

ESDRAS. No. I put my son's life in your hands.
When you're gone,
that may come to your mind.

MIO. Don't count on it.

ESDRAS. Oh,
I count on nothing. (*He turns to go.* MIRI-
AMNE *runs over to him and silently kisses
his hands.*)
Not mine, not mine, my daughter!
They're guilty hands. (*He goes out.* GARTH'S
violin is heard within.)

MIO. There was a war in heaven
once, all the angels on one side, and all
the devils on the other, and since that time
disputes have raged among the learned,
  concerning
whether the demons won, or the angels.
  Maybe
the angels won, after all.

MIRIAMNE. And again, perhaps
there are no demons or angels.

MIO. Oh, there are none.
But I could love your father.

MIRIAMNE. I love him. You see,
he's afraid because he's old. The less one has
to lose the more he's afraid.

MIO. Suppose one had
only a short stub end of life, or held
a flashlight with the batteries run down
till the bulb was dim, and knew that he
  could live
while the glow lasted. Or suppose one knew
that while he stood in a little shelter of time
under a bridgehead, say, he could live, and
  then,
from then on, nothing. Then to lie and turn
with the earth and sun, and regard them not
  in the least
when the bulb was extinguished or he
  stepped beyond
his circle into the cold? How would he live
that last dim quarter-hour, before he went,
minus all recollection, to grow in grass
between cobblestones?

MIRIAMNE. Let me put my arms round you,
  Mio.
Then if anything comes, it's for me, too.
(*She puts both arms round him.*)

MIO. Only suppose
this circle's charmed! To be safe until he
  steps
from this lighted space into dark! Time
  pauses here
and high eternity grows in one quarter-hour
in which to live.

MIRIAMNE. Let me see if anyone's there—
there in the shadows. (*She looks toward
the right.*)

MIO. It might blast our eternity—
blow it to bits. No, don't go. This is forever,
here where we stand. And I ask you,
  Miriamne,
how does one spend a forever?

MIRIAMNE. You're frightened?

MIO. Yes.
So much that time stands still.

MIRIAMNE. Why didn't I speak—
tell them—when the officers were here? I
  failed you
in that one moment!

MIO. His life for mine? Oh, no.
I wouldn't want it, and you couldn't give it.
And if I should go on living we're cut
  apart
by that brother of yours.

MIRIAMNE. Are we?

MIO. Well, think about it.
A body lies between us, buried in quicklime.
Your allegiance is on the other side of that
  grave
and not to me.

MIRIAMNE. No, Mio! Mio, I love you!

MIO. I love you, too, but in case my life
  went on
beyond that barrier of dark—then Garth
would run his risk of dying.

MIRIAMNE. He's punished, Mio.
His life's been torment to him. Let him go,
for my sake, Mio.

MIO. I wish I could. I wish
I'd never seen him—or you. I've steeped too
  long
in this thing. It's in my teeth and bones. I
  can't
let go or forget. And I'll not add my lie
to the lies that cumber his ground. We live
  our days
in a storm of lies that drifts the truth too
  deep
for path or shovel; but I've set my foot on
  a truth
for once, and I'll trail it down! (*A silence.*
MIRIAMNE *looks out to the right.*)

MIRIAMNE. There's someone there—
I heard—(CARR *comes in from the right.*)

MIO. It's Carr.

CARR. That's right. No doubt about it.
Excuse me.

MIO. Glad to see you. This is Miriamne.
Carr's a friend of mine.

CARR. You're better employed
than when I saw you last.

MIO. Bow to the gentleman,
Miriamne. That's meant for you.

MIRIAMNE. Thank you, I'm sure.
Should I leave you, Mio? You want to talk?

MIO. Oh, no,
we've done our talking.

MIRIAMNE. But—

CARR. I'm the one's out of place—
I wandered back because I got worried about
  you,
that's the truth.—Oh—those two fellows
  with the hats
down this way, you know, the ones that ran
after we heard the shooting—they're back
  again,
lingering or malingering down the bank,
revisiting the crime, I guess. They may
mean well.

MIO. I'll try to avoid them.

CARR. I didn't care
for the way they looked at me.—No luck, I
  suppose,
with that case history? The investigation
you had on hand?

MIO. I can't say. By the way,
the stiff that fell in the water and we saw
  swirling
down the eddy, he came trudging up, later
  on,
long enough to tell his name. His name was
  Shadow,
but he's back in the water now. It's all in an
  evening.
These things happen here.

CARR. Good God!

MIO. I know.
I wouldn't believe it if you told it.

CARR. But—
the man was alive?

MIO. Oh, not for long! He's dunked
for good this time. That's all that's happened.

CARR. Well,
if you don't need me—

MIRIAMNE. You had a message to send—
have you forgotten—?

MIO. I?—Yes, I had a message—
but I won't send it—not now.

MIRIAMNE. Then I will—!

MIO. No.
Let it go the way it is! It's all arranged
another way. You've been a good scout,
  Carr,
the best I ever knew on the road.

CARR. That sounds
like making your will.

MIO. Not yet, but when I do
I've thought of something to leave you. It's
  the view
of Mt. Rainier from the Seattle jail,
snow over cloud. And the rusty chain in my
  pocket
from a pair of handcuffs my father wore.
  That's all
the worldly goods I'm seized of.

CARR. Look, Mio—hell—
if you're in trouble—

MIO. I'm not. Not at all. I have
a genius that attends me where I go,
and guards me now. I'm fine.

CARR. Well, that's good news.
He'll have his work cut out.

MIO. Oh, he's a genius.

CARR. I'll see you then.
I'll be at the Grand Street place. I'm lucky tonight,
and I can pay. I could even pay for two.

MIO. Thanks, I may take you up.

CARR. Good night.

MIO. Right, Carr.

CARR (to MIRIAMNE). Good night.

MIRIAMNE (after a pause). Good night.
(CARR goes out to the left.)
Why did you do that? He's your genius, Mio,
and you let him go.

MIO. I couldn't help it.

MIRIAMNE. Call him.
Run after him and call him!

MIO. I tried to say it
and it strangled in my throat. I might have known
you'd win in the end.

MIRIAMNE. Is it for me?

MIO. For you?
It stuck in my throat, that's all I know.

MIRIAMNE. Oh, Mio,
I never asked for that! I only hoped
Garth could go clear.

MIO. Well, now he will.

MIRIAMNE. But you—
It was your chance!

MIO. I've lost
my taste for revenge if it falls on you. Oh, God,
deliver me from the body of this earth
I've dragged behind me all these years! Miriamne!
Miriamne!

MIRIAMNE. Yes!

MIO. Miriamne, if you love me
teach me a treason to what I am, and have been,
till I learn to live like a man! I think I'm waking
from a long trauma of hate and fear and death

that's hemmed me from my birth—and glimpse a life
to be lived in hope—but it's young in me yet, I can't
get free, or forgive! But teach me how to live
and forget to hate!

MIRIAMNE. He would have forgiven.

MIO. He?

MIRIAMNE. Your father. (A pause.)

MIO. Yes. (Another pause.)
You'll think it strange, but I've never remembered that.

MIRIAMNE. How can I help you?

MIO. You have.

MIRIAMNE. If I were a little older—if I knew
the things to say! I can only put out my hands
and give you back the faith you bring to me
by being what you are. Because to me
you are all hope and beauty and brightness drawn
across what's black and mean!

MIO. He'd have forgiven—
Then there's no more to say—I've groped long enough
through this everglades of old revenges— here
the road ends.—Miriamne, Miriamne,
the iron I wore so long—it's eaten through
and fallen from me. Let me have your arms.
They'll say we're children—Well—the world's made up
of children.

MIRIAMNE. Yes.

MIO. But it's too late for me.

MIRIAMNE. No. (She goes into his arms, and they kiss for the first time.)
Then we'll meet again?

MIO. Yes.

MIRIAMNE. Where?

MIO. I'll write—
or send Carr to you.

MIRIAMNE. You won't forget?

MIO. Forget?
Whatever streets I walk, you'll walk them, too,

from now on, and whatever roof or stars
I have to house me, you shall share my roof
and stars and morning. I shall not forget.

MIRIAMNE. God keep you!

MIO. And keep you. And this to remember!
if I should die, Miriamne, this half-hour
is our eternity. I came here seeking
light in darkness, running from the dawn,
and stumbled on a morning.

(*One of the* YOUNG MEN IN SERGE *strolls in
casually from the right, looks up and down
without expression, then, seemingly having
forgotten something, retraces his steps and
goes out.* ESDRAS *comes in slowly from the
left. He has lost his hat, and his face is bleeding
from a slight cut on the temple. He
stands abjectly near the tenement.*)

MIRIAMNE. Father—what is it? (*She goes
towards* ESDRAS.)

ESDRAS. Let me alone. (*He goes nearer to*
MIO.)
He wouldn't let me pass.
The street's so icy up along the bridge
I had to crawl on my knees—he kicked
  me back
three times—and then he held me there—
  I swear
what I could do I did! I swear to you
I'd save you if I could.

MIO. What makes you think
that I need saving?

ESDRAS. Child, save yourself if you can!
He's waiting for you.

MIO. Well, we knew that before.

ESDRAS. He won't wait much longer. He'll
  come here—
he told me so. Those damned six months
  of his—
he wants them all—and you're to die—
  you'd spread
his guilt—I had to listen to it—

MIO. Wait—(*He walks forward and looks
casually to the right, then returns.*)
There must be some way up through the
  house and out
across the roof—

ESDRAS. He's watching that. But come in—
and let me look.—

MIO. I'll stay here, thanks. Once in
and I'm a rat in a deadfall—Ill stay here—
look for me if you don't mind.

ESDRAS. Then watch for me—
I'll be on the roof—(*He goes in hurriedly.*)

MIO (*looking up*). Now all you silent powers
that make the sleet and dark, and never yet
have spoken, give us a sign, let the throw
  be ours
this night, on this longest night, when the
  winter sets
his foot on the threshold leading up to spring
and enters with remembered cold—let fall
some mercy with the rain. We are two lovers
here in your night, and we wish to live.

MIRIAMNE. Oh, Mio—
if you pray that way, nothing good will
  come!
You're bitter, Mio.

MIO. How many floors has this building?

MIRIAMNE. Five or six. It's not as high as
  the bridge.

MIO. No, I thought not. How many pome-
  granate seeds
did you eat, Persephone?

MIRIAMNE. Oh, darling, darling,
if you die, don't die alone.

MIO. I'm afraid I'm damned
to hell, and you're not damned at all. Good
  God,
how long he takes to climb!

MIRIAMNE. The stairs are steep. (*A slight
pause.*)

MIO. I'll follow him.

MIRIAMNE. He's there—at the window—
  now.
He waves you to go back, not to go in.
Mio, see, that path between the rocks—
they're not watching that—they're out at
  the river—
I can see them there—they can't watch
  both—
it leads to a street above.

MIO. I'll try it, then.
Kiss me. You'll hear. But if you never
  hear—
then I'm the king of hell, Persephone,
and I'll expect you.

MIRIAMNE. Oh, lover, keep safe.

MIO. Good-bye. (*He slips quickly between the rocks. There is a quick machine gun rat-tat. The violin stops,* MIRIAMNE *runs toward the path.* MIO *comes back slowly, a hand pressed under his heart.*)
It seems you were mistaken.

MIRIAMNE. Oh, God, forgive me! (*She puts an arm round him. He sinks to his knees.*)
Where is it, Mio? Let me help you in! Quick, quick,
let me help you!

MIO. I hadn't thought to choose—this—ground—
but it will do. (*He slips down.*)

MIRIAMNE. Oh, God, forgive me!

MIO. Yes?
The king of hell was not forgiven then,
Dis is his name, and Hades is his home—
and he goes alone—

MIRIAMNE. Why does he bleed so? Mio, if you go
I shall go with you.

MIO. It's better to stay alive.
I wanted to stay alive—because of you—
I leave you that—and what he said to me dying:
I love you, and will love you after I die.
Tomorrow, I shall still love you, as I've loved
the stars I'll never see, and all the mornings
that might have been yours and mine. Oh, Miriamne,
you taught me this.

MIRIAMNE. If only I'd never seen you
then you could live—

MIO. That's blasphemy—Oh, God,
there might have been some easier way of it.
You didn't want me to die, did you, Miriamne—?
You didn't send me away—?

MIRIAMNE. Oh, never, never—

MIO. Forgive me—kiss me—I've got blood on your lips—
I'm sorry—it doesn't matter—I'm sorry— (ESDRAS *and* GARTH *come out.*)

MIRIAMNE. Mio—
I'd have gone to die myself—you must hear this, Mio.

I'd have died to help you—you must listen, sweet,
you must hear it—(*She rises.*)
I can die, too, see! You! There!
You in the shadows!—You killed him to silence him! (*She walks toward the path.*)
But I'm not silenced! All that he knew I know,
and I'll tell it tonight! Tonight—
tell it and scream it
through all the streets—that Trock's a murderer
and he hired you for this murder!
Your work's not done—
and you won't live long! Do you hear?
You're murderers, and I know who you are!
(*The machine gun speaks again. She sinks to her knees.* GARTH *runs to her.*)

GARTH. You little fool! (*He tries to lift her.*)

MIRIAMNE. Don't touch me! (*She crawls toward* MIO.)
Look, Mio! They killed me, too. Oh, you can believe me
now, Mio. You can believe I wouldn't hurt you,
because I'm dying! Why doesn't he answer me?
Oh, now he'll never know! (*She sinks down, her hand over her mouth, choking.* GARTH *kneels beside her, then rises, shuddering. The* HOBO *comes out.* LUCIA *and* PINY *look out.*)

ESDRAS. It lacked only this.

GARTH. Yes. (ESDRAS *bends over* MIRIAMNE, *then rises slowly.*)
Why was the bastard born? Why did he come here?

ESDRAS. Miriamne—Miriamne—yes, and Mio,
one breath shall call you now—forgive us both—
forgive the ancient evil of the earth
that brought you here—

GARTH. Why must she be a fool?

ESDRAS. Well, they were wiser than you and I. To die
when you are young and untouched, that's beggary
to a miser of years, but the devils locked in synod
shake and are daunted when men set their lives

at hazard for the heart's love, and lose. And
  these,
who were yet children, will weigh more
  than all
a city's elders when the experiment
is reckoned up in the end. Oh, Miriamne,
and Mio—Mio, my son—know this where
  you lie,
this is the glory of earth-born men and
  women,
not to cringe, never to yield, but standing,
take defeat implacable and defiant,
die unsubmitting. I wish that I'd died so,
long ago; before you're old you'll wish
that you had died as they have. On this star,
in this hard star-adventure, knowing not
what the fires mean to right and left, nor
  whether
a meaning was intended or presumed,
man can stand up, and look out blind, and
  say:
in all these turning lights I find no clue,
only a masterless night, and in my blood
no certain answer, yet is my mind my own,
yet is my heart a cry toward something dim
in distance, which is higher than I am
and makes me emperor of the endless dark
even in seeking! What odds and ends of life
men may live otherwise, let them live, and
  then
go out, as I shall go, and you. Our part
is only to bury them. Come, take her up.
They must not lie here.

(LUCIA *and* PINY *come near to help.* ESDRAS
and GARTH *stoop to carry* MIRIAMNE.)

CURTAIN

High Tor

BY MAXWELL ANDERSON

Guthrie McClintic presented Maxwell Anderson's HIGH TOR for the first time on any stage in the Hanna Theater, Cleveland, Ohio, Wednesday night, December 30, 1936, with this cast:

THE INDIAN	Harry Irvine	A SAILOR	William Casamo
VAN DORN	Burgess Meredith	DeWITT	Charles D. Brown
JUDITH	Mab Maynard	DOPE	Leslie Gorall
ART. J. BIGGS	Harold Moffet	ELKUS	Hume Cronyn
JUDGE SKIMMERHORN	Thomas W. Ross	BUDDY	John Drew Colt
LISE	Peggy Ashcroft	PATSY	Charles Forrester
CAPTAIN ASHER	Byron McGrath	A. B. SKIMMERHORN	John M. Kline
PIETER	John Philliber	BUDGE	Jackson Halliday

DUTCH CREW OF THE ONRUST

The play was staged by Mr. McClintic and the settings were designed by Jo Mielziner.

NOTE

HIGH TOR

ACT ONE

SCENE I

SCENE: *A section of the broad flat trap-rock summit of High Tor, from which one looks out into sky and from which one might look down a sheer quarter mile to the Tappan Zee below. A cluster of hexagonal pillared rocks masks the view to the left and a wind-tortured small hemlock wedges into the rock floor at the right. Light from the setting sun pours in from the left, and an ancient* INDIAN, *wearing an old greatcoat thrown round him like a blanket, stands in the rays from a cleft, making his prayer to the sunset.*

THE INDIAN. I make my prayer to you, the falling fire,
bearing in mind the whisper in my ears
from the great spirit, talking on the wind,
whispering that a young race, in its morning,
should pray to the rising sun, but a race that's old
and dying, should invoke the dying flame
eaten and gulfed by the shark-toothed mountain-west,
a god that dies to live. As we have died,
my race of the red faces and old ways,
and as we hope to rise. I give you thanks
for light, for the coming summer that will warm
my snake's blood, cold and crawling; for the rain
that fed the ripe May apples in the woods
in secret for me; for the waterfall
where the trout climb and pause under my hand,
taken in silence; for quiet on the hills
where the loud races dare not walk for fear
lest they be lost, where their blind hunters pass
peering with caps and guns, but see no game,
and curse as they go down, while the raccoon waits,
the woodchuck stands erect to catch the wind,
the partridge steps so lightly over leaves
the listening fox hears nothing, the possum hangs
head down, looking through his hands, and takes no breath,
the gray squirrel turns to stone against the rock,
watching the owl, the rabbit holds his ears
steady above the trembling of his heart
and the crow mocks down the shellbark. I am fed
and sheltered on this mountain where their hands
are helpless. But I am old as my race is old;
my eyes hunt day and night along the ground
the grave where I shall lie; my ears have heard
dead women calling upward from the earth,
mother and wife and child: "You are welcome here;
you are no longer welcome where you walk,
but here you are most welcome." I shall go,
and lie and sleep, and I shall give you thanks,
O God that dies, that my last night is dark
and long, for I am tired, but yet I ask
one summer more, that I may be warm again
and watch the nestlings grown upon the crag,
and hear the wild geese honking south by night,
if this may be, but if it may not be
then is my prayer, that when I lie to sleep
I may lie long, sleep soundly, hear no step,
hear only through the earth your step in spring,
O God of the dying fire!
(VAN DORN *and* JUDITH *come in right.*)

VAN DORN. Evening, John.

THE INDIAN. Evening.

VAN DORN. Had any luck so far?

THE INDIAN. Yes. Plenty of luck.

VAN DORN. Found it?

THE INDIAN. Yes.

VAN DORN. O.K., John, let me know. Let me know in time.

THE INDIAN. I will. Good night.

VAN DORN. Good night. (*The* INDIAN *slips away through the rocks to the left.*)

JUDITH. Who is it, Van?

VAN. Just an Indian.

JUDITH. Are there Indians?
I didn't know there were any Indians left.

VAN. Well, there's one. There's not much left of him,
and he's the last around here.

JUDITH. He's hunting something?
You asked him if he's found it.

VAN. Um—yes, you see,
he's looking for a place to make his grave,
and he's kind of captious about it—folks get that way
along toward the end, wanting their bones done up
in some particular fashion. Maybe because
that's all you've got to leave about that time
and you want it the way you want it.

JUDITH. Did he tell you this?

VAN. We've got an understanding. When he feels it
coming over him he's going to die
he'll let me know, and I'll go dig him in
so the crows and foxes can't get at him. See,
he's all alone in the world. We fixed this up
a couple of years ago.

JUDITH. But you couldn't, Van,
without a permit. A burial permit.

VAN. Oh,
I guess you could. This getting old and dying
and crawling into the ground, that was invented
back before medical examiners
and taxes and all that. The old boy's clean.
He'll go right back to dirt.

JUDITH. But, Van, you can't!
People can't die that way!

VAN. I guess they can.
What the hell good's being wrapped in cellophane?
You don't keep anyway.

JUDITH. You're impossible
to live with! Why do you say such things? If I
should die—you'd get a pine box!—

VAN. If you should die
the old boy that drives the sun around up there,

he'd unhitch, and put the cattle out
to grass, and give it up. He'd plumb lose interest
if you should die. Maybe I would myself,
I don't say. Maybe I would.—Fetch out that supper.
We want to see what we eat.

JUDITH (*opening a lunch box*). It's dinner, Van,
not supper.

VAN. That's what I said. Fetch out that dinner.
When it gets a little darker what's black's pepper
and what's green's parsley; still you can't be sure.
It might be ants.

JUDITH. Just the same we'll quarrel.
We'll always quarrel.

VAN. Oh, no, We've both got sense.
What's the sense fighting? (*He looks at a paper that was round the lunch.*)

JUDITH. And you shouldn't read at table.

VAN. I never do. The Nanuet bank's been robbed.
My God, there's not enough money in Nanuet
to buy their gas for a get-away. One night
pap and me sat in on a poker game
in Nanuet and took twenty-seven dollars
out of town. Next day they couldn't do business.
The place was clean.

JUDITH. There were troopers at the train
tonight, and sirens going through Haverstraw,
but the robbers got away.

VAN. They took twenty-five thousand.
How'd twenty-five thousand get to Nanuet?
It's against nature.

JUDITH. It didn't stay there long.

VAN. No—I understand that.
But just to have it there in passing, just
to look at, just to fool the customers,
how do they do it?

JUDITH. Maybe it wasn't real.

VAN. Federal money, that's it. Some of the stuff

Jim Farley prints in Washington with the stamps
to pay you for voting straight. Only now you see it
and now you don't.

JUDITH. They say it buys as much
as if you earned it.

VAN. Bad for the stomach, though,
to live on humble pie.

JUDITH. I'd rather work.

VAN. Well, as I said, don't work if you don't feel like it.
Any time you want to move up in the hills
and sleep with me, it's a bargain.

JUDITH. Van!

VAN. Why not?
We'll get married if that's what you mean.

JUDITH. You haven't any job. And you make it sound
like animals.

VAN. I'm fond of animals.

JUDITH. You shoot them all the time.

VAN. Well, I get hungry.
Any man's liable to get hungry.

JUDITH. Van,
I want to talk to you seriously.

VAN. Can't be done.
Listen, things get serious enough
without setting out to do it.

JUDITH. Van, this spring
you had three weeks' work, laying dry wall.
You could have had more, but you didn't take it.
You're an expert mason—

VAN. I'm good at everything.

JUDITH. But you work three weeks in the year—

VAN. That's all I need—

JUDITH. And all the rest of the year you hunt or fish
or sleep, or God knows what—

VAN. Ain't it the truth?

JUDITH. Last fall I came looking for you once, and you

were gone—gone to Port Jervis hunting—deer,
you said on the postcard—

VAN. Sure, I was hunting deer—
didn't I bring you half a venison?

JUDITH. But not a word to me till I got the postcard
ten days later—

VAN. Didn't have a minute—

JUDITH. Then last winter there's a note nailed to a tree
and you're in Virginia, down in the Dismal Swamp
tracking bear. Now, for God's sake, Van, it's no way to live.

VAN. Jeez, it's a lot of fun.

JUDITH. Maybe for you.

VAN. You want me to take that job.

JUDITH. Why don't you, Van?

VAN. Porter in a hotel, lugging up satchels, opening windows, maybe you get a dime.
I'd choke to death.

JUDITH. I'd see you every day.

VAN. Yeah, I could see you on the mezzanine, taking dictation from the drummer boys,
all about how they can't get home. You can stand it,
a woman stands that stuff, but if you're a man
I say it chokes you.

JUDITH. We can't live in your cabin
and have no money, like the Jackson Whites over at Suffern.

VAN. Hell, you don't need money.
Pap worked that out. All you need's a place to sleep
and something to eat. I've never seen the time
I couldn't find a meal on the mountain here,
rainbow trout, jugged hare, something in season
right around the zodiac.

JUDITH. You didn't like
the Chevrolet factory, either?

VAN (*walking toward the cliff edge*). Look at it, Judy.
That's the Chevrolet factory, four miles down,

and straight across, that's Sing Sing. Right
from here
you can't tell one from another; get inside,
and what's the difference? You're in there,
and you work,
and they've got you. If you're in the factory
you buy a car, and then you put in your time
to pay for the goddam thing. If you get in
a hurry
and steal a car, they put you in Sing Sing
first,
and then you work out your time. They
graduate
from one to the other, back and forth, those
guys,
paying for cars both ways. But I was smart.
I parked at a polis station and rung the bell
and took to the woods. Not for your Uncle
Dudley.
They plugged the dice.

JUDITH. But one has to have a car.

VAN. Honest to God now, Judy, what's the
hurry?
Where in hell are we going?

JUDITH. If a man works hard,
and has ability, as you have, Van,
he takes a place among them, saves his
money,
works right out of the ruck and gets above
where he's safe and secure.

VAN. I wouldn't bet on it much.

JUDITH. But it's true.

VAN. All right, suppose it's true. Suppose
a man saves money all his life, and works
like hell about forty years, till he can say:
good-bye, I'm going, I'm on easy street
from now on. What's he do?

JUDITH. Takes a vacation.

VAN. Goes fishing, maybe? I'm on vacation
now.
Why should I work forty years to earn
time off when I've got it?

JUDITH. It's not always easy,
you know it's not. There was that time last
winter
when I helped you out.

VAN. Why, sure, you helped me out.
Why wouldn't you? But if you didn't help
me
I'd get along.

JUDITH. Yes, you would. I know you would.
But you don't even seem to want money.
You won't take it
when they bring it to you.

VAN. When did they bring me any?

JUDITH. And what if there was a child?

VAN. Why, he'd be fine—
the less they have the better they like it.—
Oh,
you mean the trap-rock company, wanting
to buy
High Tor? They offered seven hundred
dollars—
and they offered pap ten thousand before
he died,
and he wouldn't sell.

JUDITH. He wouldn't?

VAN. They wanted to chew
the back right off this mountain, the way
they did
across the clove there. Leave the old palisades
sticking up here like billboards, nothing left
but a false front facing the river. Not for
pap,
and not for me. I like this place.

JUDITH. But, Van Van Dorn!
Ten thousand dollars!

VAN. Well, it's Federal money.
Damn stuff evaporates. Put it in a sock
along with moth balls, and come back next
year,
and there's nothing left but the smell. Look,
Judy, its
a quarter mile straight down to the Tappan
Zee
from here.—You can see fifteen miles of
river
north and south. I grew up looking at it.
Hudson came up that river just about
three hundred years ago, and lost a ship
here in the Zee. They say the crew climbed
up
this Tor to keep a lookout for the fleet
that never came. Maybe the Indians got
them.
Anyway on dark nights before a storm,
they say you sometimes see them.

JUDITH. Have you seen them?

VAN. The Dutchmen? Maybe I have. You
can't be sure.
It's pretty wild around here when it storms.

That's when I like it best. But look at it now.
There was a Jaeger here from Switzerland
last year. He took one squint at this and said
they could keep their Alps, for all him.
  Look at the willows
along the far breakwater.

JUDITH. It's beautiful.

VAN. Every night I come back here like the
  Indian
to get a fill of it. Seven hundred dollars
and tear it down? Hell, no. (BIGGS and SKIM-
MERHORN *come in from the right, a bit bedraggled, and wiping their brows.* SKIMMER-
HORN *carries a brief-case. It is growing
darker.*)

BIGGS. Hey listen, Mac, any houses round
here?

VAN. Guess you're off the beat, buddy; never
heard of any houses on the mountain.

SKIMMERHORN. Come on, Art; we're doing
well if we're down at the road before dark.

BIGGS. Look, Mac, maybe you can help us
out. You familiar with this region, at all?

VAN. I've been around here some.

BIGGS. Well, we're all afternoon hunting a
cabin that's somewhere along the ridge. Ever
hear of it?

VAN. Anybody live in it?

BIGGS. Fellow named Van Dorn.

VAN. Oh, yes, sure.

BIGGS. You know where it is?

VAN. Sure. You climb down the face of the
cliff here and keep left along the ledge about
a hundred yards, then you turn sharp left
through a cleft up the ridge. Follow the trail
about half a mile and there you are.

SKIMMERHORN. Down the face of the cliff?

VAN. Down through the rocks there, then
turn left—

SKIMMERHORN. A monkey couldn't go down
there, hanging on with four hands and a
tail!

VAN. Well, you can always walk along back
toward Little Tor, and cut down from there
through the gulch. There's a slough at the

bottom of the ravine, but if you get through
that you can see the cabin up on the side-
hill. About four miles that way.

SKIMMERHORN. Yeah, we'll set right out. I
always did want to get lost up here and
spend a night in the hills.

VAN. Oh, you'll get lost, all right.

BIGGS. Any snakes?

VAN. No, you might see a copperhead, or a
timber rattler.

SKIMMERHORN. Coming back down?

BIGGS. Yeah, we'd better go down. Thanks.

VAN. Don't mention it. (BIGGS *and* SKIMMER-
HORN *go out to the right.*)

JUDITH. But they were looking for you?

VAN. Yeah.

JUDITH. Why didn't you tell them?

VAN. What?

JUDITH. Who you were!

VAN. They didn't ask about that.

JUDITH. But out of common courtesy!

VAN. Well, you see, I know who they are.

JUDITH. Who are they?

VAN. Art J. Biggs, Junior, and Skimmerhorn,
Judge Skimmerhorn.

JUDITH. But why not talk to them?

VAN. Oh, we communicate by mail. I've got
a dozen letters stacked up from the firm:
Skimmerhorn, Skimmerhorn, Biggs and
  Skimmerhorn,
and maybe two or three Skimmerhorns I left
  out
printed across the top. They're realtors,
whatever that is, and they own the trap-rock
  company,
and one of the Skimmerhorns, he's probate
  judge,
and goes around condemning property
when they want to make a rake-off. Take
  a letter:
Dear Skimmerhorn—

JUDITH. But they're the trap-rock men!

VAN. That's what I said.

JUDITH. I'll call them!

VAN. Oh, no; oh, no!
I've got nothing to say to those two buzzards
except I hope they break their fat-back necks
on their own trap-rock.

JUDITH. You take a lot for granted.

VAN. Do I?

JUDITH. You think, because I said I loved
  you once,
that's the end; I'm finished.

VAN. Oh, far from it.

JUDITH. Oh, yes—you think because a girl's
  been kissed
she stays kissed, and after that the man
does her thinking for her.

VAN. Hell, it's all I can do
to handle my own thinking.

JUDITH. If we're married
I'll have to live the way you want to live.
You prefer being a pauper!

VAN. Get it straight!
I don't take money nor orders, and I live
as I damn well please.

JUDITH. But we'd live like paupers!
And you could have a fortune!

VAN. Seven hundred dollars?

JUDITH. You could get more!

VAN. I don't mean to sell at all.

JUDITH. You see; it's your place, and your
  thinking! You decide,
but I'd have to stand it with you!

VAN. What do you want?

JUDITH. Something to start on; and now,
  you see, we could have it,
only you won't!

VAN. I can't, Judy, that's the truth.
I just can't.

JUDITH. They'll get it anyway.
They've worked right up to where your land
  begins,
and they won't stop for you. They'll just
  condemn it
and take it.

VAN. They'll be in trouble.

JUDITH. You can't make trouble
for companies. They have a dozen lawyers
and ride right over you. I've worked for
  them.
It's never any use.

VAN. Well, I won't sell.

JUDITH. We'll call it off then.

VAN. What?

JUDITH. Between you and me.

VAN. Only you don't mean it.

JUDITH. I know I do, though.
You haven't thought about it, and so you
  think
I couldn't do it. But it's better now
than later.

VAN. You don't know what it means to me
if you can say it.

JUDITH. It means as much to me,
but I look ahead a little.

VAN. What do you see?

JUDITH. Two people growing old
and having children, running wild in the
  woods
with nothing.

VAN. There's no better place to run.
But I've been counting on you. More than
  you know.
More than—Judy, this is the kind of night
we've been in love most.

JUDITH. Yes, we could be in love,
but that's not everything.

VAN. Well, just about.
What else do we get?

JUDITH. I think I'd better go.
It's getting dark.

VAN. You could find your way by the beacon.

JUDITH. I'd better go. (BIGGS *and* SKIMMER-
HORN *come back from the right.*)

BIGGS. Listen, Mac, would you do something
for us?

VAN. I don't know.

BIGGS. Could you take a paper round to Van
Dorn and leave it with him?

VAN. A summons?

BIGGS. A sort of notice.

VAN. Yeah, a notice to appear. No, I couldn't.

BIGGS. It's worth a dollar to me.

VAN. I'd be cheating you.

SKIMMERHORN. Make it two dollars.

VAN. You'd be throwing away money.

SKIMMERHORN. Never mind that part of it. Will you do it?

VAN. You'll take a running jump over the edge of the cliff and think things over on the way down before I serve any papers for you.

BIGGS. What's the matter with us?

VAN. Might be hoof and mouth disease, for all I know. You certainly brought an awful stench up here with you.

SKIMMERHORN. Not much on manners, these natives.

VAN. My rule in life is keep away from skunks.

BIGGS. You'll get the tar kicked out of you one of these days.

VAN. Make it today.

JUDITH. If you gentlemen care to know, this is Mr. Van Dorn.

BIGGS. Say, are you Van Dorn?

VAN. Sure I am.

BIGGS (*extending a hand*). Oh, in that case, forget it—you're the fellow we want to see!— Boy, we apologize—(*He uncovers.*) and to the lady, too! Listen, I don't know what to say but you've got us all wrong. We want to buy this place!

VAN. You like the view, I suppose?

BIGGS. Certainly is a view.

VAN. You wouldn't spoil it, of course? You wouldn't move in with a million dollars' worth of machinery and cut the guts out of the mountain, would you?

SKIMMERHORN. We always leave the front— the part you see from the river.

VAN. But you take down all the law allows.

SKIMMERHORN. Well, we're in business.

VAN. Not with me.

JUDITH. Do you mind if I ask how much you're offering?

BIGGS. We said seven hundred, but I'll make it a thousand right here and now.

SKIMMERHORN. As a matter of fact, we'll make it two thousand.

BIGGS. Yeah, all right. Two thousand for the hundred and seven acres.

JUDITH. But you offered Mr. Van Dorn's father ten thousand before he died.

SKIMMERHORN. His father had a clear title, right down from the original Dutch patroon to the original Van Dorn. But unfortunately the present Mr. Van Dorn has a somewhat clouded claim to the acreage.

VAN. My father's title was clear, and he left it to me.

SKIMMERHORN. The truth is he should have employed a lawyer when he drew his will, because the instrument, as recorded, is faulty in many respects. It was brought before me in my capacity as probate judge at Ledentown.

VAN. And in your capacity as second vice-president of the trap-rock company you shot it full of holes.

SKIMMERHORN. Sir, I keep my duties entirely separate.

VAN. Sure, but when your left hand takes money your right hand finds out about it. And when there's too much to carry away in both hands you use a basket. You're also vice-president of the power company, and you stole right-of-ways clear across the country north and south—

SKIMMERHORN. We paid for every foot of land—

VAN. Yes, at your own price.

BIGGS. Let's not get in an argument, Mr. Van Dorn, because the fact that your father's will was improperly drawn means he died intestate and the land goes to his heirs. Now we've found twenty-seven Van Dorns living at Blauvelt, all claiming relationship and all willing to sign away their rights for a consideration.

VAN. The best you can do you'll need my name in your little paper, and you won't have it.

SKIMMERHORN. To put it straight, you'll take three thousand dollars, and I'll hold the will valid.

VAN. Oh, it's three thousand, now?

BIGGS. You'll say that's crooked, but it's not. It's perfectly legal—and it's what you get.

VAN. I'm still waiting to hear what you do about my signature.

SKIMMERHORN. It's quite possible you'll be held incompetent by the court and a guardian appointed.

VAN. Me, incompetent.

SKIMMERHORN. But I've got the validation in my pocket, naming you executor, if you'll sell.

BIGGS. And by God, anybody that won't take money when it's offered to him is incompetent! And you'll take it now or not at all! I don't go mountain-climbing every day with a blank check in my pocket! (*A pause.*) Come on: It's bad enough sliding down that trail by daylight.

VAN. Well, I wouldn't want to make you nervous,
a couple of eminent respectables
like you two—but a dog won't bite a Dutchman—
maybe you've heard that—and the reason is
a Dutchman's poison when he don't like you. Now,
I'm Dutch and I don't like you.

SKIMMERHORN. That's a threat?

VAN. Not at all. Only don't try to eat me or you'll curl up. I'm poison to a hound-dog, and you're both sons-of-bitches.

BIGGS. Come on. (*The daylight is now gone. The airplane beacon lights the scene from the right.*)

VAN. What's more
there's something funny about this mountain-top.
It draws fire. Every storm on the Tappan Zee
climbs up here and wraps itself around

High Tor, and blazes away at what you've got,
airplane beacon, steam-shovels, anything
newfangled. It smashed the beacon twice. It blew
the fuses on your shovel and killed a man
only last week. I've got a premonition
something might happen to you.

BIGGS. God, he's crazy.

SKIMMERHORN. Yeah, let him talk. (*There is a sudden rumbling roar of falling rock.*)

BIGGS. What's that?

VAN. That's nothing much.
That's just a section of the cliff come down
across the trail. I've been expecting it
this last two years. You'd better go down this way.

BIGGS. This way?

VAN. Yeah.

BIGGS. No, thanks.

VAN. Just as you say.
But there's something definitely hostile here
toward you two pirates. Don't try that trail in the dark.
Not if you want to be buried in your vaults
in Mount Repose. Your grieving families
might have to move two thousand tons of rock
to locate your remains. You think High Tor's
just so much raw material, but you're wrong.
A lot of stubborn men have died up here
and some of them don't sleep well. They come back
and push things round, these dark nights. Don't blame me
if anything falls on you.

SKIMMERHORN. Oh, what the hell!
Let's get out of here. (*Another long rumble of falling rock.*)

VAN. Another rock-fall.
Once they start there's likely to be more.
Something hanging round in the dark up here
doesn't like you boys. Not only me.
Better go down this way.

BIGGS. Thanks. (BIGGS *and* SKIMMERHORN *go out to the right.*)

JUDITH. What do you mean?

VAN. I don't **know.**

JUDITH. They'll say you threatened them. Good-bye, Van.

VAN. You'll be up tomorrow?

JUDITH. No. (*She steps down into a cleft.*)

VAN. You'd better let me see you down.

JUDITH. Oh, no.
I can climb. Stay here and guard your rock—
you think so much of it.

VAN. When will I see you?

JUDITH. Never.
We'll forget about it. You had a choice
and you chose High Tor. You're in love with
  your mountain.
Well, keep your mountain.

VAN. All right.

JUDITH. Good night.

VAN. Good night.
(*She disappears down the rocks.* VAN *sits in the shadows, looking into darkness. After a moment a barely perceptible* FIGURE *enters from the gloom at the right and crosses the stage toward the rocks at the left. At the foot of the climb he pauses and his face is caught in the light of the beacon. He is seen to be young or middle-aged, bearded, and wearing the costume of a Dutch sailor of the sixteen hundreds. He climbs the rocks, and* ANOTHER SAILOR, *a small cask strapped to his shoulders, follows.* THREE MORE *cross the stage similarly, then the* CAPTAIN *and* HIS WIFE *pause, like the others, in the light of the beacon. The* CAPTAIN *is like his men, only younger perhaps;* HIS WIFE *is a tiny figure, with a delicate girlish face looking out from under the Dutch bonnet. They too pass up the rocks, and are followed by a rolling* SILENUS *in the same garments. As they vanish* VAN *rises, looking after them.*)
Uh—huh—going to rain.

CURTAIN

SCENE II

SCENE: *The curtain goes up on complete darkness enfolding the summit of the Tor. There is a long cumbrous rolling, as of a ball going down a bowling alley, a flash of white light, a crackling as of falling pins and a mutter dying into echo along the hills. The flash reveals the outline of the Tor, black against the sky, and on it the figures of the* DUTCH CREW. *Again the roll, the flash, the break and the dying away. The beam of the airplane beacon steals into the scene sufficiently to suggest the bowlers, some of them standing, some sitting about the keg, the* CAPTAIN'S WIFE *a little apart from the rest. Beyond the peak is a moving floor, the upper side of blown cloud.*

THE CAPTAIN'S WIFE. I'm weary of it, Martin!
  When you drink
there should be one on guard to watch the
  river
lest the ship come, and pass, and we must
  haunt
the dark another year!

THE CAPTAIN. To humor her,
Pieter, old son, climb down and post the Zee,
and mind you keep good lookout.

PIETER. Ships, aye, ships—
when the ball's rolling and there's gin in
  hand
I go to post. My luck!

THE CAPTAIN. When you shipped with me
you signed the voyage.

PIETER. Is this sea or land?
I'm no foot soldier!

THE CAPTAIN. March!

PIETER. Aye, aye. I'm going. (PIETER *detaches himself from the group and goes down the rocks.*)

THE CAPTAIN. Are you content?

THE CAPTAIN'S WIFE. When the *Half Moon* returns
and we have boarded her, and the wind
  scuds fair
into the east—yes, when we see the wharves
of Texel town across the Zuyder Zee,
with faces waiting for us, hands and cries
to welcome our returning, then perhaps
I shall be content.

A SAILOR. Now God, for Texel town.

ANOTHER SOLDIER (*rising*). I'll drink no more.

DEWITT (*the Silenus*). Drink up, lads, and forget.
It's a long way to the Texel. Drink your drink
and play your play.

THE CAPTAIN. Drink up and play it out.

THE CAPTAIN'S WIFE. Have you forgotten how the cobbled street
comes down by cranks and turns upon the quay,
where the *Onrust* set sail? The traders' doors
under the blowing signs, bright colors hung
to catch unwary eyes? The bakers' ovens
and the long, hot brown loaves? The red-coal fires
and silver under candles? There your wives
wait for you, their sharp roofs in Amsterdam
cut on a rainy sky.

THE CAPTAIN. Be quiet, Lise.
You were so much in love you must come with me;
you were so young that I was patient with you,
but now day long, night long you carp and quarrel,
a carping wife.

LISE. We stay so long—so long;
Asher, at first the days were years, but now
the years are days; the ship that set us down
to watch this river palisades becomes
alike with supper-stories round a hearth
when we were children. Was there this ship at all,
was there a sailor-city, Amsterdam,
where the salt water washed the shallow piers
and the wind went out to sea? Will the ship return,
and shall I then see the Netherlands once more,
with sabots clattering homeward from the school
on winter evenings?

ASHER. Aye, there was a ship,
and we wait here for her, but she's long away,
somewhere up-river.

LISE. And now you drink and drink,
distill your liquor on the mountain-top
and bowl against the light. But when you break it
these new strange men come build it up again;
and giant shovels spade the mountain down,
and when you break them still the new strange men
rig them afresh and turn them on the rock,
eating the pillored stone. We must go back.
There's no safety here.

A SAILOR. We must go back.

ASHER. These muttering fools!

LISE. Oh, Asher, I'm afraid!
For one thing I have known, and never told
lest it be true, lest you be frightened, too,
lest we be woven of shadow! As the years
have gone, each year a century, they seem
less real, and all the boundaries of time,
our days and nights and hours, merge and are one,
escaping me. Then sometimes in a morning
when all the crew come down the rocks together,
holding my breath, I see you in the light,
and back of you the gray rock bright and hard,
seen through figures of air! And you, and you,
and you were but cloud-drift walking, pierced by the light,
translucent in the sun.

DEWITT. Now damn the woman!

LISE. Love, love, before our blood
be shadow only, in a dark fairyland
so far from home, we must go back, go back
where earth is earth, and we may live again
and one day be one day!

ASHER. Why, then, I knew it,
and I have known it, now that you know it, too.
But the old Amsterdam of our farewells
lies in another world. The land and sea
about us on this dark side of the earth
is thick with demons, heavy with enchantment,
cutting us off from home.

LISE. Is it enchantment?
Yes, it may be. At home there were tulips growing
along my bordered path, but here the flowers

are strange to me, not one I knew, no trace
of any flower I knew; no, seedling set
upon a darkened, alien outer rim
of sea, blown here as we were blown, enchanted,
drunken and blind with sorcery.

ASHER. And yet
what we're to have we shall have here.
   Years past
the demons of this air palsied our hands,
fixed us upon one pinnacle of time,
and on this pinnacle of stone, and all
the world we knew slid backward to the
   gulf,
stranding us here like seaweed on the
   shingle,
remembering the sea. In Texel town
new houses have gone up, after new
   fashions;
the children of the children of our days,
lying awake to think of what has been,
reach doubtfully beyond the clouds of years
back to our sailing out of Texel. Men
are like the gods, work miracles, have power
to pierce the walls with music. Their beacon
   light
destroys us. You have seen us in the sun,
wraithlike, half-effaced, the print we make
upon the air thin tracery, permeable,
a web of wind. They have changed us. We
   may take
the fire-balls of the lightning in our hands
and bowl them down the level floor of cloud
to wreck the beacon, yet there was a time
when these were death to touch. The life we
   keep
is motionless as the center of a storm,
yet while we can we keep it; while we can
snuff out to darkness their bright sweeping
   light,
melt down the harness of the slow machines
that hew the mountain from us. When it
   goes
we shall go too. They leave us this place,
   High Tor,
and we shall have no other. You learn it last.
A long while now we've known.

A SAILOR. Aye, aye, a long while.

ASHER. Come, we'll go down. (*The* CAPTAIN
and his MEN *go out, leaving only* DEWITT
with LISE.)

LISE. That's why they drink.

DEWITT. It's enough to drive a sailor-man
to drink, by the great jib boom, marooned

somewhere on the hinder parts of the earth
and degenerating hourly to the status of
a flying Dutchman, half-spook and half God-
knows-what. Maps and charts we have, compass and sextant, but the ship these days are
bewitched like ourselves, spanking up and
down the Mauritius with sails struck, against
wind and tide, and on fire from below.
Drink? Why wouldn't we drink? A pewter
flagon of Hollands gin puts manhood into
the remnants and gives a sailor courage to
look out on these fanciful new devils that
ride sea, land and air on a puff of blue
smoke. They're all witches and mermaids,
these new-world devils, dancing around on
bubbles, speaking a language God never
heard, and nothing human about them except when they fall they break like the rest
of us.

LISE. If I had known. It's too late. The sun
still rises in the east and lays a course
toward the old streets and days. These are
   my hands
as when I was a child. Some great magician,
binding a half-world in his wiles, has laid
a spell here. We must break it and go home.
I see this clearly.

DEWITT. Lise, little heart, the devils are too
much for us. God knows it's a hard thing
to say, and I'd help you if I could help myself, but all hell wouldn't know where we
are nor where we ought to go. The very
points of the compass grow doubtful these
latter years, partly because I'm none too
sober and partly because the great master
devil sits on top of the world stirring up
north and south with a long spoon to con-
fuse poor mariners. I've seen him at it, a
horned bull three times the size of Dunden-
berg and with more cloven feet than the
nine beasts in Revelations. Very clearly I saw
him, too, as clear as you see the east and a
path across the waters.

LISE. Are we to wait till all the color steals
from flower and cloud, before our eyes; till
   a wind
out of the morning from the Tappan Zee
lifts us, we are so light, for all our crying,
and takes us down the valleys toward the
   ·west,
and all we are becomes a voiceless cry
heard on the wind?

DEWITT. We'll see the time, if they continue
to work on us, when we'll be apparent in a

strong light only by the gin contained in our interior piping. The odor itself, along with that of church-warden tobacco, should be sufficient to convince a magistrate of our existence.—You tremble, little Lise, and you weep, but look now, there's a remedy I've had in mind. Fall in love with one of them. Fall in love with one of these same strange new-world magicians. I shall choose me out one of their female mermaid witches, and set my heart on her, and become a man again. And for God's sake let her love me strongly and hold on, lest I go down the brook like a spring freshet in the next pounding rain.

LISE. I gave my love long ago, and it's no help.
I love enough.

DEWITT. Aye, but he's in a worse case than you are, the Captain. Saving his captaincy, there's not enough belief in him to produce half a tear in a passion of sobbing. You'll make me weep, little one, and what tears I have I shall need, lest my protestation turns out to be a dry rain.

LISE. Aye, we were warned before we came away
against the cabalistic words and signs
of those who dwell along these unknown waters;

never to watch them dance nor hear them sing
nor draw their imprecations—lest their powers
weave a weird medicine throughout the air,
chilling the blood, transfixing body and mind
and we be chained invisibly, our eyes darkened,
our wrists and breasts pulseless, anchored in time
like birds blown back in a wind. But we have listened,
and we are stricken through with light and sound,
empty as autumn leaves, empty as prayers
that drift in a godless heaven. Meaningless,
picked clean of meaning, stripped of bone and will,
the chrysalids of locust staring here
at one another.

DEWITT. If it's true it's enough to make a man weep for himself, Lise, and for all lost mariners, wherever they are, and for us more than any, here on these spellbound rocks, drawing up water from time past— the well growing deeper, and the water lower, till there be none. (*He turns to go down the path.*)

CURTAIN

SCENE III

SCENE: *Another section of the Tor, in darkness save for the airplane beacon. A large steam shovel reaches in from an adjacent excavation and hangs over the rock, the control cables dangling.* VAN *is alone on the stage looking at the machinery. He reaches up, catches a cable, and swings the shovel a little.* BIGGS *and* SKIMMERHORN *enter from the right.*

BIGGS. Hey, what are you doing with that shovel?

VAN. Did you know you're trespassing? Also when a man owns land he owns the air above it and the rock below. That means this damn shovel of yours is also trespassing.

BIGGS. Oh, it's Van Dorn. We'll have that moved tomorrow, Mr. Van Dorn. Somebody's made a miscue and left it hanging over the line.

SKIMMERHORN. By the way, that trail's gone out completely, Mr. Van Dorn; there's a fifty foot sheer drop there now, where it was.

Now we've got to get off, if you can think of any way to manage it.

VAN. I'm not worrying about it. Spend the night. No charge.

SKIMMERHORN. The truth is I have to be in court early tomorrow, and a man needs his sleep.

VAN. Afraid you'd doze off on the bench and somebody else might take a trick? Oh, you'd wake up before they got far with anything. The Skimmerhorns are automatic that way.

BIGGS. You don't know any other trail down?

VAN. I showed you the one I knew, and you both turned green looking at it. What am I supposed to do now? Pin wings on you? (*He goes out to the right.*)

SKIMMERHORN. I think I'll swear out a warrant for the squirt. He's too independent by half.

BIGGS. On what ground?

SKIMMERHORN. He threatened us, didn't he?

BIGGS. And where'll that get us?

SKIMMERHORN. He might be easier to talk to in jail.

BIGGS. That's true.

SKIMMERHORN (*sitting on a rock*). This is a hell of a mess.

BIGGS. You're explaining to me?

SKIMMERHORN. What did we ever come up here for?

BIGGS. Twenty-two thousand dollars.

SKIMMERHORN. Will we get it?

BIGGS. It'll look all right on the books.

SKIMMERHORN. It's not good enough, though.

BIGGS. What are you grousing about?

SKIMMERHORN. Because I want my dinner, damn it! And because I'm tired of taking forty per cent and giving you sixty on all the side bets! I want half!

BIGGS. You're a damn sight more likely to get your dinner. You're overpaid already.

SKIMMERHORN. The will's perfectly good. I could find holes in it, but I've probated plenty much the same.

BIGGS. What of it?

SKIMMERHORN. A judge has some conscience, you know. When he sets a precedent he likes to stick to it.

BIGGS. I never knew your conscience to operate except on a cash basis. You want half.

SKIMMERHORN. Yes, I want half.

BIGGS. Well, you don't get it. Any other judge I put in there'd work for nothing but the salary and glad of the job. You take a forty per cent cut and howl for more. The woods are full of shyster lawyers looking for probate judgeships and I'll slip one in at Ledentown next election.

SKIMMERHORN. Oh, no, you won't, Art; oh, no, you won't. You wouldn't do that to an old friend like me; because if you did, think what I'd do to an old friend like you.

BIGGS. Well, maybe I wouldn't. Not if you're reasonable. Look, what's the difference between forty per cent and fifty per cent? Practically nothing!

SKIMMERHORN. Then why don't you give it to me?

BIGGS. Because, try and get it!—

SKIMMERHORN. Damn it, I'm hungry.—I ought to telephone my wife, too.

BIGGS. Why don't you?

SKIMMERHORN. Maybe it's fun for you— nothing to eat, no place to sleep, cold as hell, black as Tophet and a storm coming up! Only I'm not used to it!

BIGGS. You're pulling down forty per cent of twenty-two thousand dollars for the night's work. I say it's worth it.

SKIMMERHORN. Think we could slide down one of those cables?

BIGGS. Maybe you could, Humpty-Dumpty, but not me.

SKIMMERHORN. I'm going to look at it.
(*He goes out left,* BIGGS *following. After a moment* THREE MEN *climb in through the rocks at the right, one of them carrying a small zipper satchel. They throw themselves down wearily on the rock. They are, in brief, the Nanuet bank robbers,* ELKUS, DOPE *and* BUDDY.)

DOPE. God, I got no wind. (*A siren is heard faintly, far down on the road.*)

ELKUS. Sons a' bitches a' troopers.

DOPE. What'd you want to wreck the car for?

ELKUS. Want to get caught with the stuff on you?

BUDDY. We'll get four hundred years for this

ELKUS. Shut up!

DOPE. You didn't need to wreck the car, though.

ELKUS. Didn't you hear the trooper slam on the brakes when he went by? You'd be wearing bracelets right now if I hadn't dumped the old crate over the embankment! The way it is he thinks he's following us, and he'll blow that fire alarm all the way to Bear Mountain Bridge. Only hope he meets something solid head-on at ninety miles an hour.

DOPE. What I want to know is where we go from here.

ELKUS. Down the other side and pick up a car. (*The siren is heard receding.*)

BUDDY. We'll get four hundred years for this.

ELKUS. What do you think you are, a chorus? Go on back to St. Thomas's and sing it to the priest. You're about as much help as a flat tire.

BUDDY. I never wanted to be in it. I was only lookout—you're both witness to that.

ELKUS. What good do you think that does you, you poor fish? Brace up and take it like a man. There's twenty-five thousand in that bag and some of it's yours.

DOPE. How do you know it's twenty-five thousand?

ELKUS. It's the Orangeburg pay roll. (BUDDY *looks off left.*)

BUDDY. Before God, it's Judge Skimmerhorn!

ELKUS. What? Where?

BUDDY. There. Coming round the rocks. Judge Skimmerhorn of Ledentown.

ELKUS. Does he know you?

BUDDY. Sure, he knows me.

ELKUS. We're out climbing, see? Hikers, see? On a picnic. (*They stand.* ELKUS *holds the satchel behind him casually.* BIGGS *and* SKIMMERHORN *come in.*)

BIGGS. Hello.

ELKUS. How are you?

BIGGS. Out walking?

ELKUS. That's right. Climbed up on a bet.

SKIMMERHORN. Isn't that Buddy?

BUDDY. Yes, sir. Evening, Judge.

SKIMMERHORN. You're a long way from home.

BUDDY. Yes, sir.

BIGGS. Think you could show us a way down? We're stuck up here.

BUDDY. There's a path down the cliff. Yes, sir.

SKIMMERHORN. No, thanks. I saw that one. Going to camp here?

ELKUS. Might as well. Sure.

SKIMMERHORN. Bring anything to eat?

ELKUS. Matter of fact, we didn't. (*He sets the satchel down behind the rock, unobtrusively.*)

SKIMMERHORN. Not a thing?

ELKUS. Not a thing.

SKIMMERHORN. That's funny. Camping wtih nothing to eat.

ELKUS. Yeah, it is kinda funny.

DOPE. We ate before we started. (*He smiles cunningly.*)

ELKUS. That's right. The Dope's right for once. We ate before we started.

SKIMMERHORN. Wish I had.

BUDDY. You—you staying up here tonight, sir?

SKIMMERHORN. Seems that way. We came up looking for somebody.

ELKUS. Looking for somebody?

SKIMMERHORN. That's what I said.

ELKUS. Who was it?

BIGGS. That's our business.

ELKUS. I see.

SKIMMERHORN (*coming near the three*) Listen, Buddy, you're young and ambitious Would you do something for me if you got well paid?

BUDDY. I guess so, Judge.

SKIMMERHORN (*sitting on the rock and incidentally over the satchel*). We're done in, traipsing around the rocks. Would you climb down the Tor and get to Haverstraw and telephone my wife I can't come home?

BUDDY. I guess so, wouldn't I, Elkus?

ELKUS. Up to you.

SKIMMERHORN. And while you're there will you buy a dozen sandwiches and some beer?

BUDDY. Yes, sir.

SKIMMERHORN. There's another thing you could do. Call up the state troopers for me, and tell them I'm here and I want them to come up and make an arrest.

BUDDY. You—want to arrest somebody?

SKIMMERHORN. You get it. What do you say?

BUDDY. I—I guess so. Is it all right, Elkus?

DOPE. Oh—no. Oh—no.

ELKUS. Sure it's O.K. Why not?

BUDDY. It'd take about five hours—to get down and back.

SKIMMERHORN. Damn it—I'll starve to death.

DOPE. What do you want to make an arrest for?

BIGGS. That's our business.

BUDDY. All right. I'll go.

SKIMMERHORN. Here's five dollars for you. And another when you get back. And make it fast, will you?

BUDDY. Yes, sir. (*He starts out right.*)

ELKUS. Just a minute, Bud. (ELKUS *and* DOPE *follow* BUDDY *out to converse with him.*)

BIGGS. You might have made it two dozen sandwiches.

SKIMMERHORN. I guess I will. (*He starts to rise, places his hand on the satchel, and jumps.*) Christ, what's that? (*He kicks the satchel, then flips it up into the rocks.*)

BIGGS. Yeah?

SKIMMERHORN. I thought it was a snake. Somebody's mouldy luggage. People are always throwing truck around. (*He calls.*) Say, for God's sake, get started, will you?

BUDDY (*outside*). Yes, sir. Right away. (ELKUS *and* DOPE *return.*)

ELKUS. I guess we'll all go. (*He looks nonchalantly where the satchel was.*)

SKIMMERHORN. Fine. Will you make it two dozen sandwiches?

ELKUS. What the hell's going on here?

SKIMMERHORN. We're hungry, that's all.

ELKUS. Are you two finnegling with us? Because if you are—!

BIGGS. What are you looking for?

ELKUS. Nothing. Who said I was looking for anything?

DOPE. Hey, Elkus! They got the troopers up here!
(DEWITT's *broad Dutch hat appears above the rocks in the rear, looking, for the moment, remarkably like that of a state trooper.* ELKUS *and* DOPE *freeze, looking at it.*)

ELKUS (*drawing a gun*). Why, you fat pimps! (DEWITT *disappears.*)

DOPE. Beat it, you fool! (ELKUS *and* DOPE *scatter out to the right.*)

BIGGS (*looking at the rocks*). What was all that about?

SKIMMERHORN. I hope they bring those sandwiches. (*He also stares toward the rear.*)

BIGGS. Sandwiches? They're not bringing sandwiches for anybody, those two. (*He calls.*) Hey! Hey, you! Anybody there?— What did he mean by troopers?

SKIMMERHORN. Want to take a look?

BIGGS. I'm plenty unhappy, right where I am. (SKIMMERHORN *climbs up on the rocks.*)

SKIMMERHORN. Wish to God I did see a trooper.

BIGGS. Nobody there?

SKIMMERHORN. Not a thing. Hey! Hey, you! (*A silence.*) Nope. Nobody.

BIGGS. Looks to me as if we just missed being stuck up by a couple of lunatics.

SKIMMERHORN. If I can't eat I'm going to sleep.

BIGGS. Maybe you've never tried adjusting yourself to igneous limestone.

SKIMMERHORN. I'm about to try it now.

BIGGS. You have my sympathy. (SKIMMERHORN *stretches out on the rock, takes off his coat for a pillow and lies down.*)

SKIMMERHORN. Thanks.

BIGGS. Beautiful shape you have. A lot of slop tied up with a piece of string.

SKIMMERHORN (*sitting up*). God it's cold. Listen, we could use one coat for a pillow and put the other one over us.

BIGGS. What other one?

SKIMMERHORN. Yours.

BIGGS. A proposition, huh?

SKIMMERHORN. You going to sit up all night?

BIGGS. In some ways it might be preferable.

SKIMMERHORN. You can't prop yourself on end forever, like a duck on a rock.

BIGGS. Pull yourself together, then. You stick out behind like a bump on a duck. All right. Move over.

SKIMMERHORN. Your coat's bigger than mine. (*They pull* BIGG's *coat around them and lie down.*)

BIGGS. Just a couple of perfect forty-nines. Where the hell am I supposed to put my hip bone?

SKIMMERHORN. You juggle your own hip bones. (DEWITT *appears on the rocks at the rear, looking down.*)

BIGGS. If you snore, you probate judge, I'll have you disbarred.

SKIMMERHORN. Go to sleep.

BIGGS. Wish I thought I could. On bed rock. Wake me early, mother dear.

SKIMMERHORN. Shut up.

(DEWITT *meanwhile has opened the satchel and now brings it down into the light to examine the contents. He sits down, takes out five packets of bills, shakes the satchel, then begins to go through the inner pockets. He finds a roll of pennies, which he breaks open into his hands.*)

DEWITT. Copper pieces, by the great jib boom, enough to purchase a new wig, if a man ever got back to a place where money was useful to him. A counting-house full of them wouldn't buy a ship from one of these semi-demi-demi-semi-devils, so that's no good. (*Two snores rise in concert from* BIGGS *and* SKIMMERHORN. DEWITT *goes over to them, dropping the money.*) What kind of demi-semi-devil do you think you are, with four legs and two faces, both looking the same direction? Jesu Maria, it's a kind of centaur, as big one way as another, no arms, and feet the size of dishpans.

BIGGS. What's that?

DEWITT (*backing away*). It's the rear end that talks, evidently, the front being fast asleep in the manner of a figure-head.

BIGGS. Who's there? Did somebody speak?

DEWITT. None too clear in the back thinker, I should say, which would be a natural result of lugging two sets of brains, fore and aft. I'd incline to communicate with the front end, but if necessary I'll converse with the posterior.

BIGGS (*sitting up, looking at* DEWITT). Skimmerhorn!

SKIMMERHORN. What's the matter?

BIGGS. I'm damned if I know.

SKIMMERHORN. Go to sleep, then.

BIGGS. Do you believe in apparitions?

SKIMMERHORN. No.

BIGGS. Well, there's a figure of fun sitting talking to me, right out of a masquerade ball.

SKIMMERHORN. You been drinking?

BIGGS. What would I find to drink?

DEWITT. If the forecastle wakes now I shall play both ends against the middle, like a marine auctioneer. I want to buy a boat.

BIGGS. You've come to the wrong shop, sailor. I'm in the real-estate business, and it's a long mile down to sea level. (SKIMMERHORN *sits up suddenly.*)

DEWITT. You have no boats?

BIGGS. No boats.

SKIMMERHORN. What in the hell?—

BIGGS. I told you I'm damned if I know.

DEWITT. And the front end has no boats?

BIGGS. You're the front end, see. He wants to know if you've got boats.

SKIMMERHORN. No, stranger, no boats.

DEWITT. Ah. (*He shakes his head mournfully, turns him about and goes to the right, still muttering.*) The great plague on them, the lying, two-headed fairies out of a witch's placket. What chance has an honest man against a two-faced double-tongued beast, telling the same tale — (*He disappears through the rocks.*)

BIGGS. Did you see what I saw?

SKIMMERHORN. Not if you saw what I saw. What I saw wasn't possible.—Did you fake that thing?

BIGGS. Fake it? I saw it.

SKIMMERHORN. Oh, no—! Nobody saw that —what I saw. I didn't either. I've got a family to support. They aren't going to put me away anywhere.

BIGGS. Whatever it was, it left a calling card. Looks as if he ate his lunch here, supposing a thing like that eats lunch. Maybe he left some for us.

SKIMMERHORN. I don't want any of that.

BIGGS (*rising and turning the package over with his foot*). There's something in it.

SKIMMERHORN. Help yourself.

BIGGS (*opening a package, tossing the cover away*). You know what this is?

SKIMMERHORN. Probably a sheaf of contracts with the devil, all ready to sign.

BIGGS. No, it's money.

SKIMMERHORN. Money! (*He leaps to his feet.*)

BIGGS. Fives and tens. (*He opens another package.* SKIMMERHORN *does the same.*)

SKIMMERHORN. Well, bless the poor little Dutchman's heart—after all we said about him, too!

BIGGS. Think he left it?

SKIMMERHORN. It wasn't there before.

BIGGS. No.

SKIMMERHORN. Were you born with a caul, or anything?

BIGGS. Always before I had to work for it, or steal it. Never till tonight have I been waked up by a little man in a big hat, fetching it to me in packages.

SKIMMERHORN. Are you asleep?

SKIMMERHORN. If you're dreaming, you're dreaming that I found money.

BIGGS. Oh, you found it now?

SKIMMERHORN. Fifty-fifty.

BIGGS. Wait a minute. You know what money this is?

SKIMMERHORN. No. (BIGGS *picks up a discarded envelope.*)

BIGGS. It came out of the Nanuet bank. (SKIMMERHORN *takes the envelope from him.*)

SKIMMERHORN. If that little guy's a bank robber he's certainly careless with the proceeds.

BIGGS. That's where it came from.

SKIMMERHORN. In that case we ought to give it back. For the reward.

BIGGS. No reward offered yet.

SKIMMERHORN. Maybe we ought to give it back anyway.

BIGGS. Think so?

SKIMMERHORN. Might be marked bills.

BIGGS. No, it's not. I was talking with the president of the bank on the 'phone. Made up for a pay roll. No marks on any of it.

SKIMMERHORN. It ought to be returned, though.

BIGGS. Sure, it should. Question is, will it be?

SKIMMERHORN. I think so, don't you?

BIGGS. I'm inclined to think so. Bank robbing's away out of my line.

SKIMMERHORN. Mine, too, as a matter of fact. The president of the bank's a friend of yours?

BIGGS. Yes, he is, in a way. Oh, he's gypped me a couple of times, same as you would.

SKIMMERHORN. He wouldn't lose anything.

BIGGS. Oh, no, he's insured.

SKIMMERHORN. Has it occurred to you the little Dutchman that was here might not mean any good to us?

BIGGS. Did you see a little Dutchman?

SKIMMERHORN. I thought I did, there for a minute.

BIGGS. I don't believe that any more.

SKIMMERHORN. Certainly doesn't sound very likely.

BIGGS. We'd better count it. Man never ought to carry money around without knowing how much it is.

SKIMMERHORN. Yeah, let's count it. It said twenty-five thousand in the paper.

BIGGS. You know, nobody in the world would ever know who had it?

SKIMMERHORN. No, they wouldn't.

BIGGS. What do you say?

SKIMMERHORN. I say fifty-fifty.

BIGGS. Damn you, Skimmerhorn, if I hadn't been in business with you for twenty years I'd say you were a crook!

SKIMMERHORN. If I wasn't a crook after twenty years with you I'd be slow in the head and hard of hearing!

BIGGS. What's fifty per cent of twenty-five thousand? Twelve thousand five hundred? And what's forty per cent? Ten thousand! Are you going to hold up the deal for two thousand five hundred?

SKIMMERHORN. I certainly am.

BIGGS. All right, take it. Fifty-fifty on this one deal.

SKIMMERHORN. And on the Van Dorn deal, too.

BIGGS. Why, you fat louse—(VAN DORN *comes in from the right out of the shadows.*)

VAN. Sorry to bother you, gentlemen, but—

BIGGS (*as they stuff the bills into their pockets*). Where the hell did you come from?

VAN. Why, you're not friends of mine, but there's a storm blowing in and it occurred to me I might show you where you could keep dry under a ledge.

BIGGS. Thanks. Much obliged.

VAN. Want me to go with you?

BIGGS. No, thanks—Let's get a little nearer the light.

SKIMMERHORN. Good idea.
(BIGGS *and* SKIMMERHORN *go out right.* VAN *looks after them, then picks up one of the discarded envelopes and studies it. He sits.* LISE *comes up the rocks in the rear and stands looking out to the river, shading her eyes from the beacon.*)

LISE. You who have watched this river in the past
till your hope turned bitterness, pity me now,
my hope gone, but no power to keep my eyes
from the mocking water. The hills come down like sand,
and the long barges bear them off to town,
to what strange market in what stranger town,
devouring mountains? but never, in all days,
never, though I should watch here without rest,
will any ship come downward with the tide
flying the flag we knew. (VAN *rises.* LISE *draws back an instant, then comes down a step toward him.*)
Do you hear my voice?

VAN. Yes, lady.

LISE. Do you see me in the light,
as I see you?

VAN. Yes.

LISE. You are one of those
the earth bears now, the quick, fierce wizard men
who plow the mountains down with steel, and set
new mountains in their sky. You've come to drive
machines through the white rock's heart.

VAN. Not I. I haven't.
I hate them all like poison.

LISE. You're against them—
the great machines?

VAN. I'd like to smash the lot,
and the men that own them.

LISE. Oh, if there were a friend
among so many enemies! I wish
I knew how to make you friend. But now
my voice
shrinks back in me, reluctant, a cold thing,
fearing the void between us.—I have seen
you.
I know you. You are kind.

VAN. How do you know?

LISE. When I have been most lonely in the
spring,
the spring rain beating with my heart, I
made
a wild flower garden; none of these I knew,
for none I knew are here, flowers of the
woods,
little and lovely, nameless. One there was
like a pink moccasin, another low
with blotted leaves, wolf-toothed, and many
more
rooted among the fern. I saw you then
come on this garden, secret as the tears
wept for lost days, and drew my breath in
dread
that you should laugh and trample it. You
smiled
and then went on. But when I came again
there was a new flower growing with the
rest,
one I'd not seen. You brought and placed
it there
only for love of gardens, ignorant whose
the garden you enriched. What was this
flower?

VAN. Wild orchid. It was your garden?

LISE. Yes. You know
the names of all the flowers?

VAN. Yes.

LISE. But then
you'd teach them to me?

VAN. Yes.

LISE. Teach me the names.
What is the tall three-petaled one that's black
almost, the red's so dark?

VAN. That's trillium.
Speaking of flowers, tell me your name.

LISE. It's Lise,
or used to be.

VAN. Not now?

LISE. I'm weary of it,
and all things that I've been. You have a
lover?
She'll be angry?

VAN. She's angry now. She's off
and gone. She won't come back.

LISE. Love me a little,
enough to save me from the dark. But if
you cannot give me love, find me a way!
The seas lie black between your harbor
town
and mine, but your ships are quick. If I
might see
the corner where the three streets come to
an end
on sundial windows, there, a child by a
fire—
no, but it's gone!

VAN. I've seen you on the hills
moving with shadows. But you're not
shadow.

LISE. No.
Could one live and be shadow?

VAN. Take my hand.

LISE. I dare not.

VAN. Come, let me see your garden.

LISE. No.
I dare not. It is your race that thins our
blood
and gathers round, besieging us with charms
to stay the feet of years. But I know you
kind.—
Love me a little. Never put out your hand
to touch me, lest some magic in your blood
reach me, and I be nothing. What I am
I know not, under these spells, if I be cloud
or dust. Nor whether you dream of me, or I
make you of light and sound. Between this
stone
and the near constellations of the stars
I go and come, doubting now whence I
come
or when I go. Cling to me. Keep me still.
Be gentle. You were gentle with the
orchid—

VAN. You're cold.

LISE. Yes.

VAN. Here on the Tor
the sun beats down like murder all day long
and the wind comes up like murder in the
night.
I'm cold myself.

LISE. How have I slipped so far
from the things you have? I'm puzzled
here and lost.
Is it so different for you? Keep my hand
and tell me. In these new times are all men
shadow?
All men lost?

VAN. Sometimes I stand here at night
and look out over the river when a fog
covers the light. Then if it's dark enough
and I can't see my hands or where the rock
leaves off against the cloud, and I'm alone,
then, well I'm damned if I know who I am,
staring out into that black. Maybe I'm cloud
and maybe I'm dust. I might be old as time.
I'd like to think I knew. A man gets that
way
standing staring at darkness.

LISE. Then—you do know.
It's better now.—Somewhere along a verge
where your life dips in dusk and my gray
days
lift to the light a moment, we walk there
and our eyes meet.—Look, when the wizards
come
to tear the mountain down, I'll have no
place.
I'll be gone then.

VAN. Child, they won't get our mountain!
Not if I have to shoot them as they come
they won't get our mountain! The mountain's mine,
and you're to make your garden where you
like;
their feet won't step across it! All their
world's
made up of fat men doing tricks with laws
to manage tides and root up hills. The hills
can afford to laugh at them. A race of grubs
bred down from men!

LISE. Is it the light I feel
come flooding back in me? Light or their
charms
broken here, seeing your face?

VAN. Your hands are warm.

LISE. I'm not cold now; for an instant I'm
not cold,
seeing your face. This is your wizardry.
Let me stand here and see you.

ELKUS (*outside*). Somewhere around here
it was. Over toward the crane.

DOPE (*outside*). What's you go and put
down the satchel for?

ELKUS (*outside*). How did I know he'd sit
on top of it? (VAN *and* LISE *slip out through
the rocks at the rear.* ELKUS *and* DOPE *come
in furtively from the right.*)

DOPE. That's where. Under that rock.

ELKUS. Keep your eye peeled. They're probably beating the woods for us.

DOPE. What's that? (*He picks up an envelope.*)

ELKUS. They got it.

DOPE. God damn the rotten business! Now
we will get four hundred years.

ELKUS. Now you're saying it—

DOPE. What are we going to do?

ELKUS. I'm going to send Buddy back with
sandwiches to see if the Judge got the
money. If he did we'll stick him up.

DOPE. Hey, how about the troopers?

ELKUS. If that was troopers I'm Admiral
Dewey. Troopers would a' used the artillery.
Come on.

DOPE. O.K. Some pennies here.

ELKUS. To hell with 'em. (DOPE *flings the
pennies to the left along the ledge.*)

DOPE. Get going. (ELKUS *and* DOPE *go out
right.* BIGGS *and* SKIMMERHORN *come in along
the ledge.*)

BIGGS. Now it's raining money. I got the
price of a morning paper square in the eye.

SKIMMERHORN. I've got two thousand five
hundred in a breast pocket, five thousand
in a side pocket, and five thousand in the
billfold. (*He slaps his rear.*) How do I look?

BIGGS. No different. Just a lot of slop tied
up with string. I've got five thousand in
each side pocket and two thousand five
hundred in the back. How do I look?

SKIMMERHORN. You? All you need now's a pair of wings.

BIGGS. Wish I could find the little guy with the big heart that gave us the money. Maybe he'd help us down off this devil's belfry.

SKIMMERHORN. How about that shovel? Any possibility of making it pick us up and set us down below there?

BIGGS. Well—if anybody was running it, sure. If it swung us over on that dump we could slide the rest of the way. You might wear out that last five thousand of yours, the five thousand that's bringing up the rear there.

SKIMMERHORN. When do they come to work in the morning?

BIGGS. They won't come to work tomorrow. They can't do any more till we buy this land.

SKIMMERHORN. That's fine. That's just dandy.

BIGGS. Nice idea though. Somebody might come along that could run the engine.

SKIMMERHORN. You don't think that boy's coming back with the sandwiches?

BIGGS. No, I don't.

SKIMMERHORN. The way I feel inside I may never live to spend the money.

BIGGS. Who you going to leave it to?

SKIMMERHORN. Yeah?

BIGGS. Oh, all right. Nothing personal. (*They sit facing the audience. The* CAPTAIN *and* HIS CREW, *including* DEWITT, *seep in through the rocks about them and stand quietly looking on.*) There was something in that— what you said about needing a pair of wings.

SKIMMERHORN. I should say that wings was the last thing likely to grow on you. You might grow horns, or a cloven hoof, or a tail, but wings, no. Not unless somebody slipped up behind you and bashed you over the head.

BIGGS. You know, you'd murder me for what I've got in my pockets?

SKIMMERHORN. You thought of it first. Who am I going to leave it to, you said.

BIGGS. Just the same I wouldn't feel right if you were standing behind me with a rock in your hand. (*The* CREW *move in a little.*)

SKIMMERHORN. You wouldn't?

BIGGS. No. At the moment I wouldn't like to think anybody was creeping up behind me. (*He stiffens.*) And by God there is somebody behind me.

SKIMMERHORN (*without turning*). What makes you think so?

BIGGS (*running a hand over his hair*). I just feel it. Turn around, will you? Take a look.

SKIMMERHORN (*shivering*). I will not.—Now you've got me worried.—Or else I'm getting light-headed for lack of food.

(BIGGS *ducks suddenly, as if from an imaginary blow.* SKIMMERHORN *dodges in sympathy, and with their heads drawn in like turtles they creep forward on hands and knees.*)

BIGGS. See anything?

SKIMMERHORN. There's nothing there, you ass! What are you dodging? Want to scare me to death? Go on, turn around and face it like a man!

BIGGS. Now!

SKIMMERHORN. Now! (*They whirl in concert, on their knees, facing the* CREW. *They look at each other.*)

BIGGS. You're crazy!

SKIMMERHORN. I certainly am. And so are you.

BIGGS. That isn't there at all. There's nothing there.

SKIMMERHORN. All right, you go up and hit it. I'll stay right here, and you go punch it in the nose. (BIGGS *stands up.*)

BIGGS. Uh—how do you do?—Maybe you— wanted to give us something, huh? (*To* DEWITT.) Uh—I see you brought your friends with you.—If you want the money back you can have it, you know. We don't want the money. (*He sticks a hand in his pocket.*) How much was it now? (*The* CREW *look at each other gravely, tapping their foreheads.*)

SKIMMERHORN *rises.*) Anything we could do, you know, we'd be glad to do. We're just trying to get down off here.

SKIMMERHORN. You know what it is, Art; it's a moving picture company. And have they got the laugh on us? Thinking they're real. It's all right, boys, we're onto you.

BIGGS. Is that so? Say, I guess that's so. Was that moving picture money, you gave us, you fellows? We thought that was real. Ha ha! That's a good one. I guess you must have thought we were pretty funny, backing up that way and jumping around. You had us scared stiff! (*The* CREW *shake their heads at each other.*)

SKIMMERHORN. Come on, now, you aren't bluffing us at all. We've seen the pictures work over at Suffern. We were right out on location there with actors and producers and everything. Some of those girls didn't care whether they wore clothes or not. You're probably used to that where you come from, but I certainly got a kick out of pictures. Fifty chorus girls changing clothes in the bushes over there. (*A silence.* DEWITT *goes over to the* CAPTAIN *and whispers in his ear.*)

ASHER. Lay a hand to it. (DEWITT *catches hold of the dangling cable.*)

DEWITT. Lay a hand to it, lads. Heave. (*The* CREW *catch the rope and haul on it, sailor-fashion. The shovel begins to descend.*)

THE CREW (*pulling down*). Heave! Heave! Heave! Heave!
Coming a blow, coming a blow;
Sea runs black; glass runs low;
Heave! Heave!
Yardarm dips; foam's like snow!
Heave! (*The shovel touches ground.*)

BIGGS. Say, that's an act if I ever saw one. What kind of picture you putting on? (*The* CAPTAIN *points to the interior of the shovel, looking at* BIGGS *and* SKIMMERHORN.) What's up, anyway? Want us to go aboard? You know, we were just saying if somebody could run that thing we might get across to the dump and slide down out of here. Think you could swing it across there? (*The* SAILORS *maneuver behind the two, edging them into the machine.*) You might haul us up there and not be able to get us down, you know. It's mighty friendly of you to try it, but you'll have your work

cut out. Sure, I'll get in. I'll try anything once. (*He steps in,* SKIMMERHORN *follows reluctantly. The* CAPTAIN *and* DEWITT *guard their retreat. The* SAILORS *catch hold of the cable.*) Take it easy, now.

THE CREW. Hoist! Hoist! Hoist! Hoist!
Tar on a rope's end, man on a yard.
Wind through an eye-bolt, points on a card;
Hoist! Hoist!
Weevil in the biscuit, rats in the lard,
Hoist!

(*They haul the two up as far as seems necessary, and swing the crane out over the abyss. Then they stop to contemplate their handiwork.*)

BIGGS. I'll tell you what—if you catch that line over there some of you can hold back while the rest pull and that'll swing it around.—If that don't work you'd better pull it down again and we'll just wait till morning. (*The* CREW *continue to stare silently.*)

SKIMMERHORN. I'm getting sick at my stomach, boys; you better make it snappy. It gives me the megrims to look down this way. (*He draws his feet up suddenly.*)

BIGGS. Hey, don't rock the boat, you fool! It's a thousand miles straight down!

SKIMMERHORN. I'm going to be sick.

BIGGS. You better take us down, fellows. It's no good. You can't make it.

DEWITT. How about a game of bowls? (*The* CAPTAIN *nods.*)

PIETER. Aye, a game of bowls. (*Led by the* CAPTAIN, *the* CREW *begin to file out.*)

BIGGS. Hey, you wouldn't leave us up here, would you? Hey, listen! You! You can have that money back, you know! We don't want the money! What in the name of time?—Listen, what did we ever do to you?—A joke's a joke, after all, but this thing might let go any minute! What's more you're responsible if anything happens to us! There's such a thing as laws in this country! (*But they have all gone.*)

SKIMMERHORN. I'm sick.

BIGGS. You'll be sicker before you're out of this mess.—What do you think they meant by that?

SKIMMERHORN. I don't know.—Quit kicking me, will you? I'm sick.

BIGGS. Well, keep it to yourself.

SKIMMERHORN. I wish I thought I could.

BIGGS. Help, somebody! Help! We're stuck up here!

SKIMMERHORN. What good's that going to do?

BIGGS. You don't think they'll leave us here, do you?

SKIMMERHORN. I don't know. I don't care. I wish I was dead!—Say, keep away from me, will you? What are you trying to do, pick my pocket?

BIGGS. Pick your pocket, you fish? All I ask is keep your feet out of my face.

SKIMMERHORN. Well, where in hell's my bill-fold?

BIGGS. How do I know? Do you think I took it?

SKIMMERHORN. Come on, now. Where is it? (*He searches his clothes frantically.*)

BIGGS. You're probably sitting on it.—You are sitting on it. There it is.

SKIMMERHORN (*finding it*). Jeez, I might have lost it.

BIGGS. Now you'd better count it. Just to make sure it's good.

SKIMMERHORN. I think I will. (*He begins to count the bills.*) It's good money, Art. Look at it.

BIGGS. Not a bad idea, either. (*He takes out money and counts it. There is a flash, a long roll and a crash of thunder. Then another and another.*) Isn't that coming pretty close?

SKIMMERHORN. What?

BIGGS. The lightning, you fool! Put your money away before you get it wet. You know what I think?

SKIMMERHORN. No.

BIGGS. There's something up there taking pot shots at us.

SKIMMERHORN. There's one thing about money you find. You don't have to pay income tax on it.

BIGGS. That's true. (*There is a terrific flash, a crash, and the stage is in darkness.*) That one got the beacon! (*Another flash runs right down the crane.*) Good God, will you quit that? That's close enough!—Say, do you know any prayers?

SKIMMERHORN. I know one.

BIGGS. Say it, will you?

SKIMMERHORN. Matthew, Mark, Luke and John,
Bless the bed that I lie on.

BIGGS. That's not much good, that one.

SKIMMERHORN. It's the only one I know.— Hey, catch it—hey!

BIGGS. What? (*The lightning is now an almost perpetual illumination, the thunder a constant roll.*)

SKIMMERHORN. I dropped fourteen ten dollar bills!

BIGGS. Do you know we're going to die here?

SKIMMERHORN. We're going to what?

BIGGS. Will you quit counting money? We're going to be killed! We're going to die right here in our own steam shovel!

SKIMMERHORN. Oh, no. I can't die now. I'm not ready to die!

BIGGS. I wish you'd put up your money, then, and pray!

SKIMMERHORN. I don't know how to pray. (*A crash.*)

BIGGS (*on his knees*). Oh, God, I never did this before, and I don't know how, but keep me safe here and I'll be a better man! I'll put candles on the altar, yes, I'll get that Spring Valley church fixed up, the one that's falling down! I can do a lot for you if you let me live! Oh, God—(*A crash.*)

SKIMMERHORN (*on his knees, his hands full of money*). Oh, God, you wouldn't do a thing like that, hang us up in our own steam shovel, wet through, and then strike us with lightning! Oh, God, you've been kind to us tonight, and given us things we never expected to get so easy; don't spoil it now!—God damn it, there goes another batch of bills! (*He snatches at the falling money, and is hauled back by* BIGGS.) I don't know how to pray! What makes you think there's anybody up there, anyway? (*Another crash.*)

BIGGS. Say the one you know then, for God's sake—say it!

SKIMMERHORN. Matthew, Mark, Luke and John,
Bless the bed that I lie on!

BIGGS. Matthew, Mark, Luke and John,
Bless the bed—Oh, God, I've got an old

mother dependent on me; please let me live! Why don't you tell him you'll give the money back?

SKIMMERHORN. Because I won't! And you won't, either! (*A crash.*)

BIGGS. Now you've done it! Can't you keep anything to yourself? There's such a thing as being politic, even when you're talking to God Almighty! (*Thunder again.*)

CURTAIN

ACT TWO

SCENE I

SCENE: *The Tor and the steam shovel as before, only five or six hours later. It's still pitch dark, and* BIGGS *and* SKIMMERHORN *are still in the shovel. They are, however, fast asleep in much the same postures they took formerly on the ground. Under the shovel sits* DEWITT, *picking up and smoothing on his knee a few bills which he has found blowing loose on the rock. The beacon light flashes into the scene.*

DEWITT. There comes on the light again, too, the sweeping light that withers a body's entrails. No sooner out than lit again.—(*Two snores rise from the sleeping pair.*) Aye, take your ease and rest, you detachable Doppelgangers, swollen with lies, protected by the fiends, impervious to lightning, shedding rain like ducks—and why wouldn't you shed rain? your complexions being pure grease and your insides blubber? You can sleep, you can rest. You of the two-bottoms. You make nothing of the lightning playing up and down your backbones, or turning in on cold iron, but a poor sailor out of Holland, what rest has he?—(*He smooths a bill.*) These will be tokens and signs, these will, useful in magic, potent to ward off evil or put a curse on your enemies. Devil's work or not, I shall carry them on me, and make myself a match for these fulminating latter-day spirits. (*He pouches the bills.*) I'm hanged if it's not noticeable at once, a sort of Dutch courage infused into the joints and tissues from the mere pocketing up of their infernal numbered papers. (*He takes out a bill and looks at it.*) That's sorcery, that's witchcraft, that's black art for you— that's a trick after the old one's heart; why, this stuff would make a man out of a cocked hat and a pair of crutches! (*He slaps his chest.*) Now I shall face destiny and take it like a pinch of snuff! Which reminds me I could use a pinch of snuff. (*He takes out his snuffbox.*) Snuff? When have I reached for snuff? It would seem to me I haven't gone after snuff in something like two hundred years! (*He ladles into both nostrils and sneezes violently.*) Aha, DeWitt! You're a man and a devil! And what shall we wish for now that we have wishing papers in the pockets of our pantaloons? What but a woman, one of these new female furies of theirs, wearing pants like a man, and with nothing to indicate her sex but the general conformation! (*He draws out bills.*) Let my woman appear, god of the numbered papers, and let her wear what she likes, so long as a man can make out how she's made. Let her appear within this next three minutes, for God knows how long this mood will last in an old man! (*He takes another pinch of snuff.*)Aha! Destiny, present occasions! (BUDDY *enters carrying beer and sandwiches.*)

BUDDY. Hello.

DEWITT. What answer would a man make to that now? That's a strange greeting.

BUDDY. Seen a couple of old fat men around anywhere?

DEWITT. Boy, I have seen nothing else all night.

BUDDY. Where are they?

DEWITT. You wish to find a couple of old fat men?

BUDDY. That's right.

DEWITT. I begin to doubt the supernal powers of these new angel-demons. Here he stands in their presence and asks very foolishly if old DeWitt has seen them.

BUDDY. What's foolish about that?

DEWITT. A very cheap, witless little cabin boy unless all signs fail. One who carries packages and lives very badly by the day on half a skilling. A cabin boy.

BUDDY. What's the matter with you?

DEWITT. What do you carry in the bag?

BUDDY. That's my business.

DEWITT. He has a business then. He is not perhaps so witless as he appears.

BUDDY. Are you going to tell me where those two are or do you want me to blow your brains out?

DEWITT. Is my carcass so thin you think to puff my brains out with a breath? Look, 'prentice devil, I am one of you. I bear your signs and symbols. Here you see your own countersign, a cabalistic device of extreme rarity and force. What have you in the bag?

BUDDY. Nothing but sandwiches. What do you mean, you're one of us?

DEWITT (waving a sheaf of bills). You should recognize the insignium.

BUDDY. Where'd you get it?

DEWITT. It blew away from these same two fat men, 'prentice devil, but now I have it, and it's mine and I obtain power over you. Let me see these sandwiches.

BUDDY. It blew away from the fat men, huh? All right, that's what I want to know. It's mine, see? Hand it over.

DEWITT. You reveal yourself a very young and tender 'prentice.

BUDDY. Hand it over or I'll fill you full of holes. (He sets down his packages and draws a gun, but DEWITT is beforehand with two flintlock pistols.)

DEWITT. You will drop your child's armory on the ground, cabin boy, or I shall pull both triggers at once and blast you halfway to the water. (BUDDY drops the gun.) I tell you I am now a great devil and violent. When I wish merely I have my way.

(BUDDY suddenly takes to his heels. DEWITT pulls the triggers one after another; the hammers click but there is no explosion.) Why, this new world is not so bad. I am left in possession of the field. (He picks up the automatic and the bag and retreats to his rock.) They fight with the weapons of children. Why, this new world begins to be mine, to do as I please with. Whatever kind of witch a sandwich may be come out and let me interrogate you. (He takes out sandwiches.) If it be food eaten by witches and wizards so much the better, for I am now a wizard myself, and by the great jib boom I haven't tasted food in God knows when. (He eats.) A sweet and excellent morsel, very strong with garlic and salami, medical for the veins and bladder. (He looks at his pistols.) A little glazed powder in the priming now, and these two will speak with more authority if it becomes necessary to defend my position. (He opens his powder horn and renews the priming.) We have seen the time, these blunderbusses and myself, when we could defend a crow's nest against a whole crew in mutiny. (He pushes away the beer bottles with his foot.) I will eat your rations, cabin boy out of the new age, and I will master you all, men and maids, now that my strength comes back, but I will not drink your drink. As Pastor Van Dorf observed very wisely before we sailed; you may eat the food of the salvages, said he, when you have voyaged to the new lands overseas; you may share their rations, you may even make up to their females after the fashion of sailors when the flesh is weak, but drink none of their drink, said he, lest it prove to be Circe's liquor and turn you all to hogs. (He eats.) Now I have small inclination to be a hog, but a man I will be, and a very good man, too, of the fieriest model. (He hears JUDITH's step.) Take care now, take care! I'm an armed man and a man of blood! (JUDITH enters.)

JUDITH (at some distance). I beg your pardon, sir—

DEWITT. A woman, by the great tropical cross, a salvage woman, come in answer to my unspoken desires. (*He rises.*) Your humblest servant, lady salvage; don't run away, please. I'm a poor lost little man, wouldn't hurt a fly.

JUDITH. Who are you?

DEWITT. I'm a poor bosun, ma'am, but grown, God knows how, to something of a person this last quarter hour.

JUDITH. Are you lost?

DEWITT. Completely adrift, ma'am, on my own mountain.

JUDITH. I don't think I've seen you before.

DEWITT. That may be, though I'm by way of being one of the earliest inhabitants, not counting Indians and Patagonians.

JUDITH. You live on the mountain?

DEWITT. I maintain a residence here, though the situation eludes me at the moment.

JUDITH. Then you are acquainted with Van—Van Dorn?

DEWITT. I have seen him about.

JUDITH. Have you seen him tonight? I want to find him.

DEWITT. A mere blind, I should say, a maidenly defense, not to be too forthright; but sent by the talisman she is.

JUDITH. You have seen him?

DEWITT. God help him, I have, and in none too sanctified an attitude, saving your ladyship, for the lad was obviously a bit taken with the captain's wife, and she a married woman of some years' standing, young though she appear.

JUDITH. Where was he? (*She takes a step nearer to him.*)

DEWITT. I was never one to break in on a budding romance, sweetheart, and out of sheer delicacy I looked the other way.

JUDITH. No, but where was he, please? I can show you the path.

DEWITT. If you hunt out a very pretty little mistress in a bonnet somewhat behind the fashion, and look under the bonnet, you may chance to find him there.

JUDITH. Who are you?

DEWITT. Alpheus DeWitt, your most humble, bosun in the King's navy.

JUDITH. Forgive me—I shall look elsewhere—

DEWITT. Oh, but I assure you the lad's head over ears, ma'am, and loathe you'd be to interrupt him. Now a pretty lass like yourself should have no trouble replacing one sailor man with another in these stirring times. They come and go like a run of salmon.

JUDITH. Thank you.

DEWITT. I am myself a notionable lad. Salt tears have been wept for me by one and another.

JUDITH. No doubt.

DEWITT. I'm a blunt man, but constant and of considerable substance on my own wharf. Could you find it in your heart to love me?

JUDITH. I'm sorry, no.

DEWITT. To save a sad and desperate man from such a death as the lines of frost on a window? This is a kindly face, this of mine, and a kindly heart under a worn jerkin. These are real tears on my cheek, too, and I weep them for you, lady.

JUDITH. I've never seen you till this moment.

DEWITT. Yet you could save me from their sorcery, with one touch of your hand. I waited here for you, and you came.

JUDITH. You're horrible. Your face is horrible!

DEWITT. Is it, truly?

JUDITH. Ancient and terrible and horrible!— Tell me where he is. I must know.

DEWITT. I don't know where he is.—You will think better of it. You need only pity me a little at first, or even laugh at me— so you do it kindly—

JUDITH. I'm in no mood for laughing, though you're ridiculous enough in that get-up.

DEWITT. It's not the latest, I know. And I'm a sad and broken man, lady, lost here among the lesser known peaks on the west side of the world, and looking only for a hand to help me.

JUDITH. I don't think you're lost at all.

DEWITT. Yes, lady, quite lost.—Nevertheless they run from me! You should have seen the lad run when I snapped my pistols at him.

JUDITH (*stepping back*). I should think he would.—Isn't there someone coming there now? (*She points to the right.* DEWITT *faces about, reaching for his pistols.* JUDITH *slips away left.*)

DEWITT. If there be, watch what soldierly stand old DeWitt makes in defense of a lady! Come out, children of the new Satan, show yourselves in the light! (ELKUS *and* DOPE *appear at right.*)

ELKUS. Stick 'em up, bo! (*They train automatics on him.*)

DEWITT. More toys! Stand back, you cheap new devils!

ELKUS. Keep your hands down or I'll let you have it!

DEWITT. Watch now how a man holds off the fiends. (*He lifts his pistols.*)

ELKUS. Give it to him! (*They fire a fusillade at* DEWITT, *who stands unmoved.*)

DEWITT. Firecrackers! You think me a devil like yourselves, to be exorcised with firecrackers?

ELKUS. Give it to him! (*They fire once more.*)

DEWITT. Look, you puny devils, I'm a patient man, but in one moment I shall blow you both into the Tappan Zee!

ELKUS (*stepping up and pouring bullets into him*). Too bad about you! (*To* DOPE.) Take the money off him.

DOPE. There's something funny about this guy! I can see right through him!

ELKUS. No wonder. He's full of holes as a tennis racket.

DOPE. No, by God, I can see through him! Look! (*They step back together.*)

ELKUS. What kind of a thing are you?

DEWITT. I'm not a man to be daunted by loud noises and firecrackers, Beelzebub! Go seek your place with the new father of hell before I send you there! Wizards!

ELKUS. Where's the money?

DEWITT. I have a talisman and I ate a sandwich, devils!

DOPE. Look, he's a moving picture! He's a regular church window! Look!

DEWITT. Disperse or I fire!

ELKUS. Keep out of the way of that sawed-off shotgun! (DOPE *suddenly runs in and shoots* DEWITT *through the head, then retreats.*)

DEWITT. I warn you I begin to be annoyed!

DOPE. It's no use, chief. I blew his brains out, and he's standing right there!

BIGGS (*looking over the side of the shovel*). It's a war.

ELKUS. Who said that?

DOPE. Damned if I know.

ELKUS. Beat it.

DOPE. Yeah, beat it. Let the money hang. I'm for Canada.

ELKUS. You said it. (*They turn tail. As they are going* DEWITT *fires his pistols in the air.*)

DEWITT. Now am I master of the world of things,
a buccaneer, a devil and a rake!
Women love mastery, and they ran from me;
they ran, these minor devils, ran from De-Witt!
Look where they go there, sweetheart! (*He turns.*)
God, she's gone!
Lady! New-world lady! Are you lost? (*He follows her.*)
Look now, I've dispersed them, brats and wizards,
spawn out of hell, they ran! I'm master here,
I'm master of the world! Look, lady! (*He goes out left.*)

SKIMMERHORN. Are you awake?

BIGGS. I hope not. I hope this is a nightmare and I wake up at home in bed.

SKIMMERHORN. How did we get here?

BIGGS. It must have been something we ate.

SKIMMERHORN. I didn't eat anything.

BIGGS. There's a bag of sandwiches down there on the ground.

SKIMMERHORN. That's a pleasant thought.

BIGGS. Look for yourself.

SKIMMERHORN. You're right. It's a bag of sandwiches.

BIGGS. Didn't we send somebody for sandwiches and beer, away back there before all this started?

SKIMMERHORN. I don't know. I'm all wet, and I'm stuck to the shovel.

BIGGS. You do seem to be kind of going to pieces. What's the matter with your toupee?

SKIMMERHORN. The glue must have melted. (*He takes off his wig.*) Now I'll catch cold.

BIGGS. If any of your constituency sees you in that condition you're out of office for good.

SKIMMERHORN. I don't even care if I fall out. I feel terrible.

BIGGS. Might be more comfortable for me if you did fall out. (*He shifts his weight.*)

SKIMMERHORN. Sit down! Quit rocking the boat!

BIGGS. I've got a cramp. Ouch!

SKIMMERHORN. Don't shove me! (*He pushes* BIGGS.)

BIGGS (*pushing back*). You want to pitch me overboard?

SKIMMERHORN. Hey! You know I might have gone out?

BIGGS. What do you care?

SKIMMERHORN. I'll show you what I care! (*They lock in a deadly struggle on the verge.*)

BIGGS. Wait, Skimmer, look now! If one of us goes down the other goes too. Look at the drop. You don't want to splash on those rocks and I don't either.

SKIMMERHORN. Let go then.

BIGGS. I'll let go when you do. I'll count three and we'll both let go.

SKIMMERHORN. All right.

BIGGS. One—two—three. (*They let go and catch the ropes over the swinging basket.*) That's better. Now take it easy, buddy. You woke up feeling like poison this morning. After this you count ten when you get an impulse to push anybody.

SKIMMERHORN. Same to you.

BIGGS. Fine. (*They sit down cautiously.*)

SKIMMERHORN. How in hell did those sandwiches get there?

BIGGS. How in hell did we get here?

SKIMMERHORN. You haven't got a fishing hook on you, have you?

BIGGS. No, I haven't. (*They sit gloomily looking at the sandwiches.* LISE *and* VAN *come in from the left.*)

VAN. Nothing in all the woods
is silent as the owl; you see his shadow
but never hear his wings. The partridge now,
every time he takes off he creaks and cranks
like an old Ford. You never heard such a fuss;
but he's quiet on the ground.

LISE. And is there a squirrel
that flies, bird-fashion?

VAN. Well, there's a flying squirrel,
but he's more the glider type. No engine, see,
but he'll do thirty yards. He's on the way
to be a bat if he's not careful.

LISE. How?

VAN. He'll leave off tail and put on wings until
he's mostly wing. No doubt the bat was once
some kind of flying mouse.

LISE. Some men have wings.
I've seen them overhead.

VAN. That's all put on.
They've no more wings than a goat. When they come down.

LISE. I've hoped that it was true that men had wings.

van. Why?

lise. Oh, they've lived so long, and tried so hard,
and it all comes to nothing.

van. Having wings,
would that be something?

lise. Yes, it seems so. And yet
a bird has wings.

van. And he gets nowhere.

lise. Yes.
Nothing but just to be a bird, and fly,
and then come down. Always the thing itself
is less than when the seed of it in thought
came to a flower within, but such a flower
as never grows in gardens.

biggs. Eh—Van Dorn!

van (looking up). What are you doing on the roost, you birds?
Building a nest?

biggs. We can't get down.

van. I'd say
it ought to be just as easy to get down
as it was to get up there.

skimmerhorn. Will you help us out?

van. You look all right to me. What happened to you?

biggs. Everything.

van. How did you get there?

biggs. God,
it's a long story.

van. You've been there all night?

biggs. Yes, all night.

van. I wouldn't want to spoil it.
It's too good to be true. You see those two,
Lise, there in the scoop?

lise. They're pitiful.
Shouldn't you help them?

van. No. Since time began
there haven't been two fat-guts that deserved
a hoisting like those two. In their own machine—
that makes it perfect.

lise. What have they done?

van. They've been
themselves, that's all. Two thieves, a probate judge
and a manipulator, hand and glove
to thieve what they can get. They've got High Tor
among other things, and mean to carve it down,
at three cents a square yard.

lise. These poor old men?

van. Yes, these poor old men.

lise. Let them hang there then!

van. They'll hang there for all me. (lise and van turn to go.)

skimmerhorn. I'll tell you what,
Van Dorn, I'll let you have the validation
if you'll help me down.

van. That means I'd own the land?

skimmerhorn. Yes, you'd own it.

van. Only you'd cancel it,
once you got down.

skimmerhorn. To tell the truth I couldn't,
not if you had the paper.

van. Toss it over;
I'd like to see it. (skimmerhorn gets out an envelope and throws it to van.)

biggs. You're a simple judge!
Now the land's his.

van. There's a bond goes with this,
a bond signed by the court. Oh, I looked it up.
I've read that much law.

skimmerhorn. Yes, I'll keep the bond
till we're on your level.

van. Then I'd advise you both
to make yourself a nest with two-three sticks,
like a couple of crows, and settle down to see
what you can hatch—or maybe lay an egg—
you'll have plenty of time.

biggs. Come now, Van Dorn,
we're in a bad way. It drops off straight down
a thousand feet here, and Judge Skimmerhorn

has vertigo. Why, just to save a life,
out of common humanity, lean on that cable
and pull us in.

VAN. This one? (*He pulls. The shovel dips.*)

BIGGS. Oh, no, no! God,
do you want to dump us out!

VAN. You said to pull it.

BIGGS. Not that one! This! Pull up on that
  again!
We're sliding!

VAN. Sure. (*He rights the shovel.*)
Now you know how it feels
when you kick out the props from under
  men
and slide 'em on the relief rolls. Ever think
how that might feel?

BIGGS. You don't know what we've both
been through, Van Dorn. Rained on and
  struck by lightning,
no dinner; we're half-crazy; we've had nightmares,
funny people in hats; that's how we got
  here,
one of those nightmares!

VAN. You sound disconnected.
Maybe you've lost your minds; still I'm not
  melting
down in my shoes with compunction. The
  fact is
he's clinging to the bond, Judge Skimmerhorn;
he's not too sunk for that. Now here's my
  bargain:
You're hanging onto life by one steel cable,
but that's much safer than the spider web
most men have to trust to. Toss me the bond,
Judge Skimmerhorn, or I'll give this line a
  yank
and you won't even hang.

SKIMMERHORN. You wouldn't do it.

VAN. Oh, wouldn't I? For a two-cent lollipop
I'd pull the chain right now!

SKIMMERHORN. You wouldn't do it!

VAN. Hang on, then! Just for a taste, how's
  the incline now?
A little steep? (*He pulls the line. The shovel
tips as before.*)

BIGGS. Pull it up! Take the God damn
  bond!—
throw it to him!

SKIMMERHORN. I will not!

VAN. Try this then. (*He tips the shovel
further.*)

BIGGS. Give him his bond! I'm slipping!

SKIMMERHORN. I will not!

BIGGS. I say you will! What good's the money
  to you
if you're bologny?

SKIMMERHORN. What money?

BIGGS. You know what money!

SKIMMERHORN. Straighten it up.

VAN. Do I get the bond?

SKIMMERHORN. Hell, yes! (VAN *restores their
equilibrium.*)
You get the bond if you agree to accept
five thousand for your claim. (*He brings out
a paper.*)

VAN. Don't stall with me!
I'll never have a chance like this again,
and it's hard to resist!

SKIMMERHORN. I'm offering you five thousand!
Five thousand! Cash!

VAN (*leaping to the rope*). Keep it!

BIGGS. Give him his bond! (*He wrenches the
paper from* SKIMMERHORN *and sails it to*
VAN.)
And now you've got it how's five thousand
  sound?
You settle for it?

VAN. Bid against them, Lise. It's a game.
What would you say, Lise?
They offer me five thousand.

LISE. Pieces of silver?

VAN. Pieces of silver.

LISE (*smiling*). But I'll give you more!
Only five thousand for this crag at dawn
shedding its husk of cloud to face a sunrise
over the silver bay? For silver haze
wrapping the crag at noon, before a storm
cascading silver levin? For winter rains
that run in silver down the black rock's face
under a gray-sedge sky? For loneliness
here on this crag? I offer you nine thousand!
To be paid in silver!

VAN. You hear? I've got nine thousand;
what am I offered?

BIGGS. Make it ten thousand—
and let us down in the bargain!

VAN. Yes? Ten thousand?
A mountain for ten thousand? Hear them,
Lise,
In their despair they lift it by a grand!
Should it go for ten?

SKIMMERHORN. We'll never get it back—
but that's al' right.

VAN. Yes, Lise?

LISE. Will they pay
no more then for the piling of this stone,
set in its tall hexagonals by fire
before men were? Searching a hundred king-
doms
men will not find a site for lodge or tower
more kingly! A hundred thousand, sir, in
silver,
this is my offer!

VAN. Come now, meet it boys—
I have a hundred thousand!

BIGGS. She's a fraud!
She's no dealer; she's a ringer, primed
to put the price up! What do you mean by
silver?
She won't pay silver!

VAN. Coinage of the moon,
but it's current here!

SKIMMERHORN. Ten thousand, cash, and that's
the last. Five thousand out of my pocket, see,
and five from Biggs! (He pulls out a bundle
of bills. BIGGS does the same.)
Take a good look at cash,
see how that operates! (He tosses down the
roll. BIGGS follows suit.)

VAN. You go well-heeled
when you go mountain-climbing. Is it real?

SKIMMERHORN. Well, look it over. Count it.
(VAN takes up one packet, then another.)

VAN. Where did this come from?

SKIMMERHORN. Where would you think?

VAN. I'll say I got a shock. (He studies the
bills again.)
I don't want your money.

BIGGS. What's wrong with it?

VAN. Didn't I tell you I had a hundred thousand?
Take the stuff back. We reckon in moonlight here!
Put up your mitts! (He tosses the bundles
back.)

BIGGS. It's yours if you want it.

VAN. No,
oh, no, I thank you. It's no sale. What's more
I never meant to sell. The auctioneer's
about to take a walk.

BIGGS. Well, look, we're sitting
right where we were.

VAN. You sit there for your health,
and think it over.

SKIMMERHORN. You won't do that, Van
Dorn,
just leave us here.

VAN. Watch me, if you don't think so. (He
gives an arm to LISE.)
Let me tell you about those babes in the
wood,
did I say they were thieves? (They start
out.)

BIGGS. Make it fifteen!

VAN. Go to sleep.

SKIMMERHORN. Well, twenty! and let us
down!

VAN. Sweet dreams.

SKIMMERHORN. We'll run you out of the
state, Van Dorn!

VAN. You'll have to get down first!

SKIMMERHORN. Is he going away
and leave us sitting?

BIGGS. Looks like it. (VAN and LISE move
off.)

SKIMMERHORN. Say, Van Dorn,
will you pitch us up a sandwich?

VAN. Sure; they're soggy,
lying out in the rain. (He returns and tosses
sandwiches to them.)

BIGGS. Thanks.

VAN. Don't mention it. (He goes out right
with LISE. BIGGS and SKIMMERHORN unwrap
sandwiches.)

SKIMMERHORN. He got away with that bond.

BIGGS. Yeah.

SKIMMERHORN. Looks as if we wouldn't make anything on Van Dorn.

BIGGS. That's what it looks like.

SKIMMERHORN. Christ.

BIGGS. Well, we've still got the windfall.

SKIMMERHORN. Yeah, we've got that.

BIGGS. And here he comes again.

SKIMMERHORN. Who?

BIGGS. Our mascot, little rabbit's foot, little good-luck token, little knee-high with the big heart.

(DEWITT *comes in from the left, looks at the place where the sandwiches were and then at the two in the shovel. He mutters.*)

DEWITT. Magic again! More devil's work! And the woman
gone, slipped round a turn, and the scent was cold
for an old dog like me. By the mizzen yards,
it's wearing to the temper of a man
even if he's not choleric!—And those two,
those buzzards of evil omen, brooding there
on how they'll cut the mountain like a pie
and sell it off in slices! (*He looks at his pistols.*)

One apiece.
It should be just enough, and it's a wonder
I never thought of it. (*He lifts his pistols, the two drop their sandwiches into the void, and cower down; he clicks the hammers.*)
Damp again! Well, boys,
we'll fix that. (*He sits down to freshen the priming.*)
They'll brood over us no more,
those two sea-lions. Damn the rain and mist;
it penetrates the priming! Damn the flint,
and damn the spring! A brace of fine horse-pistols,
that's what the Jew said back in Amsterdam;
it takes a horse to cock 'em. Now then, damn you,
blow 'em off their perch! (*As he rises his eye catches something out on the Zee. He stands transfixed for a moment, watching.*)
It can't be there!
It's there! It's gone! I saw it! Captain Asher!
Captain! Captain! Captain! Captain Asher!
(BIGGS *and* SKIMMERHORN *have ducked down again.* DEWITT *rushes out to the right, firing his pistols in the air in his excitement.* BIGGS *sits up, then* SKIMMERHORN).

SKIMMERHORN. Am I hurt? Do you see blood anywhere?

BIGGS. It seems there was nothing there. (*They contemplate the place where* DEWITT *stood.*)

CURTAIN

SCENE II

SCENE: *Another part of the Tor.* LISE *is sitting high up on a ledge, looking out over the Zee.* VAN *stands near her, looking at her as she speaks. She has his old felt hat in her lap and has woven a wreath of dandelions around the brim. The beacon light strikes athwart her face.*

LISE. But nobody likes this flower?

VAN. I like it now.
I used to think it was a weed, but now,
well, it's a flower now.

LISE. The dandelion.
Where will you find another prodigal
so merry or so golden or so wasteful,
pouring out treasure down the sides of hills
and cupping it in valleys?

VAN. Buttercups
and touch-me-nots. The touch-me-not's a shoe,

a tiny golden shoe, with a hair-spring latchet
for bees to loosen.

LISE. When did you part from Judith?

VAN. Judith?

LISE. When did she go away?

VAN. Last evening.
But it seems longer.

LISE. Why?

VAN. Why, a lot's happened.—
It's almost morning.

LISE. How do you know? (*He steps up to the ledge.*)

VAN. See that star,
that heavy red star back in the west? When that
goes down, then look for the morning star across
Long Island Sound, and after that the lights
dim down in the gray.

LISE. You loved her, very much?

VAN. Yes.

LISE. I loved someone too. I love him still.

VAN. No, you're mine now. (*He sits beside her.*)

LISE. See the great gulf that lies
between the heavy red star down the west
and the star that comes with morning? It's a long way.
There's that much lies between us.

VAN. Not for me.

LISE. Even for you.—You're weary?

VAN. Well, the truth is
I sometimes sleep at night.

LISE. Put your head down.
I'll hold you. (*He lays his head on her knees and stretches out.*)
Now I'll wish that I could sing
and make you sleep. Somehow they're all forgotten,
the old songs. Over and over when the birds
begin at morning I try hard to catch
one tune of theirs. There's one that seems to say:

> Merrily, merrily, chirr, chirr,
> Lueté, lueté, stee—
> Merrily, merrily, chirr, lueté,
> Chirr, lueté, stee.

That's only what it says; for what it sings
you'll have to ask the bird.

VAN. I know it, though.
That's the song sparrow.

LISE. Have I come so near?

VAN. Say it again.

LISE. I can't. May I ask you something?

VAN. Yes.

LISE. There's so much that's changed now men can fly
and hear each other across seas, must men
still die—do they die still?

VAN. Oh yes, they die.
Why do you ask?

LISE. Because I'm still so young,
and yet I can't remember all the years
there must have been.—In a long night sometimes
I try to count them, but they blow in clouds
across the sky, the dancing firefly years,
incredible numbers.—Tell me how old you are
before you go to sleep.

VAN. Lying here now
there's not much logic in arithmetic.
Five, or six, maybe. Five or six thousand, maybe.
But when I'm awake I'm twenty-three.

LISE. No more?

VAN. No more.

LISE. Tell me why it is I am as I am
and not like you?

VAN. I don't know, Lise.

LISE. But tell me.
Have I been enchanted here? I've seen
the trap-rock men, there in the shovel, seeming
so stupid and so pitiful. Could these
use charms and rites to hold wrecked mariners
forever in a deep cataleptic spell
high on a mountain-fringe?

VAN. The trap-rock men?
They're no more wizards than I am. They buy
and sell, and when they've had their fill of dust
they die like the rest of us.

LISE. But they laid spells
about us?

VAN. There are no wizards and no spells.
Just men and women and money and the earth
the way it always was. The trap-rock men
don't know you're here.

LISE. It's not sorcery then. If I had died
and left my bones here on the mountain-top
but had no memory of it, and lived on
in dreams, it might be as it is. As children
sure we were told of living after death,
but there were angels there, and onyx stone
paving an angel city, and they sang
eternally, no darkness and no sun,
nothing of earth. Now can it be men die
and carry thence no memory of death,
only this curious lightness of the hands,
only this curious darkness of the mind,
only to be still changeless with the winters
passing; not gray, not lined, not stricken
   down,
but stamped forever on the moving air,
an echo and an image? Restless still
with the old hungers, drifting among men,
till one by one forgotten, fading out
like an old writing, undecipherable,
we lose our hold and go? Could it be true?
Could this be how men die?

VAN (*half asleep*). It may be, Lise.
I love you when you speak.

LISE. And I love you.
But I am dead, and all the crew is dead;
all of the *Onrust* crew—and we have clung
beyond our place and time, on into a world
unreal as sleep, unreal as this your sleep
that comes upon you now. Oh, you were
   cruel
to love me and to tell me I am dead
and lie here warm and living! When you
   wake
we shall be parted—you will have a world
but I'll have none! There's a chill falls on
   me,
the night-dew gathering, or my mind's death
   chill—
knowing at last I know.—You haven't
   heard.
You told me this in a half-dream. You've
   been kind.
You never thought to hurt me. Are you
   asleep?

VAN. I think I was.

LISE. Sleep, sleep. There was once a song,
if only I could call back air and words,
about a king who watched a goblet rising
and falling in the sea. It came to land
and on the rim the king's name was inscribed
with a date many years before. Oh, many
   years,

a hundred or three hundred. Then he knew
that all his life was lived in an old time,
swept out, given to the waters. What remained
was but this goblet swimming in the sea,
touching his dust by chance.— But he's
   asleep.
And very well he might be with dull stories
out of old songs.—Sleep, sweet; let me have
your head here on my knees, only this night,
and your brown hair round my finger.
(*A girl's shadowy figure comes in from the
right, walking lightly, pauses, as if at seeing
them, and turns to go, the face still unre-
vealed.*)
Are you Judith?

JUDITH. Yes.

LISE. The lad's asleep, but when he wakes
you'll have him back.

JUDITH. Do you dispose of him
just as you please?

LISE. No. It's not what I please.
It's what will happen.

JUDITH. I don't know who you are.

LISE. I'm but a friend of his. You left him
   bitter
going away so lightly. I was bitter—
and so we tried to play at being lovers,
but it won't do. He'll wake, and he'll be
   yours,
all as it was. Only if I may hold him
while he lies here asleep, it helps a little
and I'll be happier.

JUDITH. You'll keep him then
after he wakes.

LISE. No.

JUDITH. Then why are you crying?

LISE. Am I crying?
Well, they're not for him, nor you, these
   tears;
something so far away, so long ago,
so hopeless, so fallen, so lost, so deep in dust
the names wash from the urns, summons
   my tears,
not love or longing. Only when you have
   him,
love him a little better for your sake,
for your sake, knowing how bitterly
I cried, for times past and things done.

JUDITH. You're strange—
the dress you wear's strange, too.—Who are
you then?
I'm—afraid of you!

LISE. Afraid of tears
and a voice out of long ago? It's all I have.

JUDITH. No—no—I'm not afraid. Only for
him.
I've done my crying, too.—Shall I come
back?

LISE. Don't wake him now. Come back at
dawn. You'll find him
here alone.
(TWO or THREE SAILORS appear on the rocks
at the rear, looking out over the Zee.)

PIETER. Look for yourself.

A SAILOR. Aye.

PIETER. Do you make her out?

THE SAILOR. She's the square top-yards.

ANOTHER SAILOR. Now, God, if it were she!

PIETER. It's the brigantine! The Onrust from
up-river
tacking this way!

ASHER (outside). Lise! Lise! Lise! (The
CAPTAIN comes in at the rear with DEWITT.)
Lise, the ship's on the river! Quick, there's
haste!
She must catch the tide down-stream!

LISE. Hush! Hush! You'll wake him!

ASHER. But look across the Zee! The Onrust's
in
and waiting for us!

LISE. But you say it, Asher,
only to comfort me. There is no ship,
nor are we caught in spells here, or enchanted,
but spectres of an old time. The life we live
is but a lingering, a clinging on,
our dust remembering. There is no ship,
only a phantom haunting down the Zee
as we still haunt the heights.

ASHER. Look! The Onrust!
Look, Lise!

LISE. Yes, I see it.

ASHER. Will you come?

LISE. Why would I stay? Why would I go?
For go
or stay we're phantoms still.

ASHER. But will you come?
Who is this lad?

LISE. Her lad. But he was hurt
and fell asleep. (VAN wakes and lifts his
head.)

ASHER. Come quickly!

LISE. Yes, for his sake
it's better I should go.

VAN. Where must you go? (She rises.)

LISE. The Onrust's on the river
and we must catch the tide.

VAN. Would you leave me now?

LISE. Yes, I must leave you.

VAN. You'll go back with him?

LISE. Yes.

VAN. And was nothing meant of all we said?

LISE. What could we mean, we two? Your
hurt's quite cured
and mine's past curing.

VAN. Let me go with you then.

LISE. I should have told you if I'd only
known
how we stood at the tangent of two worlds
that touched an instant like two wings of
storm
drawn out of night; touched and flew off,
and, falling,
fall now asunder through a wide abyss,
not to touch again. (She steps back among
the rocks.)

VAN. Let them go if they like!
What do I care about worlds? Any world
you have
I'll make it mine!

LISE. You told me in your sleep.
There is no witchcraft. Men are as they
were;
we're parted now.

VAN. Give me your hand again!
They dare not take you from me, dare not
touch you

no matter who they are, or where they come from—
they have no hold on us!

LISE. If I could stay!
If I could stay with you. And tend my garden
only a little longer!

VAN. Put out your hand!

LISE. There were too many, many, many years.

VAN. I'll be alone here—

LISE. No, not alone. When you must walk the air,
as all must walk it sometime, with a tread
that stirs no leaf, and breathe here with a breath
that blows impalpable through smoke or cloud,
when you are as I am, a bending wind
along the grain, think of me sometimes then
and how I clung to earth. The earth you have
seems now so hard and firm, with all its colors
sharp for the eye, as a taste's sharp to the tongue,
you'll hardly credit how its outlines blur
and wear out as you wear. Play now with fire
while fire will burn, bend down the bough and eat
before the fruit falls. For there comes a time
when the great sun-lit pattern of the earth
shakes like an image under water, darkens,
dims, and the clearest voices that we knew
are sunken bells, dead sullen under sea,
receding. Look in her eyes. (VAN *looks at* JUDITH.)

ASHER. Come!

LISE. See, the dawn
points with one purple finger at a star
to put it out. When it has quite gone out
then we'll be gone. (VAN *looks at the dawn, then turns back towards* LISE.)

VAN. Lise! Lise! (*But even as he speaks* LISE *and the* CREW *have disappeared.*)

LISE (*unseen*). This is your age, your dawn, your life to live.
The morning light strikes through us, and the wind
that follows after rain tugs at our sails—
and so we go.

DEWITT (*still half-seen*). And welcome you are to the age, too, an age of witches
and sandwiches, an age of paper, an age of paper money
and paper men, so that a poor Dutch wraith's more man
than the thickest of you! (*He steps back and vanishes. It is now dawn.*)

VAN. She never said good-bye.

JUDITH. There is a ship.

VAN. Yes?

JUDITH. Tiny, with black, square sails;
low and small.

VAN (*still looking after* LISE). She'll be a phantom too
like all the rest. The canvas casts no shadow;
the light sifts through the spars. A moonlight rig
no doubt they call it.

JUDITH. I think I hear their voices
as they go down the crag.

VAN. But you won't see them.
No matter what you hear.

THE SAILORS (*a wisp of chantey in the distance*). Coming a blow, coming a blow,
sea runs black, glass runs low.

VAN. Just voices down the wind.
Why, then they were all mist, a fog that hangs
along the crevices of hills, a kind
of memory of things you read in books,
things you thought you'd forgotten. She was here,
and she was real, but she was cloud, and gone,
and the hill's barren of her.

JUDITH. There are no ghosts.

VAN. I know—but these were ghosts or I'm a ghost,
and all of us. God knows where we leave off
and ghosts begin. God knows where ghosts leave off
and we begin.

JUDITH. You were in love with her.

VAN. She leaves the mountain barren now she's gone.
And she was beautiful.

JUDITH. I came to tell you
that I was wrong—I mean about the land—
what you have here is better than one buys
down in the towns. But since I come too late
I'll say it and then go.—Your was was best.
I think it always would be.—So, good night,
Van—
or, rather, it's good morning.

VAN. Yes, it's morning.—
Is it too late?

JUDITH. Oh, Van, I think it is.
It was for Lise you were calling, not
for Judith. I can't say I blame you much,
because she is more beautiful. And yet
you love her, and not me. You'll say they're
ghosts
and won't come back. Perhaps. I'm not so
certain
about the way of ghosts. She may come back.
And you still love her.

VAN. There's no ship at all.
It faded in the dawn. And all the mists
that hung about the Tor, look how they lift,
pouring downstream with the wind. Whatever it was,
was said, or came between us, it's all gone
now it's daylight again.

JUDITH. I came to say
if only I could keep you, you should keep
the Tor, or what you wished. I'm sorry I
went.
I'm sorry this has happened. But it has.
And so—

VAN. Should I keep the Tor?

JUDITH. Yes, if you like.

VAN. God knows they haven't left me much
of it.
Look, where the new road winds along the
ledge.
Look at the jagged cut the quarries make
down to the south, and there's a boy scout
trail
running along the ridge Mount Ivy way,

where they try out their hatchets. There's
the light,
and steps cut into stone the linesmen blew
for better climbing. The crusher underneath
dumps road rock into barges all day long
and sometimes half the night. The West
Shore tunnel
belches its trains above the dead lagoons
that line the brickyards. Their damned
shovel hangs
across my line, ready to gouge the peak
we're standing on. Maybe I'm ghost myself
trying to hold an age back with my hands;
maybe we're all the same, these ghosts of
Dutchmen
and one poor superannuated Indian
and one last hunter, clinging to his land
because he's always had it. Like a wasp
that tries to build a nest above your door—
and when you brush it down he builds again,
then when you brush it down he builds
again—
but after a while you get him.

JUDITH. Then you'll sell?

VAN. I guess if you were with me then we'd
sell
for what we could, and move out farther
west
where a man's land's his own. But if I'm
here
alone, I'll play the solitary wasp
and sting them till they get me.

JUDITH. If it's your way
then it's your way.

VAN. I'll sell it if you'll stay.
Won't you stay with me, Judith?

JUDITH. I think I'd always hear you calling
Lise
while I was standing by. I took a wrong
turning
once, when I left you and went down the
hill,
and now it may not ever be the same.
(She turns.)

CURTAIN

ACT THREE

SCENE: *The shovel still hangs over the verge, and* BIGGS *and* SKIMMERHORN *still occupy it. The rising sun sends level rays across the rock, lighting their intent faces as they stare downward.* BIGGS *has torn a handkerchief into strips and tied them together into a string. He appears to be fishing for something which lies below the ledge, out of view of the audience. Over and over he tries his cast.*

SKIMMERHORN. Little to the left.

BIGGS. You don't say?

SKIMMERHORN. Little to the right.

BIGGS. Put it to a tune and sing it, why don't you?

SKIMMERHORN. There! Almost!

BIGGS. I don't need any umpire.

SKIMMERHORN. Let me try it.

BIGGS. Oh, no. You always were a butter-fingers. (*The string tightens.*) By Golly!

SKIMMERHORN. It's on!

BIGGS. You're explaining to me? (*He pulls up. A bottle of beer emerges from below.*)

SKIMMERHORN. Fifty per cent!

BIGGS. What? (*He pauses, the bottle in air.*)

SKIMMERHORN. You tore up my handker-chief! Fifty per cent. That's the natural division between capital and labor.

BIGGS. Oh, now I'm labor and you're capital. (*He pulls up carefully.*)

SKIMMERHORN. Fifty per cent!

BIGGS. I get the first pull at it. That's all I ask. (*The string parts, and the bottle descends silently into the void.*) That's that.

SKIMMERHORN. You should 'a let me handle it.

BIGGS. Yeah. No doubt.

SKIMMERHORN. Am I thirsty?

BIGGS. Wait till the sun gets up a little. We'll be pan-fried in this thing.

SKIMMERHORN. Look! (*He points down the rocks.*)

BIGGS. If it's more of those little people I give up.

SKIMMERHORN. It's a trooper.

BIGGS. What do you know? Up early for a trooper, too. Listen, about that stuff in our pockets?

SKIMMERHORN. Yeah?

BIGGS. Do we say anything about it?

SKIMMERHORN. Do you?

BIGGS. Do you?

SKIMMERHORN. No.

BIGGS. Neither do I, then.

SKIMMERHORN. Beautiful morning.

BIGGS. I always say it's worth while being up early just to catch the sunrise. (*A* TROOPER *climbs in followed by* SKIMMERHORN SENIOR.)

THE TROOPER. Hello!

BIGGS. Hello, Patsy.

PATSY. Say, you boys had the wives worried down in Ledentown. Been looking for you all night. There they are, Mr. Skimmerhorn.

SKIMMERHORN, SR. (*winded*). Good God! (*He sits, a hand to his heart.*) And I climbed up here. We thought you were under that rock slide.

SKIMMERHORN. I guess you're disappointed.

SENIOR. The next time you two go on a bat and spend a night up a tree you can stay there and sober up.

SKIMMERHORN. We haven't been drinking.

SENIOR (*pointing to a bottle*). What's that?

SKIMMERHORN. Beer. But we didn't have a drop to drink. I'd certainly appreciate a swallow of that now.

PATSY (*tossing up bottle*). Here you are. Hair of the dog that bit you.

BIGGS. We're not drunk. We're dry. We didn't have a drop to drink nor a bite to eat.

PATSY. All right. All right. Only the ground's covered with beer and sandwiches.

BIGGS. You tell 'em how it was, Skimmer.

SKIMMERHORN. You tell 'em.

BIGGS. Well, you see, the whole thing's pretty complicated.

PATSY. I know. I've been through it. You wake up in the morning and you can't believe it yourself.

BIGGS. I don't mean that. I'm sober as a judge.

PATSY. Yeah, what judge? (*He hauls at a cable.*) Can you lend me a hand with this, A.B.?

SENIOR. Give me a minute. (*The shovel tips.*)

BIGGS. Hey, not that one! The other one!

PATSY. Sorry. Not much of a mechanic.

BIGGS. Straighten it up again. (PATSY *does so.*)

SKIMMERHORN. Are we never getting off this? My legs are paralyzed sitting here.

BIGGS. So are mine.

PATSY (*hauling down*). It's too much for me alone.

SKIMMERHORN. Got your wind yet, A.B.?

SENIOR. I don't know whether I want you down yet. You had your good time, now you can put in a few minutes paying for it.

SKIMMERHORN. Oh, we had a good time, did we?

SENIOR. What were you doing? You came up here to buy Van Dorn's property; you're gone all night, and the whole damn town's up all night hunting for you! And we find you up in a steam shovel enjoying a hangover!

PATSY. And now I know what a hang-over looks like.

BIGGS. I tell you we didn't even have a drink of water!

SENIOR. I believe that!

BIGGS. And we're thirsty! Have you got an opener?

PATSY. No, I haven't.

SENIOR. Before you open anything tell me what you were doing last night. Did you see Van Dorn?

SKIMMERHORN. Sure we saw him.

SENIOR. Well, what did he say?

SKIMMERHORN. He said no.

SENIOR. And I suppose that took all night?

SKIMMERHORN. We had an argument.

SENIOR. And then he chased you up the crane, I suppose?

SKIMMERHORN. No.

SENIOR. Well, how did you get up there?

SKIMMERHORN. We were hauled up.

SENIOR. All right. Who hauled you up?

SKIMMERHORN. You tell him, Art.

BIGGS. Oh, no. You tell him.

SKIMMERHORN. As a matter of fact, I don't think it happened.

SENIOR. You're there, aren't you?

SKIMMERHORN. Yes, we're here.

SENIOR. Well, if you weren't drunk how did you get there?

SKIMMERHORN. Well, you see, first we tried to negotiate with Van Dorn.

SENIOR. And he wouldn't take the money?

SKIMMERHORN. That's right.

SENIOR. Did you tell him he didn't really own the land? Till the will was validated?

SKIMMERHORN. Yes, we told him that.

SENIOR. And he still wouldn't talk business?

SKIMMERHORN. He's stubborn. Stubborn as a mule.

SENIOR. Did you tell him you could take the land away from him?

SKIMMERHORN. Oh, yes.

SENIOR. And you offered him the twenty-five thousand?

BIGGS. We offered him a fair price.

SENIOR. You were authorized to say twenty-five thousand.

BIGGS. We didn't quite get to that. We offered ten.

SKIMMERHORN. You see, we thought we'd save the company some money.

SENIOR. I'll bet you did. You thought you'd make a little on the side, and I'd never know.

SKIMMERHORN. Oh, no.

BIGGS. Oh, no.

SENIOR. All right, you offered ten and he wouldn't take it. Then what happened?

SKIMMERHORN. Well, we couldn't get down because of the slide, so some sailors offered to let us down in this thing.

SENIOR. Sailors—up here?

SKIMMERHORN. Little men, in big hats.

BIGGS. Might have been a moving picture company.

SENIOR. Yeah? Any elephants? Or snakes?

SKIMMERHORN. We're trying to tell you the truth!

PATSY. Certainly sounds like delirium tremens, boys.

SENIOR. Never mind, you were hauled up by pink elephants, and then what?

SKIMMERHORN. Van Dorn came along and started to dump us down the cliff.

SENIOR. What's Van Dorn look like? Kind of an octopus, with long feelers?

SKIMMERHORN. Are you going to let us down out of this basket?

SENIOR. No. Not till you come across with what's been going on.

SKIMMERHORN. All right. I'll talk when I'm down.

SENIOR. Can a grown man get pie-eyed on beer?

PATSY. Must have been something stronger. (VAN DORN *comes in from the right.*)

SENIOR. Who are you?

VAN. Oh, I'm nobody. I just own the property.

SENIOR. What property?

VAN. This.

SENIOR. Are you Van Dorn?

VAN. I am.

SENIOR. I'm A. B. Skimmerhorn, Mr. Van Dorn, president of Igneous Trap rock, and I'm glad to meet you. (*He put out a hand.*)

VAN (*ignoring the hand*). Are these friends of yours?

SENIOR. One's a nephew and one's a partner. Why?

VAN. Because any friend of theirs is no friend of mine. (JUDITH *and* THE INDIAN *enter at the rear. She is leading him.*)

PATSY. Who do you think you're talking to?

VAN. A. B. Skimmerhorn, of Skimmerhorn, Skimmerhorn, Biggs and Skimmerhorn, small-time crooks and petty thieving done. Cheap.

SENIOR. Now, to be frank, there may have been some misunderstanding, Mr. Van Dorn. Those two were hardly in condition to negotiate. But I can offer you a fair price for your land, and if you don't take it we may have to push you a little, because we want this acreage and we intend to have it.

SKIMMERHORN. He's got the validation papers.

SENIOR. You gave him the validation papers?

BIGGS. We had to. He started to trip the machine.

SENIOR. That puts us in a sweet mess, that does. Will you take twenty-five thousand?

VAN. No.

SENIOR. Will you take fifty thousand?

VAN. No.

SENIOR. Then, we go home, and the machinery can rust here. That's the best I can do.

VAN. Fine. Let it rust.

JUDITH. Van?

VAN. Yes, Judith.

JUDITH. There's someone here to see you.

VAN. You want to see me, John?

THE INDIAN. But I can wait. I have time enough.

VAN. I'll be right with you.

JUDITH. I had to bring him, Van, because he said
his eyes were bad. He couldn't see the way.

VAN. Thanks, Judith.

SENIOR. Look, Van Dorn, you know the saying,
every man has his price. I've heard it said
God has his price, if you'll go high enough.
Set a figure.

VAN. I'm not thinking of prices.
I don't want to sell. Hell, fifty thousand's
too much money for me.

SENIOR. We'll give you less.

VAN. I don't want less or more. It's not a matter of money.

SENIOR. Will you take a partnership
in the company?

VAN. No.

SSENIOR. Good God, what do you want?

VAN. I want to have it back the way it was
before you came here. And I won't get that.
I know
what kind of fool I look to all of you,
all but old John there. But I'll be a fool
along with John, and keep my own, before
I let you have an inch. John, fifty thousand
or this old hill-top. Is it worth keeping?

THE INDIAN. No.

VAN. No?

THE INDIAN. It's gone already. Not worth keeping.

VAN. I thought you'd say it was. I counted on you
to be my friend in that.

THE INDIAN. It's an old question,
one I heard often talked of round the fire
when the hills and I were younger. Then as now
the young braves were for keeping what was ours

whatever it cost in blood. And they did try,
but when they'd paid their blood, and still must sell,
the price was always less than what it was
before their blood was paid.

VAN. Well, that may be.

THE INDIAN. I wish now I had listened when they spoke
their prophecies, the sachems of the tents;
they were wiser than I knew. Wisest of all,
Iachim, had his camp here on this Tor
before the railroad came. I saw him stand
and look out toward the west, toward the sun dying,
and say, "Our god is not the setting sun,
and we must follow it. For other races,
out of the east, will live here in their time,
one following another. Each will build
its cities and its monuments to gods
we dare not worship. Some will come with ships,
and some with wings, and each will desecrate
the altars of the people overthrown,
but none will live forever. Each will live
its little time, and fly before the feet
of those who follow after." Let them come in
despoiling, for a time is but a time
and these will not endure. This little hill,
let them have the little hill, and find your peace
beyond, for there's no hill worth a man's peace
while he may live and find it. But they fought it out
and died, and sleep here.

SENIOR. Why, this is a wise Indian.
A little pessimistic about the aims
of civilization, but wise anyway.
What do you say, Van Dorn?

THE INDIAN. You too will go
like gnats on the wind. An evening and a
day, but still you have your day. Build monuments
and worship at your temples. But you too will go.

SENIOR. You're on my side, so I don't mind,
but you have a damned uncomfortable way
of speaking. I'm a Republican myself,
but I don't go that far! What do you say, Van Dorn?
Can we do business?

VAN. Judith?

JUDITH. I'm out of it.
It's your decision. I'd say keep it though
if you want to keep it.

VAN. I'll sell it. Fifty thousand.
On one condition. There's a burying grouna
I want to keep.

SENIOR. Sure. That can be arranged.
It's settled, then. Come down to Ledentown
tomorrow and get your money.

VAN. Yes, I'll come.

SENIOR. Why, three cheers, boys. We're out
of the woods. Take hold,
Van Dorn, and swing these topers off the
limb.
Then they can sign the pledge. (*A* TROOPER
appears with ELKUS *and* DOPE.)

BUDGE (THE TROOPER). Help me keep an eye
on these two, will you, Patsy? I've got a
confession out of them on the Nanuet bank
robbery, and they say the money's up here.

PATSY. Up here? Whereabouts?

BUDGE. They left it in a satchel.

PATSY. There's the satchel, all right. (*He
examines it.*) Empty.

BUDGE. Looks like a stall, you guys. You
buried it.

ELKUS. Didn't keep a cent, officer. Somebody
up here got it.

BUDGE. Well, who?

ELKUS. Last time I saw it one of those birds
sat down on it. (*He points to* BIGGS *and*
SKIMMERHORN.)

PATSY. You know who they are? That's
Judge Skimmerhorn of the Probate Court,
and Arthur Biggs of the Trap-rock Company.

ELKUS. Well, one of them sat down on it.

BUDGE. Why didn't he pick it up?

ELKUS. I don't know whether he saw it.

DOPE. And then there was a little guy in a
big hat that had some of it.

PATSY. Yeah? Who?

BUDGE. That's right. Buddy said something
about a little guy in a big hat.

PATSY. You think he got away with it?

ELKUS. He had some of it, and we haven't
got a cent.

BUDGE. So now we have to look for a little
guy in a big hat. Any other description?

ELKUS. Short and fat, had two sawed-off
shotguns, and wore knee-pants.

DOPE. And you could see right through him.
(L. DGE *is writing in a notebook*.)

PATSY. What?

DOPE. You could see right through him.

BUDGE. I'm beginning to think I can see
right through you.

PATSY. Check on that. Elkus, you saw him.
Could you see through him?

ELKUS. Certainly was a funny-looking guy.
Looked as if you could see right through
him.

BUDGE. You expect me to send that out
over the country: "Look for a short, fat man
with a big hat and two sawed-off shotguns.
Dangerous. You can see right through
him."?

PATSY. They buried the money, Budge. Or
else they're screwy.

ELKUS. I thought I was screwy. You couldn't
hurt him with a gun.

BUDGE. What do you mean?

DOPE. We bored him full of holes and he
wouldn't even sit down.

BUDGE. You mean he kept on running?

DOPE. Running? He just stood there and let
us shoot him. Like shooting through a window.

BUDGE. Must have been wearing a vest.

DOPE. I shot him through the head! Two feet
away! And it just made him mad!

PATSY. Take 'em away, Budge. They're nuts.

ELKUS. But he had the money! Buddy saw
him with the money!

PATSY. They're all three nuts.

BUDGE. I never heard a line like that before.

PATSY. Who lives around here?

VAN. I guess I'm the only one that lives near-by.

PATSY. Did you hear any shooting last night?

VAN. Plenty of it.

PATSY. Did you take a look round?

VAN. Yes, I did.

PATSY. Did you see a little guy in a big hat?

VAN. Six or seven of them.

BUDGE. What!

VAN. Six or seven of them.

BUDGE. I suppose you could see right through them?

VAN. Once in a while.

BUDGE. I'm going to quit writing this down. There's enough here to get me fired already.

PATSY. If you saw six or seven where did they go?

VAN. Down the river.

PATSY. In a car?

VAN. In a ship.

PATSY. Sounds like a motor-boat gang. Well, that's something. They went down the river.

VAN. But I can tell you where there's thirty dollars of the money.

BUDGE. Where?

VAN. On the ledge there below the shovel. (BUDGE and PATSY step over to look.)

BUDGE. There it is. Three ten dollar bills. How did it get there?

VAN. I don't know. I just happened to see it.

BUDGE. Did you try to get it?

VAN. No, I thought it probably belonged to the gentlemen up there in the scoop.

PATSY. Did one of you drop some money, Judge?

SKIMMERHORN. I don't think so. Not me.

BIGGS. Not me.

PATSY. Did either of you see a little man in a big hat? (The two look at each other.)

SKIMMERHORN. Why, yes, we did. (PATSY and BUDGE look at each other.)

BUDGE. Well, if they say so he must have been here.

PATSY. What was he doing?

SKIMMERHORN. He was fighting with those two. (He points to ELKUS and DOPE.)

BIGGS. A regular war.

PATSY. Say, listen to that.

BUDGE. Do you know if he took anything out of the satchel?

SKIMMERHORN. Yes, I think he did. He had the satchel.

BUDGE. Now we're getting somewhere.

PATSY. You don't know where they went?

SKIMMERHORN. No.

PATSY. If you saw anything else that might give us a clue—?

SKIMMERHORN. No, not a thing.

PATSY. It beats me.

VAN. Want me to suggest a question?

PATSY. What?

VAN. Ask the Judge if he gained any weight during the night.

PATSY. What's the matter with you?

VAN. Looks to me like he picked up a good deal.

PATSY. I'll think up my own questions, thanks. Might as well trundle the yeggs back to pail, Budge. Whoever got the stuff it's gone.

BUDGE. That's what it looks like.

VAN. Aren't you going to help the Judge down before you go?

BIGGS. Oh, don't bother. We'll get down.

SKIMMERHORN. No hurry. We're all right. You take care of your prisoners.

PATSY. Might as well lend a hand while we're here.

BIGGS. Run along, boys. We're all right. Don't worry about us.

PATSY (*to* BUDGE). Want to wait a minute?

BUDGE. Well, I'm due back, if they can make it themselves.

BIGGS. Sure.

VAN. Oh, don't leave those poor fellows up on that crane! They've been there all night!

SKIMMERHORN. We're fine. You run along.

BUDGE. Well, take a drag on the rope, Patsy. I'll wait. (PATSY *and* VAN *haul the shovel down.*)

SKIMMERHORN. No need to go to all this trouble.

PATSY. No trouble at all.

VAN. A pleasure. Why, you were asking me all night to get you out of this. (*The shovel touches ground. The two sit still.*)

PATSY. What's the matter?

SKIMMERHORN. Guess my legs are asleep.

BIGGS. Mine too.

PATSY. I'll help you up. (*They are pulled to their feet, staggering. Their pockets are very obvious.*)

BUDGE. How about it? O.K.?

PATSY. All set. Say, you are loaded down. Carried plenty of lunch, I guess?

BIGGS. Oh, we brought plenty.

VAN (*tapping* BIGG'S *pocket*). I told you they gained weight. Something in the air up here.

ELKUS. Couldn't be money, could it?

BIGGS. As a matter of fact, some of it is. We were carrying cash to pay Van Dorn for his farm.

PATSY. Cash?

BIGGS. Yeah, cash.

PATSY. How much?

BIGGS. Just what we were authorized to pay. Twenty-five thousand.

VAN. Funny thing, too. It's got the Orangeburg pay roll stamp on it.

BIGGS. Well, hardly.

PATSY. What makes you think so?

VAN. I saw it. They offered me ten thousand.

PATSY. Just for the record, I'd better look at it, Judge.

SKIMMERHORN. I wouldn't if I were you. I'm hardly under suspicion of bank robbery.

PATSY. I'll take a look at it. (*He holds out a hand.* BIGGS *passes him a package.*)

SENIOR. I don't get this at all.

PATSY. It's got the Orangeburg stamp on it, all right.

SKIMMERHORN. Must be some mistake. They must have got the money mixed at the bank.

PATSY. Sure. Well, if that's all we can easy check on that.

VAN. Sure. You'd better check on it.

SKIMMERHORN. Are you under the impression that we robbed the bank?

VAN. You explain it. I can't.

SENIOR. You say you drew the money to pay Van Dorn?

SKIMMERHORN. That's right, A.B.

SENIOR. And it's got the Orangeburg label on it?

SKIMMERHORN. That's what they say.

SENIOR. I'll have something to say to the bank about that.

SKIMMERHORN. Oh, I'll take care of it. Just a clerical error.

PATSY. I'm afraid I'll have to take the money, though. Oh, you'll get your own money back, but if this is the Orangeburg money—

BIGGS. Sure, take it. (*They unload.*)

PATSY. And I guess I really ought to put you both under arrest.

BIGGS. What? Under arrest?

PATSY. Wouldn't you say so, Budge?

BUDGE. Don't see any way out of it. Doesn't mean anything. Just an examination.

SKIMMERHORN. I'd like to keep it out of the papers, if possible, of course. An examination might be very embarrassing—you see, I have political enemies.

BIGGS. Always ready to think the worst of a man, and print it, too.

PATSY. Still, I guess we'll have to have an examination. Just for the record.

SKIMMERHORN. You know who we are, of course?

PATSY. Yes, sir.

SKIMMERHORN. I won't submit to an examinaton! It's preposterous!

PATSY. I don't see how we can get out of it, though. Because we had a robbery, and here's the money, and we've got to explain it somehow.

SKIMMERHORN. I won't submit to it!

PATSY. You got an extra pair of handcuffs there, Budge?

BUDGE. Yeah.

SKIMMERHORN. All right. I'll go.

BIGGS. Sure. We'll go. And we'll make a lot of people sorry!

PATSY. Go on ahead, Budge. (BUDGE *starts out with his prisoners.*)

DOPE. But how about the little guy with the big hat? How about him?

BUDGE. I'll tell you about him. It's entirely possible there wasn't any little guy in a big hat.

DOPE. But we all saw him!

BUDGE. Oh, no, you didn't see him. You saw right through him. And the reason was he wasn't there. (BUDGE, ELKUS *and* DOPE *go out.*)

BIGGS. You don't think we made that up, about the man in the big hat?

PATSY. Well, you have to admit it doesn't sound exactly plausible. (PATSY, BIGGS *and* SKIMMERHORN *go out.*)

SENIOR (*as he goes*). It shakes a man's faith in evidence. (*To* VAN.) See you tomorrow.

VAN. I'll be there. (SKIMMERHORN SENIOR *goes out.*) So now—I've sold the Tor.

THE INDIAN. Yes, but it's better.

VAN. Better than living on a grudge, I guess. It might come down to that.

THE INDIAN. There's wilder land, and there are higher mountains, in the west.

VAN. Out Port Jervis way.

THE INDIAN. Perhaps. You'll find them.

JUDITH. He came to tell you, Van—this is his death-day.
I'll go now.

VAN. All right, John.

THE INDIAN. Could I keep it?
The hand I held? It's a new thing, being blind,
when you've had an Indian's eyes. (JUDITH *returns and gives him her hand again.*)

JUDITH. I'll stay a while.

THE INDIAN. When I had lost the path
halfway along the ridge, there at my feet
I heard a woman crying. We came on
together, for she led me. There'll be time
for crying later. Take her west with you.
She'll forget the mountain.

VAN. Will you come?

JUDITH. I'd remember Lise!

VAN. Was there a Lise?
I think she was my dream of you and me
and how you left the mountain barren once
when you were gone. She was my dream of you
and how you left the Tor. Say you'll come with me.

JUDITH. Yes.

THE INDIAN. It's a long day's work to dig a grave
in stony ground. But you're young and have good shoulders.
It should be done tonight.

VAN. I'll have it done
even if you don't need it. Tell me the place.

THE INDIAN. There's still an Indian burying
  ground that lies
behind the northern slope. Beneath it runs
a line of square brown stones the white
  men used
to mark their dead. Below still, in a ring,
are seven graves, a woman and six men,
the Indians killed and laid there. In the
  freshet,
after the rain last night, the leaf-mould
  washed,
and the seven looked uncovered at the sky,
white skeletons with flintlocks by their sides,
and on the woman's hand a heavy ring
made out of gold. I laid them in again.

VAN. Seven graves—a woman and six
  men—
Maybe they'll rest now.

THE INDIAN. Dig them in deeper, then.
They're covered only lightly.

VAN. I'll dig them deeper.

THE INDIAN. But you must make my grave
  with my own people,
higher, beneath the ledge, and dig it straight,
and narrow. And you must place me in the
  fashion
used by the Indians, sitting at a game,
not fallen, not asleep, And set beside me
water and food. If this is strange to you,
think only I'm an Indian with strange ways,
but I shall need them.

VAN. Don't worry. You shall have it
just the way you want it.

THE INDIAN. Shall we go?

VAN. One last look at the rock. It's too late
to hold out on the bargain. Think of the
  gouge
they'll make across these hills.

JUDITH. If it's for me
you sell, we'll have enough without it, Van.
We'll have each other.

VAN. Oh, but you were right.
When they wash over you, you either swim
or drown. We won't be here.

THE INDIAN. And there's one comfort.
I heard the wise Iachim, looking down
when the railroad cut was fresh, and the
  bleeding earth
offended us. There is nothing made, he said,
and will be nothing made by these new men,
high tower, or cut, or buildings by a lake
that will not make good ruins.

JUDITH. Ruins? This?

THE INDIAN. Why, when the race is gone, or
  looks aside
only a little while, the white stone darkens,
the wounds close, and the roofs fall, and
  the walls
give way to rains. Nothing is made by men
but makes, in the end, good ruins.

VAN. Well, that's something.
But I can hardly wait.

CURTAIN

Idiot's Delight

BY ROBERT EMMET SHERWOOD

THIS PLAY IS LOVINGLY DEDICATED TO
LYNN FONTANNE
AND
ALFRED LUNT

IDIOT'S DELIGHT

Presented by the Theatre Guild, at the National Theatre, Washington, D. C., March 9th, 1936, with the following cast:

DUMPTSY	George Meader	ELAINE	Marjorie Baglin
ORCHESTRA LEADER	Stephen Sandes	EDNA	Frances Foley
DONALD NAVADEL	Barry Thompson	MAJOR	George Greenberg
PITTALUGA	S. Thomas Gomez	FIRST OFFICER	Alan Hewitt
AUGUSTE	Edgar Barrier	SECOND OFFICER	Winston Ross
CAPTAIN LOCICERO	Edward Raquello	THIRD OFFICER	Gilmore Bush
DR. WALDERSEE	Sydney Greenstreet	FOURTH OFFICER	Tomasso Tittoni
MR. CHERRY	Bretaigne Windust	QUILLERY	Richard Whorf
MRS. CHERRY	Jean Macintyre	SIGNOR ROSSI	Le Roi Operti
HARRY VAN	Alfred Lunt	SIGNORA ROSSI	Ernestine de Becker
SHIRLEY	Jacqueline Paige	MAID	Una Val
BEULAH	Connie Crowell	ACHILLE WEBER	Francis Compton
BEBE	Ruth Timmons	IRENE	Lynn Fontanne
FRANCINE	Etna Ross		

The scene of the play, designed by Lee Simonson, is the cocktail lounge in the Hotel Monte Gabriele, in the Italian Alps, near the frontiers of Switzerland and Austria.

ACT I
Afternoon of a winter day in any imminent year.

ACT II
Scene I. Eight o'clock that evening.
Scene II. Eleven o'clock that evening.
Scene III. After midnight.

ACT III
The following afternoon.

IDIOT'S DELIGHT

ACT ONE

The cocktail lounge of the Hotel Monte Gabriele.

The hotel is a small one, which would like to consider itself a first-class resort. It was originally an Austrian sanatorium. Its Italian management has refurnished it and added this cocktail lounge and a few modern bedrooms with baths, in the hope that some day Monte Gabriele may become a rival for St. Moritz. So far, this is still a hope. Although the weather is fine, the supply of winter sports enthusiasts at Monte Gabriele is negligible, and the hotel is relying for its trade upon those itinerants who, because of the current political situation, are desirous of leaving Italy.

Near at hand are a railway line into Switzerland, highways into Switzerland and Austria, and an Italian army airport.

At the left, up-stage, is a large doorway, leading to the lobby, in which we can just see the Reception Desk.

At the upper right is a staircase. A few steps up is a landing, above which is a high window with a fine view of the Alpine scenery to the North and West. The panes are fringed with frost. From the landing, the stairs continue up to a gallery which leads to bedrooms off to the upper left.

Downstairs left is a swinging door marked with the word "BAR."

Over this bar entrance are crossed skis and the head of a mountain goat. On the wall at the right is a Fascist emblem with crossed Italian flags. About the Reception Desk, off to the left, are signs assuring the guest that this hotel has been approved by all the automobile associations of Europe and that Travellers' Cheques may be cashed here. Somewhere on the walls are pictures of the Coliseum and the S.S. "Conte di Savoia."

There are small tables and chairs about, with perhaps a couch or two. At the left is a piano, and when the first curtain rises a dismal little four-piece orchestra is playing "June in January."

Note a line in the dialogue along toward the end of Act One: there is something about this place that suggests "a vague kind of horror." This is nothing definite, or identifiable, or even, immediately, apparent. Just an intimation.

Behind the Reception Desk, PITTALUGA *is occasionally visible. He is the proprietor of the hotel—a fussy, worried little Italian in the conventional morning coat and striped pants.*

On the landing at the upper right, looking dolefully out the window, is DONALD NAVADEL, *a rather precious, youngish American, suitably costumed for winter sports by Saks Fifth Avenue. Experienced in the resort business, he was imported this year to organize sporting and social life at Monte Gabriele with a view to making it a Mecca for American tourists. He is not pleased with the way things have turned out.*

DUMPTSY *comes in from the left. He is an humble, gentle little bell-boy, aged about forty, born in this district when it was part of Austria, but now a subject of the Fascist Empire. He has come in to clean the ash-trays. He listens to the music.*

DUMPTSY. Come si chiama questa musica che suonate?

ORCHESTRA LEADER. Il pezzo si chiama: "Giugno in Gennaio."

DUMPTSY. Oh, com'e bello! Mi piace! (*To* DON.) It's good.

DON. Will you please for God's sake stop playing that same damned tiresome thing?

DUMPTSY. You don't like it, Mr. Navadel?

DON. I'm so sick of it, I could scream!

DUMPTSY. I like it. To me, it's good.

DON. Go on, and clean the ash-trays.

DUMPTSY. But they're not dirty, sir. Because there's nobody using them.

DON. There's no need to remind me of *that!* Do as you're told!

DUMPTSY. If you please, sir. (*He whistles the tune and goes out.*)

DON (*to the* LEADER). You've played enough. Get out!

94

LEADER. But it is not yet three o'clock.

DON. Never mind what time it is. There's nobody here to listen to you, is there? You can just save the wear and tear on your harpsichord and go grab yourselves a smoke.

LEADER. Very good, Mr. Navadel. (*To the other musicians*) E inutile continuare a suonare. La gente non ascolta più. Si potrà invece far quattro chiachiere e fumare una sigaretta. (*They put away instruments and music and start to go out, as* PITTALUGA *appears bristling.*)

PITTALUGA (*to* LEADER). Eh, professori? Perchè avete cessato di suonare? Non sono ancora le tre.

LEADER. Il Signor Navadel ci ha detta di andare a fumare egli ne ha avuto abbastanza della nostra musica. (*The* MUSICIANS *have gone.*)

PITTALUGA (*going to* DON). You told my orchestra it would stop?

DON (*untroubled*). I did.

PITTALUGA. My orders to them are they play in here until three o'clock. Why do you take it to yourself to countermand my orders?

DON. Because their performance was just a little too macabre to be bearable.

PITTALUGA. So! You have made yourself the manager of this hotel, have you? You give orders to the musicians. Next you will be giving orders to me—and to the guests themselves, I have no doubt. . . .

DON. The guests! (*He laughs drily.*) That's really very funny. Consult your room chart, my dear Signor Pittaluga, and let me know how many guests there are that I can give orders to. The number when last I counted . . .

PITTALUGA. And you stop being insolent, you—animale fetente. I pay you my money, when I am plunging myself into bankruptcy. . . .

DON. Yes, yes, Signor—we know all about that. You pay me your money. And you have a right to know that I'm fed to the teeth with this little pension that you euphemistically call a high-grade resort hotel.

Indeed, I'm fed to the teeth with you personally.

PITTALUGA (*in a much friendlier tone*). Ah! So you wish to leave us! I'm very sorry, my dear Donald. We shall miss you.

DON. My contract expires on March the first. I shall bear it until then.

PITTALUGA. You insult me by saying you are fed with me, but you go on taking my money?

DON. Yes!

PITTALUGA. Pezzo mascalzone farabutto prepotente canaglia . . .

DON. And it will do you no good to call me names in your native tongue. I've had a conspicuously successful career in this business, all the way from Santa Barbara to St. Moritz. And you lured me away from a superb job . . .

PITTALUGA (*as* DON *continues*). Lazzarone, briccone, bestione. Perdio.

DON. . . . with your glowing descriptions of this handsome place, and the crowds of sportlovers, gay, mad, desperately chic, who were flocking here from London, Paris, New York. . . .

PITTALUGA. Did *I* know what was going to happen? Am *I* the king of Europe?

DON. You are the proprietor of this obscure tavern. You're presumably responsible for the fact that it's a deadly, boring dump!

PITTALUGA. Yes! And I engaged you because I thought you had friends—rich friends—and they would come here after you instead of St. Moritz, and Muerren, and Chamonix. And where are your friends? What am I paying for you? To countermand my orders and tell me you are fed . . . (*Wails from warning sirens are heard from off-stage right.* PITTALUGA *stops short. Both listen.*) Che cosa succede?

DON. That's from down on the flying field.

PITTALUGA. It is the warning for the air raids! (AUGUSTE, *the barman, is heard in bar off-stage, left.*)

AUGUSTE'S VOICE. Che cosa? (PITTALUGA *and* DON *rush to the window.*)

PITTALUGA. Segnali d'incursione. La guerra e incominiciata e il nemico viene. (*Airplane motors are heard off right.*)

DON (*looking through window*). Look! The planes are taking off. They're the little ones—the combat planes. (CAPTAIN LOCICERO *enters from the lobby. He is the officer in charge of the frontier station. He is tired, quiet, nice.* AUGUSTE *enters from the bar.* DUMPTSY *follows the* CAPTAIN.)

AUGUSTE. Signor Capitano!

CAPTAIN. Buona sera! (AUGUSTE *helps him take off his coat.*)

DUMPTSY. Che cosa succede, Signor Capitano? È la guerra?

CAPTAIN. No—no—datemi cognac. (DUMPTSY *puts coat on chair right of table and goes up and exits through arch center.* CAPTAIN *sits chair left of table.*)

AUGUSTE (*as he goes out*). Si, signor Capitano. (*The* CAPTAIN *sits down at a table.* PITTALUGA *and* DON *cross to him.* DUMPTSY *goes.*)

PITTALUGA. Che cosa significano quei terribili segnali? È, forse, il nemico che arriva?

DON. What's happened, Captain? Is there an air raid? Has the war started?

CAPTAIN (*smiling*). Who knows? But there is no raid. (*The porter's hand-bell in the lobby is heard.*) They're only testing the sirens, to see how fast the combat planes can go into action. You understand—it's like lifeboat drill on a ship. (DUMPTSY *enters.*)

DUMPTSY. Scusi, padrone. Due Inglesi arrivati. (*He hurries out.*)

PITTALUGA. Scusi. Vengo subito. Presto, presto! (*He goes.*)

CAPTAIN. Have a drink, Mr. Navadel?

DON. Thank you very much—but some guests are actually arriving. I must go and be very affable. (*He goes.* DR. WALDERSEE *appears on the gallery above and comes down the stairs as* AUGUSTE *enters from the bar and serves the* CAPTAIN *with brandy and soda. The* DOCTOR *is an elderly, stout, crotchetty, sad German.*)

CAPTAIN. Good afternoon, Doctor. Have a drink?

DOCTOR. Thank you very much—no. What is all that aeroplanes? (AUGUSTE *goes.*)

CAPTAIN. This is a crucial spot, Dr. Waldersee. We must be prepared for visits from the enemy.

DOCTOR. Enemy, eh? And who is that?

CAPTAIN. I don't quite know, yet. The map of Europe supplies us with a wide choice of opponents. I suppose, in due time, our government will announce its selection—and we shall know just whom we are to shoot at.

DOCTOR. Nonsense! Obscene nonsense!

CAPTAIN. Yes—yes. But the taste for obscenity is incurable, isn't it?

DOCTOR. When will you let me go into Switzerland?

CAPTAIN. Again I am powerless to answer you. My orders are that no one for the time being shall cross the frontiers, either into Switzerland or Austria.

DOCTOR. And when will this "time being" end?

CAPTAIN. When Rome makes its decision between friend and foe.

DOCTOR. I am a German subject. I am not your foe.

CAPTAIN. I am sure of that, Dr. Waldersee. The two great Fascist states stand together, against the world.

DOCTOR (*passionately*). Fascism has nothing to do with it! I am a scientist. I am a servant of the whole damn stupid human race. (*He crosses toward the* CAPTAIN.) If you delay me any longer here, my experiments will be ruined. Can't you appreciate that? I must get my rats at once to the laboratory in Zurich, or all my months and years of research will have gone for nothing. (DON *enters, followed by* MR. *and* MRS. CHERRY—*a pleasant young English couple in the first flush of their honeymoon.*)

DON. This is our cocktail lounge. There is the American bar. We have a thé dansant here every afternoon at 4:30—supper dancing in the evening.

CHERRY. Charming.

DON. All this part of the hotel is new. Your rooms are up there. (*He crosses to the window.*) I think you'll concede that the view from here is unparalleled. We can look into four countries. (*The* CHERRYS *follow him to the window.*) Here in the foreground, of course, is Italy. This was formerly Austrian territory, transferred by the treaty of Versailles. It's called Monte Gabriele in honor of D'Annunzio, Italian poet and patriot. Off there is Switzerland and there is Austria. And far off, you can just see the tip of a mountain peak that is in the Bavarian Tyrol. Rather gorgeous, isn't it?

CHERRY. Yes.

MRS. CHERRY. Darling—*look* at that sky!

CHERRY. I say, it *is* rather good.

DON. Do you go in for winter sports, Mrs. Cherry?

MRS. CHERRY. Oh, yes—I—we're very keen on them.

DON. Splendid! We have everything here.

CHERRY. I've usually gone to Kitzbuhel. (PITTALUGA *and* DUMPTSY *appear up-stage and speak in Italian through the dialogue.*)

PITTALUGA. Dumptsy, il bagaglio è stato portato su?

DUMPTSY. Si, signore, è già sopra.

PITTALUGA. Sta bene, vattene.

DON. It's lovely there, too.

CHERRY. But I hear it has become much too crowded there now. I—my wife and I hoped it would be quieter here.

DON. Well—at the moment—it is rather quiet here.

PITTALUGA (*coming down*). Your luggage has been sent up, Signor. Would you care to see your room now?

CHERRY. Yes. Thank you.

PITTALUGA. If you will have the goodness to step this way. (*He goes up the stairs.*) 'Scuse me.

CHERRY (*pauses at the window on the way up*). What's that big bare patch down there?

DON (*casually*). Oh, that's the airport. (PITTALUGA *coughs discreetly.*) We have a great deal of flying here.

PITTALUGA. Right this way, please.

CHERRY. Oh—I see. (*They continue on up, preceded by* PITTALUGA.)

DON. And do come down for thé dansant.

MRS. CHERRY. We should love to.

PITTALUGA. Right straight ahead, please. (*They exit through gallery.*)

DON (*standing on first step*). Honeymooners.

CAPTAIN. Yes—poor creatures.

DON. They wanted quiet.

DOCTOR (*rises*). Ach Gott! When will you know when I can cross into Switzerland?

CAPTAIN. The instant that word comes through from Rome. (*The hand-bell is heard.*) You understand that I am only an obscure frontier official. And here in Italy, as in your own Germany, authority is centralized.

DOCTOR. But you can send a telegram to Rome, explaining the urgency of my position. (DUMPTSY *appears, greatly excited.*)

DUMPTSY. More guests from the bus, Mr. Navadel. Seven of them! (*He goes.*)

DON. *Good* God! (*He goes out.*)

DOCTOR. Ach, es gibt kein Ruhe hier.

CAPTAIN. I assure you, Dr. Waldersee, I shall do all in my power.

DOCTOR. They must be made to understand that time is of vital importance.

CAPTAIN. Yes, I know.

DOCTOR. I have no equipment here to examine them properly—no assistant for the constant observation that is essential if my experiments are to succeed . . .

CAPTAIN (*a trifle wearily*). I'm so sorry . . .

DOCTOR. Yes! You say you are so sorry. But what do you *do*? You have no comprehension of what is at stake. You are a soldier and indifferent to death. You say you are sorry, but it is nothing to you that hundreds of thousands, *millions,* are dying from a disease that it is within my power to cure!

CAPTAIN. Again, I assure you, Dr. Waldersee, that I . . .

DON'S VOICE. Our Mr. Pittaluga will be down in a moment. In the meantime, perhaps you and the—the others . . . (*He comes in, followed by* HARRY VAN, *a wan, thoughtful, lonely American vaudevillian promoter, press agent, book-agent, crooner, hoofer, barker or shill, who has undertaken all sorts of jobs in his time, all of them capitalizing his powers of salesmanship, and none of them entirely honest. He wears a snappy, belted, polo coat and a brown felt hat with brim turned down on all sides*) . . . would care to sit here in the cocktail lounge. We have a thé dansant here at 4:30 . . . supper dancing in the evening . . .

HARRY. Do you run this hotel?

DON. I'm the Social Manager.

HARRY. What?

DON. The Social Manager.

HARRY. Oh! American, aren't you?

DON. I am. Santa Barbara's my home, and Donald Navadel is my name.

HARRY. Happy to know you. My name's Harry Van. (*They shake hands.*)

DON. Glad to have you here, Mr. Van. Are you—staying with us long?

DOCTOR (*rising*). I shall myself send a telegram to Rome, to the German Embassy.

CAPTAIN. They might well be able to expedite matters. (*The* DOCTOR *goes.*)

HARRY. I've got to get over that border. When I came in on the train from Fiume, they told me the border is closed, and the train is stuck here for to-night and maybe longer. I asked them why, but they either didn't know or they refused to divulge their secrets to me. What seems to be the trouble?

DON. Perhaps Captain Locicero can help you. He's the commander of Italian Headquarters here. This is Mr. Van, Captain.

CAPTAIN (*rising*). Mr. Van, my compliments.

HARRY. And mine to you, Captain. We're trying to get to Geneva.

CAPTAIN. You have an American passport?

HARRY. I have. Several of them. (*He reaches in his pocket and takes out seven passports, bound together with elastic. He fans them like a deck of cards and hands them to the* CAPTAIN.)

CAPTAIN. You have your family with you?

HARRY. Well—it isn't exactly a family. (*He goes to the right.*) Come in here, girls!

SHIRLEY (*from off-stage*). Come on in, kids. Harry wants us. (*Six blonde chorus girls come in. They are named:* SHIRLEY, BEULAH, BEBE, FRANCINE, EDNA *and* ELAINE. *Of these,* SHIRLEY *is the principal, a frank, knowing fan dancer.* BEULAH *is a bubble dancer, and therefore ethereal.* BEBE *is a hard, harsh little number who shimmies.* DON *doesn't know quite how to take this surprising troupe, but the* CAPTAIN *is impressed, favorably.*)

HARRY. Allow me to introduce the girls, Captain. We call them "Les Blondes." We've been playing the Balkan circuit—Budapest, Bucharest, Sofia, Belgrade, and Zagreb. (*He turns to* DON.) Back home, that would be the equivalent of "Pan Time." (*He laughs nervously, to indicate that the foregoing was a gag.*)

CAPTAIN (*bowing*). How do you do?

HARRY. The Captain is head man, girls.

GIRLS. How do you do? . . . Pleased to meet you. . . . Etc.

HARRY. The situation in brief is this, Captain. We've got very attractive bookings at a night spot in Geneva. Undoubtedly they feel that the League of Nations needs us. (*Another laugh.*) It's important that we get there at once. So, Captain, I'll be grateful for prompt action.

CAPTAIN (*looking at the first passport*). Miss Shirley Laughlin.

HARRY. Laughlin. This is Shirley. Step up, honey. (SHIRLEY *steps forward.*)

CAPTAIN (*pleased with* SHIRLEY). How do you do?

SHIRLEY. Pleased to meet you.

CAPTAIN. This photograph hardly does you justice.

SHIRLEY. I know. It's terrible, isn't it!

HARRY (*interrupting*). Who's next, Captain?

CAPTAIN. Miss Beulah Tremoyne.

HARRY. Come on, Beulah. (*She comes forward in a wide sweep, as* SHIRLEY *goes up and joins the group.*) Beulah is our bubble dancer, a product of the æsthetic school, and therefore more of a dreamer.

CAPTAIN. Exquisite!

BEULAH. Thank you *ever* so much. (*She starts to sit down by the* CAPTAIN. *She is turning it on.*)

HARRY. That'll be all, Beulah.

CAPTAIN. Miss Elaine Messiger—

HARRY. Come on, babe.

CAPTAIN. Miss Francine Merle—

HARRY. No tricks, Francine. This is just identification.

CAPTAIN. Miss Edna Creesh—

HARRY. Turn it off, honey.

CAPTAIN. And Miss Bebe Gould.

HARRY. You'll find Bebe a very, very lovely girl.

BEBE (*remonstrating*). Harry!

HARRY. A shimmy artiste, and incorrigibly unsophisticated.

CAPTAIN (*summing up*). Very beautiful. Very, very beautiful. Mr. Van, I congratulate you.

HARRY. That's nice of you, Captain. Now, can we . . .

CAPTAIN. And I wish I, too, were going to Geneva. (*He hands back the passports to* HARRY.)

HARRY. Then it's O.K. for us to pass?

CAPTAIN. But won't you young ladies sit down?

SHIRLEY. Thanks, Captain.

BEULAH. We'd love to.

FRANCINE. He's cute.

EDNA. I'll say. (*They all sit.*)

HARRY. I don't want to seem oblivious of your courtesy, Captain, but the fact is we can't afford to hang around here any longer. That train may pull out and leave us.

CAPTAIN. I give you my word, that train will not move to-night, and maybe not to-morrow night, and maybe never. (*He bows deeply.*) It is a matter of the deepest personal regret to me, Mr. Van, but—

HARRY. Listen, pal. Could you stop being polite for just a moment, and tell us how do we get to Geneva?

CAPTAIN. That is not for me to say. I am as powerless as you are, Mr. Van. I, too, am a pawn. (*He picks up his coat and hat.*) But, speaking for myself, I shall not be sorry if you and your beautiful companions are forced to remain here indefinitely. (*He salutes the girls, smiles and goes out.*)

HARRY. Did you hear that? He says he's a pawn.

BEBE. He's a Wop.

BEULAH. But he's cute!

SHIRLEY. Personally, I'd just as soon stay here. I'm sick of the slats on those stinking day coaches.

HARRY. After the way we've been betrayed in the Balkans, we can't afford to stay any place. (*He turns to* DON.) What's the matter, anyway? Why can't decent respectable people be allowed to go about their legitimate business?

DON. Evidently you're not fully aware of the international situation.

HARRY. I'm fully aware that the international situation is always regrettable. But what's wrong now?

DON. Haven't you been reading the papers?

HARRY. In Bulgaria and Jugo-Slavia? (*He looks around at the girls, who laugh.*) No.

DON. It may be difficult for you to understand, Mr. Van, but we happen to be on the brink of a frightful calamity.

HARRY. What?

DON. We're on the verge of War.

SHIRLEY. War?

BEBE. What about?

HARRY. You mean—that business in Africa?

DON. Far more serious than that! *World* war! All of them!

HARRY. No lie! You mean—it'll be started by people like that? (*Points after the* CAPTAIN.) Italians?

DON. Yes. They've reached the breaking point.

HARRY. I don't believe it. I don't believe that people like that would take on the job of licking the world. They're too romantic. (PITTALUGA *steps forward.*)

PITTALUGA. Do you wish rooms, Signor?

HARRY. What have you got?

PITTALUGA. We can give you grande luxe accommodations, rooms with baths. . . .

HARRY. What's your scale of prices?

PITTALUGA. From fifty lira up.

DON. That's about five dollars a day.

HARRY (*wincing*). What?

DON. Meals included.

HARRY. I take it there's the usual professional discount.

PITTALUGA (*to* DON). Che cosa significa?

DON. Mr. Van and the young ladies are artists.

PITTALUGA. Ebbene?

DON (*scornfully*). In America we give special rates to artists.

PITTALUGA (*grimly*). Non posso, non posso. (*The* CHERRYS *appear on the balcony above.*)

DON. I'm sure Mr. Pittaluga will take care of you nicely, Mr. Van. He will show you attractive rooms on the *other* side of the hotel. They're delightful.

HARRY. No doubt. But I want to see the accommodations.

PITTALUGA. Step this way, please.

HARRY. Come on, girls. Now—I want two girls to a room, and a single room for me adjoining. I promised their mothers I'd always be within earshot. Put on your shoes, Beulah. (*He goes out right, followed by the* GIRLS *and* DON.)

BEULAH (*as they go*). Why's he kicking? I think this place is *attractive!*

SHIRLEY. Oh—you know Harry. He's always got to have something to worry about. (*They have gone.*)

MRS. CHERRY (*coming down*). What an extraordinary gathering!

CHERRY. There's something I've never been able to understand—the tendency of Americans to travel en masse. (*They pause to admire the view and each other. He takes her in his arms and kisses her.*) Darling!

MRS. CHERRY. What?

CHERRY. Nothing. I just said, "Darling"! (*He kisses her again.*) My sweet. I love you.

MRS. CHERRY. That's right. (*She kisses him.*)

CHERRY. I think we're going to like it here, aren't we, darling?

MRS. CHERRY. Yes. You'll find a lot to paint.

CHERRY. No doubt. But I'm not going to waste any time painting.

MRS. CHERRY. Why not, Jimmy? You've got to work and—

CHERRY. Don't ask "why not" in that laboriously girlish tone! You know damned well why not!

MRS. CHERRY (*laughing*). Now really darling. We don't have to be maudlin. We're old enough to be sensible about it, aren't we!

CHERRY. God forbid that we should spoil everything by being sensible! This is an occasion for pure and beautiful foolishness. So don't irritate me by any further mention of work.

MRS. CHERRY. Very well, darling. If you're going to be stinking about it . . . (*He kisses her again.*) (*The* DOCTOR *comes in from the right and regards their love-making with scant enthusiasm. They look up and see him. They aren't embarrassed.*)

CHERRY. How do you do?

DOCTOR. Don't let me interrupt you. (*He rings a bell and sits down.*)

CHERRY. It's quite all right. We were just starting out for a walk.

MRS. CHERRY. The air is so marvellous up here, isn't it?

DOCTOR (*doubtfully*). Yes. (DUMPTSY *comes in from the right.*)

CHERRY. Yes—we think so. Come on, darling. (*They go out at the back.*)

DOCTOR. Mineral water.

DUMPTSY. Yes, sir. (QUILLERY *comes in and sits at the left. He is small, dark, brooding and French—an extreme-radical-socialist, but still, French.*)

DOCTOR. Not iced—warm.

DUMPTSY. If you please, sir. (*He goes out, left.*) (*A group of five Italian flying corps officers come in, talking gaily in Italian. They cross to the bar entrance and go out.*)

FIRST OFFICER. Sono Americane.

SECOND OFFICER. Sono belle, proprio da far strabiliare.

THIRD OFFICER. Forse sarrano stelle cinematografiche di Hollyvood.

SECOND OFFICER. E forse ora non ci rincrescerà che abbiano cancellato la nostra licenza. (*They go into the bar.*)

HARRY (*coming in*). Good afternoon.

DOCTOR. Good afternoon.

HARRY. Have a drink?

DOCTOR. I am about to have one.

HARRY. Mind if I join you? (*He sits down near the* DOCTOR.)

DOCTOR. This is a public room.

HARRY (*whistles a snatch of a tune*). It's a funny kind of situation, isn't it?

DOCTOR. To what situation do you refer?

HARRY. All this stopping of trains . . . (DUMPTSY *enters from the bar and serves the* DOCTOR *with a glass of mineral water*) and orders from Rome and we are on the threshold of calamity.

DOCTOR. To me it is not funny. (*He rises with his mineral water.*)

HARRY. Get me a Scotch.

DUMPTSY. With soda, sir?

HARRY. Yes.

DUMPTSY. If you please, sir.

QUILLERY. I will have a beer.

DUMPTSY. We have native or imported, sir.

QUILLERY. Native will do.

DUMPTSY. If you please, sir. (*He goes out.*)

DOCTOR. I repeat—to me it is *not* funny! (*He bows.*) You will excuse me.

HARRY. Certainly. . . . See you later, pal. (*The* DOCTOR *goes.* HARRY *turns to* QUILLERY.) Friendly old bastard!

QUILLERY. Quite! But you were right. The situation *is* funny. There is always something essentially laughable in the thought of a lunatic asylum. Although, it may perhaps seem less funny when you are inside.

HARRY. I guess so. I guess it isn't easy for Germans to see the comical side of things these days. Do you mind if I join you? (*He rises and crosses to the left.*)

QUILLERY. I beg of you to do so, my comrade.

HARRY. I don't like to thrust myself forward—(*He sits down*)—but, you see, I travel with a group of blondes, and it's always a relief to find somebody to talk to. Have you seen the girls?

QUILLERY. Oh, yes.

HARRY. Alluring, aren't they?

QUILLERY. Very alluring. (DUMPTSY *comes in with the drinks and goes.*) (HARRY *takes out his chewing gum, wraps it in paper, places it in a silver snuff box, which he shows to* QUILLERY.)

HARRY. That's a genuine antique snuff box of the period of Louis Quinze.

QUILLERY. Very interesting.

HARRY. It's a museum piece. (*Puts the box in his pocket.*) You've got to hoard your gum here in Europe.

QUILLERY. You've travelled far?

HARRY. Yeah—I've been a long way with that gorgeous array of beautiful girls. I took 'em from New York to Monte Carlo. To say we were a sensation in Monte Carlo would be to state a simple incontrovertible fact. But then I made the mistake of accepting an offer from the manager of the Club Arizona in Budapest. I found that conditions in the South-East are not so good.

QUILLERY. I travelled on the train with you from Zagreb.

HARRY. Zagreb! A plague spot! What were you doing there?

QUILLERY. I was attending the Labor Congress.

HARRY. Yeah—I heard about that. The night club people thought that the congress would bring in a lot of business. They were wrong. But—excuse me—(*Rises.*) My name is Harry Van.

QUILLERY (*rises*). Quillery is my name.

HARRY. Glad to know you, Mr.—?

QUILLERY. Quillery.

HARRY. Quillery. (*Sits.*) I'm an American. What's your nationality?

QUILLERY. I have no nationality. (*Sits.*) I drink to your good health.

HARRY. And to your lack of nationality, of which I approve. (*They drink.* SIGNOR *and* SIGNORI ROSSI *come in and cross to the bar.* ROSSI *is a consumptive.*)

ROSSI. Abbiamo trascorso una bella giornata, Nina. Beviamo un po'?

SIGNORA ROSSI. Dopo tutto quell' esercizio ti farebbe male. Meglio che tu ti riposi per un'oretta.

ROSSI. Ma, no mi sento proprio bene. Andiamo. Mi riposerò più tardi. (*They go into the bar.*)

HARRY. I get an awful kick hearing Italian. It's beautiful. Do you speak it?

QUILLERY. Only a little. I was born in France. And I love my home. Perhaps if I had raised pigs—like my father, and all his fathers, back to the time when Cæsar's Roman legions came—perhaps, if I had done that, I should have been a Frenchman, as they were. But I went to work in a factory—and machinery is international.

HARRY. And I suppose pigs are exclusively French?

QUILLERY. My father's pigs are! (HARRY *laughs.*) The factory where I have worked made artificial limbs—an industry that has been prosperous the last twenty years. But sometimes—in the evening—after my work—I would go out into the fields and help my father. And then, for a little while, I would become again a Frenchman.

HARRY (*takes out his cigarette case*). That's a nice thought, pal. (*Offers* QUILLERY *a cigarette.*) Have a smoke?

QUILLERY. No, thank you.

HARRY. I don't blame you. These Jugo-Slav cigarettes are not made of the same high-grade quality of manure to which I grew accustomed in Bulgaria.

QUILLERY. You know, my comrade—you seem to have a long view of things.

HARRY. So long that it gets very tiresome.

QUILLERY. The long view is not easy to sustain in this short-sighted world.

HARRY. You're right about that, pal.

QUILLERY. Let me give you an instance: There we were—gathered in Zagreb, representatives of the workers of all Europe. All brothers, collaborating harmoniously for the United Front! And now—we are rushing to our homes to prevent our people from plunging into mass murder—mass suicide!

HARRY. You're going to try to stop the war?

QUILLERY. Yes.

HARRY. Do you think you'll succeed?

QUILLERY. Unquestionably! This is not 1914, remember! Since then, some new voices have been heard in this world—loud voices. I need mention only one of them—Lenin—Nikolai Lenin! (*A ferocious looking* MAJOR *of the Italian flying corps comes in and goes quickly to the bar. As he opens the door, he calls "Attention!" He goes into the bar, the door swinging to behind him.*)

HARRY. Yes—but what are you going to do about people like *that*?

QUILLERY. Expose them! That's all we have to do. Expose them—for what they are—atavistic children! Occupying their undeveloped minds playing with outmoded toys.

HARRY. Have you *seen* any of those toys?

QUILLERY. Yes! France is full of them. But there is a force more potent than all the bombing planes and submarines and tanks. And that is the mature intelligence of the workers of the world! There is one antidote for war—Revolution! And the cause of Revolution gains steadily in strength. Even here in Italy, despite all the repressive power of Fascism, sanity has survived, and it becomes more and more articulate. . . .

HARRY. Well, pal—you've got a fine point there. And I hope you stick to it.

QUILLERY. I'm afraid you think it is all futile idealism!

HARRY. No—I don't. And what if I did? I am an idealist myself.

QUILLERY. You too believe in the revolution?

HARRY. Not necessarily in *the* revolution. I'm just in favor of any revolution. Anything that will make people wake up, and get themselves some convictions. Have you ever taken cocaine?

QUILLERY. Why—I imagine that I have—at the dentist's.

HARRY. No—I mean, for pleasure. You know—a vice.

QUILLERY. No! I've never indulged in that folly.

HARRY. I have—during a stage of my career when luck was bad and confusion prevailed.

QUILLERY. Ah, yes. You needed delusions of grandeur.

HARRY. That's just what they were.

QUILLERY. It must have been an interesting experience.

HARRY. It was illuminating. It taught me what is the precise trouble with the world today. We have become a race of drug addicts—hopped up with false beliefs—false fears—false enthusiasms. . . . (*The four* OFFICERS *emerge from the bar, talking excitedly.*)

SECOND OFFICER. Ma, è state fatta la dichiarazone di guerra attuale?

FIRST OFFICER. Caricheremo delle bombe esplosive?

THIRD OFFICER. Se la guerra è in cominciata, allora vuol dire che noi. . . .

FOURTH OFFICER. La guerra è in cominciata

MAJOR. Silenzio! Solo il vostro commandante conosce gli ordini. Andiamo! (*All five go out hurriedly.*)

QUILLERY (*jumps up*). Mother of God! Did you hear what they were saying?

HARRY (*rises*). I heard, but I couldn't understand.

QUILLERY. It was about war. I know only a little Italian—but I thought they were saying that war has already been declared. (*He grabs his hat.*) I *must* go and demand that they let me cross the border! At once! (*He starts to go.*)

HARRY. That's right, pal. There's no time to lose.

QUILLERY. Wait—I haven't paid. . . . (*He is fumbling for money.*)

HARRY. No, no. This was my drink. You've got to hurry!

QUILLERY. Thank you, my comrade. (*He goes out quickly. Airplane motors are heard, off at the right.* HARRY *crosses to the window.* DUMPTSY *comes in to remove the empty glasses.*)

DUMPTSY. Fine view, isn't it, sir?

HARRY. I've seen worse.

DUMPTSY. Nothing quite like it, sir. From here, we look into four nations. Where you see that little village, at the far end of the valley—that is Austria. Isn't that beautiful over there?

HARRY. Are you Italian?

DUMPTSY. Well, yes, sir. That is to say, I didn't used to be.

HARRY. What did you used to be?

DUMPTSY. Austrian. All this part was Austria, until after the big war, when they decided these mountains must go to Italy, and I went with them. In one day, I became a foreigner. So now, my children learn only Italian in school, and when I and my wife talk our own language they can't understand us. (*He gets* HARRY's *drink and brings it over to him.*) They changed the name of this mountain. Monte Gabriele—that's what it is now. They named it after an Italian who dropped poems on Vienna. Even my old father—he's dead—but all the writing on the gravestones was in German, so they rubbed it out and translated it. So now he's Italian, too. But they didn't get my sister. She married a Swiss. She lives over there, in Schleins.

HARRY. She's lucky.

DUMPTSY. Yes—those Swiss are smart.

HARRY. Yeah, they had sense enough to get over there in the first place.

DUMPTSY (*laughs*). But it doesn't make much difference who your masters are. When you get used to them, they're all the same. (*The Porter's bell rings.* PITTALUGA *appears.*)

PITTALUGA. Dumptsy! Dumptsy! Una gentildonna arriva. Prendi i suoi bagagli. Affretati!

DUMPTSY. Si, Signore. Vengo subito. (*He goes.*)

PITTALUGA (*claps his hands*). Sciocco! Anna, Per Dio! Dove sei stata, va sopra a preparare la stanza. (ANNA, *the maid, enters with towels.*) Presto, presto! (ANNA *runs up the steps, exits.* PITTALUGA *goes back into the lobby.*)

IRENE'S VOICE. Vieni, Achille.

DON (*coming in*). This is our cocktail lounge, madame. (IRENE *enters. She is somewhere between thirty and forty, beautiful, heavily and smartly furred in the Russian manner. Her hair is blonde and quite straight. She is a model of worldly wisdom, chic, and carefully applied graciousness. Her name is pronounced "*EAR-RAY-NA.*" . . . She surveys the room with polite appreciation, glancing briefly at* HARRY.)

DON. Your suite is up there, madame. All this part of the hotel is quite new.

IRENE. How very nice!

DON. We have our best view from this side of the hotel. (*He goes to the window.* IRENE *follows slowly.*) You can see four countries —Italy, Switzerland, Austria and Bavaria

IRENE. Magnificent!

DON. Yes—we're very proud of it.

IRENE. All those countries. And they all look so very much alike, don't they!

DON. Yes—they do really—from this distance.

IRENE. All covered with the beautiful snow. I think the whole world should be always covered with snow. It would be so much more clean, wouldn't it?

DON. By all means!

IRENE. Like in my Russia. White Russia. (*Sighs, and goes up to the next landing.*) Oh, and—how exciting! A flying field. Look! They're bringing out the big bombers.

DON. Madame is interested in aviation?

IRENE. No, no. Just ordinary flying bores me. But there is no experience in life quite so thrilling as a parachute jump, is there!

DON. I've never had that thrill, I'm ashamed to say.

IRENE. Once I had to jump when I was flying over the jungle in Indo-China. It was indescribable. Drifting down, sinking into that great green sea of enchantment and hidden danger. (DUMPTSY *comes in.*)

DON. And you weren't afraid?

IRENE. No—no—I was not afraid. In moments like that, one is given the sense of eternity.

HARRY (*viciously*). Dumptsy! Get me another Scotch.

DUMPTSY. Yes, sir.

HARRY. And put ice in it, this time. If you haven't got any ice, go out and scoop up some snow.

DUMPTSY. If you please, sir. (*He goes into the bar.*)

IRENE (*her gaze wandering about the room*). But your place is really charming.

DON. You're very kind.

IRENE. I must tell every one in Paris about it. There's something about this design—it suggests a—an amusing kind of horror.

DON (*not knowing quite how to interpret that*). Madame is a student of decoration?

IRENE. No, no. Only an amateur, my friend. An amateur, I'm afraid, in everything. (*The siren sounds from off at the right.* IRENE, *near the top of the staircase, stops to listen.*)

IRENE. What is that?

DON. Oh—it's merely some kind of warning. They've been testing it.

IRENE. Warning? Warning against what?

DON. I believe it's for use in case of war.

IRENE. War? But there will be no war. (PITTALUGA *enters from the lobby, escorting* ACHILLE WEBER—*which is pronounced "VAYBAIR." He is a thin, keen executive, wearing a neat little mustache and excellent clothes. In his lapel is the rosette of the Legion of Honor. He carries a brief case.*)

PITTALUGA (*as they come in*). Par ici, Monsieur Weber. Vous trouverez Madame ici . . .

IRENE (*leaning over the railing*). Achille!

WEBER (*pausing and looking up*). Yes, my dear?

IRENE. Achille—there will be no war, will there?

WEBER (*amused*). No, no—Irene. There will be no war. They're all much too well prepared for it. (*He turns to* PITTALUGA.) Where are our rooms?

PITTALUGA. Votre suite est par ici, Monsieur. La plus belle de la maison! La vue est superbe!

IRENE (*to* DON). There, you see! They will not fight. They are all much too much afraid of each other. (WEBER *is going up the staircase, ignoring the view.* PITTALUGA *is following.*)

IRENE (*to* WEBER). Achille—I am mad about this place! Je rafolle de cette place!

WEBER (*calmly*). Yes, my dear.

IRENE. We must be sure to tell the Maharajah of Rajpipla, Achille. Can't you imagine how dear little "Pip" would love this? (*They go out on the landing above.*)

HARRY. Who was that?

DON (*impressed*). That was Achille Weber. One of the biggest men in France. I used to see him a lot at St. Moritz. (*There is a sound of airplane motors off at the right.*)

HARRY. And the dame? Do you assume that is his wife?

DON (*curtly*). Are you implying that she's not?

HARRY. No, no—I'm not implying a thing. (*He wanders to the piano.*) I'm just kind of —kind of baffled.

DON. Evidently. (*He goes out.*) (HARRY *at the piano strikes a chord of the Russian song, "Kak Stranna."* DUMPTSY *enters from the bar and serves* HARRY *with Scotch. The off-stage noise increases as more planes take the air.*)

DUMPTSY (*at the window*). Do you see them —those aeroplanes—flying up from the field down there?

HARRY (*glances toward window, without interest*). Yes—I see them.

DUMPTSY. Those are the big ones. They're full of bombs, to drop on people. Look! They're going north. Maybe Berlin. Maybe Paris. (HARRY *strikes a few chords.*)

HARRY. Did you ever jump with a parachute?

DUMPTSY. Why, no—sir. (*He looks questioningly at* HARRY.)

HARRY. Well, I have—a couple of times. And it's nothing. But—I didn't land in any jungle. I landed where I was supposed to—in the Fair Grounds.

DUMPTSY (*seriously*). That's interesting, sir. (*The* ROSSIS *enter from the bar. He is holding a handkerchief to his mouth. She is supporting him as they cross.*)

SIGNORA ROSSI. Non t'ho detto che dovevi fare attenzione? Te l'ho detto, te l'ho detto che sarebbe accaduto ciò. Vedi, ora ti piglia un accesso di tosse.

ROSSI. 'Scusatemi, Mina. (*Another coughing fit.*)

SIGNORA ROSSI. Va a sdraiarti. Dovresti riposarti a lungo. E adopera il termometro. Scometto che t'è aumentata la temperatura. (*They go out.*)

DUMPTSY. That Signor Rossi—he has tuberculosis.

HARRY. Is he getting cured up here? (*The* DOCTOR *appears on the landing above.*)

DUMPTSY. Ja. This used to be a sanatorium, in the old days. But the Fascisti—they don't like to admit that any one can be sick! (*He starts to go.*)

DOCTOR. Dumptsy!

DUMPTSY. Herr Doctor.

DOCTOR (*coming down*). Mineral water.

DUMPTSY. Ja wohl, Herr Doctor. (DUMPTSY *goes out, left. The* DOCTOR *sits down.* HARRY *takes one more look toward the gallery, where* IRENE *had been. He then looks at the* DOCTOR, *and decides not to suggest joining him. He starts to play* "Kak Stranna." *The* DOCTOR *turns and looks at him, with some surprise. The uproar of planes is now terrific, but it starts to dwindle as the planes depart.*)

DOCTOR. What is that you are playing?

HARRY. A Russian song, entitled "Kak Stranna," meaning "how strange!" One of those morose ballads about how once we met, for one immortal moment, like ships that pass in the night. Or maybe like a couple of trucks, side-swiping each other. And now we meet again! How strange!

DOCTOR. You are a musician?

HARRY. Certainly. I used to play the piano in picture theatres—when that was the only kind of sound they had—except the peanuts. (DUMPSTY *brings the mineral water and stops to listen, admiringly.*)

DOCTOR. Do you know Bach?

HARRY. With pleasure. (*He shifts into something or other by Bach.*)

DOCTOR (*after a moment*). You have good appreciation, but not much skill.

HARRY. What do you mean, not much skill? Listen to this. (*He goes into a trick arrangement of* "The Waters of the Minnetonka.") "The Waters of the Minnetonka"—Cadman. (*He goes on playing.*) Suitable for Scenics— Niagara Falls by moonlight. Or—if you play it this way—it goes fine with the scene where the young Indian chief turns out to be a Yale man, so it's O.K. for him to marry Lillian ("Dimples") Walker. (*Starts playing* "Boola Boola.")

DOCTOR. Will you have a drink?

HARRY. Oh! So you want me to stop playing?

DOCTOR. No, no! I like your music very much.

HARRY. Then, in that case, I'd be delighted to drink with you. Another Scotch, Dumptsy.

DUMPTSY. If you please, sir. (*He goes out.*)

DOCTOR. I'm afraid I was rude to you.

HARRY. That's all right, pal. I've been rude to lots of people, and never regretted it. (*He plays on, shifting back into* "Kak Stranna.")

DOCTOR. The fact is, I am a man who is very gravely distressed.

HARRY. I can see that, Doctor. And I sympathize with you.

DOCTOR (*fiercely*). You cannot sympathize with me, because you do not know!

HARRY. No—I guess I don't know—except in a general way.

DOCTOR. You are familiar with the writings of Thomas Mann. (*It is a challenge, rather than a question.*)

HARRY. I'm afraid not, pal. (*The* DOCTOR *opens* "The Magic Mountain," *which he has been reading.*)

DOCTOR. "Backsliding"—he said—"spiritual backsliding to that dark and tortured age —that, believe me, is disease! A degradation of mankind—a degradation painful and offensive to conceive." True words, eh?

HARRY. Absolutely! (DUMPTSY *comes in with the Scotch.* HARRY *gets up from the piano and crosses.* DUMPTSY *goes.* HARRY *sits down with the* DOCTOR.)

DOCTOR. Have you had any experience with cancer?

HARRY. Certainly. I once sold a remedy for it.

DOCTOR (*exploding*). There *is* no remedy for it, so far!

HARRY. Well—this was kind of a remedy for everything.

DOCTOR. I am within *that* of finding the cure for cancer! You probably have not heard of Fibiger, I suppose?

HARRY. I may have. I'm not sure.

DOCTOR. He was a Dane—experimented with rats. He did good work, but he died before it could be completed. I carry it on. I have been working with Oriental rats, in Bologna. But because of this war scare, I must go to neutral territory. You see, nothing must be allowed to interfere with my experiments. Nothing!

HARRY. No. They're important.

DOCTOR. The laboratory of the University of Zurich has been placed at my disposal—and in Switzerland, I can work, undisturbed. I have twenty-eight rats with me, all in various carefully tabulated stages of the disease. It is the disease of civilization—and I can cure it. And now they say I must not cross the border.

HARRY. You know, Doctor, it *is* funny.

DOCTOR. What's funny? To you, everything is funny!

HARRY. No—it's just that you and I are in the same fix. Both trying to get across that line. You with rats—me with girls. Of course—I appreciate the fact that civilization at large won't suffer much if *we* get stuck in the war zone. Whereas with you, there's a lot at stake . . .

DOCTOR. It is for me to win one of the greatest victories of all time. And the victory belongs to Germany.

HARRY. Sure it does!

DOCTOR. Unfortunately, just now the situation in Germany is not good for research. They are infected with the same virus as here. Chauvinistic nationalism! They expect all bacteriologists to work on germs to put in bombs to drop from airplanes. To fill people with death! When we've given our lives to *save* people. Oh—God in heaven—why don't they let me do what is good? Good for the whole world? Forgive me. I become excited.

HARRY. I know just how you feel, Doctor. Back in 1918, I was a shill with a carnival show, and I was doing fine. The boss thought very highly of me. He offered to give me a piece of the show, and I had a chance to get somewhere. And then what do you think happened? Along comes the United States Government and they drafted me! You're in the army now! They slapped me into a uniform and for three whole months before the Armistice, I was parading up and down guarding the Ashokan Reservoir. They were afraid your people might poison it. I've always figured that that little interruption ruined my career. But I've remained an optimist, Doctor.

DOCTOR. *You* can afford to.

HARRY. I've remained an optimist because I'm essentially a student of human nature. You dissect corpses and rats and similar unpleasant things. Well,—it has been my job to dissect suckers! I've probed into the souls of some of the God-damnedest specimens. And what have I found? Now, don't sneer at me, Doctor—but above everything else I've found Faith. Faith in peace on earth and good will to men—and faith that "Muma," "Muma" the three-legged girl, really has got three legs. All my life, Doctor, I've been selling phoney goods to people of meagre intelligence and great faith. You'd think that would make me contemptuous of the human race, wouldn't you? But—on the contrary—it has given *me* Faith. It has made me sure that no matter how much the meek may be bulldozed or gypped they *will* eventually inherit the earth. (SHIRLEY *and* BEBE *come in from the lobby.*)

SHIRLEY. Harry!

HARRY. What is it, honey? (SHIRLEY *goes to* HARRY *and hands him a printed notice.*)

SHIRLEY (*excited*). Did you see this?

HARRY. Doctor—let me introduce, Miss Shirley Laughlin and Miss Bebe Gould.

SHIRLEY. How do you do?

DOCTOR (*grunts*). How do you do.

BEBE. Pleased to know you, Doctor. (HARRY *looks at the notice.*)

SHIRLEY. They got one of those put up in every one of our rooms.

HARRY (*showing it to the* DOCTOR). Look— "What to do in case of air-raids"—in all languages.

DOCTOR. Ja—I saw that.

SHIRLEY. Give it back to me, Harry. I'm going to send it to Mama.

HARRY (*handing it to her*). Souvenir of Europe.

SHIRLEY. It'll scare the hell out of her.

BEBE. What's the matter with these people over here? Are they all screwy?

HARRY. Bebe—you hit it right on the nose! (*Turns to the* DOCTOR.) I tell you, Doctor—these are very wonderful, profound girls. The mothers of tomorrow! (*He beams on them.* BEULAH *comes in.*)

SHIRLEY. Oh—shut up!

BEULAH. Say—Harry . . .

HARRY. What is it, honey?

BEULAH. Is it all right if I go out with Mr. Navadel and try to learn how to do this ski-ing? (WEBER *comes out on the gallery and starts down.*)

HARRY. What? And risk those pretty legs? Emphatically—no!

BEULAH. But it's healthy.

HARRY. Not for me, dear. Those gams of yours are my bread and butter. (WEBER *crosses. They look at him. He glances briefly at them.*) Sit down, girls, and amuse yourselves with your own thoughts. (*The* GIRLS *sit.* WEBER, *at the left, lights his cigar. The* CAPTAIN *comes in, quickly, obviously worried.*)

CAPTAIN. I have been trying to get through to headquarters, Monsieur Weber.

WEBER. And when can we leave?

CAPTAIN. Not before to-morrow, I regret to say. (IRENE *appears on the gallery.*)

WEBER. Signor Lanza in Venice assured me there would be no delay.

CAPTAIN. There would be none, if only I could get into communication with the proper authorities. But—the wires are crowded. The whole nation is in a state of uproar.

WEBER. It's absurd lack of organization. (*The* PIANIST *and* DRUMMER *come in from the lobby. The* VIOLINIST *and* SAXOPHONIST *follow.*)

CAPTAIN (*with tense solemnity*). There is good excuse for the excitement now, Monsieur Weber. The report has just come to us that a state of war exists between Italy and France.

HARRY. What?

CAPTAIN. There is a rumor of war between Italy and France!

HARRY. Rumors—rumors—everything's rumors! When are we going to *know*?

CAPTAIN. Soon enough, my friend.

DOCTOR. And what of Germany?

CAPTAIN. Germany has mobilized. (IRENE *pauses to listen.*) But I don't know if any decision has been reached. Nor do I know anything of the situation anywhere else. But—God help us—it will be serious enough for everyone on this earth. (IRENE *joins* WEBER, *who has sat down at the left.*)

IRENE (*to* WEBER, *and straight at him*). But I thought they were all too well prepared, Achille. Has there been some mistake somewhere?

WEBER (*confidentially*). We can only attribute it to spontaneous combustion of the dictatorial ego.

IRENE (*grimly*). I can imagine how thrilling it must be in Paris at this moment. Just like 1914. All the lovely soldiers—singing—marching! We must go at once to Paris, Achille.

HARRY (*rises*). What's the matter with the music, professor? Us young folks want to dance. (ELAINE *and* FRANCINE *come in.*)

ELAINE. Can we have a drink now, Harry?

HARRY. Sure. Sit down. (DON *enters, exuding gratification at the sight of this gay, chic throng. The* ORCHESTRA *starts to play* "Valencia.")

WEBER. Will you have a drink, Irene?

IRENE. No, thank you.

WEBER. Will you, Captain Locicero?

CAPTAIN. Thank you. Brandy and soda, Dumptsy.

DUMPTSY. Si, Signor.

BEBE (*yells*). Edna! We're going to have a drink! (EDNA *comes in.*)

WEBER. For me, Cinzano.

DUMPTSY. Oui, Monsieur. (*He goes into the bar.*)

DOCTOR. It is all incredible.

HARRY. Nevertheless, Doctor, I remain an optimist. (*He looks at* IRENE.) Let doubt prevail throughout this night—with dawn will come again the light of truth! (*He turns to* SHIRLEY.) Come on, honey—let's dance. (*They dance.* DON *dances with* BEULAH. *The* ORCHESTRA *continues with its spirited but frail performance of "Valencia." There are probably "border incidents" in Lorraine, the Riviera, Poland, Czecho-Slovakia and Mongolia.*)

CURTAIN

ACT TWO

SCENE I

It is about 7:30 in the evening of the same day.
The CHERRYS *are seated, both of them dressed for dinner.* AUGUSTE *is serving them cocktails.*

CHERRY. Thank you.

AUGUSTE. Thank you, Signor.

CHERRY. Has any more news come through?

AUGUSTE. No, Signor. They permit the wireless to say nothing.

CHERRY. I suppose nothing really will happen.

AUGUSTE. Let us pray that is so, Signor. (AUGUSTE *goes into the bar.* CHERRY *leans over and kisses his wife.*)

CHERRY. My sweet . . . you're really very lovely.

MRS. CHERRY. Yes. (*He kisses her again, then lifts his glass.*)

CHERRY. Here's to us, darling.

MRS. CHERRY. And to hell with all the rest.

CHERRY. And to hell with all the rest. (*They drink, solemnly.*)

MRS. CHERRY. Jimmy—

CHERRY. What is it, darling?

MRS. CHERRY. Were you just saying that—or do you believe it?

CHERRY. That you're lovely? I can give you the most solemn assurance. . . .

MRS. CHERRY. No—that nothing is going to happen.

CHERRY. Oh.

MRS. CHERRY. Do you believe that?

CHERRY. I know this much: they can't start any real war without England. And no matter how stupid and blundering our government may be, our people simply won't stand for it.

MRS. CHERRY. But people can be such complete fools.

CHERRY. I know it, darling. Why can't they all be like us?

MRS. CHERRY. You mean—nice.

CHERRY. Yes—nice—and intelligent—and happy.

MRS. CHERRY. We're very conceited, aren't we?

CHERRY. Of course. And for good and sufficient reason.

MRS. CHERRY. I'm glad we're so superior, darling. It's comforting. (HARRY *comes in from bar.*)

CHERRY. Oh—good evening, Mr. Van.

HARRY. Good evening. Pardon me— (*He starts to go.*)

CHERRY. Oh—don't run away, Mr. Van. Let's have some music.

MRS. CHERRY. Won't you have a drink with us?

HARRY. No, thanks, Mrs. Cherry—if you don't mind. (*Sits down at the piano.*) I'm afraid I put down too many Scotches this afternoon. As a result of which, I've just had to treat myself to a bicarbonate of soda. (*Starts playing* "Some of these days.")

MRS. CHERRY. I love that.

HARRY. Thanks, pal—always grateful for applause from the discriminating. (*Finishes the chorus and stops.*)

CHERRY. Do play some more.

HARRY. No. The mood isn't right.

MRS. CHERRY. I can't tell you what a relief it is to have you here in this hotel.

HARRY. It's kind of you to say that, Mrs. Cherry. But I don't deserve your handsome tribute. Frequently, I can be an asset to any gathering — contributing humorous anecdotes and bits of homely philosophy. But here and now, I'm far from my best.

CHERRY. You're the only one here who seems to have retained any degree of sanity.

MRS. CHERRY. You and your young ladies.

HARRY. The girls are lucky. They don't know anything. And the trouble with me is that I just don't give a damn.

MRS. CHERRY. We've been trying hard not to know anything—or not to give a damn. But it isn't easy.

HARRY. You haven't been married very long, have you? I hope you don't mind my asking. . . .

CHERRY. We were married the day before yesterday.

HARRY. Let me offer my congratulations.

CHERRY. Thank you very much.

HARRY. It's my purely intuitive hunch that you two ought to get along fine.

CHERRY. That's our intention, Mr. Van.

MRS. CHERRY. And we'll do it, what's more. You see—we have one supreme thing in common:

HARRY. Yeah?

MRS. CHERRY. We're both independent.

CHERRY. We're like you Americans, in that respect.

HARRY. You flatter us.

MRS. CHERRY. Jimmy's a painter.

HARRY. You don't say!

MRS. CHERRY. He's been out in Australia, doing colossal murals for some government building. He won't show me the photographs of them, but I'm sure they're simply awful. (*She laughs fondly.*)

CHERRY. They're allegorical. (*He laughs, too.*)

HARRY. I'll bet they're good, at that. What do you do, Mrs. Cherry?

MRS. CHERRY. Oh, I work in the gift department at Fortnum's—

HARRY. Behind a counter, eh!

MRS. CHERRY. Yes—wearing a smock, and disgracing my family.

HARRY. Well, what d'ye know!

MRS. CHERRY. Both our families hoped we'd be married in some nice little church, and settle down in a nice little cottage, in a nice little state of decay. But when I heard Jimmy was on the way home I just dropped everything and rushed down here to meet him—and we were married, in Florence.

CHERRY. We hadn't seen each other for nearly a year—so, you can imagine, it was all rather exciting.

HARRY. I can imagine.

MRS. CHERRY. Florence is the most perfect place in the world to be married in.

HARRY. I guess that's true of any place.

CHERRY. We both happen to love Italy. And—I suppose—we're both rather on the romantic side.

HARRY. You stay on that side, no matter what happens.

MRS. CHERRY (*quickly*). What do you think is going to happen?

HARRY. Me? I haven't the slightest idea.

CHERRY. We've looked forward so much to being here with no one bothering us, and plenty of winter sports. We're both keen on ski-ing. And now—we may have to go dashing back to England at any moment.

MRS. CHERRY. It's rotten luck, isn't it?

HARRY. Yes, Mrs. Cherry. That's what it is—it's rotten. (QUILLERY *enters from the bar, reading a newspaper.*) So they wouldn't let you cross?

QUILLERY. No!

HARRY. Is there any news?

QUILLERY (*glaring*). News! Not in this patriotic journal! "Unconfirmed rumors"—from Vienna, London, Berlin, Moscow, Tokyo. And a lot of confirmed lies from Fascist headquarters in Rome. (*He slaps the paper down and sits.*) If you want to know what is really happening, ask *him*—up there! (*Indicates the rooms above.*)

CHERRY. Who?

QUILLERY. Weber! The great Monsieur Achille Weber, of the Comité des Forges! He can give you all the war news. Because he *made* it. You don't know who he is, eh? Or what he has been doing here in Italy? I'll tell you. (*He rises and comes close to them.*) He has been organizing the arms industry. Munitions. To kill French babies. And English babies. France and Italy are at war. England joins France. Germany joins Italy. And that will drag in the Soviet Union and the Japanese Empire and the United States. In every part of the world, the good desire of men for peace and decency is undermined by the dynamite of jingoism. And it needs only one spark, set off anywhere by one egomaniac, to send it all up in one final, fatal explosion. Then love becomes hatred, courage becomes terror, hope becomes despair. (*The* DOCTOR *appears on the gallery above.*) But—it will all be very nice for Achille Weber. Because he is a master of the one *real* League of Nations—(*The* DOCTOR *slowly comes down steps.*) The League of Schneider-Creusot, and Krupp, and Skoda, and Vickers and Dupont. The League of Death! And the workers of the world are expected to pay him for it, with their sweat, and their life's blood.

DOCTOR. Marxian nonsense!

QUILLERY. Ah! Who speaks?

DOCTOR. *I* speak.

QUILLERY. Yes! The eminent Dr. Hugo Waldersee. A wearer of the sacred swastika. Down with the Communists! Off with their heads! So that the world may be safe for the Nazi murderers.

DOCTOR. So that Germany may be safe from its oppressors! It is the same with all of you—Englishmen, Frenchmen, Marxists—you manage to forget that Germany, too, has a right to live! (*Rings handbell on the table.*)

QUILLERY. If you love Germany so much, why aren't you there, now—with your rats?

DOCTOR (*sitting.*) I am not concerned with politics. (AUGUSTE *enters from the bar.*) I am a scientist. (*To* AUGUSTE.) Mineral water! (AUGUSTE *bows and exits into the bar.*)

QUILLERY. That's it, Herr Doctor! A scientist—a servant of humanity! And you know that if you were in your dear Fatherland, the Nazis would make you abandon your cure of cancer. It might benefit too many people outside of Germany—even maybe some Jews. They would force you to devote yourself to breeding malignant bacteria—millions of little germs, each one trained to give the Nazi salute and then go out and poison the enemy. You—a fighter against disease and death—you would come a Judas goat in a slaughter house. (DON *has appeared during this.*)

CHERRY. I say, Quillery, old chap—do we have to have so much blood and sweat just before dinner?

QUILLERY (*turning on him*). Just before dinner! And now we hear the voice of England! The great, well-fed, pious hypocrite! The grabber — the exploiter — the immaculate butcher! It was *you* forced this war, because miserable little Italy dared to drag its black shirt across your trail of Europe. What do *you* care if civilization goes to pieces—as long as you have your dinner—and your dinner jacket!

CHERRY (*rising*). I'm sorry, Quillery—but I think we'd better conclude this discussion out on the terrace.

MRS. CHERRY. Don't be a damned fool, Jimmy. You'll prove nothing by thrashing him.

QUILLERY. It's the Anglo-Saxon method of proving everything! Very well—I am at your disposal.

DON. No! I beg of you, Mr. Cherry. We

mustn't have any of that sort of thing. (*He turns to* QUILLERY.) I must ask you to leave. If you're unable to conduct yourself as a gentleman, then . . .

QUILLERY. Don't say any more. Evidently I cannot conduct myself properly! I offer my apologies, Mr. Cherry.

CHERRY. That's quite all right, old man. Have a drink. (*He extends his hand. They shake.*)

QUILLERY. No, thank you. And my apologies to you, Herr Doctor.

DOCTOR. There is no need for apologizing. I am accustomed to all that.

QUILLERY. If I let my speech run away with me, it is because I have hatred for certain things. And you should hate them, too. They are the things that make us blind—and ig-norant—and—and dirty. (*He turns and goes out quickly.* DON *goes with him.*)

MRS. CHERRY. He's so right about everything.

CHERRY. I know, poor chap. Will you have another cocktail, darling?

MRS. CHERRY. I don't think so. Will you, Doctor? (*He shakes his head, indicates the mineral water. She rises.*) Let's dine.

CHERRY. It will be a bit difficult to summon up much relish. (*They go out, hand in hand.*)

HARRY. I find them very appealing, don't you, Doctor? (*The* DOCTOR *doesn't announce his findings.*) Did you know they were mar-ried only the day before yesterday? Yeah— they got themselves sealed in Florence—be-cause they love Italy. And they came here hoping to spend their honeymoon on skis. . . . Kind of pathetic, isn't it?

DOCTOR. What did you say?

HARRY. Nothing, pal. (DON *comes in.*) Only making conversation.

DOCTOR (*rising*). That Communist! Making me a criminal because I am a German!

DON. I'm dreadfully sorry, Dr. Waldersee. We never should have allowed the ill-bred little cad to come in here.

DOCTOR. Oh— It's no matter. I have heard too many Hymns of Hate before this. To be a German is to be used to insults, and in-juries. (*He goes out.* DON *starts to go out left.*)

HARRY. Just a minute, Don.

DON. Well?

HARRY. Have you found out yet who that dame is?

DON. What "dame"?

HARRY. That Russian number with Weber.

DON. I have not enquired as to her identity.

HARRY. But did he register her as his wife?

DON. They registered separately! And if it's not too much to ask, might I suggest that you mind your own damned business?

HARRY. You might suggest just that. And I should still be troubled by one of the most tantalizing of questions—namely, "Where have I seen that face before?" Generally, it turns out to be someone who was in the second row one night, yawning.

DON. I'm sure that such is the case now. (*He starts again to go.*)

HARRY. One moment, Don. There's some-thing else.

DON (*impatiently*). What is it?

HARRY. I take it that your job here is some-thing like that of a professional greeter.

DON. You're at liberty to call it that, if you choose.

HARRY. You're a sort of Y.M.C.A. secretary —who sees to it that all the guests get to-gether and have a good time.

DON. Well?

HARRY. Well—do you think you're doing a very good job of it right now?

DON (*simply furious*). Have you any sugges-tions for improving the performance of my duties?

HARRY. Yes, Don—I have.

DON. And I'd very much like to know just exactly who the hell do you think you are to be offering criticism of my work?

HARRY. Please, please! You needn't scream at me. I'm merely trying to be helpful. I'm making you an offer.

DON. What is it?

HARRY (*looking around*). I see you've got a color wheel here. (*Referring to the light.*)

DON. We use it during the supper dance. But—if you don't mind, I—

HARRY. I see—well—how would it be if I and the girls put on part of our act here, to-night? For purposes of wholesome merriment and relieving the general tension?

DON. What kind of an act is it?

HARRY. And don't say, "What kind of an act," in that tone of voice. It's good enough for this place. Those girls have played before the King of Rumania. And if some of my suspicions are correct—but I won't pursue that subject. All that need concern you is that we can adjust ourselves to our audience, and to-night we'll omit the bubble dance and the number in which little Bebe does a shimmy in a costume composed of detachable gardenias, unless there's a special request for it.

DON. Do you expect to be paid for this?

HARRY. Certainly not. I'm making this offer out of the goodness of my heart. Of course, if you want to make any appropriate adjustment on our hotel bill . . .

DON. And you'll give me your guarantee that there'll be no vulgarity? (IRENE *appears on the gallery and starts to come down. She is wearing a dinner dress.*)

HARRY. Now be careful, Don. One more word like that and the offer is withdrawn . . . (DON *cautions him to silence.*)

DON. It's a splendid idea, Mr. Van. We'll all greatly appreciate your little entertainment, I'm sure. (*To* IRENE.) Good evening, Madame.

IRENE (*with the utmost graciousness*). Good evening, Mr. Navadel. (*She pauses at the window.*) It *is* a lovely view. It's like a landscape on the moon.

DON. Yes—yes. That's exactly what it's like. (*She comes down.*)

HARRY. You understand, we'll have to rehearse with the orchestra.

DON. Oh, yes—Mr. Van. Our staff will be glad to co-operate in every way. . . . Do sit down, Madame.

IRENE (*sitting*). What became of those planes that flew off this afternoon? I haven't heard them come back. (*Takes out a cigarette.*)

DON. I imagine they were moving to some base farther from the frontier. I hope so. They always made the most appalling racket. (*Lights her cigarette for her.*)

HARRY. About eleven o'clock? (WEBER *appears on the gallery.*)

DON. Yes, Mr. Van. Eleven will do nicely. You'll have a cocktail, Madame? (HARRY *goes into the lobby.*)

IRENE. No, no. Vodka, if you please.

DON. I shall have it sent right in. (*He goes off at the left into bar.* IRENE *looks slowly off, after* HARRY. *She smiles slightly.* WEBER *comes down the stairs quickly. He is not in evening dress. He too pauses at the window.*)

WEBER. A perfectly cloudless night! They're very lucky. (*He comes on down.*)

IRENE. Did you get your call?

WEBER. Yes. I talked to Lanza.

IRENE. I gather the news is, as usual, good.

WEBER. It is extremely serious! You saw those bombers that left here this afternoon?

IRENE. Yes.

WEBER. They were headed for Paris. Italy is evidently in a great hurry to deliver the first blow.

IRENE. How soon may we leave here?

WEBER. None too soon, I can assure you. The French high command will know that the bombers come from this field. There will be reprisals—probably within the next twenty-four hours.

IRENE. That will be exciting to see.

WEBER. An air raid?

IRENE. Yes—with bombs bursting in the snow. Sending up great geysers of diamonds.

WEBER. Or perhaps great geysers of us.

IRENE (*after a moment*). I suppose many people in Paris are being killed now.

WEBER. I'm afraid so. Unless the Italians bungle it.

IRENE. Perhaps your sister—Madame d'Hilaire—perhaps she and her darling little children are now dying.

WEBER (*sharply*). My sister and her family are in Montbeliard.

IRENE. But you said the Italians might bungle it. They might drop their bombs on the wrong place.

WEBER. I appreciate your solicitude, my dear. But you can save your condolences until they are needed. (DUMPTSY *comes in from the bar and serves the vodka.* WEBER *rises.*) I must telegraph to Joseph to have the house ready. It will be rather cold in Biarritz now—but far healthier than Paris. You are going in to dinner now?

IRENE. Yes.

WEBER. I shall join you later. (*He goes out.* DUMPTSY *picks up the* CHERRYS' *glasses.*)

DUMPTSY. We will have a great treat to-night, Madame.

IRENE. Really?

DUMPTSY. That American impresario, that Mr. Harry Van—he will give us an entertainment with his dancing girls.

IRENE. Is he employed here regularly?

DUMPSTY. Oh, no, Madame. He is just passing, like you. This is a special treat. It will be very fine.

IRENE. Let us hope so. (*She downs the vodka.*)

DUMPTSY. Madame is Russian, if I may say so.

IRENE (*pleased*). How did you know that I am Russian? Just because I am having vodka?

DUMPTSY. No, Madame. Many people try to drink vodka. But only true Russians can do it gracefully. You see—I was a prisoner with your people in the war. I liked them.

IRENE. You're very charming. What is your name?

DUMPTSY. I am called Dumptsy, Madame.

IRENE. Are you going again to the war, Dumptsy?

DUMPTSY. If they tell me to, Madame.

IRENE. You will enjoy being a soldier?

DUMPTSY. Yes—if I'm taken prisoner soon enough.

IRENE. And who do you think will win?

DUMPTSY. I can't think, Madame. It is all very doubtful. But one thing I can tell you: whoever wins, it will be the same as last time—Austria will lose.

IRENE. They will all lose, Dumptsy. (*The* CHERRYS *come in. She greets them pleasantly.*) Good evening.

CHERRY. Good evening, Madame. (*The* CHERRYS *start to sit, across from* IRENE.)

IRENE. Bring some more vodka, Dumptsy. Perhaps Mr. and Mrs. Cherry will have some, too.

CHERRY. Why, thank you—we . . .

MRS. CHERRY. I'd love to. I've never tasted vodka.

IRENE. Ah—then it's high time. Bring in the bottle, Dumptsy.

DUMPTSY. Yes, Madame. (*He goes in to the bar.*)

IRENE. Come, sit down here. (*The* CHERRYS *sit by her.*) You will find vodka a perfect stimulant to the appetite. So much better than that hybrid atrocity, the American cocktail!

CHERRY. To tell you the truth, Madame—we've already dined.

IRENE. It is no matter. It is just as good as a liqueur.

MRS. CHERRY. We didn't really dine at all. We merely looked at the minestrone and the Parmesan cheese—and we felt too depressed to eat anything.

IRENE. It's the altitude. After the first exhilaration there comes a depressive reaction, especially for you, who are accustomed to the heavy, Pigwiggian atmosphere of England.

CHERRY. Pigwiggian?

IRENE. Yes, Pigwig—Oliver Twist—you know, your Dickens? (DUMPTSY *enters from bar with a bottle of vodka and two more glasses, which he places on the table. He returns to the bar.*)

CHERRY. You know England, Madame?

IRENE (*fondly*). Of course I know England! My governess was a sweet old ogre from your north country—and when I was a little girl I used to visit often at Sandringham.

CHERRY (*impressed*). Sandringham?

MRS. CHERRY. The palace?

IRENE. Yes. That was before your time. It was in the reign of dear, gay King Edward, and the beautiful Alexandra. (*She sighs a little for those days.*) I used to have such fun playing with my cousin David. He used to try to teach me to play cricket, and when I couldn't swing the bat properly, he said, "Oh, you Russians will never be civilized!" (*Laughs.*) When I went home to Petersburg I told my uncle, the Tsar, what David had said, and he was so amused! But now—you must drink your vodka. (*They rise, and lift their glasses.*) A toast! To his most gracious Majesty the King. (*They clink glasses.*) God bless him.

CHERRY. Thank you, Madame. (*All three drink and* MRS. CHERRY *coughs violently.*)

IRENE (*to* MRS. CHERRY). No—no! Drink it right down. Like this. (*She swallows it in a gulp.*) So! (*Refills the glasses from the bottle.*) The second glass will go more easily. (*They sit.*) I used to laugh so at your funny British Tommies in Archangel. They all hated vodka until one of them thought of mixing it with beer.

MRS. CHERRY. How loathsome!

IRENE. It was! But I shall be forever grateful to them—those Tommies. They saved my life when I escaped from the Soviets. For days and nights—I don't know how many—I was driving through the snow—snow—snow—snow—, in a little sleigh, with the body of my father beside me, and the wolves running along like an escort of dragoons.

You know—you always think of wolves as howling constantly, don't you?

CHERRY. Why, yes—I suppose one does.

IRENE. Well, they don't. No, these wolves didn't howl! They were horribly, confidently silent. I think silence is much more terrifying, don't you!

CHERRY. You must have been dreadfully afraid.

IRENE. No, I was not afraid for myself. It was the thought of my father. . . .

MRS. CHERRY. Please! I know you don't want to talk about it any more.

IRENE. Oh, no—it is so far away now. I shall never forget the moment when I came through the haze of delirium, and saw the faces of those Tommies. Those simple, friendly faces. And the snow—and the wolves—and the terrible cold—they were all gone—and I was looking at Kew Gardens on a Sunday afternoon, and the sea of golden daffodils—"fluttering and dancing in the breezes." (WEBER *has come in with the daffodils.*)

WEBER. Shall we go in to dinner now, Irene?

IRENE. Yes, yes, Achille. In a minute. I am coming. (WEBER *goes.* IRENE *rises.*) Now—we must finish our vodka. (CHERRY *rises.*) And you must make another try to eat something.

CHERRY. Thank you so much, Madame. (*They drink.*)

IRENE. And later on, we must all be here for Mr. Van's entertainment—and we must all applaud vigorously.

MRS. CHERRY. We shall, Madame.

CHERRY. He's such a nice chap, isn't he?

IRENE (*going*). Yes—and a real artist, too.

CHERRY. Oh—you've seen him?

IRENE. Why—yes—I've seen him, in some café chantant, somewhere. I forget just where it was. (*The three of them have gone out together. The light is dimmed to extinction. The curtain falls.*)

END OF SCENE ONE

SCENE II

About two hours later.
WEBER *is drinking brandy. The* CAPTAIN *is standing.*

CAPTAIN. I have been listening to the radio. Utter bedlam! Of course, every government has imposed the strictest censorship—but it is very frightening—like one of those films where ghostly hands suddenly reach in and switch off all the lights.

WEBER. Any suggestions of air raids?

CAPTAIN. None. But there is ominous quiet from Paris. Think of it—Paris—utterly silent! Only one station there is sending messages, and they are in code.

WEBER. Probably instructions to the frontier.

CAPTAIN. I heard a man in Prague saying something that sounded interesting, but him I could not understand. Then I turned to London, hopefully, and listened to a gentleman describing the disastrous effects of ivy upon that traditional institution, the oak.

WEBER. Well—we shall soon know. . . . There'll be no trouble about crossing the frontier to-morrow?

CAPTAIN. Oh, no. Except that I am still a little worried about madame's passport.

WEBER. We'll arrange about that. Have a cigar, Captain?

CAPTAIN. Thank you. (IRENE *comes in as the* CAPTAIN *starts to light the cigar.*)

IRENE. Do you hear the sound of airplanes? (*All stop to listen, intently. The sound becomes audible. The* CAPTAIN *shakes out the match, throws the unlit cigar on the table, and dashes to the window and looks upward.*)

CAPTAIN. It is our bombers. One—two— three. Seven of them. Seven out of eighteen. You will excuse me? (*He salutes and dashes out.*)

WEBER. Seven out of eighteen! Not bad, for Italians. (IRENE *has gone to the window to look out.*)

IRENE. I'm so happy for you, Achille.

WEBER. What was that, my dear?

IRENE. I said—I'm so happy for you.

WEBER. But—just why am I an object of congratulation?

IRENE. All this great, wonderful death and destruction, everywhere. And you promoted it!

WEBER. Don't give me too much credit, Irene.

IRENE. But I *know* what you've done.

WEBER. Yes, my dear. You know a great deal. But don't forget to do honor to Him— up there—who put fear into man. I am but the humble instrument of His divine will.

IRENE (*looking upward, sympathetically*). Yes—that's quite true. We don't do half enough justice to Him. Poor, lonely old soul. Sitting up in heaven, with nothing to do, but play solitaire. Poor, dear God. Playing Idiot's Delight. The game that never means anything, and never ends.

WEBER. You have an engaging fancy, my dear.

IRENE. Yes.

WEBER. It's the quality in you that fascinates me most. Limitless imagination! It is what has made you such an admirable, brilliant liar. And so very helpful to me! Am I right?

IRENE. Of course you are right, Achille. Had I been bound by any stuffy respect for the truth, I should never have escaped from the Soviets.

WEBER. I'm sure of it.

IRENE. Did I ever tell you of my escape from the Soviets?

WEBER. You have told me about it at least eleven times. And each time it was different.

IRENE. Well, I made several escapes. I am always making escapes, Achille. When I am worrying about you, and your career. I have to run away from the terror of my own thoughts. So I amuse myself by studying the faces of the people I see. Just ordinary, casual, dull people. (*She is speaking in a tone that is sweetly sadistic.*) That young English couple, for instance. I was watching them during dinner, sitting there, close together, holding hands, and rubbing their knees together under the table. And I saw him in his nice, smart, British uniform, shooting a little pistol at a huge tank. And the tank rolls over him. And his fine strong body, that was 'so full of the capacity for ecstasy, is a mass of mashed flesh and bones— a smear of purple blood—like a stepped-on snail. But before the moment of death, he consoles himself by thinking, "Thank God *she* is safe! She is bearing the child I gave her, and he will live to see a better world." (*She walks behind* WEBER *and leans over his shoulder.*) But I know where she is. She is lying in a cellar that has been wrecked by an air raid, and her firm young breasts are all mixed up with the bowels of a dismembered policeman, and the embryo from her womb is splattered against the face of a dead bishop. That is the kind of thought with which I amuse myself, Achille. And it makes me so proud to think that I am so close to you—who make all this possible. (WEBER *rises and walks about the room. At length he turns to her.*)

WEBER. Do you talk in this whimsical vein to many people?

IRENE. No. I betray my thoughts to no one but you. You know that I am shut off from the world. I am a contented prisoner in your ivory tower.

WEBER. I'm beginning to wonder about that.

IRENE. What? You think I could interest myself in some one else—?

WEBER. No—no, my dear. I am merely wondering whether the time has come for you to turn commonplace, like all the others?

IRENE. The others?

WEBER. All those who have shared my life. My former wife, for instance. She now boasts that she abandoned me because part of my income is derived from the sale of poison gas. Revolvers and rifles and bullets she didn't mind—because they are also used by sportsmen. Battleships too are permissible; they look so splendid in the news films. But she couldn't stomach poison gas. So now she is married to an anemic Duke, and the

large fortune that she obtained from me enables the Duke to indulge his principal passion, which is the slaughtering of wild animals, like rabbits, and pigeons and rather small deer. My wife is presumably happy with him. I have always been glad you are not a fool as she was, Irene.

IRENE. No. I don't care even for battleships. And I shall not marry an anemic Duke.

WEBER. But—there was something unpleasantly reminiscent in that gaudy picture you painted. I gather that this silly young couple has touched a tender spot, eh?

IRENE. Perhaps, Achille. Perhaps I am softening.

WEBER. Then apply your intelligence, my dear. Ask yourself: why shouldn't they die? And who are the greater criminals—those who sell the instruments of death, or those who buy them, and use them? You know there is no logical reply to that. But all these little people—like your new friends—all of them consider me an arch-villain because I furnish them with what they want, which is the illusion of power. That is what they vote for in their frightened governments—what they cheer for on their national holidays— what they glorify in their anthems, and their monuments, and their waving flags! Yes— they shout bravely about something they call "national honor." And what does it amount to? Mistrust of the motives of every one else! Dog in the manger defense of what they've got, and greed for the other fellow's possessions! Honor among thieves! I assure you, Irene—for such little people the deadliest weapons are the most merciful. (*The* CHERRYS *enter. He is whistling* "Minnie the Moocher.")

IRENE. Ah! Mr. and Mrs. Cherry!

CHERRY. Hello there. (*They come down.*)

IRENE. You have dined well!

MRS. CHERRY. Superbly!

CHERRY. We ate everything—up to and including the zabaglione.

IRENE. You can thank the vodka for that. Vodka never fails in an emergency.

CHERRY. And we can thank you, Madame, and do so.

IRENE. But—permit me to introduce Monsieur Weber. (WEBER *rises*.) Mrs. Cherry—Mr. Cherry. (*They are exchanging greetings as* DON *comes in.*)

DON. We're going to have a little cabaret show for you now, Madame.

WEBER. I don't think I shall wait for it, my dear.

IRENE. But you must—

WEBER. I really should look over Lanza's estimates—

IRENE. Please, Achille—Mr. Van is an artist. You will be so amused.

WEBER (*resuming seat*). Very well, Irene.

DON (*his tone blandly confidential*). Between ourselves, I don't vouch for the quality of it. But it may be unintentionally amusing.

IRENE. I shall love it.

CHERRY. This is the most marvellous idea, Mr. Navadel.

DON. Oh, thank you. We try to contrive some novelty each evening. If you'll be good enough to sit here— (DON *goes up to usher in the* ROSSIS *and direct them to their seats. The musicians come in and take their places. The* DOCTOR *comes in.* DUMPTSY *is busily moving chairs about, clearing a space for the act.* IRENE *and the* CHERRYS *chat pleasantly.* ANNA, *the maid, appears on the gallery above to watch the entertainment.*) (HARRY *comes in. He is wearing a tight-fitting dinner jacket, and carries a cane and a straw hat.*)

HARRY. All set, Don?

DON. Quite ready, whenever you are.

HARRY. Okey-doke. Give us a fanfare, professor. (*He goes out. The band obliges with a fanfare.* HARRY *returns, all smiles.*) Before we start, folks, I just want to explain that we haven't had much chance to rehearse with my good friend, Signor Palota, and his talented little team here. (*He indicates the orchestra with a handsome gesture.*) So we must crave your indulgence and beg you to give us a break if the rhythm isn't all kosher. (*He waits for his laugh.*) All we ask of you, kind friends, is "The Christian pearl of Charity," to quote our great American poet, John Greenleaf Whittier. We thank you. Take it away! (*He bows. All applaud. He then sings a song—The girls come on in costume and dance.*)

(*During the latter part of the act, the* CAPTAIN, *the* MAJOR, *and four flying corps* OFFICERS *come in. The latter are dirty and in a fever of heroically restrained excitement. They survey the scene with wonderment and then with delight, saying, in Italian, "What's all this?" and "What brought these blonde bambinos to Monte Gabriele?" etc.* HARRY *interrupts the act and orders the orchestra to play the Fascist anthem, "Giovinezza." The officers acknowledge this graceful gesture with the Fascist salute. The* GIRLS *wave back. The* CAPTAIN *gets the* OFFICERS *seated and then goes to order drinks.* HARRY *and the* GIRLS *resume.*)

(*At the end of the act, all applaud and the* OFFICERS *shout "Brava—Bravissima" and stamp their feet with enthusiasm. The* GIRLS *take several bows and go.* HARRY *returns for a solo bow, waving his straw hat. One of the* OFFICERS *shouts, in Italian, "We want the young ladies!"*)

CAPTAIN (*to* HARRY). My friends wish to know respectfully if the young ladies will care to join them in a little drink?

HARRY. Certainly! Come back in, girls. Get over there and join the army! (*The* GIRLS *do so.*) Now, folks—with your kind permission—I shall give the girls an interlude of rest and refreshment and treat you to a little piano specialty of my own. Your strict attention is not obligatory. (*He starts his specialty, assisted by* SHIRLEY *and* EDNA. *The* OFFICERS *don't pay much attention. Bottles of champagne are brought for them and the* GIRLS.)

(WEBER *goes and speaks to the* CAPTAIN. *He beckons him up to the landing of the stairs where they converse in low tones, the* CAPTAIN *telling him about the air-raid.*)

(HARRY's *act is interrupted by the entrance of* QUILLERY.)

QUILLERY (*to* HARRY). Do you know what has happened?

DON. I told you we didn't want you here.

PITTALUGA. We're having an entertainment here.

QUILLER. Yes! An entertainment!

HARRY. If you'll just sit down, pal. . . . (*He and the* GIRLS *continue with their singing.*)

QUILLERY. An entertainment—while Paris is in ruins!

CHERRY (*rises*). What?

DOCTOR. What are you saying?

QUILLERY. They have bombed Paris! The Fascisti have bombed Paris!

DON. What? But it can't be possible—

HARRY. Go on, Shirley. Keep on singing.

QUILLERY. I tell you—to-night their planes flew over and—

CHERRY. But how do you know this?

QUILLERY. It is on the wireless—everywhere. And I have just talked to one of their mechanics, who was on the flight, and saw, with his own eyes—

HARRY. Won't you please sit down, pal? We're trying to give you a little entertainment— (*Stops playing.*)

QUILLERY. For the love of God—listen to me! While you sit here eating and drinking, to-night, Italian planes dropped twenty thousand kilos of bombs on Paris. God knows how many they killed. God knows how much of life and beauty is forever destroyed! And you sit here, drinking, laughing, with *them*—the murderers. (*Points to the flyers, who ask each other, in Italian, what the hell is he talking about.*) They did it! It was their planes, from that field down there. Assassins! (*The* OFFICERS *make a move toward* QUILLERY—*one of them arming himself with a champagne bottle.*)

HARRY (*comes down from the piano*). We can't have any skull-cracking in this club. Hey, Captain, speak to your men before anything starts. (*The* CAPTAIN *comes down to the* OFFICERS *and pacifies them.* CHERRY *comes down to stand by* QUILLERY.)

MRS. CHERRY. Jimmy! . . . You keep out of this!

MAJOR *and* FIRST *and* THIRD OFFICERS (*jump up*). Assassini!

HARRY. Now listen, pal. . . .

SHIRLEY. Harry! Don't get yourself mixed up in this mess!

QUILLERY. You see, we stand together! France—England—America! Allies!

HARRY. Shut up, France! It's O.K., Captain. We can handle this—

QUILLERY. They don't dare fight against the power of England and France! The free democracies against the Fascist tyranny!

HARRY. Now, for God's sake stop fluctuating!

QUILLERY. England and France are fighting for the hopes of mankind!

HARRY. A minute ago, England was a butcher in a dress suit. Now we're Allies!

QUILLERY. We stand together. We stand together forever. (*Turns to* OFFICERS.) I say God damn you. God damn the villains that sent you on this errand of death.

CAPTAIN (*takes a few steps toward* QUILLERY). If you don't close your mouth, Frenchman, we shall be forced to arrest you.

QUILLERY. Go on, Fascisti! Commit national suicide. That's the last gesture left to you toy soldiers.

HARRY. It's all right, Captain. Mr. Quillery is for peace. He's going back to France to stop the war.

QUILLERY (*turns on* HARRY). You're not authorized to speak for me. I am competent to say what I feel. And what I say is "Down with Fascism! Abbasso Fascismo!" (*There is an uproar from the* OFFICERS.)

CAPTAIN (*ordinarily gentle, is now white hot with rage*). Attenzione!

QUILLERY. Vive la France! Viv—

CAPTAIN. E agli arresti.

QUILLERY. Call out the firing squad! Shoot me dead! But do not think you can silence the truth that's in me.

CAPTAIN (*grabs* QUILLERY *from the left and calls the* FIRST OFFICER). Molinari! (FIRST OFFICER *grabs* QUILLERY *from the right. They start to take him out.*)

QUILLERY (*as he is being led out*). The Empire of the Fascisti will join the Empire of the Cæsars in smoking ruins. Vive la France! Vive la France! (WEBER *goes upstairs and exits. They have gone.*)

CHERRY (*to* HARRY). You'd better carry on with your turn, old boy.

HARRY. No, pal. The act is cold. (*To the orchestra leader.*) Give us some music, Signor. (*The orchestra starts playing.*) Let dancing become general.

CHERRY. Let's dance, my sweet.

MRS. CHERRY. I can't bear to, Jimmy.

CHERRY. I think we should.

MRS. CHERRY. Very well, darling. (*They dance. The* OFFICERS *dance with the* GIRLS.)

HARRY (*goes over to* IRENE). Would you care to dance?

IRENE. Why—why, thank you. (*She stands up, and they join the slowly moving mob.*

SHIRLEY *is singing as loud as she can. The color wheel turns so that the dancers are bathed in blue, then amber, then red.*)

CURTAIN

END OF SCENE TWO

SCENE III

Later that night.
   IRENE *and* HARRY *are alone. She is sitting, telling the story of her life. He is listening with fascination and doubt.*

IRENE. My father was old. The hardships of that terrible journey had broken his body. But his spirit was strong—the spirit that is Russia. He lay there, in that little boat, and he looked up at me. Never can I forget his face, so thin, so white, so beautiful, in the starlight. And he said to me, "Irene—little daughter," and then—he died. For four days I was alone, with his body, sailing through the storms of the Black Sea. I had no food— no water—I was in agony from the bayonet wounds of the Bolsheviki. I knew I must die. But then—an American cruiser rescued me. May God bless those good men! (*She sighs.*) I've talked too much about myself. What about you, my friend?

HARRY. Oh—I'm not very interesting. I'm just what I seem to be.

IRENE. C'est impossible!

HARRY. C'est possible! The facts of my case are eloquent. I'm a potential genius—reduced to piloting six blondes through the Balkans.

IRENE. But there is something that you hide from the world—even, I suspect, from yourself. Where did you acquire your superior education?

HARRY. I worked my way through college selling encyclopædias.

IRENE. I knew you had culture! What college was it?

HARRY. Oh—just any college. But my sales talk was so good that I fell for it myself. I bought the God-damned encyclopædia. And I read it all, travelling around, in day coaches, and depot hotels, and Fox-time dressing rooms. It was worth the money.

IRENE. And how much of all this have you retained?

HARRY (*significantly*). I? I—never forget anything.

IRENE. How unfortunate for you! Does your encyclopædia help you in your dealings with the girls?

HARRY. Yes, Mrs. Weber. . . . I got considerable benefit from studying the lives of the great courtesans, and getting to understand their technique. . . .

IRENE. Forgive me for interrupting you—but that is not my name.

HARRY. Oh—pardon me, I thought . . .

IRENE. I know what you thought. Monsieur Weber and I are associated in a sort of business way.

HARRY. I see.

IRENE. He does me the honor to consult me in matters of policy.

HARRY. That's quite an honor! Business is pretty good, isn't it!

IRENE. I gather that you are one of those noble souls who does not entirely approve of the munitions industry?

HARRY. Oh, no—I'm not noble. Your friend is just another salesman. And I make it a point never to criticize anybody else's racket.

IRENE. Monsieur Weber is a very distinguished man. He has rendered very distinguished services to all the governments of the world. He is decorated with the Legion of Honor, the Order of the White Eagle, the Order of St. James of the Sword, and the Military Order of Christ!

HARRY. The Military Order of Christ. I never heard of that one.

IRENE. It is from Portugal. He has many orders.

HARRY. Have you ever been in America?

IRENE. Oh, yes—I've seen it all—New York, Washington, Palm Beach . . .

HARRY. I said America. Have you ever been in the West?

IRENE. Certainly I have. I flew across your continent. There are many White Russians in California.

HARRY. Did you ever happen to make any parachute landings in any places like Kansas, or Iowa, or Nebraska?

IRENE (*laughing*). I have seen enough of your countrymen to know that you are typical.

HARRY. Me? I'm not typical of anything.

IRENE. Oh, yes, you are. You are just like all of them—an ingenuous, sentimental idealist. You believe in the goodness of human nature, don't you?

HARRY. And what if I do? I've known millions of people, intimately—and I never found more than one out of a hundred that I didn't like, once you got to know them.

IRENE. That is very charming—but it *is* naïve.

HARRY. Maybe so. But experience prevents me from working up much enthusiasm over any one who considers the human race as just so many clay pigeons, even if he does belong to the Military Order of Christ.

IRENE. If you came from an older culture, you would realize that men like Monsieur Weber are necessary to civilization.

HARRY. You don't say.

IRENE. I mean, of course, the sort of civilization that we have got. (*She smiles upon him benevolently. It is as though she were explaining patiently but with secret enjoyment the facts of life to a backward nephew.*) Stupid people consider him an arch-villain because it is his duty to stir up a little trouble here and there to stimulate the sale of his products. Do you understand me, my friend?

HARRY. I shouldn't wonder.

IRENE. Monsieur Weber is a true man of the world. He is above petty nationalism; he can be a Frenchman in France—a German in Germany—a Greek—a Turk—whatever the occasion demands.

HARRY. Yes—that little Quillery was an Internationalist, too. He believed in brotherhood, but the moment he got a whiff of gunpowder he began to spout hate and revenge. And now those nice, polite Wops will probably have to shut him up with a firing squad.

IRENE (*takes out a cigarette from her case*). It is a painful necessity.

HARRY. And it demonstrates the sort of little trouble that your friend stirs up. (*He takes out his lighter and lights her cigarette.*)

IRENE. Do you know that you can be extremely rude?

HARRY. I'm sorry if I've hurt your feelings about Mr. Weber, but he just happens to be a specimen of the one per cent that I *don't* like.

IRENE. I was not referring to that. Why do you stare at me so?

HARRY. Have I been staring?

IRENE. Steadily. Ever since we arrived here this afternoon. Why do you do it?

HARRY. I've been thinking I could notice a funny resemblance to some one I used to know.

IRENE. You should know better than to tell any woman that she resembles somebody else. We none of us like to think that our appearance is commonplace.

HARRY. The one you look like wasn't commonplace.

IRENE. Oh! She was some one near and dear to you?

HARRY. It was somebody that occupies a unique shrine in the temple of my memory.

IRENE. That *is* a glowing tribute. The temple of your memory must be so crowded! But I am keeping you from your duties.

HARRY. What duties?

IRENE. Shouldn't you be worrying about your young ladies?

HARRY. They're all right; they've gone to bed.

IRENE. Yes—but there are several Italian officers about. Aren't you supposed to be the chaperone?

HARRY. I leave the girls to their own resources, of which they have plenty. (*He stares hard at her.*) Have you always been a blonde?

IRENE. Yes—as far as I can remember.

HARRY. You don't mind my asking?

IRENE. Not at all. And now, may I ask you something?

HARRY. Please do so.

IRENE. Why do you waste yourself in this degraded work? Touring about with those obvious little harlots?

HARRY. You mean you think I'm fitted for something that requires a little more mentality?

IRENE. Yes.

HARRY. How do you know so much about me? (*It should be remembered that all through this scene* HARRY *is studying her, trying to fit together the pieces of the jigsaw puzzle of his memory.*)

IRENE. For one thing, I saw your performance to-night.

HARRY. You thought it was punk?

IRENE. I thought it was unworthy.

HARRY. It was unfortunately interrupted. You should have seen . . .

IRENE. I saw enough. You are a very bad dancer.

HARRY. The King of Rumania thought I was pretty good.

IRENE. He is entitled to his opinion—and I to mine.

HARRY. I'll admit that I've done better things in my time. Would it surprise you to know that I was once with a mind-reading act?

IRENE. Really?

HARRY. Yeah.

IRENE. Now you're staring at me again.

HARRY. Have you ever been in Omaha?

IRENE. Omaha? Where is that? Persia?

HARRY. No. Nebraska. That's one of our states. I played there once with the greatest act of my career. I was a stooge for Zuleika, the Mind Reader. At least she called me her stooge. But I was the one who had to do all the brain work.

IRENE. And she read people's minds?

HARRY. I did it for her. I passed through the audience and fed her the cues. We were sensational, playing the finest picture houses in all the key cities. Zuleika sat up on the stage, blindfolded—and usually blind drunk.

IRENE. Oh, dear. And was *she* the one that I resemble?

HARRY. No! There was another act on the same bill. A troupe of Russians . . .

IRENE. Russians?

HARRY. Singers, mandolin players, and squat dancers. One of them was a red-headed girl. She was fascinated by our act, and she kept pestering me to teach her the code. She said she could do it better than Zuleika.

IRENE. Those poor Russians. There are so many of them all over the world. And so many of them completely counterfeit!

HARRY. This dame was counterfeit all right. In fact, she was the God-damnedest liar I ever saw. She lied just for the sheer artistry of it. She kept after me so much that I told her finally to come up to my hotel room one night, and we'd talk it over.

IRENE. I hope you didn't tell her the code.

HARRY. No. After the week in Omaha the bill split. The Russians went to Sioux Falls and we went on the Interstate Time. I played with Zuleika for another year and then the drink got her and she couldn't retain. So the act busted up. I've always hoped I'd catch up with that red-headed Russian again sometime. She might have been good. She had the voice for it, and a kind of overtone of mystery.

IRENE. It's a characteristic Gypsy quality. And you never saw her again?

HARRY. No.

IRENE. Perhaps it is just as well. She couldn't have been so clever—being duped so easily into going to your room.

HARRY. She wasn't being duped! She knew what she was doing. If there was any duping going on, she was the one that did it.

IRENE. She *did* make an impression!

HARRY (*looking straight at her*). I was crazy about her. She was womanhood at its most desirable—and most unreliable.

IRENE. And you such a connoisseur. But—it's getting late.

HARRY (*rises*). Do you know any Russian music? (*He crosses to the piano.*)

IRENE (*rises*). Oh, yes. When I was a little girl my father used to engage Chaliapin to come often to our house. He taught me many songs.

HARRY. Chaliapin, eh? Your father spared no expense. (*He sits at the piano.*)

IRENE. That was in *old* Russia. (*He plays a few bars of* "Kak Stranna.") Kak Stranna!

HARRY. Yeah! How strange! (*He starts to play* "Prostchai.") Do you know this one? (IRENE *sings some of it in Russian.*) How do you spell that name—Irene?

IRENE. I-R-E-N-E. (HARRY *pounds the piano and jumps up.*) What's the matter?

HARRY. That's it! Irene! (*He pronounces it* I-REEN.)

IRENE. But what—?

HARRY. I knew it! You're the one!

IRENE. What one?

HARRY. That red-headed liar! Irene! I knew I could never be mistaken. . . .

IRENE. Irene is a very usual name in Russia. (*She laughs heartily.*)

HARRY. I don't care how usual it is. Everything fits together perfectly now. The name—the face—the voice—Chaliapin for a teacher! Certainly it's you! And it's no good shaking your head and looking amazed! No matter how much you may lie, you can't deny the fact that you slept with me in the Governor Bryan Hotel in Omaha in the fall of 1925. (IRENE *laughs heartily again.*) All right—go ahead and laugh. That blonde hair had me fooled for a while—but now I know it's just as phoney as the bayonet wounds, and the parachute jumps into the jungle. . . .

IRENE (*still laughing*). Oh—you amuse me.

HARRY. It's a pleasure to be entertaining. But you can't get away with it.

IRENE. You amuse me very much indeed. Here we are—on a mountain peak in Bedlam. To-night, the Italians are bombing Paris. At this moment, the French may be bombing Rome, and the English bombing Germany—and the Soviets bombing Tokyo, and all you worry about is whether I am a girl you once met casually in Omaha.

HARRY. Did I say it was casual?

IRENE (*laughing*). Oh—it *is* amusing!

HARRY (*angrily*). I know you're amused. I admit it's all very funny. I've admitted everything. I told you I was crazy about you. Now when are you going to give me a break and tell me—

IRENE. You! You are so troubled—so—so uncertain about everything.

HARRY. I'm not uncertain about it any more, Babe. I had you tagged from the start. There was something about you that was indelible . . . something I couldn't forget all these years. (WEBER *appears on the gallery, wearing his Sulka dressing gown.*)

WEBER. Forgive me for intruding, my dear. But I suggest that it's time for you to go to bed.

IRENE. Yes, Achille. At once. (WEBER *treats* HARRY *to a rather disparaging glance and exits.* IRENE *starts upstairs.*) Poor Achille! He suffers with the most dreadful insomnia—it is something on his mind. (*She goes up a few more steps.*) He is like Macbeth. Good night, my friend—my funny friend.

HARRY. Good night.

IRENE. And thank you for making me laugh so much—to-night.

HARRY. I could still teach you that code.

IRENE. Perhaps—we shall meet again in—what was the name of the hotel?

HARRY. It was the Governor Bryan.

IRENE. Oh, yes! The Governor Bryan! (*Laughing heartily, she exits.* HARRY *goes to the piano, sits down and starts to play* "Kak Stranna." DUMPTSY *enters from the bar.*)

DUMPTSY. That was wonderful—that singing and dancing.

HARRY (*still playing*). Thanks, pal. Glad you enjoyed it.

DUMPTSY. Oh, yes, Mr. Van—that was good.

HARRY (*bangs a chord*). Chaliapin—for God's *sake!*

DUMPTSY. I beg your pardon, sir?

HARRY (*rises*). It's nothing. Good night, Dumptsy. (*He goes out into the lobby.*)

DUMPTSY. Good night, sir. (*He starts for the bar.*)

CURTAIN

ACT THREE

The following afternoon.
HARRY *is at the piano, idly playing the* "Caprice Viennoise," *or something similar. His thoughts are elsewhere.*
SHIRLEY *is darning some stockings and humming the tune.* BEBE *is plucking her eyebrows.*
BEULAH, ELAINE, FRANCINE *and* EDNA *are seated at a table.* BEULAH *is telling* ELAINE's *fortune with cards. The others are watching. All are intensely serious, and all chewing gum.*

SHIRLEY. What's that number, Harry?

HARRY. The "Caprice Viennoise"—Kreisler.

SHIRLEY. It's pretty.

HARRY. You think so? (*He shifts to something jazzier.*)

BEULAH. You are going to marry.

ELAINE. Again?

BEULAH. The cards indicate dis*tinctly* two marriages, and maybe a third.

ELAINE (*chewing furiously*). For *God's* sake!

SHIRLEY (*to* HARRY). We certainly need some new stockings.

HARRY. We'll renovate the wardrobe in Geneva.

BEULAH. Now—let's see what the fates tell us next.

BEBE. Say, Harry—when do we lam it out of here?

HARRY. Ask Beulah. Maybe she can get it out of the cards.

BEBE. I hate this place. It's spooky.

BEULAH (*to* HARRY). What'd you say, honey?

ELAINE. Ah—don't pay any attention to him. What else do they say about me?

BEULAH. Well . . . you'll enter upon a period of very poor health.

ELAINE. When?

BEULAH. Along about your thirty-seventh year.

SHIRLEY. That means any day now. (*She winks broadly at* BEBE, *who laughs.*)

HARRY (*vehemently*). Listen to me, you nymphs! We can't be wasting our time with card tricks. We've got to do a little rehearsing.

SHIRLEY. Why, Harry—what are you mad about now?

HARRY. Who said I was mad about anything?

SHIRLEY. Well—every time you get yourself into a peeve, you take it out on us. You start in hollering, "Listen, girls—we got to rehearse."

HARRY. I am not peeved. Merely a little disgusted. The act needs brushing up.

BEBE. Honestly, Harry—don't you think we know the routine by now?

HARRY. I'm not saying you don't know it. I'm just saying that your performance last night grieved me and shocked me. You had your eyes on those officers and not on your work. That kind of attitude went big in Rumania, but now we're going to a town where artistry counts. Some day, I'll take the whole bunch of you to watch the Russian ballet, just to give you an idea of what dancing is. (CAPTAIN LOCICERO *comes in*.)

CAPTAIN. Your pardon, Mr. Van.

HARRY. Ah, Captain. Good afternoon. . . . Rest, girls.

CAPTAIN (*to the* GIRLS). Good afternoon.

GIRLS. Good afternoon, Captain.

HARRY. You bring us news?

CAPTAIN. Good news, I hope. May I have your passports?

HARRY. Certainly. (*He gets them out of his coat and hands them to the* CAPTAIN.)

CAPTAIN. Thank you. I hope to have definite word for you very shortly. (*He salutes and starts to go*.)

HARRY. What about Mr. Quillery, Captain? What's happened to him?

CAPTAIN. Mr. Quillery was very injudicious. Very injudicious. I am glad that you are so much more intelligent. (*He goes out*.)

SHIRLEY. I don't think they could have done anything cruel to him. They're awfully sweet boys, those Wops.

HARRY. So I observed. . . . Now listen to me, girls. Geneva's a key spot, and we've got to be good. Your audiences there won't be a lot of hunkies, who don't care what you do as long as you don't wear practically any pants. These people are accustomed to the best. They're mains—big people, like prime ministers, and maharajahs and archbishops. If we click with them, we'll be set for London and Paris. We may even make enough money to get us home.

BEBE. Oh—don't speak of such a thing! Home!

EDNA. To get a real decent henna wash again!

HARRY. The trouble with all of you is, you're thinking too much about your own specialties. You're trying to steal the act, and wreck it. Remember what the late Knute Rockne said: "Somebody else can have the all-star, all-American aggregations. All *I* want is a team!" Now, you—Beulah. You've got plenty of chance to score individually in the bubble number. But when we're doing the chorus routine, you've got to submerge your genius in the mass.

BEULAH. What do I do wrong, honey?

HARRY. Your Maxie Ford is lacklustre. Here —I'll show you. . . . (HARRY *gets up to demonstrate the Maxie Ford*.)

SHIRLEY (*laughs*). If you do it that way, Beulah, you'll go flat on your face. Here— *I'll* show you.

HARRY. Just a minute, Miss Laughlin. Who's the director of this act, you or me?

SHIRLEY (*amiably*). You are, you old poop. But you just don't know the steps.

ELAINE. Don't let her get fresh, Harry.

BEBE. Slap her down!

SHIRLEY. Give us the music, Harry.

BEULAH. Please, Harry. Shirley just wants to be helpful.

HARRY. I feel I should resent this—but— (*He returns to the piano*.) Go ahead, Miss Laughlin. Carry on. (*He plays*. SHIRLEY *demonstrates*. BEULAH *tries it*.)

BEULAH. Have I got it right?

SHIRLEY. Sure! He's just shooting his face off! (*During this, the following conversation goes on*:)

ELAINE. You know that Wop that was giving me a play last night?

FRANCINE. You mean the one with the bent nose?

BEBE. I thought he was terrible. But that boy I had is a Count.

ELAINE. Well, look what he gave me.

EDNA. What is it?

BEBE. Let me see it.

ELAINE. I don't know what it is.

BEBE. Looks like money. What kind of money is that, Harry?

HARRY. It's an old Roman coin.

SHIRLEY. How much is it worth?

HARRY. I haven't looked up the latest rate of exchange on dinars. But I think, dear, you've been betrayed. Now, pay attention, girls. . . . As I said, we've got to improve the act, and with that in view, I'm going to retire from all the dance routine.

BEBE. What?

BEULAH. Why, *Harry*—we couldn't. . . .

SHIRLEY. Oh! I hurt you, didn't I! (*She rushes to him, coos over him.*) Yes, I did, you poor baby. I hurt his feelings—and I'm sorry—I'm very, very sorry.

HARRY. All right, Shirley. We can dispense with the regrets. Save your lipstick. (*He thrusts her away.*)

SHIRLEY. But why . . . ?

HARRY. I've decided that I'm a thinker, rather than a performer. From now on, I shall devote myself to the purely creative end of the act, and, of course, the negotiation of contracts.

BEULAH. But when did you make up your mind to this, honey?

HARRY. I've been considering it for a long time.

SHIRLEY. Say! What were you talking about to that Russian dame?

HARRY. We discussed world politics.

FRANCINE. Oh!

SHIRLEY. And how are politics these days?

BEBE. Did you get anywheres near to first base, Harry?

HARRY. I find it impossible to explain certain things to you girls. You're children of nature.

SHIRLEY. We're *what*?

BEULAH. He means we're natural.

HARRY. Never mind, sweetheart. You'll sing the number, Shirley.

SHIRLEY. Me?

BEBE. With that terrible voice?

HARRY. She handled it fine that time I had bronchitis in Belgrade. And with a little rehearsal, you'll have the whole League of Nations rooting for you. Now—let's have it. (*He plays,* SHIRLEY *sings,* BEBE *disapproves.*) (DON *comes in, dressed for travelling.*)

DON. Captain Locicero has got the orders to let us through and the train is due to leave about four o'clock. What a relief to be out of this foul place!

HARRY. You going too, Don?

DON. Yes. There's nothing for me here. In fact, I'm sick and tired of Europe as a whole. I was in town this morning when they shot Quillery.

BEBE. Who?

SHIRLEY. It was that little guy that bawled out the Wops.

BEULAH. They *shot* him? Why did they have to do that?

DON. Of course, he asked for it. But even so, it's pretty sickening to see one of your fellow human beings crumpled up in horrible, violent death. Well—there'll be plenty more like him, and right here, too. The French know all about this air base, and they'll be over any minute with their bombs. So—it's California here I come!

HARRY. And run right into the Japs? Better stop off at Wichita.

DON. I'll see you all on the train. (*He goes up the stairs.*)

HARRY. You girls go get yourselves ready. (*The* CHERRYS *appear on the gallery.* DON *speaks to them, then goes out. The* CHERRYS *come down.*)

ELAINE. O.K., Harry.

EDNA (going). I'm surprised at those Wops. They seemed like such sweet boys.

BEBE. Sure—when they talk they sound like opera. But they're awful excitable. (BEBE, ELAINE, EDNA and FRANCINE have gone out.)

BEULAH. But I can't understand—why did they have to shoot that poor boy?

HARRY. It's hard to explain, Beulah. But it seems there's some kind of argument going on over here, and the only way they can settle it is by murdering a lot of people.

BEBE. You don't need to tell me what it's like. I was in the Club Grotto the night the Purple Gang shot it out with the G's. And was that terrible! Blood all over everything! (She and SHIRLEY and BEULAH have gone out.)

HARRY. You heard what they did to Quillery?

CHERRY. Yes. It seems that he died like a true patriot, shouting "Vive La France."

HARRY. Better if he died like a man—sticking to what he knew was right.

CHERRY. He was a nice little chap.

MRS. CHERRY. The Italians are swine! (DON reappears on the balcony and comes down.)

CHERRY. Oh, they had a perfect right to do it.

MRS. CHERRY. But to kill a man for saying what he thinks!

CHERRY. Many people will be killed for less than that.

HARRY. I'll have to be saying good-bye pretty soon. Did you say the train goes at four, Don?

DON. Four o'clock. Correct! (He goes.)

HARRY. I hope all this unpleasantness won't spoil your winter sports.

CHERRY. Oh, that's all washed up. We're going, too—if they'll let us cross the border.

HARRY. So the honeymoon has ended already?

MRS. CHERRY. Yes—I suppose so.

CHERRY. England is coming into this business. We have to stand by France, of course. And so there's nothing for it but . . .

MRS. CHERRY. And so Jimmy will have to do his bit, manning the guns, for civilization. Perhaps he'll join in the bombardment of Florence, where we were married.

CHERRY. You know—after the ceremony we went into the Baptistery and prayed to the soul of Leonardo da Vinci that we might never fail in our devotion to that which is beautiful and true. I told you we were a bit on the romantic side. We forgot what Leonardo said about war. Bestial frenzy, he called it. And bestial frenzy it is.

MRS. CHERRY. But we mustn't think about that now. We have to stand by France. We have to make the world a decent place for heroes to live in. Oh, Christ! (She starts to sob. CHERRY rushes to her.)

CHERRY. Now, now, darling. We've got to make a pretense of being sporting about it. Please, darling. Don't cry.

HARRY. Let her cry, the poor kid. Let her sob her heart out—for all the God-damned good it will do her. You know what I often think? (He is trying to be tactful.) I often think we ought to get together and elect somebody else God. Me, for instance. I'll bet I'd do a much better job.

MRS. CHERRY. You'd be fine, Mr. Van.

HARRY. I believe I would. There'd be a lot of people who would object to my methods. That Mr. Weber, for instance. I'd certainly begin my administration by beating the can off him.

CHERRY. Let's start the campaign now! Vote for good old Harry Van, and his Six Angels! (The CAPTAIN comes in with a brief-case full of papers and passports. He takes these out and puts them on a table.)

CAPTAIN. Good afternoon, Mrs. Cherry. Gentlemen.

HARRY. Do we get across?

CAPTAIN. Here is your passport, Mr. Van— and the young ladies, with my compliments. They have been duly stamped. (He hands them over.)

HARRY. Thanks, Captain. And how about Mr. Weber and his—friend? Are they going, too?

CAPTAIN. I have their passports here. I advise you to make ready, Mr. Van. The train will leave in about forty-five minutes.

HARRY. O.K., Captain. See you later, Mr. and Mrs. Cherry. (*He goes.*)

CHERRY. O.K., Harry.

MRS. CHERRY. And what about us, Captain?

CAPTAIN. Due to a slight technicality, you will be permitted to cross the frontier. Here are your passports.

CHERRY. I can't tell you how grateful we are. (WEBER *appears on the gallery.*)

CAPTAIN. You needn't be grateful to me, Mr. Cherry. The fact that you are allowed to pass is due to the superb centralization of authority in my country. The telegram authorizing your release was filed at 11:43 today, just seventeen minutes before a state of war was declared between Great Britain and Italy. I must obey the order of Rome, even though I know it's out of date. Is your luggage ready?

CHERRY. It's all out here in the hall. We're off now, Captain. Well, good-bye and good luck!

CAPTAIN. And good luck to you—both of you.

CHERRY. I need hardly say that I'm sorry about all this. It's really a damned rotten shame.

CAPTAIN. It is. All of that. Good-bye, my friend. (*He extends his hand and* CHERRY *shakes it.*) Madame. . . . (*He extends his hand to* MRS. CHERRY.)

MRS. CHERRY. Don't call *me* your friend, because I say what Quillery said—damn you —damn your whole country of mad dogs for having started this horror.

CAPTAIN (*bows*). It is not my fault, Mrs. Cherry.

CHERRY. It's utterly unfair to talk that way, darling. The Captain is doing his miserable duty as decently as he possibly can.

CAPTAIN (*tactfully*). In this unhappy situation, we are all in danger of losing our heads.

MRS. CHERRY. I know . . . I know. Forgive me for the outburst. (*She extends her hand to the* CAPTAIN *and they shake.*) I should have remembered that it's everybody's fault.

CHERRY. That's right, my sweet. Come along. (*They go out*)

CAPTAIN (*to* WEBER). Frankly, my heart bleeds for them.

WEBER. They're young. They'll live through it, and be happy.

CAPTAIN. Will they? I was their age, and in their situation, twenty years ago, when I was sent to the Isonzo front. And people said just that to me: "Never mind, you are young —and youth will survive and come to triumph." And I believed it. That is why I couldn't say such deceiving words to them now.

WEBER. The cultivation of hope never does any immediate harm. Is everything in order?

CAPTAIN (*rises*). Quite, Monsieur Weber. Here it is. (*He hands over* WEBER'S *passport.*)

WEBER. And Madame's? (*The* CAPTAIN *picks up a document on foolscap.*)

CAPTAIN. This is an unusual kind of passport. It has given us some worry.

WEBER. The League of Nations issues documents like that to those whose nationality is uncertain.

CAPTAIN. I understand—but the attitude of Italy toward the League of Nations is not at the moment cordial.

WEBER. Then you refuse to honor Madame's passport?

CAPTAIN. My instructions are to accord you every consideration, Monsieur Weber. In view of the fact that Madame is travelling with you, I shall be glad to approve her visa.

WEBER. Madame is not travelling with me. She has her own passport.

CAPTAIN. But it is understood that you vouch for her, and that is enough to satisfy the authorities.

WEBER (*with cold authority*). Vouch for her? It is not necessary for anyone to vouch for Madame! She is entirely capable of taking care of herself. If her passport is not entirely in order, it is no affair of mine.

CAPTAIN (*genuinely distressed*). But—I must tell you, Monsieur Weber—this is something I do not like. This places me in a most embarrassing position. I shall be forced to detain her.

WEBER. You are a soldier, my dear Captain, and you should be used to embarrassing positions. Undoubtedly you were embarrassed this morning, when you had to shoot that confused pacifist, Quillery. But this is war, and unpleasant responsibilities descend upon you and on me as well. However . . . (*He sees* HARRY, *who is coming in.*) I shall attend to my luggage. Thank you, Captain. (*He goes out.*)

CAPTAIN. Don't mention it. (*To* HARRY) The young ladies are ready?

HARRY. Yes—they're ready. And some of your aviators are out there trying to talk them into staying here permanently.

CAPTAIN (*smiling*). And I add my entreaties to theirs.

HARRY. We won't have any more trouble, will we? (*The* DOCTOR *appears on the gallery with coat, hat, books done in a bundle, and umbrella. He comes downstairs.*)

CAPTAIN. Oh, no, Mr. Van. Geneva is a lovely spot. All of Switzerland is beautiful, these days. I envy you going there, in such charming company.

HARRY. Hi, Doctor. Have you got the rats all packed?

DOCTOR. Good afternoon. I am privileged to go now? (*He puts down all of his belongings and crosses.*)

CAPTAIN. Yes, Dr. Waldersee. Here is your passport.

DOCTOR. Thank you. (*He examines the passport carefully.*)

HARRY. I can tell you, Doctor—I'm going to be proud to have known you. When I read in the papers that you've wiped out cancer and won the Nobel prize, and you're the greatest hero on earth, I'll be able to say, "He's a personal friend of mine. He once admired my music."

DOCTOR (*solemnly*). Thank you very much. (*To the* CAPTAIN.) This visa is good for crossing the Austrian border?

CAPTAIN. Certainly. But you are going to Zurich?

DOCTOR (*rises*). I have changed my plans. I am going back into Germany. Germany is at war. Perhaps I am needed. (*He crosses to pick up his coat.*)

HARRY. Needed for what?

DOCTOR. I shall offer my services for what they are worth. (HARRY *goes to help him on with his coat.*)

HARRY. But what about the rats?

DOCTOR (*fiercely*). Why should I save people who don't want to be saved—so that they can go out and exterminate each other? Obscene maniacs! (*Starts to put on his gloves.*) Then I'll be a maniac, too. Only I'll be more dangerous than most of them. For I know all the tricks of death! And—as for my rats, maybe they'll be useful. Britain will put down the blockade again, and we shall be starving—and maybe I'll cut my rats into filets and eat them. (*He laughs, not pleasantly, and picks up his umbrella and books.*)

HARRY. Wait a minute, Doctor. You're doing this without thinking. . . .

DOCTOR. I'm thinking probably that remedy you sold is better than mine. Hasten to apply it. We are all diseased. . . .

HARRY. But you can't change around like this! Have you forgotten all the things you told me? All that about backsliding?

DOCTOR. No, I have not forgotten the degradation of mankind—that is painful and offensive to conceive. (*He is going out.*) I am sorry to disappoint you about the Nobel prize. (*He has gone.*)

HARRY. Good-bye, Doctor. (*He sits down, wearily.*) Why in the name of God can't somebody answer the question that everybody asks? Why? Why? Oh—I know the obvious answers, but they aren't good enough. Weber—and a million like him—they can't take the credit for *all* of this! Who is it that did this dirty trick on a lot of decent people? And why do you let them get away with it? That's the thing that I'd like to know!

CAPTAIN. We have avalanches up here, my friend. They are disastrous. They start with a little crack in the ice, so tiny that one cannot see it, until, suddenly, it bursts wide open. And then it is too late.

HARRY. That's very effective, Captain. But it don't satisfy me, because this avalanche isn't made out of ice. It's made out of flesh and blood—and—and *brains*. . . . It's God-damned bad management—that's what it is! (*This last is half to himself.*)

(IRENE *has appeared on the gallery and started to come down.*)

IRENE. Still upset about the situation, Mr. Van? Ah—good afternoon, my dear Captain Locicero.

CAPTAIN. Good afternoon, Madame.

IRENE. I have had the most superb rest here. The atmosphere is so calm, and impersonal, and soothing. I can't bear to think that we're going to Biarritz, with the dull, dismal old sea pounding in my ears. (WEBER *comes in.*)

IRENE. We are leaving now, Achille?

WEBER. I believe that some difficulties have arisen. (*He looks toward the* CAPTAIN.)

IRENE. Difficulties?

CAPTAIN. I regret, Madame, that there must be some further delay.

IRENE. Oh! Then the train is not going through, after all?

CAPTAIN. The train is going, Madame. But this passport of yours presents problems which, under the circumstances—

IRENE. Monsieur Weber will settle the problems, whatever they are. Won't you, Achille?

WEBER. There is some question about your nationality, Irene.

CAPTAIN (*referring to the passport*). It states here, Madame, that your birthplace is uncertain, but assumed to be Armenia.

IRENE. That is a province of Russia!

CAPTAIN. You subsequently became a resident of England, then of the United States, and then of France.

IRENE (*angrily*). Yes—it's all there—clearly stated. I have never before had the slightest difficulty about my passport. It was issued by the League of Nations.

WEBER. I'm afraid the standing of the League of Nations is not very high in Italy at this moment.

CAPTAIN. The fact is, Madame, the very existence of the League is no longer recognized by our government. For that reason, we can not permit you to cross the frontier at this time. (*She looks at him and then at* WEBER. *The* CAPTAIN *hands her the passport.*) I'm sure you will appreciate the delicacy of my position. Perhaps we shall be able to adjust the matter to-morrow. (*He salutes and goes out, glad to escape.* HARRY *goes with him, asking, "What's the trouble, Captain? Can't something be done about it?"*)

WEBER. I should of course wait over, Irene. But you know how dangerous it is for me to delay my return to France by so much as one day. I have been in touch with our agents. The premier is demanding that production be doubled—trebled—at once.

IRENE. Of course.

WEBER. Here—(*He takes out an envelope containing money.*) This will cover all possible expenses. (*He gives her the envelope.*) There is a train for Venice this evening. You must go there and see Lanza. I have already sent him full instructions.

IRENE. Yes, Achille. And I thank you for having managed this very, very tactfully.

WEBER (*smiles*). You are a genuinely superior person, my dear. It is a privilege to have known you.

IRENE. Thank you again, Achille. Good-bye.

WEBER. Good-bye, Irene. (*He kisses her hand.* HARRY *returns.*) Coming, Mr. Van?

HARRY. In a minute. (WEBER *goes.* IRENE *puts the money in her handbag.*) Tough luck, babe.

IRENE. It's no matter.

HARRY. I just talked to the Captain and he isn't going to be as brutal as the Bolsheviks were. I mean, you won't suffer any bayonet wounds. He'll fix it for you to get through to-morrow.

IRENE. You want to be encouraging, my dear friend. But it's no use. The Italian government has too many reasons for wishing to detain me. They'll see to it that I disappear—quietly—and completely.

HARRY. Yes—I know all about that.

IRENE. All about what?

HARRY. You're a person of tremendous significance. You always were. (SHIRLEY *appears at the left.*)

SHIRLEY. Hey, Harry! It's time for us to go.

HARRY. I'll be right out. (SHIRLEY *goes.*)

IRENE. Go away—go away with your friends. If I am to die, it is no concern of yours!

HARRY. Listen, babe—I haven't any wish to . . .

IRENE (*flaming*). And please don't call me *babe!* (*She stands up and walks away from him. He follows her.*)

HARRY. My apologies, Madame. I just call everybody "babe."

IRENE. Perhaps that's why I do not like it!

HARRY. Even if I don't believe anything you say, I can see pretty plainly that you're in a tough spot. And considering what we were to each other in the old Governor Bryan Hotel—

IRENE. Must you always be in Omaha?

HARRY. I'd like to help you, Irene. Isn't there something I can do?

IRENE. I thank you, from my heart, I thank you, for that offer. But it's useless. . . .

HARRY. You don't have to thank me. Tell me—what can I do?

IRENE. You're very kind, and very gallant. But, unfortunately, you're no match for Achille Weber. He has decided that I shall remain here and his decision is final!

HARRY. Is he responsible for them stopping you?

IRENE. Of course he is. I knew it the moment I saw that ashamed look on Captain Locicero's face, when he refused to permit me . . .

HARRY. So Weber double-crossed you, did he! What has the son of a bitch got against you?

IRENE. He's afraid of me. I know too much about his methods of promoting his own business.

HARRY. Everybody knows about his methods. Little Quillery was talking about them last night. . . .

IRENE. Yes—and what happened to Quillery? That's what happens to every one who dares to criticize him. Last night I did the one thing he could never forgive. I told him the truth! At last I told him just what I think. And now—you see how quickly he strikes back! (SHIRLEY *and* BEBE *appear.*)

SHIRLEY. Harry! The bus is going to leave.

HARRY. All right—all right!

BEBE. But we got to go this *minute!*

HARRY. I'll be with you. Get out!

SHIRLEY (*as they go*). Can you imagine? He stops everything to make another pass at that Russian. (*They have gone.*)

IRENE. Go ahead—go ahead! You can't help me! No one can! (*He picks up his coat and hat.*) But—if it will make you any happier in your future travels with Les Blondes, I'll tell you, yes—I did know you, slightly, in Omaha!

HARRY (*peering at her*). Are you lying again?

IRENE. It was Room 974. Does that convince you?

HARRY (*ferociously*). How can I remember what room it was?

IRENE (*smiling*). Well, then—you'll never be sure, Mr. Van.

BEBE's VOICE. Harry!

SHIRLEY's VOICE. For God's sake, Harry!

DON (*appearing*). We can't wait another instant! (DON *goes.*)

SHIRLEY's VOICE. Come *on!*

HARRY (*He turns and starts for the door, addressing the* GIRLS *en route*). All right, God damn it! (*He goes out.*)

(IRENE *takes out her vanity case, and does something to her face. She takes off her hat and cloak.* DUMPTSY *comes in from the back. He is wearing the uniform of a private in the Italian army, with gas mask at the alert, and a full pack on his back.*)

DUMPTSY. Good afternoon, Madame.

IRENE (*turning*). Why, Dumptsy—what is that costume?

DUMPTSY. They called me up. Look! I'm an Italian soldier.

IRENE. You look splendid!

DUMPTSY. If you please, Madame. But why didn't you go on that bus?

IRENE. I've decided to stay and enjoy the winter sports.

DUMPTSY. I don't think this is a good place any more, Madame. They say the war is very big—bigger than last time.

IRENE. Yes—I hear that on all sides.

DUMPTSY. The French will be here to drop bombs on everybody.

IRENE. It will be thrilling for us if they do. Won't it, Dumptsy?

DUMPTSY. Maybe it will, Madame. But—I came to say good-bye to Auguste, the barman, and Anna, the maid. They're both cousins of mine. They'll laugh when they see me in these clothes. (*He goes to the left.*) Can I get you anything, Madame?

IRENE. Yes, Dumptsy. I'll have a bottle of champagne. Bring two glasses. We'll have a drink together.

DUMPTSY. If you please, Madame. (DUMPTSY *goes into the bar.* IRENE *lights a cigarette and goes up to the window to look out.* PITTALUGA *comes in.*)

PITTALUGA. Your luggage is in the hall, Madame. Will you wish it taken to the same suite?

IRENE. No—I didn't really care much for those rooms. Have you anything smaller?

PITTALUGA (*in a less deferential tone*). We have smaller rooms on the other side of the hotel.

IRENE. I'll have the smallest. It will be cozier.

PITTALUGA. You wish to go to it now?

IRENE. No. You can send up the luggage. I'll look at it later. (PITTALUGA *bows and goes.* DUMPTSY *returns with the champagne.*)

DUMPTSY. I was right, Madame. Auguste laughed very much.

IRENE (*coming down*). What will happen to your wife and children, Dumptsy?

DUMPTSY. Oh—I suppose the Fascisti will feed them. They promised to feed all the families with a man who is out fighting for their country. (*He has filled her glass. She sits down.*)

IRENE. Go ahead and pour yourself one, Dumptsy.

DUMPTSY. Thank you so much, Madame. I wasn't sure I heard correctly.

IRENE. Here's to you, Dumptsy—and to Austria.

DUMPTSY. And to you, Madame, if you please.

IRENE. Thank you. (*They drink.*)

DUMPTSY. And may you soon be restored to your home in Petersburg.

IRENE. Petersburg?

DUMPTSY. Yes, Madame. Your home.

IRENE (*with a slight smile*). Ah, yes. My home! (*They drink again.*) And have no fear for the future, Dumptsy. Whatever happens—have no fear!

DUMPTSY. If you please, Madame. (*He finishes his drink.*) And now I must go find Anna, if you will excuse me.

IRENE. Here, Dumptsy. (*She hands him a note of money.*) Good-bye, and God bless you.

DUMPTSY. Thank you so much, Madame. (DUMPTSY *leans over and kisses her hand.*) Kiss die hand, Madame. (*The* CAPTAIN *and* MAJOR *come in from the lobby.* DUMPTSY *salutes, strenuously, and goes out. The* MAJOR *goes across and into the bar. The* CAPTAIN *is following him.*)

IRENE. Some champagne, Captain?

CAPTAIN. No, thank you very much.

IRENE. You needn't be anxious to avoid me, Captain. I know perfectly well that it wasn't your fault.

CAPTAIN. You are very understanding, Madame.

IRENE. Yes—that's true. I am one of the most remarkably understanding people on earth. (*She swallows her drink.*) I understand so damned much that I am here, alone, on this cold mountain, and I have no one to turn to, nowhere to go . . .

CAPTAIN. If I can be of service to you in any way . . .

IRENE. I know you'll be kind, Captain Locicero. And faultlessly polite.

CAPTAIN (*with genuine sympathy*). I realize, Madame, that politeness means nothing now. But—under these tragic circumstances —what else can I do?

IRENE (*deliberately*). What else can you do? I'll tell you what else you can do in these tragic circumstances. You can refuse to fight! Have you ever thought of that possibility? You can refuse to use those weapons that they have sold you! But—you were going into the bar. Please don't let me detain you.

CAPTAIN. You will forgive me, Madame?

IRENE. Fully, my dear Captain. . . . Fully.

CAPTAIN. Thank you. (*He salutes and goes into the bar.*)

(IRENE *pours herself another drink. Then she picks it up, goes to the piano, and starts to play a sketchy accompaniment for "Kak Stranna." She seems to be pretty close to tears. Perhaps she does cry a little, thoroughly enjoying the emotion.* HARRY *comes in wearing his snappy overcoat and his hat. He pays no attention to her, as he takes off his coat and hat and throws them down somewhere.*)

IRENE. Did you have some trouble?

HARRY. No. Whose is that champagne?

IRENE. Mine. Won't you have some?

HARRY. Thanks.

IRENE. Dumptsy used that glass.

HARRY. That's all right. (*He fills the glass and drinks.*)

IRENE. What happened? Didn't the train go?

HARRY. Yes—the train went. . . . I got the girls on board. Mr. and Mrs. Cherry promised to look out for them. They'll be O.K.

IRENE. And you came back—to me?

HARRY (*curtly*). It seems fairly obvious that I did come back. (*He refills his glass.*)

IRENE. You meant it when you said that you wanted to help me.

HARRY. You said I'd never be sure. Well—I came back to tell you I *am* sure! I got thinking back, in the bus, and I came to the conclusion that it *was* Room 974 or close to it, anyway. And somehow or other, I couldn't help feeling rather flattered, and touched, to think that with all the sordid hotel rooms you've been in, you should have remembered that one. (*He has some more champagne.*)

IRENE (*after a moment*). Bayard is not dead!

HARRY. Who?

IRENE. The Chevalier Bayard.

HARRY. Oh?

IRENE. Somewhere in that funny, music-hall soul of yours is the spirit of Leander, and Abelard, and Galahad. You give up everything—risk your life—walk unafraid into the valley of the shadow—to aid and comfort a damsel in distress. Isn't that the truth?

HARRY. Yes—it's the truth—plainly and simply put. (*He pours himself more champagne and drinks it quickly.*) Listen to me, babe —when are you going to break down and tell me who the hell are you?

IRENE. Does it matter so very much who I am?

HARRY. No.

IRENE. Give me some more champagne. (HARRY *goes to her and pours.*) My father was not one of the Romanoffs. But for many years, he was their guest—in Siberia. From him I learned that it is no use telling the truth to people whose whole life is a lie. But you—Harry—you are different. You are an honest man.

HARRY (*after a short pause*). I am—am I? (*He crosses to the bar.*) Another bottle of champagne. . . . Hi, Captain.

CAPTAIN'S VOICE (*offstage in bar*). What has happened, Mr. Van? Did you miss the train?

HARRY. No—just a God-damned fool. (*He closes the bar door.* IRENE *is gazing at him. He goes to her and kisses her.*)

IRENE. All these years—you've been surrounded by blondes—and you've loved only me!

HARRY. Now listen—we don't want to have any misunderstanding. If you're hooking up with me, it's only for professional reasons—see?

IRENE. Yes—I see.

HARRY. And what's more, I'm the manager. I'll fix it with the Captain for us to cross the border tomorrow, or the next day, or soon. We'll join up with the girls in Geneva —and that's as good a place as any to rehearse the code.

IRENE. The code! Of *course*—the code! I shall learn it easily.

HARRY. It's a very deep complicated scientific problem.

IRENE. You must tell it to me at once.

HARRY. At once! If you're unusually smart and apply yourself you'll have a fairly good idea of it after six months of study and rehearsal.

IRENE. A mind reader! Yes—you're quite right. I shall be able to do that very well! (AUGUSTE *enters from the bar with a bottle of champagne. He refills their glasses, then refills* HARRY's *glass, gives* HARRY *the bottle and goes back in to the bar.*)

HARRY. And, another thing, if you're going to qualify for this act with me, you've got to lay off liquor. I mean, after we finish this. It's a well-known fact that booze and science don't mix. (*He has another drink.* IRENE *is as one in a trance.*)

IRENE. I don't think I shall use my own name. No—Americans would mispronounce it horribly. No, I shall call myself—Namoura . . . Namoura the Great—assisted by Harry Van.

HARRY. You've got nice billing there.

IRENE. I shall wear a black velvet dress— very plain—My skin, ivory white. I must have something to hold. One white flower. No! A little white prayer book. That's it. A little white . . . (*The warning siren is heard.*) What's that?

HARRY. Sounds like a fire. (*The* CAPTAIN *and* MAJOR *burst out of the bar and rush to the big window, talking excitedly in Italian and pointing to the northwestern sky. The siren shrieks continue. The* MAJOR *then rushes out, the* CAPTAIN *about to follow him.*) What's up, Captain?

CAPTAIN. French aeroplanes. It is reprisal for last night. They are coming to destroy our base here.

HARRY. I see.

CAPTAIN. They have no reason to attack this hotel. But—there may easily be accidents. I advise the cellar. (AUGUSTE *rushes in from the bar,* PITTALUGA *from the lobby. The latter orders* AUGUSTE *to lower the Venetian blinds.*)

IRENE. Oh, no, Captain. We must stay here and watch the spectacle.

CAPTAIN. I entreat you not to be reckless, Madame. I have enough on my conscience now, without adding to it your innocent life!

IRENE. Don't worry, Captain. Death and I are old friends.

CAPTAIN. God be with you, Madame. (*He goes out.* HARRY *and* IRENE *empty their glasses.* HARRY *refills them. Airplane motors are heard, increasing. Then the sound of machine guns.*)

(*Bombs are heard bursting at some distance.* AUGUSTE *and* PITTALUGA *go.*)

IRENE Those are bombs.

HARRY. I guess so.

IRENE. We're in the war, Harry.

HARRY. What do you think we ought to do about it? Go out and say "Boo"?

IRENE. Let them be idiotic if they wish. We are sane. Why don't you try singing something?

HARRY. The voice don't feel appropriate. Too bad we haven't got Chaliapin here. (*She laughs.*) You know, babe—you look better blonde.

IRENE. Thank you. (PITTALUGA *runs in.*)

PITTALUGA. The French beasts are bombing us! Every one goes into the cellar.

HARRY. Thanks very much, Signor.

PITTALUGA. You have been warned! (*He rushes out.*)

IRENE. Ridiculous! Here we are, on top of the world—and he asks us to go down into the cellar. . . . Do you want to go into the cellar?

HARRY. Do you?

IRENE. No. If a bomb hits, it will be worse in the cellar. (*He holds her close to him. She kisses him.*) I love you, Harry.

HARRY. You do, eh!

IRENE. Ever since that night—in the Governor Bryan Hotel—I've loved you. Because I knew that you have a heart that I can trust. And that whatever I would say to you, I would never—*never* be misunderstood.

HARRY. That's right, babe. I told you I had you tagged, right from the beginning.

IRENE. And you adore me, don't you darling?

HARRY. No! Now lay off—

IRENE. No—of course not—you mustn't admit it!

HARRY. Will you please stop pawing me? (*She laughs and lets go of him.*)
(HARRY *pours more champagne, as she crosses to the window, opens the slats of the blinds, and looks out. There is now great noise of planes, machine guns and bombs.*)

IRENE. Oh, you must see this! It's superb! (*He crosses to the window with his glass and looks out. The light on the stage is growing dimmer, but a weird light comes from the window. The scream of many gas bombs is heard.*) It's positively Wagnerian —isn't it?

HARRY. It looks to me exactly like "Hell's Angels." Did you ever see that picture, babe?

IRENE. No. I don't care for films.

HARRY. I *do*. I love 'em—every one of them. (*He is dragging her to the piano—a comparatively safe retreat.*) Did you know I used to play the piano in picture theatres? Oh, sure—I know all the music there is. (*They are now at the piano—*HARRY *sitting,*

IRENE *standing close by him. She is looking toward the window. He starts to accompany the air-raid with the* "Ride of the Walkyries." *There is a loud expulosion.*)

IRENE. Harry . . .

HARRY. Yes, babe?

IRENE. Harry—do you realize that the whole world has gone to war? The *whole world!*

HARRY. I realize it. But don't ask me why. Because I've stopped trying to figure it out.

IRENE. I know why it is. It's just for the purpose of killing *us* . . . you and me. (*There is another loud explosion.* HARRY *stops playing.*) Because we are the little people—and for us the deadliest weapons are the most merciful. . . . (*Another loud explosion.* HARRY *drinks.*)

HARRY. They're getting closer.

IRENE. Play some more. (*He resumes the* "Walkyrie.") Harry—do you know any hymns?

HARRY. What?

IRENE. Do you know any hymns?

HARRY. Certainly. (*He starts to play* "Onward, Christian Soldiers" *in furious jazz time, working in strains of* "Dixie." *There is another fearful crash, shattering the pane of the big window. He drags her down beside him at the piano.* HARRY *resumes* "Onward, Christian Soldiers" *in a slow, solemn tempo.*)

HARRY (*sings*). Onward, Christian Soldiers —(IRENE *joins the loud singing.*)

BOTH (*singing*)
Marching as to war—
With the Cross of Jesus
Going on before. . . .

(*The din is now terrific. Demolition— bombs, gas-bombs, airplanes, shrapnel, machine guns.*)

CURTAIN

Johnny Johnson

The Biography of a Common Man

BY PAUL GREEN

Music by Kurt Weill

SCENES

ACT I

ACT II

ACT III

The cast of the play as presented by The Group Theatre at the Forty-Fourth Street Theatre, New York City, Thursday, November 19, 1936.

Johnny Johnson

PLAY BY	MUSIC BY
PAUL GREEN	KURT WEILL

Staged by Lee Strasberg	Musical direction, Lehman Engel
Settings by Donald Oenslager	Costumes by Paul Du Pont

CAST

(In order of their speech)

HIS HONOR, the Mayor	Played by	Bob Lewis
THE VILLAGE EDITOR	" "	Tony Kraber
MINNY BELLE TOMPKINS, the sweetheart of Johnny Johnson	" "	Phoebe Brand
GRANDPA JOE, her grandfather	" "	Roman Bohnen
A PHOTOGRAPHER	" "	Will Lee
A BICYCLE MESSENGER	" "	Curt Conway
JOHNNY JOHNSON, a tombstone cutter and private citizen	" "	Russell Collins
ANGUISH HOWINGTON, rival to Johnny in business and love and owner of the Crystal Mineral Springs	" "	Grover Burgess
AGGIE TOMPKINS, Minny Belle's mother	" "	Susanna Senior
CAPTAIN VALENTINE, a U. S. Army officer and formerly a movie stand-in	" "	Sanford Meisner
DOCTOR McBRAY, a major in the medical corps, formerly a veterinary surgeon and county health officer	" "	Lee J. Cobb
PRIVATE JESSEL, a stenographer at the recruiting office	" "	Curt Conway
SERGEANT JACKSON, the Captain's aide, an old army man and top-sergeant	" "	Art Smith
A CAMP DOLL	" "	Eunice Stoddard
CORPORAL GEORGE, formerly a waiter at Child's	All Members of Johnny Johnson's Squad	Albert Van Dekker
PRIVATE FAIRFAX, formerly a gangster		William Challee
PRIVATE GOLDBERGER, a junkman's apprentice		Will Lee
PRIVATE HARWOOD, a Texas cowpuncher		Tony Kraber
PRIVATE KEARNS, a baseball pitcher		Elia Kazan
PRIVATE O'DAY, a life-insurance salesman		Curt Conway
PRIVATE SVENSON, a Swedish farm-hand		Herbert Ratner
A WESTPOINT LIEUTENANT	" "	Joseph Pevney
AN ENGLISH SERGEANT	" "	Jules Garfield
A FRENCH NURSE	" "	Paula Miller
AN ORDERLY	" "	Paul Mann
A DOCTOR	" "	Art Smith
A SISTER, from the organization for the Delight of Soldiers Disabled in Line of Duty (ODSDLD)	" "	Ruth Nelson
THE CHIEF OF THE ALLIED HIGH COMMAND	" "	Morris Carnovsky
HIS MAJESTY, A KING	" "	Orrin Jannings
A BELGIAN MAJOR-GENERAL	" "	Luther Adler
THE BRITISH COMMANDER-IN-CHIEF	" "	John Most
A FRENCH MAJOR-GENERAL	" "	Lee J. Cobb
THE FRENCH PREMIER	" "	Bob Lewis
THE AMERICAN COMMANDER-IN-CHIEF	" "	Roman Bohnen
A SCOTTISH COLONEL	" "	Thomas C. Kennedy
A LIAISON OFFICER	" "	Jack Saltzman
A SECOND LIAISON OFFICER	" "	Joseph Pevney
AN AMERICAN PRIEST	" "	Alfred Saxe
A GERMAN PRIEST	" "	Paul Mann
A MILITARY POLICEMAN	" "	Herbert Ratner
DOCTOR MAHODAN, a phychiatrist	" "	Morris Carnovsky
HIS SECRETARY	" "	Kate Allen
DR. FREWD	" "	Elia Kazan
BROTHER THOMAS	Inmates of the forensic arena in a house of balm	Art Smith
BROTHER CLAUDE		Roman Bohnen
BROTHER GEORGE		Lee J. Cobb
BROTHER WILLIAM		Curt Conway
BROTHER HIRAM		Albert Van Dekker
BROTHER JIM		Robert Joseph
BROTHER THEODORE		Tony Kraber
BROTHER HENRY		Luther Adler
A DOCTOR	" "	William Challee
ANGUISH HOWINGTON'S SECRETARY	" "	Alfred Saxe
AN ATTENDANT	" "	Herbert Ratner
ANGUISH HOWINGTON, Jr.	" "	Eddie Ryan, Jr.
SOLDIERS	" "	Peter Ainsley / James Blake / Judson Hall

NEIGHBORS, men and women, young and old; A SQUAD OF ENGLISH SOLDIERS, A SQUAD OF GERMAN SOLDIERS, THE ENGLISH PREMIER, AN ITALIAN BRIGADIER-GENERAL, A POLISH COLONEL, THREE FIELD CLERKS, SEVERAL ORDERLIES, HOSPITAL DIRECTORS, A GUARD, and ATTENDANTS.

TIME

A few years ago as well as now.

PLACE

Somewhere in America, somewhere in France, and somewhere in a house of balm.

ACT ONE

SCENE I

"How sweetly friendship binds."

The curtain rises on the level and clean-swept top of a little hill. The ground is covered with a carpet of green grass, and at the right front a quaint young arbor-vitae tree is growing. In the middle back-ground is a funereal obelisk-like monument about ten feet high and draped in a dark low-hanging cloth. At the left is a naïve and homemade example of the Star-spangled Banner hanging down from a hoe-handle staff which stands stuck in the ground. It is a beautiful day in spring, and far beyond the obelisk and far beyond the scene stretches the blue and light-filled sky with here and there a tiny billowy cloud hanging motionless in it.

At the conclusion of the slightly mock-heroic overture the curtain goes up reveal-ing a group of villagers assembled on the little hilltop. They have just marched in and are taking their places around the monument. On the left are some eight or ten women, young and old. They are garbed in dark dresses and wear brown slat bonnets which shadow their faces, and each one holds a little United States flag in her hand. Some eight or ten men, young and old, stand on the right. They are dressed in ordinary sober clothes, and each holds his dark hat against his heart with one hand and in the other like the women a little flag. At the right front stands a little bow-legged swarthy man with a camera, and at the left front a young girl with a large wreath of flowers. To the right front and opposite the girl stands ANGUISH HOW-INGTON *with a bottle of water in his hand. He is a long gangling young man resem-bling the stage undertaker type. To the rear and at the left of the monuments stands* MINERVA TOMPKINS, *or* MINNY BELLE *to us. She is a vision of loveliness with her golden hair, baby limpid eyes, and doll-like face, and is dressed like a village May Queen. Her filmy white dress comes down to the ground to hide all except the toes of her tiny white shoes. Her shoulders are draped with a light blue scarf, and her golden hair is set off by a chaplet of pasture daisies. Clasped against her girlish bosom*

in her two white cotton-gloved hands is an object that looks like a small picture frame. MINNY BELLE *is about twenty years old. Opposite to her and to the right of the obelisk stands* JOHNNY JOHNSON, *a quiet-mannered young fellow of twenty-five or six. He is dressed in a well-worn palm beach suit, soft checked shirt, blue tie, flat-topped straw hat, and square-toed russet shoes. He is of medium height, his face roundish and clean-shaven, his nose short and snubby, his eyes blue and mild, his whole appearance denoting a gentle and complacent attitude towards both his neigh-bors and the world in which he lives. Between* MINNY BELLE *and the monument stands* GRANDPA JOE, *an old man with a scraggly graying mustache, dressed in a shrunk-up faded blue-and-gray uniform of 1865, on the breast of which is pinned a marksman's badge and some sort of brass medal about the size of an alarm clock dial. He wears an old dark felt hat turned up at one side, and around his neck a fiery red handkerchief as large as a towel, and holds a bloodthirsty looking sabre in his hand. Between* JOHNNY JOHNSON *and the obelisk stands the* EDITOR *of* The County Argus, *a nondescript middle-aged man in a dark shiny-sleeved seersucker suit, with spectacles, a grimy collar and shoestring tie. Several huge carpenter's pencils and a fountain pen resembling a small fire ex-tinguisher show in his upper outside pocket. Standing on a little platform directly behind the* EDITOR *is the* MAYOR. *He is an elderly fellow with a violet red nose, and dressed in an antediluvian swallow-tailed coat, wing collar, swollen black tie, baggy striped trousers and button shoes. In his lapel he wears a big red rose. His old top hat and a big day ledger rest on a little stand before him.*

As the music in the orchestra stops, he holds up one lean hand in a gesture that looks like a combination raspberry and Fascist salute, and begins his speech.

MAYOR. Friends and fellow-citizens,
We are met this April sixth,
In the year of our Lord nineteen hundred
    and seventeen,

On an occasion most auspicious—
(*At the pompous dignity in the* MAYOR'S
voice, JOHNNY *removes his hat, and* GRAND-
PA JOE *salutes sharply with his sabre.*)
For we are gathered to commemorate
The anniversary of the founding of our
    town—
(*Gesturing off to the left.*)
Two hundred years ago today.
'Twas on this hilltop here—
This very site—
That our forefathers met to arbitrate
And sign a treaty with the Indians
Which ended strife and war.
With this eternal stone we mark that fact.
And at this moment let me pay respect
To Johnny Johnson here,
Our gentle-hearted friend and artisan
And tombstone carver of the skilful hand—
'Twas through his kindly zeal
That we at this late date
Erect this monument of peace—
Our thanks to Johnny Johnson.
(*The villagers applaud warmly.*)

JOHNNY. (*With shy awkward acceptance
as* MINNY BELLE *looks admiringly over at
him.*) Thanks, folks, thanky.
(*Reaching out and shaking hands with a
little old lady in a black dress and bonnet.*)
Howdy, Miz Smith.

MIZ SMITH. Howdy, Johnny.

MAYOR. (*Continuing as* JOHNNY *turns
back respectfully.*) And now
Full meet it is that I speak forth my
    thoughts
Upon this vital subject—peace.
(*Leaning forward.*)
These are parlous times—
(*To the* EDITOR.)
Parlous times.
The war clouds belch and thunder over
    Europe's sky
As if to swallow up the solid earth—
Where Germany and France and half the
    world
Do battle unto death.
The question now before th' American
    people is
Shall we take part or not—
(*After an emphatic pause.*)
I point you to our glorious president—
(*He points in a general direction towards
Washington.*)
Who stands unshaken like a rock

And tells us nay—
We are too proud to fight—
For peace it is that's made our nation great
And peace that's made our village likewise
    what she is
Where each man loves his neighbor as him-
    self
And puts his money in the bank on Mon-
    day morn.
(*Cutting a sudden spasmodic step and be-
ginning to sing, his slightly cracked and
nasal voice filling the air as the orchestra
strikes up a soft and teasing accompani-
ment.*)
    Over in Europe things are bad,
    A great big war is going on,
    And every day somebody's dad
    Has shot and killed somebody's son.
    —Turr-uble—turr-uble,
    It's awful to think about,
    Oh frightful, oh shameful,
    America will stay out.

VILLAGERS. —Turr-uble—turr-uble,
    It's awful to think about.

MAYOR. They say in France a million odd
    Of souls have yielded up their lives,
    In Germany th' elect of God
    Have widowed more'n a million wives.
    —Turr-uble—turr-uble,
    The woe and ruin and rout—
    Oh monstrous, oh horrible,
    America must stay out.

VILLAGERS. —Turr-uble—turr-uble,
    The woe and ruin and rout—
    Oh monstrous, oh horrible,
    America *must* stay out.
(*With the exception of* JOHNNY *everybody
has joined in with the singing.*)

MAYOR. (*Continuing his speech.*) America
    must stay out.
(*Some of the villagers nod agreement, and
JOHNNY reaches gravely out and takes the
wreath from the girl and places it at the
foot of the monument. The* MAYOR *con-
tinues with deepening oratory.*)
What said th' immortal Washington?
No entangling alliances.
And James Monroe?
People of Europe stay over on your side,
You heard me.
(*He looks around to see if the* EDITOR *is on
the job with his pencil. He is.*)
And what does the great President of the

United States say today—
Than whom there is none whom—ahem—?
He says that neutral we must be to the
　　last ditch.
And what do I your mayor say?
I say the same.
(*Pointing to* MINNY BELLE.)
You all do well recall the matchless verse
Which lately in *The Argus* said—
(*Pulling out his handkerchief, he violently
blows his flaming red nose.*)

EDITOR. (*Intoning to his pad as he writes.*)
"Democracy Advancing"—Minerva Tomp-
　　kins.

MINNY BELLE. (*Beginning to sing from
her framed verses as the orchestra strikes
up and the others join in.*) Though Wash-
　　ington did fighting stand
　　Embattled in the fray,
My children, 'twas that this great land
　　Should know a happier day
Of peace—peace—peace—
And then his flag was furled,
　　Washington—Washington,
The leader of the world.
(*The* MAYOR *now joins in with his nasal
bleating.*)

MAYOR and the VILLAGERS. And then when
　　frightful carnage swept
　　With red and direful gleam
Across our land 'twas Lincoln kept
　　The vision and the dream
Of peace—peace—peace,
And then his flag was furled,
　　Lincoln, Abe Lincoln,
The leader of the world.

MAYOR. (*With great feeling.*) And now
　　today a mighty third
　　Proclaims that men are free,
'Tis Wilson with the golden word
　　Of peace and liberty—

MAYOR and the VILLAGERS. (*With* MINNY
BELLE's *voice fresh and clear above.*) Of
　　peace—peace—peace,
And thus his flag is furled—
　　Wilson, great Wilson,
The leader of the world.
(GRANDPA JOE *suddenly stands by the monu-
ment.*)

GRANDPA JOE. (*His eyes closed with intense
reminiscence as he babbles.*) Up Chicka-
　　mauga Hill we rode,

The bullets whizzed, and loud the shells
　　they screamed—
Hold, hold, they cried, enough!
But on we sped and straight we flew
And never stopped until
We reached the parapet and grasped the flag
And brought the victory home.
This leg was crushed that day,
(*Indicating his leg.*)
This ear was sorely hacked,
(*Indicating his ear.*)
But praises to Almighty God,
Behind us came the riding fools
Of Barlow's cavalry—
(*Letting out a sudden bloodthirsty yell.*)
Yay-eh! Yay-eh! Yay-eh!
It's victory or die!

VILLAGERS. (*Including the* MAYOR.) Yay-eh!
　　Yay-eh! Yay-eh!
It's victory or die!
(JOHNNY *touches the* MAYOR *on the arm.*)

JOHNNY. (*Quietly.*) Say, your honor, are
we for peace or war?

VILLAGERS. Peace, Johnny!

MAYOR. (*Recovering himself.*) Why, yes of
　　course—
Our hero of the Civil War
Always enthuses us—ahem—
And now before we unveil the monument
and have our pictures made, I think we
ought to hear a few words from the young
man who carved this work of art—Johnny
Johnson.

VILLAGERS. Speech, Johnny! Hooray for
Johnny!

JOHNNY. (*In hesitating embarrassment.*)
Aw shucks—I can't make a speech. I might
say though, I think we've done a mighty
good thing in putting up this monument.
It's the biggest job I've ever done.—But
then peace and arbitration's a big idea. I
side with Woodrow Wilson on that. (*He
stops.*)

MAYOR. He'll be glad to hear of it, Johnny.

JOHNNY. I reckon he's already heard of it.
I wrote him a letter— (*The villagers applaud.*)—inviting him down to the unveil-
ing—(*The applause is louder.*) But he
hasn't come—not yet—(*Helplessly he twists
his hat about in his hands.*) Well, that's
about all. I am better at working with my

hands than my tongue. (*Looking up admiringly.*) But the Mayor now—(*The* MAYOR *starts slightly.*)

MAYOR. And now we'll gather round the monument and have our picture made—

PHOTOGRAPHER. (*Hopping out in front of his camera.*) One moment, please. (*Everybody looks toward the camera and stiffens himself as the little guy runs around and sticks his head under the cloth. Immediately he bounds out again, grasps the shutter bulb and quavers.*) Here's the little bir-dee-ee! (*He presses the bulb and there is a flash, followed by a sharp explosion. A nervous shock goes through the crowd, and* MINNY BELLE *lets out a low scream.* JOHNNY *looks over at her paternally and smiles. The little guy jerks out the plate, reverses it, and grasps his bulb again.*) Once more, please. (*The villagers with the exception of* JOHNNY *all get set again. The* PHOTOGRAPHER *presses the bulb but nothing happens. He hops around in front of the camera and begins working hurriedly at one of his gadgets. And now beginning softly in the orchestra and coming rapidly nearer is the tuh-blickety-blickety-blickety-blick of a galloping horse. The villagers gradually take their eyes from the camera and begin looking at one another. The sound of the galloping horse grows louder in the orchestra. They all turn to look off at the left. Now the thundering hoofs are upon them, for it seems the scudding horse is coming into the scene. It does—a lanky bare-foot boy with a tangle of grimy hair under a coca-cola cap, riding slowly on a ramshackle bicycle and gnawing the remnant of an ice-cream cone. He skids the machine a few inches by dragging his heel on the ground, lets it fall out from under him, and then wanders over to the* MAYOR *and hands him up a big envelope, sealed with authoritative devices, which he pulls from his blouse.*)

BOY. (*In a gosling voice.*) Extry for his reverence the Mayor. (*The* MAYOR *grabs the letter and rips open the envelope. Pulling down his spectacles he peers at the unwinding sheet of paper. Back and forth he runs his eyes and then suddenly flings up his hand.*)

MAYOR. (*Bellowing.*) War is declared! (*For a moment he holds his hand so and then lets it fall with heavy finality. A low murmur runs through the villagers.*)

FIRST VILLAGER. War—war.

SECOND VILLAGER. What war? (*The* MAYOR *is peering at the paper and mumbling to himself as he tries to decipher it.*)

THIRD VILLAGER. Who're we fighting against?

MAYOR. (*Now straightens up again, his shoulders squared in the grip of a sudden military feeling.*) And in this fateful hour,
my friends,
America expects that every man shall do his duty.

GRANDPA JOE. (*Giving his sabre a trembling swish through the air.*) Forward against the enemy—
Lead on.
(*He begins hacking at an imaginary adversary before him, and* JOHNNY *steps nimbly out of the way.*)

JOHNNY. (*Looking around in dolorous amazement, at the growing excitement.*) Heigh, folks, we got to unveil the monument!

MAYOR. (*Holding up his hand again in his raspberry and Fascist gesture.*) Silence! (*Now beginning to read, his words running out in a low, voluble roll.*) Now therefore I, Woodrow Wilson, by virtue of—and so on—so on—do hereby proclaim to all whom it may concern that a state of war exists—ahem—exists—between the United States and the Imperial German government, and I do specially direct all officers, civil or military, of the United States that they exercise vigilance and zeal in the discharge of duties incident to such a state of war— (*Looking over at* GRANDPA JOE.) Our police force will take cognizance of these orders. (GRANDPA JOE *pulls out a whistle and blows a sharp and sudden blast.*)

GRANDPA JOE. (*Gazing searchingly about him, his voice hoarse with sudden ominousness.*) Be careful of what you say,
Be watchful of everyone,
All spies will be shot or hanged without mercy—
At the rising of the sun.

MAYOR. (*Rolling up the long paper.*) In such an hour as this, my friends,

'Tis not for us to question why,
'Tis but for us to do and die—
I command each and every one of you to meet me at the courthouse for a public reading.

EDITOR. (*Again talking to his pad as he writes.*) The president has called to arms—the nation answers to a man.

MAYOR. (*Calling out again.*) Our democratic institutions stand endangered. (*Shaking his fist at the* BOY.) Go ring the courthouse bell!

BOY. Sure. (*He turns and gets on his bicycle and goes rolling off.*)

MAYOR. Volunteers, hold up your hands! (*The hands of the men and women go up, with* GRANDPA JOE's *sabre showing above them all. And even* ANGUISH *gets his hand slowly hoisted, for he like Johnny is under the watchful eye of* MINNY BELLE. *But* JOHNNY *does not raise his hand. The* MAYOR *peers over at him an instant.*) Johnny Johnson, where's your good right hand?

JOHNNY. (*Hesitating.*) Why — why — I thought we were all for peace.

MAYOR. (*Bawling out.*) These exercises are adjourned! (MINNY BELLE *stares at* JOHNNY *in querying reproachment.*)

JOHNNY. But folks—heigh, people—we've got to unveil the monument! Your Honor —heigh!— (*The* MAYOR *makes no answer, for by this time he has hopped down from his perch and hurried over to the flag, pulled it up and begun waving it in the air.*)

MAYOR. Follow me to the courthouse! War! War!

MINNY BELLE. (*Starting to sing as she and the* MAYOR *begin marching at the head of the rout.*) And now the fateful hour has come— (ANGUISH, *who has been watching his chance, steps to* MINNY BELLE's *side, bows and smiles, waves his bottle and begins singing in a loud flat voice. Now they all sing, waving their little flags and swirling about the stage.*)

PEOPLE. (*With the exception of* JOHNNY.)
And now the fateful hour has come
And millions strong we rise

To fight for France and Belgium
And crush their enemies!—
—War! War! War!
Our banner flies unfurled—
(*The* MAYOR *waves the flag aloft.*)
America—America,
The leader of the world!

(*They go milling around, shouting and singing out at the right front, the little guy caught helplessly in the maelstrom and knocked this way and that as he and his camera are swept along. In an instant the scene is deserted save for* JOHNNY *who stares mournfully before him.*

And now the orchestra begins softly playing JOHNNY's *theme melody. In the distance the singing and the shouting die away. A moment passes, and then* MINNY BELLE's *voice is heard off at the right—"Johnny!"—* JOHNNY *turns quickly around as* MINNY BELLE *comes running in. The orchestra, out of deference to her, suddenly stops.*)

MINNY BELLE. (*In sharp petulance.*) Whatever is the matter with you, Johnny? (*Hurrying over and getting him by the hand.*) Come on, come on!

JOHNNY. But, Minny Belle—

MINNY BELLE. (*Wiggling her childlike form up and down in a panic of nervous haste.*) Please—please—listen to the bell ringing— (ANGUISH's *long lean figure comes hurrying in.*)

ANGUISH. The Mayor needs his ledger. (*He goes over to the monument, picks up the volume, and then turns back and slows up by* MINNY BELLE's *side.*)

MINNY BELLE. (*Taking hold of* JOHNNY's *arm with one hand and* ANGUISH's *arm with the other.*) Forward march— One—two—three—four— (*But* JOHNNY *balks.*)

JOHNNY. I can't go just now. (*Calling off to the left.*) Heigh you, Mr. Fink—we want our pictures took!

MINNY BELLE. (*Staring at him.*) Oh Johnny, surely you'll be the first to fly to the defense of your flag.

JOHNNY. But—why, I got all my work to attend to (*Softly.*) and— (*He touches her shyly and lovingly on the arm.*) I've got other things to arrange for—for you and me. I'll tell you Wednesday night.

MINNY BELLE. (*Hiding her face in her hands.*) He can't mean it. His country needs him, and now he talks of personal happiness.

JOHNNY. Good gracious, Minny Belle, you don't expect me to do that—go off and enlist—and we don't even know what it's all about.

MINNY BELLE. We've declared war on Germany, that's what.

JOHNNY. And it ain't like Woodrow Wilson to do that. Why, he's been our first leader for peace. And now— (*Shaking his head.*) I bet it's a false alarm.

ANGUISH. (*Swallowing manfully and then speaking out boldly, as he raises his clenched fist.*) I'll go—I'll be in No-Man's Land in a fortnight. Yes, that I will! (*His valor mounting.*) They'll get a taste of my smoke —them Huns and Boches that rape—mistreat French ladies. Let me at 'em.

MINNY BELLE. Ah, listen!

ANGUISH. Yeh, dod-rot their souls!

MINNY BELLE. Yes, Anguish, yes.

ANGUISH. Dod-dum 'em, I say. (*Letting out a bloodthirsty gr-r-r.*) Give me a gun and a bayonet—a gun and a bayonet is all I want.

MINNY BELLE. (*Rapturously.*) Hurrah!

JOHNNY. (*Growling.*) Yeh, hurrah! Anguish Howington won't ever see the sight of a German. He can run too fast.

ANGUISH. Here, now—

MINNY BELLE. (*Stamping her tiny foot.*) Stop it—stop it!

JOHNNY. Oh, Minny Belle, I'm sorry, but this buzzard here— (*Snapping at ANGUISH.*) Take your hand off her arm. (ANGUISH *instinctively jerks away from* MINNY BELLE, *and then reaches out to take her hand, but she denies him that. In the distance a trumpet begins blowing "The Star Spangled Banner."* JOHNNY *calls out.*) All right, Mr. Fink, we're ready for the pictures! (*Reaching out and taking* MINNY BELLE'S *hand.*) You and me, Minny Belle, one on either side of the tombstone.

MINNY BELLE. (*Pulling her hand away.*)

No—most emphatically no.

JOHNNY. But I need the pictures for advertising the business.

MINNY BELLE. (*Almost ready to weep with vexation.*) Business — business — and our country called to war.

ANGUISH. (*Taking his cue from* MINNY BELLE.) Yes, he talks of business—and at such an hour!

JOHNNY. (*Angrily again.*) Yeh? You may not be talking it right now but you're thinking it. (*Scornfully.*) And such a business!

ANGUISH. (*Likewise angry again.*) Well, selling mineral water is just as elevated as putting up tombstones. And there's a sight more money in it.

MINNY BELLE. Stop it! You boys promised not to quarrel over me again. (*She starts away at the right and then turns back.*) I'm not engaged to either of you. Remember that. (*She hurries tearfully away at the right.* ANGUISH *starts to follow after when* JOHNNY *darts in front of him.*)

JOHNNY. Now you listen to me, Anguish Howington, I want you to stay away from my girl.

ANGUISH. (*Edging back.*) Well, she's no more yours than mine.

JOHNNY. But she's gonna be.

ANGUISH. (*With weak determination.*) Not if I can help it.

JOHNNY. You — heard me — you — (*He springs at* ANGUISH *who darts around behind the monument.*)

ANGUISH. (*Defensively.*) I got a right to love her.

JOHNNY. The hell you have! I love her myself. (*He doubles up his left fist and starts towards him.*)

ANGUISH. (*Pleadingly, as he peeps out from behind the monument.*) Why—I—I thought you believed in settling things by arbitration, Johnny.

JOHNNY. This here's a different matter. (*He starts on towards* ANGUISH *and then stops and stares queryingly at the ground a moment as if suddenly confronted with a tough problem.* ANGUISH *flies out at the left front.* JOHNNY *gazes quizzically after him, and then turning in vexation, pulls the* *draw-string hanging down from the monument. The drape rolls up and reveals the single word "peace" engraved in large letters on the stone.)*

BLACK OUT.

SCENE II

"Keep the home fires burning."

The living-room of MINNY BELLE's *house a few days after Scene I. The interior is a simple one and rather typical of the American rural village home of the year 1917. At the right center is a fireplace, with a window on each side set off by clean muslin curtains. At the right rear is a door that opens into the hall, at the left rear a combination day-bed and sofa, the kind that can be got from a cheap mail-order house on the instalment plan, and at the right and left front are doors that open into other rooms. In the center is an oval table of the same style as the sofa, and placed here and there about the room are several heavy imitation oak chairs of the same suite. Between the center-table and the sofa is a sewing machine. The floor is covered with clean straw matting and the walls with a bright flower-patterned wall paper. But though the room is typical and ordinary, the arrangement of the three framed poster portraits on the rear wall is not. For here we see the touch of an individual and patriotic hand. In the center of the wall hangs a large picture of Woodrow Wilson, on the right is a smaller picture of George Washington, and on the left likewise a picture of Abraham Lincoln. Under the Washington picture is a semi-circular pasteboard slogan with these words—"He saved the colonies," under Lincoln's a second slogan—"He saved a nation," and under Wilson's portrait in larger letters—"Make the world safe for democracy." Further emphasis upon Wilson is given by a United States flag which drapes his portrait from above.*

It is early evening, and the light that comes into the scene from the windows reveals GRANDPA JOE *sitting just beyond the fireplace. He is working at some sort of contraption about two feet high which resembles a small Ferris wheel, and is dressed in a not too clean collarless white shirt, galluses and sleeve holders, a pair of dark trousers and old carpet slippers. His thin* *graying hair is pushed raggedly back from his smooth dome-like forehead, and his high ridged nose is set off with a pair of steel-rimmed spectacles which somewhat hide his dead dreamy eyes and give a homey comic touch to his face. In brief his whole get-up and personality are now no longer that of the bloodthirsty warrior but rather that of the quiet local inventor who is always on the verge of perfecting a new patent window-shade or a perpetual motion machine. In the case of* GRANDPA JOE, *it is the latter mysterious device which has him in thrall.*

When the curtain rises he is hypnotically engaged with his machine, hovering over it and fiddling with some screw, gadget, tooth or cog. AGGIE TOMPKINS, *with the responsible and somewhat harassed appearance of a housewife and bread earner, is sitting at the sewing machine. She is a stoutish middle-aged woman with a strong-jowled face, a thundering ample bosom and a pair of capable arms.*

AGGIE. (*Belching and looking angrily over at the bent back of the old man as she stops her sewing.*) Father, how you can sit there working at that old perpetual motion machine and my Minny Belle running around town stark raving mad with the war fever is more than I can see. I want you to talk to her. (GRANDPA JOE *makes no answer.*) You know what she did when she came in a while ago? (*Grimly biting off a thread.*) Why, she stood up on her tip-toes and kissed that picture. Now anybody that'll kiss Woodrow Wilson—

GRANDPA JOE. I'd rather kiss him than that bearded fellow—er—Charles Evans Hughes.

AGGIE. I hadn't.

GRANDPA JOE. That's because you're a Republican.

AGGIE. It's not— If that low-down Johnny Johnson didn't like Wilson so much maybe I wouldn't mind. (*With a loud belch.*) Ah,

Lord, why don't Anguish come on with my mineral water.

GRANDPA JOE. Yeh, and if you don't quit drinking them slops you're going to rot out your insides, Aggie.

AGGIE. It's not slops. Anguish had his spring tested by experts. It says so in *The Argus.*

GRANDPA JOE. Yeh, and Johnny says that water's plumb poison to both man, bird, and beast. I'd believe him.

AGGIE. (*Scornfully.*) Of course he'd say that. He hates the very ground Anguish walks on.

GRANDPA JOE. And I don't blame him either—in a manner of speaking.

AGGIE. You listen to me, Father Joe. Anguish Howington is going somewhere in the world. Johnny Johnson won't ever amount to a row of pins. (*Grimacing.*) Too good—wishy-washy—no backbone.

GRANDPA JOE. That's what you think. Anyhow *I* like Johnny. A lot of people do.

AGGIE. You may like him, but you all laugh at him. Now you don't catch folks laughing at Anguish.

GRANDPA JOE. That's right, they don't get much fun out of him. (*He begins hammering on his machine.*)

AGGIE. (*Singing defensively to herself as she sews, her voice suddenly grown mellifluous and free.*) My husband is dead,
  God rest the poor man,
  And I in his stead
  Do all that I can,
  Keeping body and soul
  And the house from the dole—
    —Sing treddle, trid-treddle,
    The wheel it goes around.
  I wash and I cook,
  I sweep and I clean,
  I once dreamt a dook
  Had made me his queen,
  But oh weary me,
  Such things cannot be
    —Sing treddle, trid-treddle,
    The wheel it goes round.

(*She stands up and begins fitting her corset around her.* JOHNNY *appears at the rear door with a package in his hand.*)

JOHNNY. Howdy, you all.

AGGIE. (*Dropping her corset from around her and glaring at him.*) Oh, it's you!

GRANDPA JOE. Come in, Johnny. (JOHNNY *comes on into the room. He is dressed in the same clothes as before.* AGGIE *now busily begins folding up her mending and piling it on top of the machine.*)

AGGIE. (*With a scissors snip in her voice.*) And how is your tombstone business? Guess this war will kill it off.

JOHNNY. Well, can't be fair weather all the time—as the cuckoo said. (*With finality.*) That's the way I've figured it out, Miz Tompkins. Still things are not so bad. (*Nodding gravely.*) Miz Esther Smith has just ordered a nice piece of stone work.

AGGIE. Well, I'm glad to hear that. Her poor husband has been lying there in the graveyard these ten years with nothing but a plank headboard to mark his resting place.

JOHNNY. She only wanted to put out twenty dollars for him. Then she decided to let her husband's headboard stand and take a sixty-dollar job for the cow.

AGGIE. (*Throwing up her hands.*) The cow!

JOHNNY. Yes'm, the one that used to give four gallons of milk a day, year in, year out. I had a mighty lot of respect for that cow. There's nothing like good milk for humanity, you know. (*With a genial pointed touch.*) Better'n mineral water. (*Slapping his thigh as* AGGIE *stares at him.*) Daggone, I was forgetting. I've got a little present for your birthday, Miz Tompkins. (AGGIE, *who has started out of the room at the left front, with her arms full of the clothes, turns back.*)

AGGIE. (*Somewhat mollified.*) For me?

JOHNNY. Yes ma'am. (*He is busy unwrapping the package.* AGGIE, *showing she is a bit touched by his thoughtfulness as well as curious, comes over nearer* JOHNNY.)

AGGIE. That's real nice of you, Johnny.

JOHNNY. Shucks, I was glad to do it. It's a jim-dandy piece of work, too. (*He now lifts out a small white tombstone and sets it on the center table.* AGGIE *stares at it in speechless horror.* JOHNNY *runs his hand lovingly over the carving.*) You see there's two hands a-shaking. Below that the word "Friendship." (*Looking around at her.*) What's the matter, Miz Tompkins, don't you—?

AGGIE. (*Her voice almost breaking with anger and chagrin.*) So—you're already making a tombstone for me, are you? (*Fiercely.*) Well, let me tell you, I'm not ready to die yet!

JOHNNY. Why Miz Tompkins, I didn't mean it that way—

AGGIE. (*Yelling.*) Don't Miz Tompkins me, you—you fool! (*She turns and goes storming out at the left front, carrying the clothes with her.* JOHNNY *stares forlornly after her a moment, sighs, and begins wrapping up the tombstone again. A low chuckle breaks from* GRANDPA JOE *where he works.*)

GRANDPA JOE. She don't like you, Johnny.

JOHNNY. (*Giving his shoulders a doleful shrug.*) Well, everybody to his own taste, as the goat said to the skunk.

GRANDPA JOE. It's Anguish she likes, the rising young business man. (JOHNNY *sits down with the tombstone in his lap and stares abstractedly at the floor.* GRANDPA JOE *looks over at his glum face.*) Come on now, don't worry about Aggie.

JOHNNY. I'm not worrying about her—especially. It's the war, Mr. Joe. I still can't make heads or tails of it.

GRANDPA JOE. I didn't understand the Civil War but I fought in it—just the same.

JOHNNY. Yeh, and suppose you had been killed—

GRANDPA JOE. Then they'd a-raised me up a fine tombstone the way you did to peace.

JOHNNY. But what good would it do you and you dead as a door-nail?

GRANDPA JOE. Whew—no good, that's certain. Say, you ain't afraid are you, Johnny?

JOHNNY. No, but if I had to die I'd like to know what I was dying for— (*Emphatically.* You're durn right I would.

GRANDPA JOE. You're getting sort of strong in your language, ain't you, Johnny?

JOHNNY. Yeh—I feel strong about it all, Mr. Joe. I tell you it's plain as the nose on your—my face—war is about the low-downest thing the human race could indulge in. Add up all the good in it and it's still a total loss. There ought to be some way of settling it by discussion—the way we do over in the Adelphi Debating Society, and not by killing. The more you fight and kill the worse it gets. You may conquer your enemy for a while but he or his friends only wait to grow strong again to come back at you. That's human nature. And what I can't understand about Wilson is—why all of a sudden he's willing to go out and kill a lot of people for some idea about freedom of the seas.

GRANDPA JOE. The sea has got to be free, Johnny—it's got to be free.

JOHNNY. Well, maybe it has, though after all you could look on it as nothing but a big pond. Now if I was out in a pond and Anguish passed by—

GRANDPA JOE. Anguish?

JOHNNY. Well, take anybody you don't like. And he tried to come in and contaminate the water, I'd raise a little disturbance all right, but I wouldn't try to kill him. No, we'd get out on the bank and—

GRANDPA JOE. Arbitrate, Johnny?

JOHNNY. Anyhow there would'nt be any killing, at least I don't think so. (*Glumly.*) There must be some other idea in Wilson's mind—for him and me's been seeing eye to eye all along. Maybe when *The Argus* comes out—

GRANDPA JOE. Well, you needn't worry so. You don't *have* to go fight, not yet you don't.

JOHNNY. Uh, that's just the trouble, Mr. Joe. I'm for peace and Minny Belle's for war. That's the long and short of it.

GRANDPA JOE. (*Thoughtfully.*) Uhm, you are in a kind of a jam, ain't you—in a manner of speaking? On the one hand—your principle, on the other—your—er—love?

JOHNNY. (*Fervently.*) Yes sir.

GRANDPA JOE. I'd drop principle.

JOHNNY. But I can't do what I don't believe in.

GRANDPA JOE. Then you're sunk—like the Lusitania.

JOHNNY. (*Going heavily on.*) If I could see some honest-to-God reason in this war —then I'd go quick as scat. Like if by going I could help—well—(*Deep in thought.*) put an end to—sort of like the idea of—say, a war to put down war. You know what I mean. Sometimes you have to fight fire with fire. Then I'd feel the cause was worth it. For when it was over the democratic nations maybe could league up and unite for peace and— (*His voice dies out and for a moment he is silent. Then he turns to the old man.*) What is democracy, Mr. Joe?

GRANDPA JOE. (*Hesitating and then speaking thoughtfully.*) Democracy?—Well—

JOHNNY. I asked the Mayor and he said democracy is the principle of freedom—self-government—whatever that is.

GRANDPA JOE. He's right—that's what it is —the principle of liberty—to follow your own business like I do my perpetual motion machine and—be happy.

JOHNNY. (*Staring at the portrait of Wilson.*) Yes, but suppose in order to be happy, I want something and somebody else wants it— (*He suddenly sets the package on the floor by the table and rises out of his seat just as* MINNY BELLE *enters at the right front. It is almost as if he were so sensitive to her presence that he can feel her nearness without even seeing or hearing her. She comes on into the room and* JOHNNY *holds a chair ready for her to sit down.* MINNY BELLE *is dressed in a trim blue coat-suit, the lace collar of which is fastened with a little pin, and her golden hair is combed back into a becoming bob. She comes over and sits down in the chair which he holds for her.*)

GRANDPA JOE. (*Suddenly beginning to sing in his flat cracked voice.*) When two are
    alone in a parlor at eve,
And a manly young arm waits inside of
    its sleeve
So anxious its duty to do and receive—
Then, Grandpa, it's skidoo for you—
    For you—

(*With a fond glance at the two, he goes nimbly out at the left front.* JOHNNY *in great glee, suddenly stands up, dusts off his chair, and then sits down again and begins fumbling sheepishly with his hat.*)

JOHNNY. (*Presently.*) You're—you're looking purty as a pink tonight, Minny Belle.

MINNY BELLE. (*With a slight touch of coldness.*) Thank you.

JOHNNY. (*Furtively taking a small trinket from his pocket.*) That locket come in the mail today. (*He reaches out and quickly lays it in her lap.*) When you open it— see—it's got a picture of me inside.

MINNY BELLE. (*Examining it after a moment.*) It's nice, Johnny—nice. (*She hesitates and then puts it on.*)

JOHNNY. (*Joyously.*) I knew you'd like it. (*He stares at her in speechless love and stammers.*) You—you ain't mad at me for quarrelling with that rapscallion Anguish?

MINNY BELLE. (*As she pulls a tiny snow-white handkerchief from her sleeve and puts it demurely against her lips.*) Please, Johnny—you know I can't ever stay mad with you.

JOHNNY. (*Haltingly getting out a few more words.*) You remember that night when I was here—two weeks ago?

MINNY BELLE. I remember.

JOHNNY. And I pointed out that verse in the song book. (*Looking about him.*) Where is that book? It was here on the table.

MINNY BELLE. It's up in my room.

JOHNNY. (*Gazing at her fondly, his face wreathed in a sudden beatific smile.*) In your room, Minny Belle—where you sleep at night? (*His chair moves a bit nearer.*) You must remember what the song said. Something about—about how one person feels when separated from the other. (*Pulling out a pencil he writes in the palm of his hand and holds it out to her. She reads it and drops her eyes.*) You see—see what I mean— (*Spelling.*) "L-o-n-g-ing." (*Helplessly.*) Oh, Minny Belle!

MINNY BELLE. (*Looking off before her and beginning to sing softly.*) Oh heart of love,
    The soul of all my yearning,

Come back to me,
My days are filled with pain,

JOHNNY. (*Sliding his chair still nearer.*)
You sing it—almost like—like you meant it.

MINNY BELLE. My fondest thoughts
To you are ever turning—
Wild foolish hopes
To have you back again.

JOHNNY. Why, you know it all by heart.

MINNY BELLE. Every sound along the street,
Every voice I chance to hear,
Every note of music sweet
Sets me longing for you, dear.
—Come back to me,
Oh, can't you hear me calling!
Lost is my life,
Alas, what can I do?
Shadows of night
Across my path are falling,
Frightened and lone
I die apart from you.

JOHNNY. (*Rapturously.*) Minny Belle,
Minny Belle! (*By this time his chair is
alongside of hers. He reaches over and
takes her hand.*) Minny Belle — oh — you
know what I want to say.

MINNY BELLE. (*Singing again as she looks
around at him with bright eyes and pink
cheeks.*) Every footfall on the floor,
Every tip-tap on the stair—
Open wide I fling the door,
You are never standing there.
—Come back to me,
Oh, can't you hear me calling!
Lost is my life,
Alas, what can I do?
Shadows of night
Across my path are falling,
Frightened and lone
I die apart from you.

JOHNNY. (*His words pouring out as he
stands up, his hat falling unnoticed to the
floor.*) Like the song says, Minny Belle, you
are the— (*He stutters, swallows the lump
in his throat and struggles on.*) From that
first day I saw you down there in the meat
market—yes, my heart thumps like it will
hurt when I think of you. When I'm carving my tombstones—my hammer going
whick-whack — whick-whack — it's all in
time to my heart beating out what I want
to say— (*Pulling out his handkerchief and
wiping his forehead.*) And I can't say it—

MINNY BELLE. (*Murmuring and likewise
standing up.*) Beautiful—beautiful how you
talk so. (*She leans against him, and he puts
his arms suddenly around her and stands
stupefied with joy.*)

JOHNNY. (*Brokenly.*) My little—er—bird.
(*Holding her from him he stares down
into her averted face, and then bends over
and kisses her tenderly on top of the head.*)

MINNY BELLE. (*Clinging to him an instant.*) Oh, Johnny—

JOHNNY. (*In hushed wonder.*) We're engaged. (*Spinning drunkenly about the
room.*) We're engaged. I'm the happiest
man in all the world. Yay-eh! (*Turning
ecstatically back to her.*) And now can I
ask you—ask you that other question? (*A
tiny nod of her bright head says he may.*)
When are we to be— (*His voice trembling
over the word.*) be married? What do you
say to next week? We'll get his honor the
Mayor to—to do it.

MINNY BELLE. (*With ever the slightest
movement away from him.*) But we can't
do that.

JOHNNY. Why not, Precious?

MINNY BELLE. It's the war—you've got to
enlist.

JOHNNY. (*His arms dropping down from
her with a thud.*) Great guns, I'd forgot
all about the war! (*He stands gazing
moodily at the floor.*)

MINNY BELLE. (*Her handkerchief to her
lips.*) It will be hard to be separated from
you—hard. But we both must endure it for
our country's sake.

JOHNNY. (*Wretchedly.*) But, Minny
Belle—

MINNY BELLE. At night I'll think of you
there on the battlefield—under the vast and
starry sky—think of you standing there
with your rifle, a bulwark of strength.

JOHNNY. (*Murmuring.*) A bulwark of
strength.—But, Minny Belle—

MINNY BELLE. (*Her face already touched
with the pain of woman's renunciation as
she stares off into the air.*) Like that other
song says— (*Beginning to recite.*)
Alone I'll wait

Steadfast and true,
My every thought
A thought of you—
Of you.

(*Half-singing as* JOHNNY *gazes yearningly at her.*)

So go, my dear, and quickly now,
And then the cruel deed is done,
For parting is a sharper blow
Than absence, my beloved one.

(*Her voice now rising into a plaintive melody.*)

Farewell, goodbye,
Goodbye, farewell,
No tears, no words
My love can tell—
    Farewell.

(*She buries her face tearfully against his shoulder.*)

JOHNNY. (*Pulling her tightly to him.*) Don't cry, Minny Belle. It breaks my heart —oh, don't—

MINNY BELLE. (*Gulping.*) Be careful won't you? Do be careful, Johnny, and come back safe.

JOHNNY. Sure—sure.—Oh—but look here, Minny Belle, you see I'm not really gone yet.—

MINNY BELLE. (*Mournfully.*) I know, Johnny, but what is one day, or two days? For then you are gone. It comes so quick.

JOHNNY. No, I just as well tell you, Minny Belle, I've not been able to make up my mind about this war yet. I've got some more thinking to do.

MINNY BELLE. (*Starting to speak and then staring at him in sudden and pained surprise.*) You mean—you mean you still hesitate?—(*His unhappy face betraying him.*) After all I've promised? (*With a wail.*) Oh, Johnny, you can't!

JOHNNY. (*Pleadingly.*) But, Minny Belle, listen. You know how it is. I've got to have a reason before I—

MINNY BELLE. Reason? (*Her voice almost breaking in a sob.*) And I thought you— Oh, Johnny, you don't love me—no you don't.

JOHNNY. (*With a groan.*) My Lord! (*He looks helplessly about him as if seeking aid from the empty air.*) Maybe I can figure

things out—maybe—

MINNY BELLE. Figure—figure— (*With a sob.*) Then we're not engaged, we're not. I take it all back. (*With heaving shoulders, her handkerchief stuffed against her mouth, she hurries into the room at the right and closes the door behind her.*)

JOHNNY. (*Calling piteously after her.*) Minny Belle! Minny Belle! (*But there is no answer. For a while he stands in the middle of the room crushed and desolate. Presently he picks up his tombstone and goes slowly out at the rear. A moment passes and the door at the left front opens and* ANGUISH HOWINGTON, *carrying a large glass jug full of water, stick his head in. He looks inquiringly about him and then knocks on the side of the wall.*)

ANGUISH. (*Calling.*) Mis' Agnes! Mis' Agnes! (MINNY BELLE's *grieving face looks out from the room at the right.*)

MINNY BELLE. Oh, it's you! (*She slams the door shut.*)

ANGUISH. (*Knocking and calling.*) Mis' Agnes! I've brung your mineral water at last! Mis' Agnes! (*The door at the rear opens and* AGGIE *enters. She is looking behind her.*)

AGGIE. (*Reaching out a supplicating hand as she comes across the room.*) Quick— quick—Anguish. (ANGUISH *hurries over to her with the jug. She seizes it and, like a mighty toper drinking from the bung, holds it aloft and lets the life-giving fluid trickle down her throat. Then she sets the jug down, wipes her lips with her apron, and looks over at him, the anger and grief gradually passing from her face.*)

ANGUISH. I'm sorry to be so late, but I'm trying to wind up my business before I enlist.

AGGIE. (*Sitting.*) Uh-huh, and that's what I want to talk to you about. (*She gazes at him a moment and then continues.*) You're not going to enlist, Anguish.

ANGUISH. (*With a questioning look, and then shaking his head glumly.*) Don't see any way out of it. Minny Belle's determined that I—

AGGIE. (*Leaning forward and speaking with deep confidentiality.*) In the Civil War my Uncle Heck didn't enlist. Why? He melted down a whole beeswax candle, got himself a hollow reed, and blew the stuff into a hole he'd cut into his arm. From then until Grant captured Lee at Appomattox he had a bad case of St. Vitus Dance. He shook so bad that bringing the milk from the cowbarn he'd make the butter come. Yes, and Cousin Melchisidec, he hamstrung his left leg with a butcher knife.

ANGUISH. (*Staring at her in fearful amazement as he drops down in a chair.*) Lord upon me, you mean they done damage to theirselves with knives!

AGGIE. And Bud Lauderdale, an old sweetheart of Ma's, cut off his big toe with a grass hook. He limped bad the rest of his life and wore a special made shoe.

ANGUISH. (*Aghast.*) Merciful heavens!

AGGIE. (*Shaking her head reminiscently.*) Ah, they had nerve—Uncle Heck and Cousin Melchisidec, and Bud Lauderdale. Brave men all, they were. (*Consolingly.*) But you don't have to do damage to yourself to keep out of this war, Anguish. It's your eyes. Cataracts and scales—Anguish.

ANGUISH. Huh, Mis' Agnes?

AGGIE. You can hardly see from here to the door— Almost blind. I'll swear an affidavid for you. (*She gazes at him in silence.*)

ANGUISH. (*A great ragged smile sliding around his slit of a mouth.*) I see—I see (*Suddenly rising and grasping her hand in thankfulness.*) You've saved my life— Ever since last Sunday when that English hero preached in church I haven't slept a wink— (*Stiffening sharply and croaking in a hypnotic, sepulchral voice.*)

"In Flanders Fields the poppies blow
Between the crosses row and row
That mark *my* place—"

AGGIE. (*Rising.*) I got a pair of cross-eyed glasses I used when the flues settled in my eyes. You wear 'em and if you're not blind now you will be shortly. Come on into the kitchen. (*She starts out at the left front, ANGUISH following; then suddenly she turns back, picks up the jug, and goes off drinking from it. For a moment the scene is empty except for a low note that scurries around in the orchestra like a mouse on the floor. Then there is a noise of thumping footsteps in the hall at the rear. The door is opened and JOHNNY comes running in with a newspaper in his hand.*)

JOHNNY. (*Calling out wildly.*) Minny Belle! Minny Belle, say, I've got some wonderful news for you! (MINNY BELLE *comes in at the right front, with her hair hanging down. Her eyes are red from weeping.* JOHNNY *runs over to her.*) Minny Belle, I'm going to enlist. Listen, it's all here in *The Argus.* Wilson's proclamation. And now I'm ready to go. (*Reading enthusiastically.*) "We have no quarrel with the German people. It's their leaders who are to blame. Drunk with military power and glory, they are leading the democratic people of Germany as well as the whole world into shameless slaughter." (*With deep finality.*) "This is a war to end war." Daggone, near 'bout my own words! (*He sweeps* MINNY BELLE *into his arms and kisses her on the lips.*)

BLACK OUT.

SCENE III

"Your Country needs another man—and that means you."

Interior of the recruiting office—a medium-sized room. At the right front is a door opening to the street outside, and at the left rear a door opening into an inner room. On the wall at the back is a wide flamboyant poster with the sign—"Recruiting Office 18,659." Plastered all around the walls are other flaming signs and posters calling upon American manhood to go and fight for its country. At the left front, *diagonally placed, is a bare-topped office desk, and farther back towards the rear is another and smaller desk with a typewriter, behind which* PRIVATE JESSEL, *the stenographer, sits. Just to the right of him is a tall white weighing and measuring scale, and still farther over at the right is a small table with a phonograph, the horn of which disappears through the wall toward the street. At the right front is a bench on which* CAPTAIN VALENTINE *and* SERGEANT JACKSON *sit, and in the exact center of the stage near the foot-lights a chair is placed facing outwards.*

When the curtain rises, PRIVATE JESSEL *is busily typewriting, his keys going in a whirring clatter of sound somewhat like a small mowing machine, for his typewriter is of ancient model.* CAPTAIN VALENTINE *and* SERGEANT JACKSON, *facing the front, are reading a lurid magazine which carries the picture of a male movie star on its cover.* PRIVATE JESSEL *is a slender, nervous fellow with a pale burning eye, and is about twenty years old;* CAPTAIN VALENTINE *is a handsome man, some thirty years old, with a dark matinee-idol face, and is dressed in a spick and span uniform of the United States Infantry;* SERGEANT JACKSON *is shorter, with a scrubby bull-dog face and stubby upturned nose, and is about forty years old.*

For a moment after the curtain goes up PRIVATE JESSEL *clatters away at his work, and the* CAPTAIN *and the* SERGEANT *read their magazine, the* CAPTAIN'S *fingers going tap tap on the bench. Then suddenly from the room at the left rear comes a low moaning cry. No one pays any attention to it.* SERGEANT JACKSON *bends closer to the magazine, snickers lewdly, and points to the page with extended forefinger. The* CAPTAIN *smiles and nods a languorous agreement to the joke. The* SERGEANT *now salutes the* CAPTAIN, *stretching his snaggle-toothed mouth in a grin, and drops his hand. He turns the page and the two of them read on. The* CAPTAIN'S *voice rises out of his tapping into a low croon.*

CAPTAIN VALENTINE. (*Singing abstractedly as he reads.*) What are you coming for
    Into my private boudoir
Disturbing the sleep of a lady, an innocent
        one?
    So sorry, the soldier replied,
    I'll honorably step outside,
I meant no offense in the least and 'twas
        only in fun.

(*And now the scene is suddenly split by a blood-curdling scream from the room at the left rear.* PRIVATE JESSEL *abruptly stops typing, and sits listening. The* CAPTAIN *continues his reading and singing.*)

    Up spake the lady demure,
    If fun and not robbery, sir,
Is what you intend then perchance and
        perhaps you may stay.
    Nay, nay I confess on my oath

    Most stiffly inclined to them both
Was my will, and they say with a will like
        my will there's a way.

(*And now* PRIVATE JESSEL *leans over and sets the phonograph playing, and we can hear the air in the street outside being flooded with the brassy band notes of the "Democracy March." The record has played only part way through when the door at the left rear opens and* DOCTOR MC BRAY, *a middle-aged, pot-gutted fellow wearing a medical corps major's uniform comes in, carrying a stethoscope in his hand and mopping his face exhaustedly. He gestures to the stenographer—who cuts off the record, steps swiftly back to his little desk, takes up his dictation pad and waits. The* MAJOR *stands mopping and scouring his hand around down in his coat collar. Again the door at the left rear opens and two giant private soldiers of the regular U. S. army come in bringing* ANGUISH HOWINGTON *between them. They are stripped to the waist and their great muscular torsos are tattooed most horribly, mainly with voluptuous women's figures. As for* ANGUISH, *or what there is left of him, he is stark naked except for a scanty hand-towel tied around his middle, and his bony shaking form is on the verge of collapse. His swollen red eyes are almost closed, his face is bathed in cold sweat, and he is panting hoarsely for breath. The soldiers drag him over to the chair and drop him into it, and step one to the left and one to the right and stand waiting, the while they pinch and wiggle the women's figures on their fore-arms.* ANGUISH *sits shivering and mumbling incoherently to himself.*)

DOCTOR MC BRAY. (*Barking out to the stenographer as the* CAPTAIN *and the* SERGEANT *continue to read their magazine in unconcern.*) Examination findings. (*Dictating rapidly, with a mixed jargon of veterinary and medical learning, and now and then shooting out a word of advice to* ANGUISH.) Venereal diseases—none—candidate claims virginity. Claim sustained. General diseases—none—needs feeding, short on his fodder and corn— (*Snapping his fingers.*) —Chook—nutritious food, I mean. Nervous diseases—characteristic hysteria during use of pump. Nose and throat—foul. (*To* ANGUISH.) Drench with turpentine and linseed oil. (ANGUISH *bends his head over on his arms and begins to weep softly.*) Teeth show candidate to be about twenty-eight. (*Snapping his fingers again.*) Sight—moon-eyed, almost blind. Combination diseases—leucoma, incipient cataract, granular conjunctivitis and God knows what. (*Yelling at* ANGUISH.) Get out! (ANGUISH *springs to his feet and stands cowering in terror. At a gesture from the doctor, the two giants seize him and hurl him through the door at the left rear.* MC BRAY *sits down at the desk at the left and sprawls himself forward exhaustedly on it. And now the handsome* CAPTAIN VALENTINE *is interested. He turns towards* MC BRAY *and speaks in a polite stage voice, his manner that of a cross-mixture of Sherlock Holmes and Rudolph Valentino.*)

CAPTAIN. It's all very well for you to turn down that fellow, Major, but I need another man to fill out my company.

MC BRAY. And pursuant thereof to General Order thirty-four thousand oh—oh—six, we've got to have him today. (*Grimly.*) And let me tell you—the next fellow comes in here better be a man. (*He gestures to* PRIVATE JESSEL *who sets the phonograph playing again. The two giant privates come back into the room and take up the same position and business as before.*)

PRIVATE JESSEL. (*Leaning out the door at the right and calling high above the music.*) Next man! Next man! (*Everybody waits, the record plays, but no one comes in. With a low wheezy growl, the phonograph stops.*)

MC BRAY. (*Savagely.*) Don't they love their country in this lousy dump! Only three enlistments today.

PRIVATE JESSEL. There's that same fellow walking up and down.

SERGEANT. (*Turning and looking back through the door.*) He was there an hour ago.

MC BRAY. Get the—(*Clearing his throat.*) —get him in here.

SERGEANT. That music hooked him. Here he comes. (*The* MAJOR *rubs his hands gleefully and fits his stethoscope into his ears.*)

CAPTAIN. (*Languidly, as he sits down to his magazine again.*) Pass him if you possibly can, Major.

MC BRAY. If he lives, I will. (JOHNNY JOHNSON *enters and stops just inside the door. He is in smiling good humor and wears a new blue serge suit all pressed for the occasion. A red poppy blooms in his lapel and a little United States flag is tucked into the band of his flat-topped straw hat.* MC BRAY *grunts with anticipated joy.*) Unh.—

JOHNNY. (*Removing his hat, giving them a benign smile, and beginning to shake hands around.*) Well, folks, I've decided to do what Minny Belle said and enlist. Where's the paper I sign?

MC BRAY. (*Motioning* JOHNNY *to a chair in the manner of a headwaiter welcoming an honored guest to a table.*) Come right in, sir, and make yourself at home.

SERGEANT JACKSON. We're tickled to death to see you.

JOHNNY. And I'm real glad to see you all. (*Turning towards the chair.*) I came here last night, but the office was closed.

MC BRAY. Now ain't that too bad?

JOHNNY. Yes sir. But if you don't succeed at first—you know. And so—since this a war to end war, I'm in it a hundred percent strong.

MC BRAY. You are?

JOHNNY. You bet your tintype. But it's not against the common man I'm going to fight. No-siree. It's the German leaders. As Wilson says, drunk with military power and—

MC BRAY. (*Chortling.*) Good, good. (*Growling.*) Sit down. (*The two privates step forward and, lifting him suddenly from the floor, slam him down in the chair.* JOHNNY *looks up at them in pained surprise.*)

JOHNNY. Heigh, you fellows are kinder rough, ain't you?

MC BRAY. (*Chuckling in low malevolence.*) Don't mind them, son, it's just their little way.

JOHNNY. (*Sharply.*) Well, I don't like it.

SERGEANT JACKSON. (*To the* CAPTAIN.) He don't like it.

CAPTAIN VALENTINE. (*Crooning.*) Says he don't like it, but he will—

JOHNNY. Still if that's the way you initiate folks into the army, then I suppose I'll have to stand it. It's all in the cause.

CAPTAIN VALENTINE. (*Languorous as always.*) And what cause is that, my friend?

JOHNNY. Why, democracy—world democracy—the biggest idea of modern times, including electricity. (*They all stare at him with some show of interest.* PRIVATE JESSEL *lifts a sort of tripod easel from the corner and sets it between* JOHNNY *and* MC BRAY *and slightly towards the rear, then stands waiting with his notebook in his hand.*)

MC BRAY. (*In his barking manner again.*) What's your name?

JOHNNY. Johnny Johnson.

MC BRAY. (*As* PRIVATE JESSEL *writes.*) Occupation?

JOHNNY. I'm an artist.

MC BRAY. Artist?

JOHNNY. At least that's what the Mayor called me. Artists in stone—I make tombstones—tombstones for both people and animals. You know we don't properly appreciate our pets. They are about the best friends man ever—

MC BRAY. (*Snapping.*) Place of birth?

JOHNNY. I don't know.

MC BRAY. Don't know?

JOHNNY. You see, my daddy and mammy were sort of worthless and wandered around all over—from one poorhouse to another. I don't know where I was born. I was dragged from pillar to post—

MC BRAY. (*To* PRIVATE JESSEL.) Born—between pillar and post.

JOHNNY. (*With a wide breaking laugh as he slaps his knee.*) Daggone my hide, that's good!

MC BRAY. How old are you?

JOHNNY. Well, let me see.—According to the way my pappy figured it I ought to be about twenty-six come pumpkin time. He remembered there was a big frost on the ground—

MC BRAY. (*Wagging his tired shaggy head and speaking in a soft query to the* CAPTAIN.) My God, don't tell me he's crazy!

CAPTAIN VALENTINE. (*Bored.*) Let science decide it.

MC BRAY. (*Loudly to* PRIVATE JESSEL.) Army intelligence test number one—lowest grade. (PRIVATE JESSEL *now throws back a wide sheet of paper from the easel and reveals the illustrated example in test number one.*)

PRIVATE JESSEL. Look this way, Mr. Johnson. (JOHNNY *shifts himself around and stares at the easel. As* MC BRAY *calls off the questions,* PRIVATE JESSEL'S *pencil points them out.*) First question—

MC BRAY. Cats are useful animals because —one, they catch mice; two, they are gentle; and three, because they are afraid of dogs. (*Whirling on him.*) Quick, Mr. Johnson, which is correct—one, two or three?

PRIVATE JESSEL. (*Looking at his wrist watch and counting off the seconds.*) One —two—three—four—

SERGEANT JACKSON *and* CAPTAIN VALENTINE. (*In unison.*) Make it snappy, Mr. Johnson.

JOHNNY. Well, as a matter of fact, cats *ain't* useful. They're the worst pests in the world. Once I had a mocking-bird—

MC BRAY. (*Controlling himself by grim will.*) Mr. Johnson, I want you to understand that we are trying to find out whether you've got sense enough to be a soldier.

JOHNNY. Sure I have. You ain't blind.

MC BRAY. (*Loudly—as he strikes the table with his fist.*) Problem number two! (PRIVATE JESSEL *turns another sheet.*) If you fell into a river and couldn't swim, would you—one, yell for help and try to scramble out; two, dive to the bottom and crawl out; or three, lie on your back and float until help came?

JOHNNY. How deep is the river? (MC BRAY *wipes his dripping forehead with his sleeve.* PRIVATE JESSEL *turns over another leaf.*)

MC BRAY. (*Hoarsely and with suppressed but withering scorn.*) Maybe you forget, Mr. Johnson, that these tests are prepared by the psychological experts of the United States government and you're either crazy or you're not.

CAPTAIN VALENTINE. (*Sweetly.*) Yes, Mr. Johnson, we need another man immediately. Please tell us whether you're a lunatic.

JOHNNY. (*Flaring up.*) Now look here, you folks—

MC BRAY. (*Intoning heavily.*) Why is wheat better for food than corn?—Is it, one,—because it—Chook—is it because, one —is it more nutritious, two, more expensive than nutrinsive—or because in a miller you can flound it gri-ner?—Ha-ha— (*A sickly look spreads over his face.*)

JOHNNY. I catch your drift, neighbor. It all depends. Now take a mule—he likes corn better for his food than he does wheat. Of course I like wheat better—that is, flour. But take a sheep now—he—likes grass. And a hog'll eat anything.

MC BRAY. (*Flinging up his hands.*) Po-leece! Po-leece!

JOHNNY. (*Looking about him and grinning with sudden comprehension.*) I know what you all are doing. You're playing riddles, ain't you? I'm good at that. Me and my daddy used to play 'em. (*His words snapping out with stern authority.*) Everybody get set— (*He pops his fingers dramatically, and with the exception of the two giant watchdogs everybody looks up with sudden attention. Even the exhausted MC-BRAY raises his drooping head.*) If a hen and a half lays an egg and a half in a day and a half, how many eggs will three hens lay in one day? (*Pulling out a big brass watch and staring at it.*) Quick—one —two— (*They look at one another and then almost simultaneously all jerk out their pencils and set to figuring.*) —three, four, five— You give up?—Sure you do, takes a quick mind to answer that. Well, a hen lays only one egg a day anyhow, so the answer is three eggs, that is, if they're three good hens. (*Popping his fingers.*) Here's another one. On your toes— If two snakes got hold of each other's tail and started swallowing and kept on swallowing how would they wind up?

MC BRAY. (*In a spinning rhythm.*) How would they wind-up?—How would they wind up?— (*Suddenly waked out of* JOHNNY'S *spell by his pencil breaking under his great figuring, and gasping.*) Nuts, that's how! (*Yelling.*) Throw him out!

(*The two privates start toward* JOHNNY, *but he darts around behind the easel.*)

JOHNNY. (*Staring about him.*) What you folks mean? I come here to enlist, I tell you. (*Running over to* MC BRAY, *his voice almost frantic.*) You can't turn me down, you can't. (*Aghast.*) Lord, Minny Belle wouldn't ever speak to me again. No, no, I got to go fight— I want to help end this war. I got to go—I— (*At a gesture from* MC BRAY *the guards seize* JOHNNY *and drag him through the door at the left.* MC BRAY *staggers to his feet, feels blindly about him, and goes in after them.* SERGEANT JACKSON *shrugs his shoulders hopelessly.*)

SERGEANT JACKSON. Looks like we got to spend another night in this burg.

CAPTAIN VALENTINE. (*Beginning to croon again as he looks off into space.*) The days
    went happy by,
  And the nights more merrily,
But alas like my ditty most every good
    thing has an end.
  The Colonel came home from the
    wars—
(*He breaks off.*)

SERGEANT JACKSON. (*Staring at his figuring.*) Say what *would* happen to them two snakes? (*A loud guttural cry comes from the left rear.*) That old horse doctor's giving him the works—ha-ha! (*Suddenly the door flies open and one of the tattooed giants pitches headlong into the scene and lies groaning on the floor, with his hands over his face.* JOHNNY *springs in after him, bareheaded and his torn blue serge coat in his hand.*)

JOHNNY. (*Shaking his left fist at the prostrate figure and roaring.*) So you'd tear my blue serge, would you? Well, let me tell you, I'm planning to get married in that coat—at least I was. (*They all stare at him in amazement. The giant moans and rolls on the floor.* JOHNNY *now looks down at him somewhat in sorrow.*) I got a mighty hard fist from chiseling tombstones, and I didn't mean to hit you such a blow in the face.

CAPTAIN VALENTINE. (*With a courtly bow and sweet smile.*) Crazy or not crazy, he's our man!

BLACK OUT.

SCENE IV

"A light that lighteth men their way."

It is night. A prospect looking seaward from the entrance to the harbor of New York. The tips of a few dark branches frame the scene of an infinite ocean and starless sky. Far in the background stands the STATUE OF LIBERTY, *the upper part of her figure illuminated from a hidden light, and in her hand a brightly glowing beacon. Tall and majestic she stands, immovable, and brooding over the scene like some fabled apocalyptic figure.*

When the curtain rises, the orchestra is concluding a soft, harmonious arrangement of a lullaby. And then sliding across the background from right to left, a painted thing upon a painted ocean, comes the gray ghostly shape of a great warship with its threatening guns stuck forward like the antennae of some strange, primeval crustacean. It disappears at the left ,and now in from the right and almost close enough to the ledge to be touched by an onlooker's hand come the curved rail and part of the deck of a passenger ship. Stretched out on the floor one after the other lie the sleeping forms of soldiers, their pale upturned faces bathed in the radiance of the moon, and looking like recumbent figures on a great slow-moving catafalque. Standing by the rail and partly obscured by his hanging blanket is JOHNNY JOHNSON, *dressed in an army union suit, and his rumpled hair gently caressed by a little breeze. He has just risen from his sleep and is staring in dreamy and silent awe at the faraway* STATUE.

JOHNNY. (*After a moment, his words rising at first broken and almost indistinct.*)
Think of it—
(*The motion of the rail and deck stops.*)
There you stand,
Like a picture in that history book I read.
Minny Belle said I'd see you so,
And now at last I have—
Your hand uplifted with a torch
Saying goodbye to us,
Good luck and bless you every one.
(*With hushed fervency.*)
And God bless you,
O Mother of Liberty—
That's what you are,
A sort of mother to us all,
(*Saluting sharply.*)
And we your sons.
And here tonight as we set forth

To fight the German Lords,
I raise my hand
(*He does so.*)
And swear a Bible oath
That Johnny Johnson—
That's my name,
You maybe haven't heard of me,
But some day soon you will—
I swear that neither by a look, a thought, or word,
Will I fail either you or Minny Belle.
And I will keep my character clean
And come back as I went—
Without a smirch.
(*More sternly and emphatically.*)
And furthermore I swear
That I will never see your light again
Until I've helped to bring back peace—
And win this war which ends all wars.
And yet I'm not just sure
How it will come to pass,
But I will find a way,
And if the generals and the kings don't know
I'll show them how it's done,
For never yet has Johnny Johnson failed
To get an answer when he hunted for it.
I swear!
I swear!
And once an oath is made with me,
It's same as sealed and bound.
(*Murmuring.*)
Farewell, Mother,
And peaceful be thy dreams.
(*With his hand still at salute, he pulls his blanket around him and slowly sinks back to his rest. And only when he is stretched out like the other figures does he let his hand fall. A murmurous groan seems to run among the sleepers; they turn in their hard beds and lie still again.* JOHNNY's *voice rises once more in falling drowsy syllables.*)
Starlight, star-bright—
Goodbye, Minny Belle, my darling,
I sleep with your dear—picture—'gainst— my—heart.
(*The rail and the deck slowly move away at the left and disappear in a great engulfing shadow. The illuminated* STATUE *remains alone in the depths of the night, lonely and aloof as she holds her beacon up, and following with her sightless, stony stare the progress of the boat that carries* JOHNNY JOHNSON *out to sea.*)

CURTAIN.

ACT TWO
SCENE I

"Lead, Kindly Light."

The scene is a shadowy road somewhere in France behind the front lines. It is night. A slow cortège of dark twisted and anguished French soldiers is moving like a small funeral procession across the foreground of the scene from right to left. These are the wounded men returning from the front. A few black trees show against the dim light of the sky in the background. As the figures go limping and moving painfully by, a file of American soldiers in full war gear, including gas masks at the alert, are discerned moving along the upper level of the roadbank from left to right. They are going up to the front lines as the Frenchmen are coming out. The wounded men—some blinded, some walking with the aid of crutches, some helped along by their more fortunate fellows—are chanting a low, mournful hymn of pain.

WOUNDED SOLDIERS. Nous sommes blessés,
  Ayez pitié,

Aidez, aidez,
Nous sommes blessés.

(The last of the file of American soldiers stops on the roadbank and stands looking sympathetically down as the end of the cortège moves slowly out at the left. In the dim light of approaching dawn and silhouetted as he is against the sky we recognize the form of JOHNNY JOHNSON. *He stands there in an attitude of great sorrow and sympathy as the orchestra plays out its Marche Dolorosa and the little bleating cries and mumbling words of pain break forth from the lips of the wounded men. When the last Frenchman has disappeared,* JOHNNY *straightens himself up, looks out before him, and raises his clenched fist as if making another covenant.)*

JOHNNY. *(With grim and stern emphasis.)* Lafayette, we are here! *(He turns, and with his bayoneted rifle held on left-handed guard before him, sets off running to the right.)*

BLACK OUT.

SCENE II

"There is one spot forever England."

The scene represents the front line trench, with its parapet and kneeling ledge running zig-zag across the stage at the rear. Beyond the trench and leaning awkwardly against the sky the tops of a few scattered and broken wooden crosses show themselves. On one of them a little bird is sitting.

When the curtain rises, CORPORAL GEORGE *and his squad of six men are standing on guard at an interval of a step apart with their backs to the audience, their rifles resting on the parapet and pointing out into No Man's Land. Sitting on the ledge in each of the intervals is a sleepy English soldier in full marching equipment. Standing to the front and in profile to the audience is an English* SERGEANT.
The time is late afternoon of an early autumn day.

SERGEANT. *(Showing a mouth gapped with snaggled teeth, as he continues his speech.)* It's the big push, the big push you Yanks will be facing and me risking my life in the traffic of London. Gawd help you— Some of you'll come out of it alive. *(He hoists one foot up on a broken box, spits in his palm and begins polishing his shoe.)*

CORPORAL GEORGE. *(Looking around.)* Yeh?

SERGEANT. Things is quiet up here, too quiet. You can see the little larks sitting on the crosses out there. *(He gestures towards the rear. A noise is heard off at the left like the sound of a breaking board.* PERCY FAIRFAX *at the right rear suddenly fires off his rifle into the vastness of No Man's Land, his body recoiling backwards from the kick of the gun. The little bird disappears from the cross, and the English* SERGEANT *bounds around and stares at him angrily.)* Oh, it's Percival Fairfax, the Chicago bad man.

FAIRFAX. *(Reloading his rifle and still staring straight ahead of him his voice tremulous and frightened.)* Yes sir, I—I'm nervous, I guess. If it—this was killing cops I wouldn't mind it, but this silence—I can't stand it.

PRIVATE SVENSON. (*A long horse-faced Swede.*) You scare our little bird away.

CORPORAL GEORGE. (*Softly.*) The waiting —the waiting—that's what unnerves a man.

PRIVATE GOLDBERGER. (*A little squabby Jew.*) Yeh, it says so in the books—the waiting. (*And now the musical whing of a bullet is heard flying towards the men. The Americans duck their heads down, but the English sit as they are. The bullet strikes the parapet with a plop.*)

FAIRFAX. O-ooh, and that sniper, he keeps shooting at us!

GOLDBERGER. (*Mannishly.*) Aw, what the hell! (*He whirls around and begins grubbing in the bank, then holds up a little object triumphantly and jiggles it.*) Look-a-there—that bullet's hot enough to burn your hand. (*Going over to his place at the parapet he lifts the lid of an old box and drops the bullet in.*)

PRIVATE KEARNS. (*A huge square shouldered fellow about twenty years old, chewing tobacco.*) Abie here likes this war. He was a junk man back home.

PRIVATE GOLDBERGER. Yeh, and let me tell you there's plenty of junk up here. Beats the flats of Jersey all hollow.

PRIVATE O'DAY. (*A short red-faced Irishman.*) And prowling around some of these nights you're gonna get your head blowed off.

PRIVATE HARWOOD. (*Sandy-haired and blue-eyed, about twenty-one, singing softly to himself.*) Keep your head down, Allemand,
   Late last night, by the pale moonlight—
   I saw you—
Heigh, Swede, how's your corn crop coming on?

PRIVATE SVENSON. (*Gazing dolefully down at a little potted plant on the ledge beside him.*) It can't grow—gas—too much in the air, I tank.

SERGEANT. (*Staring around.*) Is it m'ize he's got here?

PRIVATE O'DAY. (*Sarcastically.*) No, corn. He found it growing back there in a shell-hole. Reminds him of Iowa.

SERGEANT. (*Resuming his spitting and polishing.*) Bless me, what queer birds—you Americans!

PRIVATE O'DAY. (*Belligerently.*) Yeh? That's like an Englishman—everybody's queer but himself.

CORPORAL GEORGE. (*Sternly.*) Keep your shirt on, Pat.

SERGEANT. (*With a sharp grunt.*) Uhck— "Pat"—Irish be Gawd! (*The other English soldiers snicker.*)

PRIVATE O'DAY. Yes, from Boston.

SERGEANT. (*Calling loudly off at the left.*) Private Johnson!—Where is that bloody skivvy?

PRIVATE KEARNS. (*Spitting.*) He'll be back.

PRIVATE FAIRFAX. He always comes back.

SERGEANT. Queer?—Anyway me lads, England never produced a specimen like your Johnny Johnson.

PRIVATE KEARNS. You're right about that.

SERGEANT. Yesterday he offered to set me up with a nice tombstone for a shilling.

CORPORAL GEORGE. With epitaph?

SERGEANT. Cripes, that too.

PRIVATE HARWOOD. He's got epitaphs writ for everybody in the company, including the Captain and the Colonel.

PRIVATE GOLDBERGER. (*Teasingly, as he indicates* PRIVATE FAIRFAX.) Sold him one.

PRIVATE FAIRFAX. (*With timid braggadocio.*) Johnny says—he says—be prepared for the worst is the way to keep it from happening.

PRIVATE KEARNS. (*Gloomily.*) I wish there was some way of being prepared for that big battle the Sergeant talks about.

PRIVATE SVENSON. Yohnny Yohnson, he say maybe the war be over soon. (*He bends down, peers at his corn and then dipping a handful of water up out of the bottom of the trench pours it around its roots.*)

SERGEANT. (*With genial cruelty.*) This war will last ten years.

PRIVATE FAIRFAX. (*With a groan.*) We might as well be dead then.

SERGEANT. The big blighters back home don't want it to end. Who'd they sell their munitions to if we have peace? Ten years? It might last twenty.

PRIVATE O'DAY. (*Still anxious to put salt in the split tail.*) It would if you English had to win it. (*Defiantly.*) Yeh, it's me talking.

SERGEANT. (*Scornfully.*) Yeh, and if talking meant anything, the Irish would rule the world—not England.

PRIVATE O'DAY. (*Now doubling up his fists.*) Is it a fight you want? Come on!

CORPORAL GEORGE. (*Shouting.*) Can it! Can it! (*He jerks down his gun and steps between* O'DAY *and the* SERGEANT. *The* SERGEANT *tries to push by* CORPORAL GEORGE *as* JOHNNY *comes in from the left, staggering under a heavy load. In one hand he carries a huge battered tin bucket full of hot steaming tea, and over his shoulder a tow sack of provisions. Like the other soldiers he wears a helmet and gas mask at the ready, but he is stripped to the waist, grimed and muddy, and in general is a poor specimen of democracy's champion. A big hole has been torn in the top of his helmet. But though he looks somewhat dirty he seems to be the same cheerful* JOHNNY *as before.*)

JOHNNY. Old England and Ireland fighting again?—Here's something to stop it— your tea! (*At the word "tea" the English soldiers spring to their feet and along with the* SERGEANT *snap their drinking cups from their belts.* JOHNNY *drops the bag of provisions, and with a dipper in one hand and the can in the other pours each man a drink.*)

SERGEANT. (*Joyously.*) Ha-ha-ha—here's to everybody. Cheer up, Yanks, cheer up.

ENGLISH SOLDIERS. Ha-ha-ha-ha-ha—tea— tea!

SERGEANT. (*Suddenly, beginning to sing.*)
Now, England is, as we all know,
A great and mighty nation
With power big as half the world
And colonies galore.
Her army and her navy too
They quite befit her station,
The watchdogs of her flag unfurled
From Bath to Singapore.
(*The English Soldiers join in the chorus.*)
Then hail—hail—hail!

All hail Britannia and her crown!
We lift our cups to thee—
(*They do so.*)
And drink thy health in bumpers down
Of tea, strong tea.
(*They all drink.*)
'Twas tea that raised her in her might,
At least that's our opinion.
And tea that made America—
Go read your history—
And fit it is that we unite
To further the dominion
Of freedom's laws and lead the way
For England and her tea.

ALL. (*With the exception of* JOHNNY *and* PRIVATE O'DAY—*singing.*)
Then hail! hail! hail!
All hail Britannia and her crown!
We lift our cups to thee
And drink thy health in bumpers down
Of tea—strong tea.
(*Their song ended, they drain down the last drop, snap their cups back in their belts, and stand ready to march away. Suddenly as if coming from underground at the back a faint and faraway chorus of foreign voices is heard answering like an echo.*)

VOICES. "Then hail! hail! hail!
All hail Britannia and her crown!
We lift our cups to thee!—"

CORPORAL GEORGE. (*Softly, as they all listen.*) Golly, them Heinies are answering us.

SERGEANT. (*With quiet and forlorn reminiscence.*) Last Christmas up here we were singing "Holy Night," and they done the same.

JOHNNY. (*Snapping his fingers and turning inclusively around.*) See there—good scouts like us, I been telling you.

SERGEANT. Well, good or bad, our business is to lick 'em. (*Shaking his shoulders mournfully.*) Everything shipshape, mates?

ENGLISH SOLDIERS. (*Loudly as they pat their bellies.*) Aye, sir.

SERGEANT. Right-face! (*They obey.*) Hip-hip— (*They start marching off. The* SERGEANT *salutes.*) Cheerio, Yanks—we turn this war over to you. And Johnson, if you capture old Hindenburg, let me know. (*But* JOHNNY *makes no reply, for he has already gone over and sat down on a box to the right of the can of tea and begun figuring on a sheet of paper. The* SERGEANT *goes on out after his squad singing.*)

Then hail! hail! hail!
All hail Britannia and her crown!
We lift—

(*The American soldiers turn and watch them leave regretfully.*)

PRIVATE KEARNS. God, it's lonesome already!

PRIVATE O'DAY. (*Furiously.*) Just like the dirty English. As soon as they think a real fight's coming on they march out and leave us holding the bag.

JOHNNY. (*Still figuring.*) Well, every jug's got to stand on its own bottom sometime— as my mammy said.

CORPORAL GEORGE. (*Snapping.*) Don't start them old sayings again, Johnson, I'm sick of 'em.

JOHNNY. All right, sir, you're the boss, as the ox said to the yoke—

CORPORAL GEORGE. (*Yelling.*) You heard me!

JOHNNY. (*Humbly.*) Sorry, sir. (*And now the men come over and get their food out of the bag—a hunk of bread to each man and a can of bully beef. Then they turn around from their rifles and sit down on the ledge and begin eating.*)

PRIVATE KEARNS. (*Scratching himself with his elbows.*) Where did you learn them old sayings, Johnson— "As the minnow said to the whale" and "If smell was all the goat would win," and all the rest of it?

JOHNNY. Huh? Oh, just picked 'em up.

PRIVATE SVENSON. (*Throwing crumbs over the parapet.*) Chick-chick-chick!

CORPORAL GEORGE. That little bird won't come back around here, Slim. He's got too much sense. (*Yawning.*) I feel like I've stood watch forty hours. What time is it, Johnson? (JOHNNY *pulls out his big watch and looks at it, then begins to chuckle softly.*) What you laughing at?

JOHNNY. Back home there was a teamster —when you asked him what time it was he'd say— (*He stops.*)

CORPORAL GEORGE. Yeh, and what would he say?

JOHNNY. He'd say—Time all dogs was dead, ain't you sick? (*The soldiers laugh and* CORPORAL GEORGE *springs angrily to his feet.*)

CORPORAL GEORGE. Damm it, I told you not to pull any more of them cracks. (*Wagging his head, he sinks back on the parapet.*) For six years I was a head waiter in Childs', I thought I'd met every kind of a crumb—

JOHNNY. (*Now springing up.*) I won't take any more of that. I'm not a crumb. (*He seizes his bayoneted rifle which has been leaning against the bank and starts towards* CORPORAL GEORGE.) You keep picking on me—

CORPORAL GEORGE. (*With a shriek.*) Stop that left-handed fool! (PRIVATE KEARNS *and* HARWOOD *jump up and get in front of him.*)

JOHNNY. (*In a low hard voice.*) Take it back, Corporal—

PRIVATE KEARNS. (*Eyeing* JOHNNY.) You better, Corp, you better.

CORPORAL GEORGE. (*Muttering.*) All right, I take it back. And put that gun down, Johnson. You're breaking orders by touching it anyhow. (JOHNNY *waits a moment and then with a chuckle replaces the gun against the parapet, after which he sits down and sets to figuring again.*)

PRIVATE O'DAY. (*After a moment's silence.*) What you figuring on now, Old-end-the-war?

CORPORAL GEORGE. (*Satirically.*) He's writing a letter to the general, again . . . I guess . . . or is it Minny Belle this time?

JOHNNY. (*Quietly.*) I'm figuring on a sort of document addressed to the German enlisted men.

CORPORAL GEORGE. Ho-ho! Will wonders never cease as the Rabbi said to the— (*With sour distaste.*) Bah!

JOHNNY. Well, you'll never end this war if you don't try to.

CORPORAL GEORGE. And you think you can do that by writing letters. Wonderful, wonderful.

JOHNNY. Well we don't seem to be able to end it with guns. (PRIVATE HARWOOD *suddenly pushes his food away from him and picking up a rope from the ledge sits spinning it aimlessly.*)

PRIVATE HARWOOD. (*Twirling his rope.*) What I'd like to do would be to slip up on the Kaiser standing somewhere and lasso the crook. That'd stop the whole crazy business. (*He throws his lariat backward over his shoulder, jerks it, and begins pulling it in.*)

PRIVATE KEARNS. (*Scratching himself savagely.*) And what I wish is old Kaiser Bill had my cooties.

PRIVATE HARWOOD. (*Springing up from the ledge and pulling on his lariat.*) Heigh, I've hung something. (*He sticks his head quickly up and jerks it down again.*) God, it's a German soldier's leg—with a boot on! (*He drops the rope and sits staring before him. With the exception of* JOHNNY *the others shoot their heads up, then jerk them down and sit in grim silence.* PRIVATE FAIRFAX *starts to whimper and pulls a little book from his pocket and begins to read.*)

JOHNNY. Yeah, there's legs and arms scattered all around. Down there where you cross that gully you can see 'em. Young arms and legs that used to throw rocks and walk about. (*Now once more comes the musical whing of the sniper's bullet. They all, except* JOHNNY, *duck their heads and then sit a moment in silence.*)

PRIVATE FAIRFAX. (*As if to himself.*) It says here in the Bible to love your enemies. How can a man do that? (*And now off at the right the voice of* CAPTAIN VALENTINE *is heard humming. He comes drifting slowly in, immaculately dressed as ever.*)

CAPTAIN VALENTINE. (*Continuing his ballad as he gives the scene a thorough inspection.*) Woe, woe, cried the lady so fair
The while she disrupted her hair—
Ha-ha laughed the colonel, you're guilty,
   I knew I'd unearth it.
And the sergeant he too had his say
Ere the rope took his brave life away—
(*He breaks off his humming as they all stand to attention.*) At ease. (*They all relax. He continues in a fast sharp flow of words, unlike his former drawling.*) We've got orders to get this sniper. You can draw lots.

JOHNNY. (*Stepping forward.*) Is he a leader—a big man, sir?

CAPTAIN VALENTINE. Right now he's more important to us than Hindenburg himself. He's got the provision train scared off of that road down there.

JOHNNY. (*Saluting.*) I volunteer, sir.

CAPTAIN VALENTINE. (*Turning and looking at him with a smile.*) That's very nice of you, Johnson, but you're too valuable a man to risk. (*He takes a box of matches from his pocket and strikes one of them, then reverses the ends of several matches and holds them out.*) The fellow who draws the burnt match goes for the sniper at dawn.

JOHNNY. Can I draw, sir?

CAPTAIN VALENTINE. Yes—last. (*He turns and holds out his hand to* PRIVATE FAIRFAX, *who draws and lets out a glad cry.*)

PRIVATE FAIRFAX. I didn't get it! (CAPTAIN VALENTINE *holds out his hand to* PRIVATE GOLDBERGER. *He draws. From the look of relief he too is saved.*)

JOHNNY. (*Crowding up.*) I'm always lucky at such things. (CAPTAIN VALENTINE *holds his hand out to* PRIVATE HARWOOD.)

PRIVATE HARWOOD. (*Drawing.*) Ha-ha—I don't go. (*Then* PRIVATE KEARNS *draws. He strikes the match joyously on his helmet and flings it down. And now* PRIVATE SVENSON *stands up trembling. He draws.*)

PRIVATE SVENSON. (*In a nervous tittering of relief.*) Ha-ha—hee-hee—

CAPTAIN VALENTINE. (*With an ironic groan.*) I see what's coming.

JOHNNY. (*Grinning.*) I told you so. (*He draws the last match and the* CAPTAIN *shakes his head disgustedly.*)

CAPTAIN VALENTINE. I'll say this for you, Johnson, whatever your drawbacks, cowardice is not one of them. (*Angrily.*) Tomorrow night I'm going to send some of you fellows out too.

JOHNNY. Aw, you won't need to do that sir.

CAPTAIN VALENTINE. Lie down now and get some sleep—all of you. There's going to be a patrol directly in front of you. (*He gestures to the rear.*) Johnson, you can use your own judgment about the sniper.

JOHNNY. Yes, sir.

CORPORAL GEORGE. Attenshun. (*They all stand up, salute, and* CAPTAIN VALENTINE *starts away at the left. And now once more we hear the musical whinging of the sniper's bullet, followed by a loud yell off at the left. Everybody ducks, then straightens up again.* CAPTAIN VALENTINE *looks off and hurries away. They all resume their seats.*) I wonder who got hit that time? Well, Johnson, I suppose you'd better begin to wind up your earthly business.

JOHNNY. (*Now sitting down and cleaning the mud from his shoe with a stick.*) I will —about forty or fifty years from now, I hope.

PRIVATE FAIRFAX. (*Staring at him.*) You mean you're not scared?

PRIVATE KEARNS. Ever notice these nuts?— They ain't scared. (*By this time the shades of evening have begun to fall. The soldiers sit a moment in silence and then begin to make themselves comfortable on the ground and on the parapet ledge.* JOHNNY *gets his old coat, brings it over and spreads it out close beside the can of tea. With the exception of* PRIVATE FAIRFAX *and* PRIVATE HARWOOD, *they all stretch themselves out.* PRIVATE HARWOOD *pulls off his shirt and sits staring before him.*)

PRIVATE FAIRFAX. (*Beginning to read aloud from his Bible.*) "For God so loved the world that he gave his only begotten Son that whosoever believeth on Him should not perish but have everlasting life." (*He drops down on his knees in an attitude of prayer.* JOHNNY *looks around and breaks into a low chuckle.*)

CORPORAL GEORGE. (*Muttering as he lies down.*) I'll tell you this, Johnson, if I were in your shoes, I'd be praying too.

JOHNNY. Human beings are funny, ain't they?—I was just thinking how the Germans are praying to the same God on their side too. (CORPORAL GEORGE *lies down again, and with the exception of* PRIVATE HARWOOD *they all settle themselves for sleep.*)

PRIVATE HARWOOD (*Mournfully.*) Getting on towards dark—just about this time the boys are rounding up the calves back home.

CORPORAL GEORGE. Yeh, back home— Good-night everybody.

JOHNNY. (*Kissing a photograph and putting it in his shirt.*) Good-night, Minny Belle—good-night.

PRIVATE KEARNS. (*With a mock-smacking sound.*) Good-night, Minny Belle, the mighty hero is thinking of you.

JOHNNY. Thank you, Private Kearns.

PRIVATE HARWOOD. (*Beginning to unwrap his leggings and singing with wistful remembrance.*) Oh the Rio Grande—where the wind blows free
And the sun shines so clear and bright,
Where the trail is long, o'er the wide prairie
And the cowboy travels light.
Well it's saddle and boots
In sun and rain
And away, and watch me ride
Up along the canyon and over the plain.
Myself and my horse are one and the same
And one shadow runs beside.

(*The men stir and murmur sleepily to themselves.*)

Oh life was dull but it happened so
A rodeo came one day.
I took my gal to see the show—
There stood my little bay.
I jumped in the saddle and grabbed the horn
And yelled to all around,
I'm the best damn cowpuncher ever was born,
And for Texas I am bound.

(*A foggy twilight begins to envelop the scene.*)

Oh the Rio Grande—where the wind blows free—
(*He lies down on the parapet. The lights slowly die out, and the scene is gradually enveloped in the gloom of night, with the sightless eyelid of the world slowly shutting out the sky. Far away as if under the rim of the earth the low growling of the mighty guns is heard. A moment passes. The muffled forms of the soldiers are dimly discerned as they sleep. Only the smiling*

blissful face of JOHNNY *is visible. In the orchestra the low melody of* MINNY BELLE's *love song is playing, and far away from out of No Man's Land comes the faint indistinguishable whisper of her tender voice.*)

JOHNNY. (*Murmuring.*) Minny Belle— My honey-love! (*And now the gray illumination of* JOHNNY's *face begins to die out, and* MINNY BELLE's *song fades in air. As it fades the other sleepers are heard moaning and twisting in the grip of an uneasy dream. And on their now tortured faces appears the same gray illumination, but* JOHNNY's *face remains in shadow. As if embodied forth by the restless sleepers' nightmare, the round muzzles of three great cannon push themselves slowly up over the parapet and then out and out until their long threatening necks stretch above the recumbent figures.* MINNY BELLE's *song has now died out from the orchestra and is supplanted by the growling croompy notes of the guns. They begin to sing in a queer outlandish trio harmony.*)

GUNS. Soldiers, soldiers—
Sleep softly now beneath the sky,
    Soldiers, soldiers—
Tomorrow under earth you lie.
We are the guns that you have meant
For blood and death. — Our strength is
    spent
Obedient to your stern intent—
    Soldiers, masters, men.

Masters, masters,
Deep dark in earth as iron we slept,
    Masters, masters,
Till at your word to light we leapt.
We might have served a better will—
Ploughs for the field, wheels for the mill,
But you decreed that we must kill—
    Masters, soldiers, men.

Soldiers, soldiers,
Sleep darkly now beneath the sky,
    Soldiers, soldiers—
No sound shall wake you where you lie,
No foe disturb your quiet bed
Where we stand watching overhead—
We are your tools—and you the dead!—
    Soldiers, masters, men!
(*As the cannon song begins to die, the air is split by the musical tinkling of an alarm clock. As it continues to ring, the guns*

withdraw behind the parapet, their great muzzles slowly and sullenly sinking out of sight. The ringing of the clock stops, and JOHNNY *sits up looking about him. Jerking his arms above his head, he yawns and gapes and then gets to his feet.*)

CORPORAL GEORGE. (*Mumbling.*) What time is it, Johnson?

JOHNNY. (*Looking up at the sky.*) About three-thirty—by the ell and the yard. Go on and get your sleep. (*He takes an old sock from his knapsack and begins to fit it over his face like a mask. Suddenly* PRIVATE FAIRFAX *lets out a scream, sits up and begins to beat wildly about him.*)

PRIVATE FAIRFAX. Catch him, catch him! (*The other soldiers sit up and beat at something in the trenches.*)

PRIVATE GOLDBERGER. (*Lunging off to the left.*) There he goes.

PRIVATE O'DAY. Whoo!—that bugger was big as a hog!

JOHNNY. (*Still working with his mask.*) Yeah, the rats get plenty to eat up here. I saw one yesterday squatted on a dead Australian's face. (*For a while they all sit in disconsolate silence.*)

CORPORAL GEORGE. What in the devil are you doing now, Johnson?

JOHNNY. Camouflage. (*Now pulling an old poncho over his shoulders, he picks up the bread knife and begins whetting it on his palm. Then he goes over to the parapet, pulls in part of the lariat and cuts it off. The soldiers stare at him.*)

CORPORAL GEORGE. Don't tell me you're going after that sniper without a gun.

JOHNNY. This piece of rope and bread knife ought to do.

PRIVATE GOLDBERGER. Do you know where he hangs out?

JOHNNY. I've got an idea.

PRIVATE KEARNS. He's got ideas. (PRIVATE SVENSON *clambers up and comes over to* JOHNNY.)

PRIVATE SVENSON. (*Grabbing his hand, his voice choked with emotion.*) Goodbye Yohnny. Be careful—uh— (*He gulps.*)

JOHNNY. I will, Slim. (*Jauntily.*) So long. I'll be back about sun-up. (*Stopping and calling back.*) Better have some breakfast for that sniper, he'll be hungry. (*He goes away at the left.*)

PRIVATE SVENSON. (*Blubbering.*) He'll be killed!—

CORPORAL GEORGE. I hope so. Go to sleep. (*They all lie down again.*)

BLACK OUT.

SCENE III

"A new way to pay old debts."

It is near dawn, and the scene represents a shell-battered churchyard with a few broken tombstones about and a piece of ruined church tower distant in the background. The earth is covered with a thick tangle of grass about knee high. In the immediate center rear of the scene stands a huge black wooden statue of the Christ, leaning a bit awry and showing in its posture something of the beaten and agonized torture of an El Greco figure. While the orchestra continues to play the music of the stricken Redeemer, JOHNNY crawls in from the right front and secretes himself in the tall rank grass. A moment passes, the music continues, and then from the left rear the SNIPER enters, dodging behind tombstones and any bit of covering much in the manner of the Big Bad Wolf slipping upon the house of the three little pigs. He comes to the base of the statue and looks appraisingly about him. He is a slender fellow with a rather large Kaiser Wilhelm mustache and an evil-looking helmet pulled low down over his forehead. Climbing up on a little platform built behind the statue, he opens a panel in the back of the Christ, crawls in and secretes himself, the door closing after him. And now as he worms his way further up inside the dolorous figure, like an animal squeezing along inside a hollow tree, the statue shakes and wriggles with his weight. Then it grows still, the orchestra stops playing, and a moment of silence passes. And now through a great wounded hole in the breast of Christ where the heart should be, the ugly muzzle of a telescopic rifle with a silencer attached is pushed through. The muzzle comes to rest on the outstretched hand of the Redeemer. It seems to grow tense and the eye of the SNIPER can be seen shining out of the heart as he takes his sight. Suddenly the air is stricken with a muffled explosion and the bullet goes whinging on its musical way. JOHNNY bounds up out of the grass and rushing forward, flings his rope around the statue and draws it tight. Immediately a tremendous drumming sets up inside, and the wooden figure totters and sways and gesticulates like a live thing.

JOHNNY. Ha-ha— I got the dead wood on you this time— (*He ties the rope as the statue continues to shake and the drumming keeps up.*)

SNIPER. (*In a high piteous voice as the figure bobs about.*) Kamerad! Kamerad!

JOHNNY. Yeah, and I'll Kamerad you, you Proosian devil! Drop that gun. (*The statue gives a final buck and lunge.*) Drop it, I tell you. (*And now the rifle is pushed through the hole and falls to the ground.*) Pistol too! You've got one. (*A moment passes. And now a mean-looking Luger with belt attached is disgorged from the heart and falls to the ground.* JOHNNY *unwinds his rope and stands aside as he flings open the door.*) Come on out. (*The* SNIPER *comes gingerly down, and as he steps to the earth* JOHNNY *lays his knife against the back of his neck.*)

SNIPER. (*In a high treble cry.*) Ooh, um Gottes willen, tun Sie das nicht!

JOHNNY. (*Cuffing him about the head.*) You dirty stinking rascal! I've a good mind to cut your throat. Ain't you ashamed—using Jesus Christ like that!—and he a good man! (*He slaps his face again. The* SNIPER *drops down on the ground and buries his face in his hands.* JOHNNY *steps over, picks up the gun and the pistol and throws them out of reach towards the front and then stands over the* SNIPER *looking angrily down at him, wiping his sweaty face with his sleeve.*)

SNIPER. (*Looking up as* JOHNNY *takes off his mask.*) Du lieber Himmel!

JOHNNY. (*Suddenly kicking him in the shins as he pulls off his helmet.*) Look-a-there—that hole. You shot at me yesterday!

SNIPER. (*Howling.*) Ow! Ow!

JOHNNY. (*Stamping down on one of his feet and mocking him.*) Ow! Ow! I ought to get me a switch and beat the lard out of you.

SNIPER. (*With piteous pleading.*) Bitte, bitte— (*He begins sobbing.*)

JOHNNY. (*Staring at him malevolently.*) Stop that crying! (*The* SNIPER'S *sobs stop.*)

SNIPER. Yes—yes, sir.

JOHNNY. Why, you speak English.

SNIPER. Yes, sir.

JOHNNY. Smart, mean and smart, you big guys.—What's happened to your mustache? (*The* SNIPER *pushes his hanging lip piece quickly back but it comes off in his hand, revealing the lips and face of a beardless boy.*)

JOHNNY. (*Throwing up his hands.*) Great Jehosaphat! You're just a boy!

BOY. (*Pushing back his helmet and wiping his forehead with his hand, disclosing his close-cropped boyish head.*) Yes, sir. (JOHNNY *suddenly turns away and stands looking off deep in thought. The* BOY *watches him apprehensively.*)

JOHNNY. (*In anger and disgust.*) That knocks me for a row of stumps—it does! (*Turning back to him.*) Come over here by this pile of dirt. (*He goes over and sits down. The* BOY *crawls along the ground and sits a few feet away from him.*) Of all the ungodly things! How old are you?

BOY. Sixteen, sir.

JOHNNY. Sixteen— Hardly weaned. (*After a pause.*) Is your mother living?

BOY. Yes—sir. (*He bows his bare head over in his hands and begins to weep again.*)

JOHNNY. Aw, don't do that— Aw—quit it. (*He moves over a bit and puts his hand on the* BOY'S *shoulder. With the back of his other hand he furtively wipes his own eyes. Turning to him again.*) Why in the devil did you get into this war—young as you are?

BOY. (*His voice suddenly stronger.*) For Faterland and Kaiser, sir. (*He salutes the air.*)

JOHNNY. (*With an exclamation of impatience.*) Nuts, as the monkey said! But never mind that— Don't you know it's for his own power and glory that the Kaiser sends such little boys as you out to die? (*As the* BOY *makes no answer.*) Don't you believe that?

BOY. (*Lowering his voice.*) That's what Sergeant Mueller says. (*Quickly.*) But he only talks it among the soldiers— (*Murmuring.*) Sergeant Mueller.

JOHNNY. And he's right. (*After a moment's silence.*) Who is this Sergeant Miller?

BOY. (*Fervently.*) He is kind and good— The best man in the world. He was my English teacher.

JOHNNY. He is—huh?

BOY. Yes, sir.

JOHNNY. And how does he feel about this war?

BOY. (*Reluctantly.*) Yes—yes, sir, he—hates it.

JOHNNY. Like you and me—huh?

BOY. May-bee.

JOHNNY. Hmn-n. (*After a moment.*) Want some chewing gum? (*He hands the* BOY *a piece which he has drawn from his pocket.*) Put it in your mouth and chew—like me— Don't swallow it. (*The* BOY *does so.* JOHNNY *watches him with a sort of paternal geniality.*) Good? (*A tiny half-frightened smile breaks for an instant over the* BOY'S *white drawn face.* JOHNNY *pats him on the shoulder.*) What's your name, son?

BOY. Johann—Johann Lang. It means John —in English.

JOHNNY. I be jim-swingled! Why that's my name too—John. (*He reaches over and shakes the* BOY'S *limp hand.*) Don't be afraid. I'm not going to hurt you.

JOHANN. (*Now staring at him.*) But the generals tell us you Americans cut and kill and scalp and chop the German soldiers to pieces with knives.

JOHNNY. Ha-ha, they do!

JOHANN. Yes, sir, they all do— (*Hesitatingly.*) The generals and the colonels in their speeches—the newspapers too.

JOHNNY. That's because the Kaiser's crowd tells 'em what to say.

JOHANN. (*More confidingly as he chews.*) But Herr Mueller says he don't believe it —to us he says so. (*Eagerly.*) He says he thinks you soldiers are like us—in the heart good. But he don't know—he think so. (JOHNNY *sits looking off. Suddenly he slaps his knee.*)

JOHNNY. Say—it looks like me and this Miller fellow ought to get together on the war. (*He begins tapping his lip with his forefinger in deep thought. Young* JOHANN *watches him constantly, though now something of his first fright has disappeared.*)

JOHANN. Pardon me, sir, but the sun will soon rise. Then it will be very dangerous for you here.

JOHNNY. (*Turning to the* BOY.) Suppose your friend Miller knew we American soldiers wanted to end this war the way he does, what do you think he'd do?

JOHANN. (*Mournfully.*) Aber, he cannot know that.

JOHANN. Suppose he knew that we Americans deep down are the German people's friends—what do you think he'd want to do?

JOHANN. Stop fighting.

JOHNNY. He's a sensible man. (*Dumping some letters and folded papers from his pockets, he suddenly begins writing with a stub of a pencil, reading off some of the words as he does so.*) "Friend Miller, John Lang who brings this letter to you was captured by me, but I am sending him back—"

JOHANN. (*With a cry.*) You let me go! (*He springs forward and hugs* JOHNNY's *knees and then lies weeping on the ground, one of his hands touching* JOHNNY's *foot.*)

JOHNNY. (*Smiling.*) Yeah, that's right— (*Looking around towards the flaming horizon.*) and we got to hurry. (*Reading aloud again as he writes.*) "—sending him back with these messages—um—um— See the enclosed speeches of Woodrow Wilson, also some by me which come quicker to the point. You and me have the same ideas about being friends and ending this war. John will tell you more. I must close on account of the sun coming up—
> Yours in friendship,
> Johnny Johnson,
> Private soldier."
(*Touching* JOHANN *on the shoulder.*) Get up, son. (JOHANN *rises and stands wiping the tears of happiness from his eyes.*)

JOHANN. You—you really let me go?

JOHNNY. (*Shoving several papers in an envelope and sticking them into* JOHANN's *pocket.*) I'm sending you back, son, and I hope we end the war before it ends you.

(JOHANN *grabs his hand and kisses it with wild joy.*)

JOHANN. Forgive me—the Colonel, he made me do it—

JOHNNY. (*Pulling his hand sheepishly away.*) Do what?

JOHANN. (*With a gesture towards the figure of Christ.*) Hide in there and shoot at you Americans. All the time after this I shoot in the air.

JOHNNY. (*Quickly.*) That's the idea. Tell friend Miller to spread the news among his soldiers—his friends—make copies of the speeches, distribute them everywhere. You'll hear from me again—somehow. Now quick—run—we're going to save a lot of lives. (*He pushes him along.* JOHANN *grabs* JOHNNY's *hand once more, then embraces him and dashes away at the left rear.* JOHNNY *stares after him, waves his hand, and then picks up the rifle and the pistol and stands looking at the statue of Christ. He pulls off his helmet in humility and respect.* CAPTAIN VALENTINE *comes crawling in on his all-fours at the right front. He is humming softly to himself.* JOHNNY *gives a last look at the statue, gazes at the rifle and pistol in his hands, then shrugs his shoulders in a vague comment on the world ınd comes towards the front.* CAPTAIN VAL- ENTINE *calls out in a low admiring voice.*)

CAPTAIN VALENTINE. You killed him!

JOHNNY. (*In good humor.*) No.

CAPTAIN VALENTINE. (*Standing quickly up.*) What! (*Looking off and then jerking out his pistol.*) Yonder—look out! (*Raging.*) Oh, you fool!

JOHNNY. (*Springing in front of him.*) Don't you shoot him! (CAPTAIN VALENTINE *tries to dodge this way and that around* JOHNNY, *and finally gets in a shot over his shoulder.*)

CAPTAIN VALENTINE. (*Raising his pistol as if to strike* JOHNNY *with the butt of it.*) I missed him. (*Suddenly a burst of machine*

gun fire rattles out from the direction of the German trenches. The air is filled with a medley of whinging sounds and the plop of bullets striking against the earth. The CAPTAIN *throws himself flat on his belly.* JOHNNY *darts forward to drop down beside him, then suddenly slaps his hand to his rump with a howl.* CAPTAIN VALENTINE *laughs hysterically as* JOHNNY *sprawls down by him.*) Ha-ha-ha, got you, did they? There is a just God after all!

JOHNNY. (*Half-sobbing with anger and vexation, one hand still on his rump.*) Ain't that a hell of a place to get shot! (*The* CAPTAIN *starts crawling off at the right front,* JOHNNY *crawling painfully after him.*)

BLACK OUT.

SCENE IV

" 'Tis not so deep as a well—but 'tis enough. 'Twill serve."

The hospital. JOHNNY's *bed is in the fore- ground with an infinite row of beds painted on the backdrop and diminishing in the distance.* JOHNNY *is lying restless on his side with his face towards the audience. A young French* NURSE, *very chic and at- tractive in her French uniform, is trying to make him comfortable.*

NURSE. (*Sitting down by him and begin- ning to sing.*) My Madelon of Paree
　　She laugh and dance and sing
　　To cheer the weary soldier
　　　At his homecoming.
　　A little room together,
　　An hour of love to spend,
　　Comme-ça, your arm around me,
　　　Oh—mon ami, my friend.

(JOHNNY *stirs and closes his eyes.*)
　　But she—ah—she remembers
　　That other love and joy,
　　The first, the best, the dearest,
　　　Tired soldier boy—
　　A narrow room alone now,
　　Rain on the roof above,
　　And he will sleep forever,
　　　Oh—mon ami, my love.
　　My Madelon of Paree
　　She does not sit and grieve,
　　But sings away her sorrow
　　　To cheer the soldier's leave.

　　For life is short and funny,
　　And love must have an end.
　　An hour may be forever—
　　　Oh—mon ami, my friend.

(*A fat middle-aged hospital* ORDERLY *comes in from the right and starts on across the scene.*)

JOHNNY. (*Jerking up his head and calling out.*) Any mail for me?

ORDERLY. (*Chuckling.*) Not even a letter from General Pershing. (*Laughing softly.*) Hee-hee—how's the wound this morning?

JOHNNY. (*Irately.*) I've told you to lay off that subject.

ORDERLY. The doctor's coming to have an- other look at it in a minute.

JOHNNY. (*Irritably.*) Yeh—and I want to have a look at him. He's got to let me out of here.

ORDERLY. Why in blazes you want to get back to the front is more than I can see. (*Wagging his head he goes on out at left.*)

NURSE. (*Putting her hand on his fore- head.*) Forty times a day I say take it easy, bébé, you last longer.

JOHNNY. And how can I take it easy, and me with work to do in the trenches? (*He pulls a letter from under his pillow and begins reading it.*)

NURSE. (*Presently.*) Johnny.

JOHNNY. Yeh.

NURSE. (*Softly.*) Don't you love me a— you say—little bit?

JOHNNY. There you go—back on that subject. Now look here—you know I'm an engaged man.

NURSE. Oui, but your Minny Belle—she is so far away—

JOHNNY. (*Pressing the letter to his breast.*) She is here—close by— (*Reading his letter aloud to himself perhaps for the twentieth time.*) "Every night when we meet in the church I think of you and pray for victory. I am sure the despicable Hun will soon be brought to their knees." (*The warmth dying out of his voice.*) "Anguish has just come with his new motor truck to take me to the office— How many of the enemy have you killed? Goodbye till next time."

NURSE. I don't like Anguish.

JOHNNY. Nobody does.

NURSE. Maybe Minny Belle likes him?

JOHNNY. (*Rearing up in bed.*) I should say not. (*Grimacing he lies down again.*)

NURSE. (*In a flutter of sympathy.*) You must sleep—your fever will be worse.

JOHNNY. (*Gruffly.*) Fever or no fever, I got to go, I tell you. (*He turns over on his side.*)

NURSE. (*After a moment timidly.*) Johnny?

JOHNNY. Unh-hunh.

NURSE. You don't mind—me loving you— a little? Comprenez-vous?

JOHNNY. I comprenez, all right, but it don't do me no good.—You go try one of them fellows with boots and spurs. (*A middle-aged* DOCTOR *wearing a goatee and carrying a black satchel in his hand enters from the left. Close behind him comes the* ORDERLY *with a little cylinder-tank, about fifteen inches long and three inches in diameter in his hand. They stop by* JOHNNY's *bed.*)

DOCTOR. (*Gesturing with an inclination of his head towards the orderly.*) Better give him a whiff, I guess.

JOHNNY. (*As the* ORDERLY *steps to the head of his bed.*) What for?

ORDERLY. It's laughing gas—make you feel good.

JOHNNY. I don't need any gas, or whatever it is. Go ahead. And then I want you to tell me when you're going to turn me loose.

DOCTOR. (*Opening his satchel.*) Hm—m— At the proper time.

JOHNNY. (*Vexatiously.*) What time is that —as the owl said?

DOCTOR. (*Sourly.*) Maybe sooner than you expect, as the pill said—ah-oom— Turn over. (*The* ORDERLY *lays his cylinder down on the bed and rolls up his sleeve. He and the* DOCTOR *now step behind the bed, bend down and begin deftly dressing* JOHNNY's *wound. The little* NURSE *pulls a waist-high screen from under the bed and sets it up in front of* JOHNNY; *after which she moves over to the right and stands looking off. And now entering from the right comes the* SISTER *of the Organization for the Delight of Disabled Soldiers. She is a tall, rawboned, breezy woman of middle-age, over-dressed and slightly over-enthusiastic in her manner.*)

SISTER. (*Gazing about her.*) I vow! This will be bully for our show. The acoustics look good. (*Trying them.*) Tra-la-la. (*To the* NURSE.) How many brave buddies have we got here?

NURSE. Four thousand and sixty-four soldiers this morning, madame.

SISTER. That's a real break. There's nothing like a big audience to cheer the actor— I mean the soldier. I wish to speak to the head doctor.

NURSE. (*Gesturing towards the screen.*) He is busy.

SISTER. (*Looking behind the* NURSE *at the bed, her voice filling with sudden sympathy.*) Hello, how are you buddy! (*Then springing back in confusion.*) Oh—it's not decent— And I was mistaken. One of our brave buddies is a coward.

NURSE. (*Stoutly.*) Johnny Johnson is not a coward.

SISTER. Then how did he get shot where he did? (*The* DOCTOR *finishes with* JOHNNY, *straightens up and sees the* SISTER.)

DOCTOR. (*Hurrying over and shaking her hand.*) Delighted, delighted. (*To the* ORDERLY *who is covering* JOHNNY *with the sheet.*) Run—notify the Colonel. We will have entertainment this evening. The Sister from the Organization for the Delight of Soldiers Disabled in the Line of Duty is here. (*At the rigmarole of words,* JOHNNY *raises himself up. The* ORDERLY *hurries away to do the* DOCTOR's *bidding leaving the little gas cylinder behind.*)

SISTER. You got my message—

DOCTOR. Yes-yes-yes.

SISTER. The piano and the stage?

DOCTOR. All arranged.

SISTER. Good. (*Looking approvingly about.*) Wonderful hospital, doctor. Best I've seen on my tour.

DOCTOR. (*Bowing low.*) Thank you, thank you. They tell me so in higher quarters.

SISTER. Hmn-n. Everything so spick and span—so many beds. (*Sleepily.*) I could lie right down. (JOHNNY *looks up watchfully.*)

DOCTOR. (*Stiffly, as a military manner creeps over him.*) Extra facilities are being provided for the great oncoming battle, madam.

JOHNNY. (*Calling out.*) Battle?—when is it to start, sir?

DOCTOR. (*Turning to him.*) My man, the exact hour is known only to the Allied High Command, but it will doubtless be soon—perhaps tomorrow.

JOHNNY. (*Aghast.*) Tomorrow? — And here I lie. (*His face full of pain.*) And there will be thousands killed—thousands of boys killed. (*He begins fingering the little cylinder abstractedly.*)

DOCTOR. But we must be prepared to offer these sacrifices on the altar of freedom.

JOHNNY. (*Starting violently up.*) The more I hear of this freedom the less I like it.

SISTER. (*Loudly.*) I was right. He *is* a coward!

JOHNNY. (*Angrily.*) And old lady, you're full of prunes.

DOCTOR. (*Sternly.*) Lie down, young man. You do not know to whom you are talking.

JOHNNY. (*Wagging his head in pain as the* NURSE *comes over and lays her hand on his shoulder.*) When I think of the fools running this world it near'bout sets me distracted. (*Frantically.*) Can't somebody do something to put off this fight?

DOCTOR. This is the most opportune time. (*To the* SISTER.) From yesterday's prisoners we learn that a spirit of rebellion has begun to spread among the German soldiers.

JOHNNY. (*Crying out.*) What! Say that again.

DOCTOR. And we must strike while the iron is hot. (*Taking the* SISTER's *arm.*) Let me show you around.

JOHNNY. (*Wildly.*) Hooray! Hooray! It's working! Good for you, Sergeant Miller!— (*Gazing out at them in happy innocence.*) He's a German friend of mine on the other side—thinks the same way I do. He and Johann. (*The* SISTER *looks at him in horror.*)

SISTER. (*Bending down and glaring at him.*) Not only a coward, but a—traitor! (JOHNNY *in fingering the gas cylinder suddenly lets loose a spray in her face.*)

DOCTOR. Heigh! (*He starts toward* JOHNNY *then he turns and steadies the* SISTER *who seems about to fall.*)

JOHNNY. (*As he cuts off the hiss of escaping gas.*) Excuse me—I'm excited—I'm— (*A vacant look passes over the* SISTER's *countenance, and then she begins to laugh with a low infectious gurgle of fun.* JOHNNY *stares at her in amazement.*)

SISTER. (*With a sudden whoop.*) I feel good! I love everybody. I love you, my brave suffering hero!

DOCTOR. Never mind, it's only the gas. (*She suddenly grabs* JOHNNY *and begins to manhandle him in an affectionate embrace. The* DOCTOR *and the young French* NURSE *spring forward and pull her off. The* SISTER *now begins cavorting about and flinging her long shanks shamelessly before their gaze.*)

SISTER. I feel wonderful! I feel like flying. (*She begins a clattering tap dance, and then throws her arms around the* DOCTOR.) Come on, doctor, the show's ready to start.

DOCTOR. Young man, I'll attend to you later! (*The* SISTER *goes dancing off at the left, pulling the* DOCTOR *with her.* JOHNNY *and the* NURSE *sit looking off at the left as the sound of the dancing dies out. Then* JOHNNY's *gaze comes back to the cylinder and he stares at it.*)

JOHNNY. You see what happened? One minute she wanted to shoot me and the next minute eat me with love. Wonderful stuff this laughing gas.

NURSE. (*As* JOHNNY *keeps staring before him.*) You sleep now.

JOHNNY. Pity they don't use laughing gas in the war instead of poison gas. (*Snapping his fingers.*) Bring me my britches.

NURSE. (*Alarmed, as she bends over him and tries to push him back.*) No, Johnny! Mon Dieu!

JOHNNY. (*He looks at the* NURSE, *then suddenly lays himself back.*) All right— (*The* NURSE *pulls the cover up and tucks him in.*)

NURSE. (*Kissing him on the forehead.*) 'S'right—a good boy. Good-night, Johnny.

JOHNNY. (*Dreamily.*) Good-night—(*She blows him a kiss from her fingers and goes softly away at the right. A moment passes,* JOHNNY *cautiously raises his head, looks around and then slides his legs out of the bed. He pulls the sheet off and the gas tank falls to the floor.*) Guess I better take you along—might meet another fool. (*He picks it up, then crawls out, pajamas and all, through the open window ct the right.*)

BLACK OUT.

SCENE V

"In the multitude of counsellors there is safety."

The scene is a meeting of the Allied High Command in the Chateau de Cent Fontaines somewhere behind the lines. The setting is one of magnificence, mainly consisting of glass, red plush, and a flight of marble-columned stairs in the right rear. Running along the back is a glassed hall with potted palms and decorative flowers, and with a door opening inward.

When the curtain rises, the Allied High Command is sitting around a long table in the middle of the room. At the center, back of the table, sits the CHIEF OF THE COMBINED ALLIED FORCES. *He bears a striking resemblance to Marshal Foch. And at his right sits an* AMERICAN GENERAL, *the Commander of the American Expeditionary Forces, who just as obviously resembles General Pershing; and on his left sits the* COMMANDER-IN-CHIEF *of the British Expeditionary Forces, an almost exact replica of Marshal Sir Douglas Haig. On the* BRITISH COMMANDER's *left sits a* BRITISH MAJOR-GENERAL *who resembles General Rawlinson, and on the* AMERICAN COMMANDER's *right a* FRENCH MAJOR-GENERAL *who looks much like General Petain. At the left end of the table in profile to the audience sits a man in civilian clothes somewhat resembling the British Premier Lloyd George. At the other end of the table also in profile is another man in civilian clothes much like Clemenceau, the Tiger Premier of France. On the side of the table next to the audience sits a single lone figure in uniform somewhat resembling Albert, King of the Belgians, who throughout most of the military proceedings remains with bowed head, as if taking no interest in what goes on around him. At the left in the rear stand several staff officers—a* BELGIAN MAJOR-GENERAL, *a* BRITISH BRIGADIER-GENERAL, *a* SCOTTISH COLONEL *and a* POLISH COLONEL. *Behind each of the three central figures—the* CHIEF OF THE ALLIED FORCES, *the* BRITISH COMMANDER, *and the* AMERICAN COMMANDER—*stands a* FIELD CLERK *with a stenographic pad in his hand. All of the officers are dressed in most elite uniforms and are plentifully decorated with medals, crosses and orders of merit. Their field coats and caps are placed on a sofa near the stairway. Spread out on the table is a huge war map which the three military leaders are considering.*

As these mighty keepers of men's destiny speak forth their arguments and plans with puppet pomp and solemn precision, the orchestra keeps up an accompaniment of wide-spaced chords with now and then an ironic figure played by the flute or oboe in between.

CHIEF OF THE ALLIED HIGH COMMAND. (*Continuing with a slight accent as he gestures with his baton of Maréchal de France.*)
The Flanders group of armies—hmmn—
Will march as we have said
Towards Brussels on the left,
The right towards Hal—
(*Saluting and addressing the* KING.)
Your Majesty.
(*The* KING *without replying gestures with a long finger towards the* BELGIAN MAJOR-GENERAL *at the left rear.*)

BELGIAN MAJOR-GENERAL. (*With his wooden salute.*) Poor Belgium understands and quite agrees—
What little part is left of her I mean—

BRITISH COMMANDER-IN-CHIEF. (*With a low mutter.*) And plenty of her's left, I'm shuah—
Such as it is.

BELGIAN MAJOR-GENERAL. (*With his hand on his sword.*) I did not catch the gentleman's remarks—

CHIEF. (*Sternly.*) We're not concerned with private quarrels here.
The question is not reparations now,
Nor yet division of the spoils.

BRITISH COMMANDER.   My speech was purely topographical. (*The* BELGIAN MAJOR-GENERAL *bows.*)

CHIEF. (*Looking around at the* BRITISH COMMANDER.) The mission of the British army, sir,
Will be to hurl th'invader forces back
Towards Froidchapelle and Philippeville.
(*The* BRITISH-COMMANDER *looks confusedly around and then turns to the* ENGLISH MAJOR-GENERAL *at his side. The* MAJOR-GENERAL *looks uncertainly about him and then turns towards the* ENGLISH BRIGADIER-GENERAL *at the left.*)

BRIGADIER-GENERAL (*Vacuously.*) Ha-ha—quite so—
To hurl th'invader's forces back.

CHIEF. (*Briskly.*) It seems that everything goes well in hand.

(*The* FIELD CLERKS *continue writing rapidly. The one behind the* CHIEF *bends down and whispers in his ear. The* CHIEF *nods and continues.*)
—Right—goes well in hand—
Though we were much remiss in leaving out
Our allied friends—les braves Américains.

AMERICAN COMMANDER-IN-CHIEF. (*Gruffly.*)
Mistakes in such small matters will occur.

CHIEF. (*Consulting his map again.*) Th' American forces will move south
Co-operating with the French armies—
The first, the fourth, the fifth, the tenth,
Maneuvring on both wings
To catch the Boches by surprise.
(*He looks questioningly at the* AMERICAN COMMANDER *who nods his head in slothful agreement. Then as the* CHIEF *gazes about the room for confirmation, everybody nods with the exception of the* KING. *The* CHIEF *now picks up a huge stamp and with three swift and sudden blows puts the final seal upon the orders before him. Then he rises and in even more puppet dignity than before addresses the assembly, while the orchestra keeps up its mock solemn accompaniment.*)
And so, Messieurs,
The disposition of the Allied arms
Is—all—arranged,
And each man knows his task,
N'est-ce-pas?
(*They all nod.*)
And now the saddest subject possible—
The necessary loss of life
In this oncoming drive—
Are we prepared to suffer it—
As we have done so many times before?

THE ASSEMBLY. (*Like one man with the exception of the* KING *and the* AMERICAN COMMANDER.) Oui!
We are!

CHIEF. Your majesty? (*The* KING *again points his finger towards the* BELGIAN MAJOR-GENERAL *at the left.*)

BELGIAN MAJOR-GENERAL. (*In a crisp mathematical voice.*) The rivers, mud, concrete and wire,
Which Belgium's sons must struggle through
Force us to allow for heavy loss—
Some thirty thousand dead perhaps,

Some hundred and ten thousand wounded
too.
(*The* CHIEF *stamps an order with his seal.*)

CHIEF.   Your excellency of the British Isles?
(*The* BRITISH COMMANDER *leans towards the*
ENGLISH MAJOR-GENERAL, *who turns once
more and looks to the left at the* ENGLISH
BRIGADIER-GENERAL.)

BRIGADIER-GENERAL.   More than a hundred
thousand killed
And thrice as many wounded, sir.

CHIEF.   (*Hollowly.*) Vive, vive!
Proud England's glory never shall **grow**
dim
The while her sons can die so easily.
(*Once more he stamps an order.*)

BELGIAN MAJOR-GENERAL.   (*Piteously.*) But
Belgium, sir, is such a little land,
So tiny and so small—
(*Beginning to figure on a piece of paper.*)
But tiny though she is, who knows?
We may enlarge that figure some—to say—
Er—fifty thousand dead.

CHIEF.   Bravo!

OTHERS.   Bravo! (*The* BELGIAN MAJOR-GEN-
ERAL *bows and looks at the* BRIGADIER-GEN-
ERAL.)

CHIEF.   (*Continuing as he addresses the*
FRENCH MAJOR-GENERAL *at the left.*) Et vous,
mon cher brave camarade?

FRENCH MAJOR-GENERAL.   (*Rising and glanc-
ing about him.*) We bow before the mighty
English nation.
(*Pounding the table with his knuckles, his
thin face working with pent-up emotion.*)
If we lose more than eighty thousand dead
Revolt will spread and anarchy break out in
France!
(*He sits down.*)

CHIEF.   (*Stamping another order with a
bang.*) Vraiment!
(*But now the* PREMIER OF FRANCE *stands
up, his white mustache quivering with
vexation and rage.*)

FRENCH PREMIER.   Non, non, I say and
still say non!
If England gives her hundred thousand
dead,
La Belle France, my native France,

Can give her hundred thousand so the
same.
(*He collapses suddenly in his chair.*)

VOICES.   Vive la France!

FRENCH MAJOR-GENERAL.   But England has
more men to lose—
(*Loudly.*)
—and why?—
(*Now on his feet again.*)
Because the sons of France fell with their
guns
The while the English let them fall—
At Ypres, Vimy Ridge and Mons they did.

ENGLISH PREMIER.   (*Springing up.*) The
English soldiers are no fools.
They know well when to die—
(*Scornfully.*)
Unlike the French who at Verdun
Lost half a million wasteful dead—
Perhaps a million if the truth were known.
(*And now the French and Belgian staff
officers are on their feet and the* FRENCH
PREMIER *sputters like a fire cracker in his
chair.*)

OFFICERS.   We protest!

BRITISH PREMIER.   I see that's still a hornet's
nest—
So let it lie—
I only wanted to make clear my point,
And no offense was meant.
(*He sits down. The* CHIEF *bangs on the
table with his baton.*)

CHIEF.   As allies in a sacred cause
I ask you to forget what's past—
(*To the French and Belgian officers.*)
Please have no worry, mes amis,
The course of tactics and control
Is safely in French hands.
Be seated.
(*They all sit down, and the* CHIEF **now**
turns to the AMERICAN COMMANDER.)
Your estimated losses, sir?

AMERICAN COMMANDER.   (*Curtly.*) Very few,
I hope.
(*Bending over the spread-out map.*)
It seems we have right many trees
Along the sector where we fight—
I don't expect so many killed—
I say expect.
(*The generals and officers look at him in
querying displeasure. The* BRITISH PREMIER

suddenly applauds, then stares morosely at the floor.)
There's nothing better than a tree
Between you and machine gun fire—
Especially if it's big.

CHIEF. (*Airily.*) Much so the poor benighted Indians used to fight.
(*With a shrug.*)
Where are they now?

AMERICAN COMMANDER. I hear they're living peaceful in the West
And doing well with copper mines and oil.

CHIEF. (*With a more violent shrug.*)
Tant pis!
(*His voice suddenly stern and authoritative.*)
Messieurs,
At this high moment and historic hour
We all stand up—stand up—stand up—
(*Everybody does so including the unhurrying AMERICAN COMMANDER.*)
Salute—
(*They all lift their hands and salute, staring straight towards the front.*)
Salute the coming of the early dawn
That marks the zero hour of doom,
The end of Germany.

VOICES. The end of Germany! (*For a moment they all stand in silence while the orchestra continues its commenting chords. Suddenly the CHIEF barks out.*)

CHIEF. We meet upon the battlefield—
The Council is adjourned—
For breakfast—
(*They all rise and, with the exception of the AMERICAN COMMANDER, begin shaking one another's hand solemnly. JOHNNY appears on the stairway at the right rear. He is still dressed in his pajamas which are now muddy-legged. And under his arm he carries the little gas tank bundled up in the hospital sheet.*)

JOHNNY. (*Calling out.*) Say—say, you folks, don't break up just yet. (*He comes on down into the scene and stops at the right front. Everybody has whirled around and is staring at the bizarre newcomer in speechless amazement.*)

AMERICAN COMMANDER. (*Blinking.*) How did you get in here?

JOHNNY. (*With a tired disarming smile.*) Oh, but I didn't hurt your guards. They're down there in the bushes, all feeling fine. (*He chuckles and looks around at them.*) I know most of you. I've seen your pictures in the papers.

CHIEF. Arrest that man. (*The FIELD CLERKS start around the table towards him. JOHNNY steps toward the footlights, his hand on the concealed cylinder.*)

JOHNNY. Say—wait a minute.

AMERICAN COMMANDER. Gentlemen, he is one of my countrymen. I know him by his accent. (*He addresses JOHNNY.*) Young man, I ask you quietly to leave the room, otherwise these gentlemen here will have the pleasant duty of hanging you.

JOHNNY. No, they won't hang me, General. They'll thank me—all of you will—when I tell you what I've come for.

AMERICAN COMMANDER. (*With a placating gesture around him.*) And what have you come for?

JOHNNY. To help you end this war. (*Now edging closer to the footlights as the staff officers at the right and left rear take a step towards him.*) Yes sir, I've been in communication with some of the German soldiers and they're about ready to stop this fighting. (*Triumphantly.*) A rebellion is spreading.

CHIEF. (*In a low voice to the AMERICAN COMMANDER.*) Rebellion?—How did he know that?

JOHNNY. I know it all right.

AMERICAN COMMANDER. (*With a smile as he gazes around him as much as to say, "He is harmless. We can spare him a moment or two."*) You do?

JOHNNY. Yes sir, I got direct news from the German sniper I captured. (*The CHIEF and the AMERICAN COMMANDER look at each other.*)

AMERICAN COMMANDER. So you captured a German?

JOHNNY. Yes sir. He said the common soldiers wanted to be friends with us, and I sent him back with all kinds of messages saying we want to be friends too. And I tell you it's beginning to work. They're rebelling against their German war lords— already. What we got to do now is get millions of articles and speeches printed and—

AMERICAN COMMANDER. (*Abruptly.*) Is your name by any chance — Johnson — Johnny Johnson?

JOHNNY. (*With a sudden pleased grin.*) Yes sir, that's me, and you never did answer my letters.

AMERICAN COMMANDER. (*To the assembly.*) There's nothing to fear, gentlemen, he's harmless.

CHIEF. The meeting is adjourned.

JOHNNY. (*Springing frantically towards them.*) But it's the truth, the truth I'm telling you. You've got to hold up this battle. I'll make my way into the German lines— I'll prove it—I'll do anything! You and the other generals can sign an order right now stopping the offensive. Then we get busy with prop—propaganda—words—words.— Yessir, they're a lot more powerful than bullets if you speak them at the right time. And this is the right time. For the more the Germans read, the more they'll see the truth of what we say. And right now when they're worn out and sick of war they'll be glad to come to terms, and there won't be a dozen people killed. (*Turning vehemently to the* SCOTTISH COLONEL.) Ain't there some truth in what I'm saying, ma'am?

COLONEL. (*Blinking and hesitating.*) Aye, there is. (*Then wadding up his kilt nervously as his confreres stare around at him.*) I—er—mean—ha-ha-ha.

JOHNNY. That's right, you can always depend on the women folks. Now, come on, let's use our heads—that's what they're for. Let's—

CHIEF. (*Sternly to the staff officers.*) Take him away!

JOHNNY. (*Incredulously.*) You mean—you don't believe what I'm saying? (*Crying out warningly as the staff officers move towards him.*) Heigh, better not! (*Suddenly he shoots his gas cylinder out and holds it protectively in front of him.*)

KING. (*In a low horror-struck voice as he points a quivering fore-finger.*) A bomb!

VOICES. (*Softly.*) A bomb.

JOHNNY. (*Eyeing them.*) Well— (*Then quickly.*) Ho-ho, then suppose I have got a bomb. (*He takes a quick step forward and they all draw back from him and stand frightened and awed, and even the* AMERICAN COMMANDER *is stopped in his tracks.* JOHNNY *watches them in silence a moment and then continues with suppressed emotion.*) Now then maybe you'll listen to me. (*Anger creeping into his voice.*) I was standing there listening to you all right and you were speaking of a pile of dead men in tomorrow's battle higher'n that big tower in Paris—poor dumb guys like me you're sending out to die—to be blown to pieces! (*With sudden rage.*) All right, suppose I blow you to pieces with this—er—bomb. (*Yelling.*) Sit down, King! (*He lifts his bundle menacingly.*)

KING. (*Collapsing into his chair and calling piteously.*) Gendarmes! Gendarmes! (*And now all the others, with the exception of the* AMERICAN COMMANDER *who never takes his eyes off* JOHNNY, *sink down into their chairs and stare about them with fearful faces.*)

JOHNNY. So here you sit on your hind ends holy as God and make your plans— marking up your thousands of dead and dying like cold figures on a blackboard. Know what that means? I ask you—know what it means?—all these boys—young fellows like me—like what you used to be— going out to die—shot down—killed—murdered—to be dead and stiff and rotten in a trench with rats and mud? We were meant for something better, I tell you! (*Vehemently.*) We want to live, and you could let us live! We want to be let alone to do our work in peace—to have our homes—to raise our families— We want to look back someday and say our life has meant something—we have been happy and it was good to be born into this world. (*Pleadingly to the* AMERICAN COMMANDER *who has approached close to him.*) You see what I mean don't you—don't you? (*More quietly as he controls the trembling in his voice.*) When you come right down to it what sense is there in human beings trying to cut and tear and destroy one another like wild beasts in a jungle? There's no sense in it, is there? Is there! (*Stretching out his hands to all of them.*) You're our leaders— you're all-powerful over us—you tell us to die for freedom or a flag or our country or whatever crazy ideal it is—and we have to die. (*Half-sobbing as they look at him with cold authority-set faces.*) You'd rather live too, hadn't you? You'd rather be at home with your wives and children, hadn't you —living in peace the way men were meant to live? Then end this killing — end it now— (*Brokenly.*) Only a second's time— a movement of your hand—a written word —and you could stop this war. Do it! Do it! (*Staring at them aghast as they look at him with dull baleful eyes.*) But you don't listen. That Englishman was right. You don't want to end this war. (*A queer baffled grieving in his voice.*) There's something black and evil got into you—something blinded you—something— (*He drops his head. Suddenly at a gesture from the* AMER- ICAN COMMANDER *several of the staff officers spring upon him. He turns quick as a flash and starts toward the stairway at the right rear, but the* FIELD CLERKS *head him off. And now as several of the officers close in upon him he suddenly unscrews the tank of gas and sends it hissing and spraying into their faces. The officers gradually stop their pursuit, look at one another, and the expression of their faces changes. And now they begin to laugh.* JOHNNY *stares at them in astonishment, as do the great generals. Then as the latter rise and move towards him, he rushes around among them re- leasing the gas in their faces, taking time to squirt the* KING *a full dose.*)

KING. (*Throwing up his hands in a loud clapping.*) Ho-ho-ho!

OTHERS. Whoops!—Wonnerful!—Merveil- leux! (*And now the* AMERICAN COMMANDER *breaks into a roar and slaps his side. The orchestra begins to play a sprightly tune, and the scene changes from one of solemn dignity into one of humor and gaiety. Several of the officers begin dancing their native dances—the* POLISH COLONEL *at the right doing a Polonaise, the* SCOTTISH COLO- NEL *at the left a Highland Fling and the* American, English, and French officers tap

dancing, waltzing, and minuetting. JOHNNY *with the sheet wadded over his nose and mouth, stands gazing at them with ques- tioning, puckered eyes. And now the* BRIT- ISH PREMIER *and the* FRENCH PREMIER *hop out into the middle of the room, and hook- ing their arms together cut a few steps like old men at a country dance.* HIS MAJESTY THE KING *bows his head over on the table like a great ungainly puppet and begins to laugh at some secret and mysterious joke.*)

KING. Ho-ho-ho-ho!

OTHERS. Heh-heh-heh-heh| (*And now there is a general chorus of merry laughter, and even* JOHNNY *giggles a bit.*)

THE WHOLE ASSEMBLY. (*With the excep- tion of* JOHNNY. Ha-ha-ha-ho-ho-ho- Haw-haw-haw- Hey-hey-hey-hey-hey-hey- Hy-hy-hy-hee-hee-hee- Hi-hi-hi-iiiiiiiiiii-ay! (*The Frenchmen now kiss the Americans and the Americans kiss the Frenchmen, and then they all take hands and dance around the table in a circle like children around a mav-pole. As they whirl by, the* AMERICAN COMMANDER *grabs* JOHNNY's *hand and pulls him into the dance. He moves with them, holding his sheet around him. The* AMERI- CAN COMMANDER *in a benevolent outburst of feeling picks up his great-coat with its insignia and puts it around* JOHNNY *and then follows by placing his cap on his head.*)

AMERICAN COMMANDER. (*With a loud voice as he salutes.*) General Johnny Johnson! (*The dance suddenly stops, and the officers all crowd towards* JOHNNY, *click their heels and salute likewise, as they repress their laughter into bubbling giggles.*)

VOICES. Vive General Johnny Johnson! Hooray General Johnny Johnson! Hip, hip General Johnny Johnson!

CHIEF. What can we do for you, General?

JOHNNY. (*Shaking his head groggily and returning their salute with his left hand, and then after a moment's hesitation bark- ing out.*) Stop this war!

AMERICAN COMMANDER. Just as you say, General. Tee-hee-hee — so you want this fighting stopped? (*Turning around and calling to everybody.*) General Johnson's right. This war is foolish, there's nothing to it but blood and murder.

VOICES. War is foolish! Let's stop it!

AMERICAN COMMANDER. (*Embracing the* CHIEF. Old boy, we're going to stop this war. What you say?

CHIEF. (*Clapping his hands.*) Stop the war! (*A great burst of applause and cheering follows.*)

AMERICAN COMMANDER. We'll sign the order right now. (*He hurries over to the table, writes something, signs it and hands the pen to the* CHIEF *who also signs and stamps it. Then he gives the paper to* JOHNNY, *and calls out in a loud voice.*) Silence! (*The laughter dies down once more to suppressed giggles.*) We have signed an order stopping the offensive! General Johnson, see that it is carried out!

THE ASSEMBLY. Vive Johnny Johnson! Hooray Johnny Johnson! Hip, hip Johnny Johnson! (*And now the orchestra resumes playing. The officers lift* JOHNNY *on their shoulders and march around the room, then place him on the table and stand applauding him.*)

VOICES. Speech, speech!

JOHNNY. (*Blinking and passing his hand across his forehead as if to clear his mind.*)

There's not much to say, friends. Now that we're going to stop the war, we'll all be home in time for Christmas to see old Santa Claus. Ain't that fine?

VOICES. Christmas! Christmas! Merry Christmas! (*And now they all start marching around the table again and singing, with the exception of* JOHNNY, *who hops down and disappears up the stairs the way he came.*)

ALL. (*Singing as in a round.*) We'll all be home for Christmas—a merry, merry Christmas! (*A moment passes while the singing continues. The orchestra rises to a loud fortissimo and suddenly stops. Gradually the noise subsides, the generals and the others sink down in their seats and gaze about them in amazement. The* AMERICAN COMMANDER *looks at the* CHIEF'S *scattered and windblown hair and the* CHIEF *looks at his disarray.*)

CHIEF. (*In a hollow dazed voice.*) What time is it?

AMERICAN COMMANDER. (*Staring at his wrist watch.*) Ten minutes till five.

CHIEF. (*With a cry.*) The offensive!

AMERICAN COMMANDER. (*Springing out of his chair with a yell.*) My God!—We gave him an order stopping the offensive! Catch that man! (*He and the* CHIEF *tear out through the door at the rear followed by the mad scramble of the others.*)

BLACK OUT.

SCENE VI

"Still stands thine ancient sacrifice."

The scene is the edge of a great battlefield near dawn. In the foreground is a small dugout opening into a raised eyebrow of the earth. By a shaded lantern light two liaison officers are discerned, one a CAPTAIN, *talking into a field telephone, and the other a young* LIEUTENANT, *squatted by him, taking notes in a book. The orchestra accompaniment has continued.*

CAPTAIN. (*Chanting into the phone.*) North—first British army; South—British six, two, one, three, four.

LIEUTENANT. Check.

CAPTAIN. French army toward Saint-Quentin.

LIEUTENANT. Check.

CAPTAIN. On the right the American army. Code—L E, Prefix three, six S M.

LIEUTENANT. Check.

CAPTAIN. Zero hour—0 1 5 1 0.

LIEUTENANT. Check.

CAPTAIN. Three minutes now— Three minutes—

Three minutes and the western front
From Calais to Sedan will go—
Over the top—
The zero hour falls.

LIEUTENANT. (*Half-sobbing.*) Check.

CAPTAIN. May heaven help our enemies—
In such an hour!

LIEUTENANT. Check.—And help us all!
(*And now off at the left we hear the singing command "Attention," then nearer at
hand the command repeated, and then still
nearer the command repeated. The* CAPTAIN
and the LIEUTENANT *look around and suddenly spring to their feet as* JOHNNY JOHN-
son *enters wrapped in the* AMERICAN COM-
MANDER'S *overcoat, and cap.*)
CAPTAIN. (*Saluting and clicking his heels.*)
Attenshun! (*The* LIEUTENANT *quickly salutes, clicks his heels likewise.* JOHNNY'S
*hand is pushed into his coat in an attitude
somewhat resembling the popular picture
of Napoleon.*)

JOHNNY. (*In a slightly disguised voice.*)
At ease.

CAPTAIN. (*Gasping.*) General—General—
General—
The danger is too great—
Oh General!

JOHNNY. (*In a still heavy voice.*) The
General has no fear when his own men
are involved.
Are you in touch with the different com-
manders?

CAPTAIN. Everything's in order, sir—in
order, sir—
(*Jerking his wrist watch by his eyes.*)
Two minutes now—two minutes—
The barrage will begin—

LIEUTENANT. (*With a moan.*) Check.

JOHNNY. There'll be no barrage—no bom-
bardment either.
(*With a bark.*)
The war is called off!

CAPTAIN. (*With a shout.*) What!

JOHNNY. Suspended until further orders—
(*Authoritatively.*)
In the name of the Allied High Command.
Here!
(*He hands him the signed order.*)

LIEUTENANT. (*With a broken cry.*) Thank
God, thank God.
(*Slightly hysterical.*)
We'll live to get back home again!
(*Wildly.*)
We'll live!
(*He runs over and kisses* JOHNNY'S *hand,
then whirls and embraces the* CAPTAIN.)

JOHNNY. Quick—get the news on the
wire.

CAPTAIN. (*Now down on his knees and
grinding the telephone.*) Hello, hello! Sec-
ond Army Corps, Second Army Corps—
Ypres section, General Godby— Hello.
This is Varner—Varner—L-two-V-O-seven.
(*Reading from the order.*) Order urgent—
Special invoice—Allied High Command—
Cancellation. Eight-four-three-two-one.
Code— Acceptive. G. O.

JOHNNY. (*From the shadow where he
stands.*) Talk sense!

CAPTAIN. General offensive will not take
place. Indefinite suspension of hositilities.

LIEUTENANT. (*Running about and clapping his hands.*) Shall we send up the
signals?

JOHNNY. (*Shouting.*) Send 'em up! Send
'em up!

LIEUTENANT. (*Rushing off at the right.*)
Flares! Flares! (BLACK OUT. *The orchestra
plays the "Democracy March." fortissimo.
The lights come up again.* JOHNNY *is at the
back looking off and waving his sheet in
the air. And now at the left the sound
of cheering is heard, coming nearer as if
underground. From a flare somewhere off
stage the scene of No Man's Land at the
rear is lighted up. The subterranean cheering seems to pass across the stage. And now
at the back as if popping out of the ground
several American soldiers spring up on the
parapet yelling and waving their caps.*)
A SOLDIER. Hooray, the war is over! War
is over! (*Shouting across No Man's Land.*)
Heigh, Heinie, where are you?

ANOTHER SOLDIER. Come on out, you boys!
We've quit fighting!

ANOTHER SOLDIER. Kommt d'raus! Kein
Krieg mehr! (*And now as the orchestra*

plays, the figures of several German soldiers, muddy and begrimed, appear at the left and right rear. The Americans run forward and shake hands with them. They slap one another on the back and embrace affectionately, weeping with happiness. Suddenly off at the left a siren blows. The CAPTAIN *and the* LIEUTENANT *look off.* JOHNNY *hops across the trench and joins the German and American soldiers at the rear. They salute him and he goes among them shaking hands. And now rushing in from the left come three or four brigadier-generals and colonels with drawn pistols.)*

FIRST BRIGADIER. (*Yelling and pointing towards* JOHNNY.) Catch that man!

JOHNNY. (*Coming over to the trench and speaking sternly to the staff officers.*) Get back to headquarters, you fellows, or I'll slap you under arrest.

SECOND BRIGADIER. (*Raising his pistol.*) Spy! Spy! Kill him!

LIEUTENANT. (*Stepping in front of him.*) My God, would you shoot the Commander-in-Chief? (*The soldiers spring protectively around* JOHNNY.)

SECOND BRIGADIER. Commander-in-Chief!

JOHNNY. (*Pushing his way through the soldiers and turning towards them.*) Boys, do you want to stop this war?

SOLDIERS. (*With some of the Germans crying "Ja, Ja!"*) Yes, General, great God, we say so!
End it right now. And let's go home. Home—let's go home.
(*A* COLONEL *springs suddenly over, jerks* JOHNNY'S *coat from him and at the same time another officer knocks off his cap.*)

COLONEL. Look at him! (*The soldiers stare at him in silent astonishment.*)

FIRST BRIGADIER. (*To the liaison* CAPTAIN.) Command the offensive to begin at once! (*He sticks an order into his hand. The* CAPTAIN *stares at the order, then springs to the telephone and begins cranking.* JOHNNY *whirls about as the officers and soldiers start towards him, jumps down into the trench and disappears. The* FIRST BRIGADIER *yells to the soldiers.*) Back into your trenches! The battle is beginning! (*The American soldiers look helplessly about. Both brigadiers now have their pistols drawn.*)

SECOND BRIGADIER. At "three' we fire. One—two— (*He raises his pistol. The American soldiers jump down into the trenches.*)

CAPTAIN. (*At the telephone.*) G-O-eight-four-three-two-one cancelled. Forged orders. Work of spies.

LIEUTENANT. (*Now weeping as he squats with his pad and pencil.*) Check. (*The German soldiers at the back turn and flee toward their trenches. But some of them never reach there, for the American machine guns now begin their rat-tat-tat-tat-tat-tat, and they are seen falling. The* CAPTAIN *continues yelling into the telephone.*)

CAPTAIN. *At once! At once!* (*As he looks at his watch.*) It is now exactly hours— 0 5 1 0— Open fire!—Fire! (*Somewhere far away and as if beneath the earth, a great gun is fired. There is an instant of pause, and then the battle begins, with the music in the orchestra portraying its fury and violence.*)

BLACK OUT.

SCENE VII

"There's many a mangled body, a blanket for their shroud."
A SERIES OF FLASHES—by the light of bursting shells. The orchestra is now an organ playing the stately chant music of a church prayer, while in a nebulous circle of light at the extreme right front of the stage an AMERICAN PRIEST *is seen standing above the members of his congregation who are bowed in prayer, and while at the left*

front a GERMAN PRIEST *likewise stands above his praying flock. As the battle goes on and the organ plays, the two priests repeat in unison, the one in English, the other in German, the prayer "In Time of War and Tumults"*—
Almighty God, the supreme Governor of all things, whose power no creature is able to resist, to whom it belongeth justly to punish sinners, and to be merciful to those

who truly repent; save and deliver us, we humbly beseech thee, from the hands of our enemies; that we, being armed with thy defense, may be preserved evermore from all perils, to glorify thee, who art the only giver of all victory; through the merit of thy Son, Jesus Christ our Lord. *Amen.*

FLASH 1

Two squads of horrible creatures in gas masks, German and American, flying to meet each other and fighting hand to hand.

BLACK OUT

FLASH 2

Two men fighting, a German and an American, with bare fists choking and strangling each other, towering up over the footlights.

BLACK OUT

FLASH 3

Two soldiers—an American and a German —tangled in a roll of barbed wire, gasping and frothing from burning gas, clasping the hand of friendship as they die.

BLACK OUT

FLASH 4

A squad of Germans holding up their hands in surrender. An American on his belly in the foreground with a machine gun mowing them down.

BLACK OUT

FLASH 5

A squad of American soldiers holding up their hands in surrender. A German machine-gunner in the foreground mowing them down.

BLACK OUT

FLASH 6

JOHNNY JOHNSON, fleeing around in No Man's Land, bare-headed, his pajamas in tatters.

BLACK OUT

FLASH 7

A young German praying at the foot of the black wooden statue of Christ. He rises to meet an American who enters with drawn bayonet. They fight and the German is run through. An exploding shell kills the American. The statue totters and falls with a crash.

BLACK OUT

FLASH 8

JOHNNY JOHNSON, holding the head of a dying man in his lap and giving him a drink of water. (*And now the organ music and the entire scene gradually fade out with the long breathing word of the two priests—* "Amen.")

BLACK OUT

SCENE VIII

"Dulce et decorum est pro patria mori."
It is dawn over No Man's Land. In the dim light that showers a faint gray in the east we can discern the forms of dead men scattered about us as far as the eye can see, and in the background the mutilated and shattered figure of the Christ. And ever and anon from somewhere out of that vast stretch of ruined world come the feeble and begging cries of those who have not yet died. The music in the orchestra now is that of the wounded French soldiers in Scene I, Act Two, "Nous Sommes Blessés." In the middle foreground, sitting on the edge of the raised lip of a torn shell hole is* JOHNNY JOHNSON. *Stretched out at his feet is the form of a soldier, his pale face upturned in the gray light. The face is that of* JOHANN *the young sniper.* JOHNNY *is*

naked save for a torn piece of cloth tied around his middle. His body is marked with sweat and powder burns. For a while he sits staring down at the pale face, then reaching out he lays his hand on the soldier's forehead, moving the German helmet back from his head to do so.*

JOHNNY. (*In a low voice.*) Feel better now? (*There is no reply. He bends closer, puts his hand on the soldier's mouth, and then sits with his head and shoulders bowed and his hands clasped around his knees. His voice rises through his burnt swollen lips in a hoarse broken monologue.*) Two hundred thousand dead, five hundred thousand dead, a million dead.—And they have had their way, Johann. And all for what? And why? What for? (*Wagging his head.*)

Nobody knows—nobody! (*Far off in the background a voice calls piteously.*)

VOICE. Mother, mother. (JOHNNY *continues to stare before him.*)

JOHNNY. He'll quit calling soon, he'll quit calling and lie still—like you, Johann, lie still. And they killed you. I saw it happen. One of my own squad did it. He stuck a bayonet through you. (*Gasping.*) I had the war stopped once. Maybe there's no sense in that. They said so. But you wouldn't say so—no, you wouldn't would you? (*Stretching out his hands over the still figure with a loud cry.*) Would you!

(*And now two tall military police loom up in the darkness at the left. With their hands on their pistols they approach* JOHNNY.)

FIRST MILITARY POLICE. Are you Johnny Johnson?

JOHNNY. (*Without looking around.*) He's dead.

SECOND MILITARY POLICE. Are you Johnny Johnson? (*His head sags down on his breast.*)

FIRST MILITARY POLICE. In the name of the armies of Europe and America we arrest you!

BLACK OUT.

SCENE IX

"Hail, Mary full of grace."

A prospect looking out upon the entrance to New York harbor. In the distance the STATUE OF LIBERTY *stands against the evening sky, but this time she is not illuminated. And now the same gray ghostly warship slides across the back of the scene but from left to right, and from the left comes the rail and the deck of the passenger ship again.* JOHNNY *is sitting at the rail with his back to the* STATUE *and staring straight before him. A uniformed* GUARD *is standing at his side. The* GUARD *salutes and then touches* JOHNNY *on the shoulder and points to the* STATUE. *But* JOHNNY *keeps staring ahead of him. The rail and the deck pass out at the right and disappear into a great engulfing shadow without stopping.*

CURTAIN.

ACT THREE

SCENE I

"Is there no balm in Gilead? Is there no physician there?"

A psychiatrist's office in the State Hospital. At the left front is a heavy door opening into a corridor. At the left a typewriter desk and to the right of that a larger desk with telephones, papers, and so on. At the center rear another door opens to an inner room. At the right rear are several filing cases, and to the right front a third door opening towards the entrance hall. When the curtain rises DR. MAHODAN, *a melancholy middle-aged man is seated at the desk looking through several folders of newspaper clippings, letters and reports. The telephone rings. He picks up the receiver.*

DR. MAHODAN. Hello. (*Wearily.*) Yes, this is the bureau of psychiatry— (*Listening a moment and then bawling out at the unknown speaker.*) You're crazy! (*He hangs up the receiver and sits staring before him. Presently he begins to sing to himself, to a low tom-tom accompaniment in the orchestra.*)

    Back in the ages primitive
      When souls with devils were possess't,
      The witch man came and did his best
      With yell and blow and expletive
        And loudly beaten drum.
    And up and down and round about
    He whirled with fearful fetish rout
      And wild delirium.
But rarely did the patient live
    Back in the ages primitive.
(*Continuing with organ accompaniment.*)

    Back when the priests had things their way

They viewed insanity the same,
Though now they would invoke the
    name
Of heaven's hosts, and sing and pray
    In accents dolorous.
And if they failed to ease his pains,
They bound the poor soul down in
    chains,
    Condemned and infamous.
And there in dungeon cell he lay,
Back when the priests had things their
    way.

(*And now the orchestra is jazzing a bit.*)

Today psychologists agree
The insane man is only sick,
The problem is psy-chi-a-trick,
See Jung and Adler, Freud and me,
    And we will analyze.
And though it hurts, we probe the ruts
Of mental pain that drives men nuts
And heal their lunacies.
And from their devils being free,
They all take up Psychiatry.

(*The telephone rings again as a spinsterish looking stenographer appears from the rear with a glass of yellow liquid in her hand. She sets the glass down and picks up the receiver.*)

STENOGRAPHER.   Dr. Mahodan's office— Yes, we're expecting him. (*Sitting down and holding her stenographic pad in readiness.*) Take your medicine.

DR. MAHODAN.   Yes—yes— (*He gulps down some of the liquid and shudders.*)

STENOGRAPHER.   Better this morning?

DR. MAHODAN.   No, worse— (*Sadly.*) Well, my business is to cure others, and not myself. (*Picking up a photograph and staring at it.*) And this Johnny Johnson looks like a difficult case to cure. (*As the* STENOGRAPHER *writes.*) Rare, very, very rare. Only once in a generation does such a diseased personality occur. According to his record, he appears to be one of those naturals born into the world at rare intervals. You recall my monograph on Jesus, the rural prophet and will-less egocentric.— Same type, same type. (*Tapping the photograph with his finger.*) You will notice one significant fact. He holds his rifle left-handed—the others do not. (*Musingly.*)

Also notice the discrepancy between his forehead and his chin. (*The telephone on the desk rings again. The* STENOGRAPHER *picks it up.*)

STENOGRAPHER.   Dr. Mahodan.—Good—yes, send him right in.

DR. MAHODAN.   You'd better fetch the orderlies.

STENOGRAPHER.   Yes, sir. (*She rises and goes to the heavy door at the left, unlocks it with a loud click and disappears beyond.* DR. MAHODAN *picks up a hand mirror and begins studying the interior of his mouth. The door at the right opens and* JOHNNY JOHNSON *is escorted in by his former guard. He wears his old over-sized soldier's uniform, though now it is clean, and in general his whole appearance denotes his usual cheerfulness and complacency. He looks about the scene with interest as* DR. MAHODAN *rises and receives a large envelope from the guard.*)

DR. MAHODAN.   Mr.—er—? (*He consults a clipping.*)

JOHNNY JOHNSON.   Howdy, sir.

DR. MAHODAN.   Have a seat, Mr.—er—Johnson. (*JOHNNY sits down and the guard retires towards the door at the right and stands waiting.*)

JOHNNY.   (*With a gentle disarming smile.*) Yes sir, I don't mind sitting down. I had to give my seat to a lady on the train, and my feet hurt. (*The* STENOGRAPHER *re-enters. She looks keenly at* JOHNNY *and he rises out of his seat.*) Have my chair, ma'am.

STENOGRAPHER.   (*Startled.*) Oh—no, thank you. (*She sits at her desk again and takes up a writing pad.*)

DR. MAHODAN.   (*As the* STENOGRAPHER *writes.*) Were you seasick on the ocean, Mr. Johnson?

JOHNNY.   Oh no, sir. Funny, I didn't get seasick either way.

DR. MAHODAN.   (*With a slight inclination of his head toward the* STENOGRAPHER.) Perfect adjustment of sense organs as expected.

JOHNNY.   Sir?

DR. MAHODAN. I was just speaking to the young lady.

JOHNNY. Excuse me. Could I ask you a question, Mr.—Mr.?

DR. MAHODAN. (*Bowing slightly.*) My name? Er—? (*Blankly and then getting the answer.*) —Ah—Mahodan, Dr. Mahodan.

JOHNNY. Glad to know you, sir. Has Minny Belle come yet?

GUARD. (*Taking a step forward.*) That's his fiancée, Doctor. He wanted her to know he was home from the war so I let him send her a telegram.

DR. MAHODAN. Hum—hum. Question of procedure. (*To* JOHNNY *soothingly.*) No, she hasn't come yet.

JOHNNY. (*Dolefully.*) That's funny. I wonder if she'll be able to locate me here. It's such a big place.

DR. MAHODAN. Yes, it's quite large.

JOHNNY. (*Looking around him.*) It's one of the nicest jails I ever saw.

DR. MAHODAN. (*As the* STENOGRAPHER *writes away.*) This is not a jail, Mr.—er—Johnson. It's a hospital. (*And now several husky orderlies enter from the left in white uniforms. They take up their position by the door.* JOHNNY *looks at them with interest.*)

JOHNNY. Why it is a jail too. I saw some bars beyond that door. (*He stares around with quizzical eyes.*) And why is he locking up?

DR. MAHODAN. That's all right. We do that as a matter of habit. (JOHNNY *stares at the floor now, saying nothing.* DR. MAHODAN'S *voice changes to a more professional curtness as he sits down and hands the* STENOGRAPHER *the envelope he has received from the guard.*) Usual six copies of these, please. (*Then turning to* JOHNNY.) We've looked forward with interest to seeing you. You are quite a famous man in military circles.

JOHNNY. (*Looking up now with a grin.*) I'm the man that stopped the war if that's what you mean. (*Shaking his head glumly,*

the smile dying from his face.) But they wouldn't let it stay stopped. They're still killing each other and shooting over there right on. They've got everything bassackwards!

DR. MAHODAN. (*With the faintest touch of amusement beginning to show in his eyes.*) Bass what?

JOHNNY. (*Chuckling.*) Oh, shucks, that's just a word means the front part behind— (DR. MAHODAN *stares at him and gradually the dour hardness of his face begins to break up into a wrinkly smile. As if infected by* JOHNNY's *chuckle, he throws back his head and laughs and then goes off into a paroxysm of sputtering and coughing. The astonished* STENOGRAPHER *hurries to him with the remainder of the medicine which he drains off.*)

DR. MAHODAN. (*Dabbing his lips with a large white handkerchief.*) Excuse me, I am not accustomed to laughter. (*Leaning forward eagerly.*) Tell us more about your wonderful experiences.

JOHNNY. (*Humbly.*) I didn't have any experiences. I didn't even shoot my gun once.

DR. MAHODAN. (*To the* STENOGRAPHER *who jumps to her pad and starts writing rapidly.*) The superman complex through the technique of humility, which— (*Stopping and eyeing* JOHNNY *closely.*) No—Cancel that.

JOHNNY. Sir?

DR. MAHODAN. I was addressing the young lady.

JOHNNY. I know you were. But it was about me.

DR. MAHODAN. Yes, and very complimentary. (*And now the door at the right opens and* MINNY BELLE *comes in. She is dressed in a little blue coat suit and cute hat and looks adorable, though somewhat pale and worn.*)

MINNY BELLE. Johnny— (*Springing up, he whirls around and grabs her.*)

JOHNNY. (*Brokenly.*) Minny Belle, Minny Belle! (*His lips quiver with emotion, and tears come into his eyes. And now he pulls her into his arms and hugs her tight to him. Then he pushes her from him and stares at her with hungry, devouring eyes. For a moment he stands looking at her so, and then kisses her on the forehead.*)

MINNY BELLE. No—Johnny—please—these people!

JOHNNY. (*Manfully.*) Oh, it's all right. They already know we're engaged. (*Taking* MINNY BELLE *by the hand and turning towards the doctor.*) This is Minny Belle, Dr. Mahodan. Yes, that's his name, Minny Belle. He says it is. And he seems like a fine man.

MINNY BELLE. I'm sorry I'm late, sir, but we had a puncture on the way.

JOHNNY. A puncture?

MINNY BELLE. Yes, Anguish was good enough to bring me over in his new car.

JOHNNY. Oh—

MINNY BELLE. You're all dressed out in your uniform. (*Gazing at him queryingly.*) But why are you back? The war's not over yet.

JOHNNY. They decided to send me back here. (*Then quickly.*) But it weren't because I wasn't a good soldier. Maybe I was too good.

MINNY BELLE. (*Stiffly.*) But why did you come back so soon? (JOHNNY *says nothing.*) And how many Germans did you kill, Johnny?

JOHNNY. None, Minny Belle—not a single one.

MINNY BELLE. Oh, Johnny!

DR. MAHODAN. We are sorry to interrupt you, Mr.—er—

STENOGRAPHER. (*Prompting.*) —Johnson.

DR. MAHODAN. Yes—I'd like to have a word with the young lady in private. Will you kindly go with these gentlemen—to another room for a moment?

JOHNNY. (*Looking about him.*) All right, sir. I'll be right back, Minny Belle. (*The orderlies come forward and escort* JOHNNY *out at the rear and close the door behind them.*)

DR. MAHODAN. (*Gesturing* MINNY BELLE *to a seat.*) My dear young lady, I have a very sorrowful duty to perform. (*Curtly, to the* STENOGRAPHER.) You needn't write down everything I say. (*The* STENOGRAPHER *stops writing.*) Your fiancé will not be able to go home with you.

MINNY BELLE. What's the matter?

DR. MAHODAN. This is a home for mental cases. Does that mean anything to you?

MINNY BELLE. I—I thought it was strange —Johnny's being here but— (*With a sudden cry.*) You don't mean there's something wrong—wrong with his mind?

DR. MAHODAN. (*Gravely.*) The psychological experts of the United States army say so. I have their reports here.

MINNY BELLE. (*Crying out.*) No, no, Johnny—he's a little peculiar in his way but— (*Her words die out and she sits staring horrified at the doctor.*)

DR. MAHODAN. To you it may not appear that anything is wrong. But to one skilled in the science of mental diseases it is apparent that— (*The door at the rear suddenly opens and* JOHNNY *dashes in. He has been stripped of his army coat and wears in its place the blue denim jacket of an inmate of the house of balm. He is followed by the orderlies.*)

JOHNNY. (*Hotly to* DR. MAHODAN *as he tears off his jacket and throws it down.*) What's the meaning of this sir? (*He stares from the doctor to* MINNY BELLE'S *grieved face. She suddenly drops her head in her hands and begins sobbing.* JOHNNY *hurries over to her.*) Has this—this queer dick of a doctor done anything to you, Minny Belle?

MINNY BELLE. Oh—oh—oh!

DR. MAHODAN. Unfortunately I had to tell her about your condition.

JOHNNY. What condition?

DR. MAHODAN. That you are sick.

JOHNNY. Sick? Why I never felt in better

health—at least I did till I came into this place. (*Grabbing* MINNY BELLE's *hand.*) Come on, we're going out of here!

MINNY BELLE. (*With a wail.*) Oh, Johnny! You can't.

JOHNNY. We'll see about that! (*The door at the right opens and* ANGUISH *sticks his head in. He is sportingly dressed, like the rising young business man he is.*)

ANGUISH. Did you call me, Minny Belle?

MINNY BELLE. (*Looking at* JOHNNY, *wavering a moment and then pulling away from him and running over to* ANGUISH.) They're going to keep Johnny here, Anguish.

ANGUISH. (*As he takes hold of her arm.*) Well, an asylum is where he belongs.

JOHNNY. Asylum! (*Whirling around.*) Take your hand off her arm.

ANGUISH. (*As* MINNY BELLE *clings to him.*) Don't you let him get at me, folks.

DR. MAHODAN. (*Raising a gently teasing finger.*) Now, Mr.—er— Now, now—

JOHNNY. (*Stopping as the orderlies take a step towards him.*) I see. They think I'm crazy. They're going to shut me up. (*Then turning to* MINNY BELLE. *Pleadingly.*) You can't—you can't think— (MINNY BELLE *drops her head and begins to sob again.* ANGUISH *puts his arm protectingly around her. At a gesture from the doctor, he leads her away at the right and closes the door.* JOHNNY *stands staring at the floor like a man in a dream.* DR. MAHODAN *comes over and puts his hand kindly on his shoulder. Then he picks up the jacket from the floor, and* JOHNNY *slowly holds out his arm for the sleeve.*)

DR. MAHODAN. I think you'll make a very interesting patient, Mr.—er— (*Blankly, then getting the answer.*) Mr. Mahodan.

BLACK OUT.

SCENE II

"Out of the mouths of babes and sucklings."

The forensic arena in the house of balm— a sort of ordinary reading or club room with several rows of chairs at the center right and a little speaker's stand facing diagonally outward from the left rear. Above the speaker's stand hangs a beflagged picture of Woodrow Wilson and above that a big placard with the words "Adelphi Debating Society" on it. When the curtain rises some dozen or more elderly men are standing by their seats as they face the rostrum. Some of them have pencils and cheap writing tablets in their hands. They resemble the ordinary type of American business men—railroad, bank, or insurance company directors. On the rostrum sits BROTHER THOMAS, *a man who resembles a certain late Vice-President of the United States, and to his left a pale-faced clerk type of man about thirty years old. Sitting on a lower level and to the right of the rostrum is* JOHNNY JOHNSON. JOHNNY *has aged much since we saw him last. He is dressed in an old collarless white shirt and a dark sack coat much too large for him, and his hair with suspicious signs of gray-*

ness at the temples is still unruly though brushed somewhat to one side. Like the portrait above him he wears spectacles though his are of the plain steel-rimmed kind, and in an indefinite way he seems to resemble the portrait. With a small brush he is painting a wooden toy which he holds in his hand.

The scene is somewhat cut off from the footlights by a low railing which crosses the front of the stage and in the center of which is a little gate. Two uniformed hospital guards stand one on either side of the scene at the front looking straight ahead of them and with their arms folded akimbo. It is ten years after the preceding scene. As the curtain rises, the Brethren are concluding a song. With the exception of JOHNNY *everybody is singing.*

BRETHREN. (*As* BROTHER THOMAS *beats time with his rubber gavel.*) How sweetly
    friendship binds—
Our hearts in brother love
With kindness of forgiving minds—
Life's sweetest pleasures prove.

For fled are hate and harm,

No foe seeks us to kill—
To all we stretch the open arm
Of welcome and good will.
(*Ending with a churchly long-drawn chant.*)
    —Amen.
(*Then all sit down.* DR. FREWD, *an old bearded gentleman wearing a linen duster, springs up in the front row.*)

DR. FREWD. (*Piping out gently.*) Hurrah for the President of the United States! (*And now several of the other Brethren join in likewise, while* BROTHER THOMAS *thumps on the table with his soft gavel.*)

BRETHREN.   Hurrah for Johnny Johnson! (*They begin a gentle clapping.* JOHNNY *smiling kindly at them, shushes them with downward gestures of his hands.*)

THOMAS. (*Bowing to the old bearded brother.*) I'm sorry, Dr. Frewd, but you keep making the same mistake. Johnny is not the President of the United States. (*Turning to* JOHNNY.) Are you, Johnny?

JOHNNY. (*Looking up at the portrait.*) No. (*The* SECRETARY *begins writing in a huge ledger.*)

DR. FREWD. (*Sitting down.*) I stand corrected, sir. (*Then rising again.*) If Johnny Johnson's not the President of these United States, he ought to be. (*The old gentlemen nod an enthusiastic agreement.*)

ANOTHER VOICE.   That's true. As chairman of the ways and means committee I say we ought to elect him.

ANOTHER VOICE.   As ex-secretary of war, I say so.

JOHNNY. (*With kindly firmness.*) You all honor me a lot but— Maybe you'd better get on with the business. (*He resumes his painting.*)

ANOTHER VOICE.   That's right—asylum rules —get on with the business.

THOMAS.   Call the roll, sir.

SECRETARY. (*Intoning above the ledger.*) Brother Claude—

CLAUDE.   Present.

SECRETARY.   Brother George—

GEORGE.   Present.

SECRETARY.   Brother Henry— (*There is no answer, and the members look about them. A man resembling a well-known Senator from the Northwest rises.*)

WILLIAM.   The gentleman from Massachusetts is working on his speech. He will be here at any moment. (*He sits down.*)

A VOICE.   I thought he'd lost his voice in that filibuster.

THOMAS. (*Chuckling as he holds up his gavel.*) As Johnny says—who ever heard of a politician losing his voice?

VOICES.   That's right. Johnny knows.

ANOTHER VOICE.   But I thought Massachusetts had finished speaking. (*A man resembling a certain Senator from the west coast rises in pompous importance.*)

HIRAM.   Like California the old Bay State is never finished. Thar she blows—I mean stands. (*He sits down as* WILLIAM *applauds.*)

SECRETARY. (*With a questioning look at* JOHNNY *which* JOHNNY *answers with a nod.*) Brother Hiram—

HIRAM.   Present.

SECRETARY.   Brother Jim—

JIM.   Present.

SECRETARY. (*With a slight change of tone.*) Brother Theodore— (*A man resembling a certain late President of the United States, with his square teeth and mustache, rises. He has an inflated rubber stick in his hand.*)

THEODORE. (*Waving his stick.*) Both present—me and my stick. (*He bows and sits down.*)

THOMAS.   Read the minutes of the last meeting.

SECRETARY. (*Beginning to intone more sonorously.*) On December the twelfth the Adelphi Debating Society met in weekly session assembled, same being the five hundred and fifteenth meeting of the order, and proceeded to the business of voting upon their final draft of the League of

World Republics. This League was passed by an overwhelming majority—overwhelming majority— (*The door at the left rear opens and a little man resembling a certain late Senator from Massachusetts comes bustling in. Under one arm he carries a load of books and in his hand several sheets of paper.*)

HENRY. (*In a voice hoarse from too much use.*) One moment, gentlemen. (*He comes forward in front of the rostrum and drops his books with a bang. The old gentlemen spring out of their seats with a squeal, and* JOHNNY *looks out at them nodding and smiling, and under his influence they sit down again.*) This infamous league cuts at the very base of our democratic institutions. (*Someone makes a loud raspberry noise and* HENRY *glares about him.*) I am first and foremost an American. I love the American flag, a flag devoted to the principles of liberty, and the pursuit of happiness.

A VOICE. And in this asylum we're all happy.

HENRY. Not only did the great Washington tell us to keep ourselves aloof and inviolable in the service of—

SECRETARY. (*Spontaneously.*) —Liberty. (*He looks about him abashed and begins writing hurriedly in the ledger.*)

HENRY. I challenge these interruptions. (*Picking up a book, opening it and reading.*) "If this damnable document is foisted upon the American people it will mark the beginning and end of our nation." Who said that?

THEODORE. (*Rising again and bowing all around.*) I said it, and you all know me.

HENRY. (*Continuing.*) Gentlemen, if we allowed the sentimentality and romanticism of our President ex-officio—and he is the real author of this covenant— (*Reaching around and shaking hands.*) Hello, Johnny— (*Continuing.*) —allow him to involve us in responsibility for any and every unimportant quarrel in Europe, we would find our strength wasted and the great principles of—

VOICES. (*In unison.*) —Liberty! Sit down!

HENRY. (*Turning towards the members, and stretching out his hands emphatically.*) Under the rules governing this floor I have a right to speak—and I exercise that right in a last appeal to you to use your reason as—as— (*Croaking.*) My voice is failing— I have given my all in the service of my country. (*He staggers and sits down.*)

WILLIAM. Look at this martyr. (*Rising to applaud.*) In his name I move the vote be retaken.

THEODORE. (*Rising.*) Second the motion.

SEVERAL VOICES. No! No!

WILLIAM. The motion's before the house.

THOMAS. Let me speak! (*The* SECRETARY *nods.* HIRAM, THEODORE *and* WILLIAM *murmur to one another in disgruntlement.*) Gentlemen, we've passed this covenant once and let's let it stay passed. As Johnny says, don't chew your tobacco twice.

VOICES. That's right.

WILLIAM. (*Springing up under* HENRY's *urging.*) But under the Constitution we have a right to ask for a recount. (*He sits down.*)

THOMAS. Brethren, it is obvious that a majority of people everywhere want some sort of world co-operation which will bring peace and happiness to mankind—in place of wars and misery which we have had so long.

VOICES. Hear, hear!

THOMAS. The disorganized nations of the earth—frightened, suspicious, hating one another—are waiting for someone to show them the way out of their dilemma. (*Gesturing towards the ledger.*) And in this covenant we show them.

VOICES. We show them.

THOMAS. Every day the need for great statesmanship increases — (*Bowing to* JOHNNY.)—while the terrors of war hang in the air. Remember the pictures Johnny showed us yesterday?—horrible pictures— (*Some of the old gentlemen shudder.*) —Little children all over the world are leaving their toys and their playthings, their marbles and their maypoles, to learn to wear gas masks and sleep in shell- and gas-proof dungeons. In this very town they're doing it.

SEVERAL BRETHREN. (*Covering their faces with their hands.*) Horrible! Horrible!

THEODORE. (*Waving his rubber stick.*) In time of peace prepare for war.

JOHNNY. (*Chuckling.*) Same old argument, Theodore. We answered that the other day, I thought.

SECRETARY. (*Intoning.*) Article nineteen, Section six—inviolability of noncombatants.

THOMAS. Silence, Johnny's going to speak.

VOICES. (*Eagerly.*) That's right, Johnny, tell us a story.

JOHNNY. (*As they listen attentively.*) I'm no speaker. (*Lifting his hand as* THEODORE *starts to interrupt.*) And I've already said what I believe on the subject. But Brother Theodore's old argument about every country having to have a big show-off army and navy to keep peace reminds me of old Mr. Zollicoff's dog. Now that was a good dog—until one day Mr. Zollicoff dressed him up in a brass spiked collar. First thing you know that dog was showing off his spikes and fighting every other dog in the neighborhood. They finally had to kill him with a baseball bat. Now our constitution shows—

VOICES. (*With gentle laughter.*) That's right, Johnny. He speaks straight to the point, don't he?

WILLIAM. We are not talking about dogs, but civilized men. (JOHNNY *smiles, shrugs his shoulders and resumes his work.*)

THOMAS. The Chair feels that men are same as dogs—when they start fighting one another. (*He looks at* JOHNNY *for confirmation.*) History shows it.

DR. FREWD. I beg to report that in this asylum we are civilized men. Put it in the minutes. (*He sits down amid applause.*)

THEODORE. (*Doggedly.*) Let's vote.

THOMAS. (*Bowing in resignation.*) All in favor of the League of World Republics as laid down— (*Gesturing towards the ledger.*) —in our Constitution please signify the same by rising. (*The majority of the brethren rise.* JOHNNY *keeps his seat.*)

SECRETARY. (*Beginning to count.*) One— two — three — four — five — six — seven — (JOHNNY *leans over and whispers to* THOMAS.)

THOMAS. Will the gentleman from California there in the rear kindly make his vote clear? He seems to be in a crouching position.

HIRAM. (*Straightening up.*) I—I—all right, I'll vote for it, but I'll have a hard time explaining it to the folks back home.

THEODORE. (*Staring at him.*) You—you've sold Brother Henry out.

HIRAM. (*Now rising in recovered dignity.*) I was offered a price but I didn't sell.

HENRY. (*Springing up and croaking.*) As Abe Lincoln said—let the American people speak. And they won't accept your verdict. I've got a hundred postal cards— (*Feeling in his pocket.*) —and I'm going to flood the country—

VOICES. Sit down! (*He stands wavering an instant and then collapses in his chair.*)

JOHNNY. (*Gently but firmly as he stands up.*) I think now we ought to make it unanimous, boys. What do you say, Henry? (HENRY *makes no answer.*) You'd feel better if you joined in. We've done a lot of good work here, and we've got a lot more to do. We all need to pull together.

SECRETARY. Section forty-three—pull together.

JOHNNY. And you need to do it too—for your own good. Think how much happier all of us are since we started to work at something that interested us. We've forgot our own troubles and we eat better, sleep better. And besides if we don't take up these big problems, who will? In the outside world they don't seem to be interested any more. (*He looks smilingly at* HENRY.) Come on now.

HENRY. (*Croaking gruffly.*) No, no.

THOMAS. Dr. Frewd will just have to analyze him some more—I reckon. (HENRY *cowers in his seat as* DR. FREWD *steps nimbly to his side and begins a crouching down and lifting up pantomime. The brethren, with the exception of* THOMAS *and* JOHNNY, *crowd around.*)

HENRY. (*In a pleading mumble.*) No—no —I'm a free individual—I'm— (*But as if against his will he is finally lifted to his feet. He receives their plaudits and handshakings with bowed head and deep emotion.*)

THOMAS. (*Happily.*) The League of World Republics is passed unanimously. This is an historic hour. (*Loud applause.*)

DR. FREWD. (*Crying out.*) Hurrah for the League!

OLD GENTLEMEN. (*Loudly.*) Hurrah! (THOMAS *thumps with his rubber gavel.*)

THOMAS. We're making a little too much noise, brethren.

VOICES. All right.

THOMAS. The new chairman of the board is inspecting the hospital this morning and we want everything quiet.

SECRETARY. And he's a millionaire too.

VOICE. (*From the rear.*) We don't like millionaires.

ANOTHER VOICE. No, we don't.

JOHNNY. Millionaires ain't so bad, fellows. They have their troubles too as the lap dog said.

DR. FREWD. Hurrah for peace.

ANOTHER VOICE. Hurrah for peace! (DR. FREWD *stands up and lifting his arms begins to lead them in a song.*)

BRETHREN. (*Singing as in a round, with* THOMAS *and the clerk joining in.*) Come let
us hymn a hymn to peace,
Jollily, merrily we will sing—
Loudly proclaiming wars shall cease,
Hark ye, how the bells go ting-ling-ling—
(*The guard at the right front reaches out on the wall and turns on a radio. A gentle and sleepy requiem is heard playing.*

Gradually the brethren stop their singing and sit down in their seats as if feeling the drowsy spell of some opiate.)

JOHNNY. (*Resuming his work.*) That's right—rest a while—listen to the soft music —listen and rest a while—

THOMAS. (*Mumbling.*) The next question before the house is—Capital and Labor— Section one— (*He sinks down into his seat.*) —the man who works must share in—share in— (*He bows his head over on the table. And now all the old men likewise bow their heads over and go to sleep.* JOHNNY *sits working at his toy as the scene of the Adelphi Debating Society begins to dim out. The soft music continues to play for a moment and then it too dies gradually away.*

Now entering slowly and dreamily from the right come the group of hospital directors on their tour of inspection. In front walks ANGUISH HOWINGTON, *carrying a cane and wearing a top silk hat, and by his side walks a young clinical-faced* DOCTOR. *Behind* ANGUISH *and the* DOCTOR *come five or six stout and well-dressed business men, a few orderlies, and a young man secretary dressed in a Crystal Mineral Water uniform.*)

DOCTOR. (*Gesturing to the rear where only* JOHNNY *now is visible.*) —And here we have developed a little debating society where some of our elderly patients engage in harmless talk.

ANGUISH. (*Softly, mechanically, and almost dreamily.*) Interesting idea.

DOCTOR. Owing to our limited means the equipment is poor, as you see.

ANGUISH. (*To his secretary.*) Make a note of that. (*The young man writes on his pad.*)

DOCTOR. Thank you, sir, thank you, sir. You have already been very generous.

ANGUISH. And Mrs. Howington and I will continue to be so. She has a deep interest in this institution.

DOCTOR. For which we are very grateful. I may mention that all of our staff use Crystal Mineral Water nightly— Before retiring we do so. (*Slightly bowing.*) We find it very helpful.

ANGUISH. (*Stiffening with a sense of greatness.*) Millions find it helpful in these disordered times. (*Staring towards the rear.*) Adelphi Debating Society—I used to belong to a society with the same name—in the old days. It wasn't very peaceful though. There was a fellow—Johnson— He was always creating friction. (*His voice dies out.*)

DOCTOR. But the founder of this society— you see him there—seems to be able to keep peace. In fact we have finally diagnosed his disease as peace monomania.

ANGUISH. Is it dangerous?

DOCTOR. (*Gravely.*) Oh no—I shouldn't say so.

ANGUISH. (*Still gazing towards the rear.*) That fellow's face looks familiar.

DOCTOR. His name is Johnson too—Johnny Johnson.

ANGUISH. Oh yes. Yes, I remember now.

DOCTOR. We are thinking of letting him out in a few days.

ANGUISH. (*Quickly.*) Do you think it is safe?

DOCTOR. Oh quite, quite. It will be a loss to us too. He has a way with the patients— (*Hurriedly.*) I mean everybody likes him. (*Far off in the distance a musical gong begins to sound. The light comes up on the scene in the rear as if in time to the notes, and the old gentlemen rise sleepily from their chairs. The two attendants step over and stand by the little gate that opens in the railing and* JOHNNY, *carrying his basket of toys and accompanied by the* SECRETARY *with the great ledger, leads them out.* ANGUISH *and the directors move slowly on across the foreground to the left.*)

ANGUISH. (*Pointing off down the hall.*) Those bars seem rather frail and old.

DOCTOR. They are, sir.

ANGUISH. (*To the young fellow behind him with the pad.*) Make a note of that.

DOCTOR. Thank you, sir. (*At the sound of* ANGUISH'S *voice* JOHNNY *stops, and the* SECRETARY *and the old gentlemen move away at the right with the two attendants, leaving him behind. Suddenly he runs forward and pulls* ANGUISH *by the arm.*)

JOHNNY. (*As* ANGUISH *turns coldly and puppetlike around.*) Why, I hardly knew you, Anguish, in all them duds. (*The orderlies spring back and surround* ANGUISH.)

ANGUISH. (*Manfully.*) Never mind, my men—

JOHNNY. (*Hesitating.*) Tell me—have you got any news—about Minny Belle, I mean?

ANGUISH. (*Pondering a moment gravely.*) She's—er—well—very well.

JOHNNY. Golly, I'm glad to hear that. It's been so long since—I heard. (*Staring off an instant as if caught in a vague worry and then smiling around at* ANGUISH.) She must be awful busy—yeh—tell her I will be seeing her—I hope—soon.

ANGUISH. (*After a cruel and genteel pause.*) You don't keep up with what is going on, do you?

JOHNNY. Well, we get the *International Digest* and that gives us the world news.

ANGUISH. (*Coldly.*) Miss Tompkins did me the honor some years ago of accepting my hand in marriage. (*He bows and moves on accompanied by the* DOCTOR, *the directors and attendants. As he goes out he points quietly towards Wilson's portrait with his cane.*) That picture there should be removed.

DOCTOR. It shall be sir, at once. (*They all disappear at the left.* JOHNNY *stands with bent head looking at the floor. A moment passes and an* ATTENDANT *comes hurriedly in from the right.*)

ATTENDANT. Say, it's against the rules— even for you, Johnny—to fall out like this Lunch is ready. (*He takes* JOHNNY *by the arm and then stares at him.*) You look kind of sick—anything wrong? (*JOHNNY makes no answer but continues looking at the floor. The* ATTENDANT, *touched by something in his face, speaks kindly to him.*) Can I get a doctor? (*Gazing carefully about him.*) You can trust me.

JOHNNY. (*Murmuring.*) No, thanks.

ATTENDANT. (*A little more confidentially.*) I've got some good news for you, Johnny. You're going to be let out of here next week. It's a secret, but we know it. Don't it make you feel better?

JOHNNY. (*Shaking his head.*) No, I guess I'll—I'll stay here—now.

ATTENDANT. What!

JOHNNY. All—my friends—are here—my work too.

ATTENDANT. Yeh, but when they say you're ready to leave you got to leave. That's the law. (JOHNNY *says nothing, and the* ATTENDANT, *taking him by the arm, leads him away at the right.*)

BLACK OUT

SCENE III

"Whither have ye made a road?"

The scene is a street corner—projecting diagonally in at the right front. Stretching along the right towards the rear is an evergreen hedge with an imposing iron gate marked "Private." Behind the hedge in the distance and showing through the leafless winter trees is the high rim of a great pennanted stadium cutting horizontally across the sky. It is viewed from the rear, and from over this rim now and then comes the muted trumpet sound of a high hoarse hysterical voice haranguing a multitude. The words are cacophonous and are applauded now and then by a burst of martial band music, beaten drum, or the husky rainy-sounding cheers of thousands. Over at the left front is the corner of a red brick factory-like building.

When the curtain rises, JOHNNY JOHNSON— *now a man of forty-five or fifty but looking much older, though his face and manner are still cheery—is standing by a lightless iron lamp-post looking out before him. He is dressed in non-descript clothes, an old shapeless gray felt hat, a work shirt, dark coat and trousers, and heavy well-worn walking shoes. Hung by a string around his neck and held in front of him is a little tray like that with which street hawkers pursue their calling. Stray passersby on their way to the stadium go down the street at the right every now and then.*

JOHNNY. (*Keeping a watchful eye for any prospective customer as he sends his voice across the scene in a quavering call.*) Toy-ees! Toy-ees for sale! (*He waits a moment, looking about him and wiggling his feet to keep them warm. Then he calls again.*) Toy-ees! (*And now coming down through the great iron gate is a little* BOY *about twelve years old, dressed in the new uniform of a boy scout. He stops and looks behind him.*)

BOY. (*Calling.*) Can I give the old man a nickel, Mother?

A WOMAN'S VOICE. (*Beyond the gate.*) Remember, nickels make dollars—as daddy says.

BOY. But I haven't done my scout's good deed for today. (MINNY BELLE *comes suddenly out through the gate. She is wrapped in furs and somewhat stout.*) May I, Mother?

MINNY BELLE. We're already late for the parade. (*She starts on down the street at the left rear.*)

JOHNNY. (*Calling.*) Nice little toy-ees for nice little girls and boy-ees! (*As if touched by some faint and far-off remembrance* MINNY BELLE *stops. She slowly and abstractedly opens her purse.*)

MINNY BELLE. All right, give him a nickel— He looks cold. (*The* BOY *takes the nickel and comes over to* JOHNNY.)

BOY. (*Touching* JOHNNY *on the arm.*) Here's the nickel, sir.

JOHNNY. What do you want?—A monkey or a dove?—Maybe this little terrapin. See —he can wiggle his legs when you pull the string. Look.

BOY. (*Appraisingly.*) Hmn— Maybe I might take a toy soldier.

JOHNNY. (*Sternly.*) No—no—I don't make soldiers.

BOY. Then I don't want anything.

JOHNNY. Here's your nickel.

BOY. Oh no, you must keep the nickel anyway. My daddy's rich.

JOHNNY. (*Smiling.*) Is he?—That's nice. What's your name, son?

BOY. Anguish Howington, Junior.

JOHNNY. (*After a moment's silence.*) That's a nice name. (*And now as if conscious that* MINNY BELLE *is there in the distance he pulls up his coat collar and turns his face slightly away.*)

ANGUISH, JR. I'm named after my father. He's mayor of the town, you know.

JOHNNY. Is he? That's wonderful. I'm a sort of stranger here— So he's mayor of the town? And you're a boy scout?

ANGUISH, JR. Yes sir. And some day I'm going to be a soldier.

JOHNNY. (*Quickly.*) No, I wouldn't be that.

ANGUISH, JR. Why not?

JOHNNY. You could be—well, you could make things—or be a great doctor—or a good farmer—do something that would be of use to the world.

ANGUISH, JR. But daddy says that we're in for a terrible war and all the people have got to be ready to keep the enemy from destroying us.

JOHNNY. (*Staring out before him.*) Ah—

MINNY BELLE. (*Calling.*) Come on!

JOHNNY. And—and how is your mother, son?

ANGUISH, JR. Why, she's all right. She's standing right over there. (*But* JOHNNY *keeps looking before him.*) Goodbye.

JOHNNY. (*In a muffled voice.*) Goodbye, son. (*Little* ANGUISH *turns and runs back to his mother, elated by his charitable act.*

MINNY BELLE *takes him by the hand and they go away at the left rear.* JOHNNY *gazes at the nickel in his hand and then raises his voice again in a call.*) Toy-ees for sale! Nice little— (*His voice dies out and he stands staring before him. And now blaring suddenly in the air nearby, comes a sound of a brass band playing the "Democracy March."* JOHNNY *still stands gazing before him. The rat-tat-tat-tat of the drums comes near him, and crossing the scene at the extreme left rear is the American Legion Drum Corps with a few bugles and pieces of brass. Two boy scout flag-bearers go before, and behind them, several young men and women carrying banners and placards —"America First," "Be Prepared," and so forth. The parade passes on like a vision in a, dream, but* JOHNNY *still looks before him with his old man's face and unblinking eyes. He shivers a bit, and his shoulders seem to sag. By this time the gloom of approaching twilight has spread over the scene. The street lamp above his head gradually lights up, casting its nebulous halo over his shabby figure standing motionless as stone. Suddenly he begins to whistle low and aimlessly to himself—the theme melody of the play. For a moment he continues whistling; then giving his shoulders the faintest touch of a shrug, he turns and starts down the long street. He looks up now and then at the row of silent houses on his right.*) Toy-ees! Toy-ees— for nice little girls and boys! (*But nobody answers, no windows are opened, no smiling youthful faces appear, for all are gathered into the great stadium in the distance where the drear outlandish haranguer voice can still be heard continuing its queer clamor to the sky—"Gog-a-gog—Magog-a-gog." Yet even so,* JOHNNY JOHNSON *is not hushed by this strange voice booming through the world. As he disappears down the long street that leads from the great city into the country and beyond, he begins whistling his song again—a little more clearly now, a little more bravely.*)

CURTAIN.

The Green Pastures

A Fable

SUGGESTED BY ROARK BRADFORD'S SOUTHERN
SKETCHES, "OL' MAN ADAM AN' HIS CHILLUN"
BY MARC CONNELLY

TO MY MOTHER

Produced by Lawrence Rivers at the Mansfield Theatre, New York, February 26, 1930.

CHARACTERS

MR. DESHEE, the Preacher
MYRTLE
FIRST BOY
SECOND BOY
FIRST COOK
A VOICE
SECOND COOK
FIRST MAN ANGEL
FIRST MAMMY ANGEL
A STOUT ANGEL
A SLENDER ANGEL
ARCHANGEL
GABRIEL
GOD
CHOIR LEADER
CUSTARD MAKER
ADAM
EVE
CAIN
CAIN'S GIRL

ZEBA
CAIN THE SIXTH
BOY GAMBLER
GENERAL
HEAD MAGICIAN
FIRST WIZARD
SECOND WIZARD
JOSHUA
FIRST SCOUT
MASTER OF CEREMONIES
FIRST GAMBLER
SECOND GAMBLER
VOICE IN SHANTY
NOAH
NOAH'S WIFE
SHEM
FIRST WOMAN
SECOND WOMAN
THIRD WOMAN

FIRST MAN
FLATFOOT
HAM
JAPHETH
FIRST CLEANER
SECOND CLEANER
ABRAHAM
ISAAC
JACOB
MOSES
ZIPPORAH
AARON
A CANDIDATE MAGICIAN
PHARAOH
KING OF BABYLON
PROPHET
HIGH PRIEST
CORPORAL
HEZDREL
SECOND OFFICER

SCENES

Part I

1. The Sunday School
2. A Fish Fry
3. A Garden
4. Outside the Garden
5. A Roadside

6. A Private Office
7. Another Roadside and a House
8. A House
9. A Hillside
10. A Mountain Top

Part II

1. The Private Office
2. The Mouth of a Cave
3. A Throne Room
4. The Foot of a Mountain

5. A Cabaret
6. The Private Office
7. Outside a Temple
8. Another Fish Fry

PART ONE

SCENE I

A corner in a Negro church.

Ten children and an elderly preacher.

The costumes are those that might be seen in any lower Louisiana town at Sunday-School time. As the curtain rises, MR. DESHEE, the preacher, is reading from a Bible. The CHILDREN are listening with varied degrees of interest. Three or four are wide-eyed in their attention. Two or three are obviously puzzled, but interested, and the smallest ones are engaged in more physical concerns. One is playing with a little doll, and another runs his fingers on all the angles of his chair.

DESHEE. "An' Adam lived a hundred and thirty years, an' begat a son in his own likeness, after his image; an' called his name Seth. An' de days of Adam, after he had begotten Seth, were eight hundred years; an' he begat sons an' daughters; an' all de days dat Adam lived were nine hundred an' thirty years; an' he died. An' Seth lived a hundred an' five years an' begat Enos; an' Seth lived after he begat Enos eight hundred an' seven years and begat sons and daughters. An' all de days of Seth were nine hundred and twelve years; an' he died." An' it go on like dat till we come to Enoch an' de book say: "An' Enoch lived sixty an' five years and begat Methuselah." Den it say: "An' all de days of Methuselah were nine hundred an' sixty an' nine years an' he died." An' dat was de oldest man dat ever was. Dat's why we call ol' Mr. Gurney's mammy ol' Mrs. Methuselah, caize she's so ol'. Den a little later it tell about another member of de fam'ly. His name was Noah. Maybe some of you know about him already. I'm gonter tell you all about him next Sunday. Anyway dat's de meat an' substance of de first five chapters of Genesis. Now, how you think you gonter like de Bible?

MYRTLE. I think it's jest wonderful, Mr. Deshee. I cain't understand any of it.

FIRST BOY. Why did dey live so long, Mr. Deshee?

DESHEE. Why? Caize dat was de way God felt.

SECOND BOY. Dat made Adam a way back

DESHEE. Yes, he certainly 'way back by de time Noah come along. Want to ask me any mo' questions?

SECOND BOY. What de worl' look like when de Lawd begin, Mr. Deshee.

DESHEE. How yo' mean what it look like?

MYRTLE. Carlisle mean who was in N'Orleans den.

DESHEE. Dey wasn't nobody in N'Orleans on 'count dey wasn't any N'Orleans. Dat's de whole idea I tol' you at de end of de first Chapter. Yo' got to git yo' minds fixed. Dey wasn't any Rampart Street. Dey wasn't any Canal Street. Dey wasn't any Louisiana. Dey wasn't nothin' on de earth at all caize fo' de reason dey wasn't any earth.

MYRTLE. Yes, but what Carlisle wanter know is—

DESHEE......(*Interrupting and addressing little boy who has been playing with his chair and paying no attention.*) Now Randolph, if you don't listen, how yo' gonter grow up an' be a good man? Yo' wanter grow up an' be a transgressor?

LITTLE BOY. (*Frightened.*) No.

DESHEE. You tell yo' mammy yo' sister got to come wid you next time. She kin git de things done in time to bring you to de school. You content yo'self. (*The little boy straightens up in his chair.*) Now, what do Carlisle want to know?

CARLISLE. How he decide he want de worl' to be right yere and how he git de idea he wanted it?

MYRTLE. Caize de Book say, don't it, Mr. Deshee?

DESHEE. De Book say, but at de same time dat's a good question. I remember when I was a little boy de same thing recurred to me. An ol' Mr. Dubois, he was a wonderful preacher at New Hope Chapel over in East Gretna, he said: "De answer is dat de Book ain't got time to go into

192

all de details." And he was right. You know sometimes I think de Lawd expects us to figure out a few things for ourselves. We know that at one time dey wasn't anything except Heaven, we don't know jest where it was but we know it was dere. Maybe it was everywhere. Den one day de Lawd got the idea he'd like to make some places. He made de sun and de moon, de stars. An' he made de earth.

MYRTLE. Who was aroun' den, nothin' but angels?

DESHEE. I suppose so.

FIRST BOY. What was de angels doin' up dere?

DESHEE. I suppose dey jest flew aroun' and had a good time. Dey wasn't no sin, so dey musta had a good time.

FIRST BOY. Did dey have picnics?

DESHEE. Sho, dey had the nicest kind of picnics. Dey probably had fish frys, wid b'iled custard and ten cent seegars for de adults. God gives us humans lotsa ideas about havin' good times. Maybe dey were things he'd seen de angels do. Yes, sir, I bet dey had a fish fry every week.

MYRTLE. Did dey have Sunday School, too?

DESHEE. Yes, dey musta had Sunday School for de cherubs.

MYRTLE. What did God look like, Mr. Deshee?

DESHEE. Well, nobody knows exactly what God looked like. But when I was a little boy I used to imagine dat he looked like de Reverend Dubois. He was de finest looking ol' man I ever knew. Yes, I used to bet de Lawd looked exactly like Mr. Dubois in de days when he walked de earth in de shape of a natchel man.

MYRTLE. When was dat, Mr. Deshee?

DESHEE. Why, when He was gettin' things started down heah. When He talked to Adam and Eve and Noah and Moses and all dem. He made mighty men in dem days. But aldo they was awful mighty dey always knew dat He was beyond dem all. Pretty near one o'clock, time fo' you chillun to go home to dinner, but before I let you go I wan' you to go over wid me de main facts of de first lesson. What's de name of de book?

CHILDREN. Genesis.

DESHEE. Dat's right. And what's de other name?

CHILDREN. First Book of Moses.

DESHEE. Dat's right. And dis yere's Chapter One. (*The lights begin to dim.*) "In de beginnin' God created de heaven an' de earth. An' de earth was widout form an' void. An' de darkness was upon de face of de deep."

SCENE II

In the darkness many voices are heard singing "Rise, Shine, Give God The Glory." They sing it gayly and rapidly. The lights go up as the second verse ends. The chorus is being sung diminuendo by a mixed company of angels. That is they are angels in that they wear brightly colored robes and have wings protruding from their backs. Otherwise they look and act like a company of happy negroes at a fish fry. The scene itself is a pre-Creation Heaven with compromises. In the distance is an unbroken stretch of blue sky. Companionable varicolored clouds billow down to the floor of the stage and roll overhead to the branches of a live oak tree which is up left. The tree is leafy and dripping with Spanish moss and with the clouds makes a frame for the scene. In the cool shade of the tree are the usual appurtenances of a fish fry a large kettle of hot fat set on two small parallel logs, with a fire going underneath, and a large rustic table formed by driving four stakes into the ground and placing planks on top of the small connecting boards. On the table are piles of biscuits and corn bread and the cooked fish in dish pans. There are one or two fairly large cedar or crock "churns" containing boiled custard, which looks like milk. There is a gourd dipper beside the churns and several glasses and cups of various sizes and shapes from which the custard is drunk.*

The principal singers are marching two by two in a small area at the R. *of the stage. Two* MAMMY ANGELS *are attending to the frying beside the kettle. Behind the table a* MAN ANGEL *is skinning fish and passing them to the cooks. Another is ladling out the custard. A* MAMMY ANGEL *is putting fish on bread for a brood of cherubs, and during the first scene they seat themselves on a grassy bank upstage. Another* MAMMY ANGEL *is clapping her hands disapprovingly and beckoning a laughing* BOY CHERUB *down from a cloud a little out of her reach. Another* MAMMY ANGEL *is solicitously slapping the back of a girl cherub who has a large fish sandwich in her hand and a bone in her throat. There is much movement about the table, and during the first few minutes several individuals go up to the table to help themselves to the food and drink. Many of the women angels wear hats and a few of the men are smoking cigars. A large boxful is on the table. There is much laughter and chatter as the music softens, but continues, during the early part of the action. The following short scenes are played almost simultaneously.*

FIRST COOK. (*At Kettle*) (*Calling off*) Hurry up, Cajey. Dis yere fat's cryin' fo' mo' feesh.

A VOICE. (*Off stage.*) We comin', fas' we kin. Dey got to be ketched, ain't dey? We cain't say. "C'm'on little fish. C'm'on an' git fried," kin we?

SECOND COOK. (*At Table.*) De trouble is de mens is all worm fishin'.

FIRST MAN ANGEL. (*At Table*) Whut dif'runce do it make? Yo' all de time got to make out like somebody's doin' somethin' de wrong way.

SECOND COOK. (*Near Table*) I s'pose you got de per'fec' way fo' makin' bait.

FIRST MAN ANGEL. I ain't sayin' dat. I is sayin' whut's wrong wid worm fishin'.

SECOND COOK. Whut's wrong wid worm fishin'? Ever'thing, dat's all. Dey's only one good way fo' catfishin', an' dat's minny fishin'. Anybody know dat.

FIRST MAN ANGEL. Well, it jest so happen dat minny fishin' is de doggondest fool way

of fishin' dey is. You kin try minny fishin' to de cows come home an' all you catch'll be de backache. De trouble wid you, sister, is you jest got minny fishin' on de brain.

SECOND COOK. Go right on, loud mouf. You tell me de news. My, my! You jest de wisest person in de worl'. First you, den de Lawd God.

FIRST MAN ANGEL. (*To the custard ladler.*) You cain't tell dem nothin'. (*Walks away to the custard churn.*) Does you try to 'splain some simple fac' dey git man-deaf.

FIRST MAMMY ANGEL. (*To* CHERUB *on the cloud.*) Now, you heerd me. (*The* CHERUB *assumes several mocking poses, as she speaks.*) You fly down yere. You wanter be put down in de sin book? (*She goes to the table, gets a drink for herself and points out the cherub to one of the men behind the table.*) Dat baby must got imp blood in him he so vexin'. (*She returns to her position under the cloud.*) You want me to fly up dere an' slap you down? Now, I tol' you. (*The* CHERUB *starts to come down.*)

STOUT ANGEL. (*To the* CHERUB *with a bone in her throat.*) I tol' you you was too little fo' cat fish. What you wanter git a bone in yo' froat fo'? (*She slaps the* CHERUB'S *back.*)

SLENDER ANGEL. (*Leisurely eating a sandwich as she watches the back-slapping.*) What de trouble wid Leonetta?

STOUT ANGEL. She got a catfish bone down her froat. (*To the* CHERUB.) Doggone, I tol' you to eat grinnel instead.

SLENDER ANGEL. Ef'n she do git all dat et, she gonter have de bellyache.

STOUT ANGEL. Ain't I tol' her dat? (*To* CHERUB.) Come on now; let go dat bone. (*She slaps* CHERUB'S *back again. The bone is dislodged and the* CHERUB *grins her relief.*) Dat's good.

SLENDER ANGEL. (*Comfortingly.*) Now she all right.

STOUT ANGEL. Go on an' play wid yo' cousins. (*The* CHERUB *joins the* CHERUBS *sitting on the embankment. The concurrency of scenes ends here.*) I ain't see you lately, Lily. How you been?

SLENDER ANGEL. Me, I'm fine. I been visitin' my mammy. She waitin' on de welcome table over by de throne of grace.

STOUT ANGEL. She always was pretty holy.

SLENDER ANGEL. Yes, ma'am. She like it dere. I guess de Lawd's took quite a fancy to her.

STOUT ANGEL. Well, dat's natural. I declare yo' mammy one of de finest lady angels I know.

SLENDER ANGEL. She claim you de best one she know.

STOUT ANGEL. Well, when you come right down to it, I suppose we is all pretty near perfec'.

SLENDER ANGEL. Yes, ma'am. Why is dat, Mis' Jenny?

STOUT ANGEL. I s'pose it's caize de Lawd he don' 'low us 'sociatin' wid de devil any mo' so dat dey cain' be no mo' sinnin'.

SLENDER ANGEL. Po' ol' Satan. Whutevah become of him?

STOUT ANGEL. De Lawd put him some place I s'pose.

SLENDER ANGEL. But dey ain't any place but Heaven, is dey?

STOUT ANGEL. De Lawd could make a place, couldn't he?

SLENDER ANGEL. Dat's de truth. Dey's one thing confuses me though.

STOUT ANGEL. What's dat?

SLENDER ANGEL. I do a great deal of travelin' an' I ain't never come across any place but Heaven anywhere. So if de Lawd kick Satan out of Heaven jest whereat did he go? Dat's my question.

STOUT ANGEL. You bettah let de Lawd keep his own secrets, Lily. De way things is goin' now dey ain't' been no sinnin' since dey give dat scamp a kick in de pants. Nowadays Heaven's free of sin an' if a lady wants a little constitutional she

kin fly 'til she wing-weary widout gittin' insulted.

SLENDER ANGEL. I was jest a baby when Satan lef'. I don't even 'member what he look like.

STOUT ANGEL. He was jest right fo' a devil. (*An* ARCHANGEL *enters. He is older than the others and wears a white beard. His clothing is much darker than that of the others and his wings a trifle more imposing.*) Good mo'nin', Archangel. (*Others say good morning.*)

ARCHANGEL. Good mo'nin'', folks. I wonder kin I interrup' de fish fry an' give out de Sunday school cyards? (*Cries of "Suttingly!" "Mah goodness, yes"—etc. The marching* CHOIR *stops.*) You kin keep singin' if you want to. Why don' you sing "When de Saints Come Marchin' In?" Seem to me I ain' heard dat lately. (*The* CHOIR *begins "When the Saints Come Marching In", rather softly, but does not resume marching. The* ARCHANGEL *looks off left.*) All right, bring 'em yere. (*A prim looking* WOMAN TEACHER-ANGEL *enters, shepherding ten* BOY *and* GIRL CHERUBS. *The* TEACHER *carries ten beribboned diplomas, which she gives to the* ARCHANGEL. *The* CHERUBS *are dressed in stiffly starched white suits and dresses, the little girls having enormous ribbons at the backs of their dresses and smaller ones in their hair and on the tips of their wings. They line up in front of the archangel and receive the attention of the rest of the company. The* CHOIR *sings through the ceremony.*) Now den cherubs, why is you yere?

CHILDREN. Because we so good.

ARCHANGEL. Dat's right. Now who de big boss?

CHILDREN. Our dear Lawd.

ARCHANGEL. Dat's right. When you all grow up what you gonter be?

CHILDREN. Holy angels at de throne of grace.

ARCHANGEL. Dat's right. Now, you passed yo' 'xaminations and it gives me great pleasure to hand out de cyards for de whole class. Gineeva Chaproe. (*The* FIRST GIRL

CHERUB *goes to him and gets her diploma. The* CHOIR *sings loudly and resumes marching, as the* ARCHANGEL *calls out another name—and presents diplomas.*) Corey Moulter. (SECOND GIRL CHERUB *gets her diploma.*) Nootzie Winebush. (THIRD GIRL CHERUB.) Harriet Prancy. (FOURTH GIRL CHERUB.) I guess you is Brozain Stew't. (*He gives the* FIFTH GIRL CHERUB *the paper. Each of the presentations has been accompanied by hand-clapping from the bystanders.*) Now you boys know yo' own names. Suppose you come yere and help me git dese 'sorted right? (BOY CHERUBS *gather about him and receive their diplomas. The little* GIRLS *have scattered about the stage, joining groups of the adult angels. The angel* GABRIEL *enters. He is bigger and more elaborately winged than even the* ARCHANGEL, *but he is also much younger and beardless. His costume is less conventional than that of the other men, resembling more the* GABRIEL *of the Doré drawings. His appearance causes a flutter among the others. They stop their chattering with the children. The* CHOIR *stops as three or four audible whispers of "GABRIEL!" are heard. In a moment the heavenly company is all attention.*)

GABRIEL. (*Lifting his hand.*) Gangway! Gangway for de Lawd God Jehovah! (*There is a reverent hush and* GOD *enters. He is the tallest and biggest of them all. He wears a white shirt with a white bow tie, a long Prince Albert coat of black alpaca, black trousers and congress gaiters. He looks at the assemblage. There is a pause. He speaks in a rich, bass voice.*)

GOD. Is you been baptized?

OTHERS. (*Chanting.*) Certainly, Lawd.

GOD. Is you been baptized?

OTHERS. Certainly, Lawd.

GOD. (*With the beginning of musical notation.*) Is you been baptized?

OTHERS. (*Now half-singing.*) Certainly, Lawd. Certainly, certainly, certainly, Lawd. (*They sing the last two verses with equivalent part division.*)
  Is you been redeemed?
  Certainly, Lawd.
  Is you been redeemed?

  Certainly, Lawd.
  Is you been redeemed?
  Certainly, Lawd. Certainly, certainly,
    certainly, Lawd.
  Do you bow mighty low?
  Certainly, Lawd.
  Do you bow mighty low?
  Certainly, Lawd.
  Do you bow mighty low?
  Certainly, Lawd. Certainly, certainly,
    certainly, Lawd.
(*As the last response ends all heads are bowed.* GOD *looks at them for a moment; then lifts His hand.*)

GOD. Let de fish fry proceed. (EVERYONE *rises. The* ANGELS *relax and resume their inaudible conversations. The activity behind the table and about the cauldron is resumed. Some of the choir members cross to the table and get sandwiches and cups of the boiled custard. Three or four of the children in the Sunday School class and the little girl who had the bone in her throat affectionately group themselves about* GOD *as he speaks with the* ARCHANGEL. *He pats their heads, they hang to his coat-tails, etc.*)

ARCHANGEL. Good mo'nin', Lawd.

GOD. Good mo'nin', Deacon. You lookin pretty spry.

ARCHANGEL. I cain' complain. We jus' been givin' our cyards to de chillun.

GOD. Dat's good. (*A small* CHERUB, *his feet braced against one of* GOD's *shoes is using* GOD's *coat tail as a trapeze. One of the* COOKS *offers a fish sandwich which* GOD *politely declines.*)

FIRST MAMMY ANGEL. Now, you leave go de Lawd's coat, Herman. You heah me?

GOD. Dat's all right, sister. He jest playin'

FIRST MAMMY ANGEL. He playin' too rough. (GOD *picks up the* CHERUB *and spanks him good-naturedly. The* CHERUB *squeals with delight and runs to his mother.* GABRIEL *advances to* GOD *with a glass of the custard.*)

GABRIEL. Little b'iled custud, Lawd?

GOD. Thank you very kindly. Dis look nice.

CUSTARD MAKER. (*Offering a box.*) Ten cent seegar, Lawd?

GOD.....(*Taking it.*) Thank you, thank you. How de fish fry goin'? (*Ad lib. cries of* "O. K. Lawd," "Fine an' dandy, Lawd," "De best one yit, Lawd," *etc*. *To the* CHOIR.) How you shouters gittin' on?

CHOIR LEADER. We been marchin' and singin' de whole mo'nin'.

GOD. I heerd you. You gittin' better all de time. You gittin' as good as de one at de throne. Why don' you give us one dem ol' time jump-ups?

CHOIR LEADER. Anythin' you say, Lawd. (*To the others.*) "So High!" (*The* CHOIR *begins to sing* "So High You Can't Get Over It." *They sing softly, but do not march. An* ANGEL *offers his cigar to* GOD *from which He can light His own.*)

GOD. No, thanks. I'm gonter save dis a bit. (*He puts the cigar in his pocket and listens to the singers a moment. Then he sips his custard. After the second sip, a look of displeasure comes on his face.*)

GABRIEL. What's de matter, Lawd?

GOD. (*Sipping again.*) I ain't jest sure, yit. Dey's something 'bout dis custahd. (*Takes another sip.*)

CUSTARD MAKER. Ain't it all right, Lawd?

GOD. It don't seem seasoned jest right. You make it?

CUSTARD MAKER. Yes, Lawd. I put every-hin' in it like I allus do. It's' supposed o be perfec'.

GOD. Yeah. I kin taste de eggs and de cream and de sugar. (*Suddenly.*) I know what it is. It needs jest a little bit mo' firmament.

CUSTARD MAKER. Dey's firmament in it, Lawd.

GOD. Maybe, but it ain' enough.

CUSTARD MAKER. It's all we had, Lawd. Dey ain't a drap in de jug.

GOD. Dat's all right. I'll jest r'ar back an' pass a miracle. (CHOIR *stops singing.*) Let t be some firmament! An' when I say

let it be some firmament, I don't want jest a little bitty dab o' firmament caize I'm sick an' tired of runnin' out of it when we need it. Let it be a whole mess of firmament! (*The stage has become misty until* GOD *and the heavenly company are obscured. As he finishes the speech there is a burst of thunder. As the stage grows darker.*) Dat's de way I like it. (*Murmurs from the others*; "Dat's a lot of firmament." "My, dat is firmament!" "Look to me like he's created rain," *etc.*)

FIRST MAMMY ANGEL. (*When the stage is dark.*) Now, look Lawd, dat's too much firmament. De cherubs is gettin' all wet.

SECOND MAMMY ANGEL. Look at my Carlotta, Lawd. She's soaked to de skin. Dat's *plenty* too much firmament.

GOD. Well, 'co'se we don't want de chillun to ketch cold. Can't you dreen it off?

GABRIEL. Dey's no place to dreen it, Lawd.

FIRST MAMMY ANGEL. Why don't we jest take de babies home, Lawd?

GOD. No, I don' wanta bust up de fish fry. You angels keep quiet an I'll pass another miracle. Dat's always de trouble wid miracles. When you pass one you always gotta r'ar back an' pass another. (*There is a hush.*) Let dere be a place to dreen off dis firmament. Let dere be mountains and valleys an' let dere be oceans an' lakes. An' let dere be rivers and bayous to dreen it off in, too. As a matter of fac' let dere be de earth. An' when dat's done let dere be de sun, an' let it come out and dry my Cherubs' wings. (*The lights go up until the stage is bathed in sunlight. On the embankment upstage there is now a waist-high wrought iron railing such as one sees on the galleries of houses in the French quarter of New Orleans. The* CHERUBS *are being examined by their parents and there is an ad lib. murmur of,* "You all right, honey?" "You feel better now, Albert?" "Now you all dry, Vangy?" *until the* ARCHANGEL, *who has been gazing in awe at the railing, drowns them out.*)

ARCHANGEL. Look yere! (*There is a rush to the embankment accompanied by exclamations,* "My goodness!" "What's dis?"

'I declah!" etc. GABRIEL *towers above the group on the middle of the embankment* GOD *is wrapped in thought, facing the audience. The* CHOIR *resumes singing "So High You Can't Get Over It" softly. The babbling at the balustrade dies away as the people lean over the railing.* GABRIEL *turns and faces* GOD *indicating the earth below the railing with his left hand.*)

GABRIEL. Do you see it, Lawd?

GOD. (*Quietly, without turning his head upstage.*) Yes, Gabriel.

GABRIEL. Looks mighty nice, Lawd.

GOD. Yes. (GABRIEL *turns and looks over the railing.*)

GABRIEL. (*Gazing down.*) Yes, suh. Dat'd make mighty nice farming country. Jest look at dat South forty over dere. You ain't going to let dat go to waste is you, Lawd? Dat would be a pity an' a shame.

GOD. (*Not turning.*) It's a good earth. (GOD *turns, room is made for him beside* GABRIEL *on the embankment.*) Yes. I ought to have somebody to enjoy it. (*He turns, facing the audience. The others, save for the choir who are lined up in two rows of six on an angle upright, continue to look over the embankment.*) Gabriel! (GOD *steps down from the embankment two paces.*)

GABRIEL. (*Joining him.*) Yes, Lawd.

GOD. Gabriel, I'm goin' down dere.

GABRIEL. Yes, Lawd.

GOD. I want you to be my working boss yere while I'm gone.

GABRIEL. Yes, Lawd.

GOD. You know dat matter of dem two stars?

GABRIEL. Yes, Lawd.

GOD. Git dat fixed up! You know dat sparrow dat fell a little while ago? 'Tend to dat, too.

GABRIEL. Yes, Lawd.

GOD. I guess dat's about all. I'll be back Saddy. (*To the* CHOIR.) Quiet, angels. (*The* CHOIR *stops singing. Those on the embankment circle down stage.* GOD *goes to embankment. Turns and faces the company.*) I'm gonter pass one more miracle. You all gonter help me an' not make a soun' caize it's one of de most impo'tant miracles of all. (*Nobody moves.* GOD *turns, facing the sky and raises his arms above his head.*) Let there be man. (*There is growing roll of thunder as stage grows dark. The* CHOIR *bursts into "Hallelujah," and continues until the lights go up on the next scene.*)

SCENE III

(*Enclosing the stage is a heterogeneous cluster of cottonwood, camphor, live oak and sycamore trees, youpon and turkey berry bushes, with their purple and red berries, sprays of fern-like indigo fiera and splashes of various Louisiana flowers. In the middle of the stage, disclosed when the mistiness at rise grows into warm sunlight, stands* ADAM. *He is a puzzled man of 30, of medium height, dressed in the clothing of the average field hand. He is bare-headed. In the distance can be heard the choir continuing. "Bright Mansions Above." A bird begins to sing.* ADAM *smiles and turns to look at the source of this novel sound. He senses his strength and raises his forearms, his fists clenched. With his left hand he carefully touches the muscles of his upper right arm. He smiles* again, realizing his power. He looks at his feet which are stretched wide apart. He stamps once or twice and now almost laughs in his enjoyment. Other birds begin trilling and* ADAM *glances up joyfully toward the foliage.* GOD *enters.*)

GOD. Good mo'nin', Son.

ADAM. (*With a little awe.*) Good mo'nin', Lawd.

GOD. What's yo name, Son?

ADAM. Adam.

GOD. Adam which?

ADAM. (*Frankly, after a moment's puzzled groping.*) Jest Adam, Lawd.

GOD. Well, Adam, how dey treatin' you? How things goin?

ADAM. Well, Lawd, you know it's kind of a new line of wukk.

GOD. You'll soon get de hang of it. You know yo' kind of a new style with me.

ADAM. Oh, I guess I'm gonter make out all right soon as I learn de ropes.

GOD. Yes, I guess you will. Yo' a nice job.

ADAM. Yes, Lawd.

GOD. Dey's jest one little thing de matter with you. Did you notice it?

ADAM. Well, now you mentioned it, Lawd, I kind of thought dey was somethin' wrong.

GOD. Yes suh, you ain't quite right. Adam, you need a family. De reason for dat is in yo' heart you is a family man. (*Flicking the ash off his cigar.*) *I'd say dat was de main trouble at de moment.*

ADAM. (*Smiling.*) *Yes sir.* (*His smile fades and he is puzzled again.*) At de same time—dey's one thing puzzlin' me, Lawd. Could I ask you a question?

GOD. Why, certainly, Adam.

ADAM. Lawd, jest what *is* a family?

GOD. I'm gonter show you. (*Indicates a spot.*) Jest lie down dere, Adam. Make out like you was goin' to slumber.

ADAM. (*Gently.*) Yes, Lawd. (*He lies down.* GOD *stands beside him and as he raises his arms above his head the lights go down. In the darkness* GOD *speaks.*)

GOD. Eve. (*Lights go up.* EVE *is standing beside* ADAM. *She is about twenty-six, and quite pretty. She is dressed like a country girl. Her gingham dress is quite new and clean.* GOD *is now at the other side of the stage, looking at them critically.* EVE *looks at* ADAM *in timid wonder and slowly turns her head until she meets the glance of* GOD. ADAM *stands beside* EVE. *They gaze at each other for a moment.* GOD *smiles.*) Now you all right, Eve. (ADAM *and* EVE *face him.*) Now I'll tell you what I'm gonter do. I'm gonter put you in charge here. I'm gonter give you de run of dis whole garden. Eve, you take care of dis man an' Adam you take care of dis woman.

You belong to each other. I don' want you to try to do too much caize yo' both kind of experiment wid me an' I ain't sho' whether you could make it. You two jest enjoy yo'self. Drink de water from de little brooks an' de wine from de grapes an' de berries, an' eat de food dat's hangin' for you in de trees. (*He pauses, startled by a painful thought.*) Dat is, in all but one tree. (*He pauses. Then, not looking at them.*) You know what I mean, my children?

ADAM AND EVE. Yes, Lawd. (*They slowly turn their heads left, toward the branches of an offstage tree. Then they look back at* GOD.)

ADAM. Thank you, Lawd.

EVE. Thank you, Lawd.

GOD. I gotter be gittin' along now. I got a hund'ed thousan' things to do fo' you take yo' nex' breath. Enjoy yo'selves— (GOD *exits.*) (ADAM *and* EVE *stand looking after Him for a moment, then each looks down and watches their hands meet and clasp.*) (*After a moment they lift their heads slowly until they are again gazing at the tree.*)

EVE. Adam.

ADAM. (*Looking at the tree, almost in terror.*) What?

EVE. (*Softly as she too continues to look at the tree.*) Adam. (*The* CHOIR *begins singing "Turn You Round" and as the lights go down the* CHOIR *continues until there is blackness. The* CHOIR *suddenly stops. The following scene is played in the darkness.*)

MR. DESHEE'S VOICE. Now, I s'pose you chillun know what happened after God made Adam 'n' Eve. Do you?

FIRST GIRL'S VOICE. I know, Mr. Deshee.

MR. DESHEE'S VOICE. Jest a minute, Randolph. Didn't I tell you you gotta tell yo' mammy let yo' sister bring you. Carlisle, take way dat truck he's eatin'. You sit by him, see kin you keep him quiet. Now, den, Myrtle what happened?

FIRST GIRL'S VOICE. Why, den dey ate de fo'bidden fruit and den dey got driv' out de garden.

MR. DESHEE'S VOICE. An' den what happened?

FIRST GIRL'S VOICE. Den dey felt ver bad.

MR. DESHEE'S VOICE. I don' mean how dey feel, I mean how dey do. Do dey have any children or anything like dat?

FIRST GIRL'S VOICE. Oh, yes, suh, dey have Cain 'n' Abel.

MR. DESHEE'S VOICE. Dat's right, dey have Cain an' Abel.

BOY'S VOICE. Dat was a long time after dey got married, wasn't it, Mr. Deshee? My mammy say it was a hund'ed years.

MR. DESHEE'S VOICE. Well, nobody kin be so sure. As I tol' you befo' dey was jest beginnin' to be able to tell de time an' nobody was any too sure 'bout anythin' even den. So de bes' thing to do is jest realize dat de thing happened an' don't bother 'bout how many years it was. Jest remember what I told you about it gittin' dark when you go to sleep an' it bein' light when you wake up. Dat's de way time went by in dem days. One thing we do know an' dat was dis boy Cain was a mean rascal. (*The lights go up on the next scene.*)

SCENE IV

A roadside.

CAIN, *a husky young Negro, stands over the body of the dead* ABEL. *Both are dressed as laborers.* CAIN *is looking at the body in awe, a rock in his right hand.* GOD *enters.*

GOD. Cain, look what you done to Abel.

CAIN. Lawd, I was min'in' my own business and he come monkeyin' aroun' wit' me. I was wukkin' in de fiel' an' he was sittin' in de shade of de tree. He say "Me, I'd be skeered to git out in dis hot sun. I be 'fraid my brains git cooked. Co'se you ain't got no brains so you ain' in no danger." An' so I up and flang de rock. If it miss im all right, an' if it hit 'im, all right. Dat's de way I feel.

GOD. All right, but I'm yere to tell you dat's called a crime. When de new Judge is done talkin' to you you'll be draggin' a ball and chain de rest of yo' life.

CAIN. Well, what'd he want to come monkeyin' aroun' me fo' den? I was jest plowin', min'in' my own business, and not payin him no min', and yere he come makin' me de fool. I'd bust anybody what make me de fool.

GOD. Well,, I ain't sayin' you right an' I ain't sayin' you wrong. But I do say was I you I'd jest git myself down de road 'til I was clean out of de county. An' you better take an' git married an' settle down an' raise some chillun. Dey ain't nothin' to make a man fo'git his troubles iike raisin' a family. Now, you better git.

CAIN. Yessuh. (CAIN *walks off.*) (GOD *watches him from the forestage and as the lights begin to dim looks off. The* CHOIR *begins "Run, Sinner, Run."*)

GOD. Adam an' Eve you better try again. You better have Seth an' a lot mo' chillun. (*There is darkness. The* CHOIR *continues until the lights go up on the next scene.*)

SCENE V

CAIN *is discovered walking on an unseen treadmill. A middle distance of trees, hillsides and shrubbery passes him on an upper treadmill. Behind is the blue sky. He stops under the branches of a tree to look at a sign on a fence railing. Only half the tree is visible on the stage. The sign reads,* "NOD PARISH. COUNTY LINE."

CAIN. (*Sitting down with a sigh of relief under the tree.*) At las'. Phew! (*Wipes his forehead with a handkerchief.*) Feels like

I been walkin' fo'ty years. (*He looks back.*) Well, dey cain' git me now. Now I kin raise a fam'ly. (*An idea occurs to him, and suddenly he begins looking right and left.*) Well, I'll be hit by a mule! Knock me down for a trustin' baby! Where I gonter git dat fam'ly? Dat preacher fooled me (*He is quite dejected.*) Doggone!

CAIN'S GIRL. (*Off stage.*) Hello, Country Boy! (CAIN *glances up to the offstage branches of the tree.*)

CAIN. Hey-ho, Good lookin'! Which way is it to town?

CAIN'S GIRL. (*Off stage.*) What you tryin' to do? You tryin' to mash me? I be dog-gone if it ain't gittin' so a gal cain't hardly leave de house 'out some of dese fast men ain' passin' remarks at her.

CAIN. I ain' passin' remarks.

CAIN'S GIRL. (*Off stage.*) If I thought you was tryin' to mash me, I'd call de police an' git you tooken to de first precinct.

CAIN. Look yere, gal, I ast you a question, an' if you don' answer me I'm gonter bend you 'cross my pants an' burn you up.

CAIN'S GIRL. (*Off stage.*) I'm comin' down. (CAIN *takes his eyes from the tree.*)

CAIN. Yes, an' you better hurry. (CAIN'S GIRL *enters. She is as large as* CAIN, *wickedly pretty, and somewhat flashily dressed. She smiles at* CAIN.)

CAIN'S GIRL. I bet you kin handle a gal mean wid dem big stout arms of your'n. I sho' would hate to git you mad at me, Country Boy.

CAIN. (*Smiling.*) Come yere. (*She goes a little closer to him.*) Don't be 'fraid, I ain' so mean.

CAIN'S GIRL. You got two bad lookin' eyes. I bet yo' hot coffee 'mong de women folks.

CAIN. I ain' never find out. What was you doin' in dat tree?

CAIN'S GIRL. Jest coolin' myself in de element.

CAIN. Is you a Nod Parish gal?

CAIN'S GIRL. Bo'n an' bred.

CAIN. You know yo' kinda pretty.

CAIN'S GIRL. Who tol' you dat?

CAIN. Dese yere two bad eyes of mine.

CAIN'S GIRL. I bet you say dat to everybody all de way down de road.

CAIN. Comin' down dat road I didn't talk to nobody.

CAIN'S GIRL. Where you boun' for, Beautiful?

CAIN. I'm jest seein' de country. I thought I might settle down yere fo' a spell. You live wit' yo' people?

CAIN'S GIRL. Co'se I does.

CAIN. 'Spose dey'd like to take in a boarder?

CAIN'S GIRL. Be nice if dey would, wouldn' it?

CAIN. I think so. You got a beau?

CAIN'S GIRL. Huh-uh!

CAIN. (*Smiling.*) You has *now.*

CAIN'S GIRL. I guess—I guess if you wanted to kiss me an' I tried to stop you, you could pretty nearly crush me wit' dem stout arms.

CAIN. You wouldn't try too much, would you?

CAIN'S GIRL. Maybe for a little while.

CAIN. An' den what?

CAIN'S GIRL. Why don' we wait an' see?

CAIN. When would dat be?

CAIN'S GIRL. Tonight. After supper. Think you kin walk a little further now, City Boy?

CAIN. Yeh, I ain't so weary now. (*She takes his hand.*)

CAIN'S GIRL. What yo' name? (*Takes his arm.*)

CAIN. Cain.

CAIN'S GIRL. Then I'm Cain's Gal. Come on, honey, an' meet de folks. (*They exit.*) (*The* CHOIR *is heard singing "You Better Mind," as* GOD *enters.* GOD *watches the vanished* CAIN *and his girl.*)

GOD. (*After shaking his head.*) Bad business. I don' like de way things is goin' atall. (*The stage is darkened.*) (*The* CHOIR *continues singing until the lights go up on the next scene.*)

SCENE VI

GOD'S *private office in Heaven. It is a small room, framed by tableau curtains. A large window up center looks out on the sky. There is a battered roll-top desk. On the wall next to the window is a framed religious oleograph with a calendar attached to it underneath. A door is at the left. A hat rack is on the wall above the door. There are two or three cheap pine chairs beside the window, and beyond the door. In front of the desk is an old swivel armchair which creaks every time* GOD *leans back in it. The desk is open and various papers are stuck in the pigeonholes. Writing implements, etc. are on the desk. On a shelf above the desk is a row of law books. A cuspidor is near the desk and a waste basket by it. The general atmosphere is that of the office of a Negro lawyer in a Louisiana town. As the lights go up* GOD *takes a fresh cigar from a box on the desk and begins puffing it without bothering to light it. There is no comment on this minor miracle from* GABRIEL *who is sitting in one of the chairs with a pencil and several papers in his hand. The singing becomes pianissimo.*

GABRIEL. (*Looking at the papers.*) Well, I guess dat's about all de impo'tant business this mornin', Lawd.

GOD. How 'bout dat Cherub over to Archangel Montgomery's house?

GABRIEL. Where do dey live, Lawd? (*The singing stops.*)

GOD. Dat little two story gold house, over by de pearly gates.

GABRIEL. Oh, *dat* Montgomery. I thought you was referrin' to de ol' gentleman. Oh, yeh. (*He sorts through the papers and finds one he is looking for.*) Yere it 'tis. (*Reads.*) "Cherub Christina Montgomery; wings is moltin' out of season an' nobody knows what to do."

GOD. Well, now, take keer of dat. You gotter be more careful, Gabe.

GABRIEL. Yes, Lawd. (*Folds the papers and puts them in a pocket.* GOD *turns to his desk, takes another puff or two of the cigar, and with a pencil, begins checking off items on a sheet of paper before him.*

His back is turned toward GABRIEL. GABRIEL *takes his trumpet from the hat rack and burnishes it with his robe. He then wets his lips and puts the mouthpiece to his mouth.*)

GOD. (*Without turning around.*) Now, watch yo'self, Gabriel.

GABRIEL. I wasn't goin' to blow, Lawd. I jest do dat every now an' den so I can keep de feel of it. (*He leans trumpet against the wall.* GOD *picks up the papers and swings his chair around toward* GABRIEL.)

GOD. What's dis yere about de moon?

GABRIEL. (*Suddenly remembering.*) Oh! De moon people say it's beginnin' to melt a little, on 'count caize de sun's so hot.

GOD. It's goin' 'round 'cordin' to schedule, aint it?

GABRIEL. Yes, Lawd.

GOD. Well, tell 'em to stop groanin'. Dere's nothin' de matter wid dat moon. Trouble is so many angels is flyin' over dere on Saddy night. Dey git to beatin' dere wings when dey dancin' an' dat makes de heat. Tell them dat from now on dancin' 'roun' de moon is sinnin'. Dey got to stop it. Dat'll cool off de moon. (*He swings back and puts the paper on the desk. He leans back in the chair comfortably, his hands clasped behind his head.*) Is dere anythin' else you ought to remin' me of?

GABRIEL. De prayers, Lawd.

GOD. (*Puzzled, slowly swinging chair around again.*) De prayers?

GABRIEL. From mankind. You know, down on de earth.

GOD. Oh, yeh, de poor little earth. Bless my soul, I almos' forgot about dat. Mus' be three or four hund'ed years since I been down dere. I wasn't any too pleased wid dat job.

GABRIEL. (*Laughing.*) You know you don' make mistakes, Lawd.

GOD. (*Soberly, with introspective detachment.*) So dey tell me. (*He looks at* GABRIEL *then through the window again.*) So dey tell me. I fin' I kin be displeased though, an' I was displeased wid de mankind I las' seen. Maybe I ought to go down dere agin—I need a little holiday.

GABRIEL. Might do you good, Lawd.

GOD. I think I will. I'll go down an' walk de earth agin an' see how dem poor humans is makin' out. What time is it, by de sun an' de stars?

GABRIEL. (*Glancing out of the window.*) Jest exactly half-past, Lawd. (GOD *is taking his hat and stick from the hat rack.*)

GOD. (*Opening the door.*) Well, take keer o' yo'self. I'll be back Saddy. (*He exits.*) (*The stage is darkened. The* CHOIR *begins "Dere's No Hidin' Place," and continues until the lights go up on the next scene.*)

SCENE VII

GOD *is walking along a country road. He stops to listen. Church bells are heard in the distance.*

GOD. Dat's nice. Nice an' quiet. Dat's de way I like Sunday to be. (*The sound is broken by a shrill voice of a girl. It is* ZEBA *singing a "blues."*) Now, dat ain't so good. (GOD *resumes his walk and the upper treadmill brings on a tree stump on which* ZEBA *is sitting. She is accompanying her song with a ukulele.* GOD *and the treadmills stop. When the stump reaches the center of the stage, it is seen that* ZEBA *is a rouged and extremely flashily dressed chippy of about eighteen.*) Stop dat!

ZEBA. What's de matter wid you, Country Boy? Pull up yo' pants. (*She resumes singing.*)

GOD. Stop dat!

ZEBA. (*Stops again.*) Say, listen to me, Banjo Eyes. What right you got to stop a lady enjoyin' herself?

GOD. Don't you know dis is de Sabbath? Da's no kin' o' song to sing on de Lawd's day.

ZEBA. Who care 'bout de Lawd's day anymo'? People jest use Sunday now to git over Saddy.

GOD. You a awful sassy little girl.

ZEBA. I come fum sassy people! We even speak mean of de dead.

GOD. What's yo' name?

ZEBA. (*Flirtatiously.*) "What's my name?" Ain't you de ol'-time gal hunter! Fust, "What's my name?" den I s'pose, what it be like if you tried to kiss me? You preachers' is de debbils.

GOD. I ain't aimin' to touch you daughter. (*A sudden sternness frightens* ZEBA. *She looks at him sharply.*) What is yo' name?

ZEBA. Zeba.

GOD. Who's yo' fam'ly?

ZEBA. I'm de great-great gran' daughter of Seth.

GOD. Of Seth? But Seth was a good man.

ZEBA. Yeh, he too good, he die of holiness.

GOD. An' yere's his little gran' daughter reekin' wid cologne. Ain't nobody ever tol' you yo' on de road to Hell?

ZEBA. (*Smiling.*) Sho' dat's what de preacher say. Exceptin' of course, I happens to know dat I'm on de road to de picnic groun's, an' at de present time I'm waitin' to keep an engagement wid my sweet papa. He don' like people talkin' to me. (CAIN THE SIXTH *enters. He is a young buck, wearing a "box" coat and the other flashy garments of a Rampart Street swell.*)

CAIN THE SIXTH. Hello sugah! (*He crosses in front of* GOD *and faces* ZEBA.) Hello, mamma! Sorry I'm late baby, but de gals in de barrel-house jest wouldn't let me go. Doggone, one little wirehead swore she'd tear me down. (ZEBA *smiles and takes his hand.*)

GOD. What's yo' name, son?

CAIN THE SIXTH. (*Contemptuously; without turning.*) Soap 'n water, Country Boy.

GOD. (*Sternly.*) What's yo' name, son? (CAIN *slowly turns and for a moment his manner is civil.*)

CAIN THE SIXTH. Cain the Sixth.

GOD. I was afraid so.

CAIN THE SIXTH. (*His impudence returning.*) You a new preacher?

GOD. Where you live?

CAIN THE SIXTH. Me, I live mos' any place.

GOD. Yes, an' you gonter see dem all. Is de udder young men all like you?

CAIN THE SIXTH. (*Smiling.*) De gals don' think so. (*He turns towards* ZEBA *again, picks her up and sits on the stump with the laughing* ZEBA *on his lap.*)

ZEBA. Dey ain't nobody in de worl' like my honey-cake. (CAIN *kisses her and she resumes her song.*) (GOD *watches them.* ZEBA *finishes a verse of the song and begins another softly.* CAIN THE SIXTH'S *eyes have been closed during the singing.*)

CAIN THE SIXTH. (*His eyes closed.*) Is de preacher gone? (ZEBA *looks quickly at* GOD *without seeing him, and then looks off. She stops the song.*)

ZEBA. Yeh, I guess he walks fast. (CAIN *pushes her off his lap and rises.*)

CAIN THE SIXTH. (*With acid sweetness.*) Dey tell me las' night you was talkin' to a creeper man, baby.

ZEBA. Why, you know dey ain't nobody in de worl' fo' me but you.

CAIN THE SIXTH. (*Smiling.*) I know dey ain't. I even got dat guaranteed. (*Takes a revolver from his pocket.*) See dat, baby?

ZEBA. Sho' I see it, honey.

CAIN THE SIXTH. Dat jest makes me positive. (*Puts the gun back.*)

ZEBA. (*Pushing him back on the stump.*) You don' wanter believe dem stories, papa.

CAIN THE SIXTH. (*With sinister lightness.*) No, I didn't believe dem, baby. Co'se dat big gorilla, Flatfoot, from de other side of de river *is* in town ag'in.

ZEBA. Dat don' mean nothin'. Flatfoot ain't nothin' to me.

CAIN THE SIXTH. (*Sitting again.*) Co'se he ain't. Go 'head, sing some mo', baby. (ZEBA *resumes singing.*)

GOD. Bad business. (*The treadmills start turning.* GOD *resumes his walk.* ZEBA, *still singing, and* CAIN THE SIXTH *recede with the landscape.* GOD *is again alone on the country road. There is a twitter of birds.* GOD *looks up and smiles.*) De birds is goin' 'bout dere business, all right. (*A patch of flowers goes by, black-eyed Susans, conspicuously.*) How you flowers makin' out? (CHILDREN'S *voices answer,* "We O. K., LAWD.") Yes, an' you looks very pretty. (CHILDREN'S *voices*: "Thank you, Lawd." *The flowers pass out of sight.*) It's only de human bein's makes me downhearted. Yere's as nice a Sunday as dey is turnin' out anywhere, an' nobody makin' de right use of it. (*Something ahead of him attracts his attention.*) (*His face brightens.*) Well, now dis is mo' like it. Now dat's nice to see people prayin'. It's a wonder dey don' do it in de church. But I fin' I don' min' it if dey do it outdoors. (*A group of five adult Negroes and a boy on their knees in a semicircle, appears. The treadmills stop. The* BOY, *his head bent, swings his hands rhythmically up to his head three or four times. There is a hush.*)

GAMBLER. Oh, Lawd, de smoke-house is empty. Oh, Lawd, lemme git dem groceries. Oh, Lawd, lemme see dat little *six*. (*He casts the dice.*) Wham! Dere she is, frien's. (*Exclamations from the others:* "Well damn my eyes!" "Doggone, dat's de eighth pass he make." "For God's sake, can't you ever crap?" *etc. The* BOY *is picking up the money.*)

GOD. Gamblin' (*Looks over the group's shoulders.*) An' wid frozen dice!

BOY GAMBLER. Dey's a dolla' 'n' a half talkin' fo' me. How much you want of it, Riney?

FIRST GAMBLER. I take fo bits. Wait a minute. Mebbe I take a little mo'. (*He counts some money in his hand.*)

SECOND GAMBLER.. (*Glancing up at* GOD.) Hello, Liver Lips. (*To the others.*) Looka ol' Liver Lips. (*The others look up and laugh good-naturedly, repeating* "Liver Lips.")

FIRST GAMBLER. Ain't his pockets high from de groun'? Ol' High-Pockets. (*The*

others keep saying "Ole Liver Lips." "Ol'
Liver Lips don't like to see people dicin'."
"Dats a good name, 'High Pockets'.")

BOY GAMBLER. (To others.) Come on, you
gonter fade me or not? (GOD seizes the
BOY's ears and drags him to his feet. The
others do not move, but watch, amused.)

GOD. Come yere, son. Why, yo' jest a
little boy. Gamblin' an' sinnin'. (GOD looks
at the boy's face.) You been chewin' tobacco, too, like you was yo' daddy. (GOD
sniffs.) An' you been drinkin' sonny-kick-
mammy-wine. You oughta be 'shamed.
(To the others.) An' you gamblers oughta
be 'shamed, leadin' dis boy to sin.

FIRST GAMBLER. He de bes' crap shooter in
town, mister.

GOD. I'm gonter tell his mammy. I bet
she don' know 'bout dis.

FIRST GAMBLER. No, she don' know. (The
others laugh.) She don' know anythin'.

SECOND GAMBLER. Das de God's truth.

FIRST GAMBLER. See kin you beat 'im, High
Pockets. Dey's a dolla' open yere.

GOD. I ain't gonter beat 'im. I'm gonter
teach 'im. I may have to teach you all.
(He starts walking from them. The BOY
sticks out his tongue the moment GOD's'
back is turned.)

BOY GAMBLER. If you fin' my mammy you
do mo'n I kin. Come on, gamblers, see kin
you gimme a little action. Who wants any
part of dat dollar? (The treadmill carries
them off. The FIRST GAMBLER is heard saying: "I'll take anoder two bits," and the
others, "Gimme a dime's wo'th," "I ain't
only got fifteen cents left," etc. as they
disappear.)

GOD. (Walking.) Where's dat little boy's
home? (The front of a shanty appears and
GOD stops in front of the door.) Yere's de
place. It ain't any too clean, either. (Knocks
on the door with his cane.)

VOICE IN SHANTY. Who dar?

GOD. Never you min' who's yere. Open
de door.

VOICE IN SHANTY. You gotta search warrant?

GOD. I don' need one.

VOICE IN SHANTY. Who you wanter see?

GOD. I wanter see da mammy of de little
gamblin' boy.

VOICE IN SHANTY. You mean little Johnny
Rucker?

GOD. Dat may be his name.

VOICE IN SHANTY. Well, Mrs. Rucker ain't
home.

GOD. Where's she at?

VOICE IN SHANTY. Who, Mrs. Rucker?

GOD. You heerd me.

VOICE IN SHANTY. Oh, she run away las'
night wid a railroad man. She's eloped.

GOD. Where's Rucker?

VOICE IN SHANTY. He's flat under de table.
He so drunk he cain't move.

GOD. Who are you?

VOICE IN SHANTY. I'se jest a fren' an'
neighbor. I come in las' night to de party,
an' everybody in yere's dead drunk but me.
De only reason I kin talk is I drank some
new white mule I made myself, an' it burn
my throat so I cain't drink no mo'. You
got any mo' questions?

GOD. Not for you. (The shanty begins to
move off as GOD starts walking again.)

VOICE IN SHANTY. Good riddance, I say.
(Shanty disappears.)

GOD. Dis ain't gittin' me nowheres. All
I gotta say dis yere mankind I been peoplin'
my earth wid sho' ain't much. (He stops
and looks back.) I got good min' to wipe
'em all off an' people de earth wid angels.
No. Angels is all right, singin, an' playin'
an' flyin' around, but dey ain't much on
workin' de crops and buildin' de levees.
No, suh, mankind's jest right for my earth,
if he wasn't so doggone sinful. I'd rather
have my earth peopled wit' a bunch of
channel catfish, dan I would mankin' an'
his sin. I jest cain't stan' sin. (He is about
to resume his walk when NOAH enters.
NOAH is dressed like a country preacher.
His coat is of the "hammer-tail" variety.
He carries a prayer book under his arm.)

NOAH. Mo'nin', brother.

GOD. Mo'nin', brother. I declare you look like a good man.

NOAH. I try to be, brother. I'm de preacher yere. I don't think I seen you to de meetin'. (*They resume walking.*)

GOD. I jest come to town a little while ago an' I been pretty busy.

NOAH. Yeh, mos' everybody say dey's pretty busy dese days. Dey so busy dey cain't come to meetin'. It seem like de mo' I preaches de mo' people ain't got time to come to church. I ain't hardly got enough members to fill up de choir. I gotta do de preachin' an' de bassin' too.

GOD. Is dat a fac'?

NOAH. Yes, suh, brother. Everybody is mighty busy, gamblin', good-timin', an' goin' on. You jest wait, though. When Gabriel blow de horn you gonter fin' dey got plenty of time to punch chunks down in Hell. Yes, suh.

GOD. Seems a pity. Dey all perfec'ly healthy?

NOAH. Oh, dey healthy, all right. Dey jest all lazy, and mean, and full of sin. You look like a preacher, too, brother.

GOD. Well, I am, in a way.

NOAH. You jest passin' through de neighborhood?

GOD. Yes, I wanted to see how things was goin' in yo' part of de country, an' I been feelin' jest 'bout de way you do. It's enough to discourage you.

NOAH. Yes, but I gotta keep wres'lin' wid 'em. Where you boun' for right now, brother?

GOD. I was jest walkin' along. I thought I might stroll on to de nex' town.

NOAH. Well, dat's a pretty good distance. I live right yere. (*He stops walking.*) Why don' you stop an' give us de pleasure of yo' comp'ny for dinner? I believe my ol' woman has kilt a chicken.

GOD. Why, dat's mighty nice of you, brother. I don' believe I caught yo' name.

NOAH. Noah, jest brother Noah. Dis is my home, brother. Come right in. (GOD *and* NOAH *start walking towards* NOAH's *house which is just coming into view on the treadmill.*) (*The stage darkens, the* CHOIR *sings "Feastin' Table," and when the lights go up again, the next scene is disclosed.*)

SCENE VIII

Interior of NOAH's *house. The ensemble suggests the combination living-dining room in a fairly prosperous Negro's cabin. Clean white curtains hang at the window. A table and chairs are in the center of the room. There is a cheerful checked tablecloth on the table, and on the wall, a framed, highly colored picture reading "God Bless Our Home."* (NOAH's WIFE, *an elderly Negress, simply and neatly dressed,* GOD *and* NOAH *are discovered grouped about the table.*)

NOAH. Company, darlin'. (NOAH's *wife takes* NOAH's *and* GOD's *hats.*) Dis gemman's a preacher, too. He's jest passin' through de country.

GOD. Good mo'nin', sister.

NOAH's WIFE. Good mo'nin'. You jest ketch me when I'm gittin' dinner ready. You gonter stay with us?

GOD. If I ain't intrudin'. Brother Noah suggested—

NOAH's WIFE. You set right down yere. I got a chicken in de pot an' it'll be ready in 'bout five minutes. I'll go out de back an' call Shem, Ham 'n' Japheth. (*To* GOD.) Dey's our sons. Dey live right acrost de way but always have Sunday dinner wid us. You mens make yo'selves comf'table.

GOD. Thank you, thank you very kindly.

NOAH. You run along, we all right. (GOD *and* NOAH *seat themselves.* NOAH's WIFE *exits.*)

GOD. You got a fine wife, Brother Noah.

NOAH. She pretty good woman.

GOD. Yes, suh, an' you got a nice little home. Have a ten cent seegar? (GOD *offers him one.*)

NOAH. Thank you, much obliged. (*Both men lean back restfully in their chairs.*)

GOD. Jest what seems to be de main trouble 'mong mankind, Noah?

NOAH. Well, it seems to me de main trouble is dat de whol' distric' is wide open. Now you know dat makes fo' loose livin'. Men folks spen's all dere time fightin', loafin' an' gamblin', an' makin' bad likker.

GOD. What about de women?

NOAH. De women is worse dan de men. If dey ain't makin' love powder dey out beg, borrow an' stealin' money for policy tickets. Doggone, I come in de church Sunday 'fo' las' 'bout an' hour befo' de meetin' was to start, and dere was a woman stealin' de altar cloth. She was goin' to hock it. Dey ain't got no moral sense. Now you take dat case las' month, over in East Putney. Case of dat young Willy Roback.

GOD. What about him?

NOAH. Dere is a boy sebenteen years old. Doggone, if he didn't elope with his aunt. Now, you know, dat kin of goin' on is bad fo' a neighborhood.

GOD. Terrible, terrible.

NOAH. Yes, suh. Dis use' to be a nice, decent community. I been doin' my best to preach de Word, but seems like every time I preach de place jest goes a little mo' to de dogs. De good Lawd only knows what's gonter happen.

GOD. Dat is de truth. (*There is a pause. Each puffs his cigar.*) (*Suddenly* NOAH *grasps his knee, as if it were paining him, and twists his foot.*)

NOAH. Huh!

GOD. What's de matter?

NOAH. I jest got a twitch. My buck-auger I guess. Every now and den I gets a twitch in de knee. Might be a sign of rain.

GOD. That's just what it is. Noah, what's de mos' rain you ever had 'round dese parts?

NOAH. Well, de water come down fo' six days steady last April an' de ribber got so swole it bust down de levee up 'bove Freeport. Raise cain all de way down to de delta.

GOD. What would you say was it to rain for forty days and forty nights?

NOAH. I'd say dat was a *complete* rain!

GOD. Noah, you don't know who I is, do you?

NOAH. (*Puzzled.*) Yo' face looks easy, but I don' think I recall de name. (GOD *rises slowly, and as he reaches his full height there is a crash of lightning, a moment's darkness, and a roll of thunder. It grows light again.* NOAH *is on his knees in front of* GOD.) I 'should have known you. I should have seen de glory.

GOD. Dat's all right, Noah. You didn't know who I was.

NOAH. I'm jes' ol' preacher Noah, Lawd, an' I'm yo' servant. I ain' very much, but I'se all I got.

GOD. Sit down, Noah. Don' let me hear you shamin' yo'se'f, caize yo' a good man. (*Timidly* NOAH *waits until* GOD *is seated, and then sits, himself.*) I jest wanted to fin' out if you was good, Noah. Dat's why I'm walkin' de earth in de shape of a natchel man. I wish dey was mo' people like you. But, far as I kin see you and yo' fam'ly is de only respectable people in de worl'.

NOAH. Dey jest all poor sinners, Lawd.

GOD. I know. I am your Lawd. I am a god of wrath and vengeance n' dat's why I'm gonter destroy dis worl'.

NOAH. (*Almost in a whisper. Drawing back.*) Jest as you say, Lawd.

GOD. I ain't gonter destroy you, Noah. You and yo' fam'ly, yo' sheep an' cattle, an' all de udder things dat ain't human I'm gonter preserve. But de rest is gotta go. (*Takes a pencil and a sheet of paper from his pocket.*) Look yere, Noah. (NOAH *comes over and looks over his shoulder.*) I want you to build me a boat. I want you to call it de "Ark," and I want it to look like dis. (*He is drawing on the paper. Continues to write as he speaks.*) I want you to take two of every kind of animal and bird dat's in de country. I want you to take seeds an' sprouts an' everythin' like dat an' put dem on dat Ark, because dere is gonter be all dat rain. Dey's gonter to be a deluge, Noah, an' dey's goin' to be a flood. De levees is gonter bust an' everything dat's fastened down is comin' loose, but it ain't gonter float long, caize I'm gonter make a storm dat'll sink everythin' from a hencoop to a barn. Dey ain't a ship on de sea dat'll be able to fight dat tempest. Dey all got to go. Everythin'. Everythin' in dis pretty worl' I made, except one thing, Noah. You an' yo' fam'ly an' de things I said are going to ride dat storm in de Ark. Yere's de way it's to be. (*He hands* NOAH *the paper.* NOAH *takes it and reads.*)

NOAH. (*Pause. Looks at paper again.*) Yes, suh, dis seems to be complete. Now 'bout the animals, Lawd, you say you want everythin'?

GOD. Two of everythin'.

NOAH. Dat would include jayraffes an' hippopotamusses?

GOD. Everythin' dat is.

NOAH. Dey was a circus in town las' week. I guess I kin fin' dem. Co'se I kin git all de rabbits an' possums an' wil' turkeys easy. I'll sen' de boys out. Hum, I'm jest wonderin'—

GOD. 'Bout what?

NOAH. 'Bout snakes? Think you'd like snakes, too?

GOD. Certainly, I want snakes.

NOAH. Oh, I kin git snakes, lots of 'em. Co'se, some of 'em's a little dangerous. Maybe I better take a kag of likker, too?

GOD. You kin have a kag of likker.

NOAH. (*Musingly.*) Yes, suh, dey's a awful lot of differ'nt kin's of snakes, come to think about it. Dey's water moccasins, cotton-moufs, rattlers—mus' be a hund'ed kin's of other snakes down in de swamps. Maybe I better take two kags of likker.

GOD. (*Mildly.*) I think de one kag's enough.

NOAH. No. I better take two kags. Besides I kin put one on each side of de boat, an' balance de ship wid dem as well as havin' dem fo' medicinal use.

GOD. You kin put one kag in de middle of de ship.

NOAH. (*Buoyantly.*) Jest as easy to take de two kags, Lawd.

GOD. I think one kag's enough.

NOAH. Yes, Lawd, but you see forty days an' forty nights—(*There is a distant roll of thunder.*)

GOD. (*Firmly.*) One kag, Noah.

NOAH. Yes, Lawd. One kag. (*The door in the back opens and* NOAH'S WIFE *enters with a tray of dishes and food.*)

NOAH'S WIFE. Now, den, gen'lemen, if you'll jest draw up cheers. (*The stage is darkened. The* CHOIR *is heard singing "I Want to Be Ready." They continue in the darkness until the lights go up on the next scene.*)

SCENE IX

In the middle of the stage is the Ark. On the hillside, below the Ark, a dozen or more men and women, townspeople, are watching NOAH, SHEM, HAM *and* JAPHETH *on the deck of the Ark. The three sons are busily nailing boards on the cabin.* NOAH *is smoking a pipe. He wears a silk hat, captain's uniform and a "slicker."*

NOAH. (*To* SHEM.) You, Shem, tote up some ol' rough lumber, don' bring up any

planed up lumber, caize dat ain't fo' de main deck.

SHEM. Pretty near supper time, daddy.

NOAH. Maybe 'tis, but I got de feelin' we ought to keep goin'.

FIRST WOMAN. You gonter work all night, Noah, maybe, huh?

NOAH. (*Without looking at her.*) If de sperrit move me.

SECOND WOMAN. Look yere, Noah, whyn't you give up all dis damn foolishness? Don' you know people sayin' yo' crazy? What you think you doin' anyway?

NOAH. I'se buildin' a Ark. (*Other men and women join those in the foreground.*) Ham, you better stop for a while 'n see whether dey bringin' de animals up all right. (*He looks at his watch.*) Dey ought to be pretty near de foot o' de hill by dis time; if dey ain't you wait fo' dem and bring 'em yo'se'f. (HAM *goes down a ladder at the side of the ship and exits during the following scene. The newcomers in group have been speaking to some of the early arrivals.*)

SECOND WOMAN. (*To* THIRD WOMAN, *one of the newcomers.*) No, you don't mean it!

THIRD WOMAN. I do so. Dat's what de talk is in de town.

FIRST MAN. You hear dat, Noah? Dey say yo' ol' lady is tellin' everybody it's gonter rain fo' fo'ty days and fo'ty nights. You know people soon gonter git de idea you *all* crazy.

NOAH. Lot I keer what you think. (*To* JAPHETH.) Straighten up dem boards down dere, Japheth. (*Indicates floor of deck.*)

FIRST MAN. (*To* THIRD WOMAN) Was I you, I wouldn' go 'roun with Mrs. Noah anymore, lady. Fust thing you know you'll be gittin' a hard name, too.

THIRD WOMAN. Don' I know?

SECOND WOMAN. A lady cain't be too partic'lar dese days. (ZEBA *and* FLATFOOT, *a tall, black, wicked-looking buck, enter, their arms around eoch other's waist.*)

ZEBA. Dere it is baby. Was I lyin'?

FLATFOOT. Well, I'll be split in two!

FIRST MAN. What you think of it Flatfoot?

FLATFOOT. I must say! Look like a house wit' a warpin' cellar.

NOAH. Dis yere vessel is a boat.

FLATFOOT. When I was a little boy dey used to build boats down near de ribber, where de water was. (*The others laugh.*)

NOAH. Dis time it's been arranged to have de water come up to de boat. (JAPHETH *looks belligerently over the rail of the Ark at* FLATFOOT. *To* JAPHETH.) Keep yo' shirt on, son.

SECOND WOMAN. (*To* THIRD WOMAN.) Now, you see de whole fam'ly's crazy.

THIRD WOMAN. Listen, dey ain't gonter 'taminate me. It was me dat started resolvin' dem both out o' de buryin' society.

ZEBA. When all dis water due up yere, Noah?

NOAH. You won't know when it gits yere, daughter.

ZEBA. Is she goin' to be a side-wheeler, like de Bessy-Belle?

FLATFOOT. No! If she was a side-wheeler she'd get her wheels all clogged wid sharks. She gonter have jus' one great big stern wheel, like de Commodore. Den if dey ain't 'nuf water why de big wheel kin stir some up. (*General laughter. Two or three of the* GAMBLERS *enter and join the group, followed by* CAIN THE SIXTH.)

CAIN THE SIXTH. Dere's de fool an' his monument, jest like I said! (*The* GAMBLERS *and* CAIN THE SIXTH *roar with laughter, slap their legs, etc., the members of the main group talk sotto voce to each other as* CAIN THE SIXTH *catches* ZEBA's *eye.* FLATFOOT *is on her right and is not aware of* CAIN *the* SIXTH's *presence.*)

NOAH. See how dey makin' out inside, son. (*Stops hammering.*) (JAPHETH *exits into Ark.*) (NOAH *turns and gazes towards the east.*)

CAIN THE SIXTH. Hello, honey.

ZEBA. (*Frightened but smiling.*) Hello, sugah.

CAIN THE SIXTH. (*Pleasantly.*) Ain' dat my ol' frien' Flatfoot wid you?

ZEBA. Why, so 'tis! (FLATFOOT *is now listening.*) (*To* FLATFOOT.) He's got a gun.

CAIN THE SIXTH. No, I ain't. (*He lifts his hands over his head.* ZEBA *quickly advances and runs her hands lightly over his pockets.*)

ZEBA. (*Relieved.*) I guess he ain't.

CAIN THE SIXTH. No, I ain't got no gun for my ol' friend, Flatfoot. (*He walks up to him.*)

FLATFOOT. (*Smiling.*) Hi, Cain. How's de boy? (CAIN *quickly presses his chest against* FLATFOOT's, *his downstage arm sweeps around* FLATFOOT's *body and his hand goes up to the small of* FLATFOOT's *back.*)

CAIN THE SIXTH. (*Quietly, but triumphantly.*) I got a little knife fo' him. (FLATFOOT *falls dead.*) (*The laughter of the others stops and they look at the scene.* ZEBA *for a moment is terrified, her clenched hand pressed to her mouth. She looks at* CAIN THE SIXTH, *who is smiling at her. He tosses the knife on the ground and holds his hands out to her. She goes to him, smiling.*)

ZEBA. You sho' take keer of me, honey.

CAIN THE SIXTH. Dat's caize I think yo' wo'th takin' keer of. (*To the others.*) It's all right, folks. I jest had to do a little cleanin' up.

FIRST WOMAN. (*Smiling.*) You is de quickes' scoundrel.

FIRST GAMBLER. It was a nice quick killin'. Who was he?

SECOND WOMAN. (*Casually.*) Dey called him Flatfoot. From over de river. He wa'nt any good. He owed me for washin' for over a year.

THIRD WOMAN. Used to peddle muggles. Said it had a kick like reg'lar snow. Wasn't no good.

SECOND GAMBLER. Think we ought to bury him?

FIRST MAN. No, just leave him dere. Nobody comes up yere, 'cept ol' Manatee. (*Indicates* NOAH. *Cries of "Ol' Manatee! Ol' Manatee, dat's good!"*)

NOAH. (*Still looking off.*) You bettah pray, you po' chillun. (*They all laugh.*)

FIRST WOMAN. We bettah pray? You bettah pray, Ol' Manatee?

ZEBA. You bettah pray for rain. (*Laughter again.*)

NOAH. Dat's what I ain't doin', sinners. Shem! Japheth! (*To others, as he points off. Patter of rain.*) Listen!

CAIN THE SIXTH. (*Casually.*) Doggone, I believe it *is* gonter shower a little.

FIRST GAMBLER. It do looks like rain.

FIRST WOMAN. I think I'll git on home. I got a new dress on.

ZEBA. Me, too. I wants to keep lookin' nice fo' my sweet papa. (*She pats* CAIN THE SIXTH's *cheek.* CAIN THE SIXTH *hugs her.*)

NOAH. (*Almost frantically.*) Ham! Is de animals dere?

HAM. (*Off stage.*) Yes, sir, dere yere. We're comin'.

NOAH. Den bring 'em on. (SHEM *and* JAPHETH *come on deck with their hammers. The stage begins to darken.*)

THIRD WOMAN. I guess we all might go home 'till de shower's over. Come on, papa.

SECOND GAMBLER. See you after supper, Noah. (*Crowd starts moving off* R.)

NOAH. God's gittin' ready to start, my sons. Let's git dis plankin' done.

ZEBA. Put a bix Texas on it, Noah, an' we'll use fo' excursions. (*There is a distant roll of thunder, there are cries of "Good night, Admiral." "See you later." "So long, Manatee," as the crowd goes off. The thunder rumbles again. There is the sound of increasing rain. The hammers o;* SHEM *and* JAPHETH *sound louder and are joined by the sounds of other hammerers. There is a flash of lightning. The* CHOIR *begins "Dey Ol' Ark's a-Movering," the sounds on the Ark become faster and louder. The rush of rain grows heavier.*)

NOAH. Hurry! Hurry! Where are you, Ham?

HAM. (*Just off stage.*) Yere, I am, father, wid de animals.

NOAH. God's give us his sign. Send 'em up de gangplank. (*An inclined plane is thrown against the Ark from the side of the stage by* HAM, *who cracks a whip.*)

HAM. Get on dere. (*The heads of two elephants are seen.*)

NOAH. Bring 'em on board! De Lawd is strikin' down de worl'! (*The singing and* the noises reach fortissimo *as* HAM *cracks his whip again, and the rain falls on the stage.*) (*The stage is darkened. The* CHOIR *continues singing in the darkness.*)

SCENE X

When the lights go up on scene, the Ark is at sea. Stationary waves run in front of it. The hillside has disappeared. The Ark is in the only lighted area.
SHEM *is smoking a pipe on the deck, leaning on the rail. A steamboat whistle blows three short and one long blast.* SHEM *is surprised. In a moment* HAM *appears, also with a pipe, and joins* SHEM *at the rail.*

SHEM. Who'd you think you was signallin'?

HAM. Dat wasn't me, dat was daddy.

SHEM. He think he gonter git a reply?

HAM. I don' know. He's been gittin' a heap of comfort out of dat likker.

SHEM. De kag's nearly empty, ain't it?

HAM. Pretty nearly almos'. (*They look over the rail. A pause.*) Seen anythin'?

SHEM. Dis mornin' I seen somethin' over dere migh'a' been a fish.

HAM. Dat's de big news of de week.

SHEM. How long you think dis trip's gonter las'?

HAM. I don' know! Rain fo'ty days 'n' fo'ty nights an' when dat stop' I thought sho' we'd come up ag'inst a san' bar o' somethin'. Looks now like all dat rain was jest a little incident of de trip. (*The whistle blows again.*) Doggone! I wish he wouldn't do dat. Fust thing we know he'll wake up dem animals ag'in. (JAPHETH *appears.*)

SHEM. What de matter wit' de ol' man, Jape?

JAPHETH. Doggone, he say he had a dream dat we're nearly dere. Dat's why he pullin de whistle cord. See kin he git a' answer. (*He looks over the rail.*) Look to me like de same ol' territory. (MRS. NOAH *appears on deck.*)

NOAH'S WIFE. You boys go stop yo' paw pullin' dat cord. He so full of likker he think he's in a race.

JAPHETH. He claim he know what he's doin'.

NOAH'S WIFE. I claim he gittin' to be a perfec' nuisance. Me an' yo' wives cain't hardly heah ou'sel'es think. (NOAH *appears, his hat rakishly tilted on his head. He goes to the railing and looks out.*) You 'spectin' company?

NOAH. Leave me be, woman. De watah don' look so rough today. De ol' boat's ridin' easier.

NOAH'S WIFE. Ridin' like a ol' mule!

NOAH. Yes suh, de air don' feel so wet. Shem! 'Spose you sen' out 'nother dove. (SHEM *goes into the Ark.*) Ham, go git de soundin' line. Jape, keep yo' eye on de East. (JAPHETH *goes to the end of the boat.*)

NOAH'S WIFE. As fo' you, I s'pose you'll help things along by takin' a little drink.

NOAH. Look yere, who's de pilot of dis vessel?

NOAH'S WIFE. Ol' Mister Dumb Luck.

NOAH. Well, see dat's where you don' know anythin'.

NOAH'S WIFE. I s'pose you ain't drunk as a fool?

NOAH. (*Cordially.*) I feel congenial.

NOAH'S WIFE. An' you look it. You look jest wonderful. I wonder if you'd feel so congenial if de Lawd was to show up?

NOAH. De Lawd knows what I'm doin', don' you worry 'bout dat.

NOAH'S WIFE. I wouldn't say anythin' ag'inst de Lawd. He suttinly let us know dey'd be a change in de weather. But I bet even de Lawd wonders sometimes why he ever put you in charge.

NOAH. Well, you let de Lawd worry 'bout dat. (SHEM *appears with the dove.*)

SHEM. Will I leave her go, Paw?

NOAH. Leave 'er go. (*There is a chorus of "Good Luck, Dove," from the group as the dove flies off stage.* HAM *appears with the sounding line.*) Throw 'er over, Boy. (HAM *proceeds to do so.*)

NOAH's WIFE. An' another thing—

HAM. Hey!

NOAH. (*Rushing to his side.*) What is it?

HAM. Only 'bout a inch! Look! (*They lean over.*)

JAPHETH. It's gettin' light in de East. (*As* HAM *works the cord up and down,* NOAH *and* NOAH's WIFE *turn toward* JAPHETH. *The* CHOIR *begins "My Soul Is a Witness for the Lord."*)

NOAH. Praise de Lawd, so it is.

NOAH's WIFE. Oh, dat's pretty.

NOAH. (*To* HAM.) An' de boat's stopped. We've landed. Shem, go down n' drag de fires an' dreen de boiler. Yo go help 'im, Ham.

JAPHETH. Look, Paw. (*The dove wings back to the Ark with an olive branch in its mouth.*)

NOAH. 'N' yere's de little dove wid greenery in its mouth! Take 'er down, Jape, so she kin tel de animals. (JAPHETH *exits after* SHEM *and* HAM *carrying the dove. To* MRS. NOAH.) Now, maybe you feel little different.

NOAH's WIFE. (*Contritely.*) It was jes' gittin' to be so tiresome. I'm sorry, Noah.

NOAH. Dat's all right, ol' woman. (NOAH's WIFE *exits.* NOAH *looks about him. The lights have changed and the water piece is gone and the ark is again on the hillside. Two mountains can be seen in the distance and a rainbow slowly appears over the Ark. The singing has grown louder.*) Thank you, Lawd. thank you very much

indeed. Amen. (*The singing stops with the "Amen."* GOD *appears on the deck.*)

GOD. Yo' welcome, Noah. (NOAH *turns and sees him.*)

NOAH. O, Lawd, it's wonderful.

GOD. (*Looking about him.*) I sort of like it. I like de way you handled de ship, too, Noah.

NOAH. Was you watchin', Lawd?

GOD. Every minute. (*He smiles.*) Didn't de ol' lady light into you?

NOAH. (*Apologetically.*) She was kinda restless.

GOD. That's all right. I ain't blamin' nobody. I don' even min' you' cussin' an' drinkin'. I figure a steamboat cap'n on a long trip like you had has a right to a little redeye, jest so he don' go crazy.

NOAH. Thank you, Lawd. What's de orders now?

GOD. All de animals safe?

NOAH. Dey all fin'n' dandy, Lawd.

GOD. Den I want you to open dat starboard door, an' leave 'em all out. Let 'em go down de hill. Den you an' de family take all de seeds 'n de sprouts an' begin plantin' ag'in. I'm startin' all over, Noah. (NOAH *exits.* GOD *looks around.*)

GOD. Well, now we'll see what happens. (GOD *listens with a smile, as noises accompanying the debarking of the animals are heard. There are the cracks of whips, the voices of the men on the Ark, shouting: "Git along dere." "Whoa, take it easy." "Duck yo' head." "Keep in line dere," etc. Over the Ark there is a burst of centrifugal shadows, and the sound of a myriad of wings.* GOD *smiles at the shadows.*) Dat's right, birds, fin' yo' new homes. (*Bird twitters are heard again.* GOD *listens a moment and rests an arm on the railing. He speaks softly.*) Gabriel, kin you spare a minute?" (GABRIEL *appears.*)

GABRIEL. Yes, Lawd? (*The sounds from the other side of the Ark are by now almost hushed. The* LORD *indicates the new world with a wave of the hand.*)

GOD. Well, it's did.

GABRIEL. (*Respectfully, but with no enthusiasm.*) So I take notice.

GOD. Yes, suh, startin' all over again.

GABRIEL. So I see.

GOD. (*Looking at him suddenly.*) Don' seem to set you up much.

GABRIEL. Well, Lawd, you see— (*He hesitates.*) 'Tain't none of my business.

GOD. What?

GABRIEL. I say, I don' know very much about it.

GOD. I know you don'. I jest wanted you to see it. (*A thought strikes him.*) Co'se, it ain' yo' business, Gabe. It's my business. 'Twas my idea. De whole thing was my idea. An' every bit of it's my business 'n nobody else's. De whole thing rests on my shoulders. I declare, I guess *dat's* why I feel so solemn an' serious, at dis particklar time. You know *dis* thing's turned into quite a proposition.

GABRIEL. (*Tenderly.*) But, it's all right, Lawd, as you say, it's did.

GOD. Yes, suh, it's did. (*Sighs deeply. Looks slowly to the right and the left. Then softly.*) I only hope it's goin' to work out all right.

CURTAIN

PART TWO

SCENE I

GOD's *Office again.*
Somewhere the CHOIR *is singing: "A City Called Heaven." In the office are* TWO WOMEN CLEANERS. *One is scrubbing the floor, the other dusting the furniture. The one dusting stops and looks out the window. There is a whirr and a distant faint Boom. The* CHOIR *stops.*

FIRST CLEANER. Dat was a long way off.

SECOND CLEANER. (*At window.*) Yes, ma'am. An' dat must a' been a big one. Doggone, de Lawd mus' be mad fo' sho', dis mo'nin'. Dat's de fo'ty-six' thunde'-bolt since breakfast.

FIRST CLEANER. I wonder where at He's pitchin' dem.

SECOND CLEANER. My goodness, don' you know?

FIRST CLEANER. (*A little hurt.*) Did I know I wouldn't ask de question.

SECOND CLEANER. Every one of dem's bound fo' de earth.

FIRST CLEANER. De earth? You mean dat little ol' dreenin' place?

SECOND CLEANER. Dat's de planet. (*Another faint whirr and boom.*) Dere goes another.

FIRST CLEANER. Well, bless me. I didn't know dey was thunde'bolts.

SECOND CLEANER. Wha'd you think dey was?

FIRST CLEANER. (*Above desk.*) I wasn't sho', but I thought maybe He might be whittlin' a new star o' two, an' de noise was jest de chips fallin'.

SECOND CLEANER. Carrie, where you been? Don' you know de earth is de new scandal? Ever'body's talkin' 'bout it.

FIRST CLEANER. Dey kep' it from me.

SECOND CLEANER. Ain't you noticed de Lawd's been unhappy lately?

FIRST CLEANER. (*Thoughtfully.*) Yeah, He ain't been his old self.

SECOND CLEANER. What did you think was de matteh? Lumbago?

FIRST CLEANER. (*Petulantly.*) I didn't know I didn't think it was fo' me t'inquieh..

SECOND CLEANER. Well, it jest so happens dat de Lawd is riled as kin be by dat measly little earth. Or I should say de scum dat's on it.

FIRST CLEANER. Dat's mankind down dere.

SECOND CLEANER. Dey mus' be scum, too, to git de Lawd so wukked up.

FIRST CLEANER. I s'pose so. (*Another whirr and boom.*) Looks like He's lettin' dem feel de wrath. Ain' dat a shame to plague de Lawd dat way?

SECOND CLEANER. From what I hear dey been beggin' fo' what dey're gittin'. My brother flew down to bring up a saint de other day and he say from what he see mos' of de population down dere has made de debbil king an' dey wukkin' in three shifts fo' him.

FIRST CLEANER. You cain't blame de Lawd.

SECOND CLEANER. Co'se you cain't. Dem human bein's 'd make anybody bile oveh. Ev'rytime de Lawd try to do sompin' fo' dem, doggone if dey don't staht some new ruckus.

FIRST CLEANER. I take notice He's been wukkin' in yere mo' dan usual.

SECOND CLEANER. I wish He'd let us lad-ies fix it up. Wouldn't take a minute to make dis desk gold-plated.

FIRST CLEANER. I s'pose He likes it dis way. De Lawd's kind o' ol' fashioned in some ways. I s'pose He keeps dis office plain an' simple on purpose.

SECOND CLEANER. (*Finishing her work.*) I don' see why.

FIRST CLEANER. (*Looking off.*) Well, it's kind of a nice place to come to when He's studyin' somethin' impo'tant. 'Most evah-thin' else in heaven's so fin' 'n' gran', may-be ev'ry now an den He jest gits sick an' tired of de glory. (*She is also collecting her utensils.*)

SECOND CLEANER. Maybe so. Jest de same I'd like to have a free hand wid dis place for a while, so's I could gold it up. (GOD *appears in the doorway.*)

GOD. Good mo'nin', daughters.

FIRST AND SECOND CLEANERS. Good mo'-nin', Lawd. We was jest finishin'.

GOD. Go ahead den, daughters. (*Goes to the window.*)

FIRST AND SECOND CLEANERS. Yes, Lawd. (*They exeunt. Off stage.*) Good mo'nin', Gabriel (*Off stage* GABRIEL *says, "Good mo'nin', sisters," and enters immediately. He stands in the doorway for a moment watching* GOD—*a notebook and pencil in his hand.*)

GOD. What's de total?

GABRIEL. (*Consulting the book.*) Eighteen thousand nine hund'ed an' sixty for de mo'nin'. Dat's includin' de village wid de fo'tune tellers. Dey certainly kin breed fast.

GOD. (*Solemnly.*) Dey displease me. Dey displease me greatly.

GABRIEL. Want some more bolts, Lawd?

GOD. (*Looking through window.*) Look at 'em dere. Squirmin' an' fightin' an' bear-in' false witness. Listen to dat liar, dere. He don' intend to marry dat little gal. He don' even love her. What did you say?

GABRIEL. Should I git mo' bolts?

GOD. Wait a minute. (*He carefully points his finger down through the window.*) I'm goin' to git dat wicked man myself. (*From a great distance comes an agonized cry: "Oh, Lawd!"* GOD *turns from the window.*) No use gittin' mo' thunde'bolts. Dey don' do de trick. (*He goes to the swivel chair and sits.*) It's' got to be somethin' else.

GABRIEL. How would it be if you was to doom 'em all ag'in, like dat time you sent down de flood? I bet dat would make dem mind.

GOD. You see how much good de flood did. Dere dey is, jest as bad as ever.

GABRIEL. How about cleanin' up de whole mess of 'em and sta'tin' all over ag'in wid some new kind of animal?

GOD. An' admit I'm licked?

GABRIEL. (*Ashamedly.*) No, of co'se not, Lawd.

GOD. No, suh No, suh. Man is a kind of pet of mine and it ain't right fo' me to give up tryin' to do somethin' wid him. Dog-gone, mankin' mus' be all right at de core or else why did I ever bother wid him in de first place? (*Sits at desk.*)

GABRIEL. It's jest dat I hates to see you worryin' about it, Lawd.

GOD. Gabe, dere ain't anythin' worth while anywheres dat didn't 'cause somebody some worryin'. I ain't never tol' you de trouble I had gittin' things started up yere. Dat's a story in itself. No, suh, de more I keep on bein' de Lawd de more I know I got to keep improvin' things. An' dat takes time and worry. De main trouble wid mankin' is he takes up so much of my time. He ought to be able to help hisself a little. (*He stops suddenly and cogitates.*) Hey, dere! I think I got it!

GABRIEL. (*Eagerly.*) What's de news?

GOD. (*Still cogitating.*) Yes, suh, dat seems like an awful good idea.

GABRIEL. Tell me, Lawd.

GOD. Gabriel, have you noticed dat every now an' den, mankin' turns out some pretty good specimens?

GABRIEL. Dat's de truth.

GOD. Yes, suh. Dey's ol' Abraham and Isaac an' Jacob an' all dat family.

GABRIEL. Dat's so, Lawd.

GOD. An' everyone of dem boys was a hard wukker an' a good citizen. We got to admit dat.

GABRIEL. Dey wouldn't be up yere flyin' wid us if dey hadn't been.

GOD. No, suh. An' I don' know but what de answer to de whole trouble is right dere.

GABRIEL. How you mean, Lawd?

GOD. Why, doggone it, de good man is de man dat keeps busy. I mean I been goin' along on de principle dat he was something like you angels—dat you ought to be able to give him somethin' an' den jest let him sit back an' enjoy it. Dat ain't so. Now dat I recollec' I put de first one down dere to take keer o' dat garden an' den I let him go ahead an' do nothin' but git into michief. (*He rises.*) Sure, *dat's* it. He ain't' *built* jest to fool 'roun' an' not do nothin'. Gabe, I'm gonter try a new scheme.

GABRIEL. (*Eagerly.*) What's de scheme, Lawd?

GOD. I'll tell you later. Send in Abraham, Isaac an' Jacob. (*A voice outside calls: Right away, Lawd.*") You go tell dem to put dem bolts back in de boxes. I ain' gonter use dem a'gin a while.

GABRIEL. O. K., Lawd.

GOD. Was you goin' anywhere near de Big Pit?

GABRIEL. I could go.

GOD. Lean over de brink and tell Satan he's jest a plain fool if he thinks he kin beat anybody as big as me.

GABRIEL. Yes, suh, Lawd. Den I'll spit right in his eye. (GABRIEL *exits.*) (GOD *looks down through the window again to the earth below.*)

GOD. Dat new polish on de sun makes it powerful hot. (*He "r'ar back."*) Let it be jest a little bit cooler. (*He feels the air.*) Dat's nice. (*Goes to His desk. A knock on the door.*) Come in. (ABRAHAM ISAAC *and* JACOB *enter. All are very old men, but the beard of* ABRAHAM *is the longest and whitest, and they suggest their three generations. They have wings that are not quite so big as those of the native angels.*)

ISAAC. Sorry we so long comin', Lawd. But Pappy and me had to take de boy (*Pointing to* JACOB) over to git him a can of wing ointment.

GOD. What was de matter, son?

JACOB. Dey was chafin' me a little. Dey fine now, thank you, Lawd.

GOD. Dat's good. Sit down an' make yo'-selves comf'table. (*The three sit.* MEN: "*Thank you, Lawd.*") Men, I'm goin' to talk about a little scheme I got. It's one dat's goin' to affec' yo' fam'lies an' dat's why I 'cided I'd talk it over wid you, fo' it goes into ee-fect. I don' know whether you boys know it or not, but you is about de three best men of one fam'ly dat's' come up yere since I made little apples. Now I tell you what I'm gonter do. Seein' 'dat you human bein's cain't 'preciate anythin' lessen you fust wukk to git it and den keep strugglin' to hold it, why I'm gonter turn over a very valuable piece of property to yo' fam'ly, and den see what kin dey do with it. De rest of de worl' kin go jump in de river fo' all I keer. I'm gonter be lookin' out fo' yo' descendants only. Now den, seein' dat you boys know de country pretty tho'ly' where at does you think is de choice piece of property in de whole worl'? Think it over for a minute. I'm gonter let you make de s'lection.

ABRAHAM. If you was to ask me, Lawd, I don't think dey come any better dan de Land of Canaan.

GOD. (*To* ISAAC *and* JACOB.) What's yo' feelin' in de matter?

JACOB. (*After a nod from* ISAAC.) Pappy an' me think do we get a pick, dat would be it.

GOD. (*Goes to window again; looks out.*) De Land of Canaan. Yes, I guess dat's a likely neighborhood. It's all run over wid Philistines and things right now, but we kin clean dat up. (*He turns from the window and resumes his seat.*) All right. Now who do you boys think is de best of yo' men to put in charge down dere? You see I ain't been payin' much attention to anybody in partic'lar lately.

ISAAC. Does you want de brainiest or de holiest, Lawd? (MEN *look up.*)

GOD. I want de holiest. I'll make him brainy. (MEN *appreciate the miracle.*)

ISAAC. (*As* ABRAHAM *and* ISAAC *nod to him.*) Well, if you want A Number One, goodness, Lawd, I don't know where you'll git more satisfaction dan in a great- great-great-great grandson of mine.

GOD. Where's he at?

ISAAC. At de moment I b'lieve he's in de sheep business over in Midian County. He got in a little trouble down in Egypt, but t'wan't his doin'. He killed a man dat was abusin' one of our boys in brick works. Of co'se you know old King Pharaoh's got all our people in bondage.

GOD. I heard of it. (*With some ire.*) Who did you think put them dere? (*The visitors lower their heads.*) It's all right, boys. (*All rise.*) I'm gonter take dem out of it. An' I'm gonter turn over de whole Land of Canaan to dem. An' do you know whose gonter lead dem dere? Yo' great, great, great, great grandson. Moses, ain't it?

ISAAC. Yes, Lawd.

GOD. (*Smiling.*) Yes. I been noticin' *him*.

ABRAHAM. It's quite a favor fo' de fam'ly, Lawd.

GOD. Dat's why I tol' you. You see, it so happens I love yo' fam'ly, an' I delight to honor it. Dat's all, gen'lemen. (*The three others rise and cross to the door, murmuring, "Yes, Lawd," "Thank you, Lawd," "Much obliged, Lawd." etc. The* CHOIR *begins, "My Lord's A-Writin' All De Time" pianissimo.* GOD *stands watching the men leave.*) Enjoy yo'selves. (*He goes to the window. The singing grows softer. He speaks through the window to the earth.*) I'm comin' down to see you Moses, an' dis time my scheme's got to wukk.

(*The stage is darkened. The singing grows louder and continues until the lights go up on the next scene.*)

SCENE II

The tableau curtains frame the opening of a cave, which is dimly lighted. A large turkey-berry bush is somewhere near the foreground. MOSES *is seated on the grass eating his lunch from a basket in his lap.* ZIPPORAH, *his wife, stands watching him. He is about forty,* ZIPPORAH *somewhat younger. They are dressed inconspicuously.* MOSES *stutters slightly when he speaks. He looks up to see* ZIPPORAH *smiling.*

MOSES. What you smilin' at, Zipporah?

ZIPPORAH. Caize you enjoyin' yo'self.

MOSES. You is a good wife, Zipporah.

ZIPPORAH. You is a good husband, Moses, (MOSES *wipes his mouth with a handkerchief and begins putting into the basket the various implements of the meal which had been on the ground about him.*) Why you suppose it's so dark yere today? Dey's no rain in de air.

MOSES. Seems like it's jest aroun' dis cave. Yo' father's house is got de sun on it. (*He looks in another direction.*) Looks all clear down toward Egypt.

ZIPPORAH. Co'se it *would* be fine weather in Egypt. De sky looks all right. Maybe it's gonter rain jest right yere. Why don' you move de sheep over to de other pasture?

MOSES. (*A bit puzzled.*) I don' know. It got dark like dis befo' you come along wid de dinner an' I was gonter stop you on de top of de hill. Den somethin' kep' me yere.

ZIPPORAH. S'pose it could be de Lawd warnin' you dat dey's 'Gyptians hangin' 'roun'?

MOSES. Dey may have fo'gotten all about dat killin' by now. Dey got a new Pharoah down dere.

ZIPPORAH. An' I hear he's' jest as mean to yo' people as his pappy was. I wouldn't put it pas' him to send soljahs all the way up yere fo' you.

MOSES. Dat's all right. De Lawd's looked after me so far, I don' 'spect him to fall down on me now. You better be gittin' home.

ZIPPORAH. (*Taking the basket.*) I'll be worryin' about you.

MOSES. (*Kissing her and then smiling.*) 'Parently de Lawd ain't. He knows I'm safe as kin be. Lemme see you feel dat way.

ZIPPORAH. You is a good man, Moses.

MOSES. I's a lucky man. (ZIPPORAH *exits with the basket.* MOSES *looks up at the sky.*) Dat's funny. De sun seems to be shinin' everyplace but right yere. It's shinin' on de sheep. Why ain't dey no cloud dere?

GOD. (*Off stage.*) Caize I want it to be like dat, Moses.

MOSES. (*Looking about him.*) Who's dat?

GOD. (*Off stage again.*) I'm de Lawd, Moses.

MOSES. (*Smiling.*) Dat's what you say. Dis yere shadow may be de Lawd's wukk, but dat voice soun' pretty much to me like my ol' brother Aaron.

GOD. (*Off stage.*) Den keep yo' eyes open, son. (*The turkey-berry bush begins to glow and then turns completely red.* MOSES *looks at it fascinated.*) Maybe you notice de bush ain't burnin' up.

MOSES. Dat's de truth. (MOSES *is full of awe but not frightened.*)

GOD. (*Off stage.*) Now you believe me?

MOSES. Co'se I does. It's wonderful. (*The light in the bush dies and* GOD *appears from behind it.*)

GOD. No, it ain't, Moses. It was jest a trick.

MOSES. 'Scuse me doubtin' you, Lawd. I always had de feelin' you wuz takin' keer of me, but I never 'spected you'd fin' de time to talk wid me pussunly. (*He laughs.*) Dat was a good trick, Lawd. I'se seen some good ones, but dat was de beatenest.

GOD. Yo' gonter see lots bigger tricks dan dat, Moses. In fac', yo' gonter perfo'm dem.

MOSES. (*Incredulously.*) Me? I'm gonter be a tricker?

GOD. Yes, suh.

MOSES. An' do magic? Lawd, my mouth ain't got de quick talk to go wid it.

GOD. It'll come to you now.

MOSES. (*Now cured of stuttering.*) Is I goin' wid a circus?

GOD. (*Slowly and solemnly.*) Yo' is goin' down into Egypt, Moses, and lead my people out of bondage. To do dat I'm gonter make you de bes' tricker in de worl'.

MOSES. (*A little frightened.*) Egypt! You know I killed a man dere, Lawd. Won't dey kill me?

GOD. Not when dey see yo' tricks. You ain't skeered, is you?

MOSES. (*Simply and bravely.*) No, suh, Lawd.

GOD. Den yere's what I"m gonter do. Yo' people is my chillun, Moses. I"m sick and tired o' de way ol' King Pharoah is treatin' dem, so I'se gonter take dem away, and yo' gonter lead dem. You gonter lead 'em out of Egypt an' 'across de river Jordan. It's gonter take a long time, and you ain't goin' on no excursion train. Yo' gonter wukk awful hard for somethin' yo' goin' to fin' when de trip's over.

MOSES. What's dat, Lawd?

GOD. It's de Land of Canaan. It's de bes' land I got. I've promised it to yo' people, an' I'm gonter give it to dem.

MOSES. Co'se, ol' King Pharoah will do everything he kin to stop it.

GOD. Yes, an' dat's where de tricks come in. Dey tell me he's awful fond of tricks.

MOSES. I hear dat's *all* he's fon' of. Dey say if you can't take a rabbit out of a hat you cain't git in to see him.

GOD. Wait'll you see de tricks you an' me's goin to show him.

MOSES. (*Delightedly.*) Doggone! Huh, Lawd?

GOD. Yes, suh. Now de first trick—(GOD *is lifting a stick which he carries.*)

MOSES. Jest a minute, Lawd. (GOD *halts the demonstration.*) I'm gonter learn de tricks and do just like you tell me, but I know it's gonter take me a little time to learn all dat quick talkin'. Cain't I have my brother Aaron go wid me? He's a good man.

GOD. I was gonter have him help you wid de Exodus. I guess he can watch, too.

MOSES. I'll call 'im. (*He turns as if to shout.*)

GOD. Wait. (MOSES *turns and looks at* GOD.) I'll *bring* him. (*Softly.*) Aaron! (AARON *appears between* GOD *and* MOSES *in the mouth of the cave. He is a little taller than* MOSES *and slightly older. He, too, is dressed like a field hand.*)

AARON. (*Blankly.*) Hey! (MOSES *goes to him, takes his hand and leads him, bewildered, down to where* MOSES *had been standing alone.* AARON *then sees* GOD.)

MOSES. (*Almost in a whisper.*) It's all right.

GOD. Don't worry, son, I'm jest showin' some tricks. Bringin' you yere was one of dem. (AARON *stares at* GOD *as if hypnotized.*) Now den, you see dis yere rod? Looks like a ordinary walking stick, don' it?

MOSES. Yes, Lawd.

GOD. Well, it ain't no ordinary walkin' stick, caize look. (MOSES *leans forward.*) when I lays it down on de groun'—(*The stage is darkened. The* CHOIR *begins, "Go Down, Moses," and continues until the lights go up on the next scene.*)

SCENE III

The throne room of PHARAOH. *It suggests a Negro lodge room. The plain board walls are colored by several large parade banners of varying sizes, colors and materials, bordered with gold fringe and tassels on them. Some of the inscriptions on them read:*

SUBLIME ORDER OF THE HOUSE OF PHARAOH
HOME CHAPTER

MYSTIC BROTHERS OF THE EGYPTIAN HOME GUARD
LADIES AUXILIARY, NO. 1

SUPREME MAGICIANS AND WIZARDS OF THE UNIVERSE

PRIVATE FLAG OF HIS HONOR OLD KING PHARAOH

ROYAL YOUNG PEOPLE'S PLEASURE CLUB

ENCHANTED AND INVISIBLE CADETS OF EGYPT BOYS' BRIGADE

There is one door up right and a window. The throne, an ordinary armchair with a drapery over its back, is on a dais. PHARAOH *is seated on the throne. His crown and garments might be those worn by a high officer in a Negro lodge during a ritual. About the throne itself are high officials, several of them with plumed hats, clothing that suggests military uniforms, and rather elaborate sword belts, swords and scabbards. A few soldiers carrying spears are also in his neighborhood and one or two bearded ancients in brightly colored robes with the word "Wizard" on their conical hats. In the general group of men and women scattered elsewhere in the room Sunday finery is noticeable everywhere. Most of the civilians have bright "parade" ribbons and wear medals. In a cleared space immediately before the throne a* CANDIDATE MAGICIAN *is performing a sleight-of-hand trick with cards.* PHARAOH *watches him apathetically. He is receiving earnest attention from a few of the others, but the majority of the men and women are talking quietly among themselves. Beside the* CANDIDATE MAGICIAN *are several paraphernalia of previously demonstrated tricks.*

CANDIDATE MAGICIAN. (*Holding up some cards.*) Now den, ol' King Pharaoh, watch dis. (*He completes a trick. There is a murmur of "Not Bad." "Pretty Good," etc. from a few of the watchers.* PHARAOH *makes no comment.*) Now, I believe de cyard I ast you to keep sittin' on was de trey of diamonds, wasn't it?

PHARAOH. Yeah.

CANDIDATE MAGICIAN. Den kin I trouble you to take a look at it now? (PHARAOH *half rises to pick up a card he has been sitting on, and looks at it.*) I believe you'll now notice dat it's de King of Clubs?

(PHARAOH *nods and shows the card to those nearest him. The* CANDIDATE MAGICIAN *waits for an audible approval and gets practically none.*) An' dat, ol' King Pharaoh, completes de puffohmance. (*An elderly man in a uniform steps forward.*)

GENERAL. On behalf of my nephew I beg Yo' Honor to let him jine de ranks of de royal trickers and magicians.

PHARAOH. (*To the two* WIZARDS.) What do de committee think? (*The* WIZARDS *shake their heads.*) Dat's what I thought. He ain't good enough. I'd like to help you out, General, but you know a man's got to be a awful good tricker to git in de royal society dese days. You better go back an' steddy some mo', son. (*He lifts his*

voice and directs two soldiers guarding the door.) Is de head magician reached de royal waitin' room yit? (*One of the soldiers opens the door to look out.*) If he is, send him in. (*The soldier beckons to some one off stage, throws the door open, and announces to the court.*)

SOLDIER. De Head Magician of de land of Egypt. (*A very old and villainous man enters. His costume is covered with cabalistic and zodiacal signs. He advances to the* KING, *the other magician and his uncle making way for him. He bows curtly to* PHARAOH.)

HEAD MAGICIAN. Good mo'nin', ol' King Pharaoh.

PHARAOH. Mo'nin', Professor. What's de news?

HEAD MAGICIAN. Evahthing's carried out like you said.

PHARAOH. How's de killin' of de babies 'mongst de Hebrews comin' 'long?

HEAD MAGICIAN. Jes' like you ordered.

PHARAOH. (*Genially.*) Dey killed all of 'em, huh?

HEAD MAGICIAN. Do dey see one, dey kill 'im. You teachin' 'em a great lesson. Dey don' like it a-tall.

PHARAOH. (*Smilingly.*) What do dey say?

HEAD MAGICIAN. (*Pawing the air inarticulately.*) I hates to tell in front of de ladies.

PHARAOH. Dey feels pretty bad, huh?

HEAD MAGICIAN. Dat's jest de beginnin' of it. Betwixt de poleece and de soljahs we killed about a thousan' of 'em las' night. Dat's purty good.

PHARAOH. (*Thoughtfully.*) Yeh, it's fair. I guess you boys is doin' all you kin. But I fin' I ain't satisfied, though.

HEAD MAGICIAN. How you mean, Yo' Honor?

PHARAOH. I mean I'd like to make dose Hebrew chillun realize dat I kin be even mo' of a pest. I mean I hates dem chillun. An' I'm gonter think of a way of makin' 'em even mo' mizzable.

HEAD MAGICIAN. But dey *ain't* anythin' meaner dan killin' de babies, King.

PHARAOH. Dey must be sump'n. Doggone, you is my head tricker, you put yo' brains on it. (*To the others.*) Quiet, whilst de Head Magician go into de silence.

HEAD MAGICIAN. (*After turning completely around twice, and a moment's cogitation.*) I tell you what I kin do. All de Hebrews dat ain't out to de buryin' grounds or in de hospitals is laborin' in de brick wukks.

PHARAOH. Yeh?

HEAD MAGICIAN. (*After a cackling laugh.*) How would it be to take de straw away from 'em and tell 'em dey's got to turn out jest as many bricks as usual? Ain't dat nasty?

PHARAOH. Purty triflin', but I s'pose it'll have to do for de time bein'. Where's de extreme inner guard? (*One of the military attendants comes forward.*) Go on out an' tell de sup'intendent to put dat into eeffect. (*The attendant bows and starts for the door. He stops as* PHARAOH *calls to him.*) Wait a minute! Tell 'im to chop off de hands of anybody dat say he cain't make de bricks dat way. (*The attendant salutes and exits, the door being opened and closed by one of the soldiers.*) Now what's de news in de magic line?

HEAD MAGICIAN. I ain't got very many novelties today, King, I bin wukkin' too hard on de killin's. I'm so tired I don' believe I could lift a wand. (*There are murmurs of protest from the assemblage.*)

PHARAOH. Doggone, you was to 'a been de chief feature o' de meetin' dis mawnin'. Look at de turn-out you got account of me tellin' 'em you was comin'.

HEAD MAGICIAN. Well, dat's de way it is, King. Why don' you git de wizards to do some spell castin'?

PHARAOH. Dey say it's in de cyards dat dey cain't wukk till high noon. (*He glances at the* WIZARDS.) Think mebbe you kin cheat a little?

FIRST WIZARD. Oh dat cain't be done, King.

PHARAOH. Well, we might as well adjourn, den. Looks to me like de whole program's shot to pieces. (*He starts to rise, when there is a furious banging on the door.*) What's de idea, dere? See who dat is. (*The soldiers open the door.* MOSES *and* AARON *enter, pushing the two soldiers aside and coming down in front of* PHARAOH. *The soldiers are bewildered and* PHARAOH *is angry.*) Say, who tol' you two baboons you could come in yere?

MOSES. Is you ol' King Pharaoh?

PHARAOH. Dat's me. Did you heah what I asked you?

MOSES. My name is Moses, and dis is my brother Aaron. (*Murmur of "Hebrews" spreads through the room.*)

PHARAOH. (*In a rage.*) Is you Hebrews?

MOSES. Yes, suh.

PHARAOH. (*Almost screaming.*) Put 'em to de sword! (*As the courtiers approach,* AARON *suddenly discloses the rod, which he swings once over his head. The courtiers draw back as if their hands had been stung. Cries of "Hey!" "Lookout," etc.*)

MOSES. Keep outside dat circle. (*The courtiers nearest* MOSES *and* AARON *look at each other, exclaiming ad lib., "Did you feel dat?" "What is dat?" "What's goin' on, heah?" "My hands is stingin'!" etc.*)

PHARAOH. (*Puzzled but threatening.*) What's de idea yere?

MOSES. We is magicians, ol' King Pharaoh.

PHARAOH. (*To the* HEAD MAGICIAN.) Put a spell on 'em. (*The* HEAD MAGICIAN *stands looking at them bewildered. To* MOSES.) I got some magicians, too. We'll see who's got de bes' magic. (MOSES *and* AARON *laugh. Most of the courtiers are cowering. To the* HEAD MAGICIAN.) Go ahead, give 'em gri-gri.

MOSES. Sure, go ahead.

PHARAOH. Hurry up, dey's laughin' at you. What's de matter?

HEAD MAGICIAN. I cain't think of de right spell.

PHARAOH. (*Now frightened himself.*) You mean dey got even *you* whupped?

HEAD MAGICIAN. Dey's got a new kind of magic.

PHARAOH. (*Gazes at* HEAD MAGICIAN *a moment, bewildered. To the* WIZARDS.) I s'pose if de Professor cain't, you cain't.

FIRST WIZARD. Dat's a new trick, King.

HEAD MAGICIAN. (*Rubbing his fingers along his palms.*) It's got 'lectricity in it!

PHARAOH. H'm, well dat may make it a little diff'rent. So you boys is magicians, too?

MOSES. Yes, suh.

PHARAOH. Well, we's always glad to see some new trickers in de co't, dat is if dey good. (*He glances about him.*) You look like you is O. K.

MOSES. Dat's what we claims, ol' King Pharaoh. We think we's de best in de worl'.

PHARAOH. You certainly kin talk big. Jest what is it you boys would like?

MOSES. We came to show you some tricks. Den we's goin' to ask you to do somethin' for us.

PHARAOH. Well, I s'pose you know I'm a fool for conjurin'. If a man kin show me some tricks I ain't seen, I goes out of my way to do him a favor.

MOSES. Dat's good. Want to see de first trick?

PHARAOH. It ain't goin 'to hurt nobody?

MOSES. Dis one won't.

PHARAOH. Go ahead.

MOSES. Dis yere rod my brother has looks jes' like a walkin' stick, don't it? (*The courtiers now join the King in interest.*)

PHARAOH. Uh huh. Le's see. (AARON *hands the rod, which* PHARAOH *inspects and returns.*)

MOSES. Well, look what happens when he lays it on de groun'. (AARON *places the rod on the second step of the throne. It turns into a lifelike snake. There are exclamations from the assemblage.*)

PHARAOH. Dat's a good trick! Now turn it back into a walkin' stick again. (AARON *picks is up and it is again a rod. Exclamations of "Purty good!" "Dat's all right!" "What do you think of that!" etc.*) Say, you is good trickers!

MOSES. You ain't never seen de beat of us. Now I'm goin' to ask de favor.

PHARAOH. Sure, what is it?

MOSES. (*Solemnly.*) Let de Hebrew chillun go!

PHARAOH. (*Rises and stares at them. There is a murmur of "Listen to 'im!" "He's got nerve!" "I never in my life!" "My goodness!" etc.*) What did you say?

MOSES. Let de Hebrew chillun go. (PHARAOH *seats himself again.*)

PHARAOH. (*Slowly.*) Don' you know de Hebrews is my slaves?

MOSES. Yes, suh.

PHARAOH. Yes, suh, my slaves. (*There is a distant groaning.*) Listen, and you kin hear 'em bein' treated like slaves. (*He calls toward the window.*) What was dey doin' den?

MAN NEAR THE WINDOW. Dey's jest gettin' de news down in de brick-yard.

PHARAOH. I won't let them go. (*He snorts contemptuously.*) Let's see another trick.

MOSES. Yes, suh, yere's a better one.(*He lowers his head.*) Let's have a plague of de flies. (AARON *raises the rod. The room grows dark and a great buzzing of flies is heard. The courtiers break out in cries of "Get away fum me!" "Take 'em away!" "De place is filled with flies!" "Dis is terrible!" "Do sump'n, PHARAOH!"*)

PHARAOH. (*Topping the others.*) All right —stop de trick!

MOSES. Will you let de Hebrews go?

PHARAOH. Sho' I will. Go ahead stop it!

MOSES. (*Also above the others.*) Begone! (*The buzzing stops and the room is filled with light again, as* AARON *lowers the rod. All except* MOSES *and* AARON *are brushing the flies from their persons.)*

PHARAOH. (*Laughing.*) Doggone, dat was a good trick! (*The others, seeing they are uninjured, join in the laughter, with exclamations of "Doggone!" "You all right?" "Sho' I'm all right." "Didn' hurt me," etc.*) You is good trickers.

MOSES. Will you let de Hebrew chillun go?

PHARAOH. (*Sitting down again.*) Well, I'll tell you, boys. I'll tell you sump'n you didn' know. You take me, *I'm* a pretty good tricker, an' I jest outtricked you. So, bein' de bes' tricker, I don' think I will let 'em go. You got any mo' tricks yo'self?

MOSES. Yes, suh. Dis is a little harder one. (AARON *lifts the rod.*) Gnats in de mill pon', gnats in de clover, gnats in de tater patch, stingin' all over. (*The stage grows dark again. There is the humming of gnats and the slapping of hands against faces and arms, and the same protests as were heard with the flies, but with more feeling, "I'm gittin' stung to death!" "I'm all stung!" "Dey're like hornets!" "Dey's on my face!" etc.*)

PHARAOH. Take 'em away, Moses!

MOSES. (*His voice drowning the others.*) If I do, will you let 'em go?

PHARAOH. Sho' I will, dis time.

MOSES. Do you mean it?

PHARAOH. Co'se I mean it! Doggone, one just stang me on de nose.

MOSES. Begone! (*Lights come up as* AARON *lowers the rod. There is a moment of general recovery again.* PHARAOH *rubs his nose, looks at his hands, etc., as do the others.*) Now, how about it?

PHARAOH. (*Smiling.*) Well, I'll tell you, Moses. Now dat de trick's over—(MOSES *takes a step toward* PHARAOH.)

MOSES. Listen, Pharaoh. You been lyin' to me, and I'm gittin' tired of it.

PHARAOH. I ain't lyin', I'm trickin', too.

You been trickin' me and I been trickin' you.

MOSES. I see. Well, I got one mo' trick up my sleeve which I didn't aim to wukk unless I had to. Caize when I does it, I cain't undo it.

PHARAOH. Wukk it an' I'll trick you right back. I don' say you ain't a good tricker, Moses. You is one of de best I ever seen. But I kin outtrick you. Dat's all.

MOSES. It ain't only me dat's goin' to wukk dis trick. It's me an' de Lawd.

PHARAOH. Who?

MOSES. De Lawd God of Israel.

PHARAOH. I kin outtrick you an' de Lawd too!

MOSES. (*Angrily.*) Now you done it, ol' King Pharaoh. You been mean to de Lawd's people, and de Lawd's been easy on you caize you didn't know no better. You been givin' me a lot of say-so-and no do-so, and I didn' min' dat. But now you've got to braggin' dat you's better dan de Lawd, and dat's too many.

PHARAOH. You talk like a preacher, an' I never did like to hear preachers talk.

MOSES. You ain't goin' to like it any better, when I strikes down de oldes' boy in every one of yo' people's houses.

PHARAOH. Now you've given up trickin and is jest lyin'. (*He rises.*) Listen, I'm Pharaoh. I do de strikin' down yere. I strike down my enemies, and dere's no one in all Egypt kin kill who he want to, 'ceptin' me.

MOSES. I'm sorry, Pharaoh. Will you let de Hebrews go?

PHARAOH. You heard my word. (AARON *is lifting his rod again at a signal from* MOSES.) Now, no more tricks or I'll—

MOSES. Oh, Lawd, you'll have to do it, I guess. Aaron, lift de rod. (*There is a thunderclap, darkness and screams. The lights go up. Several of the younger men on the stage have fallen to the ground or are being held in the arms of the horrified elders.*)

PHARAOH. What have you done yere? Where's my boy? (*Through the door come four men bearing a young man's body.*)

FIRST OF THE FOUR MEN. King Pharaoh. (PHARAOH *drops into his chair, stunned, as the dead boy is brought to the throne.*)

PHARAOH. (*Grief-stricken.*) Oh, my son, my fine son. (*The courtiers look at him with mute appeal.*)

MOSES. I'm sorry, Pharaoh, but you cain't fight de Lawd. Will you let his people go?

PHARAOH. Let them go. (*The lights go out. The* CHOIR *begins, "Mary Don't You Weep," and continues until it is broken by the strains of "I'm Noways Weary and I'm Noways Tired." The latter is sung by many more voices than the former, and the cacophony ends as the latter grows in volume and the lights go up on the next scene.*)

SCENE IV

The CHILDREN *of* ISRAEL *are marching on the treadmill and now singing fortissimo. They are of all ages and most of them are ragged. The men have packs on their shoulders, one or two have hand carts. The line stretches across the stage. It is nearing twilight, and the faces of the assemblage are illumined by the rays of the late afternoon sun. The upper treadmill carries a gradually rising and falling middle distance past the marchers. The foot of a mountain appears: a trumpet call is heard as the foot of the mountain reaches stage center. The marchers halt. The picture now shows the mountain running up out of sight off right. The singing stops. A babel of "What's de matter?" "Why do we stop?" "Tain't sundown yet!" "What's happened?" "What's goin' on?" "What are they blowin' for?" etc. Those looking ahead begin to murmur. "It's Moses," "Moses." "What's happened to him?" The others take up the repetition of "Moses," and Moses enters, on the arm of* AARON. *He is now an old man, as is his brother, and he totters toward the center of the stage. Cries of "What's de matter, MOSES?" "You ain't hurt, is you?" "Ain't that too bad?" etc. He slowly seats himself on the rock at the foot of the mountain.*

AARON. How you feelin' now, brother?

MOSES. I'm so weary, Aaron. Seems like I was took all of a sudden.

AARON. Do we camp yere?

MOSES. (*Pathetically.*) No, you got to keep goin'.

AARON. But you cain't go no further tonight, brother.

MOSES. Dis never happened to me befo'.

A YOUNG WOMAN. But you's a ol' man, now, Father Moses. You cain't expect to go as fas' as we kin.

MOSES. But de Lawd said I'd do it. He said I was to show you de Promised Land. Fo'ty years, I bin leadin' you. I led you out o' Egypt. I led you past Sinai, and through de wilderness. Oh, I cain't fall down on you now!

AARON. Le's res' yere fo' de night. Den we'll see how you feel in de mo'nin'.

MOSES. We tol' de scouts we'd meet 'em three miles furder on. I hate fo' 'em to come back all dis way to report. 'Tis gettin' a little dark, ain't it?

AARON. It ain't dark, Brother.

MOSES. No, it's my eyes.

AARON. Maybe it's de dust.

MOSES. No, I jest cain't seem to see. Oh, Lawd, dey cain't have a blind man leadin' 'em! Where is you Aaron?

AARON. I'se right yere, Moses.

MOSES. Do you think—(*Pause.*) Oh! Do you think it's de time He said?

AARON. How do you mean, Moses? (*Crowd look from one to another in wonder.*)

MOSES. He said I could lead 'em to de Jordan, dat I'd *see* de Promised Land, and dat's all de further I could go, on account I broke de laws. Little while back I thought I *did* see a river ahead, and a pretty land on de other side. (*Distant shouts "Hoo-*

ray!" "Yere dey are!" "Dey travelled quick." etc.) Where's de young leader of de troops? Where's Joshua? (*The call "JOSHUA" is taken up by those on the right of the stage, followed almost immediately by "Yere he is!" "MOSES wants you!" etc.)* (*JOSHUA enters. He is a fine looking Negro of about thirty.*)

JOSHUA. (*Going to MOSES' side.*) Yes, suh.

MOSES. What's de shoutin' 'bout, Joshua?

JOSHUA. De scouts is back wid de news. De Jordan is right ahead of us, and Jericho is jest on de other side. Moses, we're dere! (*There are cries of "Hallelujah!" "De Lawd be praised!" "Hooray!" "De Kingdom's comin'!" etc. With a considerable stir among the marchers, several new arrivals crowd in from right, shouting "MOSES, we're dere!" JOSHUA seeing the newcomers.*) Yere's de scouts! (*Three very ragged and dusty young men advance to MOSES.*)

MOSES. (*As the shouting dies.*) So it's de River Jordan?

FIRST SCOUT. Yes, suh.

MOSES. All we got to take is de city of Jericho.

FIRST SCOUT. Yes, suh.

MOSES. Joshua, you got to take charge of de fightin' men, an' Aaron's gotta stay by de priests.

JOSHUA. What about you?

MOSES. You are leavin' me behind. Joshua, you gonter get de fightin' men together and take dat city befo' sundown.

JOSHUA. It's a big city, Moses, wid walls all 'round it. We ain't got enough men.

MOSES. You'll take it, Joshua.

JOSHUA. Yes, suh, but how?

MOSES. Move up to de 'walls 'wid our people. Tell de priests to go wid you with de rams' horns. You start marchin' 'roun' dem walls, and den—

JOSHUA. Yes, suh.

MOSES. De Lawd'll take charge, jest as he's' took charge ev'y time I've led you against a city. He ain't never failed, has he?

SEVERAL VOICES. No, Moses. (*All raise their heads.*)

MOSES. And he ain't goin' to fail us now. (*He prays. All bow.*) Oh, Lawd, I'm turnin' over our brave young men to you, caize I know you don' want me to lead 'em any further. (*Rises.*) Jest like you said, I've got to de Jordan but I cain't git over it. An' yere dey goin' now to take de city of Jericho. In a little while dey'll be marchin' 'roun' it. An' would you please be so good as to tell 'em what to do? Amen. (*To JOSHUA.*) Go ahead. Ev'ybody follows Joshua now. Give de signal to move on wid e'vything. (*A trumpet is heard.*) You camp fo' de night in de City of Jericho. (*MOSES seats himself on the rock.*)

JOSHUA. Cain't we help you, Moses?

MOSES. You go ahead. De Lawd's got his plans fo' me. Soun' de signal to march. (*Another trumpet call is heard. The company starts marching off. AARON lingers a moment.*) Take care of de Ark of de Covenant, Aaron.

AARON. Yes, Brother. Good-bye.

MOSES. Good-bye, Aaron. (*The singing is resumed softly and dies away. The last of the marchers has disappeared.*) Yere I is, Lawd. De chillun is goin' into de Promised Land. (*GOD enters from behind the hill. He walks to MOSES, puts his hands on his shoulders.*) You's with me, ain't you, Lawd?

GOD. Co'se I is.

MOSES. Guess I'm through, Lawd. Jest like you said I'd be, when I broke de tablets of de law. De ol" machine's broke down.

GOD. Jest what was it 'I said to you, Moses? Do you remember?

MOSES. You said I couldn't go into de Promised Land.

GOD. Dat's so. But dat ain't all dey was to it.

MOSES. How do you mean, Lawd?

GOD. Moses, you been a good man. You been a good leader of my people. You got me angry once, dat's true. And when you anger me I'm a God of Wrath. But I never meant you wasn't gonter have what was comin' to you. An' I ain't goin' to do you out of it, Moses. It's jest de country acrost de River dat you ain't gonter enter. You gonter have a Promised Land. I been gettin' it ready fo' you, fo' a long time. Kin you stand up?

MOSES. (*Rising, with* GOD's *help.*) Yes, suh, Lawd.

GOD. Come on, I'm goin' to show it to you. We goin' up dis hill to see it. Moses, it's a million times nicer dan de Land of Canaan. (*They start up the hill.*)

MOSES. I cain't hardly see.

GOD. Don't worry. Dat's jest caize you so old. (*They take a step or two up the hill, when* MOSES *stops suddenly.*)

MOSES. Oh!

GOD. What's de matter?

MOSES. We cain't be doin' dis!

GOD. Co'se we kin!

MOSES. But I fo'got! I fo'got about Joshua and de fightin' men!

GOD. How about 'em?

MOSES. Dey're marchin' on Jericho. I tol' 'em to march aroun' 'de walls and den de Lawd would be dere to tell 'em what to do.

GOD. Dat's all right. He's dere.

MOSES. Den who's dis helpin' me up de hill?

GOD. Yo' faith, yo' God.

MOSES. And is you over dere helpin' them too, Lawd? Is you goin' to tell dem poor chillun what to do?

GOD. Co'se I is. Listen Moses. I'll show you how I'm helpin' dem. (*From the distance comes the blast of the rams' horns, the sound of crumbling walls, a roar, and a moment's silence. The* CHOIR *begins* "Joshua Fit De Battle of Jericho" *and continues through the rest of the scene.*)

MOSES. You did it, Lawd! You've tooken it! Listen to de chillun'—dey's in de Land of Canaan at last! You's de only God dey ever was, ain't you, Lawd?

GOD. (*Quietly.*) Come on, ol' 'man. (*They continue up the hill.*) (*The stage is darkened.*)

MR. DESHEE. (*In the dark.*) But even dat scheme didn't work. Caize after dey got into the Land of Canaan dey went to de dogs again. And dey went into bondage again. Only dis time it was in de City of Babylon. (*The* CHOIR, *which has been singing* "Cain't Stay Away," *stops as the next scene begins.*)

SCENE V

Under a low ceiling is a room vaguely resembling a Negro night club in New Orleans. Two or three long tables run across the room, and on the left is a table on a dais with a gaudy canopy above it. The table bears a card marked "Reserved for King and guests."

Flashy young men and women are seated at the tables. About a dozen couples are dancing in the foreground to the tune of a jazz orchestra. The costumes are what would be worn at a Negro masquerade to represent the debauchees of Babylon.

FIRST MAN. When did yuh git to Babylon?

SECOND MAN. I jes' got in yesterday.

THIRD MAN. (*Dancing.*) How do you like dis baby, Joe?

FOURTH MAN. Hot damn! She could be de King's pet!

A WOMAN. Anybody seen my papa?

THIRD MAN. Don' fo'git de dance at de High Priest's house tomorrow. (*The dance stops as a bugle call is heard. Enter* MASTER OF CEREMONIES.)

MASTER OF CEREMONIES. Stop! Tonight's guest of honor, de King of Babylon an' party of five. (*Enter the* KING *and five girls. The* KING *has on an imitation ermine cloak over his conventional evening clothes and wears a diamond tiara. All rise as the* KING *enters, and sing, "Hail, de King of Bab—Bab—Babylon."*

KING. Wait till you see de swell table I got. (*He crosses the stage to his table. The girls are jabbering.*) Remind me to send you a peck of rubies in de mo'nin'.

MASTER OF CEREMONIES. Ev'nin', King!

KING. Good ev'nin'. How's de party goin'?

MASTER OF CEREMONIES. Bes' one we ever had in Babylon, King.

KING. Any Jew boys yere?

MASTER OF CEREMONIES. (*Indicating some of the others.*) Lot o' dem yere. I kin go git mo' if you want 'em.

KING. I was really referrin' to de High Priest. He's a 'ticlar frien' o' mine an' he might drop in. You know what he look like?

MASTER OF CEREMONIES. No, suh, but I'll be on de look-out fo' him.

KING. O. K. Now le's have a li'l good time.

MASTER OF CEREMONIES. Yes, suh. (*To the orchestra.*) Let 'er go, boys. (*The music begins, waiters appear with food and great urns painted gold and silver, from which they pour out wine for the guests. The* MASTER OF CEREMONIES *exits. The* KING'S *dancing-girls go to the middle of the floor, and start to dance. The* KING *puts his arms about the waists of two girls, and draws them to him.*)

KING. Hot damn! Da's de way! Let de Jew boys see our gals kin dance better'n dere's. (*There is an ad lib. babel of "Da's de truth,* KING*!" "I don' know—we got some good gals, too!" etc.*) Dey ain' nobody in de worl' like de Babylon gals. (*The dancing grows faster, the watchers keep time with hand-claps. The door at the left opens suddenly, and the* PROPHET, *a patriarchal, ragged figure enters. He looks belligerently about the room, and is followed almost immediately by the* MASTER OF CEREMONIES.)

PROPHET. Stop! (*The music and the dancers halt.*)

KING. What's the idea, bustin' up my party?

MASTER OF CEREMONIES. He said he was expected, King. I thought mebbe he was de—

KING. Did you think he was de High Priest of de Hebrews? Why, he's jest an ol' bum! De High Priest is a fashion plate. T'row dis ole bum out o' yere!

PROPHET. Stop! (*Those who have been advancing to seize him stop, somewhat amused.*)

KING. Wait a minute. Don't throw him out. Let's see what he has to say.

PROPHET. Listen to me, King of Babylon! I've been sent yere by de Lawd God Jehovah. Don't you dare lay a hand on de Prophet!

KING. Oh, you're a prophet, is yuh? Well you know we don' keer muh fo' prophet in dis part of de country.

PROPHET. Listen to me, sons and daughter of Babylon! Listen, you children of Israel dat's given yo'selves over to de evil ways o' yo' oppressors! You're all wallowin' like hogs in sin, an' de wrath of Gawd ain goin' to be held back much longer! I'm tellin' you, repent befo' it's too late. Repent befo' Jehovah casts down de same fire dat burned up Sodom and Gomorrah. Repent befo' de— (*During this scene yell increase as the* PROPHET *continues.*)
(*The* HIGH PRIEST *enters left. He is a fat voluptuary elaborately clothed in brightl colored robes. He walks in hand in hand with a gaudily dressed "chippy."*)

HIGH PRIEST. (*Noise stops.*) Whoa, dere What you botherin' the King fo'?

PROPHET. (*Wheeling.*) And you, de High Priest of all Israel, walkin' de town wid dirty li'l tramp.

KING. Seems to be a frien' o' yours, Jake

HIGH PRIEST. (*Crossing to the* KING *with his girl.*) Aw, he's one of dem wild men like Jeremiah and Isaiah. Don' let him bother you none. (*Pushes* PROPHET *aside a goes to* KING's *table.*)

PROPHET. You consort with harlots, an' yo' pollution in the sight of de Lawd. De Lawd God's goin' to smite you down, jest as he's goin' to smite down all dis wicked world! (*Grabs* HIGH PRIEST *and turns him around.*)

KING. (*Angrily against the last part of the preceding speech.*) Wait a minute. I'm getting tired of this. Don' throw him out. Jest kill him! (*There is the sound of a shot. The* PROPHET *falls*)

PROPHET. Smite 'em down, Lawd, like you said. Dey ain't a decent person left in de whole world. (*He dies.* MASTER OF CERE-MONIES, *revolver in hand, looks down at the* PROPHET.)

MASTER OF CEREMONIES. He's dead, King.

KING. Some of you boys take him out. (*A couple of young men come from the background and walk off with the body.*)

HIGH PRIEST. Don' know whether you should'a done that, King.

KING. Why not?

HIGH PRIEST. I don' know whether de Lawd would like it.

KING. Now, listen, Jake. You know yo' Lawd ain't payin' much attention to dis man's town. Except fo' you boys, it's tho'ly protected by de Gods o' Babylon.

HIGH PRIEST. I know, but jest de same—

KING. Look yere, s'pose I give you a couple hund'ed pieces of silver. Don' you s'pose you kin arrange to persuade yo' Gawd to keep his hands off?

HIGH PRIEST. (*Oilily.*) Well of co'se we could try. I dunno how well it would work. (*As the* HIGH PRIEST *speaks, The*

KING *claps his hands.* MASTER OF CEREMON-IES *enters with bag of money.*)

KING. Yere it is.

HIGH PRIEST. (*Smiling.*) I guess we kin square things up. (*He prays—whiningly.*) Oh Lawd, please forgive my po' frien' de King o' Babylon. He didn't know what he was doin' an'—(*There is a clap of thun-der, darkness for a second. The lights go up and* GOD *is standing in the center of the room.*)

GOD. (*In a voice of doom.*) Dat's about enough. (*The guests are horrified.*) I's stood all I kin from you. I tried to make dis a good earth. I helped Adam, I helped Noah, I helped Moses, an' I helped David. What's de grain dat grew out of de seed? Sin! Nothin' but sin throughout de whole world. I've given you ev'y chance. I sent you warriors and prophets. I've given you laws and commandments, an' you betray-ed my trust. Ev'ything I've given you, you've defiled. Ev'y time I've fo'given you, you've mocked me. An' now de High Priest of Israel tries to trifle wid my name. Listen, you chillun of darkness, yo' Lawd is tired. I'm tired of de struggle to make you worthy of de breath I gave you. I put you in bondage ag'in to cure you an' yo' worse dan you was amongst de flesh pots of Egypt. So I renounce you. Listen to the words of yo' lawd God Jehovah, for dey is de last words yo' ever hear from me. I repent of dese people dat I have made and I will deliver dem no more. (*There is darkness and cries of "Mercy!" "Have pity, Lawd!" "We didn' mean it, Lawd!" "Forgive us, Lawd!" etc. The* CHOIR *sings "Death's Gwinter Lay His Cold Icy Hands On Me" until the lights go up on the next scene.*)

SCENE VI

GOD *is writing at his desk. Outside, past the door, goes* HOSEA, *a dignified old man, with wings like* JACOB's. GOD, *sensing his presence, looks up from the paper he is examining, and follows him out of the corner of his eye. Angrily he resumes his work as soon as* HOSEA *is out of sight. There is a knock on the door.*

GOD. Who is it? (GABRIEL *enters.*)

GABRIEL. It's de delegation, Lawd.

GOD. (*Wearily.*) Tell 'em to come in. (ABRAHAM, ISAAC, JACOB, *and* MOSES *enter.*) Good mo'nin', gen'lemen.

THE VISITORS. Good mo'nin', Lawd.

GOD. What kin I do for you?

MOSES. You know, Lawd. Go back to our people.

GOD. (*Shaking his head.*) Ev'ry day fo' hund'ed's of years you boys have come in to ask dat same thing. De answer is still de same. I repented of de people I made. I said I would deliver dem no more. Good mo'nin', gen'lemen. (*The four visitors rise and exeunt.* GABRIEL *remains.*) Gabe, why do dey do it?

GABRIEL. I 'spect dey think you gonter change yo' mind.

GOD. (*Sadly.*) Dey don' know me. (HOSEA *again passes the door. His shadow shows on the wall.* GABRIEL *is perplexed, as he watches.* GOD *again looks surreptitiously over His shoulder at the passing figure.*) I don' like dat, either.

GABRIEL. What Lawd?

GOD. Dat man.

GABRIEL. He's jest a prophet, Lawd. Dat's jest old Hosea. He jest come up the other day.

GOD. I know. He's one of de few dat's come up yere since I was on de earth last time.

GABRIEL. Ain' been annoyin' you, has he?

GOD. I don' like him walkin' past de door.

GABRIEL. All you got to do is tell him to stop, Lawd.

GOD. Yes, I know. I don' want to tell him. He's got a right up yere or he wouldn' be yere.

GABRIEL. You needn' be bothered by him hangin' aroun' de office all de time. I'll tell 'im. Who's he think he—

GOD. No, Gabe. I find it ain't in me to stop him. I sometimes jest wonder why he don' come in and say hello.

GABRIEL. You want him to do dat? (*He moves as if to go to the door.*)

GOD. He never has spoke to me, and if he don' wanta come in, I ain't gonter make him. But dat ain't de worst of it, Gabriel.

GABRIEL. What is, Lawd?

GOD. Ev'y time he goes past de door I hears a voice.

GABRIEL. One of de angels?

GOD. (*Shaking his head.*) It's from de earth. It's a man.

GABRIEL. You mean he's prayin'?

GOD. No, he ain't exactly prayin'. He's jest talkin' in such a way dat I got to lissen. His name is Hezdrel.

GABRIEL. Is he on de books?

GOD. No, not yet. But ev'y time dat Hosea goes past I hear dat voice.

GABRIEL. Den tell *it* to stop.

GOD. I find I don' want to do that, either. Dey's gettin' ready to take Jerusalem down dere. Dat was my big fine city. Dis Hezdrel, he's jest one of de defenders. (*Suddenly and passionately, almost wildly.*) I ain't comin' down. You hear me? I ain't comin' down. (*He looks at* GABRIEL.) Go ahead, Gabriel. 'Tend to yo' chores. I'm gonter keep wukkin' yere.

GABRIEL. I hates to see you feelin' like dis, Lawd.

GOD. Dat's all right. Even bein' Gawd ain't a bed of roses. (GABRIEL *exits.* HOSEA'S *shadow is on the wall. For a second* HOSEA *hesitates.* GOD *looks at the wall. Goes to window.*) I hear you. I know yo' fightin' bravely, but I ain't comin' down. Oh, why don' you leave me alone? You know you ain't talkin' to me. *Is* you talkin' to me? I cain't stand yo' talkin' dat way. I kin only hear part of what you' sayin', and it puzzles me. Don' you know you cain't puzzle God? (*A pause. Then tenderly.*) Do you want me to come down dere ve'y much? You know I said I wouldn't come down? (*Fiercely.*) Why don' he answer me a little? (*With clenched fists, looks down through the window.*) Listen! I'll tell you what I'll do. I ain't goin' to promise you anythin', and I ain't goin' to do nothin' to help you. I'm jest feelin' a little low, an' I'm only comin' down to make myself feel a little better, dat's all. (*The stage is darkened.* CHOIR *begins 'A Blind Man Stood In De Middle of De Road," and continues until the lights go up on the next scene.*)

SCENE VII

*It is a shadowed corner beside the walls
of the temple in Jerusalem. The light of
camp fires flickers on the figure of* HEZ-
DREL, *who was* ADAM *in Part I. He stands
in the same position* ADAM *held when first
discovered but in his right hand is a sword,
and his left is in a sling. Around him are
several prostrate bodies. Pistol and cannon
shots, then a trumpet call. Six young men
enter from left in command of a* CORPORAL.
They are all armed.

CORPORAL. De fightin's stopped fo' de
night, Hezdrel.

HEZDREL. Yes?

CORPORAL. Dey're goin' to begin ag'in at
cockcrow. (*Man enters, crosses the stage
and exits.*) Herod say he's goin' to take
de temple tomorrow, burn de books and
de Ark of de Covenant, and put us all to
de sword.

HEZDREL. Yo' ready, ain't you?

EVERYBODY. Yes, Hezdrel.

HEZDREL. Did de food get in through de
hole in de city wall? (*Two soldiers enter,
cross the stage and exit.*)

CORPORAL. Yessuh, we's goin' back to
pass it out now.

HEZDREL. Good. Any mo' of our people
escape today?

CORPORAL. Ol' Herod's got de ol' hole
covered up now, but fifteen of our people
got out a new one we made. (*Other soldiers enter, cross the stage and exit.*)

HEZDREL. Good. Take dese yere wounded
men back and git 'em took care of.

CORPORAL. Yes, suh. (*They pick up the
bodies on the ground and carry them off-
stage as* HEZDREL *speaks.*)

HEZDREL. So dey gonter take de temple
in de mo'nin'? We'll be waitin' for 'em.
Jest remember, boys, when dey kill us we
leap out of our skins, right into de lap
of God. (*The men disappear with the
wounded; from the deep shadow upstage
comes* GOD.)

GOD. Hello, Hezdrel—Adam.

HEZDREL. (*Rubbing his forehead.*) Who
is you?

GOD. Me? I'm jest an ol' preacher, from
back in de hills.

HEZDREL. What you doin' yere?

GOD. I heard you boys was fightin'. I jest
wanted to see how it was goin'.

HEZDREL. Well, it ain't goin' so well.

GOD. Dey got you skeered, huh?

HEZDREL. Look yere, who is you, a spy
in my brain?

GOD. Cain't you see I's one of yo' people?

HEZDREL. Listen, Preacher, we ain't skeered. We's gonter be killed, but we ain't
skeered.

GOD. I's glad to hear dat. Kin I ask you a
question, Hezdrel?

HEZDREL. What is it?

GOD. How is it you is so brave?

HEZDREL. Caize we got faith, dat's why!

GOD. Faith? In who?

HEZDREL. In our dear Lawd God.

GOD. But God say he abandoned ev' one
down yere.

HEZDREL. Who say dat? Who dare say dat
of de Lawd God of Hosea?

GOD. De God of Hosea?

HEZDREL. You heard me. Look yere, you
is a spy in my brain!

GOD. No, I ain't, Hezdrel. I'm jest puz
zled. You ought to know dat.

HEZDREL. How come you so puzzled 'bout
de God of Hosea?

GOD. I don' know. Maybe I jest don' hear
things. You see, I live 'way back in de hills.

HEZDREL. What you wanter find out?

GOD. Ain't de God of Hosea de same
Jehovah dat was de God of Moses?

HEZDREL. (*Contemptuously.*) No. Dat ol'
God of wrath and vengeance? We have de

God dat Hosea preached to us. He's de one God.

GOD. Who's he?

HEZDREL. (*Reverently.*) De God of mercy.

GOD. Hezdrel, don' you think dey must be de same God?

HEZDREL. I don' know. I ain't bothered to think much about it. Maybe dey is. Maybe our God is de same ol' God. I guess we jest got tired of his appearance dat ol' way.

GOD. What you mean, Hezdrel?

HEZDREL. Oh, dat ol' God dat walked de earth in de shape of a man. I guess he lived wid man so much dat all he seen was de sins in man. Dat's what made him de God of wrath and vengeance. Co'se he made Hosea. An' Hosea never would a found what mercy was unless dere was a little of it in God, too. Anyway, he ain't a fearsome God no mo'. Hosea showed us dat.

GOD. How you s'pose Hosea found dat mercy?

HEZDREL. De only way he could find it. De only way I found it. De only way anyone kin find it.

GOD. How's dat?

HEZDREL. Through sufferin'.

GOD. (*After a pause.*) What if dey kill you in de mo'nin', Hezdrel.

HEZDREL. If dey do, dey do. Dat's all.

GOD. Herod say he's goin' to burn de temple—

HEZDREL. So he say.

GOD. And burn de Ark an' de books. Den dat's de end of de books, ain't it?

HEZDREL. (*Buoyantly.*) What you mean? If he burns dem things in dere? Naw. Dem's jest copies.

GOD. Where is de others?

HEZDREL. (*Tapping his head.*) Dey's a set in yere. Fifteen got out through de hole in the city wall today. A hundred and fifty got out durin' de week. Each of em is a set of de books. Dey's scattered safe all over de countryside now, jest waitin' to git pen and paper fo' to put 'em down agin.

GOD. (*Proudly.*) Dey cain't lick you, kin dey Hezdrel?

HEZDREL. (*Smiling.*) I know dey cain't. (*Trumpet.*) You better get out o' yere, Preacher, if you wanter carry de news to yo' people. It'll soon be daylight.

GOD. I'm goin'. (*He takes a step upstage and stops.*) Want me to take any message?

HEZDREL. Tell de people in de hills dey ain't nobody like de Lawd God of Hosea.

GOD. I will. If dey kill you tomorrow I'll bet dat God of Hosea'll be waitin' for you.

HEZDREL. I *know* he will.

GOD. (*Quietly.*) Thank you, Hezdrel.

HEZDREL. Fo' what?

GOD. Fo' tellin' me so much. You see I been so far away I guess I was jest way behin' de times. (*He exits. Pause, then trumpet sounds.*) (HEZDREL *paces back and forth once or twice. Another young soldier appears. Other men enter and stand grouped about* HEZDREL.)

SECOND OFFICER. (*Excitedly.*) De cock's jest crowed, Hezdrel. Dey started de fightin' ag'in.

HEZDREL. We's ready for 'em. Come on, boys. (*From the darkness upstage comes another group of soldiers.*) Dis is de day dey say dey'll git us. Le's fight till de last man goes. What d'you say?

CORPORAL. Le's go, Hezdrel!

HEZDREL. (*Calling left.*) Give 'em ev'ything, boys! (*There is a movement toward the left, a bugle call and the sound of distant battle. The lights go out. The* CHOIR *is heard singing, "March On," triumphantly. They continue to sing after the lights go up on the next scene.*)

SCENE VIII

*t is the same setting as the Fish Fry Scene
'n Part I. The same angels are present
but the* CHOIR, *instead of marching, is
standing in a double row on an angle upstage right.* GOD *is seated in an armchair
near center. He faces the audience. As the*
CHOIR *continues to sing,* GABRIEL *enters,
unnoticed by the chattering angels. He
looks at* GOD *who is staring thoughtfully
toward the audience.*

GABRIEL. You look a little pensive, Lawd.
(GOD *nods his head.*) Have a seegar,
Lawd?

GOD. No thanks, Gabriel. (GABRIEL *goes
to the table, accepts a cup of custard; chats
with the angel behind the table for a moment as he sips, puts the cup down and
returns to the side of* GOD.)

GABRIEL. You look awful pensive, Lawd.
You been sittin' yere, lookin' dis way, an
awful long time. Is it somethin' serious,
Lawd?

GOD. Very serious, Gabriel.

GABRIEL. (*Awed by His tone.*) Lawd, is
de time come for me to blow?

GOD. Not yet, Gabriel. I'm just thinkin'.

GABRIEL. What about, Lawd? (*Puts up
hand. Singing stops.*)

GOD. 'Bout somethin' de boy tol' me.
Somethin' 'bout Hosea, and himself. How
dey foun' somethin'.

GABRIEL. What, Lawd?

GOD. Mercy. (*A pause.*) Through *sufferin',* he said.

GABRIEL. Yes, Lawd.

GOD. I'm tryin' to find it, too. It's awful
impo'tant. It's awful impo'tant to all de
people on my earth. Did he mean dat even
God must suffer? (GOD *continues to look
out over the audience for a moment and
then a look of surprise comes into his face.
He sighs. In the distance a voice cries.*)

THE VOICE. Oh, look at him! Oh, look,
dey goin' to make him carry it up dat
hill! Dey goin' to nail him to it! Oh, dat's
a terrible burden for one man to carry!
(GOD *rises and murmurs "Yes!" as if in
recognition. The heavenly beings have
been watching him closely, and now, seeing him smile gently, draw back, relieved.
All the angels burst into "Hallelujah,
King Jesus."* GOD *continues to smile as the
lights fade away. The singing becomes
fortissimo.*

CURTAIN

You Can't Take It With You

BY MOSS HART AND GEORGE S. KAUFMAN

"You Can't Take It With You" was produced at the Booth Theatre, New York City, Monday night, December 14th, 1936, by Sam H. Harris, with the following cast:

PENELOPE SYCAMORE	Josephine Hull
ESSIE	Paula Trueman
RHEBA	Ruth Attaway
PAUL SYCAMORE	Frank Wilcox
MR. DE PINNA	Frank Conlan
ED	George Heller
DONALD	Oscar Polk
MARTIN VANDERHOF	Henry Travers
ALICE	Margot Stevenson
HENDERSON	Hugh Rennie
TONY KIRBY	Jess Barker
BORIS KOLENKHOV	George Tobias
GAY WELLINGTON	Mitzi Hajos
MR. KIRBY	William J. Kelly
MRS. KIRBY	Virginia Hammond
THREE MEN	George Leach / Ralph Holmes / Franklin Heller
OLGA	Anna Lubowe

The Scene Is the Home of Martin Vanderhof, New York.

ACT I

A Wednesday Evening

During this act the curtain is lowered to
denote the passing of several hours.

ACT II

A Week Later

ACT III

The Next Day

Copyright, 1937, by Moss Hart and George S. Kaufman

YOU CAN'T TAKE IT WITH YOU

ACT ONE

SCENE I

The home of MARTIN VANDERHOF—*just around the corner from Columbia University, but don't go looking for it. The room we see is what is customarily described as a living room, but in this house the term is something of an understatement. The every-man-for-himself room would be more like it. For here meals are eaten, plays are written, snakes collected, ballet steps practiced, xylophones played, printing presses operated—if there were room enough there would probably be ice skating. In short, the brood presided over by* MARTIN VANDERHOF *goes on about the business of living in the fullest sense of the word. This is a house where you do as you like, and no questions asked.*

At the moment, GRANDPA VANDERHOF's *daughter,* MRS. PENELOPE SYCAMORE, *is doing what she likes more than anything else in the world. She is writing a play—her eleventh. Comfortably ensconced in what is affectionately known as Mother's Corner, she is pounding away on a typewriter perched precariously on a rickety card table. Also on the table is one of those plaster-paris skulls ordinarily used as an ash tray, but which serves* PENELOPE *as a candy jar. And, because* PENNY *likes companionship, there are two kittens on the table, busily lapping at a saucer of milk.*

PENELOPE VANDERHOF SYCAMORE *is a round little woman in her early fifties, comfortable looking, gentle, homey. One would not suspect that under that placid exterior there surges the Divine Urge—but it does, it does.*

After a moment her fingers lag on the keys; a thoughtful expression comes over her face. Abstractedly she takes a piece of candy out of the skull, pops it into her mouth. As always, it furnishes the needed inspiration—with a furious burst of speed she finishes a page and whips it out of the machine. Quite mechanically, she picks up one of the kittens, adds the sheet of paper to the pile underneath, replaces the kitten.

As she goes back to work, ESSIE CARMICHAEL, MRS. SYCAMORE's *eldest daughter, comes in from the kitchen. A girl of about twenty-nine, very slight, a curious air of the pixie about her. She is wearing ballet slippers—in fact, she wears them throughout the play.*

ESSIE (*fanning herself*). My, that kitchen's hot.

PENNY (*finishing a bit of typing*). What, Essie?

ESSIE. I say the kitchen's awful hot. That new candy I'm making—it just won't ever get cool.

PENNY. Do you have to make candy today, Essie? It's such a hot day.

ESSIE. Well, I got all those new orders. Ed went out and got a bunch of new orders.

PENNY. My, if it keeps on I suppose you'll be opening up a store.

ESSIE. That's what Ed was saying last night, but I said No, I want to be a dancer. (*Bracing herself against the table, she manipulates her legs, ballet fashion.*)

PENNY. The only trouble with dancing is, it takes so long. You've been studying such a long time.

ESSIE (*slowly drawing a leg up behind her as she talks*). Only—eight—years. After all, mother, you've been writing plays for eight years. We started about the same time, didn't we?

PENNY. Yes, but you shouldn't count my first two years, because I was learning to type. (*From the kitchen comes a colored maid named* RHEBA—*a very black girl somewhere in her thirties. She carries a white tablecloth, and presently starts to spread it over the table.*)

RHEBA (*as she enters*). I think the candy's hardening up now, Miss Essie.

ESSIE. Oh, thanks, Rheba. I'll bring some in, mother—I want you to try it. (*She goes into the kitchen.*)

(PENNY *returns to her work as* RHEBA *busies herself with the table.*)

RHEBA. Finish the second act, Mrs. Sycamore?

PENNY. Oh, no, Rheba. I've just got Cynthia entering the monastery.

RHEBA. Monastery? How'd she get there? She was at the El Morocco, wasn't she?

PENNY. Well, she gets tired of the El Morocco, and there's this monastery, so she goes there.

RHEBA. Do they let her in?

PENNY. Yes, I made it Visitors' Day, so of course anybody can come.

RHEBA. Oh.

PENNY. So she arrives on Visitors' Day, and —just stays.

RHEBA. All night?

PENNY. Oh, yes. She stays six years.

RHEBA (*as she goes into the kitchen*). Six years? My, I bet she busts that monastery wide open.

PENNY (*half to herself, as she types.*) "Six Years Later." . . . (PAUL SYCAMORE *comes up from the cellar. Mid-fifties, but with a kind of youthful air. His quiet charm and mild manner are distinctly engaging.*)

PAUL (*turning back as he comes through the door.*) Mr. De Pinna! (*A voice from below. "Yah?"*) Mr. De Pinna, will you bring up one of those new sky rockets, please? I want to show them to Mrs. Sycamore. (*An answering monosyllable from the cellar as he turns toward* PENNY.) Look, Penny—what do you think of these little fire crackers? Ten strings for a nickel. Listen. (*He puts one down on the center table and lights it. It goes off with a good bang.*) Nice, huh?

PENNY. Paul, dear, were you ever in a monastery?

PAUL (*quite calmly*). No, I wasn't. . . . Wait till you see the new rockets. Gold stars, then blue stars, then some bombs, and then a balloon. Mr. De Pinna thought of the balloon.

PENNY. Sounds lovely. Did you do all that today?

PAUL. Sure. We made up—oh, here we are. (MR. DE PINNA *comes up from the cellar. A bald-headed little man with a serious manner, and carrying two good-sized sky rockets.*) Look, Penny. Cost us eighteen cents to

make and we sell 'em for fifty. How many do you figure we can make before the Fourth, Mr. De Pinna?

DE PINNA. Well, we've got two weeks yet— what day you going to take the stuff up to Mount Vernon?

PAUL. Oh, I don't know—about a week. You know, we're going to need a larger booth this year—got a lot of stuff made up.

DE PINNA (*examining the rocket in his hand*). Look, Mr. Sycamore, the only thing that bothers me is, I'm afraid the powder chamber is just a little bit close to the balloon.

PAUL. Well, we've got the stars and the bombs in between.

DE PINNA. But that don't give the balloon time enough. A balloon needs plenty of time.

PAUL. Want to go down in the cellar and try it?

DE PINNA. All right.

PAUL (*as he disappears through the cellar door*). That's the only way you'll really tell.

PENNY (*halting* DE PINNA *in the cellar doorway*). Mr. De Pinna, if a girl you loved entered a monastery, what would you do?

DE PINNA (*he wasn't expecting that one*). Oh, I don't know, Mrs. Sycamore—it's been so long. (*He goes.*)
(RHEBA *returns from the kitchen, bringing a pile of plates.*)

RHEBA. Miss Alice going to be home to dinner tonight, Mrs. Sycamore?

PENNY (*deep in her thinking*). What? I don't know, Rheba. Maybe.

RHEBA. Well, I'll set a place for her, but she's only been home one night this week. (*She puts down a plate or two.*) Miss Essie's making some mighty good candy today. She's doing something new with cocoanuts. (*More plates.*) Let's see—six, and Mr. De Pinna, and if Mr. Kolenkhov comes that makes eight, don't it? (*At which point a muffled crack, reminiscent of the Battle of the Marne, comes up from the cellar. It is the sky rocket, of course. The great preliminary hiss, followed by a series of explosions.* PENNY *and* RHEBA, *however, don't even ro-*

tice it. RHEBA *goes right on.*) Yes, I'd better set for eight.

PENNY. I think I'll put this play away for a while, Rheba, and go back to the war play.

RHEBA. Oh, I always liked that one—the war play. (ESSIE *returns from the kitchen, carrying a plate of freshly made candy.*)

ESSIE. They'll be better when they're harder, mother, but try one—I want to know what you think.

PENNY. Oh, they look awfully good. (*She takes one.*) What do you call them?

ESSIE. I think I'll call 'em Love Dreams.

PENNY. Oh, that's nice. . . . I'm going back to my war play, Essie. What do you think?

ESSIE. Oh, are you, mother?

PENNY. Yes, I sort of got myself into a monastery and I can't get out.

ESSIE. Oh, well, it'll come to you, mother. Remember how you got out of that brothel. . . . Hello, boys. (*This little greeting is idly tossed toward the snake solarium, a glass structure looking something like a goldfish aquarium, but containing, believe it or not, snakes.*) The snakes look hungry. Did Rheba feed them?

PENNY (*as* RHEBA *re-enters*). I don't know. Rheba, did you feed the snakes yet?

RHEBA. No, Donald's coming and he always brings flies with him.

PENNY. Well, try to feed them before Grandpa gets home. You know how fussy he is about them.

RHEBA. Yes'm.

PENNY (*handing her the kittens*). And take Groucho and Harpo into the kitchen with you. . . . I think I'll have another Love Dream. (MR. SYCAMORE *emerges from the cellar again.*)

PAUL. Mr. De Pinna was right about the balloon. It was too close to the powder.

ESSIE (*practicing a dance step*). Want a Love Dream, father? They're on the table.

PAUL. No, thanks. I gotta wash.

PENNY. I'm going back to the war play, Paul.

PAUL. Oh, that's nice. We're putting some red stars after the blue stars, then come the bombs and *then* the balloon. That ought to do it. (*He goes up the stairs.*)

ESSIE (*another dance step.*) Mr. Kolenkhov says I'm his most promising pupil.

PENNY (*absorbed in her own troubles*). You know, with forty monks and one girl, something ought to happen. (ED CARMICHAEL *comes down the stairs. A nondescript young man in his mid-thirties. In shirtsleeves at the moment.*)

ED. Listen! (*He hums a snatch of melody as he heads for the far corner of the room—the xylophone corner. Arriving there, he picks up the sticks and continues the melody on the xylophone. Immediately* ESSIE *is up on her toes, performing intricate ballet steps to* ED's *accompaniment.*)

ESSIE (*dancing*). I like that, Ed. Yours?

ED (*shakes his head*). Beethoven.

ESSIE (*never coming down off her toes*). Lovely. Got a lot of *you* in it. . . . I made those new candies this afternoon, Ed.

ED (*playing away*). Yah?

ESSIE. You can take 'em around tonight.

ED. All right. . . . Now, here's the finish. This is me. (*He works up to an elaborate crescendo, but* ESSIE *keeps pace with him right to the finish.*)

ESSIE. That's fine. Remember it when Kholenkhov comes, will you?

PENNY (*who has been busy with her papers*). Ed, dear, why don't you and Essie have a baby? I was thinking about it just the other day.

ED. I don't know—we could have one if you wanted us to. What about it, Essie? Do you want to have a baby?

ESSIE. Oh, I don't care. I'm willing if Grandpa is.

ED. Let's ask him. (ESSIE *goes into the kitchen as* PENNY *goes back to her manuscripts.*)

PENNY (*running through the pile*). Labor play . . . religious play . . . sex play. I know it's here some place. (ED, *meanwhile, has transferred his attention from the xylophone to a printing press that stands handily by,*

and now gives it a preliminary workout.)
(MR. DE PINNA *comes out of the cellar, bound for the kitchen to wash up.*)

DE PINNA. I was right about the balloon. It was too close to the powder.

ED. Anything you want printed, Mr. De Pinna? How about some more calling cards?

DE PINNA (*as he passes into the kitchen*). No, thanks. I've still got the *first* thousand.

ED (*calling after him*). Well, call on somebody, will you? (*He then gives his attention to* RHEBA, *who is busy with the table again.*) What have we got for dinner, Rheba? I'm ready to print the menu.

RHEBA. Cornflakes, watermelon, some of those candies Miss Essie made, and some kind of meat—I forget.

ED. I think I'll set it up in boldface Cheltenham tonight. (*He starts to pick out the letters.*) If I'm going to take those new candies around I'd better print up some descriptive matter after dinner.

PENNY. Do you think anybody reads those things, Ed—that you put in the candy boxes? . . . Oh, here it is. (*She pulls a manuscript out of a pile.*) "Poison Gas." (*The door bell sounds.*) I guess that's Donald. (*As* RHEBA *breaks into a broad grin.*) Look at Rheba smile.

ED. The boy friend, eh, Rheba?

PENNY (*as* RHEBA *disappears into the hallway*). Donald and Rheba are awfully cute together. Sort of like Porgy and Bess. (RHEBA *having opened the door, the gentleman named* DONALD *now looms up in the doorway—darkly. He is a colored man of no uncertain hue.*)

DONALD. Good evening, everybody!

ED. Hi, Donald! How've you been?

DONALD. I'm pretty good, Mr. Ed. How you been, Mrs. Sycamore?

PENNY. Very well, thank you. (*She looks at him, appraisingly.*) Donald, were you ever in a monastery?

DONALD. No-o, I don't go no place much. I'm on relief.

PENNY. Oh, yes, of course.

DONALD (*pulling a bottle out of each side pocket*). Here's the flies, Rheba. Caught a big mess of them today.

RHEBA (*taking the jars*). You sure did.

DONALD. I see you've been working, Mrs. Sycamore.

PENNY. Yes, indeed, Donald.

DONALD. How's Grandpa?

PENNY. Just fine. He's over at Columbia this afternoon. The Commencement exercises.

DONALD. My, the years certainly do roll 'round.

ED (*with his typesetting*). M — E — A — T. . . . What's he go there for all the time, Penny?

PENNY. I don't know. It's so handy—just around the corner. (PAUL *comes downstairs.*)

PAUL. Oh, Donald! Mr. De Pinna and I are going to take the fireworks up to Mount Vernon next week. Do you think you could give us a hand?

DONALD. Yes, sir, only I can't take no money for it this year, because if the Government finds out I'm working they'll get sore.

PAUL. Oh! . . . Ed, I got a wonderful idea in the bathroom just now. I was reading Trotzky. (*He produces a book from under his arm.*) It's yours, isn't it?

ED. Yah, I left it there.

PENNY. *Who* is it?

PAUL. *You* know, Trotzky. The Russian Revolution.

PENNY. Oh.

PAUL. Anyhow, it struck me it was a great fireworks idea. Remember "The Last Days of Pompeii"?

PENNY. Oh, yes. Palisades Park. (*With a gesture of her arms she loosely describes a couple of arcs, indicative of the eruption of Mt. Vesuvius.*) That's where we met.

PAUL. Well, I'm going to do the Revolution! A full hour display.

DONALD. Say!

PENNY. Paul, that's wonderful!

ED. The red fire is the flag, huh?

PAUL. Sure! And the Czar, and the Cossacks!

DONALD. And the freeing of the slaves?

PAUL. No, no, Donald— (*The sound of the front door slamming. A second's pause, and then* GRANDPA *enters the living room.* GRANDPA *is about 75, a wiry little man whom the years have treated kindly. His face is youthful, despite the lines that sear it; his eyes are very much alive. He is a man who made his peace with the world long, long ago, and his whole attitude and manner are quietly persuasive of this.*)

GRANDPA (*surveying the group*). Well, sir, you should have been there. That's all I can say—you should have been there.

PENNY. Was it a nice Commencement, Grandpa?

GRANDPA. Wonderful. They get better every year. (*He peers into the snake solarium.*) You don't know how lucky you are you're snakes.

ED. Big class this year, Grandpa? How many were there?

GRANDPA. Oh, must have been two acres. *Everybody* graduated. And much funnier speeches than they had last year.

DONALD. You want to listen to a good speech you go up and hear Father Divine.

GRANDPA. I'll wait—they'll have him at Columbia.

PENNY. Donald, will you tell Rheba Grandpa's home now and we won't wait for Miss Alice.

DONALD. Yes'm. . . . (*As he goes through the kitchen door.*) Rheba, Grandpa's home—we can have dinner.

PAUL. Got a new sky rocket today, Grandpa. Wait till you see it. . . . Wonder why they don't have fireworks at Commencements.

GRANDPA. Don't make enough noise. You take a good Commencement orator and he'll drown out a whole carload of fireworks. And say just as much, too.

PENNY. Don't the graduates ever say anything?

GRANDPA. No, they just sit there in cap and nightgown, get their diplomas, and then along about forty years from now they suddenly say, "Where am I?" (ESSIE *comes in from the kitchen, bringing a plate of tomatoes for the evening meal.*)

ESSIE. Hello, Grandpa. Have a nice day?

GRANDPA (*watching* ESSIE *as she puts the tomatoes on the table*). Hello-have-a-nice-day. (*Suddenly he roars at the top of his voice.*) Don't I even get kissed?

ESSIE (*kissing him*). Excuse me, Grandpa.

GRANDPA. I'll take a tomato, too. (ESSIE *passes the plate;* GRANDPA *takes one and sits with it in his hand, solemnly weighing it.*) You know, I could have used a couple of these this afternoon. . . . Play something, Ed.

(ED *at once obliges on the xylophone—something on the dreamy side. Immediately* ESSIE *is up on her toes again, drifting through the mazes of a toe dance.*)

ESSIE (*after a moment*). There was a letter came for you, Grandpa. Did you get it?

GRANDPA. Letter for me? I don't know anybody.

ESSIE. It was for you, though. Had your name on it.

GRANDPA. That's funny. Where is it?

ESSIE. I don't know. Where's Grandpa's letter, mother?

PENNY (*who has been deep in her work*). What, dear?

ESSIE (*dancing dreamily away*). Where's that letter that came for Grandpa last week?

PENNY. I don't know. (*Then, brightly.*) I remember seeing the kittens on it.

GRANDPA. Who was it from? Did you notice?

ESSIE. Yes, it was on the outside.

GRANDPA. Well, who was it?

ESSIE (*first finishing the graceful fluttering of the Dying Swan*). United States Government.

GRANDPA. Really? Wonder what *they* wanted.

ESSIE. There was one before that, too, from the same people. There was a couple of them.

GRANDPA. Well, if any more come I wish you'd give them to me.

ESSIE. Yes, Grandpa. (*A fresh flurry of dancing; the xylophone grows a little louder.*)

GRANDPA. I think I'll go out to Westchester tomorrow and do a little snake-hunting.

PAUL (*who has settled down with his book some time before this*). "God is the State; the State is God."

GRANDPA. What's that?

PAUL. "God is the State; the State is God."

GRANDPA. Who says that?

PAUL. Trotzky.

GRANDPA. Well, that's all right—I thought *you* said it.

ED. It's nice for printing, you know. Good and short. (*He reaches into the type case.*) G — O — D — space — I — S — space — T — H — E (*The sound of the outer door closing, and* ALICE SYCAMORE *enters the room. A lovely, fresh young girl of about twenty-two. She is plainly* GRANDPA's *grand-daughter, but there is something that sets her apart from the rest of the family. For one thing, she is in daily contact with the world; in addition, she seems to have escaped the tinge of mild insanity that pervades the rest of them. But she is a Sycamore for all that, and her devotion and love for them are plainly apparent. At the moment she is in a small nervous flutter, but she is doing her best to conceal it.*)

ALICE (*as she makes the rounds, kissing her grandfather, her father, her mother*). And so the beautiful princess came into the palace, and kissed her mother, and her father, and her grandfather—hi, Grandpa—and what do you think? They turned into the Sycamore family. Surprised?

ESSIE (*examining* ALICE's *dress*). Oh, Alice, I like it. It's new, isn't it?

PENNY. Looks nice and summery.

ESSIE. Where'd you get it?

ALICE. Oh, I took a walk during lunch hour.

GRANDPA. You've been taking a lot of walks lately. That's the second new dress this week.

ALICE. Oh, I just like to brighten up the office once in a while. I'm known as the Kay Francis of Kirby & Co. . . . Well, what's new around here? In the way of plays, snakes, ballet dancing or fireworks. Dad, I'll bet you've been down in that cellar all day.

PAUL. Huh?

PENNY. I'm going back to the war play, Alice.

ESSIE. Ed, play Alice that Beethoven thing you wrote. Listen, Alice. (*Like a shot* ED *is at the xylophone again,* ESSIE *up on her toes.*)
(GRANDPA, *meanwhile, has unearthed his stamp album from under a pile of oddments in the corner, and is now busy with his magnifying glass.*)

GRANDPA. Do you know that you can mail a letter all the way from Nicaragua for two pesetos?

PENNY (*meanwhile dramatically reading one of her own deathless lines*). "Kenneth, my virginity is a priceless thing to me."

ALICE (*finding it hard to break through all this*). Listen, people. . . . Listen. (*A break in the music; she gets a scattered sort of attention.*) I'm not home to dinner. A young gentleman is calling for me.

ESSIE. Really? Who is it?

PENNY. Well, isn't that nice?

ALICE (*with quiet humor*). I did everything possible to keep him from coming here, but he's calling for me.

PENNY. Why don't you both stay to dinner?

ALICE. No, I want him to take you in easy doses. I've tried to prepare him a little, but don't make it any worse than you can help. Don't read him any plays, mother, and don't let a snake bite him, Grandpa, because I like him. And I wouldn't dance for him, Essie, because we're going to the Monte Carlo ballet tonight.

GRANDPA. Can't do *anything*. Who *is* he—President of the United States?

ALICE. No, he's vice-president of Kirby & Co. Mr. Anthony Kirby, Jr.

ESSIE. The Boss' son?

PENNY. Well!

ALICE. The Boss' son. Just like the movies.

ESSIE. That explains the new dresses.

ED. And not being home to dinner for three weeks.

ALICE. Why, you're wonderful!

PENNY (*all aglow*). Are you going to marry him?

ALICE. Oh, of course. Tonight! Meanwhile I have to go up and put on my wedding dress.

ESSIE. Is he good-looking?

ALICE (*vainly consulting her watch*). Yes, in a word. Oh, dear! What time is it?

PENNY. I don't know. Anybody know what time it is?

PAUL. Mr. De Pinna might know.

ED. It was about five o'clock a couple of hours ago.

ALICE. Oh, I ought to know better than to ask you people. . . . Will you let me know the minute he comes, please?

PENNY. Of course, Alice.

ALICE. Yes, I know, but I mean the *minute* he comes.

PENNY. Why, of course. (ALICE *looks apprehensively from one to the other; then disappears up the stairs.*) Well, what do you think of that?

GRANDPA. She seems to like him, if you ask me.

ESSIE. I should say so. She's got it bad.

PENNY. Wouldn't it be wonderful if she married him? We could have the wedding right in this room.

PAUL. Now, wait a minute, Penny. This is the first time he's ever called for the girl.

PENNY. You only called for me once.

PAUL. Young people are different nowadays.

ESSIE. Oh, I don't know. Look at Ed and me. He came to dinner *once* and just stayed.

PENNY. Anyhow, I think it's wonderful. I'll bet he's crazy about her. It must be he that's been taking her out every night. (*The door bell rings.*) There he is! Never mind, Rheba, I'll answer it. (*She is fluttering to the door.*)

Now remember what Alice said, and be *very* nice to him.

GRANDPA (*rising*). All right—let's take a look at him.

PENNY (*at the front door; milk and honey in her voice*). Well! Welcome to our little home! I'm Alice's mother. Do come right in! Here we are! (*She reappears in the archway, piloting the stranger.*) This is Grandpa, and that's Alice's father, and Alice's sister, and her husband, Ed Carmichael. (*The family all give courteous little nods and smiles as they are introduced.*) Well Now give me your hat and make yourself right at home.

THE MAN. I'm afraid you must be making a mistake.

PENNY. How's that?

THE MAN. My card.

PENNY (*reading*). "Wilbur C. Henderson. Internal Revenue Department."

HENDERSON. That's right.

GRANDPA. What can we do for you?

HENDERSON. Does a Mr. Martin Vanderhof live here?

GRANDPA. Yes, sir. That's me.

HENDERSON (*all milk and honey*). Well, Mr. Vanderhof, the Government wants to talk to you about a little matter of income tax.

PENNY. Income tax?

HENDERSON. Do you mind if I sit down?

GRANDPA. No, no. Just go right ahead.

HENDERSON (*settling himself*). Thank you (*From above stairs the voice of* ALICE *floats down.*)

ALICE. Mother! Is that Mr. Kirby?

PENNY (*going to the stairs*). No. No, it isn' darling. It's—an internal something or other (*To Mr. Henderson.*) Pardon me.

HENDERSON (*pulling a sheaf of papers from his pocket*). We've written you several letters about this, Mr. Vanderhof, but have not had any reply.

GRANDPA. Oh, that's what those letters were

ESSIE. I told you they were from the Govern ment. (MR. DE PINNA *comes up from the cel lar, bearing a couple of giant firecrackers. He pauses as he sees a stranger.*)

DE PINNA. Oh, pardon me.

PAUL. Yes, Mr. De Pinna?

DE PINNA. These things are not going off, Mr. Sycamore. Look. (*He prepares to apply a match to one of them, as a startled income tax man nearly has a conniption fit. But* PAUL *is too quick for him.*)

PAUL. Ah—not here, Mr. De Pinna. Grandpa's busy.

DE PINNA. Oh. (MR. DE PINNA *and* PAUL *hurry into the hall with their firecrackers.*)

HENDERSON (*now that order has been restored*). According to our records, Mr. Vanderhof, you have never paid an income tax.

GRANDPA. That's right.

HENDERSON. Why not?

GRANDPA. I don't believe in it.

HENDERSON. Well—you own property, don't you?

GRANDPA. Yes, sir.

HENDERSON. And you receive a yearly income from it?

GRANDPA. I do.

HENDERSON. Of— (*He consults his records.*) —between three and four thousand dollars.

GRANDPA. About that.

HENDERSON. You've been receiving it for years.

GRANDPA. I have. 1901, if you want the exact date.

HENDERSON. Well, the Government is only concerned from 1914 on. That's when the income tax started.

GRANDPA. Well?

HENDERSON. Well—it seems, Mr. Vanderhof, that you owe the Government twenty-two years' back income tax.

ED. Wait a minute! You can't go back that far—that's outlawed.

HENDERSON (*calmly regarding him*). What's *your* name?

ED. What difference does that make?

HENDERSON. Ever file an income tax return?

ED. No, sir.

HENDERSON. What was your income last year?

ED. Ah—twenty-eight dollars and fifty cents, wasn't it, Essie? (ESSIE *gives quick assent; the income tax man dismisses the whole matter with an impatient wave of the hand and returns to bigger game.*)

HENDERSON. Now, Mr. Vanderhof, you know there's quite a penalty for not filing an income tax return.

PENNY. Penalty?

GRANDPA. Look, Mr. Henderson, let me ask you something.

HENDERSON. Well?

GRANDPA. Suppose I pay you this money—mind you, I don't say I'm going to do it—but just for the sake of argument—what's the Government going to do with it?

HENDERSON. How do you mean?

GRANDPA. Well, what do I get for my money? If I go into Macy's and buy something, there it *is*—I see it. What's the Government give me?

HENDERSON. Why, the Government gives you everything. It protects you.

GRANDPA. What from?

HENDERSON. Well—invasion. Foreigners that might come over here and take everything you've got.

GRANDPA. Oh, I don't think they're going to do that.

HENDERSON. If you didn't pay an income tax, they would. How do you think the Government keeps up the Army and Navy? All those battleships . . .

GRANDPA. Last time we used battleships was in the Spanish-American War, and what did we get out of it? Cuba—and we gave that back. I wouldn't mind paying if it were something sensible.

HENDERSON (*beginning to get annoyed*). Well, what about Congress, and the Supreme

Court, and the President? We've got to pay *them*, don't we?

GRANDPA (*ever so calmly*). Not with my money—no, sir.

HENDERSON (*furious*). Now wait a minute! I'm not here to argue with you. All I know is that you haven't paid an income tax and you've got to pay it!

GRANDPA. They've got to show me.

HENDERSON (*yelling*). We *don't* have to show you! I just told you! All those buildings down in Washington, and Interstate Commerce, and the Constitution!

GRANDPA. The Constitution was paid for long ago. And Interstate Commerce—what *is* Interstate Commerce, anyhow?

HENDERSON (*with murderous calm*). There are forty-eight states—see? And if there weren't Interstate Commerce, nothing could go from one state to another. See?

GRANDPA. Why not? They got fences?

HENDERSON. No, they haven't got fences! They've got *laws!* . . . My God, I never came across anything like this before!

GRANDPA. Well, I might pay about seventy-five dollars, but that's all it's worth.

HENDERSON. You'll pay every cent of it, like everybody else!

ED (*who has lost interest*). Listen, Essie— listen to this a minute. (*The xylophone again;* ESSIE *goes into her dance.*)

HENDERSON (*going right ahead, battling against the music*). And let me tell you something else! You'll go to jail if you don't pay, do you hear that? There's a law, and if you think you're bigger than the law, you've got another think coming! You'll hear from the United States Government, that's all I can say! (*He is backing out of the room.*)

GRANDPA (*quietly*). Look out for those snakes

HENDERSON (*jumping*). Jesus! (*Out in the hall, and not more than a foot or two behind* MR. HENDERSON, *the firecracker boys are now ready to test that little bomber. It goes off with a terrific detonation, and* MR. HENDERSON *jumps a full foot. He wastes no time at all in getting out of there.*)

PAUL (*coming back into the room*). How did that sound to you folks?

GRANDPA (*quite judicially*). I liked it.

PENNY. My goodness, he was mad, wasn't he?

GRANDPA. Oh, it wasn't his fault. It's just that the whole thing is so silly.

PENNY (*suddenly finding herself with a perfectly good Panama in her hand*). He forgot his hat.

GRANDPA. What size is it?

PENNY (*peering into its insides*). Seven and an eighth.

GRANDPA. Just right for me.

DE PINNA. Who was that fellow, anyhow? (*Again the door bell.*)

PENNY. This *must* be Mr. Kirby.

PAUL. Better make sure this time.

PENNY. Yes, I will. (*She disappears.*)

ESSIE. I hope he's good-looking.

PENNY (*heard at the door*). How do you do?

A MAN'S VOICE. Good evening.

PENNY (*taking no chances*). Is this Mr. Anthony Kirby, Jr.?

TONY. Yes.

PENNY (*giving her all*). Well, Mr. Kirby, come right in! We've been expecting you. Come right in! (*They come into sight;* PENNY *expansively addresses the family.*) This is *really* Mr. Kirby! Now, I'm Alice's mother, and that's *Mr.* Sycamore, and Alice's grandfather, and her sister Essie, and Essie's husband. (*There are a few mumbled greetings.*) There! Now you know *all* of us, Mr. Kirby. Give me your hat and make yourself right at home. (*TONY KIRBY comes a few steps into the room. He is a personable young man, not long out of Yale, and, as we will presently learn, even more recently out of Cambridge. Although he fits all the physical requirements of a Boss' son, his face has something of the idealist in it. All in all, a very nice young man.*)

TONY. How do you do? (*Again the voice of the vigilant* ALICE *floats down from upstairs. "Is that Mr. Kirby, mother?"*)

PENNY (*shouting up the stairs*). Yes, Alice. He's *lovely!*

ALICE (*aware of storm signals*). I'll be right down.

PENNY. Do sit down, Mr. Kirby.

TONY. Thank you. (*A glance at the dinner table.*) I hope I'm not keeping you from dinner?

GRANDPA. No, no. Have a tomato?

TONY. No, thank you.

PENNY (*producing the candy-filled skull*). How about a piece of candy?

TONY (*eyeing the container*). Ah—no, thanks.

PENNY. Oh, I forgot to introduce Mr. De Pinna. This is Mr. De Pinna, Mr. Kirby. (*An exchange of "How do you do's?"*)

DE PINNA. Wasn't I reading about your father in the newspaper the other day? Didn't he get indicted or something?

TONY (*smiling*). Hardly that. He just testified before the Securities Commission.

DE PINNA. Oh.

PENNY (*sharply*). Yes, of course. I'm sure there was nothing crooked about it, Mr. De Pinna. As a matter of fact— (*She is now addressing* TONY.)—Alice has often told us what a lovely man your father is.

TONY. Well, I know father couldn't get along without Alice. She knows more about the business than any of us.

ESSIE. You're awful young, Mr. Kirby, aren't you, to be vice-president of a big place like that.

TONY. Well, you know what that means, vice-president. All I have is a desk with my name on it.

PENNY. Is that all? Don't you get any salary?

TONY (*with a laugh*). Well, a little. More than I'm worth, I'm afraid.

PENNY. Now you're just being modest.

GRANDPA. Sounds kind of dull to me—Wall Street. Do you like it?

TONY. Well, the hours are short. And I haven't been there very long.

GRANDPA. Just out of college, huh?

TONY. Well, I knocked around for a while first. Just sort of had fun.

GRANDPA. What did you do? Travel?

TONY. For a while. Then I went to Cambridge for a year.

GRANDPA (*nodding*). England.

TONY. That's right.

GRANDPA. Say, what's an English commencement like? Did you see any?

TONY. Oh, very impressive.

GRANDPA. They are, huh?

TONY. Anyhow, now the fun's over, and— I'm facing the world.

PENNY. You've certainly got a good start, Mr. Kirby. Vice-president, and a rich father.

TONY. Well, that's hardly my fault.

PENNY (*brightly*). So now I suppose you're all ready to settle down and—get married.

PAUL. Come now, Penny, I'm sure Mr. Kirby knows his own mind.

PENNY. I wasn't making up his mind for him—was I, Mr. Kirby?

TONY. That's quite all right, Mrs. Sycamore.

PENNY (*to the others*). You see?

ESSIE. You mustn't rush him, mother.

PENNY. Well, all I meant was he's bound to get married, and suppose the wrong girl gets him? (*The descending* ALICE *mercifully comes to* TONY's *rescue at this moment. Her voice is heard from the stairs.*)

ALICE. Well, here I am, a vision in white. (*She comes into the room—and very lovely indeed.*) Apparently you've had time to get acquainted.

PENNY. Oh, yes, indeed. We were just having a delightful talk about love and marriage.

ALICE. Oh, dear. (*She turns to* TONY.) I'm sorry. I came down as fast as I could.

RHEBA (*bringing a platter of sliced water-melon*). God damn those flies in the kitchen. . . . Oh, Miss Alice, you look beautiful! Where you going?

ALICE (*making the best of it*). I'm going out, Rheba.

RHEBA (*noticing* TONY). Stepping, huh? (*The door bell sounds.*)

ESSIE. That must be Kolenkhov.

ALICE (*uneasily*). I think we'd better go, Tony.

TONY. All right. (*Before they can escape, however,* DONALD *emerges from the kitchen, bearing a tray.*)

DONALD. Grandpa, you take cream on your cornflakes? I forget.

GRANDPA. Half and half, Donald. (*The voice of* BORIS KOLENKHOV *booms from the outer door.*)

KOLENKHOV. Ah, my little Rhebishka!

RHEBA (*with a scream of laughter*). Yassuh, Mr. Kolenkhov!

KOLENKHOV. I am so hungry I could even eat my little Rhebishka! (*He appears in the archway, his great arm completely encircling the delighted* RHEBA. MR. KOLENKHOV *is one of* RHEBA'S *pets, and if you like Russians he might be one of yours. He is enormous, hairy, loud, and very, very Russian. His appearance in the archway still further traps* ALICE *and* TONY.) Grandpa, what do you think? I have had a letter from Russia! The Second Five Year Plan is a failure! (*He lets out a laugh that shakes the rafters.*)

ESSIE. I practiced today, Mr. Kolenkhov!

KOLENKHOV (*with a deep Russian bow*). My Pavlowa! (*Another bow.*) Madame Sycamore! . . . My little Alice! (*He kisses her hand.*) Never have I seen you look so magnificent.

ALICE. Thank you, Mr. Kolenkhov. Tony, this is Mr. Kolenkhov, Essie's dancing teacher. Mr. Kirby.

TONY. How do you do? (*A click of the heels and a bow from* KOLENKHOV.)

ALICE (*determined, this time*). And now we really *must* go. Excuse us, Mr. Kolenkhov— we're going to the Monte Carlo ballet.

KOLENKHOV (*at the top of his tremendous voice*). The Monte Carlo ballet! It *stinks!*

ALICE (*panicky now*). Yes. . . . Well—goodbye, everybody. Goodbye.

TONY. Goodbye. I'm so glad to have met you all. (*A chorus of answering "Good-byes" from the family. The young people are gone.*)

KOLENKHOV (*still furious*). The Monte Carlo ballet!

PENNY. Isn't Mr. Kirby lovely? . . . Come on, everybody! Dinner's ready!

ED (*pulling up a chair*). I thought he was a nice fellow, didn't you?

ESSIE. Mm. And so good-looking.

PENNY. And he had such nice manners. Did you notice, Paul? Did you notice his manners?

PAUL. I certainly did. You were getting pretty personal with him.

PENNY. Oh, now Paul . . . Anyhow, he's a very nice young man.

DE PINNA (*as he seats himself*). He looks kind of like a cousin of mine.

KOLENKHOV. Bakst! Diaghlieff! *Then* you had the *ballet!*

PENNY. I think if they get married here I'll put the altar right where the snakes are. You wouldn't mind, Grandpa, would you?

ESSIE. Oh, they'll want to get married in a church. His family and everything.

GRANDPA (*tapping on a plate for silence*). Quiet, everybody! Quiet! (*They are immediately silent—Grace is about to be pronounced.* GRANDPA *pauses a moment for heads to bow, then raises his eyes heavenward. He clears his throat and proceeds to say Grace.*) Well, Sir, we've been getting along pretty good for quite a while now, and we're certainly much obliged. Remember, all we ask is just to go along and be happy in our own sort of way. Of course we want to keep our health, but as far as anything else is concerned, we'll leave it to You. Thank You. (*The heads come up as* RHEBA *comes through the door with a steaming platter.*) So the Second Five Year Plan is a failure, eh, Kolenkhov?

KOLENKHOV (*booming*). Catastrophic! (*He reaches across the table and spears a piece of bread. The family, too, is busily plunging in.*)

THE CURTAIN IS DOWN

SCENE II

Late the same night. The house is in darkness save for a light in the hall.

Somewhere in the back regions an accordion is being played. Then quiet. Then the stillness of the night is suddenly broken again by a good loud BANG! from the cellar. Somewhere in the nether regions, one of the Sycamores is still at work.

Once more all is quiet, then the sound of a key in the outer door. The voices of ALICE *and* TONY *drift through.*

ALICE. I could see them dance every night of the week. I think they're marvelous.

TONY. They are, aren't they? But of course just walking inside *any* theatre gives *me* a thrill.

ALICE (*as they come into sight in the hallway*). It's been *so* lovely, Tony. I hate to have it over.

TONY. Oh, is it over? Do I have to go right away?

ALICE. Not if you don't want to.

TONY. I don't.

ALICE. Would you like a cold drink?

TONY. Wonderful.

ALICE (*pausing to switch on the light*). "I'll see what's in the ice-box. Want to come along?

TONY. I'd follow you to the ends of the earth.

ALICE. Oh, just the kitchen is enough. (*They go out. A pause, a ripple of gay laughter from the kitchen, then they return.* ALICE *is carrying a couple of glasses,* TONY *brings two bottles of ginger ale and an opener.*) Lucky you're not hungry, Mr. K. An ice-box full of cornflakes. That gives you a rough idea of the Sycamores.

TONY (*working away with the opener*). Of course, why they make these bottle openers for Singer midgets I never *was* able to—ah! (*As the bottle opens.*) All over my coat.

ALICE. I'll take mine in a glass, if you don't mind.

TONY (*pouring*). There you are. A foaming beaker.

ALICE. Anyhow, it's cold.

TONY (*pouring his own*). Now if you'll please be seated, I'd like to offer a toast.

ALICE (*settling herself*). We are seated.

TONY. Miss Sycamore— (*He raises his glass on high.*)—to you.

ALICE. Thank you, Mr. Kirby. (*Lifting her own glass.*) To you. (*They both drink.*)

TONY (*happily*). I wouldn't trade one minute of this evening for—all the rice in China.

ALICE. Really?

TONY. Cross my heart.

ALICE (*a little sigh of contentment. Then shyly*). Is there much rice in China?

TONY. Terrific. Didn't you read "The Good Earth?" (*She laughs. They are silent for a moment.*) I suppose I ought to go.

ALICE. Is it very late?

TONY (*looks at his watch*). Very. (ALICE *gives a little nod. Time doesn't matter.*) I don't want to go.

ALICE. I don't want you to.

TONY. All right, I won't. (*Silence again.*) When do you get your vacation?

ALICE. Last two weeks in August.

TONY. I might take mine then, too.

ALICE. Really?

TONY. What are you going to do?

ALICE. I don't know. I hadn't thought much about it.

TONY. Going away, do you think?

ALICE. I might not. I like the city in the summer time.

TONY. I do too.

ALICE. But you always go up to Maine, don't you?

TONY. Why—yes, but I'm sure I *would* like the city in the summer time. That is, I'd like it if—Oh, you know what I mean, Alice. I'd love it if *you* were here.

ALICE. Well—it'd be nice if you were here, Tony.

TONY. You know what you're saying, don't you?

ALICE. What?

TONY. That you'd rather spend the summer with me than anybody else.

ALICE. It looks that way, doesn't it?

TONY. Well, if it's true about the summer, how would you feel about—the winter?

ALICE (*seeming to weigh the matter*). Yes. I'd—like that, too.

TONY (*tremulous*). Then comes spring—and autumn. If you could—see your way clear about those, Miss Sycamore. . . .

ALICE (*again a little pause*). Yes.

TONY. I guess that's the whole year. We haven't forgotten anything, have we?

ALICE. No.

TONY. Well, then— (*Another pause; their eyes meet. And at this moment,* PENNY *is heard from the stairway.*)

PENNY. Is that you, Alice? What time is it? (*She comes into the room, wrapped in a bathrobe.*) Oh! (*In sudden embarrassment.*) Excuse me, Mr. Kirby. I had no idea— that is, I—(*She senses the situation.*)—I didn't mean to interrupt anything.

TONY. Not at all, Mrs. Sycamore.

ALICE (*quietly*). No, mother.

PENNY. I just came down for a manuscript— (*Fumbling at her table.*)—then you can go right ahead. Ah, here it is. "Sex Takes a Holiday." Well—good-night, Mr. Kirby.

TONY. Good-night, Mrs. Sycamore.

PENNY. Oh, I think you can call me Penny, don't you, Alice? At least I hope so. (*With*

a little laugh she vanishes up the stairs.) (*Before* PENNY's *rippling laugh quite dies,* BANG! *from the cellar.* TONY *jumps.*)

ALICE (*quietly*). It's all right, Tony. That's father.

TONY. This time of night?

ALICE (*ominously*). *Any* time of night. Any time of *day.* (*She stands silent. In the pause,* TONY *gazes at her fondly.*)

TONY. You're more beautiful, more lovely, more adorable than anyone else in the whole world.

ALICE (*as he starts to embrace her*). Don't, Tony. I can't.

TONY. What?

ALICE. I can't, Tony.

TONY. My dear, just because your mother— all mothers are like that, Alice, and Penny's a darling. You see, I'm even calling her Penny.

ALICE. I don't mean that. (*She faces him squarely.*) Look, Tony. This is something I should have said a long time ago, but I didn't have the courage. I let myself be swept away because—because I loved you so.

TONY. Darling!

ALICE. No, wait, Tony. I want to make it clear to you. You're of a different world—a whole different kind of people. Oh, I don't mean money or socially—that's too silly. But your family and mine—it just wouldn't work, Tony. It just wouldn't work. (*Again an interruption. This time it is* ED *and* ESSIE, *returning from the neighborhood movie. We hear their voices at the door, deep in an argument.* ED: "All right, have it your way. She *can't dance. That's why they pay her all that money—because she can't dance.*" *And then* ESSIE: "*Well, I don't call that dancing, what she does.*") (*They come into sight.*)

ESSIE. Oh, hello. (*There is an exchange of greetings, a note of constraint in* ALICE's *voice. But* ESSIE *goes right ahead.*) Look! What do *you* think? Ed and I just saw Fred Astaire and Ginger Rogers. Do you think she can dance, Mr. Kirby?

TONY (*mildly taken aback by this*). Why, yes—I always thought so.

ESSIE. What does she do, anyhow? Now, look—you're Fred Astaire and I'm Ginger Rogers. (*She drapes herself against* TONY, *a la Ginger Rogers.*)

ALICE. Essie, please.

ESSIE. I just want to use him for a minute. . . . Look, Mr. Kirby— (*Her arms go round his neck, her cheek against his.*)

ALICE (*feeling that it's time to take action*). Essie, you're just as good as Ginger Rogers. We all agree.

ESSIE (*triumphantly*). You see, Ed?

ED. Yeh. . . . Come on, Essie—we're butting in here.

ESSIE. Oh, they've been together all evening. . . . Good night, Mr. Kirby. (*An exchange of good-nights—it looks as though the* CAR-MICHAELS *are really going upstairs before the whole thing gets too embarrassing. Then* ED *turns casually to* ESSIE *in the doorway.*)

ED. Essie, did you ask Grandpa about us having a baby?

ESSIE (*as they ascend the stairs*). Yes—he said go right ahead.

ALICE (*when they are gone*). You see? That's what it would be like, always.

TONY. But I didn't mind that. Besides, darling, we're not going to live with our families. It's just you and I.

ALICE. No, it isn't—it's never quite that. I love them, Tony—I love them deeply. Some people could cut away, but I couldn't. I know they do rather strange things—I never know what to expect next—but they're gay, and they're fun, and—I don't know—there's a kind of nobility about them. That may sound silly, but I mean—the way they just don't care about things that other people give their whole lives to. They're—really wonderful, Tony.

TONY. Alice, you talk as though only you could understand them. That's not true. Why, I fell in love with them tonight.

ALICE. But your family, Tony. I'd want *you,* and everything about you, everything about

me, to be—one. I couldn't start out with a part of me that you didn't share, and part of you that I didn't share. Unless we were all one—you, and *your* mother and father— I'd be miserable. And they never can be, Tony—I know it. They couldn't be.

TONY. Alice, every family has got curious little traits. What of it? My father raises orchids at ten thousand dollars a bulb. Is that sensible? My mother believes in spiritualism. That's just as bad as your mother writing plays, isn't it?

ALICE. It goes deeper, Tony. Your mother believes in spiritualism because it's fashionable. And your father raises orchids because he can afford to. My mother writes plays because eight years ago a typewriter was delivered here by mistake.

TONY. Darling, what *of* it?

ALICE. And look at Grandpa. Thirty-five years ago he just quit business one day. He started up to his office in the elevator and came right down again. He just stopped. He could have been a rich man, but he said it took too much time. So for thirty-five years he's just collected snakes and gone to circuses and commencements. It never occurs to any of them— (*As if to prove her point, they are suddenly interrupted at this moment by the entrance of* DONALD *from the kitchen. It is a* DONALD *who has plainly not expected to encounter midnight visitors, for he is simply dressed in a long white nightgown and a somewhat shorter bathrobe—a costume that permits a generous expanse of white nightshirt down around the legs, and, below that, a couple of very black shins. His appearance, incidentally, explains where all that music had been coming from, for an accordion is slung over his shoulder.*)

DONALD (*surprised, but not taken aback*). Oh, excuse me. I didn't know you folks was in here.

ALICE (*resigned*). It's all right, Donald.

DONALD. Rheba kind of fancied some candy, and—(*His gaze is roaming the room.*)—oh, there it is. (*He picks up* ENNY's *skull, if you know what we mean.*) You-all don't want it, do you?

ALICE. No, Donald. Go right ahead.

DONALD. Thanks. (*He feels that the occasion calls for certain amenities.*) Have a nice evening?

ALICE. Yes, Donald.

DONALD. Nice dinner?

ALICE (*restraining herself*). Yes, Donald.

DONALD. The ballet nice?

ALICE (*entirely too quietly*). Yes, Donald.

DONALD (*summing it all up*). That's nice. (*He goes—and* ALICE *bursts forth.*)

ALICE. Now! Now do you see what I mean? Could you explain Donald to your father? Could you explain Grandpa? You couldn't, Tony, you couldn't! I should have known! I did know! I love you, Tony, but I love them too! And it's no use, Tony! It's no use! (*She is weeping now in spite of herself.*)

TONY (*quietly*). There's only one thing you've said that matters—that makes any sense at all. You love me.

ALICE. But, Tony, I know so well . . .

TONY. My darling, don't you think other people have had the same problem? Everybody's got a family.

ALICE (*through her tears*). But not like mine.

TONY. That doesn't stop people who love each other. . . . Darling! Darling, won't you trust me, and go on loving me, and forget everything else?

ALICE. How can I?

TONY. Because nothing can keep us apart. You know that. You must know it. Just as I know it. (*He takes her in his arms.*) They want you to be happy, don't they? They *must.*

ALICE. Of course they do. But they can't change, Tony. I wouldn't want them to change.

TONY. They won't have to change. They're charming, lovable people, just as they are. You're worrying about something that may never come up.

ALICE. Oh, Tony, am I?

TONY. All that matters right now is that we love each other. That's right, isn't it?

ALICE (*whispering*). Yes.

TONY. Well, then!

ALICE (*in his arms*). Tony, Tony!

TONY. Now! I'd like to see a little gayety around here. Young gentleman calling, and getting engaged and everything.

ALICE (*smiling up into his face*). What do I say?

TONY. Well, first you thank the young man for getting engaged to you.

ALICE. Thank you, Mr. Kirby, for getting engaged to me.

TONY. And then you tell him what it was about him that first took your girlish heart.

ALICE. The back of your head.

TONY. Huh?

ALICE. Uh-huh. It wasn't your charm, and it wasn't your money—it was the back of your head. I just happened to like it.

TONY. What happened when I turned around?

ALICE. Oh, I got used to it after a while.

TONY. I see . . . Oh, Alice, think of it. We're pretty lucky, aren't we?

ALICE. I know that *I* am. The luckiest girl in the world.

TONY. I'm not exactly unlucky myself.

ALICE. It's wonderful, isn't it?

TONY. Yes . . . Lord, but I'm happy.

ALICE. Are you, Tony?

TONY. Terribly . . . And now—good-night, my dear. Until tomorrow.

ALICE. Good-night.

TONY. Isn't it wonderful we work in the same office? Otherwise I'd be hanging around *here* all day.

ALICE. Won't it be funny in the office tomorrow—seeing each other and just going on as thought nothing had happened?

TONY. Thank God I'm vice-president. I can dictate to you all day. "Dear Miss Sycamore: I love you, I love you, I love you."

ALICE. Oh, darling! You're such a fool.

TON (*an arm about her as he starts toward the allway*). Why don't you meet me in the drugstore in the morning—before you go up to the office? I'll have millions of things to say to you by then.

ALICE. All right.

TONY. And then lunch, and then dinner tomorrow night.

ALICE. Oh, Tony! What will people say?

TONY. It's got to come out some time. In fact, if you know a good housetop, I'd like to do a little shouting. (*She laughs—a happy little ripple. They are out of sight in the hallway by this time; their voices become inaudible.*)

(PAUL, *at this point, decides to call it a day down in the cellar. He comes through the door, followed by* MR. DE PINNA. *He is carrying a small metal container, filled with powder.*)

PAUL. Yes, sir, Mr. De Pinna, we did a good day's work.

DE PINNA. That's what. Five hundred Black Panthers, three hundred Willow Trees, and eight dozen Junior Kiddie Bombers. (ALICE *comes back from the hallway, still under the spell of her love.*)

PAUL. Why, hello, Alice. You just come in?

ALICE (*softly*). No. No, I've been home quite a while.

PAUL. Have a nice evening? Say, I'd like you to take a look at this new red fire we've got.

ALICE (*almost singing it*). I had a beautiful evening, father.

PAUL. Will you turn out the lights, Mr. De Pinna? I want Alice to get the full effect.

ALICE (*who hasn't heard a word*). What, father?

PAUL. Take a look at this new red fire. It's beautiful. (MR. DE PINNA *switches the lights out;* PAUL *touches a match to the powder. The red fire blazes, shedding a soft glow over the room.*) There! What do you think of it? Isn't it beautiful?

ALICE (*radiant; her face aglow, her voice soft*). Yes, father. Everything is beautiful. It's the most beautiful red fire in the world! (*She rushes to him and throws her arms about him, almost unable to bear her own happiness.*)

CURTAIN

ACT TWO

A week later, and the family has just risen from the dinner table. Two or three of them have drifted out of the room, but GRANDPA *and* PAUL *still sit over their coffee cups.*

There is, however, a newcomer in the room. Her name is GAY WELLINGTON, *and, as we will presently guess, she is an actress, a nymphomaniac, and a terrible souse. At the moment she sits with a gin bottle in one hand and a glass in the other, and is having a darned good time. Hovering over her, script in hand, is a slightly worried* PENNY. ED *is watching the proceedings from somewhere in the vicinity of the printing press, and* DONALD, *leisurely clearing the table, has paused to see if* MISS WELLINGTON *can really swallow that one more drink of gin that she is about to tackle. She does, and another besides.*

PENNY *finally decides to make a try.*

PENNY. I'm ready to read the play now, Miss Wellington, if you are.

GAY WELLINTON. Just a minute, dearie—just a minute. (*The gin again.*)

PENNY. The only thing is—I hope you won't mind my mentioning this, but—you don't drink when you're acting, do you, Miss Wellington? I'm just asking, of course.

GAY. I'm glad you brought it up. Once a play opens, I never touch a drop. Minute I enter a stage door, this bottle gets put away till intermission.

GRANDPA (*who plainly has his doubts*). Have you been on the stage a long time, Miss Wellington?

GAY. All my life. I've played everything. Ever see "Peg o' My Heart"?

GRANDPA. Yes, indeed.

GAY (*with that fine logic for which the inebriated brain is celebrated*). I saw it too. Great show. (*She staggers backwards a bit, but recovers herself just in time.*) My! Hot night, ain't it?

DONALD (*ever helpful*). Want me to open a window, Miss Wellington?

GAY. No, the hell with the weather. (*She takes a second look at the dusky DONALD.*) Say, he's cute. (RHEBA, *who has entered just in time to overhear this, gives* GAY *a look that tells her in no uncertain terms to keep out of Harlem on dark nights. Then she stalks back into the kitchen,* DONALD *close on her heels.*)

DONALD (*trying to explain it all*). She's just acting, Rheba. She don't mean anything.

PENNY. Well, any time you're ready, we can go up to my room and start. I thought I'd read the play up in my room.

GAY. All right, dearie, just a minute. (*She starts to pour one more drink, then suddenly her gaze becomes transfixed. She shakes her head as though to dislodge the image, then looks again, receives verification, and starts to pour the gin back into the bottle.*) When I see snakes it's time to lay down. (*She makes for a couch in the corner, and passes right out—cold.*)

PENNY. Oh, but those are real, Miss Wellington. They're Grandpa's. . . . Oh, dear! I hope she's not going to— (*Shaking her.*) Miss Wellington! Miss Wellington!

ED. She's out like a light.

PAUL. Better let her sleep it off.

DONALD (*carrying the news into the kitchen*). Rheba, Miss Wellington just passed out. (*From the nether recesses we hear* RHEBA'S *reaction—an emphatic "Good!"*)

PENNY. Do you think she'll be all right?

GRANDPA. Yes, but I wouldn't cast her in the religious play.

PENNY. Well, I suppose I'll just have to wait. I wonder if I shouldn't cover her up.

GRANDPA. Next time you meet an actress on the top of a bus, Penny, I think I'd *send*

her the play, instead of bringing her home to read it.

ESSIE (*as* ED *starts in with the printing press*). Ed, I wish you'd stop printing and take those Love Dreams around. They're out in the kitchen.

ED. I will. I just want to finish up these circulars.

ESSIE. Well, do that later, can't you? You've got to get back in time to play for me when Kolenkhov comes.

GRANDPA. Kolenkhov coming tonight?

ESSIE. Yes, tomorrow night's his night, but I had to change it on account of Alice.

GRANDPA. Oh! . . . Big doings around here tomorrow night, huh?

PENNY. Isn't it exciting? You know, I'm so nervous—you'd think it was me he was engaged to, instead of Alice.

ESSIE. What do you think they'll *be* like—his mother and father? . . . Ed, what are you doing *now*?

ED. Penny, did you see the new mask I made last night? (*He reveals a new side of his character by suddenly holding a homemade mask before his face.*) Guess who it is.

PENNY. Don't tell me now, Ed. Wait a minute . . . Cleopatra.

ED (*furious*). It's Mrs. Roosevelt. (*He goes into the kitchen.*)

(PAUL, *meanwhile, has gone to a table in the corner of the room, from which he now brings a steel-like boat model, two or three feet high, puts it down on the floor, and proceeds to sit down beside it. From a large cardboard box, which he has also brought with him, he proceeds to take out additional pieces of steel and fit them into the model.*)

PAUL. You know, the nice thing about these Erector Sets, you can make so many different thinks with them. Last week it was the Empire State Building.

GRANDPA. What is it this week?

PAUL. The Queen Mary.

PENNY (*looking it over*). Hasn't got the right hat on. (ED *comes in from the kitchen, bringing a pile of about a dozen candy boxes, neatly wrapped, and tied together for purposes of delivery.*)

ED (*as* MR. DE PINNA *comes in from the hall*). Look. Mr. De Pinna, would you open the door and see if there's a man standing in front of the house?

ESSIE. Why, what for?

ED. Well, the last two days, when I've been out delivering, I think a man's been following me.

ESSIE. Ed, you're crazy.

ED. No, I'm not. He follows me, and he stands and watches the house.

DE PINNA. Really? (*Striding out.*) I'll take a look and see.

GRANDPA. I don't see what anybody would follow *you* for, Ed.

PENNY. Well, there's a lot of kidnapping going on, Grandpa.

GRANDPA. Yes, but not of Ed.

ED (*as* MR. DE PINNA *returns from the hall*). Well? Did you see him?

DE PINNA. There's nobody out there at all.

ED. You're sure?

DE PINNA. Positive. I just saw him walk away.

ED. You see? I told you.

ESSIE. Oh, it might have been anybody, walking along the street. Ed, will you hurry and get back?

ED (*picking up his boxes*). Oh, all right.

DE PINNA. Want to go down now, Mr. Sycamore, and finish packing up the fireworks?

PAUL (*putting the Queen Mary back on the table*). Yeh, we've got to take the stuff up to Mt. Vernon in the morning. (*They go into the cellar. Simultaneously the voice of* ALICE, *happily singing, is heard as she descends the stairs.*)

ALICE. Mother, may I borrow some paper? I'm making out a list for Rheba tomorrow night.

PENNY. Yes, dear. Here's some.

ALICE (*as she sights* MISS WELLINGTON). Why, what happened to your actress friend? Is she giving a performance?

PENNY. No, she's not acting, Alice. She's really drunk.

ALICE. Essie, you're going to give Rheba the kitchen all day tomorrow, aren't you? Because she'll need it.

ESSIE. Of course, Alice. I'm going to start some Love Dreams now, so I'll be 'way ahead. (*She goes into the kitchen.*)

ALICE. Thanks, dear . . . Look, mother, I'm coming home at three o'clock tomorrow. Will you have everything down in the cellar by that time? The typewriter, and the snakes, and the xylophone, and the printing press . . .

GRANDPA. And Miss Wellington.

ALICE. And Miss Wellington. That'll give me time to arrange the table, and fix the flowers.

GRANDPA. The Kirbys are certainly going to get the wrong impression of this house.

ALICE. You'll *do* all that, won't you, mother?

PENNY. Of course, dear.

ALICE. And I think we'd better have cocktails ready by seven-fifteen, in case they happen to come a little early. . . . I wonder if I ought to let Rheba cook the dinner. What do you think, Grandpa?

GRANDPA. Now, Alice, I wouldn't worry. From what I've seen of the boy I'm sure the Kirbys are very nice people, and if everything isn't so elaborate tomorrow night, it's all right too.

ALICE. Darling, I'm not trying to impress them, or pretend we're anything that we aren't. I just want everything to—to go off well.

GRANDPA. No reason why it shouldn't, Alice.

PENNY. We're all going to do everything we can to make it a nice party.

ALICE. Oh, my darlings, I love you. You're the most wonderful family in the world, and I'm the happiest girl in the world. I didn't know anyone could *be* so happy. He's so wonderful, Grandpa. Why, just seeing him—you don't know what it does to me.

GRANDPA. Just seeing him. Just seeing him for lunch, and dinner, and until four o'clock in the morning, and at nine o'clock *next* morning you're at the office again and there he is. You just see him, huh?

ALICE. I don't care! I'm in love. (*She swings open the kitchen door.*) Rheba! Rheba! (*She goes into the kitchen.*)

GRANDPA. Nice, isn't it? Nice to see her so happy.

PENNY. I remember when I was engaged to Paul—how happy I was. And you know, I still feel that way.

GRANDPA. I know . . . Nice the way Ed and Essie get along too, isn't it?

PENNY. And Donald and Rheba, even though they're *not* married. . . . Do you suppose Mr. De Pinna will ever marry anyone, Grandpa?

GRANDPA (*a gesture toward the couch*). Well, there's Miss Wellington.

PENNY. Oh, dear, I *wish* she'd wake up. If we're going to read the play tonight— (MR. DE PINNA *comes up from the cellar, bringing along a rather large-sized unframed painting.*)

DE PINNA. Mrs. Sycamore, look what I found! (*He turns the canvas around, revealing a portrait of a somewhat lumpy discus thrower, in Roman costume—or was it Greek?*) Remember?

PENNY. Why, of course. It's my painting of you as The Discus Thrower. Look, Grandpa.

GRANDPA. I remember it. Say, you've gotten a little bald, haven't you, Mr. De Pinna?

DE PINNA (*running a hand over his completely hairless head*). Is it very noticeable?

PENNY. Well, it was a long time ago—just before I stopped painting. Let me see—that's eight years.

DE PINNA. Too bad you never finished it, Mrs. Sycamore.

PENNY. I always meant to finish it, Mr. De Pinna, but I just started to write a play one day and that was that. I never painted again.

GRANDPA. Just as well, too. *I* was going to have to strip next.

DE PINNA (*meditatively*). Who would have thought, that day I came to deliver the ice, that I was going to stay here for eight years?

GRANDPA. The milkman was here for five, just ahead of you.

DE PINNA. Why did he leave, anyhow? I forget.

GRANDPA. He didn't leave. He died.

PENNY. He was such a nice man. Remember the funeral, Grandpa? We never knew his name and it was kind of hard to get a certificate.

GRANDPA. What was the name we finally made up for him?

PENNY. Martin Vanderhof. We gave him *your* name.

GRANDPA. Oh, yes, I remember.

PENNY. It was a lovely thought, because otherwise he never would have got all those flowers.

GRANDPA. Certainly was. And it didn't hurt *me* any. Not bothered with mail any more, and I haven't had a telephone call from that day to this. (*He catches an unwary fly and drops it casually into the snake solarium.*)

PENNY. Yes, it was really a wonderful idea.

DE PINNA (*with the picture*). I wish you'd finish this sometime, Mrs. Sycamore. I'd kind of like to have it.

PENNY. You know what, Mr. De Pinna? I think I'll do some work on it. Right tonight.

DE PINNA. Say! Will you? (*The door bell rings.*)

PENNY (*peering at the prostrate* GAY). I don't think she's going to wake up anyhow. . . . Look, Mr. De Pinna! You go down in the cellar and bring up the easel and get into your costume. Is it still down there?

DE PINNA (*excited*). I think so! (*He darts into the cellar.*)

PENNY. Now, where did I put my palette and brushes? (*She dashes up the stairs as the voice of* KOLENKHOV *is heard at the door, booming, of course.*)

KOLENKHOV. Rhebishka! My little Rhebishka!

RHEBA (*delighted, as usual*). Yassuh, Mr. Kolenkhov!

PENNY (*as she goes up the stairs*). Hello, Mr. Kolenkhov. Essie's in the kitchen.

KOLENKHOV. Madame Sycamore, I greet you! (*His great arm again encircling* RHEBA, *he drags her protestingly into the room.*) Tell me, Grandpa—what should I do about Rhebishka! I keep telling her she would make a great toe dancer, but she laughs only!

RHEBA (*breaking away*). No, suh! I couldn't get up on my toes, Mr. Kolenkhov! I got corns! (*She goes into the kitchen.*)

KOLENKHOV (*calling after her*). Rhebishka, you could wear diamonds! (*Suddenly he sights the portrait of* MR. DE PINNA.) What is that?

GRANDPA (*who has taken up his stamp album again*). It's a picture of Mr. De Pinna. Penny painted it.

KOLENKHOV (*summing it up*). It stinks.

GRANDPA. I know. (*He indicates the figure on the couch.*) How do you like that?

KOLENKHOV (*peering over*). What is *that*?

GRANDPA. She's an actress. Friend of Penny's.

KOLENKHOV. She is drunk—no?

GRANDPA. She is drunk—yes. . . . How are *you*, Kolenkhov?

KOLENKHOV. Magnificent! Life is chasing around inside of me, like a squirrel.

GRANDPA. 'Tis, huh? . . . What's new in Russia? Any more letters from your friend in Moscow?

KOLENKHOV. I have just heard from him. I saved for you the stamp. (*He hands it over.*)

GRANDPA (*receiving it with delight*). Thanks, Kolenkhov.

KOLENKHOV. They have sent him to Siberia.

GRANDPA. That so? How's he like it?

KOLENKHOV. He has escaped and gone back to Moscow. He will get them yet, if they do not get him. The Soviet Government! I could take the whole Soviet Government and—grrah! (*He crushes Stalin and all in one great paw, just as* ESSIE *comes in from the kitchen.*)

ESSIE. I'm sorry I'm late, Mr. Kolenkhov. I'll get into my dancing clothes right away.

KOLENKHOV. Tonight you will really work, Pavlowa. (*As* ESSIE *goes up the stairs.*) Tonight we will take something new.

GRANDPA. Essie making any progress, Kolenkhov?

KOLENKHOV (*first making elaborately sure that* ESSIE *is gone.*) Confidentially, she stinks.

GRANDPA. Well, as long as she's having fun. . . . (DONALD *ambles in from the kitchen, chuckling.*)

DONALD. You sure do tickle Rheba, Mr. Kolenkhov. She's laughing her head off out there.

KOLENKHOV. She is a great woman. . . . Donald, what do you think of the Soviet Government?

DONALD. The what, Mr. Kolenkhov?

KOLENKHOV. I withdraw the question. What do you think of *this* Government?

DONALD. Oh, I like it fine. I'm on relief, you know.

KOLENKHOV. Oh, yes. And you like it?

DONALD. Yassuh, it's fine. Only thing is you got to go round to the place every week and collect it, and sometimes you got to stand in line pretty near half an hour. Government ought to be run better than that—don't you think, Grandpa?

GRANDPA (*as he fishes an envelope out of his pocket*). Government ought to stop sending me letters. Want me to be at the United States Marshal's office Tuesday morning at ten o'clock.

KOLENKHOV (*peering at the letter*). Ah! Income tax! They have got you, Grandpa.

GRANDPA. Mm. I'm supposed to give 'em a lot of money so as to keep Donald on relief.

DONALD. You don't say, Grandpa? You going to pay it now?

GRANDPA. That's what they want.

DONALD. You mean I can come right *here* and get it instead of standing in that line?

GRANDPA. No, Donald. You will have to waste a full half hour of your time every week.

DONALD. Well, I don't like it. It breaks up my week. (*He goes into the kitchen.*)

KOLENKHOV. He should have been in Russia when the Revolution came. Then he would have stood in line—a bread line. (*He turns to* GRANDPA.) Ah, Grandpa, what they have done to Russia. Think of it! The Grand Duchess Olga Katrina, a cousin of the Czar, she is a waitress in Childs' restaurant! I ordered baked beans from her only yesterday. It broke my heart. A crazy world, Grandpa.

GRANDPA. Oh, the world's not so crazy, Kolenkhov. It's the people *in* it. Life's pretty simple if you just relax.

KOLENKHOV. How can you relax in times like these?

GRANDPA. Well, if they'd relaxed there wouldn't *be* times like these. That's just my point. Life is simple and kind of beautiful if you let it come to you. But the trouble is, people forget that. I know I did. I was right in the thick of it—fighting, and scratching, and clawing. Regular jungle. One day it just kind of struck me. I wasn't having any fun.

KOLENKHOV. So you did what?

GRANDPA. Just relaxed. Thirty-five years ago, that was. And I've been a happy man ever since. (*From somewhere or other* GRANDPA *has brought one of those colored targets that one buys at Schwartz's. He now hangs it up on the cellar door, picks up a handful of feathered darts, and carefully throws one at the target.*)
(*At the same time* ALICE *passes through the room, en route from kitchen to the upstairs region.*)

ALICE. Good evening, Mr. Kolenkhov.

KOLENKHOV (*bowing low over her hand*). Ah, Miss Alice! I have not seen you to present my congratulations. May you be very happy and have many children. That is my prayer for you.

ALICE. Thank you, Mr. Kolenkhov. That's quite a thought. (*Singing gayly, she goes up the stairs.*)

KOLENKHOV (*looking after her*). Ah, love! That is all that is left in the world, Grandpa.

GRANDPA. Yes, but there's plenty of that.

KOLENKHOV. And soon Stalin will take that away, too. I tell you, Grandpa— (*He stops as* PENNY *comes down the stairs—a living example of what the well-dressed artist should wear. She has on an artist's smock over her dress, a flowing black tie, and a large black velvet tam-o'-shanter, worn at a rakish angle. She carries a palette and an assortment of paints and brushes.*)

PENNY. Seems so nice to get into my art things again. They still look all right, don't they, Grandpa?

GRANDPA. Yes, indeed.

KOLENKHOV. You are a breath of Paris, Madame Sycamore.

PENNY. Oh, thank you, Mr. Kolenkhov.

DONALD (*coming in from the kitchen*). I didn't know you was working for the WPA.

PENNY. Oh, no, Donald. You see, I used to paint all the time, and then one day— (*The outer door slams and* ED *comes in.*)

ED (*in considerable excitement*). It happened again! There was a fellow following me every place I went!

PENNY. Nonsense, Ed. It's your imagination.

ED. No, it isn't. It happens every time I go out to deliver candy.

GRANDPA. Maybe he wants a piece of candy.

ED. It's all right for you to laugh, Grandpa, but he keeps following me.

KOLENKHOV (*somberly*). You do not know what following is. In Russia *everybody* is followed. I was followed right out of Russia.

PENNY. Of course. You see, Ed—the whole thing is just imagination. (MR. DE PINNA *comes up from the cellar, ready for posing. He wears the traditional Roman costume, and he certainly cuts a figure. He is carrying* PENNY's *easel, a discus, and a small platform for posing purposes.*) Ah, here we are! . . . Right here, Mr. De Pinna.

DONALD (*suddenly getting it*). Oh, is that picture supposed to be Mr. De Pinna?

PENNY (*sharply*). Of course it is, Donald. What's it look like—me?

DONALD (*studying the portrait*). Yes, it does —a little bit.

PENNY. Nonsense! What would I be doing with a discus?

KOLENKHOV. Ed, for tonight's lesson we use the first movement of Scheherazade.

ED. Okay.

DE PINNA (*about to mount the platform*). I hope I haven't forgotten how to pose. (*He takes up the discus and strikes the classic pose of the Discus Thrower. Somehow, it is not quite convincing.*)

DONALD. What's he going to do with that thing? Throw it?

PENNY. No, no, Donald. He's just posing. . . . Mr. De Pinna, has something happened to your figure during these eight years?

DE PINNA (*pulling in his stomach*). No, I don't think it's any different. (*With a sudden snort,* GAY WELLINGTON *comes to.*)

PENNY (*immediately alert*). Yes, Miss Wellington? (*For answer,* GAY *peers first at* PENNY, *then at* MR. DE PINNA. *Then, with a strange snort, she just passes right out again.*)

PENNY. Oh, dear. (ESSIE *comes tripping down the stairs—very much the ballet dancer. She is in full costume—ballet skirt, tight white satin bodice, a garland of roses in her hair.*)

ESSIE. Sorry, Mr. Kolenkhov, I couldn't find my slippers.

KOLENKHOV (*having previously removed his coat, he now takes off his shirt, displaying an enormous hairy chest beneath his undershirt*). We have a hot night for it, my Pavlowa, but art is only achieved through perspiration.

PENNY. Why, that's wonderful, Mr. Kolenkhov. Did you hear that, Grandpa—art is only achieved through perspiration.

GRANDPA. Yes, but it helps if you've got a little talent with it. (*He returns to his dart throwing.*) Only made two bull's-eyes last night. Got to do better than that. (*He hurls a dart at the board, then his eye travels to* MISS WELLINGTON, *whose posterior offers an even easier target.*) Mind if I use Miss Wellington, Penny?

PENNY. What, Grandpa?

GRANDPA (*shakes his head*). Never mind. . . . Too easy. (GRANDPA *throws another dart at the target.*)

KOLENKHOV. You are ready? We begin! (*With a gesture he orders the music started; under* KOLENKHOV's *critical eye* ESSIE *begins the mazes of the dance.*) Foutte temp el levee. (ESSIE *obliges with her own idea of foutte temp el levee.*) Pirouette! . . . Come, come! You can do that! It's eight years now. Pirouette! . . . At last . . . Entre chat . . . Entre chat! (ESSIE *leaps into the air, her feet twirling.*) No, Grandpa, you cannot relax with Stalin in Russia. The Czar relaxed, and what happened to *him?*

GRANDPA. He was too late.

ESSIE (*still leaping away*). Mr. Kolenkhov! Mr. Kolenkhov!

KOLENKHOV. If he had not relaxed the Grand Duchess Olga Katrina would not be selling baked beans today.

ESSIE (*imploringly*). Mr. Kolenkhov!

KOLENKHOV. I am sorry. (*The door bell rings.*) We go back to the pirouette.

PENNY. Could you pull in your stomach, Mr. De Pinna? . . . That's right.

KOLENKHOV. A little freer. A little freer with the hands. The whole body must work. Ed, help us with the music. The music must be free, too. (*By way of guiding* ED, KOLENKHOV *hums the music at the pace that it should go. He is even pirouetting a bit himself.*)
(*From the front door comes the murmur of voices, not quite audible over the music. Then the stunned figure of* RHEBA *comes into the archway, her eyes popping.*)

RHEBA. Mrs. Sycamore. . . . Mrs. Sycamore. (*With a gesture that has a grim foreboding in it, she motions toward the still invisible reason for her panic.*)

(*There is a second's pause, and then the reason is revealed in all its horror. The* KIRBYS *in full evening dress, stand in the archway. All three of them.* MR. *and* MRS. KIRBY, *and* TONY.)

(PENNY *utters a stifled gasp; the others are too stunned even to do that. Their surprise at seeing the* KIRBYS, *however, is no greater than that of the* KIRBYS *at the sight that is spread before them.*)

(GRANDPA, *alone of them all, rises to the situation. With a kind of old world grace, he puts away his darts and makes the guests welcome.*)

GRANDPA. How do you do?

KIRBY (*uncertainly*). How do you do? (*Not that it helps any, but* MR. DE PINNA *is squirming into his bathrobe,* KOLENKHOV *is thrusting his shirt into his trousers, and* ED *is hastily getting into his coat.*)

TONY. Are we too early?

GRANDPA. No, no. It's perfectly all right—we're glad to see you.

PENNY (*getting rid of the smock and tam*). Why—yes. Only—we thought it was to be tomorrow night.

MRS. KIRBY. Tomorrow night!

KIRBY. What!

GRANDPA. Now, it's perfectly all right. Please sit right down and make yourselves at home. (*His eyes still on the* KIRBYS, *he gives* DONALD *a good push toward the kitchen, by way of a hint.* DONALD *goes, promptly, with a quick little stunned whistle that sums up HIS feelings.*)

KIRBY. Tony, how could you possibly—

TONY. I—I don't know. I thought—

MRS. KIRBY. Really, Tony! This is most embarrassing.

GRANDPA. Not at all. Why, we weren't doing a thing.

PENNY. Just spending the evening at home.

GRANDPA. That's all. . . . Now don't let it bother you. This is Alice's mother, Mrs.

Sycamore . . . Alice's sister, Mrs. Carmichael. . . . Mr. Carmichael. . . . Mr. Kolenkhov. . . . (*At this point* MR. DE PINNA *takes an anticipatory step forward, and* GRANDPA *is practically compelled to perform the introduction.*) And—Mr. De Pinna. Mr. De Pinna, would you tell Mr. Sycamore to come right up? Tell him that Mr. and Mrs. Kirby are here.

PENNY (*her voice a heavy whisper*). And be sure to put his pants on.

DE PINNA (*whispering right back*). All right. . . . Excuse me. (*He vanishes—discus and all.*)

GRANDPA. Won't you sit down?

PENNY (*first frantically trying to cover the prostrate* GAY WELLINGTON). I'll tell Alice that you're— (*She is at the foot of the stairs.*) —Alice! Alice, dear! (*The voice of* ALICE *from above, "What is it?"*) Alice, will you come down, dear? We've got a surprise for you. (*She comes back into the room, summoning all her charm.*) Well!

GRANDPA. Mrs. Kirby, may I take your wrap?

MRS. KIRBY. Well—thank you. If you're perfectly sure that we're not— (*Suddenly she sees the snakes and lets out a scream.*)

GRANDPA. Oh, don't be alarmed, Mrs. Kirby. They're perfectly harmless.

MRS. KIRBY (*edging away from the solarium*). Thank you. (*She sinks into a chair, weakly.*)

GRANDPA. Ed, take 'em into the kitchen. (*Ed at once obeys.*)

PENNY. Of course we're so used to them around the house—

MRS. KIRBY. I'm sorry to trouble you, but snakes happen to be the one thing—

KIRBY. I feel very uncomfortable about this. Tony, how could you have done such a thing?

TONY. I'm sorry, Dad. I thought it was tonight.

KIRBY. It was very careless of you. *Very!*

GRANDPA. Now, now Mr. Kirby—we're delighted.

PENNY. Oh, now, anybody can get mixed up, Mr. Kirby.

GRANDPA. Penny, how about some dinner for these folks? They've come for dinner, you know.

MRS. KIRBY. Oh, please don't bother. We're really not hungry at all.

PENNY. But it's not a bit of bother. Ed!— (*Her voice drops to a loud whisper.*) Ed, tell Donald to run down to the A. and P. and get half a dozen bottles of beer, and— ah—some canned salmon— (*Her voice comes up again.*) —do you like canned salmon, Mr. Kirby?

KIRBY. Please don't trouble, Mrs. Sycamore. I have a little indigestion, anyway.

PENNY. Oh, I'm sorry . . . How about you, Mrs. Kirby? Do you like canned salmon?

MRS. KIRBY (*you just know that she hates it*). Oh, I'm very fond of it.

PENNY. You can have frankfurters if you'd rather.

MRS. KIRBY (*regally*). Either one will do.

PENNY (*to ED again*). Well, make it frankfurters, and some canned corn, and Campbell's Soup.

ED (*going out the kitchen door*). Okay!

PENNY (*calling after him*). And tell him to hurry! (PENNY *again addresses the* KIRBYS.) The A. and P. is just at the corner, and frankfurters don't take *any* time to boil.

GRANDPA (*as* PAUL *comes through the cellar door*). And this is Alice's father, *Mr.* Sycamore. Mr. and Mrs. Kirby.

THE KIRBYS. How do you do?

PAUL. I hope you'll forgive my appearance.

PENNY. This is Mr. Sycamore's busiest time of the year. Just before the Fourth of July— (*And then* ALICE *comes down. She is a step into the room before she realizes what has happened; then she fairly freezes in her tracks.*)

ALICE. Oh!

TONY. Darling, will you ever forgive me? I'm the most dull-witted person in the world. I thought it was tonight.

ALICE (*staggered*). Why, Tony, I thought you— (*To the* KIRBYS.) —I'm so sorry—I can't imagine—why, I wasn't—have you all met each other?

KIRBY. Yes, Indeed.

MRS. KIRBY. How do you do, Alice?

ALICE (*not even yet in control of herself*). How do you do, Mrs. Kirby? I'm afraid I'm not very—presentable.

TONY. Darling, you look lovely.

KIRBY. Of course she does. Don't let this upset you, my dear—we've all just met each other a night sooner, that's all.

MRS. KIRBY. Of course.

ALICE. But I was planning such a nice party tomorrow night . . .

KIRBY (*being the good fellow*). Well, we'll come again tomorrow night.

TONY. There you are, Alice. Am I forgiven?

ALICE. I guess so. It's just that I—we'd better see about getting you some dinner.

PENNY. Oh, that's all done, Alice. That's all been attended to. (DONALD, *hat in hand, comes through the kitchen door; hurries across the room and out the front way. The* KIRBYS *graciously pretend not to see.*)

ALICE. But mother—what are you—what did you send out for? Because Mr. Kirby suffers from indigestion—he can only eat certain things.

KIRBY. Now, it's quite all right.

TONY. Of course it is, darling.

PENNY. I asked him what he wanted, Alice.

ALICE (*doubtfully*). Yes, but—

KIRBY. Now, now, it's not as serious as all that. Just because I have a little indigestion.

KOLENKHOV (*helping things along*). Perhaps it is not indigestion at all, Mr. Kirby. Perhaps you have stomach ulcers.

ALICE. Don't be absurd, Mr. Kolenkhov!

GRANDPA. You mustn't mind Mr. Kolenkhov, Mr. Kirby. He's a Russian, and Russians are inclined to look on the dark side.

KOLENKHOV. All right, I am a Russian. But a friend of mine, a Russian, *died* from stomach ulcers.

KIRBY. Really, I—

ALICE (*desperately*). Please, Mr. Kolenkhov! Mr. Kirby has indigestion and that's all.

KOLENKHOV (*with a Russian shrug of the shoulders*). All right. Let him wait.

GRANDPA (*leaping into the breach*). Tell me, Mr. Kirby, how do you find business conditions? Are we pretty well out of the depression?

KIRBY. What? . . . Yes, yes, I think so. Of course, it all depends.

GRANDPA. But you figure that things are going to keep on improving?

KIRBY. Broadly speaking, yes. As a matter of fact, industry is now operating at sixty-four per cent. of full capacity, as against eighty-two per cent. in 1925. Of course in 1929, a peak year— (*Peak year or no peak year,* GAY WELLINGTON *chooses this moment to come to life. With a series of assorted snorts, she throws the cover back and pulls herself to a sitting position, blinking uncertainly at the assemblage. Then she rises, and weaves unsteadily across the room. The imposing figure of* MR. KIRBY *intrigues her.*)

GAY (*playfully rumpling* MR. KIRBY's *hair as she passes him.*) Hello, Cutie. (*And with that she lunges on her way—up the stairs.*) (*The* KIRBYS, *of course, are considerably astounded by this exhibition; the* SYCAMORES *have watched it with varying degrees of frozen horror.* ALICE, *in particular, is speechless; it is* GRANDPA *who comes to her rescue.*)

GRANDPA. That may seem a little strange to you, but she's not quite accountable for her actions. A friend of Mrs. Sycamore's. She came to dinner and was overcome by the heat.

PENNY. Yes, some people feel it, you know, more than others. Perhaps I'd better see if she's all right. Excuse me, please. (*She goes hastily up the stairs.*)

ALICE. It *is* awfully hot. (*A fractional pause.*) You usually escape all this hot weather, don't you, Mrs. Kirby? Up in Maine?

MRS. KIRBY (*on the frigid side*). As a rule. I had to come down this week, however, for the Flower Show.

TONY. Mother wouldn't miss that for the world. That blue ribbon is the high spot of her year.

ESSIE. I won a ribbon at a Flower Show once. For raising onions. Remember?

ALICE (*quickly*). That was a Garden Show, Essie.

ESSIE. Oh, yes. (PENNY *comes bustling down the stairs again.*)

PENNY. I'm so sorry, but I think she'll be all right now. . . . Has Donald come back yet?

ALICE. No, he hasn't.

PENNY. Well, he'll be right back, and it won't take any time at all. I'm afraid you must be starved.

KIRBY. Oh, no. Quite all right. (*Pacing the room, he suddenly comes upon* PAUL's *Erector Set.*) Hello! What's this? I didn't know there were little children in the house.

PAUL. Oh, no. That's mine.

KIRBY. Really? Well, I suppose every man has his hobby. Or do you use this as a model of some kind?

PAUL. No, I just play with it.

KIRBY. I see.

TONY. Maybe you'd be better off if *you* had a hobby like that, Dad. Instead of raising orchids.

KIRBY (*indulgently*). Yes, I wouldn't be surprised.

ALICE (*leaping on this as a safe topic*). Oh, do tell us about your orchids, Mr. Kirby. (*She addresses the others.*) You know, they take six years before they blossom. Think of that!

KIRBY (*warming to his subject*). Oh, some of them take longer than that. I've got one coming along now that I've waited ten years for.

PENNY (*making a joke*). Believe it or not, I was waiting for an orchid.

KIRBY. Ah—yes. Of course during that time they require the most scrupulous care. I remember a bulb that I was very fond of— (DONALD *suddenly bulges through the archway, his arms full. The tops of beer bottles and two or three large cucumbers peep over the edge of the huge paper bags.*)

PENNY. Ah, here we are! Did you get everything, Donald?

DONALD. Yes'm. Only the frankfurters didn't look very good, so I got pickled pigs' feet. (MR. KIRBY *blanches at the very idea.*)

ALICE (*taking command*). Never mind, Donald—just bring everything into the kitchen. (*She turns at the kitchen door.*) Mr. Kirby, please tell them *all* about the orchids—I know they'd love to hear it. And —excuse me. (*She goes.*)

GRANDPA. Kind of an expensive hobby, isn't it, Mr. Kirby—raising orchids?

KIRBY. Yes, it is, but I feel that if a hobby gives one sufficient pleasure, it's never expensive.

GRANDPA. That's very true.

KIRBY. You see, I need something to relieve the daily nerve strain. After a week in Wall Street I'd go crazy if I didn't have something like that. Lot of men I know have yachts— just for that very reason.

GRANDPA (*mildly*). Why don't they give up Wall Street?

KIRBY. How's that?

GRANDPA. I was just joking.

MRS. KIRBY. I think it's necessary for everyone to have a hobby. Of course it's more to me than a hobby, but my great solace is— spiritualism.

PENNY. Now, Mrs. Kirby, don't tell me you fell for that. Why, everybody knows it's a fake.

MRS. KIRBY (*freezing*). To me, Mrs. Sycamore, spiritualism is—I would rather not discuss it, Mrs. Sycamore.

PAUL. Remember, Penny, you've got one or two hobbies of your own.

PENNY. Yes, but not silly ones.

GRANDPA (*with a little cough*). I don't think it matters what the hobby is—the important thing is to have one.

KOLENKHOV. To be ideal, a hobby should improve the body as well as the mind. The Romans were a great people! Why! What was their hobby? Wrestling. In wrestling you have to think quick with the mind and act quick with the body.

KIRBY. Yes, but I'm afraid wrestling is not very practical for most of us. (*He gives a deprecating little laugh.*) I wouldn't make a very good showing as a wrestler.

KOLENKHOV. You could be a *great* wrestler. You are built for it. Look! (*With a startlingly quick movement* KOLENKHOV *grabs* MR. KIRBY's *arms, knocks his legs from under him with a quick movement of a foot, and presto!* MR. KIRBY *is flat on his whatsis. Not only that, but instantaneously* KOLENKHOV *is on top of him.*) (*Just at this moment* ALICE *re-enters the room—naturally, she stands petrified. Several people, of course, rush immediately to the rescue,* TONY *and* PAUL *arriving at the scene of battle first. Amidst the general confusion they help* MR. KIRBY *to his feet.*)

ALICE. Mr. Kirby! Are you—hurt?

TONY. Are you all right, father?

KIRBY (*pulling himself together*). I—I— uh— (*He blinks, uncertainly.*) —where are my glasses?

ALICE. Here they are, Mr. Kirby. . . . Oh, Mr. Kirby, they're broken.

KOLENKHOV (*full of apology*). Oh, I am sorry. But when you wrestle again, Mr. Kirby, you will of course not wear glasses.

KIRBY (*coldly furious*). *I* do not intend to wrestle again, Mr. Kolenkhov. (*He draws himself up, stiffly, and in return gets a sharp pain in the back. He gives a little gasp.*)

TONY. Better sit down, father.

ALICE. Mr. Kolenkhov, how could you do such a thing? Why didn't somebody stop him?

MRS. KIRBY. I think, if you don't mind, perhaps we had better be going.

TONY. Mother!

ALICE (*close to tears*). Oh, Mrs. Kirby—please! Please don't go! Mr. Kirby—please! I—I've ordered some scrambled eggs for you, and—plain salad—Oh, please don't go!

KOLENKHOV. I am sorry if I did something wrong. And I apologize.

ALICE. I can't tell you how sorry I am, Mr. Kirby. If I'd been here—

KIRBY (*from a great height*). That's quite all right.

TONY. Of course it is. It's all right, Alice. We're not going. (*The* KIRBYS *reluctantly sit down again.*)
(*A moment's silence—no one knows quite what to say.*)

PENNY (*brightly*). Well! That was exciting for a minute, wasn't it?

GRANDPA (*quickly*). You were talking about your orchids, Mr. Kirby. Do you raise many different varieties?

KIRBY (*still unbending*). I'm afraid I've quite forgotten about my orchids. (*More silence, and everyone very uncomfortable.*)

ALICE. I'm—awfully sorry, Mr. Kirby.

KOLENKHOV (*exploding*). What did I do that was so terrible? I threw him on the floor! Did it kill him?

ALICE. Please, Mr. Kolenkhov. (*An annoyed gesture from* KOLENKHOV; *another general pause.*)

PENNY. I'm sure dinner won't be any time at all now. (*A pained smile from* MRS. KIRBY.)

ESSIE. Would you like some candy while you're waiting? I've got some freshly made.

KIRBY. My doctor does not permit me to eat candy. Thank you.

ESSIE. But these are nothing, Mr. Kirby. Just cocoanut and marshmallow fudge.

ALICE. Don't, Essie. (RHEBA *appears in the kitchen doorway, beckoning violently to* ALICE.)

RHEBA (*in a loud whisper*). Miss Alice! Miss Alice! (ALICE *quickly flies to* RHEBA's *side.*) The eggs fell down the sink.

ALICE (*desperately*). Make some more! Quick!

RHEBA. I ain't got any.

ALICE. Send Donald out for some!

RHEBA (*disappearing*). All right.

ALICE (*calling after her*). Tell him to run! (*She turns back to the* KIRBYS.) I'm so sorry. There'll be a little delay, but everything will be ready in just a minute. (*At this moment* DONALD *fairly shoots out of the kitchen door and across the living room, beating the Olympic record for all time.*)
(PENNY *tries to ease the situation with a gay little laugh. It doesn't quite come off, however.*)

TONY. I've certainly put you people to a lot of trouble, with my stupidity.

GRANDPA. Not at all, Tony.

PENNY. Look! Why don't we play a game of some sort while we're waiting?

TONY. Oh, that'd be fine.

ALICE. Mother, I don't think Mr. and Mrs. Kirby—

KOLENKHOV. *I* have an idea. I know a wonderful trick with a glass of water. (*He reaches for a full glass that stands on the table.*)

ALICE (*quickly*). No, Mr. Kolenkhov.

GRANDPA (*shaking his head*). No-o.

PENNY. But I'm sure Mr. and Mrs. Kirby would love this game. It's perfectly harmless.

ALICE. Please, mother. . . .

KIRBY. I'm not very good at games, Mrs. Sycamore.

PENNY. Oh, but *any* fool could play this game, Mr. Kirby. (*She is bustling around, getting paper and pencil.*) All you do is write your name on a piece of paper—

ALICE. But mother, Mr. Kirby doesn't want—

PENNY. Oh, he'll love it! (*Goes right on.*) Here you are, Mr. Kirby. Write your name on this piece of paper. And Mrs. Kirby, you do the same on this one.

ALICE. Mother, what *is* this game?

PENNY. I used to play it at school. It's called Forget-Me-Not. Now, I'm going to call out five words—just anything at all—and as I say each word, you're to put down the first thing that comes into your mind. Is that clear? For instance, if I say "grass," you might put down "green"—just whatever you think of, see? Or if I call out "chair," you might put down "table." It shows the reactions people have to different things. You see how simple it is, Mr. Kirby?

TONY. Come on, father! Be a sport!

KIRBY (*stiffly*). Very well. I shall be happy to play it.

PENNY. You see, Alice? He *does* want to play.

ALICE (*uneasily*). Well—

PENNY. Now, then! Are we ready?

KOLENKHOV. Ready!

PENNY. Now, remember—you must play fair. Put down the first thing that comes into your mind.

KIRBY (*pencil poised*). I understand.

PENNY. Everybody ready? . . . The first word is "potatoes." (*She repeats it.*) "Potatoes." . . . Ready for the next one? . . . "Bathroom." (ALICE *shifts rather uneasily, but seeing that no one else seems to mind, she relaxes again.*) Got that?

KOLENKHOV. Go ahead.

PENNY. All ready? . . . "Lust."

ALICE. Mother, this is not exactly what you—

PENNY. Nonsense, Alice—that word's all right.

ALICE. Mother, it's *not* all right.

MRS. KIRBY (*unexpectedly*). Oh, I don't know. It seems to me that's a perfectly fair word.

PENNY (*to* ALICE). You see? Now, you mustn't interrupt the game.

KIRBY. May I have that last word again, please?

PENNY. "Lust," Mr. Kirby.

KIRBY (*writing*). I've got it.

GRANDPA. This is quite a game.

PENNY. Sssh, Grandpa. . . . All ready? . . . "Honeymoon." (ESSIE *snickers a little, which is all it takes to start* PENNY *off. Then she suddenly remembers herself.*) Now, Essie! . . . All right. The last word is "sex."

ALICE (*under her breath*). Mother!

PENNY. Everybody got "sex?" . . . All right —now give me all the papers.

GRANDPA. What happens now?

PENNY. Oh, this is the best part. Now I read out your reactions.

KIRBY. I see. It's really quite an interesting game.

PENNY. I knew you'd like it. I'll read your paper first, Mr. Kirby. (*To the others.*) I'm going to read Mr. Kirby's paper first. Listen, everybody! This is Mr. Kirby. . . . "Potatoes —steak." That's very good. See how they go together? Steak and potatoes?

KIRBY (*modestly, but obviously pleased with himself*). I just happened to think of it.

PENNY. It's *very* good. . . . "Bathroom— toothpaste." Uh-huh. "Lust—unlawful." Isn't that nice? "Honeymoon—trip." Yes. And "sex—male." Yes, of course . . . That's really a wonderful paper, Mr. Kirby.

KIRBY (*taking a curtain call*). Thank you . . . it's more than just a game, you know. It's sort of an experiment in psychology, isn't it?

PENNY. Yes, it is—it shows just how your *mind* works. Now we'll see how *Mrs.* Kirby's mind works. . . . Ready? . . . This is Mrs. Kirby. . . . "Potatoes—starch." I know just what you mean, Mrs. Kirby. . . . "Bathroom—Mr. Kirby."

KIRBY. What's that?

PENNY. "Bathroom—Mr. Kirby."

KIRBY (*turning to his wife*). I don't quite follow that, my dear.

MRS. KIRBY. I don't know—I just thought of you in connection with it. After all, you *are* in there a good deal, Anthony. Bathing, and shaving—well, you *do* take a long time.

KIRBY. Indeed? I hadn't realized that I was being selfish in the matter. . . . Go on, Mrs. Sycamore.

ALICE (*worried*). I think it's a very silly game and we ought to stop it.

KIRBY. No, no. Please go on, Mrs. Sycamore.

PENNY. Where was I . . . Oh, yes. . . . "Lust —human."

KIRBY. Human? (*Thin-lipped.*) Really!

MRS. KIRBY. I just meant, Anthony, that lust is after all a—human emotion.

KIRBY. I don't agree with you, Miriam. Lust is not a human emotion. It is depraved.

MRS. KIRBY. Very well, Anthony. I'm wrong.

ALICE. Really, it's the most pointless game. Suppose we play Twenty Questions?

KIRBY. No, I find this game rather interesting. Will you go on, Mrs. Sycamore? What was the next word?

PENNY (*reluctantly*). Honeymoon.

KIRBY. Oh, yes. And what was Mrs. Kirby's answer?

PENNY. Ah—"Honeymoon—dull."

KIRBY (*murderously calm*). Did you say— dull?

MRS. KIRBY. What I meant, Anthony, was that Hot Springs was not very gay that season. All those old people sitting on the porch all afternoon, and—nothing to do at night.

KIRBY. That was not your reaction at the time, as I recall it.

TONY. Father, this is only a *game*.

KIRBY. A very illuminating game. Go on, Mrs. Sycamore!

PENNY (*brightly, having taken a look ahead*). This one's all right, Mr. Kirby. "Sex—Wall Street."

KIRBY. Wall Street? What do you mean by that, Miriam?

MRS. KLRBY (*nervously*). I don't know what I meant, Anthony. Nothing.

KIRBY. But you must have meant something, Miriam, or you wouldn't have put it down.

MRS. KIRBY. It was just the first thing that came into my head, that's all.

KIRBY. But what does it mean? Sex—Wall Street.

MRS. KIRBY (*annoyed*). Oh, I don't know what it means, Anthony. It's just that you're always talking about Wall Street, even when— (*She catches herself.*) I don't know what I meant . . . Would you mind terribly, Alice, if we didn't stay for dinner? I'm afraid this game has given me a headache.

ALICE (*quietly*). I understand, Mrs. Kirby.

KIRBY (*clearing his throat*). Yes, possibly we'd better postpone the dinner, if you don't mind.

PENNY. But you're coming tomorrow night, aren't you?

MRS. KIRBY (*quickly*). I'm afraid we have an engagement tomorrow night.

KIRBY. Perhaps we'd better postpone the whole affair a little while. This hot weather, and—ah—

TONY (*smoldering*). I think we're being very ungracious, father. Of *course* we'll stay to dinner—tonight.

MRS. KIRBY (*unyielding*). I have a very bad headache, Tony.

KIRBY. Come, come, Tony, I'm sure everyone understands.

TONY (*flaring*). Well, I don't. I think we ought to stay to dinner.

ALICE (*very low*). No, Tony.

TONY. What?

ALICE. We were fools, Tony, ever to think it would work. It won't. Mr. Kirby, I won't be at the office tomorrow. I—won't be there at all any more.

TONY. Alice, what are you talking about?

KIRBY (*to* ALICE). I'm sorry, my dear—very sorry . . . Are you ready, Miriam?

MRS. KIRBY (*with enormous dignity*). Yes, Anthony.

KIRBY. It's been very nice to have met you all. Are you coming, Anthony?

TONY. No, father. I'm not.

KIRBY. I see. . . . Your mother and I will be waiting for you at home. . . . Good-night. (*With* MRS. KIRBY *on his arm, he sweeps toward the outer door.*)

(*Before the* KIRBYS *can take more than a step toward the door, however, a new* FIGURE *looms up in the archway. It is a quiet and competent-looking individual with a steely eye, and two more just like him loom up behind him.*)

THE MAN (*very quietly*). Stay right where you are, everybody. (*There is a little scream from* MRS. KIRBY, *an exclamation from* PENNY.) Don't move.

PENNY. Oh, good heavens!

KIRBY. How dare you? Why, what does this mean?

GRANDPA. What *is* all this?

KIRBY. I demand an explanation!

THE MAN. Keep your mouth shut, you! (*He advances slowly into the room, looking the group over. Then he turns to one of his men.*) Which one is it?

ANOTHER MAN (*goes over and puts a hand on* ED's *shoulder.*) This is him.

ESSIE. Ed!

ED (*terrified*). Why, what do you mean?

ALICE. Grandpa, what is it?

KIRBY. This is an outrage!

THE MAN. Shut up! (*He turns to* ED.) What's your name?

ED. Edward—Carmichael. I haven't done anything.

THE MAN. You haven't, huh?

GRANDPA (*not at all scared*). This seems rather high-handed to me. What's it all about?

THE MAN. Department of Justice.

PENNY. Oh, my goodness! J-men!

ESSIE. Ed, what have you done?

ED. I haven't done anything.

GRANDPA. What's the boy done, Officer?

ALICE. What is it? What's it all about?

THE MAN (*taking his time, and surveying the room*). That door lead to the cellar?

PENNY. Yes, it does.

PAUL. Yes.

THE MAN (*ordering a man to investigate*). Mac . . . (MAC *goes into the cellar.*) . . . Jim!

JIM. Yes, sir.

THE MAN. Take a look upstairs and see what you find.

JIM. Okay. (JIM *goes upstairs.*)

ED (*panicky*). I haven't done anything!

THE MAN. Come here, you! (*He takes some slips of paper out of his pocket.*) Ever see these before?

ED (*gulping*). They're my—circulars.

THE MAN. You print this stuff, huh?

ED. Yes, sir.

THE MAN. And you put 'em into boxes of candy to get 'em into people's homes.

ESSIE. The Love Dreams!

ED. But I didn't mean anything!

THE MAN. You didn't, huh? (*He reads the circulars.*) "Dynamite the Capitol!" "Dynamite the White House!" "Dynamite the Supreme Court!" "God is the State; the State is God!"

ED. But I didn't mean that. I just like to print. Don't I, Grandpa? (DONALD *returns with the eggs at this point, and stands quietly watching the proceedings.*)

GRANDPA. Now, Officer, the government's in no danger from Ed. Printing is just his hobby, that's all. He prints anything.

THE MAN. He does, eh?

PENNY. I never heard of such nonsense.

KIRBY. I refuse to stay here and— (MR. DE PINNA, *at this point, is shoved through the cellar door by* MAC, *protesting as he comes.*)

DE PINNA. Hey, let me get my pipe, will you? Let me get my pipe!

MAC. Shut up, you! . . . We were right, Chief. They've got enough gunpowder down there to blow up the whole city.

PAUL. But we only use that—

THE MAN. Keep still! . . . Everybody in this house is under arrest.

KIRBY. What's that?

MRS. KIRBY. Oh, good heavens!

GRANDPA. Now look here, Officer—this is all nonsense.

DE PINNA. You'd better let me get my pipe. I left it—

THE MAN. Shut up, all of you!

KOLENKHOV. It seems to me, Officer—

THE MAN. Shut up! (*From the stairs comes the sound of drunken singing—"There was a young lady," etc.* GAY WELLINGTON, *wrapped in* PENNY'S *negligee, is being carried down the stairway by a somewhat bewildered* G-MAN.)

THE G-MAN. Keep still, you! Stop that! Stop it!

THE LEADER (*after* GAY *has been persuaded to quiet down*). Who's that?

GRANDPA (*pretty tired of the whole business*). That—is my mother. (*And then, suddenly, we hear from the cellar.* MR. DE PINNA *seems to have been right about his pipe, to judge from the sounds below. It is a whole year's supply of fireworks—bombs, big crackers, little crackers, sky rockets, pin wheels, everything. The house is fairly rocked by the explosion.*)

(*In the room, of course, pandemonium reigns.* MRS. KIRBY *screams; the* G-MAN *drops* GAY *right where he stands and dashes for the cellar, closely followed by* MR. DE PINNA *and* PAUL; PENNY *dashes for her manuscripts and* ED *rushes to save his xylophone.* KOLENKHOV *waves his arms wildly and dashes in all directions at once; everyone is rushing this way and that.*)

(*All except one. The exception, of course, is* GRANDPA, *who takes all things as they come.* GRANDPA *just says "Well, well, well!"—and sits down. If a lot of people weren't in the way, in fact, you feel he'd like to throw a few darts.*)

CURTAIN

ACT THREE

The following day.

RHEBA *is in the midst of setting the table for dinner, pausing occasionally in her labors to listen to the Edwin C. Hill of the moment—*DONALD. *With intense interest and concentration, he is reading aloud from a newspaper.*

DONALD. " . . . for appearance in the West Side Court this morning. After spending the night in jail, the defendants, thirteen in all, were brought before Judge Callahan and given suspended sentences for manufacturing fireworks without a permit."

RHEBA. Yah. Kept me in the same cell with a strip teaser from a burlesque show.

DONALD. I was in the cell with Mr. Kirby. My, he was mad!

RHEBA. Mrs. Kirby and the strip teaser— they were fighting all night.

DONALD. Whole lot about *Mr.* Kirby here. (*Reading again.*) "Anthony W. Kirby, head of Kirby & Co., 62 Wall Street, who was among those apprehended, declared he was in no way interested in the manufacture of fireworks, but refused to state why he was on the premises at the time of the raid. Mr. Kirby is a member of the Union Club, the Racquet Club, the Harvard Club, and the National Geographic Society." My, he certainly is a joiner!

RHEBA. All those rich men are Elks or something.

DONALD (*looking up from his paper*). I suppose, after all this, Mr. Tony ain't ever going to marry Miss Alice, huh?

RHEBA. No, suh, and it's too bad, too. Miss Alice sure loves that boy.

DONALD. Ever notice how white folks always getting themselves in trouble?

RHEBA. Yassuh, I'm glad I'm colored. (*She sighs, heavily.*) I don't know what I'm going to do with all that food out in the kitchen. Ain't going to be no party tonight, that's sure.

DONALD. Ain't we going to eat it anyhow?

RHEBA. Well, I'm cooking it, but I don't think anybody going to have an appetite.

DONALD. *I'm* hungry.

RHEBA. Well, *they* ain't. They're all so broke up about Miss Alice.

DONALD. What's she want to go 'way for? Where's she going?

RHEBA. I don't know—mountains some place. And she's *going,* all right, no matter what they say. I know Miss Alice when she gets that look in her eye.

DONALD. Too bad, ain't it?

RHEBA. Sure is. (MR. DE PINNA *comes up from the cellar, bearing the earmarks of the previous day's catastrophe. There is a small bandage around his head and over one eye, and another around his right hand. He also limps slightly.*)

DE PINNA. Not even a balloon left. (*He exhibits a handful of exploded firecrackers.*) Look.

RHEBA. How's your hand, Mr. De Pinna? Better?

DE PINNA. Yes, it's better. (*A step toward the kitchen.*) Is there some more olive oil out there?

RHEBA (*nods*). It's in the salad bowl.

DE PINNA. Thanks. (*He goes out the kitchen door as* PENNY *comes down the stairs. It is a new and rather subdued* PENNY.)

PENNY (*with a sigh*). Well, she's going. Nothing anybody said could change her.

RHEBA. She ain't going to stay away long, is she, Mrs. Sycamore?

PENNY. I don't know, Rheba. She won't say.

RHEBA. My, going to be lonesome around here without her. (*She goes into the kitchen.*)

DONALD. How *you* feel, Mrs. Sycamore?

PENNY. Oh, I'm all right, Donald. Just kind of upset. (*She is at her desk.*) Perhaps if I do some work maybe I'll feel better.

DONALD. Well, I won't bother you then, Mrs. Sycamore. (*He goes into the kitchen.*) (PENNY *puts a sheet of paper into the typewriter; stares at it blankly for a moment;* types in desultory fashion, gives it up. She leans back and sits staring straight ahead.) (PAUL *comes slowly down the stairs; stands surveying the room a moment; sighs. He goes over to the Erector Set; absentmindedly pulls out the flag. Then, with another sigh, he drops into a chair.*)

PAUL. She's going, Penny.

PENNY. Yes. (*She is quiet for a moment; then she starts to weep, softly.*)

PAUL (*going to her*). Now, now, Penny.

PENNY. I can't help it, Paul. Somehow I feel it's our fault.

PAUL. It's mine more than yours, Penny. All these years I've just been—going along, enjoying myself, when maybe I should have been thinking more about Alice.

PENNY. Don't say that, Paul. You've been a wonderful father. And husband, too.

PAUL. No, I haven't. Maybe if I'd gone ahead and been an architect—I don't know —something Alice could have been proud of. I felt that all last night, looking at Mr. Kirby.

PENNY. But we've been so happy, Paul.

PAUL. I know, but maybe that's not enough. I used to think it was, but—I'm kind of all mixed up now.

PENNY (*after a pause*). What time is she going?

PAUL. Pretty soon. Train leaves at half past seven.

PENNY. Oh, if only she'd see Tony. I'm sure he could persuade her.

PAUL. But she won't, Penny. He's been trying all day.

PENNY. Where is he now?

PAUL. I don't know—I suppose walking around the block again. Anyhow, she won't talk to him.

PENNY. Maybe Tony can catch her as she's leaving.

PAUL. It won't help, Penny.

PENNY. No, I don't suppose so. . . . I feel so sorry for Tony, too. (GRANDPA *comes down the stairs—unsmiling, but not too depressed by the situation.*) (*Anxiously.*) Well?

GRANDPA. Now, Penny, let the girl alone.

PENNY. But, Grandpa—

GRANDPA. Suppose she *goes* to the Adirondacks? She'll be back. You can take just so much Adirondacks, and then you come home.

PENNY. Oh, but it's all so terrible, Grandpa.

GRANDPA. In a way, but it has its bright side, too.

PAUL. How do you mean?

GRANDPA. Well, Mr. Kirby getting into the patrol wagon, for one thing, and the expression on his face when he and Donald had to take a bath together. I'll never forget that if I live to be a hundred, and I warn you people I intend to. If I can have things like that going on.

PENNY. Oh, it was even worse with Mrs. Kirby. When the matron stripped her. There was a burlesque dancer there and she kept singing a strip song while Mrs. Kirby undressed.

GRANDPA. I'll bet you Bar Harbor is going to seem pretty dull to the Kirbys for the rest of the summer. (*With a determined step,* ALICE *comes swiftly down the stairs. Over her arm she carries a couple of dresses. Looking neither to right nor left, she heads for the kitchen.*)

GRANDPA. Need any help, Alice?

ALICE (*in a strained voice*). No, thanks, Grandpa. Ed is helping with the bags. I'm just going to press these.

PENNY. Alice, dear—

GRANDPA. Now, Penny. (ED *has appeared in the hallway with a couple of hatboxes,* ESSIE *behind him.*)

ED. I'll bring the big bag down as soon as you're ready, Alice.

ESSIE. Do you want to take some candy along for the train, Alice?

ALICE. No, thanks, Essie.

PENNY. Really, Alice, you could be just as alone here as you could in the mountains.

You could stay right in your room all the time.

ALICE (*quietly*). No, mother, I want to be by myself—away from everybody. I love you all—you know that. But I just have to go away for a while. I'll be all right. . . . Father, did you 'phone for a cab?

PAUL. No, I didn't know you wanted one.

PENNY. Oh, I told Mr. De Pinna to tell you, Paul. Didn't he tell you?

ED. Oh, he told *me,* but I forgot.

ALICE (*the final straw*). Oh, I wish I lived in a family that didn't always forget *every*-thing. That—that behaved the way *other* people's families do. I'm sick of cornflakes, and—Donald, and— (*Unconsciously, in her impatience, she has picked up one of* GRAND-PA's *darts; is surprised to find it suddenly in her hand.*) —everything! (*She dashes the dart to the floor.*) Why can't we be like other people? Roast beef, and two green vegetables, and—doilies on the table, and—a place you could bring your friends to—without— (*unable to control herself further, she bursts out of the room, into the kitchen.*)

ESSIE. I'll—see if I can do anything. (*She goes into the kitchen.*)
(*The others look at each other for a moment, helplessly.* PENNY, *with a sigh, drops into her chair again.* PAUL *also sits.* GRANDPA *mechanically picks up the dart from the floor; smooths out the feathers.* ED, *with a futile gesture, runs his fingers idly over the xylophone keys. He stops quickly as every head turns to look at him.*)
(*The sound of the door opening and* TONY *appears in the archway. A worried and disheveled* TONY.)

PENNY (*quickly*). Tony, talk to her! She's in the kitchen!

TONY. Thanks. (*He goes immediately into the kitchen.*)
(*The family, galvanized, listen intently.*)
(*Almost immediately,* ALICE *emerges from the kitchen again, followed by* TONY. *She crosses the living room and starts quickly up the stairs.*) Alice, won't you listen to me? Please!

ALICE (*not stopping*). Tony, it's no use.

TONY (*following her*). Alice, you're not being fair. At least let me talk to you. (*They are both gone—up the stairs.*)

PENNY. Perhaps if I went upstairs with them ...

GRANDPA. Now, Penny. Let them alone. (ESSIE *comes out of the kitchen.*)

ESSIE. Where'd they go? (ED, *with a gesture, indicates the upstairs region.*) She walked right out the minute he came in. (MR. DE PINNA *also emerges from the kitchen.*)

MR. DE PINNA. Knocked the olive oil right out of my hand. I'm going to smell kind of fishy.

GRANDPA. How're you feeling, Mr. De Pinna? Hand still hurting you?

DE PINNA. No, it's better.

PAUL. Everything burnt up, huh? Downstairs?

DE PINNA (*nodding, sadly*). Everything. And my Roman costume, too.

GRANDPA (*to* PENNY). I told you there was a bright side to everything. All except my twenty-two years back income tax. (*He pulls an envelope out of his pocket.*) I get another letter every day.

DE PINNA. Say, what are you going to do about that, Grandpa?

GRANDPA. Well, I had a kind of idea yesterday. It may not work, but I'm trying it, anyhow.

DE PINNA (*eagerly*). What is it? (*Suddenly* KOLENKHOV *appears in the doorway.*)

KOLENKHOV (*even he is subdued*). Good evening, everybody!

PENNY. Why, Mr. Kolenkhov!

GRANDPA. Hello, Kolenkhov.

KOLENKHOV. Forgive me. The door was open.

GRANDPA. Come on in.

KOLENKHOV. You will excuse my coming today. I realize you are—upset.

PENNY. That's all right, Mr. Kolenkhov.

ESSIE. I don't think I can take a lesson, Mr. Kolenkhov. I don't feel up to it.

KOLENKHOV (*uncertainly*). Well, I—ah—

PENNY. Oh, but do stay to dinner, Mr. Kolenkhov. We've got all that food out there, and somebody's got to eat it.

KOLENKHOV. I will be happy to, Madame Sycamore.

PENNY. Fine.

KOLENKHOV. Thank you. . . . Now, I wonder if I know you well enough to ask of you a great favor.

PENNY. Why, of course, Mr. Kolenkhov. What is it?

KOLENKHOV. You have heard me talk about my friend the Grand Duchess Olga Katrina.

PENNY. Yes?

KOLENKHOV. She is a great woman, the Grand Duchess. Her cousin was the Czar of Russia, and today she is a waitress in Childs' Restaurant. Columbus Circle.

PENNY. Yes, I know. If there's anything at all that we can do, Mr. Kolenkhov ...

KOLENKHOV. I tell you. The Grand Duchess Olga Katrina has not had a good meal since before the Revolution.

GRANDPA. She must be hungry.

KOLENKHOV. And today the Grand Duchess not only has her day off—Thursday—but it is also the anniversary of Peter the Great. A remarkable man!

PENNY. Mr. Kolenkhov, if you mean you'd like the Grand Duchess to come to dinner, why, we'd be honored.

ESSIE. Oh, yes!

KOLENKHOV (*with a bow*). In the name of the Grand Duchess, I thank you.

PENNY. I can hardly wait to meet her. When will she be here?

KOLENKHOV. She is outside in the street, waiting. I bring her in. (*And he goes out.*)

GRANDPA. You know, if this keeps on I want to live to be a hundred and *fifty*.

PENNY (*feverishly*). Ed, straighten your tie. Essie, look at your dress. How do *I* look? All right? (KOLENKHOV *appears in the hallway and stands at rigid attention.*)

KOLENKHOV (*his voice booming*). The Grand Duchess Olga Katrina! (*And the* GRAND

DUCHESS OLGA KATRINA, *wheat cakes and maple syrup out of her life for a few hours, sweeps into the room. She wears a dinner gown that has seen better days, and the whole is surmounted by an extremely tacky-looking evening wrap, trimmed with bits of ancient and moth-eaten fur. But once a Grand Duchess, always a Grand Duchess. She rises above everything—Childs', evening wrap, and all.*) Your Highness, permit me to present Madame Sycamore— (PENNY, *having seen a movie or two in her time, knows just what to do. She curtsies right to the floor, and catches hold of a chair just in time.*) Madame Carmichael— (ESSIE *does a curtsey that begins where all others leave off. Starting on her toes, she merges the Dying Swan with an extremely elaborate genuflection.*) Grandpa—

GRANDPA (*with a little bow*). Madame.

KOLENKHOV. Mr. Sycamore, Mr. Carmichael, and Mr. De Pinna. (PAUL *and* ED *content themselves with courteous little bows, but not so the social-minded* MR. DE PINNA. *He bows to the floor—and stays there for a moment.*)

GRANDPA. All right now, Mr. De Pinna. (MR. DE PINNA *gets to his feet again.*)

PENNY. Will you be seated, Your Highness?

THE GRAND DUCHESS. Thank you. You are most kind.

PENNY. We are honored to receive you, Your Highness.

THE GRAND DUCHESS. I am most happy to be here. What time is dinner?

PENNY (*a little startled*). Oh, it'll be quite soon, Your Highness—very soon.

THE GRAND DUCHESS. I do not mean to be rude, but I must be back at the restaurant by eight o'clock. I am substituting for another waitress.

KOLENKHOV. I will make sure you are on time, Your Highness.

DE PINNA. You know, Highness, I think you waited on me in Childs' once. The Seventy-Second Street place?

THE GRAND DUCHESS. No, no. That was my sister.

KOLENKHOV. The Grand Duchess Natasha.

THE GRAND DUCHESS. *I* work in Columbus Circle.

GRANDPA. Quite a lot of your family living over here now, aren't there?

THE GRAND DUCHESS. Oh, yes—many. My uncle, the Grand Duke Sergei—he is an elevator man at Macy's. A very nice man. Then there is my cousin, Prince Alexis. He will not speak to the rest of us because he works at Hattie Carnegie's. He has cards printed— Prince Alexis of Hattie Carnegie. Bah!

KOLENKHOV. When he was selling Eskimo Pies at Luna Park he was willing to talk to you.

THE GRAND DUCHESS. Ah, Kolenkhov, our time is coming. My sister Natasha is studying to be a manicure, Uncle Sergei they have promised to make floor-walker, and next month I get transferred to the Fifth Avenue Childs'. From there it is only a step to Schrafft's, and *then* we will see what Prince Alexis says!

GRANDPA (*nodding*). I think you've got him.

THE GRAND DUCHESS. You are telling *me*? (*She laughs a triumphant Russian laugh, in which* KOLENKHOV *joins.*)

PENNY. Your Highness—did you know the Czar? Personally, I mean.

THE GRAND DUCHESS. Of course—he was my cousin. It was terrible, what happened, but perhaps it was for the best. Where could he get a job now?

KOLENKHOV. That is true.

THE GRAND DUCHESS (*philosophically*). Yes. And poor relations are poor relations. It is the same in every family. My cousin, the King of Sweden—he was very nice to us for about ten years, but then he said, I just cannot go on. I am not doing so well, either. . . . I do not blame him.

PENNY. No, of course not. . . . Would you excuse me for just a moment? (*She goes to the foot of the stairs and stands peering up anxiously, hoping for news of* ALICE.)

DE PINNA (*the historian at heart*). Tell me, Grand Duchess, is it true what they say about Rasputin?

THE GRAND DUCHESS. Everyone wants to know about Rasputin. . . . Yes, my dear sir, it is true. In spades.

DE PINNA. You don't say?

KOLENKHOV. Your Highness, we have to watch the time.

THE GRAND DUCHESS. Yes, I must not be late. The manager does not like me. He is a Communist.

PENNY. We'll hurry things up. Essie, why don't you go out in the kitchen and give Rheba a hand?

THE GRAND DUCHESS (*rising*). I will help, too. I am a very good cook.

PENNY. Oh, but Your Highness! Not on your day off!

THE GRAND DUCHESS. I do not mind. Where is your kitchen?

ESSIE. Right through here, but you're the guest of honor, Your Highness.

THE GRAND DUCHESS. But I love to cook! Come, Kolenkhov! If they have got sour cream and pot cheese I will make you some blintzes!

KOLENKHOV. Ah! Blintzes! . . . Come, Pavlowa! We show you something! (*With* ESSIE, *he goes into the kitchen.*)

DE PINNA. Say! The Duchess is all right, isn't she? Hey, Duchess! Can I help? (*And into the kitchen.*)

PENNY. Really, she's a very nice woman, you know. Considering she's a Grand Duchess.

GRANDPA. Wonderful what people go through, isn't it? And still keep kind of gay, too.

PENNY. Mm. She made me forget about everything for a minute. (*She returns to the stairs and stands listening.*)

PAUL. I'd better call that cab, I suppose.

PENNY. No, wait, Paul. I think I hear them. Maybe Tony has— (*She stops as* ALICE'S *step is heard on the stair. She enters—dressed for traveling.* TONY *looms up behind her.*)

ALICE. Ed, will you go up and bring my bag down?

TONY (*quickly*). Don't you do it, Ed! (ED *hesitates, uncertain.*)

ALICE. Ed, please!

TONY (*a moment's pause; then he gives up*). All right, Ed. Bring it down. (ED *goes up the stairs as* TONY *disconsolately stalks across the room. Then he faces the Sycamores.*) Do you know that you've got the stubbornest daughter in all forty-eight states? (*The door bell rings.*)

ALICE. That must be the cab. (*She goes to the door.*)

GRANDPA. If it is, it's certainly wonderful service. (*To the considerable surprise of everyone, the voice of* MR. KIRBY *is heard at the front door.*)

KIRBY. Is Tony here, Alice?

ALICE. Yes. Yes, he is. (MR. KIRBY *comes in.*)

KIRBY (*uncomfortably*). Ah—good afternoon. Forgive my intruding . . . Tony, I want you to come home with me. Your mother is very upset.

TONY (*he looks at* ALICE). Very well, father . . . Good-bye, Alice.

ALICE (*very low*). Good-bye, Tony.

KIRBY (*trying to ease the situation*). I need hardly say that this is as painful to Mrs. Kirby and myself as it is to you people. I—I'm sorry, but I'm sure you understand.

GRANDPA. Well, yes—and in a way, no. Now, I'm not the kind of person tries to run other people's lives, but the fact is, Mr. Kirby, I don't think these two young people have got as much sense as—ah—you and I have.

ALICE (*tense*). Grandpa, will you please not do this?

GRANDPA (*disarmingly*). I'm just talking to Mr. Kirby. A cat can look at a king, can't he? (ALICE, *with no further words, takes up the telephone and dials a number. There is finality in her every movement.*)

PENNY. You—you want me to do that for you, Alice?

ALICE. No, thanks, mother.

PAUL. You've got quite a while before the train goes, Alice.

ALICE (*into the phone*). Will you send a cab to 761 Claremont, right away, please? . . . That's right, thank you. (*She hangs up.*)

KIRBY. And now if you'll excuse us . . . are you ready, Tony?

GRANDPA. Mr. Kirby, I suppose after last night you think this family is crazy, don't you?

KIRBY. No, I would not say that, although I am not accustomed to going out to dinner and spending the night in jail.

GRANDPA. Well, you've got to remember, Mr. Kirby, you came on the wrong night. Now tonight, I'll bet you, nothing'll happen at all. (*There is a great burst of Russian laughter from the kitchen—the mingled voices of* KOLENKHOV *and the* GRAND DUCHESS. GRANDPA *looks off in the direction of the laughter, then decides to play safe.*) Maybe.

KIRBY. Mr. Vanderhof, it was not merely last night that convinced Mrs. Kirby and myself that this engagement would be unwise.

TONY. Father, I can handle my own affairs. (*He turns to* ALICE.) Alice, for the last time, will you marry me?

ALICE. No, Tony. I know exactly what your father means, and he's right.

TONY. No, he's *not*, Alice.

GRANDPA. Alice, you're in love with this boy, and you're not marrying him because we're the kind of people we are.

ALICE. Grandpa—

GRANDPA. I know. You think the two families wouldn't get along. Well, maybe they wouldn't—but who says they're right and we're wrong?

ALICE. I didn't say that, Grandpa. I only feel—

GRANDPA. Well, what *I* feel is that Tony's too nice a boy to wake up twenty years from now with nothing in his life but stocks and bonds.

KIRBY. How's that?

GRANDPA (*turning to* MR. KIRBY). Yes. Mixed up and unhappy, the way you are.

KIRBY (*outraged*). I beg your pardon, Mr. Vanderhof, I am a very happy man.

GRANDPA. Are you?

KIRBY. Certainly I am.

GRANDPA. I don't think so. What do you think you get your indigestion from? Happiness? No, sir. You get it because most of your time is spent in doing things you don't want to do.

KIRBY. I don't do anything I don't want to do.

GRANDPA. Yes, you do. You said last night that at the end of a week in Wall Street you're pretty near crazy. Why do you keep on doing it?

KIRBY. Why do I keep on—why, that's my *business*. A man can't give up his business.

GRANDPA. Why not? You've got all the money you need. You can't take it with you.

KIRBY. That's a very easy thing to say, Mr. Vanderhof. But I have spent my entire life building up my business.

GRANDPA. And what's it got you? Same kind of mail every morning, same kind of deals, same kind of meetings, same dinners at night, same indigestion. Where does the fun come in? Don't you think there ought to be something *more*, Mr. Kirby? You must have wanted more than that when you started out. We haven't got too much time, you know— any of us.

KIRBY. What do you expect me to do? Live the way *you* do? Do nothing?

GRANDPA. Well, I have a lot of fun. Time enough for everything—read, talk, visit the zoo now and then, practice my darts, even have time to notice when spring comes around. Don't see anybody I don't want to, don't have six hours of things I *have* to do every day before I get *one* hour to do what I like in—and I haven't taken bicarbonate of soda in thirty-five years. What's the matter with that?

KIRBY. The matter with that? But suppose we *all* did it? A fine world we'd have, everybody going to zoos. Don't be ridiculous, Mr. Vanderhof. Who would do the work?

GRANDPA. There's always people that like to work—you can't *stop* them. Inventions, and they fly the ocean. There're always people to go down to Wall Street, too—because they *like* it. But from what I've seen of you, I don't think you're one of them. I think you're missing something.

KIRBY. I am not aware of missing anything.

GRANDPA. I wasn't either, till I quit. I used to get down to that office nine o'clock sharp, no matter how I felt. Lay awake nights for fear I wouldn't get that contract. Used to worry about the world, too. Got *all* worked up about whether Cleveland or Blaine was going to be elected President—seemed awful important at the time, but who cares now? What I'm trying to say, Mr. Kirby, is that I've had thirty-five years that nobody can take away from me, no matter what they do to the world. See?

KIRBY. Yes, I do see. And it's a very dangerous philosophy, Mr. Vanderhof. It's—it's un-American. And it's exactly why I'm opposed to this marriage. I don't want Tony to come under its influence.

TONY (*a gleam in his eye*). What's the matter with it, father?

KIRBY. Matter with it? Why, it's—it's downright Communism, that's what it is.

TONY. You didn't always think so.

KIRBY. I most certainly did. What are you talking about?

TONY. I'll tell you what I'm talking about. You didn't always think so, because there was a time when you wanted to be a trapeze artist.

KIRBY. Why—why, don't be an idiot, Tony.

TONY. Oh, yes, you did. I came across those letters you wrote to grandfather. Do you remember those?

KIRBY. NO! . . . How dared you read those letters? How dared you?

PENNY. Why, isn't that wonderful? Did you wear tights, Mr. Kirby?

KIRBY. Certainly not! The whole thing is absurd. I was fourteen years old at the time.

TONY. Yes, but at *eighteen* you wanted to be a saxophone player, didn't you?

KIRBY. Tony!

TONY. And at twenty-one you ran away from home because grandfather wanted you to go into the business. It's all down there in black and white. You didn't *always* think so.

GRANDPA. Well, well, well!

KIRBY. I may have had silly notions in my youth, but thank God my father knocked them out of me. I went into the business and forgot about them.

TONY. Not altogether, father. There's still a saxophone in the back of your clothes closet.

GRANDPA. There is?

KIRBY (*quietly*). That's enough, Tony. We'll discuss this later.

TONY. No, I want to talk about it *now*. I think Mr. Vanderhof is right—dead right. I'm never going back to that office. I've always hated it, and I'm not going on with it. And I'll tell you something else. I didn't make a mistake last night. I knew it was the wrong night. I brought you here on purpose.

ALICE. Tony!

PENNY. Well, for heaven's—

TONY. Because I wanted to wake you up. I wanted you to see a real family—as they really *were*. A family that loved and understood each other. You don't understand *me*. You've never had time. Well, I'm not going to make *your* mistake. I'm clearing out.

KIRBY. Clearing out? What do you mean?

TONY. I mean I'm not going to be pushed into the business just because I'm your son. I'm getting out while there's still time.

KIRBY (*stunned*). Tony, what are you going to do?

TONY. I don't know. Maybe I'll be a bricklayer, but at least I'll be doing something I want to do. (*Whereupon the door bell rings.*)

PENNY. That must be the cab.

GRANDPA. Ask him to wait a minute, Ed.

ALICE. Grandpa!

GRANDPA. Do you mind, Alice? . . . You know, Mr. Kirby, Tony is going through just what you and I did when we were his age. I think, if you listen hard enough, you can hear yourself saying the same things to *your* father twenty-five years ago. We all did it. And we were right. How many of us would be willing to settle when we're young for what we eventually get? All those plans we make . . . what happens to them? It's only a handful of the lucky ones that can look back and say that they even came close. (GRANDPA *has hit home.* MR. KIRBY *turns slowly and looks at his son, as though seeing him for the first time.* GRANDPA *continues.*) So . . . before they clean out that closet, Mr. Kirby, I think I'd get in a few good hours on that saxophone. (*A slight pause, then* THE GRAND DUCHESS, *an apron over her evening dress, comes in from the kitchen.*)

THE GRAND DUCHESS. I beg your pardon, but before I make the blintzes, how many will there be for dinner?

PENNY. Why, I don't know—ah—

GRANDPA. Your Highness, may I present Mr. Anthony Kirby, and Mr. Kirby, Junior? The Grand Duchess Olga Katrina.

KIRBY. How's that?

THE GRAND DUCHESS. How do you do? Before I make the blintzes, how many will there be to dinner?

GRANDPA. Oh, I'd make quite a stack of them, Your Highness. Can't ever tell.

THE GRAND DUCHESS. Good! The Czar always said to me, Olga, do not be stingy with the blintzes. (*She returns to the kitchen, leaving a somewhat stunned* MR. KIRBY *behind her.*)

KIRBY. Ah—who did you say that was, Mr. Vanderhof?

GRANDPA (*very offhand*). The Grand Duchess Olga Katrina, of Russia. She's cooking the dinner.

KIRBY. Oh!

GRANDPA. And speaking of dinner, Mr. Kirby, why don't you and Tony both stay?

PENNY. Oh, please do, Mr. Kirby. We've got all that stuff we were going to have last night. I mean tonight.

GRANDPA. Looks like a pretty good dinner, Mr. Kirby, and'll kind of give us a chance to get acquainted. Why not stay?

KIRBY. Why—I'd like to very much. (*He turns to* TONY, *with some trepidation.*) What do you say, Tony? Shall we stay to dinner?

TONY. Yes, father. I think that would be fine. If— (*His eyes go to* ALICE.) —if Alice will send away that cab.

GRANDPA. How about it, Alice? Going to be a nice crowd. Don't you think you ought to stay for dinner?

ALICE. Mr. Kirby—Tony—oh, Tony! (*And she is in his arms.*)

TONY. Darling!

ALICE. Grandpa, you're wonderful!

GRANDPA. I've been telling you that for years. (*He kisses her.*)
(ESSIE *enters from the kitchen, laden with dishes.*)

ESSIE. Grandpa, here's a letter for you. It was in the ice-box.

GRANDPA (*looks at the envelope*). The Government again.

TONY (*happily*). Won't you step into the office, Miss Sycamore? I'd like to do a little dictating.

GRANDPA (*with his letter*). Well, well, well!

PENNY. What is it, Grandpa?

GRANDPA. The United States Government apologizes. I don't owe 'em a nickel. It seems I died eight years ago.

ESSIE. Why, what do they mean, Grandpa?

GRANDPA. Remember Charlie, the milkman? Buried under my name?

PENNY. Yes.

GRANDPA. Well, I just told them they made a mistake and I was Martin Vanderhof, Jr. So they're very sorry and I may even get a refund.

ALICE. Why, Grandpa, you're an old crook.

GRANDPA. Sure!

KIRBY (*interested*). Pardon me, how did you say you escaped the income tax, Mr. Vanderhof?

KOLENKHOV (*bursting through the kitchen door, bringing a chair with him*). Tonight, my friends, you are going to eat. . . . (*He stops short as he catches sight of* KIRBY.)

KIRBY (*heartily*). Hello, there!

KOLENKHOV (*stunned*). How do you do?

KIRBY. Fine! Fine! Never was better.

KOLENKHOV (*to* GRANDPA). What has happened?

GRANDPA. He's relaxing. (ED *strikes the keys of the xylophone.*) That's right. Play something, Ed. (*He starts to play.* ESSIE *is immediately up on her toes.*)

THE GRAND DUCHESS (*entering from the kitchen*). Everything will be ready in a minute. You can sit down.

PENNY. Come on, everybody. Dinner! (*They start to pull up chairs.*) Come on, Mr. Kirby!

KIRBY (*still interested in the xylophone*). Yes, yes, I'm coming.

PENNY. Essie, stop dancing and come to dinner.

KOLENKHOV. You will like Russian food, Mr. Kirby.

PENNY. But you must be careful of your indigestion.

KIRBY. Nonsense! I haven't any indigestion.

TONY. Well, Miss Sycamore, how was your trip to the Adirondacks?

ALICE. Shut your face, Mr. Kirby!

KOLENKHOV. In Russia, when they sit down to dinner . . .

GRANDPA (*tapping on his plate*). Quiet! Everybody! Quiet! (*Immediately the talk ceases. All heads are lowered as* GRANDPA *starts to say Grace.*) Well, Sir, here we are again. We want to say thanks once more for everything You've done for us. Things seem to be going fine. Alice is going to marry Tony, and it looks as if they're going to be very happy. Of course the fireworks blew up, but that was Mr. De Pinna's fault, not Yours. We've all got our health and as far as anything else is concerned, we'll leave it to You. Thank You. (*The heads come up again.* RHEBA *and* DONALD *come through the kitchen door with stacks and stacks of blintzes. Even the Czar would have thought there were enough.*)

CURTAIN

End Of Summer

BY S. N. BEHRMAN

For

MAY AND HAROLD FREEDMAN

———

END OF SUMMER was produced by the Theatre Guild, Inc., at the Guild Theatre, New York, on Monday night, February 17, 1936, with the following cast:

(in the order of their appearance)

WILL DEXTER .... Shepperd Strudwick
MRS. WYLER .... Mildred Natwick
PAULA FROTHINGHAM .... Doris Dudley
ROBERT .... Kendall Clark
LEONIE FROTHINGHAM .... Ina Claire
SAM FROTHINGHAM .... Minor Watson
DR. KENNETH RICE .... Osgood Perkins
DENNIS McCARTHY .... Van Heflin
DR. DEXTER .... Herbert Yost
BORIS, COUNT MIRSKY .... Tom Powers

———

CHARACTERS

WILL DEXTER
MRS. WYLER
PAULA FROTHINGHAM
ROBERT
LEONIE FROTHINGHAM

SAM FROTHINGHAM
DR. KENNETH RICE
DENNIS McCARTHY
DR. DEXTER
BORIS, COUNT MIRSKY

SCENE

The action of the play takes place in the living room of Bay Cottage, the Frothinghams' summer place in Northern Maine.

TIME

The present

———

SCENE: *The verandah-living room of the Frothingham estate. Bay Cottage in Northern Maine. It is a charmingly furnished room with beautiful old distinguished pieces. A chintz couch and chairs give the room an air of informality. Beyond the door back you see a spacious, more formal room. Through the series of glass windows over the curving window seat on the right wall you see the early budding lilac and sumach. Woodbine and Virginia creeper are sprawling over the fence of native stone. Silver birch and maple are beginning to put out their leaves. The tops of red pine and cedar are visible over the rocks which fall away to the sea.*

Time: The present. A lovely afternoon in May.

At Rise: MRS. WYLER, *a very old lady and* WILL DEXTER, *an attractive, serious boy, are engaged in conversation.* MRS. WYLER *is knitting.*

WILL. When you were a young girl in Cleveland, did you see much of Mr. Rockefeller?

MRS. WYLER. Not much. Of course my husband saw him every day at the office. But he never came to our house. We were young and worldly. He was strict and religious.

WILL. Did you suspect, in those days, how rich you were going to be?

MRS. WYLER. Mercy no! We debated a long time before we moved up to Cleveland from Oil City. My mother thought Oil City was no place to bring up a young girl. She finally persuaded my father to let us move up to Cleveland. But there was a lot of talk about the expense.

WILL. Was Oil City lively?

MRS. WYLER. (*Demurely.*) It was pretty rough! I remember the celebration when they ran the first pipe-line through to Pittsburgh. That was a celebration!

WILL. The oil just poured, didn't it? Gushed out of the ground in great jets, and the people swarmed from everywhere to scoop it up.

MRS. WYLER. I remember we had a gusher in our backyard. We put a fence around it to keep the cows from lapping up the oil.

WILL. Were you excited?

MRS. WYLER. Not by the oil.

WILL. I should think you would have been!

MRS. WYLER. (*Dryly.*) We weren't. Oil was smelly. We wanted to get away from it. We discovered bath-salts.

WILL. You didn't know it was the true fountain of your—dynasty?

MRS. WYLER. We left it to the men—as I look back over my life the principal excitement came from houses—buying and building houses. The shack in Oil City to the mansion on Fifth Avenue. We had houses everywhere—houses in London, houses in Paris, Newport and this—and yet, it seemed to me, we were always checking in and out of hotels.

WILL. It seems strange to think—

MRS. WYLER. What?

WILL. This golden stream — that you stumbled on so accidentally—it's flowing still—quenchless—and you on it—all you dynastic families—floating along in it—in luxurious barges!

MRS. WYLER. When I read these books about the early days of oil—these debunking books, you call them—they make me smile.

WILL. Do they? Why? I'd like to know that.

MRS. WYLER. They're so far from the truth.

WILL. Are they?

MRS. WYLER. Of course they are!

WILL. Why?

MRS. WYLER. Because they're written from a foreign point of view—not *our* point of view. We did as well as anybody could have done according to our lights.

WILL. Yes, but what sort of lights were they?

MRS. WYLER. (*Tolerantly.*) There you are!

WILL. How lucky you were!

MRS. WYLER. (*Teasing him.*) Our young men didn't moon about. They made opportunities for themselves!

WILL. Or did the opportunities make them? All you had to do was pack your week-end bag and pioneer.

MRS. WYLER. Is the world quite exhausted then?

WILL. Possibly not, but our pioneering might take a form you would find—unpalatable.

MRS. WYLER. Yes yes. (*Benevolently.*) I suppose you're one of those young radicals our colleges are said to be full of nowadays. Tell me, what do you young radicals stand for?

WILL. I haven't decided exactly what I'm for, but I'm pretty certain what I'm against.

MRS. WYLER. (*Pumping him.*) Most young people are bored by the past. You're full of curiosity. Why is that?

WILL. (*Not committing himself.*) I'm interested.

MRS. WYLER. At my age to be permitted to talk of one's youth is an indulgence. Ask me anything you like. At my age also one has no reason for restraint. I have had the bad judgment to survive most of my contemporaries.

WILL. I love talking to you, Mrs Wyler. I think you're very wise.

MRS. WYLER. (*With a sigh.*) Go on thinking so—I'll try not to disillusion you! (*A moment's pause.*) Are you staying on here at Bay Cottage?

WILL. Oh, no, I have to go back to Amherst to get my degree.

MRS. WYLER. And after that?

WILL. (*Humorously.*) The dole! (*The old lady laughs.*)

MRS. WYLER. My daughter tells me she's invited your father here.

WILL. Yes.

MRS. WYLER. I shall be so glad to meet him. He's an inventor, isn't he?

WILL. He's a physicist. Specializes in—

MRS. WYLER. Don't tell me—in spite of my great wisdom I can't keep up with science. Whenever anybody makes a scientific explanation to me I find there are two things I don't know instead of just one.

WILL. (*Cheerfully.*) Anyway, Dad's been fired.

MRS. WYLER. I am very sorry to hear that.

WILL. He's been working on a method for improving high-speed steel.

MRS. WYLER. Did he fail?

WILL. He succeeded. (MRS. WYLER *is surprised.*) They decided that his discovery, if perfected and marketed, might increase the technological unemployment. They have decided therefore to call a halt on scientific discovery — especially in those branches where it might have practical results. That is one of the differences, Mrs. Wyler, between my day—and yours—in your day, you put a premium on invention —we declare a moratorium on it. (*The old lady gives him a shrewd look.*)

MRS. WYLER. Yes, yes. I am perfectly sure that you're in for a hard time, Will.

WILL. (*Lightly, shrugging his shoulders.*) As I have been elected by my class as the one most likely to succeed, I am not worrying, Mrs. Wyler. All I have to do is bide my time.

MRS. WYLER. (*Amused.*) I am perfectly certain you'll come out! Paula tells me you and your friend, Dennis McCarthy, want to start some kind of magazine.

WILL. Yes. A national magazine for undergraduate America. You see, Mrs. Wyler, before the rift in our so-called system, college men were supposed to live exclusively in a world of ukuleles, football slogans, and petting-parties—*College Humor* sort of thing. But it was never entirely true. Now it is less true than ever. This magazine—if we can get it going—would be a forum for intercollegiate thought. It would be the organ of critical youth as opposed—to the other.

MRS. WYLER. What other?

WILL. The R.O.T.C., the Vigilantes and the Fascists—the Youth Movement of guns and sabres—

MRS. WYLER. I see. Well, I wish you luck, Will.

WILL. Thank you. (PAULA FROTHINGHAM comes in, a lovely young girl in gay summer slacks.)

PAULA. (To WILL.) Aren't you swimming? Hello, Granny.

WILL. Your grandmother and I have been discussing life.

PAULA. With a capital L, I suppose?

WILL. Enormous! I've been getting data on the pioneer age. Your grandmother thinks the reason we're in the condition we're in is because we're lazy.

MRS. WYLER. (Mildly.) Lazy? Did I say that?

WILL. In a way

MRS. WYLER. If I said it, it must be so. Everybody over seventy is infallible!

PAULA. (Nestling to her.) Darling.

MRS. WYLER. Survival is quite a knack. You children don't realize it.

WILL. Oh, don't we though! It's getting harder every day.

MRS. WYLER. Nonsense! At your age you can't help it.

WILL. In your stately opulence that's what you think, Mrs. Wyler. You just don't know!

MRS. WYLER. Nonsense! Do you think your generation has a monopoly on hard times?

WILL. Now please don't tell me we've had depressions before?

MRS. WYLER. (Rising to go.) Paula, your young man is impertinent. Don't have anything to do with him. (She goes out.)

PAULA. What a conquest you've made of Granny! Way and ahead of all my beaus!

WILL. That undistinguished mob! Who couldn't?

PAULA. As long as you admit there is a mob . . .

WILL. Why wouldn't there be? Everybody loves you for your money!

PAULA. (Confidently.) I know it! And of all the fortune-hunters I've had dangling after me you're easily the most . . .

WILL. Blatant!

PAULA. That's it! Blatant! Like my new slacks?

WILL. Love 'em.

PAULA. Love me?

WILL. Loathe you.

PAULA. Good! Kiss? (They kiss quickly.)

WILL. Funny thing about your grandmother . . .

PAULA. Now I won't have you criticising Granny . . .

WILL. I'm crazy about her. You feel she's been through everything and that she understands everything. Not this though. Not the essential difference between her times and ours.

PAULA. Oh dear! Is it the end of the world then?

WILL. The end of this world.

PAULA. (Goes to window seat right, with a sigh.) Such a pretty world. (She points through windows at the garden and sea beyond.) Look at it! Too bad it has to go! Meantime before it quite dissolves let's go for a swim. (She starts for door.)

WILL. (Abstracted.) All right . . . (Following her to window seat.)

PAULA. (She turns back.) What's on your mind?

WILL. Wanted to speak to you about something. . . .

PAULA. What?

WILL. (*Embarrassed slightly.*) Er—your mother. . . .

PAULA. What's Mother gone and done now? Out with it. Or is it you? My boy-friends are always in love with Mother. I've had to contend with that all my life. So if it's that you needn't even mention it . . . come on.

WILL. No, but really, Paula. . . .

PAULA. Well then, out with it! What is it!

WILL. This. (*He gives her note.*) Found it on my breakfast tray this morning in a sealed envelope marked "Confidential."

PAULA. (*Reading note aloud, rather bewildered.*) "To give my little girl a good time with. Leonie Frothingham."

WILL. And this! (*He hands her check.* PAULA *takes it and looks at it.*)

PAULA. A hundred dollars. Does Mother think her little girl can have a good time with *that*? She doesn't know her little girl!

WILL. But what'll I do with it? How'll I get it back to her?

PAULA. Over my dead body you'll get it back to her! You'll spend it on Mother's little girl. Now come on swimming!

WILL. Does your mother put one of these on every breakfast tray?

PAULA. Argue it out with her.

WILL. I can't. It would seem ungracious. You must give it back to her for me.

PAULA. Catch me! Don't take it too seriously. She slips all the kids something every once in a while. She knows my friends are all stony. You overestimate the importance of money, Will—it's a convenience, that's all. You've got a complex on it.

WILL. I have! I've got to have. It's all right to be dainty about money when you've lots of it as you have. . . .

PAULA. Rotten with it is the expression, I believe. . . .

WILL. I repudiate that expression. It is genteel and moralistic. You can't be rotten with money—you can only be *alive* with it.

PAULA. You and the rest of our crowd make me feel it's bad taste to be rich. But what can I do? I didn't ask for it!

WILL. I know. But look here . . . I've got a brother out of college two years who's worked six weeks in that time and is broke and here I am in an atmosphere with hundred-dollar bills floating around!

PAULA. (*With check.*) Send him that!

WILL. Misapplication of funds!

PAULA. (*Warmly.*) Mother would be only too . . .

WILL. I know she would—but that isn't the point. . . . You know, Paula—

PAULA. What?

WILL. Sometimes I think if we weren't in love with each other we should be irreconcilable enemies—

PAULA. Nothing but sex, eh?

WILL. That's all.

PAULA. In that case—(*They kiss.*)

WILL. That's forgiving. But seriously, Paula—

PAULA. Seriously what?

WILL. I can't help feeling I'm here on false pretenses. What am I doing with a millionaire family — with you? If your mother knew what I think, and what I've let you in for in college—she wouldn't touch me with a ten-foot pole. And you too—I'm troubled about the superficiality of your new opinions. Isn't your radicalism—acquired coloring?

PAULA. I hope not. But—so is all education.

WILL. l know but—!

PAULA. What are you bleating about? Didn't I join you on that expedition to Kentucky to be treated by that sovereign state as an offensive foreigner? My back aches yet when I remember that terrible bus ride. Didn't I get my name in the

papers picketing? Didn't I give up my
holiday to go with you to the Chicago
Peace Congress? Didn't I?

WILL. (*Doubtfully.*) Yes, you did.

PAULA. But you're not convinced. Will
darling, don't you realize that since knowing you and your friends, since I've, as you
say, acquired your point of view about
things, my life has had an excitement and
a sense of reality it's never had before.
I've simply come alive—that's all! Before
then I was bored—terribly bored without
knowing why. I wanted something more—
fundamental — without knowing what.
You've made me see. I'm terribly grateful
to you, Will darling. I always shall be.

WILL. You are a dear, Paula, and I adore
you—but—

PAULA. Still unconvinced?

WILL. This money of yours. What'll it
do to us?

PAULA. I'll turn it over to you. Then you
can give me an allowance—and save your
pride.

WILL. I warn you, Paula—

PAULA. What?

WILL. If you turn it over to me, I'll use
it in every way I can to make it impossible
for anyone to have so much again.

PAULA. That's all right with me, Will.

WILL. Sometimes you make me feel I'm
taking candy from babies.

PAULA. The candy is no good for the
baby, anyway. Besides, let's cross that
bridge when we come to it. (ROBERT, *the
butler, enters.*)

ROBERT. I beg your pardon, Miss Frothingham.

PAULA. Yes, Robert?

ROBERT. Telephone for you.

PAULA. Thank you, Robert. (*She crosses
to table back of sofa for telephone.*) (*At
phone.*) Yes—this is Paula—Dad!—Darling!—Where are you? . . . but how wonderful . . . I thought you were in New

York . . . well, come right over this minute. . . . Will you stay the night? . . .
Oh, too bad! . . . I'll wait right here for
you. Hurry, darling! Bye! (*She hangs up.*)
Imagine, dad! He's motoring up to Selena
Bryant's at Murray Bay—I'm dying to
have you meet him. He's the lamb of the
world.

WILL. Not staying long, is he?

PAULA. No. He wants to see Mother he
says. I wonder . . . oh, dear!

WILL. What?

PAULA. I was so excited I forgot to tell
him. . . .

WILL. What?

PAULA. That a new friend of Mother's is
coming.

WILL. The Russian?

PAULA. The Russian's here. He dates from
last winter. You're behind the times, Will.

WILL. Who's the new friend?

PAULA. I'm not sure about it all yet. Maybe Mother isn't either. But I've had some
experience in watching them come and go
and my instinct tells me Dr. Rice is elected.

WILL. Who is Dr. Rice?

PAULA. Psychoanalyst from New York.
(*Burlesquing slightly.*) The last word, my
dear—(*At this point the object of* PAULA'S
*maternal impulse comes in, running a little
and breathless, like a young girl.* LEONIE
FROTHINGHAM, *as she has a daughter of
nearly twenty, must be herself forty, but,
at this moment, she might be sixteen. She
is slim, girlish, in a young and quivering
ecstasy of living and anticipation. For*
LEONIE, *her daughter is an agreeable phenomenon whom she does not specially relate
to herself biologically—a lovely apparition
who hovers intermittently, in the wild garden of her life. There is something, for all
her gaiety, heartbreaking about* LEONIE,
*something childish and child-like—an ac-
ceptance of people instantly and uncritically
at the best of their own valuation. She is
impulsive and warm-hearted and generous
to a fault. Her own fragile and exquisite
loveliness she offers to the world half*

shyly, tentatively, bearing it like a cup containing a precious liquid of which not a drop must be spilled. A spirituelle amoureuse she is repelled by the gross or the voluptuary; this is not hypocrisy—it is, in LEONIE, *a more serious defect than that. In the world in which she moves hypocrisy is merely a social lubricant but this myopia —alas for* LEONIE!—*springs from a congenital and temperamental inability to face anything but the pleasantest and the most immediately appealing and the most flattering aspects of things—in life and in her own nature. At this moment, though, she is the loveliest fabrication of Nature, happy in the summer sun and loving all the world.)*

LEONIE. My darlings, did you ever know such a day?

WILL. (*He is a shy boy with her.*) It's nice!

LEONIE. Nice! It's . . . (*Her gesture conveys her utter inadequacy to express the beauties of the day.*) It's—radiant! It knows it's radiant! The world is pleased with herself today. Is the world a woman? Today she is—a lovely young girl in blue and white.

WILL. In green and white.

LEONIE. (*Agreeing—warmly.*) In green and white!—It depends where you look, doesn't it? I'm just off to the station to meet Dr. Rice. Will, you'll be fascinated by him.

PAULA. (*Cutting in—crisply.*) Sam telephoned.

LEONIE. Sam!

PAULA. Your husband. My father. Think back, Leonie.

LEONIE. Darling! Where is he?

PAULA. He's on his way here. He telephoned from Miller's Point.

LEONIE. Is he staying?

PAULA. No.

LEONIE. Why not?

PAULA. He's going on to Selena Bryant's.

LEONIE. What is this deep friendship between Sam and Selena Bryant?

PAULA. Now, Leonie, don't be prudish!

LEONIE. (*Appealing for protection to* WILL.) She's always teasing me. She's always teasing everybody about everything. Developed quite a vein. I must warn you, Paula—sarcasm isn't feminine. In their hearts men don't like it. Do you like it, Will? Do you really like it?

WILL. I hate it!

LEONIE. (*In triumph to* PAULA.) There you see! He hates it!

PAULA. (*Tersely.*) He doesn't always hate it!

LEONIE. (*Her most winning smile on* WILL.) Does she bully you, Will? Don't let her bully you. The sad thing is, Paula, you're so charming. Why aren't you content to be charming? Are you as serious as Paula, Will? I hope not.

WILL. Much more.

LEONIE. I'm sorry to hear that. Still, for a man, it's all right, I suppose. But why are the girls nowadays so determined not to be feminine? Why? It's coming back you know—I'm sure of it—femininity is due for a revival.

PAULA. So are Herbert Hoover and painting on china.

LEONIE. Well I read that even in Russia . . . the women . . . (*She turns again to* WILL *whom she feels sympathetic.*) It isn't as if women had done such marvels with their—masculinity! Have they? Are things better because women vote? Not that I can see. They're worse. As far as I can see the women simply reinforce the men in their —mistakes.

WILL. (*To* PAULA.) She has you there!

LEONIE. (*With this encouragement warming to her theme.*) When I was a girl the calamities of the world were on a much smaller scale. It's because the women, who, after all, are half of the human race, stayed at home and didn't bother. Now they do bother—and look at us!

PAULA. Well, that's as Victorian as any-thing I ever—

LEONIE. I'd love to have been a Victorian. They were much happier than we are, weren't they? Of course they were.

PAULA. (*Defending herself to* WILL.) It's only Mother that brings out the crusader in me—(*To* LEONIE.) When you're not around I'm not like that at all. Am I, Will? (*But* WILL *is given no chance to answer because* LEONIE *is holding a sprig of lilac to his nostrils.*)

LEONIE. Smell. (WILL *smells.*) Isn't it de-licious?

WILL. It's lovely.

LEONIE. Here . . . . (*She breaks off a sprig and pins it into his lapel. While she is doing it she broaches a delicate subject quite casually to* PAULA.) Oh, by the way, Paula . . .

PAULA. Yes, Mother?

LEONIE. Did you mention to Sam that—that Boris—

PAULA. I didn't, no. It slipped my mind.

LEONIE. It doesn't matter in the least.

PAULA. Father isn't staying anyway . . .

LEONIE. Well, why shouldn't he? You must make him. I want him to meet Dr. Rice. He's really a most extraordinary man.

PAULA. Where'd you *find him?*

LEONIE. I met him at a party at Sissy Drake's. He *saved* Sissy.

PAULA. From what?

LEONIE. From that awful eye-condition.

PAULA. Is he an oculist too?

LEONIE. (*To* WILL.) She went to every oculist in the world—she went to Balti-more and she went to Vienna. Nobody could do a thing for her—her eyes kept blinking—twitching really in the most un-accountable way. It was an ordeal to talk to her—and of course she must have un-dergone agonies of embarrassment. But Dr. Rice psychoanalyzed her and com-pletely cured her. How do you suppose? Well, he found that the seat of the trouble lay in her unconscious. It was too simple. She blinked in that awful way because actually she couldn't bear to look at her husband. So she divorced Drake and since she's married to Bill Wilmerding she's as normal as you or me. Now I'll take you into a little secret. I'm having Dr. Rice up to see Boris. Of course Boris mustn't know it's for him.

PAULA. What's the matter with Boris?

LEONIE. I'm not sure. I think he's work-ing too hard.

WILL. What's he working at?

LEONIE. Don't you know? Didn't you tell him, Paula? His father's memoirs. He's the son, you know, of the great Count Mirsky!

WILL. I know.

LEONIE. I must show you the photographs of his father—wonderful old man with a great white beard like a snow-storm—looks like Moses—a Russian Moses—and Boris is sitting on his knees—couldn't be over ten years old and wearing a fur cap and boots—boots!—and they drank tea out of tall glasses with raspberry jelly in—people came from all over the world, you know, to see his father . . . !

WILL. Isn't it strange that Count Mirsky's son should find himself in this strange house on this odd headland of Maine—Maine of all places!—writing his father's life? It's fantastic!

PAULA. (*With some malice.*) Is Dr. Rice going to help you acclimate him?

LEONIE. I hope so. You and Paula will have to entertain him—you young intel-lectuals. Isn't it a pity I have no mind? (*She rises and crosses to table right to ar-range lily-of-the-valley sprigs in a vase.*)

PAULA. (*To* WILL.) She knows it's her greatest asset. Besides she's a fake.

WILL. (*Gallantly.*) I'm sure she is.

LEONIE. Thank you, my dears. It's gal-lant of you. (*She crosses to* PAULA—*em-braces her from behind.*) But I'm not deceived. I know what Paula thinks of me—she looks down on me because I won't get interested in sociology. There never were any such things about when I was a girl. The trouble is one generation never has any perspective about another generation.

WILL. That's what your mother was saying to me just a little while ago.

LEONIE. Was she? (*She sits left of* WILL.) I'm sure though Mother and I are much closer—that is, we understand each other better than Paula and I. Don't you think so, Paula?

PAULA. (*Considering it.*) Yes. I do think so.

LEONIE. I knew you'd agree. Something's happened between my generation and Paula's. New concepts. I don't know what they are exactly but I'm very proud that Paula's got them.

PAULA. (*Laughing helplessly.*) Oh, Mother! You reduce everything to absurdity!

LEONIE. (*Innocently.*) Do I? I don't mean to. At any rate it's a heavenly day and I adore you and I don't care about anything so long as you're happy. I want you to be happy.

PAULA. (*Helplessly.*) Oh dear!

LEONIE. What's the matter?

PAULA. You're saying that!

LEONIE. Is that wrong? Will—did I say something wrong?

PAULA. You want me to be happy. It's like saying you want me to be eight feet tall and to sing like Lily Pons.

LEONIE. Is it like that? Why? Will . . .

WILL. (*Gravely feeling he must stand up for* PAULA, *but hating to.*) Paula means . . . (*Pause.*)

LEONIE. Yes . . . ?

WILL. (*Miserable.*) She means—suppose there isn't any happiness to be had? Suppose the supply's run out?

LEONIE. But, Will, really . . . ! On a day like this! Why don't you go swimming?

(*Rises.*) Nothing like sea-water for—morbidity! Run out indeed! And today of all days! Really! (*Gets gloves.*) I'm disappointed in you, Will. I counted on you especially . . .

WILL. (*Abjectly.*) I was only fooling!

LEONIE. Of course he was. (*Sits on arm of sofa beside* WILL.) Will, I rely on you. Don't let Paula brood. Can't she drop the sociology in the summer? I think in the fall you're much better—braced—for things like that. Keep her happy, Will.

WILL. I'll do my best now that—thanks to you—I have the means.

LEONIE. Oh . . . . (*Remembering.*) Oh, you didn't mind, did you? I hope you didn't mind.

WILL. (*Embarrassed.*) Very generous of you.

LEONIE. Generous! Please don't say that. After all—we who are in the embarrassing position nowadays of being rich must do something with our money, mustn't we? That's why I'm helping Boris to write this book. *Noblesse oblige.* Don't you think so, Will? Boris tells me. that the Russians—the *present* Russians—

WILL. You mean the Bolsheviks?

LEONIE. Yes, I suppose I do. He says they don't like his father at all any more and won't read his works because in his novels he occasionally went on the assumption that rich people had souls and spirits too. You don't think like that too, do you, Will—that because I'm rich I'm just not worth bothering about at all— No, you couldn't! (*The appeal is tremulous.* WILL *succumbs entirely.*)

WILL. (*Bluntly.*) Mrs. Frothingham, I love you!

LEONIE. (*Rises from arm of sofa and sits in sofa beside* WILL. *To* PAULA.) Isn't he sweet? (*To* WILL.) And I love you, Will. Please call me Leonie. Do you know how Mother happened to name me Leonie? I was born in Paris, you know, and I was to be called Ruhama after my father's sister. But Mother said no. No child of mine, she said, shall be called Ruhama. She shall have a French name. And where do you think she got Leonie?

WILL. From the French version of one of those Gideon Bibles.

LEONIE. (*As breathless as if it happened yesterday.*) Not at all. From a novel the nurse was reading. She asked the nurse what she was reading and the nurse gave her the paper book and Mother opened it and found Leonie!

WILL. What was the book?

LEONIE. Everyone wants to know that . . . But I don't know. Mother didn't know. She kept the book to give to me when I grew up. But one day she met M. Jusserand on a train—he was the French Ambassador to Washington, you know—and he picked up the book in Mother's compartment and he read a page of it and threw it out of the window because it was trash! You see what I've had to live down.

WILL. Heroic!

LEONIE. I hope you stay all summer, Will. I won't hear of your going anywhere else.

WILL. Don't worry. I have nowhere else to go!

LEONIE. Tell me—that magazine you and Dennis want to start—will it be gay?

WILL. Not exactly.

LEONIE. Oh, dear! I know. Columns and columns of reading matter and no pictures. Tell me—your father is coming to dine, isn't he? I am so looking forward to meeting him. I love scientific men. They're usually so nice and understanding. Now, I've really got to go. (*Rises and starts out.*)

PAULA. Dennis will be on that train.

LEONIE. Oh, good! I like Dennis. He makes me laugh and I like people around who make me laugh, but I do wish he'd dress better. Why can't radicals be chic? I saw a picture of Karl Marx the other day and he looks like one of those advertisements before you take something. I'll look after Dennis, Will—save you going to the station— (*To* PAULA.) And Paula, tell Sam—

PAULA. Yes?

LEONIE. (*Forgetting the message to* SAM.) You know, I asked Dr. Rice if he would treat me professionally and he said I was uninteresting to him because I was quite normal. Isn't that discouraging? Really, I must cultivate something. Good-bye, darlings. (*She runs out.*)

WILL. But what was the message to Sam? (*He sits.*)

PAULA. (*Helplessly.*) I'll never know. Neither will she. (WILL *laughs.*) What can you do with her? She makes me feel like an opinionated old woman. And I worry about her.

WILL. Do you?

PAULA. Yes. She arouses my maternal impulse.

WILL. (*Who feels he can be casual about* LEONIE *now that she is gone.*) She relies rather too much on charm!

PAULA. (*Turning on him bitterly.*) Oh, she does, does she! (*Goes over to sofa and sits right of* WILL.) You renegade. You ruin all my discipline with Mother. You're like a blushing schoolboy in front of her . . .

WILL. (*Protesting sheepishly.*) Now, Paula, don't exaggerate!

PAULA. You are! I thought in another minute you were going to ask her to the frat dance. And where was all that wonderful indignation about her leaving you the check? Where was the insult to your pride? Where was your starving brother in Seattle? Where? Where?

WILL. I don't know but somehow you can't face your mother with things like that. It seems cruel to face her with realities. She seems outside of all that.

PAULA. (*Conceding that.*) Well, you're going to be no help to me in handling Mother, I can see that!

WILL. (*Changing subject—a bit sensitive about having yielded so flagrantly to* LEONIE.) This Russian—

PAULA. What about him?

WILL. (*Gauche.*) Platonic, do you suppose?

PAULA. Don't be naïve! (*Enter* SAM FROTH-INGHAM, PAULA'S *father, a very pleasant-faced, attractive man between forty-five and fifty.*)

SAM. Oh, hello. (WILL *rises.*)

PAULA. (*Flying to him.*) Darling!—

SAM. (*They meet center and embrace.*) Hello, Paula. Delighted to see you.

PAULA. This is Will Dexter.

SAM. (*Shaking hands with* WILL.) How do you do?

WILL. I'm delighted to meet you.

PAULA. (*To* WILL.) Wait for me at the beach, will you, Will?

WILL. No, I'll run down to the station and ride back with the others.

PAULA. Okay. (SAM *nods to him.* WILL *goes out.*)

SAM. (*Crosses to front of sofa.*) Nice boy. (*Follows her.*)

PAULA. Like him?

SAM. Do you?

PAULA. I think so.

SAM. Special?

PAULA. Sort of.

SAM. Very special?

PAULA. (*Sits right end of sofa.*) Well— not sure.

SAM. Wait till you are. You've lots of time.

PAULA. Oh, he's not exactly impulsive.

SAM. Then he's just a fool.

PAULA. How are you, darling?

SAM. Uneasy.

PAULA. With me!

SAM. Especially.

PAULA. Darling, why?

SAM. I'll tell you. That's why I've come.

PAULA. Everything all right?

SAM. Oh, fine.

PAULA. (*Mystified.*) Then . . . ?

SAM. (*Switching off.*) How's Leonie?

PAULA Fine. Delighted you were coming.

SAM. Was she?

PAULA. She really was. She's off to Ells-worth to meet a doctor.

SAM. Doctor?

PAULA. Psychoanalyst she's having up to massage her Russian's complexes.

SAM. (*Laughing.*) Oh— (*With a sigh.*) What's going to happen to Leonie?

PAULA. Why? She's on the crest!

SAM. She needs that elevation. Otherwise she sinks.

PAULA. Well—you know Mother . . .

SAM. Yes. (*A moment's pause.*) Paula?

PAULA. Yes, dad.

SAM. The fact is—it's ridiculous I should feel so nervous about telling you—but the fact is . . .

PAULA. What?

SAM. I've fallen in love. I want to get married. There! Well, thank God that's out! (*He wipes his forehead, quite an ordeal.*) Romance at my age. It's absurd, isn't it?

PAULA. Selena Bryant?

SAM. Yes.

PAULA. She has a grown son.

SAM. (*Smiling at her.*) So have I — a grown daughter.

PAULA. You'll have to divorce Mother.

SAM. Yes.

PAULA. Poor Leonie!

SAM. Well, after all—Leonie—you know how we've lived for years.

PAULA. Has Leonie hurt you?

SAM. Not for a long time. If this with Selena hadn't happened we'd have gone on forever, I suppose. But it has.

PAULA. You know, I have a feeling that, in spite of everything, this is going to be a shock to Leonie.

SAM. Paula?

PAULA. Yes.

SAM. Do you feel I'm deserting you? (*She turns her head away. She is very moved.*)

PAULA. No—you know how fond I am of you—I want you to be . . .

SAM. (*Deeply affected.*) Paula . . . !

PAULA. Happy. (*A silence. She is on the verge of tears.*)

SAM. I must make you see my side, Paula.

PAULA. (*Vehemently.*) I do!

SAM. It isn't only that—you're so young—but somehow—we decided very soon after you were born, Leonie and I, that our marriage could only continue on this sort of basis. For your sake we've kept it up. I thought I was content to be an—appendage—to Leonie's entourage. But I'm not—do you know what Selena—being with Selena and planning with Selena for ourselves has made me see—that I've never had a home. Does that sound mawkish?

PAULA. I thought you loved Bay Cottage.

SAM. Of our various menages this is my favorite—it's the simplest. And I've had fun here with you—watching you grow up. But very soon after I married Leonie I found this out—that when you marry a very rich woman it's always *her* house you live in. (*A moment's pause.*)

PAULA. I'm awfully happy for you, Sam, really I am. You deserve everything but I can't help it I . . .

SAM. I know. (*A pause.*) Paula . . .

PAULA. Yes, dad?

SAM You and I get on so well together—always have—Selena adores you and really—when you get to know her . . .

PAULA. I like Selena enormously. She's a dear. Couldn't be nicer.

SAM. I'm sure you and she would get on wonderfully together. Of course, Leonie will marry again. She's bound to. Why don't you come to live with us? When you want to . . .

PAULA. Want to!

SAM. All the time then. Leonie has such a busy life.

PAULA. It's awfully sweet of you.

SAM. Sweet of me! Paula!

PAULA. Where are you going to live?

SAM. New York. Selena has her job to do.

PAULA. She's terribly clever, isn't she?

SAM. She's good at her job.

PAULA. It must be wonderful to be independent. I hope I shall be. I hope I can make myself.

SAM. No reason you can't.

PAULA. It seems to take so much—

SAM. What sort of independence?

PAULA. Leonie's independent, but that independence doesn't mean anything somehow. She's always been able to do what she likes.

SAM. So will you be.

PAULA. That doesn't count somehow. It's independence in a vacuum. No, it doesn't count.

SAM. Maybe it isn't independence you want then?

PAULA. Yes, it is. I want to be able to stand on my own feet. I want to be—justified.

SAM. (*Understandingly.*) Ah! That's something else. (*A little amused.*) That's harder!

PAULA. I mean it, really I do—(*Pause.*) It's curious—how—adrift—this makes me feel. As if something vital, something fundamental had smashed. I wonder how Mother'll take it. I think—unconsciously—she depends on you much more than she realizes. You were a stabilizing force, Sam, in spite of everything and now . . .

SAM. (*Seriously.*) *You* are the stabilizing force, if you ask me, Paula . . .

PAULA. I don't know.

SAM. What's worrying you, Paula? Is it this Russian?

PAULA. Oh, I think he's harmless really.

SAM. What then?

PAULA. That one of these days—

SAM. What?

PAULA. That one of these days—now that you're going—somebody will come along—who won't be harmless.—You know, I really love Leonie. (LEONIE *comes running in just ahead of* DR. KENNETH RICE, DENNIS *and* WILL. LEONIE *is in the gayest spirits.* DR. RICE *is handsome, dark, magnetic, quiet, masterful. He is conscious of authority and gives one the sense of a strange, genius-like intuition.* DENNIS *is a flamboyant Irishman, a little older than* WILL, *gawky, black-haired, slovenly, infinitely brash.* SAM *and* PAULA *rise.* LEONIE *comes down to center with* KENNETH *at her left.* WILL *remains back of sofa.* DENNIS *follows down to right center.*)

LEONIE. Oh, Sam, how perfectly . . . This is Dr. Rice—my husband Sam Frothingham—and my daughter Paula! Sam, Dennis McCarthy.

DENNIS. How do you do? (*No one pays any attention to him.* DR. RICE *shakes hands with* SAM *and* PAULA. LEONIE *keeps bubbling, her little laugh tinkling through her chatter.*)

LEONIE. It's courageous of me, don't you think, Dr. Rice, to display such a daughter? Does she look like me? I'll be very pleased if you tell me that she does. Sit down, sit down, everybody.

DENNIS. (*Holding up his pipe.*) You don't mind if I—?

LEONIE. No, no, not at all—(*She sits center chair,* PAULA *sits on right end sofa,* DENNIS *sinks into chair, right, by table.*) Sam! How well you're looking! Are you staying at Selena's? How is Selena?

SAM. She's very well.

LEONIE. Dr. Rice knows Selena.

KENNETH. Yes, indeed!

LEONIE. I envy Selena, you know, above all women. So brilliant, so attractive and so self-sufficient. That is what I envy in her most of all. I have no resources—I depend so much on other people. (*Turns to* RICE.) Do you think, Dr. Rice, you could make me self-sufficient?

KENNETH. I think I could.

LEONIE. How perfectly marvelous!

KENNETH. But I shouldn't dream of doing it!

LEONIE. But if I beg you to?

KENNETH. Not even if you beg me to.

LEONIE. But why?

KENNETH. It would deprive your friends of their most delightful avocation.

LEONIE. Now that's very grateful. You see, Sam, there are men who still pay me compliments.

SAM. I can't believe it!

LEONIE. You must keep it up, Dr. Rice, please. So good for my morale. (*To* PAULA.) Oh, my dear, we've been having the most wonderful argument — (*To* DENNIS.) Haven't we?

DENNIS. Yes.

LEONIE. All the way in from Ellsworth—(*To* RICE.) Really, Doctor, it's given me new courage . . .

PAULA. New courage for what?

LEONIE. I've always been afraid to say it for fear of being old-fashioned—but Dr. Rice isn't afraid.

KENNETH. (*Explaining to* SAM.) It takes great courage, Mr. Frothingham, to disagree with the younger generation.

SAM. It does indeed.

PAULA. Well, what is it about?

LEONIE. Yes—what *was* it about, Dennis?

DENNIS. Statistics and theology. Some metaphysics thrown in.

SAM. Good heavens! (*Sits.*)

DENNIS. Statistics as a symbol.

WILL. Dr. Rice still believes in the individual career.

KENNETH. I hang my head in shame!

DENNIS. He doesn't know that as a high officer of the National Student Federation, I have at my fingers' ends the statistics which rule our future, the statistics which constitute our horizon. Not your future, Paula, because you are living parasitically on the stored pioneerism of your ancestors.

PAULA. Forgive me, Reverend Father!

DENNIS. I represent, Doctor, the Unattached Youth of America—

KENNETH. Well, that's a career in itself! (*They laugh.*)

DENNIS. (*Imperturbable.*) When we presently commit the folly of graduating from a benevolent institution at Amherst, Massachusetts, there will be in this Republic two million like us. Two million helots. (*Leaning over* LEONIE.) But Dr. Rice poohpoohs statistics.

LEONIE. (*Arranging his tie.*) Does he Dennis?

DENNIS. He says the individual can surmount statistics, violate the graphs. Superman!

WILL. Evidently Dr. Rice got in just under the wire.

KENNETH. I'd never submit to statistics, Mr. Dexter—I'd submit to many things but not to statistics.

LEONIE. Such dull things to submit to—

DENNIS. You must be an atheist, Dr. Rice.

KENNETH. Because I don't believe in statistics?—the new God?

LEONIE. Well, *I'm* a Protestant and I don't believe in them either.

DENNIS. Well, Protestant is a loose synonym for atheist—and I, as an Irishman—and a—

KENNETH. Young man—

DENNIS. Yes?

KENNETH. Have you ever heard Bismarck's solution of the Irish problem?

DENNIS. No. What?

KENNETH. Oh, it's entirely irrelevant.

LEONIE. Please tell us. I adore irrelevancies.

KENNETH. Well, he thought the Irish and the Dutch should exchange countries. The Dutch, he thought, would very soon make a garden out of Ireland, and the Irish would forget to mend the dikes. (*They laugh.*)

LEONIE. That's not irrelevant—

DENNIS. It is an irrelevance, but pardonable in an adversary losing an argument.

KENNETH. (*To* PAULA.) Miss Frothingham, you seem very gracious. Will you get me out of this?

PAULA. No, I'm enjoying it.

LEONIE. Whatever you may say, Dennis, it's an exciting time to be alive.

DENNIS. That is because your abnormal situation renders you free of its major excitement—

LEONIE. And what's that, Dennis?

DENNIS. The race with malnutrition.

KENNETH. But that race, Mr.—?

DENNIS. McCarthy.

KENNETH. Is the eternal condition of mankind. Perhaps mankind won't survive the solution of that problem.

WILL. (*With heat.*) It's easy to sit in this living room—and be smug about the survival of the fittest—especially when you're convinced you're one of the fittest. But there are millions who won't concede you that superiority, Dr. Rice. There are millions who are so outrageously demanding that they actually insist on the right to live! They may demand it one day at the cost of your complacency.

LEONIE. Will! We were just chatting.

WILL. I'm sorry! The next thing Dr. Rice'll be telling us is that war is necessary also—to keep us stimulated—bloodletting for the other fellow.

KENNETH. Well, as a matter of fact, there's something to be said for that too. If you haven't settled on a career yet, Mr. Dexter, may I suggest evangelism?

DENNIS. But Dr. Rice—!

KENNETH. And now, Mrs. Frothingham, before these young people heckle me too effectively, may I escape to my room?

LEONIE. (*Rising.*) Of course. Though I don't think you need be afraid of their heckling, Doctor. You say things which I've always believed but never dared say.

KENNETH. (*As they walk out.*) Why not?

LEONIE. I don't know—somehow—I lacked the—the authority. I want to show you your rooms myself. (*Leaving the room, followed by* RICE.) I'll be right back, Sam— (RICE *nods to them and follows her out. As they go out she keeps talking to him.*) I am giving you my father's rooms—he built the wing especially so that when he wanted to work he'd be away from the rest of the house—you have the sea *and* the garden—(*They are off. A moment's pause.*)

PAULA. Well, that's a new type for Leonie!

DENNIS. There's something Rasputinish about him. What's he doing in Maine?

WILL. What, for the matter of that, are you and I doing in Maine? We should be in New York, jockeying for position on the bread-line. Let's go to the beach, Dennis. Pep us up for the struggle.

DENNIS. In that surf? It looks angry. I can't face life today.

PAULA. Swim'll do you good.

DENNIS. (*Starting for garden.*) It's not a swim I want exactly but a float—a vigorous float. Lead me to the pool, Adonais—

WILL. All right. (*As he starts to follow,* DENNIS, DR. DEXTER, WILL'S *father, comes in ushered by* ROBERT. *He is a dusty little man with a bleached yellow Panama hat. He keeps wiping his perspiring face with an old handkerchief. He doesn't hear very well.*)

DENNIS. Ah, the enemy—! (PAULA *and* SAM *rise.*)

WILL. Hello, dad. You remember Paula.

DEXTER. Yes . . . yes, I do.

WILL. (*Introducing* SAM.) My father—Mr. Frothingham.

SAM. Very glad to see you.

DEXTER. (*Shaking hands.*) Thank you.

DENNIS. (*Pointing dramatically at* DEXTER.) Nevertheless I repeat—the enemy!

PAULA. Dennis!

WILL. Oh, he's used to Dennis!

DEXTER. (*Wipes his forehead.*) Yes, and besides it was very dusty on the road.

PAULA. Won't you sit down? (DEXTER *does so, in center chair. The others remain standing.*)

WILL. How long did it take you to drive over, dad?

DEXTER. Let's see—left New Brunswick at two. . . .

WILL. (*Looks at watch.*) Three and one half hours—pretty good—the old tin Lizzie's got life in her yet.

DEXTER. You young folks having a good time, I suppose? (*He looks around him absent-mindedly.*)

PAULA. Dennis has been bullying us.

DEXTER. He still talking? (*Mildly.*) It's the Irish in him.

DENNIS. (*Nettled.*) You forgot to say shanty!

DEXTER. (*Surprised.*) Eh? Why should I say that?

WILL. Dennis is a snob. Wants all his titles.

DENNIS. You misguided children don't realize it—but here—in the guise of this dusty, innocent-seeming man—sits the enemy.

DEXTER. (*Turning as if stung by a fly—cupping his hand to his ear.*) What? What did he say?

DENNIS. The ultimate enemy, the true begetter of the fatal statistics—Science. You betray us, Paula, by having him in the house; *you* betray us, Will, by acknowledging him as a father.

DEXTER. (*Wiping his forehead.*) Gosh, it's hot!

SAM. (*Sensing a fight and urging it on—solemnly.*) Can all this be true, Dr. Dexter?

DEXTER. What be true?

SAM. Dennis's accusation.

DEXTER. I am slightly deaf and McCarthy's presence always fills me with gratitude for that affliction.

DENNIS. It's perfectly obvious. You've heard of technological unemployment. Well, here it sits, embodied in Will's father. Day and night with diabolical ingenuity and cunning he works out devices to unemploy us. All over the world, millions of us are being starved and broken on the altar of Science. We Catholics understand that. We Catholics repudiate the new Moloch that has us by the throat.

WILL. Do you want us to sit in mediaeval taverns with Chesterton and drink beer? (DEXTER *turns to* DENNIS; *as if emerging suddenly from an absent-minded daze, he speaks with great authority, casually but with clarity and precision.*)

DEXTER. The fact is, my voluble young friend, I am not the Moloch who is destroying you but that you and the hordes of the imprecise and the vaguely trained—are destroying me! I have, you will probably be pleased to learn, just lost my job. I have been interrupted in my work. And why? Because I am successful. Because I have found what, with infinite patience and concentration, I have been seeking to discover. From the elusive and the indeterminate and the invisible, I have crystallized a principle which is visible and tangible and—predictable. From the illimitable icebergs of the unknown I have chipped off a fragment of knowledge, a truth which so-called practical men may put to a use which will make some of your numbers unnecessary in the workaday world. Well—what of it, I say?—who decrees that you shall be supported? Of what importance are your lives and futures and

your meandering aspirations compared to the firmness and the beauty and the cohesion of the principles I seek, the truth I seek? None—none whatever! Whether you prattle on an empty stomach or whether you prattle on a full stomach can make no difference to anybody that I can see. (*To* PAULA *abruptly, rising.*) And now, young woman, as I have been invited here to spend the night, I'd like to see my room!

PAULA. (*Crossing to him.*) Certainly! Come with me. I'll have Robert show you your room. (*They go to door back. She calls.*) Robert! (ROBERT *enters.*) Will you take Dr. Dexter to his room? (DEXTER *follows* ROBERT *out.*)

SAM. Gosh! I thought he was deaf!

WILL. He can hear when he wants to! (*To* DENNIS.) Now will you be good!

DENNIS. I'm sorry—I didn't know he'd lost his job or I wouldn't have . . .

WILL. Oh, that's all right. Well, Dennis, how does it feel to be superfluous?

DENNIS. (*Sourly.*) The man's childish! (*He goes out, door right, through garden.*)

PAULA. Isn't he marvelous? Don't you love Will's father?

SAM. Crazy about him. He's swell.

WILL. He's a pretty good feller. He seems absent-minded but actually he's extremely present-minded. If you'll excuse me, I'm going out to soothe Dennis. (*He follows* DENNIS *out.*) (*A pause.*)

SAM. That young man appears to have sound antecedents.

PAULA. Oh, yes—Will's all right, but—oh, Sam—!

SAM. What?

PAULA. With you gone—I'm terrified for Leonie. I really am! When I think of the foolish marriages Leonie would have made if not for you!

SAM. It's a useful function, but I'm afraid I'll have to give it up!

PAULA. (*With new determination.*) Sam . . .

SAM. Yes, Paula.

PAULA. If Leonie goes Russian—

SAM. Well?

PAULA. Or if she goes Freudian—?

SAM. In any case you and this boy'll probably be getting married.

PAULA. That's far from settled yet.

SAM. Why?

PAULA. Will's scared.

SAM. Is he?

PAULA. Of getting caught in Leonie's silken web.

SAM. That's sensible of him. (LEONIE *comes back, half running, breathless.*)

LEONIE. Well! Isn't Dr. Rice attractive?

SAM. (*Rising.*) Very.

PAULA. (*Rising.*) And so depressed about himself! (*She goes out—door right.*)

LEONIE. Isn't it extraordinary, Dr. Rice having achieved the position he has—at his age? He's amazing. And think of it, Sam—not yet forty.

SAM. Anybody under forty is young to me!

LEONIE. How old are you, Sam?

SAM. Forbidden ground, Leonie.

LEONIE. I should know, shouldn't I, but I don't. I know your birthday—I always remember your birthday . . .

SAM. You do indeed!

LEONIE. It's June 14. But I don't know how old you are.

SAM. Knowledge in the right place—ignorance in the right place!

LEONIE. (*Meaning it.*) You're more attractive and charming than ever.

SAM. You're a great comfort.

LEONIE. It's so nice to see you!

SAM. And you too! (*He is not entirely comfortable—not as unself-conscious and natural as she is.*)

LEONIE. Sometimes I think Paula should see more of you. I think it would be very good for her. What do you think of her new friends?

SAM. They seem nice.

LEONIE. They're all poor and they're very radical. They look on me—my dear, they have the most extraordinary opinion of me . . .

SAM. What is that?

LEONIE. I'm fascinated by them. They think of me as a hopeless kind of spoiled Bourbon living away in a never-never land —a kind of Marie Antoinette . . . (*She laughs.*) It's delicious!

SAM. Is Paula radical too?

LEONIE. I think she's trying to be. She's a strange child.

SAM. How do you mean?

LEONIE. Well, when I was a child I was brought up to care only if people were charming or attractive or . . .

SAM. Well-connected . . .

LEONIE. Yes . . . These kids don't care a hoot about that.

SAM. I think the difference between their generation and ours is that we were romantic and they're realistic.

LEONIE. Is that it?

SAM. I think so.

LEONIE. What makes that?

SAM. Changes in the world—the war—the depression. . . .

LEONIE. What did people blame things on before—the war?

SAM. (*Smiling.*) Oh, on the tariff and on the Republicans—and on the Democrats! Leonie—

LEONIE. Yes, Sam.

SAM. I—I really have something to tell you.

LEONIE. (*Looks up at him curiously.*) What? (*Pause.*)

SAM. I am in love with Selena Bryant. We want to get married.

LEONIE. (*Pause—after a moment.*) Human nature is funny! Mine is!

SAM. Why?

LEONIE. I know I ought to be delighted to release you. Probably I should have spoken to you about it myself before long—separating. And yet—when you tell me—I feel—a pang . . .

SAM. That's very sweet of you.

LEONIE. One's so possessive—one doesn't want to give up anything.

SAM. For so many years our marriage has been at its best—a friendship. Need that end?

LEONIE. No, Sam. It needn't. I hope truly that it won't.

SAM. What about Paula?

LEONIE. Did you tell Paula?

SAM. Yes. . . .

LEONIE. Did she . . . ?

SAM. (*Rising.*) Leonie . . .

LEONIE. (*Pauses.*) Yes, Sam.

SAM. A little while ago you said—you thought Paula ought to see more of me.

LEONIE. Yes . . . I did. . . . (*She is quite agitated suddenly. The thought has crossed her mind that perhaps* PAULA *has told* SAM *that she would prefer to go with him. This hurts her deeply, not only for the loss of* PAULA *but because, from the bottom of her being, she cannot bear not to be loved.*)

SAM. Don't you think then . . . for a time at least . . .

LEONIE. (*Defeatist in a crisis.*) Paula doesn't like me! (*It is a sudden and completely accepted conviction.*)

SAM. Leonie!

LEONIE. She'd rather go with you!

SAM. Not at all—it's only that . . .

LEONIE. I know what Paula thinks of me. . . .

SAM. Paula adores you. It's only that . . .

LEONIE. It's only that what—

SAM. Well, for instance— if you should get married—

LEONIE. What if I did?

SAM. (*Coming to stand close to her left.*) It would mean a considerable readjustment for Paula—wouldn't it? You can see that.

LEONIE. (*Rising.*) But it would too with you and Selena.

SAM. (*Taking step toward her.*) She knows Selena. She admires Selena.

LEONIE. (*Rising and walking down to front of sofa.*) What makes you think she wouldn't admire—whomever I married?

SAM. (*After a moment, completely serious now.*) There's another aspect of it which I think for Paula's sake you should consider most carefully.

LEONIE. What aspect?

SAM. (*Coming down to her.*) Paula's serious. You know that yourself. She's interested in things. She's not content to be a Sunday-supplement heiress—floating along —she wants to do things. Selena's a working woman. Selena can help her.

LEONIE. I know. I'm useless.

SAM. I think you ought to be unselfish about this.

LEONIE. Paula can do what she likes, of course. If she doesn't love me . . .

SAM. Of course she loves you.

LEONIE. If she prefers to live with you and Selena I shan't stand in her way. (*Her martyrish resignation irritates* SAM *profoundly. He feels that really* LEONIE *should not be allowed to get away with it.*)

SAM. You're so vain, Leonie.

LEONIE. (*Refusing to argue.*) I'm sorry. (*This makes it worse.* SAM *goes deeper.*)

SAM. After all, you're Paula's mother. Can't you look at her problem—objectively?

LEONIE. Where my emotions are involved I'm afraid I never know what words like that mean. (*He blunders in worse, farther than he really means to go.*)

SAM. (*Flatly.*) Well, this sort of thing isn't good for Paula.

LEONIE. (*Very cold, very hurt.*) What sort of thing? (*A moment's pause. He is annoyed with himself at the ineptitude of his approach.*) Be perfectly frank. You can be with me. What sort of thing?

SAM. Well—Leonie—(*With a kind of desperate bluntness.*) You've made a career of flirtation. Obviously Paula isn't going to. You know you and Paula belong to different worlds. (*With some heat.*) And the reason Paula is the way she is is because she lives in an atmosphere of perpetual conflict.

LEONIE. Conflict? Paula?

SAM. With herself. About you.

LEONIE. (*Rising.*) That's too subtle for me, I'm afraid.

SAM. Paula's unaware of it herself.

LEONIE. Where did you acquire this amazing psychological insight? You never used to have it. Of course! From Selena. Of course!

SAM. I've never discussed this with Selena.

LEONIE. No?

SAM. She's told me she'd be happy to have Paula but . . .

LEONIE. That's extremely generous of her —to offer without discussion. . . .

SAM. (*She has him there; he loses his temper.*) It's impossible for you to consider anything without being personal.

LEONIE. I am afraid it is. I don't live on this wonderful rarefied, intellectual plane inhabited by Selena and yourself—and where you want to take Paula. I'm sorry if I've made Paula serious, I'm sorry she's in a perpetual conflict about me. I'm sorry I've let her in for—this sort of thing! I'm sorry! (*She is on the verge of tears. She runs out.*)

SAM. Leonie . . . ! (*He follows her to door back, calling.*) Leonie! (*But it is too late. She is gone. He turns back into room.*) Damn! (PAULA *comes in—from beach, door right.*)

PAULA. Where's Leonie?

SAM. She just went upstairs.

PAULA. I've been showing Dr. Rice our rock-bound coast.

SAM. What's he like?

PAULA. Hard to say. He's almost too sympathetic. At the same time—

SAM. What?

PAULA. At the same time—he is inscrutable! I can't tell whether I like him or dislike him. You say Selena knows him. What does she say about him?

SAM. Selena isn't crazy about him.

PAULA. Why not?

SAM. Brilliant charlatan, she says—also a charmer.

PAULA. I gather that, and I resent him. How'd you come out with Leonie?

SAM. I've made a mess of it. I'm a fool!

PAULA. My going with you, you mean?

SAM. Yes.

PAULA. Sam . . .

SAM. Yes?

PAULA. Will you mind very much . . .

SAM. What?

PAULA. If I don't go with Selena and you?

SAM. But I thought you said—and especially if she marries somebody—

PAULA. (*Slowly.*) That's just what I'm thinking of—

SAM. What's happened?

PAULA. There's no way out of it, Sam— I've got to stay.

SAM. But why?

PAULA. (*Simply, looking up at him.*) Somebody's got to look after Leonie. . . . (KENNETH *enters.*)

KENNETH. My first glimpse of Maine. A masculine Riviera.

PAULA. It's mild now. If you want to see it really virile—come in the late fall.

KENNETH. You've only to crook your little finger. I'll be glad to look at more of Maine whenever you have the time. (*Sits, facing her.*)

PAULA. Of course. Tomorrow?

KENNETH. Yes. Tomorrow. (*To* SAM.) You know, from Mrs. Frothingham's description— (*Looking back at* PAULA, *intently.*) I never could have imagined her. Not remotely. (ROBERT *enters.*)

SAM. What is it, Robert?

ROBERT. Mrs. Frothingham would like to see Dr. Rice in her study.

KENNETH. (*Rising.*) Oh, thank you. (*He walks to door back.*) Excuse me. (*He goes upstairs.* PAULA *and* SAM *have continued looking front. As* KENNETH *starts upstairs they slowly turn and look at one another. The same thought has crossed both their minds—they both find themselves looking suddenly into a new and dubious vista.*)

Curtain

ACT TWO
SCENE I

SCENE: *The same.*

Time: *Midsummer—late afternoon.*

At Rise: KENNETH *is at a bridge table working out a chess problem. He hears voices and footsteps approaching. Gets up, unhurried, and looks off into garden. Sees* BORIS *and* LEONIE *approaching. As they come in he strolls off—they do not see him.* LEONIE's *arms are full of flowers. She is looking for* KENNETH. COUNT MIRSKY *follows her in.*

COUNT MIRSKY, *a Russian, is very good-looking, mongoloid about the eyes. His English is beautiful, with a slight and attractive accent. He is tense, jittery—a mass of jangled nerves—his fingers tremble as he lights one cigarette after another. He is very pale—his pallor accentuated by a dark scarf he wears around his neck.*

BORIS. (*Stopping center.*) It appears he is not here either.

LEONIE. He? Who? (*Crossing to table behind sofa to put some flowers in vase.*)

BORIS. When you're in the garden with me you think—perhaps he is in the house. When you are in the house you think perhaps he is in the garden.

LEONIE. Boris, darling, you have the odd habit of referring to mysterious characters without giving me any hint who they are. Is that Russian symbolism? There will be a long silence; then you will say: He would not approve, or they can't hear us. It's a bit mystifying.

BORIS. (*Crossing to stand near her.*) You know who I mean.

LEONIE. (*Going to table right to put flowers in vase.*) Really, you flatter me. I'm not a mystic, you know, Boris. I'm a simple extrovert. When you say "he," why can't it refer to someone definite— and if possible to someone I know.

BORIS. (*Crossing to back of table, facing her across it.*) You know him, all right.

LEONIE. There you go again! *Really,* Boris!

BORIS. (*Moving closer to her around table.*) You've been divorced now for several weeks. You're free. We were only waiting for you to be free—

LEONIE. (*Moving away, sitting in chair, right.*) Now that I am free you want to coerce me. It's a bit unreasonable, don't you think? (BORIS *walks to end of window-seat and sits.*) (*Enter* KENNETH, *door back.*)

KENNETH. (*Strolling across stage toward* LEONIE.) Hello, Leonie. Count Mirsky—

LEONIE. Kenneth—I haven't seen you all day.

KENNETH. I've been in my room slaving away at a scientific paper.

LEONIE. My house hums with creative activity. I love it. It gives me a sense of vicarious importance. What's your paper on?

KENNETH. Shadow-neurosis.

LEONIE. Shadow-neurosis. How marvelous! What does it mean?

KENNETH (*Looking at* BORIS.) It is a sensation of non-existence.

LEONIE. Is it common?

KENNETH. Quite. The victim knows that he exists and yet he feels that he does not!

LEONIE. In a curious way I can imagine a sensation like that—do you know I actually can. Isn't it amusing?

BORIS. The doctor is so eloquent. Once he describes a sensation it becomes very easy to feel it.

LEONIE. That's an entrancing gift. Why are you so antagonistic to Kenneth? He wants to help you but you won't let him. I asked him here to help you.

KENNETH. (*To* BORIS.) Your skepticism about this particular disease is interesting, Count Mirsky, because, as it happens, you suffer from it.

BORIS. (*Bearing down on* KENNETH.) Has it ever occurred to you that you are a wasted novelist?

KENNETH. Though I have not mentioned you in my article I have described you.

LEONIE. (*Rising and crossing left to table behind sofa.*) You should be flattered, Boris.

BORIS. I am!

LEONIE. Another case history! I've been reading some of Kenneth's scientific textbooks. Most fascinating form of biography. Who was that wonderful fellow who did such odd things—Mr. X.? You'd never think you could get so interested in anonymous people. I'd have given anything to meet Mr. X.—though I must say I'd feel a bit nervous about having him in the house.

KENNETH. How is your book getting along, Count Mirsky?

BORIS. Very well. Oh—so—

KENNETH. Far along in it?

BORIS. Quite.

LEONIE. I'm crazy to see it. He's dedicating it to me but he hasn't let me see a word of it!

KENNETH. For a very good reason.

LEONIE. What do you mean?

KENNETH. Because there is no book. There never has been a book.

LEONIE. (*She lets flowers drop.*) Kenneth!

KENNETH. Isn't that true, Count Mirsky?

BORIS. It is not!

KENNETH. Then why don't you let us see a bit of it?

LEONIE. Oh, do! At least the dedication page.

KENNETH. A chapter—

BORIS. Because it isn't finished yet.

LEONIE. Well, it doesn't have to be finished. We know the end, don't we? The end belongs to the world.

KENNETH. Let us see it, Count.

BORIS. I can't.

KENNETH. What are you calling the book?

BORIS. I haven't decided yet.

KENNETH. May I suggest a title to you—?

LEONIE. Oh, do! What shall we call it, Kenneth?

KENNETH. "The Memoirs of a Boy Who Wanted to Murder His Father."

LEONIE. What!

BORIS. (*Gripping arms of chair.*) I am not a hysterical woman, Doctor—and I'm not your patient!

LEONIE. But Kenneth—Boris worshipped his father.

KENNETH. No, he hated him. He hated him when he was alive and he hates him still. He grew up under the overwhelming shadow of this world-genius whom, in spite of an immense desire to emulate and even surpass—he felt he could never emulate and never surpass—nor even equal — Did you worship your father, Count Mirsky?

BORIS. It's true! I hated him!

LEONIE. Boris!

BORIS. I hated him!

KENNETH. Now you can let us see the book, can't you—now that we know the point of view—just a bit of it?

LEONIE. I'm more crazy than ever to see it now. I can tell you a little secret now, Boris. I was afraid—I was rather afraid—that your book would be a little like one of those statues of an ancestor in a frock-coat. Now it sounds really exciting. You hated him. But how perfectly marvelous! I can't wait to see it now. Do run up to your study and bring it down, Boris—do!

BORIS. No.

LEONIE. That's very unpleasant of you.

BORIS. You might as well know it then. There isn't any book. There never will be. Not by me.

LEONIE. But I don't understand—every day—in your room working—all these months!

BORIS. (*Facing her.*) One wants privacy! Possibly you can't realize that. You who always have to have a house full of people.

LEONIE. (*Goes back to flowers at table.*) Boris!

KENNETH. (*Rising.*) Why don't you write the book anyway, Count Mirsky? There is a vogue these days for vituperative biography.

BORIS. I am not interested in the vogue.

KENNETH. We are quite used nowadays to children who dislike their fathers. The public—

BORIS. To titillate the public would not compensate me for forcing myself to recall the atmosphere of saintly sadism in which my childhood was spent—I can still smell that living room, I can still smell those stinking, sexless pilgrims who used to come from all over the world to get my saintly father's blessing. I used to sit with my mother in a room no bigger than a closet to get away from the odor of that nauseating humanitarianism. There was no privacy in the Villa Mirskovitch. Oh, no—it was a Mecca—do you understand—a Mecca!

KENNETH. Yes, I think I understand.

BORIS. Well, I have been paying the haloed one back. I have been getting privacy at his expense at last.

LEONIE. Why have you never told me before that you felt this way about your father?

BORIS. I never said anything about him. It was you who did the talking. You always raved about the great man with that characteristic American enthusiasm for what you don't know.

LEONIE. Nevertheless, the world recognizes your father as a great man. The books are there to prove it. There they are. You can't write books like that without greatness—no matter what you say. You are a petulant child. Your father was a great man.

BORIS. It makes no difference how great he was—those pilgrims stank! (LEONIE *turns away.*)

KENNETH. I suggest that to write that book, even if no one ever sees the manuscript but you, might amuse you—a kind of revenge which, when you were a boy, you were in no position to take.

BORIS. Are you trying to cure me, Doctor? Please don't trouble. I don't need your particular species of professionalism. I do not need any help from you. (*He goes to door back, turns to* LEONIE. LEONIE *looks bewilderedly at* KENNETH. BORIS *goes out.*)

LEONIE. How did you know? You're uncanny!

KENNETH. All in the day's work.

LEONIE. Why is it I always get myself involved with men weaker than myself? I certainly am no tower of strength.

KENNETH. Possibly not—but you are generous and impulsive. You have a tendency to accept people at the best of their own valuation.

LEONIE. I want to help them. I do help them. After they get used to my help, after they get to count on my help, I get impatient with them. Why, I ask myself, can't people help themselves?

KENNETH. And very natural.

LEONIE. I seem to attract people like that!

KENNETH. Leonie—you are the last woman on earth Count Mirsky should marry. He would only transfer his hatred of his father to you.

LEONIE. I don't think I understand you, Kenneth—really I don't—and I do so want to understand things.

KENNETH. Well—your charm, your gaiety, your position, your wealth, your beauty—these would oppress him. Again, he cannot be himself.—Or, if he is himself, it is to reveal his nonentity, his inferiority—again the secondary rôle—Leonie Frothingham's husband—the son of Count Mirsky—the husband of Leonie Frothingham. Again the shadow—again, eternally and always—nonexistence. Poor fellow. (*Pause*.)

LEONIE. I'm so grateful to you, Kenneth.

KENNETH. Nonsense. You mustn't be grateful to me because I—exercise my profession.

LEONIE. I want to express my gratitude—in some tangible form. I've been thinking of nothing else lately. I can't sleep for thinking of it.

KENNETH. Well, if it gives you insomnia, you'd better tell me about it.

LEONIE. I want to make it possible for you to realize your ambition.

KENNETH. Ambition? What ambition?

LEONIE. Ah! You've forgotten, haven't you? But you let it slip out one day—you pump me professionally—but I do the same to you—non-professionally.

KENNETH. You terrify me!

LEONIE. That night last winter when we went to dinner in that little restaurant where you go with your doctor friends... you told me your dream.

KENNETH. My censor must have been napping.

LEONIE. He was. Or she was. What sex is your censor?

KENNETH. That's none of your business.

LEONIE. I'm sorry.

KENNETH. Which of my dreams was I so reckless as to reveal to you?

LEONIE. To have a sanatorium of your own one day—so you can carry out your own ideas of curing patients.

KENNETH. Oh, that! Out of the question.

LEONIE. Why?

KENNETH. To do it on the scale I visualize, would cost more than I'm ever likely to save out of my practice.

LEONIE. I'll give you the sanatorium. I've never given anyone anything like that before. What fun!

KENNETH. Will I find it all wrapped up in silver foil on Christmas morning?

LEONIE. Yes. You will! You will! We'll have a suite in it for Mr. X.—for all your anonymous friends—we'll entertain the whole alphabet!

KENNETH. You see, Leonie!

LEONIE. What do you mean? I thought you'd be—

KENNETH. Of course, it's terribly generous of you. I'm deeply touched. But . . .

LEONIE. But . . . ?

KENNETH. I'm a stranger to you.

LEONIE. Kenneth!

KENNETH. Outside of my professional relation—such as I have with scores of patients—little more than that.

LEONIE. I thought—

KENNETH. And yet you are willing to back me in a venture that would cost a sizeable fortune—just on that. Leonie! Leonie!

LEONIE. It would be the best investment I've ever made. Paula's always telling me I have no social consciousness. Well, this would be.—It would keep me from feeling so useless. I do feel useless, Kenneth. Please!

KENNETH. I'm sorry. I couldn't hear of it. Of course, it's out of the question.

LEONIE. It isn't. I can afford it. Why shouldn't I? It would be helping so many people—you have no right to refuse. It's selfish of you to refuse.

KENNETH. I distrust impulsive altruism. You will forgive me, Leonie, but it may often do harm.

LEONIE. How do you mean, Kenneth?

KENNETH. I gather you are about to endow a radical magazine for the *boys*—

LEONIE. Will and Dennis! I thought it would be nice to give them something to do!

KENNETH. Yes. You are prepared to back them in a publication which, if it attained any influence, would undermine the system which makes you and your people like you possible.

LEONIE. But it never occurred to me anyone would read it.

KENNETH. There is a deplorably high literacy in this country. Unfortunately it is much easier to learn to read than it is to learn to think.

LEONIE. Well, if you don't think it's a good idea, Kenneth, I won't do it. But this sanatorium is different.

KENNETH. Why?

LEONIE. Because, if you must know it, it would be helping you—and that means everything in the world to me. There, I've said it. It's true! Kenneth—are you terrified?

KENNETH. You adorable child!

LEONIE. It's extraordinary, Kenneth—but you are the first strong man who's ever come into my life—(*Enter* PAULA, DENNIS, WILL, *door back.*) Oh, I'm very glad to see you! Will! Hullo, Dennis. You all know Dr. Rice. Mr. Dexter, Mr. McCarthy. Sit down, everybody. Well, children, how is New York? (DENNIS *crosses down front of them to chair left by sofa and sits.*)

WILL. Stifling, thank you.

LEONIE. Any luck yet?

WILL. I am available, but New York is dead to its chief opportunity.

LEONIE. Then you can stay here for a bit. You can both stay here.

DENNIS. That was all right when we were in college, Mrs. Frothingham. Can't do it now.

LEONIE. Oh, you're working. I'm so glad!

DENNIS. I beg your pardon. Did you say working?

LEONIE. Well, then! I don't see why you can't stay here and take a holiday.

WILL. From what?

LEONIE. Since none of you are doing anything in town, you might as well stay here and do nothing and be comfortable.

DENNIS. Yes, but it's an ethical question. When we're in New York doing nothing, we belong to the most respectable vested group going! The unemployed. As such we have a status, position, authority. But if we stay here doing nothing—what are we? Low-down parasites.

KENNETH. No jobs about anywhere, eh?

WILL. Extinct commodity.

DENNIS. I did pretty well last week.

LEONIE. Really?

DENNIS. I was rejected by seven newspapers—including the *Bronx Home News* and the *Yonkers Herald*—six magazines and trade papers—a total of twenty-eight rejections in all, representing a net gain over the previous week of seven solid rejections. I submit to you, gentlemen, that's progress—pass the cigars, Will.

LEONIE. Couldn't you stay here and be rejected by mail?

DENNIS. Doesn't give you that same feeling somehow—that good, rich, dark-brown sensation of not being wanted!

LEONIE. You know, Kenneth, in a curious way, Dennis reminds me a bit of Mr. X.

DENNIS. And who's X.?

LEONIE. A sporting acquaintance.

DENNIS. There's one thing I'd like to ask Dr. Rice. . . . Do you mind?

KENNETH. At your service

DENNIS. (*Turning chair and facing* KENNETH *upstage.*) In the psychoanalytic hierarchy Freud is the god, isn't he?

KENNETH. Of one sect, yes.

DENNIS. Well, the original sect—

KENNETH. Yes. . . .

DENNIS. Now, every psychoanalyst has to have himself analyzed. That's true, isn't it, Doctor?

KENNETH. Generally speaking—yes.

DENNIS. As I understand it, the highest prices go to those nearest the Master himself.

KENNETH. This boy is irreverent . . .

DENNIS. I know whereof I speak. I prepared an article on the subject for *Fortune.*

WILL. Rejection number three hundred.

DENNIS. I am afraid, Will, that you are a success worshipper!

LEONIE. Dennis is an *enfant terrible,* and he exhausts himself keeping it up!

DENNIS. I have examined the racket with a microscopic patience and this I find to be true: at the top of the hierarchy is the Great Pan Sexualist of Vienna. To be an orthodox and accepted Freudian, you must have been analyzed by another of the same. Now what I am burning to know is this: Who analyzed Sig Freud himself? Whom does he tell his repressions to? Why, the poor guy must be lonely as hell!

LEONIE. What would you do with him, Kenneth? He has no repressions whatever!

KENNETH. He needs some badly.

LEONIE. I wonder what Dennis would confess to his psychoanalyst that he isn't always shouting to the world?

DENNIS. I'd make the psychoanalyst talk. (*To* KENNETH. *Beckoning.*) Tell me, Doctor, what did you dream last night?

KENNETH. (*Behind his cupped hand.*) Not in public.

DENNIS. (*Rises and crosses straight right.*) You see—he's repressed! I tell you these psychoanalysts are repressed. They've got nobody to talk to! I'm going swimming. It's pathetic! (*He goes out.*)

LEONIE. I'm going too. He makes me laugh. How about you, Kenneth?

KENNETH. Oh, I'll watch.

LEONIE. (*To others.*) Come along with us. There's plenty of time for a swim before dinner. (KENNETH *starts out with* LEONIE.....*stops on the way.*)

KENNETH. I suppose you and your Irish friend edited the comic paper at college?

WILL. No, we edited the serious paper.

KENNETH. Just the same it must have been very funny. (*He goes out after* LEONIE.)

WILL. Don't think that feller likes me much.

PAULA. You're psychic.

WILL. Well, for the matter of that I'm not crazy about him either.

PAULA. Don't bother about him. Concentrate on me!

WILL. How are you, darling?

PAULA. Missed you.

WILL. (*Pulls her to sofa and sits with her.* PAULA *left end sofa.*) And I you. Pretty lousy in town without you.

PAULA. Oh, poor darling!

WILL. Although my star is rising. I did some book-reviews for the New York *Times* and the *New Masses.*

PAULA. What a gamut!

WILL. I made, in fact, a total of eleven dollars. The student most likely to succeed in the first four months since graduation has made eleven dollars.

PAULA. Wonderful!

WILL. My classmates were certainly clairvoyant. As a matter of fact, I shouldn't have told you. Now I'll be tortured thinking you're after me for my money.

PAULA. You'll never know!

WILL. (*Putting arm around her shoulders and drawing her to him.*) What've you been doing?

PAULA. Lying in the sun mostly.

WILL. Poor little Ritz girl.

PAULA. Wondering what you do every night.

WILL. Forty-second Street Library mostly. Great fun! Voluptuary atmosphere!

PAULA. Is your life altogether so austere?

WILL. Well, frankly, no. Not altogether.

PAULA. Cad!

WILL. What do you expect?

PAULA. Loyalty.

WILL. I am loyal. But you go around all day job-hunting. You find you're not wanted. It's reassuring after that to find a shoulder to lean on, sort of haven where you *are* wanted. Even the public library closes at ten. You have to go somewhere. If I'm ever Mayor of New York, I'll have the public libraries kept open all night ... the flop-houses of the intellectuals!

PAULA. Is it anyone special . . . ?

WILL. Just a generalized shoulder.

PAULA. Well, you're going to have a special one from now on—mine! You know, the way you're avoiding the issue is all nonsense.

WILL. You mean my gallant fight against you?

PAULA. I've decided that you are conventional and bourgeois. You're money-ridden.

WILL. Eleven dollars. They say a big income makes you conservative.

PAULA. I don't mean your money. I mean —my money. It's childish to let an artificial barrier like that stand between us. It's also childish to ignore it.

WILL. (*Rising.*) I don't ignore it. That's what worries me. I count on it. Already I find myself counting on it. I can't help it. Sitting and waiting in an office for some bigwig who won't see me or for some underling who won't see me I think: "Why the Hell should I wait all day for this stuffed shirt?" I don't wait. Is it because of you I feel in a special category? Do I count on your money? Is that why I don't wait as long as the other fellow? There's one consolation: the other fellow doesn't get the job either. But the point is disquieting!

PAULA. What a Puritan you are!

WILL. (*Sitting beside her again.*) Will I become an appendage to you—like your mother's men?

PAULA. You're bound to—money or no money.

WILL. (*Taking her into his arms.*) I suppose I might as well go on the larger dole—

PAULA. What?

WILL. Once you are paid merely for existing—you are on the dole. I rather hoped, you know—

PAULA. What?

WILL. It's extraordinary the difference in one's thinking when you're in college and when you're out—

PAULA. How do you mean?

WILL. Well, when I was in college, my interest in the—"movement"—was really impersonal. I imagined myself giving my energies to the poor and the downtrodden in my spare time. I didn't really believe I'd be one of the poor and downtrodden myself. In my heart of hearts I was sure I'd break through the iron law of Dennis's statistics and land a job somewhere. But I can't—and it's given a tremendous jolt to my self-esteem.

PAULA. But you'll come through. I'm sure of it. I wish you could learn to look at my money as a means rather than an end.

WILL. I'd rather use my own.

PAULA. You're proud.

WILL. I am.

PAULA. It's humiliating but I'm afraid I've got to ask you to marry me, Will.

WILL. It's humiliating but considering my feelings I see no way out of accepting you.

PAULA. You submit?

WILL. (*Kissing her hand.*) I submit.

PAULA. After a hard campaign—victory!

WILL. You *are* a darling.

PAULA. (*Getting up and crossing to center.*) I can't tell you what a relief it'll be to get away from this house.

WILL. Why?

PAULA. I don't know. It's getting very complicated.

WILL. Leonie?

PAULA. *And* Boris. *And* Dr. Rice. Funny thing how that man . . .

WILL. What?

PAULA. Makes you insecure somehow.

WILL. Supposed to do just the opposite.

PAULA. He answers every question—and yet he's secretive. I've never met a man who—who—

WILL. Who what?

PAULA. Really, I can't stand Dr. Rice.

WILL. I believe he fascinates you.

PAULA. He does. I don't deny that. And I can't tell you how I resent it. Isn't it silly? (*The old lady* WYLER *in a wheel chair is propelled in by a nurse. The old lady is much wasted since the preceding summer; she is touched with mortality.*) Granny!

MRS. WYLER. Paula! How are you, my dear?

PAULA. I came up to see you before, but you were asleep.

MRS. WYLER. Nurse told me. (*Exit* NURSE, *door left.*)

PAULA. You remember Will?

WILL. How do you do, Mrs. Wyler?

MRS. WYLER. Of course. How do you do, young man?

PAULA. Well, this is quite an adventure for you, isn't it, Granny?

MRS. WYLER. You're the boy who was always so curious about my youth.

WILL. Yes.

MRS. WYLER. I've forgotten most of it. Now I just live from day to day. The past is just this morning. (*A moment's pause.*) And I don't always remember that very well. Aren't there insects who live only one day? The morning is their youth and the afternoon their middle age. . . .

PAULA. You don't seem yourself today. Not as cheerful as usual.

MRS. WYLER. Can't I have my moods, Paula? I am pleased to be reflective today. People are always sending me funny books to read. I've been reading one and it depressed me.

PAULA. Well, I'll tell you something to cheer you up, Granny—Will and I are going to be married.

MRS. WYLER. Have you told your mother?

PAULA. Not yet. It's a secret. (*Enter* KENNETH.)

KENNETH. Well, Mrs. Wyler! Wanderlust today?

MRS. WYLER. Yes! Wanderlust!

KENNETH. Paula, if you're not swimming, what about our walk, and our daily argument?

MRS. WYLER. What argument?

KENNETH. Paula is interested in my subject. She hovers between skepticism and fascination.

PAULA. No chance to hover today, Kenneth. Will's improving his tennis. Sorry.

KENNETH. So am I.

MRS. WYLER. I've a surprise for you, Paula.

PAULA. What?

MRS. WYLER. Your father's coming.

PAULA. No!

MRS. WYLER. Yes.

PAULA. But how—! How do you know?

MRS. WYLER. Because I've sent for him, and he wired me he's coming. He's driving from Blue Hill. He should be here now.

PAULA. That's too—! Oh, Granny, that's marvelous! Will, let's drive out to meet him, shall we? Does Mother know?

MRS. WYLER. I only had Sam's wire an hour ago.

PAULA. Granny, you're an angel.

MRS. WYLER. Not quite yet. Don't hurry me, child.

PAULA. Come on, Will. (*Exit* PAULA *and* WILL.)

MRS. WYLER. I can see you are interested in Paula. You are, aren't you, Dr. Rice?

KENNETH. Yes. She's an extraordinary child. Adores her father, doesn't she?

MRS. WYLER. How would you cure that, Doctor?

KENNETH It's quite healthy.

MRS. WYLER. Really? I was hoping for something juicy in the way of interpretation.

KENNETH. Sorry!

MRS. WYLER. What an interesting profession yours is, Dr. Rice.

KENNETH. Why particularly?

MRS. WYLER. Your province is the soul. Strange region.

KENNETH. People's souls, I find are, on the whole, infinitely more interesting than their bodies. I have been a general practitioner and I know.

MRS. WYLER. These young people—don't they frighten you?

KENNETH. Frighten!

MRS. WYLER. They are so radical—prepared to throw everything overboard—every tradition—

KENNETH. Paula's friends have nothing to lose, any change would be—in the nature of velvet for them.

MRS. WYLER. What do you think of Will?

KENNETH. I'm afraid I've formed no strongly defined opinion on Will.

MRS. WYLER. Oh, I see— That is a comment in itself.

KENNETH. He's nondescript.

MRS. WYLER. Do you mean to point that out to Paula?

KENNETH. I don't think so. That won't be necessary.

MRS. WYLER. Why not?

KENNETH. Blood will tell.

MRS. WYLER. That's very gracious of you, Doctor. (*Pause.*) And what do you think of Leonie?

KENNETH. Very endearing—and very impulsive.

MRS. WYLER. For example—I mean of the latter—

KENNETH. She offered to build me a sanatorium—a fully equipped modern sanatorium.

MRS. WYLER. Did she? Convenient for you.

KENNETH. Except that I refused.

MRS. WYLER. Wasn't that quixotic?

KENNETH. Not necessarily. (PAULA *and* SAM *enter, door back.*)

PAULA. Here he is!

MRS. WYLER. Sam!

SAM. Louise!

PAULA. He wouldn't come if I'd ask him. He said so shamelessly. You know Dr. Rice?

SAM. Of course.

KENNETH. Excuse me. (KENNETH *goes out*)

SAM. Well, Louise!

MRS. WYLER. Hello, Sam. (SAM *kisses her.*)

SAM. How's she behaving?

PAULA. Incorrigible. Dr. Prentiss tells her to rest in her room You see how she obeys him. She'll obey you though.

SAM. Well, I'll sneak her away from Dr. Prentiss and take her abroad.

MRS. WYLER. I want to go to Ethiopia. Run along, dear. I want to talk to Sam.

PAULA. Keep him here, Granny. Pretend you're not feeling well.

MRS. WYLER. I'll try. (*Exit* PAULA *door back*.) Well, Sam—

SAM. I got your wire last night. Here I am.

MRS. WYLER. It's nice of you.

SAM. Oh, now, Louise. You know you're the love of my life.

MRS. WYLER. Yes, Sam, I know—but how is Selena?

SAM. Flourishing.

MRS. WYLER. You're all right then?

SAM. Unbelievably.

MRS. WYLER. I knew you would be.

SAM. And you?

MRS. WYLER. I'm dying, Sam.

SAM. Not you—

MRS. WYLER. Don't contradict me. Besides, I'm rather looking forward to it.

SAM. Is Dr. Prentiss—?

MRS. WYLER. Dr. Prentiss soft-soaps me. I let him. It relieves his mind. But that's why I've sent for you.

SAM. You know, my dear—

MRS. WYLER. Yes, Sam. I know I can count on you. I'm dying. And I'm dying alone. I have to talk to somebody. You're the only one.

SAM. Is anything worrying you?

MRS. WYLER. Plenty.

SAM. What, dear?

MRS. WYLER. The future. Not my own. That's fixed or soon will be. But Leonie's—Paula's—

SAM. Aren't they all right?

MRS. WYLER. I am surrounded by aliens. The house is full of strangers. That Russian upstairs; this doctor.

SAM. Rice? Are you worried about him?

MRS. WYLER. What is he after? What does he want? He told me Leonie offered to build him a sanatorium—

SAM. Did he accept it?

MRS. WYLER. No. He refused. But something tells me he will allow himself to be persuaded.

SAM. I don't think Rice is a bad feller really. Seems pretty sensible. Are you worried about this boy—Dexter, and Paula?

MRS. WYLER. Not in the same way. I like the boy. But Paula—I'm worried about what the money'll do to her. We know what it's done to Leonie. You know, Sam, in spite of all her romantic dreams Leonie has a kind of integrity. But I often wonder if she's ever been really happy.

SAM. Oh, now, Louise, this pessimism's unlike you—

MRS. WYLER. This money we've built our lives on—it used to symbolize security—but there's no security in it any more.

SAM. Paul'll be all right. I count on Paula.

MRS. WYLER. In the long run. But that may be too late. One can't let go of everything, Sam. It isn't in nature. That's why I've asked you to come. I want you to remain as executor under my will.

SAM. Well, I only resigned because—since I'm no longer married to Leonie—

MRS. WYLER. What has that got to do with it?

SAM. All right.

MRS. WYLER. Promise?

SAM. Certainly.

MRS. WYLER. I feel something dark ahead, a terror—

SAM. Now, now, you've been brooding.

MRS. WYLER. Outside of you—Will is the soundest person I'll leave behind me, the healthiest—but in him too I feel a reckless-ness that's just kept in—I see a vista of the unknown—to us the unknown was the West, land—physical hardship—but he's hard and bitter underneath his jocularity—he isn't sure, he says, what he is— Once he is sure, what will he do?—I want you to watch him, Sam, for Paula's sake.

SAM. I will.

MRS. WYLER. They're all strange and dark . . . And this doctor. A soul doctor. We didn't have such things—I am sure that behind all this is a profound and healing truth. But sometimes truths may be per-verted, and this particular doctor—how are we to know where his knowledge ends and his pretension begins? Now that I am dy-ing, for the first time in my life I know fear. Death seems easy and simple, Sam—a self-indulgence—but can I afford it? (*She smiles up at him. He squeezes her hand.*)

SAM. Everything will be all right. Trust me.

MRS. WYLER. I do. (*A pause.*) You'll stay the night?

SAM. Of course.

MRS. WYLER. Now I feel better.

SAM. That's right. (*Pause.*)

MRS. WYLER. I'd like to live till autumn.

SAM. Of course you will. Many autumns.

MRS. WYLER. Heaven forbid. But this au-tumn. The color— the leaves turn. (*Look-ing out window.* SAM *looks too.*) The ex-pression seems strange. What do they turn to?

SAM. (*Softly, helping her mood.*) Their mother. The earth.

MRS. WYLER. I'm happy now. I'm at peace.

SAM. (*Puts arm around her and draws her to him.*) That's better.

MRS. WYLER. (*Smiling up at him.*) It's very clever of me to have sent for you, Sam. I'm pleased with myself. Now, Sam, let 'em do their worst—

SAM. (*Smiling back at her and patting her hand.*) Just let 'em . . . !

Curtain

SCENE II

SCENE: *The same.*

Time: A few hours later—before dinner. LEONIE *is standing in doorway looking out.* BORIS *center; he is fatalistically quiet at first.*

BORIS. What it comes to is this then! You're through with me. You want me to go!

LEONIE. I'm no good to you! I can no longer help you.

BORIS. Frustrated altruist!

LEONIE. You hate me!

BORIS. That would be encouraging!

LEONIE. We have nothing more for each other.

BORIS. Less than we had in the beginning!

LEONIE. Less than I thought we had.

BORIS. (*Walking toward her.*) And the man of science?

LEONIE. What?

BORIS. (*Still bearing down on her.*) This intricate man of science. You fluctuate so, Leonie. (*Facing her.*)

LEONIE. Please, Boris. I've failed. Can't we part—beautifully?

BORIS. What do you want to do? Go out on the bay and say farewell before the villagers in a barge drawn by a flock of swans? Shall we have a little orchestra to play—with the strings sobbing—and the bassoon off key?

LEONIE. You are bitter and cruel. Why? I've tried to help you. Why are you bitter?

BORIS. (*Moving close to her.*) At least I'm honest. Can you say the same?

LEONIE. (*Breaking away from him.*) I don't know what you mean by that.

BORIS. (*Getting in front of her.*) Yes, you do.

LEONIE. You're eating yourself up. You're killing yourself. There's the great lovely world outside and you sit in your room hating—

BORIS. What do you recommend? Cold showers and Swedish massage? What does the man of science prescribe for me?

LEONIE. Why do you hate Kenneth so?

BORIS. I'm jealous, my dear!

LEONIE. Poor Boris. You're beyond a simple emotion like that, aren't you?

BORIS. I envy you, Leonie. All like you.

LEONIE. Do you?

BORIS. I envy all sentimental liars who gratify their desires on high principle. It makes all your diversions an exercise in piety. You're sick of me and want to sleep with the man of science. (LEONIE *turns away. He seizes her arms and turns her to him.*) Does this suffice for you? No. It must be that you can no longer help me. (*Little silent laugh.*) My sainted father was like that! God!

LEONIE. This is the end, Boris.

BORIS. Of course it is. I tell you this though: Beware of him, Leonie. Beware of him.

LEONIE. Your hatred of Kenneth—like all your hatreds—they're unnatural, frightening. I'm frightened of you. (*Turning from him.*)

BORIS. (*Crossing before her, closing door so she can't escape.*) Much better to be frightened of him. You know what I think. What does he think? Does he tell you? Do you know?

LEONIE. Yes, I know.

BORIS. You know what he tells you. This clairvoyant who gets rich profoundly analyzing the transparent. (*Enter* KENNETH, *door back.*)

KENNETH. Your mother would like to see you, Leonie.

LEONIE. Is she all right? (BORIS *goes upstage to small table. Gets cigarette.*)

KENNETH. Oh, very chipper. Mr. Frothingham is with her.

LEONIE. She sent for Sam, didn't she? I wonder why.

BORIS. Perhaps she felt the situation too complicated—even for *you,* Dr. Rice.

KENNETH. I don't think so.

BORIS. You are so Olympian, Dr. Rice. Would it be possible to anger you?

KENNETH. Symptoms, my dear Count, never anger me. I study them.

BORIS. Really, you are in a superb position. I quite envy you. One might cut oneself open in front of you—and it would be a symptom. Wouldn't it?

LEONIE. Boris, please—what's the good?

BORIS. (*Crossing slowly to* LEONIE.) You are quite right, my dear, no good—no good in the world. Give your mother this message for me. Tell her that under the circumstances I shall simplify the situation by withdrawing.

LEONIE. You make me very unhappy, Boris.

BORIS. How agreeable then that you have Dr. Rice here—to resolve your unhappiness. (*Crosses quickly to table behind sofa and puts out cigarette.*)

LEONIE. (*Following him.*) Where will you be in case I—in case you—Boris?

BORIS. Don't worry about me. A magazine syndicate has offered me a great deal for *sentimental* reminiscences of my father. Imagine that, sentimental! They have offered me—charming Americanism—a ghost-writer. It will be quaint—one ghost collaborating with another ghost. (*Raising hand like Greek priest.*) My blessings, Leonie. (*Kisses her hand.*) You have been charming. Dr. Rice— (*He bows formally. Exit* BORIS.)

LEONIE. Poor Boris— (*She sinks into a chair, overcome.*)

KENNETH. He's part of the past. You must forget him.

LEONIE. Poor Boris!

KENNETH. You will forget him.

LEONIE. I'll try.

KENNETH. Exorcised!

LEONIE. You know, Kenneth, I feel you are the only one in the world I can count on.

KENNETH. Not me.

LEONIE. Whom else?

KENNETH. Yourself!

LEONIE. Light reed! Fragile! Fragile!

KENNETH. Pliant but unbreakable.

LEONIE. No. Don't think much of myself, Kenneth. Really I don't. My judgment seems to be at fault somehow. Paula thinks so too. She's always lecturing me. (*Sits right end of sofa.*)

KENNETH. Paula can't abide me.

LEONIE. It's not true!

KENNETH. You know, Leonie, I have an instinct in these matters—so, also, has your daughter.

LEONIE. Don't you like Paula?

KENNETH. I love her. Everyone connected with you.

LEONIE. Kenneth! How dear of you! Of course Paula and I are poles apart. Look at her friends!

KENNETH. Raffish!

LEONIE. (*A little taken aback by this.*) Oh, do you think so? All of them? Don't you like Will?

KENNETH. Nice enough. Clever in his way. With an eye to the main chance.

LEONIE. Really?

KENNETH. Naturally—penniless boy.

LEONIE. I've always encouraged Paula to be independent. I've never tried to impose my ideals or my standards on her. Have I done wrong to give her her own head this way? She's such a darling, really. She's killing, you know. So superior, so knowing. The other day—the other day, Ken-

neth . . . I took her to lunch in town and she criticized me—now what do you think about?

KENNETH. (*Sitting on arm of chair.*) For once my intuition fails me.

LEONIE. About my technique with men. She said it was lousy. Isn't it delicious?

KENNETH. Not more specific than simply lousy?

LEONIE. She said I threw myself at men instead of reversing the process.

KENNETH. But I should think she would have approved of that. She makes such a fetish of being candid!

LEONIE. That's just what I said—exactly. I said I couldn't pretend—that I couldn't descend to—technique. I said that when my feelings were involved I saw no point in not letting the other person see it. I reproached her for deviousness. Strange ideas that child has—strange!

KENNETH. I'm afraid her generation is theory-ridden! (*Pause.*)

LEONIE. Kenneth?

KENNETH. Yes, Leonie?

LEONIE. It's true of course.

KENNETH. What?

LEONIE. Paula's—criticism. I can't conceal my feelings. Least of all—from you. (*Slight pause.*)

KENNETH. Why should you?

LEONIE. Oh, Kenneth, I'm so useless! You know how useless I am!

KENNETH. I know only that you are gracious and lovely—and that you have the gift of innocence.

LEONIE. I hate my life. It's been so scattered—emotionally.

KENNETH. Whose isn't?

LEONIE. You are such a comfort. Really it's too much now to expect me to do without you. Kenneth?

KENNETH. Yes . . . Leonie.

LEONIE Will you be a darling—and marry me?

KENNETH. Leonie?

LEONIE. (*Returning his gaze.*) Yes, Kenneth.

KENNETH. Have you thought this over?

LEONIE. It's the first time—the very first time—that I've ever been sure.

KENNETH. You are so impulsive, Leonie.

LEONIE. Kenneth, don't you think we'd have a chance—you and I—don't you think? (*Enter* PAULA, *door back.*)

PAULA. (*Realizes she has interrupted a tête-à-tête.*) Oh, sorry—!

LEONIE. Paula dear, have you been with Mother?

PAULA. Yes. Granny wants to see you, as a matter of fact.

LEONIE. Oh, I forgot! Is she all right? Cheerful?

PAULA. Oh, very.

LEONIE. I'll be right there. Stay and talk to Kenneth, Paula. He thinks you don't like him. Prove to him it isn't true. Do you think you could be gracious, Paula? Or is that too old-fashioned? (*Exit* LEONIE *door back. In the following scene* PAULA *determines to get rid of the tantalizing and irritating mixed feelings she has about* KENNETH, *her sense of distrusting, disliking and simultaneously being fascinated by him—she feels he has something up his sleeve; she is playing a game to discover what it is and yet she becomes increasingly conscious that game is not unpleasant to her because of her interest in her victim.*)

PAULA. Leonie's all a-flutter. What is it?

KENNETH. She was just telling me—she envies you your poise.

PAULA. Your intentions are honorable, I hope.

KENNETH. Old hat, Paula.

PAULA. I beg your pardon.

KENNETH. Undergraduate audacity. Scott Fitzgerald. Old hat.

PAULA. We don't like each other much, do we?

KENNETH. That's regrettable.

PAULA. And yet—I'm very curious about you.

KENNETH. What would you like to know?

PAULA. Your motive.

KENNETH. Ah!

PAULA. And yet even if you told me—

KENNETH. You wouldn't believe it?

PAULA. (*Facing him.*) No. Now why is that? Even when you are perfectly frank, your frankness seems to me—a device. Now why is that?

KENNETH. I'll tell you.

PAULA. Why?

KENNETH. Because you yourself are confused, muddled, unsure, contradictory. I am simple and co-ordinated. You resent that. You dislike it. You envy it. You would like such simplicity for yourself. But, as you are unlikely to achieve it, you soothe yourself by distrusting me.

PAULA. You say I'm muddled. Why am I muddled?

KENNETH. You've accepted a set of premises without examining them or thinking about them. You keep them like jewels in a box and dangle them. Then you put them back in the box, confident that they belong to you. But as they don't you feel an occasional twinge of insecurity—

PAULA. Do you mind dropping the parables—?

KENNETH. Not at all—

PAULA. Why am I muddled? For example—

KENNETH. You're a walking contradiction in terms—

PAULA. For example?

KENNETH. For example—for example—your radicalism. Your friends. Your point of view. Borrowed. Unexamined. Insincere.

PAULA. Go on.

KENNETH. You are rich and you are exquisite. Why are you rich and exquisite? (*Walking back to face her.*) Because your forbears were not moralistic but ruthless. Had they been moralistic, had they been concerned, as you pretend to be, with the "predatory system"—this awful terminology—you'd be working in a store somewhere wrapping packages or waiting on querulous housewives with bad skins or teaching school. Your own origins won't bear a moralistic investigation. You must know that. Your sociology and economics must teach you that.

PAULA. Suppose I repudiate my origins?

KENNETH. That takes more courage than you have.

PAULA. Don't be so sure.

KENNETH. But why should you? If you had a special talent or were a crusader there might be some sense in it. But you have no special talent and you are not a crusader. Much better to be decorative. Much better for a world starving for beauty. Instead of repudiating your origins you should exult in them and in that same predatory system that made you possible. (*Crossing to table behind sofa for cigarette.*) (*Pause.*)

PAULA. What were your origins?

KENNETH. (*Lighting cigarette.*) Anonymous.

PAULA. What do you mean?

KENNETH. I was discovered on a doorstep.

PAULA. Really?

KENNETH. Like Moses.

PAULA. Where were you brought up?

KENNETH. In a foundling asylum in New England. The place lacked charm. This sounds like an unpromising beginning but actually it was more stimulating than you might imagine. I remember as a kid of twelve going to the library in Springfield and getting down the *Dictionary of National Biography* and hunting out the bastards. Surprising how many distinguished ones there were and are. I allied myself early with the brilliant and variegated company of the illegitimate.

PAULA. You don't know who your parents were?

KENNETH. No.

PAULA. Did you get yourself through college?

KENNETH. *And* medical school.

PAULA. Did you practice medicine?

KENNETH. For a bit. I devoted myself—when the victims would let me—to their noses and throats. It was a starveling occupation. But I gave up tonsilectomy for the soul. The poor have tonsils but only the rich have souls. My instinct was justified—as you see.

PAULA. You've gone pretty far.

KENNETH. Incredible journey!

PAULA. Having come from—from—

KENNETH. The mud—?

PAULA. Well—I should think you'd be more sympathetic to the under-dogs.

KENNETH. No, why should I? The herd bores me. It interests me only as an indication of the distance I've travelled.

PAULA. Will would say that you are a lucky individual who—

KENNETH. Yes, that is what Will would say. It always satisfies the mediocrity to call the exceptional individual lucky.

PAULA. You don't like Will?

KENNETH. I despise him.

PAULA. Why?

KENNETH. I detest these young firebrands whose incandescence will be extinguished by the first job! I detest radicals who lounge about in country-houses.

PAULA. You're unfair to Will.

KENNETH. I have no interest in being fair to him. We were discussing you.

PAULA. You are too persuasive. I don't believe you.

KENNETH. My advice to you is to find out what you want before you commit yourself to young Mr. Dexter.

PAULA. But I have committed myself.

KENNETH. Too bad.

PAULA. For him or for me?

KENNETH. For both of you; but for him particularly.

PAULA. Why?

KENNETH. I see precisely the effect your money will have on him. He will take it and the feeling will grow in him that in having given it you have destroyed what he calls his integrity. He will even come to believe that if not for this quenching of initiative he might have become a flaming leader of the people. At the same time he will be aware that both these comforting alibis are delusions—because he has no integrity to speak of nor any initiative to speak of. Knowing they are lies he will only proclaim them the louder, cling to them the harder. He will hate you as the thief of his character—petty larceny, I must say.

PAULA. (*Jumping up, taking several steps away from him.*) That's a lie.

KENNETH. Will is an American Puritan. A foreigner—Boris, for example—marries money, feeling that he gives value received. Very often he does. But young Dexter will never feel that—and maybe he'll be right.

PAULA. You hate Will.

KENNETH. You flatter him.

PAULA. How did you get to know so much about people? About what they feel and what they will do?

KENNETH. I began by knowing myself—but not lying to myself. (*A silence. He looks at her. He takes in her loveliness. He speaks her name, in a new voice, softly.*) Paula—

PAULA. (*She looks at him fixedly.*) What?

KENNETH. Paula—

PAULA. What?

KENNETH. Do you know me any better now? Do you trust me any better now?

PAULA. I don't know. (*Enter* WILL.)

KENNETH. Paula, Paula, Paula— (PAULA *starts toward door back.*) Don't go, Paula!

WILL. Oughtn't you to be changing for dinner? (PAULA *stops upstage.*) Hello, Doctor. What's the matter?

KENNETH. May I congratulate him?

WILL. What's he been saying?

KENNETH. Paula told me she is going to marry you.

PAULA. The doctor is a cynic.

KENNETH. We were discussing the European and American points of view toward money marriages—There's a great difference. The European fortune-hunter, once he has landed the bag, has no more twinge of conscience than a big-game hunter when he has made his kill. The American—

WILL. Is that what you think I am, Doctor?

KENNETH. (*To* PAULA *amiably.*) You see. He resents the mere phrase. But my dear boy, that is no disgrace. We are all fortune-hunters—

PAULA. (*Pointedly.*) Not all, Kenneth—!

KENNETH. But I see no difference at all between the man who makes a profession of being charming to rich ladies—or any other—specialist. The former is more arduous.

PAULA. Are you defending Will or yourself?

KENNETH. I am generalizing. (*To* WILL.) Congratulations! I admit that to scatter congratulations in this way is glib, but we live in a convention of glibness. Good God, we congratulate people when they marry and when they produce children— we skim lightly over these tremendous hazards— Excuse me. (*Exit* KENNETH.)

WILL. God damn that man!

PAULA. Will!

WILL. I can't stand him—not from the moment I saw him—because he's incapable of disinterestedness himself, h e c a n't imagine it in others. He's the kind of cynical, sneering— He's a marauder. The adventurer with the cure-all. This is just the moment for him. And this is just the place!

PAULA. I've never seen you lose your temper before, Will.

WILL. You know why, don't you?

PAULA. Why?

WILL. Because he's right! While he was talking I felt like hitting him. At the same time a voice inside me said: Can you deny it? When I came in here he was saying your name. He was looking at you —it seems he hasn't quite decided, has he?

PAULA. I'm worried about him and Leonie—

WILL. He's got Leonie hook, line and sinker. That's obvious.

PAULA. She mustn't! Will, she mustn't!

WILL. You can't stop it—you can't do anything for Leonie. Nobody can do anything for anybody. Nobody should try.

PAULA. Will—you mustn't go back to New York. You must stay and help me.

WILL. Sorry. Nothing doing.

PAULA. Will!

WILL. I have a feeling you'll rather enjoy saving Leonie from the doctor.

PAULA. Will! That's not fair, Will!

WILL. It may not be fair but it is obvious. Also, it is obvious that the doctor won't mind being saved.

PAULA. It's lucky for both of us that one of us has some self-control.

WILL. No, I won't stay here. I hate the place, I hate Dr. Rice, I hate myself for being here!

PAULA. Don't let me down, Will—I need you terribly just now—

WILL. (At white heat.) I haven't quite the technique of fortune hunting yet—in the European manner. Which of the two is he after—you or Leonie? Will he flip a coin?

PAULA. I hate you! I hate you!

WILL. Well, we know where we are at any rate.

PAULA. Yes. We do! (LEONIE comes running in. She wears an exquisite summer evening frock. She is breathless with happiness.)

LEONIE. Paula! Why aren't you dressed? I want you to wear something especially lovely tonight! Do you like this? It's new. I haven't worn it before. (She twirls for them.) I've a surprise for you, Will. You'll know what it is in a minute. I was thinking of you and it popped into my mind. You know, Will, I'm very, very fond of you. And I think you are equally fond of me. I can't help liking people who like me. I suppose you think I'm horribly vain. But then, everybody's vain about something. (BUTLER comes in with cocktails and sandwiches, to table right of fireplace.) If they're not, they're vain about their lack of vanity. I believe that's a mot! Pretty good for a brainless— Here, Will, have a cocktail— (WILL takes cocktail.) Paula— what's your pet vanity? She thinks mine's my looks but it's not. If I had my way I shouldn't look at all the way I look. (Enter DR. DEXTER, door back. He wears a sea-green baggy dinner-suit; he looks as "hicky" and uncertain as ever.)

DEXTER. Good evening, Mrs. Frothingham.

LEONIE. Dr. Dexter—how good of you to come. Delighted to see you.

DEXTER. Good evening. Hello, Will.

WILL. Dad!

DEXTER. Mrs. Frothingham invited me. Didn't you know?

LEONIE. (Takes DEXTER's arm and goes to WILL.) You told me you had to leave tomorrow to visit your father in Brunswick so I just called him up in Brunswick—

DEXTER. She sent the car all the way for me. Nice car. Great springs.

LEONIE (To WILL.) Now you won't have to leave tomorrow. You can both spend the week-end here.

WILL. (Walking away a little right.) Awfully nice of you, Leonie.

LEONIE. (*Following him.*) (DEXTER *sits on sofa.*) You see, Will, I leave the big issues to the professional altruists. I just do what I can toward making those around me happy. And that's *my* vanity! (*Enter DENNIS, door back.*)

DENNIS. Well! Well! **Fancy** that now, Hedda!

LEONIE. Oh, hello, Dennis, just in time for a cocktail. (LEONIE *leads him over to sofa.* WILL *is isolated down right center.*)

DENNIS. (*To* DEXTER.) How are you?

DEXTER. (*Not friendly.*) I'm all right.

DENNIS. Complicated week-end! You and the Healer! Faraday and Cagliostro. That'll be something.

LEONIE. (*Takes* DENNIS's *arm.*) Everybody tells me to like you, Dennis. I'm in such a mood that I'm going to make the effort.

DENNIS. I've been waiting for this. I'm thrilled!

LEONIE. (*Strolling with him across stage front.*) Something tells me you could be very charming if you wanted to. Tell me, Dennis, have you ever tried being lovable and sweet?

DENNIS. For you, Mrs. Frothingham, I would willingly revive the age of chivalry!

LEONIE. But there's no need of that. I just want you to be nice. Here, have a cocktail. Give you courage.

DENNIS. Just watch me from now on, Mrs. Frothingham.

LEONIE. I will. Passionately. (*Hands him cocktail.*) I'll be doing nothing else. (BUTLER *crosses back of sofa, offers* DEXTER *and* PAULA *cocktails.* DR. RICE *comes in.*)

DENNIS. (*Stage sigh.*) A-h-h! The doctor! Just in time to look at my tongue, Doctor.

KENNETH. That won't be necessary, young man. I can tell— It's excessive.

LEONIE. (*Crossing to* KENNETH.) Kenneth —you remember Will's father—Dr. Dexter.

KENNETH. How do you do? (*They shake hands. A second* BUTLER *has come in and he and* ROBERT *are passing cocktails and*

hors d'oeuvres. LEONIE *keeps circulating among her guests.* KENNETH *and* DEXTER *are in the center—*DENNIS, *obeying a malicious impulse, presides over them. Announces a theme on which he eggs them on to utter variations.*)

DENNIS. A significant moment, ladies and gentlemen—the magician of Science meets the magician of Sex—The floating libido bumps the absolute! What happens?

DEXTER. (*Cupping his hand to his ear.*) What? (WILL *crosses to door and looks out moodily.*)

DENNIS. The absolute hasn't got a chance. Isn't that right, Dr. Rice?

KENNETH. I shouldn't venture to contradict a young intellectual. Especially a very young intellectual.

LEONIE. (*Crosses front of* KENNETH, *to* DENNIS.) There, you see, I'm afraid, after all, I'll have to give you up, Dennis. You can't be lovable. You can't be sweet.

DENNIS. But I didn't promise to be winsome to everybody, only to you.

LEONIE. You really must treat him, Kenneth. He has no censor at all.

DENNIS. My censor is the Catholic tradition. We Catholics anticipated both Marx and Freud by a little matter of nineteen centuries. Spiritually, we have a Communion in the Holy Ghost—Communion. As for Dr. Rice, he offers confession without absolution. He is inadequate. (LEONIE *returns with tray of canapes.*)

LEONIE. It seems such bad taste to discuss religion at cocktail time. Try a stuffed olive.

DEXTER. By the time you got your beautiful new world, true science will have perished.

LEONIE. Aren't you too pessimistic, Dr. Dexter? Too much science has made you gloomy. Kenneth, the depression hasn't stopped your work, has it? Depression or no depression— (WILL *springs up.*)

WILL. (*Tensely.*) That's right, Leonie. (*Everyone faces* WILL.) Depression or no depression—war or peace—revolution or reaction—Kenneth will reign supreme! (KENNETH *stares at him.* WILL *confronts him.*)

LEONIE. Will!

WILL. Yes, Leonie. His is the power and the glory!

LEONIE. Dennis, this is your influence—

WILL. I admire you unreservedly, Doctor. Of your kind you are the best. You are the essence.

KENNETH. You embarrass me.

WILL. Some men are born ahead of their time, some behind, but you are made pat for the instant. Now is the time for you—when people are unemployed and distrust their own capacities—when people suffer and may be tempted—when integrity yields to despair—now is the moment for you!

KENNETH. (*Strolling closer to him so they are face to face.*) When, may I ask, is the moment for you—when if ever?

WILL. After your victory. When you are stuffed and inert with everything you want, then will be the time for me. (*He goes out.*)

PAULA. (*Running after* WILL.) Will . . . Will . . . Will . . . (*She follows him out.*)

LEONIE. (*Devastated by this strange behavior.*) What is it? I don't like it when people stand in the middle of the floor and make speeches. What's the matter with him? Dennis, do you know?

DENNIS. (*With a look at* KENNETH.) I can guess.

LEONIE. Has he quarreled with Paula? Paula is so inept. She doesn't know how to . . . At the same time, if he had a grievance, why couldn't he have kept it until after dinner? (*Enter* ROBERT.)

ROBERT. Dinner is served. (*Exit* ROBERT.)

LEONIE. Well, we'll do what we can. Sam is dining with Mother in her room, Boris has a headache. Dennis, you and Dr. Dexter—

DENNIS. You've picked me, Dr. Dexter. I congratulate you.

DEXTER. Thank God, I can't hear a word you say. (*Exit* DEXTER, *door back.*)

DENNIS. (*Sadistically.*) Oh, yes, he can. And we'll fight it out on these lines if it takes all dinner. (*He follows* DEXTER *out.*)

LEONIE. What extraordinary behavior! What do you suppose, Kenneth—shall I go after them?

KENNETH. I wouldn't. It's their problem. Give them time.

LEONIE. (*Reassured.*) You are so wise, Kenneth. How did I ever get on without you? I have that secure feeling that you are going to be my last indiscretion. When I think how neatly I've captured you—I feel quite proud. I guess my technique isn't so lousy after all. (*She takes his arm and swings along beside him as they waltz in to dinner.*)

Curtain

ACT THREE

SCENE: *The same.*
Time: *Late that fall. The trees have turned. The sumach have put out the brilliant red flowers of autumn.*

At Rise: WILL *and* DENNIS *have just arrived, and are standing at fireplace, back.* LEONIE *comes in to greet them.* SAM *strolls in with her.*

LEONIE. I'm so glad to see you! (*She shakes hands with each of them warmly.*) Will! How are you? (*To* DENNIS.) It's so good of you to come.

SAM. (*Shaking hands with* WILL.) Very glad to see you.

WILL. Thanks. (SAM *shakes hands with* DENNIS.)

LEONIE. Sam drove over for a few hours from Blue Hill to talk business to me. He hasn't had much luck so far. It's simply wonderful having you boys here—it's like old times. I didn't tell Paula. (*To* SAM.) I did all this on my own. It's a surprise for Paula.

DENNIS. She'll be overcome when she sees me. Maybe you should prepare her.

WILL. Where is Paula?

LEONIE. Isn't it provoking! She and Kenneth went for a walk. They should have been back long before this. (*Turning back to them.*) Paula hasn't been at all herself, Will. I thought you would cheer her up.

DENNIS. I will be glad to do what I can, of course. Several very stubborn cases have yielded to my charm.

LEONIE. I'm sure! Do sit down. (*She sits.*)

DENNIS. (*Taking out his pipe.*) Do you mind? (WILL *sits.*)

LEONIE. Oh, please—I can't tell you how I appreciate your coming—

DENNIS. (*The harassed business man.*) Well, as a matter of fact, Leonie, it wasn't easy to get away from the office—

LEONIE. Are you in an office?

DENNIS. Sometimes as many as fifteen in a day. (LEONIE *laughs.*) But when I got your appealing letter — *and* the return tickets—I'm chivalrous at heart, you know, Leonie—

LEONIE. I know you are!

SAM. How's town?

WILL. Very hot.

SAM. I'm just on my way down. Stopped by to go over several things with Leonie—

LEONIE. Poor Sam's been having an awful time with me. He keeps putting things in escrow. Where is escrow?

DENNIS. It's where squirrels put nuts in the winter-time.

LEONIE. I see! Dennis is much more lucid than you, Sam.

DENNIS. I have a knack for making the abstruse translucent. Especially in economics. Now, would you like to know why England went off gold?

LEONIE. No, I wouldn't.

DENNIS. I shall yield to your subconscious demand and tell you.

LEONIE. (*To others.*) Help!

DENNIS. I see that there is no audience for my peculiar gift.

LEONIE. You know, Will, I've thought perhaps you were angry with us.

WILL. Why?

LEONIE. You haven't been here for so long. (*To* SAM.) Since Granny died—none of them have been here. Did Paula write you about Granny's funeral?

WILL. No. She didn't.

LEONIE. Of course I hate funerals—I can't bear them—but this was so—natural. Mother wanted to live till the fall and she did. It was a dreaming blue sky and there was that poignant haze over the hills and over the bay, and the smell of burning wood from somewhere. Burning wood never smells at any other time the way it does in Indian summer. And the colors that day! Did you ever, Sam, see such a day?

SAM. It was beautiful.

LEONIE. They say the colors of autumn are the colors of death, but I don't believe that. They were in such strength that day. I cried—but not on account of Mother— that kind of day always makes me cry a little bit anyway. You couldn't cry over consigning anyone you loved to an earth like that—on a day like that. I put some blazing leaves over her, but when I passed there the other day, they were withered and brown—

SAM. (*Chiding her.*) Now Leonie—

LEONIE. Sam thinks I shouldn't talk about Mother. But I don't see why. She doesn't depress me. I think of her with joy. She had a wonderful life.

SAM. She was a wonderful woman.

LEONIE. (*To* WILL.) Imagine, Will—when Sam was here last time—you were here that week-end—she *knew*. She asked Sam to be executor of her will.

SAM. (*Very annoyed at her for bringing this up.*) Leonie—

LEONIE. Why didn't you tell me, Sam, then?

SAM. Seemed no point.

LEONIE. She didn't want me to know, did she?

SAM. No. She didn't want to distress you. (*A moment's pause.*)

LEONIE. What can be keeping Paula? (*She glances out of the window.*) Sam, do you want to talk business to me some more?

SAM. I'd like to talk to Will a minute.

LEONIE. Oh—yes. Well, Dennis, wouldn't you like me to show you to your room? (*She rises, goes to door into hallway.* DENNIS *follows.*)

DENNIS. Thanks, I've got to answer a chain letter.

LEONIE. I've given you a room you've never had. The tower room.

DENNIS. Is it ivory? I won't be comfortable if it isn't ivory.

LEONIE. Well just this once you're going to be uncomfortable — and like it! (*She goes out.*)

DENNIS. (*Tragically.*) And for this I gave up a superb view of the gas-house on 149th Street. (*He goes out.*)

SAM. (*Rises and goes up toward fireplace.*) Will—

WILL. Yes, Mr. Frothingham.

SAM. Oh—call me Sam.

WILL. All right.

SAM. I'll have to be pushing off in an hour or so. I rather wanted to talk to you.

WILL. Yes—

SAM. (*Wipes his forehead.*) Gosh, Leonie's a difficult woman to talk business to. (*Sits.*)

WILL. I can imagine that. She's not interested in business

SAM. She —is—not!!!

WILL. What do you want to speak to me about?

SAM. Paula.

WILL. What about Paula?

SAM. As I'm her father—I hope you won't think me—

WILL. Of course not—

SAM. It's not altogether easy—

WILL. Do you want me to help you?

SAM. Yes. I wish you would!

WILL. You're worried about Paula and me, aren't you? So was her grandmother. You think me irresponsible. Less responsible for example—(*As if making a random comparison*) than Dr. Rice?

SAM. Well, as a matter of fact, I've rather gotten to know Dr. Rice, and in many respects. he's a pretty sound feller. (*Rising and going to stand above* WILL.) Hang it all, Will, I like you, and I don't like to preach to you, you know.

WILL. Go on.

SAM. Well, there are—from my point of view at least—a lot of nonsensical ideas knocking about. I'd like to point out just one thing to you. Your radicalism and all that— Well, the point is this—if you marry Paula—and I hope you do, because I like you—and, what is more important, Paula likes you—you'll have responsibilities. Paula will be rich. Very rich. Money means responsibility. Now, I shouldn't, for example, like you to start radical magazines with it. I shouldn't like you to let money drift through your fingers in all sorts of aimless, millennial directions that won't get anywhere.

WILL. Who told you that was my intention?

SAM. A little bird.

WILL. With a black moustache?

SAM. Does that matter?

WILL. No.

SAM. (*Putting hand on* WILL's *shoulder.*) As a matter of fact, I'm not worried about you at all. Money, I expect, will do to you what getting power does to radical opposition, once it gets office—

WILL. Emasculate me, you mean?

SAM. Well, hardly. Mature you. Once

you're rich yourself, I have no doubt you'll be—

WILL. Sound.

SAM. Yes. Sound. But your friends—this McCarthy boy—

WILL. Well, I can easily cut Dennis—all my poor and unsound friends—

SAM. (*Quietly.*) I'm sorry you're taking this tone with me, Will. I'm the last person in the world to ask you to drop anybody. I'd be ashamed of you if you did. Only—

WILL. Only?

SAM. I must tell you that I am in position—by virtue of the will left by Mrs. Wyler—to keep Paula's money from being used for any purpose that might be construed as—subversive.

WILL. From whose point of view?

SAM. (*Quietly.*) From mine.

WILL. I see.

SAM. Possibly you may not believe this—but I trust you, Will. Mrs. Wyler trusted you.

WILL. You needn't worry. Paula seems to have other interests apparently.

SAM. What do you mean?

WILL. Sounder interests— (DENNIS *enters, through door back.*)

DENNIS. The tower room lets in light on four sides, but nothing to look at. Just the sea and the landscape.

SAM. What did you do with Leonie?

DENNIS. She's gone to her mother's room to potter around.

SAM. Maybe I can get her attention while she's pottering. Excuse me. (SAM *goes out.*)

DENNIS. Poor Leonie—she's the last of the lovely ladies. The inheritance taxes'll get 'em soon. You know we were by way of getting our magazine from Leonie when Dr. Rice spiked our guns. So I'm leaving. My time is too valuable. But the Healer won't last forever, and when he goes, I shall return. Take heart, my good man. I know you feel a little tender about this, but remember, my lad, it's the Cause that counts. Remember what Shaw says: "There is no money but the devil's money. It is all tainted and it might as well be used in the service of God." (*A moment—*WILL *is obviously thinking of something else.*) What's the matter?

WILL. Nothing.

DENNIS. (*Bringing down chair to sit left of* WILL *he imitates* RICE'S *manner.*) Now you must speak, young man—how can I sublimate your subconscious troubles, if you won't speak? Are you unhappy about Paula, my lad? (*No answer.*) Tell me what's happened between you—relieve your soul, and, as a reward, I may make you co-editor of our magazine. (*No response. He rises and walks to opposite side of table.*) No? Assistant editor you remain. I may even fire you. Yes, I think I will fire you. (*Crossing in front of* WILL *to fireplace.*) Dexter—you're through. Go upstairs and get your check. (*Rubs his hands together in glee.*) God, it gives me a sense of power to fire a man—especially an old friend! (PAULA *and* KENNETH *come in door right from the garden.*)

PAULA. (*Amazed to see them.*) Will! But how—! Dennis!

WILL. (*Rather coolly.*) Hello, Paula.

DENNIS. We came to surprise you. Now that we have surprised you, we can go home.

WILL. Leonie asked me to come.

PAULA. Oh. Well, it's very nice to see you.

WILL. Thanks.

PAULA. When I wired you to come a few weeks ago, you were too busy. It takes Leonie, doesn't it?

DENNIS. You should have tried me, Paula. Hello, Dr. Rice. How's business? Any suppressions today?

KENNETH. (*Significantly.*) Apparently not.

DENNIS. Well, come on up to my room, Doctor, and we'll play Twenty Questions. (*He goes out.*)

WILL. Hello, Dr. Rice.

KENNETH. How are you?

PAULA. Will—I'm awfully glad to see you. I was just going to write you to thank you for the 'sweet letter 'you sent me after Granny died.

KENNETH. I'm afraid it's my fault, Dexter. I do my best to keep Paula so busy that she finds no time to write letters.

WILL. I was sure I could count on you, Doctor. (WILL goes out.)

PAULA. You enjoy hurting Will, don't you?

KENNETH. When there is an obstacle in my path, I do my best to remove it.

PAULA. What makes you think it is only Will that stands between us— That if left to myself I—

KENNETH. Because it is true. Were it not for the squids of idealistic drivel spouted around you by Will and his friends, there would be no issue at all between us. I resent even an imputed rivalry with someone I despise.

PAULA. Rivalry?

KENNETH. Paula— There's no reason any longer why I shouldn't tell you the truth.

PAULA. What is it, Kenneth?

KENNETH. (*After a moment—slowly.*) Do you know what I feel like? I feel like a man on a great height, irresistibly tempted to jump over. Do 'you want the truth really? (*She says nothing. Somehow his words, his voice, his attitude make her feel that really now he may reveal something which before he wouldn't have revealed. He is in a trance-like state almost; she feels it; she is rather horribly fascinated—somehow, though she distrusts him utterly, some instinct tells her that, at this moment actually he is tempted by a force, disruptive to himself, to tell her the truth.*) Don't you know it? Don't you feel it? (*Pause.*) Haven't you known it? Haven't you felt it? (*A moment's pause.*) I love you.

PAULA. What?

KENNETH. I love you. (*A pause. She is too stupefied to speak. She too is under a spell. She is fascinated by him—by the enormity of this. She rises, walks away from him to stand by sofa.*)

PAULA. I suppose I should be afraid of you. I'm not afraid of you.

KENNETH. I am afraid of you. You tempt me to venture the impossible. That is impractical. And I have always been eminently practical.

PAULA. I'm sure you have. (*She feels herself talking automatically, as if out of a hypnotic state—at the same time some vanity and shrewdness keeps pounding inside her: "See how far he will go—see how far he will go!"*)

KENNETH. I have lived by a plan. The plan has matured. But I have yearned for a face that would give me joy, for the voice that would soothe me. It is your face. It is your voice. (*PAULA is fighting not to scream; at the same time she is caught in a nightmarish fascination.*)

PAULA. (*Very faintly.*) Don't you love Mother?

KENNETH. No. (*A moment's pause.*) You are the youth I have never had, the security I have never had—you are the home I have hungered for. (*Moves toward her—stands over her and a little back.*) That I am standing near you now, that I have achieved a share in your life, that you are listening to me, that you are thinking of me and of what I am, to the exclusion of everything else in the whirling universe—this is a miracle so devastating, that it makes any future possible—Paula—

PAULA. What?

KENNETH. Paula?

PAULA. What *is* it!

KENNETH. (*Bending over her.*) Paula ... (*It is as if he got a sexual joy from saying her name.*) I love your name. I love to say your name.

PAULA. I *am* afraid of you. I'm sorry for you.

KENNETH. Do you think me insane?

PAULA. Yes.

KENNETH. Because I am ambitious, because I am forthright, because I deal scientifically with the human stuff around me—you think me insane. Because I am ruthless and romantic, you think me insane. This boy you think you love—who spends his time sniveling about a system he is not strong enough to dominate—is he sane?

PAULA. I don't expect you to—

KENNETH. When I hear the chatter of your friends, it makes me sick. While they and their kind prate of co-operative commonwealths, the strong man takes power, and rides over their backs—which is all their backs are fit for. Never has the opportunity for the individual career been so exalted, so infinite in its scope, so horizonal. House-painters and minor journalists become dictators of great nations. (*With puckish humor—leaning on arm of her chair.*) Imagine what a really clever man could do! See what he has done! (*He smiles, makes a gesture of modest self-assertion, indicating the room as part of his conquest. She laughs, rather choked and embarrassed. He goes on.*) And this I have done alone. From an impossible distance—I have come to you, so that when I speak, you can hear. What might we not do together, Paula—you and I—(*To her surprise,* PAULA *finds herself arguing an inconceivable point. She loathes the strange fascination she feels in this man, and yet is aware that it might turn to her advantage.*)

PAULA. We don't want the same things.

KENNETH. You want what everyone wants who has vitality and imagination—new forms of power—new domains of knowledge—the ultimate sensations.

PAULA. You *are* romantic, aren't you?

KENNETH. Endlessly. And endlessly—realistic. (*Staring at her.*) What are you thinking?

PAULA. (*Shrewd against him—against herself.*) I keep thinking—what you want now—what you're after now?

KENNETH. (*Moving toward her.*) You don't believe then—that I love you?

PAULA. (*Leaning back in chair—not looking at him.*) You are a very strange man.

KENNETH. I am simple really. I want everything. That's all!

PAULA. And you don't care how you get it.

KENNETH. Don't be moralistic, Paula—I beg you. I am directly in the tradition of your own marauding ancestors. They pass now for pioneers—actually they fell on the true pioneers, and wrested what they had found away from them, by sheer brutal strength. I am doing the same thing—but more adroitly.

PAULA. Why are you so honest with me?

KENNETH. (*With his most charming smile.*) Perhaps because I feel that, in your heart, you too are an adventurer. (*A pause. During these half-spell-bound instants a thought has been forming slowly in* PAULA's *mind that crystallizes now. This man is the enemy. This man is infinitely cunning, infinitely resourceful. Perhaps—just the possibility—he really feels this passion for her. If so, why not use this weakness in an antagonist so ruthless? She will try.*)

PAULA. I shouldn't listen to you— (*A moment. He senses her cunning. He looks at her.*)

KENNETH. You don't trust me?

PAULA. Have I reason to trust you?

KENNETH. What reason would you like? What proof would you like?

PAULA. Aren't you going to marry Mother?

KENNETH. Only as an alternative.

PAULA. Will you—tell her so? Will you give up the alternative?

KENNETH. And if I do?

PAULA. What shall I promise you?

KENNETH. Yourself.

PAULA. (*Looks at him—speaks.*) And if I do?

KENNETH. Then . . .

PAULA. (*Taking fire.*) You say you love me! If you feel it—really feel it— You haven't been very adventurous for all your talk! Taking in Mother and Sam! Give up those conquests. Tell her! Tell Mother! Then perhaps I will believe you.

KENNETH. And then?

PAULA. Take your chances!

KENNETH. (*Quietly.*) Very well.

PAULA. You will?

KENNETH. I will.

PAULA. You'll tell Mother—you love me?

KENNETH. Yes.

PAULA. (*Going to the foot of the stairs, calls:*) Mother! Mother!

LEONIE. (*Offstage.*) Yes, Paula. I'm coming right down! I've the most marvelous surprise for you! Wait and see! (PAULA *walks to end of sofa—looking at* KENNETH. LEONIE *comes in. She is wearing an exquisite old-fashioned silk wedding-dress which billows around her in an immense shimmering circle. She is a vision of enchantment.*)

LEONIE. (*In a great flurry of excitement.*) Children, look what I found! It's Mother's. It's the dress she was married in. I was poking around in Granny's room while Sam was talking to me about bonds, and I came upon it. Do you like it, Kenneth? Isn't it adorable? Have you ever . . . What's the matter? Don't you like it?

PAULA. It's very pretty.

LEONIE. (*Overwhelmed by the inadequacy of this word.*) Pretty! Pretty! (*She hopes for more from* KENNETH.) Kenneth. . . ?

KENNETH. It's exquisite.

LEONIE. Isn't it? (*She whirls around in the dress.*) Isn't it? Yes. Exquisite. Can you imagine the scene? Can you imagine Granny walking down the aisle—and all the august spectators in mutton-chop whiskers and Prince Alberts? We've lost something these days—a good deal—oh, I don't miss the mutton-chops—but in ceremony, I mean—in punctilio and grace. . . .

PAULA. (*Cutting ruthlessly through the nostalgia.*) Mother!

LEONIE. What is it, Paula?

PAULA. Kenneth has something to tell you.

LEONIE. Kenneth?

PAULA. Yes. He has something to tell you.

LEONIE. Have you, Kenneth?

KENNETH. Yes.

LEONIE. What is it?

KENNETH. (*Quietly.*) I love Paula. I want to marry Paula. (*A pause. Granny's wedding dress droops.*)

LEONIE. Do you mean that, Kenneth?

KENNETH. Yes.

LEONIE. (*Piteously.*) This isn't very nice of you, Paula.

PAULA. I had nothing to do with it. I loathe Kenneth. But I wanted you to know him. Now you see him, Mother, your precious Lothario—there he is! Look at him!

LEONIE. These clothes are picturesque, but I think our modern ones are more comfortable. I think—I feel quite faint—isn't it ridiculous? (*She sways.*)

PAULA. I'm sorry, Mother. I had to. But I love you. I really do.

LEONIE (*Very faint.*) Thank you, Paula.

PAULA. You'd better go up and lie down. I'll come to you in a moment.

LEONIE. Yes. I think I'd better. Yes. (*She begins to sob; she goes out, hiding her face in the lace folds of her dress.* PAULA, *having gone with her to the door, rings bell for* ROBERT, *turns to* KENNETH.)

PAULA. I suppose you're going to tell me this isn't cricket. Well, don't, because it will only make me laugh. To live up to a code with people like you is only to be weak and absurd.

KENNETH. (*His voice is low and even but tense with hate.*) You, Miss Frothingham, are my *last* miscalculation. I might even say my first. Fortunately, not irreparable! (ROBERT *enters.*)

PAULA. Robert.

ROBERT. Yes, Miss Frothingham.

PAULA. (*Still staring fixedly at* KENNETH.) Dr. Rice is leaving. Will you see that his bags are packed, please?

ROBERT. Yes, Miss. (*He goes out.*)

KENNETH. Forgive me—for having overestimated you. (*He goes out door right.* PAULA *comes slowly down and sits on sofa. She gets a reaction herself now from all she has been through; this game hasn't been natural to her; she is trembling physically; she is on the verge of tears.* WILL *comes in.*)

PAULA. Will—Will darling— (*She clings to* WILL.)

WILL. (*Worried.*) Paula!

PAULA. Put your arms around me, Will— hold me close— (WILL *obeys.*)

WILL. What's happened?

PAULA. I've tricked him. I made him say in front of Mother that he loved me, that he wanted to marry me. Poor Leonie! But it had to be done! And do you know, Will —at the end I felt—gosh, one has so many selves, Will. I must tell you—for the—well, for the completeness of the record—

WILL. (*Curious.*) What?

PAULA. At the end I felt I had to do it— not only to save Leonie—but to save myself. Can you understand that? I felt horribly drawn to him, and by the sordid thing I was doing— But it's over. Thank God it's over. Will, darling, these six weeks have been hell without you. When I got your letter about Granny, I sat down and cried. I wanted to go right to New York to be with you. And yet I couldn't. How could I? But now, Will—I don't want to wait for you any longer. I've done what I can. It's cost me almost— Will—I need you terribly—

WILL. And I you, Paula. But listen, darling—I've decided during the weeks I've been away from you— I can't marry you now— I can't face what I'd become—

PAULA. But Will, I— (*Springing up.*) But Will, I'll give up the money. I'll live with you anywhere.

WILL. I know that, Paula. But I mustn't. You mustn't let me. I've thought it all out. You say you'd live with me anywhere. But what would happen? Supposing I didn't get a job? Would we starve? We'd take fifty dollars a week from your grandmother's estate. It would be foolish not to. Taking fifty, why not seventy-five? Why not two hundred? I can't let myself in for it, Paula. (*A long pause.*) Paula, darling— do you hate me?

PAULA. No.

WILL. Supposing you weren't rich? Is it a world in which, but for this, I'd have to sink? If it is, I'm going to damn well do what I can to change it. I don't have to scrabble for the inheritance of dead men. That's for Kenneth—one robber baron— after the lapse of several generations—succeeding another. I don't want this damn fortune to give me an unfair advantage over people as good as I am who haven't got it. (*Torn with pity for her.*) Paula— my dearest—what can I do?

PAULA. I see that you can't do anything. I quite see. Still—

WILL. I love you, Paula, and I'll be longing for you terribly, but I can't marry you—not till there's somebody for you to marry. When I've struck my stride, I won't care about Sam, or the money, or anything, because I'll be on my own. If you feel the way I do, you'll wait.

PAULA. (*Very still voice.*) Of course, Will. I'll wait.

WILL. (*Overcome with gratitude and emotion—seizes her in his arms passionately.*) Darling—darling— (LEONIE *comes in.* WILL, *overcome with emotion, goes out.*)

LEONIE. It's easy to say "lie down." But what happens then? Thoughts assail you. Thoughts . . .

PAULA. Mother . . .

LEONIE. Kenneth's going. He's leaving. I suppose you're happy. It's the end—the end of summer.

PAULA. (*Herself shaken with emotion.*) Mother— (*She wants to talk to* LEONIE, *to tell her what has happened, but* LEONIE *is lost in her own maze.*)

LEONIE. It's cold here. I hate this place. I'm going to sell it. (*She sits, in chair, right of fireplace.*) I've always wanted things around me to be gay and warm and happy. I've done my best. I must be wrong. Why do I find myself this way? With nothing. With nothing.

PAULA. (*Running to her mother and throwing herself on her knees beside her.*) Mother—Mother darling—

LEONIE. (*Not responding, reflectively.*) I suppose the thing about me that is wrong is that love is really all I care about. (*A moment's pause.*) I suppose I should have been interested in other things. Good works. Do they sustain you? But I couldn't somehow. I think when you're not in love— you're dead. Yes, that must be why I'm... (*Her voice trails off rather.* PAULA *drops her head in her mother's lap and begins to cry.*)

LEONIE. (*Surprised.*) Paula—what is it? What's the matter? Are you sorry? It's all right, child.

PAULA. (*Through her tears.*) It's Will—

LEONIE. Will?

PAULA. He's going away.

LEONIE. Why don't you go with him?

PAULA. He doesn't want me.

LEONIE. That's not true. It must be something else.

PAULA. The money.

LEONIE. Oh, the money. Yes, the money. The money won't do anything for you. It'll work against you. It's worked against me. It gives you the illusion of escape— but always you have to come back to yourself. At the end of every journey—you find yourself.

PAULA. What shall I do, Mother?

LEONIE. You and Will want the same things. In the end you will find them.

But don't let him find them with someone else. Follow him. Be near him. When he is depressed and discouraged, let it be your hand that he touches, your face that he sees.

PAULA. (*Breathless.*) Mother—you're right —he told me last summer—"you must have a shoulder to lean on"—

LEONIE. Let it be your shoulder, Paula; follow him. Be near him.

PAULA. Thank you, Mother.

LEONIE. (*Ruefully.*) I am telling you what *I* should do. It must be bad advice.

PAULA. (*Gratefully.*) Darling! (DENNIS *and* WILL *come in.*)

DENNIS. Here you are! We're off to the boat! Thirty minutes! Why don't you and Paula come too? What do you say, Leonie?

LEONIE. You know, all these years I've been coming up here, and I've never been on the Bar Harbor boat.

DENNIS. It may be said, Mrs. Frothingham, if you have never been on the Bar Harbor boat, that you have not lived!

LEONIE. Really! I'd always heard it was poky.

DENNIS. Poky! The *Normandie* of the Kennebec poky! Mrs. Frothingham!

LEONIE. It's fun, is it? But doesn't it get into New York at some impossible hour?

DENNIS. At seven A.M.

LEONIE. Seven! (*She shudders.*)

DENNIS. (*The brisk executive.*) Seven! Yes, sir! At my desk at nine! All refreshed and co-ordinated and ready to attack my South American correspondence.

LEONIE. I must learn not to believe him, mustn't I?

DENNIS. I am my own master, Leonie. All day for nine mortal hours I grind out escape fiction for the pulp magazines. But one day I shall become famous and emerge into the slicks and then I doubt very much whether I shall come here.

LEONIE. I shall miss you.

DENNIS. **Then I'll come.**

LEONIE. I hate to have you go, Dennis. You cheer me up. Why don't you stay?

DENNIS. Impossible, Leonie. I must go to New York to launch the magazine. But for the moment, good-bye, Leonie. As a reward for your hospitality I shall send you the original copy of one of my stories. Would you like to escape from something?

LEONIE. (*Smiling wanly.*) I would indeed!

DENNIS. Think no more about it. You're as good as free. The story is yours, typed personally on my Underwood. Those misplaced keys—those inaccuracies—how they will bemuse posterity! (*He goes out.*)

WILL. (*Awkwardly.*) Good-bye, Leonie.

LEONIE. Good-bye, Will. (*He goes out without looking at* PAULA. *In pantomime,* LEONIE *urges* PAULA *to go after him.* PAULA *kisses her quickly and runs out after* WILL. *Left alone,* LEONIE *walks to the chair in which her mother sat so often—she looks through the glowing autumn at the darkening sea.* KENNETH *comes in. There is a pause.*)

KENNETH. Leonie—

LEONIE. Yes, Kenneth.

KENNETH. I don't expect you to understand this. I shall not try to make you understand it.

LEONIE. Perhaps I'd better not.

KENNETH. Really I am amused at myself—highly entertained. That I should have almost had to practice on myself what hitherto I have reserved for my patients—that I who have made such a fetish of discipline and restraint so nearly succumbed to an inconsistency. I must revise my notion of myself.

LEONIE. And I too.

KENNETH. Why? Why you?

LEONIE. I seem to be a survival—Paula's directness—and your calculations—they are beyond me.

KENNETH. Nevertheless, it's curious how you and Paula are alike—no wonder that, for a moment at least, you seemed to me—interchangeable.

LEONIE. Did you know it from the beginning—that it was Paula?

KENNETH. I was attracted by her resemblance to you—for exercising this attraction I hated her. She felt it too—from the beginning and she must have hated me from the beginning. Between us there grew up this strange, unnatural antagonism—

LEONIE. What?

KENNETH. This fused emotion of love and hate. It had to be brought out into the open. It's a familiar psychosis—the unconscious desire of the daughter to triumph over the mother.

LEONIE. But I don't understand—

KENNETH. There is so much in these intricate relationships that the layman can't understand—

LEONIE. You mean that you—felt nothing for Paula?

KENNETH. No, I don't mean that at all. But I saw that what I felt for her was some twisted reflection of what I felt for you. And I saw there was only one way out of it—to let her triumph over you. I told her that I loved her. But this was not enough. I must repeat it in front of you. You must witness her triumph. I made it possible. I gave her her great moment. Well, you see what it's done. It freed her so beautifully that she was able to go to Will. They've gone away together. Perfect cure for her as well as for myself. (*A moment's pause.*)

LEONIE. It all sounds almost too perfect, Kenneth.

KENNETH. I said I didn't expect you to understand it—you have lived always on your emotions You have never bothered to delve beneath them. You are afraid to, aren't you?

LEONIE. I know this, Kenneth. I heard you say that you loved Paula. I heard your voice. No, I can't accept this, Kenneth! It's not good enough. I've never done that before. I'd only think now that everything you did, everything you said, was to cover what you felt. And I'd end by telling myself that I believed you. I'd end by taking second best from you. No, I must guard myself from that. I felt this a month ago —that's why I sent for Will.

KENNETH. Some day, Leonie, you will learn that feeling is not enough.

LEONIE. But I trust my instinct, Kenneth.

KENNETH. That, Leonie, is your most adorable trait—

LEONIE. What?

KENNETH. That trust—that innocence. If it weren't for that, you wouldn't be you— and everyone wouldn't love you—

LEONIE. Oh, no, Kenneth— (DENNIS comes in.)

DENNIS. Oh, excuse me. But I left my brief-case. Oh, here it is. (He picks it up.) Without my brief-case I am a man without a Destiny. With it I am—

KENNETH. A man with a brief-case.

LEONIE. (Crossing rather desperately to DENNIS—this straw in the current.) What's in it—your stories?

DENNIS. Stories—no, that wouldn't matter. I am fertile; I can spawn stories. But the plans for the magazine are in here—the future of Young America is here—

LEONIE. Will you stay and have a whiskey and soda?

DENNIS. Thanks, but if I do, I shall miss the boat.

LEONIE. Suppose you do?

KENNETH. Leonie—that would delay the millennium one day.

DENNIS. The doctor's right. That would be selfish.

LEONIE. Be selfish. Please stay.

DENNIS. No. Once you are enlisted in a cause, you can't live a personal life. It is a dedication.

LEONIE. Kenneth is leaving. I shall be lonely, Dennis. I can't bear to be alone.

KENNETH. Your need for people is poignant, isn't it, Leonie?

LEONIE. Stay for dinner. After dinner we can talk about your magazine.

DENNIS. Oh, well—that makes it possible for me to stay. Thank you, Kenneth. (He goes to sofa, sits, busying himself with brief-case.) (She goes to console to make highball.)

KENNETH. Send me your magazine, Dennis. I shall be honored to be the first subscriber.

DENNIS. I'll be glad to. Your patients can read it in the waiting-room instead of the National Geographic.

KENNETH. Your first subscriber—and very possibly your last. (He crosses to door and turns back.) Good-bye, Leonie. Good luck, Dennis. We who are about to retire— salute you. (She does not look at him. He bows formally to DENNIS's back, makes a gesture of "good luck" and exits.)

DENNIS. Trouble with that fellow is—he lives for himself. No larger interest. That's what dignifies human beings, Leonie—a dedication to something greater than themselves.

LEONIE. (Coming down to hand him his highball.) Yes? Here's your whiskey and soda. I envy you, Dennis. I wish I could dedicate myself to something—something outside myself.

DENNIS. (Rising to sit beside her.) Well, here's your opportunity, Leonie—it's providential. You couldn't do better than this magazine. It would give you a new interest —impersonal. It would emancipate you,

Leonie. It would be a perpetual dedication to Youth—to the hope of the world. The world is middle-aged and tired. But we—

LEONIE. (*Wistfully.*) Can you refresh us, Dennis?

DENNIS. Refresh you? Leonie, we can rejuvenate you!

LEONIE. (*Grateful there is some one there —another human being she can laugh with.*) That's an awfully amusing idea. You make me laugh.

DENNIS. (*Eagerly selling the idea.*) In the youth of any country, there is an immense potentiality—

LEONIE. You're awfully serious about it, aren't you, Dennis?

DENNIS. Where the magazine is concerned, Leonie, I am a fanatic.

LEONIE. I suppose if it's really successful— it'll result in my losing everything I have—

DENNIS. It'll be taken from you anyway. You'll only be anticipating the inevitable.

LEONIE. Why—how clever of me!

DENNIS. Not only clever but grateful.

LEONIE. Will you leave me just a little to live on—?

DENNIS. Don't worry about that—come the Revolution—you'll have a friend in high office. (LEONIE *accepts gratefully this earnest of security. They touch glasses in a toast as the curtain falls.*)

The Animal Kingdom

BY PHILIP BARRY

TO GILBERT MILLER AND LESLIE HOWARD

"THE ANIMAL KINGDOM" was first produced by Gilbert Miller and Leslie Howard at the Broadhurst Theatre in New York City on January 12, 1932. It was directed by Gilbert Miller and the settings were designed by Aline Bernstein.

CHARACTERS

RUFUS COLLIER

TOM COLLIER

CECELIA HENRY

DAISY SAGE

JOE FISK

FRANC SCHMIDT

OWEN ARTHUR

GRACE MACOMBER

RICHARD REGAN

ACTION AND SCENE

The action of the Play takes place in the course of about eighteen months, last year and this. The Scenes are as follows:

ACT ONE

Scene 1. At Tom Collier's, in Connecticut. An evening in April.
Scene 2. At Daisy Sage's, on Thirty-eighth Street.
Later the same evening.

ACT TWO

Scene 1. At Tom Collier's. An evening in January.
Scene 2. At Daisy Sage's. An afternoon in May.

ACT THREE

Scene 1. At Tom Collier's. A Sunday morning in October.
Scene 2. At Tom Collier's. Later the same evening.

ACT ONE

SCENE I

The library of TOM COLLIER's *house in the country near New York. About seven o'clock on an April evening, two years ago. The library is a fair-sized, comfortable room in a small, partially converted farmhouse, situated in a countryside which is neither fashionable nor suburban. There is an entrance from the hall at left and one into the dining-room through another hall at back right. In the center wall at back, there is a fine old fire place, framed with pine panelling. The side walls are of white plaster, windows in the one at right, with bookshelves around them. At left, a small staircase leads to the upper floor. The furniture, of no particular period, is well chosen and, in the case of chairs and sofa, invitingly comfortable. It is a cheerful room, now filled with the late evening sun.*

Upon the sofa, sits OWEN ARTHUR. *In an easy chair, turned away from him, is* RUFUS COLLIER. CECELIA HENRY *is seated in a straight chair beside a table at right center.* OWEN *is about thirty-five, well built, well dressed, agreeable looking.* RUFUS *is in his early fifties, small, slight and gray. He wears silver-rimmed spectacles, which add to his picture of himself as the man of decision.* CECELIA *is twenty-eight, lovely of figure, lovely of face, beautifully cared for, beautifully presented.*
For some moments, all sit staring in front of them, saying nothing. Finally OWEN *clears his throat, waits a moment, and without turning, ventures:*

OWEN. There's quite a fine view from the hill behind the house. (*A silence.*) —Or did I tell you that?

RUFUS. Yes.

OWEN. Sorry. (*Another silence. Then* CECELIA *speaks.*)

CECELIA. You've really never been here before?

RUFUS. I?

CECELIA. Yes.

RUFUS. Never.

CECELIA. It seems a little strange.

RUFUS. I've never been asked before. (*He glances about him.*) What anyone wants with a place at the end of the world like this, is beyond me anyhow.

OWEN. I make it in less than an hour, as a rule.

RUFUS. Oh, you come often, do you?

OWEN. Fairly. I find there's nothing like it after a stiff week in Court. I'm a new man since Friday.

RUFUS. You seem to be a fixture with him. I'm surprised he hasn't given you the go-by, as well.

OWEN. I'm too fond of him. I won't allow it.

RUFUS. But you're well-off, you work hard, you live like a gentleman—his natural enemy, I should say.

OWEN. We make few demands on each other. And he knows how I love this place.

RUFUS. But there's nothing *here!* No social life, no—

OWEN. Exactly.

CECELIA. His press is in the Village, isn't it?

RUFUS. Press? What press?

CECELIA. The Bantam Press. (*He stares.*) You know—for books.

RUFUS. Oh, so it's publishing now, is it?

CECELIA. I think it has been, for some time.

RUFUS. (*To* OWEN.) How's it going, do you know?

OWEN. Very well. Last year he only lost something like—

RUFUS. —Don't tell me! (*He rises and goes to the window.*)

CECELIA. You're not awfully fond of your son, are you, Mr. Collier? (RUFUS *turns to her.*)

326

RUFUS. Miss—I beg your pardon—you said your name was—?

CECELIA. Henry. Cecelia Henry.

RUFUS. Miss Henry, if you had spent the time and money and effort I have to make that young man realize who he is and what he ought to be doing in the world—how long have you known him?

CECELIA. I'm comparatively new, I'm afraid.

RUFUS. (*To* OWEN.) Perhaps, from longer experience, you might enlighten her.

OWEN. I presume what Mr. Collier means is that on ordinary terms, Tom doesn't seem to have got very far.

CECELIA. There's still time, isn't there?

RUFUS. Thirty-one—thirty-two in October —and he's wasted his life from the cradle.

CECELIA. It must have been pathetic to see him wasting it at three.

RUFUS. I assure you, his genius for it showed even then. I send him to Harvard, and he lasts two years there. I send him to Oxford, and he commutes from Paris. I put him in the Bank, and he— (*He sighs profoundly.*) —The world at the feet of that boy, the whole world. And all he's ever done is to run from it.

OWEN. Tom has his own ideas about what he wants to do with his life. (RICHARD REGAN *has come into the room. He is about thirty-two, with the figure of an athlete, red hair, and a genial, ugly Irish face that appears at some time to have been thoroughly mauled. He wears dark trousers and a white linen jacket, and carries a slip of paper in his hand.*) —Yes, Regan?

REGAN. There's a radio-message came by phone for him.

OWEN. You can leave it here. I'll tell him. (REGAN *folds the message and places it upon the table.*)

REGAN. Right. (*He turns and beams upon them.*)—Everything satisfactory?

OWEN. Yes, thanks.

REGAN. Comfortable, Miss?

CECELIA. Quite, thank you.

REGAN. Like a drink, anyone?

RUFUS. (*Exasperated.*) No, no! Nothing! We were talking!

REGAN. (*With a wave of his hand.*) Go right ahead. Make yourselves to home. He'll be along. (*He goes out.* CECELIA *laughs.*)

CECELIA. —The butler? But he's charming!

RUFUS. He looks like a prize-fighter.

OWEN. He was. (RUFUS *begins to hover curiously about the radio-message, wanting to read it, not quite able to bring himself to.*)

RUFUS. Why did he send me word to come out here tonight? Exceedingly important? Don't let anything interfere?

OWEN. I don't know. I found a message asking me to get Miss Henry at my Aunt's in New Canaan, and come back on the run. He had to go to town for something.

RUFUS. Well, I'll tell you what's in my mind—God knows I don't want it there.— That girl he's been living with for the last three years— (OWEN *glances quickly at* CECELIA.)

OWEN. Just a minute, Sir.

CECELIA. It's all right, Owen.

RUFUS. Good Lord, it's no secret, is it? (*To* CECELIA.) —You're not her are you?

CECELIA. Not that I know of.

RUFUS. (*To* OWEN.) Who is she, anyhow? What is she?

OWEN. —An extremely nice girl—hard-working, talented. She draws for the fashion magazines, and very successfully.

RUFUS. Admirable.—We'll, I believe he's got me out here to tell me he wants to marry her—or has already.—I've no doubt he'll bring her with him.

OWEN. Seriously—can you see Tom marrying anyone?

RUFUS. I can see her marrying him. It has happened before, and to better men. (*Again he hovers about the radio-message.*)

OWEN. If it was going to them, it would have long before this. Besides, she left for her magazine's Paris office three months ago, for an indefinite stay.

RUFUS. Maybe she's coming back.—In fact, I'm certain that she's why we're here. It offers the perfect opportunity to cut himself off finally and completely from the life he was born to. I'm surprised he has missed it as long as he has. Well—I've stood for his rowdy friendships, I've put up with his idleness, his ill-mannered insolence, his— (CECELIA *rises and faces him.*)

CECELIA. I'm sorry, Mr. Collier, but I'll have to ask you to let it go at that.

RUFUS. Ah? Why so?

CECELIA. —Because it so happens that *I'm* why we're here.

RUFUS. How's that?

CECELIA. It's me Tom's going to marry, and I've heard enough against him to last me quite a while. (RUFUS *stares.* OWEN *starts forward.*)

OWEN. —You that Tom's—?!—Good Lord, C, what are you talking about?

CECELIA. Marrying. On May first, to be exact. (*To* RUFUS.) He asked you out here to tell you, and, I imagine, to receive your good wishes. (RUFUS *still stares.*) —Thanks so much. (*She reseats herself,* OWEN *continues to gaze at her, speechless.*)

RUFUS. What did you say your name was? I'm sorry, but I—

CECELIA. Cecelia Henry. My mother was Cecelia Bond, of Baltimore. She married Stephen Henry, also of Baltimore. Except for a few distant cousins, such as Owen here, I'm alone now—poor, but quite respectable. Will it do?

RUFUS. Tom has very little of his own, you know.

CECELIA. It will be ample, thank you.

RUFUS. (*After a moment.*) Miss Henry, I'm inclined to like you. I think you have what I call "character."

CECELIA. Really? You're too kind.

RUFUS. You'll need it with him.

CECELIA. I don't agree wih you. Tom is the most interesting, most attractive man I've ever known. I consider myself shot with luck. And you make me a little tired with your abuse of him.

RUFUS. —Very loyal.

CECELIA. Not at all. I simply believe in him.—Not in his so-called "past" perhaps—I'm not quite a fool—but certainly in what's to be.

RUFUS. Faith is a beautiful thing.

CECELIA. *I* think so.

RUFUS. Well, if you can make a respectable citizen of Tom Collier at this date, you'll have nothing but praise from me, my dear. (*He picks up the radio-message and draws it through his fingers.*)

CECELIA. It seems not to occur to you that when Tom has someone who really understands him to work and care for—

OWEN. Understands him!

CECELIA. Yes. Completely. (*Again to* RUFUS.) —He'll make what you call "a citizen" of himself. (RUFUS *adjusts his spectacles and reads the message.*)

RUFUS. You think?

CECELIA. I know.—And if what you laughingly refer to as my "faith" is of any use to him—

RUFUS. "Love will conquer all." Yes, yes—of course— (*He sighs and refolds the message.*) —But forgive me a few doubts. (OWEN *leans forward.*)

OWEN. Oh? How's that, Sir?

RUFUS. "Darling. Am coming back. Arrive on 'Paris' at eight tonight. Much love Daisy." (*He looks at* CECELIA. *There is a slight pause. Then:*)

CECELIA. Well? (RUFUS *rises, and regards her intently.*)

RUFUS. —Yes, you seem to be a first-rate girl.

CECELIA. I've heard some rather agreeable things about *you,* now and then. It would be pleasant sometime to—

RUFUS. (*Smiling.*) —To see one or two of them? Well, my dear, perhaps some day you shall.—And now if you'll let me have Mr.—er—Mr. Arthur to myself for a moment— (*He moves toward the doorway.*) —There are a few dull but practical facts about—er—about your fiancé, I should like to— (*He turns to* OWEN.) —Would you mind? (OWEN *moves to follow him.* RUFUS *goes out.*)

CECELIA. Wait a minute, Owen, will you please? (OWEN *stops and turns.*)

OWEN. Well?

CECELIA. I'm sorry you had to learn about it so—abruptly.

OWEN. It doesn't matter much, does it?

CECELIA. I don't know.

OWEN. Perhaps I was supposed to hear it with little cries of pleasure.

CECELIA. The point is, that I intended to tell you on the way over, but somehow couldn't.

OWEN. I'm touched by your reluctance to deliver the blow.

CECELIA. Don't be nasty, Owen.

OWEN. It was kind of me to bring you together, wasn't it?

CECELIA. In inspiration. I'm sure I'm most grateful.

OWEN. I can't make it out. You aren't in the least the sort of girl I'd expect Tom to be interested in. (*She laughs.*)

CECELIA. Thanks!

OWEN. You know what I mean.

CECELIA. Perhaps it's the artist in him. You see, he has the charming illusion that I'm a real beauty.

OWEN. —And I can't make *you* out, either.

CECELIA. It's quite simple: I'm in love at last.

OWEN. Have you the remotest idea of what you're letting yourself in for?

CECELIA. I think so.

OWEN. I'm the one friend you and Tom have in common.

CECELIA. —But such a lovely friend, Owen. Don't ever leave me—us.

OWEN. There's not a taste, not an attitude—

CECELIA. Perhaps there will be. Give us time.

OWEN. C—how on earth did it happen?

CECELIA. Very suddenly, very sweetly.— Yesterday. (*He turns away.*) I'm sorry. You asked. (*A moment. Then:*)

OWEN. —I'll see what it is Mr. Collier wants, if you don't mind. (OWEN *goes out.* CECELIA *looks after him for a moment, then removes her hat, seats herself in a large chair, hidden from the doorway, and thoughtfully lights a cigarette. A moment, then* TOM COLLIER *appears in the doorway,* REGAN *close behind him.* TOM *is in his early thirties, slim, youthful, with a fine, sensitive, humorous face. He carries several packages in his arms.*)

TOM. Where are they?

REGAN. Well—they were. (CECELIA *rises and turns.*)

CECELIA. ....Hello, Tom.

TOM. (*To* REGAN.) Take my hat. (REGAN *removes it from his head.*) Thanks. Now get out.

REGAN. I just wanted to tell you that—

TOM. Later. (*He is gazing fondly at* CE-CELIA.)

REGAN. But there's a—

TOM. Get, will you, Red? (REGAN *goes out, murmuring.*)

REGAN. —Radio-message come for you. (*But* TOM *scarcely hears him. Suddenly he drops his parcels upon the table, goes to* CECELIA *and takes her in his arms.*)

TOM. Darling, darling— (*He is about to kiss her, but she averts her head.*)

CECELIA. No. You're late. I'm furious with you.

TOM. (*Blankly.*) Late? (*She looks at him for a moment, then smiles and kisses him lightly.*)

CECELIA. There.—All right?

TOM. Terrible. I've taken up with a thrifty spinster.

CECELIA. It's all you deserve. (*He laughs.*)

TOM. How do you like it?—I mean the place.

CECELIA. I love it.

TOM. I call it "the house in bad taste."— Look out for taste, C. There's too much of it in the world. (*He goes to the packages on the table.*) See here—what I fetched from town for you.

CECELIA. What are they?

TOM. A celebration: good things to eat and drink.—Where are they? Father? Owen?

CECELIA. In the other room.

TOM. What do you think of Father?

CECELIA. Well—

TOM. Keep a civil tongue in your head.

CECELIA. It may take a little time.

TOM. You can learn to like him and beer together. Mother was the prize: you missed something, there. Father means well, but you have to stand him off. Give him an inch, and he takes you home in his pocket. Did you really say you'd marry me? (*He slips her arm through his and leads her to a chair.*)

CECELIA. I'm afraid I did.

TOM. Heaven help us both.—Just this one marriage please, darling. I haven't been very good about marriage. I was exposed to a very bad case of it as a baby. We must make a grand go of it.

CECELIA. We shall, never you fear. (*TOM smiles.* CECELIA *seats herself in the chair,* TOM *upon the arm of it.*)

TOM. —Just do everything I say, and it will be all right.

CECELIA. —With pleasure. (*He gazes a' her.*)

TOM. C, what a marvellous object you are. (*He picks up her hand, looks at it.*) Look at those fine small bones in your wrist.

CECELIA. What about them?

TOM. This— (*He kisses the wrist.*) —You're so cunningly contrived.

CECELIA. What?

TOM. I say, you're put together on the very best principles.

CECELIA. I don't see so many blunders in you either, Thomas.

TOM. No, mine is entirely beauty of soul. Shall I tell you about my soul, C?—With lantern-slides?

CECELIA. (*Softly.*) Put your arms around me, Tom. (*He draws her to him and kisses her. Then:*)

TOM. —Oh God, I feel good!

CECELIA. (*In a breath.*) —So do I.

TOM. —Let's have all our good things together. (*He turns and calls loudly:*) Red! Oh, Red! (*Then turns again to* CECELIA.) That's a very good rule of life, darling: all one's good things together.

CECELIA. Is it, dear? (REGAN *appears beaming.* TOM *rises from the chair.*)

REGAN. Hello. Not so loud.

TOM. —Glasses with ice, Red, and run all the way.

REGAN. O.K. (*He goes out.* TOM *calls again:*)

TOM. Owen? Father! *Then turns and regards* CECELIA *once more.*) Oh, my lovely C— you lovely thing, you.

CECELIA. Stop it, Tom. You're really embarrassing me. I feel quite naked.

TOM. That's fine. (*He goes to her and draws two fingers gently across her cheek.*) It's such a fine binding, darling—such a good book. (RUFUS *re-enters, followed by* OWEN.) Hello, Father, hello, Owen—terribly nice you're here. You've met Miss Henry. Father?

RUFUS. I've had that pleasure, yes.

TOM. It *is* a pleasure.—How are the horses?

RUFUS. Do you care? (TOM *laughs.*)

TOM. Not a bit.

RUFUS. Then why ask?

TOM. Politeness.

RUFUS. You said five o'clock. It's seven.

TOM. Did I? Is it?—Listen,—you and Owen—I want to tell you what this is all about.

RUFUS. We know. We've heard. (TOM *looks to* CECELIA.)

CECELIA. He was abusing you so, I had to tell him. (TOM *laughs delightedly.*)

TOM. And it didn't discourage you?

CECELIA. On the contrary.

TOM. Stout heart. (*Then, gravely, to* RUFUS.) Why, thank you very much, Sir, but I think *I'm* the one to be congratulated. Yes, indeed we are. Yes, I'm sure we shall be. (REGAN *comes in with a tray of glasses filled with ice.*) Oh—er—this is my father, Red.

REGAN. Glad to meet you, Sir. (RUFUS *bows slightly.* REGAN *undoes one of the packages and produces a bottle of champagne.*)

TOM. —And my fiancée, Miss Henry. (*Bottle in hand,* REGAN *stares at him, puzzled.*)

REGAN. Your—? (*Then goes to* CECELIA, *seizes her hand, shakes it warmly and goes out.* CECELIA *laughs.*)

CECELIA. He is priceless!

TOM. A magnificent fellow, Red. We box every morning. I gave him that ear—but you watch, I'll pay for it. (*To* RUFUS.) You keep pretty fit, don't you, Father?

RUFUS. Quite. Do you mind?

TOM. I'm delighted. My only wonder is that some designing woman doesn't snap you up. Look how C got me. (*To* CECELIA.) —Like rolling off a log, wasn't it?

CECELIA. Easier, much.

RUFUS. I keep my defenses well in line. (TOM *laughs, and turns to* OWEN.)

TOM. Did you hear what he said? (*To* RUFUS.) —Millions for defense, eh, Sir?— But not one cent for cab-fare. (REGAN *has come in again with the bottle, now opened, and is filling the glasses.*) That's the boy, Red. Pass them, will you? Then get dinner going. I could eat an ox. (REGAN *passes the glasses.* TOM *turns to* CECELIA.) Are you hungry too, Angel?

CECELIA. Simply famished.

TOM. Good. I like a girl who likes her food. Once I said to Daisy— (*He stops, waits a moment, then smiles and raises his glass.*) Well—here's how and why and wherefore—and you know where marriages are made. (*All drink.* REGAN *has a glass of his own, which he downs at a gulp.*) —Speaking of eating, I ran into Jim Winter —you know Jim, Owen—in town today. He wants me to go salmon-fishing in Canada in June. I think I'll take him up on it. I've never done it.—It sounds like great sport, eh, Red?

REGAN. (*Putting down his glass.*) Did you get your radio, Tom?

TOM. What radio's that?

REGAN. There on the table. (*He goes out.*)

CECELIA. In June, did you say?

TOM. Yes. It won't be for long. (*He takes a swallow from his glass and puts it down.*) My, what a noble wine. (*He picks up the radio-message.*)—I'll be back in three weeks at the outside.

CECELIA. Then we'll be married in July.

TOM. (*Turning.*) July! You said May.

CECELIA. Not if you're going straight off on a trip. (*There is a silence. He regards her soberly.*)

TOM. —That's easy, then. I won't go.

CECELIA. Perhaps you'd better think it over.

TOM. No, darling. I don't have to.

CECELIA. All right, Tom. (*She smiles and raises her glass to him.*) —To May first. (*All drink.* TOM *opens the radio-message, reads it and refolds it carefully. All are watching him. He thinks a moment, frowning, then turns to* OWEN.)

TOM. Owen—would you like to show Father the new bantam-cock? (OWEN *rises and moves toward* RUFUS.)

OWEN. The red one?—Right.—Will you come along, Sir? (OWEN *goes out.* RUFUS *does not stir.* TOM *goes to him, and slips his arm through his.*)

TOM. You must see him, Father. He's a beauty, that bird. He fights at the drop of a hat. (*He draws him toward the door,* OWEN *following.*) —Even if you don't drop it, he fights. I'm sure he'll be interested to meet you, too, Sir. (*He withdraws his arm, and* RUFUS *goes out.* TOM *closes the door after him, hesitates a moment, then returns slowly to* CECELIA.)

CECELIA. Don't tell me if you don't want to, Tom.

TOM. But I do. I intended to at the first opportunity anyhow, and— (*He glances at the radio-message once again.*) —And it seems that suddenly here it is. (*And puts it in his pocket.*)

CECELIA. Am I to be a good soldier?

TOM. No. There's no need to be.—Though I'm sure you would be, if there were.

CECELIA. Thanks, dear.

TOM. C, for quite a long time I've known —known intimately—a girl who's been very important to me—

CECELIA. Yes.

TOM. —Who always will be very important to me.

CECELIA. (*Smiling.*) —That's harder.

TOM. It shouldn't be. Because it has nothing to do with you and me, not possibly.

CECELIA. I'm relieved to hear that.

TOM. In fact, as it stands, I think she'll be glad for us.

CECELIA. I hope she will.

TOM. I'm sure of it.—C, Daisy has done more for me than anyone in this world. She's the best friend I've got. I believe she always will be. I'd hate terribly to lose her. It's been a queer sort of arrangement—no arrangement at all, really. There's never been any idea of marriage between us. It's hard to explain what there has been between us. I don't believe it's ever existed before on land or on sea. Well— (*He hesitates again.*)

CECELIA. Is she attractive, Tom?

TOM. To me, she is. She's about so high, and made of platinum wire and sand.— You wouldn't like me half so well, if Daisy hadn't knocked some good sense into me.

CECELIA. Well, someone's done a good job. (TOM *laughs.*)

TOM. I'll tell her that. (*Then seriously.*) I sent her a long cable about us this morning. She couldn't have got it, because this— (*He taps his pocket.*) this is from the boat. She lands tonight.

CECELIA. I see.

TOM. I want to be sure that you understand it—understand it both ways. I'd rather not go—terribly deeply into it if you don't mind.

CECELIA. I don't, Tom.

TOM. We've been—everything possible to each other of course, and—

CECELIA. Yes, Tom.

TOM. But at the same time, free as air. There's never been any responsibility to each other involved in it—

CECELIA. I can understand that.

TOM. Can you, C? Because I never could. —Anyhow, that's the way it's been.—We haven't been what you'd call "in love," for quite a long time, now, so—

CECELIA. (*Smiling.*) Does she know that?

TOM. She knew it first. Well— I don't know what more there is to say about it, except that there's no reason at all for you to worry, and—you won't, will you?

CECELIA. No, Tom. Not if you tell me I

needn't.

TOM. I do.—And finally, that I think she ought to know the—news about us, pretty promptly.

CECELIA. Yes. Probably.

TOM. Is whatever I do about it all right with you?

CECELIA. Absolutely.

TOM. Thanks, C.

CECELIA. There's just one thing I'd like to ask. May I?

TOM. Why of course, darling. What?

CECELIA. Are you quite sure that—? (*She sees* OWEN *and* RUFUS *coming in.*) —Poor Mr. Collier. I'm sure you loathe chickens. I quite agree with you.

RUFUS. —Vicious little beast. (REGAN *comes in beaming.*)

REGAN. Come on, everyone! Dinner!

TOM. You haven't put the car away, have you?

REGAN. Say, how many hands have I got?

TOM. Don't. I'll need it. (REGAN *goes out.* TOM *turns to his father.*)

TOM. Father, I'm afraid I'll have to ask you to do the honors at dinner.

RUFUS. The—? Why? How's that?

TOM. I find I've got to go straight back to town. (*A silence. Then:*)

OWEN. But I thought this was to be a celebration.

RUFUS. I had the same impression.

TOM. I'm sorry: it can't be helped.

OWEN. Is it so important to go in just this minute, Tom?

TOM. Yes—unfortunately. (RUFUS *is eyeing him shrewdly.*)

RUFUS. Why? What's wrong?

TOM. Nothing at all. It's simply that someone's arriving from Europe. I've missed the landing, as it is.— (*To* OWEN.) —Someone I've known a long time, and am fond of.

OWEN. Oh, I see.

TOM. (*To* RUFUS.) I must—well, the fact is, I must tell her my—my— good news.

RUFUS. Now you listen to me— (TOM *confronts him.*)

TOM. —And it seems to me extremely important that I should do it at once. In fact, I can't do otherwise. (RUFUS *bursts out:*)

RUFUS. —You have the effrontery, the colossal bad taste, on the night of celebrating your engagement to a fine trusting, loyal girl, to go from her—your fiancée— to your—to your— (TOM *smiles.*)

TOM. —The same old difficulty with words, eh, Sir?—Never mind. None of them would apply to Daisy.

RUFUS. It's beyond me. It's the confoundest impertinence I've ever known.

TOM. (*Smiling.*) But you see, for all your splendid moral judgments, you know so very little, Sir.

RUFUS. I suppose you know better.—If you leave here tonight— (TOM's *smile vanishes.*)

TOM. —Yes. Much better. (*He returns to* CECELIA, *lifts her hand and kisses it lightly.*) —Until tomorrow, my Angel. (*He nods good-night to* OWEN *and* RUFUS, *and goes out.*)

CURTAIN.

SCENE II

The sitting-room of DAISY SAGE's *flat, later the same night.*

DAISY's *flat occupies the top floor of an old house in the Murray Hill section of New York. The sitting-room also serves as a workroom for* DAISY. *Victorian in atmosphere, it is light and cheerful and has been decorated and furnished with an original and unerring feeling for the period. There is a fire place of simple design at left and above it, a door opening into the bedroom. The entrance from the hall is up right, and into the pantry, down right. The sofa and chairs are fine old Victorian pieces, but comfortable in spite of it. There are three large windows in the back wall. Below*

them stands DAISY's *work-table, piled with old magazines and sketches, drawing-boards, crayons, pens and pencils.*
Opposite TOM, JOE FISK *is seated. Between them stands* FRANC SCHMIDT, *violin under her chin, playing, and playing well, the concluding measures of a César Franck sonata. She is thirty, hard, rugged—in appearance more of a handsome farm-girl than musician.* JOE *is twenty-eight, fine Irish, nervous, intense, attractive.* FRANC *concludes the piece.*

JOE. Good!—You'll get there, Franc, if you work. (*She returns the violin to its case and seats herself near them. She speaks with a slight German accent.*)

FRANC. —Only I played it much better, much.

TOM. He just wasn't impressed, eh?

FRANC. Oh, yes.—He could book me on the Big Time, he said.

JOE. (*Incredulous.*) Vaudeville?

FRANC. —That is, if I would learn to roller-skate.

TOM. He wanted you to play on skates?

FRANC. —A sensation, he said. (JOE *and* TOM *laugh with delight.* JOE *goes to her, takes her face between his hands and kisses her resoundingly upon the brow.*)

JOE. My darling. My Dutch darling. (*She brushes him aside.*)

FRANC. Get away. (JOE *calls in the direction of the bedroom:*)

JOE. Daisy!—Did you hear about Franc and the booking-agent? (*He turns to* FRANC.) Where is she?

FRANC. —Probably taking another bath. It will be her third in six hours. That's what Europe does for you.

TOM. (*Indicating the pantry.*) —No. She's in there, I think.

JOE. (*Incredulously.*) Six hours! Two o'clock—?

FRANC. It's past it.

TOM. Will you two never go home?

JOE. (*Calling in the direction of the pantry.*) Daisy! We're going! (*To* TOM *and* FRANC.) —And I promised myself tomorrow I'd do a chapter or die.

TOM. How's it coming?

JOE. All right. At least it's begun to move.

TOM. What are you calling it?

JOE. "Easy Rider."

TOM. I like that.

FRANC. But what does it mean?

JOE. Good God, must it mean something? (*Again he calls.*) Daisy!

FRANC. Yes. Your eyes have got smaller. You should get to bed.

TOM. Both of you should—go on, will you?

JOE. Why?

TOM. I want to talk to Daisy.

JOE. Look here, Tom, what *is* on your mind?

TOM. I've got something to tell her.

JOE. News?

TOM. Yes.

JOE. Good news?

TOM. Very.

FRANC. Will she cheer?

TOM. I think so.

FRANC. Tell *us*, Tom!

TOM. No.

JOE. Why not?

TOM. I want to tell Daisy first. (*To* FRANC.) You know, I've been thinking: Johnny Bristed might get a concert for you.

FRANC. I don't want it yet. I'm not ready yet. (*Again* JOE *calls.*)

JOE. (Daisy! (DAISY SAGE *comes in from the pantry. She is twenty-six, slim, lithe, a stripling, but with dignity beyond her years and a rare grace to accompany it. In contrast to* CECELIA's *lush beauty, she is plain, but there is a certain style of her own, a presence, a manner that defies description. Instantly and lastingly attractive, like no one else one knows; in short "a person," an "original." She wears white pajamas that might as well be a dress, and carries a tray containing coffee and sandwiches.*

DAISY. —And furthermore, I don't believe I like France as much as I say I do. (*She puts down the tray.*) —And I don't for a minute believe that you're leaving.

FRANC. Joe must. So must I.

DAISY. —You stay the night, if you like, Tom. You can have my room. I've got all the work in the world to do before morning.

TOM. Why, thanks. Daisy, but—

DAISY. As you like. (*She seats herself, and gives them coffee and sandwiches.*) I had thirty sketches to get through on the boat. —Oh, what lovely intentions.

FRANC. Was it rough?

DAISY. No, but Pilard was on board and we spent hours on end in the smoking-room—talk, talk, and more talk.

JOE. He's a fine painter, Pilard.

TOM. He's a good painter.

JOE. Fine, I said.

TOM. —And last week Henry Collins could write. Hold on to your standards, Joe.

JOE. You teach me, will you, Master?

TOM. Collins' life shows in his work. He can't make up his mind whether he wants to be a writer or a man-about-town.

JOE. Why not both?

TOM. —Because, little Joe, his work is the only true mistress a real artist ever had. When he takes on the world he takes on a whore.

FRANC. That goes for all good men, not only artists.

DAISY. —But all good men are, aren't they? —Look at Tom.—You don't have to put marks on paper or dents in stone to qualify, do you?

TOM. (*To* JOE.) —Yes, and pays for her favors with something a lot more precious than twenty dollars left on the mantel-piece. (JOE *reflects.*)

JOE. I had twenty dollars once. Now, when was it?

DAISY. There's a statue in Florence that made me think of you, Tom. (TOM *laughs.*)

TOM. Me! How?

DAISY. It's a David by Donatello.

TOM. You mean with the curls and the derby hat?

DAISY. That's right! (TOM *shakes his head.*)

TOM. —No David, me. I'm just the no-account-boy. Ask Father—he'll tell you.— Hand me another sandwich, Joe. (JOE *gives him one.*)

JOE. No-account, is it?—You've done more for people than any one man I know.

TOM. Why thanks, Joe.—It's not true, of course, but thanks.

JOE. And done it in the damndest, most unassuming way I've ever heard of.

TOM. Oh, go to hell, will you?

JOE. (*To* FRANC.) I could name a dozen first-class talents that, if *he* hadn't nosed 'em out, would have—

TOM. Say, are you two going to hang around here all night?

JOE. We haven't seen her either you know. (FRANC *puts down her cup.*)

FRANC. I must teach you again how to make coffee, darling.

DAISY. Your country's the one, Franc.

FRANC. Ach! There is no more new music in Germany today than there is here.

JOE. I thought there was plenty here.

FRANC. Like what?—If someone goes— (*She hums the opening bar of the "Rhapsody in Blue."*) —at me again, I shall become mad. (DAISY *gazes at the bulging brief-case on the floor beside the work-table. Her smile fades.*)

DAISY. Oh, that work!—Look at it.

TOM. Is there much of it?

DAISY. At least eight hours.

JOE. I wish we could help.

TOM. —You can. Good-night, Joe.

DAISY. —And Briggs was at the dock.

TOM. I didn't get your radio till seven.

DAISY. That didn't matter. Anyhow I hate being met. Anyhow, I tell myself I do. Briggs was frantic. Apparently they've held the presses for two days.

TOM. You're a bad girl.

DAISY. I'm a scoundrel. I swore it would be on his desk at nine. I'll be lucky if I'm through by noon. (JOE *laughs, and rises.*)

JOE. Urge us to stay once more and we may give in.—Come along, Franc. I'll see you across the hall. (FRANC *rises and takes up her violin-case.*)

FRANC. —It is good to have you back, too, Tom. You are better than all of us, but Daisy. She is better than best. Between you, you stir up our lazy bones, you hold us together, you bind our wounds. You two are the—ach!—my blood is turned to beer.—Auf wiedersehen. Good-night. (*She goes out.*)

JOE. I'll drop in tomorrow afternoon about five, if I can.

DAISY. Fine. I ought to be up by then. (*She follows* FRANC *into the hall.*)

JOE. (*To* TOM.) Will you be here?

TOM. I'm afraid I'll have to go to the country.

JOE. Shun the country. Things come out of the ground there in Spring. (*He goes out.* TOM *is alone for a moment Then* DAISY *re-enters.*)

DAISY. —Love them as I do, I thought they'd never go.

TOM. So did I. (*She puts her arms around him and looks up at him.*)

DAISY. Hello, you dear Tom.

TOM. Hello, Daisy. (*She kisses him lightly.*)

DAISY. Now it seems I haven't been away at all. (*And leaves his arms.*) Oh, it's grand to be back!

TOM. It's grand having you.—Was the trip really all that you hoped it would be?

DAISY. It was better.—If only you'd been along. Oh Tom—the pictures! I got drunk on them every day, twice a day.

TOM. I was sure you would.

DAISY. And at night when the galleries were closed I sat around and dreamed of them.—The silly contempt I always pretended to have for painting—self-protection, of course—the stuff *I* draw.

TOM. But some of it's good.

DAISY. You're right, my boy. Some of it is. (*She goes to the table and picks up a portfolio.*) Look—full—sketches.—And not a dress, a hat, a pajama among them. A market-wagon—the angle of a doorway—an open trunk. A melon cut in half—three glasses and a corkscrew—all manner of funny objects. Oh Tom, two of the most exciting things have happened to me! Not one—two! (*She moves toward the sofa.*) Come—sit down—

TOM. What are they?

DAISY. I'm bursting with them. (*She makes room for him beside her on the sofa, looks at him lovingly, smiles contentedly, touches his arm.*) Good, this—isn't it?

TOM. But what, Daisy? Did you fall in love with Pilard?

DAISY. Well I should say not! (*She laughs.*) Pilard! (*Then.*) What's that? (*From the distance the strains of a violin are heard, playing variations on the scales.*) Oh—Franc. Still working.—Guess what I found in my room when I came in? (*He looks at her questioningly. She laughs.*) —It seems the Swede maid Franc got me doesn't approve of you:—Four shirts, three socks, five ties and a razor, all done up in a great big white handkerchief.

TOM. You'd better go back to colored ones. —Maids, I mean.—

DAISY. —Remember Gladys?

TOM. Remember Hannah?

DAISY. Remember Marietta? (*They laugh together happily. She slips her arm through his, and for a moment drops her head upon his shoulder.*) Oh Tom, God love you.

TOM. God love you, my dear. (*For a moment there is silence, except for the sound of* FRANC's *violin. Then she raises her head and they speak simultaneously.*) Daisy—

DAISY. Darling— (*She laughs.*) What?

TOM. No—you tell me—

DAISY. Well, my heavy sledding ought to be over in a few weeks—by the first of May, anyway. What have you got on the fire—much?

TOM. Yes. A great deal. The fact is—

DAISY. (*In a rush.*) —Work night and day until May. Then come to Mexico for a month with Daisy. I'm dying to go. Pilard was full of it. I know it's what I need for awhile, because—well, first—oh, I feel like a fool. You mustn't breathe a word of it. (*He shakes his head.*)—Tom, I think I can paint.

TOM. But that's no surprise. I've always thought if only you'd—

DAISY. (*Quickly.*) Then you've always been wrong!—It's new. It's since these two months.—I believe that if I work my eyes out, and my fingers to the bone, someday I may paint.—You must be hard with me— no parties—no hell-raising—*work.*—And you mustn't let me show until you know I'm ready to. Is that agreed?

TOM. All right.

DAISY. You have a funny instinct about such things. I count on you.—As for the second thing—(*She hesitates.*)—You know —suddenly I feel shy with you. (*She rises.*) I don't like it. I don't like it a bit.

TOM. We've—it's been a long time. (DAISY *goes again to the work-table.*)

DAISY. Too long.—Perhaps I'd better wait to tell you the second thing.

TOM. No. Tell me now.

DAISY. Oh, my dear—what's wrong with us? Come here to me. (*He goes to her,*

takes her hands in his.) That's better. Now I don't feel it so much. (*But still she looks at him anxiously. Finally she releases her hands, turns and fumbles among her work-materials, picks up a pencil.*)—These are German pencils. They can't touch ours. You'd think they could, but they can't. Give me a "Venus-6B," every time. (*She stares fixedly at the pencil for another moment, then puts it down and turns to him.*) You're a free man, Tommy. You always have been, with me. No questions asked. But please, Mexico in May together, because listen—No! Don't look at me. Look the other way— (*He averts his head. She goes on, rapidly.*) —I stayed three days with the Allens at Vevey and they've got the sweetest small boy about two and I got crazy about him and I want one, I want one like the devil. I'm crazy for one, and would you please be good enough to marry me, and—

TOM. Daisy, I—!

DAISY. Oh, it needn't be terribly serious!— It's not a life-sentence—just for a short while, if you like—it'd be such a dirty trick on him, if we didn't.—After I get my stuff through for the June issue—then Mexico for a month—I love you so much, I was a fool ever to think I didn't, and— ah, come on, Tom—be a sport—. (*She is breathless.*) —Give me a cigarette—(*But he does not.*)

TOM. Daisy—

DAISY. (*Quickly.*) All right. No go. Let's forget about it. What a foul necktie that is. The colors are awful.

TOM. Daisy, I—Oh God, God Almighty—

DAISY. Well, what is it? (*He covers her hand with his.*) —You're going to tell me something terrible.—What is it?

TOM. I'm going to be married.

DAISY. (*Incredulously.*) To be—?! (*Then silence. She averts her head.*)

TOM. Listen to me, darling, listen: you don't really care so much. You can't. It's simply that we—you and I—after all this time, naturally we'd feel—

DAISY. It must have happened pretty quickly.

TOM. It did. A month ago we hadn't even met. It was—

DAISY. You can spare me the details, please. I don't even want to know who she is. (*He moves away from her.* FRANC's *violin begins to be heard again.*)

TOM. —Her name is Cecelia Henry.

DAISY. It sounds familiar. I've heard or read that somewhere. Where?—Well, well, will, wonders never cease? —If I'd thought you were in a marrying mood, I might have thrown my own— (*She picks up a small limp hat from the table.*) —could you call it a hat?—in the ring a bit sooner. (*She drops the hat upon the table.*) —Behold, the Bridegroom cometh—and no oil for my lamp, as usual.—A foolish virgin, me—well, foolish, anyway.—When's it to be? Soon?

TOM. —About the first of May, we planned.

DAISY. I see.—Of course, in that event Mexico *would* be out, wouldn't it?

TOM. —But I never dreamed you'd—oh God, I feel so awful.

DAISY. Does she know about us?

TOM. Yes.

DAISY. Honest Tom.

TOM. Oh, shut up.

DAISY. Remember me, Tom.

TOM. Oh my dear—as if ever in this world I— (*Suddenly, fearfully.*) Daisy!—There's to be no nonsense about not seeing each other as friends again, or any of that, you know—

DAISY. No?

TOM. No. We're grown-up human beings. We're decent and we're civilized. We—

DAISY. But there *will* be that nonsense. Oh yes—there'll be that, all right.—"Cecelia Henry"—Now I know where it was! (*She picks up a magazine and begins to run through it.*)

TOM. —But I don't understand it. I don't see why we shouldn't. I thought for a long

time we'd been out of danger so far as— well, so far as— (*He cannot finish it, but* DAISY *can.*)

DAISY. —Wanting each other goes?

TOM. But haven't we?

TOM. Speak for yourself, Tom. (*He looks at her, waits a moment, then speaks.*)

TOM. —You too, Daisy.—You first, I thought.

DAISY. (*Slowly, thoughtfully.*) It's true, that side of it was never so much to us, was it? Not in comparison—not after those first crazy months. But I thought that was natural. I was even glad of it—glad to find it was—other needs that held us together. (*She looks away.*) —Closely—without claims —not a claim—but so closely. (*A moment. Then suddenly, sharply.*) Tom—do you have to marry her?

TOM. I want to marry her.

DAISY. (*Into the magazine.*) I was just thinking—perhaps you simply want her— want her most awfully.

TOM. It's more than that, much more.

DAISY. I don't see how you can tell quite yet.—For all our big talk, we still belong to the animal kingd— (*She stops and looks closely at a photograph in the magazine.*) Here she is!—Oh, these neat, protected women. I've drawn so many of them, dressed so many more.

TOM. If you knew her—

DAISY. But I don't, you see.— (*She holds the magazine at arm's length, gazing at the photograph.*) Such a pretty face—lovely eyes, Tom. She's a prize, my boy. (*She closes the magazine and replaces it upon the table.*) —But look out for that chin.

TOM. Why?

DAISY. Just look out for it. (*She goes to him.*) —Does she love you? *Will* she love you, head over heels, regardless, as I— shall I say "as I once did"? Would you rather?

TOM. Daisy—don't—

DAISY. I hold you dear, Tom—*you*—for what you are— just *as* you are. I thought it was my special gift. But maybe she has it too. I hope, I hope— (*He gropes for her hand, raises it to his lips kisses it.*)

TOM. There's no one like you—never will be. *I* know that.—But this—it's the damndest thing—I can't tell you—

DAISY. Don't try. I'll pray for you every night, Tom. I really shall, you know I do that.

TOM. Oh, my sweet dear—

DAISY. Yes—be good enough to remember me kindly, if you will. (*She returns to the table.*)

TOM. (*Wretchedly.*) Oh, don't *talk* that stuff! (*He goes to the fire place. She takes up her work-board.*)

DAISY. Now just stand like that a minute, will you? Erect!—Will you stand erect, please? (*He turns. She looks at him keenly.*)

TOM. What's all this about "remembering"? You sound as if we were— (*She draws one strong line upon the paper and lets the work-board drop.*)

DAISY. There! That's all I want of you, all I shall keep of you. So goodbye, you Tom Collier. (*He looks at her, puzzled.*)

TOM. "Goodbye"?—Until when—?

DAISY. (*So lightly.*) Doomsday, my darling.

TOM. Daisy, what *are* you talking about!

DAISY. Just that. (*He advances to her, takes her shoulders in his hands.*)

TOM. Now you listen to me: If you think I'm going to allow two people as important to each other as you and I are, to be separated by any such false, ridiculous notion as this, you're mistaken. Just you try it.

DAISY. Tell me goodbye!

TOM. I'll do nothing of the sort.

DAISY. Yes! You have to.—Sharp, decent, clean—no loose ends between *us* two!

TOM. But it's not decent!—It's soft. It's sentimental. It's the sort of thing you've never had any use for—taught *me* never to.

DAISY. Goodbye!

TOM. I will not say it

DAISY. Goodbye!

TOM. No.

DAISY. You must!

TOM. You'll never get me to. So give up. (DAISY *throws back her head and closes her eyes in pain.*)

DAISY. Oh, sweet heaven, what a world! I could do better by people than this—

TOM. Daisy dear—listen to me—

DAISY. —And I want you to take those things of yours—you hear? I don't want them hanging around the place, not me.—That new maid had a very fine hunch about us, didn't she?—Packed you all up, yes. Second sight—well, she gets the gate for it, the big Swede. (*He stands gazing at her.*)

TOM. I don't believe in this. I don't believe in any of it. (*She indicates the bedroom.*)

DAISY. —Go in and get them, will you? Fetch, Thomas. It's quite a neat, tidy little bundle. You won't be ashamed of it.—But if it stays around—well, I don't quite see myself crying into an old shirt, do you?—I have work to do, my son—a great deal of it. (*He does not move.*) No? Won't fetch?—Then kindly permit me to— (*She moves toward the bedroom.*) —And then you must say goodbye to me—you will, won't you? You've said it so many times, so brightly—Say it this time sadly.—We'll make it an *un*-marriage ceremony, to keep it all quite regular. You must grasp my hand in yours—one splendid gesture—and murmur "Goodbye, my Daisy. Thanks very much. A charming association." (*She goes into the bedroom.*) —And may we never, never meet again so long as we two shall live.—You will, won't you? (*He has been staring fixedly after her. Suddenly he straightens.*)

TOM. —No. (*He moves swiftly to the hall doorway, picks up his hat and goes out. A moment. Then* DAISY *comes in again, with a small bundle tied up in a large white handkerchief.*)

DAISY. —See?—The wash is back.—Now do as Daisy says, and say— (*She sees that he has gone. She moves toward the door, stops against the work-table. The bundle* *droops in her hand, drops upon the table. There she stands, staring at the door. Again,* FRANC'S *violin is heard, playing the scales.*)

CURTAIN.

ACT TWO

SCENE I

At TOM COLLIER'S. *About half-past seven on a Saturday night the following January.*
The living-room has undergone a certain change. Small, feminine touches, such as new lamps, cretonne curtains at the windows and slip-covers of the same material on chairs and sofa, have made a woman's room of it.

CECELIA *and* GRACE MACOMBER *are seated near the fire place having after-dinner coffee. Grace is just over thirty. Without a single feature to remark upon except a slim and well-kept body, she manages, with the aid of coiffeurs, dressmakers and manicurists, to impress one as an attractive woman. She puts down her coffee cup and moves closer to the fire.*

GRACE. My dear, I'm congealed. I can't say I envy you the trip into town.

CECELIA. It's not my idea. (*She takes up a piece of needlepoint and begins to work upon it.*)

GRACE. But why do you do it? It's so grim.

CECELIA. Tom wants to.

GRACE. Such devotion.

CECELIA. It's her first big concert and he thinks for some reason we ought to be there.

GRACE. Who is she, anyway?

CECELIA. Schmidt, her name is. (GRACE *laughs.*)

GRACE. My dear! Not really!

CECELIA. Franc Schmidt, at that.—Tom says she's supreme.

GRACE. Oh—she's a friend, then.

CECELIA. She used to be.

GRACE. (*With meaning.*) I see. (CECELIA *smiles.*)

CECELIA. No, Grace. I doubt if you do.

GRACE. I suppose publishers have to hob-nob with all sorts of queer people.

CECELIA. We see very few people of any description any more.

GRACE. Don't tell me about the hermit life you live! I think the least you could do would be to come to my Sunday breakfasts now and then. Tomorrow's will be such fun. Do, C.

CECELIA. Perhaps we shall.

GRACE. —Not if you go in tonight.

CECELIA. Perhaps we shan't go in.

GRACE. (*Knowingly.*) Ah-ha! (*She looks about her.*) —You know, you could do so much with this house.

CECELIA. —If we weren't so poor.

GRACE. Don't be funny. Your name's Collier, isn't it?

CECELIA. Somehow that doesn't seem to make the difference it might.

GRACE. Well, I think it's brutal the way old Rufus K. hangs onto it.

CECELIA. We seem to manage somehow.

GRACE. I'd take *knives,* my dear, and gouge it out. (*A moment. Then*) —What would he be doing now, for instance? Tom, I mean.

CECELIA. Didn't he say he had letters to write? (GRACE *seats herself again.*)

GRACE. He's really extraordinary. He defeats me. (CECELIA *laughs.*)

CECELIA. What's so extraordinary about writing letters?

GRACE. The minute dinner's finished? Before coffee, even?—I guess I'm just not familiar with publishers' eccentricities. (*Again* CECELIA *laughs.*)

CECELIA. He's a little worried tonight, poor dear.—Some more coffee?— (*She gives* GRACE *a second cup.*) —He has a rather difficult ordeal to face.

GRACE. The concert?

CECELIA. No. Discharging Regan.

GRACE. Reg—?

CECELIA. —When, as and if he gets back from his weekly bat in town.

GRACE. You mean that desperate butler? Oh my dear, I'm so glad! He must have embarrassed you to death,—But how did you manage to persuade Tom to let him go?

CECELIA. I had nothing to do with it.

GRACE. No? (*She laughs gaily.*) I believe that! (TOM *comes in from the other room, with two or three magazines, which he is unwrapping.*) Ah! With us again.

TOM. With you again. (*He looks at his watch.*) Look here, C—hadn't we better be getting under way?

CECELIA. We've got hours. Let's not sit and wait in a stuffy theater. (*A silence. Then:*)

GRACE. (*Brightly.*) I read the new book you published last week, Tom.

TOM. (*Without interest.*) Yes? What did you think of it?

GRACE. Superlative, my dear. I was simply ravished!

TOM. Well, that's something, isn't it? (GRACE *laughs.*)

GRACE. —Isn't he beyond words? (*To* TOM.) You're the world's funniest man. You couldn't possibly be funnier.

TOM. You don't know me.

GRACE. Oh yes I do! Don't *you* adore it, C? The book, I mean—

CECELIA. I like it very much, (*She glances at* TOM.) In fact I'm afraid it was I who made Tom do it.

TOM. And I'm afraid I still think it's the worst tripe The Bantam ever published.

GRACE. —But my dear! Everyone's simply devouring it!

TOM. There'll be a lot of sickness this winter.

CECELIA. You're so foolish about it, Tom. (*To* GRACE.) —He'll make enough on that one book to bring out ten he really cares for. (TOM *unwraps a second magazine.*)

TOM. I suppose that's the way it works.

CECELIA. Of course it is. It's simply common sense.

TOM. I suppose so.

CECELIA. Besides, I don't care what you say, it really is amusing.

TOM. It's tripe.

GRACE. Isn't there such a thing as having too high a standard?

TOM. No, there's not. (*She looks at him, startled.*)

CECELIA. What Grace means—

TOM. (*More emphatically still.*) No, C. There is not.

CECELIA. All right, darling. (*He looks over one of the magazines. A moment. Then.*) Oh—I meant to tell you: your father wants us to dine with him Wednesday and spend the night. (GRACE *pricks up her ears.*)

TOM. Get us out of it, won't you?

CECELIA. Again? How can I?

TOM. Oh, say I'm up to my ears in work, or something else he won't believe. Say the old boat is frozen stiff.

GRACE. I could easily send you in, in the closed car. Sammy and I might even join you.

TOM. Thanks. We cannot accept your sacrifice.

GRACE. But this weather—in that *racer!* It couldn't be more sobbing.

TOM. Oh yes it could! (GRACE *rises.*)

GRACE. Well, I guess I'd better be "barging along," as they say. I'm sure it's getting colder by the minute.

TOM. Yes—I think we'd best bring the brass monkeys in tonight. (*He returns to his magazine.*)

GRACE. The—? Oh, by the way, do you happen to know a stage-director named Prentice Frith?

TOM. You know, I'm awfully afraid I don't?

GRACE. He's supposed to be the absolute top in amateur dramatics.

TOM. I can't imagine how I've missed him.

GRACE. He's coming out especially for my Sunday breakfast tomorrow—

TOM. That's perfectly fine. That's just what Sunday breakfast needs, isn't it?—Of course the coffee must be very hot, as well. (GRACE *stares.* CECELIA *rises quickly. Finally* GRACE *turns to her.*)

GRACE. Good-night, C.

CECELIA. Good-night, Grace. Must you really?

GRACE. (*Moving toward the hall door.*) Yes. I'm afraid I must. (*She goes out, followed by* CECELIA. TOM *lights a cigarette, seats himself upon the stairs and continues to glance through the magazine. A door is heard to close in the hall. A moment, then* REGAN *comes in and makes his way quietly, but only fairly steadily, toward the dining-room door. He has almost reached it, when* TOM *turns.*)

TOM. Hi, Red.

REGAN. 'Evening.

TOM. Did you have a good day in town?

REGAN. Fine, thanks.

TOM. Lots of beer?

REGAN. No.

TOM. No?

REGAN. —Ale.

TOM. Why ale?

REGAN. It's quicker.

TOM. It's bitter.

REGAN. It's bitter and quicker.

TOM. You don't seem to be in very good shape.

REGAN. I'm in awful shape.

TOM. You'd better get to bed.

REGAN. —Just where I'm headed. (*He moves toward the door again.*)

TOM. —See here a minute first, Red— (*He turns.* TOM *goes to him and confronts him sternly.*)

REGAN. Yes? (*Tom hesitates. Then.*)

TOM. The fact is, that— (*He stops, and concludes.*) —Bring a couple of bottles of beer, will you?

REGAN. Right. (*He goes out.* TOM *draws a deep breath of smoke, sinks down upon the sofa, and exhales it slowly.* CECELIA *comes in from the hall.*)

CECELIA. You ought to be ashamed, Tom.

TOM. Why?

CECELIA. You were terrible to Grace.

TOM. Why we should be exposed to a woman like that at all, is more than I can make out.

CECELIA. She's perfectly kind and friendly.

TOM. She's a silly, idle, empty, destructive woman. And the woods are full of her.

CECELIA. Grace destructive?—She doesn't know enough to be.

TOM. It's pure instinct with her. If she were malicious, that might be interesting.— Come on—it's nearly eight.

CECELIA. She thought you were trying to insult her.

TOM. Do you have to change or are you ready?

CECELIA. It seemed to *me* you were unnecessarily rude.—I have to change.

TOM. (*Rising.*) I'll warm up the car.

CECELIA. Now we've simply got to go to her breakfast in the morning.

TOM. Not me.

CECELIA. But you'll have to make *some* gesture toward her.

TOM. I only know one.

CECELIA. Tom—please be serious.

TOM. Darling, I've spent my life trying to get away from her kind of people.

CECELIA. Just what do you call her kind?

TOM. Well—people utterly without stature, without nobility of any sort.

CECELIA. It takes all kinds to make a world, doesn't it?

TOM. Yes—and then what have you got? (*He laughs, takes her face between his hands, and kisses her.*) Go get dressed.

CECELIA. All the same, I insist that if—. What did you say to Regan?

TOM. Why, I— (*He stops and smiles.*) —I told him to bring some beer, but I expect he's forgotten it.

CECELIA. Oh, I see.

TOM. —Anyhow, I've been thinking: He never drinks on duty. Why shouldn't he have a right to get slightly mellow on his one day off?

CECELIA. "Slightly mellow"!—When he came back last week, he could hardly stand. When I said "Good evening" to him he didn't even answer.

TOM. Maybe he couldn't speak.

CECELIA. Probably not.—I said "Don't forget the furnace, Regan," and all he did was to bow like this, with a foolish grin— so low he nearly toppled over.

TOM. It's pretty hard to gauge a bow under those conditions.

CECELIA. Of course *I* think it's selfish of us to keep him.

TOM. Selfish?

CECELIA. We're certainly depriving him of any chance he ever had to make anything of himself.

TOM. But hang it, C—he broke his hand. He'll never fight again.

CECELIA. I don't mean fighting.

TOM. These are hard times: I don't know what else there is for him. (CECELIA *shrugs and rises*)

CECELIA. All right. Do as you like about him. I'll leave it to you.

TOM. —And anyhow, I feel for some reason that Red's good luck for me. He's—I don't know—we understand each other. I'm awfully fond of him.

CECELIA. You must be, to ruin whatever chance in life he might have. (*A moment. Then:*)

TOM. I wouldn't do that, C. You know I wouldn't.

CECELIA. You're doing it, though. What possibly could be more degrading to a man than housework?

TOM. You're making a regular Simon Legree of me. Where's my whip?

CECELIA. No, it's simply that in your delightful, casual way, you've never thought of his side of it.

TOM. (*Thoughtfully.*) —I wouldn't do that to Red. I really wouldn't. (*A moment. Then:*) Ring for him, will you?

CECELIA. Not me. I have nothing to do with it. (TOM *stares in front of him for a moment, then goes to a bell in the wall, presses it and returns to the fire place.*)

TOM. I don't know how I'll tell him. (*A silence. He ponders it. Then:*)

CECELIA. I suppose you feel we really must go into town tonight—

TOM. Why, yes. Why?

CECELIA. She'll play again, won't she?

TOM. I hope so—and often. But the first concert's an occasion, you know.

CECELIA. I suppose all your old friends will be there, en masse.

TOM. Without a doubt. (*Then, to himself.*) —All week long I've been trying to tell Red—

CECELIA. —The one you were so fond of— the Daisy something—

TOM. —Daisy Sage.

CECELIA. What's *she* doing now?

TOM. Painting, I believe.

CECELIA. Well?

TOM. I don't know. But I should imagine so.—I haven't seen her.

CECELIA. Don't you see any of them anymore?

TOM. No.

CECELIA. But why not, dearest? (*A moment. Then:*)

TOM. They won't see me.

CECELIA. —Won't see *you!*

TOM. No.—Go on now, please, like a good girl, and get ready. (*She turns, passing her hand over her eyes, and moves toward the stairs.*) What's the matter?

CECELIA. Nothing.

TOM. But dear—what is it?

CECELIA. Just this blasted headache, that's all. I've had it all day.

TOM. What a shame.—The cold air will fix you up.

CECELIA. It's that that gave it to me. I'm—honestly, Tom, I don't think I can face it. Why not telegraph, instead? Best wishes, and all that.

TOM. It wouldn't do.

CECELIA. I'm sure she'd be every bit as glad to have a telegram.

TOM. You don't understand, C. Franc has been working for years for this. She— (*REGAN comes in with bottles of beer and two glasses on a tray.*) —Just put them there, will you? (*He does so, and turns to go.*) —And wait a minute. What's the rush? Stick around.

REGAN. Certainly. (*He waits, steadying himself in the doorway.* TOM *turns again to* CECELIA.)

TOM. —Sorry, darling, a telegram wouldn't do. I've got to be there. But there's no particular reason why you should come. I can go alone.

CECELIA. I'll come.

TOM. No, you hop into bed with a flock of aspirin. I'll be out again bright and early.

CECELIA. —I'll come, too. (*She goes out, up the stairs.* TOM *waits a moment, then turns to* REGAN.)

TOM. —Drag up a chair. (*REGAN brings a chair to the table.*)

REGAN. One more's about all I need. (*TOM opens the beer and fills the glasses.*) This morning if all the bad heads in the world'd been put together in a row, my head would've got up and sneered at the rest of them. (*TOM laughs and raises his glass.*)

TOM. Here's how. (*REGAN raises his.*)

REGAN. How. (*He drinks, and beams.*) That's the stuff.

TOM. It builds you up.

REGAN. Yo! (*He takes an old pack of cards from his pocket.*) —Seen this one?

TOM. I don't think so. (*REGAN holds the pack before him and releases one card after another with his thumb.*)

REGAN. —Tell me where to stop, and remember the card.

TOM. All right.

REGAN. Got it?

TOM. I've got it. (*REGAN makes a concealed "pass," shuffles the pack rapidly and hands it to him.*)

REGAN. Where is it? (*TOM looks through the pack.*)

TOM. Gone, of course.

REGAN. Feel in your pocket. (*TOM feels in his breast-pocket.*)

TOM. Not this time.

REGAN. No? (*He reaches into the pocket, draws out a card and shows it to him.*) That it?

TOM. Marvellous. (*REGAN gloomily returns the pack to his pocket.*)

REGAN. I paid five dollars for that one. I'll let it go for two ninety-eight.

TOM. Not interested. (*A moment.*) —Was it cold in town, today?

REGAN. —I don't envy those guys selling apples on the corners.

TOM. (*Soberly.*) No.—Not much of a job, that.

REGAN. Women's work.

TOM Pretty tough times, all right.

REGAN. —Some of 'em, by God, are down to selling those white flowers that stink so. (*Again he raises his glass.*) Two hundred for steel! (*They drink.*)

TOM. I'm feeling the pinch a bit myself.

REGAN. —Say, look here, Tom—

TOM. What?

REGAN. If I— (*But he thinks better of it and concludes.*) —nothing. (*They finish their glasses.* TOM *refills them.*)

TOM. (*Suddenly.*) Red, I might as well tell you straight off—

REGAN. What?

TOM. (*After a moment.*) —Nothing. (*They drink.*)

REGAN. —All goes to show you ought to put something by.

TOM. It certainly does.

REGAN. —Clean up while you're young and close your mitts on it.

TOM. That's it. (*A silence. Then:*)

REGAN. How's your father these days?

TOM. Never better. (REGAN *shakes his head.*)

REGAN. Tsch-tsch-tsch.

TOM. Red, do you ever think of your future?

REGAN. (*Ruefully.*) I guess I'll go to hell, all right. (TOM *laughs.*) Oh—you mean here.—Now that's a funny thing, because listen, Tom—

TOM. What?

REGAN. I've been thinking: maybe I— (*He falters, and cannot go on.*) —Oh, what the hell—

TOM. But what? (REGAN *holds out his glass.*)

REGAN. Fill her up, will you? (TOM *refills both glasses.*)

TOM. Not much future in buttling, eh, Red?

REGAN. (*With a deprecatory gesture.*) Oh, well—

TOM. I'm—I'm certainly very grateful for all you've done.

REGAN. (*Uncomfortably.*) Ah!—Be still, will you?

TOM. I am, though.

REGAN. That's fine, from you.—I'll never forget, when I was—and you— (*He gulps.*) I'll never forget it. (*He sniffs, and drinks.*)

TOM. Put it there, old man. (*They clasp hands across the table.*) You're a fine fellow.

REGAN. You're the top, boy. I don't know what you'll think of me, when I— (*Again, he is unable to continue.*)

TOM. When you what?

REGAN. When I—well, what would you say, for instance, if I— (*He looks at him, then looks away.*) Nope, it's no good—

TOM. (*Anxiously.*) You're not in trouble, are you?

REGAN. Trouble? Me? What trouble? (TOM *once more refills the glasses. Then, steeling himself:*)

TOM. —Then look here, Regan—

REGAN. Well, Chief? (TOM *looks at him. The steel melts.*)

TOM. —Good old Red. (REGAN *raises his glass.*)

REGAN. Tom Collier for President. The People's Choice.

TOM. Listen a minute—

REGAN. Wait! (*He takes another deep draught.*) Tom, I've just got to tell you. I've—I've— (*He grasps for* TOM's *hand and misses it.*) —Don't hold it against me, Tom, but I'm quitting you. I've took another job.

(TOM *half-rises in astonishment.*)

TOM. You've—?!

REGAN. Oh, I know what you'll say! (TOM *drops into his chair again, and stares.*)

TOM. Holy cats, Red—

REGAN. I couldn't stand it any longer. She don't like my ways. I mean the Missus. I get on her nerves.—Last week Moe Winters told me he wanted to open a country gym and would I run it with him, on the order of Muldoon's, but with a little bar attached and, well, God help me, I give him my word.

TOM. What's there in it for you?

REGAN. Don't put it that way, Tom.

TOM. But I really want to know.

REGAN. Two hundred a month, and a smell at the gate, if any.

TOM. It sounds like a good deal.

REGAN. Ah, the hell with it!—Let's let it go. I'll phone him.

TOM. (*Alarmed.*) No! (REGAN *looks at him.*) When do you start?

REGAN. He wanted me last Wednesday. I've been trying all week to get up the nerve to tell you. But—

TOM. How long will it take you to pack? (REGAN *grins.*)

REGAN. Well, there's my hat-trunk and my shoe-trunk, and the trunk for my fancy-dress ball-clothes—

TOM. (*Firmly.*) You leave by noon tomorrow, you hear? Not a minute later. (REGAN's *grin fades.*)

REGAN. O.K., Chief.—I'm sorry you had to take it this way.

TOM. Don't be a fool. I'm overjoyed for you.

REGAN. (*Uncertainly.*) Fact?

TOM. Absolute. (*He raises his glass.*) Here's to the new job.

REGAN. —Take it from me, boy, you're the goods.

TOM. You've got your points, too, you know. (REGAN *rises, swaying slightly, and raises his glass.*)

REGAN. Anyhow— (TOM *rises and raises his.*)

TOM. Anyhow. (*They drain their glasses put them down and again clasp hands.*)

REGAN. You'll explain to the Missus?

TOM. Of course.

REGAN. Tell her I'm sorry—hope no inconvenience—but—

TOM. I'll explain.

REGAN. So long, Tom.

TOM. Good-bye, Red.

REGAN. So long, Tom.

TOM. Good-bye, Red.

REGAN. I'll give you a ring how it goes.

TOM. Do that.

REGAN. Keep your bib clean.

TOM. I will, old boy. (*Suddenly* REGAN *sobers, looks at him intently for a long moment, then touches him on the shoulder and says:*)

REGAN. Good luck, Tom. (*Turns abruptly, and swiftly and steadily goes to the door and out.* TOM *takes a deep breath and seats himself at the table, with his back to the stairs, in utter dejection. He picks up* REGAN's *pack of cards and moodily glances through it.* CECELIA *comes down the stairs in a lovely negligee. A moment, then she speaks lowly.*)

CECELIA. Tom—

TOM. (*Without turning.*) Hello. Ready?

CECELIA. Did you tell him?

TOM. I'll miss that guy. I'll miss having him around. (*She goes to him.*)

CECELIA. I know, dear. But it's for the best. I'm sure of it. (TOM *puts down the cards.*)

TOM. I've got a feeling that my luck's going with him.

CECELIA. No, no!—I'm your luck. (*She*

draws him into her arms and takes his head against her breast. A moment. Then:)

TOM. You feel good, C.

CECELIA. Do I, dear?

TOM. You haven't any clothes on. Go on —dress—dress quickly—we've got to run. (*She moves from him toward the stairs, where she turns again.*)

CECELIA. —Come and help me? (*He looks at her for an instant, then goes to her. She turns into his arms. He holds her to him for a moment, then she leans away from him, provocatively.*) No, you'd better not. (*She glances down at the negligee, arms out.*) Look—I came across it in the bottom drawer, and my spine simply melted.—Do you remember it? (*He picks up the edge of the loose sleeve and kisses it.*)

TOM. —Quebec.

CECELIA. Then you do!—That funny little French hotel—

TOM. (*Gazing at her.*) Yes.

CECELIA. —Darling place.—Wasn't it cold that morning?—Frost on the windows an inch thick.—Remember?

TOM. —We couldn't see out—

CECELIA. We didn't want to.

TOM. No one else could see in.

CECELIA. Breakfast before the fire—shivering.—Remember—?

TOM. I remember.

CECELIA. We didn't finish it—

TOM. No.

CECELIA. (*With a little laugh.*) There was only one way to keep warm. (*He moves toward her.*)

TOM. Oh C, darling— (*She retreats, up one step of the stairs.*)

CECELIA. No.—You'll make us late.

TOM. What of it?

CECELIA. It's late already. It's—we might miss the concert altogether.

TOM. What if we do?

CECELIA. Tom, you're the limit! Ten minutes ago you said—. (*A moment. Then, in another voice.*) Tom—

TOM. Oh yes, darling. What—

CECELIA. You go in alone. I've decided to stay here.

TOM. You've—?

CECELIA. Yes. It's too cold. I'm going to tuck myself into my warm bed, and—you'll need your heavy coat, won't you? It's here— (*She goes into the hall, returning with an overcoat which she leaves upon a chair.*) Good-night, love. I'll miss you— (*He is about to take her in his arms, but she retreats, with the same provocative smile and an admonitory gesture.*) No, no!— Good-night, dear. Keep warm. (*He turns from her. She mounts the stairs, turns once, smiles down upon him curiously, and goes out leaving the door open. A moment. Then he takes up his coat, crosses the room, puts out the lights, and is returning to the hall doorway, when he hears* CECELIA *singing lowly to herself from upstairs. He stops, listens a moment, then moves slowly to the side table, where he leaves his coat upon a chair and takes up the telephone.*)

TOM. Western Union, please. (*A moment.*) Western Union? (*The curtain begins to fall.*) I want to send a telegram.

CURTAIN.

SCENE II

At DAISY SAGE'S. *Late afternoon on a fine bright day the following May. The sitting-room is as before, excepting for the painting-materials upon the work-table, and a large easel, turned away from the front, at the window.*

JOE *is seated upon the sofa, smoking.* FRANC *stands at the window, looking out. A moment, then she turns abruptly to* JOE.

FRANC. —But what if *she* doesn't come?

JOE. She'll come. (FRANC *leaves the window and seats herself, tense, upon a chair near him.*)

FRANC. My nerves are like that.

JOE. Have a cigarette?

FRANC. No.

JOE. It ought to be quite a meeting. Only that once, months ago—think of it.

FRANC. And in a speakeasy!

JOE. —Like old times, though, like a re-union. That is, until *they* came for him.—You know, I think the last thing he wanted to do was to go on to that party with them.

FRANC. She is a pretty, the wife.—But did you notice? In his top hat, when he put it on, suddenly he looked like only anybody.

JOE. Domestication works fast, when it works.

FRANC. —Well, Daisy has not spoke of him one time since. Never, never will she forgive us this.—Give me a cigarette. What did he say to you? (*He gives her a cigarette and lights it for her.*)

JOE. He just telephoned that he wanted to see me, said it seemed years.—Your hand's shaking.

FRANC. I know it.—What did you tell him?—Why shouldn't it shake?

JOE. I said I'd be back at five. Then I left a note on the door: "Had to go to Daisy's. Come there."—It wouldn't if you smoked less.

FRANC. At five. (*She looks at her watch.*) Ach, Gott!

JOE. You're getting emotional in your old age, Frankie.

FRANC. —But why did you do it? It was well enough left alone.

JOE. I like Tom, and he sounded pathetic. I imagine he saw her exhibition, and—

FRANC. What makes you think he did?

JOE. He said he was telephoning from the Overton Gallery.—I wonder what he thought of it.

FRANC. What did you?

JOE. I know so damn little about painting.

FRANC. I know less.—But it all seemed to me so fresh—done with such spirit.

JOE. That's it!

FRANC. —Bold—what-you-call it—un—in —without compromising.

JOE. Yes.—And the real stuff. No fakiness.

FRANC. —Every one of them Daisy. No little Matisses or Picassos. (*A moment.*)

JOE. But Franc—

FRANC. (*Nerves again.*) Yes? All right. What?

JOE. What really did you think of them? (*She shrugs.*)

FRANC. I tell you I am not—what-you-say —competent to judge.

JOE. What did they do to you, Franc? (*She looks at him sharply, hesitates. Then:*)

FRANC. —Nothing. I am sorry. But noth-ing—

JOE. Nor to me. (*She grasps his arm.*)

FRANC. —But we must believe in her, Joe!

JOE (*In pain.*) We do, don't we?—Oh Lord, if only all my friends made shirts for a living.

FRANC. Yes. You could say "That is not a good shirt" quite easily.

JOE. This afternoon—after a few minutes we duck out on them, understand?

FRANC. Joe, I don't like it. I am afraid of this. I think it is not wise.

JOE. —If only they'd have one of their good old-time rows. I'll bet he and that wife of his never had a decent scrap in their lives.

FRANC. (*Thoughtfully.*) —And still, may-be seeing him, Daisy finds it is all over—finished—cold. Sometimes that is so. I hope for her it will be so.

JOE. Listen, child: it's May, and the trees are in bloom.

FRANC. (*Scornfully.*) You should write in German.

JOE. Poor Tom. Poor guy. He's up against it for fair now, Franc.

FRANC. Why now more than usual?

JOE. Well, I ran into Hal Foster today, and—

FRANC. Foster—?—The one who did those stories?

JOE. That's the boy. He's finished a new novel that's even better, they say. Apparently Tom thinks he can grab it for The Bantam, and stage a comeback on the strength of it. A sort of a last straw. He's to meet him this afternoon.

FRANC. Oh, good! (JOE *shakes his head.*)

JOE. No, not so: Foster told me that hard up as he is, he'd be damned before he'd go with a house that was responsible for "Young Ecstasy" and—

FRANC. But you should have talked to him, Joe!

JOE. I did, till I was blue in the face. He just kept saying "Then how about *you?*" It was no use explaining how Tom thought I'd do better with— (JOE *glances quickly at the door, and rises.*) Look out!

FRANC. Him?

JOE. Yes, or— (DAISY *comes in.*) Oh, hello, Daisy! (DAISY *pulls off her hat and gloves and looks at them.*)

DAISY. My, you're hearty. (*To* FRANC.) What's the matter?

FRANC. With me?

DAISY. Yes. You look queer.

FRANC. I don't like the Spring. I don't like May and the trees in bloom.

DAISY. No? Nor do I. I say it's maple-syrup, and I say the hell with it. (*She seats herself near them.*) Well, the show's over. It's been a fine week. I've learned a lot about new painters, the so-called Public and the so-called Press.

FRANC. There are no judges of one's work but oneself, Daisy.

DAISY. Then you don't by any chance agree with them?

FRANC. I would sooner sleep with an art critic than agree with him.

DAISY. It's touching the way my friends have rallied round. Stout hearts. Thanks, thanks.—But oh heaven!—If only someone I love and trust would be honest with me!

JOE. And what do you call what we've been?

DAISY. Friendly, Joe, very friendly.

JOE. *I* tell you: let's all get drunk.

DAISY. No thanks. (*For a brief moment she covers her face with her hands, then looks up again.*) It's all right. It's over. Let's talk about something. Who knows anything? (*A silence.* DAISY's *head sinks again. Finally* FRANC *ventures:*)

FRANC. Jim and Nancy Peters are going to have a baby.

DAISY. (*Absently.*) A boy?

FRANC. I think so.

DAISY. Good for them. (*Another silence. Then:*)

JOE. —Er—Tom Collier rang me up this afternoon. (*A moment. Then:*)

DAISY. Oh? How is he?

JOE. He sounded sunk.

DAISY. That's too bad. (*She cools her wrists. Then, to* FRANC.) —You know, it's *hot.*

FRANC. It *is* hot.—Don't be bitter, Daisy.

DAISY. I heard grand things about Nova Scotia yesterday.—Why should I be bitter?

FRANC. You shouldn't. — About what? Where is it?

DAISY. North, way north.—Bitter! Me!— They say it's beautiful beyond words, and you can live there on oh, so little.

JOE. He said—I mean Tom did—that—

DAISY. Joe, you seem to have an idea that I might be interested in what he'd say—

JOE. Well—

DAISY. But as it happens, I'm not. (*To* FRANC.) There are miles of green meadows and a seacoast that's nobody's business.

Woods, as well. (*To* JOE.) —I suppose he was full of explanations about those choice eggs The Bantam Press has been laying lately.

JOE. No, he didn't mention them. He only said—

DAISY. Why tell me? (*To* FRANC.) The only out's the swimming. It's too cold. But other things make up for it. (*To* JOE.) —He always gets colds in the Spring—I suppose his voice was gone entirely—

JOE. It didn't seem to be.

DAISY. (*To* FRANC.) It's like Maine, they say. Only better, much.

FRANC. Not too many people? (DAISY *closes her eyes.*)

DAISY. No people. Gloriously, happily, mercifully, no people. (*The buzzer at the door sounds.*) Joe—will you? (*To* FRANC.) —Speaking of no people. (JOE *presses a button to open the door.* DAISY *continues to* FRANC.) Imagine Joe thinking that at this date *I* should give a damn what— (TOM *comes in with a brief-case in his hand.*)

TOM. Joey! How are you? (*He drops the brief-case upon the work-table.*) Franc!

FRANC. Tom, you look fine. (*He turns to* DAISY.)

TOM. Hello, Daisy.

DAISY. (*So coolly.*) Hello. How have you been?

TOM. In rude health, thanks.—And you?

DAISY. Never better.

TOM. Oh, it's fine to see you! I've been starving for you—all of you.

DAISY. Thanks.

TOM. How's the job?

DAISY. The magazine job?

TOM. Yes.

DAISY. I gave it up last winter.—A trifle— shall we say "quixotic"?—of me?

TOM. Shall we? (*He looks from one to the other of them.*) Listen: I love you three, I love you. (*He takes* FRANC's *head in his hands and kisses her brow.*) Oh Lord! (*Gives* JOE *a friendly shove.*) Lord Almighty— (*Laughs joyfully, seats himself and gazes fondly at them. There is a long silence. Finally:*) Holy cats! Talk to me, will you?—Am I a leper? (*Silence. He leans forward.*) Now listen, the lot of you: I've had enough of this nonsense. For months you've been avoiding me like the plague and I won't stand for it. You're important to me and by heaven, I'm going to hang onto your coat-tails, dog your footsteps, sit on your doorsteps, until you're ready to grant that a man can marry, and go on being a friend.—Is that understood? —Well, then: who's seen Sandy Patch? (*Then, in a rush:*)

JOE. I have.

FRANC. So have I.

DAISY. We all have.

TOM. What's he doing?

JOE. A war group in bronze for some town in Texas. He's making them look like sheep.

TOM. Good boy!

DAISY. —Except that they'll probably throw it back at him.

JOE. He'll get paid, though. Sam Frankl sees to that for him now.

TOM. How's your book doing?

JOE. Fair.—Of course nothing like The Bantam's "Indian Summer" or "Young Ecstasy."

TOM. Ouch.

JOE. What the devil made you take them on?

TOM. Money.—Ah, but Joey, I'm reforming! Did you know it?

JOE. In time, I hope.—How?

TOM. Williamson, Warren can have those bright boys now, and welcome.

JOE. It's about where they belong.

TOM. Wait till you see The Bantam's new list.

JOE. I'm waiting.

TOM. —That was certainly a foul format Brandon gave your book.

JOE. The words are there.

TOM. If you can read them. What's the stock they printed it on—paper-towelling? —I hear you're a hit, Franc.

FRANC. It has gone well enough. (*He looks at* DAISY, *hesitates. Then:*)

TOM. I—I saw your exhibition today.

DAISY. Oh really?—Funny I missed you. What did you think of it?

TOM. Well—

DAISY. (*Suddenly, eagerly.*) Tell me!

TOM. I don't think you were ready to show yet. How did it happen?

DAISY. Saunders and Munn arranged it.

TOM. Your old editors? The fashion boys?

DAISY. What about it? (TOM *shakes his head.*)

TOM. Daisy, Daisy.—How were the notices?

DAISY. Appalling.

TOM. I suppose their reasons were all wrong—

DAISY. Of course.—What are yours? (*A moment. Then:*)

TOM. Well, you've been painting less than a year—

DAISY. Yes.

TOM. —And yet you had about thirty canvases to show. (*Now* DAISY *is well on her mettle.*)

DAISY. Thirty-two.

TOM. It's a lot, Daisy.

DAISY. So you didn't care for any of them.

TOM. Oh yes!—One I loved particularly: the one of the doorstep, with the milk-bottles. I'd like to own that one.

DAISY. —Number Seven.—Sorry, it's not for sale.

TOM. Two hundred—?

DAISY. Nope?

TOM. Two-fifty!

DAISY. Nope.

TOM. Seventy-five—

DAISY. Nope.

TOM. Four hundred and one—

DAISY. Nope.

TOM. I wouldn't take it as a gift.

DAISY. That's all right, then.

TOM. Of course your drawing's a marvel. Lord, how that's come along!

DAISY. —Only what?

TOM. Good draughtsmanship's not to be sneezed at, is it?

DAISY. Certainly not. Look at Belcher.

TOM. No—at Goya.

DAISY. Thanks so much.

TOM. Of course it depends on what you want to be. I thought it was a painter. (FRANC *rises.*)

DAISY. So did I.—Goya painted pretty well, too, I thought.

TOM. In the first year? I doubt it.

DAISY. I wasn't aware it took a definite length of time.

TOM. —And living in cities all your life, you know.

DAISY. Perhaps I'd better hie me to some sylvan dell.

TOM. I don't think it would hurt a bit.

DAISY. —Listen, you: if you can show me a purer cobalt than the winter sky over the East River any afternoon at four—

TOM. That's not the point. (DAISY's *voice is higher.*)

DAISY. What is?

TOM. Fever—rush—hysteria—all day, every day. (DAISY *turns away.*)

DAISY. Oh, go to hell, will you? (FRANC *moves toward the door.*)

TOM. Sure. When do we start?

FRANC. Come along, Joe. (JOE *follows her.*)

DAISY. —And leave me with this moss-back? This— (*Again she turns upon* TOM.) —So I'm to sit under a parasol and paint tight little cows in streams, am I?

TOM. That's not what I said. (*Unnoticed by* DAISY, JOE *and* FRANC *have gone out.*)

DAISY. —Something suitable as an over-mantel for the Home of Her Dreams, I suppose.

TOM. Now you're being bull-headed.

DAISY. (*Turning.*) Bull-headed!—He calls me bull— (*She sees that* FRANC *and* JOE *are no longer there.*) Oh, you snakes—

TOM. (*With a gesture.*) Well—

DAISY. Well? What more, Teacher?

TOM. All I said and all I'm saying is, you can't expect, the first crack out of the box, to—you've got to *work*, Daisy.

DAISY. Sweet heaven! What else have I been doing? What have I done but?

TOM. —But differently—with such pains. You're turning out too much, you know it. (*Suddenly the fight goes out of her.*)

DAISY. Maybe, maybe. — Anything's too much.

TOM. Ah, darling—

DAISY. No!—Don't soften on me. Stay tough!

TOM. I do believe that's it, though. I be-lieve it's the whole story: still hung over from the old job. Pressure, pressure all the time. Still rushing countless sketches through against a magazine's deadline. (*She looks away from him. Her hand gropes blindly for his and finds it.*)

DAISY. —Anyway, against some deadline—

TOM. Daisy—darling—

DAISY. You're cruel, inhuman. You're a brute.

TOM. Oh Daisy—

DAISY. Thanks for being.

TOM. If you mean it—

DAISY. From my heart— (*She looks at him, smiling now.*) Oh, you skunk— (*He laughs, relieved.*)

TOM. Worse. Much worse.

DAISY. (*Serious again.*) Who but you, Tom? (*She points her finger at him.*) Look: only you and strangers honest with me ever. (*He draws her down beside him on the sofa.*)

TOM. —The country's the place to work, Daisy. Listen: There's a grand little house about six miles from us. Woods, hills, meadows — you can get it for almost nothing.

DAISY. That's about my price.

TOM. It could easily be painted up. What about a white roof for it?

DAISY. Oh, lovely idea!

TOM. C discovered it. She can find out all about it. I'll tell her who it's for. (*But at this,* DAISY's *mood changes.*)

DAISY. Don't dream of it.

TOM. Why not?

DAISY. I've got other places in mind.

TOM. Anyhow, go somewhere.

DAISY. Sure—somewhere.

TOM. You're going to be good, Daisy, don't think I don't think you're good.

DAISY. I won't. I won't think anything.

TOM. This is a big day for me, do you know it?

DAISY. How?

TOM. Well, I've been seeing the folly of my ways here lately. Poor C—I must have been sweet to live with this past week. She's been grand about it, though.

DAISY. I'm sure she has.

TOM. I—suddenly, for some reason, I saw that I'd got off the track—my track. It was pretty painful— But I'm getting back on, I think.

DAISY. I'm glad, Tom. You must, you know.

TOM. Did you ever hear of a fellow named Hal Foster?

DAISY. No. What does he do?

TOM. Writes. My God, how he writes!— And nobody knows it—not yet—

DAISY. Have you got him?

TOM. I'm getting him. He's done a fine, poisonous short novel that makes Candide look sick. (*In growing excitement.*) I'm going to make a grand type-job of it, advertise it all over the place, and sell it at two bucks. I don't care if I lose my shirt on it.—I'm to meet him at six this afternoon, to make arrangements.

DAISY. It must be nearly that now. You'd better go.

TOM. —Daisy.—Have you missed me, Daisy?

DAISY. You? Well, I'll tell you, it's this way: I— (*But she stops and looks at him, drops her bantering tone, and nods, dumbly.*)

TOM. Much? (*Again she nods, and adds, under her breath:*)

DAISY. —Skunk, skunk.

TOM. Oh, and I you!—It's a lot of nonsense, this. It's ridiculous. (*She looks at her watch.*)

DAISY. It *is* six.

TOM. Hell.

DAISY. You'd better run.

TOM. We need each other, we two do.

DAISY. You think?

TOM. Most terribly. I'm convinced of it. There never were such friends as you and me. It's wicked to give that up, to lose anything so fine for no good reason.—Why you, of all people, for a shabby, lowdown question of convention, fit only to be considered by shabby, lowdown—

DAISY. Wait a minute!

TOM. A hundred times I'd given my eyes to see you, to talk to you—

DAISY. Well—here I am—

TOM. (*Eagerly.*) Daisy—may I come again?—Just now and then, you know?

DAISY. (*After a moment.*) —If you like— just now and then.

TOM. Oh my sweet dear—thanks!

DAISY. But don't say "sweet dear." That belongs to another life, years ago.

TOM. Oh—there are to be rules, are there?

DAISY. One or two. One strict one— (*She hesitates.*)

TOM. What?

DAISY. Never secret. Never hidden.

TOM. No, no!

DAISY. —Always open, as before.

TOM. But of course, of course!

DAISY. I couldn't go it otherwise.

TOM. Why should a friendship be hidden? What's there to hide?

DAISY. It gets misunderstood.

TOM. It won't, it can't, or the whole world's rotten.

DAISY. It's been pretty ripe for a long time, Tommy.

TOM. "Tommy"! (*He laughs exultantly and draws her into his arms. They stand rocking back and forth, laughing in delight.*) Oh my darling, how grand this is!

DAISY. I see you run to tweeds this season.

TOM. I even have a horse now—practically a county squire.

DAISY. Look out for it.

TOM. Oh, it's tame.

DAISY. I mean going county.

TOM. Never you fear! I wouldn't be let. I'm a terribly queer duck to them.

DAISY. "Lit'ry," I suppose.

TOM. "Very artistic."

DAISY. Are they good and dull?

TOM. Crashing.

DAISY. —And respectable.

TOM. My God, how!

DAISY. *We* aren't respectable.

TOM. Not a bit. Never shall be.

DAISY. For which, praise heaven.

TOM. Heaven, I praise you that Daisy and I are not—. Kiss the boy, Daisy.

DAISY. No.—You've got to go.

TOM. Why? Would it take long? (*She laughs, and pecks his cheek.*)

DAISY. There.

TOM. Ask me am I happy—

DAISY. It's all right, isn't it?

TOM. Magnificent.—All as before.

DAISY. Yes.—But for one thing.

TOM. What? (*She leaves his arms.*)

DAISY. We aren't in love any more.—Now run. You might miss what's-his-name.

TOM. How about lunch tomorrow?

DAISY. It's fine with me.

TOM. The old place?

DAISY. I'd love it.

TOM. One o'clock?

DAISY. One o'clock.

TOM. —And we'll dine at John Donovan's. He's opened a new place on Forty-eighth Street.

DAISY. Dine?

TOM. Why not?

DAISY. All right.

TOM. The next day's Wednesday, isn't it? I said I'd drive out in the morning to see Pat Atkins. He's been sick again.

DAISY. Poor dear. I'm sorry.

TOM. He's better now.—Come along with me, Daisy.

DAISY. Wednesday? No— Wednesday, I—

TOM. If it's a good day we'll take a picnic. What do you say?

DAISY. I—I guess so.

TOM. Fine!—We'll get back in time to—let's see, can I stay in town Wednesday night? Yes, of course, I can. I want to see that black woman dance.

DAISY. Which one?

TOM. Down on Grand Street.

DAISY. Oh yes, I've heard about her!

TOM. We can look in, anyway.—Thursday I'm at the Press all day. But Friday—

DAISY. Wait a minute, Tom.—You said only now and—

TOM. I'll bring Hal Foster in about four on Friday. Will you be here?

DAISY. I—I think so.

TOM. Good-bye then, darling. Till tomorrow!

DAISY. Good-bye, Tom. (*He takes her face in his hands, kisses it several times, then her mouth, briefly:*)

TOM. Sweet dear, sweet dear—. (*He releases her.*) One o'clock?

DAISY. One o'clock. (*He goes swiftly to the door, where he turns once more.*)

TOM. —*Ten minutes* to one! (*He is gone, his footsteps heard upon the stairs. She stands rigid, exalted, her eyes shining. Then she sees his brief-case, left behind him upon the work-table. She stares at it for a long time, apprehension growing in her eyes. Then she murmurs "Franc," runs to the door, flings it open and calls in terror:*)

DAISY. Franc! (*Then returns, puts* TOM's *brief-case upon a chair, then places a work-box upon her table and begins filling it with tools and materials.* FRANC *comes in.*)

FRANC. Daisy?—What is it? Your voice frightened me.

DAISY. Franc, you're the one woman I know who can hold her tongue. (FRANC *shrugs.*)

FRANC. What is not my business— (*She sees what* DAISY *is doing, and her casual air is replaced by a real anxiety.*) Packing? What's this? What for? You and—? Oh Daisy, hold on a minute. Wait, Liebchen Think, are you wise, Daisy—

DAISY. I'm going alone—a long way, for a long time.

FRANC. To that place you said?

DAISY. (*A sudden idea.*) Yes!

FRANC. Wait! I come with you—

DAISY. No, I don't want anyone now. Later, maybe.

FRANC. But what is it, dear?

DAISY. I guess I'm running for my life, Franc.

FRANC. —Tom again.

DAISY. —Still.

FRANC. It's no better—

DAISY. (*Packing furiously.*) —It's worse.

FRANC. Poor child.

DAISY. No, no! I'm glad.—But I've got to get out.

FRANC. Yes, that is wise.

DAISY. No one's to know where I've gone to.

FRANC. No.

DAISY. No mess—it's to avoid one I'm going.

FRANC. —But compose yourself, Daisy. Be calm.

DAISY. I can't! Look— (*She points to the brief-case.*) He went without it. He'll come back for it. And if I see him again for one minute I'll die.

FRANC. He loves you, Daisy?

DAISY. I don't know. I don't believe *he* knows. But— (*She looks up from her packing.*) Oh Franc—he's so young!—Did you notice how young he looked?

FRANC. Yes, like a child.

DAISY. All slim and brown and sandy.

FRANC. Quick, Daisy!

DAISY. (*Far away.*) He'll always be like that—even when he's old. I know!—And the way he stands—that funny way—stiff—with his feet out—

FRANC. —What they call duck-footed, eh?

DAISY. (*Indignantly.*) Not at all. It's a perfectly natural way to stand. It's a fine, strong way to stand.

FRANC. Hurry, darling. Run quick!

DAISY. Yes, yes, I must. (*She resumes her packing.*)

FRANC. Will you take a trunk?

DAISY. The small one.

FRANC. How do you go—by train?

DAISY. I don't know. Boat, I think.

FRANC. But when? From where?

DAISY. I guess Boston. (*A moment.*) Perhaps I'd better see him just once more. Maybe if I can explain to him how impossible it is for us to—

FRANC. No!—And you go to Boston to-night.

DAISY. Yes. Yes, that's right. (FRANC *goes into the bedroom.* DAISY *continues to pack for a moment, then calls:*) Franc!

FRANC. What now?

DAISY. When those things come back from the Gallery, cover them, will you?

FRANC. Yes, dear.

DAISY. —Number Seven—do you hear me, Franc?

FRANC. I hear.

DAISY. Pack Number Seven and send it to him at the Press. (FRANC *re-enters.*)

FRANC. All right, dear.

DAISY. You're lunching with him tomorrow.

FRANC. So?

DAISY. At the old place, at one o'clock.

FRANC. One o'clock.

DAISY. Franc—

FRANC. Yes, darling? (DAISY *gathers up some paint-tubes.*)

DAISY. When you see him—

FRANC. Yes, darling—

DAISY. Kiss him for me. (*She realizes what she has said, and murmurs:*) Kiss him for me— (*Then hurls a tube into the box, in fury.*) Kiss him for me! (*The buzzer sounds imperatively.* DAISY *starts in alarm.* FRANC *takes her arm.*)

FRANC. Come—and don't speak— (*She leads her toward the bedroom, stopping to press the button at the fire place. They go out.* TOM *is heard running up the stairs. He hurries in, calling:*)

TOM. Daisy—? (*There is no answer. He goes to the table, and calls again:*) Daisy!

(*A moment. Then* DAISY's *voice is heard faintly from the next room.*)

DAISY. Hello—

TOM. I forgot my case. (*He finds it upon the chair and picks it up.*) It's all right. I've got it. (*At the door he turns once more and calls:*) Don't be late tomorrow! Remember! Twelve-thirty! (*And goes out. Again footsteps are heard upon the stairs, and a door slams below.*)

CURTAIN.

ACT THREE

SCENE I

At TOM COLLIER's, *six months later. Ten o'clock of a bright Sunday morning. Alterations have been made, and the old library has become a chaste dining-room. Now, at last,* TOM's *house is* CECELIA's *house, which is to say, The House in Good Taste.*

The door beside the fire place at right opens, through the hall, upon a large new living-room. The library furniture has been replaced with a dining-room table, sideboard, serving-table and chairs. The large table is set for breakfast and there are various breakfast dishes being kept hot upon the serving-table.

CECELIA *and* OWEN *are at breakfast,* CECELIA *seated and* OWEN *standing, napkin in hand, half turned in the direction of the serving-table, toward which* GRACE *is moving with a coffee-cup.*

GRACE. Oh no, thanks! I love to serve myself. It's so English. (OWEN *reseats himself.* GRACE *refills her cup and returns to the table with it.* CECELIA *presses a button upon the table.*)

CECELIA. I'll order some more hot. (OWEN *takes a swallow of water, puts down his napkin and pushes back his chair.*)

OWEN. Well, for the morning after a party, I feel pretty good. Where's the birthday-boy?

CECELIA. Still recovering upstairs.

GRACE. He was never more amusing. Honestly, when he did that skit from his new magazine, I thought I couldn't stand it. I was in stitches.

OWEN. —What's happened to the artistic element? Still asleep?

CECELIA. Miss Sage and Fisk insisted upon walking to the station with La Schmidt. It turned out that she had to take an early train.

GRACE. I've never known a musician to make such difficulties about playing.

CECELIA. She's used to her own violin.

GRACE. But is there any differ—? (*Then, thoughtfully.*) Yes—I suppose there is.— The Sage is rather a number, isn't she? Do you know she actually spent six months in Tierra del Fuego?

OWEN. Nova Scotia.

GRACE. I mean Nova Scotia.

CECELIA. Yes, I'd heard.

GRACE. The places they go!—C, I wish I knew how you get hold of such interesting people.

CECELIA. I asked them as a particular favor, for Tom's birthday. I insisted on it. It was part of the surprise party. (GRACE *sighs.*)

GRACE. —They invariably *say* they'll come to me, and then at the last minute something always happens.

CECELIA. —Besides they're very old friends of his. I said he was longing to see them.— I think he really has missed them a little.

OWEN. Clever Cecelia.

CECELIA. Why?

OWEN. Real security at last, eh?

CECELIA. Do you object (GRACE *looks at them suspiciously.*)

GRACE. What are you talking about? (*There is no answer. She rises.*) Oh, you subtle people! I wish I were subtle. (CECELIA *presses the bell again.*)

CECELIA. I wish someone would answer this bell. (GRACE *looks about her.*)

GRACE. Darling, you *have* done wonders with this house. It's all in such perfect taste, now.

CECELIA. I wish Tom was as enthusiastic about it as you are.

GRACE. Oh, men never like changes.

CECELIA. Unless they think of them themselves.—We're having a charming time about the roof.

OWEN. The roof?

CECELIA. It's got to be fixed—and ever since he came back from Bermuda last winter he's been saying he wanted a white roof—been wanting to whitewash it white.

GRACE. What!?

OWEN. (*Simultaneously.*) The roof here?

CECELIA. Yes. They're all white in Bermuda.

OWEN. But this isn't Bermuda.

CECELIA. I've tried to explain that to him.

OWEN. (*To* GRACE.) But I don't think I've ever seen a white roof around here, have you?

GRACE. Let me think. (*She thinks, painfully. Then:*) —No.

CECELIA. He says, What does that matter? He wants one. He thinks they're pretty. He thinks— (*In sudden irritation.*) Oh, he can be exasperating! (*To* OWEN.) His father

sent him a check for his birthday: he may accept it, he may not.

GRACE. Not accept a *check?*

CECELIA. —Because it's from him.

GRACE. Well, I'm amazed.—A whopper, too, I'll bet.

CECELIA. I don't know. I didn't see it.

OWEN. I thought he'd got over the nonsense about his father.

CECELIA. So did I. Everything has been simply beautiful for months. He's been so pleased with Tom, and the way business has been going. Apparently someone told him about it.

OWEN. Williamson, probably.

CECELIA. —Or Warren. I don't know which.

GRACE. Are they the ones that want to buy The Bantam Press?

CECELIA. —To buy into it, yes.

GRACE. How does Tom feel about that? (CECELIA *shrugs.*)

OWEN. He's made the price so high they'll have to refuse it.

CECELIA. Not if *you* tell them not to, Owen!

OWEN. I thought I'd explained all that to you. (*A moment. Then:*)

CECELIA. —I suppose I'll have to get the coffee myself. (*She rings again.*) I told Tom that with *him* back, the maids would do nothing.

OWEN. It does seem funny, seeing him around again.

GRACE. I was overcome last night.—How did it happen, C?

CECELIA. The new job didn't pan out. Tom ran into him somewhere and telephoned to ask if he could bring him out for a day or two, he'd been ill. There was nothing to do but say yes. Now, of course, he wants to keep him.

GRACE. Why not—you know—just give him something, and—?

CECELIA. He won't take anything without earning it. Tom swears he'll teach him manners—at least to the extent of calling us "Sir" and "Madam." He said it was the one birthday-present he really— (*She sees* REGAN *standing, beaming, in the doorway.*) Oh.

REGAN. Did someone ring?

CECELIA. Several times. Will you bring some hot coffee, please?

REGAN. Sure thing. (*He takes the coffeepot and goes out with it.* GRACE *laughs.*)

GRACE. Manners!

CECELIA. I'm afraid he's hopeless.

GRACE. You know, I can't get over old Rufus K. actually sending checks. He can be nice, can't he?

CECELIA. Extremely. Did I tell you? He's invited us to spend the winter with him in town.

GRACE. Not in the big house?

CECELIA. Yes.

GRACE. But it's the most unheard-of thing I've ever heard of!

CECELIA. We may not go. Tom's not too keen for that, either.

GRACE. He's mad!—Of course you can persuade him. It will *be such*— (TOM *comes down the stairs, a trifle white and wan.*) Ah! Good morning, host!

TOM. Is it?—How are you, Grace? Hello, Owen. (*He seats himself and eyes the food distrustfully.*) Did Franc get her train?

CECELIA. I imagine so.

TOM. I meant to get up. Where are Joe and Daisy?

CECELIA. They went walking. (TOM *settles back painfully in his chair.*)

GRACE. Oh come now! It's not as bad as that.

TOM. Lady, you don't know. (*To* CECELIA.) Was I dreadful?

CECELIA. You were delightful.

TOM. Oh, don't say that!—That means I put on an act.

GRACE. You were the life of the party. (TOM *cringes.*)

TOM. Good Grace. (REGAN *comes in with the coffee-pot and a glass of what appears to be milk.*)

REGAN. (*Heartily.*) How're'ye, Tom, my boy!

TOM. —'Morning, Red. (REGAN *puts the coffee-pot upon the serving-table.* TOM *looks guiltily at* CECELIA, *who turns away.* REGAN *comes beaming from the serving-table, the glass in hand.*)

REGAN. Look what Baby brought you— (TOM *rises and goes to him.*)

TOM. —Just a minute. (*He puts his arm through his, turns him away from the others and low enough to be heard by no one but him, murmurs:*) Look, Red—if you don't mind, I think you'd better be "Regan" from now on, and us "Sir" and "Madam."—You're a pretty good actor. (REGAN *stiffens into the Perfect Butler.*)

REGAN. (*Audibly.*) Right, Sir. H'I knows me place, Sir. (TOM *laughs, and returns to the table.*)

TOM. Don't lay it on.

REGAN. Oh no, Sir. (*He offers the glass obsequiously.* TOM *takes it.*)

GRACE. Milk?!

TOM. —Punch. (*He makes a face over it and returns it to* REGAN.) Could you possibly brush the nutmeg off?

REGAN. I think so, Sir.

TOM. Try. Move heaven and earth. (REGAN *returns to the serving-table with the glass and removes the nutmeg.* DAISY *comes in from the hall.*)

GRACE. Oh, hello!

DAISY. Good morning.

CECELIA. How was the walk?

DAISY. Very pleasant, thanks. We went miles. It's a lovely village.

CECELIA. It is nice.

DAISY. Whose house is the pretty white one on the Square?

CECELIA. Near the Post Office? (*To* GRACE.) Isn't that Judge Evans's?

GRACE. Yes.

DAISY. (*To* TOM.) I hope you remembered to find the new magazine-proofs for me. (TOM *takes some folded proof-sheets from his pocket.*)

TOM. Right here. (DAISY *extends her hand.*)

DAISY. Please—

TOM. If you'd really like to—

DAISY. I should, very much. (*She takes the proofs and goes to the stairs, where she seats herself upon the bottom step.* REGAN *returns the glass of punch to* TOM.)

TOM. That's better. (JOE *comes in from the hall.* REGAN *coughs discreetly behind his hand.*)

REGAN. (*Not presuming to look directly at his master.*) Beg pardon, Sir—

TOM. Yes?

REGAN. —If I may so, Sir—it has always seemed to me that life is like a sailboat—

TOM. (*Smiling.*) Ah?

REGAN. In good weather, no better ridin' anywhere—but the very deuce, Sir, in a storm, Sir. (TOM *laughs and waves him away.*)

TOM. Get out! (REGAN *bows gravely.*)

REGAN. Very good, Sir. (*And goes out.* CECELIA's *fixed smile leaves her face. She takes a deep breath.* DAISY *laughs softly,* JOE *loudly.* GRACE *turns to* JOE.)

GRACE. Oh hello! (JOE *recovers himself and advances into the room.*)

JOE. How are you?

GRACE. Pleasant walk?

JOE. If you like the country.

GRACE. I'll bet you made a good plot, too.

JOE. A good—?

GRACE. I know you writer-men!

DAISY. (*From the stairs.*) —Remember your prescription for me, Tom?

TOM. Prescription?

DAISY. "The country's the place to work," you said.

JOE. Something did it for you, Daisy.

TOM. —Daisy herself.—You can spend the night, can't you, Joe?

JOE. It's up to Daisy.

DAISY. I'm not certain, yet. Must we say straight off?

CECELIA. Of course not.—Do, though. We'd so love having you.

TOM. I've got to run over to Greenwich to see one C. B. Williamson, but I'll be back this evening.

JOE. The publisher?

TOM. Yes. Why?

JOE. What have *you* got to do with that old pirate? (TOM *smiles.*)

TOM. Shh?—It's a secret. (JOE *stares.*)

JOE. My God!

GRACE. You're coming to my house for Sunday breakfast, you know.

JOE. Thanks, we've had it.

GRACE. Oh, but mine is a very special breakfast!—

JOE. (*To* TOM.) —I liked the old Press building better.

TOM. We needed more room.

CECELIA. (*To* TOM.) Don't you want some coffee or something?

TOM. This is fine. Will you join me in a milk-punch, Daisy?

DAISY. Would you mind awfully if I didn't?

TOM. I'm not sure.

GRACE. Not disapproving, is she? (DAISY *laughs pleasantly.*)

DAISY. Not in the least.

TOM. (*To* JOE.) —You couldn't publish a magazine in that old shack.

JOE. Don't tell me it's that smart.

GRACE. *I* think it's going to be a sensation. I'm practically a collaborator, aren't I, Tom? (TOM *laughs.*)

TOM. Grace is my reaction-agent. She submits to tests. (DAISY *stares at the proofs.*)

DAISY. Is this all of it?

TOM. —The dummy for the first number.

DAISY. No name yet—

TOM. No.

JOE. —Any Sunday papers, by any chance?

TOM. —In the living-room. I'll send for them.

JOE. It's all right. I'll read them there. (*He goes out.* TOM *looks after him.* GRACE *rises.*)

TOM. Extraordinary fellow, Fisk.

GRACE. My people will be arriving. Who's going to run me home? (*She holds out her hand to* TOM. *He takes it and rises.*)

TOM. We'll go in Joe's Ford, and shock the village.

GRACE. Divine!

DAISY. Bring it back, Tom.

TOM. You bet.—How about your coming with us? (DAISY *rises upon the stairs.*)

DAISY. Thanks, but I want to finish this.

TOM. Be sure to like it.

DAISY. I'm afraid I'm no judge.

GRACE. Tom, I've got to tell you: *I* think the idea of a white roof in this country is idiotic. (*She tucks his hand under her arm and they move toward the door.*)

TOM. (*As they go out.*) So do I. It's insane. Whatever made you think of it? (DAISY *mounts the stairs and goes out,* CECELIA *watching her.* OWEN *moves toward the living-room.* CECELIA's *low voice stops him.*)

CECELIA. Owen—

OWEN. What, C?

CECELIA. Why did she come?

OWEN. Daisy? I thought you wanted her, for all those highly special reasons.

CECELIA. —First she said she couldn't. Then she telephoned back she would.

OWEN. Well?

CECELIA. I believe she came for some special reason of her own.

OWEN. Quite possibly.

CECELIA. What, though?

OWEN. Search me.

CECELIA. Twice last night I caught her watching me in the most curious way. Once when I was with Fisk, once with you.— But you know, I'm not the least bit jealous any more. I'm even inclined to like her.

OWEN. That's big of you.

CECELIA. I suppose Fisk is one of hers, too.

OWEN. (*Frowning.*) How do you mean?

CECELIA. Sweet innocent!

OWEN. How's that?

CECELIA. I should think by this time you'd know a promiscuous little— (*She sees his frown deepen, and with a gesture, concludes:*) —Oh, well—

OWEN. You're a strange girl, C.—And a pretty cruel one.

CECELIA. —Not at all. I tell you I don't mind in the least. In fact I really don't see why Tom and she shouldn't be as good friends now as—well, as you and I are.

OWEN. Their history is a little different.

CECELIA. Why? Don't you like our history?

OWEN. What there is of it.—A trifle uneventful, don't you think?—Or shall we simply call it lacking in excitement? (*A moment. Then:*)

CECELIA. —You've been so strange, lately. So remote, Owen.

OWEN. I wasn't aware of it.

CECELIA. —Refusing to help us one bit with Mr. Williamson.

OWEN. But Tom doesn't want to be helped!

CECELIA. I do.

OWEN. C, I've told you. I simply can't do it. (CECELIA *turns from him coldly.*)

CECELIA. Very well.

OWEN. Certainly, you must realize—

CECELIA. Of course. (*She moves toward the living-room.*) Come on—shall we?

OWEN. I've told you a dozen times, I'm counsel for Williamson's, and— (CECELIA *stops and turns to him.*)

CECELIA. Exactly.—And so they do whatever you tell them to.

OWEN. Tom's price is out of all reason.

CECELIA. Not if they really want it.

OWEN. But hang it, he made it that to stand them off! He doesn't want them to have it.

CECELIA. Tom doesn't know what he wants. (*Coaxing.*) —Just one little word to them from you—on the telephone—before he goes over this afternoon—now—before he gets back from Grace's.

OWEN. There's something called legal ethics you seem not to understand, C.

CECELIA. And something called friendship? (*He turns away. A moment. Then she looks at him sideways.*) Owen— (*He gestures "What?"*) "Lacking in excitement," you said.—For you?

OWEN. For you, I meant.

CECELIA. I suppose you're the judge of that, too.

OWEN. I don't know who else.

CECELIA. Of course you couldn't possibly be wrong.

OWEN. Could I?

CECELIA. (*Softly.*) —And I'm not a human being at all, of course. (*He advances toward her.*)

OWEN. C—!

CECELIA. (*Quickly.*) Do one thing for me: just tell them it *might* be a good thing for them.—It might, mightn't it?

OWEN. But even so, I—don't think I can.

CECELIA. —That it *is* high—admit that—but it might be a good thing. (*He ponders it, frowning.*) —Owen—telephone him—just one little word, Owen— (*He is about to protest again, but is stopped by her even gaze and her hand upon his arm. Finally he nods assent. She breathes:*) You darling— (*He inclines toward her, but she leans away from him. Suddenly he glances up at the staircase. She senses that someone is coming, and begins to talk rapidly, in a different voice:*) —And of course it will be the most marvellous thing for Tom if Williamson agrees. You can imagine what it will mean to him.

OWEN. Yes, of course. (DAISY *comes down the stairs, the magazine-proofs still in hand.*)

CECELIA. His father will be pleased as Punch, too, but the main thing is— (*She looks at* DAISY *in pretended surprise.*) Oh, hello! Owen and I were just talking about The Bantam Press combining with Williamson's. Owen engineered it.

OWEN. Oh no, C. If there's any credit due— (CECELIA *laughs, and exclaims:*)

CECELIA. Never mind! (*Then again to* DAISY.) —I'm so excited about it, I can hardly speak. (*Then, to* OWEN.) —Why, Owen—do you realize?—But you wanted to telephone, didn't you?

OWEN. Why, er—why—yes, yes, I did. (CECELIA *moves toward the living-room.*)

CECELIA. It's in here, now. (*He follows. She speaks over her shoulder to* DAISY.) Coming along?

DAISY. In just a moment. (OWEN *and* CECELIA *go out, encountering* JOE *coming in.* DAISY *gazes after them.*)

JOE. (*To* CECELIA.) I thought I'd get ready for breakfast—lunch—whatever it is.

CECELIA. But you look lovely! (*She follows*

OWEN *out, into the living-room.* DAISY *moves to the table, where she sits, staring in front of her, slowly comprehending.* JOE *approaches her, as* REGAN *comes in.*)

JOE. (*To* DAISY.) What do you say we— (REGAN *clears his throat portentously.*) —God, Red, get that fixed, will you? (REGAN *lifts a lemon in two fingers.*)

REGAN. Have you seen this one?

JOE. I had grapefruit.

REGAN. Give me a five-dollar bill. (JOE *finds one for him.* REGAN *folds it and closes his hand upon it.*) Which hand?

JOE. That one. (REGAN *opens both hands.* DAISY *is still staring, wrapt in thought.*) Good!—Only where does the lemon come in? (REGAN *beckons him nearer, cuts the lemon with a fruit-knife, extracts a five-dollar bill from it, shows it to him, picks up a tray, and moves toward the door.*)

REGAN. Thank you, sir. (*He goes out with the tray and* JOE'S *five dollars.* JOE *turns to* DAISY *about to speak, but she speaks first.*)

DAISY. Are you packed, Joe?

JOE. Not yet. Why?

DAISY. I want to go.

JOE. What's the rush?

DAISY. I want to get out of this house.

JOE. But why all of a sudden?

DAISY. I want to get out, that's all.

JOE. Tom?

DAISY. Yes.

JOE. Poor devil—

DAISY. Yes.

JOE. Of course he's terribly on the defensive: you can see that.

DAISY. (*Dully.*) Can you?

JOE. Of course. He felt us disapproving, and simply gave us the works.

DAISY. Maybe.

JOE. He was awful last night, all right.

DAISY. Go and pack, Joe.

JOE. And what an outfit they were!—I give you Grace Macomber in your Christmas stocking.

DAISY. Thanks.

JOE. I'll even throw her husband in, for good measure.

DAISY. That would be too divine.

JOE. And all those pitiful second-hand opinions of Tom's! What's happened to him? What do you suppose has done it, for God's sake—

DAISY. That's what I came to find out.

JOE. Have you?

DAISY. Yes.

JOE. What?

DAISY. The most pitiful thing that can happen to any man.

JOE. But what?

DAISY. Go and pack, Joe.

JOE. It won't take a minute.—It certainly can't be C. *I* think she's a fine girl, don't you? I talked with her for quite awhile last night. She made great sense. I think she's a damned nice, attractive woman. (DAISY *moves away from him.*)

DAISY. So was Delilah.

JOE. Deli—? Oh come on, Daisy!

DAISY. —And bring my bag down with yours.

JOE. But I don't get you at all.

DAISY. (*Turning.*) Will you go and pack?

JOE. Honestly, Daisy, you're the damndest girl. (TOM *comes in from the pantry, a whisky-and-soda in hand.*)

TOM. A drink anyone?

JOE. At this hour? I should say not. (TOM *seats himself at the end of the table, facing them.*)

TOM. Too bad.

JOE. Besides, we've got to go.

TOM. So soon? Too bad. (*He takes a swallow of his drink, and smiles at them.*) Godspeed—

JOE. (*After a moment.*) —There was a fellow once told me drink was in a way to becoming my own personal Hollywood—

TOM. Really? How amusing.

JOE. You, by a strange coincidence.

TOM. Oh not possibly!

JOE. —And it was you, incidentally, who taught me how to drink moderately.

TOM. No mean feat, I'm sure.

JOE. (*With a gesture.*) Well, physician— (TOM *raises his glass again, still smiling.*)

TOM. Similia similibus curantur. Translated, the hair of the dog that—

DAISY. Go get ready, will you, Joe? (JOE *stares at* TOM *a moment, then mounts the stairs and goes out.*)

TOM. —So solemn—all so solemn. (*He puts down his glass, unfinished.*) I'm sorry you don't like my friends.

DAISY. Your—?

TOM. They are, however.—Did you read the magazine?

DAISY. Most of it.

TOM. Couldn't finish it, eh?

DAISY. No. I didn't care for it.

TOM. Why not?

DAISY. It seemed to me that one oh-so-bright weekly was enough, without more of the same.

TOM. —Not sufficiently solemn. I see.

DAISY. Not half!—And so *cheap,* Tom! Oh, how can you? (*A moment. Then:*)

TOM. You can't please everybody.

DAISY. Never mind. It doesn't matter. (TOM *drops his cynical tone and speaks genuinely:*)

TOM. Doesn't it, Daisy?

DAISY. Tom, ever since I got home I've heard from all sides how you've changed. I came here to find out if it was true, and if so why.

TOM. Well, is it?

DAISY. Tom—

TOM. And if so why? Why?

DAISY. (*A sudden cry.*) Oh, Tom—I pity you with all my heart! (*He is at her side in an instant, her wrists in his hands.*)

TOM. Pity me! What are you talking about?

DAISY. I came to find out. I've found out. Now I'm going. (*She calls.*) Joe!

TOM. Found out what? Pity me why? (DAISY *looks down at her wrists.*)

DAISY. Would you mind? (*He releases her. A moment. They gaze at each other. Her eyes soften.*) —And love you, Tom—love you with all my heart, as well. Remember that.

TOM. (*Brokenly.*) Daisy, I— (*He recovers himself, and with the recovery the cynical smile returns. He advances, one hand out, his voice coaxing.*) Give us a kiss, Daisy. (*She takes a step back from him, in horror. Her call is almost a scream:*)

DAISY. Joe! Are you ready? (JOE'S *voice is heard from the stairs.*)

JOE. Coming! (JOE *comes down the stairs with the bags.* CECELIA *comes in from the living-room.*)

CECELIA. Did someone call? (*She sees the bags.*) Why, what's all this?

DAISY. I'm sorry, but we've got to leave.

CECELIA. But what's happened?

DAISY. I suddenly remembered something. Please don't bother—

CECELIA. But I never heard of such a—

DAISY. I'm terribly sorry, but it can't be helped.

CECELIA. But can't you at least wait until after luncheon?

DAISY. I'm afraid not. (*She turns to* JOE.)

JOE. (*To* CECELIA.) Good-bye. Thanks very much.

CECELIA. Good-bye. I must say it all seems very strange. (*Then to* DAISY.) —And when we've so loved having you.

DAISY. You were kind to ask us.

CECELIA. Well, if you insist, I suppose there's no help for it. Good-bye. Do come again when you can really stay.—Your coat's here, isn't it? (*She goes out into the hall.*)

JOE. Give me a ring sometime, Tom.

TOM. Right. (JOE *looks at* DAISY. *She nods her head in the direction of the door. He goes out.*)

DAISY. Good-bye, Tom.

TOM. —Once I wouldn't say it, would I?

DAISY. Once you wouldn't—

TOM. Well, good-bye.

DAISY. —This time you do.—

TOM. Good-bye. (*She gestures helplessly, turns and goes out. For a moment he is alone. A door is heard to close, then* CECELIA *re-enters.*)

CECELIA. Honestly! If that wasn't the rudest thing! (*He is silent.*) —I presume you agree, don't you?

TOM. I don't know what it was. (*He stares in front of him, unseeing. She looks at him intently for a moment. Then:*)

CECELIA. Well—if we're going to Grace's—

TOM. I'll get my hat. (*He moves toward the hall. She follows.*)

CURTAIN.

SCENE II

At TOM COLLIER'S. *Ten o'clock the same night.*
The dining-room is dimly lighted from the hall and living-room. There is a small fire burning in the fire place. Leaves have been removed from the table, which is now at its smallest. Two chairs are at the table, the others against the wall.

REGAN *comes in from the hall with an armful of wood, some of which he places upon the fire, making it burn brighter. This done, he lights a small candle-lamp upon the table. Two places have been set and a light supper prepared: a platter of cold meat, a bowl of salad, sandwiches, fruit. There is a champagne glass at each place. A moment, then* CECELIA *calls from upstairs:*

CECELIA. Regan?

REGAN. —Right here, Ma'am.

CECELIA. I thought I heard a car.

REGAN. Yes, Madam.

CECELIA. Is Mr. Collier's supper ready?

REGAN. Yes, Madam. (*He lights a small lamp on the serving-table, pokes the fire again, and goes out into the hall. A moment, then* CECELIA *comes down the stairs, in another charming negligee, this time more severe in cut and somber in color. She examines the table, rearranges a few things*

and puts out the lamp upon the serving-table. Now the room is lit only by the candle-lamp and the fire upon the hearth. A door closes in the hall. She turns toward it, calling:)

CECELIA. Tom? (TOM *comes in.*)

TOM. Hello. (*He looks at the table.*) What's all this?

CECELIA. I thought you might be hungry. I know what you think of Williamson's food. (*He looks at the fire, then around him, curiously.*) What's the matter?

TOM. —Lighted this way, it reminds me of some place.

CECELIA. Where?

TOM. I don't know. (*His voice is strange, as if speaking from a distance.*)

CECELIA. Do eat something, dear. (*Again he looks about him, puzzled.*)

TOM. —I came back the long way, over the Pound Ridge road, through Middle Patent.

CECELIA. What made you do that, Silly—

TOM. I don't know, I wanted to drive. (*Now it is her he looks at curiously.*)

CECELIA. Tom—what *is* the matter? (*He shakes his head, as if to shake something out of it, and laughs shortly.*)

TOM. Sorry!

CECELIA. (*Anxiously.*) Everything went all right, didn't it?

TOM. Oh yes, perfectly. (*A moment. Then:*) In fact, it's settled.

CECELIA. Not already!

TOM. Yes. They've signed. All I have to do is to dig up a notary in the Village and write my name under theirs.

CECELIA. Oh, Tom!

TOM. Are you pleased?

CECELIA. Aren't you?

TOM. I think something's happened to my nervous system. I feel awfully light.

CECELIA. You're famished. Come and sit down and eat— (*She draws him to the table. He seats himself there, and for a moment drops his head in his hands.*) —And tired, too, poor darling.

TOM. No—just light. So awfully light.— Thinking too much. (*She puts meat and salad upon a plate and sets it before him.*)

CECELIA. Here.

TOM. C—

CECELIA. Yes, dear?

TOM. I think it's time we had a child or two, C. (*A moment. Then:*)

CECELIA. We'll talk about that.

TOM. Yes. We must. (*Another moment.*) —The trees along the road stood out like— (*He rubs his eyes and looks up again.*) —like whatever it is trees stand out like.

CECELIA. You've been going much too hard, you know.

TOM. It's good for me. I'm having visions. (*Again he looks around him.*) —What *is* it it reminds me of? (*She seats herself near him at the table.*)

CECELIA. —Nothing. You're just tired and hungry.

TOM. Please let me have my visions. (REGAN *comes in with a pint of champagne.*) Good evening, Mr. Regan.

REGAN. Good evening, Sir.

TOM. —Those buttons on your coat—you know, they're terribly bright.

REGAN. I'll try to bring 'em down.

TOM. Do. It's essential.—Champagne, is it?

CECELIA. I thought you might feel like celebrating.

TOM. Well—

CECELIA. A little wine won't hurt you, Tom.

TOM. (*To himself.*) —The little more, and how much it is— (*Rousing himself.*) —Fill them, Mr. Regan. (REGAN *looks at him oddly, then fills the glasses.* TOM *raises his and squints at it.*) —Infinite riches, in a little room. (CECELIA *laughs.*)

CECELIA. You've got the quotes badly.

TOM. Little lamb, who made thee?—Regan —dost thou know who made thee? (*He holds out the glass to him.*) —And a little more, old son. (REGAN *refills the glass and goes out.* TOM *watches him, curiously.*) The discreet withdrawal—I've seen that before, too. (*Looks around him again, then cries, suddenly:*) I know! The Florentine! —A private room at the Florentine.

CECELIA. What's that?

TOM. A kind of a hotel. Flora Conover's place.

CECELIA. It sounds wicked.

TOM. It used to be the best twenty-guinea house in London.

CECELIA. Twenty-guinea? What are you talking about?

TOM. In advance, at that. (CECELIA *glances at him.*)

CECELIA. Rather expensive, wasn't it?

TOM. But one went to Flora's to celebrate. —And the food was good, the waiter discreet, the wines excellent, the lady most artful.

CECELIA. Tom! How revolting—

TOM. But we must send the boys back happy, you know.

CECELIA. I don't care to hear about it, thank you.

TOM. Very well, my dear. (*A moment. He stares at his glass. Then:*)

CECELIA. Weren't they difficult at all, Tom?

TOM. Who? Williamson's?—Easy.

CECELIA. And you actually got your own terms?

TOM. Except for their right to pass on my selections

CECELIA. That's probably just a form.

TOM. Probably.

CECELIA. They want to feel they have *some* say.

TOM. That's all.—C, What have you done to your hair?

CECELIA. Why, nothing, why?

TOM. It looks lighter.

CECELIA. It isn't. (*He gazes at it for a moment longer, then eats a little, disinterestedly.*)

TOM. I quashed the announcement they'd prepared for the papers.

CECELIA. Why? What was it?

TOM. "Williamson, Warren and Company have absorbed The Bantam Press, formerly owned by—"

CECELIA. "Absorbed"!

TOM. Yes. Like a sponge. I quashed it. For "absorbed" read "bought a controlling interest in."

CECELIA. Well—that's more like it.

TOM. —Poor little Bantam.—For "Bantam" read small little, plucked little capon.

CECELIA. Oh, don't Tom! You know it's a good thing for you—it's a grand thing for you.

TOM. —Increased scope.

CECELIA. Of course.

TOM. —Perfect distribution facilities.

CECELIA. But aren't they?

TOM. Williamson, Warren Books Girdle the Globe. Hear the eagle scream.—Poor little Bantam—peep, peep—

CECELIA. —And I thought you'd be beside yourself for joy. (*He gazes at her. She is.*)

TOM. C, your eyes are so bright. (*She laughs shortly.*)

CECELIA. Eat, you. You're seeing things. (*He looks at his plate.*)

TOM. C—

CECELIA. Yes, dear?

TOM. —Little love is no love.

CECELIA. —Meaning what, precisely?

TOM. It wasn't necessary to lock your door against me last night. (*A moment. Then:*)

CECELIA. But I didn't.—I mean—not against—

TOM. Then why?

CECELIA. I'm—it's just that sometimes I'm afraid, alone at night. (*He is watching her.*)

TOM. I don't believe you. (*She laughs nervously.*)

CECELIA. Well, really!

TOM. I don't believe you, C. (*She averts her head.*) —Only I'd like you to know that that isn't necessary, ever.

CECELIA. Very well. (*Suddenly he reaches for her hand and takes it.*)

TOM. Why was it? Tell me instantly why it was.

CECELIA. Is that an order?

TOM. Tell me. (*She tries to meet his gaze, but cannot.*)

CECELIA. (*With difficulty.*) You mean—why I—why I didn't want you near me--

TOM. Yes.

CECELIA. —And you don't know—

TOM. No.

CECELIA. Well, if you don't, you ought to.

TOM. Tell me, I say.

CECELIA. You'd been so—consistently disagreeable, that's all.

TOM. About what? — Wanting Regan back?

CECELIA. No.

TOM. What, then?

CECELIA. Your father, chiefly. (*She rises and goes to the serving-table.*) He telephoned this afternoon. (*A moment.*) He wanted to know if you'd got the birthday-check. (*Another moment.*) I told him that you had, and had tried to call him. (*He turns away.*) Well, I had to say something! (*She reseats herself at the table with a plate for herself.*)

TOM. I don't know whether to send it back, or just not to cash it. (*He finds a check among the letters in his pocket, and looks at it frowning.*)

CECELIA. —Of course, you simply can't allow yourself to show any kind of graciousness toward him.

TOM. No.

CECELIA. —As a way of telling you how pleased with you he is, he sends you a small check,—and you have the extraordinary bad taste to— (*He holds the check out for her to see. Her eyes widen.*) What! —Good heavens—I don't believe it!

TOM. There it is.

CECELIA. But there isn't that much money in the world!

TOM. In Father's world there is. He feels he can afford it, to get us to come and live with him.

CECELIA. Of course, I don't understand your attitude about that, either.

TOM. Don't you, C?

CECELIA. He knows how inconvenient it is here in winter,—and having that great, huge, lovely house in town, it's perfectly sweet and natural of him to—to, well to ask—

TOM. Yes—you, to preside night after night at his deadly dinners, me to listen eternally to his delphic advice on what to do and how to live—in short, to allow him to own us. Of course, he's willing to pay. He always is.

CECELIA. Oh, how ridiculous you are, really!—His whole life long he's tried to help you, to do things for you—

TOM. —In order to own me. I tell you I know him.

CECELIA. You're the only child he's got, and he's an old man and a very lonely man. I think it's horrible beyond belief, the way you treat him. How you can be so hard, I don't know.

TOM. Hard!—I'm not hard enough. All my life I've been trying to harden. I was born soft, that's the trouble with me.

CECELIA. You soft!

TOM. Yes. Born it.—And then brought up to refuse to face any truth that was an unpleasant truth, in myself or anyone else— always be the little gentleman, Tommy— charming and agreeable at all costs—give no pain, Tommy.

CECELIA. You seem to have outgrown it nicely.

TOM. Not yet, I haven't. No, not by a long shot. The inclination's still there, all right. Still going strong.

CECELIA. Don't be discouraged.

TOM. (*Wearily.*) All right, C.

CECELIA. —It's nothing but your old self-consciousness about money, again. It simply defeats me.—Honestly, has everyone who lives well sold his soul to the devil?

TOM. (*Rising.*) "Lives well"!—I'd give my eyes to live well. That's all I want for us. (*He goes to a chair at the window.*)

CECELIA. Oh—definitions again.—We being so weak, of course, that a little luxury would completely ruin us.

TOM. —Little—little—everything's so little. Add it up, though. (*His head sinks upon his breast.*) —Add it up.

CECELIA. To my way of thinking, if a person can't stand—

TOM. Let's drop it.

CECELIA. (*Coldly.*) Very well. We shall. (*He looks up again.*)

TOM. —Now you've gone from me again—

CECELIA. A lot you care.

TOM. Oh C—my lovely C— Where are you? What's become of you?

CECELIA. There's something you call your damned integrity— (TOM *rises from his chair.*)

TOM. (*Suddenly, sharply.*) That's the word! (CECELIA *rises also.*)

CECELIA. I see it's no use talking. (*A silence. He looks at her intently.*)

TOM. —This is what you call "being disagreeable."

CECELIA. Yes. Very. (*He returns to her.*)

TOM. —But how to be otherwise, when—

CECELIA. (*In a burst.*) Possibly by being the fine, kind, generous man you ought to be!

TOM. To Father?

CECELIA. You might begin there.

TOM. —Accept the check with thanks— and go to live with him—

CECELIA. It's only for a few months—and I think to refuse his present would be extremely bad manners—just about in a class with those of your little lady of easy virtue, this morning. If— (*She sees she has gone too far.*) I'm sorry to have said that about her. I didn't mean—

TOM. Never mind. (*A long moment. Then:*) —Suppose I should do as you say about Father—

CECELIA. Oh, Tom—do be the darling I know you are!

TOM. Would you like me better?

CECELIA. Much.

TOM. How much?

CECELIA. Oh—very much. (*He leans forward, watching her, hardly believing it possible.*)

TOM. No locked doors, anymore?

CECELIA. (*Lowly.*) Not one—ever—

TOM. That sounds—most inviting. (*She smiles.*)

CECELIA. Does it? (*Again he seats himself at the table.*)

TOM. —And suddenly I'm beginning to see with an awful clearness— (*He stops.*)

CECELIA. (*Smiling.*) What? How stupid you've been?—And what I am to you?

TOM. (*After a moment.*) Yes.

CECELIA. —And so you *are* going to be nice again?

TOM. You'll see. (*Again* CECELIA's *smile.*)

CECELIA. —But how am I to be sure?

TOM. You've told me ways to convince you.

CECELIA. I do so hate us not to agree, Tom.

TOM. I know. (*She brings her chair closer and sits at his side.*)

CECELIA. I want so to feel—I don't know —together again, as we used to be. (*Once more,* TOM *looks incredulously around him, at the room. Then:*)

TOM. You're very pretty, you know—

CECELIA. Why, thank you, Sir.

TOM. —Very exciting, too. (*His manner has changed. From now on, he is no longer the husband sitting before the fire with his wife, but a host at supper with a pretty girl, whom later he will know better.*)

CECELIA. I don't know whether it's you or the wine speaking.

TOM. —Me.

CECELIA. Shall we have a little more?

TOM. Why not? (*She presses the button.*)

CECELIA. It's a party, then.

TOM. It's a party.

CECELIA. Sometimes you're so thrilling, Tom.

TOM. You think? (*A moment. Then:*)

CECELIA. Put your arms around me, Tom— (*He inclines toward her, does not touch her, but looks full into her eyes, searching for something he still cannot believe he will find.*)

TOM. Are they around?

CECELIA. (*In a breath.*) Oh—yes—yes— (REGAN *comes in.*)

TOM. Another small bottle. (REGAN *goes out.* CECELIA *laughs a little throaty, excited laugh.*)

CECELIA. We shouldn't. You know we shouldn't.

TOM. But we seem to be—

CECELIA. I feel—all at once I feel terribly naughty, somehow—

TOM. I suppose you're the prettiest girl I've ever seen—

CECELIA. (*Archly.*) So nice of you to think so, Sir.

TOM. —So very attractive—

CECELIA. I like to be attractive.

TOM. So very seductive—

CECELIA. There, there! That's enough! (*He has found it. Coldly he salutes it:*)

TOM. You're a strange woman. Your lips drop honeycomb, your mouth is smoother than oil.

CECELIA. Now what are you quoting? (REGAN *comes in with the wine.*)

TOM. —Give the lady some, waiter. (REGAN *fills* CECELIA'S *glass, then* TOM'S *without a word.*) You can leave the bottle. (REGAN *places it upon the table, near him.*) —And that will be all. (REGAN *bows and goes out.* CECELIA *raises her glass and smiles invitingly. He raises his, murmuring:*) —To the pleasant ways of life. (*She drinks. He does not.*)

CECELIA. —Such pleasant ways. (*She smiles at her glass.*)

TOM. Is it good?

CECELIA. So good.—I'm feeling it a little.

TOM. That's what it's for, eh?

CECELIA. It must be.

TOM. "Champagne, the friend of lovers"— (*Her face inclines to him, then she averts her head.*)

CECELIA. (*Softly.*) No—not yet—

TOM. Artful child.

CECELIA. You think?

TOM. —Lovely, alluring thing—

CECELIA. I like you too, now.

TOM. Pleasant here, isn't it?

CECELIA. So pleasant. (*She refills her glass and finds that his is still full.*) —But you aren't taking any—

TOM. It makes me see almost too clearly.

CECELIA. Take a little more, and everything will get so—lovely and vague and—the way I feel now.

TOM. —A good feeling, is it?

CECELIA. (*A whisper.*) Delicious— (*She gropes for his hand, holds it against her breast.*) Oh—Tom— (*He looks at her. She smiles again.*) —One last toast? (*He draws her to her feet, glass in hand.*) But to what —what to?

TOM. You name it. (*A moment. Then:*)

CECELIA. To love— (*She comes against him, steadies her glass in both hands against his breast, bends her head and takes it. He raises his glass, holds it for a moment near his lips, then sets it down, untouched, upon the table. She replaces hers beside it, and murmurs:*) And darling—

TOM. Yes?

CECELIA. You—you *are* going to be an angel about—about things, aren't you?

TOM. You'll see.

CECELIA. Oh, I knew you would!—I'm so happy— (*She smiles, moves slowly toward the stairs, and mounts them, opening the door at the top. There she turns and whispers.*) Don't be long— (*And goes out.* TOM'S *eyes following her. Then he turns and stares down at the table. Finally his hand finds the bell and presses it. A moment then* REGAN *enters, in a business suit.*)

TOM. See here, Red, I—

REGAN. (*Sharply.*) Never mind! (TOM *looks up.* REGAN *gestures.*) All I mean is— well, I'm out for good, this time.

TOM. Why?

REGAN. I just don't like it here, that's all.

TOM. When do you want to go?

REGAN. As soon as I can.

TOM. To-night, then.

REGAN. That's all right with me. I'm packed.

TOM. Look in and say good-bye as you're leaving.

REGAN. I'm leaving now.

TOM. Look in, anyhow. (REGAN *turns to go.*) —Have you got a fountain-pen? (REGAN *finds a pen and gives it to him.*) —Don't let me forget to return it. (REGAN *goes out. Slowly, methodically,* TOM *opens the pen, shakes it, spreads the check upon the table and writes upon its back. Then, as carefully, he replaces the top of the pen, picks up the check and waves it back and forth, to dry it.* REGAN *re-enters with a traveling-bag.* TOM *returns the pen to him.*) —Here you are. Thanks.

REGAN. Well—good-bye—

TOM. Get into the car.

REGAN. I can walk to the train all right.

TOM. Bring my coat and hat, will you? (REGAN *does not stir.*) —Will you bring my coat and hat, please? (REGAN *puts down his bag and goes into the hall for them.* TOM *folds the check carefully, goes to the fire place and places it upon the mantel-piece, one corner under a vase.* REGAN *re-enters with his overcoat and hat.* TOM *puts on the hat.* REGAN *holds the coat for him.* TOM *gets into it. He takes a cigarette from the pocket and puts it in his mouth.*)

REGAN. What's the idea?

TOM. —Light, please— (REGAN *holds a match for him.* TOM *pulls on his gloves.*) Now, then—

REGAN. I can walk, I tell you.

TOM. Not at all. We'll drive in.

REGAN. *We* will—?

TOM. (*Very gently.*) I'm going back to my wife, Red.

REGAN. To your—? (*Puzzled,* REGAN *looks toward the lighted doorway at the top of the stairs.*)

TOM. —To my wife, I said. (REGAN *picks up his bag, and goes out, into the hall.* TOM *looks once around him, draws a deep breath of smoke, exhales it slowly, then turns and follows him.*)

CURTAIN.

Boy Meets Girl

BY BELLA AND SAMUEL SPEWACK

To
JO DAVIDSON
WHOSE HOSPITALITY AND
ENCOURAGEMENT DELAYED THE COMPLETION OF
THIS PLAY THREE MONTHS

BOY MEETS GIRL was produced by George Abbott at the Cort Theatre, New York City, Wednesday evening, November 27, 1935. The production was directed by Mr. Abbott; the settings designed by Arne Lundborg.

THE CAST

ROBERT LAW ....Allyn Joslyn	SUSIE ....Joyce Arling
LARRY TOMS ....Charles McClelland	A NURSE ....Helen Gardner
J. CARLYLE BENSON Jerome Cowan	DOCTOR ....Perry Ivins
ROSETTI ....Everett H. Sloane	CHAUFFEUR ....Edison Rice
MR. FRIDAY (C.F.)...Royal Beal	YOUNG MAN ....Philip Faversham
PEGGY ....Peggy Hart	STUDIO OFFICER ...George W. Smith
MISS CREWS ....Lea Penman	CUTTER ....Robert Foulk
RODNEY BEVAN .....James MacColl	ANOTHER NURSE ...Marjorie Lytell
GREEN ....Garson Kanin	MAJOR THOMPSON ..John Clarke
SLADE ....Maurice Sommers	

SCENES

ACT ONE
Mr. Friday's Office, the Royal Studios in Hollywood.

ACT TWO
Scene   I.   A Neighborhood Theatre. Seven months later.
Scene   II.   Mr. Friday's Office.
Scene III.   The same. Several hours later.

ACT THREE
Scene   I.   A hospital corridor. Three weeks later.
Scene   II.   In your home.
Scene III.   Mr. Friday's office.

COPYRIGHT, 1936, BY BELLA AND SAMUEL SPEWACK

BOY MEETS GIRL

ACT ONE

The room we see is one of a suite of three, comprising the sanctum of MR. C. ELIOT FRIDAY, *a supervisor, sometimes called a producer, who is engaged in manufacturing motion pictures in Hollywood, California.*

In its present state the room is a happy combination of the Regency and Russell Wright periods—given over to pale green, mauve and canary yellow, with Rodier-cloth-covered easy chairs and couch. A magnificent, be-French-phoned desk is at one end of the room. On it rests the inner-office dictograph, over which in the course of the play we hear the voice of the great B.K., chief executive of the studio. Beside it, appropriately, stands an amiable photograph of MRS. C. Eliot Friday, *a cultured if fatuous lady; a copy of "Swann's Way" (leaves uncut), a bronze nude astride an ash tray, a bottle of Pyramidon and a copy of "Variety." In the trash basket is a copy of "Hollywood Reporter." (It was very unkind to* MR. FRIDAY.) *On the wall back of the desk are bookshelves with pots of hanging ivy on the top shelf, the rest given over, curiously enough, to books—and occasional bric-a-brac. There are a few end tables with ash trays and boxes of cigarettes, for it is the unwritten law in Hollywood that supervisors must provide cigarettes for writers during conferences and other times of stress. The two windows, although of the old-fashioned, non-casement kind, are framed by tasteful, expensive drapes and are partially concealed by half-drawn Venetian blinds. (A supervisor would lose caste without Venetian blinds.) The door left leads to an anteroom where sits* MISS CREWS, *secretary to* MR. FRIDAY. *The door at right rear leads to a smaller office where* MR. FRIDAY *sometimes thinks in solitude. This room contains* MR. FRIDAY'S *Commencement Day photograph (Harvard '19), snapshots of B.K.'s wedding, at which* MR. FRIDAY *served as an usher, and a huge picture of Pola Negri inscribed "Sincerely yours." There are other photographs with more florid inscriptions upon faces once famous and since vanished in film dust. The room is also memorable for the fact that* MR. FRIDAY—*a bit of a diplomat in his way—sometimes keeps earnest writers here while he submits their scripts to other writers in his inner office. At times as many as fifteen bright minds are thus let loose upon a C. Elliot Friday production, with sometimes startling results.*

All this, however, is very much by the by. It is really more important to note that through those Venetian blinds you can feel the sweet sterility of the desert that is so essentially Southern California. The sun is bright, of course, and it pours endlessly through the windows. The time is two o'clock, and the boys have been at it since noon.

One of the boys is BENSON—J. CARLYLE BENSON, *whom we discover prone on a couch. He is in his thirties and in his flannels. Years ago, as he will tell you, he worked as a scene painter and a property boy. He became a writer because he learned how bricks were made and laid. He knows every cliché, every formula, and in his heart of hearts he really believes the fairy tale is a credo of life. And he's a damned nice guy; handicapped somewhat by the fact that he married a beautiful but extravagant young woman who obviously doesn't love him. They live in a gorgeous home, have four dogs, two cars and, as* MR. FRIDAY *would put it, "a menage."*

The other member of the writing team is ROBERT LAW *whom you will find listed in O'Brien's "Best Short Stories" of five years ago. He came to Hollywood to make a little money and run right back to Vermont where he could really write. He is rather handsome, a little round-shouldered; smokes incessantly. He's a damned nice guy, too.*

There is a deep and abiding affection between the two men, even though LAW'S *nostalgia for realism and sincerity and substance finds no echoing response in* MR. BENSON. *They have one great thing in common—their mutual love of a great gag, a practical joke to enliven the monotony of the writing factory.*

For we are dealing here with a factory that manufactures entertainment in approved sizes; that puts the seven arts right on the belt. And it is this very quality tha makes MR. FRIDAY'S *office as fascinating as a power house and a good deal more entertaining.*

The other inmates of the room are LARRY TOMS—*you know* LARRY TOMS—*a Western star, and one* ROSETTI, *an agent. It is* MR. ROSETTI'S *business to see to it that* MR. TOMS *is profitably employed, for* MR. ROSETTI *collects ten per cent of* MR. TOM'S *weekly salary which, despite the star's fading popularity, is still a respectable sum.* MR. TOMS *is handsome, of course. He is also parsimonious. He leads a completely righteous life, and if you don't like him it isn't our fault; in all respects he is an extremely admirable character.*

As the curtain goes up we see that LAW *is on his feet and obviously he has been telling a story to* MR. TOMS—*a story that* MR. TOMS *is expected to re-enact before the camera.*

LAW. And this bozo comes up to you and you look him straight in the eye and you say, "Why, damn your soul, I loved her before you ever married her." And then in walks the bitch, and she cries, "Larry, I heard everything you said." And you just look at her, and there's a long pause—a *long* pause. And then finally you say, "Did you?" That's all. Just a plain, quiet, simple "Did you?" Boy, what a moment! (*He lies down on the couch beside* BENSON.)

LARRY. But what's the story about?

BENSON (*rolling over*). Love!

LAW (*singing*). "Love is the sweetest thing—"

LARRY. Now, come on, boys—get off the couch. This ain't fair. I got a lot at stake in this picture. It's the last one in my contract. If I get a poor story I'm out in the cold.

LAW. Shivering with a million dollar annuity.

ROSETTI. Now, gentlemen, don't let's get personal.

LARRY (*rises and crosses to couch*). When they told me I was getting the star team of writers on the lot, I was all for it. But you've done nothing but clown around, and the shooting date's only two weeks off. I've got to play this picture.

LAW. Why?

LARRY (*swallowing*). Tell me the story in a few simple words.

LAW. Mr. Benson, what's our story?

BENSON. How the hell do I know?

LAW (*sits up*). Didn't you listen?

BENSON. No. We ought to have a stenographer.

LAW. But they won't wear tights. And I can't dictate to a stenographer who won't wear tights.

LARRY. Now listen, boys—

LAW. Don't speak to me. You don't like our story.

LARRY. I didn't say I didn't like it. I couldn't follow it. (*He slumps in disgust.*)

BENSON (*indignantly*). You couldn't follow it? Listen, I've been writing stories for eleven years. Boy meets girl. Boy loses girl. Boy gets girl.

LAW. Or—girl meets boy. Girl loses boy. Girl gets boy. Love will find a way. Love never loses. Put your money on love. You can't lose. (*Rises and saunters to window.*) I'm getting hungry.

BENSON. It's a sorry state of affairs when an actor insists on following a story. Do you think this is a golf tournament?

ROSETTI (*earnestly*). If I may make a point, I don't think you're showing the proper respect to one of the biggest stars in this studio. A man who's not only captivated millions of people but is going to captivate millions more—

BENSON (*wearily*). With his little lasso—

LARRY. Just because I don't get Gable's fan mail don't mean I ain't got his following. A lot of those that want to write me ain't never learned how.

LAW. Benson, injustice has been done. We've been lacking in respect for the idol of illiteracy.

BENSON. Do we apologize?

LAW. No!

ROSETTI. Well, let me tell you something. Before I became an agent I taught diction for years, and Larry Toms is potentially the greatest actor I've ever met. And I can prove it with X-rays. I was just taking them up to show B.K. He's got the Barrymore larynx. I'll put his larynx against John Barrymore's and I defy you to tell me which is which. (*Takes X-rays from brief-case. Gives one to* BENSON, *one to* LAW.)

LARRY. I couldn't tell it myself and it's my own larynx.

BENSON (*drawling*). Say—are you sure this is his *larynx?*

ROSETTI (*the diplomat; retrieving X-rays*). Gentlemen, I wouldn't be surprised with the proper training if Larry couldn't sing. That opens up the whole field of musicals. (*Puts brief-case on chair.*)

BENSON (*to* LAW). What are we waiting for?

LAW. Lunch.

LARRY (*angrily rising*). I'm getting fed up with this. I got writers who are just plain crazy—a producer who can't concentrate—and ain't even here—and—(*Throws hat on floor and starts for* BENSON *and* LAW. LAW *moves to back of couch and* BENSON *goes up to door.*)

ROSETTI (*crossing down on* LARRY's *left*). Now . . . now . . . Larry . . . don't lose your temper.

LARRY (*righteously*). The idea of writers getting fifteen hundred a week for acting like hoodlums.

LAW. I agree with you.

LARRY. Huh?

LAW. We're not writers. We're hacks. If we weren't would I be sitting here listening to your inarticulate grunts?

LARRY. Huh?

LAW. That's exactly what I mean. For two cents, Benson, I'd take the next train back to Vermont.

LARRY. That's all right with me.

BENSON. Will you forget Vermont?

LAW. At least I wouldn't have to sit around with *that* in Vermont. I'd write—really write. My God, I wrote once. I wrote a book.

A darn good book. I was a promising young novelist. O'Brien reprinted three of my stories. 1928-1929-1930. And in 1935 I'm writing dialogue for a horse!

LARRY (*enraged*). Now, listen—

ROSETTI (*pleading*). Larry—Larry, take a deep breath. The boys mean no harm. . . . Exhale!

LAW (*sniffing*). I smell carbon monoxide.

LARRY. One more crack, that's all—just one more crack! (*Phone rings.*)

ROSETTI (*at phone*). Hello . . . oh, yes . . . just a minute. For you, Benson.

BENSON (*taking up phone*). Yes, speaking. Who? Of course, Mrs. Benson's check is good! How much is it for? Thirty-five hundred? Oh! I hope it was real ermine. . . . Certainly it's all right. You put the check through tomorrow. (*Hangs up; dials phone.*)

ROSETTI (*with a feline purr*). Ermine is a nice fur. (MISS CREWS *enters regally; puts letters on desk.*)

LARRY (*grumbling*). Miss Crews, what's keeping C.F.?

MISS CREWS. He's still up with B.K. (*She exits regally.*)

BENSON (*into phone*). Jim? Benson. Listen, sell three of my Municipal Fives this afternoon, will you? And put it in my joint account in the Security. I've got a check to meet. Never mind about that. I'll talk to her. Right. (*Hangs up.*)

LAW. Pearl is certainly spreading prosperity.

BENSON. What the hell? She's only a kid. She's having a good time. What's money for? (C.F. *enters.* C.F. *is, of course, C.* ELLIOT FRIDAY.)

C.F. (*briskly*). Good morning.

ROSETTI (*rises*). Good morning, C.F.

LARRY (*rises and sits*). Hello, C.F. (BENSON *lies on sofa.* LAW *rises and salaams Hindu fashion, as popularized by Mr. De Mille.*)

C.F. Boys, no antics, please. We've got a heavy day ahead of us. (*Sits at desk; picks up phone. Into phone*) I don't won't to be disturbed by anybody—understand? And order some lunch. A plate of raw carrots, and a bottle of certified, raw milk. See that it's raw. Bring enough for everybody. (*About to hang up.*)

LAW (*rises*). Just a moment. (*Takes phone.*) Mr. Benson and Mr. Law want two cups of chicken broth—some ham hocks—cabbage—lemon meringue pie—and some bicarbonate of soda. (*Hangs up; returns to couch.*)

C.F. You're slaughtering yourselves, boys. You won't be able to think with that poison in your stomachs, and we've got to think. I've just seen the front office. Boys, we're facing a crisis.

ROSETTI (*eagerly*). Any truth in the report, C.F., that Gaumont British wants to buy the studio?

C.F. You know as much about it as I do, Rosetti.

LAW. Why sell? I thought we were sitting pretty. We're in receivership.

ROSETTI. Well, I'm going up to see B.K. I hope you boys get a good story for Larry.

C.F. (*ignoring him; C.F. can ignore beautifully*). As a matter of fact, you may as well know it. There may be a reorganization.

BENSON. Again?

C.F. And you know my position. I'm the only college-bred man in the studio. They resent me.

LAW. The big snobs.

C.F. Just because I've always tried to do something fine, something dignified, something worth while, I'm being hammered on all sides. Boys, if my next picture fails, I'm out. And you're out, Larry. And it won't do you boys any good either. Of course you can always write plays.

LAW. I don't see why not. We never wrote any.

C.F. I have an idea for a play I want to discuss with you some time. You'll be wild about it. Just one set, too—simple to produce, and practically anybody can play it. Katharine Cornell would be marvelous for the girl. She dies in the first act.

LARRY. Listen here, C.F., I ain't in the theatre. What about my picture?

C.F. Boys, we need a big picture. Not just a good story. I want to do something fine—with sweep, with scope—stark, honest, gripping, adult, but with plenty of laughs and a little hokum.

LARRY (*bitterly*). And no "Did you?" scenes.

C.F. Something we'll be proud of. Not just another picture, but the picture of the year. A sort of Bengal Lancer, but as Kipling would have done it. Maybe we could wire Kipling and get him to write a few scenes. It would be darned good publicity. (PEGGY *enters;* PEGGY *is the manicurist on the lot.*) Oh, come in . . . come in, Peggy. (PEGGY *puts tray of manicurist's paraphernalia on desk; moves small chair at* C.F.'s *side; takes bowl and exits for water.*)

BENSON (*in astonishment*). He doesn't think we're as good as Kipling.

C.F. (*quickly*). Mind you, not that I think Kipling is a great writer. A story-teller, yes. But greatness? Give me Proust any time. Now, boys, how about a story?

LAW. Nestling on your desk for two weeks there's a script we wrote for Larry Toms.

BENSON. A beautiful script. That one with my fingerprints on the cover.

C.F. (*picking up script, holding it in his hands as if weighing it*). This? This won't do.

LAW. That's where you're wrong. I had it weighed at the A. & P. and the manager went wild over it. (C.F. *puts script on top of dictograph.* MISS CREWS *enters.*)

MISS CREWS. Excuse me, Mr. Friday, but Casting wants to know how many midgets you'll need.

C.F. (*irritably*). Midgets? I don't need any midgets.

MISS CREWS. Casting says you ordered midgets and they've got them.

C.F. They're crazy. I'm not doing a horror story. (*Phone rings; at phone.*) Hello. . . . It's for you, Benson.

BENSON. For me?

C.F. I think it's Mrs. Benson. Listen, Miss Crews, we're in conference. Please don't disturb us again.

MISS CREWS. Yes, Mr. Friday. (*She exits.*)

BENSON (*into telephone*). Oh, hello, darling. . . . Yes, I know you've been shopping. . . . Why don't you try Woolworth's? . . . No, I'm not mad. . . . Oh, you're taking the dogs for a walk? That's good. . . . Oh, no, I can't take you to lunch. I'm in a story conference. . . . But look, darling, I'm in a story conference. . . . Hello . . . (*He mops his brow and tries to shake off his gloom.*)

C.F. How is Mrs. Benson?

BENSON. Swell.

C.F. I must get Mrs. Friday to invite her over to her French class. All the wives are taking it up very seriously. Gives them something to do, and as I said to Mrs. Friday: I'm a linguist—why shouldn't you be? That's the great thing in marriage—mutual interests. (BENSON *crosses to couch.*) Of course, Mrs. Benson isn't the studious type, is she? Beautiful girl, though. . . . Where were we? What was I saying?

BENSON (*crosses back to desk; sighs; indicates script*). You were saying that this is one of the greatest picture scripts ever written.

C.F. (*with a superior smile*). Now, just a minute—

LAW (*quickly*). And do you know why? Because it's the same story Larry Toms has been doing for years.

BENSON. We *know* it's good.

LAW. Griffith used it. Lubitsch used it. And Eisenstein's coming around to it.

BENSON. Boy meets girl. Boy loses girl. Boy gets girl.

LAW. The great American fairy tale. Sends the audience back to the relief rolls in a happy frame of mind.

BENSON. And why not?

LAW. The greatest escape formula ever worked out in the history of civilization. . . .

C.F. Of course, if you put it that way . . . but, boys, it's hackneyed.

LAW. You mean classic.

C.F. (*triumphantly*). *Hamlet* is a classic—but it isn't hackneyed!

LAW. *Hamlet* isn't hackneyed? Why, I'd be ashamed to use that poison gag. He lifted that right out of the Italians. (PEGGY *enters and crosses to her chair and sits.*) Ask Peggy. (PEGGY *puts the bowl now half-filled with water down on the desk.*)

BENSON. Yes, let's ask Peggy . . . if she wants to see Larry Toms in a different story. She's your audience.

PEGGY. Don't ask me anything, Mr. Benson. I've got the damnedest toothache. (*She takes* C.F.'s *hand and looks up at him suddenly.*) Relax! (*She begins filing.*)

BENSON (*wheedling*). But, Peggy, you go to pictures, don't you?

PEGGY. No.

BENSON. But you've seen Larry's pictures and enjoyed them?

PEGGY. No.

BENSON. . . . As millions of others have . . .

LAW. Why, one man sent him a rope all the way from Manila—with instructions.

C.F. Boys. this isn't getting us anywhere.

BENSON (*assuming the manner of a district attorney; barking at* PEGGY). Peggy, do you mean to sit there and tell me you haven't seen *one* Larry Toms picture?

PEGGY. I saw one.

BENSON. Ah!

PEGGY. *Night in Death Valley.*

BENSON. This isn't getting us anywhere, eh? How would you like to see *Night in Death Valley* again—with a new title?

PEGGY. I wouldn't.

BENSON. That's all. Step down. (*Crosses to couch; slaps* LAW *on shoulder.*) May I point out to this court that the body was found only two feet away, in an open field, with every door and window shut? (*To* LAW) Your witness. (*He exits.*)

LAW (*rises*). I've got to see a man about a woman. (*He exits. Our writers have vanished. They love to vanish from story conferences.*)

C.F. (*rises*). Come back here! (*Picks up phone.*)

LARRY. That's what I mean—clowning.

C.F. (*at phone*). Miss Crews, leave word at the gate Benson and Law are not to be allowed off the lot. They're to come right back to my office. (*Hangs up.*)

LARRY. Why do you stand for it?

C.F. Larry, those boys are crazy, but they've got something.

LARRY. They've been fired off every other lot.

C.F. I'll fire them off this one, after they've produced a story. I've made up my mind to that. Meanwhile, patience.

LARRY. That's easy to say.

C.F. You can't quibble with the artistic temperament when it produces.

LARRY (*grumbling*). They've been producing nothing but trouble around here. (*YOUNG ACTOR enters in the resplendent uniform of the Coldstream Guards. His name is RODNEY. Both uniform and actor explain themselves as the play proceeds.*)

MISS CREWS. Right in here.

RODNEY. How do you do.

C.F. What do *you* want?

RODNEY. Why, Wardrobe sent me. Do you approve the uniform?

C.F. Uniform for what?

RODNEY. *Young England.*

C.F. You see, Larry—three pictures in production—all going on at the same time—I'm standing on my head—and then they wonder what's wrong with the industry. (*Rises; barks at RODNEY.*) Stand over there. (*MISS CREWS exits. C.F. surveys the actor judicially.*) I can't say I like the hat. (*He is referring, of course, to the awe-inspiring busby.*)

RODNEY (*mildly*). The hat is authentic, sir.

C.F. I still don't like it. You can't photograph it. (*Phone rings.*) Yes?—What midgets? I didn't send out any call for midgets. Get rid of them. (*Hangs up. He jiggles the phone.*) Get me Wardrobe. (*Hubbub is heard outside window.*) Who's making all that noise? (*PEGGY goes to the window.*) This is C.F.—I don't like the hat.—I don't care if it's authentic or not— Who's making all that noise?

PEGGY (*at window*). Midgets.

C.F. (*into phone*). Change the hat. . . . You can't photograph it. . . . We want to see faces, not hats. (*Hangs up. Stone crashes through the window left.*) Good God! Somebody's thrown a rock through my window. (*To RODNEY.*) Here, you—pull down those blinds.

RODNEY (*always the little gentleman*). Yes, sir.

C.F. (*in phone*). Get me Casting. . . . This is C.F. . . . Somebody's thrown a rock through my window. One of the midgets. Of course they're indignant! Sour grapes! I'm telling you to get rid of them. (*Hangs up.*)

RODNEY. What shall I tell Wardrobe, sir?

C.F. Tell them I don't like the hat.

RODNEY (*smiles diffidently*). Well, it's very peculiar that you should take umbrage at the hat as it happens to be the only correct item in the entire outfit.

C.F. What's that?

RODNEY. This coat doesn't hang properly— these buttons are far too large. These shoulder straps are absurd, of course. And the boots . . . if I may say so . . . are too utterly fantastic. Any Guardsman would swoon away at the sight of them.

C.F. So!

RODNEY. The hat, however, *is* authentic.

C.F. It is, eh? What's your salary?

RODNEY. As I understand it, I'm to receive seven dollars a day Monday and Tuesday, when I speak no lines, and fifteen dollars a day Thursday, Friday and Saturday, when I propose a toast.

C.F. And you're telling a fifty-thousand-dollar-a-year man how to run his picture. Look here—I spent two weeks in London, my man, at the Savoy, and I watched them change the Guards, personally.

RODNEY. At the Savoy?

C.F. Young man, we have a technical adviser on this picture. And it doesn't happen to be you.

RODNEY. Quite. He's a splendid fellow, but he's a third generation Canadian. He's never even been to London.

C.F. So you don't like the uniform and you don't like the technical expert. (*Smoothly*) What's your name?

RODNEY. Rodney Bevan. Of course, it's a sort of nom de plume, or nom de guerre—

C.F. Rodney Bevan. (*Picks up phone.*) Give me Casting. . . . This is C.F. . . . Extra here by the name of Rodney Bevan doesn't like his uniform. Fire him.

RODNEY (*aghast*). Fire? Have you given me the sack?

C.F. I've enough trouble without extras telling me how to make pictures. That's the trouble with this business. A man spends his life at it, and anybody can walk in and tell him how to run it.

RODNEY. But I merely suggested— (MISS CREWS *enters.*)

MISS CREWS. Mr. Green and Mr. Slade are outside, Mr. Friday. They want you to hear the song.

RODNEY. I've waited a long time for this opening—

C.F. Get out! (*To* MISS CREWS) I'm in no mood for *music*. (GREEN *and* SLADE *enter.*)

GREEN. We've got it, and you're going to listen. If you don't like it, Schulberg's nuts about it. (SLADE *crosses to piano and starts playing the song.*) We wrote it for *Young England,* but it's flexible— Flexible as hell. (MISS CREWS *exits.* RODNEY *turns forlornly and fades out through the door. What else can he do?*)

C.F. Boys, I'm in no mood for—

GREEN. It's a touching little thing, but, boy, what power! There's a "Pain in My Heart, and My Heart's on My Sleeve." Like the

title? (SLADE *is one of those who glues himself to a piano. He's all pasted together now, and his fingers fly.* GREEN *sings with all the fervid sincerity of Georgie Jessel with a cold.*)

You promised love undying,
And begged me to believe;
Then you left, and left me crying
With a pain in my heart, and my heart
　　on my sleeve.

It isn't right to show it,
To flaunt the way I grieve;
But the world will quickly know it,
For the pain's in my heart and my heart
on my sleeve.

I confess that I'm a mess—
The way I lived my life,
But what does it matter?
Yes, I guess that happiness
Is only for a wife;
Sorrow isn't served on a silver platter.

I really shouldn't blame you
Because you chose to leave;
But one thing forever will shame you—
It's the pain in my heart, and my heart
　　on my sleeve.

(*During the song* MISS CREWS *enters with glass of orange juice. She crosses around desk, puts glass in front of* C.F., *gets book from lower drawer.*)

C.F. (*as* GREEN *finishes song*). Miss Crews, get hold of Benson and Law! (MISS CREWS *exits.*)

LARRY (*as the din grows*). I've worked for Biograph. . . . I've worked for Monogram. . . . I've worked for Columbia. . . . I've worked for Warners. . . . I've worked for Metro . . . but a screwier outfit I never did see! (BENSON *and* LAW *enter in costume of beefeaters. They, too, wear busbies.*)

C.F. (*whose nails are being buffed*). What do you want? (*At the musicians.*) Quiet! (*At the busbies, for* C.F. *doesn't deign to look at actors' faces.*) I told Wardrobe I don't like the hats.

BENSON. He doesn't like the hats.

LAW. Call Jock Whitney. We want to be in color.

C.F. (*exasperated*). For God's sake! This is a fine time to be masquerading.

BENSON (*leaping into character; picking up stone*). Wait! What a pretty stone! I wonder where that came from.

LAW (*in his own big scene*). I wonder.

BENSON (*transporting himself to the desert*). I think we've found gold, partner.

LAW (*grabbing for it*). Gold!

BENSON. Stand back—you desert rat!

LAW. Gold—after all these years! I'm going mad . . . mad . . . mad . . .

C.F. Oh, stop it, boys.

LARRY (*suddenly inspired. To* C.F.) I wouldn't be surprised if they threw that there rock through the window.

BENSON. What an innuendo!

C.F. You didn't do that, did you, boys? Smash my Vita-glass?

LAW. To think—after all these years of loyal, faithful service— Larry Toms, you ought to be ashamed!

BENSON. The man with the poison-pen mind. We're going to tell Louella Parsons on you.

C.F. (*impatiently*). Very well . . . very well. . . . But I still have my suspicions. (*Snaps.*) Now what about our story?

BENSON. Right here. (*Indicating script on desk.*)

LAW (*takes a statuette from top of desk*). Mr. Benson, for the most brilliant script of the year, the Academy takes great pleasure in presenting to you this little gargoyle—

BENSON. Wrap it up, please. (LAW *drops it in* LARRY'S *hat and stands back of couch. Music plays.*)

LARRY (*rising in a dither*). Now, listen— (C.F. *crosses below desk, retrieves statue, places it back on desk.*)

GREEN (*to* SLADE *at piano*). What do you say to this, Otto, for the second chorus:

> Yes, I've been kissed,
> But like Oliver Twist,
> I'm still crying for more.

(*Without waiting for an answer, to* C.F.) How did you like the song, C.F.?

LAW. Darn good. Can you play *Over the Waves?*

C.F. Boys, can't you be sensible for a moment? You're trying my patience. What about our story?

LAW. What about it? It's a rich, protean part for Larry.

LARRY. It just don't make sense.

LAW. I resent that as a gentleman and a grammarian.

C.F. Now really, boys, I'm tolerant, but I've got to see results. I'm not one to put the creative urge in a strait-jacket. But you've been fired off every other lot in this industry for your pranks. Perhaps you've forgotten, Benson, but when I hired you for this job you promised me to behave in no uncertain terms. And you promised me Law would toe the line. Now, I'm warning you, boys. Let's get to work. Let's concentrate. (*Crosses above desk to chair back of desk.*) Do you realize you boys are making more than the President of the United States?

LAW. But look at the fun he's having!

LARRY (*angrily*). Now looka here—

GREEN. How do you like the song, C.F.?

C.F. It lacks body.

LAW. No breasts.

C.F. That's exactly it— Pallid.

GREEN. Come on, Otto.

SLADE (*starts for door*). This isn't my idea of a fair audition.

GREEN. Wait'll they hear it at the Cocoanut Grove. They'll be sorry. (GREEN *and* SLADE *exit.* PEGGY *enters and* LAW, *humming "Merry Widow," intercepts her, dances a few measures with her.*)

C.F. Listen, boys—we've had enough of this. (SUSIE *enters carrying a tray.* SUSIE *is a waitress. We worship* SUSIE. *Why describe her? We'll tell you what she wears—the full-blown costume of a Hollywood waitress. Of her blonde fragility, her intricate but blameless sex life, and the ineffable charm of her touching naïveté we won't say a word.*)

LAW. *Lunch!*

BENSON. Grub! Susie, I love you. (PEGGY *exits. She never comes back. Why should she?*)

c.f. Wait a minute—wait a minute— (LAW *gets end table and places it in front of couch.* BENSON *takes tray from* SUSIE.)

SUSIE (*weakly*). Please, Mr. Benson, be careful.

LAW. Put that tray right down here.

SUSIE (*quavering*). Thanks. . . . It's not very heavy . . . (*She then collapses neatly on the floor.*)

c.f. Good Lord!

LAW (*bending over her*). Susie—Susie—

BENSON (*grabbing phone*). Get the doctor over here—right away——

LAW. Somebody give me water. (BENSON *takes glass from tray on table.*)

c.f. (*disapprovingly*). This is a nice thing to happen in my office. . . . Who is this girl, anyway?

LAW (*putting water to her as he kneels beside her*). Come on, Susie. (*Lifting her head up to glass.*)

LARRY (*whose father wrote letters to the papers*). That commissary shouldn't employ people with epilepsy.

c.f. (*bitter, still*). I had an actor who did that to me once. Held up my shooting schedule fourteen days.

LAW. She's all right. Here.

SUSIE. Did you all get napkins? (*Opens her eyes for the first time.*)

BENSON. Now, Susie—get into this chair.

SUSIE. Thanks. (*She sits.*)

c.f. (*sharply*). What's wrong with you, young woman?

SUSIE (*still quavering*). Nothing. . . . I'm much better now. . . . Thanks.

c.f. Where's that doctor?

SUSIE. Did you call for a doctor? You didn't have to.

c.f. Do you get these epileptic fits often?

SUSIE. I didn't have an epileptic fit.

c.f. Then what's wrong with you?

SUSIE. There's nothing wrong . . . it's only natural.

c.f. Only natural for you to come into my office and collapse on the floor.

SUSIE. Oh, no, sir . . . it's only natural for you to feel sick when you're going to have a baby.

LAW. A baby!

BENSON. Susie, you're not going to have a baby!

SUSIE. That's what they told me. . . .

BENSON. Susie's going to have a baby!

LAW. Let's get drunk!

c.f. (*into phone*). Tell that doctor not to come. You heard me. I don't want him. (*He hangs up.*) I won't have my office converted into a maternity ward! (*He turns on* SUSIE.) I don't think much of your husband—letting you work at a time like this!

SUSIE. Oh, but I haven't got a husband.

c.f. Huh?

SUSIE (*rises*). You'd better eat your lunch before it gets cold. Have you all got napkins?

LAW (*humbly*). The new generation! Faces the facts of nature without squeamishness, without subterfuge. "I haven't got a husband," she says. "It's only natural," she says. "I'm going to have a baby." . . . Susie, you're magnificent.

SUSIE. I'm quitting at the end of the week so I thought I'd tell everybody why. I wouldn't want them to think I was discontented.

LAW. Our little mother!

SUSIE. Oh, don't make fun of me.

LAW (*rises*). Fun? I've never been so touched in my life. Susie, I feel purified.

BENSON. Susie—can we be godfather?

SUSIE. Do you mean it?

BENSON. Do we mean it? We haven't got a baby. And we've been collaborating for years.

susie. Oh, I think that would be wonderful for Happy to have writers for a godfather.

benson Happy?

susie. I'm going to call him Happy—even if he's a girl. Because I want him to be happy—even if he's a girl.

benson. Beautiful! A beautiful thought! Where are you going to have this baby, Susie?

susie. In the County Hospital. It's all fixed. I was very lucky because I've only lived in the county three months and I'm not eligible.

c.f. Now, listen, boys—enough of this.

law (*into phone*). Give me the Cedars of Lebanon Hospital—and make it snappy.

benson (*jubilant*). We've got a baby!

c.f. Just a minute. Hang up that phone. (benson *good-naturedly brushes his arm down.*)

law. Dr. Marx, please. . . . Willy, this is Law of Benson and Law. Reserve the best suite in the house for us. I'm serious. Dead serious. A little friend of ours is going to have a baby and we want the goddamnedest confinement you've got in stock. . . .

benson. Day and night nurse.

law (*to* benson). And not the one with the buck teeth either. She's dynamite. (*Into phone*) We want everything that Gloria Swanson had—only double. What's that? Bill? Bill the studio, of course. (*He hangs up.*)

c.f. You'll do no such thing! What kind of a gag is this? (miss crews *enters.*)

miss crews. Do you want to hear the trumpet call? The men are here. Music Department wants your O.K.

c.f. Trumpets?

miss crews. For *Young England.*

c.f. Look here—I haven't time to listen to them now. Come back here at two o'clock. And give it to me from out there. I don't want them blasting in my ear. (*Meanwhile* benson *and* law *have been in whispered conference.*)

miss crews. Yes, Mr. Friday. (*Exits.*)

c.f. Now, boys—let's get together on this. (*Turns on* susie *from below desk.*) And you—what are you sitting here for? Get out! (susie *tries to rise.*)

law. Sit right where you are. (*Crosses to front of desk.*) Don't you bark at our inspration! We've got it!

c.f. What?

law (*with mounting excitement*). A baby!

c.f. Boys, I'm a patient man, but you're trying me.

benson (*awed*). *Larry Toms and a baby!*

law (*to* c.f.). Do you see it?

larry (*bellowing*). Wait a minute—wait a minute!

law (*quickly*). He finds a baby—in the Rockies—

benson (*inspired; quickly to* c.f.). Girl with a no good gambler—out of Los Vegas—has a baby . . . gambler is killed. Girl leaves baby on the ranger's door step. Larry is the ranger.

law (*dramatizing it all*). My God, he says—a baby!

benson (*awed*). A baby!

law. The most precious thing in life. The cutest, goddam little bastard you ever saw.

benson. Tugging at every mother's heart. And every potential mother.

law. And who isn't!

benson. A love story between Larry and the baby—

law. The two outcasts! Get it?

benson. And then he meets the mother!

law. She wants her baby back.

benson. She's been through the fires of hell.

law. The man she loved . . . let her down. . . .

benson. She hates men . . . all men. . . .

law. She won't look at Larry.

BENSON (*to* LARRY). No. There she sits . . . bitter, brooding, cynical, but underneath— a mother's heart.

LAW. Out on the Rockies—

BENSON. The hell with the Rockies—back to the Foreign Legion!

LAW. Right! Larry's joined to forget. He's out on the march. We can use all that stock stuff—and he finds a baby!

BENSON. He's gone off to fight the Riffs.

LAW. The hell with the Riffs! Ethiopians!

BENSON. Stick to the Riffs. We don't want any race problem.

LAW. Right! She doesn't know if he's coming back.

BENSON. She's waiting—waiting!

LAW. We cut to the Riffs—

BENSON. Cut back—

LAW (*to* BENSON). Right into the battle.

BENSON (*really inspired now*). His father's the Colonel!

LAW. Talk about Kipling—

BENSON. Talk about scope—sweep—what a set-up!

LAW. A love story!

BENSON. A great love story!

LAW. Mary Magdalen of the Foreign Legion and the West Point man who wanted to forget!

BENSON (*rises*). The baby brings them together, splits them apart, brings them together—

LAW. Boy meets girl—

BENSON. Boy loses girl—

LAW. Boy gets girl!

C.F. (*rising in excitement*). Boys, I think you've got something! Let's go up and try it on B.K. while it's hot.

LAW. Let's go! (*They move forward.*)

LARRY (*crosses to behind couch*). Wait a minute—you can't act with a baby. They steal every scene— Look what happened to Chevalier.

LAW. Are you selling motherhood short? (LAW, BENSON *and* C.F. *exit through next speech.*)

LARRY. They'll be looking at the baby when they should be looking at me. I tell you—I won't play it. (*Follows off.* SUSIE *tries to rise, now she is left alone. She sits down again.* RODNEY, *in the Coldstream Guards uniform, enters.* SUSIE *turns.*)

RODNEY. Oh, I'm sorry. I hope I didn't startle you.

SUSIE. Oh, no. (*Then, as he looks at* C.F.'s *desk*) They all stepped out—and they didn't even touch their lunch.

RODNEY (*licking his lips involuntarily*). Lunch?—You don't happen to know when Mr. Friday is coming back?

SUSIE. No, I don't.

RODNEY. I did want to see him. It's rather urgent. Do you mind if I wait here?

SUSIE. No, of course not. (*He seats himself on couch, near a tray. There is an awkward silence.* SUSIE *stares straight ahead.* RODNEY *plays with a cracker. Finally* SUSIE *breaks the silence.*) What are you supposed to be?

RODNEY. Eh? Oh! That's just it. . . . I'm supposed to be a Buckingham Palace Guard, sergeant major—(*He pops the cracker into his mouth and swallows it.* SUSIE *looks at him rather intently.*) Good Lord! What am I doing?

SUSIE. You're eating Mr. Friday's cracker.

RODNEY. I'm awfully sorry. I don't understand how I—

SUSIE. You must be very hungry.

RODNEY. Not a bit. Not at all.

SUSIE. You *look* hungry.

RODNEY. Do I?

SUSIE. Why don't you have something? They'll never eat it. They're always sending things back they order—never even touched.

RODNEY. Really?

SUSIE. You'll only be doing me a favor.

RODNEY. Oh?

SUSIE. I won't have so much to carry back to the commissary. Sometimes I think I carry back more than I bring.

RODNEY. You're pulling my leg, of course.

SUSIE. What did you say?

RODNEY. You're not really a waitress.

SUSIE. Sure I am.

RODNEY (*triumphantly*). Waitresses don't usually sit in producer's offices.

SUSIE. They do when they don't feel well.

RODNEY. You don't feel well? Oh, I'm sorry. Is there anything I can do?

SUSIE. No, thanks.

RODNEY. But what's wrong?

SUSIE. Oh, there's no use telling you. I told Mr. Friday and he made such a fuss about it I guess I better keep it to myself.

RODNEY. I'm afraid I don't quite understand.

SUSIE. Try the chicken soup. It's very good.

RODNEY. Are you seriously suggesting that I filch some of this broth?

SUSIE. We make it special for B.K. with nine chickens.

RODNEY. Well, dash it, I will eat it. Just to make the joke good! (*He laughs weakly and picks up the bowl and puts it to his lips, and sips it.*)

SUSIE (*warningly*). It's hot!

RODNEY (*now quite gay*). So I've learned.

SUSIE. When did you eat last?

RODNEY (*lying, of course*). I had my lunch an hour ago.

SUSIE. Have some crackers with it.

RODNEY. Thanks.

SUSIE. You're English, aren't you?

RODNEY. Yes, of course.

SUSIE. So is Ronald Colman.

RODNEY (*bolting his food*). So he is.

SUSIE. I like the way the English talk.

RODNEY. Do you?

SUSIE. It's very soothing.

RODNEY. What an idea!

SUSIE. Of course, that's only *my* idea. I'm very ignorant.

RODNEY. Oh, please don't say that. I think you're very intelligent.

SUSIE. Oh, I'm intelligent. But I don't know anything.

RODNEY. You're an extraordinary girl.

SUSIE. I've never been to high school.

RODNEY (*gallantly*). May I say that's the high school's loss?

SUSIE. But some day I'll go to high school. That's my secret ambition. Try the ham hocks. The cook eats them himself. He comes from Czechoslovakia.

RODNEY. Does he really? Look here—I feel an awful swine guzzling by myself. Won't you join me?

SUSIE. Well, I'm not very hungry, but I can eat.

RODNEY. Good! (*He rises and adjusts a chair for her.*)

SUSIE. It's funny how I keep on eating.

RODNEY. Some ham hocks?

SUSIE. No. Happy doesn't like ham. He likes milk.

RODNEY (*mystified*). I beg your pardon? (*But he doesn't press the point.*) Did you say milk?

SUSIE. Yes. Milk.

RODNEY (*as he pours*). There you are.

SUSIE. Thanks.

RODNEY. Cozy, this—what?

SUSIE. It's good milk. Have some.

RODNEY. Do you know, I think you're the most extraordinary girl I ever met.

SUSIE. Why?

RODNEY. You're so kind. You're so direct, so sincere. Most girls one meets play about with words so. They're so infernally smart. They make one feel like a worm.

SUSIE. Of course, I'm different on account of my condition. Most girls aren't in my condition.

RODNEY. Your condition?

SUSIE. The minute I found out about Happy I said to myself: I'm going to be very good and very sincere, because then Happy will be very good and very sincere.

RODNEY. I'm afraid I don't quite follow.

SUSIE (*sighing*). Nobody does.

RODNEY. Eh? Oh, yes. . . . As I was saying— What was I saying?

SUSIE (*looking into his eyes and feeling strangely stirred*). Have some mustard.

RODNEY. Do you know, I must confess. I was hungry. As a matter of fact, I was close to wiring home for funds today. But I didn't. (*Looks very determined, righteous.*)

SUSIE. You mean you need money, and you can get it—and you won't wire for it?

RODNEY. I can't—and keep my pride. I told *them* I was on my own. You see, my family didn't want me to act. Not that they've any prejudices against the stage—or the films. Not at all. In fact, one of my aunts was a Gaiety girl. Quite all right. But they don't think I *can* act. That's what hurts.

SUSIE. Can you act?

RODNEY. No.

SUSIE. Not at all?

RODNEY. Not at all. I'm awful!

SUSIE. Oh, that's too bad.

RODNEY. But I only realized it in the stock company . . . out in Pasadena. I was the worst member of the company. At first I thought it was because they were always giving me character parts—American gangsters—and that sort of thing. And then one week I played a Cambridge undergraduate. And, mind you, I've been a Cambridge undergraduate. And do you know that I was utterly unconvincing?

SUSIE. Then why don't you give it up?

RODNEY. Pride.

SUSIE. I can understand that— Pride.

RODNEY. Can you really?

SUSIE. Sure I can.

RODNEY. That's why I simply must see Mr. Friday. (*Suddenly*) Look here— (*He takes a book from couch and opens it.*) Look at this color plate. Does this uniform remotely resemble the one I'm wearing? (*He crosses down right.*)

SUSIE (*looks at book; then at* RODNEY). Yes, I think so.

RODNEY (*crosses to her left*). But, my dear girl, look at the coat and the buttons—and the boots—note the heels—and look at mine. (*Steps back.*)

SUSIE. Well, come to think of it. I guess it is different.

RODNEY. Of course. And I've taken this book right out of their own research department. When I show this to Mr. Friday he's bound to be sporting enough to admit an error.

SUSIE. Oh, sure.

RODNEY (*leaning over her*). You see, all I want is to appear in *one* picture—and then I can tell the family: "I've done it." But it's not good enough. I'm chucking it. But I'll have my pride.

SUSIE (*gazing at him*). I see.

RODNEY. Oh . . . I say . . . I'm not boring you?

SUSIE. Oh, no. Finish your ham.

RODNEY. Eh? Oh! Don't mind if I do. A bit of pie for you? (*He extends plate with fork.*)

SUSIE (*brightly. Almost flirting*). Well, I'll try. (*She smiles at him and he at her, fork poised in mid-air.*)

RODNEY. Do you know, I've never enjoyed a lunch quite as much as this one—thanks to you. (*Suddenly*) Would it bore you if I tried out my lines—in *Young England*, you know.

SUSIE. Oh, no.

RODNEY. Very well. (*He rises, holding glass of milk.*) Gentlemen, the Queen— (*He waits.*)

SUSIE. Is that all?

RODNEY. That's all. But of course I could say: "Gentlemen, I give you the Queen." Fatten up the part a bit, what? . . . Gentlemen, I give you the Queen! . . . Sounds rather better, doesn't it? (*Then with profound bass*) Gentlemen, I give you the Queen! (LARRY *enters followed by* C.F. C.F. *stares.*)

LARRY. I don't cotton to the whole idea, and if B.K.'s got any sense, he won't listen to those maniacs.

C.F. What's going on here?

RODNEY. How'd you do. . . . I . . . I . . . (*Puts glass of milk back on tray.*)

C.F. What is this? A tete-à-tete in my office! Good Gad! You've been drinking my milk!

SUSIE. It's all right, Mr. Friday. I told him he could have it.

C.F. *You* told him?

RODNEY. I'm awfully sorry. I owe you an apology, and money, of course. Will you accept my I.O.U.? And I have the book— from Research. I can show you the really authentic uniform. I'm sure if you study this— (SUSIE *finds the page and hands book to* RODNEY.)

C.F. I've a good mind to call the studio police.

SUSIE (*rises*). Oh, please don't do that, Mr. Friday.

LARRY. That's what you get for having foreign actors around. Take the food right out of your mouth!

RODNEY. I'm terrible sorry, of course.

C.F. Get out!

RODNEY. I realize there's nothing I can say— (*He turns to* SUSIE) except—my eternal gratitude. (*He grabs her by the hand and shakes it. Exits.*)

SUSIE. Oh, you shouldn't have done that. He's been having a terrible time.

C.F. (*glaring at* SUSIE). Get these dishes out of here.

SUSIE (*meekly*). Yes, sir. (*She begins piling up dishes on tray.*)

LARRY. The idea of a baby! The more I think of it, the less I like it.

C.F. (*crosses to chair at desk*). Larry, you're driving me into a nervous breakdown. I had to take you out of B.K.'s office so you'd stop arguing before he could make a decision.

LARRY. There's nothing to decision. I won't play it.

C.F. If B.K. likes the idea, you'll play it.

LARRY. Maybe—and maybe not. I'm willing to bet ten to one right now B.K. kicks the whole story in the ash can. He's no fool. (BENSON *and* LAW *enter in shirt sleeves. They've obviously had a hot session with* B.K.)

BENSON. Sold! Lock, stock and baby! B.K. says it's the best mother-love story he's heard in years.

LARRY. What? What's that?

LAW (*magnificently*). Susie, put that tray down!

SUSIE. Please, Mr. Law, I've got to get back to the commissary.

LARRY. You sold him that story, huh?

BENSON. Lie down, actor!

LARRY. I'll see about this. (*He exits.*)

BENSON. Now listen, Susie—and listen carefully.

LAW. Let me tell her, will you? (*He faces her.*) Susie, nature meant you for a sucker. You were designed to get the short end of the stick. The girl who gets slapped.

BENSON (*quickly*). But we're changing all that.

LAW. Susie, in real life, you'd have your baby in the County Hospital . . . get yourself a job, if lucky, with a philanthropic Iowa family of fourteen adults and twelve minors for twenty bucks a month. And when your grateful son grew up he'd squirt tobacco juice in your eye and join the Navy.

BENSON. There you go with your goddamn realism. (*Turns to* SUSIE *with paper and pencil.*) Sign, please—

SUSIE. Here? (*She signs; and then turns brightly.*) What is it?

BENSON. Just a power of attorney authorizing us to deal for you in all matters with this studio.

c.f. What power of attorney? What are you boys up to?

LAW. We said to ourselves upstairs—why shouldn't Susie have the good things of life?

BENSON. After all, we're godfathers.

SUSIE. I—don't feel very good.

LAW. Get this, Susie. We've just sold a story about a baby.

BENSON. Sweetest story ever told!

LAW. A new-born baby.

BENSON. Brand new.

LAW. We're going to watch that baby—the first hair—the first tooth—the first smile—

BENSON. The same baby. No switching—first time in the history of pictures. That baby's going to grow before your eyes.

LAW. Open up like a flower. . . . Just like the Dionne quintuplets.

BENSON. Minute he's born we set the camera on him. We stay with him—

LAW. That baby's going to gurgle and google and drool his way to stardom!

SUSIE. But—

LAW. And that baby, Susie, is Happy. Upstairs in B.K.'s office we put your unborn child into pictures.

SUSIE (*transported*). Happy—in pictures! Oh —that's wonderful— (*Then, with a sudden gasp.*) Oh!

LAW (*quickly*). Susie! What's the matter?

SUSIE. *I don't know . . . I . . . I . . . I don't feel so good . . . I think . . . I . . . (In these broken words,* SUSIE *tells all.* BENSON *helps* SUSIE *to lie on couch.* LAW *looks over* SUSIE'S *shoulder; whistles; runs to phone.*)

LAW (*into phone*). *Emergency! Get the ambulance over to Mr. Friday's office right away—get the doctor—get the nurse. . .*

c.f. (*staring*). What is it? In *my* office. Good Gad! Miss Crews! (*Door opens.*)

MISS CREWS (*at door*). The trumpets are here! (*Trumpets sound their triumphant clarion call.*)

LAW (*through the Wagnerian brass, to* BENSON, *awed*). Happy's on his way!

CURTAIN

ACT TWO

SCENE I

We are in your neighborhood theatre, seven months later.

As the curtain rises we face a motion picture screen, and to the sound-track accompaniment of "Home on the Range," these glaring titles pop out at us:

IF YOU LIKED HAPPY

IN

"WANDERING HEARTS"
YOU'LL ADORE HIM

IN

"GOLDEN NUGGET"

This is what is known as a trailer, in technical terms. It is shown at neighborhood theatres prior to the release of the picture so that the customers will be teased into returning the following week.

There are, of course, beautifully composed shots of horses, men and open spaces, and finally we come upon a series of close-ups of HAPPY, *over which these titles dance:*

Happy!
HAPPY!
HAPPY!

The sound track blares forth "Ride of the Valkyries."

Crown Prince of Comedy!
King of Tragedy!
Emperor of Emotion!

Just prior to these titles we have seen a Chinese, who has emerged from God knows where, but what is a ranch without a Chinese? The general idea is that the Chinese finds HAPPY *on the doorstep and communicates his discovery to* LARRY TOMS. *There follows a title which explains all:*

The Desert Waif Who Made
a Softie of a Bad Man

The picture is further described as:

The Big Gold Strike
of Mother Love

We see horses galloping, men falling, revolvers barking, and nice, big, wavy

Thrills
Chills

The credit card is as follows:

From a Story by H. G. Wells
Adapted by J. Carlyle Benson and Robert Law
Directed by Serge Borodokov

and, appropriately enough, in solitary grandeur:

Produced by C. Elliot Friday

SCENE II

The screen lifts, and once more we are in Mr. Friday's office.
C.F. is at his desk, Miss Crews *is seated upstage and at desk;* Benson *is on the couch beside* Larry. Rosetti *is seated on the piano bench.*

benson. Read those figures, Miss Crews.

miss crews. Eighty-two thousand at the Music Hall. Forty-eight thousand five hundred and thirty-eight in Des Moines.

benson. Without a stage show.

larry. I always went big in Des Moines.

miss crews. Twenty-eight thousand in Newark.

larry. That's one of my big towns.

miss crews. Forty-two thousand three hundred and eighty-four in San Francisco.

larry. I'm big there, too.

miss crews. Twenty-six thousand eight hundred and seventy-five in Detroit.

benson (*to* c.f.). And you sit there and tell me Happy isn't worth thirty-five hundred a week?

c.f. But, Benson, be reasonable. I can't go to B.K. with any such fantastic figure.

benson (*sighing*). Read that list again, Miss Crews.

c.f. Never mind, Miss Crews.

larry. What about me? *Wandering Hearts* was my picture, wasn't it? Folks came to see me. They didn't come to see Happy.

benson (*taking "Variety" from his pocket*). Let me read "Variety" to the assembled multitude. *Wandering Hearts* socko in Minneapolis despite Larry Toms . .

larry. Huh?

BENSON. Mexico nuts about Happy but no like Larry Toms—

LARRY. Where? Where does it say that? (*He takes paper.* ROSETTI *rises and looks over* LARRY'S *shoulder.*)

BENSON. This is an accidental business in an accidental world. Happy is going to get it while it's hot.

C.F. Benson, you owe me something.

BENSON. What?

C.F. Gratitude. . . . After all, the idea of a baby was mine—more or less.

BENSON. More or less.

C.F. I made that baby act.

BENSON. All right, Svengali.

C.F. Shall we say three hundred a week for Happy?

BENSON. Shall we say thirty-five hundred a week for Happy?

C.F. I've a good mind to have you thrown out of this studio.

BENSON. All right. Happy goes with us. We've still got that power of attorney.

C.F. Of course, I didn't mean that literally.

BENSON. I did. (*Telephone rings.*)

C.F. Hello. . . . Yes, Miss Goodwin. . . . What? You can't write about Brussels because you've never been there? My dear girl, why do you think we have a research department? After all, Bernard Shaw wrote *Don Juan* and he never went to Bulgaria. Imagination, my dear girl—imagination. (*Hangs up.*) Look here, Benson, I knew I couldn't deal with Law. I thought I could with you. After all, you're in no position to antagonize this studio. Some day you may need my friendship.

BENSON. I'm supposed to be working with our Mr. Law on a story. To wit: *Tiger Tamer.* Do you mind if I join my partner in a little English composition?

C.F. Some day you may be very sorry for this, Benson.

BENSON. What do you think, Miss Crews?

MISS CREWS. I think Happy ought to get it while it's hot.

C.F. Get back to your desk.

MISS CREWS. Yes, Mr. Friday. (*She exits.*)

LARRY (*waving "Variety"*). I said that baby'd ruin me! Well, he ain't going to steal no more pictures! I won't play that new scene.

C.F. (*irritably*). What new scene?

LARRY. I'm supposed to wash Happy.

C.F. That's a cute scene. I read it.

LARRY. Am I the type that washes babies?

C.F. Why not?

LARRY. 'Tain't manly!

BENSON. No. You want the baby to wash you!

LARRY. Listen!

BENSON. Any further business before the house? (*Turns to* LARRY.) By the way, I saw you with Susie at the Trocadero last night. We don't approve of you as an escort. Remind me to speak to her about that.

C.F. Benson, I'm asking you once more. Be fair—be reasonable.

BENSON. I am. We're asking thirty-five hundred a week. We'll consider three thousand and settle for twenty-five hundred. But not a penny less. Incidentally, Fox'll pay twenty-five hundred for Happy. We promised to let them know by Saturday. No hurry, of course. (*Exits.*)

C.F. Have you ever seen anything more damnably unfair? Imagine *writers* holding up this studio at the point of a gun. It's nothing but blackmail.

ROSETTI (*rises*). I've got a hunch, C.F. When did you sign Happy? Do you remember?

C.F. Of course I remember . . . July fourteenth . . . Fall of the Bastille. I remember my wife pointing out the coincidence at the time. Why?

ROSETTI (*crosses to desk*). I've got a hunch that power of attorney expires pretty soon. I want to be prepared.

c.f. Rosetti, I'm not interested in the future. I'm interested in signing Happy right now— before we lose him to Fox. (*Phone rings.*)

ROSETTI. You've got to have vision in this business, C.F. (*He reaches for other phone, changes his mind, and then exits.*)

c.f. (*into phone*). Hello. . . . Yes, listen, Gregg. . . . I ran the sound track on *Young England* last night. I don't like the trumpets. They're sour. They spoil the whole mood. . . . What? . . . What's that? You can't walk out on a picture like that. What kind of a director are you if you can't take constructive criticism . . . hello . . . hello . . . (*Hangs up.*) Gregg is walking out on *Young England,* I can't sign Happy—

LARRY. What about me?

c.f. Ten thousand feet of film sick—and he walks out. I'll have to run the picture all the afternoon and sit up all night cutting it. (MISS CREWS *enters.*)

MISS CREWS. Happy's through for the day.

NURSE (*wheeling in a stream-lined baby carriage*). Through for the day.

DOCTOR (*as he enters*). Through for the day. Is his mother here?

MISS CREWS. No, Doctor, but she should be here very soon.

NURSE (*backing carriage in front of desk*). Say da-da to Mr. Friday.

c.f. (*waving obediently*). Da-da, Happy.

DOCTOR. Nurse, take the little trouper out into the garden and keep him in the sunshine.

LARRY. He's through for the day and I'm working until eight. He's sure got it soft. (NURSE *exits with* HAPPY. ROSETTI *enters.*)

DOCTOR. They've been overworking you, have they?

LARRY. I ain't feeling so hearty, doc. I wish you'd look me over.

c.f. (*rises and goes below desk*). Just your imagination. I wish I had your constitution. I've got to see B.K. (*He exits.*)

DOCTOR. All you picture people are hypochondriacs. However, come up to my office and I'll look you over. (*He exits.*)

LARRY. I'm a star. I've been a star for ten years. I've worked hard to get where I'm at— (*He rises. Phone rings.*)

ROSETTI (*at phone*). Hello. . . . Yes . . . speaking—

LARRY. I don't drink. I don't smoke. I don't swear. I don't get into no scandal. And the girls I passed up!

ROSETTI (*into phone*). Oh, you've got that, Mr. Williams? Fine. When does it expire? . . . It *did* expire? Last week? . . . No, don't do that. I'll tell the boys. . . . You see, I may be handling Happy's new contract. Right. (*He hangs up.*)

LARRY. They ain't making pictures here no more. They're shooting nothing but close-ups of babies. Happy laughing! Happy crying! Happy! . . . Happy! . . .

ROSETTI. Larry, I've just checked with the Legal Department. The boys' power of attorney expired last week. And they don't even know it.

LARRY. What's that got to do with me?

ROSETTI. Larry, there's been something developing in the back of my mind for some weeks. Why do you think I asked you to take Susie to the Trocadero?

LARRY. She talked me deaf, dumb, and blind about going to high school. She set me back fourteen bucks. Lucky she don't drink.

ROSETTI (*the dreamer*). I wanted you to get friendly with her because I visualized a way for you and me to get Happy—for life.

LARRY. Huh?

ROSETTI (*with Napoleonic intensity*). Larry, here's the tactical move. You marry Susie.

LARRY. Marry her?

ROSETTI. That's what I said.

LARRY. I won't do it.

ROSETTI (*who knows his client*). All right, suit yourself.

LARRY. We got community property in California. If there's a bust-up the woman gets half.

ROSETTI. Larry, I don't want to hurt your feelings, but I can't get you a new contract the way things are now. B.K. is dickering to borrow Clark Gable or Gary Cooper for Happy's next picture.

LARRY (*touched to the quick*). What?

ROSETTI. I'd marry her myself if I was free. Show me a girl with a better heart—with more culture—

LARRY. You don't expect me to believe what the studio hands out—her husband was a prominent portrait painter who went down on the *Morro Castle?*

ROSETTI (*indignantly*). Who are you to cast the first stone?

LARRY. I don't want to marry nobody. Anyways, there's no sense to it.

ROSETTI (*patiently*). If you marry her, you're Happy's legal guardian and we control the situation. A father and son team off the screen as well as on! Is that practical or am I just an idealist? Look at Guy Lathrop! He argued with me when I told him to marry Betty Bird. But he finally had the sense to play along with me and we've been drawing top money ever since.

LARRY. I don't want to marry nobody.

ROSETTI. Larry, you're at the crossroads right now. One road leads to stardom and big pictures, with Happy and me. The other leads to Poverty Row and cheap Westerns. Will you put your hand in mine and let me guide you? (MISS CREWS *enters.*)

MISS CREWS. Mr. Toms, you're wanted on the set.

LARRY (*growling.*) All right.

MISS CREWS. Oh, hello, Mrs. Seabrook . . . how nice you look. (*For* SUSIE *enters. She wears a white middy-blouse and a navy blue, pleated skirt.*)

SUSIE. We had gym today. . . . Hello, Larry. . . . Hello, Mr. Rosetti. . . . I hope I didn't interrupt anything important.

ROSETTI. Not at all. . . . (*Significantly*) I'll be in the Legal Department, Larry. (*He exits.*)

SUSIE. Where's Happy?

MISS CREWS. Happy's in the garden with his nurse. He's all through for the day.

SUSIE. Oh, that's wonderful. I don't get to see him very much. He's working and I'm going to high school. (CHAUFFEUR *enters.*)

CHAUFFEUR. Excuse me, Miss.

SUSIE. What is it, Simpson?

CHAUFFEUR. You forgot your algebra book, Miss.

SUSIE. Oh, thank you, Simpson. That was very thoughtful. (CHAUFFEUR *exits.*)

MISS CREWS. And I have a new batch of fan mail for you and Happy. (*Exits.*)

SUSIE. It's wonderful to get mail. Nobody used to write me before. Now I even get letters from Japan. (MISS CREWS *enters with letters.*) All those letters? Thank you, Miss Crews.

LARRY (*sighs*). Miss Crews, call the set and tell 'em I may be a little late.

MISS CREWS. Very well. (*She exits.*)

SUSIE (*sitting on desk, poring over her hand-written, moronic literature*). Here's one from North Carolina. Oh, the poor thing! There's so much sadness in this world. (LARRY *sighs; she looks up at him.*) You look sad, too, Larry. What's the matter?

LARRY. Well—(*He rises and crosses to* SUSIE.)—uh—I been waiting a long time to talk to you, Susie. I couldn't go to the high school. All those girls would mob me for autographs, especially when I tell them who I am.

SUSIE. All the girls are crazy about Clark Gable.

LARRY (*clears his throat*). Susie—I can get two tickets for the opening at the Chinese— the De Mille picture.

SUSIE. Can you?

LARRY. I knew that'd knock you over.

SUSIE. Oh, it'll be wonderful!

LARRY. I'm always thinkin' of little things to make life wonderful—for you.

SUSIE (*nods*). Everybody is.

LARRY (*bridling*). What do you mean— everybody?

SUSIE. Only the other day Mr. Benson said something very true. He said: "Susie, you're Cinderella." And that's just what I feel like. And you know what else he said? He said: "All you need now is a Prince Charming."

LARRY. He did, huh? Who did he have in mind?

SUSIE. Oh, nobody.

LARRY. He didn't mention me, did he?

SUSIE. Oh, no. (LARRY *grunts.*) Of course I've never met a Prince Charming. I wouldn't know what he looks like. Although, one day an awful nice boy came in here.

LARRY. Who?

SUSIE. I don't even know his name. He was in uniform and I was in my condition—I've never seen him since.

LARRY. You shouldn't be thinking of him. You should be thinking of Happy.

SUSIE. But I do . . . only sometimes it gets lonesome for me, especially at night. And of course, Mr. Benson and Mr. Law are busy all the time. Happy used to say good night to them every night on the telephone. Not really good night—just goo-n'—just like that. But they're so busy they won't come to the telephone any more.

LARRY. Happy needs a father.

SUSIE. Do you think so?

LARRY. Well, you want him to be able to look the whole world in the face, don't you?

SUSIE (*twinkling*). He does!

LARRY. I mean when he grows up. He's gonna be ashamed when he finds out he never had a father.

SUSIE. Of course he had a father.

LARRY. I mean—a married father.

SUSIE. He was married—but I didn't know it. (LARRY *winces.*)

LARRY. Uh—listen, Susie—I'm mighty fond of you and Happy. (*He tries playing the bashful Western hero.*) Mighty fond.

SUSIE. Are you really, **Larry?**

LARRY. Mighty fond.

SUSIE. Who would have thought six months ago that I'd be sitting in the same room with Larry Toms and he'd be saying to me he was—

LARRY. Mighty fond.

SUSIE. Do you know something very odd? When I first came to California, it was raining very hard—oh, it rained for three weeks —it was very unusual—and I was looking for a job, and I couldn't find one—and I had fifteen cents—and I just had to get out of the rain—and I went into a theatre and there you were—on the screen—

LARRY. Mighty fond—

SUSIE (*awed*). That's just what you were saying to Mary Brian—and now you're saying it to me.

LARRY. What was the picture?

SUSIE. *Thunder over Arizona*. It was a beautiful picture. I don't remember what it was about, but I saw it four times. Until I got dry.

LARRY. Susie, soon's this picture's over, how'd you like to come up to my ranch? You and Happy—

SUSIE (*rises*). Ranch? Oh, that would be lovely! Maybe Mr. Benson and Mr. Law could come, too?

LARRY. Maybe they could, but they won't.

SUSIE. But I couldn't go alone—without a chaperon.

LARRY. Susie—you and Happy'll love that ranch. I got a mighty nice house, big and rambling. I got plenty of barns and a corral and plenty of live stock. But no baby.

SUSIE. I know Happy'll just love it.

LARRY. Susie—I know you don't expect this, and I don't want you to get too excited—but, Susie, I been thinkin' about you and Happy —thinkin' a lot. Ever since the day you come into this office and fell on that there floor, I said to myself: Larry, there's your leadin' lady—for life.

SUSIE. Me?

LARRY. Nobody else.

SUSIE. But I don't—you won't get mad?—but I'm not in love with you.

LARRY. You shouldn't be thinking of yourself—I'm not thinking of myself—you should be thinking of Happy.

SUSIE. I guess you're right. I don't know what to say. (*Pauses.*) I'll ask Mr. Benson and Mr. Law—

LARRY. Huh?

SUSIE. They've been so good to me.

LARRY. I'm not proposing to them!

SUSIE. I know, but—

LARRY. You don't mean nothing to them. Before you came along they had a Spanish snake charmer until they got tired of her. And before that they had a broken-down pug who wiggled his ears. They was groomin' him for my place. There ain't nothin' holy to them!

SUSIE. But they've done everything for me.

LARRY (*crosses to* SUSIE). I'm offering you my ranch—my name—and a father Happy'll be proud of!

SUSIE. I know, but—

LARRY. Don't give me your answer now. Think it over. (*Pats her arm.*) Only don't think too long. I'll be waiting for your answer in the Legal Department. You know where that is?

SUSIE. Oh, yes. (MISS CREWS *opens the door.*)

LARRY. I'll be there. (*He exits.* SUSIE *looks a little dazed.*)

MISS CREWS. Oh, Mrs. Seabrook—I've located that young man you were looking for. He's outside.

SUSIE. Oh, you have? Really?

MISS CREWS (*at door*). Come in. (SUSIE *tenses herself. A strange* YOUNG MAN *enters and stops.*)

SUSIE (*staring at him*). Oh! Oh, no, that's not him—I mean—he.

YOUNG MAN (*earnestly*). Won't I do? I've just finished a short for Hal Roach—I'm making a test for Metro tomorrow, and—

MISS CREWS (*firmly escorting him out*). Thank you for coming! (YOUNG MAN *shrugs and exits, and* MISS CREWS *closes the door.*)

SUSIE. He's not English.

MISS CREWS. English? We didn't have any English actors in *Young England.*

SUSIE. This boy was an extra.

MISS CREWS. Does he owe you a lot of money?

SUSIE. Oh, no. It was nothing like that.

MISS CREWS (*as it dawns on her*). Oh, I see! A personal matter! Well, I'll try again. (*Brightly.*)

SUSIE. I guess it's no use, Miss Crews. (*Sighs.*) He probably swallowed his pride and went back to England. (BENSON *and* LAW *enter.* BENSON *carries paper and pencil.* BENSON *sits upstage end of desk.* LAW *crosses to front of couch.*)

LAW. Hi, Susie! How's the little mother? Clear out. We're trying to work and a hundred chorus boys are practicing fencing underneath our windows. (*Turns to* MISS CREWS.) Miss Crews, leave a note for C.F. He's got to change our office. We can't work with fencing fairies! (*Sits on couch.*)

MISS CREWS. Yes, Mr. Law. (*She exits.*)

SUSIE. Are you very busy?

BENSON. We still need an opening.

LAW. Fade-in. . . . A zoo!

SUSIE (*crossing to* BENSON). I just wanted to thank you, Mr. Benson, for the beautiful white teddy bear.

BENSON. What teddy bear?

SUSIE. Mrs. Benson brought it herself.

BENSON (*looking up from typewriter*). Oh, she did?

SUSIE. She played with Happy, too. And even after he went for his nap, she stayed and looked at him.

BENSON (*to* LAW—*covering*). Where were we?

SUSIE. When she left, she was crying. I think she ought to have a baby of her own,

BENSON (*angered*). Come on, Law—come on—fade-in on the zoo.

LAW. I've got it! Larry's carrying a hunk of meat for his pet tiger. He's crossing the road. Bang! The dame comes tearing down ninety miles an hour.

BENSON. Give her a little character.

LAW. She's a high-handed rich bitch Bang! She almost runs the bastard down. . . . Where the hell do you think you're going? . . . She burns. . . . Society girl. . . . She's never been talked to like that before. . . . Why, you lousy bum, she snarls. . . . Listen, here's a cute piece of business. She bawls the hell out of him and he throws the hunk of meat right in her puss!

BENSON (*enthusiastically*). That's charming!

LAW. Listen, Susie, what are you standing there for? Go home and write in your diary.

SUSIE. Boys, I wanted to ask you something . . .

BENSON. Fade-out!

LAW. Fade-in!

SUSIE. . . . and then I'll go.

LAW (*wearily*). What is it?

SUSIE. Do you think I should marry Larry Toms?

LAW. Who?

SUSIE. Larry Toms.

LAW (*rises, crosses below couch*). No. . . . Fade-in. . . .

BENSON. Better get a different background. We've been staying in the zoo too long.

LAW. Right! Girl's home—a Pan shot—fifteen hundred butlers with white socks. . . . (*Turns to* SUSIE.) Did he ask you to marry him?

SUSIE. Yes.

LAW. Did you spit in his face?

SUSIE. He's taking me to the opening tonight. He says he's mighty fond of Happy and me.

LAW (*crosses to back of couch*). Why shouldn't he be? His contract depends on it.

Even Wilkes Barre doesn't want him and they're still calling for Theda Bara—

SUSIE. Don't you think he'd be good for Happy? He's an outdoor man.

LAW. So is the fellow who collects my garbage.

BENSON. Listen, let's get on with this. Introducing the fiancé. A pale anemic louse. A business man!

LAW. Right! The minute the audience sees him they yell: Don't marry that heel.

SUSIE. I know you're very busy. . . .

LAW. Go away, Susie.

SUSIE. You boys were so sweet to me. I felt I had somebody. But lately I've been awfully alone. . . .

LAW. Sure! Everybody's alone. What do you think life is? Why do you have crowds? Because everybody's alone. (*Stops; crosses above couch to front.*) That's a thought. That's what I should be writing instead of this titivating drivel. Life as it is. People as they are.

SUSIE. But that would be terrible. You don't know, Mr. Law; you don't know how awful life can be.

BENSON. When you philosophers are through I'd like to get on with this story.

SUSIE (*eagerly, to* BENSON). You wouldn't like to come out and say hello to Happy? He's in the garden. (LAW *waves her away; crosses and sits on couch.* SUSIE *is quite defeated now.*)

BENSON (*ignoring her*). I've got it. (*To* SUSIE) Don't bother me! (SUSIE *crosses to desk, gets mail, and fades from the scene.*) I've got it! Introducing Happy! Back to the zoo—Larry gets up in the morning and there, curled up with his pet tiger cub, is a baby! Happy!

LAW. Not bad!

BENSON. Larry looks at him. "How'd you get here?" (*He mimics* LARRY'S *voice.*)

LAW. The baby can't answer. The tiger begins to growl. Happy cries. Larry takes the baby to his hut.

BENSON. We meet Larry's drunken pal, the comic. (*Rises and crosses to* LAW.) That's where we have swell business. Two clumsy men pinning up his diapers—

LAW (*his enthusiasm gone*). Formula 284 . . . Diapers gag.

BENSON (*exulting*). Ah, yes, but the tiger runs away with the diapers! Fade-out! Now we need excitement. The tigers are loose—

LAW. How did they get loose?

BENSON (*crosses to* LAW). The comic's drunk. He opens the cages by accident. Christ! I see it! The city in uproar—the police—National Guard—the girl's come down to the zoo—she's trapped with Larry—and the baby. Fifty tigers snapping at Happy's throat.

LAW. And where does my priceless dialogue come in? (*Rises and crosses to chair back of desk.*) That's the worst of hack writing. It's hard work.

BENSON. Suppose—Larry—thinks—it's—the girl's baby?

LAW. Society girls go around leaving foundlings in the zoo? (*Drinking.*) Prostitution of a God-given talent! (*Sits.*) Pasteboard pictures of pasteboard people.

BENSON. Will you shut up? I've got to get this line-up today. Pearl expects me to take her to the opening.

LAW (*fiddling with the dictograph*). Eenie . . . Meenie . . . Mina . . . Mo . . . (*Dictograph buzzes.*) Music Department?

GREEN'S VOICE. Yes, this is the Music Department. This is Mr. Green.

LAW (*mimics* C.F.'s *voice*). Not Mr. Green! This is C.F. . . . Can you write me a roundelay with a symphonic undertone in about fifteen minutes? . . . Do it! (*Dictograph buzzes.*) Yes?

GREEN'S VOICE. Look, Mr. Friday, did you say a lullaby?

LAW. No, I didn't say a lullaby. I said a roundelay. The sort of thing Beethoven dashes off. (*He clicks the dictograph off.* ROSETTI *enters.*)

ROSETTI (*genially*). Hello, boys . . . have a cigar.

LAW. Hello, buzzard. What's the occasion?

BENSON. Fade-out, stooge, we're busy.

ROSETTI. Same old boys! Anything for a gag! Well, I'm feeling pretty good myself. I've just set Larry to a long-term contract. And he didn't have to take a cut, either. I got him a nice little set-up. A joint contract with Happy!

BENSON. With Happy?

LAW (*rises*). Huh? You're crazy!

ROSETTI. Well, the mother came to me just now and said you two were tired of her. And I happened to look up your power of attorney, and it seems you didn't even care to get a new one when it expired.

BENSON. Is this on the level?

LAW. Where's that power of attorney?

BENSON. I thought you had it.

LAW (*aghast*). What'd you get for Happy?

ROSETTI. Three hundred!

LAW. Why, we turned down fifteen hundred from Fox!

ROSETTI. You should have taken it. But three hundred's a lot of money. Anyway, what's the difference? It's all in the family—now.

LAW. Where's Susie?

ROSETTI. She went out with Larry. They're going to the opening tonight. They're celebrating.

LAW. Who thought this up—you?

ROSETTI. Sure.

LAW. Why, you scavenging son of a—

ROSETTI. You better be careful how you talk to me. And you'd better be careful how you talk to Larry from now on. He's fed up with your gags and insults. You got away with a lot of stuff around here because you had Happy. Well, Larry's got him now, and he's going to have plenty to say around here. I'm warning you. He'd like to see you boys off this lot. And he's in a position to do it—now. So be careful. If you want to keep your jobs. (*Turns away to door.*) And if I had a wife who was throwing my money away before I even made it, I'd be plenty careful.

BENSON. Why, you— (ROSETTI *exits quickly.* BENSON *crosses to door, then turns to* LAW.) Why the hell didn't you keep track of that power of attorney?

LAW. Why didn't *I?*

BENSON. Why the hell didn't you talk to Susie? She was in here.

LAW. Yeah.

BENSON. I see it—I see it now. Larry—Rosetti—and we let her walk right into it. Do you realize what this means? We're on our way out. (*Crosses to piano.*)

LAW. That's fine.

BENSON. Fine?

LAW. Now I'll have to go back to Vermont. Now I'll have to write.

BENSON. Pearl doesn't like Vermont.

LAW. The whims of your wife don't interest me. I've got a book—all planned.

BENSON. Listen—I want to stay in pictures. I love pictures. I'm knee-deep in debts. We've got to bust this Larry thing wide open. We've got to get Happy back.

LAW. But it's closed.

BENSON. Well, what of it? We'll open it. We've got to get Happy back.

LAW. How?

BENSON. Suppose we get Larry Toms to break that joint contract.

LAW. All right—but how?

BENSON. He's scared green of scandal. Suppose we snow up at the opening tonight with a drunken dame. *Larry's deserted wife!*

LAW. Has he got one?

BENSON. We'll get one of your tarts.

LAW. That's too damned obvious.

BENSON. Can you top it?

LAW. Let me think.

BENSON. How about a poor deserted mother? I'll bet he's got one.

LAW (*rises, carried away*). I know! *Happy's father!*

BENSON. Huh?

LAW. We're going to produce Happy's father on the air—tonight. (*Crosses to phone.*)

BENSON. Happy's father! That's swell! That's marvellous. . . . (*Pause.*) But where'll we get a father?

LAW (*into phone*). Central Casting, please. . . . Hello. I want a handsome young extra, a gentleman, a little down at the heel, not too well fed, neat business suit—shiny but well pressed; quiet manner . . . (*Door opens and* RODNEY *enters.*)

BENSON. What do you want?

RODNEY. I received a message from Miss Crews but apparently she's stepped out. Is Mr. Friday here? I assume I've been called for a part.

LAW (*into phone, as his eyes refuse to leave* RODNEY). Never mind—cancel it. (*Hangs up.*)

BENSON. Will you shut the door, please? (RODNEY *complies.*) So you're an actor, my boy? (*Paternally.*)

RODNEY. Of course, I haven't had much experience. As a matter of fact, I never appeared in a picture. I almost did. Since then I've been out of the profession, so to speak. Odd jobs—barbecue stand, and when that closed I offered to show tourists homes of the movie stars. Unfortunately I haven't a motor car and they won't walk. . . . I don't mind saying this call was an extremely pleasant surprise.

LAW. He's perfect!

RODNEY. Do you really think I'll do?

LAW (*inspired*). Benson, take these lines. . . . (BENSON *goes to chair.*)

RODNEY. Oh, are there lines? Then the fee will be fifteen dollars, I assume?

LAW. Fifteen? One hundred for you.

RODNEY. I'm afraid I'm not worth that.

LAW. This is a trailer we're making tonight. We pay more for trailers.

RODNEY. Oh, I say!

BENSON (at desk, with paper and pencil.) We're going to shoot this at Grauman's Chinese in the lobby. There'll be a girl at the microphone. Her name is Susie. You come running up . . . you say . . .

LAW (at downstage end of desk). "Susie, why did you leave me?" . . . Say it.

RODNEY. Susie, why did you leave me?

BENSON. With feeling.

RODNEY (with feeling). Susie, why did you leave me?

LAW. I'm Happy's father.

RODNEY. I'm Happy's father.

BENSON. Louder.

RODNEY. I'm Happy's father.

LAW. I did not go down on the Morro Castle. . . . Susie, I've searched for you in the four corners of the earth. . . . Susie, why did you leave me?

RODNEY (who has been repeating the ends of the phrases in LAW's speech.) Susie, why did you leave me?

BENSON (jubilant). Right!

BLACKOUT and CURTAIN

SCENE III

A radio voice is heard in the theatre before the rise of the curtain. We're right in Grauman's Chinese Theatre in Hollywood.

RADIO ANNOUNCER. Folks, this is the première of Cecil B. DeMille's super-spectacle of Egyptian life—King Saul—at Grauman's Chinese. Your favorite stars, folks, in person—and the crowds. They're pushing and shoving and yelling for autographs, but it's all in good-natured fun. Only two hurt and they've refused medical treatment. There's Constance Bennett, folks, with her husband, the Marquise de la Falaise. No, I'm wrong. Sorry. It's not the Marquis . . . it's not Constance Bennett. It's Mary Pickford. By the way, I've been reading our Mary's book, folks. She's selling God, folks, and that's something we all ought to be in the market for. Give a thought to God and He'll give a thought to you. That's the big lesson in King Saul, folks. Oh, there's Leotta Marvin. . . .
As the curtain rises, the booming voice softens to the normal tone of a radio.
Again we are in MR. FRIDAY's office, later in the evening. At the rise of the curtain, C.F. is seated with A CUTTER, and BENSON sits a little apart from him, in chair back of couch, near the radio, which is on.

RADIO ANNOUNCER. . . . And if you've seen her on the screen, I don't have to tell you she's blonde, beautiful and gorgeous. Folks, I want to tell you that this is the most thrilling première it's been my privilege to cover. King Saul, de Mille's super-spectacle of Egyptian life at Grauman's Chinese—

C.F. Benson, turn down that radio. We've got to get three thousand feet of Young England. It's a sick picture, Benson. Where's Law? I left word at his hotel.

BENSON. He'll be here. I'm inside man tonight. He's outside.

C.F. (to CUTTER). Cut the coronation scene—it drags. And give me an underlying something that means something. I want a stirring Britannic quality. (BENSON turns up the radio.)

RADIO ANNOUNCER. . . . And that, folks, was Mr. Stanley Oswald, veteran of old silent films. . . . This is the première of King Saul, Cecil B. de Mille's super-spectacle at Gauman's Chinese . . .

C.F. Benson, turn to page 94 and read that scene. I want to lap dissolve through Queen Victoria. Simmons, you're supposed to be a cutter. Give me some ideas.

RADIO ANNOUNCER. . . . And now, folks, I'm told that none other than Larry Toms is with us tonight. And he's not altogether by his lonesome for hanging on his manly arm is none other than Mrs. Susan Seabrook, mother of America's Crown Prince—Happy!

BENSON. Hooray!

CUTTER. I got a way of cutting all that Boer War stuff so you won't even miss it.

RADIO ANNOUNCER. . . . And now I have the honor to present Mrs. Seabrook, the mother of Happy . . .

C.F. Will you turn that infernal thing off? (*To* CUTTER) I can't cut the Boer War. It's historically valuable.

RADIO ANNOUNCER. . . . And now I have the honor to present Mrs. Seabrook, the mother of Happy—

SUSIE'S VOICE. But I don't know what to say!

BENSON. Susie's on the air.

RADIO ANNOUNCER. Is it true, Mrs. Seabrook, that you and Larry have been window shopping?

SUSIE'S VOICE (*and it's very nervous indeed*). Well—

RADIO ANNOUNCER. The microphone is yours.

SUSIE'S VOICE. I would like to thank all of you for the thousands of letters and gifts that you've sent my baby Happy. I read all your letters and some of them make me cry —they're so pathetic. I would like to send all of you money only I haven't got that much and the studio won't let me. I'd like to say a few words about the letters asking about Happy's diet. You read a lot of advertisements of what he eats but if Happy ate everything they said he ate I guess he'd be a giant, and he's really got a very little stomach.

BENSON. Good for Susie! Truth in advertising!

C.F. (*struck by appalling thought*). Benson, was Queen Victoria alive during the Boer War?

BENSON. If she's alive in the picture, she was.

RADIO ANNOUNCER (*through this*). Folks, this is the première of Cecil B. De Mille's super-spectacle of Egyptian life, *King Saul,* at Grauman's Chinese—

SUSIE'S VOICE. Can I say hello to all my girl friends at the Julia Marshall High School? . . . *Hello!*

C.F. Benson—

BENSON. Sssh . . . Susie's talking.

SUSIE'S VOICE. A lot of you wonder in your letters how a grown woman can go to high school. Well, it's not easy. I'm a mother, and the other girls aren't . . .

BENSON. Let's hope not.

SUSIE'S VOICE (*brightly*). . . . although some of the girls are very developed.

RADIO ANNOUNCER (*quickly*). Folks, this is the première of *King Saul,* Cecil B. De Mille's super-spectacle of Egyptian life. . . .

C.F. Shut that infernal thing off. (BENSON *lifts hand like traffic signal "Stop."*)

SUSIE'S VOICE. I didn't finish. I wanted to explain that I'm going to high school so I can keep up with Happy when he goes to college. Because I'm the only one Happy can go to. He hasn't got a father, and—

RADIO ANNOUNCER (*very, very firmly*). That was Happy's mother, folks. . . . She was wearing a white evening gown. And folks, meet Larry Toms, the lucky man.

C.F. Benson, can we lap-dissolve through, do you think, on page 94?

LARRY'S VOICE. I know this is going to be a wonderful picture.

RADIO ANNOUNCER. A little bird has whispered to me that you and Mrs. Seabrook are contemplating marriage, Larry.

BENSON. Well, what do you know about that!

C.F. Will you come here, Benson, with that script?

LARRY'S VOICE. Well, to tell you the truth—

BENSON. He's blushing.

LARRY'S VOICE. I kinda missed the little fella after the day's work was done. So I guess pretty soon I'll be Happy's father off the screen as well as on—

BENSON. Who wrote his speech? You or Rosetti?

RODNEY'S VOICE. Stop! I'm Happy's father!

C.F. (*rises*). What's that?

RODNEY'S VOICE. I did not go down on the *Morro Castle.* I've searched for you in the four corners of the earth. Susie, why did you leave me?

C.F. (*excitedly*). Did you hear that?

BENSON (*softly*). Yes. I wonder what that was ... (*Cries are heard of "Here, Officer"—inarticulate shouts—a siren.*)

RADIO ANNOUNCER. Folks, there was a slight interruption. That voice you heard was a young man ... he ... well, he threw his arms about Mrs. Seabrook and kissed her. There's some confusion—a police officer is making his way through—they've got the young man ... no, they haven't got him. ... Folks, this is the opening of Cecil B. De Mille's super-spectacle of Egyptian life, *King Saul,* at Grauman's Chinese ... (BENSON *turns it off.*)

C.F. (*stunned*). Good Gad! (*Phone rings. He moves to it.*)

BENSON (*shakes his head*). Strangest thing I ever heard.

C.F. Oh, hello, B.K. ... Yes, I've just heard it over the radio ... (*Miserable*) I'm sitting here trying to cut *Young England* ... what? ... But, B.K., ... yes, of course, it's a serious situation ... I agree with you ... yes, ... yes ... of course ... I'll get hold of the mother immediately. (*He rises; hangs up, still dazed. To* BENSON) B.K.'s coming down to the studio! (*Phone rings*) Yes ... Look here, I've nothing to say to the press. It's a canard. (*He hangs up.*) (*Phone rings again.*) I won't answer it. (MISS CREWS *enters.*)

MISS CREWS. Doctor Tompkins is calling you, Mr. Friday. He says it's important.

C.F. What's he want? I'm not in. Call Mrs. Seabrook's house and have her ring me the minute she comes in.

MISS CREWS. Yes, Mr. Friday. (*She exits.*)

C.F. Benson, do you think that young man was genuine?

BENSON (*rises, crosses around downstage end of couch*). Search me.

C.F. Well, we'll soon find out. B.K.'s set the police after him.

BENSON (*a little disturbed*). Why do that? Best thing the studio can do is ignore it.

C.F. We can't ignore it. This has brought up the whole paternity issue.

BENSON. What of it?

C.F. Suppose Happy has a skeleton in his closet?

BENSON (*lies on couch*). I don't even know if he's got a closet.

C.F. Save your gags for your pictures. They need them. I've never heard B.K. so excited. (*Crosses to window.*) What do you think the reaction will be in the sticks—in the provinces? An illegitimate baby!

BENSON. This is 1935.

C.F. To me, yes. But how many intellectuals have we in America?

BENSON. One.

C.F. You don't seem to realize—

BENSON. Why, this is going to send Happy's stock up one hundred per cent. From now on he's not only cute, he's romantic.

C.F. He's illegitimate! I know America!

CUTTER (*studying the script*). What about Prince Albert? I can cut him out of the picture and you won't even miss him.

C.F. (*crossing below desk*). Yes, yes, Simmons. You go to the cutting room and do the best you know how. (SIMMONS *rises and puts chair up against wall.*) I've something more urgent right now. (*Crosses to* SIMMONS.) And, for God's sake, Simmons, get me some trumpets that sound like trumpets.

CUTTER (*not gruffly, but politely*). You sure you don't mean a trombone, C.F.?

C.F. No. I mean trumpets. I'm not a musician but I know what I mean. Trumpets—that slide. (*He pantomimes a trombone, of course.*)

BENSON (*to* CUTTER). He wants a slide trumpet. (CUTTER *exits.*) (*Simultaneously through other door* GREEN *and* SLADE *appear.*)

GREEN. Well, we've got that roundelay.

C.F. What do you want? What roundelay? (*Phone rings.*)

GREEN. Park it, Otto. (*Both go to piano.*)

C.F. (*at phone*). Yes—yes—no, Mr. Friday is not here. He has nothing to say to the press. (*He hangs up.*)

GREEN. You're going to be enthusiastic about this. We've been up all night working on it. (SLADE *starts playing Beethoven's Turkish March. As* C.F. *starts toward the piano, the phone rings*). Smooth, ain't it?

C.F. (*at phone*). Miss Crews? Where's Mrs. Seabrook? Why haven't you got her? (*To* GREEN) I will not listen to any more music.

GREEN. Get a load of this. It's the real McCoy.

C.F. (*at phone*). Yes—I'm holding the line—all right, never mind. Call me. (*Hangs up. To* SLADE *and* GREEN) I'll call the studio guards if you don't stop that infernal din. I'll report you to B.K. for insubordination. I'll have your contracts torn up!

GREEN. Are you kidding, or is this on the level?

C.F. Get out!

GREEN. O.K. Don't get tough! Come on, Otto. (*Crosses back of couch to door.*) But it's a fine how-do-you-do when you call up a couple of artists late at night and put 'em to work going through Beethoven's symphonies for a little inspiration and then give them the bum's rush just because you ain't in the mood. (GREEN *and* SLADE *exit.*)

(LARRY *and* ROSETTI *enter, both in tails and toppers.*)

ROSETTI. Now calm down, Larry, calm down—

LARRY. I'm not saying a word.

C.F. Where's Mrs. Seabrook? What did you do with her?

LARRY. I don't know, and I don't care.

BENSON (*mockingly*). "I kinda missed the little fella after the day's work was done—"

C.F. (*quickly*). Look here, Larry, I want to know what Susie said. Did she know the young man? What did she say?

LARRY. You listen to what *I* gotta say. I ain't goin' to go through with no contract to play with no unbaptized baby!

ROSETTI (*placatingly*). Just a moment, Larry—

LARRY. I'm through! (*Overwhelmed with the memory.*) On the air—with all my fans listening in! I'm serving you notice now.

I ain't marrying her. I ain't doing no more pictures with Happy.

ROSETTI. Larry, will you listen to reason?

LARRY. There's only one thing you can do for me, Rosetti. Get me a doctor. I'm going up to my dressing room. I need a sedative. (LAW *enters quietly.*)

BENSON. Don't stand there. Get him a doctor—

LAW. Take me. I'm a qualified veterinary. (ROSETTI *exits with* LARRY.)

C.F. Law— (BENSON *sits up.*)

LAW. Hello, C.F. I just got your message at the hotel. *Young England* in trouble? Well, the old salvaging crew will pitch in. (*Takes off his coat.*)

C.F. Were you there?

LAW. Where? At the opening? Yes. Extraordinary, wasn't it?

BENSON (*significantly*). *We* heard it over the radio.

LAW (*casually*). How'd it come over?

BENSON (*admiringly*). Clear as a bell!

LAW. It certainly broke Larry up. You should have seen our chivalrous hero running from the rescue. Why, the wind whistled right past me!

C.F. Law, do you think that fellow was a crank, or do you think he was really—

LAW (*judicially*). Hard to say. He had a sinister underlip.

C.F. (*into phone*). Miss Crews, did you get Mrs. Seabrook's house? No one answers? Someone *must* answer—she has a ménage! (*Hangs up. Dictograph buzzes.*) Hello?

B.K.'s VOICE. Look here, Friday . . .

C.F. Yes, B.K.

B.K.'s VOICE. Did you get any dope on that young man?

C.F. No. I can't get any information. No one seems to know.

B.K.'s VOICE. Why not? I ask you to do the simplest little thing and, as usual, you fall down on me.

C.F. (*piteously*). Why blame me? I was sitting here cutting *Young England.*

B.K.'s VOICE. Don't bother me with *Young England.* You come up here—I want to talk with you.

C.F. Yes, B.K. I'll be right up. (*He moves to the door; sighs.*) Sometimes I wonder if this industry is worth the sacrifice. (*He exits.*)

BENSON (*smiles*). What'd you do with him?

LAW. Put him in an office across the hall.

BENSON (*aghast*). What? Why here?

LAW. They won't look for him here.

BENSON. Why didn't you dump him somewhere else?

LAW. And leave him free to roam—and blab? Listen, Benson, B.K.'s called the Chief personally and the whole damn police department is scouring the town for Rodney. (*Crosses to liquor cabinet; pours a drink.*) And you don't know what I've been up against with Rodney. (*He drinks.*) In his own peculiar English fashion, he's not entirely nitwitted. I had to shove him at the mike, and he's been demanding explanations ever since.

BENSON. One question: What'll we do with him?

LAW (*crossing back to couch; sits*). Frankly, I planned everything but Rodney's disposal. I don't know. But given a little time we'll work this problem out.

BENSON (*really aghast now*). Time?

LAW. Rodney's all right. He doesn't know it, but I've locked him in.

BENSON. Listen: I've got a wife to support! I've got a job to keep! I haven't got Vermont on my mind! I *like* writing pictures! I'm no goddamn realist!

LAW (*soothingly*). Easy, there, easy—

BENSON. If B.K. even dreamed we had anything to do with this we'd be blacklisted in the industry.

LAW (*rising*). Give me a chance to think, will you? Why the panic? I'll admit I've overlooked a few details.

BENSON. Get that guy out of the studio. Put him on a plane to Mexico. Strangle him! I don't care what you do.

LAW. No—no. Murder leads to theft and theft leads to deceit. Haven't you read De Quincey?

BENSON. C.F. may breeze in here any minute. Will you get going!

LAW. Very well, my sweet—I go. (*He starts for door, remembers that he had a coat, looks around room and finally locates it on couch. Gets it and exits. Phone rings.*)

BENSON (*into phone*). Hello . . . Yes. Right here. Oh, hello, darling. How are you feeling? (*Tenderly*) Of course I recognized your voice . . . Pearl, I'll be home in half an hour. . . . Less . . . Well, what are you crying about? . . . But I told you I couldn't take you to the opening. Well, if Louise was going why didn't you go with them? They'd be tickled to have you . . . Listen, darling . . . I know . . . I know . . . Yes, I'm listening . . . (LAW *re-enters—a changed* LAW. *He goes right to the second telephone.*)

LAW (*picking up the second telephone*). Give me the front gate!

BENSON (*into phone*). Yes, darling . . . yes . . . (*Sincerely*) Darling, please—please don't say that.

LAW. Smitty, this is Mr. Law. Any stranger go through the gate in the last ten minutes? . . . No?

BENSON (*sighs*). Yes, darling. . . .

LAW. Well, listen. The fellow that was on the air tonight—Happy's father—yes! He's loose in the studio . . . Yeah. . . .

BENSON (*turns to* LAW, *still holding the phone*). What?

LAW. Grab him and hold him. Don't let anyone come near him. Report to me personally . . . yeah . . .

BENSON. Darling, I'll call you back. (*Slams down the phone.*)

LAW (*hangs up*). The damn cleaning woman let him out!

BENSON (*apoplectic*). I told you, didn't I? I told you you shouldn't have brought him here! (SUSIE *enters. She has been magnifi-*

cently decked out for the opening, but despite her splendor she seems extremely unhappy.)

SUSIE. Oh, Mr. Benson . . . I tried to get you at your house but Mrs. Benson said you were here. I tried to get you, too, Mr. Law, at the hotel.

LAW. Now, now, Susie—I know—I know.

SUSIE. Oh, I should never have gone to that opening. I didn't want to go. When I was dressing I put my slip on the wrong side. I knew something terrible was going to happen. And then in the nursery when I went to say good night to Happy, he wouldn't eat his formula. And he wouldn't say good night to me. He was so cross. I told Larry I didn't want to leave Happy—but he insisted—and then the way Larry ran out on me—

LAW (*consolingly*). Now, now—

SUSIE. Why should he do that? Oh, I was so ashamed . . . I didn't even see the picture. And then when I got home—I knew I shouldn't have gone—I should never have left Happy. When I went to the hospital. . . .

LAW. Hospital?

BENSON. Hospital?

SUSIE. They won't let me in . . . not for two weeks.

BENSON (*crosses to* SUSIE). Happy's in the hospital?

SUSIE (*puzzled*). Happy's got the measles.

LAW. What?

SUSIE. And they won't let me come near him.

BENSON. Measles!

LAW. He certainly picked the right time for it!

SUSIE. That's why he wouldn't eat his formula.

C.F.'s VOICE (*off-stage; grimly*). Well, we'll see— (*As he opens the door*) I brought you some visitors, boys. Come in. (RODNEY *enters with* STUDIO OFFICER. *To* RODNEY) Are these the men?

RODNEY. They most certainly are.

SUSIE (*crosses to* RODNEY). You know you're not Happy's father.

RODNEY. Of course not, but—

SUSIE. You couldn't be!

RODNEY. Of course not! My dear, I'm very sorry. Look here, we always seem to meet under extraordinary circumstances . . . I never dreamt . . . I'd no idea . . . It was all so spectacular . . . And to do this to you— You were so kind to me . . . They said it was a trailer . . . I didn't realize until I was in the midst of it . . . And then I found myself in a car . . . with him . . . (*Indicates* LAW.) I asked him to bring me to you at once. Instead, he locked me in a dusty office.

C.F. So you boys put him up to it!

LAW. Before you say anything you'll be sorry for, C.F. . . . (*Turns to officer*) Smitty, who called you tonight to tell you this unfortunate young man was loose in the studio?

OFFICER. *You* did, Mr. Law.

LAW (*grandly*). That's all.

BENSON. Take him away.

LAW. It's an obvious psychiatric case, C.F.

BENSON (*to* C.F.). I wouldn't be surprised if he's the boy that's been springing out of bushes.

LAW. Certainly. Look at the way he kissed Susie!

RODNEY (*appalled*). But you coached me for hours. Both of you. Wait—here are my lines. (*He fumbles in his pocket.*) I know I have them—unless I've lost them.

LAW. So you're an author, too! And I thought it was extemporaneous.

RODNEY. Here—here they are! My dear, will you please read these lines? (*He hands the paper to* SUSIE.) They're the very words I spoke over the radio.

SUSIE (*reads and backs away from* RODNEY). You never said *these* lines. You *must* be a crank. Maybe you do spring out of bushes.

RODNEY (*stares*). Oh, I beg your pardon. My lines are on the other side.

LAW (*grabs for paper*). I'll take that! Susie—

C.F. (*taking paper out of* SUSIE's *hand, brushes* LAW *aside*). Just a minute. (*Reads*)

"She's a high-handed rich bitch."—*Tiger Tamer!*—There it is in the corner. *Tiger Tamer* by J. Carlyle Benson and Robert Law!

LAW (*hurt to the quick*). It's a forgery. Benson, we've been framed!

C.F. (*grimly*). This is the last prank you'll ever play. (*Clicks the dictograph.*)

MISS CREWS (*enters*). The new trumpets are here. (*For once,* C.F. *is not interested. The trumpets blare out.*)

C.F. (*into dictograph*). B.K.? I just found out—Benson and Law put that young man on the radio.

B.K.'s VOICE. Are you sure of that?

C.F. I have the proof. The young man is in my office.

B.K.'s VOICE. All right, fire them. I don't want them on this lot. If they think they can get away with that—

C.F. Fire them? Of course I'll fire them. (LARRY's VOICE *is heard as he enters.*)

LARRY. Don't tell me nothing—let go of me. (DOCTOR *and* ROSETTI *enter, following* LARRY *and struggling with him.*)

C.F. Quiet there—

LARRY. Let go of me!

C.F. Larry, I have neither the time nor the patience to pander to actors!

LARRY (*bellowing with the hurt roar of a wounded bull*). No? Babies, huh . . . (*Turns on* SUSIE) You—you—

SUSIE (*frightened; runs to* BENSON). What do you want?

LARRY. What do I want? That goddamn baby of yours has given me the measles!

CURTAIN

ACT THREE

A hospital corridor. Several weeks later. Facing us are several doors, punctuated by the little white cards identifying the patients within.

As the curtain rises, a white-clad NURSE *is walking down the corridor bearing a covered tray. Before she disappears,* BENSON *enters. He knocks on the door of the room where* HAPPY *is ensconced.* SUSIE *opens the door.*

SUSIE. Oh, hello, Mr. Benson. I'd ask you to come in but Happy's still sleeping. The doctor says he can be discharged tomorrow or the day after, he's getting along so fine. Where's Mr. Law?

BENSON. I don't know. We haven't been patronizing the same bar-rooms.

SUSIE. You look as if you didn't get much sleep.

BENSON (*slumping into a wheel chair*). I didn't.

SUSIE (*pityingly*). Why don't you go home?

BENSON. Home?

SUSIE. Is there anything wrong?

BENSON. Not a thing! Everything's fine.

SUSIE. How's Mrs. Benson?

BENSON. She's fine.

SUSIE. That's good. I called your house to thank her for the radio for Happy but they said you moved.

BENSON. We *were* moved.

SUSIE. You mean you were thrown out?

BENSON. If you want to be technical about it, yes.

SUSIE. Oh, I'm sorry.

BENSON (*broodingly*). What hurts is Aggrafino Jesus.

SUSIE. Who?

BENSON. My favorite Filipino butler. He slapped a lien on my brand-new Packard.

SUSIE. Oh!

BENSON. That's what the missionaries taught *him!*

SUSIE. You boys shouldn't have played that joke on me. You only hurt yourselves. Please don't drink any more, Mr. Benson.

BENSON. So it's come to that! You're going to reform me.

SUSIE. Well, I feel just like a sister to you boys. That's why I couldn't stay mad at you. Please, Mr. Benson, if you need money— I can give you some. I mean—when the studio sends Happy's checks. They haven't sent them yet.

BENSON (*looking up*). They haven't? How many do they owe you?

SUSIE. Two. I called Mr. Friday but he wouldn't talk to me. Do you think they're docking Happy?

BENSON. They can't do that. Measles are an act of God. (NURSE *enters with box of flowers.*)

NURSE. Some flowers for you, Mrs. Seabrook.

SUSIE (*extending her hand for it*). Oh, thank you.

NURSE. And he'd like to know if he can come up to see you. He's downstairs.

SUSIE (*embarrassed*). Oh . . .

BENSON. Who's downstairs? Who's sending you flowers?

SUSIE (*reluctantly*). It's Mr. Bevan. You know—

BENSON. You haven't been seeing our Nemesis?

SUSIE. Oh, no. But he's been writing me every day and sending me flowers. I didn't tell you. I didn't want to get you excited.

BENSON (*to* NURSE; *sweetly*). Tell him to come up, Nurse. And stand by.

SUSIE (*quickly*). Oh, no, Nurse. He's not to come up. I don't want to see him. Ever. And give him back his flowers. (*She hands box back to* NURSE.)

NURSE (*taking it*). Very well. (*She exits.*)

BENSON. Why deprive me of the pleasure of kicking an actor?

SUSIE. It wasn't his fault. After all, you put him up to it.

BENSON (*outraged*). Are you defending him?

SUSIE. Oh, no, I'm just as disappointed in him as you are. But I'm trying to be fair. (*She pauses.*) He writes very nice letters. (*A far-away look comes into her eyes.*)

BENSON (*suspiciously*). What kind of letters do you write him?

SUSIE (*hastily*). Oh, I don't write *any* letters.

BENSON. Good!

SUSIE. I'm afraid of my spelling. (LAW *enters. There's an air of on-my-way about him.*)

LAW. Hello, Susie. . . . And good-bye, Susie.

SUSIE. Hello, Mr. Law. Are you going away?

LAW. I am.

SUSIE. Where?

LAW. Where I belong. Vermont. Where you can touch life and feel life, and write it! (*Glares at* BENSON.)

BENSON. When does the great exodus begin?

LAW. In exactly thirty-five minutes. I'm flying back to my native hills, like a homing pigeon. No stopping in New York for me! I've chartered a plane—right to Vermont.

BENSON. Chartered a plane! Where'd you get the money?

LAW (*grudgingly*). Well, there are twelve Rotarians coming along.

BENSON. You'll be back in a week.

SUSIE (*eagerly*). Will you, Mr. Law?

LAW (*scornfully*). Back to what? Sunshine and psyllium seed? Listen, I've got me a little shack overlooking the valley . . . I'm going to cook my own food, chop my own wood, and *write*—

BENSON (*sardonically*). At twenty below?

LAW (*rapturously*). Snow! . . . God, how I love snow! (*He raises his eyes to Heaven.*)
 And since to look at things in bloom
 Fifty springs are little room,
 About the woodlands, I will go
 To see the cherry—hung with snow!

SUSIE. That's poetry.

LAW. A. E. Housman! *Shropshire Lad.* (*He pats the book in his pocket.*)

BENSON. There's plenty of snow in Arrowhead.

LAW. Yeah; they deliver it in trucks. And even when it's real you think it's cornflakes.

SUSIE. You won't drink too much in Vermont, will you, Mr. Law?

LAW. Only the heady wine air that has no dregs!

SUSIE. Because you're crazy enough without drinking.

LAW (*defensively*). I drank for escape . . . escape from myself . . . but now I'm free! I've found peace!

SUSIE. You'll say good-bye to Happy before you go? I want him to remember you.

LAW. Right now!

SUSIE. Wait! I'll see if he's awake. (*She enters* HAPPY's *room.*)

BENSON. Will you send me a copy of the book—autographed?

LAW. You get copy number one—first edition.

BENSON. What's the book about?

LAW. I'm going to bare my soul . . . I'm going to write life in the raw. I've got the opening all planned—two rats in a sewer!

BENSON. Sounds delightful.

LAW (*scornfully*). You wouldn't appreciate real writing. You've been poisoned. On second thought, I won't send you a book.

BENSON. Tell me more about the rats. What's your story?

LAW (*slightly patronizing*). This isn't a picture that you paste together, Mr. Benson. I'm going to write Life. Life isn't a story . . . it's a discordant overture to death!

BENSON. Well, if you want people to read it, the boy had better meet the girl.

LAW. There is no girl. There is no boy. These are people—real, live people—listen! I'm not even going to use a typewriter! I'm going to weigh every word—with a pencil!

BENSON. Well, maybe you're on the right track. You've got something to say—and the talent to say it with.

LAW. It's finally penetrated!

BENSON. You're probably doing the right thing.

LAW. The only thing. It's different with you —you've got a wife.

BENSON. I had.

LAW. Huh?

BENSON. Oh—uh—Pearl left last night.

LAW. No! I'm sorry.

BENSON (*shrugs*). You can't blame her. She wasn't wild about marrying me in the first place. I coaxed her into it. I painted some pretty pictures for her. It just didn't pan out.

LAW. You still want her?

BENSON (*almost to himself*). I guess I do.

LAW. Personally, I'd say the hell with her.

BENSON (*smiles bitterly*). The trouble is I don't mean it when I say it. (ROSETTI *enters.*)

ROSETTI. Hello, boys.

LAW (*cheerily*). Hello, louse. Get Benson a job, will you? He wants to stay in this God-forsaken hole.

ROSETTI. Listen! I'm not handling second-hand writers. Chicken feed! Right now I'm immersed in a three million dollar deal.

LAW (*interested*). Yeah?

ROSETTI. Yeah. With Gaumont British, and I'm underestimating when I say three million because B.K.'s turned down three million. Why should I bother with writers on the blacklist? So don't go calling me a louse! (SUSIE *enters.*)

SUSIE (*gaily*). Happy has his eyes open. You want to come in now, Mr. Law?

LAW. Coming, Susie. (*He follows* SUSIE *into* HAPPY's *room.*)

BENSON. Rosetti—(*going to him, whispering*)—Law wants to leave. He's flying in half an hour. Can you call up the studios?

Can you get us a one-picture contract? We'll make you our agent for life. *He's leaving!*

ROSETTI. Sure, he's leaving. Nobody wants him.

BENSON. How do you know? You haven't tried.

ROSETTI. I've tried. I don't let my personal feelings interfere with commissions.

BENSON. Listen, I've been a scene painter, prop boy, camera man, director, producer . . . I even sold film in Australia . . . they can't throw me out of this business!

ROSETTI (*crosses to a door and throws it back*). They won't touch you with a ten-foot pole. You, Law, or Happy.

BENSON. Or Happy?

ROSETTI. I gave B.K. a swell angle. Listen in on KNX this afternoon.

BENSON. Huh?

ROSETTI. The world is full of babies. You can get them two for a nickel. (*He opens inner door and meets* LARRY *coming out.*) Hello, Larry. I was just coming in to see you. (NURSE *pushes* LARRY *in wheel chair into corridor.*)

LAW'S VOICE. Good-bye, Happy. (*He enters with* SUSIE.) Good-bye, Susie.

SUSIE. Good-bye, Mr. Law.

LAW. Hello, Larry. How's every little spot?

LARRY. What's the idea?

LAW. What idea?

LARRY. What's the idea of sending me a box of dead spiders?

LAW. Didn't you like the box?

LARRY. You wait until I'm through convalescing!

NURSE. Now, don't excite yourself. You heard what the doctor said. You're going for your sun bath now. (*She wheels him out.*)

ROSETTI. I'll go along with you, Larry. I've got some great news for you. B.K.'s lending you out to Mascot! (*He exits.*)

LARRY (*as he goes out*). What?

LAW. Well, Susie, take good care of Happy.

SUSIE. Oh, I will.

LAW. Continue your education.

SUSIE. I'm doing that.

LAW (*quickly*). What's the capital of Nebraska?

SUSIE. Lincoln.

LAW. Who hit Sir Isaac Newton on the bean with an apple?

SUSIE. The law of gravity.

LAW. Who said, "Don't give up the ship?"

SUSIE. Captain James Lawrence in the battle of Lake Erie, 1813.

LAW. Don't give up the ship, Susie. I'll write you. (*He kisses her on the forehead.*)

SUSIE. Good-bye, Mr. Law. I've got to go back to Happy. (*Her voice breaks.*) I feel awful funny—your going away. (*Exits.*)

BENSON (*finally*). Well, you bastard—get out of here.

LAW. I'm going, stinker. (*Crosses to* BENSON. *They look at each other. A pause. Then* LAW *extends hand. They shake.* LAW *moves to go.*)

BENSON (*without turning*). Say— (LAW *stops.*) I don't suppose you'll be interested —Rosetti finally admitted Paramount wants us. Two thousand bucks a week to save Dietrich. We can close the deal in three or four days.

LAW (*turns slowly*). My plane leaves in twenty-five minutes. And you're a liar!

BENSON. I'm not trying to hold you back. But I figured this time you might *save* your money and—

LAW. I can live on twelve dollars a week in Vermont—in luxury!

BENSON. It would kind of help *me* out— If I could lay my hands on some ready dough Pearl might listen to reason.

LAW (*casually*). Well, we loaned out a lot of money in our time. Collect it. And send me my share.

BENSON. I thought of that. The trouble is I don't remember just who it was—and how much. The only one I remember is Jascha Simkovitch.

LAW. Who?

BENSON. Jascha Simkovitch. The fellow that came over with Eisenstein. Don't you remember? You made a wonderful crack about him. He said "There's a price on my head in Russia." And you said, "Yeah—two rubles." (*Laughs. He is flattering* LAW *smoothly.*)

LAW (*laughs with him*). Sure, I remember him. Why, we gave that bed-bug three thousand bucks! Get hold of him and collect it.

BENSON. He's in Paris. What's-his-name came over and said Jascha was living at the Ritz bar.

LAW. Then you can't collect it. Well, I'm off. (*He moves to exit once more.*)

BENSON (*as if struck with sudden thought*). Wait a minute! I've got a great gag for you! Let's call Jascha up in Paris—on Larry's phone! (*Chuckles, throws arms around* LAW. *Both laugh.*) Can you imagine Larry's face when he gets the bill? A farewell rib!

LAW (*hesitates*). Have I got time?

BENSON (*reassuringly; looks at his watch*). You've got plenty of time.

LAW. I'll work fast. Stand guard, Benson. (*He enters* LARRY's *room.* BENSON *follows and partly closes door.*)

LAW'S VOICE. I'm talking for Mr. Toms. I want to put a call through to Paris, France. . . . I want Jascha Simkovitch . . . Hotel Ritz, Paris. . . . Listen, don't worry about the charges . . . That's right—Jascha, as in Heifetz . . . S-i-m-k-o-v-i-t-c-h. (BENSON *closes door on* LAW. NURSE *enters with registered letter, knocks on* SUSIE's *door.* BENSON *looks at his watch.* SUSIE *appears.*)

NURSE. Registered letter for you, Mrs. Seabrook.

SUSIE. For me?

NURSE. You'll have to sign for it. There's a return receipt on it. (SUSIE *signs.*)

SUSIE. Now what do I do?

NURSE. Now you give me the receipt back and I'll give it to the postman. He's waiting for it. Here's your letter. (NURSE *exits.* SUSIE *opens letter.*)

SUSIE (*cheerily*). Why—it's from Mr. Friday. (LAW *emerges, as she opens the letter.*)

LAW. The service had better be good or there'll be no farewell rib. I haven't got much time.

SUSIE. Oh, didn't you go yet, Mr. Law?

LAW. I'm on my way!

SUSIE (*reading letter*). What does Mr. Friday mean when he says they're taking advantage of Clause 5A?

LAW. What? Let me see that. (*He reads the letter.* BENSON *looks over his shoulder.*) Well, this is the goddamest . . .

SUSIE. You mustn't swear so much. I don't mind—I'm used to it—but Happy might hear you. What does it mean?

LAW (*reading*). Clause 5A—when an artist through illness—for a period of more than fourteen days—

BENSON. They're just using that for an excuse. It's the paternity issue!

SUSIE. What paternity issue?

BENSON. They're crazy! That kid's going to be as good as he ever was—better.

SUSIE. What does it mean?

LAW. It means, Susie—Happy is out.

SUSIE. Out?

BENSON. Yeah. Finished—done. At the age of eight months—In his prime!

SUSIE. Out of pictures?

BENSON (*turning on* LAW). And there's the man who did it. It was your brilliant idea!

SUSIE (*such a nice girl!*). Oh, no. After all, it was just like a dream. I had to wake up some time.

LAW (*as phone rings*). I guess that's Paris

SUSIE. What's Paris? (*Phone still rings.*)

BENSON. Go ahead and have your farewell rib, and get out, author! (*Phone still rings.* LAW *enters room.*)

SUSIE. What's Paris?

BENSON (*going to door of* LARRY's *room*). A city in France.

LAW (*in room*). Hello—right here.—Yes—yes—I'm ready. Hello! . . . Hello—Jascha? Jascha Simkovitch? This is Bobby Law. Is it raining in Paris? . . . well, it's not raining here!

BENSON. Wonderful age we're living in!

LAW (*in room*). Listen, Jascha, are you sober? . . . How come? . . . Oh, you just got there! . . . You're going to London? . . . Today? . . . Hold the wire. (LAW *enters.*) I've got an idea! *Let's buy the studio!*

BENSON. What?

LAW. You heard Rosetti. Gaumont British is offering three million. Let's get Jascha to send a cable—sign it Gaumont British—offering four!

BENSON. Why be petty? Offer five!

LAW (*judicially*). Right! (*Exits into room.*)

SUSIE. You boys are very peculiar.

LAW (*in room*). Jascha—got a pencil and paper? Fine. Listen, Jascha, we want you to send a cable from London as follows: Quote. . . . (LARRY *enters in his wheel chair.* BENSON *closes the door hurriedly.*)

LARRY. Hey, that's my room!

BENSON (*firmly shutting the door*). A private conversation should be private.

LARRY. What's the idea of using my phone?

BENSON. Do you object?

LARRY. Certainly I object. I ain't gonna pay for your calls.

BENSON. All right, if that's the way you feel about it—here's your nickel!

BLACKOUT *and* CURTAIN

SCENE II

In Your Own Home. That is, if you have one, and if you listen to the radio.

RADIO ANNOUNCER. Ladies and Gentlemen, this is Station KNX—the Voice of Hollywood. At this time we take great pleasure in announcing the winner of the Royal Studios' Baby Star Contest to find the successor to Happy who retired from the screen after his illness. Ladies and Gentlemen, the lucky baby is Baby Sylvester Burnett, infant son of Mr. and Mrs. Oliver Burnett of Glendale, California. Congratulations, Mr. and Mrs. Burnett. Contracts for your baby are waiting in Mr. C. Elliot Friday's office at the Royal Studios. Incidentally, Mr. Friday asks that you bring your baby's birth certificate and your marriage licence. This is KNX, the Voice of Hollywood. (*Chimes are heard.*)

SCENE III

MR. FRIDAY's *office, the following day.* MR. FRIDAY *is sitting at his desk, dictating to* MISS CREWS.

C.F. My dear Mr. Pirandello. . . . On second thought, you'd better make that Signor Pirandello. . . . I am writing to ascertain if possibly you have something in your trunk —every author has—which would be suitable as a vehicle for our new baby star, Baby Sylvester Burnett. It can be either a short story or sketch or a few lines which you can jot down at your leisure and which we can whip up into suitable material. I am writing of my own volition as both Mrs. Friday and I are great admirers of you. Very truly yours. . . . Now take a letter to Stark Young. (*Dictograph buzzes.*) Yes?

B.K.'S VOICE. Listen, Friday—

C.F. What, B.K.?

B.K.'s VOICE. Come right up here. I want to see you. We've got a new cable from Gaumont British.

C.F. Gaumont British? Yes, sir, I'll be right up. (*He rises.*) Miss Crews, have you the contracts for the Burnett baby?

MISS CREWS. Right on your desk, Mr. Friday. And the parents are in the commissary.

C.F. Good. I've got to go up and see B.K. (*Exits.*)

GREEN (*who enters almost simultaneously, followed by* SLADE.) Where is he? Where's C.F.?

MISS CREWS. You can't shoot him today.

GREEN. It's a wonder we don't. We're walking up and down in front of the projection room developing an idea when we hear a number—our number— We go in, and it's in *Young England!* Our song! They don't even tell us about it—they murdered it! They run dialogue over it. You got to spot a song—we ask for Guy Lombardo and they give us a six-piece symphony orchestra!

MISS CREWS. If you buy me a handkerchief I promise to cry. Lace, if you don't mind.

GREEN. Lissen—play her the number the way it should be.

MISS CREWS. Must you?

SLADE. Oh, what's the use?

GREEN. Give her the chorus.

SLADE. I'm losing my pep.

GREEN. You might as well hear it. Nobody else will. (SLADE *plays.*) Will you listen to that? Ain't it a shame?

You promised love undying,
And begged me to believe;
Then you left, and left me crying
With pain in my heart, and my heart
  on my sleeve.

I really shouldn't blame you
Because you chose to leave;
But one thing forever will shame you—
It's the pain in my heart, and my heart
  on my sleeve.

(C.F. *has entered.*)

C.F. Miss Crews!

MISS CREWS. Yes, Mr. Friday?

C.F. Miss Crews, get hold of Benson and Law right away!

MISS CREWS. Who?

C.F. Have Benson and Law come here—immediately.

MISS CREWS. Yes, Mr. Friday.

GREEN (*as* SLADE *pounds away*). That's the chorus! That's the chorus that you murdered!

C.F. Wait a minute, Miss Crews! Get me the hospital. I want to talk to Happy's mother.

MISS CREWS. Yes, Mr. Friday. (*She exits.*)

C.F. Miss Crews! Call my florist and tell him to send Happy a bouquet of roses. And some orchids for his mother, right away. (*He turns to* GREEN.) Will you stop that noise! (*He picks up telephone.*)

GREEN. Noise? The song that you murdered? We just wanna see if you got a conscience.

C.F. (*into phone*). Miss Crews, call up Magnin's and tell them to send a radio to the hospital for Happy. One of those slick, modernistic sets in white. And don't forget to have my card put in with the flowers. Did you get Benson and Law? . . . Well, did you get Happy's mother? . . . Well, get them! (*Hangs up.*)

GREEN. Is that a song that you run dialogue over, C.F.?

C.F. What are you babbling about, Green? I haven't used any of your songs in *Young England!*

GREEN (*outraged*). How about *Westminster Abbey in the Moonlight?* They wasn't our lyrics, but it was our tune!

C.F. I used an old Jerome Kern number we've had for years, out of the library.

GREEN (*crestfallen*). You did? (*To* SLADE) I thought you said it came to you in the middle of the night. Where? In the library?

C.F. Will you get out of my office?

GREEN (*with sudden enthusiasm*). We got a new number you'll be crazy about.

C.F. I've got too much on my mind to listen to your tinny effusions. I told the studio to hire Richard Strauss and no one else. One great composer is worth twenty of your ilk! (ROSETTI *enters with* LARRY.)

LARRY. Looka here, C.F., I just got out of a sick bed to see you.

c.f. What do you want, Larry? (SLADE *plays on.*) What do you want? I'm very busy. (*Turns to* GREEN.) Will you please go? I will not listen!

GREEN (*as the worm turns*). . . . O.K., music lover! (GREEN *and* SLADE *exit.*)

LARRY. I shouldn't be here. I should be on my ranch convalescing. I'm weak.

c.f. Come to the point, Larry. Come to the point.

LARRY (*bitterly*). What's the idea of lending me out to Mascot? I'm a star! I ain't goin' to degrade myself by playing in no undignified thirty-thousand-dollar feature.

c.f. Larry, face the facts—you're through.

LARRY. That's a nice thing to tell a sick man.

ROSETTI. Now, Larry, I told you. Your attitude is all wrong.

LARRY. Never mind about my attitude.

c.f. (*at the phone*). Miss Crews, have you got Benson and Law? . . . Who's gone to Vermont? . . . What about Susie? . . . What? They left the hospital? (*He hangs up.*)

ROSETTI (*eagerly*). What's up, C.F.?

c.f. (*finally*). This is confidential, Rosetti. (*Lowers his voice.*) Gaumont British wants to buy the company intact.

LARRY. Gaumont British?

c.f. They want all our stars, including Happy. Naturally they want him. He's the sensation of London.

ROSETTI. But B.K. turned down three million. I've been handling that deal myself.

c.f. They've raised it. They've just cabled an offer of five million.

ROSETTI. They did? Say, that's marvellous. I'm in on that!

LARRY. Well, you better get me back from Mascot quick. Gaumont British wants *me.* Why, they made me an offer a year ago, only I was tied up.

c.f. They make no mention of you.

LARRY. What?

c.f. Rosetti, we've got to sign Happy immediately. Get hold of Susie and let's close.

ROSETTI. You can sign the three of 'em for a hundred a week. They're broke. And they're low. I'm going right after it. (*He starts for door.*)

LARRY. Come back here. You're supposed to be *my* agent! What are you going to do about *me?*

ROSETTI. You're all right where you are— with Mascot. I'll call you later, C.F. (*Exits.*)

LARRY (*to c.f.*). My agent! I been distrustin' that guy for years. (*Exits.*)

c.f. (*who can balance a budget, picks up phone*). Miss Crews, you didn't send those flowers off, did you? . . . What? . . . But they've left the hospital. What about the radio? . . . Well, call them up right away and cancel it. . . . Who? . . . She's here? Send her right in! (*He crosses to greet* SUSIE. *He is now cordial; hearty, a thing of beauty and a joy forever.*) Well, Susie, I'm delighted to see you. You're looking well. I must say we've missed you. I hear the boys are in Vermont.

SUSIE (*stands in door*). Mr. Law was going but he missed the plane.

c.f. (*taken aback*). Well, where are they?

SUSIE. They're in B.K.'s office, getting the contracts.

c.f. Without consulting me?

SUSIE. They said they don't trust you, Mr. Friday.

c.f. Gad! After all I've done for them!

SUSIE (*seating herself on the couch*). Do you mind if I sit here and do my homework? I'm way behind and I don't want to be left back. I'm supposed to wait here until they get B.K.'s signature, and then I'm going to sign.

c.f. I'm going right up to see B.K. (MISS CREWS *enters.*)

MISS CREWS. Mr. and Mrs. Burnett have had their coffee and now they want their contracts.

c.f. What contracts?

MISS CREWS. The parents of the other infant.

C.F. What other infant? What other infant is there except Happy?

MISS CREWS. But what'll I do with them?

C.F. Send them away. (*Now he sees* RODNEY *looking in through door.* RODNEY *has a large box of flowers.*) What do you want?

RODNEY. Here's the check for the milk—and other odd items.

C.F. Check.

RODNEY. I think you'll find it correct. I verified it at the commissary. And of course I included a service charge—and interest at six per cent. The total is two dollars and eighty-four cents. Thank you. (*Dictograph buzzes.*)

C.F. (*into dictograph*). Hello—

B.K.'S VOICE. Listen, Friday, you might as well be here. I'm settling the Happy contract with Benson and Law.

C.F. Yes, B.K. I'm coming right up. (*Phone rings; into phone*) What? . . . I never asked for trumpets in the first place. I don't want any trumpets. I want a period of utter silence. See that I get it. (*Hangs up. To* RODNEY) You get out!

RODNEY (*firmly*). I've something to say to Mrs. Seabrook. (SUSIE *turns away. Softly*) I brought you some flowers.

C.F. Give her her flowers, and get out. And don't let me find you here when I come back. Miss Crews, I'll be up in B.K.'s office. (*He exits.*)

RODNEY. I know you don't want to see me. (*Extends flowers.*) Won't you take them? (MISS CREWS *exits.*) I wrote, you know. I explained everything.

SUSIE (*still not facing him*). Happy's not allowed to have flowers.

RODNEY. Oh, but they're for Happy's mother —from Happy's father.

SUSIE (*turning; aghast*). Are you joking about what you did?

RODNEY. I'm not joking. Lord, no. I mean it. Look here—will you marry me? (SUSIE *stares*

at him.) I've thought it all out. I owe it to you. Shall we consider it settled?

SUSIE. Did Mr. Law and Mr. Benson put you up to this, too?

RODNEY. Good Lord, no. I haven't seen them and, what's more, I don't intend to.

SUSIE. Then why do you want to marry me?

RODNEY. I owe it to you.

SUSIE (*angrily*). That's no reason.

RODNEY. My visa's expired—I've two days' grace. I must get a train this afternoon. Are you coming with me?

SUSIE. I don't think you'd make a very sensible father for Happy. I don't think so at all.

RODNEY. I'm not at all sensible. I'm frightfully stupid — impulsive — emotional — but I'm not really at my best these days. Most people aren't when they're infatuated.

SUSIE. You couldn't be infatuated with me!

RODNEY. But I am. Look here, it's no good debating. My mind's made up. I don't frequently make it up, but when I do, I stick to the end.

SUSIE. But you don't know about my past.

RODNEY. I've been through all that, in my mind. It doesn't matter.

SUSIE. But it does. I'm ashamed to tell you.

RODNEY. Please don't, then.

SUSIE. Happy's father was a bigamist.

RODNEY. Eh?

SUSIE. He married twice.

RODNEY. Is that it?

SUSIE. What did you think?

RODNEY. It doesn't really matter.

SUSIE. I didn't know he was married before.

RODNEY. But, good Lord, nobody can blame you.

SUSIE. His wife did.

RODNEY. Naturally.

SUSIE. How was I to know? And it wasn't his fault, either. He got a Mexican divorce and he didn't know it wasn't good.

RODNEY. Oh!

SUSIE (*drawing herself up à la Fairfax*). So I said to him, "Your duty is to your first wife." And I ran away. I didn't know I was going to have Happy, then.

RODNEY. Have you—heard from him?

SUSIE. Oh, no. Of course, he should have told me in the first place. But he was infatuated, too, and I didn't know any better.

RODNEY. Well, have you divorced him?

SUSIE. No.

RODNEY. You'll have to clear that matter up, I think—immediately.

SUSIE. I can't clear it up. He's dead.

RODNEY. Oh!

SUSIE. She shot him.

RODNEY. His wife?

SUSIE. Yes.

RODNEY. Good Lord!

SUSIE. I hear from her sometimes. She's awfully sorry.

RODNEY (*brightly*). Well then, you're free to marry, aren't you?

SUSIE. Oh, I'm free, but the point is—do I want to? After all, I don't know you very well, and every time we meet something terrible happens. I didn't know Jack very well, either, and look what happened to him. I've got to be careful.

RODNEY. But I'm not a bigamist.

SUSIE. Maybe not. You may be something else.

RODNEY. But the British Consul'll vouch for me. He knows my family. I haven't had much of a life, but it's an open book.

SUSIE. Oh, I believe you. But I can't listen to my heart. I've got to listen to my head.

RODNEY. Of course, I haven't much to offer you. I've just come into a little money, and on my thirtieth birthday I come into a great deal more. We can have a flat in London and one of my aunts is going to leave me a place in the country.

SUSIE. That's in Europe, isn't it?

RODNEY. Yes, of course.

SUSIE. Oh, I couldn't go to Europe.

RODNEY. But why not?

SUSIE. The boys want to put Happy back in pictures.

RODNEY. I wouldn't hear of it. That's no life for a baby. Thoroughly abnormal. And, furthermore, I don't like the California climate. Now in England we have the four seasons.

SUSIE. You have?

RODNEY (*ardently*). Summer, winter, spring and fall.

SUSIE (*finally*). I want to ask you something.

RODNEY. Certainly.

SUSIE. When I come into a room—does something happen to you?

RODNEY. Eh? Of course—very much so.

SUSIE (*rises and turns away*). Well, I'll think it over.

RODNEY (*rises and takes* SUSIE's *arm*). Look here, I couldn't possibly take no for an answer.

SUSIE. Of course, when you come into a room, something happens to me, too.

RODNEY. Does it really? (SUSIE *nods. He takes her in his arms. They kiss. Door opens and* LAW *enters with* BENSON.)

LAW. Susie, did my eyes deceive me? Were you kissing an actor?

BENSON. What's that?

LAW (*to* BENSON). An English actor!

BENSON. What? Didn't I tell you—?

SUSIE. Boys, I've been thinking it over—

BENSON (*wearily drops down to piano;* LAW *down to end of couch*). With what?

SUSIE. I'm going to marry Rodney and I'm going to Europe. They've got the four seasons over there, and Happy'll be normal.

RODNEY. Well put, my dear. (C.F. *enters.*)

SUSIE. So I don't think I'd better sign the contract.

RODNEY. Most certainly not!

C.F. You're not going to sign Happy?

LAW. Susie, I've just given up Vermont for a whole year—for you. A whole year out of my life—because B.K. begged me to stay and handle Happy. I've sacrificed a great book—for what? A paltry fifteen hundred dollars a week? I didn't want it!

C.F. If she doesn't sign, we'll break that contract with you, Law.

LAW. Try and do it.

SUSIE. I'm going to Europe with Rodney.

LAW. Do you want to tell Happy he's out of pictures? Do you want to break his little heart?

SUSIE. He'll understand!

BENSON (*suddenly*). Do you know who Rodney is? English Jack! Confidence man.

LAW (*quickly*). Yes! Ship's gambler, petty racketeer and heart-breaker. (RODNEY *tries to speak.*)

BENSON. Served two terms for bigamy!

SUSIE. Bigamy?

RODNEY. But that's absurd.

BENSON (*bitterly*). I've seen hundreds of your kind in Limehouse.

C.F. So have I!

BENSON (*quietly*). Listen, C.F., stay off our side!

RODNEY (*to* SUSIE). You don't believe this, of course. They can't possibly believe it themselves.

LAW. Brazening it out, eh? As sure as God made little green apples—and He did—you're not coming near Susie. We'll have you in the can and out of the country by morning.

BENSON. No sooner said— (*into phone*) Get me the Department of Justice.

SUSIE (*to* RODNEY). You see? Something terrible always happens when you come.

LAW (*to* SUSIE). And you—sign that contract immediately.

RODNEY. She'll do nothing of the sort. You're not to intimidate her. Do you hear? (*Door opens and* LARRY *enters, accompanied by middle-aged English gentleman.*)

LARRY. Come on in here, Major.

C.F. What do you want, Larry? I'm busy.

BENSON (*into telephone*). Department of Justice? I want two of your best operatives to come down to the Royal Studios immediately. Report to Mr. Friday's office.

SUSIE. Oh, but you can't do that—

LARRY (*angrily*). Just a minute. Major Thompson is the representative here of Gaumont British.

C.F. Oh! I'm sorry. We've been rather upset. How do you do, Major. I'm Mr. Friday.

MAJOR. How do you do, sir. I won't be a moment. Mr. Toms suggested I come down here. He told me you'd received a cable from my home office.

C.F. Yes—yes—

MAJOR. He was rather upset because his name wasn't mentioned.

C.F. Yes, yes—

MAJOR. I called my home office, and they assure me they never sent such a cable.

C.F. What?

LARRY. That's what! It was a phony.

RODNEY (*who has been trying to attract attention for some time*). Major!

MAJOR. Well! Aren't you— Why, how do you do. I thought I recognized you. Met you with your brother. By the way, I saw him a few weeks ago just before I sailed. Particularly asked me to look you up.

RODNEY. Is my name English Jack? Am I a ship's gambler? Have I served sentences for bigamy?

MAJOR. Good Gad, no!

RODNEY. Will you vouch for me?

MAJOR (*a bore of bores*). Vouch for Puffy Bevan? Delighted! His brother—splendid chap— I met him first in India—he's a captain in the Coldstream Guards. His father is Lord Severingham. His sister is Lady Beasley—lectures, I believe. Now, let me see—

LAW (*interrupting*). Did you say—Lord Severingham?

MAJOR. Yes.

BENSON. I beg your pardon, sir—*his* father? (*He indicates* RODNEY.)

MAJOR. Yes. (BENSON *shakes his head in wonder.*)

SUSIE. Is your father a lord?

RODNEY. It doesn't matter, does it?

SUSIE. If you don't care, I don't care.

MAJOR. If I can be of any further service—

RODNEY. No. I think we'll sail along beautifully now. Thanks.

MAJOR. Good afternoon. (*Shakes hands with* RODNEY.)

C.F. Who sent that cable? That's all I want to know! Who sent that cable! (MAJOR *and* LARRY *exit.*) Who perpetrated this hoax? Who's responsible for this outrage? By Gad, I'll find out. (*Exits.*)

RODNEY (*turns to* SUSIE). Shall we go?

SUSIE. Good-bye, boys. Take care of yourselves.

LAW (*bows; bitterly*). Thank you, milady.

SUSIE. Don't drink too much.

LAW. Thank you, milady.

SUSIE. You were awful good to me. Yes, they were, Rodney. They were awful good to me sometimes.

RODNEY. In that case, I don't mind shaking hands with you. (*Starts toward* LAW.)

LAW (*quickly*). Don't shake hands. Just go. Dissolve—*slow fade-out!*

BENSON (*pantomiming*). Shimmer away!

RODNEY. Eh? (*Shrugs.*) Well—come, Susie.

SUSIE (*waving a delicate little hand*). Good-bye, boys. (*Pause. They exit in silence.*)

LAW (*tense*). I wonder what C.F.'s up to?

BENSON (*struck all of a heap*). The hell with that. Look at it—it checks! Cinderella—Prince Charming—Boy meets girl. . . . Boy loses girl. . . . Boy gets girl! Where's your damned realism now? (C.F. *enters. He looks grimly at the boys.*)

C.F. (*firmly*). Well—it's a good thing you boys are not mixed up in this! (*He goes to desk.*)

BENSON (*slowly*). What?

LAW (*slowly*). What happened, C.F.?

C.F. I don't understand it at all. The cable was sent from London all right. But B.K. should have known it was a fake. It was sent collect. (*He picks up phone.*)

LAW. Jascha always sends collect.

C.F. Huh? (*Into phone.*) Miss Crews, get hold of the Burnett baby immediately. . . . Who? . . . the *what* is here? (*Puzzled. The answer comes in the clarion call of the trumpets, blaring their gay, lilting notes through the windows. Ta-ra-ta-ta-ta-ta-tata-tata-tata! So much pleasanter than a factory whistle, don't you think?*)

CURTAIN

The Women

BY CLARE BOOTHE

To BUFF COBB *with Love*

THE WOMEN

Produced by Max Gordon at the Ethel Barrymore Theatre, New York City, December 26, 1936, with the following cast:

(IN ORDER OF THEIR APPEARANCE)

JANE	Anne Teeman	HEAD SALESWOMAN	Lucille Fenton
SYLVIA (Mrs. Howard Fowler)	Ilka Chase	FIRST MODEL	Beryl Wallace
NANCY BLAKE	Jane Seymour	THIRD SALESWOMAN	Martina Thomas
PEGGY (Mrs. John Day)	Adrienne Marden	CRYSTAL ALLEN	Betty Lawford
EDITH (Mrs. Phelps Potter)	Phyllis Povah	A FITTER	Joy Hathaway
MARY (Mrs. Stephen Haines)	Margalo Gillmore	SECOND MODEL	Beatrice Cole
MRS. WAGSTAFF	Ethel Jackson	PRINCESS TAMARA	Arlene Francis
OLGA	Ruth Hammond	EXERCISE INSTRUCTRESS	Anne Hunter
FIRST HAIRDRESSER	Mary Stuart	MAGGIE	Mary Cecil
SECOND HAIRDRESSER	Jane Moore	MISS WATTS	Virgilia Chew
PEDICURIST	Ann Watson	MISS TRIMMERBACK	Mary Murray
EUPHIE	Eloise Bennett	A NURSE	Lucille Fenton
MISS FORDYCE	Eileen Burns	LUCY	Marjorie Main
LITTLE MARY	Charita Bauer	COUNTESS DE LAGE	Margaret Douglas
MRS. MOREHEAD	Jessie Busley	MIRIAM AARONS	Audrey Christie
FIRST SALESWOMAN	Doris Day	HELENE	Arlene Francis
SECOND SALESWOMAN	Jean Rodney	SADIE	Marjorie Wood
		CIGARETTE GIRL	Lillian Norton

Directed by ROBERT B. SINCLAIR   Settings designed by JO MIELZINER
Costumes supervised by JOHN HAMBLETON

SYNOPSIS OF SCENES

ACT ONE

Scene 1. Mary Haines' living room. A winter afternoon.
Scene 2. A hairdresser's. An afternoon, a few days later.
Scene 3. Mary's boudoir, an hour later.
Scene 4. A fitting room. An afternoon, two months later.

ACT TWO

Scene 1. An exercise room, two weeks later.
Scene 2. Mary's kitchen, midnight, a few days later.
Scene 3. Mary's living room, a month later.
Scene 4. A hospital room, a month later.
Scene 5. A Reno hotel room, a few weeks later.

ACT THREE

Scene 1. Crystal's bathroom, early evening, two years later.
Scene 2. Mary's bedroom, eleven-thirty, the same night.
Scene 3. The Powder Room at the Casino Roof, near midnight, the same night.

THE WOMEN

ACT ONE

SCENE I

Mary Haines' living room. Today, Park Avenue living rooms are decorated with a signifi-
cant indifference to the fact that ours is still a bi-sexual society. Period peacock alleys,
crystal-hung prima-donna roosts, they reflect the good taste of their mistresses in everything
but a consideration of the master's pardonable right to fit in his own home decor. Mary
Haines' living room is not like that. It would be thought a comfortable room by a man.
This, without sacrificing its own subtle, feminine charm. Above the fireplace, there is
a charming portrait of Mary's children—a girl of 11, a boy of 5 or 6. Right, a door to the
living quarters. Left, another to the hall. Center, a sofa, armchair, tea-table group; and
in the good light from the window, a bridge-table group.

As the curtain rises, JANE, *a pretty, and quite correct little Irish-American maid, is*
arranging the tea-table. FOUR WOMEN *are playing bridge in a smoking-car cloud of smoke.*
They are:

NANCY, *who is sharp, but not acid; sleek but not smart; a worldly and yet virginal 35.*
And her partner—

PEGGY, *who is pretty, sweet, 25.* PEGGY's *character has not, will never quite "jell." And—*
SYLVIA, *who is glassy, elegant, feline, 34. And her partner—*

EDITH, *who is a sloppy, expensively dressed (currently, by Lane Bryant) matron of*
33 or 34. Indifferent to everything but self, EDITH *is incapable of either deliberate malicious-*
ness or spontaneous generosity.

SYLVIA. So I said to Howard, "What do you expect me to do? Stay home and darn your socks? What do we all have money for? Why do we keep servants?"

NANCY. You don't keep them long, God knows— (*Placing the pack of cards.*) Yours, Peggy.

PEGGY. Isn't it Mrs. Potter's? I opened with four spades. (SYLVIA *firmly places the pack before* PEGGY. PEGGY *wrong again, deals.*)

SYLVIA. Second hand, you did. And went down a thousand. (*Patronizingly.*) Peggy, my pet, you can't afford it.

PEGGY. I can too, Sylvia. I'm not a pauper.

SYLVIA. If your bridge doesn't improve, you soon will be.

NANCY. Oh, shut up, Sylvia. She's only playing till Mary comes down.

SYLVIA (*querulously*). Jane, what's Mrs. Haines doing up there?

JANE (*reproachfully*). It's that lingerie woman *you* sent her, Mrs. Fowler.

SYLVIA. I didn't expect Mrs. Haines to buy anything. I was just trying to get rid of the creature. (JANE *exits.*) Peggy, bid.

PEGGY. Oh, mine? By.

SYLVIA (*looking at* PEGGY). She won't concentrate.

NANCY. She's in love, bless her. After the child's been married as long as you girls, she may be able to concentrate on vital matters like bridge.

SYLVIA (*bored*). Another lecture on the Modern Woman?

NANCY. At the drop of a hat. By.

SYLVIA. I consider myself a perfectly good wife. I've sacrificed a lot for Howard Fowler—two spades. I devote as much time to my children as any of my friends.

NANCY. Except Mary.

SYLVIA. Oh, Mary, of course. Mary is an exception to all of us.

NANCY. Quite right. (*They are waiting for* PEGGY *again*). Peggy?

PEGGY (*uncertainly*). Two no trumps? (EDITH *rises suddenly. Plainly, she feels squeamish.*)

SYLVIA (*wearily*). Edith, not *again*?

EDITH. I shouldn't have eaten that alligator pear. Morning sickness! I heave the whole darn day. This is positively the last time I go through this lousy business for any man! Four spades. If men had to bear babies, there'd never be—

NANCY. —more than one child in a family. And he'd be a boy. By. (EDITH *sinks on the edge of her chair, lays down her cards.*)

PEGGY. I wish *I* were having a baby. We can't afford one now.

SYLVIA. And you'll never be able to, until you know Culbertson. (*Arranging* EDITH'S *cards.*) Honestly, Edith! Why didn't you show a slam?

EDITH (*rising hurriedly*). Oh, I *have* got to unswallow. Wait till you've had three, Peggy. You'd wish you'd never gotten past the bees and flowers. (*Exits precipitously.*)

NANCY (*disgusted*). Poor, frightened, bewildered madonna!

SYLVIA. I'm devoted to Edith Potter. But she does gets me down. You'd think she had a hard time. Dr. Briggs says she's like shelling peas. She ought to go through what *I* went through. Nobody *knows!*

NANCY. No clubs, partner?

SYLVIA. So when Cynthia came, I had a Cæsarian. You should see my stomach— It's a slam!

NANCY. Are you sure?

SYLVIA. Got the king, Peggy? (PEGGY *obligingly plays the king.*) Thanks, dear, it's a slam. And the rubber. (*Rises, lights a fresh cigarette, goes to armchair and perches.*) But I've kept my figure. I must say, I don't blame Phelps Potter for playing around.

PEGGY. Oh, does her husband . . . ?

SYLVIA. Oh, Phelps has made passes at all us girls. I do think it's bad taste for a man to try to make his wife's friends, *especially* when he's bald and fat. I told him once, "Phelps Potter," I said, "the next time you grab at me, I'm going straight to Edith."

NANCY. And did you?

SYLVIA. Certainly not. I wouldn't say anything to hurt Edith for the world. Well, you can't blame the men. But I'll say one thing

for Edith. She's not as dumb as *some* of my friends. She's on to her husband.

PEGGY (*bravely*). Do you think *he* is on to her?

SYLVIA. What do you mean?

PEGGY. If he could only hear her talk about him!

SYLVIA. Listen, Peggy, do we know how men talk about us when we're not around?

NANCY. I've heard rumors.

SYLVIA. Exactly. Peggy, you haven't been married long enough to form a private opinion of your husband.

PEGGY. Well, if I had one, I'd keep it to myself. Do you think I'd tell anybody in the world about the quarrels John and I have over money? I'd be too proud! (*Enter* EDITH. *Goes to tea-table, and gathers a handful of sandwiches.*)

SYLVIA. All over, dear?

EDITH. Oh, that was a false alarm. What happened?

SYLVIA. Only a slam, dear. You do underbid.

EDITH. I'll bet you had me on the pan.

SYLVIA. I never say behind my friends' backs what I won't say to their faces. I said you ought to diet.

EDITH. There's no use dieting in my condition. I've got to wait until I can begin from scratch. Besides, I've got the most wonderful cook. She was with Mary. She said Mary let her go because she was too extravagant. I think this cook Mary has is too, too homey. (*Examines sandwich.*) Water cress. I'd just as soon eat my way across a front lawn.

SYLVIA. I think Mary's gone off terribly this winter. Have you noticed those deep lines, here? (*Draws her finger around her mouth.*)

NANCY. Smiling lines. Tragic, aren't they?

SYLVIA. Perhaps they *are.* Maybe a woman's headed for trouble when she begins to get too—smug.

NANCY. Smug? Don't you mean, happy?

PEGGY. Mr. Haines adores her so!

SYLVIA (*snickering and flashing* EDITH *a significant glance*). Yes, doesn't he?

NANCY (*coldly*). You just can't bear it, Sylvia, can you?

SYLVIA. Bear what?

NANCY. Mary's happiness. It gets you down.

SYLVIA. Nancy Blake, if there's one thing I can say for myself, I've never been jealous of another woman. Why should I be jealous of Mary?

NANCY. Because she's contented. Contented to be what she is.

SYLVIA. Which is what?

NANCY. A woman.

EDITH. And what, in the name of my revolting condition, are we?

NANCY. Females.

SYLVIA. Really. And what are you, pet?

NANCY. What nature abhors, I'm—a virgin —a frozen asset.

EDITH. I wish I were a virgin again. The only fun I ever had was holding out on Phelps. Nancy, you ought to thank God every night you don't have to make sacrifices for some man.

PEGGY. I wish I could make a little money, writing the way you do, Miss Blake.

NANCY. If you wrote the way I do, that's just what you'd make.

SYLVIA. You're not exactly a popular author, are you, dear?

NANCY. Not with you. Well, good news, Sylvia. My book is finished and once again I'm about to leave your midst.

PEGGY. Oh, I wish we could afford to travel. Where do you go this time, Miss Blake?

NANCY. Africa, shooting.

SYLVIA. Well, darling, I don't blame you. I'd rather face a tiger any day than the sort of things the critics said about your last book. (*Enter* MARY. *She is a lovely woman in her middle thirties. She is what most of us think our happily married daughters are like. She is carrying several white boxes.*)

MARY. Sorry, girls. (*Teasing.*) Sylvia, must you always send me woe-begone creatures like that lingerie woman? It's been a very expensive half hour for me.

PEGGY (*looking at* SYLVIA). For me too, Mrs. Haines.

MARY (*laughing*). Nonsense, Peggy, you were playing for me. Here. (*Hands* PEGGY *a box.*) Don't open it now. It's a bed-jacket. Or a tea cozy. Or something padded. I wouldn't know. I was crying so hard.

SYLVIA. You didn't believe that woman's sob story?

MARY. Of course I did. (*She really didn't.*) Anyway, she's a lot worse off than you and I. (*Putting down another box.*) Edith, wee garments—

EDITH. Darling, how sweet! (*It comes over her again.*) Oh, my God! I'm sick as a cat. (*Sits.*)

SYLVIA. It's a girl. Girls always make you sicker.

NANCY. Even before they're born?

EDITH. I don't care what it is. I've lost everything including my curiosity. Why did God make it take nine months?

NANCY (*helpfully*). It takes an elephant seven years.

EDITH. I wish I were an elephant. I'll look like one anyway before I'm finished. And it would be heaven not to worry for seven years.

MARY (*laughing*). Oh, Edith, it is rather trying. But when it's all over, isn't it the grandest thing in the world to have them?

EDITH. Well, I'd love mine just as much if they came out of cabbages.

NANCY. And I dare say your husband would hardly notice the difference.

JANE (*entering with tea-kettle*). Ma'am, Mr. Haines would like to speak to you on the phone.

MARY. Oh, I can feel what it is in my bones, Jane. (*To the others.*) Stephen's going to be kept at the office again tonight. (*Exits.*)

SYLVIA. Give him my love, pet.

MARY (*offstage*). I will.

SYLVIA (*she never lets anything pass*). Nancy, you couldn't be more wrong about me and Mary.

NANCY. Still rankling?

SYLVIA. Jealous? As a matter of fact, I'm sorry for her.

NANCY. Oh-ho? Why?

SYLVIA (*mysteriously*). Well, for all *we* know she may be living in a fool's paradise with Stephen.

NANCY. Let's check that one for a moment, Sylvia. Jane, are the children in?

JANE. Yes, Miss. Just back from the Park. (EDITH *rises*—SYLVIA, *in pantomime, signals her not to leave room. This is not lost on* NANCY. *For a moment she hesitates at the door.*)

PEGGY. Oh, I'd love to see Mrs. Haines' little girl, Miss Blake—

NANCY (*following* PEGGY). Come along, child. Anyway, it's our turn to go on the pan. But we don't have to worry. You've got a poor man. I've got no man at all. (*They exit.*)

EDITH (*goes to tea-table—pours two cups.* JANE *empties ash-trays*). This is positively the last time I play bridge with Nancy. She never misses a chance to get in a dig. What has a creature like her got but her friends? (JANE *exits, closing door, left.* SYLVIA *stealthily closes door, right.*) The way she kept at you about Mary made me so nervous, I thought I'd scream. And in my condition—

SYLVIA. Edith, I've got to tell you! I'll burst if I wait!

EDITH. I *knew* you had something! (*She brings her well-laden plate and tea-cup and settles herself happily beside* SYLVIA *on the sofa.*)

SYLVIA. You'll die!

EDITH. Mary?

SYLVIA. No, Stephen. Guess!

EDITH. You couldn't mean . . . ?

SYLVIA (*nodding*). Stephen Haines is cheating on Mary!

EDITH. I don't believe you; is it true?

SYLVIA. Wait till you hear. (*Now she is into it.*) You know I go to Michael's for my hair. You ought to go, pet. I despise whoever does yours. Well, there's the most wonderful new manicurist there. (*Shows her scarlet nails.*) Isn't that divine? Jungle Red—

EDITH. Simply divine. Go on.

SELVIA. It all came out in the most extraordinary way, this morning. I tried to get you on the phone—

EDITH. I was in the tub. Go on.

SYLVIA. This manicurist, she's marvelous, was doing my nails. I was looking through *Vogue,* the one with Mary in the Beaux Arts Ball costume—

EDITH. —in that white wig that flattered her so much?

SYLVIA (*nodding*). Well, this manicurist: "Oh, Mrs. Fowler," she said, "is that that Mrs. Haines who's so awfully rich?"

EDITH. Funny how people like that think people like us are awfully rich.

SYLVIA. I forget what she said next. You know how those creatures are, babble, babble, babble, babble, and never let up for a minute! When suddenly she said: "I know the girl who's being *kept* by Mr. Haines!"

EDITH. No!

SYLVIA. I swear!

EDITH (*thrilled*). Someone *we* know?

SYLVIA. No! That's what's so awful about it. She's a friend of this manicurist. Oh, it wouldn't be so bad if Stephen had picked someone in his own class. But a blonde floosie!

EDITH. But how did Stephen ever meet a girl like that?

SYLVIA. How do men ever meet girls like that? That's what they live for, the rats!

EDITH. But—

SYLVIA. I can't go into all the details, now. They're utterly fantastic—

EDITH. You suppose Mary knows?

SYLVIA. Mary's the kind who couldn't help showing it.

EDITH (*nodding, her mouth full of her third cake*). No self-control. Well, she's bound to find out. If a woman's got any instincts, she feels when her husband's off the reservation. I know *I would.*

SYLVIA. Of course you do, darling. Not Mary— (*Rises, and walks about the room, wrestling with* MARY'S *sad problem.*) If only there were some way to *warn* her!

EDITH (*horrified, following her*). Sylvia! You're not going to tell her?

SYLVIA. Certainly not. I'd *die* before I'd be the one to hurt her like that!

EDITH. Couldn't someone shut that manicurist up?

SYLVIA. A good story like that? A lot those girls care whose life they ruin.

EDITH. *Isn't* it a dirty trick?

SYLVIA. Isn't it *foul?* It's not as though only Mary's friends knew. We could keep our mouths shut.

EDITH. I know plenty that I never *breathe* about my friends' husbands!

SYLVIA. So do I? (*They exchange a sudden glance of sharp suspicion.*) Anyway, the whole thing's disgustingly unfair to Mary. I feel like a disloyal skunk, just knowing abut it—

EDITH. I adore her—

SYLVIA. I *worship* her. She's my dearest friend in all the world— (*Voices, off-stage. They sit down at the card-table and begin to play solitaire hastily. Enter* NANCY *and* PEGGY.)

NANCY. Well, Sylvia, feeling better?

SYLVIA (*innocently*). Meaning what?

NANCY. Must've been choice. You both look so *relaxed.*

SYLVIA. Nancy, were you listening at that door?

PEGGY. Oh, Mrs. Fowler, we were in the nursery. (MARY *enters.*)

SYLVIA (*quickly*). Well, darling, how is Stephen, the old dear? And did you give him my love?

MARY. I did. Stephen's not so well, Sylvia.

SYLVIA. Oh? What's the trouble?

MARY. Nervous indigestion. That's why I have such a plain cook now.

EDITH. Phelps has had indigestion for years. You should hear that man rumble in the night. Like a truck on cobblestones.

SYLVIA. There's nothing—worrying Stephen?

MARY. Oh, no, he's just been working late. He's not coming home tonight. Oh, I wish— (*Abruptly, with an indulgent laugh.*) Well, man's love is of man's life a thing apart, 'tis woman's whole—et cetera.

SYLVIA. Are you sure it's *work*, darling, and not a beautiful blonde?

MARY. Stephen? (*Laughing, and perhaps a little smugly, too.*) Oh, Sylvia.

EDITH (*afraid that* SYLVIA *will go too far*). Sylvia, let's play!

SYLVIA. Stephen's a very attractive man.

MARY. Isn't he? I can't imagine why he hasn't deserted me for some glamorous creature long ago.

NANCY (*alarmed*). Mary, you *do* sound smug.

MARY. Oh, let me be, Nancy. How can you be too sure of what you believe in most?

SYLVIA. I wouldn't be sure of the Apostle Paul. I always tell Howard, "If you ever manage to make a fool of me, I'll deserve what I get."

NANCY. You certainly will. (*Faces* SYLVIA *squarely.*) Now, Sylvia, let's have it.

SYLVIA. Have what?

NANCY. Just what did you mean when you said Mary was living in a fool's paradise?

MARY. What?

SYLVIA (*angrily*). Nancy, don't be absurd. (*A pause. Then, wriggling out of it.*) Oh, Mary, I was just trying to make a typical Nancy Blake wisecrack about marriage. I said, "A woman's paradise is always a fool's paradise!"

MARY. That's not bad, is it, Nancy? Well, Sylvia, whatever I'm living in, I like it. Nancy, cut.

SYLVIA (SYLVIA *examines her nails minutely, suddenly shows them to* MARY). Mary, how do you like that?

NANCY (*not looking*). Too, too adorable.

SYLVIA. You can't imagine how it stays on. I get it at Michael's—you ought to go, Mary!

EDITH (*protestingly*). Oh, Sylvia—

SYLVIA. A wonderful new manicurist. Olga's her name. She's marvelous.

EDITH. Will you cut, Sylvia?

SYLVIA. Look, Jungle Red.

NANCY. Looks as if you'd been tearing at somebody's throat.

SYLVIA. I'll be damned, Nancy, if I'll let you ride me any more!

MARY. Now, Sylvia, Nancy's just being clever, too.

SYLVIA. She takes a crack at everything about me. Even my nails!

MARY (*laughing*). Well, I like it. I really do! It's new and smart. (*Pats her hand.*) Michael's, Olga, Jungle Red? I'll remember that. (*Cuts cards.*) You and I, Sylvia. I feel lucky today.

SYLVIA (*with a sweet, pitying smile.*) Do you, darling? Well, you know what they say, "Lucky in cards"—

CURTAIN

SCENE II

An afternoon, a few days later. A hairdressing booth in Michael's. An elegantly functional cubby-hole. Right, a recessed mirror in the wall. Left, from the high partition pole, a curtain to the floor. The rear wall is a plain partition. Center, a swivel hairdressing chair. Above it, from an aluminum tree, the hanging thicket of a permanent-wave machine. In the wall, gadgets for curling irons, electric outlets which connect with wires to the drying machines, the hand drier, the manicurists' table-light, stools for the pedicurist, the manicurist, OLGA.*
As the curtain rises, the booth is, to put it mildly, full.*
MRS. WAGSTAFF, *a fat, elderly woman is in the chair, undergoing the punishment of a permanent. Wires and clamps, Medusa-like, rise from her head, to the cap of the machine.*
OLGA, *at her right, is doing her nails. Her fat bare feet rest in the lap of the* PEDICURIST. *The* FIRST HAIRDRESSER *cools her steaming locks with a hand-drier. The* SECOND HAIRDRESSER, *watch in hand, fiddles with the wires, times the operation. When the machine is working, a small red, light glows among the wires.*
MRS. WAGSTAFF, *apparently inured to public execution, smokes, reads a magazine on her lap, occasionally nibbles a sandwich which the* MANICURIST *passes her from a tray near her instruments. The drier, whenever it is on, makes a loud noise, drowning out voices, which must be harshly raised above it. Now the drier is on, the voices loud.*

MRS. WAGSTAFF. It's burning my neck!

SECOND HAIRDRESSER. Be brave! One minute more!

MRS. WAGSTAFF (*in pain*). O-o-oo!

FIRST HAIRDRESSER. It's going to be so worth it, Mrs. Wagstaff.

MRS. WAGSTAFF. My ears!

SECOND HAIRDRESSER. Be brave!

MRS. WAGSTAFF. O-o-o-o! My nerves— Oo—my God! (*To* PEDICURIST) My sandwich— (OLGA *hands her sandwich.*)

SECOND HAIRDRESSER. Ten seconds. We must suffer to be beautiful. (*The curtain parts; A* FIGURE *in flowing white half-enters. It is, judging by the voice, a woman, but its face is completely obliterated by a mud-mask.*)

MUD-MASK. Oh, pardon—I thought I was in here. Why, hello, Mrs. Wagstaff. (*Coyly.*) Guess who I am? (*A second* FACE *appears over this intruder's shoulder. At first, it looks like another mud-mask. It's not. It's the* COLORED MAID, EUPHIE. *She clutches the shoulder of the mud-mask.*)

EUPHIE. Mustn't talk, ma'am. You'll crack yo'self. (*Exit* MUD-MASK *followed by* EUPHIE.)

MRS. WAGSTAFF. Who was it?

FIRST HAIRDRESSER. Mrs. Phipps— (*Switches off the drier. Now they all lower their voices to a normal pitch.*) There, dear, the agony's over. (*They take the permanent clamps off* MRS. WAGSTAFF's *hair. A drier is on in the next booth. A voice is heard off-stage, screaming above it.*)

VOICE. —so I feel awful. I ate a lobster at the opening of the Ritz— (*The drier goes off.*)

OLGA (*To* MRS. WAGSTAFF). Mrs. Mordie Barnes. She's been in the hospital. It wasn't ptomaine at all. It was a mis—

SECOND HAIRDRESSER. Olga! She'll hear you—

MRS. WAGSTAFF (*thoughtfully*). I think I'll have a mud-mask.

SECOND HAIRDRESSER (*calling outside*). Euphie! Tell the desk Mrs. Wagstaff's working in a mud!

MRS. WAGSTAFF (*enviously*). Mrs. Phipps has such a lovely skin.

FIRST HAIRDRESSER. Not lovelier than yours, Mrs. Wagstaff.

CHORUS (SECOND HAIRDRESSER, OLGA, PEDICURIST). Oh, yours is lovely! Why, not nearly as lovely! Lovelier than yours?

MRS. WAGSTAFF (*coyly*). I do think it's rather good for a woman my age.

FIRST HAIRDRESSER. You talk as if you were an old woman, dear.

MRS. WAGSTAFF (*lying*). I'm 42.

SECOND HAIRDRESSER. Mustn't tell anyone. You don't look a day over 35!

CHORUS (SECOND HAIRDRESSER, PEDICURIST, OLGA). Why, no one would believe it! Why, not a day! Oh, you don't look it!

SECOND HAIRDRESSER. —now you've gotten so much slimmer!

MRS. WAGSTAFF. I have slimmed down, haven't I?

CHORUS (PEDICURIST, OLGA, FIRST HAIRDRESSER). Oh, thin as a shadow! Why, terribly thin! Oh, just right, now!

MRS. WAGSTAFF (*admiring her nail polish*). That's lovely.

OLGA. Jungle Red. Everybody loves it. Do you know Mrs. Howard Fowler?

PEDICURIST (*rising, gathering up her things*). Don't put your stockings on yet, Mrs. Wagstaff, you'll smear your beautiful big toe— (*Exits.*)

OLGA. They say Mr. Fowler made a fortune in some stock. But one of the ladies Mrs. Fowler sent in was telling me Mr. Fowler does like to drink! Only the other day—

FIRST HAIRDRESSER (*sharply*). We're ready now, Mrs. Wagstaff. (*Gets* MRS. WAGSTAFF *up.*) We'll unwind you in the shampoo (*Calling.*) Euphie!

SECOND HAIRDRESSER (*taking* MRS. WAGSTAFF *to door*). This way, dear. How does your permanent feel? And it's going to look lovely, too— (SECOND HAIRDRESSER *herds* MRS. WAGSTAFF *out of the booth,* MRS. WAGSTAFF *walking on her heels, her toes still wadded with cotton. Enter* EUPHIE, *who, during the ensuing dialogue, cleans up the debris on the floor of the booth*).

OLGA. That old gasoline truck! Fifty-two if she's a day!

FIRST HAIRDRESSER. One more permanent and she won't have a hair left on her head.

OLGA. There's plenty on her upper lip.

EUPHIE. She sho' does shed, don't she?

OLGA. Any woman who's fool enough to marry a man ten years younger! Know what a client told me? Her husband's a pansy! (HAIRDRESSER *exits followed by* OLGA.)

SECOND HAIRDRESSER (*entering*). Ready?

EUPHIE. Yes, ma'am. (*The* SECOND HAIRDRESSER *holds back the curtain.*)

MARY (*off-stage*). So I woke up this morning and decided for no reason at all to change the way— (*She enters, followed by* NANCY.) I do my hair. (*Exit* EUPHIE.)

SECOND HAIRDRESSER. Mr. Michaels will be ten minutes, ma'am. Anyone in particular for your manicure?

MARY. Who does Mrs. Fowler's nails?

HAIRDRESSER. Olga. I'll see. (*Exits.*)

NANCY. God, I'd love to do Mrs. Fowler's nails, right down to the wrist, with a nice big buzz saw.

MARY. Sylvia's all right. She's a good friend underneath.

NANCY. Underneath what?

MARY. Nancy, you don't humor your friends enough.

NANCY. So that's the big idea coming here? You're humoring Sylvia?

MARY. Oh, you did hurt her. I had it all over again at lunch. (*She catches a glimpse of herself in the mirror.*) Nancy, am I getting old?

NANCY. Who put that in your head? Sylvia?

MARY. Tell me the truth.

NANCY. Beauty is in the eye of the beholder, and twaddle to that effect.

MARY. But it's such a scary feeling when you see those little wrinkles creeping in.

NANCY. Time's little mice.

MARY. And that first gleam of white in your hair. It's the way you'd feel about autumn if you knew there'd never be another spring—

NANCY (*abruptly*). There's only one tragedy for a woman.

MARY. Growing old?

NANCY. Losing her man.

MARY. That's why we're all so afraid of growing old.

NANCY. Are you afraid?

MARY. Well, I was very pretty when I was young. I never thought about it twice then. Now I know it's why Stephen loved me.

NANCY. Smart girl.

MARY. Now I think about it all the time.

NANCY. Love is not love which alters when it alteration finds. Shakespeare.

MARY. Well, he told me, on my birthday, I'd always look the same to him.

NANCY. Nice present. No jewels?

MARY. It rained that day. He brought me a bottle of perfume called "Summer Rain."

NANCY. How many ounces?

MARY. Nancy, you've never been in love.

NANCY. Says who?

MARY (*surprised*). Have you?

NANCY. Yes.

MARY. You never told me.

NANCY. You never asked— (*Wistfully.*) Neither did *he*. (OLGA *enters with fresh bowl of water.*) Here, innocent. (*Gives a book to* MARY.) The book my readers everywhere have been waiting for with such marked apathy.

MARY. "All the Dead Ladies"?

NANCY. Originally called, "From the Silence of the Womb." My publisher thought that would make too much noise.

MARY. What's it about? (OLGA *begins to file* MARY's *nails.*)

NANCY. Women I dislike: "Ladies"—

MARY. Oh, Nancy!

OLGA. Don't soak it yet. (*Taking* MARY's *hand out of the water.*)

NANCY. No good? Too bad. It's a parting shot. I'm off.

MARY. Off?

NANCY. Africa.

MARY. But not today?

NANCY. I knew if I told you you'd scurry around and do things. A party. Steamer baskets of sour fruit. Not nearly as sour as the witty cables your girl friends would send me— So don't move. No tears. For my sake —just soak it? Good-bye, Mary—

MARY. Good-bye, Nancy. I'll miss you.

NANCY. I doubt it. Practically nobody ever misses a clever woman. (*Exits.*)

OLGA. Funny, isn't she?

MARY. She's a darling.

OLGA (*filing* MARY's *nails*). She's a writer? How do those writers think up those plots? I guess the plot part's not so hard to think up as the end. I guess anybody's life'd make a interesting plot if it had a interesting end— Mrs. Fowler sent you in? (MARY, *absorbed in her book, nods.*) She's sent me three clients this week. Know Mrs. Herbert Parrish that was Mrs. Malcolm Leeds? Well, Mrs. Parrish was telling me herself about her divorce. Seems Mr. Parrish came home one night with lipstick on his undershirt. Said he always explained everything before. But *that* was something he just wasn't going to try to explain. Know Mrs. Potter? She's awful pregnant—

MARY (*she wants to read*). I know.

OLGA. Soak it, please. (*Puts* MARY's *hand in water. Begins on other hand.*) Know Mrs. Stephen Haines?

MARY. What? Why, yes, I—

OLGA. I guess Mrs. Fowler's told you about that! Mrs. Fowler feels awfully sorry for her.

MARY (*laughing*). Oh, she does! Well, I don't. I—

OLGA. You would if you knew this girl.

MARY. What girl?

OLGA. This Crystal Allen.

MARY. Crystal Allen?

OLGA. Yes, you know. The girl who's living with Mr. Haines. (MARY *starts violently.*) Don't you like the file? Mrs. Potter says it sets her unborn child's teeth on edge.

MARY (*indignant*). Whoever told you such a thing?

OLGA. Oh, I thought you knew. Didn't Mrs. Fowler—?

MARY. No—

OLGA. Then you will be interested. You see, Crystal Allen is a friend of mine. She's really a terrible man-trap. Soak it, please. (MARY, *dazed, puts her hand in the dish.*) She's behind the perfume counter at Saks'. So was I before I got fi—left. That's how she met him.

MARY. Stephen Haines?

OLGA. Yeah. It was a couple a months ago. Us girls wasn't busy. It was an awful rainy day, I remember. So this gentleman walks up to the counter. He was the serious type, nice-looking, but kind of thin on top. Well, Crystal nabs him. "I want some perfume," he says. "May I awsk what type of woman for?" Crystal says, very Ritzy. That didn't mean a thing. She was going to sell him Summer Rain, our feature anyway. "Is she young?" Crystal says. "No," he says, sort of embarrassed. "Is she the glamorous type?" Crystal says. "No, thank God," he says. "Thank God?" Crystal says and bats her eyes. She's got those eyes which run up and down a man like a searchlight. Well, she puts perfume on her palm and in the crook of her arm for him to smell. So he got to smelling around and I guess he liked it. Because we heard him tell her his name, which one of the girls recognized from Cholly Knickerbocker's column—Gee, you're nervous—Well, it was after that I left. I wouldn't of thought no more about it. But a couple of weeks ago I stopped by where Crystal lives to say hello. And the landlady says she'd moved to the kind of house where she could entertain her gentleman friend— "What gentleman friend?" I says. "Why, that Mr. Haines that she's had up in her room all hours of the night," the landlady says—Did I hurt? (MARY *draws her hand away.*) One coat, or two? (*Picks up a red bottle.*)

MARY. None. (*Rises and goes to the chair, where she has left her purse.*)

OLGA. But I thought that's what you came for? All Mrs. Fowler's friends—

MARY. I think I've gotten what all Mrs. Fowler's friends came for. (*Puts coin on the table.*)

OLGA (*picks up coin*). Oh, thanks—Well, good-bye. I'll tell her you were in, Mrs. —?

MARY. Mrs. Stephen Haines.

OLGA. Mrs. —? Oh, gee, gee! Gee, Mrs. Haines—I'm sorry! Oh, isn't there something I can do?

MARY. Stop telling that story!

OLGA. Oh, sure, sure, I will!

MARY. And please, don't tell anyone— (*Her voice breaks*) that you told it to *me*—

OLGA. Oh, I won't, gee, I promise! Gee, that would be kind of humiliating for you! (*Defensively.*) But in a way, Mrs. Haines, I'm kinda *glad* you know. Crystal's a terrible girl—I mean, she's terribly clever. And she's terribly pretty, Mrs. Haines—I mean, if I was you I wouldn't waste no time getting Mr. Haines away from her— (MARY *turns abruptly away.*) I mean, now you *know*, Mrs. Haines!

(OLGA *eyes the coin in her hand distastefully, suddenly puts it down on the table and exits.* MARY, *alone, stares blankly in the mirror, then suddenly focusing on her image, leans forward, searching her face between her trembling hands. A drier goes on in the next booth. A shrill voice rises above its drone.*)

VOICE. —Not too hot! My sinus! So *she* said: "I wouldn't want anybody in the world to know," and *I* said: "My dear, you know you can trust *me*!"

CURTAIN

SCENE III

An hour later. MARY's *boudoir. Charming, of course. A door to bedroom, right. A door to the hall, left. A chaise-longue; next to it, a table with books, flowers, a telephone. A dressing table.*

As the curtain rises, MARY *is discovered on the chaise-longue, trying to read.* JANE *enters from the hall. She is upset about something. She keeps daubing at her eyes.*

MARY. Tea, Jane?

JANE. It's coming, ma'am.

MARY. My mother will be here in a few minutes. A cup for her.

JANE. Yes, ma'am. (*Sniffling.*) Ma'am—

MARY. And tell Cook please, dinner on time. We're going to the theatre. Mr. Haines likes to be there for the curtain. I'll wear my old black, Jane.

JANE (*looking nervously at the door behind her*). Yes, ma'am.

MARY. No, I'll wear my new blue, Jane.

JANE. Ma'am, it's Cook. She wants to see you. (*Defensively.*) It's about *me*. She says I—

MARY. Later, Jane.

JANE. Don't you believe a word she says, ma'am. It's all his fault.

MARY (*aware of* JANE's *distress for the first time*). Whose fault?

JANE. Her husband's. Ford's.

MARY (*surprised*). What's the matter with Ford? He's a very good butler.

JANE. Oh, he does his work, ma'am. But you don't know how he is in the pantry. Always kidding around with us girls. He don't mean any harm, but Cook— (*Enter* COOK *abruptly with* MARY's *tea tray. She is a fat, kind woman, with a strong Scandinavian accent. At the moment she is very mad.*)

COOK. *Afternoon, ma'am.* (*Glaring at* JANE.) I'd like to talk to you alone, ma'am.

JANE. I told you, it isn't my fault.

COOK. You led him on!

JANE. I didn't. (*Bursting into tears.*) I've been with Mrs. Haines seven years. She knows I never make trouble downstairs. (*Exits to hall.*)

MARY. Yes, Ingrid?

COOK. Ma'am, you're the nicest I ever had. But I go. I got to get Ford away from that bad girl.

MARY (*very firmly*). Jane is not a bad girl.

COOK (*bursts into tears*). Oh, course she ain't. He was always like that! Sometimes I could die, for the shame!

MARY (*kindly*). I'll send him away. You can stay.

COOK (*more soberly*). No, I don't do that, ma'am.

MARY. I'll give you a hundred dollars. That's more than half of what you make together.

COOK. Thank you, ma'am. We both go.

MARY. Is that sensible?

COOK. No. It's plain dumb.

MARY. Then why?

COOK (*she pauses, rocking from foot to foot*). I guess nobody understand. Sure it was no good to marry him. My mother told me he's a lady-killer. Don't marry them, she said. His wife is the lady he kills. Oh, he's terrible. But except for women he's a good man. He always says, "Ingrid, you take the money. You manage good." Oh, he don't want nobody but me for his wife! That's an awful big thing, ma'am.

MARY. Is that the thing that really matters?

COOK. With women like us, yes, ma'am— You give us references? (MARY *nods*.) And don't say nothing about his ways?

MARY. I won't.

COOK (*moving to the door*). Black bean soup, a fricassee, fried sweets and apple pie for dinner, ma'am—(*She opens the door.* JANE *has been eavesdropping*.)

COOK (*in a low, fierce voice*). Slut! (*Exit* COOK.)

JANE (*entering with extra cup on tray*). Did you hear what she called me, Mrs. Haines?

MARY. Please, Jane.

JANE (*cheerfully*). I'd rather be that any day than have some man make a fool of me! (*Enter* MISS FORDYCE. *She is a raw-boned, capable English spinster of 32.*)

MISS FORDYCE. May I see you, Mrs. Haines?

MARY. Of course, Miss Fordyce.

MISS FORDYCE. It's about little Mary—Really, Mrs. Haines, you'll have to talk to your child. She's just smacked her little brother, hard. Pure temper.

MARY. What did little Stevie do to her, Miss Fordyce?

MISS FORDYCE. Well, you see, it happened while I was down getting my tea. When I came up, she'd had such a tantrum, she'd made herself ill. She positively refuses to discuss the incident with me. But I'm quite sure the dear boy hadn't done a thing.

MARY. You're very apt to take the boy's side, Miss Fordyce.

MISS FORDYCE. Not at all. But in England, Mrs. Haines, our girls are not so wretchedly spoiled. After all, this *is* a man's world. The sooner our girls are taught to accept the fact *graciously*—

MARY (*gently*). Send her in to me, Miss Fordyce. (*Exit* MISS FORDYCE.) Oh, Jane, I don't understand it. Miss Fordyce really prefers Mary, but she insists we all make a little god of Stevie. (*Exits to bedroom, leaving the door open.*)

JANE. Them English ones always hold out for the boys. But they say since the War, ma'am, there's six women over there to every man. Competition is something fierce! Over here, you can treat the men the way they deserve—Men aren't so scarce. (*Enter* LITTLE MARY. *She is a broad-browed, thoughtful, healthy, little girl, physically well developed for her age.*)

LITTLE MARY. Where's Mother?

JANE. You're going to catch it. Smacking your little brother. (*Mimicking* MISS FORDYCE.) Such a dear, sweet little lad—shame. (LITTLE MARY *does not answer*.) I'll bet you wish you were Mother's girl, instead of Daddy's girl today, don't you? (LITTLE MARY *doesn't answer*.) What's the matter, the cat got your tongue? (*Enter* MARY, *wearing a negligée*.)

MARY. Hello, darling—Aren't you going to kiss me? (LITTLE MARY *doesn't move*.) What red eyes!

LITTLE MARY. I was mad. I threw up. When you throw up, doesn't it make you cry?

MARY (*smiling*). Stevie tease you? (LITTLE MARY, *embarrassed, looks at* JANE. JANE *snickers, takes the hint and goes out.*) Well, darling?

L'TTLE MARY. Mother, I don't know how to begin.

MARY (*sitting on the chaise-longue, and putting out her hand*). Come here. (LITTLE MARY *doesn't budge.*) Would you rather wait until tonight and tell Dad?

LITTLE MARY (*horrified*). Oh, Mother, I couldn't tell him! (*Fiercely.*) And I'd be killed to death before I'd tell skinny old Miss Fordyce—

MARY. That's not the way for my dear little girl to talk.

LITTLE MARY (*setting her jaw*). I don't want to be a dear little girl. (*She suddenly rushes to her mother's outstretched arms in tears.*) Oh, Mother dear, Mother dear!

MARY. Baby, what?

LITTLE MARY. What brother said!

MARY. What did he say, the wretched boy?

LITTLE MARY (*disentangling herself*). He said I had bumps!

MARY. Bumps? You don't mean mumps?

LITTLE MARY. No, bumps. He said I was covered with disgusting bumps!

MARY (*alarmed*). Mary, *where?*

LITTLE MARY (*touching her hips and breasts with delicate, ashamed finger tips*). Here and *here!*

MARY. Oh— (*Controlling her relieved laughter, and drawing her daughter to her side.*) Of course you have bumps, darling. Very pretty little bumps. And you have them because—you're a little girl.

LITTLE MARY (*wailing*). But, Mother dear, I don't want to be a little girl. I hate girls! They're so silly, and they tattle, tattle—

MARY. Not really, Mary.

LITTLE MARY. Yes, Mother, I know. Oh, Mother, what *fun* is there to be a lady? What can a lady do?

MARY (*cheerfully*). These days, darling, ladies do all the things men do. They fly aeroplanes across the ocean, they go into politics and business—

LITTLE MARY. You don't, Mother.

MARY. Perhaps I'm happier doing just what I do.

LITTLE MARY. What do you do, Mother?

MARY. Take care of you and Stevie and Dad.

LITTLE MARY. You don't, Mother. Miss Fordyce and the servants do.

MARY (*teasing*). I see. I'm not needed around here.

LITTLE MARY (*hugging her*). Oh, Mother, I don't mean that. It wouldn't be any fun at all without *you*. But, Mother, even when the ladies *do* do things, they stop it when they get the lovie-dovies.

MARY. The what?

LITTLE MARY. Like in the movies, Mother. Ladies always end up so *silly*. (*Disgusted.*) Lovey-dovey, lovey-dovey all the time!

MARY. Darling, you're too young to understand—

LITTLE MARY. But, Mother—

MARY. "But Mother, but Mother!" There's one thing a woman can do, no man can do.

LITTLE MARY (*eagerly*). What?

MARY. Have a child. (*Tenderly.*) Like you.

LITTLE MARY. Oh, that! Everybody knows that. But is that any fun, Mother dear?

MARY. Fun? No. But it is—joy. (*Hugging her.*) Of a very special kind.

LITTLE MARY (*squirming away*). Well, it's never sounded specially exciting to me—I love you, Mother. But I bet you anything you like, Daddy has more *fun* than you! (*She slips away from* MARY. *Then sees her mother's dispirited face, turns and kisses her warmly.*) Oh, I'm sorry, Mother. But you just *don't understand!* (*A pause.*) Am I to be punished, Mother?

MARY (*she is thinking about something else*). What do you think?

LITTLE MARY. I smacked him awful hard— Shall I punish myself?

MARY. It will have to be pretty bad.

LITTLE MARY (*solemnly*). Then I won't go down to breakfast with Daddy tomorrow, or the next day—O.K., Mother?

MARY. O.K. (LITTLE MARY *walks, crestfallen, to the door as* JANE *enters.* LITTLE MARY *sticks out her tongue.*)

LITTLE MARY. There's my tongue! So what? (*Exits skipping.*)

JANE (*laughing*). She never lets anybody get the best of her, does she, Mrs. Haines?

MARY. My poor baby. She doesn't want to be a woman, Jane.

JANE. Who does?

MARY. Somehow, I've never minded it, Jane. (*Enter* MRS. MOREHEAD. *She is a bourgeois aristocrat of 55.* MARY *rises, kisses her.*)

MRS. MOREHEAD. Hello, child. Afternoon, Jane.

JANE. Afternoon, Mrs. Morehead. (*Exits to bedroom.*)

MARY. Mother, dear! (*She walks slowly to the dressing-table.*)

MRS. MOREHEAD (*cheerfully*). Well, what's wrong? (*Sits.*)

MARY (*turning*). How did you know something's wrong?

MRS. MOREHEAD. Your voice on the phone. Is it Stephen?

MARY. How did you know?

MRS. MOREHEAD. You sent for *Mother.* So it must be he. (*A pause.*)

MARY. I don't know how to begin, Mother.

MRS. MOREHEAD (*delighted to find that her instincts were correct*). It's a woman! Who is she?

MARY. Her name is Crystal Allen. She—she's a salesgirl at Saks'. (*Her mother's cheerful and practical manner discourages tears, so she begins to cream and tonic her face instead.*)

MRS. MOREHEAD. She's young and pretty, I suppose.

MARY. Well, yes. (*Defensively.*) But common.

MRS. MOREHEAD (*soothingly*). Of course—Stephen told you?

MARY. No. I—I found out—this afternoon.

MRS. MOREHEAD. How far has it gone?

MARY. He's known her about three months.

MRS. MOREHEAD. Does Stephen know you know?

MARY (*shaking her head*). I—I wanted to speak to you first. (*The tears come anyway.*) Oh, Mother dear, what am I going to say to him?

MRS. MOREHEAD. *Nothing.*

MARY. Nothing? (*Enter* JANE *with the new dress.*)

JANE. I'll give it a touch with the iron.

MARY. Look, Schiaparelli—(JANE *holds dress up.*) It's rather trying, though, one of those tight skirts with a flared tunic—

MRS. MOREHEAD. Personally, I always thought you looked best in things not too extreme. (*Exit* JANE.)

MARY. But, Mother, you don't really mean I should say nothing?

MRS. MOREHEAD. I do.

MARY. Oh, but Mother—

MRS. MOREHEAD. My dear, I felt the same way twenty years ago.

MARY. Not Father?

MRS. MOREHEAD. Mary, in many ways your father was an exceptional man. (*Philosophically.*) That, unfortunately, was not one of them.

MARY. Did you say nothing?

MRS. MOREHEAD. Nothing. I had a wise mother, too. Listen, dear, this is not a new story. It comes to most wives.

MARY. But Stephen—

MRS. MOREHEAD. Stephen is a man. He's been married twelve years—

MARY. You mean, he's tired of me!

MRS. MOREHEAD. Stop crying. You'll make your nose red.

MARY. I'm not crying. (*Patting tonic on her face.*) This stuff stings.

MRS. MOREHEAD (*going to her*). Stephen's tired of himself. Tired of feeling the same things in himself year after year. Time comes when every man's got to feel something new —when he's got to feel young again, just because he's growing old. Women are just the same. But when *we* get that way we change our hair dress. Or get a new cook. Or redecorate the house from stem to stern. But a man can't do over his office, or fire his secretary. Not even change the style of his hair. And the urge usually hits him hardest just when he's beginning to lose his hair. No, dear, a man has only one escape from his old self: to see a different self—in the mirror of some woman's eyes.

MARY. But, Mother—

MRS. MOREHEAD. This girl probably means no more to him than that new dress means to you.

MARY. But, Mother—

MRS. MOREHEAD. "But Mother, but Mother!" He's not giving anything to her that belongs to you, or you would have felt that yourself long ago.

MARY (*bewildered*). Oh, I always thought I would. I love him so much.

MRS. MOREHEAD. And he loves you, baby. (*Drawing MARY beside her on the chaise-longue.*) Now listen to me: Go away somewhere for a month or two. There's nothing like a good dose of another woman to make a man appreciate his wife. Mother knows!

MARY. But, there's never been a lie between us before.

MRS. MOREHEAD. You mean, there's never been a *silence* between you before. Well, it's about time. Keeping still, when you *ache* to talk, is about the only sacrifice spoiled women like us ever have to make.

MARY. But, I'd forgive him—

MRS. MOREHEAD. Forgive him? (*Impatiently.*) For what? For being a man? Accuse him, and you'll never get a chance to forgive him. He'd have to justify himself—

MARY. How can he!

MRS. MOREHEAD (*sighing*). He can't and he *can*. Don't make him try. Either way you'd lose him. And remember, dear, it's being together at the *end* that really matters. (*Rising.*) One more piece of motherly advice: Don't confide in your girl friends!

MARY. I think they all know.

MRS. MOREHEAD. They think you don't? (*MARY nods.*) Leave it that way. If you let them advise you, they'll see to it, in the name of friendship, that you lose your husband and your home. I'm an old woman, dear, and I know my sex. (*Moving to the door.*) I'm going right down this minute and get our tickets.

MARY. Our—tickets?

MRS. MOREHEAD. You're taking me to Bermuda, dear. My throat's been awfully bad. I haven't wanted to worry you, but my doctor says—

MARY. Oh, Mother darling! Thank you!

MRS. MOREHEAD. Don't thank me, dear. It's rather—*nice* to have you need Mother again. (*Exits. The telephone rings.* MARY *answers it.*)

MARY. Yes?—Oh, Stephen—Yes, dear?— (*Distressed.*) Oh, Stephen! Oh, no—I'm not angry. It's—it's just that I wanted to see the play. Yes, I can get Mother. Stephen, will you be very—late? (*It's a bit of a struggle, but she manages a cheerful voice.*) Oh, it's— all right. Have a good time. Of course, I know it's just business—No, dear—I won't wait up—Stephen. I love— (*A click. The other end has hung up.* JANE *enters.* MARY *turns her back. Her face would belie the calmness of her voice.*) Jane—The children and I will have dinner alone—

CURTAIN

SCENE IV

Two months later. A dressmaker's shop. We see two fitting booths, the same in appointment: triplex pier glasses, dress-racks, smoking stands, two small chairs. They are divided by a mirrored partition. At the rear of each booth, a curtain and a door, off a corridor, which leads to "the floor."

As the curtain rises the booth on the left is empty. The other booth is cluttered with dresses. Two SALESGIRLS *are loading them over their arms.*

FIRST GIRL (*with vivid resentment against a customer who has just departed*). Well, now we can put them all back again. Makes you drag out everything in the damn store, and doesn't even buy a brassiere!

SECOND GIRL. And that's the kind who always needs one.

FIRST GIRL. This isn't her type. That isn't her type. I'd like to tell her what her type is.

SECOND GIRL. I'd like to know.

FIRST GIRL. It's the type that nobody gives a damn about! Gee, I'd like to work in a men's shop once. What can a man try on?

SECOND GIRL. Ever see a man try on hats? What they go through, you'd think a head was something peculiar. (*Both* GIRLS *exit.* FIRST SALESWOMAN *enters the booth on the right, hereafter called "Mary's Booth."*)

FIRST SALESWOMAN. Miss Myrtle, step in here a moment. (*A handsome wench, in a slinky negligée, enters.*)

MODEL. Yes, Miss Shapiro.

FIRST SALESWOMAN. If I've told you once, I've told you a thousand times, when you're modelling that dress, your stomach must lead. If you walk like this (*Pantomimes.*) you take away all the seduction. *This* is seduction! (*Shows* MISS MYRTLE *her rather unconvincing conception of a seductive walk.*)

MODEL. I'll try, Miss Shapiro. (*Tearfully.*) But if you had my appendix!

FIRST SALESWOMAN. Well, Miss Myrtle, you can take your choice: You will either lose your job or lose your appendix! (*Exit* MODEL. *In right booth, hereafter called "Crystal's Booth," enter* SECOND SALESWOMAN.)

SECOND SALESWOMAN (*to the* FIRST *and* SECOND GIRLS *who have returned for another load of dresses*). Quickly, please. I have a client waiting. (SECOND GIRL *exits with last* of clothes as enter CRYSTAL, *followed by* SALESWOMAN. THIRD SALESWOMAN *is seen crossing corridor from right to left.*)
(*Mary's Booth.*)

FIRST SALESWOMAN (*giving little white slip to the* SALESWOMAN *who passes*). Bring down Mrs. Haines' fittings. (*Exits, leaving booth empty.*)
(*Crystal's Booth.*)

SECOND SALESWOMAN. Will you open a charge?

CRYSTAL (*taking off her gloves and hat*). Please.

SECOND SALESWOMAN. May I have the name?

CRYSTAL (*she is quite self-assured*). Allen. Miss Crystal Allen. The Hotel Waverly.

SECOND SALESWOMAN. May I have your other charges? Saks, Bergdorf, Cartier—?

CRYSTAL (*putting it on*). Oh, I'll be opening those, in the next few days—

SECOND SALESWOMAN. Then may I have your bank?

CRYSTAL. I've no checking account either, at the moment. (*Enter* MARY *in her booth, with* FITTER *and* FIRST SALESWOMAN, *who carries her try-on gown. During the following scene* MARY *undresses, gets into gay evening gown, fits.*)

FIRST SALESWOMAN (*to* MARY, *as they enter*). Shall we show the things that came in while you were away?

MARY. Please. But I'd like to see some younger things than I usually wear.
(*Crystal's Booth.*)

SECOND SALESWOMAN. I'm sorry, Miss Allen. But we *must* ask for one business reference—

CRYSTAL (*lightly; she was prepared for this*). Oh, of course. Mr. Stephen Haines, 40 Wall. He's an old friend of my family.

SECOND SALESWOMAN (*writing*). That will do. Mrs. Haines is a very good client of ours.

CRYSTAL (*unprepared for that*). Oh?

SECOND SALESWOMAN. Will you try on now, or finish seeing the collection?

CRYSTAL. By the way, I've never met Mrs. Haines.

SECOND SALESWOMAN. She's lovely.

CRYSTAL. So—I'd rather you didn't mention to her, that I gave her husband as reference. (*Beguiling.*) Do you mind?

SECOND SALESWOMAN (*with a faint smile*). Oh, of course not, Miss Allen. (*Indulgently.*) We understand.

CRYSTAL (*angrily*). Do you! What do you understand?

SECOND SALESWOMAN (*flustered*). I mean—

CRYSTAL (*very injured*). Never mind.

SECOND SALESWOMAN. Please, I hope you don't think I meant—

CRYSTAL (*laughing and very charming again*). Of course not. Oh, it's dreadful, living in a strange city alone. You have to be so careful not to do anything people can misconstrue. You see, I don't know Mrs. Haines yet. So I'd hate to get off on the wrong foot, before I've met her *socially*.

SECOND SALESWOMAN (*she sounds convinced*). Naturally. Women are funny about little things like that.
(*Mary's Booth—Enter* SYLVIA.)

SYLVIA. Yoo-hoo! May I come in?

MARY (*not at all pleased to see her*). Hello, Sylvia.
(*In Crystal's Booth.*)

SECOND SALESWOMAN. What are you most interested in, Miss Allen, evening gowns?

CRYSTAL. Until I—I organize my social life —I won't have much use for evening gowns.

SECOND SALESWOMAN. I'll show you some smart daytime things. (*Deliberately toneless.*) And we have very *exciting* negligées—
(*They exit.*)
(*Mary's Booth.*)
(SYLVIA *circles around* MARY, *appraising her fitting with a critical eye.*)

MARY. Oh, sit down, Sylvia.

SYLVIA (*to the fitter*). I don't like that underslung line. (*Demonstrating on* MARY.) It cuts her across the fanny. Makes her look positively duck-bottomed.

MARY (*pulling away*). It's so tight, Mrs. Fowler can't sit down.

FIRST SALESWOMAN. Mrs. Fowler, shall I see if your fittings are ready?

SYLVIA. They'll call me.

MARY (*pointing to dress* FIRST SALESWOMAN *has over her arm*). Have you seen that?

FIRST SALESWOMAN (*holding up dress*). It's a lovely shape on. It doesn't look like a thing in the hand. (*Hands dress to someone outside and calls.*) Show this model, girls.

SYLVIA (*settling in a chair and smoking a cigarette*). So you had a marvelous time in Bermuda.

MARY. I had a good rest.

SYLVIA (*with unconscious humor*). Howard wants *me* to take a world cruise. By the way, dear, how is Stephen.

MARY. Splendid. (*Smiling, and very glad to be able to tell* SYLVIA *this*). He's not nearly so busy. He hasn't spent an evening—in the office, since I've come home. (*Enter* FIRST MODEL *in an elaborate negligée.* MARY *shakes her head, very practical.*) Pretty, but I never need a thing like that—

SYLVIA. Of course *you* don't. A hot little number, for intimate afternoons. (*Exit* FIRST MODEL.) Howard says nobody's seen Stephen in the Club, in the afternoon, for months—

MARY (*the thought flashes across her mind that* STEPHEN *could, of course, have revised his extra-marital schedule, from an evening to an afternoon one, but she quickly dismisses it;* STEPHEN *has never let anything interfere with his hours downtown*). Don't worry so much about Stephen, Sylvia. He's my concern. (*Enter* SECOND MODEL *in a corset. She is prettily fashioned from head to toe. She does a great deal for the wisp of lace she wears. It does nothing that nature didn't do better for her.*)

SECOND MODEL. This is our new one-piece lace foundation garment. (*Pirouettes.*) Zips up the back, and no bones. (*She exits.*)

SYLVIA. Just that uplift, Mary, you need. I always said you'd regret nursing. Look at me. I don't think there's another girl our age who has bazooms like mine. I've taken care of them. Ice water every morning, camphor at night.

MARY. Doesn't it smell like an old fur coat? (PRINCESS TAMARA *passes in the corridor.*)

SYLVIA. Who cares?

MARY. Howard?

SYLVIA (*laughing harshly*). Howard!

FIRST SALESWOMAN (*calling out door*). Princess Tamara, show here. (*Enter* PRINCESS TAMARA *in a very extreme evening gown. She is Russian, regal, soignée.*)

MARY. Oh, Tamara, how lovely!

TAMARA. You must have it. Stephen would be amazed.

MARY. He certainly would. It's too extreme for me.

SYLVIA (*rises*). And you really haven't the figure. (*Yanks at gown.*) Tamara, you wear it wrong. I saw it in *Vogue.* (*Jerks.*) Off here, and down there.

TAMARA (*slapping* SYLVIA's *hand down*). Stop mauling me!

FIRST SALESWOMAN. Princess!

TAMARA. What do you know how to wear clothes?

SYLVIA. *I* am not a model, Tamara, but no one disputes how *I* wear clothes!

TAMARA. No one has mistaken you for Mrs. Harrison Williams yet!

FIRST SALESWOMAN. Princess Tamara, you'd better apologize.

MARY (*to* SALESWOMAN). It's just professional jealousy. They're really good friends!

SYLVIA (*maliciously*). You mean Tamara and *Howard* are friends.

TAMARA (*disgusted at the thought*). Do you accuse me of flirting with *your* husband?

SYLVIA (*pleasantly*). Go as far as you can, Tamara! If *I* know Howard, you're wasting valuable time.

TAMARA (*very angry*). Perhaps I am. But perhaps somebody else is not! (*The* SALESWOMAN *gives her an angry shove.*) You are riding for a fall-off, Sylvia dear! (*Exit* TAMARA *angrily, followed by* SALESWOMAN.)

SYLVIA. Did you get that innuendo? I'd like to see Howard Fowler put anything over on me. Oh, I've always hated that girl, exploiting her title the way she does! (CRYSTAL *and* SECOND SALESWOMAN *enter Crystal's Booth.*)

SECOND SALESWOMAN (*calling down the corridor*). Princess Tamara, show in here, to Miss Allen. (MARY's SALESWOMAN *enters Mary's Booth, picking up the call.*)

FIRST SALESWOMAN. Girls, show in Number 3 to Miss Allen.

SYLVIA (*alert*). Did you say Miss Allen?

FIRST SALESWOMAN. Yes.

SYLVIA. Not—Crystal Allen?

FIRST SALESWOMAN. Why, yes—I just saw her on the floor. She's so attractive I asked her name.

SYLVIA (*watching* MARY *closely*). Oh, so Crystal Allen gets her things here? (MARY *sits down suddenly.*)

FIRST SALESWOMAN. She's a new client— Why, Mrs. Haines, are you ill? (MARY *has caught* SYLVIA's *eye in the mirror.* SYLVIA *knows now that* MARY *knows.*)

MARY. No, no. I'm just tired. (TAMARA *enters Crystal's Booth.*)

FITTER. We've kept you standing too long—

FIRST SALESWOMAN. I'll get you a glass of sherry. (*Exit* MARY's FITTER *and* SALESWOMAN. SYLVIA *closes door.*)
(*Crystal's Booth.*)

CRYSTAL (*admiring* TAMARA's *extreme evening gown*). I'm going to have that, if I have to wear it for breakfast.

SECOND SALESWOMAN. Send it in here, Princess. (TAMARA *exits.*)
(*Mary's Booth.*)

SYLVIA. Mary, you do know! (*Deeply sympathetic.*) Why didn't you confide in me?

MARY. Sylvia, go away.

SYLVIA (*fiercely*). Stephen is a louse. Spending your money on a girl like that.

MARY. Sylvia, please mind your own affairs.

SYLVIA. She's already made a fool of you before all your friends. And don't you think the salesgirls know who gets the bills?

MARY (*distraught*). I don't care, I tell you. I don't care!

SYLVIA. Oh, yes, you do. (*Pointing to* MARY's *stricken face in the mirror.*) Don't be an ostrich, Mary. (*A pause.*) Go in there.

MARY. Go in there? I'm going home. (*She rises and begins to dress.*)

FIRST SALESWOMAN (*half enters*). Mrs. Haines' sherry—

SYLVIA (*taking it from her, and closing the door in her face*). All right.

SYLVIA. You've caught her cold. It's *your* chance to humiliate her. Just say a few *quiet* words. Tell her you'll make Stephen's life *hell* until he gives her up.

MARY. Stephen will give her up when he's tired of her.

SYLVIA. When he's tired of her? Look where she was six months ago. Look where she is now.

MARY. Stephen's not in love with that girl.

SYLVIA. Maybe not. But you don't know women like that when they get hold of a man.

MARY. Sylvia, please let me decide what is best for me, and my home. (CRYSTAL, *in her booth, has been undressing, admiring herself as she does so in the mirror. Now she slips into a "really exciting" negligée.*)

SYLVIA. Well, she may be a perfectly marvelous influence for Stephen, but she's not going to do your children any good.

MARY (*turning to her*). What do you mean?

SYLVIA (*mysteriously*). Never mind.

MARY (*going to her*). Tell me!

SYLVIA. Far be it from *me* to tell you things you don't care to hear. I've known this all along. (*Nobly.*) Have I *uttered?*

MARY (*violently*). What have my children to do with this?

SYLVIA (*after all,* MARY's *asking for it*). It was while you were away. Edith saw them. Stephen, and that tramp, and your children —together, lunching in the Park.

MARY. It's not true!

SYLVIA. Why would Edith lie? She said they were having a hilarious time. Little Stevie was eating his lunch sitting on that woman's lap. She was kissing him between every bite. When I heard that, I was positively *heart-sick,* dear! (*Sees she has scored. Celebrates by tossing down* MARY's *sherry.*)
(*Crystal's Booth.*)

CRYSTAL. Oh, go get that evening gown. This thing bores me.

SECOND SALESWOMAN. Right away, Miss Allen. (*Exits.*)
(*Mary's Booth.*)

SYLVIA. But, as you say, dear, it's your affair, not mine. (*Goes to the door, looking very hurt that* MARY *has refused her good advice.*) No doubt that girl will make a perfectly good *step-mamma* for your children! (*Exits.* MARY, *now dressed, is alone. She stares at the partition which separates her from that still unmeasured enemy to her well-ordered domesticity, "the other woman." Her common sense dictates she should go home, but now she violently experiences the ache to talk. She struggles against it, then goes, bitterly determined, to the door. Exits. A second later, there is a knock on* CRYSTAL's *door.* CRYSTAL *is alone.*)

CRYSTAL. Come in! (*Enter* MARY. *She closes door.*) I beg your pardon?

MARY. I am—Mrs. Stephen Haines.

CRYSTAL (*her poise is admirable*). Sorry—I don't think I know you!

MARY. Please don't pretend.

CRYSTAL. So Stephen finally told you?

MARY. No. I found out. (SECOND SALESWOMAN *half enters.*)

CRYSTAL. Stay out of here! (*Exit* SALESWOMAN.)

MARY. I've known about you from the beginning.

CRYSTAL. Well, that's news.

MARY. I kept still.

CRYSTAL. Very smart of you. (SECOND SALES-WOMAN *pantomimes down the corridor, to another girl to join her. Enters* MARY's *booth. One by one, during the rest of this scene, the* FITTERS, SALESWOMEN *and* MODELS *tip-toe into* MARY's *booth and plaster their ears against the partition.*)

MARY. No, not smart. I wanted to spare Stephen. But you've gone a little too far—You've been seeing my children. I won't have you touching my children!

CRYSTAL. For God's sake, don't get hysterical. What do I care about your children? I'm sick of hearing about them.

MARY. You won't have to hear about them any more. When Stephen realizes how humiliating all this has been to me, he'll give you up instantly.

CRYSTAL. Says who? The dog in the manger?

MARY. That's all I have to say.

CRYSTAL. That's plenty.

MARY (*more calmly*). Stephen would have grown tired of you anyway.

CRYSTAL (*nastily*). Speaking from your *own* experience? Well, he's not tired of me yet, Mrs. Haines.

MARY (*contemptuous*). Stephen is just amusing himself with you.

CRYSTAL. And he's amusing himself plenty.

MARY. You're very hard.

CRYSTAL. I can be soft—on the *right* occasions. What do you expect me to do? Burst into tears and beg you to forgive me?

MARY. I found exactly what I expected!

CRYSTAL. That goes double!

MARY (*turning to the door*). You'll have to make other plans, Miss Allen.

CRYSTAL (*going to her*). Listen, I'm taking my marching orders from Stephen.

MARY. Stephen doesn't love you.

CRYSTAL. He's doing the best he can in the circumstances.

MARY. He couldn't love a girl like you.

CRYSTAL. What do you think we've been doing for the past six months? Crossword puzzles? What have you got to kick about? You've got everything that matters. The name, the position, the money—

MARY (*losing control of herself again*). Nothing matters to me but Stephen—!

CRYSTAL. Oh, can the sob-stuff, Mrs. Haines. You don't think this is the first time Stephen's ever cheated? Listen, I'd break up your smug little roost if I could. I have just as much right as you have to sit in a tub of butter. But I don't stand a chance!

MARY. I'm glad you know it.

CRYSTAL. Well, don't think it's just because he's *fond* of you—

MARY. *Fond?*

CRYSTAL. You're not what's stopping him—You're just an old *habit* with him. It's just those brats he's afraid of losing. If he weren't such a sentimental fool about those kids, he'd have walked out on *you* years ago.

MARY (*fiercely*). That's not true!

CRYSTAL. Oh, yes, it is. I'm telling you a few plain truths you won't get from Stephen.

MARY. Stephen's always told me the truth—!

CRYSTAL (*maliciously*). Well, look at the record. (*A pause.*) Listen, Stephen's satisfied with this arrangement. So don't force any issues, unless you want plenty of trouble.

MARY. You've made it impossible for me to do anything else—!

CRYSTAL (*rather pleased*). Have I?

MARY. You haven't played fair—!

CRYSTAL. Where would any of us get if we played fair?

MARY. Where do you hope to get?

CRYSTAL. Right where *you* are, Mrs. Haines!

MARY. You're very confident.

CRYSTAL. The longer you stay in here, the more confident I get. Saint or no saint, Mrs. Haines, you are a hell of a *dull woman!*

MARY (MARY *stares at her wide-eyed at the horrid thought that this may be the truth. She refuses to meet the challenge. She equi-*

vocates). By your standards, I probably am. I— (*Suddenly ashamed that she has allowed herself to be put so pathetically on the defensive.*) Oh, why am I standing here talking to you? This is something for Stephen and me to settle! (*Exits.*)

CRYSTAL (*slamming the door after her*). Oh, what the hell!
(*Mary's Booth.*)

SECOND SALESWOMAN. So that's what she calls meeting Mrs. Haines *socially*.

FIRST SALESGIRL. Gee, I feel sorry for Mrs. Haines. She's so nice.

NEGLIGEE MODEL. She should have kept her mouth shut. Now she's in the soup.

FIRST SALESWOMAN. It's a terrible mistake to lay down ultimatums to a man.

FIRST MODEL. Allen's smart. She's fixed it so anything Mr. Haines says is going to sound wrong.

FIRST SALESGIRL. She'll get him sure.

FIRST FITTER. Look at that body. She's got him now.

SECOND SALESGIRL. You can't trust any man. *That's* all they want.

CORSET MODEL (*plaintively, her hands on her lovely hips*). What else have we got to give?

CURTAIN

ACT TWO

SCENE I

Two weeks later. A small exercise room in Elizabeth Arden's beauty-salon. Right, a mirrored wall. Rear, a door. Left, a cabinet victrola beneath an open window. On the floor, a wadded pink satin mat. As the curtain rises, SYLVIA, *in a pair of shorts, is prone on the mat, describing lackadaisical arcs with her legs, to the sensuous rhythm of a tango record. The* INSTRUCTRESS, *a bright, pretty girl, in a pink silk bathing suit, stands above her, drilling her in a carefully cultured voice. Until the cue "stretch," the* INSTRUCTRESS' *lines are spoken through* SYLVIA'S *prattle, which she is determined, for the honor of the salon, to ignore, and, if possible, to discourage. From the word "up," this is a hopeless task.*

INSTRUCTRESS. Up—over—up—down. Up—stretch—up—together. Up—stretch—up—

SYLVIA. Of course, my sympathies are for Mrs. Haines. They always are for a woman against a man—

INSTRUCTRESS (*louder*). Up—over—up—down. Up—stretch—up—together. Up—

SYLVIA. But she did behave like an awful idiot—

INSTRUCTRESS. Stretch—up—together. Please don't try to talk, Mrs. Fowler.

SYLVIA. But you know how some women are when they lose their heads—

INSTRUCTRESS (*grimly*). Stretch—up—together—up—

SYLVIA. They do things they regret all their lives—

INSTRUCTRESS (*grabs* SYLVIA'S *languid limb and gives it a corrective yank*). Ster-retch!

SYLVIA. Ouch, my scars!

INSTRUCTRESS (*callously*). This is very good for adhesions. Up—

SYLVIA (*resolutely inert*). It's got me down.

INSTRUCTRESS. Rest. (SYLVIA *groans her relief*). And relax your diaphragm muscles, Mrs. Fowler, (*bitterly*) if you can. (*Goes to the victrola, changes the record for a foxtrot*).

SYLVIA. Of course, I do wish Mrs. Haines would make up her mind if she's going to get a divorce. It's terrible on all her friends, not knowing. Naturally, you can't ask them anywhere—

INSTRUCTRESS. Of course not. Now, on your side. (SYLVIA *rolls to her side, reclining on her elbow.*) Ready? Up—down—up—down —(*Snaps her fingers.* SYLVIA *flaps a limp leg up, down—*) Don't bend the knee—

SYLVIA (*thoughtfully*). Of course, for the children's sake, I think Mrs. Haines ought to stay. (*Piously*) I know I would. (*Her knees look bent, not to say broken.*)

INSTRUCTRESS (*imploring*). Don't crook it, please.

SYLVIA. And she ought not to have faced Mr. Haines with the issue. When a man's got himself in that deep he has to have time to taper it off—

INSTRUCTRESS (*straightening out* SYLVIA'S *offending member with considerable force*). Thigh in, not out.

SYLVIA (*pained, but undaunted*). But Mrs. Haines never listens to any of her friends. She is a very peculiar woman.

INSTRUCTRESS. She must be. Now, please— up—down—up—down—

SYLVIA (*redoubling her efforts, and her errors*). Oh, I tell everybody whatever she wants to do is the right thing. I've got to be loyal to Mrs. Haines, you know . . . Oh, I'm simply exhausted. (*Flops over, flat on her stomach, panting.*)

INSTRUCTRESS. Then suppose you try something simple—like crawling up the wall? (SYLVIA *lifts a martyred face. The* INSTRUCTRESS *changes the record for a waltz.*)

SYLVIA (*scrambling to her feet*). What I go through to keep my figure! Lord, it infuriates me at dinner parties when some fat lazy man asks, "What do you do with yourself all day, Mrs. Fowler?" (*Sits alongside the rear wall.*)

INSTRUCTRESS. You rotate on your buttocks. (SYLVIA *rotates, then lies back, her knees drawn up to her chin, the soles of her feet against the wall*). Arms flat. Now you crawl slowly up the wall.

SYLVIA (*crawling*). I wish you wouldn't say that. It makes me feel like vermin—

INSTRUCTRESS (*kneeling beside her*). Don't talk.

SYLVIA. There's a couple of people I'd like to exterminate. too—

INSTRUCTRESS. Let's reverse the action. (SYLVIA *crawls down, as* PEGGY *enters in an exercise suit. The* INSTRUCTRESS *brightens.*)

INSTRUCTRESS. How do you do, Mrs. Day? (*To* SYLVIA.) Down slowly—

PEGGY (*gaily*). How do you do? Hello, Sylvia.

SYLVIA. You're late again, Peggy.

PEGGY (*crestfallen*). I'm sorry.

SYLVIA (*sitting up*). After all, dear, I am paying for this course.

PEGGY. You know I'm grateful, Sylvia—

SYLVIA. Well, don't cry about it. It's only fifty dollars.

PEGGY. That's a lot to me—

SYLVIA (*sweetly*). To you, or just to your husband, dear?

INSTRUCTRESS. Please, ladies. Let us begin with posture. (SYLVIA *rises*). A lady always enters a room erect.

SYLVIA. Lots of my friends exit horizontally. (PEGGY *and* SYLVIA *go to the mirrored wall, stand with their backs to it.*)

INSTRUCTRESS. Now—knees apart. Sit on the wall. (*They sit on imaginary seats.*) Relax. (*They bend forward from the waist, fingertips brushing the floor.*) Now, roll slowly up the wall . . . pressing each little vertebra against the wall as hard as you can . . . shoulders back, and where they belong. Heads back. Mrs. Fowler, lift yourself behind the ears. Pretend you're just a silly little puppet dangling on a string. Chin up. (*She places her hand at the level of* PEGGY'S *straining chin.*) No, Mrs. Day, your chin is resting comfortably on a little table. Elbows bent—up on your toes—arms out—shove with the small of your back—you're off! (SYLVIA *and* PEGGY, *side by side, mince across the room.*)

PEGGY (*whispering*). Oh, Sylvia, why do you always insinuate that John is practically a—miser?

INSTRUCTRESS (*she refers to* PEGGY'S *swaying hips*). Tuck under!

SYLVIA. You have your own little income, Peggy. And what do you do with it? You give it to John—

INTRUCTRESS. Now, back, please! (*They mince backwards across the room.*)

PEGGY (*staunchly*). John makes so little—

INSTRUCTRESS (*she refers to* SYLVIA's *relaxed tummy*). Steady center control!

SYLVIA. Peggy, you're robbing John of his manly sense of responsibility. You're turning him into a gigolo. A little money of her own she lets no man touch is the only protection a woman has. (*They are against the mirror again.*)

INSTRUCTRESS. Now, are you both the way you were when you left the wall?

SYLVIA (*brightly*). Well, I am.

INSTRUCTRESS. No, Mrs. Fowler, you're not. (*She imitates* SYLVIA's *posture, showing how* SYLVIA's *posterior protrudes, against the dictates of fashion, if not of nature.*) Not *this*, Mrs. Fowler—("*Bumps*") That! (*She leads* SYLVIA *forward.*) Try it, please. (*Facing one another, they do an elegant pair of "bumps."*) Now, relax on the mat.

(*This piece of business defies description, but to do the best one can: the* GIRLS *stand side by side, arms straight above their heads. At the* INSTRUCTRESS' *count of "one," each drops a hand, limp, from the wrist. At "two," the other hand drops, then their heads fall upon their breasts, their arms flap to their sides, their waists cave in, their knees buckle under, and they swoon, or crumble like boneless things, to the mat.*)

INSTRUCTRESS (*she has changed the record*). Now, ready? Bend—stretch, you know. Begin— (*They do another leg exercise on the mat.*) Bend—stretch—bend—down—plenty of pull on the hamstrings, please! Bend—stretch—bend—down— (*Enter* EDITH. *She is draped in a white sheet. Her head is bound in a white towel. Her face is undergoing a "tie-up," that is, she wears broad white straps under her chin and across her forehead. She appears very distressed.*)

EDITH. Oh, Sylvia! Hello, Peggy—

SYLVIA (*sitting up*). Why, Edith, what are you doing up here?

EDITH. Having a facial, downstairs. Oh, Sylvia. I'm so glad you're here. I've done the most *awful* thing, I—

INSTRUCTRESS. We're right in the middle of our exercises, Mrs. Potter—

SYLVIA (*To* INSTRUCTRESS). Will you tell them outside—I want my paraffine bath now? There's a dear.

INSTRUCTRESS. But, Mrs. Fowler—

SYLVIA (*cajoling*). I'm simply exhausted.

INSTRUCTRESS. You've hardly moved a muscle.

SYLVIA (*with elaborate patience*). Look, whose carcass is this? Yours or mine?

INSTRUCTRESS. It's yours, Mrs. Fowler, but I'm paid to exercise it.

SYLVIA. You talk like a horse-trainer.

INSTRUCTRESS. Well, Mrs. Fowler, you're getting warm. (*Exits.*)

EDITH. I've done the most *ghastly* thing. Move over. (PEGGY *and* SYLVIA *move over;* EDITH *plumps between them on the mat.*) But it wasn't until I got here, in the middle of my facial, that I realized it—I could bite my tongue off when I think of it—

SYLVIA. Well, what is it, Edith?

EDITH. I was lunching with Frances Jones, and—

SYLVIA. Edith Potter, I know exactly what you're going to say!

EDITH. I forgot she—

SYLVIA. You forgot she's Dolly de Peyster.

EDITH. But I never read her awful column—

SYLVIA (*fiercely*). You told her something about me? What did you tell her?

EDITH. Oh, darling, you know I never give you away. (*Remorsefully.*) I—I—told her all about Stephen and Mary—

SYLVIA (*relieved*). Oh! That!

EDITH. It wasn't until the middle of my facial—

PEGGY. Oh, Edith! It will be in all those dreadful tabloids!

EDITH. I know—I've been racking my brains to recall what I said—I think I told her that when Mary walked into the fitting room, she yanked the ermine coat off the Allen girl—

SYLVIA. You didn't!

EDITH. Well, I don't know whether I said ermine or *sable*—but I know I told her that Mary *smacked* the Allen girl!

PEGGY. Edith!

EDITH. Well, that's what Sylvia told me!

SYLVIA. I didn't!

EDITH. You did, too!

SYLVIA (*hurt*). Anyway, I didn't expect you to tell it to a cheap reporter—

EDITH. Well, it doesn't really make much difference. The divorce is practically settled—

SYLVIA (*eagerly*). Who says so?

EDITH. You did!

SYLVIA (*patiently*). I said, Mary couldn't broadcast her domestic difficulties, and not expect them to wind up in a scandal.

PEGGY. Mary didn't broadcast them!

SYLVIA. Who did?

PEGGY. *You* did. You—you're all making it impossible for her to do anything now but get a divorce!

SYLVIA. You flatter us. We didn't realize how much influence we had on our friends' lives!

PEGGY. Everybody calling her up, telling her how badly she's been treated—

SYLVIA. As a matter of fact, I told her she'd make a great mistake. What has any woman got to gain by a divorce? No matter how much he gives her, she won't have what they have together. And you know as well as I do, he'd marry that girl. What he's spent on her, he'd have to, to protect his investment. (*Sorrowfully.*) But, I have as much influence on Mary as I have on *you,* Peggy. (*The* INSTRUCTRESS *re-enters.*)

INSTRUCTRESS. The paraffine bath is ready, Mrs. Fowler.

SYLVIA (*rises*). Well, don't worry, Edith, I'll give de Peyster a ring. I can fix it.

EDITH. How?

SYLVIA (*graciously*). Oh, I'll tell her you were lying.

EDITH. You'll do no such thing!

SYLVIA (*shrugging*). Then let the story ride. It will be forgotten tomorrow. You know the awful things they printed about—what's her name?—before she jumped out the window? Why, I can't even remember her name, so who cares, Edith? (*Exits.*)

INSTRUCTRESS. Mrs. Potter, you come right back where you belong.

EDITH. Why, you'd think this was a boarding school!

INSTRUCTRESS. But, Mrs. Potter, it's such a foolish waste of money—

EDITH. Listen, relaxing is part of my facial.

INSTRUCTRESS (*coolly*). Then you should relax completely, Mrs. Potter, from the chin up. (*Exits.*)

EDITH. Honestly, the class feeling you run into these days! (*Struggles to her feet.*) I'm so tired of paying creatures like that to insult me—

PEGGY (*going to her*). Edith! Let's call Mary up and warn her!

EDITH. About what?

PEGGY. The newspapers!

EDITH. My dear, how could we do that, without involving Sylvia—

PEGGY. But it's *her* fault— Oh, she's such a dreadful woman!

EDITH. Oh, she can't help it, Peggy. It's just her tough luck she wasn't born deaf and dumb. But what can we do about it? She's always gotten away with murder. Why, she's been having an affair for a year with that young customers' man in Howard's office.

PEGGY (*shocked*). Edith!

EDITH. Right under Howard's nose! But Howard doesn't care! So what business is it of yours or mine? (*Earnestly.*) Peggy, take a tip from me—keep out of other women's troubles. I've never had a fight with a girl friend in all my life. Why? I hear no evil, I see no evil, I speak no evil!

CURTAIN

SCENE II

A few days later.

MARY's *pantry, midnight. Left, a swinging door, to the kitchen. Rear, a sink under a curtained window. A small, built-in refrigerator. Center, a table, two chairs.*

As the curtain rises, JANE, *the maid, and* MAGGIE, *the new cook, are having a midnight snack.* MAGGIE, *a buxom, middle-aged woman, wears a wrapper and felt bedroom slippers.*

JANE (*folding a tabloid newspaper which she has been reading to* MAGGIE.) So *he* says, "All you can do with a story like that, is live it down, Mary."

MAGGIE. I told you they'd begin all over. Once a thing like that is out between a married couple, they've got to fight it out. Depends which they get sick of first, each other, or the argument.

JANE. It's enough to make you lose your faith in marriage.

MAGGIE. Whose faith in marriage?

JANE. You don't believe in marriage?

MAGGIE. Sure I do. For women. (*Sighs.*) But it's the sons of Adam they got to marry. Go on.

JANE. Well, finally he said to the madam, "I gave her up, didn't I? And I was a swine, about the way I did it." How do you suppose he did it, Maggie?

MAGGIE. Maybe he just said, "Scram, the wife is onto us."

JANE. Well, the madam didn't believe him. She says, "Stephen, you really ain't seen her?"

MAGGIE. He lied in his teeth—

JANE. Oh, the way he said it, I kind of believed him. But the madam says, "Oh, but can I ever trust you again?"

MAGGIE. You can't trust none of 'em no further than I can kick this lemon pie.

JANE. Oh, it was terrible sad. He said, "Mary, dear Mary, Mary, dear Mary, Mary—"

MAGGIE. Dear Mary. But it ain't exactly convincing.

JANE. Then, I guess he tried to kiss her. Because she says, "Please don't. I'll never be able to kiss you again, without thinking of her in your arms."

MAGGIE (*appreciatively*). Just like in the movies— Imagine him taking up with a girl like that.

JANE. He was telling the madam: She's a virgin.

MAGGIE. She *is?* Then what's all the rumpus about?

JANE. Oh, she ain't a virgin now. She was.

MAGGIE. So was Mae West—once.

JANE. He told the madam he'd been faithful for twelve years.

MAGGIE. Well, that's something these days, that beats flying the Atlantic. Did the madam believe him?

JANE. She said, "How do I know you've been faithful?"

MAGGIE. She don't.

JANE. But the way he said it—

MAGGIE. Listen, if they lay off six months, they feel themselves busting out all over with haloes.

JANE. Anyway, he says this girl was really a nice girl. So sweet and interested in him and all. And how it happened one night, unexpected, in her room—

MAGGIE. Did he think it was going to happen in Roxy's?

JANE. He said she wouldn't take nothing from him for months—

MAGGIE. Only her education. Oh, that one knew her onions. She certainly played him for a sucker.

JANE. That's what the madam said. She said, "Stephen, can't you see that girl's only interested in you for your money?"

MAGGIE. Tch, tch, tch. I'll bet that made him sore. A man don't like to be told no woman but his wife is fool enough to love him. It drives 'em nutty.

JANE. Did it! "Mary, I told you what kind of girl she is," he says. You know—I just told you—

MAGGIE. I had her number. You didn't convey no information.

JANE. Well, then they both got sore.

MAGGIE (*rises, goes out for coffee*). I knew it.

JANE. So, he began to tell her all over, what a good husband he'd been. And how hard he'd worked for her and the kids. And she kept interrupting with what a good wife she'd been and how proud she was of him. Then they began to exaggerate themselves—

MAGGIE (*enters with coffee pot*). Listen, anybody that's ever been married knows that line backwards and forwards. What happened?

JANE. Well, somewhere in there the madam says, "Stephen, you do want a divorce. Only you ain't got the courage to ask it." And he says, "Oh, my God, no I don't, Mary. Haven't I told you?" And she says, "But you don't love me!" And he says, "But oh, my God, Mary, I'm awful *fond* of you." And she says, very icy, "Fond, fond? Is that all?" And he says, "No Mary, there's the children." Maggie, that's the thing I don't understand. Why does she get so mad every time he says they've got to consider the children? If children ain't the point of being married, what is?

MAGGIE. A woman don't want to be told she's being kept on just to run a kindergarten. (*Goes to the ice box for a bottle of cream.*)

JANE. Well, the madam says, "Stephen, I want to keep the children out of this. I haven't used the children. I ain't asked you to sacrifice yourself for the children." Maggie, that's where he got so terrible mad. He says, "But why, in God's name, Mary? You knew about us all along. Why did you wait until now to make a fool of me?"

MAGGIE. As if he needed her help.

JANE. So, then, suddenly she says, in a awful low voice, "Stephen, oh, Stephen, we can't go on like this. It ain't worthy of what we been to each other!" And he says, "Oh, no, it's not, Mary!"

MAGGIE. Quite a actress, ain't you?

JANE. My boy friend says I got eyes like Claudette Colbert's.

MAGGIE. Did he ever say anything about your legs? Have a cup of coffee. (*Pours coffee.*)

JANE. That's when the madam says what you could have knocked me down with a feather! The madam says, "Stephen, I want a divorce. Yes, Stephen, *I* want a divorce!"

MAGGIE. Tch. Tch. Abdicating!

JANE. Well, Maggie, you could have knocked him down with a feather!

MAGGIE (*waving coffee pot*). I'd like to knock him down with this.

JANE. "My God! Mary," he says, "you don't mean it!" So she says, in a funny voice, "Yes, I do. You've killed my love for you, Stephen."

MAGGIE. He's just simple-minded enough to believe that.

JANE. So he says, "I don't blame you. My God, how can I blame you?"

MAGGIE. My God, he can't!

JANE. So then she said it was all over, because it was only the children he minded losing. She said that made their marriage a mockery.

MAGGIE. A mockery?

JANE. Something funny.

MAGGIE. I ain't going to die laughing.

JANE. He said she was talking nonsense. He said she was just upset on account of this story in the papers. He said what else could she expect if she was going to spill her troubles to a lot of gabby women? He said she should go to bed until she could think things over. He was going out for a breath of fresh air.

MAGGIE. The old hat trick.

JANE. So the madam says, "You're going to see that girl." And he says, "Oh, for God's sake, Mary, one minute you never want to see me again, the next I can't even go out for a airing!"

MAGGIE. You oughtn't to let none of 'em out except on a leash.

JANE. And she says, "Are you going to see her, or ain't you?" And he says, "Well, what difference does it make, if you're going to divorce me?" And she says, "It don't make no difference to *you,* I guess. Please go, Stephen. And don't come back *ever.*" (*Begins to cry.*)

MAGGIE (*impatiently*). Yes?

JANE. I didn't hear his last words. Because naturally, when he said he was going, I scooted down the hall. But I heard her call, "Stephen?" And he stops on the landing and says, "Yes, Mary?" and she says, "Nothing. Just don't slam the front door— The servants will hear you!" So I came down here. Oh, Maggie, what's going to happen?

MAGGIE. She's going to get a divorce.

JANE. Oh, dear. I'm so sad for her.

MAGGIE. I ain't.

JANE. What?

MAGGIE. She's indulging a pride she ain't entitled to. Marriage is a business of taking care of a man and rearing his children. It ain't meant to be no perpetual honeymoon. How long would any husband last if he was supposed to go on acting forever like a red-hot Clark Gable? What's the difference if he don't love her?

JANE. How can you say that, Maggie!

MAGGIE. That don't let her off her obligation to keep him from making a fool of himself, does it?

JANE. Do you think he'll marry that girl?

MAGGIE. When a man's got the habit of supporting some woman, he just don't feel natural unless he's doing it.

JANE. But he told the madam marrying her was the furthest thing from his mind.

MAGGIE. It don't matter what he's got in his mind. It's what those two women got in theirs will settle the matter.

JANE. But the madam says it's up to *him.* She said, "You love her, or you love me, Stephen."

MAGGIE. So what did he say to that?

JANE. Nothing for a long time. Just walked up and down—up and down—up and—

MAGGIE. He was thinking. Tch—tch. The first man who can think up a good explanation how he can be in love with his wife *and* another woman, is going to win that prize they're always giving out in Sweden!

CURTAIN

SCENE III

A month later.

MARY'S *living room. The room is now denuded of pictures, books, vases, etc. The rug is rolled up. The curtains and chairs are covered with slips.*

As the curtain rises, MARY, *dressed for traveling, is pacing up and down.* MRS. MOREHEAD, *dressed for the street, watches her from the sofa.*

MRS. MOREHEAD. What time does your train go?

MARY (*looking at her wrist watch*). An hour. His secretary ought to be here. I never knew there could be so many papers to sign.

MRS. MOREHEAD. You showed everything to your lawyers—

MARY. They always say the same thing! I'm getting a "raw deal"—

MRS. MOREHEAD (*alarmed*). But, Mary—

MARY. Oh, I know it's not true. Stephen's been very generous.

MRS. MOREHEAD. Oh, I wouldn't say that. If Stephen is a rich man now, he owes it largely to you.

MARY. Stephen would have gotten where he is, with or without me.

MRS. MOREHEAD. He didn't have a penny when you married him.

MARY. Mother, are you trying to make me bitter, too?

MRS. MOREHEAD (*helplessly*). I'm sure I don't know what to say. If I sympathize with Stephen, you accuse me of taking his side.

And when I sympathize with you, I'm making you bitter. The thing for me to do is keep still. (*There is a pause. Then, emphatically.*) You're both making a terrible mistake!

MARY. Mother, please!

MRS. MOREHEAD. But the children, Mary. The children—

MARY. What good will it do them to be brought up in a home full of quarrelling and suspicion? They'll be better off just with me.

MRS. MOREHEAD. No, they won't. A child needs both its parents in one home.

MARY. A home without love?

MRS. MOREHEAD. He's terribly fond of you—

MARY. Mother, don't use that word! Oh, Mother, please. Every argument goes round in circles. And, it's too late now—

MRS. MOREHEAD. It's never too late when you love. Mary, why don't you call this thing off? I'm sure that's what Stephen's waiting for.

MARY (*bitterly*). Is it? He hasn't made any sign of it to me. Isn't he the one to come to me?

MRS. MOREHEAD. You're the one, Mary, who insisted on the divorce.

MARY. But don't you see; if he hadn't wanted it, he'd have fought me—

MRS. MOREHEAD. Stephen's not the fighting kind.

MARY. Neither am I.

MRS. MOREHEAD. Damn these modern laws!

MARY. Mother!

MRS. MOREHEAD. Damn them, I say! Fifty years ago, when women couldn't get divorces, they made the best of situations like this. And sometimes, out of situations like this they made very good things indeed! (*Enter* JANE, *right.*)

JANE. Mr. Haines' secretary, ma'am.

MRS. MOREHEAD. Tell her to come in. (*Exit* JANE.) Now, go bathe your eyes. Don't let that adding-machine see you like this. And don't be long. Remember, you have one more unpleasant task.

MARY. Mary?

MRS. MOREHEAD. The child must be told.

MARY (*miserably, and a little guiltily*). I have been putting it off. Because—

MRS. MOREHEAD. Because you hope at the last minute a miracle will keep you from making a mess of your life. Have you thought: Stephen might marry that girl?

MARY (*very confident*). He won't do that.

MRS. MOREHEAD. What makes you so sure?

MARY. Because, deep down, Stephen does love me— But he won't find it out, until I've—really gone away— (*At the door.*) You'll take good care of the children, Mother? And make them write to me to Reno, once a week? And please, Mother, don't spoil them so. (*Exits left.*)

MRS. MOREHEAD. Gracious! You'd think I'd never raised children of my own! (*Enter* MISS WATTS *and* MISS TRIMMERBACK, *right. They are very tailored, plain girls.* MISS WATTS, *the older and the plainer of the two, carries a brief-case.*) How do you do, Miss Watts?

MISS WATTS. How do you do, Mrs. Morehead? This is Miss Trimmerback from our office.

MISS TRIMMERBACK. How do you do?

MISS WATTS. She's a notary. We have some papers for Mrs. Haines to sign.

MRS. MOREHEAD. Anything I can do?

MISS WATTS. The children will be with you? (MRS. MOREHEAD *nods.*) Any incidental bills, Mrs. Morehead, send to the office. But you understand, bills arriving after the divorce will be assumed by Mrs. Haines under the terms of the settlement.

MRS. MOREHEAD. Mrs. Haines will be with you in a minute. Please don't bother her with unnecessary details. She's—she's pressed for time. (*Exits right.*)

MISS TRIMMERBACK. Gee, don't you feel sorry for Mrs. Haines?

MISS WATTS (*bitterly*). I don't feel sorry for any woman who thinks the world owes her breakfast in bed.

MISS TRIMMERBACK. You don't like her.

MISS WATTS. Oh, she never interfered at the office.

MISS TRIMMERBACK. Maybe that's why he's been a success.

MISS WATTS. He'd have gotten further without her. Everything big that came up, he was too cautious, because of her and the kids. (*Opens the brief-case, takes out papers and pen, arranges the papers, for signing, on the table.*) Well, thank heaven it's almost over. He and I can go back to work. (*Sits.*)

MISS TRIMMERBACK. What about Allen?

MISS WATTS (*guardedly.*) What about her?

MISS TRIMMERBACK. Is he going to marry her?

MISS WATTS. I don't butt into his private affairs. Oh, I hold no brief for Allen. But I must say knowing *her* gave him a new interest in his work. Before her, he was certainly going stale. That had me worried.

MISS TRIMMERBACK (*sinking on the sofa*). Well, she's lucky, I'll say.

MISS WATTS. Oh?

MISS TRIMMERBACK. I wish I could get a man to foot my bills. I'm sick and tired, cooking my own breakfast, sloshing through the rain at 8 A.M., working like a dog. For what? Independence? A lot of independence you have on a woman's wages. I'd chuck it like that for a decent, or an indecent, home.

MISS WATTS. I'm sure you would.

MISS TRIMMERBACK. Wouldn't you?

MISS WATTS. I have a home.

MISS TRIMMERBACK. You mean Plattsburgh, where you were born?

MISS WATTS. The office. That's my home.

MISS TRIMMERBACK. Some home! I see. The office-wife?

MISS WATTS (*defiantly*). He could get along better without Mrs. Haines or Allen than he could without me.

MISS TRIMMERBACK. Oh, you're very efficient, dear. But what makes you think you're indispensable?

MISS WATTS. I relieve him of a thousand foolish details. I remind him of things he forgets, including, very often these days, his good opinion of himself. I never cry and I don't nag. I guess I *am* the office-wife. And a lot better off than Mrs. Haines. He'll never divorce me!

MISS TRIMMERBACK (*astonished*). Why, you're in love with him! (*They both rise, face each other angrily.*)

MISS WATTS. What if I am? I'd rather work for him than marry the kind of a dumb cluck I could get— (*Almost tearful*) just because he's a *man*— (*Enter* MARY, *left.*)

MARY. Yes, Miss Watts.

MISS WATTS (*collecting herself quickly*). Here are the inventories of the furniture, Mrs. Haines. I had the golf cups, the books, etchings, and the ash stands sent to Mr. Haines' club. (*Pauses.*) Mr. Haines asked if he could also have the portrait of the two children.

MARY (*looking at the blank space over the mantel*). Oh, but—

MISS WATTS. He said it wouldn't matter, if you really didn't *care* for him to have it.

MARY. It's in storage.

MISS WATTS (*laying a paper on the table*). This will get it out. Sign there. The cook's letter of reference. Sign here. (MARY *sits, signs.*) The insurance papers. You sign here. (MISS TRIMMERBACK *signs each paper after* MARY.) The transfer papers on the car. What do you want done with it?

MARY. Well, I—

MISS WATTS. I'll find a garage. Sign here. What do you want done if someone meets your price on this apartment?

MARY. Well, I thought—

MISS WATTS. This gives us power of attorney until you get back. Sign here.

MARY. But—I—

MISS WATTS. Oh, it's quite in order, Mrs. Haines. Now, Mr. Haines took the liberty of drawing you a new will. (*Places a blue, legal-looking document before* MARY.)

MARY (*indignantly*). But—really—

MISS WATTS. If anything were to happen to you in Reno, half your property would revert to him. A detail your lawyers overlooked. Mr. Haines drew up a codicil cutting himself out—

MARY. But, I don't understand legal language, Miss Watts. I—I must have my lawyer—

MISS WATTS. As you please. (*Stiffly.*) Mr. Haines suggested this for *your* sake, not his. I'm sure you realize, he has nothing but your interests at heart. (*A pause.*) Sign here. (MARY *signs*, MISS WATTS *signs*.) We need three witnesses. (*Enter* JANE, *right, with a box of flowers.*) Your maid will do.

MARY. Jane, please witness this. It's my will.

JANE (*in tears*). Oh, Mrs. Haines! (*Signs.*)

MISS WATTS (*gathering all the papers*). You can always make changes, in the event of your remarriage. (MARY *rises.*) And don't hesitate to let me know at the office, if there is anything *I* can ever do for you.

MARY (*coldly*). There will be nothing, Miss Watts.

MISS WATTS (*cheerfully*). Oh, there are always tag ends to a divorce, Mrs. Haines. And you know how Mr. Haines hates to be bothered with inconsequential details. Good day, Mrs. Haines, and pleasant journey to you! (*Exit* MISS WATTS *right, followed by* MISS TRIMMERBACK.)

JANE (*sniveling as she places the box on the table*). Mr. Haines said I was to give you these to wear on the train. (*Exits abruptly.* MARY *slowly opens the box, takes out a corsage of orchids and a card. Reads aloud:* "What can I say? Stephen." *Then throws them violently in the corner. Enter* MRS. MOREHEAD, LITTLE MARY, *dressed for street.*)

MRS. MOREHEAD. All set, dear?

MARY (*grimly*). All set—Mary, Mother wants to talk to you before she goes away.

MRS. MOREHEAD. Brother and I will wait for you downstairs. (*Exit* MRS. MOREHEAD.)

MARY. Mary, sit down, dear. (LITTLE MARY *skips to the sofa, sits down. A pause.* MARY *discovers that it's going to be even more painful and difficult than she imagined.*) Mary—

LITTLE MARY. Yes, Mother?

MARY. Mary—

LITTLE MARY (*perplexed by her mother's tone, which she feels bodes no good to her*). Have I done something wrong, Mother?

MARY. Oh, no, darling, no. (*She sits beside her daughter, and takes her two hands.*) Mary, you know Daddy's been gone for some time.

LITTLE MARY (*sadly*). A whole month.

MARY. Shall I tell you why?

LITTLE MARY (*eagerly*). Why?

MARY (*plunging in*). You know, darling, when a man and woman fall in love what they do, don't you?

LITTLE MARY. They kiss a lot—

MARY. They get married—

LITTLE MARY. Oh, yes. And then they have those children.

MARY. Well, sometimes, married people don't stay in love.

LITTLE MARY. What, Mother?

MARY. The husband and the wife—fall out of love.

LITTLE MARY. Why do they do that?

MARY. Well, they do, that's all. And when they do, they get unmarried. You see?

LITTLE MARY. No.

MARY. Well, they do. They—they get what is called a divorce.

LITTLE MARY (*very matter of fact*). Oh, do they?

MARY. You don't know what a divorce is, but—

LITTLE MARY. Yes, I do. I go to the movies, don't I? And lots of my friends have mummies and daddies who are divorced.

MARY (*relieved, kisses her*). You know I love you very much, don't you, Mary?

LITTLE MARY (*a pause*). Of course, Mother.

MARY. Your father and I are going to get a divorce. That's why I'm going away. That's why— Oh, darling, I can't explain to you quite. But I promise you, when you are older you will understand. And you'll forgive me. You really will! Look at me, baby, please!

LITTLE MARY (*her lips begin to tremble*). I'm looking at you, Mother—Doesn't Daddy love you any more?

MARY. No, he doesn't.

LITTLE MARY. Don't you love him?

MARY. I—I—no, Mary.

LITTLE MARY. Oh, Mother, why?

MARY. I—I don't know—But it isn't either Daddy's or Mother's fault.

LITTLE MARY. But, Mother, when you love somebody I thought you loved them until the day you die!

MARY. With children, yes. But grown-ups are different. They can fall out of love.

LITTLE MARY. I won't fall out of love with you and Daddy when I grow up. Will you fall out of love with me?

MARY. Oh, no, darling, that's different, too.

LITTLE MARY (*miserable*). I don't see *how*.

MARY. You'll have to take my word for it, baby, it is. This divorce has nothing to do with our love for you.

LITTLE MARY. But if you and Daddy—

MARY (*rising and drawing her daughter up to her*). Darling, I'll explain it better to you in the taxi. We'll go alone in the taxi, shall we?

LITTLE MARY. But, Mother, if you and Daddy are getting a divorce, which one won't I see again? Daddy or you?

MARY. You and Brother will live with me. That's what happens when—when people get divorced. Children must go with their mothers. But you'll see Daddy—sometimes. Now, darling, come along.

LITTLE MARY. Please, Mother, wait for me downstairs.

MARY. Why?

LITTLE MARY. I have to go to the bathroom.

MARY. Then hurry along, dear— (*Sees the orchids on the floor, and as she moves to the door stoops, picks them up, goes out.* LITTLE MARY *stands looking after her, stricken. Suddenly she goes to the back of the chair, hugs it, as if for comfort. Then she begins to cry and beat the back of the chair with her fists.*)

LITTLE MARY. Oh, please, please, Mother dear— Oh! Daddy, Daddy darling! Oh, why don't you do something—*do something*—Mother dear!

CURTAIN

SCENE IV

A month later.

A room in a lying-in hospital. Left, a door to the corridor. Right, a window banked to the sill with expensive flowers. Center, a hospital bed, in which EDITH, *propped up in a sea of lace pillows, lies with a small bundle at her breast. A white-uniformed nurse sits by the window. The droop of her shoulders is eloquent:* EDITH *is a trying patient. As the curtain rises,* EDITH *reaches across the bundle to the bedside table for a cigarette. She can't make it.*

EDITH (*whining*). Nurse!

NURSE (*rising wearily*). Yes, Mrs. Potter.

EDITH. Throw me a cigarette.

NURSE. Can't you wait, at least until you're through nursing?

EDITH. How many children have you nursed? I've nursed four. (NURSE *lights her cigarette;* EDITH *shifts the bundle slightly.*) Ouch! Damn it! It's got jaws like a dinosaur. (*Enter* PEGGY *with a box of flowers.*)

PEGGY. Hello, Edith.

EDITH (*in a faint voice*). Hello, Peggy.

PEGGY (*putting flowers on bed*). Here—

EDITH. How thoughtful! Nurse, will you ask this damn hospital if they're equipped with a decent vase? (NURSE, *takes the box, opens flowers and arranges them, with others, in the window.*)

PEGGY (*leans over baby*). Oh, let me see. Oh, Edith, isn't he divine!

EDITH. I hate that milky smell.

PEGGY (*alarmed*). What's that on his nose?

EDITH. What nose? Oh, that's an ash. (*Blows away the ash. Hands* PEGGY *a letter from bedside table.*)

PEGGY. Mary?

EDITH (*nodding*). All about how healthy Reno is. Not a word about how she feels. I thought she cared more about Stephen than that. She sends her love to you and John. (PEGGY *reads. The wail of a new-born is heard outside.*)

EDITH. Nurse, close that door. (*The* NURSE *closes the door.*) I can't tell you what that new-born yodel does to my nerves. (*To* PEGGY.) What're you so down in the mouth about? I feel as badly about it as you do, but it was the thing Mary wanted to do, or she wouldn't have done it. Judging by that, she's reconciled to the whole idea.

PEGGY. She's just being brave!

EDITH. Brave? Why should she bother to be brave with her friends? Here, Nurse, he's through. (*The* NURSE *takes the bundle from her.*) I told Phelps to be sure to tell Stephen that Mary's perfectly happy. It will cheer Stephen up. He's been going around like a whipped dog.

PEGGY. Oh, Edith, please let me hold him! (*The* NURSE *gives* PEGGY *the baby.*)

NURSE (*smiling*). Careful of his back. Mrs. Day.

PEGGY (*goes to the window, hugging the bundle*). Oh, I *like* the feeling so!

EDITH. You wouldn't like it so much if you'd just had it. (*Whimpering.*) I had a terrible time, didn't I, Nurse?

NURSE. Oh, no, Mrs. Potter. You had a very easy time. (*She is suddenly angry.*) Why, women like you don't know what a terrible time is. Try bearing a baby and scrubbing floors. Try having one in a cold filthy kitchen, without ether, without a change of linen, without decent food, without a cent to bring it up—and try getting up the next day with your insides falling out, to cook your husband's—! (*Controls herself.*) No, Mrs. Potter, you didn't have a terrible time at all— I'll take the baby, please. (*Sees the reluctant expression on* PEGGY'S *face.*) I hope

some day you'll have one of your own, Mrs. Day. (*The* NURSE *exits with the baby.* PEGGY *breaks into tears.*)

EDITH. Well, for God's sake, Peggy, that old battle-axe didn't hurt my feelings a bit! They're all the same. If you don't get peritonitis or have quintuplets, they think you've had a picnic—(PEGGY *sits beside the bed, crying.*) What's the matter?

PEGGY. Oh, Edith—John and I are getting a divorce!

EDITH (*patting her hand*). Well, darling, that's what I heard!

PEGGY (*surprised*). But—but we didn't decide to until last night.

EDITH (*cheerfully*). Oh, darling, everybody could see it was in the cards. Money, I suppose?

PEGGY (*nodding*). Oh, dear! I wish Mary were here—

EDITH. Well, she'll be there. (*Laughs.*) Oh, forgive me, dear. I do feel sorry for you. But it is funny.

PEGGY. What's funny?

EDITH. It's going to be quite a gathering of the clan. (*Sitting up in bed, full of energy to break the news.*) Howard Fowler's bounced Sylvia out right on her ear! He's threatened to divorce her right here in New York if she doesn't go to Reno. And name her young customer's man—

PEGGY. But—Howard's always known—

EDITH. Certainly. He hired him, so he'd have plenty of time for his own affairs. Howard's got some girl he wants to marry. But nobody, not even Winchell, knows who she is! Howard's a coony cuss. (*Laughing.*) I do think it's screaming. When you remember how Sylvia always thought she was putting something over on us girls! (*She laughs so hard, she gives herself a stitch. She falls back among her pillows, limp and martyred.*)

PEGGY (*bitterly*). Life's awfully unattractive, isn't it?

EDITH (*yawning*). Oh, I wouldn't complain if that damned stork would take the Indian sign off me.

CURTAIN

SCENE V

A few weeks later. Mary's living room in a Reno hotel. In the rear wall, a bay window showing a view of Reno's squat roof-tops and distant Nevada ranges. Left, doors to the kitchenette, the bedroom. Right, a door to the corridor. A plush armchair, a sofa. In the corner, MARY's *half-packed trunks and bags. It is all very drab and ugly. As the curtain rises,* LUCY, *a slatternly middle-aged, husky woman in a house-dress, is packing the clothes that are strewn on the armchair and the table. She is singing in a nasal falsetto.*

LUCY.
Down on ole Smokey, all covered with snow,
I lost my true lov-ver, from courtin' too slow.
Courtin' is pul-leasure, partin' is grief,
Anna false-hearted lov-ver is worse thanna thief—
(PEGGY *enter, right. She wears a polo-coat and a wool tam. She is on the verge of tears.*)

PEGGY. Lucy, where's Mrs. Haines?

LUCY. Down waiting for the mail. You'll miss her a lot when she goes tomorrow? (PEGGY *nods, sinks, dejected, on the sofa.*) Mrs. Haines is about the nicest ever came here.

PEGGY. I hate Reno.

LUCY. You didn't come for fun. (*Goes on with her packing and singing.*)
The grave'll de-cay you, an' change you tuh dust,
Ain't one boy outta twenty, a poor gal kin trust—

PEGGY. You've seen lots of divorcees, haven't you, Lucy?

LUCY. Been cookin' for 'em for ten years.

PEGGY. You feel sorry for us?

LUCY. Well, ma'am, I don't. You feel plenty sorry enough for yourselves. (*Kindly.*) Lord, you ain't got much else to do.

PEGGY (*resentfully*). You've never been married, Lucy.

LUCY (*indignant*). I've had three—

PEGGY. Husbands?

LUCY. Kids!

PEGGY. Oh, then, you're probably very happy—

LUCY. Lord, ma'am, I stopped thinking about being happy years ago.

PEGGY. You don't think about being happy?

LUCY. Ain't had the time. With the kids and all. And the old man such a demon when he's drinking— Them big, strong, red-headed men. They're fierce.

PEGGY. Oh, Lucy, he beats you? How terrible!

LUCY. Ain't it? When you think what a lot of women in this hotel need a beating worse than me.

PEGGY. But you live in Reno. You could get a divorce overnight.

LUCY. Lord, a woman can't get herself worked up to a thing like that overnight. I had a mind to do it once. I had the money, too. But I had to call it off.

PEGGY. Why?

LUCY. I found out I was in a family way. (*There is a rap on the door.*)

PEGGY (*going to her*). Lucy, tell Mrs. Haines I must talk to her—alone—before supper— (*Enter* COUNTESS DE LAGE, *left. She is a silly, amiable, middle-aged woman, with carefully waved, bleached hair. She wears a gaudily checked riding habit, carries an enormous new sombrero and a jug of corn liquor.*)

COUNTESS. Ah, Peggy, how are you, dear child?

PEGGY. All right, Countess de Lage.

COUNTESS. I've been galloping madly over the desert all day. Lucy, here's a wee juggie. We must celebrate Mrs. Haines' divorce.

PEGGY. Oh, Countess de Lage, I don't think a divorce is anything to celebrate.

COUNTESS. Wait till you've lost as many husbands as I have, Peggy. (*Wistfully.*) Married, divorced, married, divorced! But where Love leads I always follow. So here I am, in Reno.

PEGGY. Oh, I wish I were anywhere else on earth.

COUNTESS. My dear, you've got the Reno jumpy-wumpies. Did you go to the doctor? What did he say?

PEGGY. He said it was—the altitude.

COUNTESS. Well, la, la, you'll get used to that. My third husband was a Swiss. If one lives in Switzerland, Peggy, one has simply got to accept the Alps. As I used to say to myself, Flora, there those damn Alps are, and there's very little even you can do about it.

PEGGY. Yes, Countess de Lage. (*Exits, hurriedly, left.*)

COUNTESS. Oh, I wish she hadn't brought up the Alps, Lucy. It always reminds me of that nasty moment I had the day Gustav made me climb to the top of one of them. (*Sits in armchair.*) Lucy, pull off my boots. (LUCY *kneels, tugs at her boots.*) Anyhow, there we were. And suddenly it struck me that Gustav had pushed me. (*Tragically.*) I slid halfway down the mountain before I realized that Gustav didn't love me any more. (*Gaily.*) But Love takes care of its own, Lucy. I slid right into the arms of my fourth husband, the Count.

LUCY (*rises, with boots.*) Ain't that the one you're divorcing now?

COUNTESS. But, of course, Lucy. (*Plaintively.*) What could I do when I found out he was putting arsenic in my headache powders. Ah! L'amour! L'amour! Lucy, were you ever in love?

LUCY. Yes, ma'am.

COUNTESS. Tell me about it, Lucy.

LUCY. Well, ma'am, ain't much to tell. I was kinda enjoyin' the courtin' time. It was as purty a sight as you ever saw, to see him come lopin' across them hills. The sky so big and blue and that hair of his, blazing like the be-jesuss in the sun. Then we'd sit on my back fence and spark. But, ma'am,

you know how them big, strong, red-headed men are. They just got to get to the point. So we got married, ma'am. And natcherly, I ain't had no chanct to think about love since—

COUNTESS (*she has not been listening*). The trouble with me, Lucy, is I've been marrying too many foreigners. I think I'll go back to marrying Americans. (*Enter* MIRIAM, *right. She is a breezy, flashy red-head, about 28 years old. She is wearing a theatrical pair of lounging pajamas.*)

MIRIAM. Hya, Lucy?

LUCY. Evening, Mrs. Aarons. (*Exits, right.*)

MIRIAM. Hya, Countess, how's rhythm on the range? (*Sees the jug on the table, pours the* COUNTESS *and herself drinks.*)

COUNTESS. Gallop, gallop, gallop, madly over the sagebrush! But now, Miriam, I'm having an emotional relapse. In two weeks I'll be free, free as a bird from that little French bastard. But whither, oh, whither shall I fly?

MIRIAM. To the arms of that cowboy up at the dude ranch?

COUNTESS (*modestly*). Miriam Aarons!

MIRIAM. Why, he's nuts for you, Countess. He likes you better than his horse, and it's such a damn big horse.

COUNTESS (*rises, and pads in her stocking-feet to the sofa*). Well, Buck Winston is nice. So young. So strong. Have you noticed the play of his muscles? (*Reclining.*) Musical. Musical.

MIRIAM. He could crack a coconut with those knees. If he could get them together. Say, Countess, that guy hasn't been arousing your honorable intentions, has he?

COUNTESS. Yes, Miriam, but I'm different from the rest of you. I've always put my faith in love. Still, I've had four divorces. Dare I risk a fifth?

MIRIAM. What are you risking, Countess, or maybe I shouldn't ask?

COUNTESS. I mean, Miriam, I could never make a success of Buck at Newport.

MIRIAM. Even Mrs. Astor would have to admit Buck's handsome. If I had your dough,

I'd take him to Hollywood first, then Newport.

COUNTESS. Hollywood? Why *not?* I might turn him into a picture star. After all, my second husband was a gondolier, and a month after I married him, a Duchess eloped with him. Ah! L'amour! (*Enter* SYLVIA, *right. She is wearing a smart dinner dress. Her trip to Reno has embittered her, but it has not subdued her.*)

MIRIAM. Hya, Sylvia? Going to a ball?

SYLVIA (*pours a drink*). Doing the town with a boy friend.

MIRIAM. Where'd you pick him up?

SYLVIA. The Silver State Bar. I'm not going to sit around, moping, like Mary.

COUNTESS. Poor Mary. If her husband gave her the flimsiest excuse, she'd take him back.

SYLVIA. She has no pride. I'd roast in hell before I'd take Howard Fowler back. Kicking me out like that! After all I sacrificed!

MIRIAM. Such as what?

SYLVIA. I gave him my *youth!*

COUNTESS (*dreamily*). Hélas, what can a woman do with her youth, but give it to a man?

MIRIAM. Hélas, she can't preserve it in alcohol.

COUNTESS (*practical*). But, Sylvia, how could your husband kick you out, if you were a femme fidèle.

SYLVIA. Of course, I was a faithful wife. (MIRIAM *snorts.*) What are you laughing at?

MIRIAM. Two kinds of women, Sylvia, owls and ostriches. (*Raises her glass.*) To the feathered sisterhood! To the girls who *get* paid and paid. (*Parenthetically.*) And you got paid *plenty!*

SYLVIA. You bet I got plenty! The skunk!

COUNTESS. I never got a sou from any of my husbands, except my first husband, Mr. Straus. He said the most touching thing in his will. I remember every word of it. "To my beloved wife, Flora, I leave all my estate

in trust to be administered by executors, because she is an A No. 1 *schlemeil."* (*Touched anew.*) Wasn't that sweet?

MIRIAM (*Enter* MARY, *right. She is subdued. She is carrying some letters*). Hya, queen?

MARY. Fine.

MIRIAM. Ya lie.

COUNTESS. Mary, I'm starved. (LUCY *enters, left, takes* MARY's *hat.*)

MARY. Supper's nearly ready. As my last official act in Reno, I cooked the whole thing with my hands, didn't I, Lucy?

LUCY. All but the steak and tomatoes and dessert, Mrs. Haines. (*Exits, left.*)

MARY (*gives a letter to* SYLVIA, *glancing as she does so, at the inscription*). For you, Sylvia. From Edith?

SYLVIA. You couldn't miss that infantile handwriting. (*Pointedly.*) You didn't hear from anyone?

MARY. No.

SYLVIA. Well, darling, Stephen's hardly worth a broken heart.

MARY. The less you have to say about me and Stephen the better I like it!

SYLVIA. I'm only trying to cheer you up. That's more than you do for me.

MARY. I'm doing enough, just being pleasant to you.

SYLVIA. My, you have got the jitters, dear.

MIRIAM. Hey, Sylvia, we're all out here in the same boat. Mary's laid off you. Why don't you lay off her?

SYLVIA. Oh, I'm just trying to make her see life isn't over just because Stephen let her down. (*Opens her letter. A batch of press-clippings falls out. The* COUNTESS *picks them up, reads them idly, as* SYLVIA *goes on with the letter.*)

COUNTESS. You see, Miriam? What else is there for a woman but l'amour?

MIRIAM. There's a little corn whiskey left. (*She pours another drink.*)

COUNTESS. Cynic, you don't believe in Cupid.

MIRIAM. That double-crossing little squirt! Give me Donald Duck. (*To* MARY.) Have a drink? (MARY *shakes her head.*) Listen, Babe, why not—give out? You'd feel better—

MARY (*laughing*). Miriam, you're not very chatty about your own affairs.

COUNTESS (*suddenly engrossed by the clippings from* SYLVIA'S *letter*). Miriam, you sly puss, you never told us you even knew Sylvia's husband.

SYLVIA (*looking up from her letter*). What?

COUNTESS (*rises*). Sylvia, listen to this: "Miriam Vanities Aaron is being Renovated. Three guesses, Mrs. Fowler, for whose Ostermoor?" (SYLVIA *snatches the clippings from her.*)

MIRIAM. Why can't those lousy rags leave a successful divorce alone?

COUNTESS (*reading another clipping*). "Prominent stockbroker and ex-chorine to marry."

SYLVIA (*To* MIRIAM). Why, you little hypocrite! (*During this,* PEGGY *has entered and goes back of the sofa. She listens but does not join the group.*)

MARY (*going to her*). Now, Sylvia—

SYLVIA. Did you know this?

MARY. Oh, Sylvia, why do you care? You don't love Howard—

SYLVIA (*brushing her aside*). That has nothing to do with it. (*To* MIRIAM, *fiercely.*) How much did he settle on you?

MIRIAM. I made Howard pay for what he wants; you made him pay for what he doesn't want.

SYLVIA. You want him for his money.

MIRIAM. So what do you want him for? I'll stay bought. That's more than you did, Sylvia.

SYLVIA. Why, you dirty little trollop!

MIRIAM. Don't start calling names, you Park Avenue push-over! (SYLVIA *gives* MIRIAM *a terrific smack. In the twinkling of an eye, they are pulling hair.* MARY *seizes* SYLVIA'S

arm; SYLVIA *breaks loose. The* COUNTESS *tugs at* MIRIAM'S *belt, as* LUCY *comes in, looks at the fight with a rather professional eye, and exits for the smelling-salts.*)

COUNTESS. Tiens! Miriam. Don't be vulgar (*Her interference enables* SYLVIA *to slap* MIRIAM *unimpeded.*)

MIRIAM (*shoving the* COUNTESS *on the sofa*). Out of the way, you fat old—! (SYLVIA *grabs* MIRIAM'S *hair.*) Ouch, let go! (SYLVIA *is about to use her nails.* MARY *takes a hand.*)

MARY. I won't have this, you hear! (MARY'S *interference allows* MIRIAM *to give* SYLVIA *a terrific kick in the shins.*)

SYLVIA (*routed, in sobs*). Oh, you hurt me, you bitch, you! (*As she turns away,* MIRIAM *gives her another well-placed kick, which straightens* SYLVIA *up.*)

MIRIAM. Take that! (SYLVIA, *shrieking with rage and humiliation, grabs* MIRIAM *again, sinks her white teeth into* MIRIAM'S *arm. At this mayhem,* MARY *seizes her, shakes her violently, pushes her sobbing into the armchair.*)

MARY (*to* MIRIAM). That's enough.

MIRIAM. Where's the iodine? (MARY *points to bedroom.*) Gotta be careful of hydrophobia, you know. (*Exits, right.*)

SYLVIA (*blubbering, nursing her wounds*). Oh, Mary, how could you let her do that to me!

MARY (*coldly*). I'm terribly sorry, Sylvia.

SYLVIA. The humiliation! You're on her side. After all I've done for you!

MARY. What have you done for me?

SYLVIA. I warned *you!*

MARY (*bitterly*). I'm not exactly grateful for that.

SYLVIA (*hysterical*). Oh, aren't you? Listen to me, you ball of conceit. You're not the object of pity you suppose. Plenty of the girls are tickled to death you got what was coming to you. You deserved to lose Stephen, the stupid way you acted. But I always stood up for you, like a loyal friend. What thanks do I get? You knew about that woman, and you stood by, gloating, while she—

MARY. Get out of here! (LUCY *enters from the bedroom, with a bottle of spirits of ammonia, as* SYLVIA *gives way completely to hysteria, and, screaming with rage, picks up ash-trays, glasses, and cigarette boxes, and hurls them violently against the wall.*)

SYLVIA (*at the top of her lungs*). I hate you! I hate you! I hate *everybody*—

LUCY (*takes* SYLVIA *firmly by the shoulders, forces the bottle under her nose*). Listen, Mrs. Fowler! You got the hy-strikes! (*Rushes her gasping, sobbing, to the door.*)

SYLVIA. You wait. Some day you'll need a woman friend. Then you'll think of me— (*Exit* LUCY *and* SYLVIA, *struggling helplessly, right.*)

COUNTESS (*rising from the sofa*). Poor creatures. They've lost their equilibrium because they've lost their faith in love. (*Philosophically.*) L'amour. Remember the song Buck made up, just for me? (*Pours herself a drink, sings.*) "Oh, a man can ride a horse to the range above, But a woman's got to ride on the wings of love, Coma a ti-yi-yip-pi." (*Throws the jug over her shoulder, and exits right, still singing, as* MIRIAM *enters, the ravages of her fight repaired.*)

MIRIAM. The coast clear?

PEGGY. Oh, that was the most disgusting thing I ever saw.

MIRIAM. Right, kid, we're a pair of alley cats—

MARY. You should not be here, Peggy, to see it at all. (*She picks up the ash-trays, etc.*)

MIRIAM. What the hell are you doing here?

MARY. Peggy wanted to buy a car.

PEGGY. With my own money!

MARY. John said they couldn't afford a car.

PEGGY. He couldn't. I could.

MARY. What was his—is yours. What is yours—is your own. Very fair.

PEGGY. A woman's best protection is a little money of her own.

MARY. A woman's best protection is—the right man. (*With gentle sarcasm.*) Obvious-

ly, John isn't the right man and Peggy will forget all about him in another month.

PEGGY. No, I won't. I can't. Because—because— (*Bursts into tears.*) Oh, Mary, I'm going to have a baby. Oh, Mary, what shall I do?

MARY. Peggy, what's his telephone number?

PEGGY (*quickly*). Eldorado 5-2075. (MIRIAM *goes at once to the phone. Gets the operator, gives the number.*) But, oh, Mary, I can't tell him!

MIRIAM. Why? Isn't it his?

PEGGY. Oh, of course!

MIRIAM. And make it snappy, operator.

PEGGY. I always wanted it. But what can I do with it now?

MIRIAM. Land it with the Marines—

MARY. Peggy, you've shared your love with him. Your baby will share your blood, your eyes, your hair, your virtues—and your faults— But your little pin-money, that, of course, you could not share.

PEGGY. Oh, Mary, I know I'm wrong. But, it's no use—you don't know the things he said to me. I have my pride.

MARY (*bitterly*). Reno's full of women who all have their pride.

PEGGY. You think I'm like them.

MIRIAM. You've got the makings, dear.

MARY. Love has pride in nothing—but its own humility.

MIRIAM (*at telephone*). Mr. Day, please. Reno calling—Mr. Day? My God, he must live by the phone. Just hold the— (PEGGY *leaps to the phone.*)

PEGGY. Hello, John. (*Clears her throat of a sob.*) No, I'm not sick. That is, I am sick! That is, I'm sick to my stomach. Oh, John! I'm going to have a baby— Oh, darling, are you?— Oh, darling, do you?— Oh, darling, so am I! So do I! Course, I forgive you.— Yes, precious. Yes, lamb. On the very next train! John? (*A kiss into the phone. It is returned.*) Oh, Johnny, when I get back, things are going to be so different—! John do you mind if I reverse the charges? (*Hangs up.*) I can't stay for supper. I've got to pack.

MARY. When you get back—don't see too much of the girls.

PEGGY. Oh, I won't, Mary. It's all their fault we're here.

MARY. Not—entirely.

PEGGY. Good-bye! Oh, I'm so happy, I could cry. (*Exits, right.*)

MIRIAM. Getting wise, aren't you?

MARY. Know all the answers.

MIRIAM. Then, why're you here?

MARY. I had plenty of advice, Miriam. (*The telephone rings.* MIRIAM *goes to it.*)

MIRIAM. Hello. No, we completed that call, operator. (*Hangs up.*)

MARY. Cigarette?

MIRIAM (*suddenly*). Listen.

MARY. There's nothing you can say I haven't heard.

MIRIAM. Sure? I come from a world where a woman's got to come out on top—or it's just too damned bad. Maybe I got a new slant.

MARY (*wearily*). All right, Miriam. Talk to me about my—lawful husband. Talk to me about security— What does it all come to? Compromise.

MIRIAM. What the hell? A woman's compromised the day she's born.

MARY. You can't compromise with utter defeat. He doesn't want me.

MIRIAM. How do you know?

MARY. How do I know—why else am I here?

MIRIAM (*a pause. Then, mock-tragically*). Because you've got no guts, Mary Haines. It happened to me—I lost my man, too.

MARY (*smiling*). You?

MIRIAM. Oh, it only happened once. Got wise to myself after that. Look, how did I lose him? We didn't have enough dough to get married. I wouldn't sleep with him until we did. I had ideals—God knows where I got 'em. I held out on him—(*Sighs.*) Can you beat it? I liked him a lot better than I've ever liked anybody since. I never held out again— What'd my Romeo do? Got himself another girl. I made a terrible stink. Why shouldn't I? I should. But what I ought not to have done was say—good-bye. I was like you.

MARY. I don't understand.

MIRIAM. Then get a load of this. I should of licked that girl where she licked me—in the hay.

MARY. Miriam!

MIRIAM. That's where you win in the first round. And if I know men, that's still Custer's Last Stand. (MARY *walks away from her.*) Shocked you? You're too modest. You're ashamed. O.K., sister. But my idea of love is that love isn't ashamed in nothing.

MARY (*turning to her*). A good argument, Miriam. So modern. So simple. Sex the cause, sex the cure. It's too simple, Miriam. Your love battles are for—lovers—or professionals. (*Gently.*) Not for a man and woman who've been married twelve quiet years! Oh, I don't mean I wouldn't love Stephen's arms around me again. But I wouldn't recapture, if I could, our—young passion. That was the wonderful young thing we had. That was part of our youth, like the—babies. But not the thing that made him my husband, that made me his wife—Stephen needed me. He *needed* me for twelve years. Stephen doesn't need me any more.

MIRIAM. I get it. (*Phone rings.*) That's why I'm marrying this guy Fowler. He needs me like hell. If I don't marry him he'll drink himself to death in a month, the poor dope.

MARY (*at the telephone*). Yes? No, operator, we completed—you say, New York is calling Mrs. Haines? I'll take that call— (*To* MIRIAM.) Stephen!

MIRIAM. Listen, make him that speech you just made me!

MARY (*radiant*). I knew he'd call. I knew when the last moment came, he'd realize he needed me.

MIRIAM. For God's sake, tell him that *you* need him!

MARY. Hello—hello? Stephen? Mary. Yes. I'm very cheerful. It's so good to hear your voice, Stephen. I—why, yes, it's scheduled for tomorrow at 12—but, Stephen, I can— (*Frightened*) but, Stephen! No—of course —I haven't seen the papers. How could I, out here? (*There is a long pause.*) Yes, I'd rather *you* told me. Of course I understand the position you're both in. No, I'm not bitter, not bitter at all—I—I hope you'll both be very happy. No, I have no plans, no plans at all—Stephen, do you mind if I hang up? Good-bye, Stephen—Good-bye—

MIRIAM. He's marrying her?

MARY. Oh, God, why did I let this happen? We were married. We were one person. We had a good life. Oh, God, I've been a *fool!*

MIRIAM. Sure you have. Haven't we all, sister?

MARY. But she doesn't love him. I *do*. That's the way it is. (*She goes to the window, and looks out. There is a pause. Then, violently*) But it's not ended if your heart doesn't say so. It's not ended!

CURTAIN

ACT THREE

SCENE I

Early evening, two years later. CRYSTAL's *bathroom. Left, a black marbleized tub with frilled shower-curtains. In a niche, back of the tub, a gilded French telephone. Right, a satin-skirted dressing table, covered with glittering toilet bottles and cosmetic jars. Towel-racks piled with embroidered bath-towels. Center, a door to* CRYSTAL's *bedroom. As the curtain rises,* CRYSTAL *is lolling in the bath, reading a magazine, smoking as* HELENE, *a chic French maid, enters.*

HELENE. Madame has been soaking an hour.

CRYSTAL (*rudely*). So what?

HELENE. But, monsieur—

CRYSTAL. Monsieur is going out with me and my friends, whether he likes it or not. Has that kid gone home yet?

HELENE. Mademoiselle Mary has just finished the supper with her daddy. Madame, monsieur is so anxious that you say good night to her.

CRYSTAL. Listen, that kid doesn't want to bid me beddy-bye any more than I do. He's tried for two years to cram us down each other's throats. Let her go home to her mommer. (*Passes* HELENE *a brush.*) Here—scrub —Some day I'm going to slap that kid down. She's too— (*As* HELENE *scrubs too hard.*) Ow! You're taking my skin off—Oh, I'm so bored I could—(*Hurls the soap across the room.*) Helene, never marry a man who's deserted a "good woman." He's as cheerful as a man who's murdered his poor old mother. (*Telephone rings.*) Get out! And,

Helene, when Mrs. Fowler comes, keep her downstairs, if you have to *sit* on her. (*Exit* HELENE. CRYSTAL *picks up the telephone. Her voice melts.*) Hello, darling, I'm in the tub. I'm shrivelled to a peanut waiting for this call. No, I'm not afraid of a shock. You ought to know— Oh, Buck, I'm going to miss you like nobody's business. I can't tell you what it did to me, locking the door on our little apartment— I'll say we had fun! Coma ti-yi-yippy, what? Oh, no, say anything you like. This is the one place where I have some privacy— (CRYSTAL's *back is to the door. She does not hear a brief rap.*) Listen, baby, must you really go to the coast? Oh, the hell with Mr. Goldwyn. (*Enter* LITTLE MARY. *She stands hesitantly against the door.*) Listen, you don't have to tell me what you sacrificed to have a movie career. I've seen that cartoon you married. If Flora was ever a Countess, I'm the Duchess of Windsor. Well, Buck, maybe she's not such a half-wit, but— (*Sees* LITTLE MARY.) Oh—call me back in two minutes. I've had a small interruption. (*Hangs up.*) Who told you to come in here?

LITTLE MARY (*politely*). Daddy. Good night. (*Turns to go.*)

CRYSTAL (*sweetly*). Oh, don't go, darling. Hand me that brush.

LITTLE MARY (*gently*). Please?

CRYSTAL. Please. (LITTLE MARY *gives her the brush.*)

LITTLE MARY. Good night. (*Goes to the door.*)

CRYSTAL. My, you're in a hurry to tell Daddy about it.

LITTLE MARY. About what?

CRYSTAL. My talk on the telephone.

LITTLE MARY. I don't understand grown-ups on the telephone. They all sound silly. Good night.

CRYSTAL. Good night, who? (*A pause.*) You've been told to call me Aunty Crystal. (*A pause.*) Why don't you do it?

LITTLE MARY (*still edging to the door*). Yes.

CRYSTAL. Yes, what?

LITTLE MARY (*lamely*). Yes, good night.

CRYSTAL (*angry*). You sit down!

LITTLE MARY. Oh, it's awfully hot in here. I've got my coat on.

CRYSTAL. You heard me! (LITTLE MARY *sits on the stool before the dressing table, squirms.*) We're going to have this out. I've done my damn—my level best to be friends with you, but you refuse to co-operate.

LITTLE MARY. What?

CRYSTAL. Co-operate.

LITTLE MARY (*nodding mechanically*). Co-operate.

CRYSTAL (*exasperated*). Answer my question. You don't like me. Why?

LITTLE MARY (*rising*). Well, good night, Crystal—

CRYSTAL. I said, why?

LITTLE MARY (*very patiently*). Listen, Crystal, my mother told me I wasn't to be rude to you.

CRYSTAL. For the last time, young lady, you give me one good reason why you don't like me.

LITTLE MARY. I never said I didn't like you, Crystal.

CRYSTAL. But you don't like me, do you?

LITTLE MARY. No, but I never *said* so. I've been very polite, Crystal, considering you're something awful!

CRYSTAL. Wait till your father hears this!

LITTLE MARY (*suddenly defiant*). Listen— Daddy doesn't think you're so wonderful any more!

CRYSTAL. Did he tell you that?

LITTLE MARY. No. Daddy always pretends you're all right, but he's just ashamed to have Mother know what a mean, silly wife he's got. And I don't tell Mother what *we* think, because you've made her cry enough, Crystal. So I'm not going to co-operate *ever!*

CRYSTAL. Get out!

LITTLE MARY (*goes to the door, then turns, rather superior*). And *another* thing, I think this bathroom is perfectly ridiculous! Good night, Crystal! (*Exits. The telephone rings.* CRYSTAL *grabs it, irritable.*)

CRYSTAL. Yes, darling— That Haines brat. God, she gets under my skin!— No, she didn't hear anything. What good would it do her, anyhow? You're off in the morning, and Lord knows we've been discreet— What? You are? (*Giggling.*) Dining with the first Mrs. Haines?— Well, darling, lay off the gin. It makes you talk too much— Well, just be careful, darling. (*Enter* SYLVIA, *without knocking. She wears an elaborate evening gown, and carries a cocktail. These two years have had no appreciable effect on* SYLVIA. *She is her old Act One self again.*)

SYLVIA. Yoohoo! May I come in?

CRYSTAL (*in the telephone*). No, this is not the Aquarium. It's Grand Central Station. (*Hangs up.*)

SYLVIA. Who was that?

CRYSTAL. A wrong number.

SYLVIA. You were talking to a man

CRYSTAL. Pass me that sponge.—Please.

SYLVIA (*waiting on* CRYSTAL). Oh, Crystal, you know you can trust me.

CRYSTAL. And that eye cup.

SYLVIA. There must be someone. After all, I've known Stephen for years. He's really not your type. I often wonder how you two got together. I was telling my psycho-analyst about it. You know, I've got to tell him everything.

CRYSTAL. That must be an awful effort.

SYLVIA. I don't mind discussing myself. But talking about my friends does make me feel disloyal. He says Stephen has a Guilt Complex.

CRYSTAL. What?

SYLVIA (*cheerfully*). He says men of Stephen's generation were brought up to believe that infidelity is a sin. That's why he allowed Mary to divorce him, and that's why he married you, Crystal. He had to marry you just to convince himself he was not a sexual monster.

CRYSTAL. Yes? Well, if Stephen is a sexual monster, psycho-analysis is through.

SYLVIA. And he says you've got a Cinderella Complex. He says most American women have. They're all brought up to believe that marriage to a rich man should be their aim in life. He says we neither please the men nor function as child-bearing animals—

CRYSTAL (*bored and angry*). Will you function yourself into the bedroom?

SYLVIA (*hurt*). I don't think that's the way to talk to me, after all I've done for you. When you married Stephen you didn't know a soul. It wasn't easy to put *you* over. Everybody was on Mary's side.

CRYSTAL. They still are. They never miss a chance to remind me what a noble, useful woman Mary has become since she left Stephen.

SYLVIA (*comforting.*) My dear, she's miserable! Why, she never sees a soul.

CRYSTAL. She's having a dinner party tonight.

SYLVIA. Edith told me. She's going. And Flora.

CRYSTAL. Flora?

SYLVIA. The Countess de Lage. Mrs. Buck Winston? My God, I have to laugh when I think of Flora actually turning that cowboy into a movie star. Of course he's not my type, but he's positively the Chambermaid's Delight—

CRYSTAL (*fiercely*). Will you shut up?

SYLVIA. But, Crystal—

CRYSTAL. I said shut up— (*Calling.*) Helene!

SYLVIA. Well, I think you're very ungrateful!

CRYSTAL. Well, take it up with your psycho-analyst. (HELENE *enters.*) Helene, draw the curtains. I want to take a shower. (SYLVIA *goes to the door as* HELENE *draws the curtains.*) That's right, Sylvia—wait in the bedroom.

SYLVIA (*sees the scales, decides to weigh herself*). Oh, dear, I've lost another pound. I must remember to tell my analyst. You know, everything means something. (*The shower goes on.* HELENE *exits.* SYLVIA *gets off the scales. During the following monologue, she goes to* CRYSTAL's *dressing-table, where she examines all the bottles and jars.*) But even my analyst says no woman should try to do as much as I do. He says I attach too much value to my feminine friendships. He says I have a Damon and Pythias Complex. I guess I have given too much of myself to other women. He says women are natural enemies— (*Picks up bottle.*) Why, Crystal, I thought you didn't touch up your hair— (*Sniffing perfume.*) My dear, I wouldn't use this. You smell it on every tart in New York. That reminds me—(*Going to the shower-curtains*)—if you do have an affair, Crystal, for heaven's sake, be discreet. Remember what Howard did to me, the skunk. (*Peeking in.*) My, you're putting on weight. (*Going back to dressing-table, she sits down, and begins to pry in all the drawers.*) But men are so mercenary. They think they own you body and soul, just because they pay the bills— I tried this cream. It brought out pimples— Of course, Crystal, if you were smart, you'd have a baby. It's the only real hold a woman has—(HELENE *enters.*)

HELENE. Monsieur says will madame be long?

SYLVIA. Can't you see she's rushing?—(HELENE *exits. The shower goes off.*) Men are so selfish! When you're only making yourself beautiful for them. (*Opens another drawer.*) I wish I could find a man who would understand my need for a companion—(*Finds a key, examines it.*) Why, Crystal, what are *you* doing with a key to the Gothic Apartments? (CRYSTAL's *head pops from behind the curtain.*)

CRYSTAL. What?— Oh— (*Nervously.*) Oh, that! (*Playing for time.*) Throw me a towel, Sylvia!

SYLVIA (*bringing her towel*). That's where Howard had me followed. The doorman there is a professional blackmailer! (CRYSTAL *has wrapped herself in a big towel, now steps from behind the shower-curtains and sits on the rim of the tub to dry her legs.*) I asked my psycho-analyst about him, and he said blackmailers are really perverts who can't think of a good perversion. So they blackmail people instead.

CRYSTAL (*going to the dressing-table.*) Really? Well, he can't blackmail me now. (*As she passes* SYLVIA, *she lightly snatches the key from her.*) The Gothic Apartments are where Stephen and I had to go before the divorce. I keep it for sentimental reasons. (*Smiling, she drops the key back in the drawer, locks it.*)

SYLVIA. Poor Stephen! My dear, I thought to-night how tired he looked, and old. Crystal, I've told you everything. Tell me: how long do you think you can be faithful to Stephen?

CRYSTAL (*making up her face*). Well, life plays funny tricks. The urge might hit me tomorrow.

SYLVIA. I doubt it, pet. You're a typical blonde.

CRYSTAL. So what?

SYLVIA (*loftily*). Most *blondes* are frigid.

CRYSTAL. Really? Well, maybe that's just a dirty piece of *brunette* propaganda!

CURTAIN

SCENE II

Eleven o'clock the same night. MARY's *bedroom. A charming, simple room. Left, a door to the dressing-room. Right, a door to the hall. As the curtain rises,* JANE *is arranging a number of evening wraps on the bed.* MIRIAM, MARY *and* NANCY *are entering.*

MIRIAM. Thanks, baby, a lot! I never was at a wetter dinner.

MARY. It was a success. I left Reno two years ago today. This was a memorial dinner for you old Renoites, and your new husbands.

MIRIAM. I get it. Listen, there's no soap eating out your heart, sister!

NANCY. Mary, if I had a heroine in one of my books who behaved the way you do, my two readers would never believe it. No one man is worth it.

MIRIAM. Say, the whole Racquet Club's not worth it— Speaking of my dear husband Howard—the skunk—can I have a whiskey and soda?

NANCY. Make it two. (JANE *exits, right.*)

MIRIAM. I lay off when Howard's around. I'm weaning him from the bottle by easy stages. He's in the secondary stage now.

NANCY. What stage is that?

MIRIAM. He puts ice in.

MARY. How's matrimony, Miriam? Making a go of it?

MIRIAM. I'm doing a reconstruction job that makes Boulder Dam look like an egg-cup. (*Enter* PEGGY, *right.*)

PEGGY. Oh, Mary, can't we get off to the party? I have to get home early. Little John always wakes up. Little John said the cutest thing the other day. (*A dramatic pause.*) He said da-da—!

NANCY. When does he enter Columbia? (*Enter* JANE *with tray and highballs.*)

MARY. Jane, tell Mrs. Winston the ladies are ready to go.

JANE. Mrs. Winston, ma'am, is drinking with the gentlemen.

MARY. Well, tell her to come up. (*Exit* JANE.)

MIRIAM. What's the hurry? Two more snootfuls, and Flora will float up on her own breath. (*Enter* EDITH, *right.*)

EDITH (*petulantly*). Mary, I wish you had an elevator in this house. It's so difficult to walk upstairs in my condition.

MARY. Edith, are you Catholic or just careless?

EDITH. Mary, isn't this your old furniture?

MARY. Yes.

EDITH. I think you should get rid of it. There's nothing that keeps a woman so in the dumps as sleeping in a bed with old associations. Mary, you're carrying this nunnery business too far. How do you expect to find anyone else, if you don't make an effort?

MARY. I don't want anyone, Edith. (*Mock cynical.*) I hate men! Men are awful—

EDITH. Oh, they're not all like Stephen, dear.

MARY. I saw plenty of men when I came back from Reno. They're all alike. They never leave you at your own front door without a wrestling-match.

EDITH. You know I asked Phelps about that once. I said, "Why does a man always act like a Don Juan in a taxi?" And he said it was a hang-over from their bachelor days when a man's sex life was conditioned by the click of the meter.

MIRIAM. It beats me how in a taxi, the nicest guy turns into Harpo Marx.

EDITH. Mary, want to hear something about Sylvia? (MARY, MIRIAM, NANCY *and* PEGGY: *chorus, No!"*) Well, Sylvia's going to a psycho-analyst. She says you destroyed all her faith in friendship.

MARY. As if any woman needed to go to a psycho-analyst to find out she can't trust women.

EDITH. Mary, you've grown awfully hard since you deserted your old friends.

MARY. Isn't "wise" the word? I'm beginning to understand women.

NANCY. Too bad! It's the beginning of woman's inhumanity to woman.

EDITH (*moving to door, left*). Oh, they're going to talk philosophy, Peggy. Come on in here while I powder my nose.

PEGGY. Edith, did I tell you how little John said da-da?

EDITH. Listen, I wouldn't care if *this* one stood up and sang the Star-Spangled Banner! (*They exit, as enter* MRS. MOREHEAD, *in street clothes, right.*)

MRS. MOREHEAD. Oh, hello, girls! Hello, dear. Party over?

MARY. Enjoy the movies, Mother?

MRS. MOREHEAD. I wish I could make up my mind whether or not I like Shirley Temple. (*Enter the* COUNTESS DE LAGE, *right. She is a tangle of tulle and jewels. She has a slight "edge" on.*)

COUNTESS. Such a lovely dinner! It's so wonderful to see all our lives temporarily settled!

MARY. My mother, Mrs. Morehead, Mrs. Winston. Mrs. Buck Winston.

MRS. MOREHEAD (*trying to place the name*). Buck Winston?

MARY. The movie star.

MRS. MOREHEAD. Ah, yes! (*Pleasantly.*) My granddaughter adores your son on the screen.

COUNTESS (*good-naturedly*). I daresay the public does see Buck as just a boy. And it is a trifle absurd *me* being married to a movie star. But, Mrs. Morehead, you wouldn't believe how many of my Newport friends who ridiculed Buck when I married him positively claw for invitations to Hollywood. Mais là, East is East and West is West, but I always say Le Cinema is the Great Leveller!

MRS. MOREHEAD. You don't say! (*Edges to the hall-door.*)

COUNTESS. Mrs. Morehead, do whip into something, and come along with Mary to my party. The Casino Roof. Everyone's clamored to come. I have no idea who's going to be there.

MRS. MOREHEAD. Well, you're sure to know somebody. (*To* MARY.) Later, dear? (MARY *nods,* MRS. MOREHEAD *escapes, right.*)

COUNTESS (*gathering her wrap*). Mary, you're not coming?

MARY. I'm very tired, Flora.

COUNTESS. Oh, you're cross because Buck's had a wee droppie.

MIRIAM. Don't be modest, Flora. Your ducky is stinko.

COUNTESS. I do wish he wouldn't drink straight gin. You know, he's not allowed to. Mr. Goldwyn put that in the new contract.

MIRIAM. I wish I'd had my marriage license drawn up by Mr. Goldwyn.

COUNTESS. Mary, do come. This is *really* our farewell party. I'm never coming back to New York.

MARY. What's wrong with New York, Flora?

COUNTESS. Well, when Buck isn't working we're not going to live anywhere. (*Whispering.*) Mary, can I trust you?

MARY. Of course, Flora!

COUNTESS (*to the others*). You will keep this just between the four of us?

MIRIAM. Shoot, Flora, it's a nationwide hookup!

COUNTESS (*settling herself beside* MARY *on the foot of the bed*). Well, you know how Buck was? (*Wistfully*) So—so impassioné?

MIRIAM. The boy had something.

COUNTESS (*tartly*). Well, he hasn't got it any more, Miriam! First, I thought it was just gin interfering with his libido— (*Tear-*

fully) But now I think Buck is deceiving me—

NANCY. How incredible!

COUNTESS. Well, I have no proof. Except he comes home every afternoon smelling of a strange perfume.

MARY. Where does he say he's been?

COUNTESS. Visiting his horse. But Trixie was shipped to Hollywood last week. You remember, I was photographed with her in the baggage-car? Now he says he's been going to the Grand Central Gymnasium. But I telephoned today. Some great oaf answered. I said: "Is Buck Winston there?" He said: "Who? No." So I said: "My dear good man, he comes every day." So he said: "My mistake, lady, he's inside now boxing with Rudolph Valentino."

MARY. Poor Flora!

COUNTESS (*practical*). That's why I think it's safer just to keep floating around.

MARY. I understand—l'amour.

COUNTESS. L'amour, yes, but jamais, (*she has her lucid moments*) jamais *lopsided* amour!

MARY (*laughing*). Lopsided amour is better than no amour at all. Flora, let him make a fool of you. Let him do anything he wants, as long as he stays. He's taking the trouble to deceive you. (*Half to herself.*) And if he took the trouble, he really must have cared—

NANCY. The Voice of Experience.

MIRIAM (*to* COUNTESS). Come on, chin up.

NANCY. That's right. Both of them! (*Enter* PEGGY *and* EDITH.)

COUNTESS (*rising*). Oh, cheries, you missed it! I was just saying—now will you keep this just among the six of us?—I suspect Buck of being unfaithful. Of course, it's my own fault. I should have had him watched. The way I did all the others. I wish I'd found out where he's had that apartment!

PEGGY. An apartment—?

COUNTESS. Where would you expect him to go? Central Park? Why, it's winter.

PEGGY. Oh, I've always heard people went to hotels.

COUNTESS. But, cherie, *Buck* couldn't go to a hotel. You know what would happen. At the most inopportune moment someone would say: "Mr. Winston, may I have your autograph?" It happened to us on our wedding night. I would have sent for the manager, but it was the manager asking for the autograph. Ah, well, off to Hollywood in the morning! That's safe! (*Moving to door.*) Dear Mr. Hays will protect me from Dietrich and Harlow. (*Exits, right.*)

EDITH (*getting her wrap*). Darling, you really won't come to Flora's party?

MARY. No, Edith!

EDITH. Then I can tell you. Of course, I know how you feel about your Ex—and his New Deal—though I think you'd be glad he's so happy.

MARY. I am.

EDITH. Sylvia telephoned tonight. She and Crystal and Stephen are going on to the Roof with a theatre party. Well, darling, I don't feel much like going myself. I loathe this dress. My husband says I look as though I were going to sing in it. (*Exits, right.*)

NANCY. Think I'll go, too, Mary! It's a good chance to study Park Avenue's flora and fauna. And I'm writing a new book. It's called "Gone with the Ice-man," or "Sex Has No Place in the Home." (*Exits with* PEGGY.)

MIRIAM (*to* MARY). Listen, Queen, change your mind! Let's go on to the party!

MARY. No, Miriam.

MIRIAM. Well, I'm going. Wish you could see the cooing-fest Howard and I put on for Sylvia— Shall I spit in Crystal's eye for you? (MARY *shakes her head.*) You're passing up a swell chance, sister! Where I spit no grass grows ever! (*Exits.* JANE *enters, right.* MARY *begins to unfasten her dress, takes off her jewels, lays them on the dresser.*)

MARY. Jane, turn down my bed.

JANE. Yes, ma'am. (MARY *goes into the boudoir, left.*)

MARY (*off-stage*). Did Mary have a nice time with her father?

JANE (*turning down the bed*). Well, ma'am, you know how she is when she comes home.

MARY (*off-stage*). I'm afraid she's never going to get used to it.

JANE. She takes after you, ma'am, if you'll pardon me. Always brooding. Sometimes, ma'am, I think it would be better if she didn't see her father. Or maybe, ma'am— though it's none of my business—if you could find some nice man—(*Enter* MRS. MOREHEAD, *right, in a wrapper and slippers.*)

MRS. MOREHEAD. Going to bed, darling?

MARY (*off-stage*). Yes, Mother.

MRS. MOREHEAD. Shall we chat for a moment? Jane, I'll have a cigarette.

JANE (*surprised*). Mrs. Morehead!

MRS. MOREHEAD. Those dreadful women made me nervous. Why Mrs. Haines tolerates them even once a year is beyond me!

MARY (*entering, in a nightgown*). An object lesson. Smoking, Mother?

MRS. MOREHEAD. Oh, you, too?

MARY. Me, too?

MRS. MOREHEAD. I just felt that spooky pinch. You'd think after ten years your father's ghost might have grown more tolerant.

JANE. Good night, ma'am. (*Switches off side-lights.*)

MARY *and* MRS. MOREHEAD. Good night, Jane. (*Exit* JANE. MARY *gets into bed, opens a book, flips through it.*)
MRS. MOREHEAD (*sitting on the bed*). Good book?

MARY. Don't know. Nancy just gave it to me. It's about—love. Poetry. All about love. (*Reads*) "When love beckons to you, follow him, though his ways are hard and steep. And when his wings enfold you, yield to him— Though his voice may shatter your dreams as the North Wind lays waste the garden."

MRS. MOREHEAD. Well, all I can say is, that's very tactless of Nancy. (*Suddenly*) Oh, Mary, I wish you could find—

MARY (*slams book shut*). Some nice man. We've been all over that before, Mother. I had the only one I ever wanted, I lost him—

MRS. MOREHEAD. It wasn't entirely your fault.

MARY. If I hadn't listened to everyone, everything but my own heart!

MRS. MOREHEAD. He loved her.

MARY. He still does. Though you know, Mother, I'm just beginning to doubt it.

MRS. MOREHEAD. Why?

MARY. Because so many people, like Edith, make a point of telling me how much he loves her. Oh, Mother, I'm terribly tired.

MRS. MOREHEAD. Well, do cheer up, darling. Living alone has its compensations. You can go where you please, wear what you please and eat what you please. I had to wait twenty years to order the kind of meal I liked! Your father called it bird-food— And, heaven knows, it's marvelous to be able to sprawl out in bed, like a swastika. Good night, darling.

MARY. Good night, Mother.

MRS. MOREHEAD. Don't read by that light. You'll hurt your eyes. (*Exits.* MARY *props herself against the pillows, begins to read.*)

MARY. "But if in your fear you would seek only love's peace and love's pleasure, then it is better for you to pass out of love's threshing-floor, into the seasonless world; where you shall laugh, but not all of your laughter, and weep, but not all of your tears." (*Enter* LITTLE MARY, *in a nightgown, barefooted, and very sleepy.*)

LITTLE MARY. Mother?

MARY. Darling, what's the matter?

LITTLE MARY (*goes to the bed*). I had a bad dream!

MARY. Darling, what was it?

LITTLE MARY. I forget. Let me crawl in with you, Mother.

MARY (*helping her in*). I'm so restless.

LITTLE MARY. I don't mind if you kick me. You know, that's the only good thing about divorce; you get to sleep with your mother. (*She kisses her. A pause.*) I taste lip-stick.

MARY. I haven't washed yet. Good night, darling.

LITTLE MARY. You know, you're a very sympathetic mother.

MARY. Am I?

LITTLE MARY. Oh, yes. So would you just tickle my back?

MARY. All right. But go to sleep— (*A pause.*)

LITTLE MARY. She's so silly!

MARY. Who?

LITTLE MARY. Crystal.

MARY. Ssh—

LITTLE MARY. I told Daddy so tonight.

MARY. Oh, you mustn't hurt Daddy's feelings.

LITTLE MARY. Mother?

MARY. Ssh!

LITTLE MARY. I think Daddy doesn't love her as much as you any more.

MARY. What makes you think so, Mary?

LITTLE MARY. He told me so after I saw Crystal.

MARY. What?

LITTLE MARY. But he said I mustn't tell you because, naturally, why do you care how he feels. (*A pause*) Oh, don't stop tickling, Mother. (*A pause*) Mother?

MARY. Yes.

LITTLE MARY. What's anyone want with a telephone in the bathroom?

MARY. I don't know. Sssh!

LITTLE MARY. Crystal has one. She was awful mad when I walked in on her while she was talking.

MARY. Sleep, Mary!

LITTLE MARY. Mother, who's the Duchess of Windsor?

MARY. What a question!

LITTLE MARY. Well, Crystal said on the telephone if somebody else was a Countess, she was the Duchess of Windsor!

MARY. Really!

LITTLE MARY. Good night, Mother.

MARY. Good night, baby. (*A pause.*)

LITTLE MARY. I wonder if it was the same man you had for dinner.

MARY. Maybe, ssh!
LITTLE MARY. I thought so.

MARY (*curiously*). If who was the same man?

LITTLE MARY. Crystal was talking to, so lovey-dovey.

MARY (*protestingly*). Oh, Mary!

LITTLE MARY. Well, the front part was the same, Mother.

MARY (*a pause*). The front part of what?

LITTLE MARY. His name, Mother!

MARY (*taking her by the shoulders*). What are you talking about?

LITTLE MARY. That man Crystal was talking to in the bathtub.

MARY (*half shaking her*). Mary, what do you mean?

LITTLE MARY. I mean his front name was *Buck*, Mother! (MARY *gets quickly out of bed, rings bell on table.*) Oh, Mother, what are you doing?

MARY. Go to sleep, darling. (*Begins to pull on her stockings.*)

LITTLE MARY. Grown-ups are so sudden. Are you dressing?

MARY. Yes, Mary.

LITTLE MARY. You forgot you were invited to a party?

MARY. Almost, Mary.

LITTLE MARY. What are you going to do when you get there, Mother?

MARY. I don't know yet. But I've got to do something.

LITTLE MARY. Well, have a good time! (*Rolls over. Then suddenly sits up.*) Mother!

MARY. Yes?

LITTLE MARY. I remember now I had something to tell you!

MARY (*eagerly*). Yes?

LITTLE MARY (*dolefully*). I was awfully rude to Crystal.

MARY. I'll forgive you this time. (*Enter* JANE.)

JANE. You ring, ma'am?

MARY. Yes. My evening dress, Jane, and a taxi—and don't stand there gaping! Hurry! Hurry!

CURTAIN

SCENE III

Later, the same night. The Powder Room at ↙he Casino Roof. The decoration ıs rich, tawdry and modernistic. Right, a swinging door from the lobby. Left, another to the washrooms. The rest of the wall-space, left and right, is taken up by counter-like dressing-tables and mirrors. The rear wall is a great window overlooking the glitter of midnight Manhattan. An over-stuffed sofa and an armchair upholstered in modernistic fabric. Near the door, right, a screen hides the coat-rack. By this, a chair for SADIE, *a little old woman in a black maid's uniform and apron. As the curtain rises,* SADIE, *a reading a tabloid, which she puts down when two flashily dressed* GIRLS *enter from the lobby. They check their wraps.*

FIRST GIRL. It's jammed.

SECOND GIRL. Oh, my boy-friend'll get a table. (*Enter two* SOCIETY WOMEN. *They move directly across the stage to the washroom.*)

FIRST WOMAN. My dear, won't he let you?

SECOND WOMAN. No, he won't.

FIRST WOMAN. How incredibly foul!

SECOND WOMAN. I'm heartbroken. But I have to be philosophical; after all, missing one winter in Palm Beach really won't kill me. (*Enter* "CIGARETTES," *a pretty girl in a white satin blouse and short black skirt. She carries a tray of cigarettes.*)

FIRST GIRL (*moving left*). Thought you and the boy-friend had a row?

SECOND GIRL. We did.

FIRST GIRL. What about?

SECOND GIRL. His wife.

FIRST GIRL. His wife? What right has she got to butt in?

SECOND GIRL. He's got some cockeyed idea that after twenty years he can't kick her out. (*They exit, left.*)

CIGARETTES. Jeepers, why don't they get sick of this joint night after night! Same music, same act, same faces.

SADIE. They like familiarity. It gives them confidence.

CIGARETTES. I'll say they like familiarity. Most of them shoving around that floor would be more comfortable with each other in bed.

SADIE. In bed? If they was to get that over, what would they use for conversation? (*En-*

ter a DOWAGER *and a* DEBUTANTE, *right. They move directly across stage.*)

DOWAGER. —dancing like that! What can those boys think of you?

DEBUTANTE (*wearily*). Oh, Mother.

DOWAGER. Guzzling champagne like that! After all I spent on your education!

DEBUTANTE. Oh, Mother.

DOWAGER. It's one thing to come out. It's quite another to go under the table! (*They exit, left.*)

SADIE. —Getting married, dearie?

CIGARETTES (*sinking, very tired, on the arm of a chair*). As soon as Mike gets a job. It ain't fair! Why, we could get married and have a family on that coat— Sadie, wh'd'ya say if I was to tell you I'm a Commyanist?

SADIE. I'd say ya was bats. I was a Townsendite. Where'd it get me? (*Enter the* COUNTESS, *piloted by* NANCY *and* MIRIAM. *She is tight and tearful.* MIRIAM *and* NANCY *get her, with some difficulty, to the sofa.*)

COUNTESS (*tacking*). How could Buck do such a thing to me! Oh, the Dr. Jekyll! The Mr. Hyde! Which was which?

MIRIAM. Pipe down or you'll put an awful dent in his career, Flora.

COUNTESS. What of my career? I've had five husbands. Buck's the first one who ever told me what he really thought of me—in public.

NANCY. It takes all kinds of husbands to round out a career like yours, Flora.

COUNTESS. He told me he'd been deceiving me for months. Right in the middle of the

Organ-Grinder. (*Kicks off shoes.*) Oh, I feel so—superfluous!

MIRIAM (*to* SADIE). A bromo-seltzer.

COUNTESS. Bromo-seltzer? Qu'-est-que c'est que ca?

NANCY. It will settle your—superfluity. Flora, did he tell you the lady's name?

COUNTESS (*indignant*). Certainly not, Nancy. He's not that drunk.

MIRIAM (*as* SADIE *exits, right*). And another drink for Mr. Winston!

COUNTESS. No, Miriam. He wouldn't tell me her name, because she's a married woman. Buck is very proletarian, but he's not a bounder. He just said *she* was a natural blonde.

NANCY. That ought to narrow down the field considerably.

COUNTESS. He said she was pretty as a painted wagon.

MIRIAM. Oh, you're not such a bad calliope. Snap out of it, Flora. You know, you're going to forgive him.

COUNTESS (*firmly*). I'd forgive unfaithfulness, but not base ingratitude. I rescued him from those prairies. I married him. What thanks do I get? (*Wailing.*) He says he'll be a cockeyed coyote if he'll herd an old beef like me back to the coast!

NANCY. Let this be your lesson. Don't let your next husband become financially independent of you.

COUNTESS. Now, don't lecture me, Nancy. Every time I marry I learn something. This has taught me once and for all—you can't expect *noblesse oblige* from a cowboy—(*sitting up*) Ohhh, my eyes! They're full of mascara.

NANCY (*helping her off the couch. To* MIRIAM). We've got to get her home. Get Buck, and meet us in the lobby.

MIRIAM (*exits, right*). We're headin' for the last round-up!

COUNTESS. If there's a telephone in here I'm going to call up Mr. Goldwyn. (*Exits, left, with* NANCY, *as* SADIE, *with a bromo-seltzer, enters, right, followed by* CIGARETTES.)

CIGARETTES. What's it all about?

SADIE (*picks up* COUNTESS' *shoes, as she crosses, left*). Some man.

CIGARETTES. Bet he isn't worth it.

SADIE. You can always collect on that one. (*Exits, left, as re-enter, left, the* DOWAGER *and the* DEBUTANTE.)

DOWAGER. —Laughing and joking with those boys like that!

DEBUTANTE. Yes, Mother.

DOWAGER. What can they think of you?

DEBUTANTE. Yes, Mother.

DOWAGER. And don't think I didn't overhear that Princeton boy call me an old drizzlepuss, either! (*Exits, right.*)

SADIE (*enters, left; to* CIGARETTES). She wants gin in her bromo-seltzer. (*Enter* MARY *and* MIRIAM, *right.*)

MIRIAM (*protesting*). Crystal's not in here. I don't think she's in the joint.

MARY. She's coming. I know it.

MIRIAM. So what are you going to do when you find her? (SADIE *takes* MARY's *wrap.*)

MARY. I don't know. But I've got to find her tonight. Buck's going to Hollywood in the morning.

MIRIAM. Say, why don't you settle this matter with Stephen?

MARY. I have no proof, I tell you! But if Buck is as drunk as you say, he'll give away something.

MIRIAM. Listen, he's been trying all night to give Flora away to the doorman. Got a twenty-dollar bill?

MARY. Yes.

MIRIAM. That'll lock him in the men's room till we need him. (*Exits, right, with* MARY, *as enter, left, the two* SOCIETY WOMEN. *They cross the stage.*)

FIRST WOMAN. Not three pounds?

SECOND WOMAN. Three pounds!

FIRST WOMAN. How divine! Aren't you ecstatic?

SECOND WOMAN. Yes, but it's the moral satisfaction. Just bananas and milk for one whole week! That called for enormous character! (*They exit, right.*)

CIGARETTES (*to* SADIE). Enormous character! Well, she'll need it, all right. Comes the Revolution, she'll diet plenty! (*Enter* PEGGY *and* EDITH, *right. They powder, at the mirror, right.*)

PEGGY. I wish I hadn't come.

EDITH. Well, your husband didn't want you to.

PEGGY (*goes for her wrap*). Flora was disgusting!

EDITH. But it was funny. Even the kettle drummer was laughing.

PEGGY. You never miss anything. (SADIE *gives* EDITH *and* PEGGY *their wraps.*)

EDITH. My dear, who could stand the life we lead without a sense of humor? But Flora is a fool. Always remember, Peggy, it's matrimonial suicide to be jealous when you have a really good reason.

PEGGY. Edith, don't you ever get tired of giving advice?

EDITH. Listen, Peggy, I'm the only happy woman you know. Why? I don't ask Phelps or any man to understand me. How could he? I'm a woman. (*Pulls down her corset.*) And I don't try to understand them. They're just animals. Who am I to quarrel with the way God made them? I've got security. So I put my faith in the law. And I say: "What the hell?" And let nature take its course —it's going to, anyway. (*They exit, right, as enter the two* GIRLS, *left.*)

SECOND GIRL (*powdering at the mirror, left*). —So there we were on Sattiday night and it's Atlantic City. And he says: "I gotta go home tomorrow, baby!" And I says: (*Pulls up her stockings.*) "Why dja got to?" And he says: "My wife always expects me home on Easter Sunday." So I says: "What's she expect ya to do? Lay an egg?"

FIRST GIRL. They got no sentiment. (*Enter, right, a* GIRL, *in distress. The shoulder strap of her very low décolletage has broken.*)

GIRL IN DISTRESS (*to* SADIE). Have you got a safety pin? I was never so embarrassed! (SADIE *gets pin.*)

SECOND GIRL (*crossing, right*). So I told him, "I had a great career until you made me give up the stage, you lunkhead. For what? A couple of cheesy diamond bracelets? A lousy car, which every time it breaks down you got to have the parts shipped over from Italy. (*The* GIRLS *exit.*)

GIRL IN DISTRESS. So he says, "Don't look now, you've just dropped something!" (*Enter* CRYSTAL *and* SYLVIA, *right. They move to check their wraps with* SADIE.)

SADIE. Just a minute, please.

SYLVIA (*they go to mirror, left*). Stephen is in a mood.

CRYSTAL. He can take it and like it.

GIRL IN DISTRESS (*to* SADIE). Does it show now?

SADIE. Not what it did before, miss.

GIRL IN DISTRESS. Thank you. (*She exits, right.* SADIE *takes* CRYSTAL'S *and* SYLVIA'S *wraps.*)

CRYSTAL. Is my mouth on straight?

SYLVIA. Crystal, you didn't come here to see somebody, did you?

CRYSTAL. Oh, Sylvia, can't you lay off that for a minute? (*Enter* MARY *and* MIRIAM, *left.*)

MARY (*moving forward resolutely*). Mrs. Haines, this is a great pleasure!

CRYSTAL (*turning*). I beg your pardon?

MARY. Such a lovely party! I was afraid you weren't coming. (*Introducing* CRYSTAL *and* MIRIAM, MIRIAM *and* SYLVIA) Mrs. Fowler, Mrs. Haines, Mrs. Fowler, Mrs. Fowler.

MIRIAM (*graciously*). Chawmed.

SYLVIA (*bridling*). This is humiliating.

MARY. Modern life is complicated. When you came in I was just telling Miriam—

CRYSTAL. Oh, come along, Sylvia. The lady is tight.

SYLVIA. Mary, when did you begin drinking?

MARY (*to* CRYSTAL). Early in the evening, with Mr. Winston. You *know* Mr. Winston, don't you?

CRYSTAL (*at the door*). I'm afraid I don't.

SYLVIA. Of course you do, Crystal. I introduced you to him. Don't you remember?

CRYSTAL. Oh, yes, a cocktail party.

MARY. Well, he's in the lobby now, waiting for someone, Mrs. Haines, and drunker than you can possibly imagine. You'd find him very difficult to handle, in front of Stephen. (CRYSTAL *suddenly changes her mind about going into the lobby, moves toward the washroom.*)

SYLVIA. Crystal, where are you going?

CRYSTAL. I won't stand here and listen to drivel!

MARY. I wouldn't go in there, either, Mrs. Haines. His wife's in there now, having hysterics. She's found out that Buck has been deceiving her.

CRYSTAL. Really! What has that to do with me?

MARY. A good deal, I'm afraid. You seem to be the woman.

SYLVIA (*delighted*). Why, Crystal!— *Are* you?

CRYSTAL. If he used my name, it's a lie! He's just the cheap sort— I'll tell my husband.

MARY. You'll have to. Tomorrow it will be common gossip. I don't think Stephen will like it.

SYLVIA. Oh, Crystal, he's going to loathe it! But my psycho-analyst is going to adore it.

CRYSTAL (*going to her*). What are you trying to do? Pin something on me, in front of witnesses?

SYLVIA. Whatever she's driving at, Crystal— (*Pointing to* MIRIAM)—that little tramp put her up to it!

CRYSTAL (*to* SYLVIA). Keep out of this!

MIRIAM. Yeah, check it, Sylvia, we're minor league this evening.

CRYSTAL. All right, Mrs. Haines, you've been listening to the ravings of a conceited fool. What did he tell you?

MARY (*playing for time, or inspiration*). Really, Mrs. Haines, this is very embarrassing.

CRYSTAL (*brazening it out*). Yes, Mrs. Haines, isn't it? Exactly what do you think you know about me?

MARY. Everything! (*A pause.* CRYSTAL *laughs.*)

CRYSTAL. Then why are you standing here talking to me? You ought to be outside spilling it to Stephen. You're bluffing. Come along, Sylvia!

MARY (*also moving to door.* CRYSTAL *stops*). That's very good advice. I will tell Stephen.

CRYSTAL. Oh, he wouldn't believe you.

SYLVIA. Oh, you can't tell, Crystal! He's terribly fond of Mary.

CRYSTAL. Now get this straight, Mrs. Haines. I like what I got, and I'm going to keep it. You handed me your husband on a silver platter. (*Enter* NANCY, *left.*) But I'm not returning the compliment. I can't be stampeded by gossip. What you believe and what Stephen believes will cut no ice in a divorce court. You need proof and you haven't got it. When Mr. Winston comes to his senses, he'll apologize. And Stephen will have no choice, but to accept—my explanations. Now that's that! Good night!

MARY (*desperately*). I hope Mrs. Winston will accept your explanations.

CRYSTAL. What have I got to explain to her?

MARY (*with a conviction she does not feel*). What about the apartment?

CRYSTAL. What apartment?

MARY. You know as well as I do.

CRYSTAL. Oh, stop trying to put two and two together—

MARY. Oh, Mrs. Winston did that. She had you watched—she's seen you both.

CRYSTAL (*defiantly*). Where?

MARY. Going in, and coming out!

CRYSTAL. Going in and coming out *where*? (*A pause.*) You're lying!

SYLVIA (*warningly*). I wouldn't be so sure, Crystal!

MIRIAM. Sounds like the McCoy to me, Crystal.

CRYSTAL. Shut up!

SYLVIA. Oh, Crystal, why didn't you confide in me? (CRYSTAL *turns to the door again, triumphant.*)

MARY (*dismayed*). Sylvia, didn't she?

SYLVIA. Certainly *not!* (CRYSTAL *smiles, very pleased with herself.*) She's the cat that walks alone. (*Goes to* CRYSTAL.) Why, Crystal, I could have told you some place *much safer* than the Gothic Apartments!

CRYSTAL (*exploding*). Why, you big, loud-mouthed idiot!

SYLVIA. How dare you!

CRYSTAL. I'd like to slap your stupid face.

SYLVIA (*backing up*). Oh, Mary, how dare she?

MIRIAM. Oh, I've got a job to do on Flora. (*She pats* SYLVIA *affectionately.*) Kiss you when I get back, Sylvia. (*Exits, left.*)

NANCY. And I'll explain the facts of life to Stephen. (NANCY *exits, right.*)

CRYSTAL (*to* MARY, *fiercely*). You're trying to break up my marriage!

SYLVIA. The way you did hers, you floosie!

CRYSTAL (*nasty*). Well, maybe you're welcome to my—left-overs.

MARY (*calmly*). I'll take them, thank you.

SYLVIA. Why, Mary, haven't you any *pride*?

MARY. That's right. No, no pride; that's a luxury a woman in love can't afford. (*Enter* COUNTESS *and* MIRIAM, *left.* MIRIAM *goes to* SADIE, *gets the* COUNTESS' *and her own wraps.*)

COUNTESS (*rushing for* CRYSTAL). Oh, mon Dieu, mon Dieu!

MARY (*stopping her*). Flora, it's really too bad—

COUNTESS (*to* CRYSTAL). You—you painted wagon!

CRYSTAL. So you're determined to have a scandal, Mrs. Haines.

COUNTESS. I'm the one who's going to have the scandal. Why, Mary, she's no more a blonde naturelle than I am. What's the creature's name? Miriam forgot to tell me.

MARY. Mrs. Stephen Haines, currently.

COUNTESS. Is that the thing Stephen left you for? Well, cherie, all I can say is, you're an idiot! I hope I never live to see the day when an obvious piece like that conquers *me* on the champs d'amour! (*She exits, right, followed by* MIRIAM.)

CRYSTAL (*to* MARY). That damn fool didn't know. (SADIE *gives* MARY *her wrap.*)

MARY. I'm afraid she didn't. (*Enter* NANCY *right.*)

NANCY. There's a gentleman called Mr. Haines. He says he's been waiting a long time for his wife— (CRYSTAL *moves to get her wrap.*)

MARY (*stepping between her and* SADIE). Tell him, *I* am coming. (*Exit* NANCY *quickly.*)

SYLVIA. Mary, what a dirty female trick!

CRYSTAL. Yes! From the great, noble little woman! You're just a cat, like all the rest of us!

MARY. Well, I've had two years to sharpen my claws. (*Waves her hand gaily to* SYLVIA.) Jungle-red, Sylvia! Good night, ladies! (*Exits.*)

CURTAIN

Yes, My Darling Daughter

BY MARK REED

To

ANN AND FRANK

CAST OF CHARACTERS

(In order of appearance)

As produced at the Playhouse, New York City, on February 9, 1937, by Alfred de Liagre, Jr.

ELLEN MURRAY	Peggy Conklin
LEWIS MURRAY	Charles Bryant
CONSTANCE NEVINS	Violet Heming
MARTHA	Margaret Curtis
ANN WHITMAN MURRAY	Lucile Watson
TITUS JAYWOOD	Nicholas Joy
DOUGLAS HALL	Boyd Crawford

The play was staged by Mr. de Liagre. The settings were by Raymond Sovey. The poem in Act II was written for the play by Abby Shute Merchant.

SCENES

ACT ONE: Living-room of the Murray summer home, New Canaan, Conn. A Friday afternoon in late June.

ACT TWO: Ann's "Office." The same afternoon.

ACT THREE: The living-room again. The following Monday morning.

ACT ONE

SCENE: *There is no gilt-letter sign or bronze plaque at the entrance to the Murrays' summer home. It is not known as "Rosebank," "Triple Oaks," or even "Nineacres." Your car, turning from the main highway, passes under a quarter-mile arch of beeches and maples, then draws up to what was once a plain rectangular stone manor house. Wings, thrown out on either end, take care of the modern necessities of housing and feeding week-end guests. At the front of the house the century-old trees give way to a broad lawn, and beyond, across several misty ridges, Long Island Sound is visible. A guest, on the particular day this play starts, would see, on the edge of the lawn, the somewhat disturbing sight of three Italian labourers constructing a cement dam at the end of a lily pond . . . the object apparently being, when the water backs up, to form a pool for swimming.*

Entering the house, this same guest would pass along a wide central hall, papered with old-fashioned "landscape" paper, and step through an archway into the living-room. It is dignified, hospitable. The woodwork throughout is painted a soft green; and the formal soapstone fireplace, set in the panelled wall (actor's right), suggests at once that this room is in the old part of the house.

The fireplace is filled with June flowers, and backed against it, not too close for free passage behind, is a library table and a long comfortable couch. Facing the couch is a large stuffed chair. Both wear summer covers of a soft-toned cretonne. Balancing this furniture group, left center, is a drum table flanked on either side with arm chairs. Right and left of the arch, stand two very large mahogany bookcases. Upstage from the fireplace, a door leads to the dining-room and rear of house. Left, two French windows open out upon the terrace; the draperies, like those of the arch, are a delicate yellow and intensify the afternoon sunlight which floods the terrace and the hall.

The furnishings and ornaments are the accretion of taste and travel. Books and magazines are scattered about, not by servants, but by people who have enjoyed reading them. Above all else, you feel the room has been lived in; the furniture has been hauled about for charades, the fireplace has known a thousand fires, while men and women have gathered around, sipped good liquor, and talked out their thoughts vigorously, if not always intelligently. In brief, a room which has associated long enough with human beings to acquire a mellow and gracious humanity of its own.

At Rise: ELLEN *is discovered sitting on the couch, hunting up references in a very scholarly-looking book. An alert, slender, well-built girl of twenty-two, her charms are rather obscured by her dress and posture. She wears blue denim overalls, red sandals, tortoise-shell glasses. Her bobbed hair is at loose ends. On a tea table before the sofa are several books and a pad and pencil. After the curtain rises, she goes to the bookcase, gets two additional books and comes back to the sofa.* LEWIS MURRAY *enters from the hall.*

LEWIS *is genial, well-tanned, tall, about forty-eight. His outstanding characteristic is a hearty, playful bluntness which ordinarily is amusing; but occasionally, when it takes the form of questions, can lead to embarrassing moments. He wears an informal yachting costume and hat preparatory to departure*

LEWIS. Oh, hello, Ellen.

ELLEN. (*Without looking up.*) Hello, Dad. Had your lunch?

LEWIS. I had lunch in town. Your mother's not in her office.

ELLEN. No?

LEWIS. Where the devil is she?

ELLEN. Where she can't be disturbed. (LEWIS *crosses to upper French window, takes a look around the terrace, then returns.*)

LEWIS. What you reading?

ELLEN. I'm brushing up on my Constitution. (*She lifts her glasses to her forehead and looks up.*) You know, Dad, those fifteen judges have me worried. Do you think he can get away with it?

LEWIS. I suppose so. He generally does. (*With considerable feeling.*) I wish he'd spend more time on his stamp collection. (*He opens door, right, and calls.*) Ann! Oh, Annie! I'm back! (*Then, coming down to* ELLEN:) Where the hell is she?

ELLEN. Mother's simply got to get that story finished before people begin to arrive.

LEWIS. Who'll come on a Friday?

ELLEN. A Mr. Jaywood for one. Peter's already gone to meet him.

LEWIS. Jaywood? Never heard of him.

ELLEN. He's an important literary agent.

LEWIS. (*Getting the significance of this.*) Huh! By the way, your Aunt Connie is back East. She phoned this morning she'd be out.

ELLEN. I suppose she wants to tell us about her latest divorce.

LEWIS. Your mother ought to be told. If Connie's coming out to tell us about her divorce, somebody ought to be here to listen to her.

ELLEN. I'll be here, Dad. Now will you please go sail your boat?

LEWIS. Thought you were going to Hartford.

ELLEN. I am, but not until five o'clock.

LEWIS. In that case, I'd better give you a kiss. (*He does so.*) Good-bye, pet. Have a good time, and behave yourself.

ELLEN. (*Affectionately.*) Thanks, Dad. The same to you.

LEWIS. (*Starts to go, stops.*) Aw, be a good sport. Come across. . . .

CONNIE. (*In hallway, outside.*) Hello! Is anybody home?

LEWIS. Damn! There's Connie already. (*In a low hoarse whisper.*) Quick, so I can sneak out. Where's your mother?

ELLEN. Never you mind. Go say Hello to your sister.

LEWIS. (*Not moving.*) Hi, Connie! (CON-

NIE NEVINS *enters. She is stylish, chic, still young-looking at thirty-five. Basically a gay, affectionate, fun-loving sort of woman, she has not let a rather embittering marital career get her down.*)

CONNIE. Hello, Lewis! (*She goes to him.*)

LEWIS. Hello, Connie!

CONNIE. I didn't expect to find you here.

LEWIS. Been waiting an hour, especially to see you. (*He kisses her perfunctorily, then begins to fire questions without much regard for her answers.*) How are you anyway?

CONNIE. Pretty well, considering. . . .

LEWIS. Have a nice judge?

CONNIE. A dear.

LEWIS. Hotel good?

CONNIE. The food was terrible. I had to keep reminding myself I didn't go to Reno to eat.

LEWIS. Who you going to marry next?

CONNIE. (*With slightly embarrassed laugh.*) That's the problem. . . .

ELLEN. (*Flat on couch.*) Oh, Dad, shut up! You're nothing but a question mark.

CONNIE. (*Aware of* ELLEN *for the first time.*) Ellen darling! (*She expects to kiss* ELLEN, *but the latter keeps on reading and only raises a hand for her to shake.*) You look well. (*Inspects her more closely.*) Or don't you look well?

ELLEN. (*Tersely.*) I don't know how I look; I feel fine.

CONNIE. (*To* LEWIS.) I called up Ann after I called you, but Martha said I couldn't talk to her.

LEWIS. Oh, absolutely out of the question!

CONNIE. (*Startled.*) Ann's not sick?

LEWIS. (*Lugubriously.*) I'm afraid Ann's lost to me forever.

CONNIE. Why, Lewis! What's happened?

ELLEN. Nothing! Mother's hid herself to write a love story, that's all.

CONNIE. I'm glad she's gone back to love. I never can understand her articles about Women in Business, and Women in Marriage, and Women out of Marriage . . . except I've a vague idea they're all aimed at me. What made her go back to fiction after all these years?

ELLEN. (*Pointing to* LEWIS.) That! He felt Mother was getting too independent, so he's disciplining her.

LEWIS. Ellen! Play fair!

ELLEN. Why not tell the truth? You are.

LEWIS. Connie. it's this way. Last week my own sweet, dutiful, loving Annie ordered our duck pond made into a swimming pool. After I expressly told her we couldn't afford it. So this week she's writing a love story to pay the bill.

CONNIE. Can't you afford a swimming pool?

LEWIS. This is a matter of principle. I don't have to be firm with my Annie very often; but when I am firm, by God! I'm granite.

CONNIE. One minute you men go broke to give us a pearl necklace, the next you tell us our extravagance has ruined you . . . a woman doesn't know where she gets off.

LEWIS. My Annie knows where she gets off . . . don't forget that!

CONNIE. I'll admit you two seem to get along.

LEWIS. We're celebrating our twenty-third anniversary next week. Drop around.

CONNIE. Think of it! Remember Father said you and a woman like Ann wouldn't last it out a month. . . .

LEWIS. My father was an old-fashioned man.

ELLEN. Lord, Father, what's so modern about you?

LEWIS. The brilliant way I handle the modern woman. (MARTHA *enters. She is a demure and noiseless Scotch maid in a green dress.*)

MARTHA. Pardon, sir.

LEWIS. What's on your mind, Martha?

MARTHA. I've brought in Mrs. Nevins' bags.

CONNIE. Where do you suppose Ann will want to put me?

LEWIS. Oh, why not take your regular room!

MARTHA. That's for Mr. Jaywood, sir.

LEWIS. How about the room next to ours?

MARTHA. Folks are expected for that, too.

LEWIS. Hang around, Connie, we'll put you somewhere. (CONNIE *looks at her watch.*)

CONNIE. I must have a place to change now. I've an appointment for four . . . in my very best dress.

LEWIS. Ellen, what room *can* she have?

ELLEN. I don't know what Mother's plans are.

CONNIE. Maybe I better go back to the Waldorf.

LEWIS. You'll do no such thing. A sister of mine, just back from Reno, you rate the best room in the house. (*To* MARTHA.) Tell Mrs. Murray she must come here at once.

MARTHA. I don't know where she is, sir. Nobody's seen her this whole day.

LEWIS. (*Angrily, to* ELLEN.) This damn nonsense must stop! Produce your mother! (ELLEN *consults her wrist watch and decides her mother has worked long enough.*)

ELLEN. (*To* MARTHA.) She's out between the vegetable garden and the pump house under a beach umbrella.

LEWIS. (*To* MARTHA.) Don't you come back here without her!

MARTHA. (*As she exits to terrace.*) All right, sir.

CONNIE. (*Apologetically.*) I'm sorry to upset . . .

LEWIS. (*Interrupting, heartily.*) No, you're not either. Sit down. Rest your French heels! Want a highball? (ELLEN *rises with armful of books.*)

CONNIE. No thanks. (*Then to* ELLEN.) Darling, what are all those books for?

ELLEN. (*Taking books back to bookcase.*) I just carry them around for exercise.

CONNIE. (*Sitting on sofa.*) I'm crazy to hear about your graduation.

ELLEN. (*Prosaically, as she puts books away.*) Oh, the weather was fine, except one day it rained possibly an hour. I was handed a diploma. That's about all there was to it.

CONNIE. I hoped to get back East in time to be there.

ELLEN. Sorry you didn't. (*She returns and sits on couch.*)

CONNIE. What man did you take? (*To* LEWIS.) That sweet Jackie Whipple, I'll bet.

ELLEN. I didn't take a man.

CONNIE. You didn't take a man?

ELLEN. Nope.

CONNIE. Why, when I graduated from Miss Spence's I asked seven and eleven came. Seven, come eleven! Remember, Lewis?

LEWIS. (*With a touch of weariness.*) Yes, I remember.

ELLEN. Men in droves don't interest me.

CONNIE. But, darling, I can't understand. A girl at Commencement simply has to have a man to walk with under the Campus elms in the moonlight. . . .

ELLEN. I didn't feel the necessity.

CONNIE. Lewis, I'm worried. It's not normal.

ELLEN. (*Turning angrily.*) Connie, you worry about *your* love life, and I'll worry about *mine*.

LEWIS. (*Sharply, though amused.*) Mind your manners, daughter. (*He moves to left, to watch for* ANN.)

ELLEN. Sorry.

CONNIE. *You* forgive *me*. I didn't mean to hurt you.

ELLEN. You didn't. I daresay I *am* peculiar. Personally, I think a woman's a fool to try and build her happiness around a man.

CONNIE. (*A trace too sweetly.*) Really, Ellen, do tell me. I'm in a position this minute where I yearn to know. What else can the average woman build her happiness around?

ELLEN. Plenty of things! (ANN *enters from the terrace. The name "*ANN WHITMAN MURRAY*" has for years carried considerable prestige in the newspaper and feminist world; but in appearance* ANN *looks merely a very comfortable, human, motherly sort of person . . . with a growing tendency to be stout. At the moment she wears a cotton blouse and garden skirt, neither any too clean, a large sun hat and old straw sandals. Her face is streaked with dirt, and strands of loose hair tend to get in her eyes. Yet despite this external untidiness, she strikes one instantly as a personality and a profoundly charming woman.*)

LEWIS. (*Heartily, in a rich Irish brogue.*) Well, well, Mrs. Lewis Murray, and is it gardening you have been? (ANN *crosses, ignoring her husband as though he did not exist.*)

ANN. Connie! This is grand!

CONNIE. (*Sincere affection in her voice.*) Ann, my dear!

ANN. Don't kiss me. I'm filthy. I've been writing a love story with one hand and weeding parsnips with the other. Did you have a terrible time?

CONNIE. Not so bad!

LEWIS. She looks a lot better than she did after her last divorce.

ANN. The main point is: did you get it?

CONNIE. I'm free as air.

ANN. (*Sinking into stuffed chair and lighting a cigarette.*) I'd like to be free as air myself.

LEWIS. Not if I know it. You haven't a chance!

ELLEN. Mother, do go change, please. You're a sight.

CONNIE. I don't mind.

LEWIS. Yes, Annie, as soon as you wash your face I'd like to kiss you good-bye and go to Larchmont.

ANN. (*Indicating* LEWIS.) Who is that odd-looking man over in the sailor suit who keeps interrupting?

LEWIS. (*Grinning broadly.*) Let me introduce myself. It's me, Annie. Your husband.

ANN. What are you hanging around here for?

LEWIS. For my wife to kiss me good-bye. I'm a very eccentric man. I love my wife. . .

ANN. (*Interrupting.*) Oh, we can't talk till I get rid of him. (*She goes to* LEWIS *and kisses him lightly.*) Good-bye, Commodore.

LEWIS. Good-bye, Annie.

ANN. Hope you get a good ducking!

LEWIS. You peeved at me?

ANN. I am . . . extremely peeved.

LEWIS. Kiss me again. I may get drowned.

ELLEN. Father, will you stop making a sentimental idiot of yourself? You come along with me. (*She takes him by the arm and leads him into the hall.*)

LEWIS. (*Calling back.*) See you at dinner, Connie.

CONNIE. If I can get back in time. (LEWIS *and* ELLEN *disappear,* ANN *settles back comfortably in her chair.*)

ANN. Light yourself a cigarette, Connie, and tell me everything.

CONNIE. (*Lighting cigarette.*) Ann, it's been a tremendous experience. Tremendous! I've come back full of ideas. You know during my first divorce how I got all weepy and hurt; then the next time when Ted went off with that mouse-coloured blonde, of course I got bitter and drank a lot, and was all kinds of a damn fool. Well, this time I took myself in hand and did some thinking.

ANN. Grand!

CONNIE. I studied those women out there. Ann, ninety percent of them, one look and you'd see why they couldn't hold a man six months unless they had money. There was even more drinking this time than last.

ANN. Really?

CONNIE. I said to myself: Connie Nevins, you don't belong in this gang.

ANN. You don't, you know, Connie.

CONNIE. That's why it's been such an experience. I've found myself. At last I know what I want and why I haven't been happy. From now on I'm going to simplify my life.

ANN. I see.

CONNIE. I'm going to live in the country and have a garden and enjoy all the simple pleasures the way you do. Look, Ann, you and Lewis haven't had a row?

ANN. Not a serious one.

CONNIE. He's a beast to make you write a love story.

ANN. It was my own mistake.

CONNIE. He has money enough for fifty swimming pools. I wouldn't stand for it.

ANN. Well, he said he couldn't afford it . . . we've had extra expenses with both Roger and Ellen . . . then I saw Jim Bambarra weeping around without any work and nine children, and got soft-hearted.

CONNIE. All the same, I'd be furious with Lewis.

ANN. I'd been furious with him if he had let himself be coaxed into paying the bill . . . when I was wrong. I wouldn't want a husband I could twist around my little finger.

CONNIE. If he's around your little finger, you know where he is. (*She consults her wrist watch.*) Ann, is it all right if I fly . . . shortly?

ANN. Of course.

CONNIE. I'm having tea at the club . with Glen.

ANN. (*Trying to be enthusiastic.*) Are you? Glen Williams?

CONNIE. You've probably guessed I would anyway . . . but I want you to be the first to know. Glen and I are going to be married next week.

ANN. Next week? I thought you were going to simplify your life?

CONNIE. I am.

ANN. But you said you'd found yourself?

CONNIE. I have.

ANN. Suppose you lose yourself again?

CONNIE. It isn't as though I didn't know Glen awfully well . . . I mean *awfully well.*

ANN. I know you mean *awfully well.* So why the rush? Wait a bit before you marry again. Take a trip. Enjoy a vacation from the masculine sex.

CONNIE. I've just had a six months' vacation. If I dangle Glen any longer, I might lose him.

ANN. If he mislays as easily as that, maybe it would be just as well.

CONNIE. We're so in love.

ANN. Wait. See if you are.

CONNIE. I don't need to. I told you. I've analyzed myself. I've dug into my character with knives. I'm a very affectionate person at heart. Don't you think so?

ANN. Yes, I do. It's made me overlook a lot.

CONNIE. I know. You've stood by the old *divorcée*. Most sisters-in-law wouldn't.

ANN. You see, I like you.

CONNIE. Ann, can I be married here?

ANN. Why not?

CONNIE. (*She crosses to the fireplace.*) If I were married in a happy home . . . right here in front of your fireplace . . . it might bring me luck. I can't endure the thought of any more church weddings.

ANN. (*Drily.*) It's certainly worth a try.

CONNIE. Maybe next Wednesday or Thursday. Glen and I will make definite arrangements this afternoon.

ANN. Just let me know a day in advance. (*The phone rings.*)

ELLEN. (*Offstage, rear.*) I'll take it, Mother.

ANN. I'm trying to persuade Ellen to be my secretary for a while. (ELLEN *enters and picks up receiver on small table, left of arch.*)

ELLEN. (*Into phone.*) Hello. Yes, this is Ann Whitman Murray's residence. I'm very sorry. Mrs. Murray is not in right now. I'm her secretary . . . suppose you give me the message. I see. Yes. The fifteenth. (*Makes a note.*) Yes. Yes. I'll ring back and give you an answer as soon as I have talked with Mrs. Murray. (*She hangs up the receiver and comes down to* ANN.) It's a Mr. Henry Folsom. He wants to know will you talk ten minutes at a rally on July fifteenth.

ANN. What's the rally around?

ELLEN. It's the League against War and Fascism.

ANN. All right . . . if I'm free.

ELLEN. Your calendar's in the office. I'll go look. (*She goes out.*)

ANN. (*Calling after her.*) Find out who the other speakers are . . . and if I better wear armour plate.

ELLEN. All right, Mother.

CONNIE. Is Ellen going blind?

ANN. Not to my knowledge.

CONNIE. Why the hideous glasses?

ANN. They're just study glasses. She doesn't wear them all the time.

CONNIE. She looks so pale and intellectual. Heaven knows a woman nowadays needs all the brains she can muster up; but that's no reason she shouldn't continue to look dumb. The poor child said she didn't have a single man at her Commencement.

ANN. She could have.

CONNIE. (*Incredulously.*) And didn't!

ANN. She did invite one boy, I believe, but at the last minute he didn't come.

CONNIE. Why not?

ANN. Don't ask me. She is keeping her own counsel this spring . . . at times to the point of being sullen.

CONNIE. You'd be sullen if you weren't popular with men.

ANN. (*Amused.*) Would I?

CONNIE. Ann, I have too much respect for your judgment to think of interfering, but do you mind a suggestion?

ANN. I'd welcome one.

CONNIE. If she were my daughter I'd rush her tomorrow to some good beauty consultant, then to a really intelligent dressmaker.

ANN. (*Vaguely.*) I think she has several Schiaparelli's.

CONNIE. You'd never guess it to look at her. After all, our family does have some position. Why shouldn't Ellen have the benefit of it? Seriously, Ann, why don't you have her come out?

ANN. She has just come out of college. Can she go back in and come out again?

CONNIE. Why not? It's too terrible for her to become a private secretary. If you're going to be nursemaid to a man, you might as well be married to him. (ANN *smiles.*) Smile if you want. I'm telling you God's solemn truth. You take off Ellen's glasses, show her a few attractive men, and in six months she'd bloom like a tea rose.

ANN. Connie, you're grand. After all you've been through, you still advocate the sly, primitive female hunt for man.

CONNIE. I don't care whether Ellen hunts.

All I say is that it's a shame to let a girl with so many possibilities develop into a freak, maybe a crank.

ANN. Like her mother.

CONNIE. (*Conscience-stricken.*) Ann, dear, I didn't mean that. You're not.

ANN. My good woman, if I had a dime for every time I'd been called a crank, I could balance the national budget.

CONNIE. Anyway, you're not *now*. Since you married Lewis you've been growing more feminine steadily.

ANN. (*Delighted.*) You encourage me. Maybe by the time I'm seventy-five, I'll be sex-y. (ELLEN *enters hurriedly.*)

CONNIE. Er, do think over what I've said.

ANN. (*Studying* ELLEN *thoughtfully.*) I already am.

ELLEN. (*Who has waited for them to stop talking.*) Mother, you simply must dress. Peter's back. I think with your Mr. Jaywood. He looks horribly English and ultra. (*Both* ANN *and* CONNIE *rise.*)

CONNIE. Where you going to bunk me?

ANN. Ellen's away till Monday. You can have her room.

CONNIE. (*To* ELLEN.) Do you mind?

ELLEN. Of course not. Move right in. I'm all packed.

ANN. Tell Mr. Jaywood I'll be down in a jiffy.

ELLEN. Mother, give me fifteen minutes alone with him.

ANN. Why should I?

ELLEN. Because I've always wanted to meet an International Literary Agent.

ANN. Let's go this way. (CONNIE *and* ANN *start, right.*)

ELLEN. (*Running after them.*) Here! (*She hands* ANN *her garden hat.*) And, Mother, for Heaven's sake wash behind your ears!

ANN. (*Meekly.*) I generally do, dear.

(CONNIE *and* ANN *exit.* ELLEN *leisurely removes her glasses and puts them in case; pulls down her skirt; then crosses to mirror, left, and arranges her hair. The result is not style, but she does possess a certain breathless charm.* MARTHA *enters.*)

MARTHA. Miss Ellen, Mr. Jaywood.

ELLEN. Show him in. And Martha: bring us whiskey and soda at once. (MARTHA *nods and goes out.* ELLEN *waits eagerly.* JAY *appears followed by* MARTHA. *He is a quietly alert Englishman in his early forties. He wears a conservative business suit.* MARTHA *sees him safely through the archway, then disappears from sight.*)

ELLEN. I suppose we'll have to introduce ourselves. I'm Ellen Murray.

JAY. (*As they shake hands.*) I'm Titus Jaywood. How do you do?

ELLEN. (*Briskly, quite unabashed.*) Swell you came early. I've been hoping desperately you would.

JAY. I'm flattered.

ELLEN. Do sit down. There are cigarettes at your elbow.

JAY. (*Taking cigarette*) Thanks.

ELLEN. (*Offering him light.*) Mother says you are an old friend of hers.

JAY. Not so old. About five weeks. I met your mother in May at a literary tea.

ELLEN. (*Somewhat taken back.*) In May! I got the impression . . . Oh well, it doesn't matter. (*She stops, then says briskly.*) If you'll forgive me, I'm going to plunge right ahead.

JAY. By all means. Let's not stop now... (MARTHA *enters with tray.*)

ELLEN. Place it here, Martha. (MARTHA *puts tray beside* ELLEN *and goes out.*) I ordered us whiskey and soda, or would you prefer something else?

JAY. Whiskey and soda suits me perfectly.

ELLEN. Two fingers or three? (*She pours whiskey.*)

JAY. (*Smiling at her intense eagerness.*) I think I shall need three. (ELLEN *starts to put ice in drink.*) No ice, thanks.

ELLEN. (*Pouring soda.*) Mother said you were English. (*Hands him glass.*)

JAY. Thanks

ELLEN. Comfortable?

JAY. I'm enjoying all the sensations of the prodigal son.

ELLEN. Then I'm coming straight to the point.

JAY. Point? Is there a point?

ELLEN. Mr. Jaywood, I've just graduated from college. The customary thing would be for me to play up to you all this week-end, put myself across as hard as I could . . . then just before you leave, ask you to help me get a job.

JAY. I wish, Miss Murray, you'd stick to your American customs. I'd much prefer to be "played up to" till Monday.

ELLEN. But I'm not going to be home this week-end.

JAY. Oh, that's too bad.

ELLEN. I've got to visit a classmate in Hartford. Her father runs a paper there. I'd a lot rather stay here and talk with you. I've a million questions to ask you about Maugham, and Priestly and all the other authors you handle. Unfortunately I made this date before I knew Mother had asked you out.

JAY. Naturally **you** can't look for work in two places the same week-end.

ELLEN. No, not very well. Will you excuse me if I talk about myself?

JAY. I think it would be charming.

ELLEN. Of course, I was editor of the "Lit" and all that sort of junk, and of course, I've learned all I can from Mother. You see, I want to be one of the best all-round newspaper women that ever drew breath, like Anne O'Hare McCormick or Dorothy Thompson.

JAY. Splendid.

ELLEN. You needn't if you don't want to, but I thought perhaps you'd give me let-

ters to two or three editors. I wouldn't
mind going on a magazine . . . anything
to get a start. You don't have to say anything very good about me . . . just enough
so I can get one foot inside an editor's
door.

JAY. That will make it easier.

ELLEN. I wish you'd stop looking so
amused. After all, I have already sold stuff.

JAY. (*Surprised.*) You have? What?

ELLEN. Oh, a few poems . . . at the large
sum of two dollars each. I wish there was
money in poetry.

JAY. A lot of poets wish that.

ELLEN. Then, of course, I've sold quite a
few articles on education and politics.

JAY. Politics? How's your thousand-page
novel?

ELLEN. Fine. How's yours? (JAY *smiles.*)
Really, it's no credit to me. Mother and
I get into awful arguments. She sells what
she says to liberal papers, and I sell what
I say to conservatives.

JAY. Haven't you your viewpoints reversed?

ELLEN. When it comes to being liberal,
Mother's got me licked six ways. She's
just as radical as when she wrote for the
Masses in Greenwich Village and headed
Suffrage Parades. You know, she used to
be a famous feminist when she was young.
Incidentally, Mr. Jaywood, Mother's been
in jail nineteen times.

JAY. That's a very nice record.

ELLEN. I suppose the reason I'm conservative is on account of Father. He's half
Dutch. Have you ever met him?

JAY. No, I never have.

ELLEN. I think you'll like him. Can you
imagine? Mother an Iowa hog and corn
farmer and Father Dutch Social Register!
What do you suppose that makes me?

JAY. Let's hope it makes you a good all-
round newspaper woman.

ELLEN. You mean you'll really help me
get a job? (JAY *nods.*) Look, Mr. Jaywood,

I want to get this job on my own. You
won't mention who my mother is, will
you?

JAY. A g r e e d. There's one question,
though, before I commit myself to a series
of introductory letters. . . .

ELLEN. Ask me anything.

JAY. Are you engaged?

ELLEN. (*With unexpected vehemence.*) I
should hope not!

JAY. I've introduced girls to jobs before.
Almost invariably within a year or two, I
get an irate phone call: "Dammit, Jay!"
they say, "just as I got that woman trained, she's up and leaving me to have a
child!"

ELLEN. Oh, I don't think I'll have a
child.

JAY. Well, you watch your step! (MARTHA
enters.)

MARTHA. Miss Ellen, there's a Mr. Douglas Hall outside that says . . .

ELLEN. (*Interrupting angrily.*) What's
that man doing here?

MARTHA. (*Prosaically.*) He's waiting on
the steps.

ELLEN. Tell him I can't see him. I have
to leave the house immediately. (MARTHA
exits. ELLEN *turns to* JAY. *She has lost her
poise. Her one desire is to flee.*) I simply
must go. You've been awfully helpful. I
wish I could stay and get really well
acquainted.

JAY. My ambition is to be asked out
again.

ELLEN. If Mother doesn't ask you, you
come out and see *me.* (*Extends hand, nervously.*) Good-bye. It's been grand. . . .

JAY. Hasn't it? Your indomitable youth
refreshes me.

ELLEN. (*Stopping abruptly.*) I bet *you*
wrote poetry once.

JAY. Did I? Why?

ELLEN. I don't know. There was something about that line. And you seem so

impressed by the word "youth." (DOUGLAS HALL *enters.* "DOUG" *is an attractive, forceful young man of around twenty-five. His clothes are of good material and cut, but well-worn.* MARTHA *hovers in the background.*)

DOUG. (*With touch of defiance.*) Hi, Ellen! (*She does not answer.*) Forgive my barging in.

ELLEN. (*Recovering.*) Mr. Jaywood, much as I regret the necessity, may I introduce Mr. Hall?

JAY. How do you do.

DOUG. How are you, sir. (*A pause. Neither* ELLEN *nor* DOUGLAS *can find anything to say.* JAY *senses he is between two belligerents who yearn to open fire.*)

JAY. (*Blandly.*) Perhaps this would be an excellent moment for me to unpack.

ELLEN. Do you mind?

JAY. Not at all.

ELLEN. Martha, you know Mr. Jaywood's room?

MARTHA. Your mother said he was to have the Sound view.

ELLEN. (*To* JAY.) Mother will be down very soon.

JAY. (*Bowing gravely.*) Mr. Hall, it's been a rare pleasure.

DOUG. Thank you. (JAY *exits after* MARTHA.)

ELLEN. (*With cool sarcasm.*) So you *are* able to leave Boston?

DOUG. Listen, Ellen, we've no time to be sore.

ELLEN. I'm not sore. I merely commented on the fact that though you couldn't possibly leave Boston last week, you are able to leave this week.

DOUG. Yes? Well, let me comment on the fact that when I tell a girl I can't get to a place, I don't care to be insulted with a wire for twenty-five dollars.

ELLEN. Insulted?

DOUG. I said "insulted"!

ELLEN. But I thought we were friends.

DOUG. So did I.

ELLEN. Well, then . . . didn't you understand?

DOUG. Why didn't you do a little understanding yourself? You knew I was strapped.

ELLEN. Obviously, else why wire you money?

DOUG. Yes, and you know why I wired it back.

ELLEN. Frankly, I don't.

DOUG. I'm no paid escort.

ELLEN. That's pretty cheap.

DOUG. The letter you wrote me was pretty cheap too. (*Fumbles in his pocket.*) Maybe you'd like to refresh your memory.

ELLEN. I kept a carbon copy.

DOUG. You say you understand people's psychology.

ELLEN. I try to.

DOUG. Good God, then! Didn't you realize I couldn't come because I wasn't in the mood? I'd have been a gloom in all that Commencement gaiety. It wasn't the actual carfare. Lord, I'd have pawned my watch and hitch-hiked.

ELLEN. Exactly! You didn't want to come.

DOUG. Sure I wanted to come.

ELLEN. Then why didn't you?

DOUG. I told you.

ELLEN. You were too proud.

DOUG. Damn right I was too proud. Think I'd humiliate you?

ELLEN. I'd rather be humiliated than . . . than disappointed.

DOUG. I felt you'd have enough other men.

ELLEN. Oh, I had plenty.

DOUG. Then what are you sore about?

ELLEN. I'm not sore. Is that what you came to find out?

DOUG. No, I came to say good-bye.

ELLEN. Good-bye. Awfully glad you dropped in. (*She sits on couch and turns her back.*)

DOUG. Listen, Ellen, for God's sake, be a human being, will you? I've come to say good-bye, because I'm going to Belgium.

ELLEN. (*Blankly.*) Belgium?

DOUG. Yes. You remember Belgium, don't you?

ELLEN. What are you talking about? How can you leave your job?

DOUG. Oh, it wasn't so hard to leave ... especially after I got your twenty-five-dollar wire. I've chucked architecture.

ELLEN. Doug! That's terrible!

DOUG. The hell with it! What do I want with that profession? After six years' study and work, it won't pay me enough even to go and see the girl I love graduate! (*At the words "I love," ELLEN gives him a surprised look, then turns away.*) Well, it's out! My idea was to tell you later ... a little more romantically. Ellen, you've looked right to me from the day I met you. I love you. I'm heart-sick over you. That's why that damn telegram burned me up. (*He studies her face anxiously.*)

ELLEN. That's what I couldn't understand. Why should my telegram burn you up? I mean if we *both* cared for each other.

DOUG. Say, you mean you actually do? Oh, darling! (*She nods. He takes her into his arms. They kiss, shyly, then more eagerly.*)

ELLEN. Oh, Doug, this past month has been pure hell.

DOUG. I'll say it has.

ELLEN. Anyway, everything is all right now.

DOUG. Well, it's better. (*She breaks away from him.*)

ELLEN. That's so. You're leaving. You don't have to go for some time, do you?

DOUG. I sail Monday at midnight.

ELLEN. Monday! Can't you put it off?

DOUG. Impossible. I've got to start work July first. It's a ten-day boat. I can just make it.

ELLEN. But we've everything to talk over. We haven't made any plans yet.

DOUG. We can do a lot of planning between now and Monday night.

ELLEN. But I'm catching a train in less than an hour.

DOUG. Where you going?

ELLEN. Edith Colby's. I agreed to stay till Monday. Say, I might get you invited, too.

DOUG. Swell!

ELLEN. No, that wouldn't be so good. There's going to be masses of people about. We couldn't be by ourselves. I guess I'd better call it off. . . .

DOUG. Well, if you don't mind. . . .

ELLEN. You can stay here. No, there'll be a crowd here. I've given up my room to Connie, already. The house will seethe. How long will you have to be gone?

DOUG. I've signed up for two years.

ELLEN. Two years? Do you feel it's wise to stay away from . . . from America so long?

DOUG. I couldn't get the job if I didn't.

ELLEN. Do you realize that just when we've discovered we care, we're about to be separated. It might be forever.

DOUG. Oh, no, it won't.

ELLEN. Well, I'm not going to Hartford, that's settled!

DOUG. Good girl! (*She crosses thoughtfully.*)

ELLEN. I have it. I *will* go to Hartford.

DOUG. Say, make up your mind.

ELLEN. I mean suppose I *start* for Hartford, then you join me, and I won't go.

DOUG. Won't they expect you?

ELLEN. I'll wire them I can't come. That would give us three whole days together.

DOUG. (*Uneasily.*) Together? Er, where?

ELLEN. I don't know. Somewhere! Some little cottage maybe . . . with a lake and a canoe. We could cook our own meals, and smoke and talk, and plan our whole life together.

DOUG. I don't know about that. (*He crosses to left, worried and uncomfortable.*)

ELLEN. What's the matter? Have I shocked you?

DOUG. No, it's not that.

ELLEN. In marriage everything depends on getting off to a right start.

DOUG. This might not be such a swell start.

ELLEN. I mean we've been separated so much and had so many misunderstandings. Before you go, I think it's terribly important we settle every point we could possibly fight about after you're gone.

DOUG. Something to that.

ELLEN. I know a little lake outside Lancsville. We used to drive over from college. There are several darling cottages on it. I know we could hire one. The season doesn't start till the Fourth. There wouldn't be three people around the entire lake.

DOUG. Three people is plenty sometimes. I don't want you to lose your reputation.

ELLEN. I won't . . . if we plan things carefully.

DOUG. I still don't quite like the idea.

ELLEN. Maybe you think I've done something like this before.

DOUG. Of course not.

ELLEN. (*Solemnly.*) Doug, this is an emergency measure.

DOUG. God, I wish we could marry.

ELLEN. Well, if we can't, we can't! And I do think we're entitled to something . . . something beautiful and set apart. Something we can cling to after you're gone! Don't you?

DOUG. Yes, but . . .

ELLEN. Doug, be frank. What do you really feel? Does . . . does my willingness to go like this make me seem cheap?

DOUG. What do you think I am? (*He rises and takes her by the shoulders affectionately.*) Makes you seem precious. What I don't like is . . . it's a bit underhanded.

ELLEN. Whose earthly business is it, except yours and mine?

DOUG. You've got a mother, you know.

ELLEN. I don't think she'd mind particularly. . . .

DOUG. (*Surprised.*) Why not?

ELLEN. I mean, under the circumstances. Mother's tremendously advanced. Not, of course, that I'd want her to know. . . .

DOUG. I wish we had more time to think it over.

ELLEN. So do I, but we haven't. Well, what shall we do?

DOUG. I think you're right, Ellen. We'll go.

ELLEN. Oh, I'm glad.

DOUG. So am I. (*Their voices lower, and take an a brisk secretive quality.*)

ELLEN. How'd you get here?

DOUG. I borrowed my cousin's car. I'm making my headquarters with him till I sail.

ELLEN. When does he expect you back?

DOUG. When he sees me. I've got a couple of visits to make. How far is a place called Silver Mine from here?

ELLEN. About six miles.

DOUG. (*Looking at watch.*) Your train goes at five? (ELLEN *nods.*) I can just make it. There's a Yale man lives at Silver Mine said he'd buy my drafting instruments.

ELLEN. Oh, Doug, you must let me pay.

DOUG. No, I'm financing this little expedition.

ELLEN. Let's both finance it. . . .

DOUG. No.

ELLEN. Fifty-fifty, I insist. . . .

DOUG. No.

ELLEN. I just received a twenty-dollar check for writing an article.

DOUG. Well, all right. I'll be right back. (*He kisses her.*) Darling, it seems impossible you and I should have scrapped so.

ELLEN. (*Very seriously.*) Maybe our love was clarifying itself.

DOUG. Maybe. Good-bye. (*He starts up to door.*)

ELLEN. (*Stopping him.*) Doug, I do think we can work this out, don't you?

DOUG. Of course we can, darling. A college education must be good for something. (*He hurries out.* ELLEN *follows and calls after him.*)

ELLEN. Drive carefully! We haven't time to get arrested! (*He disappears.* ELLEN *comes back, center and stands for a moment, getting her feet on solid ground again. Then she utters a contented sigh, and starts around the drum table towards the hall.* ANN *enters from right. She has changed into afternoon dress and done her hair. The result is a well-groomed, much more sophisticated-looking woman.*)

ANN. What have you done with Mr. Jaywood?

ELLEN. (*Starting, as though caught with the family jewels.*) Oh, hello, Mother! He . . . he went to his room. (*She regains her poise.*) We had a grand talk. I asked him for some letters of introduction. . . .

ANN (*In disapproving tone.*) The moment he stepped inside the house?

ELLEN. I know. I apologized. I told him I'd have waited till Monday if I hadn't been going away.

ANN. Ellen, we don't use our guests.

ELLEN. (*In joking tone.*) Mother, suppose Mr. Jaywood thought you were entertaining him this week-end in order to sell your story. Aren't you worried stiff?

ANN. (*With calm assurance.*) No, dear, I am not.

ELLEN. Anyway, I invited him out again to see me. . . . (JAY *enters. He has changed to grey flannel trousers and sport coat.*)

ANN. Oh, how do you do, Mr. Jaywood. I'm so glad you could come this afternoon. Please forgive me for not being down.

JAY. That's quite all right. Your daughter has been entertaining me.

ANN. Ellen tells me she asked you for some letters.

JAY. I'll be glad to help her.

ANN. I'm sorry. She shouldn't have done it.

JAY. I liked her frankness.

ANN. Well, I don't. I'm out of patience with this current mania for frankness. It's just a cold-blooded excuse to say what you please, do what you please, and get what you please, without regard for the common decencies.

ELLEN. (*Eagerly.*) Mother, there's an article in that. Here I am, just out of college. It's terribly hard to get a job. A nice important person like Mr. Jaywood comes along . . . should I, or should I not, tell him frankly how good I am and ask his help? And if I don't tell him how good I am, and ask his help, would I, or would I not, be a spineless idiot who ought to end her days in the gutter?

ANN. Suppose you change your clothes and start for Hartford.

ELLEN. Okay. (*In archway she turns. Her manner is most innocent and casual.*) By the way, Mother, I've altered my plans slightly. Doug Hall showed up just now out of the blue.

ANN. Really? I wish I'd got a look at him.

ELLEN. He said he'd come back and take me to the train.

ANN. Did you tell Peter he won't be needed?

ELLEN. Not yet. I will. See you both before I go. . . . (*She exits.*)

JAY. I like her, Ann.

ANN. I do myself . . . most of the time. Occasionally, when that brain of hers gets too active, I wish I'd given birth to a nice fluffy-headed little moron . . . with a lisp!

JAY. I doubt if you could. (*Lightly.*) Of course I haven't seen your husband yet. (ANN *laughs.*)

ANN. (*Impulsively.*) Jay, it's grand you could get out this afternoon. Will you have a drink?

JAY. I've still part of what Ellen gave me.

ANN. Did that daughter of mine ply you with whiskey?

JAY. She was jolly hospitable.

ANN. What do they teach them at college nowadays . . . to be night-club hostesses? No one else is coming till tomorrow. It'll give us time for a real talk.

JAY. (*With mock solemnity.*) Frankly, Ann, I'm afraid this week-end will be something of an ordeal for me.

ANN. (*Surprised.*) Ordeal? Indeed?

JAY. It's not easy to visit an old sweetheart. A chap looks about, and realizes this happy home, this gracious wife and lovely daughter might . . . with better luck . . . have been his. It makes for melancholy in a single man at times.

ANN. I imagine it might.

JAY. (*Brightly.*) On the other hand, it may work the other way. A man realizes what he has escaped. Why only last Monday morning, I left a home over in Jersey . . . laughing like a hyena.

ANN. Don't you start any hyena laughs around here!

JAY. No danger!

ANN. You said you never married, didn't you?

JAY. Yes. I've had a few flutters, but you were the big palpitation.

ANN. I must have been. I meet you accidentally at a tea, and find you've been in America three years . . . without looking me up.

JAY. I made inquiries the day I landed. Unfortunately, not in the right social sphere. I asked around Washington Square. One person told me positively you were dead.

ANN. What did I die of?

JAY. It was no joke, I can tell you. I walked slowly under the Arch and started up Fifth Avenue. The next I knew I was on Riverside Drive. There, in the twilight, I buried my youth . . . and my love . . . right next to Grant's Tomb! Later on, of course, I heard you'd married a wealthy banker. It seemed better to let it go at that.

ANN. (*With faint sarcasm.*) Oh, much better.

JAY. (*After a pause.*) Er, you never got to England?

ANN. Several times.

JAY. Without looking me up?

ANN. I tried to. I decided probably you didn't get through the war.

JAY. Yes, I got through.

ANN. When we were in London, several years ago, Lewis dragged me to the Tomb of the Unknown Soldier. Know what I thought as I stood there?

JAY. I can't imagine.

ANN. I thought: "My heavens! for all I know, this may be Jay!" I burst into tears. Lewis was thoroughly irritated. He made me walk ten paces behind . . . so I wouldn't disgrace him. (*A pause.*)

JAY. (*Drily.*) We both seem to have shed some unnecessary tears!

ANN. Oh, I loathe sentiment.

JAY. (*Briskly.*) We must stop. It's aging me rapidly.

ANN. Yes, it's aging me, too. I want to show you the farm. Let's stroll, shall we?

JAY. (*Rising.*) Delighted.

ANN. Jay, I can't get used to you . . . not in a corduroy suit.

JAY. I say, do you remember that corduroy suit? It popped into my head upstairs just now. I wore it from 1908 to 1913 inclusively. The pants moaned when I walked.

ANN. And whistled when you ran!

JAY. Jove, that was a pair of pants.

ANN. Oh, sentiment again . . . !

JAY. Where is this farm?

ANN. Oh, it's just occurred to me. (*She goes to archway and looks up-stairs.*) I really must wait and say good-bye to Ellen. Do you mind?

JAY. Of course not. (*Sees photograph on table between windows.*) Is this your son?

ANN. Yes, that's Roger. I'm sorry you won't see him. He left on Monday for Canada to be a counsellor in a boys' camp.

JAY. Nice manly chap.

ANN. Yes, he's like his father.

JAY. Tell me, Ann, your husband . . . this Lewis, who dragged you away from my tomb . . . does he know about me?

ANN. Jay! As if that sort of thing mattered among adult people today.

JAY. Lewis is quite adult?

ANN. Of course he is. I know you'll like him. He's out playing with his boat right now. He'll be back before long.

JAY. I shall look forward to meeting the man who domesticated Ann Whitman.

ANN. (*With unexpected sharpness.*) I don't like that word "domesticated." Do I look domesticated?

JAY. Yes, you've mellowed, Ann. You're . . . softer.

ANN. You're the second person today to tell me I'm soft. I know what's done it. It's that accursed love story.

JAY. How's it coming?

ANN. I've been out in the garden since eight this morning trimming it with moonlight.

JAY. Gray dawn is better, Ann. Gray dawn is frightfully popular in fiction this season.

ANN. I'll run my moonlight into dawn. But what has me tearing my hair is love . . . the 1939 model.

JAY. That shouldn't be so difficult, with two children.

ANN. They're no help at all. Ellen and I argue ourselves hoarse over everything else, but when it comes to love, she seems indifferent. Children nowadays don't seem to want to discuss it.

JAY. Maybe all the love problems are settled.

ANN. I hope so. (CONNIE *enters hurriedly. She has changed into a very smart dress.* JAY *rises.*)

CONNIE. Ann, darling, I'm off.

ANN. What in the world is keeping Ellen upstairs?

CONNIE. She seems to be finding it a problem what to pack.

ANN. Oh, you two haven't met. Mrs. Nevins, may I introduce Mr. Jaywood?

JAY. Mrs. Nevins, how do you do.

CONNIE. How do you do.

ANN. Mr. Jaywood has come out to brighten up our week-end.

CONNIE. How thrilling!

MARTHA. (*Entering from right.*) Excuse me, Mrs. Murray.

ANN. Yes, Martha?

MARTHA. Peter wants to know is Miss Ellen nearly ready.

ANN. Tell Peter he won't be needed, Martha. A friend is driving Miss Ellen to Stamford. (MARTHA *exits.*)

CONNIE. (*Unaccountably interested.*) Really, Ann? Who?

ANN. A boy from Boston.

CONNIE. (*Thoughtfully.*) I see (*She looks towards door, right with mounting sus-*

picion.) Ann, do you mind walking out to my car with me?

ANN. (*Settling herself comfortably.*) I most certainly do. Why should I?

CONNIE. It's about Ellen.

JAY. Shall I . . . ? (*He starts for the terrace.*)

ANN. Nonsense, Mr. Jaywood. Connie's always being mysterious.

CONNIE. Ann, please!

ANN. It can't be as important as all that!

CONNIE. There's no time to argue. Ann, you've simply got to do something. I'm sure Ellen isn't going to Hartford at all. She's going off somewhere with this boy . . . right now!

ANN. Connie Nevins, do you know what you're saying?

JAY. (*Starting to go.*) If you'll excuse me . . .

ANN. No, you've heard part. I prefer that you hear the rest. (JAY *comes back.*)

CONNIE. When I came back into Ellen's room just now, she had started to re-pack her bags completely.

ANN. What of it? I always pack the things I don't want first.

CONNIE. She'd taken out her party dresses and her white evening coat, and was putting in riding breeches and heavy shoes. She said she thought she'd probably do more hiking than dancing.

ANN. Why get suspicious over that?

CONNIE. I didn't, until I put this boy and the riding breeches together . . . well, er, you know what I mean.

ANN. I still see nothing to justify . . .

CONNIE. Ann, I may not know much, but I do know a week-end date when I see one. Her expression had completely changed. Her eyes were all shining and starry. She had that look, you know . . .

ANN. I know. Anticipatory.

CONNIE. Exactly. I felt you ought to know about it at once. (*She turns to* JAY.) No doubt you think I'm a meddling old aunty.

JAY. Quite the contrary.

CONNIE. (*To* ANN.) I've got to fly. I don't know when I'll be back. I imagine Glen will want to go on somewhere for dinner. (*Turning back in archway.*) Good-bye, Mr. Jaywood. Don't wait up for me, Ann. (*She exits.*)

ANN. (*Calling after her.*) You know where the key is?

CONNIE. (*Outside.*) Yes, I know. Good-bye.

ANN. (*Turning to* JAY, *after a pause.*) You must have seen this boy. Did he look like a week-ender?

JAY. He looked like a very decent chap.

ANN. This thing does have a kind of plausibility to it. An affair's the one subject on earth on which Connie is a final authority. (*Getting worked up, she rises.*) Maybe Ellen thinks she's being modern. Maybe she's just a love-sick child. Jay, what shall I do?

JAY. I'm hardly qualified to say. . . .

ANN. You've been around, haven't you?

JAY. My dear Ann, not to the point of being a mother.

ANN. I'm going upstairs to ask a few questions. Make yourself comfortable. (*She turns in archway.*) And pray for me. (*She goes out.* JAY *shrugs his shoulders expressively.*)

CURTAIN

ACT TWO

Scene: A comfortable and much-used upstairs room commonly known in the MURRAY *family as "Mother's Office." There are many shelves of books and bound magazines. Upstage, right center, is a large old-fashioned desk on which are two phones and a typewriter. Left, is a fireplace with a couch in front of it. Rear,*

*two dormer windows open out with a
view into the lower branches of a large
maple tree. Sunlight filters through the
green leaves. Right, is the only entrance.
About the room are pictures, photographs,
artistic knick-knacks, such as might be
collected in a lifetime. The door and windows are open, with a breeze blowing
through. The abstract effect is of a cool,
mellow, summer-time interior in an old
house set among large trees.*

ANN. (*Speaking offstage, right.*) Ellen,
come and say good-bye before you go.

ELLEN. (*Faintly, in distance.*) Of course,
Mother.

ANN. I'll be in the office. (ANN *enters.
She has just come up-stairs from receiving* CONNIE'S *news. For a moment she
stands by her desk, trying to decide what
to do; then she lights a cigarette and
waits, looking towards the door expectantly. The suspense becomes too much;
she moves about the room, finally ending
up at the window. The fear assails her
that* ELLEN *may leave without coming in.
She crosses to the door and listens.*)

ANN. (*At length.*) Ellen! You aren't going to forget that I want to see you.

ELLEN. (*In distance.*) I'll be right there,
Mother. (ANN *returns to desk, snubs out
her cigarette nervously and waits.* ELLEN
*enters. She wears a light summer travel-
ling suit and appears extremely piquant
and self-possessed.* ANN *watches her cross
anxiously without speaking.*) Good-bye,
old dear. (*She kisses* ANN, *who does not
respond. If* ELLEN *notes this she does not
show it. Her voice is gay.*) Think you'll
be able to protect yourself from interruptions without me?

ANN. I think so.

ELLEN. That idiotic story's about done,
isn't it?

ANN. Almost.

ELLEN. Crazy to read it. Well, see you
Monday. . . .

ANN. Ellen, I'd like to talk to you a moment.

ELLEN. I haven't much time.

ANN. Your Mr. Hall hasn't returned yet,
has he?

ELLEN. He'll be here in a minute.

ANN. (*In tone of authority.*) Well, close
the door, and wait for him here, please.

ELLEN. Why, if you wish. . . . (*She closes
the door and returns, doing plenty of
thinking on the way.* ANN *watches her
with a troubled expression. Catching* EL-
LEN'S *glance she tries to smile reassuringly, then she nerves herself, and takes the
plunge.*)

ANN. Ellen, I . . . I dislike to be obliged
to talk seriously . . . especially when you're
about to leave . . . but . . .

ELLEN. (*Nervously, hoping to beat her
to it.*) If it's about hitting up Mr. Jaywood
for those letters, I'm sorry. I suppose I
was cold-blooded and not at all polite . . .
but I don't think he minded. You heard
him say my frankness made a hit.

ANN. I want *you* to be frank with me,
too.

ELLEN. I always am.

ANN. And I hope you always will be. (*A
pause. She moves articles on desk about
nervously.*) You know, dear, up to the
present moment, you and I have always
got along very well without my ever having to fall back on the fact . . . the fact
that I'm your mother. . . .

ELLEN. Dear, you act hurt about something!

ANN. No.

ELLEN. I admit I'm trying every way I
know to get a job, but you must see I'd not
get much experience sticking around the
house here as your secretary . . .

ANN. I see it perfectly.

ELLEN. I'd really love to work with you
. . . if it were practical.

ANN. That's not what I asked you in for.
Ellen, hasn't there been an unexpected
change in your plans this past half hour?

ELLEN. (*Looking away from* ANN.) Why,
no! What plans?

ANN. To visit Edith in Hartford.

ELLEN. No, why should there be?

ANN. You were all packed. Then you rush up-stairs, throw out your party gowns and put in riding breeches and what seems to be a costume for an extremely rough week-end.

ELLEN. (*Crossing to behind couch.*) Good night, Mother! Can you see around corners and through walls?

ANN. No, but I'm blessed with a sister-in-law who can.

ELLEN. Connie?

ANN. Yes.

ELLEN. (*Angrily.*) Why doesn't Connie mind her own business?

ANN. (*Gently.*) I appreciate it is a great deal to ask you to confide in anyone, but if you are facing a problem . . . can't we talk it over?

ELLEN. I think one's private life is one's private life, and I felt you thought so, too.

ANN. I do, only . . .

ELLEN. Only Connie got to work on you . . . with her nasty mind!

ANN. That's not fair. . . .

ELLEN. You know perfectly well that every time Connie looks at a man her I. Q. goes down to ten!

ANN. (*Taken back by the truth of this remark.*) If you feel that way about Connie's, er . . . life, I am rather surprised that you . . .

ELLEN. (*Indignantly, crossing to right.*) There's no comparison.

ANN. I'm glad.

ELLEN. The way she flits from one male to another is positively biological!

ANN. She is trying desperately hard to find . . . love.

ELLEN. Of course, if that's *your* idea of love!

ANN. It's not. I am trying to find out

yours. (*A pause.*) You *are* planning not to go to Hartford, aren't you? (*A pause. ELLEN studies the carpet, then in one pent-up outburst.*)

ELLEN. Mother, Doug and I've had a terrible time. We've both been at cross purposes and only making each other miserable, then suddenly we got a complete understanding and realized how much we mean to each other . . . and bang! Just like that, Doug announced that Monday he had to go away and I wouldn't see him for two years!

ANN. Where has he got to go?

ELLEN. Belgium.

ANN. Why Belgium?

ELLEN. He has a job there.

ANN. Two years is not so long.

ELLEN. Sometimes it's forever.

ANN. Of course, there is the quaint old custom of marriage.

ELLEN. How could *we* marry? Mother, there's just no use discussing it. My mind is made up. We talked it over. This is absolutely the only chance we may ever have to be together . . . and nothing's going to stop us. I'm sorry if you're going to let yourself get upset, but you have Connie to blame for that, and really deep down in your heart, Mother, I think you do understand, don't you?

ANN. Suppose you meet someone who recognizes you?

ELLEN. We'll look out. We're going to a little lake in Lanesville. There won't be a soul there.

ANN. Ellen, it's not as simple for you as you make it sound, unless . . .

ELLEN. Unless what?

ANN. Unless this is not the first time. . . .

ELLEN. Put your mind to rest. It is.

ANN. (*Rising.*) That makes my duty all the more clear to me. I'm sorry, I know how miserably unhappy it will make you at first.

ELLEN. (*Interrupting.*) Mother, I simply won't be stopped by you or anybody else!

ANN. What do you think your father would say?

ELLEN. Does he have to know?

ANN. We have shared your virtues and your sins equally so far.

ELLEN. I know I must sound awfully underhanded and tricky but, you know, I did intend to tell you eventually.

ANN. (*Gently sarcastic.*) Oh, did you?

ELLEN. Sometime when we were alone and feeling confidential over a cocktail, or late some night by the fire . . .

ANN. That would have been considerate. You could tell me too, if I didn't like it, I could lump it!

ELLEN. After all it's none of your business.

ANN. You just get that idea out of your head, Ellen. You are my business. You and Roger. True, I've puttered around a little the past twenty years at writing and lecturing; but my real thought and my real concern have been over you and Roger. You're all I have to show for my life. That's why, when half my business gets it into its head to go into bankruptcy, I feel I do have something to say about it.

ELLEN. It's so funny to hear *you* get sentimental.

ANN. I'm sorry if what I've said strikes you as humorous.

ELLEN. I used the wrong word. I mean odd . . . because usually you're so rational.

ANN. No matter how you meant it . . . even if I do appear just an old-fashioned mother . . . you can't go off with this boy, and that's the end of it!

ELLEN. You mean you're going to take a moral stand?

ANN. If you wish to call it that.

ELLEN. I'm sorry. There's one thing I thought you could never be, and that's a hypocrite.

ANN. Darling, please! Let's not start calling names!

ELLEN. (*Going up to book-shelves, right of desk.*) I said I didn't think you could be one . . . if you stopped and thought it over. (*She selects a small thin book.*)

ANN. I'm afraid I don't know quite what you mean.

ELLEN. Listen, Mother! (*She comes down to* ANN, *finds a page, and begins to read.*) It was blustering March but a song of Spring
Piped high through the Village. Our hungering
Hearts revolted from sidewalk meetings;
From park-bench trysts; from corner greetings.
All we asked of the gods above.
Was a place we could be alone with our love.
Yet there's always a moment the fates relent.
Some optimistic editor sent
Me thirty dollars . . . enough for rent.
Oh, that was the moment our fortunes were blessed,
For Twenty-one Barrows Street got dispossessed!
While I bearded the landlord, you hurried to borrow,
Tony the Iceman's two-wheeled barrow,
And we trundled my Japanese prints and your chair,
Clothes, books and brass candlesticks over the Square. . . .
Oh yes, I smile now that I write of it,
Only . . . I'll never forget the delight of it!
How you'd come rushing in of nights
Burning with zeal for Woman's Rights,
To find me, probably, just as hot
Over Capital's errors and Labour's lot.
We took our life strong, in Barrows Street.
And did we love it? And wasn't it sweet?
For the Spring Song piped high, while our busy tongues flew,
That you were with me and I was with you!
Ah, we had it all, then, all of Love's delight;
Good talk, good food, good fire bright,
And peace . . . and a kind bed at night.
(*A pause.* ELLEN *looks to see the effect the poem has had upon* ANN.) It's still alive and beautiful, isn't it?

ANN. (*Evasively.*) In a way.

ELLEN. I think it's one of John Bliss's best poems. (ANN *doesn't answer.* ELLEN *sits on couch.*) The Village meant something in those days, didn't it? Oh, Mother, I can imagine what it must have been! You all together for a table d'hôte at the Griffou . . . John Reed, and Max, and maybe Dreiser and "Jig" Cook or perhaps you were all broke so you were at Polly's . . . or maybe they were all there except you . . . and someone rushes in and says: "What do you know? John Bliss just called up from Paterson! The police knocked Ann Whitman down and they've thrown her in jail!" Then everybody got as excited as anything, and they all rushed around trying to borrow money to bail you out!

ANN. (*Sharply.*) Where'd you hear all this?

ELLEN. I didn't hear it. I imagined it.

ANN. You didn't imagine those names.

ELLEN. Oh, I had to read up, of course.

ANN. What do you mean: you had to read up, *of course?*

ELLEN. For my thesis in Senior English.

ANN. I don't quite get the connection, Ellen.

ELLEN. You see, I didn't want to write about one of the conventional cut-and-dried literary topics, so I talked it over with Chop-sticks . . . of course he knows you're my mother. . . .

ANN. Chop-sticks?

ELLEN. Professor Lingley. He always carries his own chop-sticks in a little case when he goes to a Chinese restaurant. He said by all means write about what I was most interested in.

ANN. Did he, indeed?

ELLEN. So I wrote on "The Contribution of Greenwich Village to the Cause of Freedom in American Art and Morals." It's a lousy title, don't you think?

ANN. Extremely lousy.

ELLEN. (*Excitedly.*) I've been dying to talk it over, but you've been so busy since I came home. You know I got thrill after thrill. Almost everything we've got now, that we take as a matter of course . . . bobbed hair, tea-rooms, better art, poetry, votes for women, freedom of speech and sex . . . is due to you pioneer women.

ANN. Maybe not all to our credit!

ELLEN. That's what I meant . . . it's so ridiculous for you to start going back on yourself now.

ANN. At my age we know more about the world's limitations than at twenty.

ELLEN. I was referring specifically to Doug and me.

ANN. Oh!

ELLEN. Because after all, I suppose you and John Bliss . . . (ANN *turns sharply.*) I mean you did face the same problem . . . only, of course, in a prudish Victorian society . . . now, didn't you?

ANN. (*Swallowing, uncomfortably.*) Well.

ELLEN. Mother, you idiot, don't look so fussed. Suppose you and he did live together . . . what of it? (ANN *rises and moves to right.*) I think you were absolutely justified. (ANN *pulls herself together.*)

ANN. I'm afraid your sources of information were rather unreliable.

ELLEN. (*Coolly.*) I don't think so. I checked up pretty thoroughly.

ANN. (*Weak tone.*) Checked up!

ELLEN. John Bliss wrote "Twenty-one Barrows Street" in 1911 at the time he was living there; and from other sources I found at least a dozen references to John and Ann. There was no other important Ann in the village but you, and his name was never linked with that of any other girl.

ANN. (*Angrily.*) Look here, Ellen, do you think it was quite cricket to prowl around in your mother's past with a college professor?

ELLEN. What kind of an egg do you think I am?

ANN. I'm beginning to wonder.

ELLEN. I didn't put your affair in the thesis.

ANN. I daresay I should render you thanks.

ELLEN. Mother, you're taking this oddly.

ANN. I . . . I feel odd.

ELLEN. All you've got to do is be consistent.

ANN. Er, I see.

ELLEN. After all, we're just a couple of females discussing woman's problems.

ANN. (*With great patience.*) Ellen, this whole talk of ours must stop. Whether I am consistent or not has nothing to do with what you are planning to do. It's totally different. You don't know what you are talking about.

ELLEN. (*Rising, indignantly.*) Of course I know what I'm talking about. Mother, what's come over you? You sound like some ordinary conventional matron who doesn't know the facts of life! Why, you and Aunt Connie have done all the pioneer work that makes what I want to do not worth a passing comment!

ANN. Now I know you're a little fool if you think your Aunt Connie is a pioneer.

ELLEN. Is that so? Connie came out of school in 1919. The aviators were coming back from France. Speakeasies had begun to open up. I'll bet Connie was flaming youth!

ANN. Connie's private life is her private life.

ELLEN. Exactly, and mine is mine! (*Going to* ANN *eagerly.*) That's the whole point, Mother! That's the principle you fought and struggled for! That's what Connie and all the rest put in practice! And now when a perfectly decent emergency arises, when I want to take advantage of the very thing you worked for, you say "naughty-naughty"! (*A horn sounds outside.*) Mother, there he is!

ANN. (*Desperately.*) How can I make you see the difference? Maybe I did lead a pretty free life. But I had left home . . . my mother was dead . . . and I was a lot older than you.

ELLEN. You were exactly . . . (*She calculates rapidly.*) twenty-four when you lived with John Bliss. What's two years?

ANN. I was ten years more mature.

ELLEN. Oh, I don't know.

ANN. (*Ignoring this.*) What's more, Ellen, you're still dependent on your father for support. At that time I was a reporter on the old *World*. As soon as you get a job, why then I suppose you can do what you want, even if your father and I don't approve. . . .

ELLEN. Mother, of all the illogical poppycock! If I was two years older, and you were dead, and I had a job . . . ! (*The horn sounds again.*) Yes, yes, I'm coming!

ANN. (*Moving between* ELLEN *and the door.*) Ellen, you're not to stir one step out of this room.

ELLEN. It . . . it's going to be awful if we quarrel, isn't it?

ANN. It is!

ELLEN. When I'm so in love and have been so unhappy, how you can be so utterly, inhumanly lacking in sympathy . . . !

ANN. I do sympathize.

ELLEN. You don't! You're like all the other blue-noses. Everything is just ducky for you to do, but all wrong for everybody else!

ANN. Ellen, please!

ELLEN. If there's one thing I loathe it's a hypocrite . . . and now you . . . I thought you stood for something! Plenty of mothers would be stupid, I know, but I . . . (*She breaks down, sits in desk chair and begins to cry.*) I counted on you.

ANN. (*Also near tears.*) Please, dear, please . . . don't cry! We . . . we'll work this out together some way.

ELLEN. Sorry . . . I said . . . what I said.

ANN. Forget it. (*Horn again.* ELLEN *wipes her eyes and blows her nose.*)

ELLEN. How are my eyes?

ANN. Fine! How are mine?

ELLEN. (*Coldly, ignoring this invitation to fraternize.*) I'll call up Monday. Meanwhile you and Dad talk it over and decide whether you ever want me in the house again. (ANN *puts her hand on* ELLEN'S *shoulder and forces her back into the chair.*)

ANN. Ellen you're running the risk of a terrible disillusionment. I wonder if I can explain. You know, we women have considerable moral sense when we *don't* love a man. Mighty little when we *do*. With a man, it's the opposite. If he *doesn't* care for a girl, he's without scruples. If he *does* care, he is likely to develop a moral code only the angels can live up to. Suppose Doug gets moral and turns against you?

ELLEN. He won't!

ANN. How do you know he isn't just taking advantage of . . . of your generosity?

ELLEN. (*Rising, impatiently.*) Oh, that's old-fashioned! He's not taking advantage of me any more than I'm taking advantage of him.

ANN. Do you realize I've never so much as seen this boy?

ELLEN. He's a man, not a boy. And I never saw your lover!

ANN. Dear, at least introduce him to me. That's not much to ask.

ELLEN. It would only be awkward.

ANN. Are you ashamed of him . . . or of me?

ELLEN. You're just trying to work on me. You know perfectly well I've always been proud of you . . . until today.

ANN. Until today.

ELLEN. Now you're hurt! Mother, there's no use keeping this up.

ANN. Do me one last favour, dear. Bring him up for five minutes.

ELLEN. But he thinks you don't know.

ANN. I won't know.

ELLEN. He might suspect. He thinks you think he's taking me to the train at Stamford.

ANN. I shall do nothing to shatter that illusion. I promise.

ELLEN. Word of honour?

ANN. My word of honour.

ELLEN. Well, very well. (*Turning at door.*) But this will make absolutely no difference in my intentions. (ELLEN *exits.*)

ANN. Oh, oh . . . ! (*She crosses to the desk quickly and speaks into the house phone.*) Martha? Martha, will you please serve tea at once. In the office! And Martha, before you do that, find Mr. Jaywood and ask him to come up. He was in the living-room. And Martha, tea will be for four. That's right! Hurry! (ANN *takes books and cigarettes from the tea table and puts them on mantel. She picks up book of poems from the couch and starts to cross, right. Midway she stops, and glances at the poem* ELLEN *read, then shuts the book sharply and replaces it on the shelf. A knock at the door finds her by the couch again.*) Come in quickly and close the door. (JAY *enters.*) Jay, I'm at my wits' end.

JAY. (*After closing door.*) There was some truth in the week-end clue?

ANN. Plenty! Boston has a job in Belgium. They've apparently had a series of quarrels with a reconciliation this afternoon, and he has to sail Monday to be gone two years!

JAY. The poor devils.

ANN. Jay, what am I going to do?

JAY. You can't let her go, of course.

ANN. How can I stop her?

JAY. You and your husband will have to stand firm.

ANN. Lewis is in the middle of Long Island Sound . . . he can't stand firm there . . . and they're about to start.

JAY. You're top hole with her, Ann. I can't believe she'll go against your express wishes.

ANN. I tried my express wishes. They failed utterly. Jay, in this room, not five minutes ago, I stood before my daughter a fallen woman. She knows . . . how shall I put it? . . . that I, too, have had unhallowed moments.

JAY. That's not possible!

ANN. She has done research on my past . . . with the help of a college professor.

JAY. Good Lord, Ann!

ANN. To make my ignominy complete, she even read me "Twenty-one Barrows Street" . . . and read it beautifully.

JAY. Does she link you with me?

ANN. Heavens, no! (*She sits on the couch behind tea table.*) Look, Jay, I fought for time. She's bringing the boy up to see me. I want you to stand by.

JAY. Of course, though, frankly, I don't see . . .

ANN. I'm serving tea. That'll take time.

JAY. And nerves of steel!

ANN. It's to be a perfectly respectable tea. I promised. Nobody knows anything about anyone. I thought maybe some way we could show him up, or show free love up, or show something up! (*Someone knocks, right.*) Don't stand there, looking helpless! Open the door! (JAY *opens the door.* ELLEN *enters, followed by* DOUG.)

ELLEN. (*Much relieved to see a third party.*) Oh, hello, Mr. Jaywood. This is grand.

JAY. Er, I dropped up, er . . . to read your mother's story.

ELLEN. Mother, I want you to meet Mr. Douglas Hall.

ANN. How do you do, Mr. Hall. I asked Ellen to invite you in for a moment. It seemed extremely inhospitable to let you wait outside . . . like a taxi, or something.

DOUG. I'm afraid I did honk like a taxi. I thought perhaps Ellen didn't hear me.

ANN. She had some last-minute packing to do. (ELLEN *flashes* ANN *an angry look.* MARTHA *enters with tray on which are tea things.*) Do sit down, children. Mr. Jay-wood, being very English, insisted I serve him some tea. Perhaps you'll join us, Mr. Hall. Will you sit over here? (ANN *sits on couch, left.*)

ELLEN. Really, Mother, we haven't time.

ANN. (*Placidly.*) When does your train leave, dear?

ELLEN. (*Sulkily.*) Five-fifteen.

ANN. You've oceans of time. (DOUG *and* ELLEN *exchange looks. He crosses to stool before fireplace and sits.* JAY *sits right of couch.*) Come along. Sit by me. (ELLEN *sits right of* ANN.) Lemon, Mr. Hall?

DOUG. Thanks . . . and two lumps! (ANN *prepares tea throughout the next speeches until all are served.*)

ANN. Ellen?

ELLEN. No, thanks, Mother.

ANN. Mr. Jaywood?

JAY. Just plain, thanks.

ANN. (*Politely, to* DOUG.) Is your home near here?

DOUG. I haven't any home. I'm making my cousin's home my headquarters this week-end.

ANN. Oh, are you? How pleasant!

DOUG. Yes, very pleasant . . . it's very central. I have a lot of errands in this vicinity.

ANN. Errands?

DOUG. (*Nervously.*) Before I sail for Belgium.

ANN. Belgium?

DOUG. I'm sort of liquidating my education. I've already sold my Encyclopaedia Britannica and my drafting instruments. And I still have two pairs of skiis, a Phi Beta Kappa key, and about a thousand architectural plates that I hope to cash in on before Monday night.

ANN. Doesn't an architect need plates?

DOUG. I'm through with that trade. Two years ago I got fifteen dollars a week; this spring I'm working for nothing; next year my boss admitted he'd expect me to pay him a salary. (JAY *chuckles*.)

ANN. What work do you expect to take up in Belgium?

DOUG. (*Embarrassed at having to mention it*.) I . . . I'm going over to represent a razor blade concern.

ANN. Oh! That's splendid!

JAY. The Belgians could do with a few more razor blades.

DOUG. That's my idea, sir. I'm trying to give the job a social significance.

ANN. It seems a pity to give up architecture.

DOUG. (*He looks at* ELLEN.) Not if a man wants a home and a wife.

ANN. Marriage interests you, Mr. Hall?

DOUG. (*Cautiously*.) In a general sort of way. You can't expect a woman to wait around forever.

ANN. Yes, the girls today are extremely impatient.

ELLEN. Some of them were impatient in your day, too, Mother.

ANN. Imprudent was the word then, dear.

ELLEN. (*Who can face no more*.) Doug, we ought to get started. (DOUG *rises to go.* ANN *stops him*.)

ANN. Mr. Hall, I've been running over my criminal record.

DOUG. (*Gasping*.) Oh, really?

ANN. There was a Judge Hall once in Providence. . . .

DOUG. That was my father. At one time, Dad was Police Court Judge. Later he became Supreme Court Justice.

ANN. I knew it! It all comes back. Mr. Hall, once your father gave me thirty days.

DOUG. I'm awfully sorry.

ANN. Nonsense! I deserved it. I was as unconventional as Bernard Shaw and I went to jail at the drop of a hat! Hasn't Ellen told you?

DOUG. (*Much embarrassed*.) Why, er . . . no.

ELLEN. (*Hastily*.) Mother, we haven't time . . . I'll miss my train.

ANN. Mr. Hall, this has been so nice. Do feel free to drop in any time.

DOUG. I'm afraid I'll be pretty far away for that. Anyway, thanks. (*To* JAY.) Good-bye. (JAY *shakes hands with him*.)

JAY. Good-bye.

ELLEN. Good-bye, Mother.

DOUG. (*To* ELLEN.) Did you have any bags?

ELLEN. They're in my room. I'll show you.

ANN. Oh, Mr. Hall! Why can't you stay with us over Sunday? Ellen would love to have you.

ELLEN. Mother, I'm going to Hartford.

ANN. Oh, so you are.

DOUG. Good-bye, Mrs. Murray. Good-bye, sir. (*He bows awkwardly then exits after* ELLEN.)

ANN. Wasn't I a nice muddle-headed old fool of a mother!

JAY. Ann, why that speech about getting arrested in Providence?

ANN. Did you notice how troubled the boy was at taking my daughter out from under my very nose?

JAY. Yes.

ANN. I was trying to put his conscience at ease . . . by sounding a liberal note!

ELLEN. (*Outside*.) I'll be right down, Doug. (*She enters, and stands by the door*.) So long, Mother.

ANN. Come in, dear. (ELLEN *comes forward reluctantly*.) Ellen, I liked him. I liked his courage. I forgot to ask: is he a Communist?

ELLEN. No, he isn't!

ANN. (*With a smile at her vehemence*.) Well, even so, I still like him. He's attempting to pull through on his own initiative. Ellen, I'm a fool; but then I always was. I'm going to stick to my principles. Go off with this boy. (*A pause; then huskily.*) My dear, I give you my blessing.

ELLEN. Mother, do you realize Mr. Jaywood is here?

ANN. Oh, dear, so he is . . . well, anyway he was also present when Connie came down and told me.

ELLEN. Couldn't she use a little tact! It's a nice state of affairs when private and sacred things have to be blurted out before everybody. Mother, you're not fair . . . serving tea in that Park Avenue manner, and then . . . (*She looks at* JAY *and stops.*)

JAY. I assure you, Ellen, your romance will lie, er . . . tenderly and close within my breast. (*She stares at him. Silently her lips and forefinger accentuate the words "tenderly and close within my breast."*) What's the matter?

ELLEN. That line scans. Several of the things you said downstairs . . . ! You're a poet. You're John Bliss.

ANN. Nonsense!

ELLEN. I might have known it. I felt you two had known each other a long time!

JAY. My name is Titus Jaywood. Want to see my baptismal certificate?

ELLEN. Who'd write poetry under a name like Jaywood! (*To* ANN, *with simple frankness.*) I certainly am glad to get this point cleared up. You know, I worked my head off trying to find out what had become of him. I bet I wrote a dozen letters.

JAY. What did they reply?

ELLEN. They said you were missing.

JAY. I am . . . poetically.

ELLEN. Why'd you change your name back.

JAY. You were on the correct scent. No New York editor would bother to read poems of American mines and steel mills written by an Englishman named Titus Jaywood; whereas, he would jump at the opportunity to buy an English novel from Jaywood, Ltd.

ELLEN. Naturally. Mother, you don't intend to stop me now do you?

ANN. I told you I didn't. Besides, this boy may never come back. Anything may happen in Europe in the next two years.

ELLEN. That's what I meant.

ANN. Well, then go quickly before I regain my commonsense. Go. Climb hills. Walk hand in hand under the stars. Make love. This may be your one great hour on earth. Go. I'll stand by you.

ELLEN. Oh, Mother, I won't go . . . if you say I shouldn't!

ANN. Get out of here . . . quick!

ELLEN. (*To* JAY.) It's been grand meeting you . . . especially since I know who you really are.

JAY. I've enjoyed meeting you.

ELLEN. (*to* ANN, *kissing her.*) Good-bye. (*Then, impulsively.*) Oh, Mother, I never realized how much I loved you! (ANN *clasps her fiercely in her arms.*)

ANN. Ellen, dear . . . it's all right. It's all right. Don't let a thing worry you. I'll stand by you.

ELLEN. Don't *you* worry.

ANN. I won't. Good-bye. (ELLEN *goes. A pause.* ANN *looks at* JAY.) Say it, say it! I'm not a fit mother to bring up a decent girl.

JAY. Now, Ann, I wouldn't go as far as that.

ANN. But you think it.

JAY. On the contrary, I think you did the wise thing. The boy's good stuff. He won't let her down.

ANN. (*Sitting.*) Jay, give me a cigarette. I'm going to bawl.

JAY. Pull yourself together. (*He lights cigarette for her. She takes handkerchief from his breast pocket, dabs her eyes.*) You know perfectly well that a high-minded romance, conceived more in the spirit of poetry than of legality, is just about the noblest work of man . . . and woman! If this had to come, I think you are to be congratulated that when it did come, your daughter acted with so much dignity and fine feeling.

ANN. Oh, shut up your Mayfair cynicism! Now it's all over, I realize l haven't acted as I have just because I'm a liberal thinker. More likely it's because I'm a selfish coward.

JAY. Now, really, Ann . . . !

ANN. When we first talked she got angry. She called me a hypocrite and a look came into her eyes. I couldn't endure the thought of losing her respect . . . of deliberately shoving myself off the pedestal on which she had placed me!

JAY. (*With a protesting gesture.*) Now, Ann . . .

ANN. (*From behind her handkerchief.*) She's like her father. When she turns, she turns hard! Oh, it's all such a mess. I'm such a mess! You're such a mess!

JAY. (*Sharply, in a gay tone.*) I resent that. I'm a well-ordered human being, thinking clearly, a good judge of correct artistic values . . . both in fiction and in life! And so are you!

ANN. Oh, stop trying to cheer me up . . . ! (CONNIE's *voice is heard outside.*)

CONNIE. Ann, are you there?

ANN. Heavens! What's *she* back for?

CONNIE. (*Still outside.*) May I come in?

ANN. I suppose so. . . . (CONNIE *enters, much excited.*)

CONNIE. Do you realize what has happened?

ANN. Aren't they serving tea at the club any more?

CONNIE. Glen left word he was tied up in Court. He's going to phone me here.

ANN. Oh!

CONNIE. (*Returning to the subject.*) I meant happened to Ellen. Driving back I passed a most rattly-looking car and in it was Ellen and that young man. I couldn't believe my eyes. I supposed, of course, you had brought her to her senses by this time.

JAY. (*When* ANN *doesn't answer.*) But we have.

CONNIE. Really?

JAY. Mr. Hall was merely driving Ellen to her train at Stamford. They lost their nerve. It was a complete victory for law and order.

CONNIE. They were headed north, not towards Stamford.

JAY. Naturally. They missed the train at Stamford . . . so they . . . (*He sees her smiling, and ends lamely.*) Oh, I can't lie!

CONNIE. You can lie all right, but not well. (*To* ANN.) You poor dear! I'd never believed Ellen . . . deliberately against your will . . .

ANN. (*Smiling wanly.*) Not just now . . . please!

CONNIE. I was so amazed to see them driving past me . . . wouldn't you like me to bathe your head?

ANN. No, thanks!

CONNIE. Maybe some spirits of ammonia . . . ?

ANN. No, really, I'm all right. . . .

JAY. (*To* ANN's *rescue.*) Connie! (CONNIE *turns.*) Do you mind if I call you Connie?

CONNIE. I've had so many last names it's the only one I'm sure to answer to.

JAY. How about a cup of tea?

CONNIE. I'd love one. (*She sits on couch, to right of* JAY.)

JAY. How many lumps?

CONNIE. Merely lemon. (*Watches* JAY *pour.*) You handle a tea pot with exquisite skill. Are you a bachelor?

JAY. I suppose I am.

CONNIE. Don't you *know?*

JAY. I am . . . definitely.

CONNIE. Well, I won't hold it against you. I always enjoy tea poured by contented bachelors.

JAY. (*Indicating* ANN's *untouched cup.*) Freshen you up?

ANN. No, thanks. Connie, I don't think we will tell Lewis anything about what has happened this afternoon.

CONNIE. It would be a terrible blow. He adores Ellen.

ANN. I'd like it to be a private secret between us three. . . .

CONNIE. Suppose Lewis should start hurling questions that awful way he does. . . . I'd never be able to keep it from him.

ANN. I know you wouldn't. But he won't have any reason to hurl questions if nothing is said.

CONNIE. Heaven knows I don't want to say anything more.

ANN. Then it's agreed?

CONNIE. Of course. As a matter of fact, I called myself names all the way into Greenwich. I never peached on a person before in my life. But Ann, she's such a kid, and we'd been talking about her, I did feel you ought to know . . . then you could do as you please.

ANN. You were dead right. You told me, and I have done as I please!

CONNIE. (*Startled.*) Done as you please! Ann Murray, do you mean to sit there and tell me you deliberately . . . ?

JAY. Cake, Connie!

CONNIE. (*Accepting both the cake and the hint.*) You're right; you're both right. I'm getting straight-laced. (*She sees cake is rich and puts it back on plate.*) No, thanks. I swear another trip to Reno and I'll be positively conventional. . . . (*The phone rings.*)

ANN. Excuse me.

CONNIE. (*Rising excitedly.*) It's probably for me, Ann.

ANN. (*Into phone.*) Hello. Yes. Yes, she's here. I'll call her.

CONNIE. (*Eagerly.*) Is it Glen?

ANN. It talks like a lawyer.

CONNIE. (*Into phone.*) Hello. Hello, dear. Oh, that's quite all right. Of course! I can't wait to see you. (*Pause.*) Your voice does sound tired. (*Pause; during next speeches,* CONNIE's *tone changes from enthusiasm to a dull, stunned quality.*) Glen, you're joking. I see. I've heard that alibi before. Oh, much better not to see each other at all. A real inspiration on your part, and so much easier for you. (*Long pause.*) Well, you might have been man enough to meet me as you promised and tell me to my face! Oh, you're right! The telephone does lessen the shock. Yes. Goodbye. (*Mechanically she hangs up the phone. A pause. Her lips quiver, as she fights for self-control, then she laughs.*) Well, well, Connie, take that on the chin!

ANN. (*Going to her.*) You poor dear! That's a rotten dirty trick to play!

CONNIE. God, Ann! And I thought this was the real thing at last!

ANN. Perhaps it's better to find it out now than later.

CONNIE. It saves flying to Reno. (*A pause; she wipes her eyes.*) Ann, it just can't be done. You can't give your love to too many men. They hold you cheap. (LEWIS *appears in doorway. Her voice begins to get shrill and hysterical.*) That's why I know I was so absolutely right in telling you about Ellen. You ought to have stopped her. You ought to have prevented her making the damn fool stinking mess of her life that I have made of mine! (*She breaks down completely.*)

LEWIS. Well, well, what kind of a tea party is this?

CONNIE. (*Rushing past him.*) Excuse me. (*She exits.* ANN *goes to* LEWIS.)

ANN. (*Trying to appear casual.*) You're home early, dear.

LEWIS. (*Also trying to appear casual.*) Just had to get back to my Annie! (*He kisses her.*)

ANN. That means the wind died down?

LEWIS. Enough so I could use it for an excuse.

ANN. Mr. Jaywood, this is my husband. He looks like an admiral but under the disguise he's just a banker.

JAY. (*As they shake hands.*) How do you do.

LEWIS. How do you do. You the chap who's going to sell Ann's love story?

JAY. Well, I hope so.

LEWIS. How long you and Ann known each other?

JAY. Let's see. We met sometime in May.

LEWIS. Huh! She's in a bad money jam. Sure you can sell it?

JAY. A good yarn by a well-known name rarely fails to find a market.

LEWIS. My Annie should write a wicked love story.

JAY. (*Turns and looks at* ANN.) Er, quite. (ANN *hands* LEWIS *a cup of tea.*)

ANN. Will you have some tea, dear?

LEWIS. Thanks. (*Her hand trembles as he takes the cup.*) Ann, you're upset. And Connie in tears! What's happened since I left my happy home two hours ago?

ANN. Not much.

LEWIS. Well, let's hear it!

JAY. I've had my tea, Ann. If you'll excuse me, I'll dress for dinner.

ANN. Don't bother to dress. Stay and chat. . . . (*She signals him to stay.*)

LEWIS. (*Turning, heartily to* JAY.) Hell no, old man, we're informal here. Don't bother to dress. (*He smiles engagingly.*) Just give me five minutes alone with my wife, that's all. (*At the door,* JAY *turns and shakes his finger warningly to* ANN *behind* LEWIS' *back and says silently.*)

JAY. I wouldn't tell him . . . at least no more than you have to. (LEWIS *turns in time to notice.* JAY *changes his gesture into a farewell wave and exits.*)

LEWIS. Annie, old girl, what is all this? (*A pause; she does not answer.*) Come on now. (*He leans over couch and kisses her.*) Tell Papa all about it.

ANN. Connie's lawyer friend just broke off with her over the phone. It was pretty cruel.

LEWIS. Hasn't he seen her since she came back?

ANN. No.

LEWIS. My Lord! Won't we ever get Connie permanently married?

ANN. We don't seem to.

LEWIS. (*Sitting, right of couch.*) Well, Glen Williams was no fatal loss. He plays a filthy game of golf.

ANN. I think she counted on improving his golf after they were married.

LEWIS. Oh, did she? (*He looks at* ANN *sharply.*) How is Ellen mixed up in all this?

ANN. Ellen?

LEWIS. Connie was telling you it was absolutely necessary Ellen should be told so she wouldn't make a mess of her life. Or something like that. I don't see any connection, do you?

ANN. Maybe, remotely. Sort of the horrible example idea, I suppose.

LEWIS. Apparently she'd already told Ellen . . . as I recall.

ANN. Had she? I didn't catch all Connie said, she was so hysterical.

LEWIS. But Ellen's already gone, hasn't she?

ANN. Yes.

LEWIS. Then if Connie just got this message over the phone, how could she tell Ellen?

ANN. Oh, Lord, Lewis, I don't know. Does it matter so much right now?

LEWIS. Annie, you don't have secrets from me very often . . . but when you do, they stick out all over you.

ANN. I'll tell you sometime.

LEWIS. (*In a level, determined tone.*) I think I'd prefer to know now. (*A pause; she does not answer.*) Something serious has happened, I can tell. If you don't feel like discussing it right now, suppose I talk with Connie . . . (*He rises and starts to go.*)

ANN. (*In alarm.*) No, don't do that!

LEWIS. Why not?

ANN. Connie doesn't know the real situation. If you must wring the truth out of anyone, you'd better wring it out of me. Sit down! (*She beckons and he sits beside her on the couch.*) There! Lewis, during our entire married life, I think what has endeared you to me more than anything else, has been your broadmindedness and sympathy with my . . . my liberal ideas.

LEWIS. Oh, get on, Ann. I know I'm broadminded.

ANN. I just thought I'd remind you.

LEWIS. Ann, come to the point.

ANN. I'm trying to.

LEWIS. Well, what is it?

ANN. Oh, God, I can't tell you!

LEWIS. (*Getting worried.*) It can't be so serious. Ann; you tell me, or I'll bat you one.

ANN. Lewis, that Boston boy who failed Ellen at Commencement turned up this afternoon. They've gone off together for the week-end.

LEWIS. Well, what of it? Whose house? Someone we know, isn't it?

ANN. They're not going to anybody's house. They're just going off together alone. (*Pause. He looks blank.*) You know the meaning of the phrase, don't you, Lewis?

LEWIS. You mean they're going off *together . . . alone?*

ANN. That's what I mean.

LEWIS. Ellen's not that kind. A vulgar cheap week-end!

ANN. This is on a very high plane. Really, it is, dear. They didn't find out they loved each other till this afternoon . . . and the young man's leaving for two years.

LEWIS. How did *you* learn so much about it?

ANN. The young man called for a moment. His name is Hall.

LEWIS. Oh, you're imagining this! He probably took her to the train.

ANN. Ellen told me they were going.

LEWIS. Why didn't you stop her?

ANN. I did try.

LEWIS. You mean she defied you?

ANN. Why, no . . . not exactly. Naturally I tried to talk it over calmly with her.

LEWIS. Ann, we've got to find them . . . before it's too late. (*He starts for the door.*)

ANN. (*Going to him hastily.*) Lewis, you can't go rushing after her. You'd only be ridiculous . . .

LEWIS. (*Stopping.*) Well, we must do something.

ANN. Dear, I know how you love to spring into action, but this is one occasion where if nothing is done, nothing will happen.

LEWIS. Do you mean Ellen deliberately told you, and then walked out of the house?

ANN. Lewis, will you please stop feeling you've got to do something about it? I think our duty is to be sympathetic and understanding, and let them work out their own destiny . . . !

LEWIS. Don't tell me you were sympathetic!

ANN. Not at first, perhaps!

LEWIS. Ann, are you crazy? Did you let a girl of twenty-two talk you into a thing like this? You should have stopped her, if you had to tie her. Don't you love her?

ANN. Of course I love her.

LEWIS. That's a pretty way to show it.

ANN. (*Quietly.*) Ellen has exactly as much right to love as you have yourself. All we can do, as parents, is prepare her to exercise that right intelligently and decently. In fact, our work is over.

LEWIS. Did she *say* that?

ANN. (*Turning away.*) No, I did.

LEWIS. Well, how did she win you over? (ANN *doesn't answer.*) What did she say? You didn't talk about the weather, did you? (ANN, *back to him. busies herself behind couch with her hair.*) You're too anxious to drop this matter. I think I *will* talk to Connie. (*Again he starts for the door.*)

ANN. Lewis, wait a minute! Maybe you're right. We've faced everything together so far. We might as well continue.

LEWIS. My God! What else is there to face?

ANN. (*Taking his arm.*) When you married me . . . *before* you married me . . . you had no illusions you were the first man in my life, did you? You took me for what I was.

LEWIS. Of course I did.

ANN. Well, then . . .

LEWIS. But you were different . . . you were *you.*

ANN. Exactly.

LEWIS. What do you mean, "exactly"?

ANN. I mean I was in rather an inconsistent position when it came to stopping Ellen.

LEWIS. If there's one thing a parent doesn't have to be . . . it's consistent!

ANN. It's wiser with a girl of Ellen's mentality.

LEWIS. She wouldn't know. . . . (*Struck with a sudden idea.*) You mean she does know?

ANN. More about me than I do myself.

LEWIS. I see. How'd she ever hear?

ANN. She's been writing a thesis on "The Contribution of Greenwich Village to the Cause of Freedom in American Art and Morals" . . . and naturally, she discovered that I, among others, had contributed my bit.

LEWIS. This is a hell of a time to be funny.

ANN. I didn't mean to be.

LEWIS. But you admit it's right.

ANN. Right or wrong, I don't know. Justifiable anyway!

LEWIS. (*Exploding.*) By God, my father spoke the truth! He warned me. He was a wiser bird than I was.

ANN. You know your father was a conservative old fool. You've told me so a hundred times.

LEWIS. Huh! I can hear him now. (*Quotes in severe hard tone.*) "So, Lewis, you don't mind if the mother of your children is a woman of loose morals!" (*He strides to behind couch, and back.*)

ANN. (*Angrily, following him.*) My morals aren't loose. I've never looked at another man since I married you. You've got to be fair. You're not going to take any high and mighty attitude with me and get away with it.

LEWIS. I can't understand. I should think when Ellen found she had a mother like you . . .

ANN. (*Interrupting, coolly.*) I took care I had a rather beautiful love affair. . . .

LEWIS. (*Savagely.*) I don't want to hear about it.

ANN. I don't intend to tell you. It's pretty late in the day, Lewis, for you to be jealous over a twenty-five-year-old romance!

LEWIS. I suppose you helped your daughter pick out a pleasant place to go.

ANN. I wasn't consulted in the matter.

LEWIS. She told you where she was going though, didn't she? (ANN *does not answer.*) I see she did.

ANN. Lewis, they won't be discovered. I don't think there's a chance.

LEWIS. Where is this place? (*A pause.*) I said: where is this place?

ANN. I don't know . . . exactly. I won't tell you anyway.

LEWIS. Naturally, I suppose not! (*Balked, he crosses to the desk. He stands for a moment, thinking, then he returns to* ANN.) I'll ask you once more. Will you tell me where Ellen was going?

ANN. No, I won't. At least, not till you've cooled off.

LEWIS. Very well. (*He turns to go.*)

ANN. Where are you going? Dinner's at seven.

LEWIS. I certainly don't intend to sit opposite *you* at dinner tonight. (*She runs to him, and seizes his coat by both lapels furiously, as though to shake him.*)

ANN. Darling, you big fool, will you come to your senses! I didn't want to tell you. You insisted. Now the least you can do is stand by me, so we can help Ellen over this tough spot . . . ! (*He frees himself from her grasp.*)

LEWIS. I'm going to talk with Connie . . . after that I can be reached at my Club.

ANN. Oh, don't be such a stuffed shirt! Run off to your Club to sulk! I'm ashamed of you!

LEWIS. With your perverted moral sense, I daresay you are. (*He goes out, slamming the door. For a moment* ANN *stands motionless, then she mutters a disgusted "Oh!" She sees the untidy tea tray. Mechanically she picks it up and starts for the door.*)

ANN. (*Angry and unhappy, through a suggestion of tears.*) Oh, goddamn sex anyway!

CURTAIN

ACT THREE

Scene: The living-room again. It is ten o'clock the following Monday morning. A bright sunlight floods the terrace outside. The curtains blow about briskly in quite a stiff breeze.
At Rise: JAY *enters from the terrace followed by* MARTHA *with a breakfast tray.* JAY *wears a blue coat with gray trousers, and a vivid crimson scarf around his throat. He stands by the table, left, wets his finger and sticks it up above his head to test the breeze.*

JAY. This seems a quiet spot. I'll finish here. (MARTHA *puts tray on table.* JAY, *about to sit, notices a music-box on table between windows. He winds it and sets it going. The strains of a sprightly waltz begin to tinkle off.*)

MARTHA. Is there anything else?

JAY. Have you a copy of *The Times* knocking about?

MARTHA. Yes, there's one knocking about over here. (*She goes to table before the fireplace and brings back a newspaper.*)

JAY. Thanks, that's fine! (JAY *watches* MARTHA *exit, then he opens his paper, and begins to read while he sips his coffee, a picture of unruffled contentment.* CONNIE *enters from the hall, in smart white costume with trousers and bolero jacket effect. She looks cheerfully seductive.*)

CONNIE. Good morning, Jay. Don't get up.

JAY. Hello. Excellent morning!

CONNIE. Why breakfast in here?

JAY. I started on the lawn, but the wind raised a surf on my coffee. (*A pause. He begins to whistle an accompaniment to the music. She studies him thoughtfully. He steals a sly glance at his newspaper.*)

CONNIE. You're a maddening man.

JAY. I beg your pardon. Will you have some coffee!

CONNIE. I mean being so disagreeably cheerful, when everybody else in the house is practically in mourning.

JAY. Perhaps my orchestra is a bit gay. I'll turn it off. (*He turns off the music-box, and for the first time gets a square look at* CONNIE.) As a matter of fact, you look moderately cheerful yourself.

CONNIE. I've made it a rule not to have more than one good cry over any man.

JAY. (*Not caring to pursue this subject.*) Let's see: you said you didn't want any coffee?

CONNIE. No, I didn't. (*She picks up the coffee pot.*) May I pour you some more?

JAY. No, thanks.

CONNIE. Do you mind if I use your cup?

JAY. Not at all. (*She pours herself some coffee.*)

CONNIE. There, aren't we cozy?

JAY. (*Changing subject.*) Have you seen Ann this morning?

CONNIE. I went in before I came down. She is terribly upset at Lewis' attitude. Do you suppose Ellen will bring that young man home with her?

JAY. Er, it's not customary, is it?

CONNIE. It may be. This younger generation is too much for me. In my days we had at least a shred of decency. (*She removes outside jacket, revealing a well-tanned back, then puts jacket on couch, right.*) At least we *knew* we were kicking over the traces. But Ellen apparently thinks what she is doing is all in the day's work. (JAY *smiles.*) Frankly, don't you find it rather shocking?

JAY. Other people's affairs of the heart never shock me. Sometimes they bore me; sometimes they nauseate me; but they never shock me.

CONNIE. Don't my three husbands shock you?

JAY. Not in the slightest.

CONNIE. (*Coquettishly.*) Oh, just a tiny bit.

JAY. (*Firmly.*) Not one iota. (*A pause.* JAY *sips glass of water.* CONNIE *studies him, getting up courage to ask a personal question. She seats herself opposite him.*)

CONNIE. Jay, how have you solved your love life?

JAY. (*Choking slightly.*) Well, n o w, really . . .

CONNIE. I'm envious. Here the rest of us are, embroiled in sex up to our necks . . . while you loll about and enjoy life. How do you get that way? You really *never* married?

JAY. No, never.

CONNIE. Don't you get desperately lonesome? Don't you feel you just must have somebody who thinks you're wonderful . . . even if you know you're not?

JAY. I manage to struggle along without admiration.

CONNIE. You live alone?

JAY. Yes. I've a very small penthouse in the East Fifties.

CONNIE. Without even a mother or a canary.

JAY. Not even a guppy.

CONNIE. How appalling!

JAY. Oh, I forgot to mention it; I do have a Filipino chap who comes in and cooks for me.

CONNIE. (*Seductively.*) No love in your life at all?

JAY. Oh, plenty of love! I manage to read from twenty to thirty love stories a day. That's about all the love I can endure. By night I'm ready for a prize fight . . . or maybe to sit on the terrace and watch the sunset and the East River shipping!

CONNIE. Reading love stories doesn't affect me that way.

JAY. You should read bad ones!

CONNIE. But you're missing so much, Jay. A family and children . . . romance . . . passion!

JAY. I know. One pays a price for everything . . . even contentment!

CONNIE. There! I knew you must have a philosophy. I've tried "a short life and a gay one" and "love is all." Now I believe I'll try yours. Contentment! A bachelor woman living in a penthouse with her books and her sunsets and her friends.

JAY. I recommend it highly.

CONNIE. The only problem is friends. They're not so easy.

JAY. True!

CONNIE. Jay, I'd like you for a friend.

JAY. Er, that's awfully nice of you . . . !

CONNIE. I need a wise well-poised friend terribly . . . someone to watch the East River shipping with . . . someone who isn't interested in love, at least actively. Jay, do me a favour . . . ask me up to your terrace some evening.

JAY. Why, er . . . of course.

CONNIE. You're not conventional?

JAY. God forbid!

CONNIE. Maybe you're clandestine!

JAY. No, I'm not that either.

CONNIE. Then do please, like a good fellow . . . give me a ring . . . some evening when you're not going to a prize fight.

JAY. Why, that'll be fine!

CONNIE. My number is Rhinelander 4-3333.

JAY. That's an interesting number.

CONNIE. Doesn't it interest you enough to take it down?

JAY. I can remember it.

CONNIE. It's very easy to remember. Four times three. It's the only four of a kind in the book that adds up to an even dozen. You can't forget it.

JAY. (*Gloomily.*) I'm sure I can't. . . .

CONNIE. More coffee, darling? (*He looks up, startled. She is embarrassed.*) Oh! Sorry. It slipped out . . . from long habit. (ANN *enters. She appears gay and casual, but underneath she is heavy-hearted and worried.*)

ANN. Good morning.

JAY. Hello, Ann.

ANN. Have you both had breakfast?

JAY. Just finished.

ANN. I'll take away the tray.

CONNIE. Let me do it, Ann. (*She picks up tray and starts, right.*)

ANN. Was everything satisfactory, sir?

JAY. Fine, thanks.

CONNIE. (*Excitedly.*) Ann, I've an idea, I believe I've reached that stage in a woman's life where she starts a tea-room. (*She kicks door open, like a waitress, and exits with a flourish.*)

ANN. How is she taking *her* tragedy?

JAY. (*Drily.*) I'm afraid she has fully recovered.

ANN. I know. She always does, poor dear! Yet, Jay, she would make the right man a splendid wife, and when it comes to running a house . . .

JAY. May I interrupt?

ANN. (*Smiling.*) If you must. . . .

JAY. I don't want to marry her, if you don't mind.

ANN. No?

JAY. No.

ANN. Oh.

JAY. Look here, did you "sic" her on me this morning?

ANN. No.

JAY. Oh.

ANN. Yet you'll have to admit . . .

JAY. I do. I also admit she has given me her phone number. It adds up to an even dozen.

ANN. (*With a chuckle.*) The minx! (*She sits right of table.*)

JAY. Now tell me your troubles.

ANN. My troubles aren't speaking to me unless a third person is present.

JAY. I say, that's carrying it a bit far.

ANN. Have you seen the man this morning?

JAY. A moment. He's gone to Greenwich for a minister.

ANN. The devil he has!

JAY. Also to see about a marriage license.

ANN. The dear, befuddled lamb! And I suppose in case Ellen refuses to be made a good woman, he'll bring along a snowstorm, too, to cast her out into!

JAY. I don't think he means it that way. He feels . . .

ANN. He feels moral, that's what he feels . . . superior, capable of leading the entire female sex back to the Gay Nineties. The idea of his trying to marry Ellen off like some wanton! (*She begins to walk back and forth.*) I feel the old malignant spirit surging within! I'm going to strike a blow for feminine emancipation on the top of Lewis' head that will . . .

JAY. (*Sharply.*) Ann!

ANN. (*Subsiding meekly.*) You're right. Whacking Lewis won't help Ellen. Tell me, has your Paris man telephoned you yet?

JAY. He was out. He's to call me here as soon as he gets back.

ANN. I'm awfully sorry you had to be mixed up in all this. Go back to town. If the call comes, I'll relay it on to you. . . .

JAY. Frothingham's in this country for only a couple of days. We can't risk missing him.

ANN. Ellen might blurt out something about you and me.

JAY. She'll be loyal.

ANN. You can't tell . . . if she gets excited. Lewis would be sure to make a fool of himself. Why should you stay and be humiliated?

JAY. I'll wait for the phone call . . . if it's all the same?

ANN. Oh, *I'd* prefer to have you here. I'm getting in a mood in which I'd like to confront Lewis with all my lovers.

JAY. You never had any besides me, Ann. Don't get boastful.

ANN. Then, I'm in a mood in which I *wish* I'd had more!

JAY. You're in a mood in which you're going to spill the fat in the fire if you don't take care. (LEWIS *enters. He wears a plain business suit, and appears very busy and self-righteous.*)

LEWIS. Hello, Jaywood. (JAY *waves an acknowledgment.*)

ANN. (*Sweetly.*) Good morning, Lewis.

LEWIS. (*Looking squarely at her.*) Huh!

ANN. Huh . . . yourself!

JAY. (*Diplomatically, to* LEWIS.) Er, what luck?

LEWIS. Not bad. I talked with the Mayor. He called up the License Bureau and arranged to have the five-day ruling overlooked.

ANN. (*Pleasantly.*) So you are going to insult your daughter as soon as she enters your house?

LEWIS. What do you mean, insult my daughter?

JAY. I say . . . ! I suspect I'm in the way again.

LEWIS. Nonsense. (*He signals him to stay.*)

ANN. (*At the same time.*) A clergyman and a marriage license waiting on the doorstep sounds like an insult to me.

LEWIS. I'm merely helping her out.

ANN. I'd wait till she asks for your help.

LEWIS. If she loves him, she must want to marry him.

ANN. The young man's salary won't be thirty a week.

LEWIS. I'll put him in the bank.

ANN. He has signed a contract.

LEWIS. My lawyer can get him out of that.

ANN. Lewis, let him have his adventure with the razor blades. It's much bigger.

LEWIS. He's had adventure enough. This morning he assumes his responsibilities. . . .

ANN. Provided he appears. . . .

LEWIS. George! Well, I can get him on the phone . . . or at the boat.

ANN. Lewis, you look like a man I never met before.

LEWIS. You've looked pretty much of a stranger yourself these past few days. (*He glares at* ANN. *A pause.*)

JAY. (*Uncomfortably.*) Er, I'll stroll out and see how the roses are getting along. . . .

LEWIS. Don't go, old man. Glad to have you around. Mighty helpful!

JAY. Even so, I think I'll take a breathing spell. (*He exits to terrace.*)

ANN. You see. You embarrass everybody. You're emotionally *gauche!*

LEWIS. Huh!

ANN. Lewis, dear, don't you realize Ellen has undergone a rather . . . how shall I put it for your correct ears . . . a rather revolutionary physical experience since Friday?

LEWIS. (*Squirming.*) I don't know anything about that.

ANN. No, I don't suppose you do. That's why I'm telling you. I think it's only fair we give Ellen a little time to . . . to brood and dream, before she takes her next step.

LEWIS. Meanwhile this young man leaves the country.

ANN. Well, what of it? Ellen can sail later . . . if she still wants to.

LEWIS. If she *still* wants to! Exactly! It's phrases like that I can't understand, Ann. You've got the goddamnedest attitude.

ANN. I'm only trying . . .

LEWIS. Know what you remind me of? The way I was last fall when Roger made the football team . . . just like his old man. By Jingo, you're proud of Ellen.

ANN. I am. She's beginning to be a person in her own right.

LEWIS. You're swaggering all over the place because she has made the free-love team.

ANN. (*Bursts out laughing.*) Just like her old woman! Look out, Lewis, you'll smile.

LEWIS. (*Refusing to smile.*) What you never did get through your head is that this is basically a conventional world. Always has been, always will be. Buck the conventions and you pay for it sooner or later.

ANN. Did *I* pay for it? I was rewarded.

LEWIS. How?

ANN. I got *you.*

LEWIS. There's no use arguing with you. At any rate, you know where I stand.

ANN. You don't stand anywhere. You're lying down, back in the Dark Ages.

LEWIS. (*Starting on a new tack.*) Damn it, Ann, take our own case. This old lover of yours bobbing up has nearly got us on the rocks, and you know it!

ANN. (*Startled, in a small voice.*) Which old lover?

LEWIS. I don't know. Any of 'em! All of 'em!

ANN. I don't think my old lovers need bother you.

LEWIS. They make me want to wring your neck!

ANN. Well that's a risk a woman has to run if she marries a man with a narrow mind.

LEWIS. Thanks!

ANN. You're quite welcome. (CONNIE *enters hurriedly from the hall.*)

CONNIE. (*Crossing to* ANN *in suppressed excitement.*) Hello, Lewis..

LEWIS. Hello, Connie.

CONNIE. (*Whispers audibly to* ANN.) Ellen is back. She came in a taxi.

ANN. (*Coolly, in normal tone.*) Is she alone?

CONNIE. Yes. Er, if you'll excuse me, I'll go up and pack. (*She starts for the door, right.*)

LEWIS. Connie, I want you here.

CONNIE. Frankly, Lewis, I'd prefer not to meet her. I hate scenes. . . .

LEWIS. I want the family here. There may be a great deal to do, and we'll have only a short time in which to do it.

CONNIE. Do what?

ANN. Lewis feels he'd enjoy marrying Ellen off over my dead body.

CONNIE. (*To* LEWIS.) You'll break up your whole family.

LEWIS. I assure you, if a wedding takes place it will be in an atmosphere of family love and effection.

CONNIE. (*Yearning to flee.*) Really, Ann . .

ANN. Stay, dear. There's safety in numbers. (ELLEN *enters.*)

ELLEN. Hello, everybody! (ELLEN *starts at the sight of* LEWIS, *then tries to appear casal. She drops her suitcase by the bookcase, right.*) Hello, Mother.

ANN. Hello darling. (*She puts her arms around* ELLEN *and holds her close.*)

ELLEN. Dad, why aren't you at the office?

LEWIS. I had a few things at home to attend to.

ELLEN. Did you have a good week-end, Mother?

ANN. Very pleasant. Did you?

ELLEN. Deadly!

CONNIE. (*Drily.*) That's too bad!

ELLEN. The Colbys may run a newspaper, but Lord! They are antiques. Prayers before Sunday dinner! Dad, can you imagine?

LEWIS. No, dear, but I see you can. (ELLEN *hesitates for a split second, then plunges on.*)

ELLEN. Anyway the *Hartford Register* is definitely out.

ANN. (*Affecting keen interest.*) Really, dear? Why?

ELLEN. It's all births and deaths and local politics. It doesn't give half a page to world affairs. I want to get on a more sophisticated sheet.

LEWIS. (*Scornfully at word "sophisticated."*) Huh!

ELLEN. Gee, I'm hungry. (*To* ANN.) Wonder if I can have some bacon and eggs.

ANN. Of course.

ELLEN. I had to grab breakfast at seven to make my train. (ELLEN *starts for door, right.*)

LEWIS. (*Sharply.*) Ellen!

ELLEN. Yes?

LEWIS. You come back here.

ELLEN. Why, Dad, what's the matter?

LEWIS. You didn't go to Hartford. (*A pause.* ELLEN *comes back and looks from* ANN *to* LEWIS.)

ELLEN. Does Dad know?

ANN. He does, I regret to say.

ELLEN. But, Mother, you said you'd stand by.

ANN. And I intend to. But you see, dear, after you left things became so involved. . . .

ELLEN. Connie, you ought to be taken out and shot!

LEWIS. That's enough of that attitude.

CONNIE. Ellen, I'm frightfully sorry. I felt . . .

ELLEN. Couldn't you think back a bit? In your day you did a little pioneering yourself.

CONNIE. (*Trying to laugh it off.*) I've never even seen a covered wagon in my life.

ELLEN. You're a fine one to talk! If you weren't rich, and Dad's sister, and too old, you'd have been put in a home for delinquent girls years ago!

CONNIE. (*Explosively.*) Well . . . !

ANN. Ellen Murray . . . !

ELLEN. She had it coming to her.

LEWIS. Ellen, I told you . . . !

ELLEN. Okay, I see my mistake. I just shouldn't have come back to this house. I had too much confidence in my family, that's all! (*She starts to go.*)

LEWIS. (*Stops her and puts his arm around her waist.*) Now, Ellen, hold on. No, you didn't. Your old Dad wants to help. He's taking all the circumstances into consideration. In fact, he is mighty sympathetic.

ELLEN. (*Looking at him doubtfully.*) Are you sure you are?

LEWIS. Positive. Now tell me . . . deep down in your heart . . . are you quite happy about this situation?

ELLEN. Yes, I am.

LEWIS. You two are both deeply in love, aren't you?

ELLEN. Of course we are. (*Indignantly.*) What do you think?

LEWIS. I think maybe I can help you.

ELLEN. I don't know what you can do... unless you start rebuilding the economic system, and a lot of people are ahead of you on that already.

LEWIS. Have you considered marrying this Mr. Douglas . . . ?

ANN. (*Helpfully.*) Mr. Hall, Lewis.

LEWIS. Mr. Hall . . . before he sails?

ELLEN. Of course, I haven't! We don't even dare consider it until after he gets back.

LEWIS. By the way, where is your, er . . . friend?

ELLEN. You mean Doug? He stopped in Stamford for a shave. He still doesn't know that any of you know, and he's terribly sunk over leaving. Will you all be generous enough to act as though our miserable little romance hadn't been flaunted before the general public?

LEWIS. Huh!

ELLEN. Mother, do make Father behave himself, won't you?

ANN. I hope we can all behave.

ELLEN. I've got to dress. I'm going in town to help Doug shop. You know, that man hasn't but two pairs of socks to his name. . . . (*The phone rings.* LEWIS *answers it.*)

LEWIS. (*Into phone.*) Hello. . . . Yes. One minute. I'll put him on the wire. . . . (LEWIS *crosses to terrace.* ELLEN *goes behind table to pick up gloves and purse, then starts for hall.*)

ANN. Ellen!

ELLEN. Yes?

ANN. I think this may concern you, dear.

ELLEN. (*Coming back to* ANN.) Me?

LEWIS. (*Calling.*) Oh, Jaywood! New York calling! (JAY *enters.*)

LEWIS. They're holding the line for you.

JAY. (*Spotting* ELLEN.) Cheerio!

ELLEN. Hello!

JAY. (*Into phone.*) Hello. Hello, Froth, old bean! What I called about particularly was this. Have you a place in your Paris office for an A-1 American girl?

LEWIS. Good idea. (*He comes to table and listens eagerly.*)

JAY. (*Into phone.*) No favour to me; I'm doing you the favour. No, but she has been published. Has a decided flair for newspaper work. Speaks French. Two summers in Europe. She is Ann Whitman Murray's daughter. . . .

ELLEN. You promised not to tell.

JAY. (*Into phone.*) But understand this! She won't take the job unless she gets it on her own. Perfectly satisfactory, I should say. Fine! I'll bring her in for lunch. . . .

ELLEN. I'm lunching with Doug.

JAY. (*Into phone.*) Oh, Froth! She can't wait till lunch. We'll be in your office at twelve. Righto! (*He hangs up the receiver, and turns to* ELLEN.) The Paris edition of the *Herald Tribune*. Office dog. About twenty dollars a week. Would you be interested?

ELLEN. I might. What do you think, Mother?

ANN. Decide as you think best, dear. It's your own problem.

LEWIS. (*Briskly, beaming with satisfaction.*) This fits right into my plan . . . (*He catches her expression, then quickly.*) subject, of course, to your approval. We'll all motor to Greenwich about four and have a quiet family wedding. Dr. Whittacker is available, he tells me, at that hour. Then a nice quiet little supper which your loving mother will arrange . . . and you're off on the *Queen Mary* at midnight! Now isn't that neat?

ELLEN. (*With sarcasm.*) Very neat. Doug is sailing *steerage* on the *Laconia*.

LEWIS. Oh! Well I'll give you a bridal suite for a wedding present.

ELLEN. So that's the angle? The wayward daughter has returned, and you're going to make an honest woman of her.

LEWIS. (*Patient, with effort.*) Now, now . . . no such idea entered my head . . . nor your mother's.

ANN. It certainly didn't.

LEWIS. We merely realized how miserable you'd be separated from Mr. Douglas. . . .

ELLEN. (*Interrupting.*) Mr. Hall, Dad!

LEWIS. . . . Mr. Hall for two years; then your mother intimated to Mr. Jaywood . . .

ELLEN. (*Again interrupting.*) Dad, it doesn't listen right.

LEWIS. Well, you wanted a newspaper job . . . so there you are: exactly what you wanted.

ELLEN. I tell you what I think I'll do, Father. I'll take the *job*. (ANN *smiles broadly to* CONNIE.)

LEWIS. (*Squirming uncomfortably.*) Er, I'm not sure that would be wise unless you were married.

ELLEN. Dad, don't you see? I can't hang myself around Doug's neck. Suppose I should get sick or get fired. He'd worry himself to death over a wife he couldn't support!

CONNIE. After all, your father would be glad . . .

ELLEN. (*Interrupting.*) To dole out money to us! Not on your life! When we marry we'll be independent.

CONNIE. You might consider your mother.

ELLEN. You see what I'm fighting for, don't you, Mother?

ANN. Indeed I do, dear. Make your own decisions.

ELLEN. I intend to.

ANN. Of course you must realize that in Paris you'll be working alone at a difficult job in a foreign background. What's more, you may at any moment be plunged into a revolution or a war!

ELLEN. (*Eagerly.*) That's just what I want . . . a chance to study, to see why the world is so cock-eyed.

LEWIS. Why not stay home and study your mother?

ANN. Or your father!

ELLEN. (*Turning to* JAY.) Where'll I meet you for that twelve o'clock appointment? (*She crosses to him by drum table.*)

LEWIS. They won't give you the job, unmarried.

ELLEN. (*To* JAY.) Your man didn't ask if I was "Mrs." did he?

JAY. (*Evasively.*) Single girls, you know! Paris! They are a bit of a risk!

ELLEN. So you advocate marriage, too?

JAY. Well, er . . . it does sound so.

ELLEN. You of all people!

JAY. I know. I know.

LEWIS. (*Suspiciously.*) See here, Ellen, why attack Mr. Jaywood? (ELLEN *realizes she has said too much. She steals a quick look at* ANN.)

ELLEN. No reason. I guess I'm attempting to think things out too honestly for my own good or anybody else's. Please forgive me.

ANN. Ellen, I thought you said you had to go up and dress.

ELLEN. It's all right, Mother. Don't worry, I'm just going. (*She exits.*)

LEWIS. (*To* ANN.) You actually encouraged her to take that job. Are you crazy?

ANN. I think it's an excellent opportunity . . . whether she marries, or whether she doesn't.

LEWIS. My God! First you help her to a week-end affair, now you help her to continue it all over Europe!

CONNIE. Lewis, you only irritate Ann . . . and make things worse.

ANN. (*Placidly, rising.*) I wouldn't allow such a superficial thinker to irritate me. (*To* LEWIS.) I know what I'm about. I've seen this boy and you haven't. (*She goes upstairs.*)

LEWIS. (*Wearily to* JAY.) I could do with a drink. How about you? (*He goes to his private hiding-place in book-case, right, and produces bottle of whiskey and two glasses.*)

JAY. I feel I should be getting into town.

CONNIE. (*Eagerly.*) Jay, I'm driving in town myself. Why don't you go with me? I'd love company.

JAY. Kind of you, but . . .

CONNIE. I drive beautifully. I'll go tell Peter to drive my car around. I'll be ready in ten minutes. (*She exits right.*)

JAY. I think I will take a drink. (*Indicating* LEWIS *has poured enough.*) Whoa! (LEWIS *pours himself a glass.*)

LEWIS. Nice of you, old man, to wangle Ellen that Paris job.

JAY. Glad to be of service. (*They drink.*)

LEWIS. Er, now she's got it, do us one more favour, will you?

JAY. Of course . . . what?

LEWIS. See she doesn't get it.

JAY. (*Looking in direction* ANN *departed.*) Well, I don't know . . .

LEWIS. Your friend is particular whom he hires, isn't he?

JAY. You mean call him up and say I've discovered your daughter is, er . . . a bit of a frip? (*He sits on lower end of couch.*)

LEWIS. (*With a groan.*) God, no, that won't do. (*He takes a drink.*) Jaywood, I'm a confused and unhappy man. (*Sits on couch.*) Tell me: is morality dead and I don't know it?

JAY. On the contrary, if I were a father, I suspect I'd have feelings much like yours. (*Warming to the subject.*) You know, it's always been a pet theory of mine that men are much more moral than women.

LEWIS. (*Bluntly.*) Are you moral?

JAY. (*Cheerfully.*) Oh, rather!

LEWIS. Huh! (*He glances at* JAY *shrewdly.*) I noticed both Ellen and Ann appeared surprised when you came out in support of this marriage. "You of all people!" Ellen said.

JAY. (*Affecting surprise.*) Did Ellen say that? I didn't notice.

LEWIS. You know damn well you noticed. You got red as a turkey cock.

JAY. (*Embarrassed.*) Er, well, the truth is, I have been rather a gay dog in my time.

LEWIS. (*Suspiciously.*) Indeed?

JAY. (*Hastily.*) In London, you know.

LEWIS. How would Ellen hear about that?

JAY. About what?

LEWIS. About your being a gay dog in London?

JAY. Er, I fear my reputation may have been somewhat international.

LEWIS. Huh! (*He rises and crosses to center.* MARTHA *enters from the hall.*)

MARTHA. Excuse me, sir.

LEWIS. What do you want?

MARTHA. There's a Mr. Hall to see Miss Ellen, sir.

LEWIS. (*With mounting anger.*) Show him in here, Martha.

MARTHA. Yes, sir. (*She exits.*)

JAY. Easy does it, old boy!

LEWIS. I intend to be diplomatic. (DOUG *enters. At sight of* LEWIS, *he stops dead in his tracks. He would like to run. Then he sees* JAY *and crosses to him, much relieved.*)

DOUG. Oh, hello, Mr. Haywood. Nice to see you again.

JAY. (*As they shake hands.*) Nice to see you. Mr. Hall, may I introduce Mr. Murray . . . Ellen's father.

DOUG. (*He hesitates, then gives* LEWIS *a hearty athletic hand-shake.*) It's a privilege to meet you, sir.

LEWIS. Huh! Thanks.

DOUG. I dropped in to see if Ellen had returned from Hartford yet.

LEWIS. Yes, she's back. (*An awkward pause.*)

DOUG. Has she been back long?

LEWIS. About 'fifteen minutes, I should say, shouldn't you, Jaywood?

JAY. (*Coming out of his revery.*) Er, what? Oh, about fifteen or twenty. (*Looks at watch.*) Nearer twenty. (LEWIS *consults his watch.*)

LEWIS. Yes, nearer twenty. (DOUG *consults his watch. It is a large-sized popular brand.* LEWIS *and* JAY *bend forward to compare his time with theirs.* DOUG *hastily pockets his watch. An awkward pause.*)

JAY. Will you have a drink?

DOUG. No, thanks. (*To* LEWIS.) I'm wondering if Ellen has had time to tell you yet . . . or maybe she phoned.

LEWIS. No, she didn't phone.

DOUG. (*He looks at* JAY, *then decides to take the plunge.*) You see, Mr. Murray, I've fallen pretty deeply in love with Ellen, and before I left Friday, we decided to become engaged . . . of course with your consent. . . .

LEWIS. Frankly, Mr. Hall, in your particular case don't you feel the word engagement is a slight, er . . . error in terminology?

DOUG. You mean on account of my going away for so long?

LEWIS. I had in mind the fact you'd been away.

DOUG. Been away?

LEWIS. I said "been away."

JAY. (*With warning gesture.*) Easy.

LEWIS. Mr. Hall, unfortunately I wasn't at home when you dropped in for tea.

DOUG. (*Politely.*) I was disappointed to find you away.

LEWIS. (*Explosively.*) How in the name of heaven can a well-born, clean-cut, apparently decent young chap like you stand there and look me in the eye . . . (*Noticing* JAY's *worried expression.*) No, suppose we drop that phase of the matter. . . .

DOUG. I'd prefer you continue.

LEWIS. I . . . you . . . (*The subject is too difficult for him. He gives up.*) Nothing important, my boy. Some other time . . . when we're better acquainted.

DOUG. (*Coolly.*) I'm driving in town directly with Ellen, sir, and I sail at midnight. If you have anything to say, I wish you'd say it now.

LEWIS. Er, Mr. Hall, my daughter's happiness means a great deal to me. I don't want to jeopardize it. Probably I am, as my wife frequently reminds me, narrow-minded. Anyway, my personal opinion is that you behaved like a . . .

JAY. (*Warningly.*) Easy does it.

LEWIS. (*In a milder tone.*) . . . damn cad.

JAY. (*To* DOUG.) In brief, he knows you spent the week-end with his daughter.

DOUG. I thought that was what he was driving at.

LEWIS. Correct! That's it.

DOUG. Did Ellen just tell you?

LEWIS. No, I've known it for some time.

DOUG. Some time? That's impossible.

LEWIS. I knew it last Friday.

DOUG. Then why didn't you stop us?

LEWIS. I didn't get the news until after you had gone.

DOUG. (*Thoroughly mystified.*) But Ellen assured me . . . why we all had tea together . . . nobody knew then.

JAY. A few of us were in on it.

DOUG. Did Mrs. Murray know?

JAY. Oh, definitely.

DOUG. Before we started?

JAY. Yes.

DOUG. Do you mean to say that Mrs. Murray sat there all the time, served tea and talked nonsense . . . ?

JAY. That's right.

DOUG. Did *you* know?

JAY. Oh, yes!

DOUG. What kind of a family is this?

JAY. They're extremely nice people, Mr. Hall.

DOUG. (*To* LEWIS.) Say, why didn't some of you raise a row? Then naturally, I wouldn't have thought of going.

LEWIS. Not much courage, eh?

DOUG. Oh, I've plenty of courage. I admit if a person didn't know the facts, my conduct might seem kind of rotten; but frankly, I think you have only yourselves to blame. You know I'm beginning to get pretty good and sore about this!

LEWIS. By God! You needn't get sore . . . ! (CONNIE *enters right. She notices the general air of suppression and tension.*)

CONNIE. Oh, excuse me. I'm just after my cigarette case. I'm going right up to pack. (*She takes case from table, and starts for archway, only to find herself face to face with* DOUG.)

JAY. Mrs. Nevins, may I introduce Mr. Hall?

CONNIE. Mr. Hall?! Oh, how do you do. I've often heard the family speak of you.

DOUG. You're Aunt Connie?

CONNIE. I am Connie.

DOUG. (*Bluntly to* CONNIE.) I suppose *you* know, too.

CONNIE. Know what?

DOUG. About our trip to Lanesville.

CONNIE. Er, just vaguely. . . .

DOUG. And you didn't tell your own niece what you know, and advise her not to go!

CONNIE. Why, no!

DOUG. I can only repeat: what a family!

LEWIS. (*Angrily.*) If you don't like this family, you're at liberty to leave. There's the door.

DOUG. Oh no, I don't go yet. What would that make *me*?

CONNIE. That's hard to say. At the moment you seem an extremely impossible young man. . . . (ANN *enters from the hall.*)

ANN. Oh, good morning, Mr. Hall.

DOUG. (*Tersely, a stag at bay.*) Good morning.

ANN. (*Chattily.*) We saw you drive in. Ellen will be right along. Won't you sit down?

DOUG. No!

ANN. (*Offended by his tone.*) I beg your pardon.

DOUG. Mrs. Murray, I'm afraid we're beyond the point where we can be polite to each other. I'll tell you frankly: I am pretty mad.

ANN. Lewis is exasperating, but . . .

DOUG. (*Interrupting.*) I'm not so mad at him. It's you. . . .

ANN. Me?

LEWIS. (*Gloatingly.*) You, Mrs. Murray.

ANN. (*To* DOUG.) My dear boy, I've tried to be sympathetic. . . .

DOUG. (*Interrupting.*) What kind of a woman are you to serve a man tea when all the time you know he is running off with your daughter? Where were your motherly instincts?

ANN. Under control, Mr. Hall!

DOUG. Don't you think it's pretty tough for Ellen and me to be let in for any such exhibition as this?

ANN. (*All sympathy.*) Of course I do, bless your heart. Lewis! Ellen begged you not to tell him we knew.

LEWIS. I didn't. He dragged it out of me.

DOUG. Yes, and another point you've overlooked. My reputation!

ANN. *Your* reputation? Oh, I see. (ANN *sits end of sofa, right.*)

LEWIS. News of your reputation won't travel any farther.

DOUG. Everybody I've met so far seems to know it. . . . (ELLEN *enters, furious. She has changed hurriedly.*)

ELLEN. So you have told him . . . the moment my back was turned! Oh, darling, they're just trying to spoil everything. I'm ready. Let's get out of here. . . . .

DOUG. Oh, no!

ELLEN. (*Stopped short by his tone.*) What do you mean, "Oh, no!"?

DOUG. We talk this out right here and now.

ELLEN. Not before everybody. (JAY *and* CONNIE *murmur apologies.*)

CONNIE. Come, Jay. . . . (*They start to go.*)

DOUG. Don't one of you leave this room. I want them all here.

CONNIE. Oh!

LEWIS. See here . . .

ELLEN. Why, Doug, what's come over you?

DOUG. I want them to hear me propose to you.

ELLEN. But, Doug, you ought to know you don't have to propose to me.

DOUG. Darling, they think I've misled you.

ELLEN. What do we care what they think?

DOUG. Don't you understand, it's the wrong way to look at it. I care too much for you to . . . to . . . to . . .

ELLEN. We don't need to go into that now. Listen, Doug, we've had a grand piece of luck. Through Mr. Jaywood, I may be able to get a job on the *Paris Herald.* Isn't that a break? A newspaper job one week out of college! Aren't you excited?

DOUG. Say, it might work out at that. (*He turns to* LEWIS.) We could get married and Ellen could come over later.

LEWIS. We thought she might even sail with you.

DOUG. I see no objection.

ELLEN. I see plenty. It's out of the question. Anyway, we can talk it over on the boat.

DOUG. Ellen, I'm sorry. I can't let you take the same boat with me. . . .

ELLEN. Why not? You didn't buy it, did you?

DOUG. Ellen, you and I are going to be married here, right now, today, where your family can watch . . . or you're not going to see me for two years. . . . .

ELLEN. Darling, you're just having a moral spasm. It'll pass. (*He makes gesture of protest.*)

DOUG. Ellen, I'll have to insist. Either you marry me today, or it's good-bye for *more* than two years.

ELLEN. I won't be forced . . . by you, or any of the rest of you. I know: you've all been working on him.

CONNIE. I'd say he's been working on us.

ELLEN. (*Turning back.*) Doug, I can't marry you like this.

DOUG. Ellen!

ELLEN. In fact, I *won't* marry you like this.

DOUG. (*Weakly, overwhelmed.*) That sounds final.

ELLEN. It is.

DOUG. Then good-bye.

ELLEN. Good-bye.

DOUG. (*Turning to* LEWIS.) Sorry. At least you'll admit I've tried. . . .

LEWIS. Hall, you've acted mighty fine. No father could ask more. (DOUG *backs toward archway. He takes one final look at* ELLEN *to see if there is chance of her relenting.*)

DOUG. (*Awkwardly.*) Pleased to have met you all. (*He hurries out.*)

CONNIE. Good-bye, Mr. Hall.

JAY. Good-bye, old boy. (*A pause. No one knows what to say.* ELLEN, *miserably unhappy, turns to* ANN *in appeal.*)

ELLEN. Mother, what do you think?

ANN. (*In pleasantly vigorous tones.*) I think, when a man makes such a fuss over being seduced . . . a nice girl ought to marry him. (*It is the tiny filip needed to decide* ELLEN.)

ELLEN. Maybe you're right. (*Calling.*) Doug! Doug, wait a minute! (*She turns and runs out.*) (ANN *turns to* LEWIS *and gives a nod of profound satisfaction, a nod that says:* "There you are, I handled her in my own way. What are you kicking about?" *She extends her arms. He hesitates, then extends his. They embrace in hearty congratulation as the Curtain Falls.*)

END OF PLAY

Three Men On A Horse

BY JOHN CECIL HOLM AND GEORGE ABBOTT

*"To Equipoise,
that good old horse."*

"THREE MEN ON A HORSE" was first produced by Alex Yokel at The Playhouse in New York City on January 30, 1935. The play was staged by Mr. Abbott, the settings were designed by Boris Aronson, and the cast was as follows:

AUDREY TROWBRIDGE	Joyce Arling
THE TAILOR	J. Ascher Smith
ERWIN TROWBRIDGE	William Lynn
CLARENCE DOBBINS	Fleming Ward
DELIVERY BOY	Nick Wiger
HARRY	James Lane
CHARLIE	Millard Mitchell
FRANKIE	Teddy Hart
PATSY	Sam Levene
MABEL	Shirley Booth
MOSES	Richard Huey
GLORIA	Edith Van Cleve
AL	Garson Kanin
HOTEL MAID	Margaret Mullen
MR. CARVER	Frank Camp

SCENES

ACT I

Scene 1. The living room of the Trowbridge House, Ozone Heights, New Jersey.
Scene 2. A bar room in the basement of the Lavillere Hotel, New York City.

ACT II

Scene 1. Ozone Heights.
Scene 2. A room in the Lavillere Hotel.

ACT III

Scene 1. Ozone Heights.
Scene 2. The Hotel Room.

ACT ONE

SCENE I

Scene: The living room of the Trowbridge house, Ozone Heights, New Jersey.

A typical standardized house. There is a stairway leading up, a door to the kitchen and a front door.

ORCHESTRA *plays "Just a Love Nest."*

At rise: AUDREY TROWBRIDGE *enters from the kitchen. She carries a plate of toast which she places on a bridge table. We also see coffee, orange-juice, etc.* AUDREY *is wearing a red print house-dress. She is about twenty-five. As she crosses to the foot of the stairs she examines the sole of one bedroom slipper.*

AUDREY. (*Calling.*) Erwin.

ERWIN. (*Off.*) Yes.

AUDREY. The paint you put on the kitchen floor isn't dry yet.

ERWIN. Well, I didn't expect it would be. It says on the can it takes forty-eight hours.

AUDREY. Oh. Anyway I set up the bridge table in the living room. Breakfast is all ready.

ERWIN. All right. (*Buzzer rings.* AUDREY *opens door, admits the* TAILOR.)

AUDREY. Oh, yes. Just a minute. (*Calls.*) Erwin.

ERWIN. (*Off.*) Yes.

AUDREY. The man is here for your suit. Will you bring it down?

ERWIN. All right. Just a second.

AUDREY. (*Over her shoulder.*) Just a second!

ERWIN. (*Pause.*) Here it comes. (*Suit lands at* AUDREY's *feet.* AUDREY *cleans out pockets of pocket-handkerchief, pipe, matches and a little note-book.*)

AUDREY. The last time I sent this suit I forgot to take out a white handkerchief with a blue border and it never came back.

TAILOR. I'll tell him about it.

AUDREY. (*As the* TAILOR *is leaving.*) It was a good handkerchief. (*She looks through note-book—is shocked and distressed—looks up stairs—goes to phone cautiously. Picks up phone.*) Give me forty-two W—Ring four. (*Sits.*) Hello, Clarence . . . (*Weakly.*) I wonder if you could come over for a minute. I just found something that's upset me. . . . You will. . . . Oh, thanks. (*Hangs up. Wipes tear away, blows nose, then calls.*) Erwin, breakfast is ready.

ERWIN. (*Upstairs.*) All right, dear. (AUDREY *blows nose and looks straight ahead.* ERWIN *comes quickly down the stairs and into room. He is dressed, except for his necktie. He is the model little commuter.*) I thought of another verse while I was shaving. Darned good, too— (*Sits at table.*) What's the matter, dear, something get in your eye?

AUDREY. I'll be all right.

ERWIN. Gee, that's too bad. It's this dry spell we're having. Dust everywhere.

AUDREY. Better drink your coffee before it's too cold.

ERWIN. (*Sits.*) Oh, yes. (*Starts eating. Pause.*)

AUDREY. You forgot your necktie.

ERWIN. (*Looks.*) Necktie? So I have. Oh, I couldn't decide which tie to wear.

AUDREY. You need new ones, I guess.

ERWIN. No, no. I have plenty. Gee, I'm late— (*Looking at wrist watch.*)

AUDREY. (*Crossing to the table.*) You told me you'd stay home from the office one day this week.

ERWIN. I know I did, sweetheart— But not today. How in the name of Heaven can I turn out sixty-seven Mother's Day greetings?

AUDREY. (*Suddenly; hopefully.*) You could write them in the country. We could go for a drive. (*Sits.*)

ERWIN. No. No. I know I couldn't. I've never been able to write in the country— the birds and the butterflies, distract me— (*Suddenly.*) —wait— (*Writing.*) "The

512

birds and the butterflies send you a greeting. It's spring and today in mem'ry we're meeting." Mother's Day Number Eleven. Yes, that's all right—well, that's another one. I'll call that "To Mother on Mother's Day"— (*Starts gulping breakfast. She goes to window.*) What's the matter?

AUDREY. I'm expecting Clarence, that's all.

ERWIN. I wish you'd have him visit when I'm not here; he gets me upset—he laughs at me—calls me the Poet of Dobbins Drive.

AUDREY. He doesn't understand. He's a business man.

ERWIN. Business man? Every time I look out the window, I see forty-six empty houses that he's built and can't sell. My greeting card verses are read from Asbury Park to Seattle, Washington.

AUDREY. Well, I'm not going to be happy in Ozone Heights—after today.

ERWIN. (*Looks.*) Why, has something happened?

AUDREY. Yes—something has. Erwin—

ERWIN. I wish you wouldn't say Erwin in that tone of voice, Audrey. I know my name is Erwin, but it makes me feel whatever has happened has something to do with me.

AUDREY. It has.

ERWIN. Why, Audrey—

AUDREY. I discovered it before you came down.

ERWIN. About me? (AUDREY *nods.*) Why —why, what is it?

AUDREY. I'm going to wait until brother gets here.

ERWIN. Do you have to have him here to tell me what it is?

AUDREY. Yes . . . Erwin, you don't love me any more. (*Sits—cries.*)

ERWIN. (*Crosses right.*) Why, Audrey, of course I love you. Maybe I don't walk up and say, "Audrey, I love you," every time I see you . . . (*Sits.*) but you know how I feel. Gosh, I don't know how other husbands act. But I always do the best I can

and we seem to get along all right. If I've done anything that's wrong I'd rather have you tell me than tell your brother. (*Turns front.*) I wish you wouldn't start the day off like this. It's hard to write my verses if I'm in the wrong mood, you know that. Come on, dear, tell Erwin what it is so he can explain and get to the office. . . .

AUDREY. Well, this morning the man came for your blue suit—and I gave it to him.

ERWIN. Well . . . why are we so excited about it? You were the one who said it needed cleaning. (CLARENCE *enters room. Looks at tie-less collar on* ERWIN. CLARENCE *is about thirty-five. A small town business man. A check book, pen and pencil in his breast pocket and when the jacket is open we see several lodge emblems.*)

CLARENCE. Well, good morning, what's happened? Oh, just getting up?

AUDREY. Good morning—Clarence.

CLARENCE. Hello, sis—you look all upset. Has he been doing anything to you?

ERWIN. I haven't done a thing that I know of. I was just having breakfast. It's something about my suit. My blue suit. Audrey sent it out to be cleaned.

CLARENCE. You being funny?

ERWIN. Maybe you think it's funny. I don't. I should be at the office and my wife tells me I don't love her any more.

CLARENCE. What has that got to do with a blue suit?

AUDREY. I sent it out to be cleaned, and— (*Takes notebook from pocket and crosses to* CLARENCE.) I found this note-book in the coat pocket.

ERWIN. Oh, that book. Is that what upset you . . .

AUDREY. (*Holds up hand; goes to* CLARENCE. *Flips pages through.*) Look at those names . . . Shirley, May, Lena Wee, Bambola, Nell McClatchy, Squeeze . . . not one or two, Clarence, but pages of them . . . look at those telephone numbers . . . Jamaica six-three-two-one. . . .

ERWIN. (*As* AUDREY *returns to davenport.*) But darling!

CLARENCE. My gosh, say. What are you keeping . . . a harem?

ERWIN. Wait, dear. (*Meekly.*) I can explain. It's only a hobby.

AUDREY. Only a hobby. Oh— (*Sits—cries.*)

ERWIN. They're horses.

CLARENCE. Horses, huh—

AUDREY. Horses!

ERWIN. Horse racing.

CLARENCE. Oh, is that it?

ERWIN. Yes!

CLARENCE. (*Stalking toward* ERWIN.) I always knew you had some secret vice. I was telling Audrey just the other day . . .

ERWIN. I don't play them.

CLARENCE. Then what do you do?

ERWIN. I dope them out.

CLARENCE. For who? For what?

ERWIN. For fun. I do it on the bus on the way to the office to pass the time. Like some people do cross-words. . . .

CLARENCE. Oh, you do?

ERWIN. Yes—one day I came across a racing paper on the bus and I found out that the fellow who doped them out wasn't so good. So the next day I did it myself for fun . . . and I've been keeping track of them in that book.

AUDREY. (*Stands.*) But Erwin, you haven't explained all these numbers.

ERWIN Certainly I have, sweetheart. (*Takes book.*) Listen, here, I wrote on one page Jamaica—six—that's the sixth race. And then two-three-one. The two, three, and one was in the order I thought the entries would finish. On this other page is the way they did finish. (*Turning page.*)

CLARENCE. (*Looking at book.*) You mean you guessed them right?

ERWIN. (*Like a little boy.*) Sure.

AUDREY. But that doesn't explain this number. (*Looking at book.*) This eight ninety-six point fifty—

ERWIN. It isn't a number. That's what I made the week of January twentieth—at two dollars a bet. Eight hundred and ninety-six dollars and fifty cents.

AUDREY. You made that and never told me?

ERWIN. Only on paper, sweetheart. Oh, I'd never bet on a horse. You know we couldn't afford that. (*To* CLARENCE.) Look —in the back of the book is what I would have made on a four horse parlay, playing two dollars a day fourteen thousand dollars and fifty cents since January first. It's what you call mental betting.

CLARENCE. (*Looking in book; business-like.*) So you win on paper. (*Takes book.*)

ERWIN. (*Going back to his breakfast.*) But I wouldn't bet on a horse with real money.

CLARENCE. But on paper with two dollar bets you've made a few thousand dollars. Suppose you did put two dollars on a horse? And the horse paid three to one . . . you would have six dollars besides the original two dollars you bet.

ERWIN. Yes. But suppose the horse didn't win, I'd be out two dollars. Two dollars is a lot of money to us, Clarence.

CLARENCE. (*Slowly as he crosses to fire-place.*) But according to your little book here, you couldn't have picked many horses that lost or you wouldn't have run up those figures.

ERWIN. Oh! yes. I have. Now last Tuesday, going to town, I went through the entries in the morning paper and picked out horses one-two-three in all the races and the one I picked in the fourth race, fell down and finished out of the money and one lost his rider and three were scratched.

CLARENCE. How about the other horses?

ERWIN. (*Eating.*) Oh, they finished all right.

CLARENCE. One-two-three?

ERWIN. One-two-three.

CLARENCE. (*Turning away.*) How long have you been doing this, Erwin?

ERWIN. Only since the first of the year.

CLARENCE. Well, that's long enough.

ERWIN. That isn't very long—

CLARENCE. I mean that's long enough to sock it away.

ERWIN. Sock what away?

CLARENCE. (*Going to the table.*) Come on now, Erwin. I've been around. I can see through you.

ERWIN. I don't know what you mean, Clarence.

CLARENCE. How many savings accounts have you, Erwin?

ERWIN. You mean banks?

CLARENCE. Yes, banks.

ERWIN. Only one. The Bowery Savings Bank.

CLARENCE. How much you got in there?

ERWIN. It's down to twenty-two dollars now.

CLARENCE. Say, Erwin, you're as plain as pie to me. You've been playing the horses since January—you've won a pile of money —you don't want anyone to know about it—so what do you do? You cry poor. So we'll think you're broke.

ERWIN. I am broke.

CLARENCE. I'll bet you've got about six different bank accounts under "non de plums."

AUDREY. Why Erwin—

ERWIN. But I haven't, honest, I wish I had.

CLARENCE. (*Sits.*) Now listen—you might die tomorrow, Erwin, and nobody knows about those bank accounts but you. Think of Audrey.

ERWIN. But honest, Clarence, I haven't any money. I don't know how you can think up things like this. Gee—if I had a brain like yours, I'd write detective stories. I only do this for fun—it's just a hobby— like—like—like golf—or—or tropical fish.

CLARENCE. Is that the truth?

ERWIN. That's the truth, Clarence!

CLARENCE. Great grief, man. Why don't you bet?

ERWIN. That would spoil it all.

CLARENCE. (*Baffled.*) Do you mean to tell me you can pick horses, that win every day, and be satisfied with paper profits?

ERWIN. Yes.

CLARENCE. Why?

ERWIN. Because I did bet once.

AUDREY. Why, when was that, Erwin?

ERWIN. Well, that was a long time ago . . . I guess it doesn't hurt to tell about it now. We'd only been married a little while. You wanted something and I wanted to get it for you . . . you said it was too expensive. . . .

CLARENCE. What happened to the horse?

ERWIN. Oh, he lost.

AUDREY. Oh.

ERWIN. He was a good horse, though. One of the fellows at the office showed me a telegram right from the jockey who was going to ride in the race, saying, "It's a sure thing and to play right on the nose. . . ." So I did. I took ten dollars out of my envelope. . . . That was the time I told you my pocket was picked—remember? I was only making thirty then—

CLARENCE. So you thought the race was fixed, huh?

ERWIN. I didn't know anything about that. But he sure was a good horse . . . maybe something went wrong. Just as the race was about to start . . . this horse broke the barrier and ran all the way around the track before they could catch him . . . so they brought him back to the post . . . when the race started he was so tired he just stayed there.

CLARENCE. How do you pick these horses, Erwin?

ERWIN. When I get on the bus, I just look through the entries and pick out the ones I like. I guess you'd call it playing hunches.

CLARENCE. Just for the fun of it. I guess a lot of people do that. I'll bet you even know what's going to win today.

ERWIN. Sure. I figured it out last night on the bus coming home—but I only figured the first race—Brass Monkey—is going to win it.

CLARENCE. Brass Monkey—

ERWIN. Sure, he's a good horse.

AUDREY. I'm awfully sorry, Erwin, I suspected you of anything wrong.

ERWIN. (*Going to her.*) That's all right, darling. I'd never do anything behind your back, you know that.

CLARENCE. But great grief, Erwin, you don't seem to have any initiative. No other man would have let a chance like that slip through his fingers—why don't you bet?

ERWIN. (*Turning.*) I don't think it would be moral for me to bet—we haven't enough money—

CLARENCE. That's ridiculous—why don't you make some? I told you I'd give you a percentage if you sold one of my houses—

AUDREY. That's sweet of you, Clarence.

ERWIN. I don't think I could sell one. Maybe Audrey could. I don't like them. (*Turns and goes toward door.*)

CLARENCE. What do you mean you don't like them?

ERWIN. I don't like them, that's all, and I couldn't sell anything I don't like.

AUDREY. (*Rising.*) What's wrong with them?

ERWIN. (*Trapped.*) There isn't anything wrong with them exactly, but well—there is too much water in the cellar.

CLARENCE. (*Going to* ERWIN.) Now I don't want any minor criticisms from you after that porch you tacked on the house—I built a beautiful row of houses all alike, and you tacked that thing on. You put this house out of step, you know that?

ERWIN. Now listen, Clarence— (*Changing his mind as* CLARENCE *turns.*) Never mind, I'm late. (*Starts.*)

AUDREY. Wait a minute, Erwin.

ERWIN. What's the matter, darling? I have to go to work.

AUDREY. Don't you think you better apologize to Clarence before you go?

ERWIN. Apologize? For what?

AUDREY. For being so rude.

ERWIN. Rude?

AUDREY. Yes. About the houses. Erwin!

ERWIN. Well, I apologize—but I don't like water in the cellar—I don't think it adds anything to a house. (*Buzzer rings.* ERWIN *opens door.*)

BOY. Number one Dobbins Drive?—

ERWIN. That's right.

BOY. Package for Mrs. Trowbridge. (*Handing* ERWIN *package.*)

ERWIN. There she is there. . . . (*Starts out.*)

BOY. C. O. D. Forty-eight dollars.

ERWIN. What?

AUDREY. I bought some dresses, darling.

ERWIN. C. O. D. Forty-eight dollars? How are we going to pay it—what made you do that?

CLARENCE. I told her she needed some decent clothes. That's why, and since I've found out a few things today, I guess I was right.

ERWIN. We can't afford it— (*To* BOY.) Take them back, son. (*Giving him package.*)

BOY. I can't take them back. They've been altered.

AUDREY. That's right, Erwin. It was a sale. They'd cost sixty-five next week. I saved you seventeen dollars. Darling, you know I didn't have anything to wear.

ERWIN. Nothing to wear! All I seem to do is pay for dresses and hats . . . and my life insurance. (*Crosses to cabinet, takes out "Household Budget Book." Looks through book.*)

CLARENCE. Don't yell at my sister like that.

ERWIN. Nothing to wear. (*Reads.*) Listen —Nineteen twenty-nine—six dresses—four hats—Nineteen thirty—seven dresses—five hats—Nineteen thirty-one, thirty-two and thirty-three—eight, nine, and ten dresses and five, four, and eight hats respectively, altogether, that's forty dresses and thirty-two hats. I should be in the hat business instead of trying to get some place.

AUDREY. Darling, it does sound like a lot, I know, but that's since Nineteen twenty-nine—some of those hats I couldn't wear because my hair was growing back and they didn't fit.

ERWIN. Here's my hat—five dollars it cost me in Nineteen thirty-one and it's good enough for me, Fall, Winter, Spring and Summer— (*Puts on hat.*) and look at it.

CLARENCE. Women's things are different— Some women buy—

ERWIN. Well, look at it.

AUDREY. I'm looking. I have a right to have a dress or two. I've saved a little money from the budget and anyway how do I know you haven't been betting on the horses.

CLARENCE. Yes, there's a lot of things about you I'd like to know—

ERWIN. My Gosh, don't I bring home my salary every week? You know I never bet on a horse or anything.

AUDREY. (*Going to* CLARENCE.) Oh, Clarence, let's not argue any more—

CLARENCE. (*Enfolding* AUDREY.) Don't worry, Audrey. I'll pay for the dresses.

ERWIN. Oh, no you won't. I don't want you to pay for anything. (*Goes to cabinet, takes tobacco tin. He takes out bills.*) Here, this is for your dresses. This ten was going to be for a split bamboo weakfishing outfit. These three tens were going to be for a motor trip for the two of us and this ten was supposed to become a panama and a pair of sport shoes—but pay for the dresses. Don't forget to get a receipt. (*Picks up box and puts it back in cabinet.*)

AUDREY. Where are you going?

ERWIN. To the office—I'm late.

AUDREY. You've forgotten your necktie.

ERWIN. What's the difference. Who cares how I look? To Hell with the tie.

AUDREY. Erwin.

ERWIN. And to Hell with this house.

CLARENCE. What?

AUDREY. Erwin! You'll hurt Clarence's feelings.

ERWIN. And I won't apologize. (*Rushing past delivery boy and out door.*)

AUDREY. (*Calls.*) Erwin.

BLACKOUT AND CURTAIN.

SCENE II

Scene: A bar-room in the Lavillere Hotel. The bar is upstage, two thirds the distance. Telephone booth to the right. Elevator door diagonally across from booth. Door to men's room off right out of view. Stairs up center leading to the street. This is really the basement of the Lavillere Hotel.

Time: About three in the afternoon.

At Rise: HARRY *the bartender is behind the bar.* CHARLIE *and* FRANKIE *seated at table down right. They have racing sheets spread out on table.* FRANKIE *is about half the size of* CHARLIE. *His feet just touch the floor. He wears a derby and is smoking a large cigar.* CHARLIE *is smoking a cigarette. His grey hat is pushed back off his forehead.*

HARRY. What'll you have, the same?

CHARLIE. Just make it one beer this time. (*Counts change.*) We'll split it, Frankie. (*To* HARRY.) We don't want to break a bill if we can help it—maybe we can figure out a horse to play on in this third race.

HARRY. That's all right by me.

FRANKIE. Geez, you'd think Patsy would call up or somethin'.

CHARLIE. It don't take all day to hock a belt buckle.

FRANKIE. Maybe it wasn't gold after all.

CHARLIE. He paid enough for it.

HARRY. (*As he brings beer to table.*) It just goes to show you how the luck will go. Lobster one day—beans the next. You three fellows were sittin' pretty—how much was it you ran up to last month?

CHARLIE. About four hundred bucks. Aw —we'll have it again.

FRANKIE. Sure.

HARRY. Geez, I could almost open my own place with that. I was tellin' the manager the other day—now the trouble with this place is—it looks too much like a speakeasy—if a thing is legal it should look legal —that's what I say—and another thing— when anybody takes a room at this hotel they don't come in here much—if they want to have a party—they take the bottle to the room. (*The phone rings.* HARRY *goes into booth.*)

CHARLIE. (*Counting money.*) Two, three, four, five, six. Well, I know how I'm goin' to play my six bucks.

FRANKIE. Yeah?

CHARLIE. Yeah, I'm playin' the surest thing I know . . . three bucks on Rose Cross to show.

FRANKIE. But Charlie, Rose Cross won't pay back anything much even if she wins . . . if you lay three bucks to place, you'd only get about ninety cents—so if she shows, you're lucky to get two bits.

CHARLIE. Listen, we got to reserve our capital. Two bits is breakfast money anyways. How d'ya think we're going to eat? We can't get credit for a bet any more— let alone feed money. You know that!

FRANKIE. But, you're puttin' up half your roll. Suppose Rose Cross don't come in?

CHARLIE. There's only five horses in the race. She ought to show at least— This is a Hell of a spot to be in. I wish Patsy would come back. Sometimes he gets some good ideas. Even Mabel ain't in her room. Did she go out with Patsy?

FRANKIE. No, she's doin' the same thing— she took out all her dresses and a parasol that's got a gold top. It's a good thing Patsy's got Mabel—he got forty-five bucks on that bracelet of hers yesterday.

CHARLIE. What do you mean "it's a good thing Patsy's got Mabel"? He bought all that stuff for her, didn't he?

FRANKIE. What I mean is—she's a good investment. (HARRY *goes to bar.* ERWIN *enters slowly down the stairs.*) She's a nice kid, Mabel.

CHARLIE. Yeah, she's all right—well, the Hell with all that. I got to bet.

HARRY. That was Gus on the phone. He wanted to find out if anybody wanted to bet the third race.

CHARLIE. Who copped that second?

HARRY. Fairweather.

CHARLIE. Brass Monkey took the first. He paid eight to one. (*Looks at paper.*)

HARRY. (*Looks at slip of paper.*)

CHARLIE. Musta been a sleeper.

HARRY. What'll it be?

ERWIN. (*Looking around.*) I don't think I'll meet anybody here—

HARRY. What'll you have?

ERWIN. Scotch.

FRANKIE. I don't think I want to bet today.

CHARLIE. Now listen, we didn't play yesterday nor the day before—we got to bet today. We might as well break the ice.

ERWIN. (*To* HARRY.) Hey, I should be at the office.

HARRY. Takin' a couple hours for lunch, huh?

ERWIN. No. I mean I should have been at the office this morning.

HARRY. Oh.

CHARLIE. We could play it like this—say we put two dollars on Rose Cross to win— then we put—now let's see . . .

HARRY. I guess you can always do what you like when you're in business for yourself.

ERWIN. Gosh, sometimes I wish I was in business for myself.

HARRY. I thought you was.

ERWIN. No, that's the trouble. I should have been at the office a long time ago. Let me have another drink.

HARRY. It's none of my business, brother, but don't you think you should go to the office while you're able to navigate?

ERWIN. (*Waves idea aside.*) I don't think I'll ever go to the office again. (*Rests chin on elbow at bar as his attention is drawn to table.*)

HARRY. Oh. (*As if to say "It's as bad as that."*)

CHARLIE. Maybe we should pass up the third. Does anything look good in the fourth?

HARRY. (*To* ERWIN.) They been sittin' there for an hour tryin' to decide on a horse to play.

ERWIN. Do you know them?

HARRY. Sure. They live in this hotel.

ERWIN. Do you think they'd mind if I gave them a horse?

HARRY. What's that again?

ERWIN. I said, do you think they would mind if I gave them a tip on the third race?

HARRY. Do you play the horses, too?

ERWIN. Me? No.

HARRY. Oh. Well, you see they're down to twelve bucks and I think it might be better if they made a choice themselves—because if they lost they wouldn't feel so good.

ERWIN. You mean they wouldn't like me?

HARRY. That's it.

FRANKIE. (ERWIN *turns. Throws down racing paper.*) Aw, Hell, do what you like, Charlie. I don't see anything good. I think I'll wait for Patsy. He might have somethin'.

CHARLIE. All right. I'm playin' Rose Cross.

ERWIN. (*Looks in book. Weaves to table.*) Excuse me, gentlemen, I see you're interested in horses. You should play Semester in the third race.

CHARLIE. Yeah.

FRANKIE. Wheredja get that?

ERWIN. Oh, I have it right here.

FRANKIE. Semester ain't rated much with the boys.

HARRY. Hey! You better come back here and finish your drink.

CHARLIE. One of them long shot guys.

FRANKIE. Looks like a nut.

CHARLIE. Say, Harry, you better see if he can pay for his drinks. He might want to pay you with a tip.

ERWIN. You fellows have the wrong opinion of me. I was just trying to do you a favor. (*Pulls bill out of wallet.*) Look, twenty dollars. I can pay for more drinks than I ever drank in my whole life. (*To* HARRY.) Don't get me wrong. I don't drink much. But, did you ever feel blue?

HARRY. Sure. Lots of times.

ERWIN. That's just the way I feel today. I got off the bus—and I just didn't care any more—I should be at the office—but my wife and brother-in-law—you married?

HARRY. No.

ERWIN. Then you haven't got a brother-in-law. I got off the bus and I started for the office—and then I just didn't care any more.

CHARLIE. I'll put a dollar to win and one to show. Rose Cross.

FRANKIE. It's your six bucks, not mine. (CHARLIE *starts for booth.*)

ERWIN. You should really play Semester.

CHARLIE. If it's all the same to you, Pal, I'll play Rose Cross. (*Goes into booth.*)

ERWIN. (*Back to* HARRY.) That's the trouble. Nobody pays much attention to me. I think I'll have another drink. (HARRY *pours drink.*) Say, Harry . . . your name is Harry, isn't it?

HARRY. Yes.

ERWIN. (*Patting* HARRY *on shoulder.*) You are a very understanding sort of fellow— How would *you* like to play Semester in the third race just to see what would happen?

HARRY. (*Laughs.*) I know what would happen.

ERWIN. Don't you bet on horses?

HARRY. Say, I wouldn't bet on a horse if I was ridin' him myself.

CHARLIE. Just got it down in time. (*Returns to table.*)

ERWIN. Harry, you're a gentleman. I'd like to see you make some money.

HARRY. So would I.

ERWIN. (*Takes out book.*) Now let's see what I have for the fourth race.

PATSY. (*Enters from street. He is very dapper in a blue suit, grey suede shoes and light hat. He has an air of authority.*) Hello, Harry.

HARRY. Hello, Patsy. The boys was worried about you.

PATSY. (*Sits.*) I been all over town. Interestin' how many guys never heard of you before when they know you lost your roll. Well, Frankie, what did you do?

FRANKIE. Nothin'.

CHARLIE. Frankie was waitin' to see if you knew somethin' good. I just played two bucks on Rose Cross.

PATSY. Two bucks?

CHARLIE. We only got twelve between us. Did you get much on your buckle?

PATSY. Couple bucks. Mabel come in yet?

CHARLIE. No—an' I called her room for you.

PATSY. Thanks. She's trying to raise something too.

ERWIN. (*Weaving to table.*) I was telling them they should play Semester in the third race.

PATSY. (*To boys.*) Who's he?

CHARLIE. Just some drunk.

ERWIN. (*Standing in the middle of the room. More to himself.*) Semester in the third. Hasty Belle in the fourth. (*Suddenly he feels sick.*)

HARRY. Hey—right back in there, brother.

ERWIN. Oh. (*Heads for lavatory. Exits. Phone rings.* HARRY *shuts door after him.*)

HARRY. Geez, the country's full of amateurs. That guy shouldn't drink much.

CHARLIE. That's Gus. (*Goes into booth.*)

PATSY. He don't look like a drinker to me.

FRANKIE. He looks like a goof.

HARRY. No. He's a nice guy.

CHARLIE. (*Comes out of booth.*) Well, I'll be hit on the nose.

PATSY. What's the matter?

CHARLIE. Guess who won that race—Semester.

PATSY. Well, what about it?

CHARLIE. Didn't you hear him? He's been trying to give us Semester for the last ten minutes.

FRANKIE. Say, how did that guy know?

HARRY. He kept looking in a little book—

PATSY. What book?

HARRY. Here it is. This book.

PATSY. (*Crosses to bar.*) Let's see. (*Takes book.* CHARLIE *and* FRANKIE *follow.*) Geez —he's got them all figured out.

CHARLIE. What do you mean figured out?

PATSY. Here's yesterday's winners, and the day before—pages of races— My God, he's got Brass Monkey for today—he come in— so did Fairweather and Semester.

FRANKIE. Aw, he maybe wrote them down after the races was run.

HARRY. Wrote them down nuts. I heard him tell you to bet Semester before you got the result.

CHARLIE. Yeah, that's right.

FRANKIE. (*Leans on bar.*) Maybe he's a handicapper.

PATSY. Now you know he don't look like a handicapper.

HARRY. He said somethin' about workin' in an office.

CHARLIE. What's he got for the fourth?

PATSY. Hasty Belle. He's got the fourth, fifth, sixth, seventh and eighth figured out.

FRANKIE. Hasty Belle, huh, maybe we ought to lay two bucks on him.

PATSY. Two bucks, nothin'. We'll play the works. (FRANKIE *takes book.*)

CHARLIE. Wait a minute! Maybe it's a new kind of a racket.

PATSY. To Hell with that. How much you got?

CHARLIE. I still got four bucks. I ain't been any place.

FRANKIE. I got six left.

PATSY. And I got eight. (*Pulls out money.*) You put up your ten between you, that's eighteen bucks altogether. You take it around to Gus, Frankie, while this guy's in there.

FRANKIE. But we don't know anything about him.

PATSY. Maybe he runs a service or somethin'. You go on around and I'll go in and talk to him.

HARRY. I'll bet he's sick as a pup.

PATSY. What the Hell do I care.

FRANKIE. But suppose the horse loses.

PATSY. If he does Mabel will be in with some dough in time for the next race. It wouldn't be the first time we ever lost, would it? Now you go on around and I'll keep this guy busy in here. (*Going toward* "MEN.")

FRANKIE. (*Up steps.*) All right. What's the name of the horse again?

PATSY. Hasty Belle.

FRANKIE. (*On landing.*) I'll lay the eighteen bucks, but I ain't responsible if this goat don't come in. (*He goes.*)

HARRY. He kept tryin' to give *me* a horse.

PATSY. I'll see if he's still conscious. (*Exits.*)

HARRY. (CHARLIE *sits at table.*) It will be interestin' to know what the Hell this is all about. He kept askin' me if I was married—now what would that have to do with horses? Hey, I don't want to forget to collect for those drinks.

MABEL. (*Enters from street. She is an ex-Follies girl. A little faded and quite dumb.*) Hello, boys.

CHARLIE. H'ya Mabel.

MABEL. Patsy told me to meet him here. We had some business to talk over.

CHARLIE. That's all right, Mabel, we know where you been.

MABEL. (*Sitting at the table.*) Kinda embarrassing, isn't it, to always be hockin' things. Well, it's all over now. I haven't anything left to hock except the dress I got on. It wouldn't be worth much. . . . I couldn't hock it anyway because I haven't anything else left to wear . . . you know in case I had to go out some place.

CHARLIE. Oh, I think you can keep that, Mabel.

MABEL. Hasn't Patsy come in yet?

CHARLIE. Sure, he's come in. He's in there. (*Gestures with thumb.*)

MABEL. Oh! I'll wait for him then.

CHARLIE. He's pretty busy.

MABEL. Sure, I guess he is.

CHARLIE. I mean he's got somebody with him.

MABEL. Somebody with him—in the—in there?

CHARLIE. Yeah—some guy.

MABEL. What kind of a guy, Charlie?

CHARLIE. Oh, he's all right. He's a friend of Patsy's.

MABEL. Do I know him?

CHARLIE. I don't think so. You see—he knew Patsy in the old days—you know—and he heard how the luck was—and . . . and—he just dropped in to tip Patsy off on some fixed races so Patsy could get straightened out. Isn't that right, Harry?

HARRY. That sounds all right, Charlie.

MABEL. You mean he fixes them?

CHARLIE. Yeah, that's it . . . he fixes them.

MABEL. But why are they in the Johnnie?

CHARLIE. Well, he got sick from the heat and some bum liquor. . . . I mean he ain't used to drinkin'. Patsy used to be his best friend— He's holding his head. (MOSES *stops elevator and steps out.* MOSES *is the colored elevator boy. He is quite a big boy. About twenty-eight.*)

FRANKIE. (*Enters.*) I put in that bet. Hello, Mabel.

MABEL. Hello—

FRANKIE. Where are they?

MABEL. They're in the Johnnie.

MOSES. One pint rye, bottle ginger ale. (*Looks at table.*) Good afternoon.

FRANKIE. (*Sitting at table.*) Hello, Moses—

MOSES. How is the horses?

CHARLIE. O. K. How are the numbers?

MOSES. (*As he goes to bar.*) Fine and dandy. I is playin' a combination I seen on a two dollar bill today. I just see it.

HARRY. (*Gives him order.*) Somebody havin' a party?

MOSES. The couple in three twelve just wakin' up— (*Going back with tray.*) Mr. Charlie, I was on the third floor and the maid asked me if it was all right to make up your room and I said yeah— (*Goes into elevator.*)

CHARLIE. Thanks, Moses.

PATSY. (*Enters.*) He's pretty sick. Did you lay the bets, Frankie?

FRANKIE. On the nose.

PATSY. That's right. Well, Mabel, how did you make out.

MABEL. (*Rising and crossing to* PATSY.) I went down to this place on Eighth Avenue like you told me and I unwrapped the dresses . . .

PATSY. Yeah?

MABEL. . . . which were very good as you recall . . . and he said they wasn't so good and I told him they was and then he said they was out of style and I showed him the price tags with the date on which was only last week and he said, "How much do you want?" and I said, "How much do you think they're worth?" and he said that isn't the question, he said he might be able to sell them for forty dollars but that they was only worth eight dollars to him and I said that wasn't the right attitude to take and he said, "The Hell with the attitude, will you take the eight bucks?"

PATSY. Did you take it?

MABEL. Yes.

PATSY. Good.

MABEL. (*Gives him money.*) Then I asked somebody on the street where I could sell a parasol with a gold head and they said I would have to go to the assay office and I said I wouldn't do that. (*Crosses; pushes elevator bell.*)

CHARLIE. Ertznay . . . you can sell that any place.

FRANKIE. Gold? Certainly you can sell that any place. That's the basic metal, ain't it?

PATSY. Frankie, take this eight bucks and put it on More Anon in the fifth.

CHARLIE. More Anon?

FRANKIE. (*As he crosses to* PATSY.) But we don't know the results of the fourth yet or anything. How do we know—

PATSY. I know a lot now. I been talkin' to him.

FRANKIE. All right then, if you're sure. (*Starts to go.*) The fourth is on pretty soon.

PATSY. We'll call up. (FRANKIE *goes up the stairs. Elevator door opens.*)

MOSES. Goin' up?

MABEL. Yeah, my feet are tired. I'm goin' up to change my shoes, Patsy. Gee, honey, I think it's swell about this friend of yours fixin' the races for us so we can get a roll again.

PATSY. Yeah . . . yeah. . . . Sweetheart, ain't that somethin'. We'll see you later then.

MABEL. All right. (*Goes. Elevator rises.*)

PATSY. What didja tell her, Charlie, so I'll know?

CHARLIE. I told her he was a friend of yours who was fixin' some races for you because he heard how you was broke . . . you two is old buddies . . . he used to be your best friend.

PATSY. (ERWIN *enters.* PATSY *goes to him.*) How do you feel now, Erwin? (*Turns to boys.*) His name is Erwin.

HARRY. I knew it would be somethin' like that.

ERWIN. (PATSY *leads him to chair.*) I think I feel a little bit better now.

PATSY. (CHARLIE *rises.*) Sit down in this nice chair.

CHARLIE. I hope he don't have to leave soon.

PATSY. He's not leavin'. He's stayin' here 'til he gets straightened out.

ERWIN. I forgot to pay for the drinks.

HARRY. (*Coming around to him.*) Aw, that's all right.

ERWIN. How much is it?

HARRY. One dollar, even.

ERWIN. Can you break a twenty?

HARRY. Sure. (*Takes bill to register.*)

FRANKIE. (*Enters. Crosses right to phone booth; speaks while he dials.*) The bets are in. I'm calling Gus. It's post time for the fourth. (*Dials phone leaving booth door open.*)

PATSY. We had a long talk. His name is Erwin somebody. He picks those horses for fun. He says it's a hobby.

CHARLIE. Hobby, huh?

FRANKIE. Hello, Gus . . . this is Frankie. Hasty Belle is four to one . . . yeah, Gus . . . ?

HARRY. (*Brings change to* ERWIN.) Gee, I hope he's not a nut, you know how a guy can get about horses.

FRANKIE. Yeah, Gus, I'm here . . . they're at the quarter—

HARRY. Here's your change.

ERWIN. Thanks. (HARRY *goes back to bar.*)

FRANKIE. Yeah, Yeah, Joybird . . . Little Lie . . . Post Script I got it . . . Hasty Belle in that order . . .

PATSY. This is the fourth.

CHARLIE. The one Hasty Belle is in.

PATSY. He ain't done much this season.

CHARLIE. Yeah, I know.

ERWIN. (*Opens eyes.*) What's the matter?

PATSY. (*Crosses to both.*) Horse race.

FRANKIE. Joybird up at the half . . . Who comes up? . . . Little Lie . . . Now Post Script . . . neck and neck . . . yes . . . still that way? . . . They're in the stretch . . . yes, yes . . . He's past (*Turning to others.*) he's past . . . (*Back to telephone.*) who's past? . . . Joybird? Hasty Belle . . . passes Joybird . . . she does. (*Hangs up, turns to others.*) Hasty Belle wins!!

CHARLIE. Hasty Belle wins.

PATSY. Huh?

ERWIN. What's the matter?

CHARLIE. Hasty Belle wins.

ERWIN. What do you know about that.

CHARLIE. (*Looks at sheet.*) He ran out of the money last five starts.

PATSY. (*Crossing to bar. Looks at ceiling.*) Boy! (*Suddenly* FRANKIE, CHARLIE *and* PATSY *look at* ERWIN.)

ERWIN. (*Embarrassed.*) Well, he won. (*Searches pocket.*) Where is my little book?

FRANKIE. (*Across table.*) I was holdin' it for you.

ERWIN. Just make a check beside Hasty Belle.

HARRY. Here, I'll buy you a drink. (*Puts glass on bar.*)

ERWIN. I'm not sure I can drink any more.

PATSY. Sure you can. Frankie, collect and put it all on Rip Van Winkle.

FRANKIE. I'll put up the same amount for the three of us. (*Exits.*)

PATSY. (*Pacing back and forth.*) That's the idea—that bracelet don't suit Mabel so hot anyways. I think I'll get her a platinum wrist watch. Don't you want to bet, Erwin?

ERWIN. I never bet.

PATSY. You don't?

ERWIN. No.

ERWIN. I just spent forty-eight dollars.

HARRY. No in here.

ERWIN. No, before I left home. Forty-eight dollars. Now I'm not going fishing. Forty-eight dollars and he's going to buy a platinum rich wast. Women. It's all the same, isn't it, no matter how you look at it?

HARRY. Sure, it's all the same.

ERWIN. (*Rises.*) Well, I think I'll go.

PATSY. Where you goin'?

ERWIN. Oh, I have to be at the office.

CHARLIE. (*Rises to them.*) You can't go to any office like that. (*Turning* ERWIN.)

HARRY. You'll lose your job.

PATSY. Sure. You work, huh? Everybody's goin' to go home pretty soon.

ERWIN. Huh?

PATSY. People who work in offices will be goin' home pretty soon.

ERWIN. Mr. Carver would still be there. He'll be waiting for me.

PATSY. (*Sits. Seats* ERWIN. CHARLIE *stands.*) Sit down a second, I want to talk to you— How much do you make a week?

ERWIN. Well, I get regular forty dollars and then there's extra. At fifty cents a line sometimes I sell stuff and that brings it up to forty-six or fifty some weeks not counting the postage stamps and the envelopes and maybe this week it might come to forty-nine.

CHARLIE. (*Sits.*) Don't you want to wait and see how these races come out?

ERWIN. Oh, no. I can look at the results on my way home.

PATSY. (*Sits.*) So you make about fifty bucks a week. That's eight-fifty a day. Now why don't you stay here and I'll give you ten per cent on everything I play and Charlie and Frankie will too.

CHARLIE. Sure.

ERWIN. That sounds all right as far as the money is concerned—

PATSY. What's the matter? We bet on horses, that's our business, but you like to pick them—so we pay you for it—if we bet, say, twenty dollars on a horse and he pays back say, eight to one . . . we get one hundred and sixty dollars—you get sixteen dollars . . . ten per cent . . . that's about twice as much as you'd make if you worked all day.

CHARLIE. You see—we take a chance too, suppose the horse loses?

ERWIN. (*Rises.*) Yes . . . but I don't think I want to stay here.

PATSY. Why not . . you can't go to the office like that. We'll call up.

CHARLIE. What's the number, Erwin? I'll call him—

ERWIN. B. O. four six seven five two.

PATSY. I'll call your boss and tell him you won't be in.

HARRY. I guess he knows that by now.

CHARLIE. We'll tell him anyway.

PATSY. We'll tell him you don't feel good. (*Going to phone.*) Charlie. (*Dialing.*) Who shall I ask for?

ERWIN. Mr. J. G. Carver.

CHARLIE. (*Into phone.*) Mr. Carver please Oh, you're Mr. Carver—well, Mr. Carver, (*To* ERWIN.) What's your last name. Erwin?

ERWIN. Trowbridge.

CHARLIE. (*Into phone.*) Erwin Trowbridge won't be in today . . . (ERWIN *rises—*PATSY *seats him.*) he got sick on his way to the office . . . yeah . . . terrible . . . he's in the drug store now . . . been here for a long time . . . we been workin' over him . . . Me! I'm the pharmacist . . . yeah . . . What . . . I'll tell him. Goodbye. (*Hangs up—sits left of* ERWIN.) He says that's O. K. because there wouldn't be no use comin' in this late anyways. He says as long as you can get your work done by tomorrow that's jake by him. If you don't feel so hot tomorrow you better send them anyways. Does that make sense to you?

ERWIN. Yes. I should get those verses written.

PATSY. You a song writer?

ERWIN. No. Greeting verse. I'm late for Mother's Day.

PATSY. You're what?

ERWIN. I have to catch up on Mother's Day.

PATSY. We understand, Erwin. You got an aspirin, Harry? (*Turning to bar.*)

HARRY. (*Passes aspirin.*) Sure.

PATSY. Now you just sit there and relax.

HARRY. On the house. (*As he gives* PATSY *an aspirin and glass of water.*)

CHARLIE. I'll give it to him. (*Takes them.*)

FRANKIE. (*Runs in.*) Hey, listen, what do you think—I played the fifth . . . one-two-three . . . like in the book.

PATSY. Yeah . . . yeah . . . so what?

FRANKIE. They come in.

PATSY. One-two-three?

FRANKIE. One-two-three.

CHARLIE. Can you top that?

PATSY. You hear that, Erwin? Go on take it down. What's a headache to you, eh, Erwin? You're makin' money. (*Pounding* ERWIN *on back.*)

ERWIN. Have I made eight-fifty yet? (*Almost choking.*)

PATSY. Eight-fifty! About eighty-eight-fifty. (CHARLIE *returns to bar with glass and sips as he crosses.*) How much you bet altogether, Frankie?

FRANKIE. (*Looking in book.* PATSY *with* FRANKIE.) Let's see—I got back on the fifth at ten each eighty-four and forty-one and fifteen, that's one hundred and forty dollars each, plus what we got on Hasty Belle, that we played on More Anon. Altogether that brings a total of two hundred and forty-five dollars each.

CHARLIE. There ain't that much money. Harry, could you make up a turkey sandwich?

HARRY. (*At bar.*) I haven't sold a turkey sandwich in a week. How about cheese?

PATSY. We ain't got time to fool around with food.

FRANKIE. We ought to play all the races one-two-three.

PATSY. Erwin's only got the fifth figured that way. Let's see the sheets, Frankie. (*They start looking at the handicap sheets.*)

ERWIN. (*Who has been sitting with head in hands.*) Could I have a pencil?

PATSY. (*First looking at boys.*) Sure, sure, Erwin, here's a pencil.

CHARLIE. Here's some paper—

ERWIN. (*Searching through clothes.*) Thanks, I have some paper. (ERWIN *goes to work writing rapidly.*)

PATSY. Got a flash, hey Erwin?

CHARLIE. (*Tapping* PATSY's *arms as the three retreat upstage.*) We better not talk much.

FRANKIE. (*Whispering.*) I been looking through the book and I see Erwin has a record of parlays but he ain't got none for today.

CHARLIE. (*Holds up hand.*) Look, he's got somethin' hot.

PATSY. What you got, Erwin?

ERWIN. (*More to himself.*) I got one.

FRANKIE. Let's have it.

ERWIN. What?

PATSY. (*Slowly returning.*) Let's hear what you got.

ERWIN. Oh. No. You wouldn't be interested in this.

CHARLIE. (*Coming down.*) Sure we would. Let's hear it.

ERWIN. (PATSY *and* CHARLIE *sink down into chairs on each side.*) Well, I think it will do. Here it is.
   "At Christmas Tide your hair was grey
   But memories chased your cares away
   Now lovingly in my simple way
   I send you love on Mother's Day."
Mother's Day Number Sixteen.

PATSY. Yeah . . . yeah . . . that's all right, Erwin. That's elegant — what is that, Erwin?

ERWIN. That's a Mother's Day verse.

PATSY. You mean you just thought that up?

ERWIN. Yes.

PATSY. Since you been sittin' there?

ERWIN. Sure.

PATSY. Geez, can you imagine that, Frankie?

FRANKIE. (*Turns to* HARRY.) Weird, ain't it?

CHARLIE. (*Stands.*) Why don't you ask him about the horses?

PATSY. We thought you was figurin' some parlay. You know, like you have in your book.

ERWIN. No, sir. I have work to do. (*Rises.*) I have fifty more of those to do. How did that one sound? All right?

CHARLIE. (*Pats him.*) That was the nuts. I wish you'd dope out some parlays . . . you know . . . just for fun.

PATSY. (*Knocks* CHARLIE's *arm down.*) Leave him alone—leave him alone—let him do whatever he wants. (*Seats him down— pushes down.*) You go ahead, Erwin, write some more of them Mother's Day gags. . . . Where's the roll, Frankie? (*Sits.*)

FRANKIE. Here. (*Puts bills on table.*)

CHARLIE. (*Muses.*) You know I like that. (*Sits.*) "At Christmas Tide your hair was grey."

PATSY. Suppose you run down and wait around and get paid off on the sixth.

FRANKIE. O. K. Patsy. I don't mind at all. (*He goes off street door.* MABEL *enters from elevator.*)

PATSY. (MABEL *crosses to* PATSY.) Mabel, guess what I got for you. Look. (*Gives her money.*) You can go next door and get your bracelet out of hock.

MABEL. No foolin'. Are you sure if I get it out I won't have to put it back in the morning? I only hocked it yesterday and I'd feel so funny if I put it back in to-morrow.

PATSY. Sugar, you won't ever have to hock that bracelet again. Oh, Mabel, this is Erwin. Erwin is here to give us a helping hand.

MABEL. Pleased to meet you.

ERWIN. How do you do?

MABEL. (*Sits on* PATSY's *knees.*) Charlie was telling me about you, how you're going to fix the races just for us. I think it's just wonderful.

HARRY. Hey, Patsy, how about settin' 'em up. I'm supposed to work here.

PATSY. Sure, Harry, rye for me, same for Erwin.

CHARLIE. Same here.

MABEL. Rye with plenty of ginger ale—I haven't been eatin' regular lately—I don't want to get tight.

PATSY. You're going to eat tonight, Mabel.

MABEL. (*Goes to* ERWIN.) Gee, I'm glad you looked us up.

ERWIN. "When I was young and on your knee—"

MABEL. What?

CHARLIE. Sh-sh.

PATSY. Did you say somethin', Erwin?

ERWIN. How does that sound?
"When I was young and on your knee
You told a nursery rhyme to me
But now I've grown a man to be
I send my Love in rhyme to Thee."
(*Writes it down.*) Mother's Day Number Seventeen.

MABEL. What is that?

PATSY. (*Both rise, cross down right.*) It's kind of hard to explain. (*Embarrassed to think he is associating with a sentimental verse writer.*) That's a sort of a code. (*Rise.*)

HARRY. There yuh are.

MABEL. Huh!

PATSY. A message.

MABEL. Gee, Patsy, this is swell—it's like —it's like spies talk in that magazine story I was readin'— (HARRY *puts drink on bar.*) now what was the name of that—

HARRY. Here we are. (*Serves drinks.*)

PATSY. Mabel, how would you like to go to the Follies tonight?

MABEL. I don't know. Let's go somewheres else. There's none of the old crowd in it at all any more.

PATSY. Bet you could get back if you wanted to.

MABEL. Do you really think so, Patsy?

PATSY. Sure— (*Pats her hip.*) Take off a few pounds—you know—here and there. It would be a cinch. Here you are, Harry. (*Gives him bill.*) But I got other plans for you, Mabel. You don't want to be tied down. How do we know where we'll be— New Orleans, Lexington, Chicago— (HARRY *rings cash register.*)

MABEL. How do you mean, Patsy? (*Crosses to* PATSY.)

PATSY. That depends on what agreement me and Erwin can come to. (*Walks to street door with* MABEL.) Now you run upstairs and get your bracelet out and we'll celebrate tonight. Just you and me. How would that be? We'll get dressed and have dinner at Moore's and make a night of it.

MABEL. Get dressed—all right—but this is the only dress I got.

PATSY. Get another one. (*Pats her behind. Gives her money.*) Happy days are here again, huh, Mabel. (MABEL *goes out the street door.* PATSY *returns to bar.*) She's as happy as a kid. Buy Erwin another drink, Harry—on me.

CHARLIE. (*Watching* ERWIN *write.*) How many of them things do you have to write?

ERWIN. Fifty more.

CHARLIE. This week?

ERWIN. By tomorrow.

PATSY. Do you think you can do it?

ERWIN. I have to—my job.

PATSY. Job—huh—say, I bet you'll retire on these ten per cents. (*He crosses—pushes elevator bell.*)

FRANKIE. (*Runs in.*) I got the sixth.

CHARLIE. The sixth. (*Ad lib.*)

FRANKIE. He come in— (*Tosses bills on table.*)

PATSY. It ain't true. Look at that, Erwin. Your brains did that. Don't that make you excited? (*Sits at the table down left.*)

ERWIN. There's a lot of money there, I guess. I can see some twenty-dollar bills.

FRANKIE. (HARRY *starts left with drink for* ERWIN *and change for* PATSY.) Twenties, huh? I bet ten each like I said. My Blaze paid back six-sixty for two so that was thirty-three dollars each and Rip Van Winkle paid seven-forty for two. That comes to— (HARRY *sets drink before* ERWIN.)

PATSY. Five times seven-forty.

CHARLIE. (*Excited.*) Thirty-seven . . .

FRANKIE. Altogether it comes to seventy dollars each.

PATSY. Now you get seven dollars from me plus what you got before and you get the same from Frankie and Charlie too. That's as much as you'd make in a week writing them Mother's Day Number Fifteens. (*Elevator stops.*)

MOSES. Goin' up?

PATSY. You count out the dough, Charlie, I'll be right back. I'm going to celebrate and pay my bill. (*Exits into elevator.*)

CHARLIE. (*Crosses bar.*) That's ten for Frank—ten for Patsy—ten for me. (*Continues this silently as* MABEL *comes in from street.*)

MABEL. (*Enters, sits right.*) I got my bracelet out. (*Holding up arm.*) Hello! Where's Patsy?

CHARLIE. He'll be right back. He went to pay the hotel bill.

MABEL. What bank was all this in?

CHARLIE. Horses.

MABEL. (*Sits and looks at* ERWIN *with genuine admiration. He sips drink.*) You mean you won all this since I left, Erwin?

CHARLIE. This is just from the sixth race.

MABEL. Gee, that must take a lot of nerve —to fix races.

ERWIN. Oh, I don't know.

MABEL. How long did it take you?

ERWIN. About an hour.

MABEL. (*Sits.*) How did you get in this racket, Erwin? On account of Repeal? I'll bet you were making out all right before. I'd never think you were in rackets if I didn't see you here with Patsy and the boys and that roll there. I'll bet you never have to worry about making a living.

FRANKIE. (*Going to bar.*) How about a drink for everybody?

MABEL. Sure.

CHARLIE. O. K.

ERWIN. I don't think I could drink any more.

FRANKIE. I'm buying them. We ought to celebrate.

ERWIN. But I don't feel so good.

MABEL. It wouldn't be any fun if you don't drink too—on account of we'll really be drinking to you—you know what I mean —fixing the races and all that.

ERWIN. All right then. (*Elevator opens.*)

FRANKIE. Four drinks.

PATSY. (*Enters from elevator.*) Make it five. (*Points to bills.*) How's that look to you, Mabel? This mine, Charlie? (*Picking pile off table.*)

CHARLIE. That's yours.

PATSY. (*Going to* MABEL.) That's fine. Mabel, let's see your bracelet. You and me is going to be back in circulation tonight. How's about it?

HARRY. (*Serves drinks.*) Here we are.

MABEL. It feels like old times again, huh, Patsy? I was just saying we ought to drink this to Erwin because he's helping us out like this. Come on, Erwin . . . bottoms up. (*They all drink.*)

ERWIN. Oh, sure. (*He drinks.*)

PATSY. Sugar, suppose you go along and start to get dolled up, and knock on my door when you're ready.

MABEL. All right, Patsy. Well, goodbye. . . . (*As she starts to elevator* ERWIN *rises, attempts to bow, collapses again.*) Oh, Patsy, I saw a dress in a window I want to show you later on.

PATSY. Anything you say goes, Mabel . . . dress, coat, hat . . . I might even name a horse after you.

MABEL. Goodbye, Erwin. (*Elevator door closes.*)

PATSY. Say, do you guys realize how lucky we are? Twenty-four hours ago we owed ourselves money . . . now look at us . . . we got the makings of a million-dollar bank roll. But we got to keep our mouths shut and Erwin has to play along with us. You hear that, Erwin? (*Drops arm.*) Geez, he's passed out.

HARRY. What did you think he was, a sponge?

PATSY. Listen, Harry. He's staying here with us tonight. Then he can pick the entries for tomorrow's races, get it?

HARRY. Sure, I get it.

CHARLIE. (*Rises and fans* ERWIN *with racing sheets.*) Hey, you don't think we'll get in any trouble, do you?

PATSY. Trouble? We're doing him a favor. My God, he's been working for fifty cents a line and here he's already made as much as he would in a week. Ring for the elevator, Charlie.

FRANKIE. But suppose something . . . (ERWIN *topples from chair, they grab him.*) Is he all right? (HARRY *goes to* ERWIN.)

PATSY. He's all right. He just passed out. Hey Harry?

HARRY. Yeah. Yeah. He'll be O. K. He'll be all right.

PATSY. (*Catching* HARRY'S *arm.*) Say, you're not going to say anything about this, are you, Harry?

HARRY. Hell, no. I just want you to play this five bucks for me on the last race. This is the first time I ever came face to face with a sure thing.

FRANKIE. But suppose somebody finds out about it?

PATSY. Say, what's the matter with you guys? You got a yellow streak all of a sudden? He should be tickled to death. We're giving him a break. Suppose Leo's crowd had ever discovered him? He'd never see his wife again. They'd take him from track to track like a horse.

CHARLIE. I guess that's right.

PATSY. All we want to do is run up a bank roll, then to hell with the bookies . . . I'm going to get myself a stable and do this thing right.

MOSES. Goin' up.

PATSY. Here, give us a hand, will you, boys? (*Ad libs.*) Moses, he's a friend of ours just passed out. He's staying in my room tonight. (*Ad libs as they put* ERWIN *in the elevator.*)

CURTAIN.

ACT TWO

SCENE I

Place: Ozone Heights.

Time: The next morning.

ORCHESTRA *plays "Just a Love Nest" before curtain goes up and as it rises.*

At Rise: AUDREY *sits alone, trying not to cry. She wipes her eyes, bites her lip, hits the pillow of divan with her fist. The phone rings. She leaps to her feet and rushes to it.*

AUDREY. (*In phone.*) Hello. (*Disappointedly.*) Oh, yes, good morning, Mrs. Marple. We'd be delighted—at least I think we would—well, I can't ask him just now —he isn't here— Well, he didn't come home last night—oh, no—nothing wrong (*Sniff.*) —only he just didn't come home— business of course. . . . He and Mr. Carver . . . that's his boss—they have so many things to talk over, I suppose . . . and I'll ask him if he comes home today— Oh, yes, of course he'll be here—I just slipped. Thank you, Mrs. Marple. (*Hangs up.*) Oh, Erwin—where are you? (CLARENCE *enters aggressively.*)

CLARENCE. Showed up yet? (*She shakes her head.*) Didn't even phone. (*Shakes her head.*) Didn't hear from him at all, huh?

AUDREY. (*Between sobs.*) Mrs. Marple phoned . . .

CLARENCE. Yes?

AUDREY. Invited us to a party, but he may not even be here. (*Sobs.*)

CLARENCE. Well, if he isn't, I'll go with you.

AUDREY. Oh, dear. (*Sobs worse.*)

CLARENCE. (*Walks.*) He's the last fellow in the world I'd expect to do such a thing.

AUDREY. Do what thing?

CLARENCE. But in a way, I always knew he was that kind.

AUDREY. What are you talking about?

CLARENCE. Did you phone him at the office?

AUDREY. Erwin doesn't like me to phone his office.

CLARENCE. (*To phone.*) That's just a gag. What's his number? Huh. I can see through that. (*At desk.*) This it?

AUDREY. He won't like it.

CLARENCE. (*Grimly.*) This is just one of the things he isn't going to like. (*In phone.*) Bogardus four six seven five two. I've got quite a few surprising revelations for you.

AUDREY. I don't want any revelations. I just want Erwin.

CLARENCE. (*Sits. In phone.*) I'd like to speak to Mr. Trowbridge—please—Erwin Trowbridge. No? Is that so? . . . Oh, he didn't. I thank you very much—

AUDREY. What did they say?

CLARENCE. (*Rising.*) Mr. Carver isn't there.

AUDREY. Oh, Clarence—I don't care anything about Mr. Carver.

CLARENCE. Neither is Erwin. What's more he didn't come to work at all yesterday.

AUDREY. It's all my fault.

CLARENCE. What do you mean? It's all your fault?

AUDREY. I shouldn't have bought those dresses. I knew he wouldn't like it.

CLARENCE. Oh, what right has a worm like that to object anyhow?

AUDREY. (*With tearful dignity.*) Erwin is not a worm—I don't like you to say such things about him.

CLARENCE. I told you not to marry him. Didn't I? Remember what I said to you? I said—"Don't marry him." You were stubborn. All right. I won't say anything about it. It's all past now. You could have married Charley Blanchard, don't forget that—I spotted him as a comer at the first Kiwanis luncheon and where is he now? Seventy-five dollars a week and one per cent of all sales on his hardware accessories in greater New York and northern New Jersey. And where is Erwin?

AUDREY. (*Sobbing.*) I don't know—I wish I did— Oh, Erwin!

CLARENCE. I'll tell you then—he's left you.

AUDREY. He has not.

CLARENCE. I had a feeling there was something funny about him when he went out of here. He wouldn't look me in the eye.

AUDREY. That wasn't it at all.

CLARENCE. He kept turning away from me.

AUDREY. He doesn't like to look at you—he told me so.

CLARENCE. I might have known he'd treat us like that. I help him along—I let him have a house on easy payment plan—do everything I can for him—does he come to me with a good thing? No—just quietly makes his little cleaning and then leaves us all flat.

AUDREY. What are you talking about?

CLARENCE. Brass Monkey won yesterday.

AUDREY. Who's Brass Monkey?

CLARENCE. The horse— He had a sure tip. That little book of his was full of sure tips. He's been cleaning up. (*Crossing to AUDREY.*) All the time he's been playing poor and talking about how he couldn't afford things, he's been rich—he's had winnings enough in the last few weeks to spend the rest of his life loafing— He's got deposits in a dozen banks—when I saw that little book yesterday it all came across me clear—in fact I went down to the bookies in the afternoon to put a thousand dollars on Brass Monkey and then I was afraid of some trickery and I changed my mind. God damn it.

AUDREY. Why Clarence, I never heard you swear before.

CLARENCE. But the worm had his roll on that race—he had every cent—and he cleaned up and you'll never see him again.

AUDREY. You don't understand him—you don't understand him at all.

CLARENCE. Why couldn't he have come to me as man to man and told me about it? That would have been the thing to do— No, but he's selfish—keeps it all to himself —wouldn't look me in the eye—I knew something was wrong— Eight to one it paid—but that worm held out on me.

AUDREY. He's not a worm. (*Violent.*) You shut up. You treat him awful. (*Telephone rings.* AUDREY *crosses to it.*) And I don't blame him for getting mad—and he never liked living in your old house anyhow. (AUDREY *answers it.*) Yes?—Oh, oh Mr. Carver—yes, this is Mrs. Trowbridge— No, I—haven't. I don't know.

CLARENCE. Do you want me to talk to him?

AUDREY. He had the verses with him—a drug store? . . .

CLARENCE. What did he say?

AUDREY. Yes, of course I will. (*Hangs up.*) Mr. Carver is awful mad (*Rises.*) because the verses aren't there yet. He says Erwin telephoned him yesterday from a drug store

and said he didn't feel well— (*Looks up suddenly.*) He's lying in some hospital—sick—or in the back of some drug store. (*Picks up phone.*)

CLARENCE. What are you going to do?

AUDREY. (*In phone.*) Give me the Ozone Heights Police Department.

CLARENCE. Audrey!

AUDREY. Leave me alone. This is Mrs. Erwin Trowbridge. Number one Dobbins Drive. . . . I wish to report a missing person . . . yes, my husband . . . he didn't come home last night.

BLACKOUT.

Orchestra plays "All Alone."

SCENE II

Place: The hotel room.

Time: Noon next day. Room in the Lavillere Hotel. Door to elevator and hall up stage to left. Door to bathroom up stage right. Bed up stage right. Window above head of bed. Night table next to bed. Chifferobe down stage right. Closet down stage left. Telephone on table down stage left. Chairs, etc.

At Rise: ERWIN *is discovered in bed. He has on union suit. He sits up and groans.* CHARLIE *enters from bathroom with wet towel.*

CHARLIE. (*Crossing to* ERWIN.) How are you?

ERWIN. Where did everybody go?

CHARLIE. (*Places wet towel on* ERWIN's *forehead.*) Don't worry—they'll be back. How's that feel?

ERWIN. Pretty good—but I don't feel so good.

FRANKIE. (*Enters from door with tomato juice.* PATSY *follows him a beat later.*) Here, drink this.

PATSY. Drink it. (ERWIN *is bewildered.*) Drink all you can.

ERWIN. I don't think I can drink anything. (*Sighs.*) Oh, my head. What are all those papers on the floor?

CHARLIE. (*Picking them up.*) Those jingles of yours. Don't you remember? You wrote half the night.

FRANKIE. (*Picking too.*) Three-four-five.

ERWIN. How many did I do?

CHARLIE. I got twenty-two here.

FRANKIE. Six-seven-eight.

PATSY. There's about ten more in the bathroom.

ERWIN. I must have written nearly the whole sixty-seven.

CHARLIE. You certainly did.

ERWIN. I don't remember anything about it.

CHARLIE. You kept me awake the whole night.

PATSY. Feel better now?

ERWIN. (*Nods.*) Say, I must have gotten drunk. (*Looking around.*) Where am I?

PATSY. You're in the Lavillere Hotel. You passed out on us last night. We had to bring you up here.

ERWIN. What time is it?

CHARLIE. It's after twelve o'clock.

ERWIN. What! Thought you said it was daybreak. . . . I must go to the office. (*Starts to get out of bed.* PATSY *pushes him back, giving* CHARLIE *a dirty look.*)

CHARLIE. You can't get up now.

FRANKIE. Easy now, pal.

PATSY. You can't go to the office like that. You look like the devil. You'll lose your job.

ERWIN. But Mr. Carver must have these verses today.

PATSY. He'll have 'em today. One of us will take 'em around. There's nothin' to worry about— (*Winks at boys.*) —I just had him on the phone. He said if you don't feel good—you can stay in bed all day.

ERWIN. I guess I was in a bad way—you see I never drink. Where are my clothes?

CHARLIE. In the bathroom.

ERWIN. (*Looks at bathroom.*) I must go in there a minute. I feel better now that I know the verses are practically done. Do they look all right? (*Sits up.*)

CHARLIE. They're swell. I wish I could say things like that in poetry . . . especially if you're with a gal. It makes it romantic-like—sort of breaks the ice.

ERWIN. Oh, yes.

CHARLIE. You know, you don't want to start right off and say, "How about it, Baby?"

ERWIN. You better get a big envelope and put all the verses in and take them personally to Mr. Carver—he's waiting for them.

PATSY. You take them, Frankie.

FRANKIE. Where is the joint?

ERWIN. The Holly Cheer Greeting Company Incorporated in the Wedgewood Building. You walk down Sixth Avenue—

FRANKIE. I know where it is. I used to know a tomato on the tenth floor.

ERWIN. Our office is Nine Hundred and Nine.

PATSY. (*Going to window.*) O. K. Now get dressed and wash up and you'll feel like a new man.

ERWIN. Frankie, be sure Mr. Carver gets the verses himself.

PATSY. Don't worry about it.

ERWIN. Oh, but it's very important.

PATSY. Listen, you're going to make more money dopin' horses than you ever made. Now go on and get under a cold shower so you'll be in shape to pick the horses today. (*Gets out of bed, goes to bathroom door.*)

ERWIN. (*Suddenly. Coming to* PATSY.) Horses? Oh, I don't think I'll have time. I have to call my wife and I must see Mr. Carver later on—

CHARLIE. You can do all that afterwards.

PATSY. Go on, get straightened up. Meantime I'll count out that money I owe you.

ERWIN. Money?

PATSY. A hundred and twelve dollars—I think it is. Yeah, that's right.

ERWIN. You owe me?

PATSY. Certainly. Don't you recall the agreement? We said we'd give you ten per cent of all we won.

ERWIN. I remember something like that. (*Sits on foot of bed stage right.*) . . . but I thought you said eight dollars and fifty cents . . . you mean I made one hundred and twelve dollars—on horses!

CHARLIE. That's right.

ERWIN. Well — Gee — I — you mean if I picked them again today I might make that much again—?

FRANKIE. Maybe more. (*Sits end bed next* ERWIN.)

ERWIN. But even that much again. That would be two hundred and twenty-four dollars . . . why with that I could tell Clarence to go to Hell.

CHARLIE. Who's Clarence?

ERWIN. My brother-in-law.

FRANKIE. You could tell a lot of people.

ERWIN. It's just Clarence that I've been thinking about.

PATSY. Then you mean you'll pick them?

ERWIN. Yes, (*Rises.*) I—I'd like to very much. I'll get dressed. (*Goes into bathroom, starts to close door.*)

PATSY. We're set.

FRANKIE. Sure. (*Sits.*)

CHARLIE. (*Walks to desk.*) I don't know. I wouldn't be too certain. I'm worried.

PATSY. You're always crabbing. If it's rainin' you're afraid of wet feet; if it's shinin', the sun gets in your eyes.

FRANKIE. What you worried about now? Everything is going fine, ain't it?

CHARLIE. That's the trouble. Everything is going too good. I'm worried. How do we know? (*Turns.*) For instance, how long it takes him to dope 'em out? Maybe he has to work on 'em for a couple of weeks ahead of time.

PATSY. (*Alarmed, goes to bathroom and opens door.*) Say—

ERWIN. Huh!

PATSY. Oh, excuse me—say, how long does it take you to dope 'em out? (ERWIN *mumbles.*) Oh. O. K. (*Shuts door and turns to the others triumphantly. Sits arm chair.*) About an hour. We got plenty of time.

FRANKIE. There's some good races, too.

CHARLIE. If he can only pick 'em like yesterday. (MABEL *enters.*)

MABEL. (*Crosses, kisses* PATSY, *sits on end of bed.*) Hello, I didn't think you'd be up so early, Pats.

PATSY. Hello, sugar.

MABEL. Where's the boy friend?

FRANKIE. Gettin' dressed—

PATSY. Say, here's another one of them verses. (*Reads it.*) Listen, fellows, do you know we're associatin' with a genius?

MABEL. What's that?

PATSY. Poetry. Erwin's poetry

MABEL. Oh, Gee, I thought he was a guy who fixed horse races.

PATSY. He does. He just does poetry for a hobby.

FRANKIE. Yeah, I better get those around for him. Room Nine-O-Nine he said. We don't want him to lose his job. (*Crosses to desk.*)

PATSY. You know, I feel sorry for that guy. Slavin' everyday. Doin' the same things over and over.

FRANKIE. I can't find a big envelope. (*Looking through desk.*)

CHARLIE. (*At desk.*) They have 'em downstairs.

PATSY. Listen to this:
"Why was it that I chose to roam
Cross Land and Sea so far from home?
If that be Life— My Mother Dear,
I send this card of Love and Cheer."
Mother's Day Number Thirty-seven. That touches you—you know that—right here.

MABEL. Yeah . . . like when you're seein' a good sad movie . . . geez—

PATSY. You know, this Erwin guy ain't bein' appreciated.

CHARLIE. You mean he's better than he is?

PATSY. I mean he's better than forty bucks . . . do you know any other guys who could sit down and write them gems for forty bucks a week?

FRANKIE. Well, I guess there is some guys . . .

PATSY. You don't know any off hand?

FRANKIE. No.

PATSY. That's just it. We ought to do somethin'. (*Crosses to window.*)

MABEL. Like what?

PATSY. (*Crosses up right.*) Like somethin', anyway. It gets me sore to think a nice guy like him is workin' for a guy like this here fellow he's tellin' about all the time—J. G. Carver. Look up the Holly Cheer Greeting Company. I don't know Mr. Carver, but he's probably a louse. . . .

CHARLIE. What are you goin' to do, anyways? (*Crossing and sitting on bed.*)

PATSY. I'm goin' to get Erwin a raise. I feel for him like my own brother. That's the trouble with people in this world—they get a good thing like him and they take advantage of it.

FRANKIE. Give me Bogardus Four six seven five two. . . . I'll get it for you.

PATSY. Let me have it Let me talk to . . . Mr. Carver . . . just say it's important . . . Hello, Carver . . . this is a very good friend of Mr. Erwin Trowbridge . . . in fact, I'm his manager . . . since yesterday . . . Oh, they're all written . . . they're gems . . . that's what they are . . . well, before I sent them around I thought we'd discuss terms. Those verses are the best verses I have ever read and I've read a lot of verses . . . what I thought was this . . . we might as well talk man to man . . . you're gettin' away with murder . . . forty bucks a week . . . Yeah . . . yeah . . . that's what I call a steal . . . Hello . . . hello . . . he hung up . . . Is that polite? (*Crosses right and turns.*) Is that the way to talk to me that's manager of a poet practically?

CHARLIE. Maybe one of us should go down and punch him in the nose.

FRANKIE. (*Going to* CHARLIE.) No—let's not start any fights . . . not till we make some money.

PATSY. I don't like him. (*Sits arm chair.*) It ain't what he said to me, you understand, but he said for Erwin to go to Hell too.

FRANKIE. (*Sits at desk.*) It looks like Erwin stayed up all night for nothin'.

PATSY. Like Hell he has. The world should see art like that . . . those gems should be put in bar-rooms . . . railroad stations . . . on calendars . . . wait, I got it.

FRANKIE. We ought to have somethin' because if Erwin finds out I haven't taken—

PATSY. Liebowitz!

MABEL. The printer.

PATSY. Jake Liebowitz who did all the classy postal cards for that smoker last month.

FRANKIE. He prints lots of stuff.

PATSY. Suppose it cost us a hundred bucks . . . get a couple o' guys to go around sell 'em to factories, clubs, the Y.M.C.A. . . . the Y.W.C.A. . . . the Y.M.H.A. and all the railroad stations then . . . railroad stations! (*Crossing left.*) Frankie, have you ever been in a washroom in a railroad station?

FRANKIE. Sure. Haven't you?

PATSY. Lot of times. Well, in those railroad stations . . . not only railroads, but all over . . . you've seen those verses like . . . "A man's ambition must be small to write his name . . ." (*At phone.*) Kitty . . . Patsy . . . tell Moses to come right up here and bring a big envelope. (*Hangs up.*)

MABEL. . . . and the one about sittin' and thinkin'.

PATSY. Sure. Well, nobody's thought to commercialize that kind of poetry . . . they're gems. That's what that guy can do. If he can write serious stuff like he has here, he can write funny stuff too.

FRANKIE. Gee, that's a swell idea. (*Knock on the door.*)

CHARLIE. Come in. (MOSES *enters.*)

FRANKIE. I'll bet he never thought of that.

MOSES. This all right, Mr. Patsy?

PATSY. Yeah. That's what I want.

FRANKIE. Here, give it to me.

PATSY. Here you are, Moses. Frankie, take those around to Jake Liebowitz, I'll call him and tell him you're coming.

FRANKIE. O. K. I'll shoot right over.

PATSY. Come around later and I'll give you a horse. Pennsylvania six seven eight one one.

MOSES. If it's all the same to you, Mr. Patsy, I'd sooner have a number.

PATSY. Mr. Erwin only has horses.

MOSES. All right then, I guess I'll have to take a horse. (*Exits.*)

PATSY. (*In phone.*) Hello . . . Jake? This is Patsy. How are you? . . . Well, say listen, you ain't so busy . . . yeah, I know . . . but listen, I want a special job done on verses . . . no, not singin' verses . . . poetry verses . . . you know—"Roses are Red" . . . yeah . . . shiney paper, with lace maybe. They'll be there in a couple of minutes. Don't leave before you get them. O. K. (*Hangs up.*)

MABEL. If you're going to do this, what's Erwin going to get out of it?

PATSY. All of it . . . we're only helping him out.

MABEL. Oh, like bein' in business for himself, huh?

PATSY. Sure. All he has to do is write 'em. When it gets going good . . . he just stays home and picks horses and the verses sell themselves . . . because they're good.

MABEL. That's what I call givin' him a break.

ERWIN. (*Enters and sees* MABEL.) Oh, good morning.

MABEL. Hello. I hope you feel better than yesterday.

ERWIN. Well, I guess I do. Maybe I ought to go out and get a little breakfast. (*Crossing to bureau.*)

PATSY. (*Going to* ERWIN.) I was just talking to Mr. Carver on the phone.

ERWIN. You were?

PATSY. I don't think that he likes you so much. I could tell by his voice.

ERWIN. Why, what's happened?

PATSY. Somethin' good . . . we're settin' you up in business on your own.

ERWIN. But what about Mr. Carver?

PATSY. To Hell with him. He don't appreciate you.

ERWIN. Doesn't he like my verses?

PATSY. I told him I wouldn't even let him see them.

ERWIN. Why not? What right have you to do a thing like that? I'll lose my job. Where are my verses?

PATSY. Wait a minute, Erwin, this is for your good.

ERWIN. (*Rushing past* PATSY.) Where are they? Where are my verses?

PATSY. (*Clutching* ERWIN's *arm.*) Listen, Erwin, we sent them over to Liebowitz.

ERWIN. Who is Liebowitz?

PATSY. He's one of our best friends. He's going to print your verses so they'll be sold all over the country. See.

ERWIN. Please don't. You can't do this to me . . . you fellows might think this is funny, but I'm going to lose my job . . . you don't know what it means to have a job, fifty-two weeks in the year—forty dollars a week.

PATSY. Don't you know you rate more than that? Don't you know that big crook is cheating Hell out of you? Here you are starving along on forty a week, while that big piece of salami is living high with high offices in the Wedgewood Building. Sure. And he made it all off you. Now Liebowitz is going to print your verses so that every home . . .

ERWIN. I don't want Liebowitz to print my verses. All I want is to work for Mr. Carver.

PATSY. But he's a louse.

ERWIN. He is not. Don't you say that about Mr. Carver . . . he's the only boss I ever had and I like to work for him. Get me back my verses. (FRANKIE *enters.*)

FRANKIE. Well, everything's O. K.

PATSY. Frankie, you'll have to get the verses back.

FRANKIE. What the Hell is this?

PATSY. You're careless, that's all.

FRANKIE. I can't get 'em back now.

ERWIN. What's happened to my verses?

FRANKIE. Nothing's happened to them. Liebowitz was waitin' for me at the door when I got there and he said, "Congratulate me, Frankie, my daughter is having a baby at the Beth Israel Hospital and my son is being confirmed at the synagogue . . ." so

I congratulated him and he took the verses with him in a taxicab. Say, it's gettin' late, don't you think Erwin ought to start pickin' the horses.

ERWIN.   Horses . . I can't even think of horses.

PATSY.   (*Going to* FRANKIE.) Erwin can't pick any horses until he gets the verses back.

FRANKIE.   Well, what the Hell are we going to do about it?

PATSY.   We gotta do something. We gotta get 'em back.

ERWIN.   Working hard all my life . . . trying to get some place, trying to build a reputation. (*Sits in chair right.*)

MABEL.   (*Rises.*) Don't worry, Erwin. It'll be all right. Boys, you got to find Liebowitz . . . it's a cinch he's in one of two places, his daughter is havin' a baby at the Beth Israel Hospital and his son is being confirmed at the synagogue.

FRANKIE.   But suppose he's gone to his home? He said he had to get dressed.

PATSY.   I'll take care of that. Mabel is right. We got to find him. We got to keep Erwin happy so his mind can work good and pick the horses. Frankie, you go to the Beth Israel Hospital. And Charlie, you look for him in the synagogue. Come on, boys, get moving . . . and don't forget the name, Frankie, Beth Israel Hospital.

CHARLIE.   Why should I have to go to the synagogue? All right. If you say so that makes it right. (*Goes.*)

FRANKIE.   Beth Israel . . . Beth Israel . . . (*Goes.*)

PATSY.   There now . . . we'll get the verses right back, see, Erwin. . . . Wait till I look up where he lives.

MABEL.   You see, Erwin, now there isn't anything to worry about. (*Going to* ERWIN.) Erwin, say look, Patsy . . . he's all pale . . . Erwin . . . I think he's fainted or something.

PATSY.   Fainted? Geez.

MABEL.   Should I phone down for a doctor?

PATSY.   Doctor? No! Give me a hand. Put him on the bed. We don't want any doctors around. (*They take him over to the bed.*) We'll get him a drink—a couple o' drinks will fix him up. (*Rushes to telephone.*)

MABEL.   Maybe that's all he needs—just a pick-me-up.

PATSY.   (*In telephone.*) Hello—get me the bar. (ERWIN *opens eyes for a moment.*)

MABEL.   Oh, Patsy, look, he just opened his eyes.

PATSY.   Say, his health is important now— remember that—we got to take good care of him.

MABEL.   You bet—

PATSY.   (*In phone.*) Hello, Harry—Patsy. Are you very busy? Well, bring up a bottle of rye right away. Yeah. (*Hangs up. Picks up telephone book.*)

MABEL.   (*To* ERWIN.) How do you feel now? (ERWIN *nods.*) Sure—sure, just a teensie hangover, that's all.

PATSY.   Sure, he'll be all right— Geez, there's about a million Liebowitz's—Abraham—Benjamin—David—Herman—Isaac —Jacob— (*Picks up receiver.*) Chelsea three seven four four four.

HARRY.   (*Enters.*) You sounded like you was in a hurry. (*Looks at* ERWIN.) Geez, ain't he come to yet?

PATSY.   Yeah, but he passed out again.

MABEL.   He's about half to, now—but I'm makin' him rest.

HARRY.   Do you think he can stand another drink?

PATSY.   Sure, that's just what— Hello, Jake—

HARRY.   (*To* MABEL.) Got a corkscrew?

MABEL.   Yeah. (*Goes into bathroom.*)

PATSY.   Jake, I gotta have those verses back —never mind why— Oh—well, how long you goin' to be there? —The Hell with the baby. This is a matter of life and death— I'll be right over for them— Wait for me. (*Hangs up; grabs hat.*) Work on him,

Harry—he's got to pick those horses. Mabel, don't let Erwin get out of here and don't let him call anybody up till I get back. (PATSY *exits.* HARRY *pours drink.*)

MABEL. (*Bringing another glass from bathroom.*) Pour me one, too, Harry. I feel kind of faint myself. (HARRY *pours one for* MABEL.) I never seen so much excitement. (*Drinks it down.*)

HARRY. I wish he'd hurry up and come to. I want another horse today.

ERWIN. (*Groans.*) Oh—

MABEL. Quick, Harry!

HARRY. (*Forces drink down* ERWIN's *throat.*) Here, drink this.

ERWIN. (*Sitting up.*) Audrey! . . . (*Sees* Harry.) Oh, gosh.

HARRY. Now, how do you feel?

ERWIN. (*Rises.*) I don't know.

HARRY. Better get him under the covers. Get his pants off.

ERWIN. (*Alarmed.*) What?

MABEL. (*Going to* ERWIN.) Sure. (*Starts to unbutton his pants.*)

ERWIN. Hey, don't—no, no, no. Please.

MABEL. What's the matter?

ERWIN. It tickles.

HARRY. Better let me do it. (*Pulls his pants off—puts* ERWIN *in bed. Phone rings.*)

ERWIN. I'm all right.

HARRY. Sure you are.

MABEL. (*Answering phone.*) Hello . . . yeah . . . he's here—well he just got here—he's helpin' me—he's—all right—I'll tell him. (*Hangs up.*) You got some customers at the bar, Harry—you better go down.

HARRY. (*Tucking* ERWIN *in.*) Who was that?

MABEL. Mac.

HARRY. Ah—nuts to him. (*To* ERWIN.) What do you think of Mad Hatter in the first race today, Erwin?

ERWIN. I don't know.

HARRY. Well, take your time. But don't forget me, will you?—and if there's any little thing I can do for you, you let me know.

MABEL. You better hop down there or Mac'll be yappin' some more. (MABEL *goes to dresser, gets drink, crosses to bed.*)

HARRY. That damn bar—it's a nuisance. (*Exits.*)

MABEL. Gee, it's awful nice of you to stay here and help Patsy like you been doin'.

ERWIN. I was desperate or I wouldn't have done such a thing.

MABEL. But if you know how much we liked to have you here—I don't mean just the boys, I mean more particularly just myself personally.

ERWIN. Give me back my pants.

MABEL. What's the matter?

ERWIN. I ought to call up my wife.

MABEL. Not just now, Erwin—I don't want you to get out of bed. You might faint again.

ERWIN. I ought to call her. I've punished her enough. She'll be worried.

MABEL. But listen now, pet, just wait till Patsy gets back, will you? 'Cause I promised him I wouldn't let you call anybody.

ERWIN. Yes, but I haven't been home all night.

MABEL. She must be used to that.

ERWIN. Oh, no, she isn't.

MABEL. You're a good deal different than most men then. God knows Patsy's liable to disappear for a week at a time. But he's awfully good to me though— You ought to see all the swell things he gave me when I quit the Follies for him! . . . Two weeks later they tried a four horse parlay at Saratoga and we lost everything—I didn't have a nightgown left, to my name.

ERWIN. Oh! That must have been terrible.

MABEL. Well, it's just the breaks. Now, it looks as though things is brightening up again since you come into my life.

ERWIN. Where's my pencil—quick— (*He writes.*)

MABEL. What is it? You got the first race? (ERWIN *shakes his head.*) Let's see. (*She takes the paper and reads.*)
"My soul was sad as darkest night.
But now the world seems fair and bright
Because you came so true and fine.
Oh, stay and be my Valentine."

ERWIN. Valentine's Day Number One. It doesn't do any hurt to get ahead of schedule.

MABEL. Yeah. If you're ahead then you're a fast worker, is that it?

ERWIN. What?

MABEL. Never mind. (*Reads.*) "Stay and be my Valentine." Gee, that's wonderful! . . . I'm crazy about poetry.

ERWIN. I don't get much time to write real poetry. I've been so busy with my Mother's Day verses.

MABEL. Oh . . . gee, I haven't heard from Mom in a long time—of course I haven't written to her lately—maybe I ought to send her one of them . . . a verse . . . it might make her feel good . . . you see, I ain't sure she's my mother. (*Business of taking drink.*)

ERWIN. Oh, but she'd feel good anyway.

MABEL. I guess so. I haven't seen her since I came to New York to go on the stage.

ERWIN. Did you really used to be on the stage?

MABEL. Yeah, I used to be in the Follies. I'd like to get back in show business but Patsy doesn't think I look as good as I used to. (*Stands up and pats her hips.*) Don't you think I could get back if I worked hard?

ERWIN. Sure, I'll bet you could. Of course I've never seen a Follies girl close to before —only from the balcony. You look all right to me.

MABEL. Do I really, Erwin?

ERWIN. Why yes—yes—you're beautiful.

MABEL. Gee, I like you . . . just think— maybe I have read one of your poems in a magazine—like a movie magazine—and

here I am standing talking to you . . . I guess that's what you call romantic. Gee, I'm pretty jealous of your wife, you know it?

ERWIN. You are? Why?

MABEL. Havin' you all to herself—I'm just thinkin' how wonderful it would be to travel around the country with you—listenin' to your poetry and helpin' you make a lot of money bettin' on the horses.

ERWIN. Oh, but I wouldn't bet—that would spoil everything.

MABEL. Well, I mean—just enough for a fur coat and stuff like that.

ERWIN. But I don't think I could tell what ones are going to win if I ever started betting on them.

MABEL. Well anyhow, you could make a lot of money if you wanted to just with words for songs like they have in shows . . . lyrics.

ERWIN. You think so?

MABEL. Sure. Say, lots of times I sang words in the chorus that wasn't half as good as that.

ERWIN. Did you sing in the Follies?

MABEL. Yeah— did a specialty once. Want me to show you? (*He nods.*) Say, I'd do anything for you. (*Goes to radio.*) 'Cause I'm crazy about poetry, that's why. (*Turns radio on. Tries a few steps.*) I may not be so good till I get limbered up. (*Radio begins to talk.*) I'll see if I can get my dress off— I guess among friends it's all right, huh? (*Starts to take off dress.*)

ANNOUNCER. Two tablets daily and assure yourself a perfect health and a happy old age— The Press Radio News Report will be brought to you at five P. M. At this time we present Ivan Aronson and his jazzy cossacks in a program of dance music —"Take it away Ivan!" (*Music.*)

ERWIN. What is? (MABEL *crosses right.*) Maybe I ought to telephone my wife.

MABEL. Don't you want to see my dance?

ERWIN. Yes, I do.

MABEL. (*Gets music.*) Here we go. Now, you're the audience. I come out, you see, with a big spot on me. (*Dances.*) The other girls are jealous 'cause I got a specialty— (*She kicks, exposing all.*) Of course this is just a rough idea—

ERWIN. Say, that's good!

MABEL. This is my finish. (*Whirls across stage. Turns off radio. Leans against bureau.*)

ERWIN. What's the matter?

MABEL. (*Breathless.*) Out of practice . . . haven't done this for so long . . . got dizzy.

ERWIN. (*Jumps out of bed and helps* MABEL *to bed where she sits.*) I'll give you a drink. (*Pours drink.* PATSY *enters while* ERWIN *is giving* MABEL *a drink. He stands at door and looks. He has the verses in his hand.*)

PATSY. What the Hell's this?

ERWIN. Have you got my verses?

PATSY. Yeah.

ERWIN. She was doin' a dance—and all of a sudden—she got dizzy.

PATSY. Oh yeah.

ERWIN. Yes.

PATSY. (*Walks slowly toward* MABEL.) You get your dress on and go back to your room.

MABEL. What's the matter, Patsy?

PATSY. I said get your dress on and go back to your room.

MABEL. He wanted to phone his wife and— (*She rises and takes dress from bed.*)

PATSY. All right, never mind the lip— get back to your room. (*As* MABEL *backs up to door.*) You're just good and lucky I don't take a poke at you. Go on.

MABEL. But, Patsy—

PATSY. Get out. Get out before I kick your teeth in—you crooked little punk.

MABEL. Geez, you never talked to me like this before. (*She goes out almost in tears carrying dress.*)

ERWIN. I hope you don't think—(PATSY *tears verses.*) Hey, stop that—

PATSY. Get those on and take yourself out of here.

ERWIN. Hey, my verses!

PATSY. (*Throws pants at him.*) Get your pants on and get out of here before I lose my temper . . . you double-crossin' little . . .

ERWIN. My verses! (*He goes to bathroom; locks door.*) (PATSY, *in a rage, tears verses some more.* CHARLIE *and* FRANKIE *enter together.*)

CHARLIE. Hey, what the Hell did you do to Mabel? She's cryin' in the hall.

FRANKIE. Geez, I never seen a girl cry so much.

PATSY. I didn't do a thing to her, but I should have. (*Points toward bathroom, keeps one verse to tear.*) Can you imagine?

FRANKIE. What?

PATSY. And me thinkin' he was a sap.

CHARLIE. Well what's happened?

PATSY. What the Hell do you think?

FRANKIE. (*Crossing to center.*) She said she was just tryin' to be nice to him till you got back.

PATSY. Yeah. Nice is right. Took three weeks and a diamond bracelet to get her that nice to me.

CHARLIE. Well, you told her to hold him didn't you?

FRANKIE. Yeah—maybe she didn't like it no better than you did. Maybe she just seen her duty, that's all.

PATSY. Aw—it's my fault, I suppose, for leavin' them alone together.

CHARLIE. No, but you can trust Mabel— geez, I never could get nowhere with her—

PATSY. What?

CHARLIE. I mean—if I'd tried. No, you just mistook the looks of things.

FRANKIE. Where's Erwin?

PATSY. In there.

CHARLIE. What didja do to him?

PATSY. I told him to get dressed and get the Hell out of here.

FRANKIE. (*Crossing up to door.*) He ain't gone yet, is he?

PATSY. No. But he will as soon as he gets dressed.

CHARLIE. How about the horses for today?

PATSY. We'll select our own.

CHARLIE. (*Closes in.*) And lose our shirts! Now listen, wise guy, he's just as much ours as he is yours.

FRANKIE. (*Coming down to* PATSY.) That's what I say. You can't throw him out—just because you think your girl happened to go for him. And you ain't even sure—you couldn't prove it in a court of law.

PATSY. How would you feel if your girl happened to do that?

FRANKIE. To do what?—how do you know she did anything?—and suppose she did— what I mean is—well, Gee—you know, a guy like Erwin. That wouldn't be much of anything. (PATSY *slams chair and crosses left.*)

CHARLIE. Sure— Gee, you don't mean to tell me you're worried about a guy like him.

PATSY. Worried? What's that got to do with it? God! there's such a thing like decency, ain't there? It don't look right to me to come back and find some guy in his underpants passin' my girl drinks—it don't look right.

CHARLIE. She was just stallin' for time. (PATSY *paces back and forth.*)

FRANKIE. (*Following him.*) Sure, she was just trying to keep him from phoning his wife. Geez, she was willin' to come through for you and you don't even appreciate it. Ain't that the kind of a girl you want— ain't that loyalty, huh?

CHARLIE. What more do you want? She's always played ball with you.

PATSY. Yeah—but—

CHARLIE. What more do you want? She's only tryin' to keep this guy on the fire so's you can make enough money to buy a house and settle down with her.

PATSY. Yeah?

CHARLIE. That's what she said.

FRANKIE. And besides, Harry helped take his pants off, you know that, don't you?

PATSY. No.

CHARLIE. Sure. That don't sound very sensual to me.

FRANKIE. You sap. You ought to be busted right in the nose for makin' her cry that way.

PATSY. Was she really crying?

CHARLIE. Was she cryin'— Geez!

PATSY. (*Goes right to phone.*) Hello— give me Mabel's room. (FRANKIE *takes drink.* CHARLIE *sees verses on floor, picks them up.*)

CHARLIE. What the Hell happened to the verses?

PATSY. Oh, I got sore. . . . Hello, Mabel. . . . Now listen, honey, stop crying. . . . Well, I didn't mean it—but I couldn't help it—you know how I feel about you . . . I just didn't like the looks of things. . . . Well, it did look bad to me when I come in. . . . Now listen, I want you to dry your eyes and forget all about it . . . Yeah . . . I'll tell you what I want to do. . . . Put on that pretty dress I bought you yesterday and go out and look at apartments. . . . All right, look at a house, what the Hell do I care . . . Papa wouldn't treat you that way, it's just 'cause Papa loves you.

CHARLIE. Papa gives me a pain in the— hang up, will you, you said enough.

PATSY. (*Hangs up.*) Gee, she *was* cryin'.

FRANKIE. Listen, boys, quit foolin' around about women and all that sort of tripe— let's get down to something important— now, how about those horses?

CHARLIE. Yeah, it's after one o'clock.

PATSY. Aw, it only takes him about an hour.

CHARLIE. Well, we ought to get him started. (*Bathroom door opens.* ERWIN *enters, crosses to bureau. Puts on coat.*)

FRANKIE. Hey, where you goin'?

ERWIN. I'm goin' to the office.

FRANKIE. (*Rushing to* ERWIN. *Shocked.*) Oh, you wouldn't do a thing like that!

ERWIN. (*Heading for* PATSY.) Where's my verses?

CHARLIE. (*Stops him.*) No, but wait a minute—let's talk it over, that's all.

ERWIN. (*Passing him.*) I haven't time.

PATSY. Now, listen, Erwin, I'm sorry I spoke to you the way I did. It did look a little bad—but I'm goin' to square everything. I just been talking to Mabel.

ERWIN. (*To* PATSY.) You ought to be ashamed of yourself. She's too good for you.

PATSY. It's all right pal, it's all right—only I just forgot myself.

ERWIN. Where'd you put my verses?

CHARLIE. After all, Erwin, you got nothing against Frankie and me, have you?

ERWIN. No, no, I haven't, but—

FRANKIE. Geez, we nursed you back to health and everything like you was a baby almost—

PATSY. You wouldn't walk out on us after the way we took care of you. (*Takes him by lapels.*) Listen, Erwin, didn't you ever lose your temper?

ERWIN. Yes, I did.

PATSY. Well, that's me—and I'm sorry. If you walk out on us now the boys will hold it against me for the rest of my life. They'll say I insulted you and that's why you left us.

ERWIN. I have to get to the office. I'm late now. And Mr. Carver is going to be upset. Maybe he won't even give me my job back after the way you talked to him—

PATSY. (*Tough.*) He'll give it to you, if I have to go down and—

CHARLIE. Nix, nix. (FRANKIE *goes up right.*)

PATSY. We'll buy the joint and let you run it.

ERWIN. I don't want to run it—I just want to work for Mr. Carver. Anyhow, I have to go and explain to him.

CHARLIE. Couldn't you just dope out the horses before you go?

ERWIN. No.

FRANKIE. I'm disappointed in you, Erwin, I thought we could trust you. I certainly did.

ERWIN. (*Worried.*) Well, I'd like to help you. . . .

PATSY. (*Acting the martyr while the others gesture encouragements.*) It's all right, Erwin—I must give you your ten per cent before you go. (*Counts out money.*)

ERWIN. What, Well—I—

PATSY. If you feel like letting us down I wouldn't want to be the one to interfere. Here you are. A hundred and twelve bucks! Sorry it ain't more, but I thought we was going to have longer to work on it. Might have got up into some real coin if you would have stayed with us today.

CHARLIE. Yes, I guess your share today would have been a thousand dollars or so.

FRANKIE. Yeah—it's too bad. (*Knock.*)

PATSY. (*Tough.*) Who is it?

MABEL. (*Sticks her head in.*) Did you say come in?

PATSY. (*Sweet loud kiss.*) Oh, come in, honey. (*She enters in new dress.*) You're just in time to say good-bye to Erwin.

MABEL. (*Alarmed.*) Goodbye?

PATSY. He thinks I didn't treat you right, so he's walking out on us.

MABEL. (*Rushing to* ERWIN.) Aw.

ERWIN. I'd like to stay, honest, I would, I feel terrible about it, but—

MABEL. Oh, Erwin, I can't bear to have you go.

FRANKIE. If you'd just dope out a couple of horses before you go.

PATSY. I tell you what, Erwin; here's the solution to the whole proposition: you can't take these verses back to the office like this, they're all torn—you just sit down and wait a few minutes while we copy 'em for you.

ERWIN. Well—

CHARLIE. (*Picks up verses and sits.*) Sure, we'll do it—then we can all part the best of friends.

FRANKIE. Sure—move over—give me a couple of those.

PATSY. And while you're waiting for us to do it you can just pass the time figuring a couple of horses.

ERWIN. I can help copy verses.

PATSY. No, no, we tore 'em up, we'll copy 'em. You figure horses— Give me some of those, will you— You figure horses. Give him a pencil, Mabel.

MABEL. Sure. Here's a pencil—Erwin. And there's the *Telegraph*.

ERWIN. Well, all right—I'll try.

MABEL. I knew you would—now—sit right here.

PATSY. That's the boy.

CHARLIE. I always said he was a regular fellow.

PATSY. You bet, you can count on Erwin.

MABEL. Oh yeah, he'll come through all right.

CHARLIE. Good Old Erwin!

FRANKIE. All right boys, don't talk so much. Let him concentrate. (ERWIN *thinks, crosses legs.*)

MABEL. Is there anything I can do?

CHARLIE. Yeah, go into your dance.

PATSY. Shut up.

CHARLIE. Well, don't be bustin' up his thoughts.

PATSY. Well, who's talkin'—you are.

MABEL. Yeah, he's doin' all the—

FRANKIE. Shut up, all of you.

CHARLIE. Come on now, let's not argue so much, get busy on these verses. (ERWIN *tears off slip of paper.*)

FRANKIE. Sure. (ERWIN *looks at paper, shaking head.*) No good, huh, Erwin? (*As* ERWIN *crams paper under pillow.*)

PATSY. Leave him alone. Leave him alone.

FRANKIE. No, but he wrote one down. He put it under the pillow.

ERWIN. It isn't anything. It's no good.

CHARLIE. (*Reading slip, gets prop from* ERWIN.) Equipoise.

PATSY. Equipoise. Runs in the fourth, huh?

FRANKIE. Equipoise. That's the one I was going to pick.

ERWIN. But it doesn't count, I tell you.

CHARLIE. Why don't it?

ERWIN. I don't know.

CHARLIE. It's no good?

ERWIN. No!

CHARLIE. (*They all rise.*) He ain't going to come through—I can feel it.

PATSY. (*Going to* ERWIN.) He is so. You wouldn't let me down, would you, Erwin?

ERWIN. It's no use.

PATSY. What do you mean, it's no use? Now, Erwin, you ain't going to get discouraged?

ERWIN. I can't figure them out just sitting here. I've always done them on a bus.

CHARLIE. Well, just imagine you're on a bus.

PATSY. Geez, no wonder he couldn't think of 'em sittin' there on that lousy bed—come over here by the window, Erwin. This is more like a bus. (*Rushing* ERWIN *over to window.* ERWIN *demurs.*) Slip that chair under him, Frankie. Give him that pencil and paper. Just try—just concentrate. Now, just pretend you're on the bus, see. Just concentrate. (*He concentrates. They watch him.* CHARLIE *is in rear of* ERWIN.)

CHARLIE. (*Gently, to give atmosphere but not to break the spell.*) Fares, please—have your fares ready— (PATSY *wants to swing on him.* ERWIN *jumps up.*)

ERWIN. (*Steps down.*) It's no use. I can't do it. (CHARLIE *follows to the right of* ERWIN.)

PATSY. But you don't try, Erwin.

ERWIN. I've tried before. I'm not kidding. They only come to me on a bus.

CHARLIE. Would a taxi do? A nice taxi with a radio?

ERWIN. No.

PATSY. Hell, a taxi is better than a bus any time. And we can get one quicker.

ERWIN. (*Shakes his head.*) Only on a bus.

PATSY. All right. Frankie, go down and reserve the rear seat of the Coney Island bus. Tell them to throw out all them stooges. Get the best lookin' bus you can.

ERWIN. Now, wait a minute. . . . I hope you're not going to think I'm awfully particular—but you see, I couldn't do them on the Coney Island bus.

PATSY. For God's sake—why not?

ERWIN. Because I've always done them on the bus that goes to Ozone Heights.

CHARLIE. Where do you get one of them?

PATSY. (*Crossing to* CHARLIE.) No— No—

FRANKIE. We could just change the sign.

PATSY. (*Yelling.*) No— No— No—

MABEL. If you fellows would let him do it his own way—

PATSY. Yeah, that's what we're going to do. Now shut up!

ERWIN. Why—(ERWIN *looks up at them, shocked by the sharp tone.*)

PATSY. Well, ain't that right—they're getting you flustered, ain't they, kid?

ERWIN. I am getting kind of mixed up. You see, usually, just for fun, I figure them out going home.

PATSY. All right—that's easy—now you'd like to go home, wouldn't you?

ERWIN. Yes, I would.

PATSY. All right, that's what you're going to do.

CHARLIE. (*Going down right. Sotto voce.*) Goodbye, we'll never see him again.

PATSY. You're going out and get on your regular bus just like you always do. Mabel and Frankie, they'll go with you. We'll be copying verses—but in the meantime—you'll be taking a nice ride and then you can drop in and see the wife . . . tell her everything is fine.

ERWIN. Yes, I'd like to do that.

PATSY. But just before you tell her, see, phone us what horses to bet on. We'll be right here copying your verses and waiting for the dope.

ERWIN. (*Crossing left.*) All right. Let's get started. Come on, Frankie—

CHARLIE. And Erwin, no looking out of windows—just horses.

PATSY. Unless you hurry we ain't going to make the first race as it is.

ERWIN. Where's my necktie?

CHARLIE. You never had none.

FRANKIE. Take mine.

PATSY. Keep it on. I got plenty. (*Takes ties from bureau drawer—throws on bed.*) Help yourself.

ERWIN. Oh, thanks.(*As he selects a brilliant red tie.*)

PATSY. Frankie, take the *Telegraph*.

FRANKIE. Where the Hell is it?

MABEL. Here it is on the bed. Erwin was sittin' on it.

PATSY. Have you got a pencil, Erwin?

CHARLIE. Have you got your little black book?

PATSY. Yeah!

FRANKIE. I've got it right here.

PATSY. Stick it in his pocket.

ERWIN. I'll bet my wife will be surprised when she sees this necktie.

PATSY. Get going. Get going.

ERWIN. Where's my hat?

CHARLIE. Here you are—

FRANKIE. (*Dashes to dresser; gets hat.*) I'll get it for you. Ring for the elevator, Mabel. (CURTAIN *starts down.*)

MABEL. (*They rush him out.*) All right, but hurry.

ERWIN. Seems as if I'd been away forever.

PATSY. Get on the right bus, Erwin.

CHARLIE. Treat him nice. Buy him a soda.

CURTAIN

ACT THREE

SCENE I

Place: Ozone Heights.
ORCHESTRA *plays "Just A Love Nest."*
At Rise: GLORIA *and* AL *cross downstage left off left. The room is littered with newspapers.* CLARENCE *is peeking out the door. He jumps to the window to watch someone outside.* AUDREY *comes downstairs in a new dress.*

CLARENCE. They took a picture of the house. (AUDREY *dry-eyed and repressed, walks across room and sits.*) Wouldn't it be wonderful if they'd put that in the paper? (*Points to paper on floor.*) That *Newark Star* gave us a very bad write-up. . . . Nothing about Dobbins Drive . . . just said a versifier of Ozone Heights is missing. (*Notices* AUDREY.) You didn't need to get all dressed up—she said she'd take your picture just as you were.

AUDREY. I got dressed up for Mr. Carver, not for her. I'm sure that Erwin would want me to look as well as I can.

CLARENCE. Well, from time to time I've said things against J. G. Carver, but I take 'em all back. His heart is in the right place or he wouldn't be coming out here. Gee, I wonder if I could interest him in a house.

AUDREY. He isn't coming out here about houses he's coming out about Erwin.

CLARENCE. Well, if I've got to support you the rest of my life, the least I can get out of this is maybe a sale or two. (*Snaps fingers and sits.*) Or a tip on a horse. Doggone, if Erwin was going to walk out that way you would have thought he could at least have left a *hot tip.* He's probably out at some bookie's right now putting his money on the winners—gosh, what wouldn't I give to know which ones!

AUDREY. You don't have to support me the rest of your life, so don't say that again. And if you must keep on making remarks that Erwin has run away, then I'll have to ask you not to come in my house any more.

CLARENCE. Why, sis! (*Front door opens and* GLORIA GRAY, *reporter on the "Newark Gazette" enters, followed by* AL, *the photographer.*)

GLORIA. Now, Mrs. Trowbridge, if you'll just stand over here. (AUDREY *crosses to davenport.*) Have you got a handkerchief?

AUDREY. (*Turning.*) Handkerchief?

GLORIA. Yes, you ought to be crying, you know—

AUDREY. I'm not going to cry any more.

CLARENCE. She cried terrible this morning. But she's a brave little woman.

GLORIA. "Brave little woman." There's a very trenchant phrase—remind me to use that, will you, Al?

CLARENCE. Want me in the picture? (GLORIA *favors him with a cold smile and then turns away.*)

AL. Still—(*Snaps picture.*)

GLORIA. That's fine. Now just one more. We'll take another one brave. That's just as good. We've had half a dozen weeping wives this week anyhow—(*To* CLARENCE.) You're the brother of the missing man, are you?

CLARENCE. No, I'm the brother of the wife of the missing man, and I'm the owner of this row of houses here.

GLORIA. They're very attractive.

CLARENCE. They're all alike.

GLORIA. I noticed that.

AL. Still—

GLORIA. (*Giving* CLARENCE *a look.*) All right, Al, shoot him just for luck.

CLARENCE. Let's see where'll we a—(*Picks up chair planning to sit for the picture.*)

AL. Still—

CLARENCE. (*Holding chair in the air.*) Oh, I wasn't ready—

GLORIA. That's all right—you looked worried—just the right expression.

CLARENCE. I am worried—he was a fine fellow—

AUDREY. (*Crossing to telephone table.*) Now, here's the picture of Erwin—I hate to part with it— It's the only one I've got—

GLORIA. Oh, we'll send it back in good condition— (*Writes on the face.*) Here you are, Al— (*Tosses it to* AL.)

AUDREY. But of course, if it'll help to find Erwin . . .

GLORIA. Sure it will. Somebody might recognize him—and—you'll get a lot of people who think they do. I'll promise you that—

CLARENCE. If you'd print a description I should think it might help. When he left here he was wearing a grey suit, brown hat, black shoes. . . .

AUDREY. And no necktie.

GLORIA. No necktie—(AUDREY *shakes head.*) Why was that?

AUDREY. He was in a hurry. He was late.

GLORIA. Often do that, does he?

AUDREY. (*Shakes head.*) No—it's the first time.

GLORIA. And—this the first time he ever stayed away from home overnight? (AUDREY *nods.*) And the first time he ever went to work without a necktie?

AL. Doesn't look like a date—

GLORIA. Who asked you? (*Changes tone.*) Any suspicious letters or phone calls from women?

AUDREY. Erwin wasn't like that. He was different!

GLORIA. Different—

AL. Hey, Toots. (AL *shows* GLORIA ERWIN'S *picture as though to prove he wasn't like that.*)

GLORIA. Oh— (*Buzzer rings.*)

AUDREY. (*Helplessly to* CLARENCE.) If that's the neighbors—

CLARENCE. Let me— (*Opens door.* CARVER, *an irascible old gentleman, stands there, wearing seedy Prince Albert and grey striped trousers.*) Yes.

CARVER. (*Handing* CLARENCE *his hat and coming center.*) How do you do? My name is Carver— *Where's Erwin?*

AUDREY. (*Clutching his hand and shaking it.*) Oh, Mr. Carver, it's so nice of you to come out here. This is my brother, Mr. Dobbins, and this is Miss Gloria Gray of the *Newark Gazette,* and that's—I don't believe I know your—name—

GLORIA. Just Al, pay no attention to him.

AUDREY. Mr. Carver is my husband's boss.

CARVER. (*Recovering from the handshakes of* GLORIA *and* CLARENCE.) Where's Erwin?

GLORIA. (*Making notes.*) Oh sure—J. G. Carver— Right?

CARVER. What's the difference? Where is Erwin?—that's the point.

CLARENCE. Well, I'll tell you my theory, J. G.

CARVER. Who?

CLARENCE. J. G.? Isn't that correct?

CARVER. My name is Carver—call me Carver, Mr. Carver, or Hey You—but don't call me J.G.

GLORIA. (*Offering hand.*) My pal.

CARVER. (*Waving it away.*) No. No.—No nonsense— Where's Erwin?

AUDREY. The detective was here this morning and he said he thought they could trace him. He said lots of men disappear every day—especially married men about Erwin's age.

CARVER. Foolish talk. Foolish talk.

AUDREY. He said they generally turned up in hospitals saying they lost their memory—

CARVER. A lot of pish-posh— Now here's a man that's a reliable citizen, see—worth more than you or you or any of you—in his way. He's gone!! Where? Nobody knows. It's a silly country. Man phones me, says he's Erwin's manager— Why don't they trace him. 'Cause they're a lot of fools. Make a lot of mystery out of nothing—I know where he is.

GLORIA. Where?

CARVER. (*Shakes finger.*) Writing verses for a rival concern.

AUDREY. Oh, but Mister—

CARVER. Don't talk. Don't argue. I've figured it out. Thought I didn't appreciate him just 'cause I didn't pat him on the back every minute—along comes some sneak—gives him a lot of sugar and steals him away—no justice anywhere—never was —never will be.

GLORIA. But he'd hardly keep it a secret from his wife.

CARVER. 'Fraid of his wife?

AUDREY. Oh, no.

CARVER. Don't argue. Afraid of you. 'Fraid of that man over there—don't know who he is.

CLARENCE. Why, Mr. Carver, I'm—

CARVER. And I don't care. 'Fraid of everybody—just a poet. Just lives in himself. (*Taps forehead.*) Afraid of me, even. The fact is, that none of you can deny, he's gone—(*Shakes finger.*) and Mother's Day deadline is tomorrow. But I happen to know my rights. I've fought competitors before and I can do it again. (*Phone rings.*) Answer that. And if it's for me, I'm out. (AUDREY *starts for phone, but* CLARENCE *takes it.* CLARENCE *goes to phone and is seen but not heard talking.*)

CARVER. (*Coming down stage.*) Erwin wasn't so good at first. He had the feeling, the warmth and the inspiration to be a top-notch greeting card man, but he didn't have the technique. I taught him all I knew—I worked and struggled to bring him up, up the ladder and then someone steals him from me. (*Goes to the foot of divan.*)

CLARENCE. (*In phone.*) Well, you can if you want to.

AUDREY. What is it?

CLARENCE. (*In phone.*) Well, we know he took the bus for New York, but go ahead if you want to. (*Hangs up.*)

AUDREY. What was that?

CLARENCE. The Boy Scouts at Eagleville.

CARVER. What do they want?

CLARENCE. They want to drag the Eagleville Pond for Erwin.

AUDREY. What?

CLARENCE. I told them he wouldn't be there—but they said they'd never dragged a pond before and they wanted to do it anyway.

GLORIA. The Eagleville Pond—where is that?

CLARENCE. It's right down the street.

GLORIA. Come on, Al. We might use that —(*Starts for door.*)

CLARENCE. It's right next to my property —(GLORIA, CLARENCE *and* AL *go out.*)

AUDREY. (*Crosses right.*) I'm sure Erwin wouldn't want to work for anybody but you Mr. Carver—he was always saying how he liked being in your office and how wonderful you were.

CARVER. I didn't come here to listen to a lot of sentimental nonsense.

AUDREY. No, sir.

CARVER. What I want to know is—did he leave any verses around?

AUDREY. He took them with him—

CARVER. I mean any old ones? Things he was going to throw away maybe?

AUDREY. He wouldn't let me touch his desk—he was very particular about that.

CARVER. Stuff—stuff—stuff — nonsense—who cares? Did he leave any papers around?

AUDREY. He had a little room way up in the attic where it would be quiet and his desk is all covered with papers—

CARVER. All right—all right—show me.

AUDREY. But I don't know—

CARVER. Anything he did while working for me is my property. (AUDREY *starts up* —*he follows.*)—Go ahead with you (AUDREY *starts up the stairs*) Easter—I wouldn't care—got a man can write good Easter stuff—but Mother's Day is Erwin's specialty—nobody in the office has got his touch—(*They go out of sight and we hear him continue to grumble as the voices grow farther away.*) Printers have to have the proof way in advance—if I'm late then they charge me overtime . . . overtime, double time, all kinds of time . . . bunch of crooks—can't plan anything—raise prices —pay 'em more every year, get less work every year—the whole country is going to the dogs as fast as it can go. (*Upstairs a door slams, shutting off the then distant voice.*) (ERWIN *enters, followed by* MABEL *and* FRANKIE.)

MABEL. This the place?

ERWIN. Dearie. (ERWIN *opens front door.*)

MABEL. Oh, it's cute.

ERWIN. Dearie.

FRANKIE. Ain't she to home?

ERWIN. (*Sad.*) I guess not.

MABEL. (*Crossing right.*) Most likely went to a movie.

ERWIN. Guess so. Thought maybe she'd be worried about me, but—

FRANKIE. No—no—she wouldn't be worried.

ERWIN. Of course, maybe she's upstairs and can't hear me—(*Starts up.*)

FRANKIE. (*Grabbing* ERWIN.) No, wait—listen—before you do anything else, you got to phone Patsy.

ERWIN. Well.

FRANKIE. You promised, didn't he, Mabel?

MABEL. (*Crossing to door.*) Sure you did.

FRANKIE. What's the matter, Erwin? You got them selections, ain't you?

ERWIN. (*Coming back.*) Yes, I told you I had—Dearie.

FRANKIE. Well, you're acting kind of funny.

ERWIN. No, I'm not: honest I'm not.

FRANKIE. Where's your phone? (ERWIN *points to it.*)

MABEL. (*At door.*) Hey, look—there's a lot of people up there.

FRANKIE. (*Pulls her in.*) Never mind what anybody's doing—keep working on him, will you?

MABEL. (*Shaking him off.*) Well, Erwin's going to phone.

ERWIN. Sure, I'm going to—I just wonder where my wife is, that's all.

FRANKIE. Well, geez, this phoning is much more important, you know that, Erwin—you can look for your wife later. Shall I call the number for you?

ERWIN. No. I'll do it. (*Going to phone.*) You don't see a note around for me, do you? (MABEL *and* FRANKIE *look about.*) You'd think she'd have left a note. (*In phone.*) Hello—I want— (*Rises.*)

FRANKIE. What's the matter?

MABEL. (*In phone.*) Pennsylvania six five eight nine two—

ERWIN. (*Running to* FRANKIE.) Suppose Audrey's mad! Suppose she's gone back to live with her mother.

FRANKIE. She hasn't. She don't even like her mother—she likes you better—what the Hell—

MABEL. Hello—Kitty, give me Patsy's room—

FRANKIE. (*Exasperated.*) Look—everything is around here, ain't it? If she'd gone away she'd pack up, wouldn't she? Sure.

MABEL. (*In phone.*) This is me. He's here. Get a paper and pencil.

ERWIN. Well. I guess that's right.

FRANKIE. She's just gone out to get a little fresh air— that's all. You want her to be healthy don't you?

MABEL. (*Passes phone.*) Here you are. Patsy's waiting.

ERWIN. (*Taking phone from* MABEL.) Hello—yes, this is Erwin— What? Oh—oh, yes. Just a minute. I've got them— (*Gets out book to read list.* FRANKIE *pulls a paper out of his pocket to compare lists.*) For the first race Sunador—second Frolic —third Motto—fourth Mr. Khayyam— Well, that's all . . . yes, I know, but I didn't figure the rest of them yet . . . I thought I'd get the others on the way back.

FRANKIE. (*To* MABEL—*holding his list.*) I missed every one.

MABEL. What do you mean?

FRANKIE. I thought I'd see if there was anything in this bus business for me, too, maybe—so you know when I went to the rear seat and sat by myself?—I was trying to dope 'em, and I wrote 'em down all right but, I didn't hit a single one— (*Crumples paper, throws it on floor and walks to window.*) well, that shows it ain't just the bus anyhow.

ERWIN. Certainly I will—but I have my verses to think of too, you know—and— (AUDREY *enters from stairs.*)

FRANKIE. (*Seeing* AUDREY.) Oh—how are you?

AUDREY. Erwin.

ERWIN. (*Grins.*) Hello, dear—I was looking for you. I yoo-hooed a couple of times but— (*In phone.*) Well, goodbye, I want to talk to my wife. Dearie— (*Hangs up, rises and crosses to her.*) These are my friends.

AUDREY. Oh, Erwin— (*Rushes to his arms.* ERWIN *looks at the others pleased.* FRANKIE *gestures I-told-you-so.*) I've worried so—I couldn't imagine— (*Draws back.*) Where have you been?

ERWIN. Up at the hotel with them— (*As* AUDREY *looks at* MABEL.) him. Oh Dearie —I've got so much to tell you—

FRANKIE. Listen Erwin—them last two races. (*Coming between* ERWIN *and* AUDREY.)

ERWIN. Oh yes, of course—I can't tell you everything now, because we have to hurry right back again.

MABEL. Well, don't you think we better get started—

AUDREY. Is anything wrong?

ERWIN. No, no, everything's fine. And I'm going to give you a lot of money— over a hundred dollars.

AUDREY. I don't need any money, Erwin.

ERWIN. I'm going to give it to you anyhow. (*Searches through clothes.*)

AUDREY. Where'd you get it?

ERWIN. (*They start to drag* ERWIN *out.*) The horses.

AUDREY. Horses?

ERWIN. Yes. In my little book, you know. It's been quite a source of revenue just for advising. (CLARENCE *appears in center door.*)

CLARENCE. Well, well, well—

ERWIN. But don't tell him.

CLARENCE. (*Coming down.*) Don't tell me what?

MABEL. (*Going to* AUDREY.) I think your house is swell, Mrs. Trowbridge. I'd just like to own it myself. (*Going up center.*)

FRANKIE. (*Grabs him.*) Say, I don't want to rush you, Erwin, but—

ERWIN. Yes, we must get started.

CLARENCE. You going away already? Where you been?

AUDREY. Erwin, you'll be back?

ERWIN. Oh sure.

FRANKIE. He'll be back on the bus— every day—back and forth—you know . . . (*Grabbing him by arm.*)

ERWIN. Audrey.

FRANKIE. Remember your promise, Erwin.

ERWIN. Yes, yes, I know. I know. Oh, wait a minute. (*Breaks away. Rushes back to kiss* AUDREY.) See you tomorrow— (MA-BEL, FRANKIE *and* ERWIN *hurry out.*)

CLARENCE. Where's he gone?

AUDREY. (*Rushes to window, calling.*) Erwin.

CLARENCE. (*Follows.*) Where'd he get the money? What'd he say? What's he doing? What did he mean—don't tell me?

AUDREY. Oh, dear—

CLARENCE. Where's he gone? Where's he living? Who are those people with him?

AUDREY. (*Starts.*) He didn't even tell me where he was . . .

CLARENCE. (*Stops her.*) And why did he say "don't tell me"?—what is it he doesn't want me to know? He's got a horse, that's it—and he won't tell me.

CARVER. (*Enters from above.*) I found a few odds and ends that Erwin had apparently discarded as not good enough— but I think I can use them—I'll have to.

AUDREY. Oh, Mr. Carver—I forgot to tell him—

CARVER. What do you mean?

AUDREY. Erwin was here—he just left.

CARVER. Where? Where's he gone? (*Rushes out.*)

AUDREY. (*Starts after.*) They went up that way, I think. (*Outside.* CARVER *and* AUDREY *exeunt.* CLARENCE *goes to door, then turns and sees paper left on floor by* FRANKIE. *He picks it up, unfolds and reads, his eyes bulge with excitement.* CARVER *re-enters, followed by* AUDREY.)

CLARENCE. Huh.

CARVER. (*Coming down.*) It's your fault— it's all your fault. You should have called me. No wonder Erwin isn't farther ahead in the world. He's got an incompetent wife—that's what's the matter. You don't know where he is. Let him get away without finding out where he is.

CLARENCE. I know where he is.

CARVER. What? What'd you say?

CLARENCE. He's at the Lavillere Hotel.

CARVER. Where's that? Whoever heard of such a place? What are you talking about? How do you know?

CLARENCE. They dropped this paper.

CARVER. They? Who's they?

CLARENCE. There was a man and woman with him.

CARVER. Oh, so that's it—unscrupulous competitors—trying to ruin my Mother's Day output—I'll show 'em—I can fight for my rights—I'll show 'em— (*He jams on his hat and goes.*)

CLARENCE. He thinks they want Erwin's verses, but I know better. Look— (*Shows paper.*)

AUDREY. What's that?

CLARENCE. Horses. That's what he didn't want you to tell me, isn't it?

AUDREY. Yes, but—

CLARENCE. I found this on the floor— It's their list of the winning horses— Thought he'd hold out on me, did he—well, I'll show him— (*Stands.*)

AUDREY. What are you going to do?

CLARENCE. (*Gets phone.*) I'm going to bet my shirt.

BLACKOUT

ORCHESTRA *plays "Horses."*

SCENE II

Place: The hotel room.

Time: The same afternoon.

At Rise: HARRY, MOSES, PATSY, CHARLIE *and a* CHAMBERMAID *are copying verses. The maid is a Swede.*

CHARLIE. (*Rising from bed and looking over* PATSY's *shoulder.*) I ain't so sure Mr. Carver is going to like your handwriting.

PATSY. (*At desk.*) What's the matter with it?

CHARLIE. Plenty.

PATSY. To Hell with Carver.

CHARLIE. (*Pointing to* CHAMBERMAID.) Why don't you do it like her?

PATSY. Aw—she writes like a pansy.

CHARLIE. That's the way you're supposed to write. (*Sarcastic.*) The idea is so that somebody else can read it, see?

PATSY. The idea is get 'em done by the time Erwin gets back, that's all.

CHARLIE. (*Walking toward bed.*) Yeah, but we want him to like the job, don't we? We got to keep him contented? My God—look at what Moses is doing—what language you writing that in? African?

PATSY. Who appointed you foreman anyhow? (*Goes to phone.*) Get busy instead of criticizing so much. The thing is to be able to say they are copied.

CHARLIE. (*Sits.*) Get to work yourself, you tore 'em up. I'm tired—

PATSY. What're you so tired about?

CHARLIE. Do you think it's easy to find a synagogue?

PATSY. (*Suddenly.*) Geez, we forgot all about the second race— (*In phone.*) Let me talk to Gus. (*Sharply, in phone.*) Well, listen, Kitty, keep this wire open all the time, will you? This is important. To Hell with Mr. Shapiro—which is more important—cloaks and suits or horses?—well, I'm tellin' you—

MOSES. (*Looking up from bed where he has been seated.*) Lord a' mercy. (MOSES *starts out.*)

PATSY. Where you going?

MOSES. Somebody is pushin' that bell right through the elevator, Mr. Patsy, but I'll be back. (*Gives* CHARLIE *paper.*) I got this one all straight exceptin' one word down there in the corner. (*Exits.*)

HARRY. I got an extra word here. What does he need?

CHARLIE. Something to rhyme with—let me see— (*Reading.*) "We trudged our way on Sundays"—something to rhyme with Sundays.

HARRY. (*Looking at his piece of paper.*) No. The word I have here is "blue-birds."

CHARLIE. The only word I can think of is "undies" but I don't suppose Erwin would want to use that.

PATSY. (*In phone.*) Gus, how is it—over? (*Turning to others.*) "Frolic" in the second race. (*They all cheer.*)

HARRY. Atta baby. (*Jumps up, spilling papers.*)

CHARLIE. Hey, look out for them poems.

HARRY. I'm one hundred and four dollars to the good. Yeah—

PATSY. Pipe down, will you. (*In phone.*) That all goes on Motto in the third. Sure, it's a parlay. What the Hell do you think —we're pikers? . . . What are you crawlin' about? . . . Well, don't forget you ain't the only bookie . . . What's the matter? You yellow?

CHARLIE. Come on, Harry, help me pick them up. (*Starts to pick up papers.*)

HARRY. I got to listen.

CHARLIE. Suppose Erwin comes back and finds they ain't ready. He's liable to dry up on us before we get the last races out of him.

HARRY. Geez, that's right. We got to think about the future. (*Stooping to pick up verses.*)

PATSY. (*Back to phone.*) Sure we got a system—but he ain't here now. We sent him out to get some air. . . . How much? (*To others.*) He wants to buy a piece of Erwin.

CHAMBERMAID. (*Alarmed.*) What? (CHARLIE and HARRY *are amused by the* CHAMBERMAID's *expression.*)

PATSY. (*Into phone.*) Never mind how we got him—we own him, that's all. What's your offer for ten per cent? . . . Well, he ain't missed yet, has he? Wait till you pay up on this four horse parlay and you'll think so. . . . We wouldn't even consider an offer like that. (*Hangs up.*) A lousy two grand for ten per cent of Erwin.

CHARLIE. Maybe we ought to take it.

PATSY. What for?

CHARLIE. Well, supposing something went wrong?

PATSY. What're you talking about?

CHARLIE. Supposing this guy Erwin's holding out on us.

PATSY. Why you . . .

CHARLIE. No, but listen, what does he give us over the phone . . . Mr. Khayyam . . . and what does he give us under the pillow . . . Equipoise.

PATSY. What of it? Maybe that's the way he warms himself up. (*Phone.*)

HARRY. There's your poetry. Geez, a hundred and four dollars. I think I'll buy Erwin a necktie.

CHARLIE. He's got a necktie.

PATSY. (*In phone.*) Yeah? (*Turns to* HARRY.) It's Mac, he wants you to come right down.

HARRY. Huh. Tell him I took the day off. Tell him I've resigned.

PATSY. He's quit. He's too rich to work.

HARRY. (*Strolling back and forth.*) I can't be bothered with that small time stuff . . . all I want is to be able to follow Erwin around for the rest of my life.

PATSY. (*In phone.*) . . . and don't keep callin' us up, we want this wire open. (*Hangs up.*)

HARRY. I guess that surprised him, huh? I don't think I was meant to be a barkeep anyway.

PATSY. Now to Hell with all that. Let's get this stuff copied.

HARRY. Sure. All right. I'm just as anxious as you are. After all I got some rights to Erwin ain't I? Who discovered him in the first place?

MOSES. (*Enters.*) Yes sir, but I don't know if they . . .

CARVER. (*Enters.*) Never mind about that boy . . . Who's in charge here?

PATSY. Who are you?

CARVER. My name's J. G. Carver in case you're interested . . . and I'm here to tell you I know my rights.

CHARLIE. I guess you got the wrong room, brother.

CARVER. Don't try to shilly-shally with me. I've had the call traced. I know all about what's been going on here from A to Z. You kept him here all right . . .

HARRY. We what?

CARVER. (*Crossing to* HARRY.) You've been stealing his verses, the very verses he'd been working on under my instructions. I know what you're doing . . . all of you . . . Yes, and you too. (*To* MAID.)

MAID. I tink I better go now.

PATSY. Stay where you are, keep copying. (MAID *sits.*)

CARVER. You can all hear what I have to say . . . and if I don't get action any other way, the United States court will hear about it, let that be understood . . .

PATSY. What the Hell is it you want?

CARVER. I want Erwin Trowbridge.

HARRY. (*Jumps up.*) What?

CHARLIE. (*Pulls him back.*) Take it easy.

CARVER. I want him back in his office by tomorrow morning, or I'll have supoenas enough flying around here to make your eyes water. (*Phone rings.*) If that's for me, I'm out— There's no individualism in an organization like this . . . it's a bad thing for him.

PATSY. It's the third race, boys. Bounce him out of here.

CARVER. I ain't afraid of you fellows or any other greeting card company in the United States.

PATSY. Pipe down, will you.

CARVER. (*Struggles.*) I'll fight all of you.

PATSY. Did you hear us, pipe down . . . get him out of here, will you, boys? The bum's rush. Want me to miss this race? (CHARLIE and HARRY *grab him by the seat of his pants, knocking his hat off.* MOSES *picks up hat.*)

CHARLIE. Come on, Bo . . . scram.

HARRY. Leave him to me, I can handle him.

CARVER. Take your hands off me.

MOSES. Here's your hat.

PATSY. (*At phone.*) Coming down the stretch, eh? Who's in the lead?

CARVER. I'll have you blackguards in jail. Every one of you.

HARRY I've thrown out tougher guys than you.

CHARLIE. Don't hold back . . . I'll give you the boot.

MOSES. Better take your hat. (CHARLIE *and* HARRY *rush* CARVER *out door.*)

MAID. I've found the last line.

PATSY. (*Rises. In phone.*) Motto huh?

HARRY. (*Re-entering.*) He won't be back.

PATSY. Motto wins.

HARRY. Motto?

PATSY. We won . . . we won. Hold on a minute, Gus.

HARRY. (*As* CHARLIE *returns.*) Motto wins, Charlie.

CHARLIE. He won, huh?

CARVER. (*Throws open door.*) I've been in business since eighteen ninety-eight. (CHARLIE *slams door shut.*)

CHARLIE. Out and stay out.

MAID. That's the last one. Is there anything else?

PATSY. (*Extracting five dollar bill.*) Yeah. Here's a fin for you. Go down and put it on Mr. Khayyam in the fourth race.

MAID. Please Mr.—if it's all the same by you—I got a place that's much safer. (*Sticks it down shirt front.*)

CARVER. (*At door.*) Don't forget what the code says about unfair competition.

PATSY. Harry, take that guy downstairs and throw him in the street. Give him a hand, will you, Moses? (HARRY *exits.*)

MOSES. Mr. Patsy, I wish you wouldn't mix me up in this thing on account of the race problem.

PATSY. Maybe you're right. (MOSES *and* MAID *exit.*)

PATSY. (*Back to phone.*) Listen, Gus, it all rides on Mr. Khayyam—the works— what? . . . All right—then half of it— what do I care—I'll bet the rest with Eddie . . . No, I'm not crazy. (*With hand over phone; to* CHARLIE.) Go down and place half the dough with Eddie.

CHARLIE. Maybe we oughtn't to bet that half, Patsy, what d'ya say? Equipoise is a pretty good horse, Patsy, what about it? Well, I'm only thinkin'—

PATSY. Has Erwin missed yet?

CHARLIE. No-o-o, but—

PATSY. Then do what I tell you and collect on the straight bets—get going.

CHARLIE. Just the same— (*Goes to door.*) But I'm worried. (*Exits.*)

PATSY. (*Back to phone.*) . . . Yeah, that kind of money don't interest us. Erwin is a gold mine . . . we ain't selling shares

for chicken feed . . . all right, all right—
you know my number. (*Hangs up.* MABEL
has entered before the end of PATSY'S
speech.)

MABEL. (*Coming down to* PATSY.) I seen
it, Patsy—I seen it.

PATSY. Seen what?

MABEL. Our little dream house.

PATSY. Oh. Where's Erwin?

MABEL. He's downstairs with Frankie. Oh,
Patsy—it's gorgeous—you ought to been
there—there was the nicest curtains and
little pictures and a real garden and a
porch to sit on—and a second floor—only
I didn't go up and Erwin says he wants
to sell it.

PATSY. (*Going to the right away from
her.*) O. K. Buy it. Just don't bother me,
that's all.

MABEL. Patsy, don't you think we ought
to get married if we're going to live in
a house?

PATSY. We'll get married. You can get
married any day— (*Going to phone.*) but
I got a four horse parlay on the fire and
they don't come up often.

MABEL. They come up too often—they
come up and hit you right in the face.

PATSY. What do you mean by that?

MABEL. I mean I want you to buy this
house before everything goes back into
hock.

FRANKIE. (*Enters followed by* ERWIN.)
What's the matter with the elevator? We
had to walk up.

ERWIN. Are my verses copied?

PATSY. I think you'll find everything in
A-1 condition, Erwin.

FRANKIE. (PATSY *crosses to* FRANKIE.) Who
won the first race?

PATSY. (ERWIN *goes to the bed.*) We won
the first three. Charlie's out collectin' the
straight bets now. We got a parlay—ridin'
to Mr. Khayyam. (*Going back to desk.*)

FRANKIE. (*Sits on end bed.*) Did you hear
that, Erwin—we copped the first three.

ERWIN. (*He is looking at verses.*) What?

FRANKIE. The first three come in.

ERWIN. Oh.

MABEL. I was tellin' Patsy about the house,
Erwin, he says we'll buy it.

ERWIN. (*Looking at verses.*) Gee, I can
hardly read these. (*Telephone.*)

PATSY. (MABEL *goes right of* ERWIN. *Answering it.*) Hello— Oh, hello, Gus, now
you're talkin' turkey . . . we can close the
deal on those terms . . . sure . . . well,
Erwin is worth that much . . . he's just
like money in the bank. . . . All right—
we'll incorporate—but listen, I'm president.
(*Hangs up.*) That was Gus. They've come
around. I made them guys appreciate Erwin's true value.

FRANKIE. I'll bet we'll make a half million with him.

ERWIN. Oh, this is terrible.

PATSY. What's the trouble?

MABEL. What's the matter, Erwin?

ERWIN. Look at this!

MABEL. The handwriting?

ERWIN. No. The words. Those aren't my
words at all. (CHARLIE *enters.*)

PATSY. Well.

CHARLIE. I collected the straight bets and
the parlay stands. Geez, they certainly are
afraid of us—Gus had to lay off with three
bookies.

ERWIN. Oh, Mr. Carver would die if he
saw this—I'd lose my job.

MABEL. Looks like one of yours, Charlie.

CHARLIE. What's the trouble? (*Coming
down left.*)

ERWIN. I couldn't write anything like
this—

CHARLIE. Write what? Let's see.

ERWIN. It doesn't even scan.

PATSY. (*At desk.*) Well, come on boys, let's not have any fuss—let's just fix it, that's all.

CHARLIE. I did fix it.

ERWIN. I don't want anything fixed—I just wanted them copied.

CHARLIE. But we lost the last line.

PATSY. (*Comes center.*) What is it? (*Takes verses. Reads.*)
   "I wonder if the old church stands
   Where we trudged our way on Sundays;
   I recall how we sat with folded hands"

ERWIN. That part's all right—see—but the rest of it.

PATSY. (*Takes paper and reads.*) "So now I don't ever get drunk no more on Tuesdays or Mondays." (*Looks at Erwin.*) That's no good, huh?

ERWIN. It's awful.

CHARLIE. It's the right idea, ain't it? He's thinkin' of his mother, see—

ERWIN. It's no good—

FRANKIE. (*Going to CHARLIE.*) Yeah, you got a crust monkeying with Erwin's verses.

CHARLIE. I was only tryin' to help out—

PATSY. (*Crossing to the right.*) Well, come on, Erwin—just put in your words. What's the stew about?

ERWIN. I can't think what it was myself now. You got me so upset.

FRANKIE. There, you see—you got him all upset, you mug.

MABEL. What you cheap-skates ought to do is hire some first-class poet to do Erwin's verses for him—then he wouldn't have to worry so much.

PATSY. (*Crossing back to desk.*) When this four-horse parlay comes in we'll hire Longfellow.

MABEL. You couldn't hire Longfellow— 'cause he's dead—I think he is.

CHARLIE. Here. It all comes to thirty-three hundred dollars. That's on the straight bets. I'm keeping mine. Here's twenty-two hundred.

PATSY. (*Taking money.*) O.K. Now Erwin gets three hundred and thirty.

ERWIN. I do? All that?

PATSY. (*Going to ERWIN.*) That ain't nothin'. Wait till Mr. Khayyam comes through to make that four-horse parlay. Here you are, Erwin—three hundred and thirty dollars.

ERWIN. It doesn't seem right. (*Stuffing bills into pocket.*)

MABEL. The way you got to figure it out is, Erwin, that we wouldn't have this money if it wasn't for you.

PATSY. Well, we might have—

MABEL. Yeah, we might—but we probably wouldn't. You helped, that's sure.

PATSY. Erwin is always going to get his cut, don't worry. And when this fourth race comes through—

CHARLIE. *If* this fourth race comes through—

ERWIN. (*Turns and looks at him. ERWIN and PATSY look at CHARLIE, then at each other.*) Yes. I see what you mean. That's pretty good. (*Laughs.*)

PATSY. (*Alarmed.*) Wait a minute.

ERWIN. (*Looking at verses.*) It's funny how one line could get lost that way.

PATSY. Never mind about that poetry for just a minute, will you, Erwin?

ERWIN. (*Absently, pieces of paper in his hand.*) What?

PATSY. Let's just concentrate on this—the fourth race, I mean—

ERWIN. Of course.

PATSY. We can't lose. Can we, Erwin?

ERWIN. No—I don't think so.

PATSY. Mr. Khayyam is your selection, isn't he?

ERWIN. Oh, yes—that's the horse. (*Sees paper.*) There!—the line—there's the verse.

PATSY. Stop changing the subject.

CHARLIE. (*Crossing to* ERWIN.) Do you think we should shift to Equipoise?

ERWIN. No.

CHARLIE. Then why did you write his name on a piece of paper?

ERWIN. I didn't—

CHARLIE. Oh, you didn't—what about this? (*Flashes paper.*)

ERWIN. (*Takes paper.*) Oh, that?

CHARLIE. Yeah, that. Why did you hide it under the pillow?

ERWIN. Oh, that was when I was sitting on the bed trying to dope them and I wasn't sure I could do it—so I wrote Equipoise two or three times just to see how it would look—but I didn't think it looked so good.

PATSY. Oh, you wasn't sure.

ERWIN. No— Don't you see— I'm surprised at you fellows—you were all right yesterday, when I was sick and you took care of me and all that—but now you're getting greedy.

PATSY. I notice you took your ten per cent.

ERWIN. Oh, yes indeed.

PATSY. You wouldn't by any chance be thinkin' of crossin' us, would you, Erwin?

ERWIN. No—of course not— Oh no—

PATSY. All right, boys, everything goes on Mr. Khayyam.

CHARLIE. How much you betting, Erwin?

ERWIN. Oh, I wouldn't bet.

PATSY. What do you mean? Which way wouldn't you bet?

ERWIN. No. I wouldn't bet on anything. That would spoil it.

MABEL. Sure. Erwin explained that to me.

PATSY. Shut up. (*To* ERWIN.) I thought maybe you ought to bet on this nag, Erwin—you doped him.

ERWIN. But don't you see, if I did—

PATSY. No, I don't see a thing except that if he's good enough for us to put our shirts on—he's good enough for you too. Just give your bet to Frankie and he'll take it over with him. (FRANKIE *rises.*)

ERWIN. Well it'll spoil all my fun— (CHARLIE *crosses to window.*) but of course —if you buy the house—then I won't be riding on the bus anymore anyway— Well, I think I'll bet two dollars.

CHARLIE. Two dollars!

PATSY. What are you doing—kidding?

ERWIN. No, I'm serious— I think he'll win. I want to bet two dollars.

PATSY. Well, this is a Hell of a joke. We got eleven thousand dollars on Mr. Khayyam and you want to bet a deuce. You can't think much of the horse.

ERWIN. I certainly do—I picked him.

PATSY. Well, then play something worth while.

ERWIN. Oh, I see what you mean. Here Frankie—put ten dollars on his nose. (*Counts it.*)

PATSY. Frankie didn't hear you.

CHARLIE. No, he's deaf.

FRANKIE. They think you ought to put up some real dough, Erwin.

MABEL. I don't think you ought to make him bet, boys.

PATSY. Well, we're going to, whether you think so or not. I wouldn't go so far as to say that Charlie's right about you, but a good-sized bet from you would make me think his heart is in the right place.

ERWIN. All right—here—put a hundred dollars on Mr. Khayyam to show.

PATSY. To show, huh—he's good enough for us to have all we got on his nose and you want to play a louzy century note to show. (*Knocks* ERWIN's *arm down.*)

FRANKIE. You better hurry up if you want to get this down.

PATSY. Shut up. You're goin' to play what you got—on the nose.

ERWIN. You mean all my ten per cents?

PATSY. All your ten per cents. Hand it over.

ERWIN. (*Hands roll to* PATSY.) Well—all right—here you are.

PATSY. (*Gives him money.*) Put that on Mr. Khayyam for Erwin—right on the nose.

ERWIN. Hey, wait—my money from the Bowery Savings Bank is in that.

PATSY. The Hell with it. If he's good enough for us he's good enough for you— every nickel. Go on, Frankie.

FRANKIE. O.K. I got to hurry. (*Goes out.*) (*When* FRANKIE *opens door to go out we see* CLARENCE *standing in hall. He looks in and sees* ERWIN.)

CLARENCE. (*Entering. To* ERWIN. *Comes in.*) There he is. Hiding from me, you sneak. You low down cheat. You couldn't come out and fight like a man. You had to trick me—you crook.

PATSY. Hey, wait a minute.

CLARENCE. He pretends he knows all about horse races. He's got a list. He's got a little black book.

PATSY. Yeah—we know all about that.

CLARENCE. He cleaned me out. He tricked me. He left a list on the floor—knew I'd find it—

ERWIN. That's not the facts at all.

CLARENCE. You double-crossing, Mother's Day crook—I went to the bank—drew all my money out— I'm cleaned—lost every cent.

PATSY. Who is this guy?

ERWIN. He's my brother-in-law.

CLARENCE. Yesterday he had them right— all winners—just to lead me on— (HARRY *enters.*) just to make me bet.

PATSY. You're just in time, Harry. Push this guy downstairs, will you?

HARRY. Be glad to oblige, Mr. Patsy. (*To* CLARENCE.) Come on— (*Takes his arm.*)

CLARENCE. Now just a minute, I don't know who you gentlemen are but I'd like to introduce myself.

HARRY. Tough guy, huh— (*Grabs him by pants and rushes him out.*)

CLARENCE. What's the idea? (*As they exit.*)

PATSY. So you'd double-cross your own brother-in-law?

ERWIN. No, I didn't—honestly. He just made a mistake, that was all I wouldn't cheat anybody—(*Pause—they look at him.*) You fellows believe me, don't you?

PATSY. (*Drily.*) Sure.

CHARLIE. (*Disregarding* ERWIN.) I told you we shouldn't put everything on Mr. Khayyam—(*Pause.*) Well, what are we going to do?

PATSY. It's too late to do anything. (*Looks at watch.*) It's past time. I'll go down to Gus's so I can collect as soon as—I mean if Mr. Khayyam comes in. You stay here.

CHARLIE. Don't worry—I'll take care of him. (*Crosses and sits near desk.*) (PATSY *exits.*)

ERWIN. Gee, you fellows are getting pretty serious. I haven't missed yet, have I?

CHARLIE. (*More to himself.*) Eleven thousand dollars.

ERWIN. Well, I suppose Mr. Carver is waiting for me—I better get my verses together and—Get over there—

CHARLIE. You stay here.

ERWIN. But I can't, I—

CHARLIE. Until after the race.

ERWIN. But Charlie.

CHARLIE. (*Makes a gesture of finality and sits by the door.*) After the race.

ERWIN. (*Poetic.*) After the race (*sits*) after the race—
That ought to lead to something. (*Takes pencil and paper.*) Oh, I can't even think any more.

MABEL. (*Turns on radio.*) Maybe I can get the race on here. (MABEL turns on *wrong stations.*)

ERWIN. It's WMCA at the top of the dial —I think. (*She gets the station.*)

ANNOUNCER. . . . and took the first turn in that order. War Glory, Good Advice, Ladies' Man and Mr. Khayyam.

CHARLIE. (*At the same time.*) That's it— hold it.

MABEL. (*To* CHARLIE.) Is this our race?

CHARLIE. Yeah—they're on their way.

ANNOUNCER. At the quarter . . . War Glory, Good Advice, Mr. Khayyam there in that order now. Lady's Man going up . . . yes, past Farino. Good Advice is holding that lead, jockey Meade using his head. There they are at the half, Good Advice, War Glory, Mr. Khayyam. Mr. Khayyam driving now—rushing in there. Ah, there's a tumble, a spill. Chase Me stumbled, throwing the jockey, Slate. Slate's all right. That's the three quarter pole. Mr. Khayyam now leading with Lady's Man coming up and War Glory right behind. There they come fast into the stretch. Looks like a little shoving there . . . no, all right. At the stretch coming down there with a rush, Equipoise passes Mr. Khayyam, Sun Archer right behind. Yes, yes, that's the finish. Equipoise wins. Equipoise, the Whitney horse with Workman up. Mr. Khayyam second and Sun Archer closed fast to get third and in the money. Those who backed Equipoise had something to be thankful for today.
(MABEL *turns off radio.*)

ERWIN. Well, that's too bad.

CHARLIE. Yes, it's just too bad.

MABEL. (*Slowly crosses to window.*) Ah, geez, I'm just sick—you know it—I'm just sick to the stomach.

ERWIN. Well, the handicappers were right —they all thought Equipoise would win. Well, that's what makes it interesting. (FRANKIE *enters. Crosses to radio.*)

CHARLIE. Where's Patsy?

FRANKIE. He's coming.

CHARLIE. You guys wouldn't listen to me. Didn't I tell you all along—I had a hunch something like this would happen. (PATSY *enters, comes toward* ERWIN.)

ERWIN. (*Rises.*) I suppose you want your necktie back now.

PATSY. I want more than that.

ERWIN. I feel awfully sorry for you fellows,

PATSY. You better start feeling sorry for yourself.

CHARLIE. He tried to beat it off to the office and leave us holding the bag.

FRANKIE. What his brother-in-law said about him was all true.

CHARLIE. The crook.

MABEL. (*Terrified.*) Boys, what are you going to do?

PATSY. We'll give him something to remember us by. He knew damn well Equipoise was going to win.

ERWIN. I didn't. That's not so.

PATSY. Well, I'll tell you one thing . . . he'll never forget that Mr. Khayyam lost. (*Bing. He hits* ERWIN.)

MABEL. Patsy.

ERWIN. Now wait a minute.

PATSY. Learn you to cross us. (*Grabs him by the coat and hits again.*)

FRANKIE. Give one for me.

MABEL. Don't—don't.

ERWIN. Don't you think this is a little drastic?

PATSY. I'll show you what's drastic.

MABEL. Patsy . . . Patsy . . .

PATSY. You keep out of it. (*Shoving her aside.*)

MABEL. Don't hit him again.

PATSY. I ain't started yet. Get a loud station, Frankie.
(FRANKIE *turns on radio.*)

CHARLIE. (*Grabs* MABEL *and holds her.*) Here. Don't try to interfere. That ain't going to do any good.

MABEL. No . . . No . . .

PATSY. Listen, I ain't even begun. (*Radio is heard.*)

CHARLIE. Wait a minute.

ANNOUNCER. Something going on down at the judges stand and no bets are being paid until the official announcement. Looks like a disqualification to me.

PATSY. What?

CHARLIE. Listen.

ANNOUNCER. . . . I was all wrong, folks,— I was all wrong. Equipoise did not win after all—the judges have been in a huddle down there at the stand—what excitement —wait a minute folks,—what is it, Perry? —here's the latest announcement—I just got it—Equipoise disqualified—Mr. Khayyam declared the official winner—Sun Archer second and Lady's Man third. Mr. Khayyam paid twelve to one (FRANKIE *snaps it off. He turns to the others with a naive grin.*

PATSY. We won. (*They look at* ERWIN. PATSY *goes to him apologetically.*) Gee, I'm awfully sorry, Erwin—

ERWIN. You—(ERWIN *hits him a belt in the jaw.* PATSY *staggers back more from surprise than force.*)

PATSY. Hey, what's the idea?

MABEL. You had it coming to you.

CHARLIE. (*Pushing him about.*) Yeah, I don't blame Erwin. What's the idea of hitting him that way?

ERWIN. Yes, what's the idea? You make me good and mad. (*Takes a swing at* PATSY. PATSY, *mad, would defend himself.*)

CHARLIE. (*Pushing him away.*) Don't hit him, Patsy—he'll quit us.

(CLARENCE *opens center door and comes in, ad libbing. He sees* ERWIN *swinging on* PATSY, *who is apparently afraid of him. He is astounded.* ERWIN *turns and sees* CLARENCE—*full of new-born confidence he*

rushes at him. CLARENCE *runs out in fear and slams door.* ERWIN *turns and gets his breath, leaning against door. Hercules has cleaned the Aegean Stables.*)

PATSY. (*At desk.*) Come on, Erwin, don't be sore. Announcers don't make mistakes like that often—and geez, we had our shirts up.

AUDREY. (*Opens door, sees* ERWIN.) Thank you very much—Erwin! I want to talk to you—It's very important. What did you do to Clarence?

ERWIN. Oh, that big—

AUDREY. Please forgive him—he's lost all his money—he's so upset— (CLARENCE *and* CARVER *appear center.*)

ERWIN. Oh, Mr. Carver—

AUDREY. And, Erwin, will you do me a favor—?

ERWIN. Sure!

AUDREY. Will you speak to Mr. Carver?

ERWIN. Why—

CARVER. (*Coming left of* ERWIN.) Erwin—

ERWIN. Yes, Mr. Carver—I'm sorry I—

CARVER. Have these men a contract with you?

ERWIN. Oh no—no—they just—

CARVER. Who gave you your start?

ERWIN. You did, Mr. Carver.

CARVER. Who taught you the business? (HARRY *enters, goes between* CARVER *and* PATSY.)

HARRY. What do I do for the fifth?

CARVER. Don't interrupt!

HARRY. What do you mean, don't interrupt? (*Slaps* CARVER.) Who do you think you are?

ERWIN. Don't talk to Mr. Carver that way.

HARRY. (*Meek.*) Oh, all right, Erwin, if you say so. But what do I do in the fifth?

PATSY. Shut up.

MOSES. (*Enters with sheaf of money.*) Boy, did I ride home on a cloud of glory.

ERWIN. Get back on your elevator.

MOSES. Oh . . . yes sir, Mr. Erwin.

AUDREY. (*In admiration.*) Erwin.

ERWIN. I'm sorry we've been interrupted, Mr. Carver.

CARVER. I'm going to have the room with the north light repainted and redecorated and you can have that to work in, and I'm going to get you a new desk and put your name on the door and I'll give you sixty dollars a week.

ERWIN. Sixty?

CARVER. Seventy-five. (*Phone rings.*) I'm in conference . . . telephones, telephones . . . all day long . . . haven't I had enough trouble . . . I'm sorry, Erwin, I'm sorry. (*Phone rings again.*)

PATSY. O.K. for me to answer that call, Erwin?

ERWIN. Sure, go ahead. (PATSY *does so.*)

AUDREY. Erwin, please do me a favor . . . go back to Mr. Carver. I know you'll be happier that way.

PATSY. They want to buy twenty per cent of you, Erwin. They've doubled their offer.

ERWIN. Yes. That's all right, except I won't be able to dope them anymore.

PATSY. Why not, why won't you?

ERWIN. Cause you made me bet.

PATSY. What's the difference?

ERWIN. Well, you can't dope them for money. You just have to do it for fun. I told you that. I wouldn't have any idea who was going to win now. (*Puts hand to his head.*)

AUDREY. What's the matter, Erwin? Do you want Clarence to leave the room?

ERWIN. Mr. Carver, have you got a pencil?

CARVER. (*Hurrying to get it.*) Yes, Erwin, yes, my boy, what is it?

ERWIN. Take this down:
  The race is o'er
  We've won my lad
  Love and kisses
  to dear ol' Dad.
(*Raises one finger indicating Father's Day Number One.*)

CURTAIN AND MUSIC

The Children's Hour

BY LILLIAN HELLMAN

FOR

D. HAMMETT

WITH THANKS

THE CHILDREN'S HOUR was produced and directed by Herman Shumlin at Maxine Elliott's Theatre, New York, on November 20, 1934. The settings were designed by Aline Bernstein.

CAST

(In the order of their speech)

PEGGY ROGERS	Eugenia Rawls
MRS. LILY MORTAR	Aline McDermott
EVELYN MUNN	Elizabeth Seckel
HELEN BURTON	Lynne Fisher
LOIS FISHER	Jacqueline Rusling
CATHERINE	Barbara Leeds
ROSALIE WELLS	Barbara Beals
MARY TILFORD	Florence McGee
KAREN WRIGHT	Katherine Emery
MARTHA DOBIE	Anne Revere
DOCTOR JOSEPH CARDIN	Robert Keith
AGATHA	Edmonia Nolley
MRS. AMELIA TILFORD	Katherine Emmet
A GROCERY BOY	Jack Tyler

ACT I

Living-room of the Wright-Dobie School.
Late afternoon in April.

ACT II

Scene I. Living-room at Mrs. Tilford's. A few hours later.
Scene II. The same. Later that evening.

ACT III

The same as Act I. November.

THE CHILDREN'S HOUR

ACT ONE

SCENE: A room in the Wright-Dobie School for girls, a converted farm-house eighteen miles from the town of Lancet. It is a comfortable, unpretentious room used as an after-noon study-room and at all other times as the living-room.

A large door Left Center faces the audience. There is a single door Right. Against both back walls are bookcases. A large desk is at Right; a table, two sofas, and eight or ten chairs.

It is early in an afternoon in April.

AT RISE: MRS. LILY MORTAR is sitting in a large chair Right Center, with her head back and her eyes closed. She is a plump, florid woman of forty-five with obviously touched-up hair. Her clothes are too fancy for a class-room.

Seven girls, from twelve to fourteen years old, are informally grouped on chairs and sofa. Six of them are sewing with no great amount of industry on pieces of white material. One of the others, EVELYN MUNN, is using her scissors to trim the hair of ROSALIE, who sits, nervously, in front of her. She has ROSALIE's head bent back at an awkward angle and is enjoying herself.

The eighth girl, PEGGY ROGERS, is sitting in a higher chair than the others. She is reading aloud from a book. She is bored and she reads in a singsong, tired voice.

PEGGY (*reading*). "It is twice blest; it blesseth him that gives and him that takes: 'tis mightiest in the mightiest; it becomes the throned monarch better than his crown; his sceptre shows the force of temporal power, the attribute to awe and majesty, wherein . . ." (MRS. MORTAR *suddenly opens her eyes and stares at the hair-cutting. The children make efforts to warn* EVELYN. PEGGY *raises her voice until she is shouting.*) "doth sit the dread and fear of kings; but mercy is above . . ."

MRS. MORTAR. Evelyn! What are you doing?

EVELYN (*inanely. She lisps*). Uh—nothing, Mrs. Mortar.

MRS. MORTAR. You are certainly doing something. You are ruining the scissors, for one thing.

PEGGY (*loudly*). "But mercy is above. It . . ."

MRS. MORTAR. Just a moment, Peggy. It is very unfortunate that you girls cannot sit quietly with your sewing and drink in the immortal words of the immortal bard. (*She sighs.*) Evelyn, go back to your sewing.

EVELYN. I can't get the hem thtraight. Honeth, I've been trying for three weekth, but I jutht can't do it.

MRS. MORTAR. Helen, please help Evelyn with the hem.

HELEN (*rises, holding up the garment* EVELYN *has been working on. It is soiled and shapeless, and so much has been cut off that it is now hardly large enough for a child of five. Giggling.*) She can't ever wear *that*, Mrs. Mortar.

MRS. MORTAR (*vaguely*). Well, try to do something with it. Make some handkerchiefs or something. Be clever about it. Women must learn these tricks. (*To* PEGGY.) Continue. "Mightiest in the mightiest."

PEGGY. "'Tis mightiest in the mightiest; it becomes the throned monarch better than his crown; his sceptre—his sceptre shows the force of temporal power, the attribute to awe and majesty, wherein—"

LOIS (*from the back of the room chants softly and monotonously through the previous speech*). Ferebam, ferebas, ferebat, ferebamus, ferebatis, fere, fere—

CATHERINE (*two seats away, the book propped in front of her*). Fere*bant*.

LOIS. Ferebamus, ferebatis, fere*bant*.

MRS. MORTAR. Who's doing that?

PEGGY (*the noise ceases. She hurries on*). "Wherein doth sit the dread and fear of kings; but mercy is above this sceptred sway,

562

it is enthroned in the hearts of kings, it is an attribute to God himself—"

MRS. MORTAR (*sadly, reproachfully*). Peggy, can't you imagine yourself as Portia? Can't you read the lines with some feeling, some pity? (*Dreamily.*) Pity. Ah! As Sir Henry said to me many's the time, pity makes the actress. Now, why can't *you* feel pity?

PEGGY. I guess I feel pity.

LOIS. Ferebamus, ferebatis, fere—fere—fere—

CATHERINE. Fere*bant,* stupid.

MRS. MORTAR. How many people in this room are talking? Peggy, read the line again. I'll give you the cue.

PEGGY. What's a cue?

MRS. MORTAR. A cue is a line or word given the actor or actress to remind them of their next speech.

HELEN (*softly*). To remind *him* or *her.*

ROSALIE (*a fattish girl with glasses*). Weren't you ever in the movies, Mrs. Mortar?

MRS. MORTAR. I had many offers, my dear. But the cinema is a shallow art. It has no—no— (*vaguely.*) no fourth dimension. Now, Peggy, if you would only try to submerge yourself in this problem. You are pleading for the life of a man. (*She rises and there are faint sighs from the girls, who stare at her with blank, bored faces. She recites hammily, with gestures.*) "But mercy is above this sceptred sway; it is enthroned in the hearts of kings, it is an attribute to God himself; and earthly power doth then show likest God's when mercy seasons justice."

LOIS (*almost singing it*). Utor, fruor, fungor, potior, and vescor take the dative.

CATHERINE. Take the *ablative.*

LOIS. Oh, dear. Utor, fruor, fung—

MRS. MORTAR (*to LOIS, with sarcasm*). You have something to tell the class?

LOIS (*apologetically*). We've got a Latin exam this afternoon.

MRS. MORTAR. And you intend to occupy the sewing and elocution hour learning what should have been learnt yesterday?

CATHERINE (*wearily*). It takes her more than yesterday to learn it.

MRS. MORTAR. Well, I cannot allow you to interrupt us like this.

CATHERINE. But we're finished sewing.

LOIS (*admiringly*). I bet you were good at Latin, Mrs. Mortar.

MRS. MORTAR (*conciliated*). Long ago, my dear, long ago. Now, take your book over by the window and don't disturb our enjoyment of Shakespeare. (CATHERINE *and* LOIS *rise, go to window, stand mumbling and gesturing.*) Let us go back again. "It is an attribute of—" (*At this point the door opens far enough to let* MARY TILFORD, *clutching a slightly faded bunch of wild flowers, squeeze cautiously in. She is fourteen, neither pretty nor ugly. She is an undistinguished-looking girl, except for the sullenly dissatisfied expression on her face.*) "And earthly power doth then show likest God's when mercy seasons justice. We do pray for mercy, and that same prayer doth teach—"

PEGGY (*happily*). You've skipped three lines.

MRS. MORTAR. In my entire career I've never missed a line.

PEGGY. But you did skip three lines. (*Goes to* MRS. MORTAR *with book.*) See?

MRS. MORTAR (*seeing* MARY *sidling along wall toward other end of the room, turns to her to avoid* PEGGY *and the book*). Mary!

HELEN (*in whisper to* MARY). You're going to catch it now.

MRS. MORTAR. Mary!

MARY. Yes, Mrs. Mortar?

MRS. MORTAR. This is a pretty time to be coming to your sewing class, I must say. Even if you have no interest in your work you might at least remember that you owe me a little courtesy. Courtesy is breeding. Breeding is an excellent thing. (*Turns to class.*) Always remember that.

ROSALIE. Please, Mrs. Mortar, can I write that down?

MRS. MORTAR. Certainly. Suppose you all write it down.

PEGGY. But we wrote it down last week. (MARY *giggles*.)

MRS. MORTAR. Mary, I am still awaiting your explanation. Where have you been?

MARY. I took a walk.

MRS. MORTAR. So you took a walk. And may I ask, young lady, are we in the habit of taking walks when we should be at our classes?

MARY. I am sorry, Mrs. Mortar. I went to get you these flowers. I thought you would like them and I didn't know it would take so long to pick them.

MRS. MORTAR (*flattered*). Well, well.

MARY (*almost in tears*). You were telling us last week how much you liked flowers, and I thought that I would bring you some and—

MRS. MORTAR. That was very sweet of you, Mary; I always like thoughtfulness. But you must not allow anything to interfere with your classes. Now run along, dear, and get a vase and some water to put my flowers in. (MARY *turns, sticks out her tongue at* HELEN, *says* "A-a-a," *and exits Left*.) You may put that book away, Peggy. I am sure your family need never worry about your going on the stage.

PEGGY. I don't want to go on the stage. I want to be a lighthouse-keeper's wife.

MRS. MORTAR. Well, I certainly hope you won't read to him. (*The laughter of the class pleases her.* PEGGY *sits down among the other girls, who are making a great show of doing nothing.* MRS. MORTAR *returns to her chair, puts her head back, closes her eyes*.)

CATHERINE. How much longer, O Cataline, are you going to abuse our patience? (*To* LOIS.) Now translate it, and for goodness' sakes try to get it right this time.

MRS. MORTAR (*for no reason*). "One master passion in the breast, like Aaron's serpent, swallows all the rest." (*She and* LOIS *are murmuring during* KAREN WRIGHT'S *entrance.* KAREN *is an attractive woman of twenty-eight, casually pleasant in manner, without sacrifice of warmth or dignity. She smiles at the girls, goes to the desk. With her entrance there is an immediate change* in the manner of the girls: they are fond of her and they respect her. She gives MORTAR, whose quotation has reached her, an annoyed look.)

LOIS. "Quo usque tandem a*butere*. . . . "

KAREN (*automatically*). "Abutere." (*Opens drawer in desk*). What's happened to your hair, Rosalie?

ROSALIE. It got cut, Miss Wright.

KAREN (*smiling*). I can see that. A new style? Looks as though it has holes in it.

EVELYN (*giggling*). I didn't mean to do it that bad, Mith Wright, but Rothalie'th got funny hair. I thaw a picture in the paper, and I wath trying to do it that way.

ROSALIE (*feels her hair, looks pathetically at* KAREN). Oh, what shall I do, Miss Wright? (*Gesturing*.) It's long here, and it's short here and—

KAREN. Never mind. Come up to my room later and I'll see if I can fix it for you.

MRS. MORTAR. And hereafter we'll have no more haircutting.

KAREN. Helen, have you found your bracelet?

HELEN. No, I haven't, and I've looked everywhere.

KAREN. Have another look. It must be in your room somewhere. (MARY *comes in Right, with her flowers in a vase. When she sees* KAREN, *she loses some of her assurance.* KAREN *looks at the flowers in surprise*.)

MARY. Good afternoon, Miss Wright. (*Sits down, looks at* KAREN, *who is staring hard at the flowers*.)

KAREN. Hello, Mary.

MRS. MORTAR (*fluttering around*). Peggy has been reading Portia for us. (PEGGY *sighs*.)

KAREN (*smiling*). Peggy doesn't like Portia?

MRS. MORTAR. I don't think she quite appreciates it, but—

KAREN (*patting* PEGGY *on the head*). Well, I didn't either. I don't think I do yet. Where'd you get those flowers, Mary?

MRS. MORTAR. She picked them for me. (*Hurriedly.*) It made her a little late to class, but she heard me say I loved flowers, and she went to get them for me. (*With a sigh.*) The first wild flowers of the season.

KAREN. But not the very first, are they, Mary?

MARY. I don't know.

KAREN. Where did you get them?

MARY. Near Conway's cornfield, I think.

KAREN. It wasn't necessary to go so far. There was a bunch exactly like this in the garbage can this morning.

MRS. MORTAR (*after a second*). Oh, I can't believe it! What a nasty thing to do! (*To* MARY.) And I suppose you have just as fine an excuse for being an hour late to breakfast this morning, and last week— (*To* KAREN.) I haven't wanted to tell you these things before, but—

KAREN (*hurriedly, as a bell rings off stage*). There's the bell.

LOIS (*walking toward door*). Ad, ab, ante, in, de, inter, con, post, præ— (*Looks up at* KAREN.) I *can't* seem to remember the rest.

KAREN. Præ, pro, sub, super. Don't worry, Lois. You'll come out all right. (LOIS *smiles, exits.* MARY *attempts to make a quick exit.*) Wait a minute, Mary. (*Reluctantly* MARY *turns back as the girls file out.* KAREN *moves the small chairs, clearing the room as she talks.*) Mary, I've had the feeling—and I don't think I'm wrong—that the girls here were happy; that they liked Miss Dobie and me, that they liked the school. Do you think that's true?

MARY. Miss Wright, I have to get my Latin book.

KAREN. I thought it was true until you came here a year ago. I don't think you're very happy here, and I'd like to find out why. (*Looks at* MARY, *waits for an answer, gets none, shakes her head.*) Why, for example, do you find it necessary to lie to us so often?

MARY (*without looking up*). I'm not lying. I went out walking and I saw the flowers and they looked pretty and I didn't know it was so late.

KAREN (*impatiently*). Stop it, Mary! I'm not interested in hearing that foolish story again. I *know* you got the flowers out of the garbage can. What I do want to know is why you feel you have to lie out of it.

MARY (*beginning to whimper*). I *did* pick the flowers near Conway's. You never believe me. You believe everybody but me. It's always like that. Everything I say you fuss at me about. Everything I do is wrong.

KAREN. You know that isn't true. (*Goes to* MARY, *puts her arm around her, waits until the sobbing has stopped.*) Look, Mary, look at me. (*Raises* MARY's *face with her hand.*) Let's try to understand each other. If you feel that you *have* to take a walk, or that you just *can't* come to class, or that you'd like to go into the village by yourself, come and tell me—I'll try and understand. (*Smiles.*) I don't say that I'll always agree that you should do exactly what you want to do, but I've had feelings like that, too—everybody has—and I won't be unreasonable about yours. But this way, this kind of lying you do, makes everything wrong.

MARY (*looking steadily at* KAREN). I got the flowers near Conway's cornfield.

KAREN (*looks at* MARY, *sighs, moves back toward desk and stands there for a moment*). Well, there doesn't seem to be any other way with you; you'll have to be punished. Take your recreation periods alone for the next two weeks. No horseback-riding and no hockey. Don't leave the school grounds for any reason whatsoever. Is that clear?

MARY (*carefully*). Saturday, too?

KAREN. Yes.

MARY. But you said I could go to the boat-races.

KAREN. I'm sorry, but you can't go.

MARY. I'll tell my grandmother. I'll tell her how everybody treats me here and the way I get punished for every little thing I do. I'll tell her, I'll—

MRS. MORTAR. Why, I'd slap her hands!

KAREN (*turning back from door, ignoring* MRS. MORTAR's *speech. To* MARY) Go upstairs, Mary.

MARY. I don't feel well.

KAREN (*wearily*). Go upstairs now.

MARY. I've got a pain. I've had it all morning. It hurts right here (*pointing vaguely in the direction of her heart.*) Really it does.

KAREN. Ask Miss Dobie to give you some hot water and bicarbonate of soda.

MARY. It's a bad pain. I've never had it before.

KAREN. I don't think it can be very serious.

MARY. My heart! It's my heart! It's stopping or something. I can't breathe. (*She takes a long breath and falls awkwardly to the floor.*)

KAREN (*sighs, shakes her head, kneels beside* MARY. *To* MRS. MORTAR). Ask Martha to phone Joe.

MRS. MORTAR (*going out*). Do you think—? Heart trouble is very serious in a child. (KAREN *picks* MARY *up from the floor and carries her off Right. After a moment* MARTHA DOBIE *enters Center. She is about the same age as* KAREN. *She is a nervous, high-strung woman.*)

KAREN (*enters Right*). Did you get Joe?

MARTHA (*nodding*). What happened to her? She was perfectly well a few hours ago.

KAREN. She probably still is. I told her she couldn't go to the boat-races and she had a heart attack.

MARTHA. Where is she?

KAREN. In there. Mortar's with her.

MARTHA. Anything really wrong with her?

KAREN. I doubt it. (*Sits down at desk and begins to mark papers.*) She's a problem, that kid. Her latest trick was kidding your aunt out of a sewing lesson with those faded flowers we threw out. Then she threatened to go to her grandmother with some tale about being mistreated.

MARTHA. And, please God, Grandma would believe her and take her away.

KAREN. Which would give the school a swell black eye. But we ought to do something.

MARTHA. How about having a talk with Mrs. Tilford?

KAREN (*smiling*). You want to do it? (MARTHA *shakes her head.*) I hate to do it. She's been so nice to us. (*Shrugging her shoulders.*) Anyway, it wouldn't do any good. She's too crazy about Mary to see her faults very clearly—and the kid knows it.

MARTHA. How about asking Joe to say something to her? She'd listen to him.

KAREN. That would be admitting that we can't do the job ourselves.

MARTHA. Well, we can't, and we might as well admit it. We've tried everything we can think of. She's had more attention than any other three kids put together. And we still haven't the faintest idea what goes on inside her head.

KAREN. She's a strange girl.

MARTHA. That's putting it mildly.

KAREN (*laughs*). It's funny. We always talk about the child as if she were a grown woman.

MARTHA. It's not so funny. There's something the matter with the kid. That's been true ever since the first day she came. She causes trouble here; she's bad for the other girls. I don't know what it is—it's a feeling I've got that it's wrong somewhere—

KAREN. All right, all right, we'll talk it over with Joe. Now what about our other pet nuisance?

MARTHA (*laughs*). My aunt the actress? What's she been up to now?

KAREN. Nothing unusual. Last night at dinner she was telling the girls about the time she lost her trunks in Butte, Montana, and how she gave her best performance of Rosalind during a hurricane. Today in the kitchen you could hear her on what Sir Henry said to her.

MARTHA. Wait until she does Hedda Gabler standing on a chair. Sir Henry taught her to do it that way. He said it was a test of great acting.

KAREN. You must have had a gay childhood.

MARTHA (*bitterly*). Oh, I did. I did, indeed. God, how I used to hate all that—

KAREN. Couldn't we get rid of her soon, Martha? I hate to make it hard on you, but she really ought not to be here.

MARTHA (*after a moment*). I know.

KAREN. We can scrape up enough money to send her away. Let's do it.

MARTHA (*goes to her, affectionately pats her head*). You've been very patient about it. I'm sorry and I'll talk to her today. It'll probably be a week or two before she can be ready to leave. Is that all right?

KAREN. Of course. (*Looks at her watch.*) Did you get Joe himself on the phone?

MARTHA. He was already on his way. Isn't he always on his way over here?

KAREN (*laughs*). Well, I'm going to marry him some day, you know.

MARTHA (*looking at her*). You haven't talked of marriage for a long time.

KAREN. I've talked of it with Joe.

MARTHA. Then you *are* thinking about it—soon?

KAREN. Perhaps when the term is over. By that time we ought to be out of debt, and the school should be paying for itself.

MARTHA (*nervously playing with a book on the table*). Then we won't be taking our vacation together?

KAREN. Of course we will. The three of us.

MARTHA. I had been looking forward to some place by the lake—just you and me—the way we used to at college.

KAREN (*cheerfully*). Well, now there will be three of us. That'll be fun, too.

MARTHA (*after a pause*). Why haven't you told me this before?

KAREN. I'm not telling you anything we haven't talked about often.

MARTHA. But you're talking about it as *soon* now.

KAREN. I'm glad to be able to. I've been in love with Joe a long time. (MARTHA *crosses to window and stands looking out, her back to* KAREN. KAREN *finishes marking papers and rises.*) It's a big day for the school. Rosalie's finally put an "l" in could.

MARTHA (*in a dull, bitter tone, not turning from window*). You really *are* going to leave, aren't you?

KAREN. I'm not going to leave, and you know it. Why do you say things like that? We agreed a long time ago that my marriage wasn't going to make any difference to the school.

MARTHA. But it will. You know it will. It can't help it.

KAREN. That's nonsense. Joe doesn't want me to give up here.

MARTHA (*turning from window*). I don't understand you. It's been so damned hard building this thing up, slaving and going without things to make ends meet—think of having a winter coat without holes in the lining again!—and now when we're getting on our feet, you're all ready to let it go to hell.

KAREN. This is a silly argument, Martha. Let's quit it. You haven't listened to a word I've said. I'm not getting married tomorrow, and when I do, it's not going to interfere with my work here. You're making something out of nothing.

MARTHA. It's going to be hard going on alone afterwards.

KAREN. For God's sake, do you expect me to give up my marriage?

MARTHA. I don't mean that, but it's so— (*Door Center opens and* DOCTOR JOSEPH CARDIN *comes in. He is a large, pleasant-looking, carelessly dressed man of about thirty-five.*)

CARDIN. Hello, darling. Hi, Martha. What's the best news?

MARTHA. Hello, Joe.

KAREN. We tried to get you on the phone. Come in and look at your little cousin.

CARDIN. Sure. What's the matter with her now? I stopped at Vernie's on the way over to look at that little black bull he bought. He's a baby! There's going to be plenty of good breeding done in these hills.

KAREN. You'd better come and see her. She says she has a pain in her heart. (*Goes out Right.*)

CARDIN (*stopping to light a cigarette*). Our little Mary pops up in every day's dispatches.

MARTHA (*impatiently*). Go and see her. Heart attacks are nothing to play with.

CARDIN (*looks at her*). Never played with one in my life. (*Exits Right.*)

(MARTHA *walks around room and finally goes to stare out window.*)
(MRS. MORTAR *enters Right.*)

MRS. MORTAR. *I* was asked to leave the room. (MARTHA *pays no attention.*) It seems that I'm not wanted in the room during the examination.

MARTHA (*over her shoulder*). What difference does it make?

MRS. MORTAR. What difference does it make? Why, it was a deliberate snub.

MARTHA. There's very little pleasure in watching a man use a stethoscope.

MRS. MORTAR. Isn't it natural that the child should have me with her? Isn't it natural that an older woman should be present? (*No answer.*) Very well, if you are so thick-skinned that you don't resent these things—

MARTHA. What are you talking about? Why, in the name of heaven, should *you* be with her?

MRS. MORTAR. It—it's customary for an older woman to be present during an examination.

MARTHA (*laughs*). Tell that to Joe. Maybe he'll give you a job as duenna for his office.

MRS. MORTAR (*reminiscently*). It was I who saved Delia Lampert's life the time she had that heart attack in Buffalo. We almost lost her that time. Poor Delia! We went over to London together. She married Robert Laffonne. Not seven months later he left her and ran away with Eve Cloun, who was playing the Infant Phenomenon in Birmingham—

MARTHA. Console yourself. If you've seen one heart attack, you've seen them all.

MRS. MORTAR. So you don't resent your aunt being snubbed and humiliated?

MARTHA. Oh, Aunt Lily!

MRS. MORTAR. Karen is consistently rude to me, and you know it.

MARTHA. I know that she is very polite to you, and—what's more important—very patient.

MRS. MORTAR. Patient with me? *I*, who have worked my fingers to the bone!

MARTHA. Don't tell yourself that too often, Aunt Lily; you'll come to believe it.

MRS. MORTAR. I *know* it's true. Where could you have gotten a woman of my reputation to give these children voice lessons, elocution lessons? Patient with me! Here I've donated my services—

MARTHA. I was under the impression you were being paid.

MRS. MORTAR. That small thing? I used to earn twice that for one performance.

MARTHA. The gilded days. It was very extravagant of them to pay you so much. (*Suddenly tired of the whole thing.*) You're not very happy here, are you, Aunt Lily?

MRS. MORTAR. Satisfied enough, I guess, for a poor relation.

MARTHA (*makes a motion of distaste*). But you don't like the school or the farm or—

MRS. MORTAR. I told you at the beginning you shouldn't have bought a place like this. Burying yourself on a farm! You'll regret it.

MARTHA. We like it here. (*After a moment.*) Aunt Lily, you've talked about London for a long time. Would you like to go over?

MRS. MORTAR (*with a sigh*). It's been twenty years, and I shall never live to see it again.

MARTHA. Well, you can go any time you like. We can spare the money now, and it will do you a lot of good. You pick out the boat you want and I'll get the passage. (*She has been talking rapidly, anxious to end the whole thing.*) Now that's all fixed. You'll have a grand time seeing all your old friends, and if you live sensibly I ought to be able to let you have enough to get along on. (*She begins to gather books, notebooks, and pencils.*)

MRS. MORTAR (*slowly*). So you want me to leave?

MARTHA. That's not the way to put it. You've wanted to go ever since I can remember.

MRS. MORTAR. You're trying to get rid of me.

MARTHA. That's it. We don't want you around when we dig up the buried treasure.

MRS. MORTAR. So? You're turning me out? At my age! Nice, grateful girl you are.

MARTHA. Oh, my God, how can anybody deal with you? You're going where you want to go, and we'll be better off alone. That suits everybody. You complain about the farm, you complain about the school, you complain about Karen, and now you have what you want and you're still looking for something to complain about.

MRS. MORTAR (*with dignity*). Please do not raise your voice.

MARTHA. You ought to be glad I don't do worse.

MRS. MORTAR. I absolutely refuse to be shipped off three thousand miles away. I'm not going to England. I shall go back to the stage. I'll write to my agents tomorrow, and as soon as they have something good for me—

MARTHA. The truth is I'd like you to leave soon. The three of us can't live together, and it doesn't make any difference whose fault it is.

MRS. MORTAR. You wish me to go tonight?

MARTHA. Don't act, Aunt Lily. Go as soon as you've found a place you like. I'll put the money in the bank for you tomorrow.

MRS. MORTAR. You think I'd take your money? I'd rather scrub floors first.

MARTHA. I imagine you'll change your mind.

MRS. MORTAR. I should have known by this time that the wise thing is to stay out of your way when *he's* in the house.

MARTHA. What are you talking about now?

MRS. MORTAR. Never mind. I should have known better. You always take your spite out on me.

MARTHA. Spite? (*Impatiently.*) Oh, don't let's have any more of this today. I'm tired. I've been working since six o'clock this morning.

MRS. MORTAR. Any day that he's in the house is a bad day.

MARTHA. When *who* is in the house?

MRS. MORTAR. Don't think you're fooling me, young lady. I wasn't born yesterday.

MARTHA. Aunt Lily, the amount of disconnected unpleasantness that goes on in your head could keep a psychologist busy for years. Now go take your nap.

MRS. MORTAR. I know what I know. Every time that man comes into this house, you have a fit. It seems like you just can't stand the idea of them being together. God knows what you'll do when they get married. You're jealous of him, that's what it is.

MARTHA (*her voice is tense and the previous attitude of good-natured irritation is gone*). I'm very fond of Joe, and you know it.

MRS. MORTAR. You're fonder of Karen, and I know that. And it's unnatural, just as unnatural as it can be. You don't like their being together. You were always like that even as a child. If you had a little girl friend, you always got mad when she liked anybody else. Well, you'd better get a beau of your own now—a woman of your age.

MARTHA. The sooner you get out of here, the better. Your vulgarities are making me sick and I won't stand for them any longer. I want you to leave— (*At this point there is a sound outside the large doors Center.* MARTHA *breaks off, angry and ashamed. After a moment she crosses to the door and opens it.* EVELYN *and* PEGGY *are to be seen on the staircase. For a second she stands still as they stop and look at her. Then, afraid that her anger with her aunt will color anything she might say to the children, she crosses the room again and stands with her back to them.*)

MARTHA. What were you doing outside the door?

EVELYN (*hurriedly*). We were going up-thtairth, Mith Dobie.

PEGGY. We came down to see how Mary was.

MARTHA. And you stopped long enough to see how we were. Did you deliberately listen?

PEGGY. We didn't mean to. We heard voices and we couldn't help—

MRS. MORTAR (*fake social tone*). Eavesdropping is something nice young ladies just don't do.

MARTHA (*turning to face the children*). Go upstairs now. We'll talk about this later. (*Slowly shuts door as they begin to climb the stairs.*)

MRS. MORTAR. You mean to say you're not going to do anything about that? (*No answer. She laughs nastily.*) That's the trouble with these new-fangled notions of discipline and—

MARTHA (*thoughtfully*). You know, it's really bad having you around children.

MRS. MORTAR. What exactly does that mean?

MARTHA. It means that I don't like them hearing the things you say. Oh, I'll "do something about it," but the truth is that this is their home, and things shouldn't be said in it that they can't hear. When you're at your best, you're not for tender ears.

MRS. MORTAR. So now it's my fault, is it? Just as I said, whenever he's in the house you think you can take it out on me. You've got to have some way to let out steam and— (*Door opens Right and* CARDIN *comes in.*)

MARTHA. How is Mary? (MRS. MORTAR, *head in air, gives* MARTHA *a malicious half-smile and makes what she thinks is majestic exit Center.*)

MRS. MORTAR. Good day, Joseph.

CARDIN. What's the matter with the Duchess? (*Nods at door Center.*)

MARTHA. Just keeping her hand in, in case Sir Henry's watching her from above. What about Mary?

CARDIN. Nothing. Absolutely nothing.

MARTHA (*sighs*). I thought so.

CARDIN. I could have managed a better faint than that when I was six years old.

MARTHA. Nothing the matter with her at all, then?

CARDIN (*laughs*). No, ma'am, not a thing. Just a little something she thought up.

MARTHA. But it's such a silly thing to do. She knew we'd have you in. (*Sighs.*) Maybe she's not so bright. Any idiots in your family, Joe? Any inbreeding?

CARDIN. Don't blame her on me. It's another side of the family. (*Laughs.*) You can look at Aunt Amelia and tell: old New England stock; never married out of Boston; still thinks honor and dinner's at eight thirty. Yes, ma'am, we're a proud old breed.

MARTHA. The Jukes were an old family, too. Look, Joe, have you any idea what is the matter with Mary? I mean, has she always been like this?

CARDIN. She's always been a honey. Aunt Amelia's spoiling hasn't helped any, either.

MARTHA. We're reaching the end of our rope with her. This kind of thing—

CARDIN (*looking at her*). Aren't you taking this too seriously?

MARTHA (*after a second*). I guess I am. But you stay around kids long enough and you won't know what to take seriously, either. But I do think somebody ought to talk to Mrs. Tilford about her.

CARDIN. You wouldn't be meaning me now, would you, Miss Dobie?

MARTHA. Well, Karen and I were talking about it this afternoon and—

CARDIN. Listen, friend, I'm marrying Karen, but I'm not writing Mary Tilford in the contract. (MARTHA *moves slightly.* CARDIN *takes her by the shoulders and turns her around to face him again. His face is grave, his voice gentle.*) Forget Mary for a minute. You and I have got something to fight about. Every time anything's said about marrying—about Karen marrying me—you —(*She winces.*) There it is. I'm fond of you. I always thought you liked me. What is it? I know how fond you are of Karen, but our marriage oughtn't to make a great deal of difference—

MARTHA (*pushing his hands from her shoulders*). God damn you. I wish— (*She puts her face in her hands.* CARDIN *watches her in silence, mechanically lighting a cigarette. When she takes her hands from her face, she holds them out to him. Contritely.)* Joe, please, I'm sorry. I'm a fool, a nasty, bitter—

CARDIN *(takes her hands in one of his, patting them with his other hand).* Aw, shut up. *(He puts an arm around her, and she leans her head against his lapel. They are standing like that when* KAREN *comes in Right.)*

MARTHA *(to* KAREN, *as she wipes her eyes).* Your friend's got a nice shoulder to weep on.

KAREN. He's an admirable man in every way. Well, the angel child is now putting her clothes back on.

MARTHA. The angel child's influence is abroad even while she's unconscious. Her room-mates were busy listening at the door while Aunt Lily and I were yelling at each other.

KAREN. We'll have to move those girls away from one another. *(A bell rings from the rear of the house.)*

MARTHA. That's my class. I'll send Peggy and Evelyn down. You talk to them.

KAREN. All right. *(As* MARTHA *exits Center,* KAREN *goes toward door Right. As she passes* CARDIN *she kisses him.)* Mary! *(*MARY *opens door, comes in, stands buttoning the neck of her dress.)*

CARDIN *(to* MARY*).* How's it feel to be back from the grave?

MARY. My heart hurts.

CARDIN *(to* KAREN*).* Science has failed. Try a hairbrush.

MARY. It's *my* heart, and it hurts.

KAREN. Sit down.

MARY. I want to see my grandmother. I want to— *(*EVELYN *and* PEGGY *timidly enter Center.)*

KAREN. Sit down, girls, I want to talk to you.

PEGGY. We're awfully sorry, really. We just didn't think and—

KAREN. I'm sorry too, Peggy. *(Thoughtfully.)* You and Evelyn never used to do things like this. We'll have to separate you three.

EVELYN. Ah, Mith Wright, we've been together almotht a year.

KAREN. It was evidently too long. Now don't let's talk about it. Peggy, you will move into Lois's room, and Lois will move in with Evelyn. Mary will go in with Rosalie.

MARY. Rosalie hates me.

KAREN. That's a very stupid thing to say. I can't imagine Rosalie hating anyone.

MARY *(starting to cry).* And it's all because I had a pain. If anybody else was sick they'd be put to bed and petted. You're always mean to me. I get blamed and punished for everything. *(To* CARDIN.) I do, Cousin Joe. All the time for everything. *(*MARY *by now is crying violently and as* KAREN *half moves toward her,* CARDIN, *who has been frowning, picks* MARY *up and puts her down on the couch.)*

CARDIN. You've been unpleasant enough to Miss Wright. Lie here until you've stopped working yourself into a fit. *(Picks up his hat and bag, smiles at* KAREN.) I've got to go now. She's not going to hurt herself crying. The next time she faints, I'd wait until she got tired lying on the floor. *(Passing* MARY, *he pats her head. She jerks away from him.)*

KAREN. Wait a minute. I'll walk to the car with you. *(To girls.)* Go up now and move your things. Tell Lois to get her stuff ready. *(She and* CARDIN *exit Center. A second after the door is closed,* MARY *springs up and throws a cushion at the door.)*

EVELYN. Don't do that. She'll hear you.

MARY. Who cares if she does? *(Kicks table.)* And she can hear that, too. *(Small ornament falls off table and breaks on floor,* EVELYN *and* PEGGY *gasp, and* MARY's *bravado disappears for a moment.)*

EVELYN *(frightened).* Now what are you going to do?

PEGGY *(stooping down in a vain effort to pick up the pieces).* You'll get the devil now. Dr. Cardin gave it to Miss Wright. I guess it was kind of a lover's gift. People get awfully angry about a lover's gift.

MARY. Oh, leave it alone. She'll never know we did it.

PEGGY. *We* didn't do it. You did it yourself.

MARY. And what will you do if I say *we* did do it? (*Laughs.*) Never mind, I'll think of something else. The wind could've knocked it over.

EVELYN. Did you really have a pain? one.

MARY. Oh, stop worrying about it. I'll get out of it.

EVELYN. Yeh. She'th going to believe that

MARY. I fainted, didn't I?

PEGGY. I wish I could faint sometimes. I've never even worn glasses, like Rosalie.

MARY. A lot it'll get you to faint.

EVELYN. What did Miss Wright do to you when the clath left?

MARY. Told me I couldn't go to the boat-races.

EVELYN. Whew!

PEGGY. But we'll remember everything that happens and we'll give you all the souvenirs and things.

MARY. I won't let you go if I can't go. But I'll find some way to go. What were *you* doing?

PEGGY. I guess we shouldn't have done it, really. We came down to see what was happening to you, but the doors were closed and we could hear Miss Dobie and Mortar having an awful row. Then Miss Dobie opens the door and there we were.

MARY. And a lot of crawling and crying you both did too, I bet.

EVELYN. We were thort of thorry about lithening. I gueth it wathn't—

MARY. Ah, you're always sorry about everything. What were they saying?

PEGGY. What was who saying?

MARY. Dobie and Mortar, silly.

PEGGY (*evasively*). Just talking, I guess.

EVELYN. Fighting, you mean.

MARY. About what?

EVELYN. Well, they were talking about Mortar going away to England and—

PEGGY. You know, it really wasn't very nice to've listened, and I think it's worse to tell.

MARY. You do, do you? You just don't tell me and see what happens. (PEGGY *sighs.*)

EVELYN. Mortar got awful thore at that and thaid they juth wanted to get rid of her, and then they thtarted talking about Dr. Cardin.

MARY. What about him?

PEGGY. We'd better get started moving; Miss Wright will be back first thing we know.

MARY (*fiercely*). Shut up! Go on, Evelyn.

EVELYN. They're going to be married.

MARY. Everybody knows that.

PEGGY. But everybody doesn't know that Miss Dobie doesn't want them to get married. How do you like that? (*The door opens and* ROSALIE WELLS *sticks her head in.*)

ROSALIE. I have a class soon. If you're going to move your things—

MARY. Close that door, you idiot. (ROSALIE *closes door, stands near it.*) What do you want?

ROSALIE. I'm trying to tell you. If you're going to move your things—not that I want you in with me—you'd better start right now. Miss Wright's coming in a minute.

MARY. Who cares if she is?

ROSALIE (*starts for door*). I'm just telling you for your own good.

PEGGY (*getting up*). We're coming.

MARY. No. Let Rosalie move our things.

ROSALIE. You crazy?

PEGGY (*nervously*). It's all right. Evelyn and I'll get your things. Come on, Evelyn.

MARY. Trying to get out of telling me, huh? Well, you won't get out of it that way. Sit down and stop being such a sissy. Rosalie, you go on up and move my things and don't say a word about our being down here.

ROSALIE. And who was your French maid yesterday, Mary Tilford?

MARY (*laughing*). You'll do for today. Now go on, Rosalie, and fix our things.

ROSALIE. You crazy?

MARY. And the next time we go into town, I'll let you wear my gold locket and buckle. You'll like that, won't you, Rosalie?

ROSALIE (*draws back, moves her hands nervously*). I don't know what you're talking about.

MARY. Oh, I'm not talking about anything in particular. You just run along now and remind me the next time to get my buckle and locket for you.

ROSALIE (*stares at her a moment*). All right, I'll do it this time, but just 'cause I got good disposition. But don't think you're going to boss me around, Mary Tilford.

MARY (*smiling*). No, indeed. (ROSALIE *starts for door.*) And get the things done neatly, Rosalie. Don't muss my white linen bloomers— (*The door slams as* MARY *laughs.*)

EVELYN. Now what do you think of that? What made her tho agreeable?

MARY. Oh, a little secret we got. Go on, now, what else did they say?

PEGGY. Well, Mortar said that Dobie was jealous of them, and that she was like that when she was a little girl, and that she'd better get herself a beau of her own because it was unnatural, and that she never wanted anybody to like Miss Wright, and that was unnatural. Boy! Did Miss Dobie get sore at that!

EVELYN. Then we didn't hear any more. Peggy dropped a book.

MARY. What'd she mean Dobie was jealous?

PEGGY. What's unnatural?

EVELYN. Un for not. Not natural.

PEGGY. It's funny, because everybody gets married.

MARY. A lot of people don't—they're too ugly.

PEGGY (*jumps up, claps her hand to her mouth*). Oh, my God! Rosalie'll find that copy of *Mademoiselle de Maupin*. She'll blab like the dickens.

MARY. Ah, she won't say a word.

EVELYN. Who getth the book when we move?

MARY. You can have it. That's what I was doing this morning—finishing it. There's one part in it—

PEGGY. What part? (MARY *laughs.*)

EVELYN. Well, what wath it?

MARY. Wait until you read it.

EVELYN. Don't forget to give it to me.

PEGGY. It's a shame about being moved. I've got to go in with Helen, and she blows her nose all night. Lois told me.

MARY. It was a dirty trick making us move. She just wants to see how much fun she can take away from me. She hates me.

PEGGY. No, she doesn't, Mary. She treats you just like the rest of us—almost better.

MARY. That's right, stick up for your crush. Take her side against mine.

PEGGY. I didn't mean it that way.

EVELYN (*looks at her watch*). We'd better get upthtairth.

MARY. I'm not going.

PEGGY. Rosalie isn't so bad.

EVELYN. What you going to do about the vathe?

MARY. I don't care about Rosalie and I don't care about the vase. I'm not going to be here.

EVELYN *and* PEGGY (*together*). Not going to be here! What do you mean?

MARY (*calmly*). I'm going home.

PEGGY. Oh, Mary—

EVELYN. You can't do that.

MARY. Can't I? You just watch. (*Begins to walk around the room.*) I'm not staying here. I'm going home and tell Grandma I'm not staying any more. (*Smiles to herself.*) I'll tell her I'm not happy. They're scared of Grandma—she helped 'em when they first started, you know—and when she tells 'em something, believe me, they'll sit up and listen. They can't get away with treating me like this, and they don't have to think they can.

PEGGY (*appalled*). You just going to walk out like that?

EVELYN. What are you going to tell your grandmother?

MARY. Oh, who cares? I'll think of something to tell her. I can always do it better on the spur of the moment.

PEGGY. She'll send you right back.

MARY. You let me worry about that. Grandma's very fond of me, on account my father was her favorite son. I can manage *her* all right.

PEGGY. I don't think you ought to go, really, Mary. It's just going to make an awful lot of trouble.

EVELYN. What'th going to happen about the vathe?

MARY. Say I did it—it doesn't make a bit of difference any more to me. Now listen, you two got to help. They won't miss me before dinner if you make Rosalie shut the door and keep it shut. Now, I'll go through the field to French's, and then I can get the bus to Homestead.

EVELYN. How you going to get to the thtreet-car?

MARY. Taxi, idiot.

PEGGY. How are you going to get out of here in the first place?

MARY. I'm going to walk out. You know where the front door is, or are you too dumb even for that? Well, I'm going right out that front door.

EVELYN. Gee, I wouldn't have the nerve.

MARY. Of course you wouldn't. You'd let 'em do anything to you they want. Well, they can't do it to me. Who's got any money?

EVELYN. Not me. Not a thent.

MARY. I've got to have at least a dollar for the taxi and a dime for the bus.

EVELYN. And where you going to find it?

PEGGY. See? Why don't you just wait until your allowance comes Monday, and then you can go any place you want. Maybe by that time—

MARY. I'm going today. *Now.*

EVELYN. You can't *walk* to Lanthet.

MARY (*goes to* PEGGY). You've got money. You've got two dollars and twenty-five cents.

PEGGY. I—I—

MARY. Go get it for me.

PEGGY. No! No! I won't get it for you.

EVELYN. You can't have *that* money, Mary—

MARY. Get it for me.

PEGGY (*cringes, her voice is scared*). I won't. I won't. Mamma doesn't send me much allowance—not half as much as the rest of you get—I saved this so long—you took it from me last time—

EVELYN. Ah, she wantth that bithycle tho bad.

PEGGY. I haven't gone to the movies, I haven't had any candy, I haven't had anything the rest of you get all the time. It took me so long to save that and I—

MARY. Go upstairs and get me the money.

PEGGY (*hysterically, backing away from her*). I won't. I won't. I won't. (MARY *makes a sudden move for her, grabs her left arm, and jerks it back, hard and expertly.* PEGGY *screams softly.* EVELYN *tries to take* MARY's *arm away. Without releasing her hold on* PEGGY, MARY *slaps* EVELYN's *face.* EVELYN *begins to cry.*)

MARY. Just say when you've had enough.

PEGGY (*softly, stiflingly*). All—all right—I'll get it. (MARY *smiles, nods her head as the Curtain falls.*)

ACT TWO

SCENE I

SCENE: Living-room at Mrs. Tilford's. *It is a formal room, without being cold or elegant. The furniture is old, but excellent. The exit to the hall is Left; glass doors Right lead to a dining-room that cannot be seen.*

AT RISE: Stage is empty. Voices are heard in the hall.

AGATHA (*off-stage*). What are *you* doing here? Well, come on in—don't stand there gaping at me. Have they given you a holiday or did you just decide you'd get a better dinner here? (AGATHA *enters Left, followed by* MARY. AGATHA *is a sharp-faced maid, no longer young, with a querulous voice.*) Can't you even say hello?

MARY. Hello, Agatha. You didn't give me a chance. Where's Grandma?

AGATHA. Why aren't you in school? Look at your face and clothes. Where have you been?

MARY. I got a little dirty coming home. I walked part of the way through the woods.

AGATHA. Why didn't you put on your middy blouse and your old brown coat?

MARY. Oh, stop asking me questions. Where's Grandma?

AGATHA. Where ought any clean person be at this time of day? She's taking a bath.

MARY. Is anybody coming for dinner?

AGATHA. She didn't say anything about you coming.

MARY. How could she, stupid? She didn't know.

AGATHA. Then what are you doing here?

MARY. Leave me alone. I don't feel well.

AGATHA. Why don't you feel well? Who ever heard of a person going for a walk in the woods when they didn't feel well?

MARY. Oh, leave me alone. I came home because I was sick.

AGATHA. You look all right.

MARY. But I don't feel all right. (*Whining.*) I can't even come home without everybody nagging at me.

AGATHA. Don't think you're fooling me, young lady. You might pull the wool over some people's eyes, but—I bet you've been up to something again. (*Stares suspiciously at* MARY, *who says nothing.*) Well, you wait right here till I tell your grandmother. And if you feel so sick, you certainly won't want any dinner. A good dose of rhubarb and soda will fix you up. (*Exits Left.*)

(MARY *makes a face in the direction* AGATHA *has gone and stops sniffling. She looks nervously around the room, then goes to a low mirror and tries several experiments with her face in an attempt to make it look sick and haggard.*)

(MRS. TILFORD, *followed by* AGATHA, *enters Left.* MRS. TILFORD *is a large, dignified woman in her sixties, with a pleasant, strong face.*)

AGATHA (*to* MRS. TILFORD, *as she follows her into the room*). Why didn't you put some cold water on your chest? Do you want to catch your death of cold at your age? Did you have to hurry so?

MRS. TILFORD. Mary, what are you doing home? (MARY *rushes to her and buries her head in* MRS. TILFORD's *dress, crying.* MRS. TILFORD *lets her cry for a moment while she pats her head, then puts an arm around the child and leads her to a sofa.*)

MRS. TILFORD. Never mind, dear; now stop crying and tell me what is the matter.

MARY (*gradually stops crying, fondling* MRS. TILFORD's *hand, playing on the older woman's affection for her*). It's so good to see you, Grandma. You didn't come to visit me all last week.

MRS. TILFORD. I couldn't, dear. But I was coming tomorrow.

MARY. I missed you so. (*Smiling up at* MRS. TILFORD.) I was awful homesick.

MRS. TILFORD. I'm glad that's all it was. I was frightened when Agatha said you were not well.

AGATHA. Did I say that? I said she needed a good dose of rhubarb and soda. Most likely she only came home for Wednesday night fudge cake.

MRS. TILFORD. We all get homesick. But how did you get here? Did Miss Karen drive you over?

MARY. I—I walked most of the way, and then a lady gave me a ride and—(*Looks timidly at* MRS. TILFORD.)

AGATHA. Did she have to walk through the woods in her very best coat?

MRS. TILFORD. Mary! Do you mean you left without permission?

MARY (*nervously*). I ran away, Grandma. They didn't know—

MRS. TILFORD. That was a very bad thing to do, and they'll be worried. Agatha, phone Miss Wright and tell her Mary is here. John will drive her back before dinner.

MARY (*as* AGATHA *starts toward telephone*). No, Grandma, don't do that. Please don't do that. Please let me stay.

MRS. TILFORD. But, darling, you can't leave school any time you please.

MARY. Oh, please, Grandma, don't send me back right away. You don't know how they'll punish me.

MRS. TILFORD. I don't think they'll be that angry. Come, you're acting like a foolish little girl.

MARY (*hysterically, as she sees* AGATHA *about to pick up the telephone*). Grandma! Please! I can't go back! I can't! They'll kill me! They will, Grandma! They'll kill me! (MRS. TILFORD *and* AGATHA *stare at* MARY *in amazement. She puts her head in* MRS. TILFORD's *lap and sobs.*)

MRS. TILFORD (*motioning with a hand for* AGATHA *to leave the room*). Never mind phoning now, Agatha.

AGATHA. If you're going to let her— (MRS. TILFORD *repeats the gesture.* AGATHA *exits Right, with offended dignity.*)

MRS. TILFORD. Stop crying, Mary.

MARY (*raising her head from* MRS. TILFORD's *lap*). It's so nice here, Grandma.

MRS. TILFORD. I'm glad you like being home with me, but at your age you can hardly— (*More seriously.*) What made you say such a terrible thing about Miss Wright and Miss Dobie? You know they wouldn't hurt you.

MARY. Oh, but they would. They—I— (*Breaks off, looks around as if hunting for a clue to her next word; then dramatically.*) I fainted today!

MRS. TILFORD (*alarmed*). Fainted?

MARY. Yes, I did. My heart—I had a pain in my heart. I couldn't help having a pain in my heart, and when I fainted right in class, they called Cousin Joe and he said I didn't. He said it was maybe only that I ate my breakfast too fast and Miss Wright blamed me for it.

MRS. TILFORD (*relieved*). I'm sure if Joseph said it wasn't serious, it wasn't.

MARY. But I did have a pain in my heart—honest.

MRS. TILFORD. Have you still got it?

MARY. I guess I haven't got it much any more, but I feel a little weak, and I was so scared of Miss Wright being so mean to me just because I was sick.

MRS. TILFORD. Scared of Karen? Nonsense. It's perfectly possible that you had a pain, but if you had really been sick your Cousin Joseph would certainly have known it. It's not nice to frighten people by pretending to be sick when you aren't.

MARY. I didn't *want* to be sick, but I'm always getting punished for everything.

MRS. TILFORD (*gently*). You mustn't imagine things like that, child, or you'll grow up to be a very unhappy woman. I'm not going to scold you any more for coming home this time, though I suppose I should. Run along upstairs and wash your face and change your dress, and after dinner John will drive you back. Run along.

MARY (*happily*). I can stay for dinner?

MRS. TILFORD. Yes.

MARY. Maybe I could stay till the first of the week. Saturday's your birthday and I could be here with you.

MRS. TILFORD. We don't celebrate my birthday, dear. You'll have to go back to school after dinner.

MARY. But— (*She hesitates, then goes up to* MRS. TILFORD *and puts her arms around the older woman's neck. Softly.*) How much do you love me?

MRS. TILFORD (*smiling*). As much as all the words in all the books in all the world.

MARY. Remember when I was little and you used to tell me that right before I went to sleep? And it was a rule nobody could say another single word after you finished? You used to say: "Wor-rr-ld," and then I had to shut my eyes tight.

MRS. TILFORD. And sometimes you were naughty and didn't shut them.

MARY. I miss you an awful lot, Grandma.

MRS. TILFORD. And I miss you, but I'm afraid my Latin is too rusty—you'll learn it better in school.

MARY. But couldn't I stay out the rest of this term? After the summer maybe I won't mind it so much. I'll study hard, honest, and—

MRS. TILFORD. You're an earnest little coaxer, but it's out of the question. Back you go tonight. (*Gives* MARY *a playful slap.*) Let's not have any more talk about it now, and let's have no more running away from school ever.

MARY (*slowly*). Then I really have to go back there tonight?

MRS. TILFORD. Of course.

MARY. You don't love me. You don't care whether they kill me or not.

MRS. TILFORD. Mary.

MARY. You don't! You don't! You don't care what happens to me.

MRS. TILFORD (*sternly*). But I *do* care that you're talking this way.

MARY (*meekly*). I'm sorry I said that, Grandma. I didn't mean to hurt your feelings. (*Puts her arms around* MRS. TILFORD'S *neck.*) Forgive me?

MRS. TILFORD. What made you talk like that?

MARY (*in a whisper*). I'm scared, Grandma, I'm scared. They'll do dreadful things to me.

MRS. TILFORD. Dreadful? Nonsense. They'll punish you for running away. You deserve to be punished.

MARY. It's not that. It's not anything I do. It never is. They—they just punish me anyhow, just like they got something against me. I'm afraid of them, Grandma.

MRS. TILFORD. That's ridiculous. What have they ever done to you that is so terrible?

MARY. A lot of things—all the time. Miss Wright says I can't go to the boat-races and— (*Realizing the inadequacy of this reply, she breaks off, hesitates, hunting for a more telling reply, and finally stammers.*) It's—it's after what happened today.

MRS. TILFORD. You mean something else besides your naughtiness in pretending to faint and then running away?

MARY. I *did* faint. I didn't pretend. They just said that to make me feel bad. Anyway, it wasn't anything that I did.

MRS. TILFORD. What was it, then?

MARY. I can't tell you.

MRS. TILFORD. Why?

MARY (*sulkily*). Because you're just going to take their part.

MRS. TILFORD (*a little annoyed*). Very well. Now run upstairs and get ready for dinner.

MARY. It was—it was all about Miss Dobie and Mrs. Mortar. They were talking awful things, and Peggy and Evelyn heard them and Miss Dobie found out, and then they made us move our rooms.

MRS. TILFORD. What has that to do with you? I don't understand a word you're saying.

MARY. They made us move our rooms. They said we couldn't be together any more. They're afraid to have us near them, that's what it is, and they're taking it out on me. They're scared of you.

MRS. TILFORD. For a little girl you're imagining a lot of big things. Why should they be scared of me? Am I such an unpleasant old lady?

MARY. They're afraid you'll find out.

MRS. TILFORD. Find out what?

MARY (*vaguely*). Things.

MRS. TILFORD. Run along, Mary. I hope you'll get more coherent as you get older.

MARY (*slowly starting for door*). All right. But there're a lot of things. They have secrets or something, and they're afraid I'll find out and tell you.

MRS. TILFORD. There's not necessarily anything wrong with people having secrets.

MARY (*coming back in the room again*). But they've got funny ones. Peggy and Evelyn heard Mrs. Mortar telling Miss Dobie that she was jealous of Miss Wright marrying Cousin Joe.

MRS. TILFORD. You shouldn't repeat things like that.

MARY. But that's what she said, Grandma. She said it was unnatural for a girl to feel that way.

MRS. TILFORD. What?

MARY. I'm just telling you what she said. She said there was something funny about it, and that Miss Dobie had always been like that, even when she was a little girl, and that it was unnatural—

MRS. TILFORD. Stop using that silly word, Mary.

MARY (*vaguely realizing that she is on the right track, hurries on*). But that was the word *she* kept using, Grandma, and then they got mad and told Mrs. Mortar she'd have to get out.

MRS. TILFORD. That was probably not the reason at all.

MARY (*nodding vigorously*). I bet it was, because honestly, Miss Dobie does get cranky and mean every time Cousin Joe comes, and today I heard her say to him: "God damn you," and then she said she was just a jealous fool and—

MRS. TILFORD. You have picked up some very fine words, haven't you, Mary?

MARY. That's just what she said, Grandma, and one time Miss Dobie was crying in Miss Wright's room, and Miss Wright was trying to stop her, and she said that all right, maybe she wouldn't get married right away if—

MRS. TILFORD. How do you know all this?

MARY. We couldn't help hearing because they—I mean Miss Dobie—was talking awful loud, and their room is right next to ours.

MRS. TILFORD. Whose room?

MARY. Miss Wright's room, I mean, and you can just ask Peggy and Evelyn whether we didn't hear. Almost always Miss Dobie comes in after we go to bed and stays a long time. I guess that's why they want to get rid of us—of me—because we hear things. That's why they're making us move our room, and they punish me all the time for—

MRS. TILFORD. For eavesdropping, I should think. (*She has said this mechanically. With nothing definite in her mind, she is making an effort to conceal the fact that* MARY'S *description of the life at school has shocked her.*) Well, now I think we've had enough gossip, don't you? Dinner's almost ready, and I can't eat with a girl who has such a dirty face.

MARY (*softly*). I've heard other things, too.

MRS. TILFORD (*abstractedly*). What? What did you say?

MARY. I've heard other things. Plenty of other things, Grandma.

MRS. TILFORD. What things?

MARY. Bad things.

MRS. TILFORD. Well, what were they?

MARY. I can't tell you.

MRS. TILFORD. Mary, you're annoying me very much. If you have anything to say, then say it and stop acting silly.

MARY. I mean I can't say it out loud.

MRS. TILFORD. There couldn't possibly be anything so terrible that you couldn't say it out loud. Now either tell the truth or be still.

MARY. Well, a lot of things I don't understand. But it's awful, and sometimes they fight and then they make up, and Miss Dobie cries and Miss Wright gets mad, and then they make up again, and there are funny noises and we get scared.

MRS. TILFORD. Noises? I suppose you girls have a happy time imagining a murder.

MARY. And we've seen things, too. Funny things. (*Sees the impatience of her grandmother.*) I'd tell you, but I got to whisper it.

MRS. TILFORD. Why must you whisper it?

MARY. I don't know. I just got to. (*Climbs on the sofa next to* MRS. TILFORD *and begins whispering. At first the whisper is slow and hesitant, but it gradually works itself up to fast, excited talking. In the middle of it* MRS. TILFORD *stops her.*)

MRS. TILFORD (*trembling*). Do you know what you're saying? (*Without answering,* MARY *goes back to the whispering until the older woman takes her by the shoulders and turns her around to stare in her face.*) Mary! Are you telling me the truth?

MARY. Honest, honest. You just ask Peggy and Evelyn and— (*After a moment* MRS. TILFORD *gets up and begins to pace about the room. She is no longer listening to* MARY, *who keeps up a running fire of conversation.*) They know, too. And maybe there're other kids who know, but we've always been frightened and so we didn't ask, and one night I was going to go and find out, but I got scared and we went to bed early so we wouldn't hear, but sometimes I couldn't help it, but we never talked about it much, because we thought they'd find out and— Oh, Grandma, don't make me go back to that awful place.

MRS. TILFORD (*abstractedly*). What? (*Starts to move about again.*)

MARY. Don't make me go back to that place. I just couldn't stand it any more. Really, Grandma, I'm so unhappy there, and if only I could stay out the rest of the term, why, then—

MRS. TILFORD (*makes irritated gesture*). Be still a minute. (*After a moment.*) No, you won't have to go back.

MARY (*surprised*). Honest?

MRS. TILFORD. Honest.

MARY (*hugging* MRS. TILFORD). You're the nicest, loveliest grandma in all the world. You—you're not mad at me?

MRS. TILFORD. I'm not mad at you. Now go upstairs and get ready for dinner. (MARY *kisses her and runs happily out Left.* MRS. TILFORD *stands staring after her for a long moment; then, very slowly, she puts on her eyeglasses and crosses to the phone. She dials a number.*) Is Miss Wright—is Miss Wright in? (*Waits a second, hurriedly puts down the receiver.*) Never mind, never mind. (*Dials another number.*) Dr. Cardin, please. Mrs. Tilford. (*She remains absolutely motionless while she waits. When she does speak, her voice is low and tense.*) Joseph? Joseph? Can you come to see me right away? Yes, I'm perfectly well. No, but it's important, Joseph, very important. I must see you right away. I—I can't tell you over the phone. Can't you come sooner? It's not about Mary's fainting—I said it's not about Mary, Joseph; in one way it's about Mary— (*Suddenly quiet.*) But will the hospital take so long? Very well, Joseph, make it as soon as you can. (*Hangs up the receiver, sits for a moment undecided. Then, taking a breath, she dials another number.*) Mrs. Munn, please. This is Mrs. Tilford. Miriam? This is Amelia Tilford. I have something to tell you—something very shocking, I'm afraid— something about the school and Evelyn and Mary—

CURTAIN

SCENE II

SCENE: The same as Scene I. The curtain has been lowered to mark the passing of a few hours.

AT RISE: MARY *is lying on the floor playing with a puzzle.* AGATHA *appears lugging blankets and pillows across the room. Almost at the door, she stops and gives* MARY *an annoyed look.*

AGATHA. And see to it that she doesn't get my good quilt all dirty, and let her wear your green pyjamas.

MARY. Who?

AGATHA. Who? Don't you ever keep your ears open? Rosalie Wells is coming over to spend the night with you.

MARY. You mean she's going to sleep *here*?

AGATHA. You heard me.

MARY. What for?

AGATHA. Do I know all the crazy things that are happening around here? Your grandmother phoned Mrs. Wells all the way to New York, three dollars and eighty-five cents and families starving, and Mrs. Wells wanted to know if Rosalie could stay here until tomorrow.

MARY (*relieved*). Oh. Couldn't Evelyn Munn come instead?

AGATHA. Sure. We'll have the whole town over to entertain you.

MARY. I won't let Rosalie Wells wear my new pyjamas.

AGATHA (*exits as the front door-bell rings*). Don't tell me what you won't do. You'll act like a lady for once in your life. (*Off-stage.*) Come on in, Rosalie. Just go on in there and make yourself at home. Have you had your dinner?

ROSALIE (*off-stage*). Good evening. Yes'm.

AGATHA (*off-stage*). Hang up your pretty coat. Have you had your bath?

ROSALIE (*off-stage*). Yes, ma'am. This morning.

AGATHA (*off-stage*). Well, you better have another one. (*She is climbing the stairs as* ROSALIE *comes into the room.* MARY, *lying in front of the couch, is hidden from her. Gingerly* ROSALIE *sits down on a chair.*)

MARY (*softly*). Whooooooo. (ROSALIE *jumps.*) Whooooooo. (ROSALIE, *frightened, starts hurriedly for the door.* MARY *sits up, laughs.*) You're a goose.

ROSALIE (*belligerently*). Oh, so it's you. Well, who likes to hear funny noises at night? You could have been a werewolf.

MARY. A werewolf wouldn't want you.

ROSALIE. You know everything, don't you? (MARY *laughs.* ROSALIE *comes over, stands staring at puzzle.*) Isn't it funny about school?

MARY. What's funny about it?

ROSALIE. Don't act like you can come home every night.

MARY. Maybe I can from now on. (*Rolls over on her back luxuriously.*) Maybe I'm never going back.

ROSALIE. Am I going back? I don't want to stay home.

MARY. What'll you give to know?

ROSALIE. Nothing. I'll ask Mamma.

MARY. Will you give me a free T. L. if I tell you?

ROSALIE (*thinks for a moment*). All right. Lois Fisher told Helen that you were very smart.

MARY. That's an old one. I don't take it.

ROSALIE. You got to take it.

MARY. Nope.

ROSALIE (*laughs*). You don't know, anyway.

MARY. I know what I heard, and I know Grandma phoned your mother in New York to come and get you right away. You're just going to spend the night here. I wish Evelyn could come instead of you.

ROSALIE. But what's happened? Peggy and Helen and Evelyn and Lois went home tonight, too. Do you think somebody's got scarlet fever or something?

MARY. No.

ROSALIE. Do *you* know what it is? How'd you find out? (*No answer.*) You're always pretending you know everything. You're just faking. (*Flounces away.*) Never mind, don't bother telling me. I think curiosity is very unladylike, anyhow. I have no concern with your silly secrets.

MARY. Suppose I told you that I just may have said that you were in on it?

ROSALIE. In on what?

MARY. The secret. Suppose I told you that I *may have* said that you told me about it?

ROSALIE. Why, Mary Tilford! You can't do a thing like that. I didn't tell you about anything. (MARY *laughs.*) Did you tell your grandmother such a thing?

MARY. Maybe.

ROSALIE. Did you?

MARY. Maybe.

ROSALIE. Well, I'm going right up to your grandmother and tell her I didn't tell you anything—whatever it is. You're just trying to get me into trouble and I'm not going to let you. (*Starts for door.*)

MARY. Wait a minute, I'll come with you.

ROSALIE. What for?

MARY. I want to tell her about Helen Burton's bracelet.

ROSALIE (*sits down suddenly*). What about it?

MARY. Just that you stole it.

ROSALIE. Shut up. I didn't do any such thing.

MARY. Yes, you did.

ROSALIE (*tearfully*). You made it up. You're always making things up.

MARY. You can't call me a fibber, Rosalie Wells. That's a kind of a dare and I won't take a dare. I guess I'll go tell Grandma, anyway. Then she can call the police and they'll come for you and you'll spend the rest of your life in one of those solitary prisons and you'll get older and older, and when you're very old and can't see anymore, they'll let you out maybe with a big sign on your back saying you're a thief, and your mother and father will be dead and you won't have any place to go and you'll beg on the streets—

ROSALIE. I didn't steal anything. I borrowed the bracelet and I was going to put it back as soon as I'd worn it to the movies. I never meant to keep it.

MARY. Nobody'll believe that, least of all the police. You're just a common, ordinary thief. Stop that bawling. You'll have the whole house down here in a minute.

ROSALIE. You won't tell? Say you won't tell.

MARY. Am I a fibber?

ROSALIE. No.

MARY. Then say: "I apologize on my hands and knees."

ROSALIE. I apologize on my hands and knees. Let's play with the puzzle.

MARY. Wait a minute. Say: "From now on, I, Rosalie Wells, am the vassal of Mary Til-

ford and will do and say whatever she tells me under the solemn oath of a knight."

ROSALIE. I won't say that. That's the worst oath there is. (MARY *starts for the door.*)

Mary! Please don't—

MARY. Will you swear it?

ROSALIE (*sniffling*). But then you could tell me to do anything.

MARY. And you'd have to do it. Say it quick or I'll—

ROSALIE (*hurriedly*). From now on, I, Rosalie Wells, am the vassal of Mary Tilford and will do and say whatever she tells me under the solemn oath of a knight. (*She gasps, and sits up straight as* MRS. TILFORD *enters.*)

MARY. Don't forget that.

MRS. TILFORD. Good evening, Rosalie, you're looking very well.

ROSALIE. Good evening, Mrs. Tilford.

MARY. She's getting fatter every day.

MRS. TILFORD (*abstractedly*). Then it's very becoming. (*Door-bell rings.*) That must be Joseph. Mary, take Rosalie into the library. There's some fruit and milk on the table. Be sure you're both fast asleep by half past ten. (*Leans down, kisses them both.* ROSALIE *starts to exit Right, sees* MARY, *stops and hesitates.*)

MARY. Go on, Rosalie. (*Waits until* ROSALIE *reluctantly exits.*) Grandma.

MRS. TILFORD. Yes?

MARY. Grandma, Cousin Joe'll say I've got to go back. He'll say I really wasn't— (CARDIN *enters and she runs from the room.*)

CARDIN. Hello, Amelia. (*Looks curiously at the fleeing* MARY.) Mary home, eh?

MRS. TILFORD (*watching* MARY *as she leaves*). Hello, Joseph. Sit down. (*He sits down, looks at her curiously, waits for her to speak.*) Whisky?

CARDIN. Please. How are you feeling? Headaches again?

MRS. TILFORD (*puts drink on table*). No.

CARDIN. Those are good powders. Bicarbonate of soda and water. Never hurt anybody yet.

MRS. TILFORD. Yes. How have you been, Joseph?

CARDIN. My good health is monotonous.

MRS. TILFORD (*vaguely, sparring for time*). I haven't seen you the last few weeks. Agatha misses you for Sunday dinners.

CARDIN. I've been busy. We're getting the results from the mating-season right about now.

MRS. TILFORD. Did I take you away from a patient?

CARDIN. No. I was at the hospital.

MRS. TILFORD. How's it getting on?

CARDIN. Just the same. No money, badly equipped, a lousy laboratory, everybody growling at everybody else— Amelia, you didn't bring me here to talk about the hospital. We're talking like people waiting for the muffins to be passed around. What's the matter with you?

MRS. TILFORD. I—I have something to tell you.

CARDIN. Well, out with it.

MRS. TILFORD. It's a very hard thing to say, Joseph.

CARDIN. Hard for you to say to *me*? (*No answer.*) Don't be worried about Mary. I guessed that she ran home to tell you about her faint. It was caused by nothing but bad temper and was very clumsily managed, at that. Amelia, she's a terribly spoilt—

MRS. TILFORD. I heard about the faint. That's not what is worrying me.

CARDIN (*gently*). Are you in some trouble?

MRS. TILFORD. We all are in trouble. Bad trouble.

CARDIN. We? Me, you mean? Nothing's the matter with me.

MRS. TILFORD. When did you last see Karen?

CARDIN. Today. This afternoon.

MRS. TILFORD. Oh. Not since seven o'clock?

CARDIN. What's happened since seven o'clock?

MRS. TILFORD. Joseph, you've been engaged to Karen for a long time. Are your plans any more definite than they were a year ago?

CARDIN. You can get ready to buy the wedding present. We'll have the wedding here, if you don't mind. The smell of clean little girls and boiled linen would worry me.

MRS. TILFORD. Why has Karen decided so suddenly to make it definite?

CARDIN. She has not suddenly decided anything. The school is pretty well on its feet, and now that Mrs. Mortar is leaving—

MRS. TILFORD. I've heard about their putting Mrs. Mortar out.

CARDIN. Putting her out? Well, maybe. But a nice sum for a trip and a promise that a good niece will support you the rest of your life is an enviable way of being put out.

MRS. TILFORD (*slowly*). Don't you find it odd, Joseph, that they want so much to get rid of that silly, harmless woman?

CARDIN. I don't know what you're talking about, but it isn't odd at all. Lily Mortar is not a harmless woman, although God knows she's silly enough. She's a nasty, tiresome, spoilt old bitch. If you're forming a Mortar Welfare Society, you're wasting your time. (*Gets up, puts down his glass.*) It's not like you to waste your time. Now, what's it that's really on your mind?

MRS. TILFORD. You must not marry Karen.

CARDIN (*shocked, he grins*). You're a very impertinent old lady. Why must I—(*imitates her*) not marry Karen?

MRS. TILFORD. Because there's something wrong with Karen—something horrible. (*The door-bell is heard to ring loud and long.*)

CARDIN. I don't think I can allow you to say things like that, Amelia.

MRS. TILFORD. I have good reason for saying it. (*Breaks off as she hears voices off-stage.*) Who is that?

KAREN (*off-stage*). Mrs. Tilford, Agatha. Is she in?

AGATHA (*off-stage*). Yes'm. Come on in.

MRS. TILFORD. I won't have her here.

CARDIN (*angrily*). What are you talking about?

MRS. TILFORD. I won't have her here.

CARDIN (*picks up his hat*). Then you don't want me here either. (*Turns to face* KAREN, *who, with* MARTHA, *has rushed in.*) Darling, what?—

KAREN (*stops when she sees him, puts her hand over her eyes*). Is it a joke, Joe?

MARTHA (*with great force to* MRS. TILFORD). We've come to find out what you are doing.

CARDIN (*kissing* KAREN). What is it?

KAREN. It's crazy! It's crazy! What did she do it for?

CARDIN. What are you talking about? What do you mean?

MRS. TILFORD. You shouldn't have come here.

CARDIN. What is all this? What's happened?

KAREN. I tried to reach you. Hasn't she told you?

CARDIN. Nobody's told me anything. I haven't heard anything but wild talk. What is it, Karen? (*She starts to speak, then dumbly shakes her head.*) What's happened, Martha?

MARTHA (*violently*). An insane asylum has been let loose. How do we know what's happened?

CARDIN. What was it?

KAREN. We didn't know what it was. Nobody would talk to us, nobody would tell us anything.

MARTHA. I'll tell you, I'll tell you. You see if you can make any sense out of it. At dinner-time Mrs. Munn's chauffeur said that Evelyn must be sent home right away. At half past seven Mrs. Burton arrived to tell us that she wanted Helen's things packed and that she'd wait outside because she didn't want to enter a place like ours. Five minutes later the Wells's butler came for Rosalie.

CARDIN. What was it?

MARTHA. It was madhouse. People rushing in and out, the children being pushed into cars—

KAREN (*quiet now, takes his hand*). Mrs. Rogers finally told us.

CARDIN What? What?

KAREN. That—that Martha and I have been —have been lovers. Mrs. Tilford told them.

CARDIN (*for a moment stands staring at her incredulously. Then he walks across the room, stares out of the window, and finally turns to* MRS. TILFORD). Did you tell them that?

MRS. TILFORD. Yes.

CARDIN. Are you sick?

MRS. TILFORD. You know I'm not sick.

CARDIN (*snapping the words out*). Then what did you do it for?

MRS. TILFORD (*slowly*). Because it's true.

KAREN (*incredulously*). You think it's true, then?

MARTHA. You fool! You damned, vicious—

KAREN. Do you realize what you're saying?

MRS. TILFORD. I realize it very well. And—

MARTHA. You realize nothing, nothing, nothing.

MRS. TILFORD. And that's why I don't think you should have come here. (*Quietly, with a look at* MARTHA.) I shall not call you names, and I will not allow you to call me names. It comes to this: I can't trust myself to talk about it with you now or ever.

KAREN. What's she talking about, Joe? What's she mean? What is she trying to do to us? What is everybody doing to us?

MARTHA (*softly, as though to herself*). Pushed around. We're being pushed around by crazy people. (*Shakes herself slightly.*) That's an awful thing. And we're standing here— (CARDIN *puts his arm around* KAREN, *walks with her to the window. They stand there together.*) We're standing here taking it. (*Suddenly with violence.*) Didn't you know we'd come here? Were we supposed to lie down and grin while you kicked us around with these lies?

MRS. TILFORD. This can't do any of us any good, Miss Dobie.

MARTHA (*scornfully imitating her*). "This can't do any of us any good." Listen, listen. Try to understand this: you're not playing with paper dolls. We're human beings, see? It's our lives you're fooling with. *Our* lives.

That's serious business for us. Can you understand that?

MRS. TILFORD (*for the first time she speaks angrily*). I can understand that, and I understand a lot more. *You've* been playing with a lot of children's lives, and that's why I stopped you. (*More calmly.*) I know how serious this is for you, how serious it is for all of us.

CARDIN (*bitterly*). I don't think you do know.

MRS. TILFORD. I wanted to avoid this meeting because it can't do any good. You came here to find out if I had made the charge. You've found out. Let's end it there. *I don't want you in this house.* I'm sorry this had to be done to you, Joseph.

CARDIN. I don't like your sympathy.

MRS. TILFORD. Very well. There's nothing I mean to do, nothing I want to do. There's nothing anybody can do.

CARDIN (*carefully*). You have already done a terrible thing.

MRS. TILFORD. I have done what I had to do. What they are may possibly be their own business. It becomes a great deal more than that when children are involved.

KAREN (*wildly*). It's not true. Not a word of it is true; can't you understand that?

MRS. TILFORD. There won't be any punishment for either of you. But there mustn't be any punishment for me, either—and that's what this meeting is. This—this thing is your own. Go away with it. I don't understand it and I don't want any part of it.

MARTHA (*slowly*). So you thought we would go away?

MRS. TILFORD. I think that's best for you.

MARTHA. There must be something we can do to you, and, whatever it is, we'll find it.

MRS. TILFORD. That will be very unwise.

KAREN. You are right to be afraid.

MRS. TILFORD. I am not afraid, Karen.

CARDIN. But you *are* old—and you *are* irresponsible.

MRS. TILFORD (*hurt*). You know that's not true.

KAREN (*goes to her*). I don't want to have anything to do with your mess, do you hear me? It makes me feel dirty and sick to be forced to say this, but here it is: there isn't a single word of truth in anything you've said. We're standing here defending ourselves—and against what? Against a lie. A great, awful lie.

MRS. TILFORD. I'm sorry that I can't believe that.

KAREN. Damn you!

CARDIN. But you can believe this: they've worked eight long years to save enough money to buy that farm, to start that school. They did without everything that young people ought to have. You wouldn't know about that. That school meant things to them: self-respect, and bread and butter, and honest work. Do you know what it is to try so hard for anything? Well, now it's gone. (*Suddenly hits the side of the table with his hand.*) What the hell did you do it for?

MRS. TILFORD (*softly*). It had to be done.

CARDIN. Righteousness is a great thing.

MRS. TILFORD (*gently*). I know how you must feel.

CARDIN. You don't know anything about how I feel. And you don't know how they feel, either.

MRS. TILFORD. I've loved you as much as I loved my own boys. I wouldn't have spared them; I couldn't spare you.

CARDIN (*fiercely*). I believe you.

MARTHA. What is there to do to you? What can we do to you? There must be something—something that makes you feel the way we do tonight. You don't want any part of this, you said. But you'll get a part. More than you bargained for. (*Suddenly.*) Listen: are you willing to stand by everything you've said tonight?

MRS. TILFORD. Yes.

MARTHA. All right. That's fine. But don't get the idea we'll let you whisper this lie: you made it and you'll come out with it. Shriek it to your town of Lancet. We'll *make* you shriek it—and we'll make you do it in a court room. (*Quietly.*) Tomorrow, Mrs. Tilford, you will have a libel suit on your hands.

MRS. TILFORD. That will be very unwise.

KAREN. Very unwise—for you.

MRS. TILFORD. It is you I am thinking of. I am frightened for you. It was wrong of you to brazen it out here tonight; it would be criminally foolish of you to brazen it out in public. That can bring you nothing but pain. I am an old woman, Miss Dobie, and I have seen too many people, out of pride, act on that pride. In the end they punish themselves.

MARTHA. And you feel that you are too old to be punished? That we should spare you?

MRS. TILFORD. You know that is not what I meant.

CARDIN (*turns from the window*). So you took a child's word for it?

MARTHA (*looks at him, shakes her head*). I knew it, too.

KAREN. That is really where you got it? I can't believe—it couldn't be. Why, she's a child.

MARTHA. She's not a child any longer.

KAREN. Oh, my God, it all fits so well now. That girl has hated us for a long time. We never knew why, we never could find out. There didn't seem to be any reason—

MARTHA. There wasn't any reason. She hates everybody and everything.

KAREN. Your Mary's a strange girl, a bad girl. There's something very awful the matter with her.

MRS. TILFORD. I was waiting for you to say that, Miss Wright.

KAREN. I'm telling you the truth. We should have told it to you long ago. (*Stops, sighs.*) It's no use.

MARTHA. Where is she? Bring her out here and let us hear what she has to say.

MRS. TILFORD. You cannot see her.

CARDIN. Where is she?

MRS. TILFORD. I won't have that, Joseph.

CARDIN. I'm going to talk to her.

MRS. TILFORD. *I won't have her go through with that again.* (*To* KAREN *and* MARTHA.) You came here demanding explanations. It was I who should have asked them from

you. You attack me, you attack Mary. I've told you I didn't mean you any harm. I still don't. You claim that it isn't true; it may be natural that you should say that, but I *know* that it is true. No matter what you say, you know very well that I wouldn't have acted until I was absolutely sure. All I wanted was to get those children away. That has been done. There won't be any talk about it or about you—I'll see to that. You have been in my house long enough. Get out.

KAREN (*gets up*). The wicked very young, and the wicked very old. Let's go home.

CARDIN. Sit down. (*To* MRS. TILFORD.) When two people come here with their lives spread on the table for you to cut to pieces, then the only honest thing to do is to give them a chance to come out whole. Are you honest?

MRS. TILFORD. I've always thought so.

CARDIN. Then where is Mary? (*After a moment she moves her head to door Right. Quickly* CARDIN *goes to the door and opens it.*) Mary! Come here. (*After a moment* MARY *appears, stands nervously near door. Her manner is shy and afraid.*)

MRS. TILFORD (*gently*). Sit down, dear, and don't be afraid.

MARTHA (*her lips barely moving*). Make her tell the truth.

CARDIN (*walking about in front of* MARY). Look: everybody lies all the time. Sometimes they have to, sometimes they don't. I've lied myself for a lot of different reasons, but there was never a time when, if I'd been given a second chance, I wouldn't have taken back the lie and told the truth. You're lucky if you ever get that chance. I'm telling you this because I'm about to ask you a question. Before you answer the question, I want to tell you that if you've l—, if you made a mistake, you must take this chance and say so. You won't be punished for it. Do you get all that?

MARY (*timidly*). Yes, Cousin Joe.

CARDIN (*grimly*). All right, let's get started. Were you telling your grandmother the truth this afternoon? The exact truth about Miss Wright and Miss Dobie?

MARY (*without hesitation*). Oh, yes. (KAREN *sighs deeply,* MARTHA, *her fists closed tight, turns her back to the child.* CARDIN *smiles as he looks at* MARY.)

CARDIN. All right, Mary, that was your chance; you passed it up. (*Pulls up a chair, sits down in front of her.*) Now let's find out things.

MRS. TILFORD. She's told you. Aren't you through?

CARDIN. Not by a long shot. You've started something, and I'm going to finish it for you. Will you answer some more questions, Mary?

MARY. Yes, Cousin Joe.

MARTHA. Stop that sick, sweet tone. (MRS. TILFORD *half rises;* CARDIN *motions her back.*)

CARDIN. Why don't you like Miss Dobie and Miss Wright?

MARY. Oh, I do like them. They just don't like me. They never have liked me.

CARDIN. How do you know?

MARY. They're always picking on me. They're always punishing me for everything that happens. No matter what happens, it's always me.

CARDIN. Why do you think they do that?

MARY. Because—because they're—because they— (*Stops, turns.*) Grandma, I—

CARDIN. All right, we'll skip that one. Did you get punished today?

MARY. Yes, and it was just because Peggy and Evelyn heard them and so they took it out on me.

KAREN. That's a lie.

CARDIN. Sssh. Heard what, Mary?

MARY. Mrs. Mortar told Miss Dobie that there was something funny about her. She said that she had a funny feeling about Miss Wright, and Mrs. Mortar said that was unnatural. That was why we got punished, just because—

KAREN. That was not the reason they got punished.

MRS. TILFORD (*to* MARTHA). Miss Dobie?

MARTHA. My aunt is a stupid woman. What she said was unpleasant; it was said to annoy me. It meant nothing more than that.

MARY. And, Cousin Joe, she said that every time you came to the school Miss Dobie got jealous, and that she didn't want you to get married.

MARTHA (*to* CARDIN). She said that, too. For God's sake, can't you see what's happening? This—this child is taking little things, little family things, and making them have meanings that— (*Stops, suddenly regards* MARY *with a combination of disgust and interest.*) Where did you learn so much in so little time?

CARDIN. What do you think Mrs. Mortar meant by all that, Mary?

MRS. TILFORD. Stop it, Joseph!

MARY. I don't know, but it was always kind of funny and she always said things like that and all the girls would talk about it when Miss Dobie went and visited Miss Wright late at night—

KAREN (*angrily*). And we go to the movies at night and sometimes we read at night and sometimes we drink tea at night. Those are guilty things, too, Mrs. Tilford.

MARY. And there are always funny sounds and we'd stay awake and listen because we couldn't help hearing and I'd get frightened because the sounds were like—

MARTHA. Be still!

KAREN (*with violence*). No, no. You don't want her still now. What else did you hear?

MARY. Grandma, I—

MRS. TILFORD (*bitterly to* CARDIN). You are trying to make her name it, aren't you?

CARDIN (*ignoring her, speaks to* MARY). Go on.

MARY. I don't know; there were just sounds.

CARDIN. But what did you think they were? Why did you frighten you?

MARY (*weakly*). I don't know.

CARDIN (*smiles at* MRS. TILFORD). She doesn't know.

MARY (*hastily*). I saw things, too. One night there was so much noise I thought somebody was sick or something and I looked through the keyhole and they were kissing and saying things and then I got scared because it was different sort of and I—

MARTHA (*her face distorted, turns to* MRS. TILFORD). That child—that child is sick.

KAREN. Ask her again how she could see us.

CARDIN. How could you see Miss Dobie and Miss Wright?

MARY. I—I—

MRS. TILFORD. Tell him what you whispered to me.

MARY. It was at night and I was leaning down by the keyhole.

KAREN. *There's no keyhole on my door.*

MRS. TILFORD. What?

KAREN. There—is—no—keyhole—on—my—door.

MARY (*quickly*). It wasn't her room, Grandma, it was the other room, I guess. It was *Miss Dobie's* room. I saw them through the keyhole in Miss Dobie's room.

CARDIN. How did you know anybody was in Miss Dobie's room?

MARY. I told you, I told you. Because we heard them. Everybody heard them—

MARTHA. I share a room with my aunt. It is on the first floor at the other end of the house. It is impossible to hear anything from there. (*To* CARDIN.) Tell her to come and see for herself.

MRS. TILFORD (*her voice shaken*). What is this, Mary? Why did you say you saw through a keyhole? *Can* you hear from your room?—

MARY (*starts to cry*). Everybody is yelling at me. I don't know what I'm saying with everybody mixing me all up. I did see it! I did see it!

MRS. TILFORD. *What* did you see? *Where* did you see it? I want the truth, now. The truth, whatever it is.

CARDIN (*gets up, moves his chair back*). We can go home. We are finished here. (*Looks around.*) It's not a pleasant place to be.

MRS. TILFORD (*angrily*). Stop that crying, Mary. Stand up. (MARY *gets up, head down, still crying hysterically.* MRS. TILFORD *goes and stands directly in front of her.*)

MRS. TILFORD. *I want the truth.*

MARY. All—all right.

MRS. TILFORD. What is the truth?

MARY. It was Rosalie who saw them. I just said it was me so I wouldn't have to tattle on Rosalie.

CARDIN (*wearily*). Oh, my God!

MARY. It *was* Rosalie, Grandma, she told us all about it. She said she had read about it in a book and she knew—

CARDIN (*picks up his hat*). We'll go now. Good night, Amelia, and good-by.

MARY (*desperately*). You ask Rosalie. You just ask Rosalie. She'll tell you. We used to talk about it all the time. That's the truth, that's the honest truth. She said it was when the door was open once and she told us all about it. I was just trying to save Rosalie, and everybody jumps on me.

MRS. TILFORD (*to* CARDIN). Please wait a minute. (*Goes to library door.*) Rosalie!

CARDIN. You're giving yourself an awful beating, Amelia, and you deserve whatever you get.

MRS. TILFORD (*stands waiting for* ROSALIE, *passes her hand over her face*). I don't know. I don't know, any more. Maybe it's what I do deserve. (*As* ROSALIE, *frightened, appears at the door, making bows to everybody, she takes the child gently by the hand, brings her down Center, talking nervously.*) I'm sorry to keep you up so late, Rosalie. You must be tired. (*Speaks rapidly.*) Mary says there's been a lot of talk in the school lately about Miss Wright and Miss Dobie. Is that true?

ROSALIE. I—I don't know what you mean.

MRS. TILFORD. That things have been said among you girls.

ROSALIE (*wide-eyed, frightened*). What things? I never—I—I—

KAREN (*gently*). Don't be frightened.

MRS. TILFORD. What was the talk about, Rosalie?

ROSALIE (*utterly bewildered*). I don't know what she means, Miss Wright.

KAREN. Rosalie, Mary has told her grandmother that certain things at school have been—er—puzzling you girls. You, particularly.

ROSALIE. History puzzles me. I guess I'm not very good at history, and Helen helps me sometimes, if that—

KAREN. No, that's not what she meant. She says that you told her that you saw certain —certain acts between Miss Dobie and myself. She says that once, when the door was open, you saw us kissing each other in a way that—(*Unable to bear the child's look, she turns her back.*) women don't kiss one another.

ROSALIE. Oh, Miss Wright, I didn't, didn't, I didn't. I *never* said such a thing.

MRS. TILFORD (*grimly*). That's true, my dear?

ROSALIE. I never saw any such thing. Mary always makes things up about me and everybody else. (*Starts to weep in excitement.*) I never said any such thing ever. Why, I never even could have thought of—

MARY (*staring at her, speaks very slowly*). Yes, you did, Rosalie. You're just trying to get out of it. I remember just when you

said it. I remember it, because it was the day Helen Burton's bracelet was—

ROSALIE (*stands fascinated and fearful, looking at* MARY). I never did. I—I—you're just—

MARY. It was the day Helen's bracelet was stolen, and nobody knew who did it, and Helen said that if her mother found out, she'd have the thief put in jail.

KAREN (*puzzled, as are the others, by the sudden change in* ROSALIE's *manner*). There's nothing to cry about. You must help us by telling the truth. Why, what's the matter, Rosalie?

MARY. Grandma, there's something I've got to tell you that—

ROSALIE (*with a shrill cry*). Yes. Yes. I did see it. I told Mary. What Mary said was right. I said it, I said it— (*Throws herself on the couch, weeping hysterically;* MARTHA *stands leaning against the door;* KAREN, CARDIN, *and* MRS. TILFORD *are staring at* ROSALIE; MARY *slowly sits down as the Curtain falls.*)

ACT THREE

SCENE: *the same as Act One. Living-room of the school.*
AT RISE: *The room has changed. It is not actually dirty, but it is dull and dark and uncared for. The windows are tightly shut, the curtains tightly drawn.* KAREN *is sitting in a large chair, Right Center, feet flat on floor.* MARTHA *is lying on the couch, her face buried against the pillows, her back to* KAREN. *It is a minute or two after the rise of the curtain before either speaks.*

MARTHA. It's cold in here.

KAREN. Yes.

MARTHA. What time is it?

KAREN. I don't know. What's the difference?

MARTHA. None. I was hoping it was time for my bath.

KAREN. Take it early today.

MARTHA (*laughs*). Oh, I couldn't do that. I look forward all day to that bath. It's my last touch with the full life. It makes me feel important to know that there's one thing ahead of me, one thing I've *got* to do. You ought to get yourself something like that. I tell you, at five o'clock every day you comb your hair. How's that? It's better for

you, take my word. You wake up in the morning and you say to yourself, the day's not entirely empty, life is rich and full: at five o'clock I'll comb my hair. (*They fall back into silence. A moment later the phone rings. Neither of them pays the slightest attention to it, until the ringing becomes too insistent. Then* KAREN *rises, takes the receiver off, goes back, and sits down.*)

KAREN. It's raining.

MARTHA. Hungry?

KAREN. No. You?

MARTHA. No, but I'd like to be hungry again. Remember how much we used to eat at college?

KAREN. That was ten years ago.

MARTHA. Well, maybe we'll be hungry in another ten years. It's cheaper this way.

KAREN. What's the old thing about time being more nourishing than bread?

MARTHA. Yeah? Maybe.

KAREN. Joe's late today. What time is it?

MARTHA (*turns to lie on her side*). We've been sitting here for eight days asking each other the time. Haven't you heard? There isn't any time any more.

KAREN. It's been days since we've been out of this house.

MARTHA. Well, we'll have to get off these chairs sooner or later. In a couple of months they'll need dusting.

KAREN. What'll we do when we get off?

MARTHA. God knows.

KAREN (*almost in a whisper*). It's awful.

MARTHA. Let's not talk about it. (*After a moment.*) What about eggs for dinner?

KAREN. All right.

MARTHA. I'll make some potatoes with onions, the way you used to like them.

KAREN. It's a week ago Thursday. It never seemed real until the last day. It seems real enough now, all right.

MARTHA. Now and forever after.

KAREN (*suddenly*). Let's go out.

MARTHA (*turns over, stares at her*). Where to?

KAREN. We'll take a walk.

MARTHA. Where'll we walk?

KAREN. Why shouldn't we take a walk? We won't see anybody, and suppose we do, what of it? We'll jus—

MARTHA (*slowly gets up*). Come on. We'll go through the park.

KAREN. They might see us. (*They stand looking at each other.*) Let's not go. (MARTHA *goes back, lies down again.*) We'll go tomorrow.

MARTHA (*laughs*). Stop kidding yourself.

KAREN. But Joe says we've got to go out. He says that all the people who don't think it's true will begin to wonder if we keep hiding this way.

MARTHA. If it makes you feel better to think there *are* such people, go ahead.

KAREN. He says we ought to go into town and go shopping and act as though—

MARTHA. Shopping? That's a sound idea. There aren't three stores in Lancet that would sell us anything. Hasn't he heard about the ladies' clubs and their meetings and their circulars and their visits and their—

KAREN (*softly*). Don't tell him.

MARTHA (*gently*). I won't. (*There are footsteps in the hall, and the sound of something being dragged.*) There's our friend. (*A* GROCERY BOY *appears lugging a box. He brings it into the room, stands staring at them, giggles a little. Walks toward* KAREN, *stops, eamines her. She sits tense, looking away from him. Without taking his eyes from* KAREN, *he speaks.*)

GROCERY BOY. I knocked on the kitchen door, but nobody answered.

MARTHA. You said that yesterday. All right. Thanks. Good-by.

KAREN (*unable any longer to stand the stare*). Make him stop it.

GROCERY BOY. Here are the things. (*Giggles, moves toward* MARTHA, *stands looking at her. Suddenly* MARTHA *thrusts her hand in the air.*)

MARTHA. I've got eight fingers, see? I'm a freak.

GROCERY BOY (*giggling*). There's a car comin' here. (*Gets no answer, starts backing out of door, still looking. Familiarly.*) Goodby. (*Exits.*)

MARTHA (*bitterly*). You still think we should go into town.

KAREN. I don't know. I don't know about anything any more. (*After a moment.*) Martha, Martha, Martha—

MARTHA (*gently*). What is it, Karen?

KAREN. What are we going to do? It's all so cold and unreal and awful. It's like that dark hour of the night when, half awake, you struggle through the black mess you've been dreaming. Then, suddenly, you wake up and you see your own bed or your own nightgown and you know you're back again in a solid world. But now it's all the nightmare; there is no solid world. Oh, Martha, *why* did it happen? *What* happened? What are we doing here like this?

MARTHA. Waiting.

KAREN. For what?

MARTHA. I don't know.

KAREN. We've got to get out of this place. I can't stand it any more.

MARTHA. You'll be getting married soon. Everything will be all right then.

KAREN (*vaguely*). Yes.

MARTHA (*looks up at the tone*). What is it?

KAREN. Nothing.

MARTHA. There mustn't be anything wrong between you and Joe. Never.

KAREN. (*without conviction*). Nothing's wrong. (*As footsteps are heard in the hall, her face lights up.*) There's Joe now. (MRS. MORTAR, *small suitcase in hand, stands in the doorway, her face pushed coyly forward.*)

MRS. MORTAR. And here I am. Hello, hello.

MARTHA (*she has turned over on her back and is staring at her aunt. She speaks to* KAREN). The Duchess, isn't it? Returned at long last. (*Too jovially.*) Come on in. We're delighted to see you. Are you tired from your journey? Is there something I can get you?

MRS. MORTAR (*surprised*). I'm very glad to see you both, and (*looks around*) I'm very glad to see the old place again. How is everything?

MARTHA. Everything's fine. We're splendid, thank you. You're just in time for tea.

MRS. MORTAR. You know, I should like some tea, if it isn't too much trouble.

MARTHA. No trouble at all. Some small sandwiches and a little brandy?

MRS. MORTAR (*puzzled finally*). Why, Martha.

MARTHA. Where the hell have you been?

MRS. MORTAR. Around, around. I had a most interesting time. Things—

MARTHA. Why didn't you answer my telegrams?

MRS. MORTAR. Things have changed in the theater—drastically changed, I might say.

MARTHA. *Why didn't you answer my telegrams?*

MRS. MORTAR. Oh, Martha, there's your temper again.

MARTHA. Answer me and don't bother about my temper.

MRS. MORTAR (*nervously*). I was moving around a great deal. (*Conversationally.*) You know, I think it will throw a very revealing light on the state of the new theater when I tell you that the Lyceum in Rochester now has a toilet back-stage.

MARTHA. To hell with the toilet in Rochester. Where were you?

MRS. MORTAR. Moving around, I tell you.

KAREN. What difference does it all make now?

MRS. MORTAR. Karen is quite right. Let bygones be bygones. As I was saying, there's an effete something in the theater now, and that accounts for—

MARTHA (*to* KAREN). Isn't she wonderful? (*To* MRS. MORTAR.) Why did you refuse to come back here and testify for us?

MRS. MORTAR. Why, Martha, I didn't refuse to come back at all. That's the wrong way to look at it. I was on a tour; that's a moral obligation, you know. Now don't let's talk about unpleasant things any more. I'll go up and unpack a few things; tomorrow's plenty of time to get my trunk.

KAREN (*laughs*). Things have changed here, you know.

MARTHA. She doesn't know. She expected to walk right up to a comfortable fire and sit down and she very carefully waited until the whole thing was over. (*Leans forward, speaking to* MRS. MORTAR.) Listen: Karen Wright and Martha Dobie brought a libel suit against a woman called Tilford because her grandchild had accused them of having what the judge called "sinful sexual knowledge of one another." (MRS. MORTAR *holds up her hand in protest, and* MARTHA *laughs.*) Don't like that, do you? Well, a great part of the defense's case was based on remarks made by Lily Mortar, actress in the toilets of Rochester, against her niece, Martha. And a greater part of the defense's case rested on the telling fact that Mrs. Mortar would not appear in court to deny or explain those remarks. Mrs. Mortar had a moral obligation to the theater. As you probably read in the papers, we lost the case.

MRS. MORTAR. I didn't think of it that way, Martha. It couldn't have done any good for all of us to get mixed up in that unpleasant notoriety— (*Sees* MARTHA's *face. Hastily*) But now that you've explained it, why, I do see it your way, and I'm sorry I didn't come back. But now that I am here, I'm going to stand shoulder to shoulder with you. I know what you've gone through, but the body and heart *do* recover, you know. I'll be here working right along with you and we'll—

MARTHA. There's an eight o'clock train. Get on it.

MRS. MORTAR. Martha.

MARTHA. You've come back to pick the bones dry. Well, there aren't even bones anymore. There's nothing here for you.

MRS. MORTAR (*sniffling a little*). How can you talk to me like that?

MARTHA. Because I hate you. I've always hated you.

MRS. MORTAR (*gently*). God will punish you for that.

MARTHA. He's been doing all right.

MRS. MORTAR. When you wish to apologize, I will be temporarily in my room. (*Starts to exit, almost bumps into* CARDIN, *steps back with dignity.*) How do you do?

CARDIN (*laughs*). Look who's here. A little late, aren't you?

MRS. MORTAR. So it's you. Now, I call *that* loyal. A lot of men wouldn't still be here. They would have felt—

MARTHA. Get out of here.

KAREN (*opening door*). I'll call you when it's time for your train. (MRS. MORTAR *looks at her, exits.*)

CARDIN. Now, what do you think brought her back?

KAREN. God knows.

MARTHA. I know. She was broke.

CARDIN (*pats* MARTHA *on the shoulder*). Don't let her worry you this time, Martha. We'll give her some money and get rid of her. (*Pulls* KAREN *to him.*) Been out today, darling?

KAREN. We started to go out.

CARDIN (*shakes his head*). Feel all right? (KAREN *leans over to kiss him. Almost imperceptibly he pulls back.*)

KAREN. Why did you do that?

MARTHA. Karen.

CARDIN. Do what?

KAREN. Draw back that way.

CARDIN (*laughs, kisses her*). If we sit around here much longer, we'll all be bats. I sold my place today to Foster.

KAREN. You did what?

CARDIN. We're getting married this week. Then we're going away—all three of us.

KAREN. You can't leave here. I won't have you do this for me. What about the hospital and—

CARDIN. Shut up, darling, it's all fixed. We're going to Vienna and we're going quick. Fischer wrote that I can have my old place back.

KAREN. No! No! I'm not going to let you.

CARDIN. It's already done. Fischer can't pay me much, but it'll be enough for the three of us. Plenty if we live cheap.

MARTHA. I couldn't go with you, Joe.

CARDIN. Nonsense, Martha, we're all going. We're going to have fun again.

KAREN (*slowly*). You don't want to go back to Vienna.

CARDIN. No.

KAREN. Then why?

CARDIN. Look: I don't want to go to Vienna; I'd rather have stayed here. But then you don't want to go to Vienna; you'd rather have stayed here. Well, to hell with that. We *can't* stay here, and Vienna offers enough to eat and sleep and drink beer on. Now don't object any more, please, darling. All right?

KAREN. All right.

MARTHA. I can't go. It's better for all of us if I don't.

CARDIN (*puts his arm around her*). Not now. You stay with us now. Later on, if you want it that way. All right?

MARTHA (*smiles*). All right.

CARDIN. Swell, I'll buy you good coffee cakes and take you both to Ischl for a honeymoon.

MARTHA (*picking up grocery box, she starts for door*). A big coffee cake with a lot of raisins. It would be nice to like something again. (*Exits.*)

CARDIN (*with a slightly forced heartiness*). I'll be going back with a pretty girl who belongs to me. I'll show you off all over the place—to Dr. Engelhardt, and the nurse at the desk, and to the fat gal in the cake shop, and to Fischer. (*Laughs.*) The last time I saw him was at the railroad station. He took me back of the baggage car. (*With an imitation of an accent.*) "Joseph," he said, "you'll be a good doctor; I would trust you to cut up my Minna. But you're not a great doctor, and you never will be. Go back where you were born and take care of your sick. Leave the fancy work to the others." I came home.

KAREN. You'll be coming home again some day.

CARDIN. No. Let's not talk about it. (*After a moment.*) You'll need some clothes?

KAREN. A few. Oh, your Dr. Fischer was so right. This is where you belong.

CARDIN. I need an overcoat and a suit. You'll need a lot of things—heavy things. It's cold there now, much colder than you'd expect—

KAREN. I've done this to you. I've taken you away from everything you want.

CARDIN. But it's lovely in the mountains, and that's where we'll go for a month.

KAREN. They—*they've* done it. They've taken away every chance we had. Everything we wanted, everything we were going to be.

CARDIN. And we've got to stop talking like that. (*Takes her by the shoulders.*) We've got a chance. But it's just one chance, and if we miss it we're done for. It means that we've got to start putting the whole business

behind us now. *Now,* Karen. What you've done, you've done—and that's that.

KAREN. What *I've* done?

CARDIN (*impatiently*). What's been done to you.

KAREN. What did you mean? (*When there is no answer.*) What did you mean when you said .What you've done....?

CARDIN (*shouting*). Nothing. Nothing. (*Then very quietly.*) Karen, there are a lot of people in this world who've had bad trouble in their lives. We're three of those people. We could sit around the rest of our lives and exist on that trouble, until in the end we had nothing else and we'd want nothing else. That's something I'm not coming to and I'm not going to let you come to.

KAREN. I know. I'm sorry. (*After a moment.*) Joe, can we have a baby right away?

CARDIN (*vaguely*). Yes, I guess so. Although we won't have much money now.

KAREN. You used to want one right away. You always said that was the way you wanted it. There's some reason for your changing.

CARDIN. My God, we *can't* go on like this. Everything I say to you is made to mean something else. We don't talk like people any more. Oh, let's get out of here as fast as we can.

KAREN (*as though she is finishing the sentence for him*). And every word will have a new meaning. You think we'll be able to run away from that? Woman, child, love, lawyer—no words that we can use in safety any more. (*Laughs bitterly.*) Sick, high-tragic people. That's what we'll be.

CARDIN (*gently*). No, we won't, darling. Love is casual—that's the way it should be. We must find that out all over again. We must learn again to live and love like other people.

KAREN. It won't work.

CARDIN. What?

KAREN. The two of us together.

CARDIN (*sharply*). Stop talking like that.

KAREN. It's true. (*Suddenly.*) I want you to say it now.

CARDIN. I don't know what you're talking about.

KAREN. Yes, you do. We've both known for a long time. I knew surely the day we lost the case. I was watching your face in court. It was ashamed—and sad at being ashamed. Say it now, Joe. Ask it now.

CARDIN. I have nothing to ask. Nothing— (*Quickly.*) All right. Is it—was it ever—

KAREN (*puts her hand over his mouth*). No. Martha and I have never touched each other. (*Pulls his head down on her shoulder.*) That's all right, darling. I'm glad you asked. I'm not mad a bit, really.

CARDIN. I'm sorry, Karen, I'm sorry. I didn't mean to hurt you, I—

KAREN. I'll say it for you. You wanted to wait until it was all over, you really never wanted to ask at all. You didn't know for sure; you thought there might be just a little truth in it all. (*With great feeling.*) You've been good to me and loyal. You're a fine man. (*Afraid of tears, she pats him, walks away.*) Now go and sit down, Joe. I have a lot of things to say. They're all mixed up and I must get them clear.

CARDIN. Don't let's talk any more. Let's forget and go ahead.

KAREN (*puzzled*). Go ahead?

CARDIN. Yes, Karen.

KAREN. You believe me, then?

CARDIN. Of course I believe you. I only had to hear you say it.

KAREN. No, no, no. That isn't the way things work. Maybe you believe me. I'd never know whether you did or not. You'd never know whether you did, either. We couldn't do it that way. Can't you see what would happen? We'd be hounded by it all our lives. I'd be frightened, always, and in the end my own fright would make me— would make me hate you. (*Sees slight movement he makes.*) Yes, it would; I know it would. I'd hate you for what I thought I'd done to you. And I'd hate myself, too. It would grow and grow until we'd be ruined by it. (*Sees him about to speak.*) Ah, Joe, you've seen all that yourself. You knew it first.

CARDIN (*softly*). I didn't mean it that way; I don't now.

KAREN (*smiles*). You're still trying to spare me, still trying to tell yourself that we might be all right again. But we won't be all right. Not ever, ever, ever. I don't know all the reasons why. Look, I'm standing here. I haven't changed. (*Holds out her hands.*) My hands look just the same, my face is the same, even my dress is old. We're in a room we've been in so many times before; you're sitting where you always sit; it's nearly time for dinner. I'm like everybody else. I can have all the things that everybody has. I can have you and a baby, and I can go to market, and we can go to the movies, and people will talk to me and —(*Suddenly notices the pain in his face.*) Oh, I'm sorry. I mustn't talk like that. That couldn't be true any more.

CARDIN. It could be, Karen. We'll make it be like that.

KAREN. No. That's only what we'd like to have had. It's what we can't have now. Go home, darling.

CARDIN (*with force*). Don't talk like that. No matter what it is, we can't leave each other. I can't leave you—

KAREN. Joe, Joe. Let's do it now and quick; it will be too hard later on.

CARDIN. No, no, no. We love each other. (*His voice breaks.*) I'd give anything not to have asked that question, Karen.

KAREN. It had to be asked sooner or later— and answered. You're a good man—the best I'll ever know—and you've been better to me than— But it's no good now, for either of us; you can see that.

CARDIN. It can be. You say I helped you. Help me now; help me to be strong and good enough to— (*Goes towards her with his arms out.*) Karen!

KAREN (*drawing back*). No, Joe! (*Then, as he stops*) Will you do something for me?

CARDIN. Anything but leave you.

KAREN. Will you—will you go away for two days—a day—and think this all over by yourself—away from me and love and pity? Will you? And then decide.

CARDIN (*after a long pause*). Yes, if you want, but it won't make any difference. We will—

KAREN. Don't say anything. Please go now. (*She sits down, smiles, closes her eyes. For a moment he stands looking at her, then slowly puts on his hat.*) And all my heart goes with you.

CARDIN (*at door, leaving*). I'll be coming back. (*Exits, slowly, reluctantly, closing door.*)

KAREN (*a moment after he has gone*). No, you won't. Never, darling. (*Stays as she is until* MARTHA *enters Right.*)

MARTHA (*goes to lamp, lights it*). It gets dark so early now. (*Sits down, stretches, laughs.*) Cooking always makes me feel better. Well, I guess we'll have to give the Duchess some dinner. When the hawks descend, you've got to feed 'em. Where's Joe? (*No answer.*) Where's Joe?

KAREN. Gone.

MARTHA. A patient? Will he be back in time for dinner?

KAREN. No.

MARTHA (*watching her*). We'll save dinner for him, then. Karen! What's the matter?

KAREN (*in a dull tone*). He won't be back any more.

MARTHA (*speaking slowly and carefully*). You mean he won't be back any more tonight.

KAREN. He won't be back at all.

MARTHA (*quickly, walks to* KAREN). What happened? (KAREN *shakes her head.*) What happened, Karen?

KAREN. He thought that we had been lovers.

MARTHA (*tensely*). I don't believe you. (*Wearily* KAREN *turns her head away.*)

KAREN. All right.

MARTHA (*automatically*). I don't believe it. He's never said a word all these months, all during the trial—(*Suddenly grabs* KAREN *by the shoulders, shakes her.*) Didn't you tell him? For God's sake, didn't you tell him it wasn't true?

KAREN. Yes.

MARTHA. He didn't believe you?

KAREN. I guess he believed me.

MARTHA (*angrily*). Then what have you done?

KAREN. What had to be done.

MARTHA. It's all wrong. It's silly. He'll be back in a little while and you'll clear it all up—(*Realizes why that can't be, covers her mouth with her hand.*) Oh, God, I wanted that for you so much.

KAREN. Don't. I feel sick to my stomach.

MARTHA (*goes to couch opposite* KAREN, *puts her head in her arms*). What's happened to us? What's really happened to us?

KAREN. I don't know. I want to be sleepy. I want to go to sleep.

MARTHA. Go back to Joe. He's strong; he'll understand. It's too much for you this way.

KAREN (*irritably*). Stop talking about it. Let's pack and get out of here. Let's take the train in the morning.

MARTHA. The train to where?

KAREN. I don't know. Some place; any place.

MARTHA. A job? Money?

KAREN. In a big place we could get something to do.

MARTHA. They'd know about us. We've been famous.

KAREN. A small town, then.

MARTHA. They'd know more about us.

KAREN (*as a child would say it*). Isn't there anywhere to go?

MARTHA. No. There'll never be any place for us to go. We're bad people. We'll sit. We'll be sitting the rest of our lives wondering what's happened to us. You think this scene is strange? Well, get used to it; we'll be here for a long time. (*Suddenly pinches* KAREN *on the arm.*) Let's pinch each other sometimes. We can tell whether we're still living.

KAREN (*shivers, listlessly gets up, starts making a fire in the fireplace*). But this isn't a new sin they tell us we've done. Other people aren't destroyed by it.

MARTHA. **They** are the people who believe in it, who want it, who've chosen it. We aren't like that. We don't love each other. (*Suddenly stops, crosses to fireplace, stands looking abstractedly at* KAREN. *Speaks casually.*) I don't love you. We've been very close to each other, of course. I've loved you like a friend, the way thousands of women feel about other women.

KAREN (*only half listening*). The fire's nice.

MARTHA. Certainly that doesn't mean anything. There's nothing wrong about that. It's perfectly natural that I should be fond of you, that I should—

KAREN (*listlessly*). Why are you saying all this to me?

MARTHA. Because I love you.

KAREN (*vaguely*). Yes, of course.

MARTHA. I love you that way—maybe the way they said I loved you. I don't know. (*Waits, gets no answer, kneels down next to* KAREN.) Listen to me!

KAREN. What?

MARTHA. *I have loved you the way they said.*

KAREN. You're crazy.

MARTHA. There's always been something wrong. Always—as long as I can remember. But I never knew it until all this happened.

KAREN (*for the first time looks up, horrified*). Stop it!

MARTHA. You're afraid of hearing it; I'm more afraid than you.

KAREN (*puts her hands over her ears*). I won't listen to you.

MARTHA. Take your hands down. (*Leans over, pulls* KAREN'S *hands away.*) You've got to know it. I can't keep it any longer. I've got to tell you how guilty I am.

KAREN (*deliberately*). You are guilty of nothing.

MARTHA. I've been telling myself that since the night we heard the child say it; I've been praying I could convince myself of it. I can't, I can't any longer. It's there. I don't know how, I don't know why. But I did love you. I do love you. I resented your marriage; maybe because I wanted you; maybe

I wanted you all along; maybe I couldn't call it by a name; maybe it's been there ever since I first knew you,—

KAREN (*tensely*). It's a lie. You're telling yourself a lie. We never thought of each other that way.

MARTHA (*bitterly*). No, of course *you* didn't. But who says I didn't? I never felt that way about anybody but you. I've never loved a man— (*Stops. Softly.*) I never knew why before. Maybe it's that.

KAREN (*carefully*). You are tired and sick.

MARTHA (*as though she were talking to herself*). It's funny; it's all mixed up. There's something in you, and you don't know it and you don't do anything about it. Suddenly a child gets bored and lies—and there you are, seeing it for the first time. (*Closes her eyes.*) I don't know. It all seems to come back to *me*. In some way I've ruined your life. I've ruined my own. I didn't even *know*. (*Smiles.*) There's a big difference between us now, Karen. You feel sad and clean; I feel sad and dirty. (*Puts out her hand, touches* KAREN'S *head.*) I can't stay with you any more, darling.

KAREN (*in a shaken, uncertain tone*). All this isn't true. We'll pretend you never said it; you'll have forgotten it tomorrow.

MARTHA. Tomorrow? That's a funny word. In all those years to come, Karen, we would have had to invent a new language, as children do, without words like tomorrow.

KAREN (*crying*). Go and lie down, Martha. You'll feel better.

MARTHA (*looks around the room, slowly, carefully. She is very quiet. Exits Right, stands at door for a second looking at* KAREN, *then slowly shuts the door behind her*). Yes. I think I will feel better. (*KAREN sits alone without moving. There is no sound in the house until, a few minutes after* MARTHA'S *exit, a shot is heard. The sound of the shot should not be too loud or too strong; the act has not been sensational. For a few seconds after the noise has died out,* KAREN *does not move. Then, suddenly, she springs from the chair, crosses the room, pulls open door Right. Almost at the same moment footsteps are heard on the staircase.*)

MRS. MORTAR. What was that? Where is it? (*Enters door Center, frightened, aimlessly moving about.*) Karen! Martha! Where are you? I heard a shot. What was— (*Stops as she sees* KAREN *reappear Right. Walks toward her, still talking. Stops when she sees* KAREN'S *face.*) What—what is it? (KAREN *moves her hands, shakes her head slightly, passes* MRS. MORTAR, *and goes toward window.* MRS. MORTAR *stares at her for a moment, rushes past her through door Right. Left alone,* KAREN *leans against the window.* MRS. MORTAR *re-enters crying. After a minute.*) What shall we do? What shall we do?

KAREN (*in a toneless voice*). Nothing.

MRS. MORTAR. We've got to get a doctor—right away. (*Goes to phone, nervously, fumblingly starts to dial.*)

KAREN (*without turning*). There isn't any use.

MRS. MORTAR. We've got to do something. Oh, it's awful. Poor Martha. I don't know what we can do— (*Puts phone down, collapses in chair, sobs quietly.*) You think she's dead—

KAREN. Yes.

MRS. MORTAR. Poor, poor Martha. I can't realize it's true. Oh, how could she—she was so—I don't know what—(*Looks up, still crying, surprised.*) I'm—I'm frightened.

KAREN. Don't cry.

MRS. MORTAR. I can't help it. How can I help it? (*Gradually the sobs cease, and she sits rocking herself.*) I'll never forgive myself for the last words I said to her. But I was good to her, Karen, and you know God will excuse me for that once. I always tried to do everything I could. (*Suddenly.*) Suicide's a sin. (*No answer. Timidly.*) Shouldn't we call somebody to—

KAREN. In a little while.

MRS. MORTAR. She shouldn't have done it, she shouldn't have done it. It was because of all this awful business. She would have got a job and started all over again—she was just worried and sick and—

KAREN. That isn't the reason she did it.

MRS. MORTAR. What—why—?

KAREN (*wearily*). What difference does it make now?

MRS. MORTAR (*reproachfully*). You're not crying.

KAREN. No.

MRS. MORTAR. What will happen to me? I haven't anything. Oh, she wouldn't have wanted me, no matter what she said, to suffer and starve. I know she wouldn't have wanted that.

KAREN. She was very good to you; she was good to us all.

MRS. MORTAR. Oh, I know she was, Karen, and I was good to her too. I did everything I could. I—I haven't any place to go.

KAREN (*without malice*). When the hawks descend, they must be fed. You'll be taken care of.

MRS. MORTAR (*after a few seconds of silence*). I'm afraid. It seems so queer—in the next room. (*Shivers.*)

KAREN. Don't be afraid.

MRS. MORTAR. It's different for you. You're young.

KAREN. Not any more. (*The sound of the door-bell ringing.* MRS. MORTAR *jumps.* KAREN *doesn't move. It rings again.*)

MRS. MORTAR (*nervously*). Who is it? (*The bell rings again.*) Shall I answer it? (KAREN *shrugs.*) I think we'd better. (*Exits down the hall through Center doors. Returns in a minute followed by* MRS. TILFORD'S *maid,* AGATHA, *who stands in the door.*) It's a woman. (*No answer.*) It's a woman to see you, Karen. (*Getting no answer, she turns to* AGATHA.) You can't come in now; we've had a—we've had trouble here.

AGATHA. Miss Karen, I've *got* to speak to you.

KAREN (*turns slowly, mechanically*). Agatha.

AGATHA (*goes to* KAREN). Please, Miss Karen. We've tried so hard to get you. I been phoning all the time. Please, please let her come in. Just for a minute, Miss Karen. Please—

MRS. MORTAR. Who wants to come in here?

AGATHA. Mrs. Tilford. (*Looks at* KAREN.) Don't you feel well? (KAREN *shakes her head.*) You ain't mad at *me*?

MRS. MORTAR. That woman can't come in here. She caused all—

KAREN. I'm not mad at you, Agatha.

AGATHA. Can I—can I get you something?

KAREN. No.

AGATHA. You poor child. You look like you got a pain somewhere. (*Hesitates, takes* KAREN's *hands.*) I only came 'cause she's so bad off. She's got to see you, Miss Karen, she's just got to. She's been sittin' outside in the car, hoping you'd come out. She can't get Dr. Joe. He—he won't talk to her any more. I wouldn't a come—I always been on your side—but she's sick. If only you could see her, you'd let her come for just a minute.

KAREN. I couldn't do that, Agatha.

AGATHA. I don't blame you. But I had to tell you. She's old. It's going to kill her.

KAREN (*bitterly*). Kill her? Where is Mrs. Tilford?

AGATHA. Outside.

KAREN. All right.

AGATHA (*presses* KAREN's *arm*). You always been a good girl. (*Hurriedly exits.*)

MRS. MORTAR. You going to allow that woman to come in here? With Martha lying there? How can you be so feelingless? (*She starts to cry.*) I won't stay and see it. I won't have anything to do with it. I'll never let that woman— (*Rushes sobbing from the room.*)
(*A second after,* MRS. TILFORD *appears in the doorway Center. She is a sick woman; an old woman. Her face, her walk, her voice have changed. She is feeble.*)

MRS. TILFORD. Karen, let me come in. (*Without turning,* KAREN *bows her head.* MRS. TILFORD *enters, stands staring at the floor.*)

KAREN. Why have you come here?

MRS. TILFORD. I had to come. (*Stretches out her hand to* KAREN, *who does not turn. She drops her hand.*) I know now; I know it wasn't true.

KAREN. What?

MRS. TILFORD (*carefully*). I know it wasn't true, Karen.

KAREN (*stares at her, shudders*). You know it wasn't true? I don't care what you know. It doesn't matter any more. If that's what you had to say, you've said it. Go away.

MRS. TILFORD (*puts her hand to her throat*). I've *got* to tell you.

KAREN. I don't want to hear you.

MRS. TILFORD. Last Tuesday Mrs. Wells found a bracelet in Rosalie's room. The bracelet had been hidden for several months. We found out that Rosalie had taken the bracelet from another girl, and that Mary— (*Closes her eyes.*) that Mary knew that and used it to force Rosalie into saying that she had seen you and Miss Dobie together. I— I've talked to Mary. I've found out. (KAREN *suddenly begins to laugh, high and sharp.*) Don't do that, Karen. I have only a little more to say. I've talked to Judge Potter. He will make all arrangements. There will be a public apology and an explanation. The damage suit will be paid to you in full and—and any more that you will be kind enough to take from me. I—I must see that you won't suffer any more.

KAREN. We're not going to suffer any more. It's all too late. Martha is dead. (MRS. TILFORD *gasps, shakes her head as though to shake off the truth, feebly falls into a chair, and covers her face.* KAREN *watches her for a minute.*) So you've come here to relieve your conscience? Well, I won't be your confessor. It's choking you, is it? (*Violently.*) And you want to stop the choking, don't you? You've done a wrong and you have to right that wrong or you can't rest your head again. You want to be "just," don't you, and you wanted us to help you be just? You've come to the wrong place for help. You want to be a "good" woman again, don't you? (*Bitterly.*) Oh, I know. You told us that night you had to do what you did. Now you "have" to do this. A public apology and money paid, and you can sleep again and eat again That done and there'll be peace for you. You're old, and the old are callous. Ten, fifteen years left for you. But what of me? It's a whole life for me. A whole God-damned life. (*Suddenly quiet, points to door Right.*) And what of her?

MRS. TILFORD (*she is crying*). You are still living.

KAREN. And I don't know why.

MRS. TILFORD (*with a tremendous effort to control herself*). I didn't come here to relieve myself. I swear to God I didn't. I came to try—to try anything. I knew there wasn't any relief for me, Karen, and that there never would be again. (*Tensely.*) But what I am or why I came doesn't matter. The only thing that matters is you and— You, now.

KAREN. There's nothing for me any more.

MRS. TILFORD. Oh, let's try to make something for you. You're young and I—I can help you.

KAREN (*smiles*). You can help me?

MRS. TILFORD (*with great feeling*). Take whatever I can give you. Take it for yourself and use it for yourself. It won't bring me peace, if that's what's worrying you. (*Smiles.*) Those ten or fifteen years you talk about! I hope it won't be that long. But however long it is, it will be in darkness. And I won't blame you if that gives you pleasure.

KAREN. It doesn't now. I'm too tired to want even that. (*Almost tenderly.*) You will have a hard time ahead, won't you?

MRS. TILFORD. Yes.

KAREN. Mary?

MR. TILFORD. I don't know.

KAREN. You can send her away.

MRS. TILFORD. No. I could never do that. Whatever she does, it must be to me and no one else. She's—she's—

KAREN. Yes. Your very own, to live with the rest of your life. They will be years of darkness; you're right. (*For a moment she watches* MRS. TILFORD's *face.*) It's over for me now, but it will never end for you. She's harmed us both, but she's harmed you more, I guess. (*Sits down beside* MRS. TILFORD.) I'm sorry.

MRS. TILFORD (*clings to her*). Then you'll try for yourself.

KAREN. All right.

MRS. TILFORD. You and Joe.

KAREN. No. We're not together anymore.

MRS. TILFORD (*looks up at her*). Did I do that, too?

KAREN. I don't think anyone did anything, any more.

MRS. TILFORD (*makes a half-movement to rise*). I'll go to him right away.

KAREN. No, it's better now the way it is.

MRS. TILFORD. But he must know what I know, Karen. You must go back to him.

KAREN (*smiles*). No, not any more.

MRS. TILFORD. You must, you must—(*Sees her face, hesitates.*) Perhaps later, Karen?

KAREN. Perhaps.

MRS. TILFORD (*after a moment in which they both sit silent*). Come away from here now, Karen. (KAREN *shakes her head.*) You can't stay with—(*Moves her hand toward door Right.*)

KAREN. When she is buried, then I will go.

MRS. TILFORD. You'll be all right?

KAREN. I'll be all right, I suppose. Good-by, now. (*They both rise.* MRS. TILFORD *speaks, pleadingly.*)

MRS. TILFORD. You'll let me help you? You'll let me try?

KAREN. Yes, if it will make you feel better.

MRS. TILFORD (*timidly*). And you—you'll take the money?

KAREN (*tired*). If you want it that way.

MRS. TILFORD (*with great feeling*). Oh yes, oh yes, Karen. (*Unconsciously* KAREN *begins to walk toward the window.*)

KAREN (*suddenly*). Is it nice out?

MRS. TILFORD. It's been cold. (KAREN *opens the window slightly, sits on the ledge.* MRS. TILFORD *with surprise*) It seems a little warmer, now.

KAREN. It feels very good. (*They smile at each other.*)

MRS. TILFORD. You'll write me some time?

KAREN. If I ever have anything to say. Good-by, now.

MRS. TILFORD. You will have. I know it. Good-by, my dear. (KAREN *smiles, shakes her head as* MRS. TILFORD *exits. She does not turn, but a minute later she raises her hand.*)

KAREN. Good-by.

CURTAIN

Tobacco Road

BY JACK KIRKLAND

From the novel by Erskine Caldwell

ORIGINAL CAST OF CHARACTERS

As they appeared in the first performance, December 4, 1933, at the Forty-Eighth Street Theatre, New York City.

DUDE LESTER .... Sam Byrd
ADA LESTER .... Margaret Wycherly
JEETER LESTER .... Henry Hull
ELLIE MAY .... Ruth Hunter
GRANDMA LESTER .... Patricia Quinn
LOV BENSEY .... Dean Jagger
HENRY PEABODY .... Ashley Cooper
SISTER BESSIE RICE .... Maude Odell
PEARL .... Reneice Rehan
CAPTAIN TIM .... Lamar King
GEORGE PAYNE .... Edwin Walter

Produced and directed by Anthony Brown

Settings by Robert Redington Sharpe

ACT I
Late Afternoon

ACT II
Next Morning

ACT III
Dawn, the Following Day.

The entire action of the play takes place at the farm of Jeeter Lester, situated on a tobacco road in the back country of Georgia.

TOBACCO ROAD

ACT ONE

TIME: *The Present.*

PLACE: *The back country, Georgia—thirty miles or so from Augusta. It is a famished, desolate land, once given over to the profitable raising of tobacco, then turned into small cotton plantations, which have been so intensively and stupidly cultivated as to exhaust the soil. Poverty, want, squalor, degeneracy, pitiful helplessness and grotesque, tragic lusts have stamped a lost, outpaced people with the mark of inevitable end. Unequipped to face a changing economic program, bound up in traditions, ties, and prejudices, they unknowingly face extinction. It is a passing scene, contemporary and fast fading, hurling the lie at nature's mercy and challenging a god who reputedly looks after his own. Grim humor pervades all, stalking side by side with tragedy on the last short mile which leads to complete, eventual elimination. The pride and hope of a once aggressive group, pioneers in a great new world, thus meet ironic conclusion. The world moves on, unmindful of their ghosts.*

SCENE: *The squalid shack of* JEETER LESTER, *where live his wife, his mother, and two children, last of a multiple brood and last of many generations of deep Georgia crackers. Left stage, angled to curtain line, is the front of the cracked and bleeding house. A small porch, one step up from the yard, projects beyond the building front. Rear, running parallel with the curtain line and disappearing—Left, behind the house, and, Right, behind a clump of bushes—is the immediate section of the Tobacco Road. Center stage, from road rear to foots, is a sandy yard. Right center stage is a leafless chinaberry tree, under which is a broken, weatherworn bench. Downstage from this, to within two feet of the curtain line, is a well structure, behind which, masking Right stage to curtain, is a broken corn crib. A sprawling, broken log fence separates the yard from the road, beyond which fields of sedge brush stretch away in the distance.*

AT RISE: JEETER, *dressed in dirty, torn overalls and dark shirt, an old, battered hat on his head, and heavy, worn boots on his feet, is sitting on the edge of the porch, trying vainly to patch a rotted inner tube. He is really concentrating on his work, but that does not hinder an almost constant run of chatter, most of it a complaining monotone. Standing in the yard and hurling a ball, which he retrieves on the rebound, against the side of the house, upstage beyond the porch, is* DUDE, *last son of* JEETER *to remain at home.* DUDE *is just sixteen, dirty, skinny, and not too bright. He is dressed like his father in dirty overalls and a shirt. Underfeeding has had its effect on both* JEETER *and* DUDE. *They are scrawny and emaciated.* DUDE *continues thumping the ball against the house and catching it on the rebound in spite of the fact that the old boards aren't capable of much resistance. The ball hits the house several times before* JEETER *complains.*

JEETER. Stop chunkin' that ball against that there old house, Dude. You've clear about got all the weatherboards knocked off already. (DUDE, *ignoring him, throws the ball three more times.*) Don't you never do what I tell you? Quit chunkin' that ball at them there weatherboards. The durned old house is going to pitch over and fall on the ground one of these days if you don't stop doing that.

DUDE (*casually*). Aw, go to hell, you dried-up old clod. Nobody asked you nothin'. (*Throws ball again.*)

JEETER (*an edge of supplication in his voice*). Now, Dude, is that a way to treat your old Pa? You ought to sort of help me out instead of always doing something contrary. You ought to be helping me fix up this old inner tube instead of chunking that ball at that old house all the time.

DUDE. That there old inner tube ain't going to stay fixed noway. You might just as well quit tryin'.

JEETER. Maybe you're right. Maybe I ought to try filling the tires with cotton hulls and drivin' on them that way. A man told me that was the way to do it.

DUDE (*between throwing the ball*). That old automobile ain't no good. It ain't got no

600

horn on it no more and there ain't no sense drivin' an automobile unless you got a horn.

JEETER. It had one of the prettiest horns in the country when it was new.

DUDE. Well, it ain't got no horn now, and it don't hardly run neither.

JEETER. It used to be one of the prettiest runnin' and prettiest soundin' automobiles you ever saw. I used to put you children in it and let you blow the horn all you liked.

DUDE. That was so long ago it ain't doing me no good now.

JEETER. That old automobile is just about the last of my goods. It looks like a man can't have any goods no more.

DUDE (*suddenly—fierce*). Some day I'm going to have me a new automobile. I'm going to have me a new automobile and a new horn on it and I'm going to ride through the country just a raisin' of hell. (GRANDMA LESTER, *an old, bent hag in ragged, black clothes comes around the far corner of the house just as* DUDE *throws his ball with particular viciousness, almost striking her. In fright, she drops to her knees and begins crawling downstage toward the porch.* DUDE *catches the ball on the rebound and prepares to hurl it again.*) Look out of the way, old woman, or I'll knock your head off. (DUDE *hurls the ball against the house just above the old woman as she crawls, whimpering, along the ground in the direction of the porch steps. He takes savage delight in her fears. She moves painfully and slowly and he has time for two throws before she reaches the comparative safety of the steps, under which she crawls.*)

JEETER. Now, Dude, is that a way to act toward your old grandma? You got her scared half to death.

DUDE. Aw, shut up. You wish she was dead just as much as anybody, even if she is your own ma.

JEETER. Now, Dude . . . I never wished no harm to nobody.

DUDE. You're a dirty old liar. You don't even give her nothing to eat.

JEETER. I don't give her nothing because there ain't nothing.

DUDE. Even when there is you don't give it to her. You needn't go telling me you don't want her dead.

JEETER. Now, Dude, is that a way to talk? It don't seem to me like that's a way a son should talk to his father.

DUDE. Then keep your mouth out of it when nobody's asked you nothing. (DUDE *throws the ball against the house, beginning his game again.* JEETER *resumes work on the inner tube, sitting on the patch.* GRANDMA *comes slowly from under the edge of the porch, rises and starts cautiously to move around* DUDE *in the direction of the Tobacco Road. She is carrying an old gunny sack.*)

DUDE (*seeing the old woman and stopping*). Where you going now? There ain't no use you picking up firewood today. There ain't going to be anything to eat. (*The* OLD WOMAN *shuffles on toward Right rear hole in the log fence.* DUDE *looks after her, the spirit of hurt in his heart and mind.*) You better run, old woman, I'm going to chunk this ball at you. (*He holds ball to throw. She sees his gesture, moves more quickly, stumbles, falls, get up.*) Look out now, I'm going to hit you in the head—I'm going to hit you in the head. (GRANDMA *stumbles again in her hurry, but this time doesn't rise, continuing her exit on hands and knees.* DUDE *is on the point of throwing the ball at her, when his eye catches the torn cover and checks him. He looks at the ball more closely.*) Goddamn, just look at that ball. Just look at what that old house done to that ball.

JEETER (*wiggling on tube to make the patch stick*). Let me see it here. (DUDE *hands him the ball. He looks at it and shakes his head.*) Yes, sir, it's plumb wore out.

DUDE (*taking back the ball, holding it up, and looking at it*). It ain't even round no more. That old house just about ruined it for good. (*Sits on ground, inspecting ball.*)

JEETER. Looks like about everything around here is wore out. Seems like the Lord just ain't with us no more at all.

DUDE. I'm going down to Fuller tomorrow and steal me a new ball. That's what I'm going to do.

JEETER. Stealing is powerful sinful, Dude. I wouldn't want you doing that. I guess stealing is about the most sinful thing a man can do.

DUDE. Go on, you old liar. You're always stealing something if you can find it.

JEETER. Now, Dude! Maybe I have been a powerful sinner in my time, but ain't nobody never been sorrier than me when he's done something against the Lord.

DUDE. You're always praying and shouting after you been stealing something, but that ain't never stopped you from doing it. I'd like to hear you tell me of one time when it stopped you. Just tell me. (*Pauses while* JEETER *fiddles with inner tube.*) You just won't tell me—that's what.

JEETER (*avoiding the issue, pulls at the patch, which comes off in his hand*). Just look at that old inner tube. . . . (*Inspects it for an instant, tosses it aside.*) Well, I guess there ain't no use trying to fix that no more. Looks to me like I got to figure some other way of getting a load of wood down to Augusta. (*Yawns, stretches.*) I got to do some thinking about that. (*Lies back on porch, tilting his hat over his eyes.* DUDE *continues to pound ball on rock.*) I know what I'm going to do. I'm going down to Fuller one of these days and borrow me a mule. I expect I could take a load of wood to Augusta almost every day that way.

DUDE (*laughs*). Ho! Ho! Ain't nobody going to loan you a mule. You can't even get seed-cotton and guano to plant a crop with.

JEETER. Never you mind now. That way I could do about everything I wanted. When I wasn't hauling wood I could cultivate the fields. That's what a man ought to be doing anyway. When February comes like this and the ground gets right for plowing a man ought to be planting in the ground and growing things. That's what the Lord intended a man should do. But he can't do much without a mule to plow with. (*Nods his head, sits up.*) Yes, sir, that's what I'm going to do. I'm going down to Fuller or maybe even McCoy one of these days and borrow me a mule. (*Lies down on his back again, tilting hat over his eyes.*) I got to do some thinking about that. (DUDE *makes no comment, concentrating on pounding the ball back into shape. Hits it twice on the ground.*)

DUDE. Goddamn that old house. This ball never will get round no more. (*Enter* ADA *through doorway on to the porch and taking in* JEETER's *recumbent form with a quick, irritated glance.* ADA *is a thin, gaunt, pellagra-ridden woman. Her shapeless dress is dirty and ragged. She was never a beauty, and pellagra and forty years of living with* JEETER *have not helped to improve her appearance. Her hair is a stringy, colorless gray-brown. She shambles rather than walks, and leans against anything strong enough to bear her weight. An inevitable snuff stick protrudes from her lips. She speaks when* DUDE *stops pounding the ball to inspect it again.*)

ADA. What are you doing laying down there on the porch, Jeeter Lester? Ain't you going to haul no wood to Augusta?

JEETER (*pushing back hat and sitting up. Even in that short time he has fallen asleep. He regards his wife vaguely*). What's that?

ADA. When you going to haul some wood to Augusta?

JEETER (*sinking back*). I'm aiming to take a load over there tomorrow or the next day.

DUDE. The hell he is, Ma. He's just trying to lie out of it.

JEETER. Now, Dude.

ADA. You're just lazy, that's what's wrong with you. If you wasn't lazy you could haul a load every day, and I'd have me some snuff when I wanted it most.

JEETER. I ain't no durn wood-chopper. I'm a farmer. The wood-choppers hauling wood to Augusta ain't got no farming to take up their time like I has. Why, I expect I'm going to grow near about fifty bales of cotton this year.

ADA. That's the way you talk every year about this time, but you don't never get started.

JEETER. This year I'm going to get at it. Dude and me'll burn the broom sedge off the fields one of these days and it won't take long then to put in a crop.

ADA. I been listening to you talk like that so long I don't believe nothing you say now. It's a big old whopping lie.

JEETER. Now leave me be, Ada. I'm going to start in the morning. Soon as I get all the fields burned off I'll go borrow me some mules. I wouldn't be surprised if me and Dude growed more than fifty bales of cotton this year, if I can get me some seed-cotton and guano.

DUDE. Who's going to give you seed-cotton and guano this year any more than they did last year or the year before, or the year before that?

JEETER. God is aiming to provide for me. I'm getting ready right now to receive His bounty.

ADA. You just lay there and see! Even the children has got more sense than you has. Didn't they go off and work in the mills as soon as they was big enough? If I wasn't so old I'd go up there right now and make me some money, myself, just like you ought to be doing.

JEETER (*intensely—sitting bolt upright*). It's wicked, you saying that, Ada. City ways ain't God-given. It wasn't intended for a man with the smell of the land in him to live in a mill in Augusta.

ADA. It's a whole lot better to live in the mills than it is to stay out here on the Tobacco Road and starve to death.

DUDE. Cuss the hell out of him, Ma.

JEETER (*sadly. Again lying down*). The Lord sends me every misery He can think of just to try my soul. He must be aiming to do something powerful big for me because He sure tests me hard. I reckon He figures if I can put up with my own people I can stand to fight back at the devil.

ADA. Humph! If He don't hurry up and do something about it, it will be too late. My poor stomach gives me a powerful pain all day long when I ain't got the snuff to calm it.

JEETER (*without moving*). Yes, I reckon you women folks is about near as hungry as I is. I sure feel right sorry for you women folks. (*Pulls hat over his eyes and dozes off again. Enter* ELLIE MAY *right on Tobacco Road.* ELLIE MAY *is eighteen, and not unattractive as to figure. Her eyes are good; her hair is brown. The outstanding feature, however, is a slit lip, red and fiery, the opening running from about the center of the lip*

to the left side of her nose. When she speaks, which is seldom, she has the garbled pronunciation and nasal emphasis of those afflicted with a harelip. She is barefoot and hatless, and her light cotton dress is old, rumpled, and streaked with dirt. She comes forward shyly, like a frightened doe, her eyes watching the three other people. She only comes in as far as the chinaberry tree, half edging behind it.)

ADA. You talk like an old fool. . . . Where you been there, Ellie May?

ELLIE MAY. No place, Ma.

ADA (*eagerly*). You didn't maybe go to see Pearl, did you?

ELLIE MAY. No, Ma.

ADA (*more to herself than to anyone*). I declare I don't know what's got into that girl. I ain't seen hide nor hair of her since she and Lov got married.

DUDE (*with deliberate cruelty*). Why should Pearl want to see you?

ADA. She loves her old Ma, that's why.

DUDE. Well, she ain't been back, has she?

ADA. Pearl is different. There ain't one of the whole seventeen she's like.

DUDE (*pointedly—leering*). She sure ain't like the rest of us, all right. . . . What was you doing, Ma, horsing around some man besides that old fool over there?

ADA. You ain't no right talking like that to your old Ma, Dude Lester. The Lord will strike you dead one of these days.

DUDE. I ain't afraid of the Lord. He ain't never done nothing for me one way or the other. . . .

ADA. If you was a good son, you wouldn't be saying things like that. You'd be helping to get rations and snuff for your old Ma. I declare to goodness I don't know when I've had enough to eat. It's getting so if I had a stylish dress to be buried in I'd like to lie down right now and die.

DUDE (*with vicious humor*). You ain't never going to get a new dress to die in. You're going to die and be buried in just what you got on. They're going to bury you in that same old dress.

ADA. Now, Dude, don't start fooling with your old Ma like that. (JEETER *is aroused and straightens up sleepily.* ELLIE MAY *moves a step nearer the porch, but is still close to the chinaberry tree.* DUDE *gets to his feet, leering with joy at the effect of his cruel tormenting.* ADA *steps down from the porch, but one hand still holds the upright.*)

DUDE. I ain't fooling. I guess I know . . . Yeh, and they're going to bury Pa just like he is, too. They're going to lay you in the corn crib and then they're going to bury you both just like you is.

JEETER (*plaintively*). What are you saying, Dude? You're always saying that when you know how I feel about it. They ain't going to lay me in no corn crib. Lov swore to me he'd dig a hole and put me right in it.

DUDE. What do I care what Lov promised? I know what they're going to do.

ADA. Make him say they ain't, Jeeter.

JEETER. Dude, you can't let them do that. My Pa was laid in the corn crib before they buried him and the rats ate off half his face. You can't let them do that to me.

DUDE. What you so worried about? You'll be dead, anyhow.

JEETER. My old Pa was dead and I know he minded.

DUDE. There ain't no rats in that old corn crib no more. There ain't been no corn in there for five years. They've all gone away.

JEETER. They'll come back, when they know I'm layin' there. They got it in good and heavy for me because there ain't been no corn in that old crib all this time. They'll just be waitin' to come back when I'm dead and eat off me when I can't do nothing to keep 'em away.

DUDE. What do I care about that?

ADA. You're the only boy left to see your old Ma is buried in a stylish dress. You got to swear to me, Dude.

DUDE (*getting up*). I ain't going to swear to nothing.

JEETER (*coming forward a few steps*). Now, Dude, boy—

DUDE. Aw, go to hell. What do I care about you? (*Turns—starts to chant*). You're going to die and get laid in the corn crib—you're going to die and get laid in the corn crib.

JEETER (*threateningly*). You shut up, Dude Lester. You shut up your mouth.

DUDE (*continuing chant, walking toward gate*). You're going to die and get laid in the corn crib—you're going to die, etc. (JEETER *rushes at* DUDE.)

JEETER (*striking weakly at* DUDE's *back*). Shut up. You hear me—shut up!

DUDE (*turning—blocking blows easily*). What you trying to do, you old fool? Get away from me. (*Pushes* JEETER, *who stumbles back, falling.*) You keep away from me when I tell you. (*Turns—breaks again into chant.*) You're going to die and get laid in the corn crib . . . etc. (*Exits.*)

ADA (*plaintively*). Dude, you come back here. You can't go off like that without making a promise to your old Ma. (ADA *is answered only by* DUDE's *grim chant, diminishing in the distance.* JEETER *gets up, goes back to the porch and sits, abstractedly picking up the inner tube and working on it.* ADA *at bench.*)

JEETER (*after a pause*). I reckon Dude is about the worst child of the whole lot. Seems like a boy would have the proper respect for his old Pa.

ADA. I know Lizzie Belle'd help me get a stylish dress if I could find out where she is at. She used to love her old Ma a heap. Clara might help some, too. She used to tell me how pretty I looked when I combed my hair mornings and put on a clean apron. I don't know if the others would want to help none or not. It's been such a long time since I saw the rest of them I've just about forgot what they was like. Seems like I can't recall their names even.

JEETER. Lizzie Belle might be making a lot of money over in the mills. Maybe if I was to find her and ask her about it, she might come sometime and bring us a little money. I know Bailey would. Bailey was just about the best of all the boys.

ADA. Reckon any of the children is dead?

JEETER. Some, I reckon. . . . But Tom ain't dead. I know that for sure. I ain't got around to doing it yet, but one of these days I'm going over to Burke County and see him. Everybody in Fuller tells me he's hauling cross ties out of the camp by the wagon load day and night. From what people say about him he's a powerful rich man now. He sure ought to give me some money.

ADA. When you see Tom tell him that his old Ma would like to see him. You tell him that I said he was near about the best of the whole seventeen. Clara and Lizzie Belle was about the best, I reckon, but Tom and Bailey led the boys when it came to being good children. You tell Tom I said he was the best and maybe he'll send me some money for a stylish dress.

JEETER. Pearl is the prettiest. Ain't none of the other gals got pretty yellow hair like she has. Nor them pale blue eyes, neither.

ADA. Pearl is my real favorite. But I wish she'd come to see me sometime. What do you think makes her stay away since she got married, Jeeter?

JEETER. There never was no telling what Pearl was going to do. You was much like her yourself in that respect when you was twelve or thirteen.

ADA. Do you think she's happy married to Lov?

JEETER. Happy? I don't know anything about that. When a gal is mated to a man that's all there is to it.

ADA. Maybe she should've gone off to Augusta like the others done, even if she was scared. That's where a pretty girl ought to be. She ought to be where there's pretty clothes and shoes to wear and windows to look at.

JEETER. I don't agree to that. People that's born on the land should stay on the land. The Lord intended such. I made her go to live with Lov because that was the best thing for her to do.

ADA. Humph! Well, it might be she's satisfied. Maybe she don't care about seeing her old Ma right now. When girls is satisfied they sometimes don't like to talk about their husbands any more than they do when they ain't satisfied.

JEETER. Pearl don't talk none anyway. Reckon she talk to Lov, Ada?

ADA. When girls sleep in the bed with their husbands they usually talk to them, I've discovered.

JEETER. By God and by Jesus you was certainly in no hurry to talk to me even then.

ADA. I'll go down to see her one of these days if she don't come to see me. You go see Lov, too. It's time you done that.

JEETER. Don't bother me about that now. I got to figure out some way to plant me a crop this year. (*Leans against upright.*) I got to do some thinking about that right away. (JEETER *pulls hat over his eyes and promptly goes to sleep.* ADA *shakes her head.* ELLIE MAY *starts out gate, but* ADA *sees her.*)

ADA. Ellie May! Hey you, Ellie May! You come inside and fix up the beds. They ain't been made all day and somebody's got to do something around here. (ELLIE MAY *turns and reluctantly starts toward house, when* DUDE *enters excitedly from Right and comes to right of porch.*)

DUDE. Hey, Lov's coming! Lov's coming down the road. (ELLIE MAY *crosses to right end of fence; looks down road.*)

JEETER (*drowsily*). What?

ADA (*kicks* JEETER). Wake up, you old fool—Lov's coming. Maybe he wants to talk about Pearl.

JEETER. What do I care about that now? By God, woman, can't you see I'm thinking?

DUDE. He's toting a croker sack that's got something in it.

JEETER (*suddenly wide awake*). A croker sack! (*Rises.*) What does it look like in that croker sack, Dude?

DUDE. He's just coming over the ridge now and I couldn't make out. But nobody carries a sack that ain't got nothing good in it. (JEETER *runs to the fence and looks over it down the road.* ELLIE MAY *also goes to the fence, but as far right stage from the others as possible. Enter* GRANDMA LESTER *with a sackful of twigs which she drags along the ground. She does not even glance at the others, who are gazing in the opposite direction down the road, but crosses to the porch, releases the sack, and sits, pressing her hands to her side in pain and swaying back and forth.*)

JEETER (*peering over fence*). By God and by Jesus, that's Lov all right. Do you think them's turnips he's toting, Dude? Do you think them's turnips in that croker sack?

DUDE. It's something all right.

JEETER (*delighted*). By God and by Jesus, I just been waiting to have me some turnips.

ADA. If them's turnips do you reckon he'll let me have some?

JEETER. I'll mention it when I talk to him, but I don't know how he'll take it. He must have paid a good stiff price if they's winter turnips.

DUDE. Lov ain't giving away nothing he paid a good stiff price for.

JEETER. I ain't concerning myself about that. Lov and me think a heap of each other.

DUDE. If he don't give you none, is you going to try and steal some?

JEETER (*admonishingly*). Now, Dude! Stealing is about the most sinful thing a man can do. The Lord don't have no truck with stealing. (ELLIE MAY *giggles foolishly.* JEETER *turns to her.*) Get away from that fence, Ellie May. Lov ain't likely to come in here at all if he sees that face of yours. (ELLIE MAY *giggles foolishly again and moves behind chinaberry tree, from where she peaks.* GRANDMA LESTER *shuffles downstage and flattens herself against the corner of the porch nearest the curtain line.* JEETER *and* DUDE *stretch far over the fence to watch* LOV's *approach.*)

ADA. Is he near about here, Jeeter?

JEETER. Near about. He's just about here now.

ADA. Is them turnips?

JEETER. By God, if they ain't, I sure is doing a hell of a lot of stretching for nothing. (JEETER *gives his full attention to the approaching man for a second, then turns and motions to the others.*)

JEETER. Get away from that fence—all of you. Come on, sit down. Act unconcerned. (JEETER *goes to side of house;* ADA *to the well;* DUDE *sits on fence. Enter* LOV BENSEY. LOV *is a man about thirty, dressed in coal-grimed overalls and wearing a dirty, floppy hat. When he removes the hat to wipe the sweat from his face a shock of unruly hair is seen rising above a sunburned face. He is not unattractive in his dull, slow way, and his body shows the result of hard work and a reasonable amount of food. He is not a big man, but he is stronger and better nourished than either* DUDE *or* JEETER. *He carries a partly filled gunny sack over his shoulder. Caution and suspicion mark his every move in dealing with the* LESTERS, *and this is in evidence now as he comes into the scene.*)

JEETER (*hiding his eagerness by trying to be casual*). Hi there, Lov.

LOV. Hi. (*He moves on beyond them toward Center stage.*)

JEETER. Ain't seen you in a long time.

LOV. No. (*He stops near the gate, and shifts bag.*)

JEETER. You must be plumb wore out toting that croker sack. Come in off the Tobacco Road and rest yourself.

LOV. I ain't tired.

JEETER. You must of come a far piece off if you come from down Fuller way.

LOV. Umm.

JEETER. Come inside and get yourself a drink.

LOV. I ain't thirsty.

JEETER (*with calculated amiability*). We was just talking about you, Lov. We ain't seen you since a way long the first of the winter. How is you and Pearl getting on down there at the coal chute?

ADA (*a trace of anxiety*). Pearl—is she all right?

LOV. Humph! (*He glances suspiciously at all of them.*) I want to talk to you, Jeeter.

JEETER. Sure. Come inside the yard and sit down. No use toting that croker sack while you're talking. (LOV *repeats his glance of suspicion, but comes hesitatingly inside and drops the sack against fence near gate. He stands in front of it, guarding it.* JEETER *tries to make his voice casual, but every eye on the stage is on that sack, giving the lie to their pretended indifference.*) What you got in that croker sack, Lov? (*Innocently, as* LOV *doesn't answer.*) I heard it said that some people has got turnips this year. (LOV'S *eyes narrow with suspicion and he backs even more protectively against the sack.*)

LOV (*shrewdly*). It's Pearl I want to talk to you about.

ADA. She ain't sick, is she?

LOV (*suddenly angry*). By God, she's something! (*He lets himself to ground, sitting beside turnips and gripping neck of sack.*)

JEETER (*archly*). Why don't you go over on the porch? That ain't no place to sit.

LOV. I'll sit right where I is.

JEETER (*agreeably*). What you got to say to me, Lov? You must have a heap to say, toting that sack all this way to do it.

LOV. I sure has. You got to talk to Pearl. That's what I got to say.

JEETER. What's that gal up to? I never could understand her. What's she done now?

LOV. It's just like she done ever since she went down to live with me at the chute, only i'm getting pretty durn tired of it by this time. All the niggers make fun of me because of the way she treats me.

JEETER. Pearl is just like her Ma. Her Ma used to do the queerest things in her time.

ADA (*sharply*). Is you treating her right?

LOV. That ain't got a goddamn thing to do with it. She's married to me, ain't she?

JEETER. You got leave of the county. I remember that all right.

LOV. Then why the hell don't she act like she ought to? Every time I want to have her around, she runs off in the broom sedge. She won't talk to me, neither, and she won't cook nothing I want to eat.

JEETER. Great day in the morning, now what do you think makes her do that?

LOV. I don't know and I don't care. But I call it a hell of a business.

JEETER. About the cooking you is just about right. But when it comes to not talking I don't see no harm in that. Ada, there, didn't used to talk neither, but, by God and by Jesus, now you can't make her shut up.

LOV (*stubbornly*). I want Pearl to talk to me. I want her to ask me if my back is sore when I come home from the chute, or if it's going to rain, or when I is going to get a hair cut. There's a hell of a lot of things she could ask me about, but she don't talk at all.

JEETER. Maybe you don't try the right way to make her.

LOV. I tried kicking her and I tried pouring water on her and chunking rocks and sticks at her, but it don't do no good. She cries a lot when she's hurt, but, by God, I don't call that talking.

ADA. Don't you dare hurt her, Lov Bensey.

LOV. You keep out of this. I guess I know my rights. (*He pauses, looking belligerently from* ADA *to* JEETER.) And they is something else she don't do neither.

JEETER. For one little gal they sure is a heap of things she don't do. What else don't she do, Lov?

LOV. She don't sleep in the bed with me, that's what. (*Viciously to* ADA.) And what you got to say about that?

JEETER (*much more interested*). Now that's something. By God and by Jesus, that's something.

LOV (*turning back to* JEETER). She ain't never slept in the bed. It's a durn pallet on the floor she sleeps on every night. Now what I say is, what the hell is the sense in me marrying a wife if I don't get none of the benefits?

ADA. If you don't like what she's doing, you send her right home and get yourself another girl. Her old Ma will look after her.

LOV. No. I ain't going to do that neither. I want Pearl. She's about the prettiest piece in the whole country and I want her.

JEETER. You give her time and she'll get in the bed.

LOV. By God. I already give her enough time. Right now I feel like I got to have me a woman. (*He looks at* ELLIE MAY. ELLIE MAY *catches his glance and giggles. She begins the wriggling movement, which at the right time brings her near* LOV.)

JEETER. I know how you feel, Lov. When the time to plow and put seed in the ground comes along a man feels just like that. Even at this day and age I could do a little of that myself.

LOV. Well, then, you go down and talk to her. You tell her to stop sleeping on that durn pallet and get in the bed—and tell her to talk to me, too, by God.

JEETER. I might do that if I felt you was ready and willing to do something for me in return.

LOV (*suspiciously*). What do you mean by that, Jeeter?

JEETER (*unable longer to restrain himself*). By God and by Jesus, Lov, what you got in that croker sack? I been looking at it ever since you been here and I sure got to know.

LOV. I don't see what that's got to do with it?

JEETER. What is they, I tell you!

LOV (*after a short pause for emphasis and a hard, proud glance around*). Turnips, by God. (*His announcement causes a noticeable reaction on everyone. Their bodies stiffen and lean forward—a look of greed appears in their faces. But wisely they refrain from taking any actual steps forward. Instinctively they wait for* JEETER *to see it through. Only* ELLIE MAY *forgets her hunger in the sharpening force of passion brought on by proximity to* LOV, *and continues her sex-conscious wriggling.*)

JEETER (*keyed up, but holding himself in*).

Turnips! Where'd you get turnips, Lov?

LOV. Wouldn't you like to know?

JEETER. Turnips is about the thing I want most of all right now. I could just about eat me a whole croker sackful between now and sundown.

LOV. Well, don't look to me to give you none because I ain't.

JEETER. That's a mean thing to say, Lov. It's a whopping mean thing to say to Pearl's old Pa.

LOV. To hell with that. I had to pay fifty cents for this many in a sack and I had to walk clear to the other side of Fuller to fetch them.

JEETER. I was thinking maybe you and me could fix up some sort of trade. I could go down to your house and tell Pearl she's got to sleep in the bed, and you could give me some of them—

LOV. No, by God. You're Pearl's Daddy and you ought to make her behave for nothing.

JEETER. By God and by Jesus, Lov, you oughtn't to talk to me like that. I just got to have me some turnips. I ain't had a good turnip since a year ago this spring. All the turnips I raised this year has got them damn-blasted green-gutted worms in them.

LOV. I don't see what that's got to do with Pearl one way or another. I gave you seven dollars when she came to live with me and that's enough.

JEETER. Maybe it was then, but it ain't now. We is about starved around here. What God made turnip-worms for I can't make out. It appears to me like He just naturally has got it in good and heavy for a poor man. I worked all the fall last year digging up a patch of ground to grow turnips in, and when they're getting about big enough to pull up and eat, along come them damn-blasted green-gutted worms and bore clear to the middle of them. (LOV *is entirely indifferent to* JEETER's *plea. Cruelly he takes a turnip from the sack and takes a big bite. Chewing the bite to the agony of the starving* LESTERS, *he points the stub of the turnip at the wriggling* ELLIE MAY, *sitting on the ground near the bench and looking at him with avid eyes. She giggles.*)

LOV. Now if Pearl was anything like Ellie May there, she wouldn't act like she does. You go down and tell her to act like Ellie May.

JEETER. Is you in mind then to make a trade with them turnips?

LOV (*eating*). I ain't trading turnips with nobody.

JEETER. That's a hell of a thing to say, Lov. I'm wanting turnips God himself knows how bad.

LOV. Go over to Fuller and buy yourself some, then. I went over there to get mine.

JEETER. Now, Lov, you know I ain't got a penny to my name. You got a good job down there at the chute and it pays you a heap of money.

LOV. I don't make but a dollar a day. House rent takes up near about all that and eating the rest of it.

JEETER. Makes no difference. You don't want to sit there and let me starve, do you?

LOV. I can't help it if you do. The Lord looks at us with equal favor, they say. He gives me mine and if you don't get yours you better go talk to Him about it.

DUDE. You give him hell, Lov. If he wasn't so durn lazy he'd do something instead of cussing about it all the time. He's the laziest son-of-a-bitch I ever seen.

JEETER. My children all blame me because God sees fit to make me poverty-ridden, Lov. They and their Ma is all the time cussing me because we ain't got nothing to eat. It ain't my fault that Captain John shut down on giving us rations and snuff, and then went away and died.

LOV (*indifferently*). It ain't my fault neither.

JEETER. I worked all my life for Captain John, Lov. I worked harder than any four of his niggers in the field; then the first thing I knowed he came down here one morning and says he can't be letting me get no more rations and snuff at the store. After that he sells all the mules and goes up to Augusta to live. He said there wasn't no use trying to run a farm no more—fifty plows or one plow. He told me I could stay on the land as long as I liked, but that ain't doing me no good. Ain't no work I can find to do for hire and I can't raise a crop of my own because I ain't got no mule and I ain't got no credit. (LOV's *attention turns from* JEETER *to* ELLIE MAY, *whose wriggling movement is bringing her inch by inch closer to*

him.) That's what I'm wanting to do powerful strong right now—raise me a crop. When the winter goes and when it gets time to burn off the broom sedge in the fields, I sort of want to cry. I reckon it is the smell of the sedge smoke this time of year near about drives me crazy. Then pretty soon all the other farmers start plowing. That's what's the worst. When the smell of that new earth turning over behind the plows strikes me, I get all weak and shaky. It's in my nature—burning broom sedge and plowing in the ground this time of year. I did it for near about fifty years, and my Pa and his Pa before him was the same kind of men. Us Lesters sure like to stir up the earth and make plants grow in it. The land has got a powerful hold on me, Lov. (LOV *is giving his full attention to* ELLIE MAY *now, a half-eaten turnip arrested on its way to his mouth.* ELLIE MAY *leans back until she rests on the ground and continues her wriggling and squealing.* LOV *begins to edge toward her.* DUDE *watches them closely.*)

DUDE. Hey, Pa.

JEETER. Shut up, Dude. It didn't always used to be like it is now, neither, Lov. I can remember a short time back when all the merchants in Fuller was tickled to give me credit. Then all of a sudden Captain John went away and pretty soon the sheriff comes and takes away near about every durn piece of goods I possessed. He took every durn thing I had, excepting that old automobile and the cow. He said the cow wasn't no good because she wouldn't take no freshening, and the automobile wasn't no good neither. I reckon he was right, too, because the automobile won't run no more and the cow died.

DUDE (*throwing a broken piece of weatherboarding at* JEETER). Hey, you.

JEETER (*angrily*). What you want, Dude? What's the matter with you—chunking weather-boarding at me like that?

DUDE. Ellie May's horsing. That's horsing from way back yonder, hey, Pa?

JEETER (*giving the action conscious attention for the first time*). By God and by Jesus, Lov, has you been paying attention to what I was saying? You ain't answered me about them turnips yet.

DUDE. Lov ain't thinking about no turnips. He's wanting to hang up with Ellie May. Look at her straining for him. She's liable to bust a gut if she don't look out. (*It's* JEETER's *turn now to be indifferent to conversation. He watches while* LOV *creeps several yards from the turnip sack up to* ELLIE MAY *and awkwardly begins to fondle her. Their backs meet and rub together in a primitive love gesture. Slowly and silently,*

JEETER *puts aside the inner tube which he has been holding and vaguely trying to fix, and gets to his feet. Inch by inch he begins edging toward the sack.* LOV *has worked his way around in back of* ELLIE MAY *and his hands are around her, stroking her arms and legs.*)

JEETER (*moves closer and closer to the sack, unseen by* LOV. *Only* ADA *and* GRANDMA LESTER *notice him.* DUDE *is too occupied watching* LOV *and* ELLIE MAY). By God, Lov ain't never got that close before. He said he wouldn't never get close enough to Ellie May to touch her with a stick. But he ain't paying no mind to that now. I bet he don't even know she's got a slit-lip on her. If he does know it, he don't give a good goddamn. (*And now* JEETER *makes his play. In one swift lunge he crosses the intervening distance and grabs up the sack.* LOV *sees him, turns swiftly, and reaches for him, but misses. He starts to rise as* JEETER *backs a step away, but* ELLIE MAY *grabs his legs, tripping him up. Before he can shake her off,* ADA *hurries from the well, picking up a stick on the way.* GRANDMA LESTER *totters from her place, also brandishing a stick. The two* OLD WOMEN *move down on* LOV *to help* ELLIE MAY.)

LOV. Drop them turnips, Jeeter! Drop them turnips. (ELLIE MAY, *quicker than* LOV, *practically leaps on top of him, holding him down. They roll and struggle.*)
(*To* ELLIE MAY).
Get off me, you. Get off me. (LOV *struggles to rise.* ADA *and* GRANDMA *slap and jab at him with their sticks.*)

JEETER (*at the gate*). You tell Pearl I said be good to you, Lov. I'll be down to see about that first thing in the morning. (*He exits, running.*)

LOV. Goddamn you! (LOV, *by dint of great effort, throws off the women, literally hurl-*

ing ELLIE MAY *to the ground and dashes to the gate. He stops there, looking down the road, trying to spy* JEETER.)

DUDE. Ain't no use trying to catch Pa. He's run off in the brush and there ain't nobody can catch Pa when he runs off in the brush. (LOV *realizes the truth of* DUDE's *statement, and, winded and panting, leans against the fence, making no effort to run.* ELLIE MAY *lies on the ground, also breathing hard, but her eyes still are on* LOV.)

ADA. Go on back to Ellie May, Lov. Don't be scared of her. You might even get to like her and let Pearl come back here to me. (LOV *doesn't answer, pulling a huge colored handkerchief from his pocket and wiping his streaming face.* DUDE *moves to the fence, center.*)

DUDE. How many scoops-full does that No. 17 freight engine empty at the chute every morning, Lov? Looks to me like them freight engines takes on twice as much coal as the passenger ones does. (LOV *pays no attention.* ADA *goes back to the porch.* GRANDMA LESTER *picks up her sack of twigs, and, groaning, goes into the house.*) Why don't the firemen blow the whistles more than they do, Lov? If I was a fireman I'd pull the whistle cord near about all the time. (DUDE *makes noise like locomotive whistle.* LOV *turns from the fence, goes back into the yard, recovers his hat, glances at* ELLIE MAY, *who lies sprawled on the ground. Then he turns and starts off.* DUDE *follows* LOV *to the gate.* LOV *finishes adjusting his overalls and crosses to the gate,* DUDE *following.*) When is you going to buy yourself an automobile, Lov? You make a heap of money at the chute. You ought to get one that has got a great big horn on it. (*Repeats locomotive sound. Ecstatically.*) Whistles and horns sure make a pretty sound. (*Ignoring* DUDE, LOV *exits through the gate and down the road.*) I reckon Lov don't feel much like talking today.

ADA. Dude, you run right out in the brush and find your Pa before he eats up all them turnips. (DUDE *starts.*) See you bring some of them back to your old Ma, too. (*Exit* DUDE. ADA *watches him through the gate, then calls.*) Ellie May . . . Ellie May!

ELLIE MAY (*looking up—blinking*). Yes, Ma.

ADA. You get inside the house and fix up them beds like I told you a long time ago. (ELLIE MAY *stretches and yawns, showing no disposition to move.*) I declare to goodness there ain't nobody around here got gumption enough to do anything. Now you get inside the house and do like I tell you. Do you hear me? Come on.

ELLIE MAY (*slowly getting to her feet*). All right—I'm coming. (*Enter* HENRY PEABODY, *a man who, except for his voice and slight difference in his dress, might well be* JEETER. HENRY *in very excited. He doesn't come into the yard, but hangs over the fence.* ELLIE MAY *promptly sits again.*)

HENRY. Hey you, Ada. Is Jeeter home?

ADA (*shaking her head negatively*). He went out into the brush a little while back. I'm expecting him pretty soon, but I ain't certain.

HENRY. You tell him I was here.

ADA. What's got you so excited, Henry Peabody? I ain't seen you hurry like that since you was a boy.

HENRY. I ain't got time to tell you about it now, but you tell Jeeter I been here and I'll stop again on my way home. (*Enter* SISTER BESSIE RICE, *a rather portly woman of about forty, She is dressed in a faded apron and wears a sunbonnet over her large, round face.* BESSIE *is one of the brood of itinerant women preachers peculiar to certain sections of the deep South. She owes allegiance to no church, and her creed and method of divine teaching are entirely her own. She is loud and sure of voice, and is generally accepted at her own value by the God-fearing innocents among whom she moves. She enters by way of the gate, coming inside the yard, and takes off her sunbonnet, fanning herself, as she gives her greeting.*)

BESSIE. Good evening, Brother Henry—good evening, Sister Ada. The Lord's blessing be with you.

HENRY. Good evening, Sister Bessie. . . . Well, I got to be rushing off. (*Starts off.*)

BESSIE. What's hurrying you, Brother Henry? You been sinning against the Lord?

HENRY. No, praise God, but I got to hurry. (*Exits.*)

BESSIE (*calling after him*). I'm coming down to your house for preaching and praying one of these days, Brother Henry. (*There is no answer and she turns to* ADA.) Now what do you suppose that Henry Peabody's been up to? I bet he's been a powerful wicked man here of late to hurry off like that. Looks like the devil's got into him sure.

ADA. Come inside, Bessie. I reckon Jeeter will be right glad to see you.

BESSIE. I'll be right pleased to, Sister. I reckon I walked near about three miles getting here. (*Walks to the porch, stands for a second.*)

ADA. Set down.

BESSIE. Has you got a chair, Sister? My poor back's so weary it feels like it's mighty near breaking in half.

ADA. H'mm. (*She exits into house.* BESSIE, *looking around and fanning herself, sees* ELLIE MAY. ELLIE MAY *giggles.*)

BESSIE. How is you, child? God be with you. (*She goes onto the porch singing the hymn "Shall We Gather at the River." Midway in the song* ADA *returns from the house dragging an old rocking chair which she thumps down.* BESSIE *abruptly stops singing. To* ADA.) Bless you, Sister. (*She sits, rocking back and forth, fanning herself.* ADA *stands on the ground, leaning against the porch upright, chewing on her snuff stick.*) Where is Jeeter at this time of day, Sister Ada? Has that man been up to something sinful again?

ADA. He's out in the broom sedge, eating up turnips he stole from Lov a while back.

BESSIE. Lord, O Lord, he's been stealing again. Jeeter's a powerful sinful man. Ain't no sin like stealing. . . . Was they good eating winter turnips, Sister?

ADA. I reckon.

BESSIE. Lord forgive us our sins, and particularly forgive Jeeter. . . . Is he coming back with any of them turnips, Ada?

ADA. I told Dude to fetch him before he eats them all up. Maybe he will and maybe he won't.

BESSIE. Dude will do right by the Lord. Dude's a mighty fine boy, Sister.

ADA. Humph.

BESSIE. We got to be careful against delivering him to the Hardshell Baptists, though. They're sinful people. They don't know the working of the Lord like I does.

ADA. What do you call your religion, Sister Bessie? You ain't never said what name you called it.

BESSIE. It ain't got a name. I generally just call it "Holy." It's just me and God. God talks to me in prayer and I answer Him back. I get most things done that way.

ADA. I want you to say a prayer for Pearl before you go away, Bessie. I reckon Lov's mad about Jeeter stealing his turnips and he might beat Pearl more than he ought to.

BESSIE. I'll be right happy to say a prayer for Pearl. But she ought to pray for herself, too. That sometimes helps a lot with the Lord.

ADA. Pearl don't talk to nobody except me— not even the Lord. I reckon what praying's done for her has got to be done by somebody else.

BESSIE. I'll mention that to the Lord and see if he'll let loose her tongue. There's sin someplace in her or she'd talk like everybody else. The Lord didn't intend for a woman not to talk.

ADA. Ellie May don't talk much, either. But that's because of her lip. It sounds funny when she talks.

BESSIE. There's been a powerful lot of sinning among you Lesters, or Ellie May wouldn't have that lip. One way or another I reckon you Lesters is about the most sinful people in the country. (*They are interrupted by the offstage sound of* JEETER *and* DUDE *quarreling.*)

DUDE (*offstage*). You ain't the only one that likes turnips. I ain't had no more to eat this week than you has.

JEETER (*offstage*). You had five already.
DUDE. Give me some more. Do you hear me?

JEETER. You don't need no more.

DUDE. I'll wham you. (*At this point* JEETER *comes running to the gate. He has his pockets filled with turnips.* DUDE *is right on his heels and catches him in the gate, throws one arm around him from behind and holds him as he extracts turnips from his pockets with his right hand.*)

JEETER (*trying to free himself*). Stop that, Dude, you stop that!

DUDE (*laughing at him*). Ho! Ho! You can't hurt nobody. You're as weak as an old cat. (*Pushes* JEETER, *who falls on the ground near the corner of the house.* DUDE *crosses to right of gate eating a turnip.*)

JEETER (*lying on ground*). Now that's all you're going to git. (*Picks himself up.*)

BESSIE (*oracularly*). You been sinning again, Jeeter Lester.

JEETER (*seeing* BESSIE *for the first time*). Sister Bessie! The good Lord be praised. (*He rushes to the porch.*) I knowed God would send His angel to take away my sins. You come just at the right time.

BESSIE. The Lord always knows the right time. I was at home sweeping out the kitchen when He come to me and said, "Sister Bessie, Jeeter Lester is doing something evil. You go to his house and pray for him right now before it's too late." I looked right back at the Lord and said, "Lord, Jeeter Lester is a powerful sinful man, but I'll pray for him until the devil goes clear back to hell." That's what I told Him and here I is.

JEETER (*dancing ecstatically in front of* BESSIE's *chair on the porch*). I knowed the good Lord wouldn't let me slip and fall in the devil's hands. I knowed it! I knowed it!

BESSIE. Ain't you going to give me a turnip, Jeeter? I ain't had much to eat lately. Times is hard for the good and bad alike.

JEETER. Sure, Bessie. (JEETER *selects several of the largest, gives them to* BESSIE. *Turns to* ADA.) Here you is, Ada. (*Gives her some. As others get theirs,* GRANDMA *enters, comes to* JEETER, *and starts pulling at his coat. To* BESSIE.) I wish I had something to give you to take home, Sister. When I had plenty, I uesd to give Brother Rice a whole armful of chickens and potatoes at a time. Now I ain't got nothing but a handful of turnips, but I ain't ashamed of them. The Lord growed them and His doings is good enough for me.

BESSIE (*with full mouth*). Praise be the Lord.

JEETER *and* ADA. Amen, Sister! Amen.

BESSIE (*finishing her turnip with a sigh*). I feel the call of the Lord. Let's have a little prayer. (BESSIE *gets up and crosses to the center of the yard,* JEETER *following, as does* ADA *and* GRANDMA LESTER, *who groans as she moves.* ELLIE MAY *and* DUDE *sit on the porch, eating the turnips and watching.*) Some people make an objection to kneeling down and having prayer out of doors. They say, "Sister Bessie, can't we go in the house and pray just as good?" And do you know what I do? I say, "Brothers and Sisters, I ain't ashamed to pray out here in the open. I want folks passing along the road to know that I'm on God's side. It's the old devil that's always whispering about going in the house out of sight." That's what I tell them. That's the way I stick up for the Lord.

JEETER. Praise the Lord.

BESSIE. Let's get ready to pray. (*They all kneel.*) Sister Ada, is you still suffering from pleurisy?

ADA. All the time. (JEETER *and* ADA *bow their heads and close their eyes, but* GRANDMA LESTER *stares straight ahead, her eyes open, her head raised a bit.* BESSIE *nods to* ADA, *then prays.*)

BESSIE. Dear God, here I is again to offer a little prayer for sinful people. Jeeter Lester and his family want me to pray for them again. The last time helped a whole lot, but Jeeter let the devil get hold of him today and he went and done a powerful sinful thing. He stole all of Lov's turnips. They're just about all et up now, so it's too late to take them back. That's why we want to pray for Jeeter. You ought to make him stop stealing like he does. I never seen a more stealing man in all my days. Jeeter wants to quit, but it seems like the devil gets hold of him as soon as we get through praying for him. You ain't going to let the old

devil tell You what to do, is You? The Lord ought to tell the devil what he should do. . . . And Sister Ada has got the pleurisy again. You ought to do something for her this time sure enough. The last time didn't help none too much. If You'll make her well of it she'll quit the devil for all time. Won't you, Sister Ada?

ADA. Yes, Lord.

BESSIE. And old Mother Lester has got a misery in her sides. She's in pain all the time with it. She's kneeling down right now, but she can't do it many more times. . . . You ought to bless Ellie May, too. Ellie May has got that slit in her lip that makes her an awful sight to look at. (ELLIE MAY *buries her face in her hands.* DUDE *looks at her and grins.*)

JEETER. Don't forget to pray for Pearl, Sister Bessie. Pearl needs praying for something awful.

BESSIE. I was just going to do that. Sister Ada told me to pray Lov wouldn't beat her too hard because of them turnips you stole.

JEETER. It ain't that. It's what Pearl's done herself.

BESSIE. What has Pearl done sinful, Brother Jeeter?

JEETER. That was what Lov spoke to me about today. He says Pearl won't talk to him and she won't let him touch her. When night comes she gets down and sleeps on a durn pallet on the floor, and Lov has got to sleep in the bed by himself. That's a pretty bad thing for a wife to do, and God ought to make her quit it.

BESSIE. Brother Jeeter, little girls like Pearl don't know how to live married lives like we grown-up women do. So maybe if I was to talk to her myself instead of getting God to do it, she would change her ways. I expect I know more about what to tell her than He does, because I been a married woman up to the past summer when my former husband died. I expect I know all about it. God wouldn't know what to tell her.

JEETER. Well, you can talk to her, but maybe if you asked God about it He might help some, too. Maybe He's run across gals like that before, though I don't believe there's another durn gal in the whole country who's as contrary-minded about sleeping in the bed as Pearl is. (DUDE *stands up and takes his ball from his pocket.*)

BESSIE. Maybe it wouldn't hurt none if I was to mention it.

JEETER. That's right. You speak to the Lord about it, too. Both of you together ought to get something done. (DUDE *hurls the ball against the house and catches it.* JEETER *speaks angrily*). Quit chunking that there ball against that old house, Dude. Don't you see Sister Bessie's praying. I declare I wish you had more sense.

DUDE. Aw, go to hell.

BESSIE. Now, Dude. . . . (*Waits until he stops.*) Now, Lord, I've got something special to pray about. I don't ask favors unless they is things I want pretty bad, so this time I'm asking for a favor for Pearl. I want You to make her stop sleeping on a pallet on the floor while Brother Lov has to sleep by himself in the bed. I was a good wife to my former husband. I never slept on no pallet on the floor. Sister Ada here don't do nothing like that. And when I marry another man, I ain't going to do that neither. I'm going to get in bed just as big as my new husband does. So You tell Pearl to quit doing that.

JEETER. What was that you was saying, Sister Bessie? Didn't I hear you say you was going to marry yourself a new husband?

BESSIE. Well, I ain't made up my mind yet. I been looking around some, though.

JEETER. Now if it wasn't for Ada there . . .

BESSIE (*giggling*). You hush up, Brother Jeeter. How'd you know I'd take you anyway? You're pretty old, ain't you?

JEETER. Maybe I is and maybe I ain't, but if I is I ain't too old for that.

ADA (*stiffly*). I reckon you'd better finish up the prayer. You ain't done like I asked you about Pearl yet.

BESSIE. So I ain't. . . . Please, Lord, Sister Ada wants me to ask You not to let Lov beat up Pearl too much. And I guess that's about all. . . . Save us from the devil and—

JEETER. Hey, wait a minute. You clear forgot to say a little prayer for Dude. You left Dude out all around.

DUDE. No, sir, not me, you don't. I don't want no praying. (BESSIE *jumps up and runs to* DUDE. *Clutching him by the arm she starts dragging him back to the praying circle.*)

BESSIE. Come on, Dude. Come and kneel with me.

DUDE (*angrily*). I don't want to do that. I don't want no praying for me. (BESSIE *puts one arm around his waist, holding him very close, and with her free hand strokes his shoulder.*)

BESSIE (*tenderly*). I got to pray for you, Dude. The Lord didn't leave you out no more than He did Ellie May. (*She kneels, but keeps his legs encircled in her arms.*) Come on now. All of us has got to have prayer some time or another. (DUDE *finds the pressure of her arms on his legs quite stimulating and exciting, and he begins giggling and squirming.*)

JEETER. Quit that jumping up and down, Dude. What ails you? (DUDE *puts his arm around her neck and begins rubbing her as she is rubbing him.*)

BESSIE. You kneel down beside me and let me pray for you. You'll do that, won't you, Dude?

DUDE (*snickering*). Hell, I don't give a damn if I do. (*He kneels, continuing to keep his arms about her, and she keeps her arms around him.*)

BESSIE. I knowed you would want me to pray for you, Dude. It will help you get shed of your sins like Jeeter did. (*Closes her eyes, lifts her head.*) Dear God, I'm asking You to save Brother Dude from the devil and make a place for him in heaven. That's all. Amen.

JEETER. Praise the Lord, but that was a durn short prayer for a sinner like Dude. (*He gets to his feet.* BESSIE *and* DUDE *continue to hold each other.*)

BESSIE (*smiling fondly at* DUDE.) Dude don't need no more praying for. He's just a boy, and he's not sinful like us grown-ups is.

JEETER. Well, maybe you're right. But I sort of recollect the Bible says a son shouldn't cuss his Ma and Pa like he does other people.

BESSIE (*stroking* DUDE's *hair*). Dude won't do that again. He's a fine boy, Dude is. He would make a handsome preacher, too. He's mighty like my former husband in his younger days. (*She and* DUDE *stop kneeling, but sit on the ground and continue to hold each other.*)

JEETER. Dude's about sixteen years old now. That makes him two years younger than Ellie May. He'll be getting a wife pretty soon, I reckon. All my other male children married early in life, just like the gals done. It it wasn't for Ellie May's lip she'd been married as quick as any. Men here around Fuller all want to marry gals about eleven or twelve years old, like Pearl was. Ada, there, was just turning twelve when I married her.

BESSIE. The Lord intended all of us should be mated. He made us that way. My former husband was just like the Lord in that respect. They both believed in the same thing when it came to mating.

JEETER. I reckon the Lord did intend for us all to get mated, but He didn't take into account a woman with a slit in her mouth like Ellie May's got.

BESSIE. The Lord's ways is wise, Jeeter.

JEETER. Well, maybe, but I don't believe He done the right thing by her when He opened up her lip. That's the only contrary thing I ever said about the Lord, but it's the truth. What use is a slit like that for? You can't spit through it, and you can't whistle through it, now can you? It was just meanness on His part when He done that—just durn meanness.

BESSIE. You shouldn't talk about the Lord like that. He knows what He done it for. He had the best reason in the world for doing it.

JEETER. What reason?

BESSIE. Maybe I ought not to say it, Jeeter.

JEETER. You sure ought to tell me if you tell anybody. I'm her Pa.

BESSIE. He done that to save her pure body from you, Brother Jeeter.

JEETER. From me?

BESSIE (*nodding*). He knowed she would be safe in this house when He made her like that. He knowed that you was once a powerful sinner, and that you might be again.

JEETER. That's the truth. I used to be a powerful sinful man in my time. I reckon at one time I was the most powerful sinful man in the whole country. Now you take them Peabody children over across the field. I reckon near about all of them is half mine, one way or another.

BESSIE. You wait till I finish accusing you, Jeeter, before you start lying out of it.

JEETER. Praise God, I ain't lying out of it. I just told you how powerful sinful I once was.

BESSIE. Don't think the Lord didn't know about it.

JEETER (*chuckles; crossing to well*). Henry Peabody didn't know nothing about it, though.

ADA. Humph.

JEETER (*turns Left; really noticing* BESSIE's *and* DUDE's *goings on*). Say, Sister Bessie, what in hell is you and Dude doing? You and him has been squatting there, hugging and rubbing of the other, for near about half an hour. (BESSIE *manages as much of a blush as she is capable of.*)

BESSIE (*removing* DUDE's *arm from around her waist, trying to rise*). The Lord was speaking to me. (DUDE *replaces his arm about her waist.*) He was telling me I ought to marry a new husband.

JEETER. He didn't tell you to marry Dude, did he?

BESSIE. Dude would make a fine preacher. He would be just about as good as my former husband was, maybe better. He is just suitable for preaching and living with me. Ain't you, Dude?

DUDE (*quickly*). You want me to go home with you now? (*Takes a step toward her.*)

BESSIE. Not now, Dude. I'll have to ask the Lord if you'll do. (*Crosses Left of* DUDE.) He's sometimes particular about his male preachers, especially if they is going to marry women preachers. I got to pray over it first—(*with a knowing glance at* DUDE) and Dude, you pray over it, too.

DUDE (*giggles in embarrassment*). Aw, like hell I will. (*Crosses to Left of gate.*)

JEETER (*crossing to* DUDE). What's the matter with you, Dude? Didn't you hear Sister Bessie tell you to pray over that? You is the luckiest man alive. What's the matter with you, anyway? Great day in the morning, if you ain't the goddamdest boy I ever heard tell of. (JEETER *starts down Left;* DUDE *crosses to Right of gate. Enter* HENRY PEABODY. *He comes running to the gate.*)

PEABODY (*coming to gate*). Hey, you, Jeeter —Jeeter.

JEETER (*crosses to* PEABODY). What's the matter, Henry?

PEABODY. Didn't Ada tell you nothing?

JEETER. She didn't tell me nothing.

PEABODY. Didn't she tell you I was here before?

JEETER (*impatiently*). No. What is it you've got to say?

PEABODY. It's big news, Jeeter.

JEETER. Well, start telling it. It ain't going to do me no good keeping it to yourself.

PEABODY (*impressively*). Captain John's coming back.

JEETER (*shocked*). Captain John! Captain John's dead.

PEABODY. Well, not Captain John, but his boy is.

JEETER. He is! (*Turning on* ADA.) Do you heart that, Ada? Captain John's coming back!

ADA. He didn't say Captain John. He said Captain John's boy.

JEETER. That don't make no difference. Captain Tim is Captain John's boy, ain't he? (*To* PEABODY.) He figures on giving credit to the farmers again, don't he?

PEABODY. I reckon so. That's what everybody thinks. He's down in Fuller now, but he'll be around about here tomorrow.

JEETER. God be praised. I knowed the Lord was aiming to provide (*To* ADA.) Well, what has you got to say now, woman? Didn't I tell you I was going to plant me a crop this year? (*To* DUDE, *as* ADA *shrugs and doesn't answer.*) Hey, you, Dude. Get out in the fields and start burning off that broom sedge. You go to the far side and I'll go to the near. We're going to burn off all the fields this year. We're going to grow us the biggest crop you ever seen.

PEABODY. Well, I got to be going, Jeeter. I reckon I'll burn off my own fields now myself. (JEETER *nods and he exits.*)

JEETER. Good-by, Henry. . . . Now you go in that house, Ada, and fix us something to eat. We're going to be hungry when we come back.

ADA. There ain't nothing to fix.

JEETER. You're the contrariest woman I ever seen. By God and by Jesus, if you ain't. You do like I tell you and quit saying all them damn fool things. . . . Come on, Dude, Captain John's boy has got to see we is all ready when he comes around tomorrow. Hurry up now . . . come on. (JEETER *climbs over fence, Left, in his hurry, exiting down the Tobacco Road.* DUDE *gives a hungry glance at* BESSIE, *then hurries to the gate and exits.* BESSIE *runs to fence and calls after* DUDE.)

BESSIE. Hey, you, Dude. Don't you forget. You pray like I told you and I'll be back here in the morning and let you know. (*Turns to* ADA *with a benevolent smile.*) Something tells me the Lord is going to like Dude a whole lot.

CURTAIN

ACT TWO

Scene: *Same as Act One.*

Time: *The following day.*

At Rise: *It is still early morning and the amber glow of dawning day haunts the scene. Slowly, as time passes, the light comes on fuller and brighter until full day has arrived. As the curtain rises, no one is seen, the rotting house enjoying the dawn in solitude. In a moment, however,* Bessie *enters swiftly through the gate, crosses to the porch, and hammers loudly on the door with her fists.*

BESSIE. Dude. . . . Hey, you, Dude. . . . Dude! (*She waits impatiently a few seconds, glancing first to the upstage corner of the house, then to the window downstage of the porch. Then she flings open the door and yells inside.*) Where is you, Dude? (JEETER, *yawning and scratching, sticks his head out of the window and rubs his mouth with the back of his hand before speaking. He is still sleepy but is wearing, already, his tattered hat, although the rest of his body is, apparently, as naked as a blue jay.*)

JEETER. What you want with Dude this time of day, Bessie?

BESSIE. Never you mind. I want Dude. . . . Hey, you, Dude. (*She exits through the door, calling.*) Dude. . . . You, Dude. (JEETER *draws back from the window, looking inside, as* BESSIE'S *voice continues, off.*) Where is you, Dude? . . . (*For an instant the stage is empty. Then* DUDE *enters Left down Tobacco Road and crosses yard to the well, where he draws up water and drinks. He pays no attention to* BESSIE'S *occasionally repeated cry for him. Enter* JEETER *through the house door. He is getting into his overalls, and is carrying his shirt, also socks and shoes in his hands. He sees* DUDE.)

JEETER. Hey, you, Dude, where you been? Bessie's been looking all over for you. (DUDE *doesn't answer, continuing to drink water.* JEETER *drops shoes and socks and slips into overalls.*) She just about tore up every bed in the house. Why don't you tell her where you is?

DUDE. Aw, to hell with her. (*Drinks.*)

JEETER (*dressing*). By God and by Jesus, I never seen a woman so anxious to see anybody. I reckon she wants to get married to you after all. (*Glances up as* DUDE *doesn't answer.*) Is you thinking about getting yourself married to her if that's what she wants?

DUDE. Aw, what do I want to do that for?

JEETER. You sure looked like you was set on doing that yesterday—all that hugging and rubbing of the other. What do you think about that now, Dude?

DUDE. Aw, hell, it don't always look the same to a man in the morning.

BESSIE (*off*). Dude! . . . Hey, you, Dude.

JEETER. Listen to her yelling. She must of gone clear through to the backyard by this time. Why don't you answer her, Dude? Where was you when she went looking in the bed for you? Where was you anyway?

DUDE. Out in the fields.

JEETER (*excitedly*). What about them fields? Is they finished burning?

DUDE (*nodding*). Most. Them to the north is still burning some.

JEETER. I is sure glad to hear that. We want to be ready to start the plowing and planting when Captain John's boy comes around today.

BESSIE (*off*). Dude. . . . Where is you, Dude? (BESSIE *enters around upstage corner of house, sees* DUDE.) There you is! (*Crosses swiftly to him. He glances at her, but keeps his back to her as she comes up.*) Didn't you hear me call you? (*Affectionately—putting her arms around his waist from the rear.*) Don't you know I been looking for you, Dude boy? (*Her arms tighten in a sudden and sharp squeeze that causes the water to slosh from the bucket he is holding.*)

DUDE. Hey, now look what you made me go and do.

BESSIE. Now that ain't nothing, Dude. Ain't you glad to see me? (*She presses him closer.*) Don't that make you feel good?

DUDE (*grinning*). H'mm. (*He puts down the bucket, turns and embraces her. Their posture is awkward and amusing. On the steps,* JEETER *continues to pick his feet and slowly put on shoes and socks, the while he watches the amorous couple.*)

JEETER. You must be figuring on getting married after all, Bessie. (BESSIE *starts to smooth down* DUDE's *wet hair.* ADA *appears in doorway,* ELLIE MAY *at window.*)

BESSIE (*confidentially—nodding affirmatively*). The Lord told me to do it. I asked Him about it last night and He said, "Sister Bessie, Dude Lester is the man I want you to wed. Get up early in the morning and go to the Lester place and marry Dude the first thing." That's what He said, so I got out of bed and ran up here as fast as I could, because the Lord don't like to be kept waiting. (BESSIE *affectionately regards* DUDE *who grins self-consciously.*)

JEETER. You hear what the Lord told Sister Bessie. What do you think of doing now, Dude?

DUDE. Shucks! I don't know.

JEETER. What's ailing you? Ain't you man enough?

DUDE. Maybe I is, and maybe I ain't.

BESSIE. There ain't nothing to be scared of, Dude. You'll like being married to me because I know how to treat men fine. (DUDE *hesitates.* ADA *moves forward from doorway and rests against the porch upright.* GRANDMA LESTER *appears around the upstage corner of the house but keeps crouched and hidden so as not to attract attention.*)

JEETER. Well, is you going to do it, Dude?

DUDE (*self-consciously*). Aw, hell, what do I want to go marry her for? (DUDE *pulls ball out of his pocket and throws it against house.* BESSIE *glances swiftly at* DUDE's *averted face, then plays her trump card. She turns to* JEETER.)

BESSIE (*wisely to* JEETER). Do you know what I is going to do, Jeeter?

JEETER. What?

BESSIE. I is going to buy me a new automobile. (*The effect of this on all of them is electric.* JEETER *comes quickly to his feet, and* DUDE *stops throwing ball with sudden awed interest.*)

JEETER. A new automobile? A sure enough brand-new automobile?

BESSIE (*nodding*). A brand-new one. (BESSIE *shakes her head emphatically.* DUDE *looks at her wide-eyed and unbelieving.*)

JEETER. Is you got money?

BESSIE (*proudly*). Eight hundred dollars.

JEETER. Eight hundred dollars! Where did you get all that money, Bessie?

BESSIE (*nodding*). My former husband had that in insurance and when he died I got it and put it in the bank.

JEETER. That sure is a heap of money. I didn't think there was that much real money in the whole country.

ADA. You ain't going to spend all that on a new automobile, is you?

BESSIE (*nodding*). Dude and me wants the best there is. Don't we, Dude? (DUDE *can only look at her wide-eyed.*)

ADA. It don't seem right to me. It seems to me like if you wanted to do right you'd give some of that money to Dude's old Ma and Pa. We could sure use it for snuff and food.

BESSIE. No, Sister Ada, the Lord didn't intend for it to be used like that. He intended I should use it to carry on the preaching and the praying. That's what I'm buying the new automobile for, so Dude and me can drive around when we take a notion to go somewheres in the Lord's work.

JEETER. Sister Bessie's right, Ada. There ain't nothing like working for the Lord. It don't make no difference to us about that money noway. Captain John's boy, Captain Tim, is back now and I'll get all the credit I need.

ADA. Humph. You is sure mighty high-handed with something you ain't got yet.

JEETER. Never you mind about her, Bessie. When you going to buy that new automobile?

BESSIE. I'm going over to Fuller and get it right now. (*Glances at* DUDE *eagerly.*) That is, if Dude and me gets married.

JEETER. What do you say to that now, Dude? Will you be wanting to marry Sister Bessie and ride around the country preaching and praying in a new automobile?

DUDE. Will it have a horn on it?

BESSIE. I reckon it will. Don't all new automobiles have horns?

DUDE. Can I drive it?

BESSIE. That's what I'm buying it for.

DUDE. Can I drive it all the time?

BESSIE. Sure, Dude. I don't know how to drive an automobile.

DUDE. Then why the hell not?

BESSIE (*joyfully hugging him and trying to kiss him*). Oh, Dude! (DUDE *escapes from her embrace and begins to put on his shoes.*)

ADA. When is you and Dude going to do all this riding around and preaching and praying? Is you going to get married before or after?

BESSIE. Before. We'll walk over to Fuller right now and buy the new automobile and then get married.

JEETER. Is you going to get leave of the county, or is you just going to live along without it?

BESSIE. I'm going to get the license for marrying.

JEETER. That costs about two dollars. Is you got two dollars? Dude ain't—Dude ain't got nothing.

BESSIE. I ain't asking Dude for one penny of money. I'll attend to that part myself. I've got eight hundred dollars in the bank and a few more besides. Dude and me won't have nothing to worry about. Will we, Dude?

DUDE (*impatiently*). Naw. Come on. We ain't got no time to lose. (DUDE *starts to walk away, while* BESSIE *is delayed arranging her hair, walking more slowly to the gate.*)

ADA. You'll have to make Dude wash his feet every once in a while, Bessie, because if you don't he'll dirty up the quilts. Sometimes he don't wash himself all winter long, and the quilts get that dirty you don't know how to go about the cleaning of them.

BESSIE (*pleasantly to* DUDE, *who is waiting at the gate*). Is you like that, Dude?

DUDE (*impatiently*). If we is going to buy that new automobile, let's buy it.

ADA. Dude is just careless like Pa. I had the hardest time learning him to wear his socks in the bed, because it was the only way I could keep the quilts clean. Dude is just going on the way his Pa done, so maybe you'd better make him wear his socks, too.

BESSIE. That's all right. Me and Dude'll know how to get along fine. (*Exit* DUDE. *Exit* BESSIE.)

ADA (*calling after* BESSIE *and* DUDE). If you get down around where Pearl lives, I wish you'd tell her that her Ma sure would like to see her again. (JEETER, ADA, *and* ELLIE MAY *move to fence to look after* DUDE *and* BESSIE. *Even* GRANDMA LESTER *looks from behind the trunk of the chinaberry tree.*)

JEETER (*shakes his head emphatically*). That Dude is the luckiest man alive. (*Directly to others*). Now, ain't he? . . . He's going to get a brand-new car to ride around in and he's going to get married all at the same time. There's not many men get all that in the same day, I tell you. There ain't nobody else that I know of between here and the river who has got a brand-new automobile. And there ain't many men who has a wife as fine-looking as Sister Bessie is, neither. Bessie makes a fine woman for a man— any man, I don't care where you find him. She might be just a little bit more than Dude can take care of, though. Now if it was me, there wouldn't be no question of it. I'd please Sister Bessie coming and going right from the start, and keep it up clear to the end.

ADA (*in disgust*). Huh!

JEETER (*speaks now to* ELLIE MAY). Now you, Ellie May, it's time you was finding yourself a man. All my other children has got married. It's your time next. It was your time a long while ago, but I make allowances for you on account of your face. I know it's harder for you to mate up than it is for anybody else, but you ought to get out and find yourself a man to marry right away. It ain't going to get you nowhere fooling around with Lov like you was doing, because he's married already. He might have married you if it wasn't for the way you looked, but don't show your face too much and it won't stop the boys from getting after you. (*He pauses, and to his amazement* ELLIE MAY *bursts into heartbroken sobs, hiding her face in her hands.*) What's the matter? What's the matter with you, Ellie May? (*Still sobbing,* ELLIE MAY *runs to the gate and exits down the road.* JEETER *turns helplessly to* ADA.) Now I never seen the likes of that before. I wonder what I said to make her carry on like that? (JEETER *sits on porch.*) I declare to goodness I don't know what gets into women folks sometimes. There ain't never no way to figure them out. (*Starts to lie down, but* ADA *is in the way.*) By God and by Jesus, woman, can't you move over when a man wants to lay down?

ADA. Ain't you going to take no wood to Augusta today?

JEETER. Are you going to start that talk again? Ain't I told you Captain Tim is coming and I'm going to plant me a crop? I've got to save my strength for that.

ADA. Humph! There ain't a bite in the house, and nobody never saved their strength by not eating.

JEETER. Never mind that now. Captain Tim will fix that. Anyhow, I couldn't make that old automobile go even if I wanted to.

ADA. Do you reckon Dude and Bessie will let you take a load in their new car?

JEETER. I ain't aiming to carry no more wood to Augusta. But I sure is going to take a ride in that new car. I reckon I'll be riding clear over into Burke County one of these days to see Tom.

ADA. If you see him you might mention that his old Ma sure would like a stylish dress to die in. I know he won't stand back with his money for a little thing like that.

JEETER. I'll mention it, but I don't know how he'll take it. I expect he's got a raft of children to provide for.

ADA. Reckon he has got some children?

JEETER. Maybe some.

ADA. I sure would like to see them. I know I must have a whole heap of grandchildren somewhere. I'm bound to have, with all them boys and girls off from home.

JEETER. Clara has got a raft of children, I bet. She was always talking about having them. And they say over in Fuller that Lizzie Belle has got a lot of them, too. I don't know how other folks know more about such things than I do. Looks like I ought to be the one who knows most about my own children. (*Enter* LOV, *who stands just inside gate, panting heavily and looking at* ADA *and* JEETER. JEETER *glances up and sees* LOV, *whose heaving chest and haunted eyes make him believe* LOV *has come for revenge for stealing the turnips.*) Lov, by God! (*He springs to his feet and darts for the downstage corner of the well.*)

LOV (*through quick breathing*). Never mind running, Jeeter. I ain't going to hurt you.

JEETER (*at corner of house, still ready to run*). Ain't you peeved about me stealing them turnips yesterday?

LOV (*wearily*). I don't care about that no more.

JEETER. What's the matter with you, Lov? You look like you run all the way here. What's wrong with you, anyway? (LOV *doesn't answer and sits.*) Is you sick? (LOV *nods negatively.*)

ADA (*higher note—stepping forward*). It's Pearl! That's what it is—it's Pearl! (LOV *looks at her and nods. She comes forward hysterically.*)

JEETER. What's the matter with her, Lov?

LOV. She run off.

ADA. No! She didn't! She wouldn't have done that without seeing her Ma first.

LOV (*coming forward—shaking head*). She just run off.

JEETER. How do you know, Lov? Maybe she's just hiding in the woods someplace.

LOV (*shakes his head*). Jones Peabody saw her walking along the road to Augusta this morning.

ADA. Augusta!

LOV. He said he stopped and asked her where she was going, but she wouldn't talk to him. She just kept on going.

ADA (*fiercely to* LOV). You done something to her. Don't tell me you didn't.

LOV. No, I didn't, Ada. I woke up early this morning and looked at her down on that pallet on the floor and I just couldn't stand it no longer. I got down and hugged her in my arms. I wasn't going to hurt her. I just wanted to hold her for a minute. But she got loose from me and I ain't seen her since. (ADA *rocks, heartbroken, on the porch.*)

JEETER. Well, I figured that she was going to run off to Augusta one of these days, only she was always afraid before.

LOV. Jones Peabody said she acted like she was about scared to death this morning. (*Desperately.*) I got to get her back, Jeeter. I just got to get her back.

JEETER. Ain't much use you figuring on that. All them girls went off all of a sudden. Lizzie Belle up and went to Augusta just like that. (*He snaps his fingers.*)

LOV. Ain't there something I can do, Jeeter?

JEETER. About the best thing you can do, Lov, is let her be.

LOV. If I was to go up to Augusta and find her, do you reckon she'd let me bring her back home to stay? . . . Reckon she would, Jeeter?

JEETER. I wouldn't recommend that. You'll lose your time down there at the chute while you was looking for her, and if you was to bring her back she'd run off again twice as quick.

LOV. She might get hurt up there.

JEETER. Lizzie Belle and Clara took care of themselves all right, didn't they?

LOV. Pearl ain't like them.

JEETER. In many ways she ain't, but in many she is, too. She wasn't never satified living down here on the Tobacco Road. She's just like Lizzie Belle and Clara and the other gals in that respect. I can't call all their names right now, but it was every durn one of them, anyhow. They all wanted stylish clothes.

LOV. Pearl never said nothing to me about wanting stylish clothes. She never said anything to me at all.

JEETER. It's just like I said. They're like their Ma. Ada there ain't satisfied neither,

but she can't do nothing about it. I broke her of wanting to run off, but them gals was more than I could take care of. There was too durn many of them for one man to break. They just up and went.

LOV (*thinking aloud*). I sort of hate to lose her, for some reason or another. All them long yellow curls hanging down her back always made me hate the time when she would grow up and be old.

JEETER. That sure ain't no lie. Pearl had the prettiest yellow hair of any gal I ever saw. I wish Ada had been that pretty. Even when Ada was a young gal she was that durn ugly it was a sin. I reckon I ain't never seen an uglier woman in the whole country.

LOV. I been the lonesomest man in the whole country for the longest time, Jeeter. Ain't there something you can do to get her back again?

JEETER. I might try something, but it wouldn't do no good. One way or another I've said about everything I can to that girl, but she won't even answer me. She won't talk to nobody but her Ma. It wouldn't do no good for me to do anything, even if you could find her.

LOV. Ada, will you? . . . (*Sees hopelessness of help from* ADA. *Abjectly*). Well, I've got to get back to the chute. That morning freight will be coming along pretty soon now and it always empties all the scoops. They raise hell if they ain't filled up again. (*Turns; crosses to gate; leans against post.*)

JEETER. I sure am glad you wasn't riled about the turnips, Lov. I meant to go down first thing this morning and talk to you about that, but Dude and Bessie went off to get married and I forgot all about it. Did you hear about that, Lov? Dude and Bessie went off to Fuller to get married and buy them a new automobile all at the same time. Now ain't that something! (LOV *nods.*)

LOV. If you happen to see or hear anything about Pearl, you let me know. (LOV *exits down road Left.*)

JEETER (*turning back to* ADA, *who still sits on the porch, staring blankly into space*). Lov sure is a funny one. He just can't think about anything but Pearl. It looks to me like he wouldn't want a gal that won't stay in the bed with him. I don't understand him at all. I don't understand Pearl, for that matter, neither. I'd of bet almost anything she would have come up here and told us good-by before running off. But it's like I always said. Coming or going, you can't never tell about women. (*Looks at* ADA, *hoping she'll talk to him. Crosses closer to her, but her eyes stare straight ahead. Finally he hits her gently with the back of his hand.*) That's all right, Ada. (*He crosses to fence, Left, climbs it, glances back at her.*) If Captain John's boy comes along, you tell him I'll be back soon. I'm going to look at them fields. (JEETER *exits.* ADA *sits staring ahead, her eyes holding a depth of suffering. Suddenly there is an offstage cry from* JEETER *and she turns to look toward the gate.*)

JEETER (*off—calling*). Ada—Ada! (*Lower, but still off.*) Come on, child—come on. (*He appears at the edge of the gate, pulling someone after him.* ADA, *eyes wide with wonder, stands up.*) Come on—there ain't nothing to be afraid of. Your old Pa ain't going to hurt you. (*He pulls* PEARL *through the gate.*) Look, Ada—look what I found hiding in the broom sedge.

ADA (*lifts her hands, palms turned up, toward her daughter*). Pearl!

PEARL. Ma!! (*Pulling away from* JEETER, PEARL *rushes across stage and flings herself, sobbing, into her mother's arms.* JEETER, *eager and alive with excitement and admiration, comes up to the two women.* PEARL *is a beautiful child. She looks at least sixteen, in spite of the fact that she is much less than that, and is almost as tall as* ADA. *She is barefoot, and wears only a shabby, dark gray calico dress. Her hair hangs down over her shoulders like a cloud of spun gold.* ADA *soothes her.*)

ADA. There, now—there, now, don't cry. You got your old Ma again.

JEETER (*prancing around* PEARL). Now ain't that somethin'! I was just turning to go across the fields when I saw that yellow head of hers moving in the broom sedge and there she was. If she hadn't stumbled I never would of caught her. Ain't she pretty! She's about the prettiest piece in the whole country. . . .

ADA. Go away, Jeeter.

JEETER (*who hasn't the slightest intention of going away*). Ain't she growed some in the past year, though? She's most a grown woman by now. (*Moves* PEARL's *dress the better to see her figure.*) By God and by Jesus if she ain't.

ADA (*sharply—slapping* JEETER's *hand away*). Stop that, Jeeter.

JEETER. What for? She is, ain't she? Look how white and gold she looks with that yellow hair hanging down her back. . . . What are you standing there crying for, Pearl? Why didn't you go on to Augusta like you started to anyway? Was you scared? Was that it, Pearl?

ADA. She wanted to see her old Ma first. (*To* PEARL.) That was it, wasn't it, child? (PEARL *nods, her head still on her mother's shoulder, and* ADA *speaks to* JEETER.) There, you see that, Jeeter. Now you go on away like I tell you. She ain't going to talk none while you're here.

JEETER. I got to speak to her about Lov first. Now that she ain't run away she'll have to begin treating him right.

ADA. Hush up, Jeeter. Maybe she ain't going to go back and live with Lov at all. Just because she didn't go all the way to Augusta, don't mean she's going to stay with Lov again.

JEETER. What's that? Now you wait a minute. That ain't right. When a gal is mated up with a man she's got to live with him.

ADA. Mind your own business, Jeeter.

JEETER. I is minding my own business. I'm minding my business and Lov's business, too. A gal's got no right to act like Pearl's been acting. No, sir. I say Pearl has got to go back and live in the house with Lov and let him have his rights with her.

ADA (*angrily*). Now you listen to me, Jeeter Lester. You keep out of this. If I says so Pearl can do just like she wants. You ain't got the right to tell her what she's got to do.

JEETER. What! Who you talking to, anyway? I'm her Pa, ain't I?

ADA. No, you ain't.

JEETER. What?

ADA. That's what.

JEETER. By God and by Jesus! Do you know what you're saying, woman?

ADA. I sure do. You ain't her Pa. You never was and never will be.

JEETER (*lightly amazed*). Well, by damn— now what do you think of that?

ADA. Whatever made you think you was, anyway? Do you think a lazy old fool like you could be the Daddy of a gal like Pearl?

JEETER (*without rancor*). Well, I thought about that now and then. She didn't look to me like none of the Lesters I ever heard of.

ADA. There ain't no Lester in her. Her real Pa wouldn't have no truck with any of you.

JEETER. It wasn't that Henry Peabody down the road, was it?

ADA (*with disgust*). No.

JEETER. I didn't think it was. He couldn't have a pretty piece like Pearl for a child any more than I could. Who was it, Ada?

ADA. Nobody you ever knew. He came from South Carolina and was on his way to Texas.

JEETER. H'mm. I don't remember nobody like that. I must of been in Fuller, or even maybe in Augusta at the time.

ADA. You was down seeing Captain John about a mule to plow with.

JEETER. By God and by Jesus, I remember now. I remember that old mule just like I remember that old cow I used to have. Remember that old mule, Ada?

ADA. I reckon.

JEETER. It was the last one I ever got off Captain John. Pretty soon after that he moved up to Augusta and I ain't heard a word from him since, until now when his boy is coming back. (*To* PEARL.) Did you hear about that, Pearl? Captain John's boy is coming back this morning and I'm going to plant me a crop this year sure.

ADA. Pearl ain't interested in that now.

JEETER (*indignantly*). Well, she ought to be. Everybody ought to be when they's been born and raised on the land like I was. Cap- tain John was and Captain John's boy that comes after him is interested just as much, you'll find out. You can't keep nobody like Captain John or me away from the land forever.

ADA. Shut up, Jeeter. Can't you see Pearl is all wore out? If Jones Peabody saw her on the road to Augusta she must of walked about ten miles this morning to get here. (*To* PEARL.) Is you hungry, Pearl? (PEARL *shakes her head affirmatively.*)

JEETER (*watching the girl with disapproval*). Now what's the sense to all that shaking of your head? (*Mimics her.*) What's the meaning of all that? It's plain to see you ain't no child of mine all right. Coming and going us Lesters has always talked about as much as anybody in the whole country. Can't you speak up?

ADA. Quit your nagging, Jeeter. You know what she means all right. She's hungry. You get busy and find her something to eat.

JEETER. Ain't you got no sense at all, Ada? How can I get her something to eat when there ain't even nothing for myself.

ADA. You got something yesterday from Lov when *you* was hungry.

JEETER. Is you aiming to make me steal again, woman? (ADA *shrugs.*) Well, if you is I ain't. The Lord's a wise old somebody. He's watching around the corner every minute for just such as that. You can't fool Him about stealing. . . . Besides there ain't nothing between here and Fuller to steal noway.

ADA. I heard tell Morgan Prior bought hisself a sack of corn meal down to McCoy the other day.

JEETER. Corn meal! I ain't et corn meal since—(*Checks himself.*) No, sir! Maybe he did and maybe he didn't, but I ain't going near Morgan Prior's house no matter what the circumstance. I promised the Lord—

ADA (*shrewdly*). They say he's got some bacon and fat back, too.

JEETER. Woman, you is a sinner in the eyes of God! . . . (*Whistles.*) Morgan Prior must be a powerful rich man to have all that to eat. Maybe if I went down there and asked him he might let me borrow some for a little while.

ADA. Humph! I don't build no hopes on that. Morgan Prior ain't going to let you borrow nothing.

JEETER. I don't see why he oughtn't. The Lord says the rich should share their bounty with the poor. You come along with me, Ada, and we'll see if Morgan Prior is ready to do like the Lord says.

ADA. Me? What do you want me for?

JEETER. Don't you know nothing, woman? If I want to borrow me something from Morgan Prior somebody's got to talk to him at the front door, while I go around to the back, don't they? (*A full, belligerent pause.*) Now hurry up. Morgan Prior might be out early plowing the fields and it would be an almighty temptation and a sin if we borrowed something when he wasn't at home.

ADA. You go get my old hairbrush first. Pearl ain't brushed her hair this morning.

JEETER (*eagerly*). Is she going to do that?

ADA (*with an abrupt nod*). While I'm gone off. (JEETER *exits quickly into house.*)

PEARL (*gripping* ADA). Oh, Ma, don't go off from me.

ADA (*comforting her*). There now. You don't need to worry no more. Your old Ma's looking out for you from now on. You don't have to go back and live with Lov no matter what Jeeter says.

PEARL. I don't never want to go back!

ADA. You don't have to. But one of these days you got to go down to Augusta to live. I've made up my mind to that.

PEARL. I'm scared, Ma. (JEETER *enters with hairbrush.*)

JEETER (*eagerly*). Here you is, Ada. Great day, we ought to see something now! Lov says there ain't a prettier piece in the whole country than Pearl when she's brushing her hair and I'm inclined to agree with him.

ADA (*snatching brush*). Go along, Jeeter. Don't think you're going to stay around here all day watching Pearl.

JEETER. Lord, Ada, don't get so peeved. I ain't doing nothing.

ADA. No, and you never would if I didn't make you. Hurry up now. You go along. I'll catch up with you down the road.

JEETER. Well—(*Reluctantly crossing to gate.*) Pearl, if Captain John's boy comes here, you tell him I won't be gone long. You tell him I got a little business down the way and to wait right here for me. (*Exits.*)

ADA. Now you listen to me, honey. There ain't no sense you being scared about going off to Augusta. All my other gals went there or someplace else to live and they don't regret it.

PEARL (*fervently*). I want to stay here with you.

ADA. Never you mind that. I ain't going to be here long. One of these days I'm going to die.

PEARL. No—no, you ain't!

ADA. That's all right, honey. It don't matter —only sometimes I do wish I had me a stylish dress to be buried in.

PEARL. I'll get you a stylish dress, Ma. Honest I will.

ADA. Don't you care about me. You got to look out for yourself. You got to have a hat to put on and shoes and dresses to wear like the gals in Augusta.

PEARL. I don't want none.

ADA. Sure you do. You don't want to stay here like your old Ma, raising a raft of children and no snuff to calm you when there ain't nothing to eat. None of my other children was as pretty as you, or as smart, neither, when you want to talk, and if they can do it you can do it. (JEETER *appears on Tobacco Road.*)

JEETER. Hey, you, Ada. Is you coming or ain't you?

ADA. I heard you, I'm coming. (*Gets up. Speaks to* PEARL.) Now, honey, you just think about that while I'm gone. And don't fret none. I won't be off long. (*Enter* GRANDMA LESTER *from around house, as* ADA *crosses to gate.*) Hey, you, old woman. You go out in the broom sedge and pick up some sticks for the fire. We might be wanting to cook around here pretty soon now. (*To* PEARL.) Fix up your hair now, honey. (ADA *exits and* GRANDMA LESTER *hurries to the porch and pulls her old croker sack from beneath it.* PEARL *watches her. Straightening up, the old woman looks long at* PEARL*. Hobbling forward she tries to touch the girl's hair, but* PEARL *backs away from her.* GRANDMA LESTER *stops, her eyes reflecting her deep hurt and disappointment. For a moment more she gazes at the girl, then turns and shuffles off.* PEARL *stands looking after her, and when the* OLD WOMAN *has quite gone, she goes to the well and dips her brush in the bucket. She has taken a stroke or two with the brush when she suddenly stops and listens. The audience hears nothing, but she does. Moving quickly in back of the well, she drops to her knees, listening and waiting. Presently* HENRY PEABODY *enters down the road, running. He glances inside the yard, sees nothing, and then comes through the gate to the porch. Pushing open the door he calls inside.*)

PEABODY. Jeeter—hey, you, Jeeter—Ada. . . . Aw, to hell with them. (*No answer and he comes down from the porch and goes to upstage corner of the house; he glances around. Seeing nothing, then, he moves quickly to the gate and exits. Slowly and cautiously* PEARL *now comes around from behind the well, runs to the road to see if* PEABODY *has gone, then comes back to the porch and sits, her back to the gate, brushing her hair. She is so preoccupied she does not hear* LOV *enter quietly on the Tobacco Road. He sees her. He pauses. He moves silently through the gate across the yard on the balls of his feet and stands in back of her, watching. Suddenly he reaches down and takes her hand firmly as it makes a stroke with the brush. She leaps to her feet, panic-stricken, to run off, but his hold is too strong and he pulls her back.*)

LOV (*pleading*). Don't run off, Pearl. I ain't going to hurt you. (*She won't answer or look at him.*) If you only wouldn't run away, I'd leave hold of you now and just watch you brush your hair again. I'd rather see you do that than anything I can think of. There ain't nobody got pretty hair like you. I used to sit on the porch and watch through the window when you was combing and brushing it and I just couldn't keep my eyes off it. Will you promise you won't run off again if I leave you go? (*Pause as he waits for her to answer.*) Won't you talk to me? Won't you say nothing to me at all? You don't know how I been missing you

since you run off. I didn't mean nothing by what I done this morning. It's just that you won't stay in the bed with me or talk to me. Sometimes I just shake all over, for wanting to squeeze you so hard. I keep on thinking how pretty your eyes is early in the morning. They's pretty any time of the day, but early in the morning they's the prettiest things a man could ever want to look at. Won't you come back again sometime? You won't even have to stay in the bed with me. Will you come back if I do that, Pearl? (*He waits, but still there is no answer.*) Remember that last pretty I got for you? I can remember like it was yesterday. They was green beads on a long string and when you put them around your neck I swear to God if it didn't make you about the prettiest girl I ever heard tell about. (*Pitiful enthusiasm.*) I tell you what . . . one of these days we'll ride up to Augusta and buy you a hat—and a stylish dress, too. Would you like to do that? Maybe Dude and Bessie will take us in the new automobile they're buying today. Did you know about that, Pearl? Dude and Bessie is getting married and is buying a new automobile. (*Not a flicker of interest shows in* PEARL's *impressive expression.* LOV *has a dream.*) A new automobile! That's what we'll get one of these days, and we'll ride all over the whole country faster than that old No. 7 passenger ever thought of going—(*In the excitement stimulated by imagination,* LOV *has released his hold on* PEARL's *wrist and she has sprung clear of him. His pleading, broken cry falls on unhearing ears. Swiftly—much more swiftly than his clumsiness will permit him to follow—she steps away from the porch, whirls, and dashes to the gate.*) Pearl! (*Just as* PEARL *reaches the gate,* ADA *appears and the girl throws herself into her mother's arms.*)

PEARL. Ma! Ma! (*ADA says nothing, but over* PEARL's *shoulder her eyes fasten malevolently on the innocent* LOV*. Appearances are against him, he knows it, and he is so emotionally upset his sense of guilt gains upper hand. For a full pause they regard each other.*)

LOV (*pitifully apologetic*). I didn't do nothing, Ada. We was just talking. I didn't hurt her none. (*ADA pushes* PEARL *behind her, picks up stick, and advances grimly and silently on him. He takes an involuntary step back.*) I just wanted her to come back and live in the house with me. (*ADA comes up to him, her fury blazing in her eyes. The stick falls across* LOV's *hunched shoulders. He stands his ground, but lowers his head and raises his arms to protect himself.* PEARL *is thrilled.)* Don't do that, Ada—don't do that. (*Her answer is to strike him again. Enter* JEETER, *carrying a couple of small packages. His eyes light up as he sees the action.*)

JEETER. Great day in the morning, will you look at that! What you beating Lov for, Ada? What's he done to make you beat him like that?

LOV. I ain't done nothing, Jeeter—(*He is stopped by a whack.*)

JEETER. By God and by Jesus, maybe you ain't, but you sure is getting a beating for it just the same. I don't remember when I ever seen such a good, round beating as you is getting right this minute. (LOV *gives ground slowly, so that* ADA' *misses now and again.*)

LOV. I tell you I ain't done nothing!

JEETER. That don't stand to reason to me. In my experience I found that people usually get what's coming to them in this world or the next and it looks to me like right now you is getting yours in this.

LOV. I swear to God I ain't, Jeeter.

JEETER. Do you hear that, Ada? Lov says he ain't done nothing. What have you got to say about that?

ADA. Shut up.

JEETER. By God, woman, don't talk like that. Put down that stick, do you hear me? You has already done one whopping big sin today. You ought to be mighty sorry to do another. (LOV *manages to grab* ADA's *stick and stop the attack.* JEETER *nods approval.*) I'm glad to see you do that, Lov. That was no way for Ada to treat you. But what did you do to her anyway to make her keep hitting you with that old stick all the time?

LOV. I only wanted Pearl to come back and live with me.

ADA (*holding* PEARL). Pearl ain't never going back and live with you. There ain't no use you trying to make her, either. She's going to Augusta just like she set out to do this morning and nothing you do can stop her.

LOV. I'm her husband, ain't I? I can stop her and by God I will!

ADA (*belligerently*). You just try it.

JEETER. There ain't no sense you trying to carry your point, Lov. Ada made up her mind Pearl's going to Augusta and there ain't nothing I know can change it.

LOV. You can't be letting Pearl do that. It ain't right.

JEETER. Right or wrong ain't got nothing to do with it where Ada is concerned. Just a little while ago she made me borrow something when Morgan Prior wasn't at the house. That's about the biggest sin a woman can make a man do, but she don't care none. There ain't no use talking to her about right or wrong.

LOV. Augusta ain't no place for a girl as pretty as she is.

JEETER. I sure would like to stand in her way, but I ain't got no more right than that—(*Snaps his finger characteristically.*) Ada's the one you got to talk to, about that.

LOV. Ada's her Ma, but you're her Pa, ain't you?

JEETER. By God and by Jesus, no! Ada there was horsing around big as you please with some man while I was down borrowing me a mule one time. That don't make me her Pa no more than you is.

LOV. You took care of her until she was married to me. That's the same thing.

JEETER. No, it ain't. The Lord don't take no recognition of that. The Lord is a wise old somebody. He said His flesh is His flesh. That don't make no provision for Ada horsing around while I'm down borrowing me a mule. (*Enter* ELLIE MAY, *who hides bashfully behind tree when she sees* LOV.)

ADA. You might just as well go away, Lov. I ain't lettin' Pearl go back with you no matter how much you talk, less'n she wants to. . . . And I don't reckon she wants to.

LOV. Pearl—won't you come back? (PEARL *shrinks farther back.* LOV *glances pleadingly at* ADA.) Ada—(LOV *glances helplessly from* ADA *to* PEARL, *then lowers his head and reaches down to pick up his hat, which has fallen off. He dusts it off on his knee and is starting away when* JEETER *stops him.*)

TEETER. Hold on there, Lov. No sense you going off without a gal just because Pearl don't want to go with you. Why don't you take Ellie May there? (ELLIE MAY, *behind her chinaberry tree, giggles and puts her arm over her mouth to hide the torn lip.* LOV *glances from* JEETER *to* ELLIE MAY, *then back to* JEETER *again. Without a word he pulls his hat tighter and again starts off.* JEETER *takes a step forward as he sees* LOV's *indifference.* LOV *takes another step and* JEETER *follows.*) Ellie May's got to get a man somewhere. When me and Ada's dead and gone there won't be nobody to watch after her. The niggers would haul off and come here by the dozen. The niggers would get her in no time if she was here by herself. (ELLIE MAY *sets up her giggling and wriggling again and* LOV *once more regards her objectively and solemnly.*)

LOV (*looking away from* ELLIE MAY. *He speaks stubbornly*). I want Pearl.

JEETER (*exasperated*). By God and by Jesus, you know you ain't going to get Pearl, so what's the sense going on talking about that? Now Ellie May there's got a lot of—

LOV. Ellie May's got that ugly looking face. (ELLIE MAY, *standing in* LOV's *path, giggles and squirms.* LOV *looks at her hard as* JEETER *continues.*)

JEETER. You and her was hugging and rubbing of each other to beat all hell just yesterday. Wouldn't you like to do that some more?

LOV (*still looking hard at* ELLIE MAY). No, by God! I want Pearl or nothing. (*He moves past her and exits.* JEETER *shakes his head as he watches* LOV *disappear down the road.*)

JEETER (*chiefly to* ADA). Now that's something I can't understand at all. It looks to me when a man loses one gal he'd be thankful to get another—hey, stop that! What you doing there, Ellie May? (*His sentence has been broken by* ELLIE MAY's *attack on* PEARL. *She pushes* PEARL *to the ground, picks up the stick* ADA *dropped after beating* LOV, *and belabors her pretty sister furiously.* JEETER *steps forward to stop her, but he is slower than the infuriated* ADA, *who grabs the stick away from* ELLIE MAY *and starts beating her in turn.* ELLIE MAY *fights back for a moment.* GRANDMA LESTER *enters furtively and goes behind the chinaberry tree where she observes scene.*)

ADA (*swinging stick sharply*). I'll show you—I'll show you. (ELLIE MAY *gives up the unequal fight and flees through the gate and Left down road.* PEARL *gets up and seeks protection behind her mother.*) Don't you worry none, Pearl. She won't do that no more. (*She starts dusting off* PEARL's *dress.*)

JEETER (*shaking his head*). Great day in the morning! I never seen such beating one of the other as I seen here today. What do you suppose Ellie May done that for, Ada? (ADA *shoots him a baleful glance, but the disdainful reply she is forming is checked by the sudden muffled blast of a motor car horn. All of them look up. The horn, louder, sounds again.* JEETER's *face lights up.*) That's Dude! That's Dude and Bessie in that new automobile. (JEETER *goes through gate, works to center stage, and looks down the road.* ADA *crosses to fence and looks. Even* PEARL *is moved by sudden interest and goes to the fence. Only* GRANDMA LESTER *comes further in, taking her place downstage of the well, where she huddles, listening and waiting.*) Here they come! Just look at them! It's a brand-new automobile, all right—just look at that shiny black paint! Great day in the morning! Just look at them coming yonder! (*The horn sounds again—closer.* JEETER *speaks with pride.*) Listen to Dude blow that horn. Don't he blow it pretty, though? (ELLIE MAY *enters Left and flashes down the Tobacco Road on a dead run, exiting Right to meet the car.*)

ADA. Ain't that the prettiest sight to see, Pearl? Look at that dust flying up behind. It makes it look like a big black chariot, running away from a cyclone. (*The horn sounds again, to the same rhythm of an engineer blowing a locomotive whistle.*)

JEETER. That's Dude driving it and blowing the horn, too. (*Mounting excitement.*) Hi, there, Dude! Hi, Bessie. (*Swinging down from the fence, he runs through gate and exits down road toward car. The horn continues to sound.* ADA, PEARL, *and* GRANDMA LESTER *wait, watching. We hear* JEETER *returning before we see him.*) By God, Bessie, I been seeing you come a far piece off in that new automobile. (BESSIE *and* JEETER *enter.*) In all my days I never seen a finer looking machine. Is it real brand new?

BESSIE (*vigorously and proudly*). I paid the whole eight hundred dollars for it. (*The horn sounds.*)

JEETER (*listens to* DUDE, *then speaks*). By God and by Jesus, it sure does make me feel happy again to know there's such a handsome automobile around. Don't you reckon you could take me for a little trip, Bessie? I sure would like to go off in it for a piece.

BESSIE (*looking pretentiously at marriage license she carries*). I reckon when Dude and me gets back you can go riding.

JEETER. Where is you and Dude going to, Bessie?

BESSIE (*proudly*). We're going to ride around like married folks.

ADA. Did you and Dude get married in Fuller?

BESSIE. Not all the way. I got leave of the county, however. It cost two dollars to do that little bit. (*Waves license at them.*) There's the paper to show it.

ADA. Ain't you going to get a preacher?

BESSIE. I is not! Ain't I a preacher of the gospel? I'm going to do it myself. Ain't no Hardshell Baptist going to fool with us.

JEETER. I knowed you would do it the right way. You sure is a fine woman preacher, Sister Bessie. (DUDE *blows horn again.* JEETER *smiles complacently.*) That there old Dude sure does like fooling around with that there old horn.

BESSIE (*a bit peeved*). He's been doing that about every minute all the way up from Fuller. Looks to me like he'd want to stop now that we is about to do the rest of the marrying.

ADA. Did you and Dude have any trouble getting leave from the county?

BESSIE. None to speak of. At first the man said Dude was too young and that I'd have to get the consent of his Ma and Pa. I told him the Lord said for me to marry Dude, but he told me that didn't make no difference. So I started praying right then and there, and pretty soon the man said if I would just stop he'd do anything I wanted.

JEETER. You sure is a powerful pray-er, all right, Sister Bessie. You is about the best

pray-er and Dude is about the best automobile driver in the country. Coming and going that makes you just about equal. (*Enter* DUDE *lugging, with quite some noise, a torn off, dented fender.* JEETER *whirls to look at him.*) Great day, Dude, what you got there? Ain't that a fender off your new car?

DUDE (*dropping fender without concern*). Uh-huh.

JEETER. Now how did that happen? Did you run into something?

DUDE. We was coming back from Fuller and I was looking out at a big turpentine still, and then the first thing I knowed we was smashed smack bang into the back of a two-horse wagon.

JEETER. Didn't hurt the running of the automobile, though, did it?

DUDE. Naw. It runs like it was brand new yet. The horn wasn't hurt none at all. It blows just as pretty as it did at the start.

JEETER (*nodding in agreement*). Don't pay no attention to it, Bessie. Just leave it be and you'll never know that machine was any different than when you got it.

BESSIE. That's right. I ain't letting it worry me none, because it wasn't Dude's fault. He was looking at the big turpentine still alongside the road, when the wagon got in our way. The nigger driving it ought to have had enough sense to move over.

JEETER. Was you blowing the horn then, Dude?

DUDE. Not right then I wasn't. I was busy looking at that big still. I never saw one that big nowhere. It was most as big as a corn-liquor still, only it wasn't so shiny-looking.

BESSIE (*bending down and wiping dust from fender with her skirt*). It's a shame to get the new car smashed up so soon, however. It was brand new not more than an hour ago.

DUDE. It was that damn nigger. If he hadn't been asleep on the wagon it wouldn't have happened at all. He was plumb asleep till it woke him up and threw him out in the ditch.

JEETER. He didn't get hurt much, did he?

DUDE. I don't know about that. The wagon turned over on him and smashed him some. His eyes was wide open all the time, but I couldn't make him say nothing. He looked like he was dead.

JEETER. Niggers will get killed. Looks like there just ain't no way to stop it. (DUDE *takes out ball and hurls it against house*.)

ADA. When is you and Dude going to go on with the marrying?

BESSIE (*turning from fender and resuming her aggressive manner*). Right this minute. (*Smooths her skirt. Unrolls license again*.) Come on, Dude.

DUDE (*turning impatiently with ball in hand*). What you want to do now?

BESSIE. Marry us.

DUDE. Didn't you get that all done at the courthouse in Fuller?

BESSIE (*still extending his end of license*). That wasn't all. We got to get married in the sight of the Lord.

DUDE. Humph! (*Throws ball again*.)

JEETER. By God and by Jesus, Dude, stop chunking that ball against that old house and do what Bessie tells you.

DUDE. I want to take a ride.

BESSIE. We got plenty of time to ride around after we is married.

DUDE. Will we go then?

BESSIE. Yes, Dude.

DUDE. Is you sure?

BESSIE. Sure, Dude.

DUDE. What the hell, then. Then what do I do?

BESSIE (*extending license*). You hold your end of the license while I pray. (DUDE *gingerly takes one end of license, and* BESSIE *the other.* BESSIE *lowers her head and closes her eyes for several seconds of silent prayer, while* DUDE *looks down on her with a slight, rather perplexed frown. Presently* BESSIE *lifts her head, but her eyes are still closed as she intones,*) I marry us man and wife. So be it.

That's all, God. Amen. (*She opens her eyes and smiles gently up at* DUDE.)

DUDE (*pulling away*). Come on.

BESSIE. I got to pray now. You kneel down on the ground while I make a little prayer. (BESSIE *and others all kneel and* DUDE *reluctantly follows, still watching her with his expression of bored annoyance*.)
(*Praying*). Dear God, Dude and me is married now. We is wife and husband. Dude, he is an innocent young boy, unused to the sinful ways of the country, and I am a woman preacher of the gospel. You ought to make Dude a preacher, too, and let us use our new automobile in taking trips to pray for sinners. You ought to learn him how to be a fine preacher so we can make all the goats into sheep. That's all this time. We're in a hurry now. Save us from the devil and make a place for us in heaven. Amen. (*She opens her eyes and smiles brightly at* DUDE.)

JEETER (*jumping up*). Bless the Lord, that was one of the prettiest marriages I ever seen. Dude sure got hisself good and wed, didn't he, Ada?

ADA. Humph!

JEETER (*goes to* BESSIE *and kisses her*). Praise God, Sister Bessie, that Dude is a lucky man. I'd sure like to be in his place right now.

BESSIE (*laughing coyly*). Be still, you old sinner.

JEETER (*to* DUDE). Yes, sir, Dude, boy. You sure is lucky to get a fine woman like Bessie.

DUDE (*shaking him off*). Aw, shut up, you old fool. (BESSIE *raps on the porch and* JEETER *turns to look at her*.)

JEETER. What you knocking on the porch for, Bessie? (*She raps again and* JEETER'S *face clears*.) Great day! Now, why didn't I think of that? . . . You, Dude—can't you see how bad Sister Bessie wants to go into the house?

DUDE. What for?

JEETER. Never you mind what for. (*He starts pushing* DUDE.)

BESSIE (*taking* DUDE'S *arm*). Just for now, Come on, Dude.

DUDE. You said we was going for a ride.

BESSIE. We can go after a little while.

JEETER (*pushing him harder*). What's the matter with you, Dude? Go on in with Sister Bessie. (*Slowly and grudgingly* DUDE *allows himself to be shoved and pulled on to the porch. At the door he pauses.*)

DUDE. This is a hell of a time to be going indoors. (BESSIE *and* DUDE *exit into the house, the door closing.* JEETER *stands almost center stage, his eyes shining with excitement.* ELLIE MAY *crosses quickly to the window and draws herself up on her toes, her fingers on the sill, as she tries to look into the house.* JEETER *crosses to window and pulls* ELLIE MAY *away.*)

JEETER. You got no business trying to see inside. Sister Bessie and Dude is married. (*Shoving* ELLIE MAY *aside, he promptly pulls himself up on the sill to see.* ELLIE MAY *suddenly turns and crosses swiftly toward porch, where* ADA *leans against an upright.* PEARL *stands on the ground at the edge of the porch near her mother.*)

ELLIE MAY (*passing* PEARL). Come on around to the back. (PEARL *hesitates for an instant, then joins her, and the two girls exit around upstage corner of house.* JEETER *hasn't much success seeing into the window, and he suddenly stops trying and scampers around the upstage corner of the house. He returns almost immediately with a chopping block on which he climbs to see into the room. A smile of approval beams on his weathered face.*)

JEETER. Sister Bessie sure is a fine-looking woman, ain't she, Dude?

BESSIE (*appearing at window*). Get away from there, Jeeter Lester.

JEETER. What's the matter, Bessie? I ain't done nothing.

BESSIE. Never you mind. You get away from there.

JEETER. Now don't get peeved, Bessie. This time of year puts a queer feeling into a man. I feel that way every late February and early March. No matter how many children a man's got, he always wants to get more.

BESSIE. That don't matter. I don't want to have nothing to do with you. You is an old sinner.

JEETER (*complacently*). Yes, I reckon I is. I reckon I is one of the biggest sinners in the whole country. (*Suddenly changes and roars.*) But, by God and by Jesus, woman—what's a man going to do! (DUDE *comes up to window and starts pushing at* JEETER *as enter* CAPTAIN TIM *and* GEORGE PAYNE.)

DUDE. Get away from there, you old fool, or I'll wham you one.

TIM (*amused*). Well, Jeeter, what's all the excitement?

JEETER (*turning on block*). Captain John's boy!—Captain Tim! (JEETER *steps from the box and runs swiftly to meet* TIM *at the gate, almost frantic with excitement.* ADA *stands on the porch, eying the strangers impassively and sucking on her snuff brush. The old* GRANDMOTHER *peers out from behind the protecting well.* TIM *extends his hand as* JEETER *comes running up.*)

TIM. How are you, Jeeter, how are you?

JEETER (*eagerly*). Captain Tim, I sure is glad to see you!

TIM. Jeeter, this is Mr. Payne, from Augusta.

PAYNE. How do you do, Mr. Lester?

JEETER. Morning, sir.

TIM (*seeing* ADA *on porch*). That's Ada, isn't it? Good morning, Ada.

ADA (*coldly*). Morning.

TIM (*indicating* DUDE). I don't recognize the boy, Jeeter. Which one is he?

JEETER. That's Dude.

TIM. Oh, yes. I remember Dude now. (*To* DUDE.) Hello there, Dude. Do you remember me?

DUDE (*impudently*). Naw! (*Giggles self-consciously.*)

JEETER. That there next to Dude is Sister Bessie. They just married themselves before you came.

PAYNE. Married *themselves*?

JEETER. Sister Bessie is a woman preacher and she done it.

PAYNE (*dubiously*). I see.

TIM (*to* DUDE). Well, congratulations, Dude. Congratulations, Sister Bessie. (*To* JEETER.) Is Dude the only one of your children left, Jeeter?

JEETER. Ellie May and Pearl is around someplace.

TIM (*looking about*). Well, the place hasn't changed much. What keeps it from falling down, Jeeter?

JEETER. Praise God, Captain Tim, I don't know. I expect it will one of these days. . . . Now you come on the porch and sit down. . . . Dude, you bring some chairs out here.

PAYNE. Don't bother. I'm afraid we won't be able to stay very long.

JEETER. Ain't no bother at all. Could you do with a drink of water, Captain Tim?

TIM. Thanks, Jeeter. (PAYNE *crosses up Left, glancing about the property and inspecting the house.*)

JEETER (*crossing to well for water*). Dude, you go do what I told you. (*While* JEETER *is getting the water,* PAYNE *glances around curiously. His eyes meet* TIM's *and he shakes his head to suggest his reaction to the surroundings.* DUDE *pulls a chair on to the porch.*) Here you is. (*Crossing to* TIM *with dipper of water.*)

TIM. Much obliged. (*Drinks.*)

JEETER. I sure is glad to see you back, Captain. I knowed you couldn't stay away from the land any more than your Daddy could. Maybe city ways is all right for a short time, but when they start cleaning off the fields and burning the broom sedge, a man ain't happy unless he can be seeing it and be doing it, too.

TIM. You must be getting pretty old, Jeeter. I'd think you'd be tired of it by this time.

JEETER. No, sir. I is ready to do just as big a day's work as the next one. Ada there is always saying I is lazy, but there ain't no truth in that when it comes to planting a crop.

TIM (*going to well and putting cup down*). How have crops been lately?

JEETER. Praise God there ain't been none in seven years. We just ain't been able to get credit down here on the Tobacco Road.

Ain't nobody got no mony. By God and by Jesus, I is glad ʾou came back to provide that again.

TIM (*turning—surprised*). What?

JEETER. Yes, sir, Captain Tim. I was just telling Ada a short time back that the Lord was aiming to take care of me out of His bounty. I wasn't thinking about you at the time, but soon as I heard you was here again Dude and me set to burning off the fields. Them north fields is burning some right this minute.

TIM (*after a glance at* PAYNE). Well, I don't know how that idea got around. I'm sure sorry, but I'm—well, Jeeter, I'm afraid I can't help you. I'm in pretty much the same fix you are.

JEETER (*unbelieving*). What's that, Captain Tim?

TIM (*turning to* PAYNE). You'd better tell him, Payne.

PAYNE. Well, you see, Mr. Lester, I'm from the bank in Augusta. We're down here to collect money, not lend it.

JEETER. You mean I can't have no credit to grow me a crop this year?

PAYNE. I'm afraid not.

JEETER. But I just got to have credit. Me and my folks is starving out here on the Tobacco Road.

PAYNE. Well, then you ought to be glad we came. We're ready to help you to get away from here to where you have a chance of making a living.

JEETER. I don't want to get away from here. If you mean go off and work in the mills, I say, by God and by Jesus, no!—I ain't going to do it.

PAYNE. But if you're really starving—

JEETER. That ain't got nothing to do with it. Captain John said I could live here as long as I wanted. He said he couldn't give me credit at the stores in Fuller no more, but he told me I could stay here and live until I died. You know that, Captain Tim.

TIM. Yes, Jeeter, I remember, and that was all right as long as the land was ours. But it's not any more. I had to borrow money on every farm we owned around here and now I can't pay it back. Like your grand-daddy used to own the land and Captain John took it over, the bank's doing it with me.

JEETER (*heatedly*). I don't understand that. This was my daddy's place and his daddy's before him, and I don't know how many Lesters before that. There wasn't nothing here in the whole country before they came. They made that road out there hauling tobacco kegs fifteen miles down the ridge to the river. Now I don't own it and you don't own it and it belongs to a durn bank that ain't never had nothing to do with it even.

TIM. That's the way things just seem to happen, Jeeter.

JEETER. Praise God, it ain't the way things just happen. It's the rich folks in Augusta that's doing it. They don't work none, but they get all the money us farmers make. One time I borrowed me three hundred dollars from a loan company there to grow a crop and when I gave them interest and payments and every other durn thing they could think of I didn't make but seven dollars the whole year working every day. By God, that ain't right, I tell you. God won't stand for such cheating much longer. He ain't so liking of the rich people as they think He is. God, He likes the poor.

PAYNE. Now, Mr. Lester. We don't want to be hard on you old farmers, but we're going to try putting this whole section under scientific cultivation and there wouldn't be any use for you.

JEETER. Why not? If you is going to grow things on the land, why can't I stay right here and do it, too? I'd work for you just like I did for Captain John and no nigger ever worked harder than that.

PAYNE. I'm afraid that's impossible.

DUDE. What did I tell you, you old fool? Nobody ain't going to give you nothing.

JEETER. You shut up, Dude Lester. You shut up and get away from here. Captain Tim ain't going to let them send me away. Is you, Captain Tim?

PAYNE. Be reasonable, Mr. Lester. You've proved you can't get along here. Why don't you move your family up to Augusta or

across the river in South Carolina where the mills are?

JEETER. No! By God and by Jesus, no! That's one thing I ain't never going to do. Them durn cotton mills is for the women folks to work in. I say it's a hell of a job for a man to spend his time winding strings on spools.

PAYNE. It shouldn't be any harder than trying to grow a crop here. Even if you do get one, you can't make enough out of it to live on.

JEETER. I don't care. God made the land, but you don't see Him building no durn cotton mills.

PAYNE. That hasn't anything to do with it. You old farmers are all the same. You don't realize that times have changed.

JEETER. That's no concern of mine. I is ready to look after my own like the Bible says, but that don't include no goddam mill! (*Turning to* TIM.) Please, Captain Tim, don't let them make me do that. I'm like to die pretty soon now, anyway, but up there I'd go before my time. You ain't going to let them do that to me, is you?

TIM. Lord, Jeeter, what can I do? That's up to Mr. Payne now. (*Turning to* PAYNE.) How about it, Payne? Couldn't you do something for this man?

PAYNE. I'm sorry, Mr. Harmon, but if we made an exception for one we'd have to for all of them. Of course, if he could pay rent—

JEETER. Rent! No use asking that. I couldn't pay no rent. Praise God, I hasn't even got money to buy food with.

TIM. What about your children? Couldn't one of them help you?

JEETER. I don't know where none of them is except Tom—(*A sudden idea.*) By God and by Jesus—Tom!

TIM. I remember Tom. What's Tom doing?

JEETER. They say down in Fuller he's a powerful rich man now. They tell me he hauls all the ties for the railroad. (*Turns to* PAYNE.) How much money would you be wanting for rent, mister?

PAYNE. Well—this place ought to be worth a hundred dollars a year.

JEETER. That's a heap of money, but Tom ought to be ready to help out his old Pa at a time like this. When would you be wanting that hundred dollars?

PAYNE. We ought to be starting back early tomorrow.

JEETER. I got time for that. Tom's only over in Burke County. (*Turns and calls.*) Hey, you, Dude. You and Bessie get in that new automobile and ride over and see Tom. You tell him his old Pa has got to have a hundred dollars. Don't lose no time about doing it neither.

DUDE (*jumping off porch—eager for a ride*). Come on, Bessie. We is going for a ride. (BESSIE *hesitates, glancing back into the house.*)

JEETER. You hurry up there, Bessie. Ain't no time to be thinking about going in the house now. (*With a last disappointed glance,* BESSIE *comes down off the porch.* DUDE *moves ahead of her to the gate.*)

TIM. Don't you think you ought to go and speak to Tom yourself, Jeeter?

JEETER. He might not like that so much. He might have changed some since he was a boy. He'll talk to Dude and Bessie, though. (BESSIE *and* DUDE *disappear down the road, and* JEETER *runs to the gate to call after them.*) Hey, you, Dude. You tell Tom his old Pa needs that money powerful bad. You tell him we ain't got anything to eat here, either, and his Ma needs snuff to calm her stomach with. (*Turns back to* TIM.) Tom was just about the best of all the boys. I reckon Bailey was the best, but Tom was good, too. He always said he was going to make a heap of money. (*The horn sounds off in* DUDE's *inimitable manner.* JEETER *speaks proudly.*) That's Dude doing that. Don't he blow the horn pretty, though? Just listen to it. (*The horn sounds again, somewhat fainter, and* JEETER *again smiles with pride at* TIM.) That's Dude. (*He is listening again as the* CURTAIN *falls.*)

ACT THREE

SCENE: *The same.*

TIME: *Dawn the following morning.*

AT RISE: JEETER, *shoeless, is discovered asleep on the porch, his back against one of the uprights, head slumped forward on his chest. Again the early sun spreads its soft golden glow, soon to become a fierce white glare as the morning advances.* JEETER *awakens abruptly, as one does who all night has tried to fight off sleep, and crosses swiftly to the gate, where he gazes off Right stage down the empty, silent road. Disappointed, he comes back into the yard to the well, where he performs his casual morning ablutions, using, as always, his shirt for a towel. Fingers through his hair serve as a comb for his scraggly hair; his hat goes back on his head. He is ready for the day. Again he crosses to the road, where his anxious gaze once more sweeps the horizon Right for a glimpse of* DUDE *and* BESSIE. ADA *appears on the porch, pressing her sides to ease the early morning pains of a body that sleep can no longer refresh.*

ADA. Is they coming yet?

JEETER. No. (*Comes inside to porch where he sits and starts putting on shoes.*) By God and by Jesus, I don't understand that. They been gone long enough to go to Burke County and back three times over.

ADA. It's that Bessie. She ain't going to hurry none just because you want her to.

JEETER. They must of seen Tom all right if they been gone this long. Maybe he made them stay all night. Do you think he done that, Ada?

ADA. Maybe he did and maybe he didn't. But if he asked them, you can bet that Bessie stayed all right. She ain't going to come home as long as there is any other place to go.

JEETER. What is you so peeved at Bessie for? She's a fine woman preacher.

ADA. She's a old hussy, that's what she is.

JEETER. Now what makes you say that? Sister Bessie is—

ADA. Don't tell me what she is. I know. Walking around here so uppity because she bought herself that new automobile. Why didn't she buy us some rations and snuff instead of spending all that money. That's what a good woman preacher would have done.

JEETER. She wants that new automobile to carry on the preaching and the praying. Women preachers ain't like the rest of us. They is got the Lord's work to do.

ADA. Humph. Looks to me like the Lord's work would be done better if she bought Dude's Ma a stylish dress. The Lord would understand that.

JEETER (suddenly and impatiently). Say, when is we going to eat this morning, anyway? Ain't there none of that meal left we borrowed from Morgan Prior yesterday?

ADA (crossly). There's some meal all right, but there ain't no kindling wood. Ellie May's ready to cook it as soon as she gets some.

JEETER. You tell Ma Lester to go get it then.

ADA. Ma Lester ain't here.

JEETER. Where is she?

ADA. I don't know. She didn't sleep in the bed last night.

JEETER. H'mm. Maybe she went out in the broom sedge yesterday and couldn't get back. Maybe she even died out there.

ADA. Maybe. She ain't never stayed away before.

JEETER. I'll go out and look around one of these days. . . . Well, you tell Ellie May to go out and get some wood. I sure got to have my chicory before long. . . .

ADA (calling inside house). Ellie May—Ellie May!

ELLIE MAY (off—in house). What you want, Ma?

ADA. You go out in the fields and get some sticks for the fire.

ELLIE MAY (off). Oh, make that old woman go.

ADA. She ain't here.

ELLIE MAY (complaining). Well, where is she?

ADA. She's likely dead. You go on do like I tell you. (ELLIE MAY enters yawning and scratching her head.)

ELLIE MAY. Why don't you make Pearl go? She don't never do nothing.

ADA. Never you mind now. I got other things for Pearl to do.

ELLIE MAY. Aw, gee!

JEETER. You hurry up. I is near about dying for my chicory.

ELLIE MAY (complaining). Can't I even get me a drink of water?

JEETER. All right, you get you some water, then get along. But keep away from them north fields. They might be burning some yet. That's probably what happened to your old Grandma. The fire come up on her and she couldn't get away from it. (He is filled with sudden energy, gets up, crosses to the road, and looks down it, shakes his head. ELLIE MAY drinks leisurely from the water dipper.) By God and by Jesus, they ought to be back with that money before this. First thing you know Captain Tim and that man will be along here looking for it.

ADA (calling into house—ignoring JEETER). Pearl—Pearl, git up, honey. Come out here and freshen up. We'll be having something to eat pretty soon now. Bring that old brush with you, too. I want to pretty up your hair. (ELLIE MAY hears ADA and takes the dipper slowly down from her mouth. She looks at ADA, her face livid with unspoken rage. Suddenly she flings the dipper at ADA, the water spilling. JEETER, coming through the gate, regards ELLIE MAY with anger.)

JEETER. Great day in the morning, what's the meaning of all that! (ELLIE MAY, disregarding JEETER, looks at her mother with blazing eyes, her breath coming hard. ADA returns the look with level coldness. ELLIE MAY's throat contracts with half-stifled sobs and she turns and rushes to the gate. She starts down the Tobacco Road Left when something she sees offstage stops her. For an instant she is rigid, then, with the first pronounced sob, she turns, and exits Right, running down the road. JEETER follows ELLIE MAY with a puzzled glance, then turns to ADA.)

JEETER. Now if that ain't the durndest gal. What do you suppose made her turn around like that for? (*He answers his own curiosity by crossing to the road and looking off Left. He turns back with some surprise.*) It's Lov coming down the road.

ADA. Don't you let him come in here.

JEETER. What the hell, woman. He ain't going to do no harm. He looks too durned tired.

ADA. He ain't going to have Pearl.

JEETER. Who said he was? I just said he was coming down the road.

ADA (*calling inside*). Pearl, Lov's coming. Stay where you is and get ready to run case he starts trying to get at you. (ADA *shuts the door and stands with her back to it.*)

JEETER. Great day, he's toting something again. Now whatever could be in that anyway? I bet you one thing, by God—it ain't turnips! (*Twitching with eagerness he comes inside the yard and takes his familiar place, hanging over the fence, his back to the audience, straining to see down the road.*) Whatever he's got, I sure could use some, even if I can't see it. I certainly is happy Lov and me is friends about this time.

ADA. Humph! The only way you'll ever get anything from him is stealing it.

JEETER. No, sir! The Lord forgave me for that before and I ain't going to risk his wrath again.

ADA. Humph.

JEETER (*again stretching over fence to peer down the road*). Now, Ada, don't be too hard on Lov and I might be able to prevail on him to give us a little something.

ADA. Then he better keep away from Pearl. (JEETER *waves her quiet and turns back to the fence, but he restrains his eagerness, as he did in the first act, so that* LOV *will not be frightened off.* LOV *enters disconsolately, carrying a small flour sack, the bottom of which bulges somewhat from an object the size of a brick.*)

JEETER (*casually*). Hi, there, Lov. (LOV *stops.*)

LOV (*after a pause*). I want to talk to you, Jeeter.

JEETER. Sure, Lov. Come inside and rest yourself. (LOV *slowly comes through the gate.*) What you got in that sack, Lov? What you got there anyway?

LOV (*after a significant pause and a glance from* JEETER *to* ADA *and back to* JEETER. *Knowing the bombshell effect of his words*). Salt pork.

JEETER (*electrified*). Salt pork! Lord a'-mighty! I ain't had salt pork since the Lord himself knows how long. Is you going to give me some of that, Lov? I sure could do with a small piece about this time.

LOV. Take it. (*He holds sack to the astounded* JEETER.)

JEETER (*unbelieving*). Take it? You mean take it all?

LOV. I bought it for that.

JEETER (*taking sack*). Great day in the morning, I never heard of such bounty! (*Turns.*) Did you hear that, Ada? Lov has give me all this salt pork.

ADA (*coldly*). What does he want for it?

JEETER. He don't want nothing for it. Lov just give it to me, that's all.

ADA. Ask him.

JEETER (*doubtfully*). Well now . . . What have you got to say about that, Lov? *Is* you after something from me in return for this salt pork?

LOV. I want to talk to you about Pearl.

ADA. That's just what I thought. Well, you ain't going to have her back. No use you trying to talk Jeeter into it, neither. He ain't got nothing to say about it. You give him back that salt pork, Jeeter.

JEETER. Now, Ada, there ain't no sense in being hasty about this matter. What you say is right, but there can't be no harm in talking about it.

ADA. You just want to hold on to that salt pork.

JEETER. Now, Ada—

LOV (*with sudden desperation*). I got to have Pearl back, Jeeter, no matter what you said yesterday. I just got to have her back.

JEETER. Now, Lov, we talked all about that before. I told you—

LOV. I don't care what you told me. Maybe you ain't Pearl's real Pa, but you got the right of her.

JEETER. I wish I could agree with you on that matter, Lov, but it ain't right in the eyes of God.

LOV. I'll pay you, Jeeter. I'll give you a dollar every week out of the money I make at the chute.

JEETER (*whistles*). That's a heap of money, Lov, and coming and going I might have considered it a short time back. But I ain't going to need money bad enough now to make me fly against the wrath of the Lord. Dude and Bessie is over with Tom right this minute and he'll be sending me all the money I want for my needs.

LOV. I'll give you two dollars.

JEETER. Two dollars a week! Now, Lov Bensey, you quit tempting me.

LOV (*with sudden fury*). By God, I want my wife. (ADA *plants her back more firmly against the door and the movement tells* LOV *where* PEARL *is. He takes a few steps to the edge of the porch.* ADA's *arms raise to cover the door.*)

ADA. You come any closer, and I'll call to her to run off. (LOV, *checked by the threat, stops, his sudden anger cooling.*)

LOV (*defeated*). No, don't do that. (JEETER *takes this opportunity to hide the sack behind the well.* LOV *slowly turns to* JEETER.) Jeeter, I don't see how I can make it more than two dollars every week. But that's a heap of money.

JEETER. Praise God, I know it, Lov.

ADA. Get out of here, Lov Bensey—get out. (LOV *slowly turns and crosses to the gate;* JEETER *keeps himself in front of the well to lessen any chance of* LOV *seeing and remembering the salt pork.* LOV *exits Left.* JEETER *waits until* LOV *has gone, then runs to the fence and looks after him.*)

JEETER. He's gone all right. He's gone and forgot that salt pork, too. (*Running back to the well, he picks up the sack and takes out the pork.*) Now ain't that something! That must be near about two pounds. Lov sure is a generous provider. (*Crosses to* ADA.) There you is, Ada. You fix up some of this with the corn meal when Ellie May comes back with the kindling. (ADA *takes the sack. She has moved away from the door on* LOV's *exit and is in her usual position, leaning against an upright.*) Now what do you think's happened to Ellie May, anyway? What's happened to Dude and Bessie for that matter? By God and by Jesus, they ought to be back with that money before this.

ADA. What is you going to do with that money, Jeeter?

JEETER (*pausing with foot half raised to put on other shoe. He is outraged*). What is I going to do? Is you crazy, woman! I got to give it to that man with Captain Tim.

ADA. Humph! That don't make no sense to me.

JEETER. Great day in the morning, you *is* crazy! That money's going to keep me my land, ain't it? That money's going to let me stay here and raise a crop. By God and by Jesus, what do you mean there ain't no sense in that?

ADA. You give the money to that man and what has you got left? Nothing! You ain't got no seed cotton to plant in the fields, you ain't got nothing to eat and you ain't no better off than you was before.

JEETER. I ain't aiming to be better off. I'm aiming to keep my land.

ADA. You're an old fool, Jeeter Lester. With that money we could get us a place to live up in Augusta. Maybe we could even buy us an automobile like Bessie's. (*Wisely.*) You wouldn't have to worry none about being laid in the corn crib when you die neither. Ain't no telling what's going to happen if you stay here.

JEETER. Shut up! You just say that to scare me into doing what you want. Well, I ain't going to be laid in no corn crib, and I ain't going to work in no cotton mill neither.

ADA. Maybe you wouldn't have to work none up there. (*Glances toward door.*) Maybe Ellie May and Pearl could do that. Pearl would like that a lot. She wouldn't be scared of going if her old Ma went.

JEETER. You ain't thinking about my wants when you talk like that. It's Pearl you is thinking about. Well, you can take her if that's what you want, and leave me here alone. I was born here on the land, and by God and by Jesus that's where I'll die.

ADA (*fiercely*). I hope you do. I hope you die and they lay you in the corn crib and the rats eat off your face just like they done your Pa.

JEETER (*rising—threatening and furious, raising his shoe to strike her*). Goddam you, woman! (*The horn, sounded in* DUDE's *inimitable style, checks* JEETER's *descending blow. Radiance replaces black fury in his face as he hears it again.*) Here they is. That's them, all right. That's Dude blowing that old horn. (PEARL *and* ELLIE MAY *enter on to porch. Hobbling because of the one shoe,* JEETER *crosses to the gate, where he stops and starts to pull on his shoe, while the horn continues its bleat.* JEETER's *shoe goes on with difficulty. Once or twice he starts off with it half on, but is so impeded that he stops and works on it again. The horn stops.* JEETER, *giving up the job of putting on the shoe while standing, plumps to the ground, puts it on, and gets through the gate, starting down the road Right, when* BESSIE *enters.*) Here you is, Bessie. I been waiting all night and day for you and Dude to come back. Where you been anyway?

BESSIE (*proudly*). In Augusta.

JEETER. Augusta! Didn't you go see Tom?

BESSIE. We saw Tom first. Then we rode up to Augusta and had us a honeymoon.

JEETER. Honeymoon? What the hell is that?

BESSIE. A honeymoon is when two people is married and they get in the bed together.

JEETER. Where did you do that?

BESSIE (*proudly*). At a hotel.

JEETER. Great day in the morning! Didn't that take a heap of money?

BESSIE. It took two bits.

JEETER. Hear that, Ada? Dude and Bessie stayed at a hotel in Augusta.

ADA (*dourly*). Did they bring us anything back?

BESSIE. I didn't have no money left to do that. That two bits was the last piece of money I had.

ADA. Humph! Looks to me like you might have brought some snuff back to Dude's old Ma instead of wasting money like that. (*Enter* DUDE *carrying broken headlight.*)

JEETER. Now, Ada, you let Bessie alone. (*Sees* DUDE.) Here you is, Dude. Bessie just told us about staying all night in Augusta— (*Sees headlight.*) Great day, just look at that old headlight. What done that?

DUDE. A goddam old pine tree. That's what.

JEETER (*inspecting light*). H'mm. Was you looking where you was going?

DUDE. I just looked back once and there it was—smack in front of me.

JEETER. Well, it don't look like it's going to be much good no more.

DUDE. If I had me an ax, I'd have chopped that tree down right then and there.

JEETER. I wouldn't concern myself much about it. One headlight is plenty to drive with.

DUDE. Oh, to hell with it. (*He drops light on ground, crosses to gate.*) It's just the way that pine tree got in front of me, that's all.

JEETER. Looks like they will do that sometimes. Hey, Dude. Where is the money Tom sent me?

DUDE. Tom didn't send you no money. Why the hell did you think he would anyway? (*Exits.*)

JEETER. Hey, Dude—(*Turning back to* BESSIE.) Dude's lying, ain't he, Bessie?

BESSIE (*nodding*). Tom ain't at all like he used to be, Jeeter.

JEETER (*desperately*). Now, Bessie—don't fool with me. Give me the money.

BESSIE. There ain't no money, Jeeter. Tom just didn't send any—that's all.

JEETER. You is crazy, woman. He did send it. Tom wouldn't do that to me.

BESSIE. Yes, he did, Jeeter. He's a wicked man, Tom is.

JEETER. No, sir, I don't believe it. You is got the money and I want it. Give it to me, hear me—give it to me.

BESSIE. I ain't got it, Jeeter.

JEETER. You is a liar. That's what you is—an old liar. Tom did send it. (*Enter* DUDE *rolling an auto wheel.* JEETER *rushes over to him inside the gate and grabs him.*) Dude, give me that money—hear me, give me that money.

DUDE (*shaking him off*). Didn't I tell you once! There ain't no money. Now get away from me and shut up. (*Bends over wheel, his back half to* BESSIE.)

JEETER. No. Tom wouldn't do•that. He was my special boy. You just didn't go see him.

DUDE. We saw him all right. We saw him and he said to tell you to go to hell. (BESSIE *grabs him by the neck and shakes him so that the wheel falls to the ground.* DUDE *is furious.*) Damn you, turn loose of me. (*Shakes free.*) What the hell you doing?

BESSIE. You shouldn't have told Jeeter that. That's a wicked thing to say.

DUDE. I didn't say it— Tom said it. And you keep off me. I didn't do nothing to you.

BESSIE. Praise the Lord, you won't be fit to preach a sermon next Sunday if you cuss like that. Good folks don't want to have God send them sermons by cussing preachers.

DUDE. All right, I won't cuss no more. But don't you go jumping on my neck no more neither. (*He picks up wheel and rolls it against fence near the other broken pieces of the automobile, and sits.* JEETER *sits on fence, staring blankly ahead.* PEARL *and* ELLIE MAY *exit into the house.*)

ADA. What does Tom look like now? Has he changed much?

BESSIE. He looks a lot like Jeeter. There ain't much resemblance in him and you.

ADA. Humph! There was a time when I'd have declared it was the other way around.

BESSIE. Maybe one time, but now he looks more like Jeeter than Jeeter does hisself.

ADA. What did he say when you told him you and Dude was married?

BESSIE. He didn't say nothing much. Looked to me like he didn't care one way or the other.

DUDE (*over his shoulder from where he sits, back to audience, appraising the damaged parts*). Tom said she used to be a two-bit slut when he knowed her. (*With a bound* BESSIE *is on his neck again, choking him. He jerks away from her quickly and pushes his hand at her face, getting up, threatening.*) Goddam you! You keep off me.

BESSIE (*tenderly as she backs off*). Now, Dude, you promised me you wasn't going to cuss no more.

DUDE. Then, by God, quit choking me. I'm getting damned sick and tired of you doing that.

BESSIE. You shouldn't talk like that about the woman you is mated to.

DUDE. Well, that's what Tom said. He told it right to you and you didn't do nothing. Why didn't you do something to him if he was telling a lie?

BESSIE. Tom is a wicked man. The Lord punishes wicked men like that.

DUDE. Well, then, you let the Lord punish me and keep your hands off my neck. (DUDE *pulls wheel down and begins trying to straighten spokes by pulling on them with his hands and pounding them with a hand-sized rock.*)

ADA. Did Tom say he had any children?

BESSIE. He didn't mention it if he had. He didn't seem to want to talk very much, not even when I told him you and Jeeter didn't have meal nor meat in the house.

DUDE (*looking up fro... his work*). He just said he didn't give a damn and went on driving his team of ox.

ADA (*briskly—pleased*). Well, I reckon we better be getting ready to go off, Jeeter.

JEETER. What?—(*Snapped back from his stunned silence.*) No, I ain't going, I tell you.

ADA (*exasperated*). Tom didn't send you no money. How you going to stay here?

JEETER. By God, I'm going to stay, that's all. (ADA, *realizing the uselessness of arguing with him, turns and exits into the house.* BESSIE *turns to* DUDE *and watches him work.*)

BESSIE. Do you reckon you'll ever get that wheel straight again, Dude?

DUDE (*crossly*). I'm trying, ain't I?

JEETER (*abstractedly, pointing to wheel*). What done that?

DUDE. Remember that old pine tree that busted the headlight?

JEETER Um.

DUDE. Well, I was backing away from that and some durn fool left a pile of cross ties right where I'd run smack into them.

JEETER (*easily*). Well, now what do you think?

DUDE. It busted the back of the car in, too.

BESSIE. It looks like everything's trying to ruin my new automobile. Ain't nothing like it was when I paid eight hundred dollars for it in Fuller just yesterday.

JEETER. It ain't hurt the running of it none, though, has it? It runs good yet.

BESSIE. I reckon so, but it makes a powerful lot of noise when it's running up hill—and down hill, too.

DUDE. That's because we was running it without oil. The man at the gasoline station said something was burned out inside.

JEETER. That's a pity.

DUDE. It runs pretty good, though, even if it does make all that racket.

JEETER. Some automobiles is like that. (*Jumps down from fence, suddenly his old self again.*) By God and by Jesus, now why didn't I think of that before. Quit pounding on that old wheel, Dude. You come with me.

DUDE (*still sitting*). What you want to do now? I done enough running around for one morning.

JEETER. You get up from there and do like I say. You and me is going to start hauling wood to Augusta right this minute.

DUDE. You're just an old fool. That old machine of yours can't carry no wood to Augusta.

JEETER. No, but that there new one can. You come on.

DUDE. What do I want to haul wood to Augusta for?

JEETER. So I can get me some money for the bank—that's what for.

DUDE. You ain't going to get no hundred dollars for no load of wood, or nothing else like it.

JEETER. I can get a couple of dollars maybe, and every day doing that I can get me more than a hundred.

BESSIE. You stop right where you is, Jeeter. You ain't going to use my new automobile for no such purpose.

JEETER. Now, Bessie, ain't I always shared what I had with you and your former husband? You ain't going to see me lose my land, is you?

BESSIE. That ain't no concern of mine. Hauling wood in my new machine would punch holes in the seat and the top just like it done to your old one.

JEETER. I won't let it hurt it none.

BESSIE. It's already broke up enough. I ain't going to let you do it.

JEETER. Now, Bessie—

BESSIE. You can't have it and that's all.

JEETER (*with heat*). That's a hell of a way to act toward me. You ain't got the mercy of the Lord in you. I say you is a hell of a woman preacher.

BESSIE (*angrily*). You shut up cussing at me, Jeeter Lester.

JEETER. I won't. You is an old bitch, that's what you is. You is an old bitch.

BESSIE (*with equal fury*). You is an old bitch, too. You is an old son-of-a-bitch. All you Lesters is sons-of-bitches. (DUDE *looks up amused.*)

JEETER (*coming up to her threateningly*). Get off my land. If I can't borrow me that automobile, you get off my land.

BESSIE. It ain't your land. It's the bank's land and *you* got to get off it.

JEETER. It's the old Lester place, and I ain't going to get off it while I'm alive. But durned if I can't run you off—(*Enter* PEARL *from house with small, blackened pot.*) Now git!—You hear me, gi—(JEETER *sees* PEARL, *who has hesitated on the porch at sight of the quarrel, and suddenly stops his tirade, the hand raised to strike* BESSIE *halted in midair.* PEARL *comes down from the porch and crosses to the well,* JEETER'*s eyes following her and his hand slowly lowering to his side. The fury in his eyes dies to a strange, puzzled, contemplative expression.* DUDE, *who has been amused by the quarrel, a smile wreathing his face, follows his father's glance curiously, but without enlightenment.* BESSIE *glances from* JEETER *to* PEARL *and back to* JEETER *again, a frown wrinkling her forehead.*)

BESSIE. What's the matter with you, you old fool? Has you lost your mind?

JEETER (*suddenly turning away from regarding* PEARL *at the well, smiling at* BESSIE, *and moving away a few steps*). Ain't no sense you and me fighting, Bessie. You and me always thought a heap of each other. You can stay here just as long as you has a mind to.

BESSIE. H'mm. (*Suspicious and uncompromising.*) You ain't going to have the use of my new automobile to haul wood to Augusta.

JEETER. I gave up thinking about that a long time back. Don't concern yourself about that no more. However, I might be wanting you and Dude to take a little trip for me pretty soon now. Will you do that?

BESSIE (*suspiciously*). Maybe. What you want us to do?

JEETER. Never you mind. It won't be far.

BESSIE. Well, if it ain't far.

JEETER. It won't hardly take no time. (*Crosses to* DUDE.) How is you getting on there, Dude?

DUDE (*back trying to straighten spokes*). Maybe it will be all right. It don't much matter if all the spokes ain't straight.

JEETER. Umm. (*Out of the corner of his eye* JEETER *watches* PEARL, *who, having filled the kettle, crosses back from well to house and exits.* JEETER *leaves his place at the fence and nonchalantly ambles to the porch and leans, taking out his knife and whittling on a piece of broken weather-boarding. Although he tries to appear at ease, his tenseness is apparent, and occasional swift glances at the door reveal his real interest.*)

DUDE (*hitting at spokes with a stone harder than before*). This is a hell of a job.

JEETER. Don't worry too much about that. The wheels of my old machine wasn't straight much after the first few days and it didn't hurt the running of it hardly any.

BESSIE. I don't like my new car busted up like that though. (*Indicating headlight.*) Look there, Dude. There ain't hardly a piece of glass left in that headlight.

DUDE. Don't I know it. Goddam it, can't you let me be? Can't you see I'm trying to fix this old wheel?

BESSIE. Now, Dude, is that a way to talk? Good folks don't want to go and hear a Sunday sermon by a cussing preacher. I thought you wasn't going to swear no more.

DUDE. Then don't be always poking around. Go sit down someplace. (*Enter* PEARL *with pan.* JEETER *watches her sharply as she crosses to well.*)

JEETER (*pretending interest*). When's Dude going to start being a preacher, Bessie? (*Follows* PEARL *slowly to well.*)

BESSIE. He's going to preach a little short sermon next Sunday. I is already telling him what to say when he preaches.

JEETER. Dude might make a fine man preacher at that under your direction, although I never thought he had right good sense. I used to think he was going to stay on the land like I always done, but I reckon he'll be better off riding around the country preaching and praying with you. (*Edges forward a bit as* PEARL *fills her bucket and starts back to door. With a spring* JEETER *is at* PEARL'*s side and grabs her firmly by the wrist. The bucket falls— the girl's cry rings out, as she makes a desperate effort to pull away and run.*)

PEARL. Ma! (BESSIE *and* DUDE *whirl around to look.*)

JEETER. Hey, Dude—you and Bessie ride down to the chute and get Lov. Tell him I got Pearl for him. (*The door flies open and an infuriated* ADA *takes in the scene. She rushes down on* JEETER *and begins hitting at him furiously.*)

ADA. You let her be—you let her be!

JEETER (*pushing off* ADA *with his free hand*). Hurry up there, Dude. You tell Lov if he's still ready to pay that two dollars a week I'll make Pearl go back and live with him.

BESSIE. Jeeter, that ain't the right thing to do.

JEETER (*fighting off* ADA). Maybe it wasn't right before, but it sure is now. You get the hell out of here!

DUDE (*grabbing* BESSIE). Come on. (DUDE *half pulls* BESSIE *through gate.*)

ADA (*clawing at* JEETER *and yelling at* DUDE). Don't you go, Dude—don't you go.

JEETER. Go on, Dude. You do like I tell you. (DUDE *and* BESSIE *exit Right.* ADA *strikes at* JEETER, *but when she sees* DUDE *and* BESSIE *exit, she suddenly stops her attack and runs after them.*)

ADA. Don't go, Dude. Wait! Wait! (ADA *exits.* PEARL *continues to scratch and fight against* JEETER, *her gasping sobs the only sound she utters.* JEETER *holds her, but looks off in direction the others have gone. For an instant there is silence, broken only by* PEARL's *sobs. Then the sound of an engine starting up and the blare of a horn come from the road below, and hard on this rings out the high shriek of a woman in agony. Again the scream cuts the silence, and even* PEARL's *sobs are hushed, as she and* JEETER *listen. Suddenly she again struggles to free herself in a frenzy of effort to be with her mother, but* JEETER's *hold does not relax. Nothing is spoken, no voice is heard, for a full pause. Then, on hands and knees, crawling along the Tobacco Road and whimpering like a hurt puppy, comes* ADA. PEARL's *struggles cease and she stands, horrified, still*

in JEETER's *grasp, as* ADA *continues forward. At the gate her strength deserts her, and she sinks to her side, now dragging herself along by her arms alone, until she is in the yard.*)

PEARL. Ma! . . . Let me go, goddam you— let me go. (*But* JEETER *holds fast,* DUDE *and* BESSIE *come running up to fence outside, followed by* ELLIE MAY. DUDE *leans over the fence, looking at his mother. There is no grief in his voice, only calm explanation.* JEETER *holds* PEARL, *who stands transfixed.*)

DUDE. We was backing on to the road and she got in the way. I guess the wheels ran over her. (ADA *makes a last movement forward and a stifled groan comes from her crushed, wracked body as she props herself on her arm. A sob escapes* PEARL *and she tries to pull away from* JEETER.)

ADA. Let her go, Jeeter. Let her come to me.

JEETER. Praise God, I'd like to do that for you, Ada, but she'll run away.

ADA. Just let her come close to me, that's all. (JEETER *yields several steps, so that* PEARL, *kneeling, can reach out her hand to touch* ADA. ELLIE MAY *enters and stands outside the fence.*)

PEARL (*kneeling—touching her mother— sobbing*). Ma! Ma! Don't die. You can't, Ma—you can't!

ADA. That's all right, Pearl. I was going pretty soon now anyway. (*Glances around as best she can.*) I wish I had that stylish dress to be buried in, though. Reckon you can get me one, Jeeter?

JEETER. I sure would like to promise you that, Ada, but it ain't likely.

PEARL. I'll get you one, Ma. I'll get you one.

ADA (*matter-of-factly, without either self-pity or bitterness*). Never mind, honey. I never really thought I'd get it. It would have sort of pleased me, though. (*Pauses, looks at* PEARL, *then* JEETER.) Let her go, Jeeter? I never asked for nothing before, but now I'm going to die.

JEETER. I sure would like to, Ada, but I'm going to die pretty soon myself now. I feel it inside me. But I got to die on the land. Don't you understand? If I don't hold on to her for Lov I won't be able to do that.

ADA. Please, Jeeter, don't make her go back.

JEETER. Praise God, Ada, I got to.

ADA. All my life I been working for you. I picked cotton in the fields and turned over the furrows. I took care of your house and raised your children, and now when I'm going to die you won't even do what I want you to.

JEETER. My concern is with the living. The dead has to look out for themselves.

ADA. You're a sinful man, Jeeter Lester. You're a sinful man, and you're going to hell. (*Holds out arm to* PEARL.) Come here, child. Just put your arm around me so I can sit up. (JEETER *allows* PEARL *to come close enough to* ADA, *so that her free arm goes around her mother, and* JEETER's *hand works close to* ADA's *mouth. Suddenly* ADA *leans forward the few necessary inches and her teeth sink into* JEETER's *hand. With a smothered exclamation* JEETER *jerks back his hand, releasing* PEARL. *With flashing quickness the girl is on her feet. A dash carries her through the gate before* JEETER *recovers from the shock of his pain. Pausing,* PEARL *looks back at her mother, propped on her arm in the yard.*)

PEARL. Good-by, Ma. (JEETER *springs forward toward her, but with a last wave of her hand,* PEARL *flashes down the road and is gone.* JEETER *reaches the fence, makes to run after her, then stops, realizing the hopelessness of overtaking the girl.* ADA, *holding herself up with her last strength, sees his defeat. A low laugh escapes her and she rolls forward on her face and is dead.* JEETER *slowly turns and comes back inside. He stops to look down at* ADA *for a moment and then crosses to the porch where he sits. His hand doesn't hurt much now, but he continues to hold it.* LOV *enters.*)

DUDE. Hi there, Lov. Jeeter was looking for you, but I guess it's too late now. Pearl's done gone.

LOV (*after a pause, indicating* ADA). What's the matter with her?

DUDE. Me and Bessie run over her in the new automobile a while back.

LOV. Is she hurt bad?

DUDE. Looks like she's dead. (LOV *comes inside, kneels down, looks at* ADA. *Then goes up to* JEETER.)

LOV. Ada's dead, Jeeter. (JEETER *nods, half dazed. Crossing to* ADA, *he stands over her for a long pause. At last he speaks.*)

JEETER. Lov, you and Dude go out in the fields and find the best place to bury her. Make a deep hole—Ada would like that. . . . Bessie, you do some praying, too. It would please Ada a whole lot.

BESSIE. Praise the Lord, I'll be glad to, Brother Jeeter. (LOV, DUDE, *and* BESSIE *exit.* ELLIE MAY *moves forward tentatively and* JEETER *notices her.*)

JEETER. Ellie May, you better go down to Lov's house and fix it up for him. He'll be coming home to supper tonight and you cook him what he wants. Be nice to him and maybe he'll let you stay. He'll be wanting a woman pretty bad now. (ELLIE MAY, *frantic with delight, drops her sticks and crosses on a run down the road. Just before she exits, she stops and looks back.*)

ELLIE MAY. Good-by, Pa. (JEETER *nods.* ELLIE MAY *exits, running.* JEETER *looks down at* ADA.)

JEETER. You shouldn't have done that, Ada. One way and another it didn't do anybody much good except maybe Pearl. (*For a brief second* JEETER *looks down at* ADA, *then he crosses to the porch and sits. He bends down slowly, takes a pinch of the earth between his fingers and rubs it into dust. He sits back, leaning against the upright, and tilts his hat forward over his eyes. It is the same posture he has assumed so many times before when he has suddenly and unexpectedly fallen asleep. For a moment he continues abstractedly to rub the dirt between his fingers. Then all movement ceases. Seconds of somber silence pass. A rotten shingle falls from the sagging porch, and the* CURTAIN *falls slowly.*)

THE END

Of Mice And Men

BY JOHN STEINBECK

CAST OF CHARACTERS

This play was first presented by Sam H. Harris at the Music Box Theatre
on the evening of November 23, 1937, with the following cast:

GEORGE	Wallace Ford
LENNIE	Broderick Crawford
CANDY	John F. Hamilton
THE BOSS	Thomas Findlay
CURLEY	Sam Byrd
CURLEY'S WIFE	Claire Luce
SLIM	Will Geer
CARLSON	Charles Slattery
WHIT	Walter Baldwin
CROOKS	Leigh Whipper

Staged by George S. Kaufman

Settings by Donald Oenslager

SYNOPSIS OF SCENES

ACT I

Scene   I.   A Sandy bank of the Salinas River. Thursday night.
Scene II.   The interior of a bunkhouse. Late Friday morning.

ACT II

Scene   I.   The same as Act I, Scene II. About seven-thirty Friday evening.
Scene II.   The room of the stable buck, a lean-to. Ten o'clock Saturday evening.

ACT III

Scene   I.   One end of a great barn. Mid-afternoon, Sunday.
Scene II.   Same as Act I, Scene I.

Time: The present.
Place: An agricultural valley in Southern California.

OF MICE AND MEN

ACT ONE

SCENE I

Thursday night.
A sandy bank of the Salinas River sheltered with willows—one giant sycamore right, upstage.
The stage is covered with dry leaves. The feeling of the stage is sheltered and quiet. Stage is lit by a setting sun.
Curtain rises on an empty stage. A sparrow is singing. There is a distant sound of ranch dogs barking aimlessly and one clear quail call. The quail call turns to a warning call and there is a beat of the flock's wings. Two figures are seen entering the stage in single file, with GEORGE, the short man, coming in ahead of LENNIE. Both men are carrying blanket rolls. They approach the water. The small man throws down his blanket roll, the large man follows and then falls down and drinks from the river, snorting as he drinks.

GEORGE (*irritably*). Lennie, for God's sake, don't drink so much. (*Leans over and shakes* LENNIE.) Lennie, you hear me! You gonna be sick like you was last night.

LENNIE (*dips his whole head under, hat and all. As he sits upon the bank, his hat drips down the back*). That's good. You drink some, George. You drink some too.

GEORGE (*kneeling and dipping his finger in the water*). I ain't sure it's good water. Looks kinda scummy to me.

LENNIE (*imitates, dipping his finger also*). Look at them wrinkles in the water, George. Look what I done.

GEORGE (*drinking from his cupped palm*). Tastes all right. Don't seem to be runnin' much, though. Lennie, you oughtn' to drink water when it ain't running. (*Hopelessly.*) You'd drink water out of a gutter if you was thirsty. (*He throws a scoop of water into his face and rubs it around with his hand, pushes himself back and embraces his knees.* LENNIE, *after watching him, imitates him in every detail.*)

GEORGE (*beginning tiredly and growing angry as he speaks*). God damn it, we could just as well of rode clear to the ranch. That bus driver didn't know what he was talkin' about. "Just a little stretch down the highway," he says. "Just a little stretch"—damn near four miles. I bet he didn't want to stop at the ranch gate. . . . I bet he's too damn lazy to pull up. Wonder he ain't too lazy to stop at Soledad at all! (*Mumbling.*) Just a little stretch down the road.

LENNIE (*timidly*). George?

GEORGE. Yeh . . . what you want?

LENNIE. Where we goin', George?

GEORGE (*jerks down his hat furiously*). So you forgot that already, did you? So I got to tell you again! Jeez, you're a crazy bastard!

LENNIE (*softly*). I forgot. I tried not to forget, honest to God, I did!

GEORGE. Okay, okay, I'll tell you again. . . . (*With sarcasm.*) I ain't got nothin' to do. Might just as well spen' all my time tellin' you things. You forgit 'em and I tell you again.

LENNIE (*continuing on from his last speech*). I tried and tried, but it didn't do no good. I remember about the rabbits, George!

GEORGE. The hell with the rabbits! You can't remember nothing but them rabbits. You remember settin' in that gutter on Howard Street and watchin' that blackboard?

LENNIE (*delightedly*). Oh, sure! I remember that . . . but . . . wha'd we do then? I remember some girls come by, and you says—

GEORGE. The hell with what I says! You remember about us goin' in Murray and Ready's and they give us work cards and bus tickets?

LENNIE (*confidently*). Oh, sure, George . . . I remember that now. (*Puts his hand into his side coat-pocket; his confidence vanishes. Very gently.*) . . . George?

GEORGE. Huh?

LENNIE (*staring at the ground in despair*). I ain't got mine. I musta lost it.

GEORGE. You never had none. I got both of 'em here. Think I'd let you carry your own work card?

LENNIE (*with tremendous relief*). I thought I put it in my side pocket. (*Puts his hand in his pocket again.*)

GEORGE (*looking sharply at him; and as he looks,* LENNIE *brings his hand out of his pocket.*) Wha'd you take out of that pocket?

LENNIE (*cleverly*). Ain't a thing in my pocket.

GEORGE. I know there ain't. You got it in your hand now. What you got in your hand?

LENNIE. I ain't got nothing, George! Honest!

GEORGE. Come on, give it here!

LENNIE (*holds his closed hand away from* GEORGE). It's on'y a mouse!

GEORGE. A mouse? A live mouse?

LENNIE. No . . . just a dead mouse. (*Worriedly.*) I didn't kill it. Honest. I found it. I found it dead.

GEORGE. Give it here!

LENNIE. Leave me have it, George.

GEORGE (*sternly*). Give it here! (LENNIE *reluctantly gives him the mouse.*) What do you want of a dead mouse, anyway?

LENNIE (*in a propositional tone*). I was petting it with my thumb while we walked along.

GEORGE. Well, you ain't pettin' no mice while you walk with me. Now let's see if you can remember where we're going. (GEORGE *throws it across the water into the brush.*)

LENNIE (*looks startled and then in embarrassment hides his face against his knees*). I forgot again.

GEORGE. Jesus Christ! (*Resignedly.*) Well, look, we are gonna work on a ranch like the one we come from up north.

LENNIE. Up north?

GEORGE. In Weed!

LENNIE. Oh, sure I remember—in Weed.

GEORGE (*still with exaggerated patience*). That ranch we're goin' to is right down there about a quarter mile. We're gonna go in and see the boss.

LENNIE (*repeats as a lesson*). And see the boss!

GEORGE. Now, look! I'll give him the work tickets, but you ain't gonna say a word. You're just gonna stand there and not say nothing.

LENNIE. Not say nothing!

GEORGE. If he finds out what a crazy bastard you are, we won't get no job. But if he sees you work before he hears you talk, we're set. You got that?

LENNIE. Sure, George . . . sure, I got that.

GEORGE. Okay. Now when we go in to see the boss, what you gonna do?

LENNIE (*concentrating*). I . . . I . . . I ain't gonna say nothing . . . jus' gonna stand there.

GEORGE (*greatly relieved*). Good boy, that's swell! Now say that over two or three times so you sure won't forget it.

LENNIE (*drones softly under his breath*). I ain't gonna say nothing . . . I ain't gonna say nothing. . . . (*Trails off into a whisper.*)

GEORGE. And you ain't gonna do no bad things like you done in Weed neither.

LENNIE (*puzzled*). Like I done in Weed?

GEORGE. So you forgot that too, did you?

LENNIE (*triumphantly*). They run us out of Weed!

GEORGE (*disgusted*). Run us out, hell! We run! They was lookin' for us, but they didn't catch us.

LENNIE (*happily*). I didn't forget that, you bet.

GEORGE (*lies back on the sand, crosses his hands under his head. And again* LENNIE *imitates him*). God, you're a lot of trouble! I could get along so easy and nice, if I didn't have you on my tail. I could live so easy!

LENNIE (*hopefully*). We gonna work on a ranch, George.

GEORGE. All right, you got that. But we're gonna sleep here tonight, because . . . I want to. I want to sleep out. (*The light is going fast, dropping into evening. A little wind whirls into the clearing and blows leaves. A dog howls in the distance.*)

LENNIE. Why ain't we goin' on to the ranch to get some supper? They got supper at the ranch.

GEORGE. No reason at all. I just like it here. Tomorrow we'll be goin' to work. I seen thrashing machines on the way down; that means we'll be buckin' grain bags. Bustin' a gut liftin' up them bags. Tonight I'm gonna lay right here an' look up! Tonight there ain't a grain bag or a boss in the world. Tonight, the drinks is on the . . . house. Nice house we got here, Lennie.

LENNIE (*gets up on his knees and looks down at* GEORGE, *plaintively*). Ain't we gonna have no supper?

GEORGE. Sure we are. You gather up some dead willow sticks. I got three cans of beans in my bindle. I'll open 'em up while you get a fire ready. We'll eat 'em cold.

LENNIE (*companionably*). I like beans with ketchup.

GEORGE. Well, we ain't got no ketchup. You go get the wood, and don't you fool around none. Be dark before long. (LENNIE *lumbers to his feet and disappears into the brush.* GEORGE *gets out the bean cans, opens two of them, suddenly turns his head and listens. A little sound of splashing comes from the direction that* LENNIE *has taken.* GEORGE *looks after him; shakes his head.* LENNIE *comes back carrying a few small willow sticks in his hand.*) All right, give me that mouse.

LENNIE (*with elaborate pantomime of innocence*). What, George? I ain't got no mouse.

GEORGE (*holding out his hand*). Come on! Give it to me! You ain't puttin' nothing over. (LENNIE *hesitates, backs away, turns and looks as if he were going to run. Coldly*). You gonna give me that mouse or do I have to take a sock at you?

LENNIE. Give you what, George?

GEORGE. You know goddamn well, what! I want that mouse!

LENNIE (*almost in tears*). I don't know why I can't keep it. It ain't nobody's mouse. I didn' steal it! I found it layin' right beside the road. (GEORGE *snaps his fingers sharply, and* LENNIE *lays the mouse in his hand.*) I wasn't doin' nothing bad with it. Just stroking it. That ain't bad.

GEORGE (*stands up and throws the mouse as far as he can into the brush, then he steps to the pool, and washes his hands*). You crazy fool! Thought you could get away with it, didn't you? Don't you think I could see your feet was wet where you went in the water to get it? (LENNIE *whimpers like a puppy.*) Blubbering like a baby. Jesus Christ, a big guy like you! (LENNIE *tries to control himself, but his lips quiver and his face works with an effort.* GEORGE *puts his hand on* LENNIE's *shoulder for a moment.*) Aw, Lennie, I ain't takin' it away just for meanness. That mouse ain't fresh. Besides, you broke it pettin' it. You get a mouse that's fresh and I'll let you keep it a little while.

LENNIE. I don't know where there is no other mouse. I remember a lady used to give 'em to me. Ever' one she got she used to give it to me, but that lady ain't here no more.

GEORGE. Lady, huh! . . . Give me them sticks there. . . . Don't even remember who that lady was. That was your own Aunt Clara. She stopped givin' 'em to you. You always killed 'em.

LENNIE (*sadly and apologetically*). They was so little. I'd pet 'em and pretty soon they bit my fingers and then I pinched their head a little bit and then they was dead . . . because they was so little. I wish we'd get the rabbits pretty soon, George. They ain't so little.

GEORGE. The hell with the rabbits! Come on, let's eat. (*The light has continued to go out of the scene so that when* GEORGE *lights the fire, it is the major light on the stage.* GEORGE *hands one of the open cans of beans to* LENNIE.) There's enough beans for four men.

LENNIE (*sitting on the other side of the fire, speaks patiently*). I like 'em with ketchup.

GEORGE (*explodes*). Well, we ain't got any. Whatever we ain't got, that's what you want. God Almighty, if I was alone, I could live so easy. I could go get a job of work and no trouble. No mess . . . and when the end of the month come, I could take my fifty bucks and go into town and get whatever I want. Why, I could stay in a cat-house all night. I could eat any place I want. Order any damn thing.

LENNIE (*plaintively, but softly*). I didn't want no ketchup.

GEORGE (*continuing violently*). I could do that every damn month. Get a gallon of whiskey or set in a pool room and play cards or shoot pool. (LENNIE *gets up to his knees and looks over the fire, with frightened face.*) And what have I got? (*Disgustedly.*) I got *you*. You can't keep a job and you lose me every job I get!

LENNIE (*in terror*). I don't mean nothing, George.

GEORGE. Just keep me shovin' all over the country all the time. And that ain't the worst—you get in trouble. You do bad things and I got to get you out. It ain't bad people that raises hell. It's dumb ones. (*He shouts.*) You crazy son-of-a-bitch, you keep me in hot water all the time. (LENNIE *is trying to stop* GEORGE's *flow of words with his hands. Sarcastically.*) You just wanta feel that girl's dress. Just wanta pet it like it was a mouse. Well, how the hell'd she know you just wanta feel her dress? How'd she know you'd just hold onto it like it was a mouse?

LENNIE (*in panic*). I didn't mean to, George!

GEORGE. Sure you didn't mean to. You didn't mean for her to yell bloody hell, either. You didn't mean for us to hide in the irrigation ditch all day with guys out lookin' for us with guns. Alla time it's something you didn't mean. God damn it, I wish I could put you in a cage with a million mice and let them pet *you*. (GEORGE's *anger leaves him suddenly. For the first time he seems to see the expression of terror on* LENNIE's *face. He looks down ashamedly at the fire, and maneuvers some beans onto the blade of his pocket-knife and puts them into his mouth.*)

LENNIE (*after a pause*). George! (GEORGE *purposely does not answer him.*) George?

GEORGE. What do you want?

LENNIE. I was only foolin', George. I don't want no ketchup. I wouldn't eat no ketchup if it was right here beside me.

GEORGE (*with a sullenness of shame*). If they was some here you could have it. And if I had a thousand bucks I'd buy ya a bunch of flowers.

LENNIE. I wouldn't eat no ketchup, George. I'd leave it all for you. You could cover your beans so deep with it, and I wouldn't touch none of it.

GEORGE (*refusing to give in from his sullenness, refusing to look at* LENNIE.) When I think of the swell time I could have without you, I go nuts. I never git no peace!

LENNIE. You want I should go away and leave you alone?

GEORGE. Where the hell could you go?

LENNIE. Well, I could . . . I could go off in the hills there. Some place I could find a cave.

GEORGE. Yeah, how'd ya eat? You ain't got sense enough to find nothing to eat.

LENNIE. I'd find things. I don't need no nice food with ketchup. I'd lay out in the sun and nobody would hurt me. And if I found a mouse—why, I could keep it. Wouldn't nobody take it away from me.

GEORGE (*at last he looks up*). I been mean, ain't I?

LENNIE (*presses his triumph*). If you don't want me, I can go right in them hills, and find a cave. I can go away any time.

GEORGE. No. Look! I was just foolin' ya. 'Course I want you to stay with me. Trouble with mice is you always kill 'em. (*He pauses.*) Tell you what I'll do, Lennie. First chance I get I'll find you a pup. Maybe you wouldn't kill it. That would be better than mice. You could pet it harder.

LENNIE (*still avoiding being drawn in*). If you don't want me, you only gotta say so. I'll go right up on them hills and live by myself. And I won't get no mice stole from me.

GEORGE. I want you to stay with me. Jesus Christ, somebody'd shoot you for a coyote if you was by yourself. Stay with me. Your Aunt Clara wouldn't like your runnin' off by yourself, even if she is dead.

LENNIE. George?

GEORGE. Huh?

LENNIE (*craftily*). Tell me—like you done before.

GEORGE. Tell you what?

LENNIE. About the rabbits.

GEORGE (*near to anger again*). You ain't gonna put nothing over on me!

LENNIE (*pleading*). Come on, George . . . tell me! Please! Like you done before.

GEORGE. You get a kick out of that, don't you? All right, I'll tell you. And then we'll lay out our beds and eat our dinner.

LENNIE. Go on, George. (*Unrolls his bed and lies on his side, supporting his head on one hand.* GEORGE *lays out his bed and sits cross-legged on it.* GEORGE *repeats the next speech rhythmically, as though he had said it many times before.*)

GEORGE. Guys like us that work on ranches is the loneliest guys in the world. They ain't got no family. They don't belong no place. They come to a ranch and work up a stake and then they go in to town and blow their stake. And then the first thing you know they're poundin' their tail on some other ranch. They ain't got nothin' to look ahead to.

LENNIE (*delightedly*). That's it, that's it! Now tell how it is with us.

GEORGE (*still almost chanting*). With us it ain't like that. We got a future. We got somebody to talk to that gives a damn about us. We don't have to sit in no barroom blowin' in our jack, just because we got no place else to go. If them other guys gets in jail, they can rot for all anybody gives a damn.

LENNIE (*who cannot restrain himself any longer. Bursts into speech*). But not us! And why? Because . . . because I got you to look after me . . . and you got me to look after you . . . and that's why! (*He laughs.*) Go on, George!

GEORGE. You got it by heart. You can do it yourself.

LENNIE. No, no. I forget some of the stuff. Tell about how it's gonna be.

GEORGE. Some other time.

LENNIE. No, tell how it's gonna be!

GEORGE. Okay. Some day we're gonna get the jack together and we're gonna have a little house, and a couple of acres and a cow and some pigs and . . .

LENNIE (*shouting*). And live off the fat of the land! And have rabbits. Go on, George! Tell about what we're gonna have in the garden. And about the rabbits in the cages. Tell about the rain in the winter . . . and about the stove and how thick the cream is on the milk, you can hardly cut it. Tell about that, George!

GEORGE. Why don't you do it yourself—you know all of it!

LENNIE. It ain't the same if I tell it. Go on now. How I get to tend the rabbits.

GEORGE (*resignedly*). Well, we'll have a big vegetable patch and a rabbit hutch and chickens. And when it rains in the winter we'll just say to hell with goin' to work. We'll build up a fire in the stove, and set around it and listen to the rain comin' down on the roof—Nuts! (*Begins to eat with his knife.*) I ain't got time for no more. (*He falls to eating.* LENNIE *imitates him, spilling a few beans from his mouth with every bite.* GEORGE, *gesturing with his knife.*) What you gonna say tomorrow when the boss asks you questions?

LENNIE (*stops chewing in the middle of a bite, swallows painfully. His face contorts with thought*). I . . . I ain't gonna say a word.

GEORGE. Good boy. That's fine. Say, maybe you're gittin' better. I bet I can let you tend the rabbits . . . specially if you remember as good as that!

LENNIE (*choking with pride*). I can remember, by God!

GEORGE (*as though remembering something, points his knife at* LENNIE's *chest*). Lennie, I want you to look around here. Think you can remember this place? The ranch is 'bout a quarter mile up that way. Just follow the river and you can get here.

LENNIE (*looking around carefully*). Sure, I can remember here. Didn't I remember 'bout not gonna say a word?

GEORGE. 'Course you did. Well, look, Lennie, if you just happen to get in trouble, I want you to come right here and hide in the brush.

LENNIE (*slowly*). Hide in the brush.

GEORGE. Hide in the brush until I come for you. Think you can remember that?

LENNIE. Sure I can, George. Hide in the brush till you come for me!

GEORGE. But you ain't gonna get in no trouble. Because if you do I won't let you tend the rabbits.

LENNIE. I won't get in no trouble. I ain't gonna say a word.

GEORGE. You got it. Anyways, I hope so. (GEORGE *stretches out on his blankets. The light dies slowly out of the fire until only the faces of the two men can be seen.* GEORGE *is still eating from his can of beans.*) It's gonna be nice sleeping here. Lookin' up . . . and the leaves . . . Don't build no more fire. We'll let her die. Jesus, you feel free when you ain't got a job—if you ain't hungry. (*They sit silently for a few moments. A night owl is heard far off. From across the river there comes the sound of a coyote howl and on the heels of the howl all the dogs in the country start to bark.*)

LENNIE (*from almost complete darkness*). George?

GEORGE. What do you want?

LENNIE. Let's have different color rabbits, George.

GEORGE. Sure. Red rabbits and blue rabbits and green rabbits. Millions of 'em!

LENNIE. Furry ones, George. Like I seen at the fair in Sacramento.

GEORGE. Sure. Furry ones.

LENNIE. 'Cause I can jus' as well go away, George, and live in a cave.

GEORGE (*amiably*). Aw, shut up.

LENNIE (*after a long pause*). George?

GEORGE. What is it?

LENNIE. I'm shutting up, George. (*A coyote howls again.*)

CURTAIN

SCENE II

Late Friday morning.
The interior of a bunkhouse.
Walls, white-washed board and bat. Floors unpainted.
There is a heavy square table with upended boxes around it used for chairs. Over each bunk there is a box nailed to the wall which serves as two shelves on which are the private possessions of the working men.
On top of each bunk there is a large noisy alarm clock ticking madly.
The sun is streaking through the windows. Note: Articles in the boxes on wall are soap, talcum powder, razors, pulp magazines, medicine bottles, combs, and from nails on the sides of the boxes a few neckties.
There is a hanging light from the ceiling over the table, with a round dim reflector on it.
The curtain rises on an empty stage. Only the ticking of the many alarm clocks is heard.
CANDY, GEORGE *and* LENNIE *are first seen passing the open window of the bunkhouse.*

CANDY. This is the bunkhouse here. Door's around this side. (*The latch on the door rises and* CANDY *enters, a stoop-shouldered old man. He is dressed in blue jeans and a denim coat. He carries a big push broom in his left hand. His right hand is gone at the wrist. He grasps things with his right arm between arm and side. He walks into the room followed by* GEORGE *and* LENNIE. *Conversationally.*) The boss was expecting you last night. He was sore as hell when you wasn't here to go out this morning. (*Points with his handless arm.*) You can have them two beds there.

GEORGE. I'll take the top one . . . I don't want you falling down on me. (*Steps over to the bunk and throws his blankets down. He looks into the nearly empty box shelf over it, then picks up a small yellow can.*) Say, what the hell's this?

CANDY. I don't know.

GEORGE. Says "positively kills lice, roaches and other scourges." What the hell kinda beds you givin' us, anyway? We don't want no pants rabbits.

CANDY (*shifts his broom, holding it between his elbow and his side, takes the can in his left hand and studies the label carefully*). Tell you what . . . last guy that had this bed was a blacksmith. Helluva nice fellow. Clean a guy as you'd want to meet. Used to wash his hands even *after* he et.

GEORGE (*with gathering anger*). Then how come he got pillow-pigeons? (LENNIE *puts his blankets on his bunk and sits down, watching* GEORGE *with his mouth slightly open.*)

CANDY. Tell you what. This here blacksmith, name of Whitey, was the kinda guy that would put that stuff around even if there wasn't no bugs. Tell you what he used to do. He'd peel *his* boiled potatoes and take out every little spot before he et it, and if there was a red splotch on an egg, he'd scrape it off. Finally quit about the food. That's the kind of guy Whitey was. Clean. Used to dress up Sundays even when he wasn't goin' no place. Put on a necktie even, and then set in the bunkhouse.

GEORGE (*skeptically*). I ain't so sure. What da' ya say he quit for?

CANDY (*puts the can in his pocket, rubs his bristly white whiskers with his knuckles*). Why . . . he just quit the way a guy will. Says it was the food. Didn't give no other reason. Just says "give me my time" one night, the way any guy would. (GEORGE *lifts his bed tick and looks underneath, leans over and inspects the sacking carefully.* LENNIE *does the same with his bed.*)

GEORGE (*half satisfied*). Well, if there's any grey-backs in this bed, you're gonna hear from me! (*He unrolls his blankets and puts his razor and bar of soap and comb and bottle of pills, his liniment and leather wristband in the box.*)

CANDY. I guess the boss'll be out here in a minute to write your name in. He sure was burned when you wasn't here this morning. Come right in when we was eatin' breakfast and says, "Where the hell's them new men?" He give the stable buck hell too. Stable buck's a nigger.

GEORGE. Nigger, huh!

CANDY. Yeah. (*Continues.*) Nice fellow too. Got a crooked back where a horse kicked him. Boss gives him hell when he's mad. But the stable buck don't give a damn about that.

GEORGE. What kinda guy is the boss?

CANDY. Well, he's a pretty nice fella for a boss. Gets mad sometimes. But he's pretty nice. Tell you what. Know what he done Christmas? Brung a gallon of whiskey right in here and says, "Drink hearty, boys, Christmas comes but once a year!"

GEORGE. The hell he did! A whole gallon?

CANDY. Yes, sir. Jesus, we had fun! They let the nigger come in that night. Well, sir, a little skinner name Smitty took after the nigger. Done pretty good too. The guys wouldn't let him use his feet so the nigger got him. If he could a used his feet Smitty says he would have killed the nigger. The guys says on account the nigger got a crooked back Smitty can't use his feet. (*He smiles in reverie at the memory.*)

GEORGE. Boss the owner?

CANDY. Naw! Superintendent. Big land company. . . . Yes, sir, that night . . . he comes right in here with a whole gallon . . . he set right over there and says, "Drink hearty, boys," . . . he says. . . . (*The door opens. Enter the* BOSS. *He is a stocky man, dressed in blue jean trousers, flannel shirt, a black unbuttoned vest and a black coat. He wears a soiled brown Stetson hat, a pair of high-heeled boots and spurs. Ordinarily he puts his thumbs in his belt.* CANDY, *shuffling towards the door, rubbing his whiskers with his knuckles as he goes.*) Them guys just come. (CANDY *exits and shuts the door behind him.*)

BOSS. I wrote Murray and Ready I wanted two men this morning. You got your work slips?

GEORGE (*digs in his pockets, produces two slips, and hands them to the* BOSS). Here they are.

BOSS (*reading the slips*). Well, I see it wasn't Murray and Ready's fault. It says right here on the slip, you was to be here for work this morning.

GEORGE. Bus driver give us a bum steer. We had to walk ten miles. That bus driver says we was here when we wasn't. We couldn't thumb no rides. (GEORGE *scowls meaningly at* LENNIE *and* LENNIE *nods to show that he understands.*)

BOSS. Well, I had to send out the grain teams short two buckers. It won't do any good to go out now until after dinner. You'd get lost. (*Pulls out his time book, opens it to where a pencil is stuck between the leaves. Licks his pencil carefully.*) What's your name?

GEORGE. George Milton.

BOSS. George Milton. (*Writing.*) And what's yours?

GEORGE. His name's Lennie Small.

BOSS. Lennie Small. (*Writing.*) Le's see, this is the twentieth. Noon the twentieth . . . (*Makes positive mark. Closes the book and puts it in his pocket.*) Where you boys been workin'?

GEORGE. Up around Weed.

BOSS (*to* LENNIE). You too?

GEORGE. Yeah. Him too.

BOSS (*to* LENNIE). Say, you're a big fellow, ain't you?

GEORGE. Yeah, he can work like hell, too.

BOSS. He ain't much of a talker, though, is he?

GEORGE. No, he ain't. But he's a hell of a good worker. Strong as a bull.

LENNIE (*smiling*). I'm strong as a bull. (GEORGE *scowls at him and* LENNIE *drops his head in shame at having forgotten.*)

BOSS (*sharply*). You are, huh? What can you do?

GEORGE. He can do anything.

BOSS (*addressing* LENNIE). What can you do? (LENNIE, *looking at* GEORGE, *gives a high nervous chuckle.*)

GEORGE (*quickly*). Anything you tell him. He's a good skinner. He can wrestle grain bags, drive a cultivator. He can do anything. Just give him a try.

BOSS (*turning to* GEORGE). Then why don't you let *him* answer? (LENNIE *laughs.*) What's he laughing about?

GEORGE. He laughs when he gets excited.

BOSS. Yeah?

GEORGE (*loudly*). But he's a goddamn good worker. I ain't saying he's bright, because he ain't. But he can put up a four hundred pound bale.

BOSS (*hooking his thumbs in his belt*). Say, what you sellin'?

GEORGE. Huh?

BOSS. I said what stake you got in this guy? You takin' his pay away from him?

GEORGE. No. Of course I ain't!
BOSS. Hell, I never seen one guy take so much trouble for another guy. I just like to know what your percentage is.

GEORGE. He's my . . . cousin. I told his ole lady I'd take care of him. He got kicked in the head by a horse when he was a kid. He's all right. . . . Just ain't bright. But he can do anything you tell him.

BOSS (*turning half away*). Well, God knows he don't need no brains to buck barley bags. (*He turns back.*) But don't you try to put nothing over, Milton. I got my eye on you. Why'd you quit in Weed?

GEORGE (*promptly*). Job was done.

BOSS. What kind of job?

GEORGE. Why . . . we was diggin' a cesspool.

BOSS (*after a pause*). All right. But don't try to put nothing over 'cause you can't get away with nothing. I seen wise guys before. Go out with the grain teams after dinner. They're out pickin' up barley with the thrashin' machines. Go out with Slim's team.

GEORGE. Slim?

BOSS. Yeah. Big, tall skinner. You'll see him at dinner. (*Up to this time the* BOSS *has been full of business. He has been calm and suspicious. In the following lines he relaxes, but gradually, as though he wanted to talk but felt always the burden of his position. He turns toward the door, but hesitates and allows a little warmth into his manner.)* Been on the road long?

GEORGE (*obviously on guard*). We was three days in 'Frisco lookin' at the boards.

BOSS (*with heavy jocularity*). Didn't go to no night clubs, I 'spose?

GEORGE (*stiffly*). We was lookin' for a job.

BOSS (*attempting to be friendly*). That's a great town if you got a little jack, Frisco.

GEORGE (*refusing to be drawn in*). We didn't have no jack for nothing like that.

BOSS (*realizes there is no contact to establish; grows rigid with his position again*). Go out with the grain teams after dinner. When my hands work hard they get pie and when they loaf they bounce down the road on their can. You ask anybody about me. (*He turns and walks out of bunkhouse.*)

GEORGE (*turns to* LENNIE). So you wasn't gonna say a word! You was gonna leave your big flapper shut. I was gonna do the talkin'. . . . You goddamn near lost us the job!

LENNIE (*stares hopelessly at his hands*). I forgot.

GEORGE. You forgot. You always forget. Now, he's got his eye on us. Now, we gotta be careful and not make no slips. You keep your big flapper shut after this.

LENNIE. He talked like a kinda nice guy towards the last.

GEORGE (*angrily*). He's the boss, ain't he? Well, he's the boss first an' a nice guy afterwards. Don't you have nothin' to do with no boss, except do your work and draw your pay. You can't never tell whether you're talkin' to the nice guy or the boss. Just keep your goddamn mouth shut. Then you're all right.

LENNIE. George?

GEORGE. What you want now?

LENNIE. I wasn't kicked in the head with no horse, was I, George?

GEORGE. Be a damn good thing if you was. Save everybody a hell of a lot of trouble!

LENNIE (*flattered*). You says I was your cousin.

GEORGE. Well, that was a goddamn lie. And I'm glad it was. Why, if I was a relative of yours—(*He stops and listens, then steps to the front door, and looks out.*) Say, what the hell you doin', listenin'?

CANDY (*comes slowly into the room. By a rope, he leads an ancient drag-footed, blind sheep dog. Guides it from running into a table leg, with the rope. Sits down on a box, and presses the hind quarters of the old dog down*). Naw . . . I wasn't listenin'. . . . I was just standin' in the shade a minute, scratchin' my dog. I jest now finished swamping out the washhouse.

GEORGE. You was pokin' your big nose into our business! I don't like nosey guys.

CANDY (*looks uneasily from* GEORGE *to* LENNIE *and then back*). I jest come there . . . I didn't hear nothing you guys was sayin'. I ain't interested in nothing you was sayin'. A guy on a ranch don't never listen. Nor he don't ast no questions.

GEORGE (*slightly mollified*). Damn right he don't! Not if the guy wants to stay workin' long. (*His manner changes*). That's a helluva ole dog.

CANDY. Yeah. I had him ever since he was a pup. God, he was a good sheep dog, when he was young. (*Rubs his cheek with his knuckles.*) How'd you like the boss?

GEORGE. Pretty good! Seemed all right.

CANDY. He's a nice fella. You got ta take him right, of course. He's runnin' this ranch. He don't take no nonsense.

GEORGE. What time do we eat? Eleven-thirty? (CURLEY *enters. He is dressed in working clothes. He wears brown high-heeled boots and has a glove on his left hand.*)

CURLEY. Seen my ole man?

CANDY. He was here just a minute ago, Curley. Went over to the cookhouse, I think.

CURLEY. I'll try to catch him. (*Looking over at the new men, measuring them. Unconsciously bends his elbow and closes his hand and goes into a slight crouch. He walks gingerly close to* LENNIE.) You the new guys my ole man was waitin' for?

GEORGE. Yeah. We just come in.

CURLEY. How's it come you wasn't here this morning?

GEORGE. Got off the bus too soon.

CURLEY (*again addressing* LENNIE). My ole man got to get the grain out. Ever bucked barley?

GEORGE (*quickly*). Hell, yes. Done a lot of it.

CURLEY. I mean him. (*To* LENNIE.) Ever bucked barley?

GEORGE. Sure he has.

CURLEY (*irritatedly*). Let the big guy talk!

GEORGE. 'Spose he don't want ta talk?

CURLEY (*pugnaciously*). By Christ, he's gotta talk when he's spoke to. What the hell you shovin' into this for?

GEORGE (*stands up and speaks coldly*). Him and me travel together.

CURLEY. Oh, so it's that way?

GEORGE (*tense and motionless*). What way?

CURLEY (*letting the subject drop*). And you won't let the big guy talk? Is that it?

GEORGE. He can talk if he wants to tell you anything. (*He nods slightly to* LENNIE.)

LENNIE (*in a frightened voice*). We just come in.

CURLEY. Well, next time you answer when you're spoke to, then.

GEORGE. He didn't do nothing to you.

CURLEY (*measuring him*). You drawin' cards this hand?

GEORGE (*quietly*). I might.

CURLEY (*stares at him for a moment, his threat moving to the future*). I'll see you get a chance to ante, anyway. (*He walks out of the room.*)

GEORGE (*after he has made his exit*). Say, what the hell's he got on his shoulder? Lennie didn't say nothing to him.

CANDY (*looks cautiously at the door*). That's the boss's son. Curley's pretty handy. He done quite a bit in the ring. The guys say he's pretty handy.

GEORGE. Well, let 'im be handy. He don't have to take after Lennie. Lennie didn't do nothing to him.

CANDY (*considering*). Well . . . tell you what, Curley's like a lot a little guys. He hates big guys. He's alla time pickin' scraps with big guys. Kinda like he's mad at 'em because *he* ain't a big guy. You seen little guys like that, ain't you—always scrappy?

GEORGE. Sure, I seen plenty tough little guys. But this here Curley better not make no mistakes about Lennie. Lennie ain't handy, see, but this Curley punk's gonna get hurt if he messes around with Lennie.

CANDY (*skeptically*). Well, Curley's pretty handy. You know, it never did seem right to me. 'Spose Curley jumps a big guy and licks him. Everybody says what a game guy Curley is. Well, 'spose he jumps 'im and gits licked, everybody says the big guy oughta pick somebody his own size. Seems like Curley ain't givin' nobody a chance.

GEORGE (*watching the door*). Well, he better watch out for Lennie. Lennie ain't no fighter. But Lennie's strong and quick and Lennie don't know no rules. (*Walks to the square table, and sits down on one of the boxes. Picks up scattered cards and pulls them together and shuffles them.*)

CANDY. Don't tell Curley I said none of this. He'd slough me! He jus' don't give a damn. Won't ever get canned because his ole man's the boss!

GEORGE (*cuts the cards. Turns over and looks at each one as he throws it down*). This guy Curley sounds like a son-of-a-bitch to me! I don't like mean little guys!

CANDY. Seems to me like he's worse lately. He got married a couple of weeks ago. Wife lives over in the boss's house. Seems like Curley's worse'n ever since he got married. Like he's settin' on a ant-hill an' a big red ant come up an' nipped 'im on the turnip. Just feels so goddanm miserable he'll strike at anything that moves. I'm kinda sorry for 'im.

GEORGE. Maybe he's showin' off for his wife.

CANDY. You seen that glove on his left hand?

GEORGE. Sure I seen it!

CANDY. Well, that glove's full of vaseline.

GEORGE. Vaseline? What the hell for?

CANDY. Curley says he's keepin' that hand soft for his wife.

GEORGE. That's a dirty kind of a thing to tell around.

CANDY. I ain't quite so sure. I seen such funny things a guy will do to try to be nice. I ain't sure. But you jus' wait till you see Curley's wife!

GEORGE (*begins to lay out a solitaire hand, speaks casually*). Is she purty?

CANDY. Yeah. Purty, but—

GEORGE (*studying his cards*). But what?

CANDY. Well, she got the eye.

GEORGE (*still playing at his solitaire hand*). Yeah? Married two weeks an' got the eye? Maybe that's why Curley's pants is fulla ants.

CANDY. Yes, sir, I seen her give Slim the eye. Slim's a jerkline skinner. Hell of a nice fella. Well, I seen her give Slim the eye. Curley never seen it. And I seen her give a skinner named Carlson the eye.

GEORGE (*pretending a very mild interest*). Looks like we was gonna have fun!

CANDY (*stands up*). Know what I think? (*Waits for an answer.* GEORGE *doesn't answer.*) Well, I think Curley's married himself a tart.

GEORGE (*casually*). He ain't the first. Black queen on a red king. Yes, sir . . . there's plenty done that!

CANDY (*moves towards the door, leading his dog out with him*). I got to be settin' out the wash basins for the guys. The teams'll be in before long. You guys gonna buck barley?

GEORGE. Yeah.

CANDY. You won't tell Curley nothing I said?

GEORGE. Hell, no!

CANDY (*just before he goes out the door, he turns back*). Well, you look her over, mister. You see if she ain't a tart! (*He exits.*)

GEORGE (*continuing to play out his solitaire. He turns to* LENNIE). Look, Lennie, this here ain't no set-up. You gonna have trouble with that Curley guy. I seen that kind before. You know what he's doin'. He's kinda feelin' you out. He figures he's got you scared. And he's gonna take a sock at you, first chance he gets.

LENNIE (*frightened*). I don't want no trouble. Don't let him sock me, George!

GEORGE. I hate them kind of bastards. I seen plenty of 'em. Like the ole guy says: "Curley don't take no chances. He always figures to win." (*Thinks for a moment.*) If he tangles with you, Lennie, we're goin' get the can. Don't make no mistake about that. He's the boss's kid. Look, you try to keep away from him, will you? Don't never speak to him. If he comes in here you move clear to the other side of the room. Will you remember that, Lennie?

LENNIE (*mourning*). I don't want no trouble. I never done nothing to him!

GEORGE. Well, that won't do you no good, if Curley wants to set himself up for a fighter. Just don't have nothing to do with him. Will you remember?

LENNIE. Sure, George . . . I ain't gonna say a word. (*Sounds of the teams coming in from the fields, jingling of harness, croak of heavy laden axles, men talking to and cussing the horses. Crack of a whip and from a distance a voice calling.*)

SLIM'S VOICE. Stable buck! Hey! Stable buck!

GEORGE. Here come the guys. Just don't say nothing.

LENNIE (*timidly*). You ain't mad, George?

GEORGE. I ain't mad at you. I'm mad at this here Curley bastard! I wanted we should get a little stake together. Maybe a hundred dollars. You keep away from Curley.

LENNIE. Sure I will. I won't say a word.

GEORGE (*hesitating*). Don't let 'im pull you in—but—if the son-of-a-bitch socks you—let him have it!

LENNIE. Let him have what, George?

GEORGE. Never mind. . . . Look, if you get in any kind of trouble, you remember what I told you to do.

LENNIE. If I get in any trouble, you ain't gonna let me tend the rabbits?

GEORGE. That's not what I mean. You remember where we slept last night. Down by the river?

LENNIE. Oh, sure I remember. I go there and hide in the brush until you come for me.

GEORGE. That's it. Hide till I come for you. Don't let nobody see you. Hide in the brush by the river. Now say that over.

LENNIE. Hide in the brush by the river. Down in the brush by the river.

GEORGE. If you get in trouble.

LENNIE. If I get in trouble.
(*A brake screeckes outside and a call: "Stable buck, oh, stable buck!" "Where the hell's that goddamn nigger?" Suddenly* CURLEY'S WIFE *is standing in the door. Full, heavily rouged lips. Wide-spaced, made-up eyes, her fingernails are bright red, her hair hangs in little rolled clusters like sausages. She wears a cotton house dress and red mules, on the insteps of which are little bouquets of red ostrich feathers.* GEORGE *and* LENNIE *look up at her.*)

CURLEY'S WIFE. I'm lookin' for Curley!

GEORGE (*looks away from her*). He was in here a minute ago but he went along.

CURLEY'S WIFE (*puts her hands behind her back and leans against the door frame so that her body is thrown forward*). You're the new fellas that just come, ain't you?

GEORGE (*sullenly*). Yeah.

CURLEY'S WIFE (*bridles a little and inspects her fingernails*). Sometimes Curley's in here.

GEORGE (*brusquely*). Well, he ain't now!

CURLEY'S WIFE (*playfully*). Well, if he ain't, I guess I'd better look some place else. (LENNIE *watches her, fascinated.*)

GEORGE. If I see Curley I'll pass the word you was lookin' for him.

CURLEY'S WIFE. Nobody can't blame a person for lookin'.

GEORGE. That depends what she's lookin' for.

CURLEY'S WIFE (*a little wearily, dropping her coquetry*). I'm jus' lookin' for somebody to talk to. Don't you never jus' want to talk to somebody?

SLIM (*offstage*). Okay! Put that lead pair in the north stalls.

CURLEY'S WIFE (*to* SLIM, *offstage*). Hi, Slim!

SLIM (*voice offstage*). Hello.

CURLEY'S WIFE. I—I'm trying to find Curley.

SLIM'S VOICE (*offstage*). Well, you ain't tryin' very hard. I seen him goin' in your house.

CURLEY'S WIFE. I—I'm tryin' to find Curley. and LENNIE). I gotta be goin'! (*She exits hurriedly.*)

GEORGE (*looking around at* LENNIE). Jesus, what a tramp! So, that's what Curley picks for a wife. God Almighty, did you smell that stink she's got on? I can still smell her. Don't have to see *her* to know she's around.

LENNIE. She's purty!

GEORGE. Yeah. And she's sure hidin' it. Curley got his work ahead of him.

LENNIE (*still staring at the doorway where she was*). Gosh, she's purty!

GEORGE (*turning furiously at him*). Listen to me, you crazy bastard. Don't you even look at that bitch. I don't care what she says or what she does. I seen 'em poison before, but I ain't never seen no piece of jail bait worse than her. Don't you even smell near her!

LENNIE. I never smelled, George!

GEORGE. No, you never. But when she was standin' there showin' her legs, you wasn't lookin' the other way neither!

LENNIE. I never meant no bad things, George. Honest I never.

GEORGE. Well, you keep away from her. You let Curley take the rap. He let himself in for it. (*Disgustedly.*) Glove full of vaseline. I bet he's eatin' raw eggs and writin' to patent-medicine houses.

LENNIE (*cries out*). I don't like this place. This ain't no good place. I don't like this place!

GEORGE. Listen—I don't like it here no better than you do. But we gotta keep it till we get a stake. We're flat. We gotta get a stake. (*Goes back to the table, thoughtfully.*) If we can get just a few dollars in the poke we'll shove off and go up to the American River and pan gold. Guy can make a couple dollars a day there.

LENNIE (*eagerly*). Let's go, George. Let's get out of here. It's mean here.

GEORGE (*shortly*). I tell you we gotta stay a little while. We gotta get a stake. (*The sounds of running water and rattle of basins are heard.*) Shut up now, the guys'll be comin' in! (*Pensively.*) Maybe we ought to wash up. . . . But hell, we ain't done nothin' to get dirty.

SLIM (*enters. He is a tall, dark man in blue jeans and a short denim jacket. He carries a crushed Stetson hat under his arm and combs his long dark damp hair straight back. He stands and moves with a kind of majesty. He finishes combing his hair. Smoothes out his crushed hat, creases it in the middle and puts it on. In a gentle voice*). It's brighter'n a bitch outside. Can't hardly see nothing in here. You the new guys?

GEORGE. Just come.

SLIM. Goin' to buck barley?

GEORGE. That's what the boss says.

SLIM. Hope you get on my team.

GEORGE. Boss said we'd go with a jerk-line skinner named Slim.

SLIM. That's me.

GEORGE. You a jerk-line skinner?

SLIM (*in self-disparagement*). I can snap 'em around a little.

GEORGE (*terribly impressed*). That kinda makes you Jesus Christ on this ranch, don't it?

SLIM (*obviously pleased*). Oh, nuts!

GEORGE (*chuckles*). Like the man says, "The boss tells you what to do. But if you want to know how to do it, you got to ask the mule skinner." The man says any guy that can drive twelve Arizona jack rabbits with a jerk line can fall in a toilet and come up with a mince pie under each arm.

SLIM (*laughing*). Well, I hope you get on my team. I got a pair a punks that don't know a barley bag from a blue ball. You guys ever bucked any barley?

GEORGE. Hell, yes. I ain't nothin' to scream about, but that big guy there can put up more grain alone than most pairs can.

SLIM (*looks approvingly at* GEORGE). You guys travel around together?

GEORGE. Sure. We kinda look after each other. (*Points at* LENNIE *with his thumb.*) He ain't bright. Hell of a good worker, though. Hell of a nice fella too. I've knowed him for a long time.

SLIM. Ain't many guys travel around together. I don't know why. Maybe everybody in the whole damn world is scared of each other.

GEORGE. It's a lot nicer to go 'round with a guy you know. You get used to it an' then it ain't no fun alone any more. (*Enter* CARLSON. *Big-stomached, powerful man. His head still drips water from scrubbing and dousing.*)

CARLSON. Hello, Slim! (*He looks at* GEORGE *and* LENNIE.)

SLIM. These guys just come.

CARLSON. Glad to meet ya! My name's Carlson.

GEORGE. I'm George Milton. This here's Lennie Small.

CARLSON. Glad to meet you. He ain't very small. (*Chuckles at his own joke.*) He ain't small at all. Meant to ask you, Slim, how's your bitch? I seen she wasn't under your wagon this morning.

SLIM. She slang her pups last night. Nine of 'em. I drowned four of 'em right off. She couldn't feed that many.

CARLSON. Got five left, huh?

SLIM. Yeah. Five. I kep' the biggest.

CARLSON. What kinda dogs you think they gonna be?

SLIM. I don't know. Some kind of shepherd, I guess. That's the most kind I seen around here when she's in heat.

CARLSON (*laughs*). I had an airdale an' a guy down the road got one of them little white floozy dogs, well, she was in heat and the guy locks her up. But my airedale, named Tom he was, he et a woodshed clear down to the roots to get to her. Guy come over one day, he's sore as hell, he says, "I wouldn't mind if my bitch had pups, but Christ Almighty, this morning she slang a litter of Shetland ponies. . . ." (*Takes off his hat and scratches his head.*) Got five pups, huh! Gonna keep all of 'em?

SLIM. I don' know, gotta keep 'em awhile, so they can drink Lulu's milk.

CARLSON (*thoughtfully*). Well, looka here, Slim, I been thinkin'. That dog of Candy's is so goddamn old he can't hardly walk. Stinks like hell. Every time Candy brings him in the bunkhouse. I can smell him two or three days. Why don't you get Candy to shoot his ol' dog, and give him one of them pups to raise up? I can smell that dog a mile off. Got no teeth. Can't eat. Candy feeds him milk. He can't chew nothing else. And leadin' him around on a string so he

don't bump into things . . . (*The triangle outside begins to ring wildly. Continues for a few moments, then stops suddenly.*) There she goes! (*Outside there is a burst of voices as a group of men go by.*)

SLIM (*to LENNIE and GEORGE*). You guys better come on while they's still somethin' to eat. Won't be nothing left in a couple of minutes. (*Exit SLIM and CARLSON, LENNIE watches GEORGE excitedly.*)

LENNIE. George!

GEORGE (*rumpling his cards into a pile*). Yeah, I heard 'im, Lennie . . . I'll ask 'im!

LENNIE (*excitedly*). A brown and white one.

GEORGE. Come on, let's get dinner. I don't know whether he's got a brown and white one.

LENNIE. You ask him right away, George, so he won't kill no more of 'em!

GEORGE. Sure! Come on now—le's go. (*They start for the door.*)

CURLEY (*bounces in, angrily*). You seen a girl around here?

GEORGE (*coldly*). 'Bout half an hour ago, mebbe.

CURLEY. Well, what the hell was she doin'?

GEORGE (*insultingly*). She *said* she was lookin' for you.

CURLEY (*measures both men with his eyes for a moment*). Which way did she go?

GEORGE. I don't know. I didn't watch her go. (CURLEY *scowls at him a moment and then turns and hurries out the door.*) You know, Lennie, I'm scared I'm gonna tangle with that bastard myself. I hate his guts! Jesus Christ, come on! They won't be a damn thing left to eat.

LENNIE. Will you ask him about a brown and white one? (*They exeunt.*)

CURTAIN

ACT TWO

SCENE I

About seven-thirty Friday evening.
Same bunkhouse interior as in last scene.
The evening light is seen coming in through the window, but it is quite dark in the interior of the bunkhouse.
From outside comes the sound of a horseshoe game. Thuds on the dirt and occasional clangs as a shoe hits the peg. Now and then voices are raised in approval or derision: "That's a good one." . . . "Goddamn right it's a good one." . . . "Here goes for a ringer. I need a ringer." . . . "Goddamn near got it, too."
SLIM and GEORGE come into the darkening bunkhouse together. SLIM reaches up and turns on the tin-shaded electric light. Sits down on a box at the table. GEORGE takes his place opposite.

SLIM. It wasn't nothing. I would of had to drown most of them pups anyway. No need to thank me about that.

GEORGE. Wasn't much to you, mebbe, but it was a hell of a lot to him. Jesus Christ, I don't know how we're gonna get him to sleep in here. He'll want to stay right out in the barn. We gonna have trouble keepin' him from gettin' right in the box with them pups.

SLIM. Say, you sure was right about him. Maybe he ain't bright—but I never seen such a worker. He damn near killed his partner buckin' barley. He'd take his end of that sack (*a gesture*) pretty near kill his partner. God Almighty, I never seen such a strong guy.

GEORGE (*proudly*). You just tell Lennie what to do and he'll do it if it don't take no figuring. (*Outside the sound of the horseshoe game goes on:* "Son of a bitch if I can win a goddamn game." . . . "Me neither. You'd think them shoes was anvils.")

SLIM. Funny how you and him string along together.

GEORGE. What's so funny about it?

SLIM. Oh, I don't know. Hardly none of the guys ever travels around together. I hardly never seen two guys travel together. You know how the hands are. They come in and get their bunk and work a month and then they quit and go on alone. Never seem to give a damn about nobody. Jest seems kinda funny. A cuckoo like him and a smart guy like you traveling together.

GEORGE. I ain't so bright neither or I wouldn't be buckin' barley for my fifty and found. If I was bright, if I was even a little bit smart, I'd have my own place and I'd be bringin' in my own crops 'stead of doin' all the work and not gettin' what comes up out of the ground. (*He falls silent for a moment.*)

SLIM. A guy'd like to do that. Sometimes I'd like to cuss a string of mules that was my own mules.

GEORGE. It ain't so funny, him and me goin' round together. Him and me was both born in Auburn. I knowed his aunt. She took him when he was a baby and raised him up. When his aunt died Lennie jus' come along with me, out workin'. Got kinda used to each other after a little while.

SLIM. Uh huh.

GEORGE. First I used to have a hell of a lot of fun with him. Used to play jokes on him because he was too dumb to take care of himself. But, hell, he was too dumb even to know when he had a joke played on him. (*Sarcastically.*) Hell, yes, I had fun! Made me seem goddamn smart alongside of him.

SLIM. I seen it that way.

GEORGE. Why, he'd do any damn thing I tole him. If I tole him to walk over a cliff, over he'd go. You know that wasn't so damn much fun after a while. He never got mad about it, neither. I've beat hell out of him and he could bust every bone in my body jest with his hands. But he never lifted a finger against me.

SLIM (*braiding a bull whip*). Even if you socked him, wouldn't he?

GEORGE. No, by God! I tell you what made me stop playing jokes. One day a bunch of guys was standin' aroun' up on the Sacramento river. I was feelin' pretty smart. I turns to Lennie and I says, "Jump in."

SLIM. What happened?

GEORGE. He jumps. Couldn't swim a stroke. He damn near drowned. And he was so nice to me for pullin' him out. Clean forgot I tole him to jump in. Well, I ain't done nothin' like that no more. Makes me kinda sick tellin' about it.

SLIM. He's a nice fella. A guy don't need no sense to be a nice fella. Seems to be sometimes it's jest the other way round. Take a real smart guy, he ain't hardly ever a nice fella.

GEORGE (*stacking the scattered cards and getting his solitaire game ready again*). I ain't got no people. I seen guys that go round on the ranches alone. That ain't no good. They don't have no fun. After a while they get mean.

SLIM (*quietly*). Yeah, I seen 'em get mean. I seen 'em get so they don't want to talk to nobody. Some ways they got to. You take a bunch of guys all livin' in one room an' by God they got to mind their own business. 'Bout the only private thing a guy's got is where he come from and where he's goin'.

GEORGE. 'Course Lennie's a goddamn nuisance most of the time. But you get used to goin' round with a guy and you can't get rid of him. I mean you get used to him an' you can't get rid of bein' used to him. I'm sure drippin' at the mouth. I ain't told nobody all this before.

SLIM. Do you want to git rid of him?

GEORGE. Well, he gets in trouble all the time. Because he's so goddamn dumb. Like what happened in Weed. (*He stops, alarmed at what he has said.*) You wouldn't tell nobody?

SLIM (*calmly*). What did he do in Weed?

GEORGE. You wouldn't tell?—No, 'course you wouldn't.

SLIM. What did he do?

GEORGE. Well, he seen this girl in a red dress. Dumb bastard like he is he wants to touch everything he likes. Jest wants to feel of it. So he reaches out to feel this red dress. Girl lets out a squawk and that gets Lennie all mixed up. He holds on 'cause that's the only thing he can think to do.

SLIM. The hell!

GEORGE. Well, this girl squawks her head off. I'm right close and I hear all the yellin', so I comes a-running. By that time Lennie's scared to death. You know, I had to sock him over the head with a fence picket to make him let go.

SLIM. So what happens then?

GEORGE (*carefully building his solitaire hand*). Well, she runs in and tells the law she's been raped. The guys in Weed start out to lynch Lennie. So there we sit in an irrigation ditch, under water all the rest of that day. Got only our heads stickin' out of water, up under the grass that grows out of the side of the ditch. That night we run outa there.

SLIM. Didn't hurt the girl none, huh?

GEORGE. Hell, no, he jes' scared her.

SLIM. He's a funny guy.

GEORGE. Funny! Why, one time, you know what that big baby done! He was walking along a road—(*Enter* LENNIE *through the door. He wears his coat over his shoulder like a cape and walks hunched over.*) Hi, Lennie. How do you like your pup?

LENNIE (*breathlessly*). He's brown and white jus' like I wanted. (*Goes directly to his bunk and lies down. Face to the wall and knees drawn up.*)

GEORGE (*puts down his cards deliberately*). Lennie!

LENNIE (*over his shoulder*). Huh? What you want, George?

GEORGE (*sternly*). I tole ya, ya couldn't bring that pup in here.

LENNIE. What pup, George? I ain't got no pup. (GEORGE *goes quickly over to him, grabs him by the shoulder and rolls him over. He picks up a tiny puppy from where* LENNIE *has been concealing it against his stomach.*)

LENNIE (*quickly*). Give him to me, George.

GEORGE. You get right up and take this pup to the nest. He's got to sleep with his mother. Ya want ta kill him? Jes' born last night and ya take him out of the nest. Ya take him back or I'll tell Slim not to let you have him.

LENNIE (*pleadingly*). Give him to me, George. I'll take him back. I didn't mean no bad thing, George. Honest I didn't. I jus' want to pet him a little.

GEORGE (*giving the pup to him*). All right, you get him back there quick. And don't you take him out no more. (LENNIE *scuttles out of the room.*)

SLIM. Jesus, he's just like a kid, ain't he?

GEORGE. Sure he's like a kid. There ain't no more harm in him than a kid neither, except he's so strong. I bet he won't come in here to sleep tonight. He'll sleep right alongside that box in the barn. Well, let him. He ain't doin' no harm out there. (*The light has faded out outside and it appears quite dark outside. Enter* CANDY *leading his old dog by a string.*)

CANDY. Hello, Slim. Hello, George. Didn't neither of you play horseshoes?

SLIM. I don't like to play every night.

CANDY (*goes to his bunk and sits down, presses the old blind dog to the floor beside him*). Either you guys got a slug of whiskey? I got a gut ache.

SLIM. I ain't. I'd drink it myself if I had. And I ain't got no gut ache either.

CANDY. Goddamn cabbage give it to me. I knowed it was goin' to before I ever et it. (*Enter* CARLSON *and* WHIT.)

CARLSON. Jesus, how that nigger can pitch shoes!

SLIM. He's plenty good.

WHIT. Damn right he is.

CARLSON. Yeah. He don't give nobody else a chance to win. (*Stops and sniffs the air. Looks around until he sees* CANDY's *dog.*) God Almighty, that dog stinks. Get him outa here, Candy. I don't know nothing that stinks as bad as ole dogs. You got to get him outa here.

CANDY (*lying down on his bunk, reaches over and pats the ancient dog, speaks softly*).

I been round him so much I never notice how he stinks.

CARLSON. Well, I can't stand him in here. That stink hangs round even after he's gone. (*Walks over and stands looking down at the dog.*) Got no teeth. All stiff with rheumatism. He ain't no good to you, Candy. Why don't you shoot him?

CANDY (*uncomfortably*). Well, hell, I had him so long! Had him since he was a pup. I herded sheep with him. (*Proudly.*) You wouldn't think it to look at him now. He was the best damn sheep dog I ever seen.

GEORGE. I knowed a guy in Weed that had an airedale that could herd sheep. Learned it from the other dogs.

CARLSON (*sticking to his point*). Lookit, Candy. This ole dog jus' suffers itself all the time. If you was to take him out and shoot him—right in the back of the head . . . (*Leans over and points.*) . . . right there, why he never'd know what hit him.

CANDY (*unhappily*). No, I couldn't do that. I had him too long.

CARLSON (*insisting*). He don't have no fun no more. He stinks like hell. Tell you what I'll do. I'll shoot him for you. Then it won't be you that done it.

CANDY (*sits up on the bunk, rubbing his whiskers nervously, speaks plaintively*). I had him from a pup.

WHIT. Let 'im alone, Carl. I ain't a guy's dog that matters. It's the way the guy feels about the dog. Hell, I had a mutt once I wouldn't a traded for a field trial pointer.

CARLSON (*being persuasive*). Well, Candy ain't being nice to him, keeping him alive. Lookit, Slim's bitch got a litter right now. I bet you Slim would give ya one of them pups to raise up, wouldn't ya, Slim?

SLIM (*studying the dog*). Yeah. You can have a pup if you want to.

CANDY (*helplessly*) Mebbe it would hurt. (*After a moment's pause, positively.*) And I don't mind taking care of him.

CARLSON. Aw, he'd be better off dead. The way I'd shoot him he wouldn't feel nothin'. I'd put the gun right there. (*Points with his toe.*) Right back of the head.

WHIT. Aw, let 'im alone, Carl.

CARLSON. Why, hell, he wouldn't even quiver.

WHIT. Let 'im alone. (*He produces a magazine.*) Say, did you see this? Did you see this in the book here?

CARLSON. See what?

WHIT. Right there. Read that.

CARLSON. I don't want to read nothing. . . . It'd be all over in a minute, Candy. Come on.

WHIT. Did you see it, Slim? Go on, read it. Read it out loud.

SLIM. What is it?

WHIT. Read it.

SLIM (*reads slowly*). "Dear Editor: I read your mag for six years and I think it is the best on the market. I like stories by Peter Rand. I think he is a whing-ding. Give us more like the Dark Rider. I don't write many letters. Just thought I would tell you I think your mag is the best dime's worth I ever spen'." (*Looks up questioningly.*) What you want me to read that for?

WHIT. Go on, read the name at the bottom.

SLIM (*reading*). "Yours for Success, William Tenner." (*Looks up at* WHIT.) What ya want me to read that for?

CARLSON. Come on, Candy—what you say?

WHIT (*taking the magazine and closing it impressively. Talks to cover* CARLSON). You don't remember Bill Tenner? Worked here about three months ago?

SLIM (*thinking*). Little guy? Drove a cultivator?

WHIT. That's him. That's the guy.

CARLSON (*has refused to be drawn into this conversation*). Look, Candy. If you want me to, I'll put the old devil outa his misery right now and get it over with. There ain't nothing left for him. Can't eat, can't see, can't hardly walk. Tomorrow you can pick one of Slim's pups.

SLIM. Sure . . . I got a lot of 'em.

CANDY (*hopefully*). You ain't got no gun.

CARLSON. The hell, I ain't. Got a Luger. It won't hurt him none at all.

CANDY. Mebbe tomorrow. Let's wait till tomorrow.

CARLSON. I don't see no reason for it. (*Goes to his bunk, pulls a bag from underneath, takes a Luger pistol out.*) Let's get it over with. We can't sleep with him stinking around in here. (*He snaps a shell into the chamber, sets the safety and puts the pistol into his hip pocket.*)

SLIM (*as* CANDY *looks toward him for help*). Better let him go, Candy.

CANDY (*looks at each person for some hope.* WHIT *makes a gesture of protest and then resigns himself. The others look away, to avoid responsibility. At last, very softly and hopelessly*). All right. Take him.
(*He doesn't look down at the dog at all. Lies back on his bunk and crosses his arms behind his head and stares at the ceiling.* CARLSON *picks up the string, helps the dog to its feet.*)

CARLSON. Come, boy. Come on, boy. (*To* CANDY, *apologetically.*) He won't even feel it. (CANDY *does not move nor answer him.*) Come on, boy. That's the stuff. Come on. (*He leads the dog toward the door.*)

SLIM. Carlson?

CARLSON. Yeah.

SLIM (*curtly*). Take a shovel.

CARLSON. Oh, sure, I get you.
(*Exit* CARLSON *with the dog.* GEORGE *follows to the door, shuts it carefully and sets the latch.* CANDY *lies rigidly on his bunk. The next scene is one of silence and quick staccato speeches.*)

SLIM (*loudly*). One of my lead mules got a bad hoof. Got to get some tar on it. (*There is a silence.*)

GEORGE (*loudly*). Anybody like to play a little euchre?

WHIT. I'll lay out a few with you. (*They take places opposite each other at the table but* GEORGE *does not shuffle the cards. He ripples the edge of the deck. Everybody looks over at him. He stops. Silence again.*)

SLIM (*compassionately*). Candy, you can have any of them pups you want. (*There is no answer from* CANDY. *There is a little gnawing noise on the stage.*)

GEORGE. Sounds like there was a rat under there. We ought to set a trap there. (*Deep silence again.*)

WHIT (*exasperated*). What the hell is takin' him so long? Lay out some cards, why don't you? We ain't gonna get no euchre played this way.
(GEORGE *studies the backs of the cards. And after a long silence there is a shot in the distance. All the men start a bit, look quickly at* CANDY. *For a moment he continues to stare at the ceiling and then rolls slowly over and faces the wall.* GEORGE *shuffles the cards noisily and deals them.*)

GEORGE. Well, let's get to it.

WHIT (*still to cover the moment*). Yeah . . . I guess you guys really come here to work, huh?

GEORGE. How do you mean?

WHIT (*chuckles*). Well, you come on a Friday. You got two days to work till Sunday.

GEORGE. I don't see how you figure.

WHIT. You do if you been round these big ranches much. A guy that wants to look over a ranch comes in Saturday afternoon. He gets Saturday night supper, three meals on Sunday and he can quit Monday morning after breakfast without turning a hand. But you come to work on Friday noon. You got ta put in a day and a half no matter how ya figure it.

GEORGE (*quietly*). We're goin' stick around awhile. Me and Lennie's gonna roll up a stake. (*Door opens and the Negro stable buck puts in his head. A lean-faced Negro with pained eyes.*)

CROOKS. Mr. Slim.

SLIM (*who has been watching* CANDY *the whole time*). Huh? Oh, hello, Crooks, what's the matter?

CROOKS. You tole me to warm up tar for that mule's foot. I got it warm now.

SLIM. Oh, sure, Crooks. I'll come right out and put it on.

CROOKS. I can do it for you if you want, Mr. Slim.

SLIM (*standing up*). Naw, I'll take care of my own team.

CROOKS. Mr. Slim.

SLIM. Yeah.

CROOKS. That big new guy is messing round your pups in the barn.

SLIM. Well, he ain't doin' no harm. I give him one of them pups.

CROOKS. Just thought I'd tell ya. He's takin' 'em out of the nest and handling 'em. That won't do 'em no good.

SLIM. Oh, he won't hurt 'em.

GEORGE (*looks up from his cards*). If that crazy bastard is foolin' round too much jus' kick him out. (SLIM *follows the stable buck out.*)

WHIT (*examining his cards*). Seen the new kid yet?

GEORGE. What kid?

WHIT. Why, Curley's new wife.

GEORGE (*cautiously*). Yeah, I seen her.

WHIT. Well, ain't she a lulu?

GEORGE. I ain't seen that much of her.

WHIT. Well, you stick around and keep your eyes open. You'll see plenty of her. I never seen nobody like her. She's just workin' on everybody all the time. Seems like she's even workin' on the stable buck. I don't know what the hell she wants.

GEORGE (*casually*). Been any trouble since she got here? (*Obviously neither man is interested in the card game.* WHIT *lays down his hand and* GEORGE *gathers the cards in and lays out a solitaire hand.*)

WHIT. I see what you mean. No, they ain't been no trouble yet. She's only been here a couple of weeks. Curley's got yellow jackets in his drawers, but that's all so far. Every time the guys is around she shows up. She's lookin' for Curley. Or she thought she left somethin' layin' around and she's lookin' for that. Seems like she can't keep away from guys. And Curley's runnin' round like a cat lookin' for a dirt road. But they ain't been no trouble.

GEORGE. Ranch with a bunch of guys on it ain't no place for a girl. Specially like her.

WHIT. If she's give you any ideas you ought to come in town with us guys tomorrow night.

GEORGE. Why, what's doin'?

WHIT. Just the usual thing. We go in to old Susy's place. Hell of a nice place. Old Susy is a laugh. Always cracking jokes. Like she says when we come up on the front porch last Saturday night: Susy opens the door and she yells over her shoulder: "Get your coats on, girls, here comes the sheriff." She never talks dirty neither. Got five girls there.

GEORGE. What does it set you back?

WHIT. Two and a half. You can get a shot of whiskey for fifteen cents. Susy got nice chairs to set in too. If a guy don't want to flop, why, he can just set in them chairs and have a couple or three shots and just pass the time of day. Susy don't give a damn. She ain't rushin' guys through, or kicking them out if they don't want to flop.

GEORGE. Might go in and look the joint over.

WHIT. Sure. Come along. It's a hell of a lot of fun—her crackin' jokes all the time. Like she says one time, she says: "I've knew people that if they got a rag rug on the floor and a kewpie doll lamp on the phonograph they think they're runnin' a parlor house." That's Gladys's house she's talkin' about. And Susy says: "I know what you boys want," she says: "My girls is clean," she says. "And there ain't no water in my whiskey," she says. "If any you guys want to look at a kewpie doll lamp and take your chance of gettin' burned, why, you know where to go." She says: "They's guys round here walkin' bowlegged because they liked to look at a kewpie doll lamp."

GEORGE. Gladys runs the other house, huh?

WHIT. Yeah. (*Enter* CARLSON. CANDY *looks at him.*)

CARLSON. God, it's a dark night. (*Goes to his bunk; starts cleaning his pistol.*)

WHIT. We don't never go to Gladys's. Gladys gits three bucks, and two bits a shot and she don't crack no jokes. But Susy's place is clean and she got nice chairs. A guy can set in there like he lived there. Don't let no Manila Goo-Goos in, neither.

GEORGE. Aw, I don't know. Me and Lennie's rollin' up a stake. I might go in and set and have a shot, but I ain't puttin' out no two and a half.

WHIT. Well, a guy got to have some fun sometimes. (*Enter* LENNIE. LENNIE *creeps to his bunk and sits down.*)

GEORGE. Didn't bring him back in, did you, Lennie?

LENNIE. No, George, honest I didn't. See?

WHIT. Say, how about this euchre game?

GEORGE. Okay. I didn't think you wanted to play. (*Enter* CURLEY *excitedly.*)

CURLEY. Any you guys seen my wife?

WHIT. She ain't been here.

CURLEY (*looks threateningly about the room*). Where the hell's Slim?

GEORGE. Went out in the barn. He was goin' put some tar on a split hoof.

CURLEY. How long ago did he go?

GEORGE. Oh, five, ten minutes. (CURLEY *jumps out the door.*)

WHIT (*standing up*). I guess maybe I'd like to see this. Curley must be spoilin' or he wouldn't start for Slim. Curley's handy, goddamn handy. But just the same he better leave Slim alone.

GEORGE. Thinks Slim's with his wife, don't he?

WHIT. Looks like it. 'Course Slim ain't. Least I don't think Slim is. But I like to see the fuss if it comes off. Come on, le's go.

GEORGE. I don't want to git mixed up in nothing. Me and Lennie got to make a stake.

CARLSON (*finishes cleaning gun, puts it in his bag and stands up*). I'll look her over. Ain't seen a good fight in a hell of a while. (WHIT *and* CARLSON *exeunt.*)

GEORGE. You see Slim out in the barn?

LENNIE. Sure. He tole me I better not pet that pup no more, like I said.

GEORGE. Did you see that girl out there?

LENNIE. You mean Curley's girl?

GEORGE. Yeah. Did she come in the barn?

LENNIE (*cautiously*). No—anyways I never seen her.

GEORGE. You never seen Slim talkin' to her?

LENNIE. Uh-uh. She ain't been in the barn.

GEORGE. Okay. I guess them guys ain't gonna see no fight. If they's any fightin', Lennie, ya get out of the way and stay out.

LENNIE. I don't want no fight. (GEORGE *lays out his solitaire hand.* LENNIE *picks up a face card and studies it. Turns it over and studies it again.*) Both ends the same. George, why is it both ends the same?

GEORGE. I don't know. That jus' the way they make 'em. What was Slim doin' in the barn when you seen him?

LENNIE. Slim?

GEORGE. Sure, you seen him in the barn. He tole you not to pet the pups so much.

LENNIE. Oh. Yeah. He had a can of tar and a paint brush. I don't know what for.

GEORGE. You sure that girl didn't come in like she come in here today?

LENNIE. No, she never come.

GEORGE (*sighs*). You give me a good whorehouse every time. A guy can go in and get drunk and get it over all at once and no messes. And he knows how much it's goin' set him back. These tarts is jus' buckshot to a guy. (LENNIE *listens with admiration, moving his lips, and* GEORGE *continues.*) You remember Andy Cushman, Lennie? Went to grammar school same time as us?

LENNIE. The one that his ole lady used to make hot cakes for the kids?

GEORGE. Yeah. That's the one. You can remember if they's somepin to eat in it. (*Scores up some cards in his solitaire playing.*) Well, Andy's in San Quentin right now on account of a tart.

LENNIE. George?

GEORGE. Huh?

LENNIE. How long is it goin' be till we git that little place to live on the fat of the land?

GEORGE. I don't know. We gotta get a big stake together. I know a little place we can get cheap, but they ain't givin' it away. (CANDY *turns over and watches* GEORGE.)

LENNIE. Tell about that place, George.

GEORGE. I jus' tole you Jus' last night.

LENNIE. Go on, tell again.

GEORGE. Well, it's ten acres. Got a windmill. Got a little shack on it and a chicken run. Got a kitchen orchard. Cherries, apples, peaches, 'cots and nuts. Got a few berries. There's a place for alfalfa and plenty water to flood it. There's a pig pen. . . .

LENNIE (*breaking in*). And rabbits, George?

GEORGE. I could easy build a few hutches. And you could feed alfalfa to them rabbits.

LENNIE. Damn right I could. (*Excitedly.*) You goddamn right I could.

GEORGE (*his voice growing warmer*). And we could have a few pigs. I'd build a smokehouse. And when we kill a pig we could smoke the hams. When the salmon run up the river we can catch a hundred of 'em. Every Sunday we'd kill a chicken or rabbit. Mebbe we'll have a cow or a goat. And the cream is so goddamn thick you got to cut it off the pan with a knife.

LENNIE (*watching him with wide eyes, softly*). We can live off the fat of the land.

GEORGE. Sure. All kinds of vegetables in the garden and if we want a little whiskey we can sell some eggs or somethin'. And we wouldn't sleep in no bunkhouse. Nobody could can us in the middle of a job.

LENNIE (*begging*). Tell about the house, George.

GEORGE. Sure. We'd have a little house. And a room to ourselves. And it ain't enough land so we'd have to work too hard. Mebbe six, seven hours a day only. We wouldn't have to buck no barley eleven hours a day. And when we put in a crop, why we'd be there to take that crop up. We'd know what come of our planting.

LENNIE (*eagerly*). And rabbits. And I'd take care of them. Tell how I'd do that, George.

GEORGE. Sure. You'd go out in the alfalfa patch and you'd have a sack. You'd fill up the sack and bring it in and put it in the rabbit cages.

LENNIE. They'd nibble and they'd nibble, the way they do. I seen 'em.

GEORGE. Every six weeks or so them does would throw a litter. So we'd have plenty rabbits to eat or sell. (*Pauses for inspiration.*) And we'd keep a few pigeons to go flying round and round the windmill, like they done when I was a kid. (*Seems entranced.*) And it'd be our own. And nobody could can us. If we don't like a guy we can say: "Get to hell out," and by God he's got to do it. And if a friend come along, why, we'd have an extra bunk. Know what we'd say? We'd say, "Why don't you spen' the night?" And by God he would. We'd have a setter dog and a couple of striped cats. (*Looks sharply at* LENNIE.) But you gotta watch out them cats don't get the little rabbits.

LENNIE (*breathing hard*). You jus' let 'em try. I'll break their goddamn necks. I'll smash them cats flat with a stick. I'd smash 'em flat with a stick. That's what I'd do. (*They sit silently for a moment.*)

CANDY (*at the sound of his voice, both* LEN-NIE *and* GEORGE *jump as though caught in some secret*). You know where's a place like that?

GEORGE (*solemnly*). S'pose I do, what's that to you?

CANDY. You don't need to tell me where it's at. Might be any place.

GEORGE (*relieved*). Sure. That's right, you couldn't find it in a hundred years.

CANDY (*excitedly*). How much they want for a place like that?

GEORGE (*grudgingly*). Well, I could get it for six hundred bucks. The ole people that owns it is flat bust. And the ole lady needs medicine. Say, what's it to you? You got nothing to do with us!

CANDY (*softly*). I ain't much good with only one hand. I lost my hand right here on the ranch. That's why they didn't can me. They give me a job swampin'. And they give me two hundred and fifty dollars 'cause I lost my hand. An' I got fifty more saved up right in the bank right now. That's three

hundred. And I got forty more comin' the end of the month. Tell you what . . . (*He leans forward eagerly.*) S'pose I went in with you guys? That's three hundred and forty bucks I'd put in. I ain't much good, but I could cook and tend the chickens and hoe the garden some. How'd that be?

GEORGE (*his eyes half closed, uncertainly*). I got to think about that. We was always goin' to do it by ourselves. Me an' Lennie. I never thought of nobody else.

CANDY. I'd make a will. Leave my share to you guys in case I kicked off. I ain't got no relations nor nothing. You fellas got any money? Maybe we could go there right now.

GEORGE (*disgustedly*). We got ten bucks between us. (*He thinks.*) Say, look. If me and Lennie work a month and don't spend nothing at all, we'll have a hundred bucks. That would be four forty. I bet we could swing her for that. Then you and Lennie could go get her started and I'd get a job and make up the rest. You could sell eggs and stuff like that. (*They look at each other in amazement. Reverently.*) Jesus Christ, I bet we could swing her. (*His voice is full of wonder.*) I bet we could swing 'er.

CANDY (*scratches the stump of his wrist nervously*). I got hurt four years ago. They'll can me pretty soon. Jest as soon as I can't swamp out no bunkhouses they'll put me on the county. Maybe if I give you guys my money, you'll let me hoe in the garden, even when I ain't no good at it. And I'll wash dishes and little chicken stuff like that. But hell, I'll be on our own place. I'll be let to work on our own place. (*Miserably.*) You seen what they done to my dog. They says he wasn't no good to himself nor nobody else. But when I'm that way nobody'll shoot me. I wish somebody would. They won't do nothing like that. I won't have no place to go and I can't get no more jobs.

GEORGE (*stands up*). We'll do 'er! God damn, we'll fix up that little ole place and we'll go live there. (*Wonderingly.*) S'pose they was a carnival, or a circus come to town or a ball game or any damn thing. (CANDY *nods in appreciation.*) We'd just go to her. We wouldn't ask nobody if we could. Just say we'll go to her, by God, and we would. Just milk the cow and sling some grain to the chickens and go to her.

LENNIE. And put some grass to the rabbits. I wouldn't forget to feed them. When we gonna to do it, George?

GEORGE (*decisively*). In one month. Right squack in one month. Know what I'm gonna do? I'm goin' write to them ole people that owns the place that we'll take 'er. And Candy'll send a hundred dollars to bind her.

CANDY (*happily*). I sure will. They got a good stove there?

GEORGE. Sure, got a nice stove. Burns coal or wood.

LENNIE. I'm gonna take my pup. I bet by Christ he likes it there. (*The window, center backstage, swings outward.* CURLEY'S WIFE *looks in. They do not see her.*)

GEORGE (*quickly*). Now don't tell nobody about her. Jus' us three and nobody else. They'll liable to can us so we can't make no stake. We'll just go on like we was a bunch of punks. Like we was gonna buck barley the rest of our lives. And then all of a sudden, one day, bang! We get our pay and scram out of here.

CANDY. I can give you three hundred right now.

LENNIE. And not tell nobody. We won't tell nobody, George.

GEORGE. You're goddamn right we won't. (*There is a silence and then* GEORGE *speaks irritably.*) You know, seems to me I can almost smell that carnation stuff that goddamn tart dumps on herself.

CURLEY'S WIFE (*in the first part of the speech by* GEORGE *she starts to step out of sight but at the last words her face darkens with anger. At her first words everybody in the room looks around at her and remains rigid during the tirade*). Who you callin' a tart! I come from a nice home. I was brung up by nice people. Nobody never got to me before I was married. I was straight. I tell you I was good. (*A little plaintively.*) I was. (*Angrily again.*) You know Curley. You know he wouldn't stay with me if he wasn't sure. I tell you Curley is sure. You got no right to call me a tart.

GEORGE (*sullenly*). If you ain't a tart, what you always hangin' round guys for? You got a house an' you got a man. We don't want no trouble from you.

CURLEY'S WIFE (*pleadingly*). Sure I got a man. He ain't never home. I got nobody to talk to. I got nobody to be with. Think I can just sit home and do nothin' but cook for Curley? I want to see somebody. Just see 'em an' talk to 'em. There ain't no women. I can't walk to town. And Curley don't take me to no dances now. I tell you I jus' want to talk to somebody.

GEORGE (*boldly*). If you're just friendly what you givin' out the eye for an' floppin' your can around?

CURLEY'S WIFE (*sadly*). I just wanta be nice. (*The sound of approaching voices:* "You don't have to get mad about it, do you?" ... "I ain't mad, but I just don't want no more questions, that's all. I just don't want no more questions.")

GEORGE. Get goin'. We don't want no trouble. (CURLEY'S WIFE *looks from the window and closes it silently and disappears. Enter* SLIM, *followed by* CURLEY, CARLSON *and* WHIT. SLIM's *hands are black with tar.* CURLEY *hangs close to his elbow.*)

CURLEY (*explaining*). Well, I didn't mean nothing, Slim. I jus' ast you.

SLIM. Well, you been askin' too often. I'm gettin' goddamn sick of it. If you can't look after your own wife, what you expect me to do about it? You lay off of me.

CURLEY. I'm jus' tryin' to tell you I didn't mean nothing. I just thought you might of saw her.

CARLSON. Why don't you tell her to stay to hell home where she belongs? You let her hang around the bunkhouses and pretty soon you're goin' to have somethin' on your hands.

CURLEY (*whirls on* CARLSON). You keep out of this 'less you want ta step outside.

CARLSON (*laughing*). Why you goddamn punk. You tried to throw a scare into Slim and you couldn't make it stick. Slim throwed a scare into you. You're yellow as a frog's belly. I don't care if you're the best boxer in the country, you come for me and I'll kick your goddamn head off.

WHIT (*joining in the attack*). Glove full of vaseline!

CURLEY (*glares at him, then suddenly sniffs the air, like a hound*). By God, she's been in *here.* I can smell— By God, she's been in here. (*To* GEORGE.) You was here. The other guys was outside. Now, God damn you— you talk.

GEORGE (*looks worried. He seems to make up his mind to face an inevitable situation. Slowly takes off his coat, and folds it almost daintily. Speaks in an unemotional monotone*). Somebody got to beat the hell outa you. I guess I'm elected. (LENNIE *has been watching, fascinated. He gives his high, nervous chuckle.*)

CURLEY (*whirls on him*). What the hell you laughin' at?

LENNIE (*blankly*). Huh?

CURLEY (*exploding with rage*). Come on, you big bastard. Get up on your feet. No big son-of-a-bitch is gonna laugh at me. I'll show you who's yellow.

(LENNIE *looks helplessly at* GEORGE. *Gets up and tries to retreat upstage.* CURLEY *follows slashing at him. The others mass themselves in front of the two contestants*: "*That ain't no way, Curley—he ain't done nothing to you.*" . . . "*Lay off him, will you, Curley. He ain't no fighter.*" . . . "*Sock him back, big guy! Don't be afraid of him!*" . . . "*Give him a chance, Curley. Give him a chance.*"

LENNIE (*crying with terror*). George, make him leave me alone, George.

GEORGE. Get him, Lennie. Get him! (*There is a sharp cry. The gathering of men opens and* CURLEY *is flopping about, his hand lost in* LENNIE's *hand.*) Let go of him, Lennie. Let go! ("*He's got his hand!*" . . . "*Look at that, will you?*" . . . "*Jesus, what a guy!*" LENNIE *watches in terror the flopping man he holds.* LENNIE's *face is covered with blood.* GEORGE *slaps* LENNIE *in the face again and again.* CURLEY *is weak and shrunken.*) Let go his hand, Lennie. Slim, come help me, while this guy's got any hand left. (*Suddenly* LENNIE *lets go. He cowers away from* GEORGE.)

LENNIE. You told me to, George. I heard you tell me to. (CURLEY *has dropped to the floor.* SLIM *and* CARLSON *bend over him and look at his hand.* SLIM *looks over at* LENNIE *with horror.*)

SLIM. We got to get him to a doctor. It looks to me like every bone in his hand is busted.

LENNIE (*crying*). I didn't wanta. I didn't wanta hurt 'im.

SLIM. Carlson, you get the candy wagon out. He'll have to go into Soledad and get his hand fixed up. (*Turns to the whimpering* LENNIE.) It ain't your fault. This punk had it comin' to him. But Jesus—he ain't hardly got no hand left.

GEORGE (*moving near*). Slim, will we git canned now? Will Curley's ole man can us now?

SLIM. I don't know. (*Kneels down beside* CURLEY.) You got your sense enough to listen? (CURLEY *nods.*) Well, then you listen. I think you got your hand caught in a machine. If you don't tell nobody what happened, we won't. But you jest tell and try to get this guy canned and we'll tell everybody. And then will you get the laugh! (*Helps* CURLEY *to his feet.*) Come on now. Carlson's goin' to take you in to a doctor. (*Starts for the door, turns back to* LENNIE.) Le's see your hands. (LENNIE *sticks out both hands.*) Christ Almighty!

GEORGE. Lennie was just scairt. He didn't know what to do. I tole you nobody ought never to fight him. No, I guess it was Candy I tole.

CANDY (*solemnly*). That's just what you done. Right this morning when Curley first lit into him. You says he better not fool with Lennie if he knows what's good for him. (*They all leave the stage except* GEORGE *and* LENNIE *and* CANDY.)

GEORGE (*to* LENNIE, *very gently*). It ain't your fault. You don't need to be scairt no more. You done jus' what I tole you to. Maybe you better go in the washroom and clean up your face. You look like hell.

LENNIE. I didn't want no trouble.

GEORGE. Come on—I'll go with you.

LENNIE. George?

GEORGE. What you want?

LENNIE. Can I still tend the rabbits, George? (*They exeunt together, side by side, through the door of the bunkhouse.*)

CURTAIN

SCENE II

Ten o'clock Saturday evening.

The room of the stable buck, a lean-to off the barn. There is a plank door upstage center; a small square window center right. On one side of the door a leather working bench with tools racked behind it, and on the others racks with broken and partly mended harnesses, collars, hames, traces, etc. At the left upstage Crooks' bunk. Over it two shelves. On one a great number of medicines in cans and bottles. And on the other a number of tattered books and a big alarm clock. In the corner right upstage a single-barreled shot-gun and on the floor beside it a pair of rubber boots. A large pair of gold spectacles hang on a nail over Crooks' bunk.

The entrance leads into the barn proper. From that direction and during the whole scene come the sounds of horses eating, stamping, jingling their halter chains and now and then whinnying.

Two empty nail kegs are in the room to be used as seats. Single unshaded small-candle-power carbon light hanging from its own cord.

As the curtain rises, we see CROOKS *sitting on his bunk rubbing his back with liniment. He reaches up under his shirt to do this. His face is lined with pain. As he rubs he flexes his muscles and shivers a little.*

LENNIE *appears in the open doorway, nearly filling the opening. Then* CROOKS, *sensing his presence, raises his eyes, stiffens and scowls.*

LENNIE *smiles in an attempt to make friends.*

CROOKS (*sharply*). You got no right to come in my room. This here's my room. Nobody got any right in here but me.

LENNIE (*fawning*). I ain't doin' nothing. Just come in the barn to look at my pup, and I seen your light.

CROOKS. Well, I got a right to have a light. You go on and get out of my room. I ain't wanted in the bunkhouse and you ain't wanted in my room.

LENNIE (*ingenuously*). Why ain't you want-ed?

CROOKS (*furiously*). 'Cause I'm black. They play cards in there. But I can't play because I'm black. They say I stink. Well, I tell you all of you stink to me.

LENNIE (*helplessly*). Everybody went into town. Slim and George and everybody. George says I got to stay here and not get into no trouble. I seen your light.

CROOKS. Well, what do you want?

LENNIE. Nothing . . . I seen your light. I thought I could jus' come in and set.

CROOKS (*stares at* LENNIE *for a moment, takes down his spectacles and adjusts them over his ears; says in a complaining tone*). I don't know what you're doin' in the barn anyway. You ain't no skinner. There's no call for a bucker to come into the barn at all. You've got nothing to do with the horses and mules.

LENNIE (*patiently*). The pup. I come to see my pup.

CROOKS. Well, God damn it, go and see your pup then. Don't go no place where you ain't wanted.

LENNIE (*advances a step into the room, remembers and backs to the door again*). I looked at him a little. Slim says I ain't to pet him very much.

CROOKS (*the anger gradually going out of his voice*). Well, you been taking him out of the nest all the time. I wonder the ole lady don't move him some place else.

LENNIE (*moving into the room*). Oh, she don't care. She lets me.

CROOKS (*scowls and then gives up*). Come on in and set awhile. Long as you won't get out and leave me alone, you might as well set down. (*A little more friendly.*) All the boys gone into town, huh?

LENNIE. All but old Candy. He jus' sets in the bunkhouse sharpening his pencils. And sharpening and figurin'.

CROOKS (*adjusting his glasses*). Figurin'? What's Candy figurin' about?

LENNIE. 'Bout the land. 'Bout the little place.

CROOKS. You're nuts. You're crazy as a wedge. What land you talkin' about?

LENNIE. The land we're goin' to get. And a little house and pigeons.

CROOKS. Just nuts. I don't blame the guy you're traveling with for keeping you out of sight.

LENNIE (*quietly*). It ain't no lie. We're gonna do it. Gonna get a little place and live on the fat of the land.

CROOKS (*settling himself comfortably on his bunk*). Set down. Set down on that nail keg.

LENNIE (*hunches over on the little barrel*). You think it's a lie. But it ain't no lie. Ever' word's the truth. You can ask George.

CROOKS (*puts his dark chin on his palm*). You travel round with George, don't you?

LENNIE (*proudly*). Sure, me and him goes ever' place together.

CROOKS (*after a pause, quietly*). Sometimes he talks and you don't know what the hell he's talkin' about. Ain't that so? (*Leans forward.*) Ain't that so?

LENNIE. Yeah. Sometimes.

CROOKS. Just talks on. And you don't know what the hell it's all about.

LENNIE. How long you think it'll be before them pups will be old enough to pet?

CROOKS (*laughs again*). A guy can talk to you and be sure you won't go blabbin'. A couple of weeks and them pups will be all right. (*Musing.*) George knows what he's about. Just talks and you don't understand nothing. (*Mood gradually changes to excitement.*) Well, this is just a nigger talkin' and a busted-back nigger. It don't mean nothing, see. You couldn't remember it anyway. I seen it over and over—a guy talking to another guy and it don't make no difference if he don't hear or understand. The thing is they're talkin'. (*He pounds his knee with his hand.*) George can tell you screwy things and it don't matter. It's just the talkin'. It's just bein' with another guy, that's all. (*His voice becomes soft and malicious.*) S'pose George don't come back

no more? S'pose he took a powder and just ain't comin' back. What you do then?

LENNIE (*trying to follow* CROOKS). What? What?

CROOKS. I said s'pose George went into town tonight and you never heard of him no more. (*Presses forward.*) Just s'pose that.

LENNIE (*sharply*). He won't do it. George wouldn't do nothing like that. I been with George a long time. He'll come back tonight. . . . (*Doubt creeps into his voice.*) Don't you think he will?

CROOKS (*delighted with his torture*). Nobody can tell what a guy will do. Let's say he wants to come back and can't. S'pose he gets killed or hurt so he can't come back.

LENNIE (*in terrible apprehension*). I don't know. Say, what you doin' anyway? It ain't true. George ain't got hurt.

CROOKS (*cruelly*). Want me to tell you what'll happen? They'll take you to the booby hatch. They'll tie you up with a collar like a dog. Then you'll be jus' like me. Livin' in a kennel.

LENNIE (*furious, walks over towards* CROOKS). Who hurt George?

CROOKS (*recoiling from him with fright*). I was just supposin'. George ain't hurt. He's all right. He'll be back all right.

LENNIE (*standing over him*). What you supposin' for? Ain't nobody goin' to s'pose any hurt to George.

CROOKS (*trying to calm him*). Now set down. George ain't hurt. Go on now, set down.

LENNIE (*growling*). Ain't nobody gonna talk no hurt to George.

CROOKS (*very gently*). Maybe you can see now. You got George. You know he's comin' back. S'pose you didn't have nobody. S'pose you couldn't 'go in the bunkhouse and play rummy, 'cause you was black. How would you like that? S'pose you had to set out here and read books. Sure, you could play horseshoes until it got dark, but then you got to read books. Books ain't no good. A guy needs somebody . . . to be near him. (*His tone whines.*) A guy goes nuts if he ain't got nobody. Don't make no difference who it is as long as he's with you. I tell you a guy gets too lonely, he gets sick.

LENNIE (*reassuring himself*). George gonna come back. Maybe George come back already. Maybe I better go see.

CROOKS (*more gently*). I didn't mean to scare you. He'll come back. I was talkin' about myself.

LENNIE (*miserably*). George won't go away and leave me. I know George won't do that.

CROOKS (*continuing dreamily*). I remember when I was a little kid on my ole man's chicken ranch. Had two brothers. They was always near me, always there. Used to sleep right in the same room. Right in the same bed, all three. Had a strawberry patch. Had an alfalfa patch. Used to turn the chickens out in the alfalfa on a sunny morning. Me and my brothers would set on the fence and watch 'em—white chickens they was.

LENNIE (*interested*). George says we're gonna have alfalfa.

CROOKS. You're nuts.

LENNIE. We are too gonna get it. You ask George.

CROOKS (*scornfully*). You're nuts. I seen hundreds of men come by on the road and on the ranches, bindles on their back and that same damn thing in their head. Hundreds of 'em. They come and they quit and they go on. And every damn one of 'em is got a little piece of land in his head. And never a goddamn one of 'em gets it. Jus' like heaven. Everybody wants a little piece of land. Nobody never gets to heaven. And nobody gets no land.

LENNIE. We are too.

CROOKS. It's jest in your head. Guys all the time talkin' about it, but it's jest in your head. (*The horses move restlessly. One of them whinnies.*) I guess somebody's out there. Maybe Slim. (*Pulls himself painfully upright and moves toward the door. Calls.*) That you, Slim?

CANDY (*from outside*). Slim went in town. Say, you seen Lennie?

CROOKS. You mean the big guy?

CANDY. Yes. Seen him around any place?

CROOKS (*goes back to his bunk and sits down, says shortly*). He's in here.

CANDY (*stands in the doorway, scratching his wrist. Makes no attempt to enter*). Look, Lennie, I been figuring something out. About the place.

CROOKS (*irritably*). You can come in if you want.

CANDY (*embarrassed*). I don't know. 'Course if you want me to.

CROOKS. Oh, come on in. Everybody's comin' in. You might just as well. Gettin' to be a goddamn race track. (*He tries to conceal his pleasure.*)

CANDY (*still embarrassed*). You've got a nice cozy little place in here. Must be nice to have a room to yourself this way.

CROOKS. Sure. And a manure pile under the window. All to myself. It's swell.

LENNIE (*breaking in*). You said about the place.

CANDY. You know, I been here a long time. An' Crooks been here a long time. This is the first time I ever been in his room.

CROOKS (*darkly*). Guys don't come in a colored man's room. Nobody been here but Slim.

LENNIE (*insistently*). The place. You said about the place.

CANDY. Yeah. I got it all figured out. We can make some real money on them rabbits if we go about it right.

LENNIE. But I get to tend 'em. George says I get to tend 'em. He promised.

CROOKS (*brutally*). You guys is just kiddin' yourselves. You'll talk about it a hell of a lot, but you won't get no land. You'll be a swamper here until they take you out in a box. Hell, I seen too many guys.

CANDY (*angrily*). We're gonna do it. George says we are. We got the money right now.

CROOKS. Yeah. And where is George now? In town in a whorehouse. That's where your money's goin'. I tell you I seen it happen too many times.

CANDY. George ain't got the money in town. The money's in the bank. Me and Lennie and George. We gonna have a room to ourselves. We gonna have a dog and chickens. We gonna have green corn and maybe a cow.

CROOKS (*impressed*). You say you got the money?

CANDY. We got most of it. Just a little bit more to get. Have it all in one month. George's got the land all picked out too.

CROOKS (*exploring his spine with his hands*). I've never seen a guy really do it. I seen guys nearly crazy with loneliness for land, but every time a whorehouse or a blackjack game took it away from 'em. (*Hesitates and then speaks timidly.*) If you guys would want a hand to work for nothin'—just his keep, why I'd come and lend a hand. I ain't so crippled I can't work like a son-of-a-bitch if I wanted to.

GEORGE (*strolls through the door, hands in pockets, leans against the wall, speaks in a half-satiric, rather gentle voice*). You couldn't go to bed like I told you, could you, Lennie? Hell, no—you got to get out in society an' flap your mouth. Holdin' a convention out here.

LENNIE (*defending himself*). You was gone. There wasn't nobody in the bunkhouse. I ain't done no bad things, George.

GEORGE (*still casually*). Only time I get any peace is when you're asleep. If you ever get walkin' in your sleep I'll chop off your head like a chicken. (*Chops with his hand.*)

CROOKS (*coming to* LENNIE'S *defense*). We was jus' settin' here talkin'. Ain't no harm in that.

GEORGE. Yeah. I heard you. (*A weariness has settled on him.*) Got to be here ever' minute, I guess. Got to watch ya. (*To* CROOKS.) It ain't nothing against you, Crooks. We just wasn't gonna tell nobody.

CANDY (*tries to change subject*). Didn't you have no fun in town?

GEORGE. Oh! I set in a chair and Susy was crackin' jokes an' the guys was startin' to raise a little puny hell. Christ Almighty—I never been this way before. I'm jus' gonna set out a dime and a nickel for a shot an' I think what a hell of a lot of bulk carrot seed you can get for fifteen cents.

CANDY. Not in them damn little envelopes—but bulk seed—you sure can.

GEORGE. So purty soon I come back. I can't think of nothing else. Them guys slingin' money around got me jumpy.

CANDY. Guy got to have *some* fun. I was to a parlor house in Bakersfield once. God Almighty, what a place. Went upstairs on a red carpet. They was big pitchers on the wall. We set in big sof' chairs. They was cigarettes on the table—an' they was *free*. Purty soon a Jap come in with drinks on a tray an' them *drinks* was free. Take all you want. (*In a reverie.*) Purty soon the girls come in an' they was jus' as polite an' nice an' quiet an' purty. Didn't seem like hookers. Made ya kinda scared to ask 'em. . . . That was a long time ago.

GEORGE. Yeah? An' what'd them sof' chairs set you back?

CANDY. Fifteen bucks.

GEORGE (*scornfully*). So ya got a cigarette an' a whiskey an' a look at a purty dress an' it cost ya twelve and a half bucks extra. You shot a week's pay to walk on that red carpet.

CANDY (*still entranced with his memory*). A week's pay? Sure. But I worked weeks all my life. I can't remember none of them weeks. But . . . that was nearly twenty years ago. And I can remember that. Girl I went with was named Arline. Had on a pink silk dress.

GEORGE (*turns suddenly and looks out the door into the dark barn, speaks savagely*). I s'pose ya lookin' for Curley? (CURLEY'S WIFE *appears in the door.*) Well, Curley ain't here.

CURLEY'S WIFE (*determined now*). I know Curley ain't here. I wanted to ast Crooks somepin'. I didn't know you guys was here.

CANDY. Didn't George tell you before—we don't want nothing to do with you. You know damn well Curley ain't here.

CURLEY'S WIFE. I know where Curley went. Got his arm in a sling an' he went anyhow. I tell ya I come out to ast Crooks somepin'.

CROOKS (*apprehensively*). Maybe you better go along to your own house. You hadn't ought to come near a colored man's room.

I don't want no trouble. You don't want to ask me nothing.

CANDY (*rubbing his wrist stump*). You got a husband. You got no call to come foolin' around with other guys, causin' trouble.

CURLEY'S WIFE (*suddenly angry*). I try to be nice an' polite to you lousy bindle bums— but you're too good. I tell ya I could of went with shows. An'—an' a guy wanted to put me in pitchers right in Hollywood. (*Looks about to see how she is impressing them. Their eyes are hard.*) I come out here to ast somebody somepin' an'—

CANDY (*stands up suddenly and knocks his nail keg over backwards, speaks angrily*). I had enough. You ain't wanted here. We tole you, you ain't. Callin' us bindle stiffs. You got floozy idears what us guys amounts to. You ain't got sense enough to see us guys ain't bindle stiffs. S'pose you could get us *canned*—s'pose you *could.* You think we'd hit the highway an' look for another two-bit job. You don't know we got our own ranch to go to an' our own house an' fruit trees. An' we got friends. That's what we got. Maybe they was a time when we didn't have nothing, but that ain't so no more.

CURLEY'S WIFE. You damn ol' goat. If you had two bits, you'd be in Soledad gettin' a drink an' suckin' the bottom of the glass.

GEORGE. Maybe she could ask Crooks what she come to ask an' then get the hell home. I don't think she come to ask nothing.

CURLEY'S WIFE. What happened to Curley's hand? (CROOKS *laughs.* GEORGE *tries to shut him up.*) So it wasn't no machine. Curley didn't act like he was tellin' the truth. Come on, Crooks—what happened?

CROOKS. I wasn't there. I didn't see it.

CURLEY'S WIFE (*eagerly*). What happened? I won't let on to Curley. He says he caught his han' in a gear. (CROOKS *is silent.*) Who done it?

GEORGE. Didn't nobody do it.

CURLEY'S WIFE (*turns slowly to* GEORGE). So *you* done it. Well, he had it comin'.

GEORGE. I didn't have no fuss with Curley.

CURLEY'S WIFE (*steps near him, smiling*). Maybe now you ain't scared of him no more.

Maybe you'll talk to me sometimes now. Ever'body was scared of him.

GEORGE (*speaks rather kindly*). Look! I didn't sock Curley. If he had trouble, it ain't none of our affair. Ask Curley about it. Now listen. I'm gonna try to tell ya. We tole you to get the hell out and it don't do no good. So I'm gonna tell you another way. Us guys got somepin' we're gonna do. If you stick around you'll gum up the works. It ain't your fault. If a guy steps on a round pebble an' falls an' breaks his neck, it ain't the pebble's fault, but the guy wouldn't of did it if the pebble wasn't there.

CURLEY'S WIFE (*puzzled*). What you talkin' about pebbles? If you didn't sock Curley, who did? (*She looks at the others, then steps quickly over to* LENNIE.) Where'd you get them bruises on your face?

GEORGE. I tell you he got his hand caught in a machine.

LENNIE (*looks anxiously at* GEORGE, *speaks miserably*). He caught his han' in a machine.

GEORGE. So now get out of here.

CURLEY'S WIFE (*goes close to* LENNIE, *speaks softly and there is a note of affection in her voice*). So . . . it was you. Well . . . maybe you're dumb like they say . . . an' maybe . . . you're the only guy on the ranch with guts. (*She puts her hand on* LENNIE's *shoulder. He looks up in her face and a smile grows on his face. She strokes his shoulder.*) You're a nice fella.

GEORGE (*suddenly leaps at her ferociously, grabs her shoulder and whirls her around*). Listen . . . you! I tried to give you a break. Don't you walk into nothing! We ain't gonna let you mess up what we're gonna do. You let this guy alone an' get the hell out of here.

CURLEY'S WIFE (*defiant but slightly frightened*). You ain't tellin' me what to do. (*The* BOSS *appears in the door, stands legs spread, thumbs hooked over his belt.*) I got a right to talk to anybody I want to.

GEORGE. Why, you—(GEORGE, *furiously, steps close—his hand is raised to strike her. She cowers a little.* GEORGE *stiffens, seeing* BOSS, *frozen in position. The others see* BOSS *too. Girl retreats slowly.* GEORGE's *hand drops slowly to his side—he takes two slow backward steps. Hold the scene for a moment.*)

CURTAIN

ACT THREE

SCENE I

Mid-afternoon Sunday.

One end of a great barn. Backstage the hay slopes up sharply against the wall. High in the upstage wall is a large hay window. On each side are seen the hay racks, behind which are the stalls with the horses in them. Throughout this scene the horses can be heard in their stalls, rattling their halter chains and chewing at the hay.

The entrance is downstage right.

The boards of the barn are not close together. Streaks of afternoon sun come between the boards, made visible by dust in the air. From outside comes the clang of horseshoes on the playing peg, shouts of men encouraging or jeering.

In the barn there is a feeling of quiet and humming and lazy warmth. Curtain rises on LENNIE *sitting in the hay, looking down at a little dead puppy in front of him. He puts out his big hand and strokes it clear from one end to the other.*

LENNIE (*softly*). Why do you got to get killed? You ain't so little as mice. I didn' bounce you hard. (*Bends the pup's head up and looks in its face.*) Now maybe George ain't gonna let me tend no rabbits if he finds out you got killed. (*He scoops a little hollow and lays the puppy in it out of sight and covers it over with hay. He stares at the mound he has made.*) This ain't no bad thing like I got to hide in the brush. I'll tell George I found it dead. (*He unburies the pup and inspects it. Twists its ears and works his fingers in its fur. Sorrowfully.*) But he'll know. George always knows. He'll say: "You done it. Don't try to put nothin' over on me." And he'll say: "Now just for that you don't get to tend no—you-know-whats." (*His anger rises. Addresses the pup.*) God damn you. Why do you got to get killed? You ain't so little as mice. (*Picks up the pup and hurls it from him and turns his back on it. He sits bent over his knees moaning to himself.*) Now he won't let me. . . . Now he won't let me. (*Outside there is a clang of horseshoes on the iron stake and a little chorus of cries.* LENNIE *gets up and brings the pup back and lays it in the hay and sits down. He mourns.*) You wasn't big enough. They tole me and tole me you wasn't. I didn't know you'd get killed so easy. Maybe George won't care. This here goddamn little son-of-a-bitch wasn't nothin' to George.

CANDY (*voice from behind the stalls*). Lennie, where you at? (LENNIE *frantically buries the pup under the hay.* CANDY *enters excitedly.*) Thought I'd find ya here. Say . . . I been talkin' to Slim. It's okay. We ain't gonna get the can. Slim been talkin' to the boss. Slim tol' the boss you guys is good buckers. The boss got to move that grain. 'Member what hell the boss give us las' night? He tol' Slim he got his eye on you an' George. But you ain't gonna get the can. Oh! an' say. The boss give Curley's wife hell, too. Tole her never to go near the men no more. Give her worse hell than you an' George. (*For the first time notices* LENNIE's *dejection.*) Ain't you glad?

LENNIE. Sure.

CANDY. You ain't sick?

LENNIE. Uh-uh!

CANDY. I got to go tell George. See you later. (*Exits.* LENNIE, *alone, uncovers the pup. Lies down in the hay and sinks deep in it. Puts the pup on his arm and strokes it.* CURLEY'S WIFE *enters secretly. A little mound of hay conceals* LENNIE *from her. In her hand she carries a small suitcase, very cheap. She crosses the barn and buries the case in the hay. Stands up and looks to see whether it can be seen.* LENNIE *watching her quietly tries to cover the pup with hay. She sees the movement.*)

CURLEY'S WIFE. What—what you doin' here?

LENNIE (*sullenly*). Jus' settin' here.

CURLEY'S WIFE. You seen what I done.

LENNIE. Yeah! you brang a valise.

CURLEY'S WIFE (*comes near to him*). You won't tell—will you?

LENNIE (*still sullen*). I ain't gonna have nothing to do with you. George tole me. I ain't to talk to you or nothing. (*Covers the pup a little more.*)

CURLEY'S WIFE. George give you all your orders?

LENNIE. Not talk nor nothing.

CURLEY'S WIFE. You won't tell about that suitcase? I ain't gonna stay here no more. Tonight I'm gonna get out. Come here an' get my stuff an' get out. I ain't gonna be run over no more. I'm gonna go in pitchers. (*Sees* LENNIE's *hand stroking the pup under the hay.*) What you got there?

LENNIE. Nuthing. I ain't gonna talk to you. George says I ain't.

CURLEY'S WIFE. Listen. The guys got a horse-shoe tenement out there. It's on'y four o'clock. Them guys ain't gonna leave that tenement. They got money bet. You don't need to be scared to talk to me.

LENNIE (*weakening a little*). I ain't supposed to.

CURLEY'S WIFE (*watching his buried hand*). What you got under there?

LENNIE (*his woe comes back to him*). Jus' my pup. Jus' my little ol' pup. (*Sweeps the hay aside.*)

CURLEY'S WIFE. Why! He's dead.

LENNIE (*explaining sadly*). He was so little. I was jus' playin' with him—an' he made like he's gonna bite me—an' I made like I'm gonna smack him—an'—I done it. An' then he was dead.

CURLEY'S WIFE (*consoling*). Don't you worry none. He was just a mutt. The whole country is full of mutts.

LENNIE. It ain't that so much. George gonna be mad. Maybe he won't let me—what he said I could tend.

CURLEY'S WIFE (*sits down in the hay beside him, speaks soothingly*). Don't you worry. Them guys got money bet on that horseshoe tenement. They ain't gonna leave it. And tomorra I'll be gone. I ain't gonna let them run over me. (*In the following scene it is apparent that neither is listening to the other and yet as it goes on, as a happy tone increases, it can be seen that they are growing closer together.*)

LENNIE. We gonna have a little place an' raspberry bushes.

CURLEY'S WIFE. I ain't meant to live like this. I come from Salinas. Well, a show come through an' I talked to a guy that was in it. He says I could go with the show. My ol' lady wouldn't let me, 'cause I was on'y fifteen. I wouldn't be no place like this if I had went with that show, you bet.

LENNIE. Gonna take a sack an' fill it up with alfalfa an'—

CURLEY'S WIFE (*hurrying on*). 'Nother time I met a guy an' he was in pitchers. Went out to the Riverside Dance Palace with him. He said he was gonna put me in pitchers. Says I was a natural. Soon's he got back to Hollywood he was gonna write me about it. (*Looks impressively at* LENNIE.) I never got that letter. I think my ol' lady stole it. Well, I wasn't gonna stay no place where they stole your letters. So I married Curley. Met *him* out to the Riverside Dance Palace too.

LENNIE. I hope George ain't gonna be mad about this pup.

CURLEY'S WIFE. I ain't tol' this to nobody before. Maybe I oughtn' to. I don't like Curley. He ain't a nice fella. I might a stayed with him but last night him an' his ol' man both lit into me. I don't have to stay here. (*Moves closer and speaks confidentially.*) Don't tell nobody till I get clear away. I'll go in the night an' thumb a ride to Hollywood.

LENNIE. We gonna get out a here purty soon. This ain't no nice place.

CURLEY'S WIFE (*ecstatically*). Gonna get in the movies an' have nice clothes—all them nice clothes like they wear. An' I'll set in them big hotels and they'll take pitchers of me. When they have them openings I'll go an' talk in the radio . . . an' it won't cost me nothing 'cause I'm in the pitcher. (*Puts her hand on* LENNIE's *arm for a moment.*) All them nice clothes like they wear . . . because this guy says I'm a natural.

LENNIE. We gonna go way . . . far away from here.

CURLEY'S WIFE. 'Course, when I run away from Curley, my ol' lady won't never speak to me no more. She'll think I ain't decent. That's what she'll say. (*Defiantly.*) Well, we really ain't decent, no matter how much my ol' lady tries to hide it. My ol' man was a drunk. They put him away. There! Now I told.

LENNIE. George an' me was to the Sacramento Fair. One time I fell in the river an' George pulled me out an' saved me, an' then we went to the Fair. They got all kinds of stuff there. We seen long-hair rabbits.

CURLEY'S WIFE. My ol' man was a sign-painter when he worked. He used to get drunk an' paint crazy pitchers an' waste paint. One night when I was a little kid, him an' my ol' lady had an awful fight. They was always fightin'. In the middle of the night he come into my room, and he says, "I can't stand this no more. Let's you an' me go away." I guess he was drunk. (*Her voice takes on a curious wondering tenderness.*) I remember in the night—walkin' down the road, and the trees was black. I was pretty sleepy. He picked me up, an' he carried me on his back. He says, "We gonna live together. We gonna live together because you're my own little girl, an' not no stranger. No arguin' and fightin'," he says, "because you're my little daughter." (*Her voice becomes soft.*) He says, "Why you'll bake little cakes for me, and I'll paint pretty pitchers all over the wall." (*Sadly.*) In the morning they caught us . . . an' they put him away. (*Pause.*) I wish we'd a' went.

LENNIE. Maybe if I took this here pup an' throwed him away George wouldn't never know.

CURLEY'S WIFE. They locked him up for a drunk, and in a little while he died.

LENNIE. Then maybe I could tend the rabbits without no trouble.

CURLEY'S WIFE. Don't you think of nothing but rabbits? (*Sound of horseshoe on metal.*) Somebody made a ringer.

LENNIE (*patiently*). We gonna have a house and a garden, an' a place for alfalfa. And I take a sack and get it all full of alfalfa, and then I take it to the rabbits.

CURLEY'S WIFE. What makes you so nuts about rabbits?

LENNIE (*moves close to her*). I like to pet nice things. Once at a fair I seen some of them long-hair rabbits. And they was nice, you bet. (*Despairingly.*) I'd even pet mice, but not when I could get nothin' better.

CURLEY'S WIFE (*giggles*). I think you're nuts.

LENNIE (*earnestly*). No, I ain't. George says I ain't. I like to pet nice things with my fingers. Soft things.

CURLEY'S WIFE. Well, who don't? Everybody likes that. I like to feel silk and velvet. You like to feel velvet?

LENNIE (*chuckling with pleasure*). You bet, by God. And I had some too. A lady give me some. And that lady was—my Aunt Clara. She give it right to me. . . . (*Measuring with his hands.*) 'Bout this big a piece. I wish I had that velvet right now. (*He frowns.*) I lost it. I ain't seen it for a long time.

CURLEY'S WIFE (*laughing*). You're nuts. But you're a kinda nice fella. Jus' like a big baby. A person can see kinda what you mean. When I'm doin' my hair sometimes I jus' set there and stroke it, because it's so soft. (*Runs her fingers over the top of her head.*) Some people got kinda coarse hair. You take Curley, his hair's just like wire. But mine is soft and fine. Here, feel. Right here. (*Takes* LENNIE's *hand and puts it on her head.*) Feel there and see how soft it is. (LENNIE's *fingers fall to stroking her hair.*) Don't you muss it up.

LENNIE. Oh, that's nice. (*Strokes harder.*) Oh, that's nice.

CURLEY'S WIFE. Look out now, you'll muss it. (*Angrily.*) You stop it now, you'll mess it all up. (*She jerks her head sideways and* LENNIE's *fingers close on her hair and hang on. In a panic.*) Let go. (*She screams.*) You let go. (*She screams again. His other hand closes over her mouth and nose.*)

LENNIE (*begging*). Oh, please don't do that. George'll be mad. (*She struggles violently to be free. A soft screaming comes from under* LENNIE's *hand. Crying with fright.*) Oh, please don't do none of that. George gonna say I done a bad thing. (*He raises his hand *from her mouth and a hoarse cry escapes. Angrily.*) Now don't. I don't want you to yell. You gonna get me in trouble just like George says you will. Now don't you do that. (*She struggles more.*) Don't you go yellin'. (*He shakes her violently. Her neck snaps sideways and she lies still. Looks down at her and cautiously removes his hand from over her mouth.*) I don't wanta hurt you. But George will be mad if you yell. (*When she doesn't answer he bends closely over her. He lifts her arm and lets it drop. For a moment he seems bewildered.*) I done a bad thing. I done another bad thing. (*He paws up the hay until it partly covers her. The sound of the horseshoe game comes from the outside. And for the first time* LENNIE *seems conscious of it. He crouches down and listens.*) Oh, I done a real bad thing. I shouldn't a did that. George will be mad. And . . . he said . . . and hide in the brush till he comes. That's what he said. (*He picks up the puppy from beside the girl.*) I'll throw him away. It's bad enough like it is.

(*He puts the pup under his coat, creeps to the barn wall and peers out between the cracks and then he creeps around to the end of the manger and disappears. The stage is vacant except for* CURLEY'S WIFE. *She lies in the hay half covered up and she looks very young and peaceful. Her rouged cheeks and red lips make her seem alive and sleeping lightly. For a moment the stage is absolutely silent. Then the horses stamp on the other side of the feeding rack. The halter chains clink and from outside men's voices come loud and clear.*)

CANDY (*offstage*). Lennie! Oh, Lennie, you in there? (*He enters.*) I been figurin' some more, Lennie. Tell you what we can do. (*Sees* CURLEY'S WIFE *and stops. Rubs his white whiskers.*) I didn't know you was here. You was tol' not to be here. (*He steps near her.*) You oughn't to sleep out here. (*He is right beside her and looks down.*) Oh, Jesus Christ! (*Goes to the door and calls softly.*) George! George! Come here . . . George!

GEORGE (*enters*). What do you want?

CANDY (*points at* CURLEY'S WIFE). Look.

GEORGE. What's the matter with her? (*Steps up beside her.*) Oh, Jesus Christ! (*Kneels beside her and feels her heart and her wrist.*

Finally stands up slowly and stiffly. From this time on through the rest of the scene GEORGE *is wooden.*)

CANDY. What done it?

GEORGE (*coldly*). Ain't you got any ideas? (CANDY *looks away.*) I should of knew. I guess way back in my head I did.

CANDY. What we gonna do now, George? What we gonna do now?

GEORGE (*answering slowly and dully*). Guess . . . we gotta . . . tell . . . the guys. Guess we got to catch him and lock him up. We can't let him get away. Why, the poor bastard would starve. (*He tries to reassure himself.*) Maybe they'll lock him up and be nice to him.

CANDY (*excitedly*). You know better'n that, George. You know Curley's gonna want to get him lynched. You know how Curley is.

GEORGE. Yeah. . . . Yeah . . . that's right. I know Curley. And the other guys too. (*He looks back at* CURLEY'S WIFE.)

CANDY (*pleadingly*). You and me can get that little place, can't we, George? You and me can go there and live nice, can't we? Can't we? (CANDY *drops his head and looks down at the hay to indicate that he knows.*)

GEORGE (*shakes his head slowly*). It was somethin' me and him had. (*Softly.*) I think I knowed it from the very first. I think I knowed we'd never do her. He used to like to hear about it so much. I got fooled to thinkin' maybe we would. (CANDY *starts to speak but doesn't.*)

GEORGE (*as though repeating a lesson*). I'll work my month and then I'll take my fifty bucks. I'll stay all night in some lousy cathouse or I'll set in a pool room until everybody goes home. An' then—I'll come back an' work another month. And then I'll have fifty bucks more.

CANDY. He's such a nice fellow. I didn't think he'd a done nothing like this.

GEORGE (*gets a grip on himself and straightens his shoulders*). Now listen. We gotta tell the guys. I guess they've gotta bring him in. They ain't no way out. Maybe they won't hurt him. I ain't gonna let 'em hurt Lennie.

(*Sharply.*) Now you listen. The guys might think I was in on it. I'm gonna go in the bunkhouse. Then in a minute you come out and yell like you just seen her. Will you do that? So the guys won't think I was in on it?

CANDY. Sure, George. Sure, I'll do that.

GEORGE. Okay. Give me a couple of minutes then. And then you yell your head off. I'm goin' now. (GEORGE *exits.*)

CANDY (*watches him go, looks helplessly back at* CURLEY'S WIFE; *his next words are in sorrow and in anger*). You goddamn tramp. You done it, didn't you? Everybody knowed you'd mess things up. You just wasn't no good. (*His voice shakes.*) I could of hoed in the garden and washed dishes for them guys. . . . (*Pauses for a moment and then goes into a sing-song repeating the old words.*) If there was a circus or a baseball game . . . we would o' went to her . . . just said to hell with work and went to her. And they'd been a pig and chickens . . . and in the winter a little fat stove. An' us jus' settin' there . . . settin' there. . . . (*His eyes blind with tears and he goes weakly to the entrance of the barn. Tries for a moment to break a shout out of his throat before he succeeds.*) Hey, you guys! Come here! Come here!
(*Outside the noise of the horseshoe game stops. The sound of discussion and then the voices come closer: "What's the matter?" . . . "Who's that?" . . . "It's Candy." . . . "Something must have happened." Enter* SLIM *and* CARLSON, *Young* WHIT *and* CURLEY, CROOKS *in the back, keeping out of attention range. And last of all* GEORGE. GEORGE *has put on his blue denim coat and buttoned it. His black hat is pulled down low over his eyes. "What's the matter?" . . . "What's happened?"*)
(*A gesture from* CANDY. *The men stare at* CURLEY'S WIFE. SLIM *goes over to her, feels her wrist and touches her cheek with his fingers. His hand goes under her slightly twisted neck.* CURLEY *comes near. For a moment he seems shocked. Looks around helplessly and suddenly he comes to life.*)

CURLEY. I know who done it. That big son-of-a-bitch done it. I know he done it. Why, everybody else was out there playing horse-shoes. (*Working himself into a fury.*) I'm gonna get him. I'm gonna get my shotgun. Why, I'll kill the big son-of-a-bitch myself.

I'll shoot him in the guts. Come on, you guys. (*He runs out of the barn.*)

CARLSON. I'll go get my Luger. (*He runs out too.*)

SLIM (*quietly to* GEORGE). I guess Lennie done it all right. Her neck's busted. Lennie could o' did that. (GEORGE *nods slowly. Half-questioning.*) Maybe like that time in Weed you was tellin' me about. (GEORGE *nods. Gently.*) Well, I guess we got to get him. Where you think he might o' went?

GEORGE (*struggling to get words out*). I don't know.

SLIM. I guess we gotta get him.

GEORGE (*stepping close and speaking passionately*). Couldn't we maybe bring him in and lock him up? He's nuts, Slim, he never done this to be mean.

SLIM. If we could only keep Curley in. But Curley wants to shoot him. (*He thinks.*) And s'pose they lock him up, George, and strap him down and put him in a cage, that ain't no good.

GEORGE. I know. I know.

SLIM. I think there's only one way to get him out of it.

GEORGE. I know.

CARLSON (*enters running*). The bastard stole my Luger. It ain't in my bag.

CURLEY (*enters carrying a shotgun in his good hand. Officiously*). All right, you guys. The nigger's got a shotgun. You take it, Carlson.

WHIT. Only cover around here is down by the river. He might have went there.

CURLEY. Don't give him no chance. Shoot for his guts, that'll double him over.

WHIT. I ain't got a gun.

CURLEY. Go in and tell my old man. Get a gun from him. Let's go now. (*Turns suspiciously on* GEORGE.) You're comin' with us, fella!

GEORGE. Yeah. I'll come. But listen, Curley, the poor bastard's nuts. Don't shoot him, he didn't know what he was doin'.

CURLEY. Don't shoot him! He's got Carlson's Luger, ain't he?

GEORGE (*weakly*). Maybe Carlson lost his gun.

CARLSON. I seen it this morning. It's been took.

SLIM (*looking down at* CURLEY'S WIFE). Curley, maybe you better stay here with your wife. (*The light is fading into evening.* CURLEY *hesitates. Seems almost to weaken, then he hardens again.*)

CURLEY. Naw, I'm gonna shoot the guts out of that big bastard, I'm gonna get him myself. Come on, you guys.

SLIM (*to* CANDY). You stay here then, Candy. The rest of us better get goin'. (*They walk out,* SLIM *and* GEORGE *last. Exeunt all but* CANDY. *He squats in the hay, watching the face of* CURLEY'S WIFE.)

CANDY. Poor bastard.

CURTAIN

ACT THREE

SCENE II

Evening.
The river bank again.
Light from the setting sun shines on the low brown hills. Among the trees by the river, the shade is deep with evening feeling.
Sounds: distant barking of dogs and the quiet call of quail.
The curtain rises on an empty stage.
There is a sudden whistle of evening wind that stirs the trees and scuds the leaves on the ground.
The stage is still again. LENNIE *enters as silently as a bear. He is bent over and wary. On stage he looks behind him. Then he takes from under his coat the dead pup, lays it on the ground and, going to the river, lies on his stomach and drinks.*
He returns to the dead pup, sits down beside it.

LENNIE. George gonna give me hell . . . I bet. I . . . won't tell him. I'll bury him. (*Begins to scoop a hole in the sand in front of him. Softly.*) But I didn't forget, you bet. I come right here. Hide in the brush an' wait for George. (*Works carefully at his little grave, shaping the hole. At last he picks up the pup and lays it in the hole. Mourning.*) He gonna give me hell. He gonna wish he was alone. (*Adjusts the puppy in the hole, turning it around to make it fit better. Defiantly.*) Well . . . I can go right up in the hills an' find a cave. 'Course I wouldn't never have no ketchup. (*Begins packing sand down carefully about the pup, patting it as he does in beat with his words.*) I'll—go—away—go--away. (*Every word a pat. Fills the grave carefully, smooths the sand over it.*) There now. (*Gathers leaves and scatters them over the place. Gets up on his knees and cocks his head to inspect the job.*) Now. I won't never tell George. (*Sinks back to a sitting position.*) He'll know. He always knows.

(*Far off sound of voices approaching. They come closer during the scene. Suddenly there is the clicking warning of a cock-quail and then the drum of the flock's wings.* GEORGE *enters silently, but hurriedly.*)

GEORGE (*in a hoarse whisper*). Get in the tules—quick.

LENNIE. I ain't done nothing, George. (*The voices are very close.*)

GEORGE (*frantically*). Get in the tules—damn you. (*Voices are nearly there.* GEORGE *half pushes* LENNIE *down among the tules. The tops rustle showing his crawling progress.*)

WHIT (*offstage*). There's George. (*Enters.*) Better not get so far ahead. You ain't got a gun. (*Enter* SLIM, CARLSON, BOSS, CURLEY, *and three other ranch hands. They are armed with shotguns and rifles.*)

CARLSON. He musta come this way. Them prints in the sand was aimed this way.

SLIM (*has been regarding* GEORGE). Now look. We ain't gonna find him stickin' in a bunch this way. We got to spread out.

CURLEY. Brush is pretty thick here. He might be lying in the brush. (*Steps toward the tules.* GEORGE *moves quickly after him.*)

SLIM (*Seeing the move speaks quickly*). Look—(*pointing*)—up there's the county road an' open fields an' over there's the highway. Le's spread out an' cover the brush.

BOSS. Slim's right. We got to spread.

SLIM. We better drag up to the roads an' then drag back.

CURLEY. 'Member what I said—shoot for his guts.

SLIM. Okay, move out. Me an' George'll go up to the county road. You guys gets the highway an' drag back.

BOSS. If we get separated, we'll meet here. Remember this place.

CURLEY. All I care is getting the bastard. (*The men move offstage right, talking.* SLIM *and* GEORGE *move slowly upstage listening to the voices that grow fainter and fainter.*)

SLIM (*softly to* GEORGE). Where is he? (GEORGE *looks him in the eyes for a long moment. Finally trusts him and points with his thumb toward the tules.*)

SLIM. You want—I should—go away? (GEORGE *nods slowly, looking at the ground.* SLIM *starts away, comes back, tries to say something, instead puts his hand on* GEORGE'S *shoulder for a second, and then hurries off upstage.*)

GEORGE (*moves woodenly toward the bank and the tule clump and sits down*). Lennie! (*The tules shiver again and* LENNIE *emerges dripping.*)

LENNIE. Where's them guys goin'? (*Long pause.*)

GEORGE. Huntin'.

LENNIE. Whyn't we go with 'em? I like huntin'. (*Waits for an answer.* GEORGE *stares across the river.*) Is it 'cause I done a bad thing?

GEORGE. It don't make no difference.

LENNIE. Is that why we can't go huntin' with them guys?

GEORGE (*woodenly*). It don't make no difference. . . . Sit down, Lennie. Right there. (*The light is going now. In the distance there are shouts of men.* GEORGE *turns his head and listens to the shouts.*)

LENNIE. George!

GEORGE. Yeah?

LENNIE. Ain't you gonna give me hell?

GEORGE. Give ya hell?

LENNIE. Sure. . . . Like you always done before. Like—"If I didn't have you I'd take my fifty bucks . . ."

GEORGE (*softly as if in wonder*). Jesus Christ, Lennie, you can't remember nothing that happens. But you remember every word I say!

LENNIE. Well, ain't you gonna say it?

GEORGE (*reciting*). "If I was alone I—could live—so easy. (*His voice is monotonous.*) I could get a job and not have no mess. . . ."

LENNIE. Go on, go on! "And when the end of the month come . . ."

GEORGE. "And when the end of the month come, I could take my fifty bucks and go to—a cat-house. . . ."

LENNIE (*eagerly*). Go on, George, ain't you gonna give me no more hell?

GEORGE. No!

LENNIE. I can go away. I'll go right off in the hills and find a cave if you don't want me.

GEORGE (*speaks as though his lips were stiff*). No, I want you to stay here with me.

LENNIE (*craftily*). Then tell me like you done before.

GEORGE. Tell you what?

LENNIE. 'Bout the other guys and about us!

GEORGE (*recites again*). "Guys like us got no families. They got a little stake and then they blow it in. They ain't got nobody in the world that gives a hoot in hell about 'em!"

LENNIE (*happily*). "But not *us*." Tell about us now.

GEORGE. "But not us."

LENNIE. "Because . . ."

GEORGE. "Because I got you and . . ."

LENNIE (*triumphantly*). "And I got you. We got each other," that's what, that gives a hoot in hell about us. (*A breeze blows up the leaves and then they settle back again. There are the shouts of men again. This time closer.*)

GEORGE (*takes off his hat; shakily*). Take off your hat, Lennie. The air feels fine!

LENNIE (*removes his hat and lays it on the ground in front of him*). Tell how it's gonna be. (*Again the sound of men.* GEORGE *listens to them.*)

GEORGE. Look acrost the river, Lennie, and I'll tell you like you can almost see it. (LENNIE *turns his head and looks across the river.*) "We gonna get a little place . . . (*Reaches in his side pocket and brings out* CARLSON's *Luger. Hand and gun lie on the ground behind* LENNIE's *back. He stares at the back of* LENNIE's *head at the place where spine and skull are joined. Sounds of men's voices talking offstage.*)

LENNIE. Go on! (GEORGE *raises the gun, but his hand shakes and he drops his hand on to the ground.*) Go on! How's it gonna be? "We gonna get a little place. . . ."

GEORGE (*thickly*). "We'll have a cow. And we'll have maybe a pig and chickens—and down the flat we'll have a . . . little piece of alfalfa. . . ."

LENNIE (*shouting*). "For the rabbits!"

GEORGE. "For the rabbits!"

LENNIE. "And I get to tend the rabbits?"

GEORGE. "And you get to tend the rabbits!"

LENNIE (*giggling with happiness*). "And live on the fat o' the land!"

GEORGE. Yes. (LENNIE *turns his head. Quickly.*) Look over there, Lennie. Like you can really see it.

LENNIE. Where?

GEORGE. Right acrost that river there. Can't you almost see it?

LENNIE (*moving*). Where, George?

GEORGE. It's over there. You keep lookin', Lennie. Just keep lookin'.

LENNIE. I'm lookin', George. I'm lookin'.

GEORGE. That's right. It's gonna be nice there. Ain't gonna be no trouble, no fights. Nobody ever gonna hurt nobody, or steal from 'em. It's gonna be—nice.

LENNIE. I can see it, George. I can see it! Right over there! I can see it! (GEORGE *fires.* LENNIE *crumples; falls behind the brush. The voices of the men in the distance.*)

CURTAIN

Dead End

BY SIDNEY KINGSLEY

"The contrast of affluence and wretchedness is like dead and living bodies chained together."

THOMAS PAINE.

CHARACTERS

GIMPTY	MR. JONES
T.B.	KAY
TOMMY	JACK HILTON
DIPPY	LADY WITH DOG
ANGEL	THREE SMALL BOYS
SPIT	SECOND CHAUFFEUR
DOORMAN	SECOND AVENUE BOYS
OLD LADY	MRS. MARTIN
OLD GENTLEMAN	PATROLMAN MULLIGAN
FIRST CHAUFFEUR	FRANCEY
"BABY-FACE" MARTIN	G-MEN
HUNK	POLICEMEN
PHILIP GRISWALD	PLAINCLOTHESMAN
GOVERNESS	INTERNE
MILTY	MEDICAL EXAMINER
DRINA	SAILOR
MR. GRISWALD	A CROWD

ACT ONE

DEAD END of a New York street, ending in a wharf over the East River. To the left is a high terrace and a white iron gate leading to the back of the exclusive East River Terrace Apartments. Hugging the terrace and filing up the street are a series of squalid tenement houses.

Beyond the wharf is the East River, covered by a swirling scum an inch thick. A brown river, mucky with floating refuse and offal. A hundred sewers vomit their guts into it. Up-town of the wharf as we float down Hell Gate, the River voices its defiant protest in fierce whirlpools and stumbling rapids, groaning. Further down, we pass under the arch of the Queensboro Bridge, spired, delicate, weblike in superstructure, powerful and brutal in the stone and steel which it plants like uncouth giant feet on the earth. In its hop, skip, and jump over the River it has planted one such foot on the Island called Welfare, once the home of hospital, insane asylum, and prison, now being dismantled, an eyesore to the fastidious who have recently become its neighbors. And here on the shore, along the Fifties is a strange sight. Set plumb down in the midst of slums, antique warehouses, discarded breweries, slaughter houses, electrical works, gas tanks, loading cranes, coal-chutes, the very wealthy have begun to establish their city residence in huge, new, palatial apartments. The East River Terrace is one of these. Looking up this street from the vantage of the River, we see only a small portion of the back terrace and a gate; but they are enough to suggest the towering magnificence of the whole structure. The wall is of rich, heavy masonry, guarded at the top by a row of pikes. Beyond the pikes, shutting off the view of the squalid street below, is a thick edging of lush green shrubbery. And beyond that, a glimpse of the tops of gaily colored sun umbrellas. Occasionally the clink of glasses and laughter filter through the shrubs. The exposed sidewall of the tenement is whitewashed and ornamented with an elaborate, ivy-covered trellis to hide its ugliness. The gate posts are crowned with brass ship lanterns, one red, one green. Through the gateway is a catwalk which leads to a floating dock, where the inhabitants of this apartment moor their boats and yachts.

Contrasting sharply with all this richness is the miseased street below, filthy, strewn with torn newspapers and garbage from the tenements. The tenement houses are close, dark and crumbling. They crowd each other. Where there are curtains in the windows, they are streaked and faded; where there are none, we see through to hideous, water stained, peeling wall-paper, and old broken-down furniture. The fire escapes are cluttered with gutted mattresses and quilts, old clothes, bread-boxes, milk bottles, a canary cage, an occasional potted plant struggling for life.

To the right is a huge, red sand hopper standing on stilts of heavy timber several stories tall. Up the street, blocking the view, is a caterpillar steam shovel. Beyond it, way over to the west, are the sky-scraping parallelepipeds of Radio City. An alleyway between two tenements, tied together by drooping lines of wash, gives us a distant glimpse of the mighty Empire State Building rearing its useless mooring tower a quarter of a mile into the clouds.

At the juncture of tenement house and terrace is a police call-box; at the juncture of the street and wharf is a police stanchion bearing the warning, "Dead End." The boards of the wharf are weather beaten and deeply grained; the piles are stained green with algae to where the water licks, and brown above. A ladder nailed to the beams dips down into the river. The sunlight tossed from the waves dances across the piles to the musical lap of the water. Other river sounds counter-point the orchestration: the bells and the whistle, the clink and the chug of passing boats.

A gang of boys are swimming in the sewerage at the foot of the wharf, splashing about and enjoying it immensely. Some of them wear torn bathing trunks, others are nude. Their speech is a rhythmic, shocking jargon that would put a truck-driver to blush.

682

There are a few onlookers. A fat, greasy WOMAN *leans out of a tenement window. She is peeling an orange and throwing the peels into the street. A sensitive-faced young* MAN, *in a patched, frayed shirt, open at the neck, is sitting on one of the piles. In his lap is a drawing board. Occasionally he will work feverishly, using pencil and triangular ruler, then he will let the pencil droop, and stare out over the river with deep-set eyes, 'dream-laden, moody.*

A tubercular-looking BOY *about sixteen is up near the hopper, pitching pennies to the sidewalk. There is a splash of water, a loud derisive laugh, and up the ladder climbs a* BOY, *lean, lithe, long-limbed, snub-nosed, his cheeks puffed with water. Reaching the top of the ladder, he leans over and squirts out the water. A yelp below. He laughs again and cries: "Gotcha dat time!"*

TWO BOYS *come running down the street toward the wharf. One, a tiny Italian with a great shock of blue-black hair, is dangling a shoe box almost as big as himself; the other, a gawky Polack, head shaven, cretinous, adenoidal, is slapping his thigh with a rolled newspaper as he runs. They shout: "Hi ya, Tommy?"*

TOMMY. H'lo Angel! H'lo Dippy! (ANGEL *unslings his box, and starts tearing off his clothes. A squat boy with a brutish face, snot bubbling from his nostrils, climbs up after* TOMMY. *As he reaches the top and sees the others, he shouts in a mocking sing-song, "Dopey Dippy, dopey Dippy, dopey Dippy!"*)

DIPPY. Shat ap, will ya, Spit!

SPIT. (*Spitting through his teeth at* DIPPY, *who is stripping his jersey over his head.*) Right inna belly-button! (*Laughs and climbs onto the wharf to sprawl next to* TOMMY. DIPPY *mumbles and wipes out his navel with his finger.*)

TOMMY. Lay off 'im, why doncha?

SPIT. I'll knock 'im innis eye!

TOMMY. Wassamattuh? Yuh a wise guy er a boy scout? C'mon in, Dippy!

ANGEL. Howza wawda, Tommy?

TOMMY. Boy! Duh nuts!

SPIT. Geeze, great!

ANGEL. Cold?

TOMMY. Nah. Swell. Jus' right. (*Wiping off some of the river filth that has clung to him.*) Boy, deah's a lot a junk inna wawda tuhday!

DIPPY. (*Pointing to some dirt on* SPIT's *back.*) Wat's at? (*He touches* SPIT, *smells his finger and makes a wry face.*) Pee—ew, whadda stink! (SPIT *plucks off a huge gob of filth and throws it at* DIPPY. DIPPY *whines.*) What yuh wanna do dat fuh?

SPIT. Aw, I'll mobilize yuh!

TOMMY. Leave 'im alone! (*To* DIPPY.) Whyn't yuh keep yuh trap shut, huh?

DIPPY. He trew dat crap on me! I wuz...

TOMMY. O.K. O.K. O.K. (*Pointing at some imaginary object near the sand hopper.*) Hey, felluhs, look! (*All look off.* TOMMY *sticks his forefinger next to* SPIT's *averted nose.*) Hey, Spit! (SPIT *turns his head and bumps his nose on* TOMMY's *finger. The boys laugh.*) Nex' time leave 'im alone, see? (*The cadaverous-looking lad picks up his pennies, and comes down to the others, boasting, "Boy I git a crack all a time!"*)

TOMMY. (*Rising.*) **Yeah? Aw right, T.B.,** I'll pitch yuh.

T.B. O.K. C'mon.

TOMMY. Lemme a couple.

T.B. Yuh ain' got 'ny?

TOMMY. Come on! I'll pay yuh back. (TOMMY *and* T.B. *go up to the hopper and pitch pennies to the sidewalk.*)

SPIT, (*Turning to* DIPPY, *makes a swipe at him.* DIPPY *backs away.*) Two fuh flinchin' ... two fuh flinchin'!

DIPPY. I di' not.

SPIT. Yuh did so.

DIPPY. I di' not.

ANGEL. Whyn't cha choose? Choose 'im! Choose fer it!

SPIT. (*Scrambling to his feet.*) O.K. Odds!

ANGEL. Go on!

DIPPY. Evens! (SPIT *and* DIPPY *match fingers.*) Once fuh me. See? Cheatin' shows!

SPIT. Come on! Once fuh me. Twice fuh me. An' tree fuh me. Cheatin' shows? Yeah. Boy, ahl knock yuh fer a loop!

ANGEL. Go on, Dippy, yuh lost. Yuh git yer lumps.

DIPPY. (*Whining.*) Hey, Tommy. . . .

SPIT. (*Grabbing* DIPPY's *rolled newspaper.*) Come on! (*He bangs* DIPPY *twice on the head.*)

DIPPY. Ow! . . . Ow! . . . Ow! Ah, yuh louse. Yuh didn't have tuh hit me so hahd. Wid all his might he hit me. Wid all his might, duh son uva bitch!

TOMMY. (*Still absorbed in pitching pennies with* T.B.) Whyn't yuh pick on a kid who kin fight back?

SPIT. Aw-ww!

TOMMY. Ah! (*The* DOORMAN, *a giant in powder-blue uniform with gilt buttons and braid, opens the gate of the apartment house, crosses to the end of the sidewalk and blows a whistle, then signals to some-one up the street to come down. He turns to speak to an aristocratic* OLD GENTLEMAN *and* OLD LADY *who appear in the gateway of the East River Terraces.*)

DOORMAN. I'm so sorry, ma'am, but it'll only be for a day or two.

OLD LADY. That's quite all right.

OLD GENTLEMAN. (*Arthritic, grumpy, walking slowly and with effort.*) It isn't at all. There's no reason why we should have to walk half a block to the car. (*A* COLORED MAN *in chauffeur's uniform comes down the sidewalk.*)

DOORMAN. I'm so sorry, sir.

OLD LADY. That's quite all right. (*She pauses a moment, surveying the boys.*) Look at this!

OLD GENTLEMAN. Humph! I've seen it from the balcony.

ANGEL. Hey, look, guys! Dey usin' a back daw.

TOMMY. I wonduh why.

DIPPY. (*Familiarly, to the young man who is sketching.*) Duh yuh know, Gimpty? Hey, Gimpty?

GIMPTY. What?

DIPPY. Duh yuh know why?

GIMPTY. Why what?

DIPPY. Why dey usin' a back daw.

GIMPTY. Are they?

DIPPY. Yeah.

GIMPTY. No . . . no, I don't. (*The* COL-ORED CHAUFFEUR *salutes the* OLD MAN *and offers him an arm to lean on.*)

CHAUFFEUR. Good afternoon sir, I'm sorry I couldn't drive the car around the . . .

OLD LADY. That's all right, Jordan. Look at these youngsters! Aren't they sweet?

OLD GENTLEMAN. Sweet? Yes . . . from a distance! (*They walk up the street, out of sight. A passing tug blasts the air with its fog horn.* TOMMY, *having won at penny-pitching, puts the pennies in the pocket of his trousers, which are hanging on the hopper.* T.B. *disconsolate, goes to* ANGEL.)

T.B. Dat cleans me. I dunno. I kin always git a crack when I'm playin' by myself. (*He watches* ANGEL, *who is fussing with a scrap of newspaper and some strange, brown substance.*) Whatcha got deah?

ANGEL. It's a dried up hawse-ball.

T.B. Whatcha doin'?

ANGEL. I'm gonna make some cigarettes. Some guy tole me—yuh kin make cigarettes outa dem.

T.B. Yeah?

ANGEL. Yeah. I'm gonna try it.

T.B. I never hoid a dat.

ANGEL. It's good. Some guy tole me.

TOMMY. Aw, yuh crazy.

ANGEL. Naw . . . it's good.

T.B. Deah wuz a guy at rifawm school once used tuh smoke marywanna. Yuh know what dat is? Dope. It's like dope. It's dope. It gives yuh dreams.

ANGEL. Didja try it?

T.B. Nah. I can't smoke on accoun' a my T.B. It gits me. I cough like anyt'ing.

ANGEL. (*Rises and crosses to* GIMPTY.) Hey, Gimpty, got a match?

T.B. (*Murmurs.*) My pratt and your face. Dat's a good match! (*Laughs to himself.*)

GIMPTY. What for?

DIPPY. He's makin' cigarettes outta hawse-balls.

GIMPTY. Out of what?

ANGEL. Hawse-balls.

GIMPTY. Throw it away, you crazy fool. You want to get sick?

ANGEL. I kin smoke. Whadda yuh tink I yam?

GIMPTY. Listen. I read about a guy once who smoked that stuff. You know what happened to him.

ANGEL. What?

GIMPTY. Great, big things grew right out of his head.

ANGEL. (*Turning away from* GIMPTY, *with disgust.*) Aw—w—w, go wan.

GIMPTY. Listen . . . if I give you a good one, will you throw that away?

ANGEL. (*Turning back eagerly.*) Sure!

GIMPTY. (*Appropriates* ANGEL's *horrible cigarette and throws it into the water; then takes a sack of tobacco from his pocket, adeptly rolls a cigarette and holds it out to* ANGEL.) Here! Stick out your tongue. (ANGEL *licks the paper.* GIMPTY *completes rolling the cigarette and gives it to him.*) There you are! Now don't try that again. You'll get sick as a dog. Remember . . . I'm tellin' you.

ANGEL. (*Proudly exhibiting his cigarette.*) Boy! Hey, felluhs, look! Gimpty gimme a butt. (*To* T.B.) Gimme a light, T.B. (T.B. *fishes some matches from his pocket and lights* ANGEL's *cigarette.*)

DIPPY. (*Dashing over to* GIMPTY.) Me too, Gimpty! Gimme! Yew know me! Yew know me! (DIPPY, TOMMY *and* SPIT *descend on* GIMPTY, *swarming over him like a horde of locusts. They hold out their hands and beg plaintively.* "Give us one! Yew know us, Gimpty.")

GIMPTY. No! No! No more! Beat it! That's all! (*They only plead the louder.*) I said that's all. Don't you understand English? You want a boot in the behind? (TWO MEN *come down the street. One, tall, young, rather good-looking in a vicious way: the other, older, shorter, squat, a sledge-hammer build. The first has thin nervous lips, narrow agate eyes, bloodshot. A peculiarly glossy face, as if the skin had been stretched taut over the cheekbones which are several sizes too large for the lean jaw underneath. Here is a man given to sudden volcanic violences that come and are gone in a breath. His movements are sharp, jerky; his reflexes exaggerated, those of a high-strung man whose nerves are beginning to snap under some constant strain. He covers it, though, with a cocky swagger. He walks leaning forward, hips thrown back, almost as if out of joint. He wears a gray, turned-down fedora, an expensive suit, sharpy style, the coat a bit too tight at the waist, pleated trousers, and gray suede shoes. His squat companion is dressed almost identically, but was not designed to wear such clothes. His trousers hang on his hips, revealing a bulge of shirt-waist between vest and trouser-top, his barrel of a chest is too thick for his jacket, his arms too long for the sleeves. His huge fingers you notice at once! Thick stubs sticking out of the shapeless bags of his hands like the teats of a cow. The two men come down almost to the edge of the wharf. The tall one lights a cigarette, looks about, smiles, shakes his head, and talks sotto voce to his companion.*)

TOMMY. (*To* GIMPTY.) Aw, ta hell wid yuh! Cheap skate! (*The boys walk away, disgusted.* GIMPTY *rolls another cigarette, lights it, and returns to his drawing-board.*)

SPIT. Yeah, ta hell wid 'im!

DIPPY. Yeah, ta hell wid 'im!

SPIT. (*Crosses to his clothes, which are hanging from a nail on the hopper.*) I dun need hisn. I gotta stack a butts I picked up I'm savin'.

TOMMY. Give us one.

DIPPY. Yeah! Give us one!

SPIT. Nah. I'm savin' 'em.

TOMMY. Don' be a miser. (SPIT *takes out a tobacco tin, opens it, exposing a rare collection of cigarette ends gleaned from the streets. Grudgingly he hands* TOMMY *and* DIPPY *a butt each, then selects a choice one for himself.*) Gimme a light, T.B. (*They all light up and puff away with huge satisfaction.*)

ANGEL. (*Suddenly aware of the two strangers.*) Shine, mistah? (*The tall fellow shakes his head and turns away.*) A good shine. Come on! (*To the other.*) Yew? (*The squat man glares at him and growls, "Yuh cockeyed? Can't yuh see we got one?"*)

ANGEL. (*Turns away, muttering.*) Aw... call at a shine? (*The* DOORMAN *comes to the gate and holds it open. A* GOVERNESS, *accompanied by a 'well-dressed, delicate-featured, little boy, comes out of the Terrace Apartments. The* GOVERNESS *talks with a marked French accent. She nods to the* DOORMAN.)

GOVERNESS. Good afternoon.

DOORMAN. Good afternoon, ma'am.

GOVERNESS. But . . . where is our chauffeur?

DOORMAN. I think he's on the corner with the cab-drivers. Shall I get him?

GOVERNESS. Never mind. (*To the little boy.*) Wait here. *Attends moi ici, mon cheri.* (*The* DOORMAN *goes in, closing the gate behind him. The little boy, surveying the curious scene, answers, a bit distracted,*

"All right, I'll . . ." *When he opens his mouth, he shows a shiny, gold orthodontic brace.*)

GOVERNESS. *Mais, Philippe! En français!*

PHILIP. (*Obediently.*) *Oui, mademoiselle, j'attendrais.*

GOVERNESS. *Très bien. J'y reviendrai de suite . . . dans deux minutes.*

PHILIP. *Oui, oui, mademoiselle.* (*She hurries up the sidewalk and out of sight.*)

TOMMY. Wee-wee! He's godda go wee-wee! (*All the boys shout with laughter.*)

DIPPY. Do a swan-dive, Tommy. At's wad I like.

TOMMY. O.K. Hole my butt. (*He hands his cigarette to* DIPPY.) Hey, kid! Hey, yew! Hey, wee-wee! (PHILIP *looks at him.*) Yuh wanna see sumpm? A swan-dive. Watch! (TOMMY *dashes off, under the hopper. We hear his "Whe-e-e" and a splash. The boys cluck approval.*)

PHILIP. What's so wonderful about that?

ANGEL. Aw, yuh fat tub a buttuh, it's more'n yew kin do.

PHILIP. That shows how much you know.

T.B. I bet a dollar he can't even swim.

PHILIP. I can too.

T.B. Ah, balonee!

PHILIP. Balonee yourself! We've a pool in there and I swim every day . . . with instruction.

SPIT. Aw, bushwah! (TOMMY *appears on the ladder.* DIPPY *hands him his cigarette.*)

DIPPY. He sez dey godda pool in ere.

TOMMY. How wuzat swan-dive?

DIPPY. He sez it wuz lousy.

TOMMY. (*Climbing over the parapet and crossing to* PHILIP, *belligerently.*) Oh, yeah? What wuza mattuh wid it? Kin yew do betta?

PHILIP. A trillion times.

TOMMY. Awright. Lessee yuh.

PHILIP. Where?

TOMMY. Heah!

PHILIP. Here?

TOMMY. Yeah, heah. Yew hoid me. Yew ain' deef. (*Turns to the others.*) His eahs ovuhlap, dat's it! (*They roar with laughter.*)

PHILIP. I wouldn't swim here.

T.B. He's yelluh, dat's what! Dat's what! He's godda yelluh streak up 'is back a mile wide.

PHILIP. It's dirty here.

DIPPY. (*Shocked.*) Doity!

T.B. (*Very indignant.*) Doity! He sez doity. He sez it's doity! I'll sock 'im!

ANGEL. Lil fairy!

SPIT. Wassamattuh? Yuh sca'd yuh git a lil doit on yuh?

PHILIP. Besides, I haven't got my suit.

TOMMY. Well, go in bareass.

T.B. Yeah, wassamattuh wid bareass?

PHILIP. And besides, I'm not allowed to.

DIPPY. (*Sing-song.*) Sissy, sissy, sucks his mamma's titty!

PHILIP. Sticks and stones may break my bones, but names will never hurt me. (*The boys crowd him back against the gate.*)

TOMMY. Ah, ahl spit in yuh eye an' drown yuh. Hey, what's at junk yuh got in yuh mout . . . like a hawse?

PHILIP. It's a brace, to make my teeth straight.

TOMMY. Wha-a-at? I could do dat wit one wallop! (*The gang roar with laughter.*)

PHILIP. You try and you'll be arrested.

SPIT. Yeah?

TOMMY. (*Contemptuously.*) Look who's gonna arrest us!

PHILIP. My uncle's a judge.

TOMMY. Balonee!

PHILIP. Did you ever hear of Judge Griswald?

ANGEL. So what? So I know a guy whose brudduh's a detective. He'll git us out.

T.B. Yeah? Did yuh evuh hear a Judge Poikins! Well, he's a frien' a mine, see? He sent me to 'ifawm school once.

DOORMAN. (*Appears, bellowing.*) What's the matter? Get away from here, you! (*They scatter, razzing him. He turns to* PHILIP.) Were they bothering you?

PHILIP. No, I don't pay any attention to them. (*The* DOORMAN *opens the gate and both he and* PHILIP *go in. The boys laugh and mock them.* DIPPY, *preoccupied with the phenomena of his body, suddenly discovers a lone hair on his chest.*)

DIPPY. Boy! Gee! Hey, I godda hair! (*He caresses it, proudly.* T.B. *comes over, inspects the hair, admires it, then suddenly plucks it out, and runs away laughing and holding up the trophy.* DIPPY *yips, first with pain, then with rage.* TOMMY *finds an old discarded broom in the litter under the hopper. He balances it skillfully on the palm of his hand.*)

SPIT. Gese, I'm hungry!

TOMMY. Me too!

ANGEL. Boy, I'm so hungry I could eat a live dog.

DIPPY. (*Looks up from his wounded chest.*) Boy, I could eat a hot dog.

ANGEL. Wid sour-kraut!

DIPPY. Yeah.

ANGEL. (*Licking his lips and patting his belly.*) Yum.

SPIT. Hey, should we go tuh Schultzie's 'n' see if we kin snitch sumpin?

TOMMY. (*Balancing the broom.*) Nah, Schultzie's wise tuh us.

ANGEL. We could try some udduh staws.

TOMMY. (*Still balancing the broom.*) Nah, dey're all wise tuh us. Duh minute we walk in 'ey ask us wadda we want. If we had some dough, while one uv us wuz buyin' sumpm de udduh guys could swipe some stuff, see? I got faw cents, but 'at ain' enough. (*He drops the broom, and becomes the man of action.*) Anybody got any dough heah? Hey, yew, Angel, yuh got some?

ANGEL. No, I ain'.

TOMMY. Come on! Don' hole out!

ANGEL. Honest! I didn' git no customah dis mawnin'.

TOMMY. Weah's' 'is pants? Look in 'is pants! (T.B. *and* SPIT *rush to the hopper, grab* ANGEL's *pants, and start rifling the pockets.* ANGEL *follows them, yelling.*)

ANGEL. Hey! Git outa deah! Git outa deah!

T.B. Nuttn but a couple a stamps 'n' a boy-scout knife.

SPIT. (*Taking the knife himself.*) Oh baby, kin I have dis?

ANGEL. (*Follows* SPIT.) No, I need it.

SPIT. No, yuh don't.

ANGEL. Aw, Spit, gimme my knife!

SPIT. (*Mocking his accent.*) Watsa ma'? Piza Taliana? (*He spits at him.*) Right inee ear! Ha!

ANGEL. (*Backs a step and wipes out his ear with a finger.*) Ah, yuh louse! Ast me fuh sumpm sometime 'n' see watcha git.

TOMMY. Giv'im 'is knife!

SPIT. Da hell I will!

ANGEL. Aw, Spit, gimme my knife! Tommy, make 'im, will yuh?

TOMMY. Gimme dat knife!

SPIT. What fuh?

TOMMY. (*Makes a fist and waves it in front of* SPIT's *nose.*) Fuh dis...right in yuh bugle! (*He grabs the knife and examines it.*) Gese, dat's a knife! Five blades! Boy, I'd like one like 'at. (*Enter from the lower tenement door, a young* BOY *of about twelve, a bit timid, neatly dressed, obvious semitic features.*)

ANGEL. Aw, Tommy, I need it. I godda use it. Honest!

TOMMY. (*Gives him his knife.*) Here! Stop squawkin'! Don' say I nevuh gave yuh nuttin'!

ANGEL. Tanks, Tommy. Dat's white.

TOMMY. (*Good-naturedly.*) Ah, shat ap! (*To* DIPPY, *who sits reflectively picking his nose.*) Hey, Dippy! Pick me a big juicy one! (DIPPY *grins, rolls the resinous matter into a little ball, and flicks it at* TOMMY. TOMMY *laughs, and trots up the street to join the others who are seated on a tenement stoop. The* TALL MAN *turns from his conversation with his companion, and calls to* DIPPY, "Hey, you!")

DIPPY. What?

THE TALL ONE. Wanna run a errand fuh me?

THE SQUAT ONE. (*Offers.*) I'll go, chief. What is it?

DIPPY. Sure. Wheah?

THE TALL ONE. (*Points to a tenement house up the block.*) 418 . . . fourth floor . . . Mrs. Martin. Tell her a friend a hers wants a see her here.

DIPPY. O.K. 418? O.K. (*He trots off.*)

GIMPTY. (*Who has looked up at the sound of* THE TALL ONE's *voice.*) Don't I know you from somewhere? (*The stranger's lips compress—"no".*) I could've sworn I . . .

SQUAT MAN. (*Comes over and mutters in a thick voice full of threat.*) He said no, didn' he? (*The other restrains him with a touch on the arm.*)

GIMPTY. Sorry. (*He looks down at his drawing. The two walk away, and stand leaning against the wall, talking in low tones. The boys on the stoop suddenly notice the little Jewish boy who is peering over the wharf.*)

T.B. Hey, look! Deah's 'at new kid 'at moved aroun' a block.

SPIT. 'At's 'at Jew kid! (*They rise and come down toward him.*)

TOMMY. Hey, kid!

ANGEL. Hey, kid!

THE JEWISH BOY. (*Looks up.*) Wadda yuh want?

SPIT. Come heah, Ikey! Come on! Don' be so slow. (*He comes over, eager to join them, yet scared.*)

TOMMY. Yew da noo kid onna block, aintcha?

THE JEWISH BOY. Yeah.

TOMMY. Watsya name?

THE JEWISH BOY. Milton. Milton Schwartz.

TOMMY. Yuh wanna belong tuh are gang?

MILTY. (*Eagerly.*) Yeah. Shuah.

TOMMY. Got 'ny dough? Yuh godda be ineetiated.

MILTY. I god tree sants.

TOMMY. Gimme it!

SPIT. (*Prodding him in the ribs.*) Give it tuh 'im!

T.B. (*Prodding him harder and pulling him around.*) Go on!

TOMMY. (*Pulling him back.*) Come on! Don' hole out! (MILTY *fishes out three cents and hands them to* TOMMY.) 'At's all yuh got?

MILTY. Yeah.

SPIT. Sure?

MILTY. Hones'.

TOMMY. Soich 'im! (*They start to go through his pockets.*)

MILTY. (*Turns his pockets inside out.*) Don'! Yuh don' haf tuh. Look!

SPIT. Ah, you punk!

TOMMY. Listen, yew! If yuh wanna belong to dis gang, yuh godda git a quatuh.

MILTY. A quatuh? Wheah ahm gonna git a quatah fum?

SPIT. Fum yuh ole lady.

MILTY. She woodn gimme no quatuh.

SPIT. Yuh know wheah she keeps huh money, doncha?

MILTY. Dat's a sin tuh steal.

SPIT. (*Mocking his accent.*) Whassamattuh, Ikey?

MILTY. Don' make fun on me. I can' help it.

SPIT. (*Contemptuously.*) Yuh scared tuh snitch a quatuh? Geese, she won' fin out.

MILTY. Yes, she would.

SPIT. (*Still mocking him.*) Oh, she counts huh money all a time, huh, Jakey Ikey?

MILTY. Stop dat! Gimme back my tree sants. I don' wanna hang out wid youse.

TOMMY. (*To* SPIT.) Yuh godda watchpocket, aincha?

SPIT. Yeah.

TOMMY. Guard dis dough! (*He hands the money to* SPIT, *who puts it in his pocket. They walk away, completely ignoring* MILTY.)

MILTY. (*Follows them, murmuring tremulously.*) Gimme back my tree sants!

SPIT. (*Whispers to the others.*) Let's cockalize him!

ANGEL. Wadda yuh say, Tommy?

TOMMY. O.K.

T.B. Come on! (ANGEL *crosses nonchalantly behind* MILTY, *then crouches on his hands and knees unnoticed. The others turn and slowly approach him. Suddenly* TOMMY *pushes* MILTY, *who stumbles backward and trips over* ANGEL, *feet flying up. They all pounce on the prostrate boy, pin his arms and legs to the ground, unbutton his pants, pull up his shirt.*)

TOMMY. Gimme some a dat doit!

SPIT. (*Scoops up a handful of dirt.*) Heah! (*They rub it into* MILTY's *groin. He kicks and screams, hysterically laughing at the sensation. When he's through rubbing in the filth,* TOMMY *coughs up a huge wad of saliva and spits on* MILTY's *organ. Each of them spit, once round the circle. The* TALL ONE *and the* SQUAT ONE *laugh. A tat-*

too of heels running down the street! A whirlwind hits the group, and the boys are dispersed right and left. The whirlwind is a girl not much bigger than TOMMY, *with a face resembling his—pushed up nose and freckles. She slaps and pulls and pushes the boys, who scatter away, laughing and shouting. She stands there, eyes blazing.*

TOMMY. Aw scram, will yuh, Drina, Scram!

DRINA. Shut up! (*She helps* MILTY *to his feet, brushes him off, and wipes his face, comforting him. On second glance she is not the child she seemed. Her simple dress, her hair combed back of the ears and held in place with a cheap celluloid clasp, her lithe, boyish figure combine to create the illusion of a very young girl. When she comforts* MILTY, *however, it is apparent in the mature quality of her solicitude that she is much older—in her earlier twenties. The* TALL ONE *grins at her. She throws him a contemptuous side glance and rebukes him sharply.*)

DRINA. You ought to be ashamed of yourself, standing there and letting them pile up on this kid.

TOMMY. Aw, Drina, will yuh butt outa dis?

DRINA. (*To the snivelling boy.*) Are you hurt? (*To the* TALL ONE.) Why didn't you stop 'em?

THE TALL ONE. What fer? It'll do 'im good.

DRINA. (*Furiously.*) Oh, yeah? I suppose it'll do you good if I crack your face, huh?

THE TALL ONE. Oh, lady, yuh scare me!

DRINA. Fresh guy, huh?

THE SQUAT ONE. (*Walks over to her, his face screwed up in disgust.*) Shut yuh big mouth or I'll . . .

THE TALL ONE. (*Sharply.*) Hunk! Cut it! (HUNK *obeys instantly. They walk away to the bulwark.*)

TOMMY. Aw, Drina, why dontcha butt outa my business?

DRINA. Wait till I get you home, I'll show you butt out of . . . (TOMMY *scratches his head. She places her hands on her hips and frowns.*) What are you scratchin' your head for? Are you buggy again? (*Her authoritative, maternal concern gives her the air of a little girl playing house.*)

TOMMY. Aw, git out a heah or I'll bust yuh one!

DRINA. That's fine talk, Tommy . . . bust you one! (*He scratches again.*) There you go again! Scratchin'! (*She crosses to him.*) Come on home! I'm gonna wash your head.

TOMMY. Aw, lemme alone. All a time yuh bodderin' me. . . . (*Runs away from* DRINA *and climbs up the hopper like a monkey, out of her reach.*)

DRINA. (*To* GIMPTY.) Pete, why didn't you stop 'em?

GIMPTY. I'm sorry, Drina. I didn't notice what was happenin'. I was thinkin' about somethin'.

DRINA. Yeah? (*She turns to* TOMMY, *dangling high on his perch.*) Tommy, did you go to school today?

TOMMY. Sure.

DRINA. If you're lying, Tommy, I'll kill you.

TOMMY. (*Wiggling his toes at her.*) Aw, nuts!

DRINA. (*To* MILTY, *who is still sobbing.*) What's the matter? Did they hurt you?

MILTY. Dey took my money.

DRINA. They did? How much?

MILTY. Tree sants.

DRINA. Tommy!

TOMMY. What?

DRINA. Did you take this boy's three cents?

TOMMY. Nope.

DRINA. You did so!

TOMMY. I di' not!

DRINA. You did so!

TOMMY. Well, I ain't got it.

DRINA. Who has? Who's got it? (*To* ANGEL.) You?

ANGEL. Not me. (DRINA *looks accusingly at* T.B.)

T.B. (*Walks away, indignantly.*) Don' look at me!

TOMMY. Go on, Spit, giv 'im back 'is tree cents.

DRINA. (*Turns on* SPIT.) Oh, so you're the one! Come on!

SPIT. (*Thumbs his nose.*) Like hell I will.

DRINA. Come on!

SPIT. Frig you!

DRINA. (*Flaring.*) I'll crack you . . . you talk like that!

SPIT. Ah, I'll sock yuh inna tit. (*She smacks him. He clenches his fist and draws it back ready to swing.*)

TOMMY. (*Jumps from the hopper and rushes at* SPIT, *fists clenched, arms raised in fighting position.*) Cut dat out yuh louse!

SPIT. Well . . . she smacked me foist. She smacked me foist. No dame kin smack me foist an' get away wid it.

TOMMY. Give 'er dat dough.

SPIT. What fuh?

TOMMY. Give her da dough. Dat's what fuh.

SPIT. Yeah?

TOMMY. Yeah.

SPIT. Ah, yuh mudduh's chooch!

TOMMY. Ah, yuh fadduh's doop!

DRINA. Keep quiet, Tommy! (*To* SPIT.) Come on! *Come on!*

TOMMY. Hurry up! Give 'er dat dough! (*Pause.* SPIT *grudgingly gives her the money.* TOMMY *drops his hands and returns to the hopper, whistling.* DRINA *hands the money back to* MILTY.)

DRINA. Here.

MILTY. Tanks!

DRINA. That's all right. You look like a nice boy. Stay away from them. They're no good. They're bums.

SPIT. (*Sullen, but seeking an ally.*) Come on, Angel. Y'ain' bin in yet. Wanna go in?

ANGEL. O.K.

SPIT. Last one in's a stinkin' rotten egg! (*They rush off and jump into the water with great splashes.* T.B. *remains near the hopper, watching. Off right voices are heard. A tall, lean, soft-spoken gentleman, middle-aged, wearing shell-rimmed glasses and carrying a pipe appears at the gate. He is followed by a plumpish man of about the same age.* PHILIP *opens the gate for them, smiling.*)

PHILIP. Hello, daddy!

PHILIP'S FATHER. Hello, son. Shoulders back! (PHILIP *straightens.*) Attaboy. Where's Jeanne?

PHILIP. She went to find Charles.

PHILIP'S FATHER. Oh? And where's he?

PHILIP. I don't know.

PHILIP'S FATHER. (*Goes up the street, looks into the tenement hallway. He shakes his head in disapproval and turns to his companion.*) Say, Jones! Look at this at our back door! (JONES *nods.*)

DRINA. (*To* GIMPTY.) You let them take his money without even interfering. Shame on you!

GIMPTY. I told you I didn't notice what was happening. My mind was on somethin' else.

DRINA. Ah, you're always sticking up for them. (*To* TOMMY.) Tommy! I'm gonna get some kerosene and clean your head right away.

TOMMY. Aw—w—w.

DRINA. Don't aw—w—w me! (*She walks up the street.* TOMMY *jumps down from the hopper and dives into the water.*)

PHILIP'S FATHER. Hm! Whose property is this?

JONES. I think J. and J. I'm not sure, Griswald.

GRISWALD. Why don't they keep it in repair?

JONES. What for? It's valuable stuff as it is. No upkeep.

GRISWALD. (*Gasps at the stench that comes out of the building.*) Phew! What do they do? Use this hallway as a latrine?

JONES. Probably.

GRISWALD. Hm! Terrible!

JONES. Well, these people have to live some place.

GRISWALD. (*Groping in his coat pockets.*) Hm. Forgot my tobacco pouch. Will you run up and get it for me, son?

PHILIP. Sure, daddy! Where is it?

GRISWALD. Now, let me see. I think it's . . . I'd better go myself. (*Turns to* JONES.)

JONES. I'll go up with you.

GRISWALD. We'll be down in a minute. Ask Charles to wait for us.

PHILIP. Certainly, daddy.

GRISWALD. Thanks, son. (*They go off into the apartment house.* DIPPY *comes running down the sidewalk.*)

DIPPY. I fuhgot. Wot wuzat name? Moitle?

THE TALL ONE. Martin! (HUNK *cautions him with a tug.* GIMPTY's *head jerks up. He stares at the* TALL ONE.)

HUNK. Maybe I better go.

THE TALL ONE. O.K. 418, fourth floor. (*To* DIPPY.) Nevuh mind, kid. (*To* HUNK.) And while yuh at it, look in at tailor's I tole yuh.

HUNK. (*Nods.*) Check! (*Exit* HUNK *up the sidewalk.*)

DIPPY. I'll go. I'll go git her.

THE TALL ONE. Beat it!

DIPPY. Don' I git nuttin'? I went part a da way.

THE TALL ONE. Nuttin' fer nuttin'. Beat it!

DIPPY. Ah, dat's a lousy trick tuh play on a kid.

THE TALL ONE. (*Raises his foot to kick* DIPPY.) Come on! . . . (DIPPY *runs to the ladder, grumbling, climbs over, yells.*)

DIPPY. Hey! Yew! (*The* TALL ONE *turns to look.*) Go tuh hell! (*And he quickly jumps into the water. The* TALL ONE *laughs, comes down to the edge of the wharf, and watches* DIPPY *splash away.*)

GIMPTY. (*Snaps his fingers. Sudden recollection.*) Martin! Baby-face Martin!

THE TALL ONE. (*Wheels to face* GIMPTY, *one hand reaching under his coat for a shoulder holster.*) I ain't Martin, you bastard!

GIMPTY. Don't you recognize me?

MARTIN. O.K. Yew asked fer it an' yuh git it!

GIMPTY. I'm Gimpty. . . . Remember?

MARTIN. Gimpty?

GIMPTY. Sure, Baby-face. I . . .

MARTIN. Sh! Shat ap! My name's Johnson. Git it? Johnson.

GIMPTY. We were kids here. Don't you remember? I was one of the gang.

MARTIN. (*Squints at him carefully for a long time.*) Yeah.

GIMPTY. You don't have to worry about me.

MARTIN. I ain't worryin' about you. I'm worryin' about me. (*His hand emerges slowly from under his coat.*) You wuz dat funny kid who used to mind my clothes when I went swimmin'.

GIMPTY. Yeah.

MARTIN. Yeah. 'At's right. Kin yuh still keep yer lips buttoned up?

GIMPTY. I guess so.

MARTIN. Yuh guess so! Yuh better find out. And God damn quick!

GIMPTY. You know me, Marty, I . . . (*A man comes out of the East River Terrace.*)

MARTIN. Sh! (MARTIN *waits till the man is out of hearing, then relaxes.*) O.K. Ony, I'm tellin' yuh, if it wuz anybody else, so help me God, I'd . . . (*Gestures with thumb and forefinger, as if reaching for his gun.*)

GIMPTY. Thanks. . . . What did you do to your face?

MARTIN. Operation. Plastic, dey call it.

GIMPTY. Oh! And you dyed your hair, too.

MARTIN. Yeah. I guess yuh read about me.

GIMPTY. Sure. You're the headliner these days.

MARTIN. God damn right; (*Pauses. Looks around reminiscently and nods toward the East River Terrace Apartments.*) Hey, dat's somethin' new, ain't it?

GIMPTY. No. It's been up a couple of years.

MARTIN. Yeah? What is it?

GIMPTY. One of the swellest apartment houses in town.

MARTIN. Yuh don' tell me! Well, what do yuh know!

GIMPTY. Yeah. You have to have blue blood, a million bucks, and a yacht to live in there, or else you have to . . . (*Breaks off, moodily.*)

MARTIN. What?

GIMPTY. Oh, nothin'.

MARTIN. Come on! I don' like 'at. If you're gonna say it, say it.

GIMPTY. It's nothin'. You see over there? They got a floatin' dock.

MARTIN. Yeah. . . . What's it doin' there? Right by de ole wharf. We used to pee over deah . . . remember?

GIMPTY. Yeah.

MARTIN. Uh-huh. (*Regards* GIMPTY *quizzically.*) What's your racket?

GIMPTY. I'm an architect.

MARTIN. What's dat?

GIMPTY. I design houses.

MARTIN. Yuh don' say! What do yuh know! Little Gimpty, an' look at 'im! An architect! Well, I always knew yuh'd come trew. Yuh had somethin' here, kid! (*Taps his head.*) Yep. Well, I'm glad tuh see yuh doin' O.K., Gimpty. Not like dese udder slobs. Yuh must be in a big dough, huh?

GIMPTY. (*Laughs.*) Nine out of ten architects are out of work.

MARTIN. Yeah?

GIMPTY. Yeah.

MARTIN. So what da hell's a good?

GIMPTY. That's the question. Don't ask me. I don't know. . . . Strictly speakin' I'm not even an architect. You see, before you're an architect, you got to build a house, an' before anybody'll let you build 'em a house, you got to be an architect.

MARTIN. Sounds screwy.

GIMPTY. Yeah, I guess it is. Besides, nobody's building any more, anyway.

MARTIN. An' fer dat yuh had to go tuh high school?

GIMPTY. College, too.

MARTIN. College? Yuh went to college?

GIMPTY. Six years.

MARTIN. Six years? Why, yuh son uv a bitch, yuh're marvelous!

GIMPTY. Well, I won a scholarship, and Mom worked like hell . . . and here I am. I was doin' a little work for the government, but . . .

MARTIN. Oh, yeah?

GIMPTY. No . . . don't get excited. . . . On a slum clearance project. But that folded up. I'm on home relief now.

MARTIN. Oh! (*A man comes down the street and enters the tenement. He bangs the door.* MARTIN *starts and looks back jerkily.*)

GIMPTY. Say, is it so smart for you to come here? With that big reward.

MARTIN. I ain' here. I'm out West. Read da papers.

GIMPTY. Have you seen your mother yet?

MARTIN. No. Dat's one reason why I come back. I ain' see dee old lady 'n seven years. I kind a got a yen. Yuh know?

GIMPTY. Sure. . . . I saw her here day before yesterday.

MARTIN. Yeah? I taught she might be aroun'. How's she look?

GIMPTY. All right.

MARTIN. Gese. Seven years! Since a day I come out a reform school. Say, yew came down 'ere wid her tuh meet, me, didn' cha?

GIMPTY. Yeah.

MARTIN. Sure. 'At's right.

GIMPTY. Well, you've gone a long way since then.

MARTIN. Yeah.

GIMPTY. You know, Marty, I never could quite believe it was you.

MARTIN. Why not?

GIMPTY. To kill eight men?

MARTIN. Say, what ta hell a yuh tryin' tuh do? Tell me off, yuh bastard. Why, I'll ...

GIMPTY. No, Marty. . . .

MARTIN. Say, maybe yuh changed, huh? Maybe yuh become a rat. Maybe yuh'd like tuh git dat faw grand at's up fuh me. . . .

GIMPTY. You know better.

MARTIN. I'm not so sure. Fawty-two hundred bucks is pretty big dough fer a joik like yew.

GIMPTY. You can trust me.

MARTIN. Den don' gimme any a dat crap! What ta hell did yuh tink I wuz gonna do, hang aroun' 'is dump waitin' fer Santa Claus tuh take care a me, fer Chris' sake? Looka yew! What a yew got? Six years

yuh went tuh college an what da hell a yuh got? A lousy handout a thoity bucks a month! Not fer me! I yain't like yew punks . . . starvin' an' freezin' . . . fuh what? Peanuts? Coffee an'? Yeah, I got mine, but I took it. Look! (*Pulls at his shirt.*) Silk. Twenty bucks. Look a dis. (*Pulls at his jacket.*) Custom tailored—a hundred an' fifty bucks. Da fat a da land I live off of. An' I got a flock a dames at'd make yew guys water at da mout'. At'd make yew slobs run off in a dark corner when yuh see dere pichure an play pocket-pool.

GIMPTY. Ain't you ever scared?

MARTIN. Me? What of? What ta hell, yuh can't live faever. Ah, I don' know. Sure! Sometimes I git da jitters. An' sometimes I git a terrific yen tuh stay put, an' . . . Ah, ta hell wid it! Say, do yew remember dat kid Francey?

GIMPTY. Francey?

MARTIN. She wuz my goil when we were kids.

GIMPTY. Oh, yeah. She was a fine girl. I remember.

MARTIN. Yew bet. Ey don' make no more like her. I know. I had 'em all. Yuh ain't seen her around, have yuh?

GIMPTY. No.

MARTIN. Hoid anythin' about her?

GIMPTY. No.

MARTIN. Gee, I got a terrific yen tuh see dat kid again. At's why I come back here. I wonder what she's doin'. Maybe she got married. Nah, she couldn'! Maybe she died. Nah, not Francey! She had too much on a ball, too much stuff . . . guts. Yeah, she wuz like me. Nuttin' kin kill Baby-face Martin an nuttin' kin kill her. Not Francey. Gese, I wonder what's become a her?

GIMPTY. She's the girl whose uncle owns a tailor shop around the corner, isn't she? (MILTY *strolls over to the parapet and stands looking into the water.*)

MARTIN. Yeah. Yuh remember her now.

GIMPTY. Sure I remember her, all right.

MARTIN. I tole Hunk, he's one a my boys, tuh look in 'ere an' see if he could git her address. Gese, I gotta see dat kid again! (SPIT *climbs out of the water, goes to* MILTY *and in one sweep of his arm, tears* MILTY's *fly open.*)

SPIT. Tree bagger!

MILTY. Stop dat!

SPIT. (*Threatening him.*) What?

TOMMY. (*Follows* SPIT *over the parapet.*) Aw, cut it out, Spit. We gave im enough fuh one time.

SPIT. I'll knock 'im intuh da middle a next week!

TOMMY. (*Tearing open* SPIT's *fly.*) Home run! (*The rest of the* KIDS *climb out of the water.* MILTY *joins them in laughing at* SPIT's *discomfiture.*)

SPIT. (*Turning on* MILTY.) What a yuh laughin' at?

DIPPY. Yeah, what?

SPIT. Sock 'im, Dippy.

DIPPY. Aw, I could lick im wid one han' tied behin' my back. (*Taps* MILTY's *shoulder with his clenched fist in rhythm to.*) Tree, six, nine, da fight is mine, I kin lick yew any ole time. Tree, six, nine, da . . .

MILTY. Git outa heah. Lemme alone. (*He swings at* DIPPY, *who retreats frightened.*)

SPIT. (*Grabbing* MILTY *roughly by his shirt.*) Oh . . . a tough guy, huh?

TOMMY. I said leave 'im alone. We give 'im enough fuh one time.

SPIT. (*Releases* MILTY *and goes to* TOMMY *threateningly.*) Wheah da hell a yuh come off, all a time tellin' me what tuh do?

TOMMY. I'll put yew out like a light.

SPIT. (*Spitting at* TOMMY.) Right inna nose!

TOMMY. (*Ducks, and the wad of saliva flies over his head.*) Miss! Now yuh git yer lumps!

SPIT. Try it! Wanna make somethin' out uv it? Come on! Come on! (*He starts*

dancing in front of TOMMY, *waves his fists and mutters dire threats.* TOMMY *suddenly gives him one terrific blow and* SPIT *collapses, his nose bleeding.*)

GIMPTY. Hey!

TOMMY. Hay fuh hosses! It wuz comin' tuh him. (*To* MILTY, *patting his back.*) O.K. kid! Yew kin stick aroun'. (HUNK *enters down the sidewalk.*)

T.B. Hey, Tommy, len' me a couple a my pennies. I wanna practice pitchin'.

TOMMY. O.K. (*They pitch pennies from the hopper to the sidewalk.*)

MARTIN. (*To* GIMPTY.) Da kids aroun' here don' change! (*Turns, meets* HUNK's *suspicious stare at* GIMPTY; *to* HUNK.) He ain' nuttin' tuh worry about.

HUNK. It's your funeral as well as mine.

MARTIN. Did yuh git huh address?

HUNK. Yuh mudder's out. Deah wuz no answer.

MARTIN. Francey. What about huh?

HUNK. Dee old joker said ee didn't know, but ee gimme da address of her aunt in Brooklyn. She might know.

MARTIN. Well, hop a cab an' git it.

HUNK. (*Making a wry face.*) Brooklyn?

MARTIN. Yeah.

HUNK. Oh, hell!

MARTIN. Come on! Stop crappin' aroun'.

HUNK. Awright. (*Exit up the sidewalk.*)

SPIT. (*To* PHILIP, *who has appeared on the terrace to watch the fight.*) Whadda yuh lookin' at, huh? Yuh nosey lil . . .

PHILIP. Nosey nothing. It's a free country, isn't it?

TOMMY. Hey, wee-wee, what ah yuh, a boy 'r a goil?

T.B. He's a goil, cantcha see?

PHILIP. I'm a man! (T.B. *razzes him loudly.* PHILIP *razzes loudly back.*)

T.B. Wassamattuh? Yew a wise guy?

PHILIP. Yes, I am.

T.B. Oh, yeah?

PHILIP. I can name all the Presidents of the United States. Can you?

T.B. What? Tommy kin . . .

PHILIP. Ah-h-h!

TOMMY. I used to be able tuh.

T.B. Ah, I bet yuh. I bet yuh a dollar ee kin. I bet yuh . . .

PHILIP. All right.

T.B. Aw right what?

PHILIP. I'll bet you a dollar.

T.B. What?

PHILIP. (*Takes a dollar bill from his pocket and proudly waves it aloft.*) Put up your dollar!

DIPPY. Gese, a buck!

T.B. (*Slaps his cheek in amazement.*) A whole real live dollar . . . my gawd! (ANGEL *and* SPIT, *impressed, exclaim and whistle.*)

PHILIP. Aw, you haven't even got a dollar.

T.B. Yeah, well . . . show 'im, Tommy, anyway. Show 'im! Jus' show 'im up, will yuh?

PHILIP. Washington, Adams, Jefferson. Go on! Name the next three!

TOMMY. Madison . . . Harrison . . . no . . ,

PHILIP. Wrong!

TOMMY. Well, I used tuh know em. I fergit.

PHILIP. Aw-w.

TOMMY. Well, who cares, anyway? Yuh li'l sissy! Let's cockalize 'im! Whadda yuh say? Come on! (*Chorus of approval. They start climbing up the wall, but the* DOORMAN *appears just in time.*)

DOORMAN. Get out of here! (*He gives them a dirty look, then exits, closing the gate.*)

TOMMY. Wait till I git yew . . . I'll fix your wagon! Come heah, guys. We gotta git dat kid away from deah. We gotta git him. . . . (*The gang all huddle about* TOMMY, *whispering. Three smaller* BOYS *straggle down the street and sit on the curb. They try to insinuate their way into the conclave.*)

TOMMY. (*To the three smaller* BOYS.) Hey, whata yew want? (*The three smaller* BOYS *don't answer, but are ready for a fight.*) Angel, tell yuh kid brudder tuh git da hell outa heah!

ANGEL. Beat it!

TOMMY. Go home and tell yuh mudder she wants yuh!

ANGEL. (*Rises, rushes the kids. The smallest stops to fight him, but* ANGEL *routs them and they flee up the sidewalk.*) Dat crazy brudduh a mine! (DRINA *enters down the street, carrying a can of kerosene.*)

MARTIN. Well, keep yer nose clean, Gimpty, an' yer lips buttoned up tight, see?

GIMPTY. Forget it! (MARTIN *exits up the sidewalk, eyeing* DRINA *as she passes him.*)

DRINA. Come on, Tommy.

TOMMY. Not now, I'm busy.

DRINA. Tommy, don't be like that, will you? You can't go around with a head full of live stock.

TOMMY. I ain't got no bugs.

DRINA. (*Grabbing him, as he pulls away.*) Let me see . . . come here! (*She examines his head.*) Whew! You ain't! You got an army witha brass band. Come on home.

TOMMY. Wassamattuh wid tuhnight?

DRINA. Tonight I got a strike meetin'. I don't know what time I'll be home.

TOMMY. Aw, yew an' yuh lousy meetin's.

DRINA. It ain't no fun for me, Tommy. Come on an' let's get you cleaned up.

TOMMY. Aw, Drina!

DRINA. I don't like it any more than you do.

TOMMY. Gese, look it! (*He points up the street, and* DRINA *relaxes her hold on him.*

TOMMY *rushes off under the hopper and dives into the water with a "Whee-ee." The other* KIDS *laugh and then straggle up the street to sit in a huddle on the doorstep of a tenement house.*)

DRINA. Tommy!

GIMPTY. (*Laughs.* DRINA *looks at him. He smiles understandingly.*) You've got a tough job on your hands, Drina.

DRINA. (*Peering over the wharf, following* TOMMY *with her eyes.*) He's really a good kid.

GIMPTY. (*Also watches* TOMMY, *whom we can hear thrashing the water with a clockwork, six-beat crawl.*) Sure.

DRINA. Just a little wild.

GIMPTY. Hey . . . Tommy's got a good crawl-kick!

DRINA. (*Calling.*) Tommy! Come on! (TOMMY *shouts under the water, making a noise like a seal.* DRINA *laughs against her will.*) What are you gonna do with a kid like that?

GIMPTY. (*Laughs.*) I don't know.

DRINA. (*Seating herself on the parapet, next to* GIMPTY.) It's not that he's dumb, either. I went to see his teacher yesterday. She said he's one of the smartest pupils she's got. But he won't work. Two weeks he played hookey.

GIMPTY. I don't blame him.

DRINA. I can't seem to do anything with him. It was different when Mom was alive. She could handle him . . . and between us we made enough money to live in a better neighborhood than this. If we win this strike, I'm gonna move, get him outa here the first thing.

GIMPTY. Yeah. That's the idea.

DRINA. (*Noticing his drawings.*) What've you got there? More drawings?

GIMPTY. Couple a new ideas in community housing. Here! see? (*He passes the drawing pad to her.*)

DRINA. (*Studies them and nods admiration.*) Yeah. Thty're beautiful houses, Pete.

But what's the good? Is anybody going to build them?

GIMPTY. No.

DRINA. (*Handing back the drawings.*) So what?

GIMPTY. All my life I've wanted to build houses like these. Well . . . I'm gonna build 'em, see? Even if it's only on paper.

DRINA. A lot of good they'll do on paper. Your mother told me you've even given up looking for a job lately.

GIMPTY. (*Suddenly bitter and weary.*) Sure. What's the use? How long have you been on strike now?

DRINA. A month.

GIMPTY. Pickeetin' an' fightin' an' broken heads. For what?

DRINA. For what? For two dollars and fifty cents a week extra. Eleven dollars a month, Pete. All toward rent. So's Tommy an' I can live in a decent neighborhood.

GIMPTY. Yeah. You're right there. I've seen this neighborhood make some pretty rough guys. You've heard about Baby-face Martin? He used to live around here.

DRINA. Yeah. I read about it.

GIMPTY. I used to know him.

DRINA. You did? What was he like? (TOMMY *climbs up out of the water, breathless. He lies on the parapet, listening.*)

GIMPTY. As a kid, all right . . . more than all right. Yeah, Drina, the place you live in is awfully important. It can give you a chance to grow, or it can twist you—(*he twists an imaginary object with grim venom*)—like that. When I was in school, they used to teach us that evolution made men out of animals. They forgot to tell us it can also make animals out of men.

TOMMY. Hey, Gimpty.

GIMPTY. Yeah?

TOMMY. What's evilushin? (*He clambers along the parapet and lies on his stomach in front of* DRINA.)

GIMPTY. (*Looks at* TOMMY *a moment, smiles, and comes out of his dark mood.*) What's evolution, Tommy? Well, I'll tell you. A thousand million years ago we were all worms in the mud, and that evolution made us men.

DRINA. And women!

GIMPTY. And women.

TOMMY. An' boys and goils?

GIMPTY. And boys and girls.

TOMMY. Ah, I wuzn't even born a tousan' million years ago.

GIMPTY. No, but your great, great, great, great grandfather and mother were; and before them their great, great, great, great great grandfather and mother were worms.

TOMMY. Blah-h-h!

DRINA. (*Impressed.*) It's like God!

GIMPTY. It is God! Once it made dinosaurs—animals as big as that house.

TOMMY. As big as at?

DRINA. Sure.

TOMMY. Wow!

GIMPTY. Then it didn't like its work and it killed them. Every one of them! Wiped 'em out!

TOMMY. Boy! I'd like tuh see one a dem babies.

GIMPTY. I'll show you a picture some time.

TOMMY. Will yuh?

GIMPTY. Sure.

TOMMY. At'll be swell, Gimpty. (SPIT *appears on the ladder and stops to listen, hanging from the top rung.*)

GIMPTY. Once evolution gave snakes feet to walk on.

TOMMY. Snakes? No kiddin'!

SPIT. (*Sings in mockery.*) Te-da-da-da-da-bushwah, te-da-da bushwah!

TOMMY. Shat ap! Right innee eye! (*He spits.* SPIT *jumps back into the water.*)

DRINA. Tommy, cut that out! See? You're like an animal.

TOMMY. Well . . . he does it tuh all ee udduh kids. . . . Anyhow, what happened tuh duh snakes' feet?

GIMPTY. Evolution took 'em away. The same as ostriches could once fly. I bet you didn't know that.

TOMMY. No.

GIMPTY. Well, it's true. And then it took away their power to fly. The same as it gave oysters heads.

TOMMY. Oysters had heads?

GIMPTY. Once, yeah.

TOMMY. Aw-w!

DRINA. Sh, listen!

GIMPTY. Then it took them away. "Now men," says Evolution, "now men"—(*nods to* DRINA, *acknowledging her contribution*)—"and women . . . I made you walk straight, I gave you feeling, I gave you reason, I gave you dignity, I gave you a sense of beauty, I planted a God in your heart. Now let's see what you're going to do with them. An' if you can't do anything with them, then I'll take 'em all away. Yeah, I'll take away your reason as sure as I took away the head of the oyster, and your sense of beauty as I took away the flight of the ostrich, and men will crawl on their bellies on the ground like snakes . . . or die off altogether like the dinosaur. (*A very attractive, smartly-groomed* YOUNG LADY *in a white linen suit comes out of the gate. She brings a clean coolness into this sweltering street. She has a distinctive, lovely face; high forehead, patrician nose, relieved by a warm, wide, generous mouth and eyes that shut and crinkle at the corners when she smiles—which she is doing now.*)

TOMMY. Gee!

GIMPTY. That scare you?

TOMMY. Wow!

ANGEL. (*Who has been sitting on the tenement steps up the streeet watching* T.B. *and* DIPPY *climb the tractor, notices the woman come out of the gate.*) Hey, Gimpty, heah's yuh goil friend!

GIMPTY. Oh, hello, Kay!

KAY. Hello, Pete. (*Her manner is simple, direct, poised and easy. She is a realist; no chichi, no pretense. And she is obviously very fond of* GIMPTY.)

DIPPY. (*To* T.B.) Hey, Gimpty's goil fren come outa deah.

T.B. (*Rising.*) No kid! No kid!

ANGEL. Gee whiz! (*The* THREE BOYS *saunter down to* KAY.)

DIPPY. Do yew live in deah?

GIMPTY. (*Embarrassed.*) Hey!

KAY. (*Laughs.*) Yes.

ANGEL. Have dey really got a swimmin' pool in at joint?

KAY. Yes. A big one.

DIPPY. Ah yew a billionairess?

KAY. No.

DIPPY. Millionairess?

KAY. No.

GIMPTY. Hey-y-y!

ANGEL. Den what a yuh doin' comin' out a deah?

DRINA. Angelo! (*To* KAY.) Don't mind him!

KAY. (*Smiling.*) Oh, he's all right.

DIPPY. I got it. She's a soivant goil.

T.B. Nah, she's too swell-dressed all a time. (KAY *laughs.*)

GIMPTY. (*Squirming with embarrassment.*) Look! Will you kids beat it? Scram! Get outa here! Go on!

DRINA. Come on, Tommy! I'm gonna wash your head.

TOMMY. (*Crawling over to the ladder.*) Nah! Hey, Gimpty . . . 'at evilushin guy . . .

GIMPTY. What about him?

TOMMY. Did he make everything?

GIMPTY. Yeah.

TOMMY. Bugs too?

GIMPTY. Yeah.

TOMMY. (*To* DRINA.) Deah yuh ah! God makes bugs an' yew wanna kill 'em. (*Gently chiding her as if she were a naughty child.*) Is 'at nice? (*He dives off the ladder into the water.*) Whee-e-e!

KAY. He's very logical.

DRINA. Yeah. That part's all right, but he's very lousy too, an' that part ain't. (*She calls.*) Tommy! Come on! (*More splashing of the water from* TOMMY.)

DIPPY. Whee! Look! He's a flyin' fish! Do dat again, Tommy! Wait, I'm comin', Tommy! (*He mounts the parapet.*) Look a me! I'm divin' . . . a backjack! (*He stands poised for a backjack, then looks back and downward, fearfully. It's awfully high.*) Wait a minute! Wait . . . wait! (*He climbs two rungs down the ladder. Looks down. Nods. This is better.*) I'm divin' a backjack! Watch out, Tommy! (*He jumps sprawling out of sight. A tremendous splash.* KAY *looks over the parapet laughing.* DIPPY *calls up.*) How wuz at?

KAY. Beautiful!

T.B. Stinks! (*He walks off toward the hopper arm in arm with* ANGEL. TWO GIRLS *come out of the Terrace, and walk up the street, chattering.* T.B. *and* ANGEL *follow them, mimicking their mincing walk, and making indecent remarks. One of the* GIRLS *stops and turns to slap* ANGEL. *The* BOYS *laugh and run off behind the hopper. The* TWO GIRLS *go up the street, one indignant, the other giggling.* KAY *has picked up* GIMPTY's *drawings and is admiring them.* DRINA *stares enviously at* KAY, *at her modish coiffure, at her smart suit, at her shoes.* KAY *becomes conscious of the scrutiny and turns.* DRINA, *embarrassed, drops her eyes, then calls to* TOMMY.)

DRINA. Tommy! Coming?

TOMMY. (*From the water.*) No-o-o!

DRINA. Well, I'm going home. I can't wait here all day. (*She goes.*)

GIMPTY. They're using the back entrance to-day. . . .

KAY. (*Handing him the drawing pad.*) Yes. There's some trouble in front. They've ripped up the whole street. (*She looks out across the River, and breathes deep.*) It's a grand day, isn't it?

GIMPTY. Yeah.

KAY. Oh! . . . I was talking to some of Jack's friends last night. I thought they could find something for you. (*Produces a business card from her pocket.*) Here's a man who said you might come up and speak to him. Here's his card.

GIMPTY. (*Takes the card from her, and reads it.*) Del Block. Oh, yeah . . . he's a good man. Thanks! Gee! Thanks!

KAY. I don't know if it'll help much.

GIMPTY. This is swell of you! (*He looks at her a moment, lost in admiration. Then, shyly, with a good deal of hesitation and groping for the right words.*) I was telling Mom about you last night. I been kind of going around the house like a chicken with its head chopped off . . . and Mom asked me why. So I told her.

KAY. What?

GIMPTY. Oh, just a little about you. How we'd got to talking here, and meeting every day, and what great friends we've become. How you've been trying to help me. And . . . that I worship you!

KAY. You didn't!

GIMPTY. Well, I do. Do you mind?

KAY. (*Deeply toched.*) Mind? You fool! What'd she say?

GIMPTY. She said you sounded like a very, real, good person.

KAY. Good? Did you tell her all about me? About Jack?

GIMPTY. Yeah.

KAY. Your mother must be a sweet woman. I'd like to meet her some time.

GIMPTY. (*Enthusiastically.*) She'd be tickled. Will you?

KAY. Right now, if you like.

GIMPTY. Well, she's out for the afternoon.

KAY. Oh!

GIMPTY. Maybe I can get her down here day after tomorrow, huh?

KAY. (*Pauses, then, a bit depressed.*) I may not be here then. I may leave tomorrow.

GIMPTY. Tomorrow?

KAY. Night. Jack's going 'on a fishing trip. He wants me with him.

GIMPTY. Isn't that sudden?

KAY. He's been planning it for some time.

GIMPTY. How long will you be gone?

KAY. About three months.

GIMPTY. That's a long time.

KAY. Yes. (*Down the street strides a well-dressed, rather handsome man in his early forties, hard lines around the eyes. At the moment he is hot and uncomfortable. He eyes the tenements curiously as he passes them. The* DOORMAN *appears as he starts to enter the gate. He asks the* DOORMAN *in a cultured, quiet voice, "What happened in front?"*)

DOORMAN. I'll tell you, Mr. Hilton. You see, the gas mains . . .

KAY. (*Rises.*) Hello, Jack!

HILTON. (*Turns around, sees* KAY. *Surprised.*) Hello! What're you doing here? (*He crosses to her.*)

KAY. Oh, I just came out.

HILTON. (*Takes off his panama, wipes the sweat band and mops his brow with a handkerchief.*) Phew! It's been a hell of a day, arranging things at the office. Well, I've made the plans for the trip. Everything's set. The boat's in shape. I've talked to Captain Swanson. (DIPPY *climbs up over the parapet, talking to himself.*)

DIPPY. Hooray fuh me! I did a backjack! (*To* GIMPTY.) Wuz 'at good, Gimpty?

GIMPTY. All right!

DIPPY. (*To* KAY.) Hey, Gimpty's goil friend, wuz at good?

KAY. Beautiful. (DIPPY, *patting his chest and gloating "Attaboy, Dippy!" goes back into the water.* HILTON *is puzzled and annoyed. He looks at* KAY.)

HILTON. What's all this about?

KAY. Nothing.

HILTON. (*His voice begins to rasp.*) Come on. Let's go in.

KAY. It's nice out. I'd like to take a walk first.

HILTON. You'll do that later. Come on.

KAY. I have a little headache. I want to stay out a few minutes more.

HILTON. Take an aspirin and you'll be all right. Come on!

KAY. Please!

HILTON. We've a million things to do,

KAY. You go ahead. I'll be right in.

HILTON. (*Casts a glance at* GIMPTY.) What's the big attraction out here?

KAY. Nothing.

HILTON. Then stop acting like a primadonna and come on in.

KAY. Plase don't make a fuss.

HILTON. (*Suddenly loses his temper and snaps.*) It's not me . . . it's you! Damn it, I've been tearing around all day like a madman, and I come home and find you behaving like a cheap . . .

KAY. Jack!

HILTON. (*Bites his lip, controls himself, and mutters curtly.*) All right. Stay there! (*He goes in.* KAY *follows him to the gate, pauses there, uncertain. Then indulges in a momentary flash of temper herself.*)

KAY. Oh . . . let him! (*She returns slowly.*)

GIMPTY. Is that the guy?

KAY. Yes. (*Then, not to be unfair.*) Don't judge him by this. He's really not so bad. He's going to be sorry in a few minutes. He's so darn jealous. His wife gave him a pretty raw deal. You can't blame him for . . .

GIMPTY. (*Suddenly inflamed.*) All right! If it were anybody else, all right! But you? He can't treat *you* like that!

KAY. (*Sits there a while in silence, thinking. Finally, she speaks, slowly, almost in explanation to herself.*) I've been living with Jack a little over a year now. He isn't usually like this. You see, he really loves me.

GIMPTY. He has a funny way of showing it.

KAY. He wants me to marry him.

GIMPTY. Are you going to?

KAY. I don't know.

GIMPTY. Do you love him?

KAY. I like him.

GIMPTY. Is that enough?

KAY. I've known what it means to scrimp and worry and never be sure from one minute to the next. I've had enough of that . . . for one lifetime.

GIMPTY. (*Intensely.*) But Kay, not to look forward to love . . . God, that's not living at all!

KAY. (*Not quite convincing.*) I can do without it.

GIMPTY. That's not true. It isn't, is it?

KAY. (*Smiles wryly.*) Of course not.

(*A very stout* LADY *with much bosom, comes out of the gate, fondling a tiny, black dog.*)

TOMMY. (*Clambering over the parapet, sees the dog and chuckles.*) Look a dat cockaroach, will yuh? Hey, lady, wheah didja git dat cockaroach?

FAT LADY. Well, of all the little! . . . (TOMMY *starts to bark. The dog yaps back, and struggles to escape. The others* BOYS *climb up and bark in various keys. The three* SMALLER BOYS *appear and join in the medley. The stout* LADY *is distraught. She shouts at them, but to no avail.*) Get away from here, you little beasts!

SPIT. In yuh hat, fat slob! (*And he continues barking.*)

FAT LADY. Wha-a-at? Doorman! (*To the frantic dog.*) Quiet, Buddy darling! Quiet! Doorman! (*The* DOORMAN *comes out on the run and chases the boys away. They run en masse to the hopper.* TOMMY *climbs up on it. The* SMALLER BOYS *retire to the steps of an upper tenement doorway.* MR. GRISWALD, PHILIP, *and* MR. JONES *come out of the East River Terrace Apartments.*)

GRISWALD. What's the matter?

DOORMAN. Those kids! They're terrible, sir.

PHILIP. They wanted to hit me, too, daddy!

GRISWALD. Oh, yes? Why? What did you do to them? (*Smiles at* JONES.)

PHILIP. Nothing.

GRISWALD. Sure?

PHILIP. Honest, daddy, I didn't say anything to them.

DOORMAN. It's all their fault, sir.

FAT LADY. They're really horrible brats. And their language! . . .

TOMMY. (*Hanging from the hopper.*) Ah, shat ap, yuh fat bag a hump!

GRISWALD. You touch him again and I'll break your necks.

TOMMY. Balls to yew, faw eyes!

GRISWALD. (*To* PHILIP, *as he takes his arm and walks him up the street.*) The next time you hit them back.

PHILIP. But they all pile up on you, daddy.

GRISWALD. Oh, is that so? Well, I think I'm going to buy you a set of gloves and teach you how to box. (*They continue up the sidewalk, followed by* JONES.)

PHILIP. Will you, daddy? (THE GOVERNESS *and a young* CHAUFFEUR *in maroon livery meet them.*)

GOVERNESS. Bonjour, monsieur!

CHAUFFEUR. (*Saluting.*) I'm sorry to keep you waiting, sir, but . . .

GRISWALD. (*Waves them ahead.*) That's all right. Never mind. (*To* PHILIP.) The next time someone attacks you, you'll be able to defend yourself.

MR. JONES. That's the idea!

TOMMY. (*Shouts up the street after them.*) Yeah! Wid ee army an' navy behin' 'im! (*Gang laughs and shouts.* TOMMY *jumps down from the hopper. The* FAT LADY *waddles across to* KAY.)

TOMMY. Come 'ere, guys, I got a scheme how we kin git dat kid an' cockalize 'im. (*They gather in a huddle.*)

ANGEL. How?

TOMMY. (*Subsiding to a whisper.*) Foist we git 'im inna hallway, an' . . .

FAT LADY. The little Indians! They oughtn't to be allowed in the street with decent people. (*Exit the* DOORMAN, *closing the gate.*)

GIMPTY. No? What would you do with them?

FAT LADY. Send them all away.

GIMPTY. Where?

FAT LADY. I'm sure I don't know.

GIMPTY. Huh! (*Great outburst of laughter from the huddle.*)

T.B. Dat'll woik! You'll see! Dat'll git 'im!

TOMMY. Wait! Shat ap! I got maw . . . ! (*The conclave becomes a whispered one again.*)

FAT LADY. The little savages! They're all wicked. It's born in them: They inherit it.

GIMPTY. (*Suddenly bursts out, a bitter personal note in his passion.*) Inheritance? Yeah. You inherit a castle thirty stories over the river, or a stinkin' hole in the ground! Wooden heads are inherited, but not wooden legs . . . nor legs twisted by rickets! (*The* FAT LADY *is completely taken aback by this unexpected antipathy. She looks at* KAY, *gasps, and walks away, head high, patting her animal.* KAY *smiles at* GIMPTY *sadly, sympathetically.*)

GIMPTY. I'm sorry.

KAY. (*Touches his hand.*) Oh, Pete! (*Another outburst. The three smaller* BOYS *have crept down and joined the fringe of the huddle.*)

TOMMY. Dey're back again! Angel, will yuh tell yuhr kid brudduh tuh git tuh hell outa heah? (ANGEL *swings at the tiniest of the* BOYS, *who kicks him in the shin, spits at him, and runs away, thumbing his nose.* ANGEL *chases the* BOYS *part of the way up the street, then returns rubbing his shin and shaking his head.*)

ANGEL. 'At crazy kid brudduh a mine, I'm gonna kill 'im when I git 'im home! (*The huddle reorganizes.*)

GIMPTY. Gosh, I wish we could be alone for a minute!

KAY. Pete, I've thought of that so many times. I've wanted to invite you inside, but . . .

GIMPTY. You couldn't, of course.

KAY. Cock-eyed, isn't it? Couldn't we go to your place?

GIMPTY. Gee, I! . . . No, you wouldn't like it.

KAY. Why not?

GIMPTY. It's an awful dump. It would depress you.

KAY. Oh!

GIMPTY. I'd love to have you, Kay, but I'm ashamed to let you see it. Honestly.

KAY. (*Rises and offers him her hand.*) Oh, Pete, that's silly. I wasn't born in a

pent house. Come on! (*With the aid of a cane he rises. They walk up the street. For the first time we notice that one of his legs is withered and twisted—by rickets.* MILTY *rises and crosses to within a few steps of the huddle.*)

MILTY. (*Timidly.*) Hey.

TOMMY. What?

MILTY. Look, I . . . (*He approaches* TOMMY *slowly.*) If yuh want, I t'ink I kin snitch 'at quatuh fuh yuh. (*The chug of an approaching tug-boat is faintly heard.*)

TOMMY. (*Thinks it over.*) O.K., Milt! O.K. Den yuhr inna gang, see? (*Turns to the others.*) Anybody gits snotty wid Milt, gits snotty wid me, see? (*To* MILTY.) Now git dat quatah. Come on, git duh lead outa yuh pants! (*The chug-chug grows louder.*)

MILTY. (*Jubilant.*) O.K., Tommy! (*Runs off into the tenement house. The chug-chug grows louder.*)

TOMMY. See? He's a good kid. He loins fast. Remember da time I moved aroun' heah? I wuz wearin' white socks an' I wouldn't coise, so yuh all taught I wuz a sissy. (*The chug-chug grows louder.*)

DIPPY. 'Cept me, Tommy.

TOMMY. Yeah, 'cept yew. Everybody else I hadda beat da pants off a first. (*Down to business again.*) Now here's how we git wee-wee. Yew, T.B.. . . . (*His voice is drowned out by the chug-chug-chug-chug—*)

CURTAIN

ACT TWO

SCENE: *The same, the following day, lit by a brilliant afternoon sun. The boys are playing poker with an ancient deck of cards, greasy and puffed, inches thick. Match sticks are their chips. Their faces are grave and intense. They handle their cards familiarly, carressing them like old gamblers.*

MARTIN *lounges against the terrace wall and watches them with grim nostalgia.*

ANGEL. (*Throwing two match sticks into the pot.*) I'll open fuh two. Hey, Spit, it's rainin'. Come on, decorate da mahogany!

T.B. (*Adds his two.*) O.K. I'm in.

SPIT. (*Follows suit.*) Heah's my two. Dippy.

DIPPY. (*Tosses in his match sticks, deliberately, one at a time.*) I'm in.

ANGEL. (*Slapping down two cards.*) Gimme . . . two.

SPIT. (*Deals.*) Aw, he's got tree uva kin'.

T.B. (*Throws away one.*) Gimme one. Make it good. (SPIT *deals him one.*)'

ANGEL. Ah, yuh ain' got nuttin'.

SPIT. He's got a monkey. I ain' takin' any. How many fuh yew, Dippy?

DIPPY. (*Studies his hand with grave deliberation.*) I'll take five.

SPIT. Yuh can' take five.

DIPPY. (*The mental effort contorts his face.*) Faw.

SPIT. Yuh kin ony take tree.

DIPPY. (*After considerable hesitation.*) Gimme one!

ANGEL. (*Inclining his head toward* T.B.) Say, T.B., feel 'at bump I got. Feel it!

T.B. (*Explores* ANGEL's *head with a finger.*) Wow! Feel 'at bump Angel's got!

DIPPY. (*Leans over and feels the bump.*) Boy! 'At's like 'n egg!

SPIT. Wheah juh git it?

ANGEL. Me ole man give it tuh me.

DIPPY. Fuh what?

ANGEL. Fuh nuttin. Just like 'at, fuh nuttin. Last night me ole man cumzin drunk.

SPIT. (*Impatiently.*) Cum on, cum on . . . whadda yuh do?

ANGEL. (*Raps his knuckles on the sidewalk.*) I blow.

T.B. (*Raps.*) I blow.

SPIT. (*Raps.*) I blow, too. Dippy?

DIPPY. (*Raps.*) I blow.

T.B. Whatcha got?

ANGEL. (*Reveals a pair of Jacks.*) A pair of Johnnies. You?

T.B. (*Exhibits two pair, twos and threes.*) Two pair. Deuces and trays. (*He reaches for the pot.*)

ANGEL. Aw hell!

SPIT. Wait a minute! (*Lays down three tens.*) Read 'em an' weep! Judge Shmuck . . . thoity days!

DIPPY. I guess I ain't got nuttin. (SPIT *gleefully rakes in the match sticks. Enter* TOMMY, *kicking a tin can before him. The* BOYS *greet him.*)

TOMMY. Hi yuh, guys. Howza wawda?

SPIT. Cold.

TOMMY. Whatcha playin' fuh?

SPIT. Owins. Wanna play?

TOMMY. (*Starts undressing.*) Deal me inna next han'. Who's winnin'?

T.B. I yam.

TOMMY. How much?

T.B. Twenty-eight matches.

TOMMY. Twenty-eight cents . . . boy, 'at's putty good! Hey, didja heah about it?

SPIT. What?

ANGEL. About what? } Together

DIPPY. What, Tommy?

TOMMY. Dincha heah? Boy, deah wuz a big fight at da Chink laundry las' night.

ANGEL. No kiddin'!

TOMMY. Yeah.

DIPPY. How did it staht, Tommy?

TOMMY. Oh . . . a couple handkuhchifs got snotty. (*They all roar with laughter.*) Did wee-wee show up yet?

DIPPY. No, Tommy.

ANGEL. Don' worry. I bin on a lookout furrim.

DIPPY. Yeah, we bin on a lookout furrim.

ANGEL. So, like I wuz tellin' yuh, las' night me old man comes in stinkin' drunk. So he stahts beatin' hell outa me ole lady Boy, he socks 'er all ovah da place! (SPIT *laughs.*)

TOMMY. What da hell a yuh laughin' at? Dat ain' so funny.

ANGEL. No, dat ain' so funny. Cause den ee picks up a chair and wants a wallop me wid it.

DIPPY. Whatcha do den?

ANGEL. So I grabs a kitchen knife . . . dat big . . . an' I sez, "Touch me, yuh louse, an' I give yuh dis."

T.B. Yeah?

ANGEL. Yeah, yeah, I did. So he laughs, so he laughs, so he falls on a flaw, an' he goes tuh sleep . . . so he snores—(*Imitates a rasping snore*)—like at. Boy, wuz ee drunk! Boy, he wuz stinkin'! (*Enter* MILTY *down the sidewalk.*)

MILTY. Hello, Tommy!

TOMMY. Hi yuh, Milty! How's evyting?

MILTY. Swell.

TOMMY. Attaboy. (MILTY *goes to* MARTIN.)

MARTIN. Well?

MILTY. She wuz deah. I tole huh. She said not tuh come up. She said tuh meet huh down heah.

MARTIN. O.K. Heah, kid, buy yerself a Rolls Royce. (*He gives* MILTY *a half-dollar.*)

MILTY. Gee!

SPIT. Whatcha git?

MILTY. Oh, momma! Haffa buck!

SPIT. (*Shouting quickly.*) Akey! Akey! Haffies!

MILTY. (*Also shouting quickly, topping* SPIT *and holding up crossed fingers.*) Fens! No akey! No akey!

SPIT. (*Throws down his cards and rises threateningly.*) I said akey. Come on, haffies.

MILTY. Yuh didn't have yuh finguhs crossed.

SPIT. Don' han' me dat balonee! Gimme two bits.

MILTY. Yuh didn't cross yuh finguhs.

SPIT. (*Thrusting his face into* MILTY'S.) Gimme two bits 'r J kick yuh ina slats.

MILTY. Yeah?

SPIT. Yeah.

MILTY. Ah, yuh mudduh's chooch!

SPIT. Ah, yuh fadduh's doop!

MILTY. Hey, Tommy, do I gotta givim?

TOMMY. Naw. He didn' have 'is finguhs crossed.

SPIT. I'll choose yuh fer it.

MILTY. Whadduh yuh tink I yam, a dope?

SPIT. Ah, yuh damn jip ahdist!

MILTY. Look who's talkin'!

SPIT. Ah, yew stink on ice!

TOMMY. Stan' up tuh him, Milty! Stan' up tuh him.

MILTY. (*Suddenly thrusts his jaw forward.*) Watsamatteh? Yew wanna fight?

SPIT. Yeah.

MILTY. Join ee ahmy! . . . Ha! (*The boys roar at* SPIT.)

SPIT. (*Raising a fist and twisting his face fiercely.*) Ah!

MILTY. (*Raising his fist and returning the grimace.*) Ah!

SPIT. (*Fiercer in grimace and growl.*) Mah!

MILTY. (*Tops him.*) Wah! (*They stand there a moment, glaring at each other in silence, fists raised, faces almost touching, then* SPIT *turns in disgust and sits down again to his cards.*)

TOMMY. (*Grins at* MILTY'S *triumph.*) Kimmeah, Milty! Yuh wanna play?

MILTY. I dunna how.

TOMMY. Kimmeah, watch me. I'll loin yuh. (*Two strange, tough-looking* BOYS *come down the street. They pause, watch a moment, confer, then wander over to the group.*)

FIRST BOY. Hey, which one a youse guys is a captain a dis gang?

TOMMY. (*Doesn't even deign to look up.*) Who wantsa know?

SECOND BOY. Weah fum da up da blocks.

TOMMY. Second Avenya gang?

FIRST BOY. Yeah.

TOMMY. (*Assorting his cards.*) Yeah? Well, go take a flyin' jump at ta moon!

SECOND BOY. Whoza leaduh?

TOMMY. Me. What about it? I pass. (*Throws down his cards, rises, turns to the enemy.*) Wanna make sumpm out uv it?

SECOND BOY. (*A bit frightened.*) Yew tell 'im.

FIRST BOY. Yuh wanna fight are gang?

TOMMY. Sure. (*Turns to his gang.*) O.K. felluhs? Yuh wanna fight da Second Aven-yoo gang? (*They approve raucously.* TOM-MY *turns back to the emissaries.*) Sure!

FIRST BOY. O.K. On are block?

TOMMY. Yeah. O.K.

SECOND BOY. Satiday?

TOMMY. (*Asks the gang.*) O.K., Satiday, felluhs? (*They shout approval.*) Faw o'clock? (*A little bickering about time, but they agree.*) O.K. We'll be up deah Satiday faw o'clock an' boy, we'll kick the stuffin's outa youse!

SECOND BOY. Yeah?

TOMMY. Yeah! No bottles 'r rocks, jus' sticks 'n' bare knucks. Flat sticks. No bats.

SECOND BOY. Sure.

TOMMY. O.K.?

SECOND BOY. O.K.!

TOMMY. O.K. Now git da hell out a heah befaw I bust yuh one! Scram! (*The two* BOYS *run off. From a safe distance they yell.*)

FIRST BOY. Nuts tuh yew! Son uva bitch! son uva bitch!

SECOND BOY. Satiday! We be waitin' faw yuh. We kick da pants offa yuh! (TOMMY *picks up a rock, hurls it after them.* DIPPY *rises, does the same.* MARTIN *laughs.*)

ANGEL. (*First noticing* MARTIN.) Shine, mistuh?

MARTIN. O.K., kid. (ANGEL *moves his box down to* MARTIN *and begins to shine his shoes.*)

SPIT. (*Sneers at* DIPPY.) Look at 'im trow, will yuh? Like a goil. Yuh godda glass ahm? Cantcha trow a rock even?

DIPPY. Yeah. Kin yew trow bettuh?

SPIT. (*Picks up a rock, rises, looks for a target. He spots a flower pot on a fire escape.*) Watch! See at flowuh pot? (*He throws the rock and breaks the pot.*)

TOMMY. Pot shot! Pot shot!

MARTIN. Say, at wuz good pitchin'. Yew kids like tuh git some dope on gang fight-in'?

ANGEL. Sure! Hey, felluhs, come heah! (*They crowd about* MARTIN.)

MARTIN. Foist ting is tuh git down ere oiliuh' an yuh. . . . (GIMPTY *enters down the sidewalk, whistling cheerfully.*) Hello, Gimpty!

GIMPTY. Hello.

MARTIN. (*Continues the lesson.* GIMPTY *stops and listens.*) Oiliuh an yuh said, see? Dey won't be ready fuh yuh. En I tell yuh kids what yuh wanna do. Git a lot of old electric bulbs, see? Yuh trow 'em, an den yuh trow a couple a milk bottles . . . an' some a dee udder kids git hoit, an' den yuh charge 'em.

TOMMY. Yeah, but we made up no milk bottles, ony bare knucks an' sticks.

MARTIN. Yuh made up! Lissen, kid . . . when yuh fight, dee idee is tuh win. It don' cut no ice how. An' in gang fightin' remember, take out da tough guys foist. T'ree aw faw a yuh gang up on 'im. Den one a yuh kin git behin' 'im an' slug 'im. A stockin' fulla sand an' rocks is good fuh dat. An' if ey're lickin' yuh, pull a knife. Give 'em a little stab in ee arm. Ey'll yell like hell an' run.

TOMMY. Yeah, but we made up no knives. Gese, 'at ain' fair. . . .

GIMPTY. What's a matter with you? What are you trying to teach these kids?

MARTIN. Yew shut yer trap. (*To* TOMMY.) Lissen. If yuh wanna win, yuh gotta make up yer own rules, see?

TOMMY. But we made up dat . . .

MARTIN. Yuh made up . . .

TOMMY. We kin lick 'em wid bare knucks . . . fair and square.

MARTIN. Lissen, kid . . . Ere ain' no fair an' ere ain' no square. It's winnah take all. An' it's easier tuh lick a guy by sluggin' 'im fum behin' 'en it is by sockin' it out wid 'im toe tuh toe. Cause if yuhr lickin' 'im, en he pulls a knife on yuh, see? En wheah are yuh?

TOMMY. Den I pull a knife back on him.

MARTIN. Yeah, but what's a good unless yuh got one an' know how tuh use it?

TOMMY. I know how tuh.

GIMPTY. Don't pay any attention to him, guys!

MARTIN. Yew lookin' fer a sock in a puss?

GIMPTY. If you kids listen to that stuff, you'll get yourselves in Dutch.

TOMMY. Aw, shat ap. (*The boys razz* GIMPTY.)

MARTIN. Git out a heah, yuh monkey! (GIMPTY, *angry but impotent, walks away.* MARTIN *turns to the boys again.*) See what I mean?

TOMMY. Yeah, well, if I had a knife . . .

MILTY. Angel's godda knife.

ANGEL. Aw, I need it. (MARTIN *hands* ANGEL *a dime for the shine.*)

TOMMY. Yuh kin jus' loan it tuh me. I'll give it back tuh yuh.

ANGEL. No, yuh won't. Honest, I need it.

SPIT. Give it tuh him! Go on, or I'll crack yuh one!

ANGEL. No!

TOMMY. Nevuh mind . . . tuh hell wid 'im!

T.B. (*To* ANGEL.) Ah, yuh stink on ice!

ANGEL. Aw, shat ap!

T.B. Shat ap yuhself!

MILTY. Look, Angel, I tell yuh what. Ahl give yuh a quarteh fuh it. Whadda yuh say?

ANGEL. Sure!

MILTY. (*To* MARTIN.) Change, Misteh?

MARTIN. Yeah. . . . (*He gives* MILTY *two quarters in exchange for the half, then rises. A newspaper in the gutter catches his attention. He frowns, picks it up, reads it, wandering off to the tenement stoop, where he sits on a step, absorbed in the newspaper item.* ANGEL *runs to the hopper, finds his trousers, fumbles in the pocket, produces the knife and returns with it. He completes the transaction with* MILTY, *who hands the knife to* TOMMY.)

MILTY. Heah, Tommy.

TOMMY. (*Rises.*) Wha' faw?

MILTY. Fuh a present.

TOMMY. Yuh mean yuh givin' it tuh me?

MILTY. Yeah. Yuh kin keep it.

TOMMY. Gee, t'anks, Milty! Gese, 'at's swell . . . t'anks!

MILTY. Aw, dat's nuttin.

TOMMY. Aw, dat's a whole lot. T'anks! Gee! (CHARLES, *the chauffeur, enters from the gate of the East River Terrace, followed by* PHILIP.)

T.B. Hey, Tommy . . . ! (*He points to* PHILIP. *The gang gathers under the hopper, in huddled consultation.*)

PHILIP. I think I'll wait here, Charles.

CHARLES. Wouldn't you rather come with me to the garage?

PHILIP. No.

CHARLES. But your mother said . . .

PHILIP. I'll wait here for them.

CHARLES. Yes, sir. (*Exit* CHARLES *up the street.* PHILIP *examines his wrist-watch os-*

tentatiously. KAY *appears on the terrace, finds a space in the shrubbery, leans over the balustrade, and signals to* GIMPTY.)

KAY. Pete!

GIMPTY. (*Rising and crossing toward her, beaming.*) Hello, Kay! How are you feeling?

KAY. All right. And you?

GIMPTY. Like a million dollars!

KAY. I'll be down in a second. (*She disappears behind the shrubs. The conclave finished, all the boys saunter off in different directions, pretending disregard of* PHILIP. TOMMY, *whistling a funeral dirge, signals* T.B. *with a wink and a nod of the head.* T.B. *approaches* PHILIP *casually.*)

T.B. Hello, what time is it?

PHILIP. Half past four.

T.B. T'anks. Gee, dat's a nice watch yuh got deah. What kine is it?

PHILIP. A Gruen.

T.B. Boy, 'at's as nice as 'n Ingersoll. (*Coughs, then proudly tapping his chest, boasts.*)—T.B. I got T.B.

TOMMY. (*On the tenement stoop.*) Hey, felluhs, come on inna hall heah. I got sumpm great tuh show yuhs. Come on, T.B. (*They all whip up loud, faked enthusiasm.*)

T.B. O.K. (*To* PHILIP.) Yuh wanna come see?

TOMMY. Nah, he can't come. Dis is ony fuh da gang. (*The others agree volubly that* PHILIP *can't join them in the mystery.*)

T.B. Aw, why not? He's a good kid.

TOMMY. (*Supported by a chorus of "Nahs".*) Nah, he can't see dis. Dis is ony fuh da gang.

PHILIP. What is it?

T.B. Gee, I can't tell yuh . . . but it's . . . gese, it's sumpm great!

TOMMY. (*To* T.B.) Come on! Git da lead out a yuh pants!

T.B. Too bad dey won' letcha see it. Boy, yuh nevuh saw anyting like dat.

PHILIP. Well, I don't care. I can't anyway. I'm waiting for my father and mother. We're going to the country.

T.B. It'll ony take a minute. . . . Hey, felluhs, let 'im come 'n' see it, will yuh? He's O.K.

TOMMY. (*Consenting with a great show of reluctance.*) Well . . . awright. Let 'im come. (TOMMY *enters the tenement, followed by the others.*)

T.B. Come on.

PHILIP. I don't know. I expect my . . .

T.B. Awright, it's yuhr loss! (T.B. *starts up the sidewalk.*)

PHILIP. Wait! Wait! I'm coming! (*Runs to catch up with* T.B. *As they reach the steps and enter,* T.B. *pushes him in the doorway, spits on his hands and follows him in.* KAY *enters.*)

GIMPTY. (*Beams. He is very happy.*) Hello!

KAY. Hello, darling. (*There is a slight strain in her voice and attitude, which manifests itself in over-kindness and too much gentleness, as if she were trying to mitigate some hurt she is about to give him. They sit on the coping.*)

GIMPTY. Well . . . I got up early this morning and went down to a stack of offices looking for a job.

KAY. That's swell. Did you find one?

GIMPTY. Not yet. But I will. Wait and see.

KAY. Of course you will.

GIMPTY. Thanks to you. (SPIT *runs from the hallway, stops a second on the sidewalk, looking about, then grabs a large barrel stave, whacks his hand with it, whistles, and runs back into the tenement hallway.*)

KAY. Did you see Del Block?

GIMPTY. Yep.

KAY. Didn't he have anything for you?

GIMPTY. Oh, we had a nice talk. He's a very interesting guy. He showed me some of his work. He's done some pretty good stuff. (*Grins.*) He asked me if I knew where *he* could find a job. (*They both have to laugh at this.*) He thinks you're pretty swell, too.

KAY. Pete . . . you've got to get something.

GIMPTY. I will.

KAY. I didn't know how important it was until yesterday.

GIMPTY. Hey, there!

KAY. I used to think we were poor at home because I had to wear a made-over dress to a prom. Yesterday I saw the real thing. If I hadn't seen it, I couldn't have believed it. I dreamt of it all night . . . the filth, the smells, the dankness! I touched a wall and it was wet. . . . (*She touches her finger-tips, recalling the unpleasant tactile sensation. She shivers.*)

GIMPTY. That house was rotten before I was born. The plumbing is so old and broken . . . it's been dripping through the building for ages.

KAY. What tears my heart out is the thought that you have to live there. It's not fair! It's not right!

GIMPTY. I's not right that anybody should live like that, but a couple a million of us do.

KAY. Million?

GIMPTY. Yeah, right here in New York . . . New York with its famous skyline . . . its Empire State, the biggest God-damned building in the world The biggest tombstone in the world! They wanted to build a monument to the times. Well, there it is, bigger than the pyramids and just as many tenants. (*He forces her to smile with him. Then he sighs, and adds, hopelessly.*) I wonder when they'll let us build houses for men to live in? (*Suddenly annoyed with himself.*) Ah, I should never have let you see that place!

KAY. I'm glad you did. I know so much more about you now. And I can't tell you how much more I respect you for coming out of that fine, and sweet . . . and sound.

GIMPTY. (*His eyes drop to his withered limb.*) Let's not get started on that.
(PHILIP *can be heard sobbing in the tenement hallway. He flings open the door and rushes out, down the street into the apartment, crying convulsively, his clothes all awry. The gang follows him from the hallway, yelling and laughing.*)

TOMMY. (*Holding* PHILIP's *watch.*) Come on, let's git dressed an' beat it!

SPIT. Let's grab a quick swim foist.

TOMMY. Nah!

SPIT. Come on!

MILTY. Betteh not. . . .

SPIT. (*Rushes off under the hopper and dives into the water.*) Las' one in's a stinkin' rotten egg!

TOMMY. (*Throws the watch to* T.B.) Guard 'at watch and lay chickee! (*All the boys except* T.B. *dive into the water.*)

GIMPTY. When I see what it's doing to those kids I get so mad I want to tear down these lice nests with my fingers!

KAY. You can't stay here. You've got to get out. Oh, I wish I could help you!

GIMPTY. But you have. Don't you see?

KAY. No. I'm not that important.

GIMPTY. Yes, you are!

KAY. I mustn't be. Nobody must. For your own good, you've got to get out of here.

GIMPTY. I will, damn it! And if I do . . . maybe I'm crazy . . . but will you marry me?

KAY. Listen!

GIMPTY. Don't get me wrong. I'm not askin' you to come and live there with me. But you see, if. . . .

KAY. Listen! First I want you to know that I love you . . . as much as I'll allow myself to love anybody. Maybe I shouldn't have gone with you yesterday. Maybe it was a mistake. I didn't realize quite how much I loved you. I think I ought to leave tonight.

GIMPTY. Why?

KAY. Yes, I'd better. (*The chug of a small boat is heard.*)

GIMPTY. Why?

KAY. I'd better get away while we can still do something about this.

GIMPTY. How will that help?

KAY. If I stay, I don't know what will happen, except that . . . we'll go on and in the end make ourselves thoroughly miserable. We'd be so wise to call it quits now.

GIMPTY. Gee, I don't see it.

KAY. I do, and I think I'm right. (*Pause. She looks out over the river.*) There's the boat.

GIMPTY. (*Pauses. Turns to look.*) Is that it?

KAY. Yes.

GIMPTY. (*Irrelevantly, to conceal his emotion. In a dull monotone.*) It's a knockout. I'm crazy about good boats. They're beautiful, because they're designed to work. That's the way houses should be built . . . like boats.

KAY. Pete, will you be here . . . tonight . . . before I leave? (MARTIN *looks up from his newspaper to eye* KAY.)

GIMPTY. Don't go, Kay. I'll do anything. Isn't there some way . . . something?

KAY. (*Hopelessly.*) What? (*Rises.*) I guess I'll go in now, and get my things ready . . . I'll see you later? (*She presses his shoulder and exits.* MARTIN *rises, throws down his newspaper and approaches* GIMPTY.)

MARTIN. (*Sucks his lips, making a nasty, suggestive sound.*) Say . . . dat's a pretty fancy lookin' broad. High class, huh? How is she? Good lay? (GIMPTY *glares at him.* MARTIN *laughs.*) Well, fer Chris' sake, what's a matter? Can't yuh talk?

GIMPTY. Cut it out, Martin. Just cut it out!

MARTIN. Lissen, kid, why don' yuh git wise tuh yerself? Dose dames are pushovers, fish fuh duh monkeys!

GIMPTY. (*Half rising, furious.*) I said cut it out!

MARTIN. (*Roughly pushes him back.*) Sit down, yew! (*A chuckle of contempt.*) Look what wantsa fight wid me! Little Gimpty wansa fight wid me! Wassamattuh, Gimpty? Wanna git knocked off? (HUNK *slouches down the street, followed in a painfully weary shuffle by a gaunt, raw-boned, unkempt woman, sloppy and disheveled. Her one garment an ancient house dress retrieved from some garbage heap, black with grease stains. Her legs are stockingless, knotted and bulging with blue, twisted, cord-like veins. Her feet show through the cracks in her house slippers. In contrast to the picture of general decay is a face that looks as if it were carved out of granite; as if infinite suffering had been met with dogged, unyielding strength.*)

HUNK. Hey! (*She comes to a dead stop as she sees* MARTIN. *There is no other sign of recognition, no friendliness on her lips. She stares at him out of dull, hostile eyes.*)

MARTIN. (*Face lights, he grins. He steps rapidly toward her.*) Hello, Mom! How are yuh? (*Pause.*) It's me. (*No recognition.*) I had my face fixed. (*There is a moment of silence. She finally speaks in an almost inaudible monotone.*)

MRS. MARTIN. Yuh no good tramp!

MARTIN. Mom!

MRS. MARTIN. What're yuh doin' here?

MARTIN. Aintcha glad tuh see me? (*She suddenly smacks him a sharp crack across the cheek.*)

MRS. MARTIN. That's how glad I am.

MARTIN. (*Rubs his cheek, stunned by this unexpected reception. He stammers.*) 'At's a great hello.

MRS. MARTIN. Yuh dog! Yuh stinkin' yellow dog yuh!

MARTIN. Mom! What kin' a talk is 'at? Gese, Mom . . .

MRS. MARTIN. Don't call me Mom! Yuh ain't no son a mine. What do yuh want from me now?

MARTIN. Nuttin'. I just . . .

MRS. MARTIN. (*Her voice rises, shrill, hysterical*) Then git out a here! Before I crack yuh goddam face again. Git out a here!

MARTIN. (*Flaring.*) Why, yuh ole tramp, I killed a guy fer lookin' at me da way yew are!

MRS. MARTIN. (*Stares at him and nods slowly. Then quietly.*) Yeah . . . You're a killer all right . . . You're a murderer . . . you're a butcher, sure! Why don't yuh leave me ferget yuh? Ain' I got troubles enough with the cops and newspapers botherin' me? An' Johnny and Martha . . .

MARTIN. What's a mattuh wid 'em?

MRS. MARTIN. None a yer business! Just leave us alone! Yuh never brought nothin' but trouble. Don't come back like a bad penny! . . . Just stay away and leave us alone . . . an' die . . .but leave us alone! (*She turns her back on him, and starts to go.*)

MARTIN. Hey, wait!

MRS. MARTIN. (*Pauses.*) What?

MARTIN. Need any dough?

MRS. MARTIN. Keep yer blood money.

MARTIN. Yuh gonna rat on me . . . gonna tell a cops?

MRS. MARTIN. No. They'll get yuh soon enough.

MARTIN. Not me! Not Martin! Huh, not Baby-face Martin!

MRS. MARTIN. (*Mutters.*) Baby-face! Baby-face! I remember . . . (*She begins to sob, clutching her stomach.*) In here . . . in here! Kickin'! That's where yuh come from. God! I ought to be cut open here fer givin' yuh life . . . murderer!!! (*She shuffles away, up the street, weeping quietly.* MARTIN *stands there looking after her for a long time. His hand goes to his cheek.*

HUNK *comes down to him, clucking sympathetically. A boat whistle is heard.*)

HUNK. How da yuh like 'at! Yuh come all away across ? country jus' tuh see yer ole lady, an' what da yuh git? Crack inna face! I dunno, my mudder ain' like dat. My mudder's always glad tuh see me. . . .

MARTIN. (*Low, without turning.*) Shut up! Gese, I must a been soft inna head, so help me!

HUNK. Yuh should a slugged 'er one.

MARTIN. Shut up! I must a bin crazy inna head. I musta bin nuts.

HUNK. Nah! It's jus' she ain't gota heart. Dat ain' . . .

MARTIN. (*Turns on* HUNK, *viciously, barking.*) Screw, willyuh? Screw! *Exit* HUNK *up the sidewalk.* Martin. (*Turns, looking after his mother. Turns slowly onto the sidewalk, then notices* GIMPTY.) Kin yuh pitchure dat?

GIMPTY. What did you expect . . . flags and a brass band?

MARTIN. (*Suddenly wheels and slaps* GIMPTY.) Why—yew—punk!

GIMPTY. What's the idea?

MARTIN. Dat's ee idea . . . fer shootin' off yer mout'. I don' like guys 'at talk outa toin. Not tuh me!

GIMPTY. Who the hell do you think you are?

MARTIN. (*Claws his fingers and pushes* GIMPTY's *face against the wall.*) Why, yuh lousy cripple, I'll . . .

GIMPTY. (*Jerks his head free of* MARTIN's *clutch.*) Gee, when I was a kid I used to think you were something, but you're rotten . . . see? You ought to be wiped out!

MARTIN. (*His face twitching, the veins on his forehead standing out, kicks* GIMPTY's *crippled foot and shouts.*) Shut up!

GIMPTY. (*Gasps in pain, glaring at* MARTIN. *After a long pause, quietly, deliberately.*) All right. O.K., Martin! Just wait!

MARTIN. What? (*Reaches for his shoulder holster.*) What's 'at?

GIMPTY. Go on! Shoot me! That'll bring 'em right to you! Go on!

MARTIN. (*Hesitates. He is interrupted by the excited voices of* GRISWALD *and* PHILIP. *Cautiously he restrains himself and whispers.*) I'll talk to yuh later. I'll be waitin' right up thuh street, see? Watch yuh step. (GRISWALD *appears behind the gate with* PHILIP, *who is sobbing. The* GOVERNESS *tries to quiet* PHILIP *while she dabs his face with her handkerchief.* MARTIN *goes up the street.*)

GRISWALD. It's all right, son! Now stop crying! What happened? Stop crying! Tell me just what happened?

GOVERNESS. *Attends, mon pauvre petit . . .* 'ere, let me wipe your face . . . *attends, attends!*

PHILIP. They hit me with a stick!

GRISWALD. A stick!

PHILIP. (*Spread-eagling his arms.*) That big!

GRISWALD. (*Furious.*) I'll have them locked up . . . I swear I'll send them to jail. Would you know them if you saw them?

PHILIP. Yes, daddy.

GRISWALD. (*To the* GOVERNESS.) You should have been with him. After yesterday . . .

GOVERNESS. I told him to stay in the garden. Madame said it was all right and she asked me to help Clara with the curtains in his room. (SPIT *starts up the ladder, followed by the other boys.* DIPPY *is frozen. He is blue and shaking with cold. His teeth are chattering.*)

DIPPY. Look, I'm shiverin'. My teet' 'r' knockin'.

TOMMY. Yeah. Yuh lips 'r' blue! Yuh bettuh git dressed quick, aw yuh'll ketch cold. (*Looks down at* MILTY *who is climbing the ladder, behind him.*) How do yuh like it, Milty?

MILTY. (*Grins from ear to ear.*) Swell! (*As the boys appear over the parapet,* T.B. *rises from under the hopper, points to* GRISWALD, *and calls the danger-cry.*)

T.B. Chikee! Putzo! Hey, felluhs! Chikee! Tommy! (PHILIP *sees the boys and points them out to* GRISWALD.)

PHILIP. There they are! They're the ones. (*Points out* TOMMY.) He's the leader!

GRISWALD. That one?

PHILIP. Yes. (SPIT, DIPPY, MILTY *and* ANGEL *dash to the hopper, all yelling "Chikee!" They gather up their clothes and run madly up the street, followed by* T.B. TOMMY, *stooping to pick up his clothes, trips, falls and is grabbed by* GRISWALD, *who shakes him violently.*)

GRISWALD. What right did you have to beat this boy? What makes you think you can get away with that?

TOMMY. (*Struggling to escape.*) Lemme go! Lemme go, will yuh? I didn' do nuttin' . . . lemme go!

PHILIP. (*Jumping up and down with excitement.*) He's the one! He's got the watch, daddy!

TOMMY. (*Tries to break away and get at* PHILIP.) I have not, yuh fat li'l bastid!

GOVERNESS. (*Frightened, screams.*) Philippe, come 'ere!

GRISWALD. (*Jerks* TOMMY *back.*) Oh, no! Not this time! I'll break your neck!

PHILIP. He's the one!

GRISWALD. Give me that watch!

TOMMY. I yain't got it!

PHILIP. He has! He's got it!

GRISWALD. (*Turns to the* GOVERNESS, *peremptorily.*) Jeanne! Call an officer! (*To* TOMMY *again.*) Give me that watch!

TOMMY. (*Frightened by the police threat.*) I yain't got it. Honest, I yain't! (*Suddenly shouts up the street for help.*) Hey, felluhs! (*The* GOVERNESS *stands there, paralyzed.*)

GRISWALD. Jeanne, *will* you call an officer! Come on! Hurry!

GOVERNESS. *Oui, oui, monsieur!* (*She runs up the sidewalk in a stiff-legged trot.*)

TOMMY. (*Stops struggling for a moment.*) Aw, Mister, don't toin me ovuh tuh da cops, will yuh? I won' touch 'im again. We do it to allee udduh kids, an 'ey do it tuh us. Dat ain' nuttin'.

GRISWALD. No? I ought to break your neck.

TOMMY. Oh, yeah? (*He suddenly pulls away, almost escaping.* GRISWALD *puts more pressure on the arm.* TOMMY *calls to the gang.*) Hey, felluhs! (GRISWALD *twists his arm double.* TOMMY *begins to cry with pain, striking at* GRISWALD.) Yuh joik! Ow, yuh breakin' my ahm! Hey, Gimpty!

GIMPTY. Have a heart! You're hurting that kid. You don't have to . . .

GRISWALD. Hurt him! I'll kill him! (MILTY *runs down the street, holding out the watch.*)

MILTY. Heah yuh ah! Heah's duh watch! Leave 'im go misteh! He didn' do nuttin'! Leave 'im go! (*He starts pounding* GRISWALD. TOMMY *frees his hand.* GRISWALD *hooks his arm around* TOMMY *in a stranglehold, and with the free arm pushes* MILTY *away.*)

GRISWALD. (*To* MILTY.) Get out of here, you . . .

TOMMY. Hey, yer chokin' me! Yer chokin' me! (*Both hands free, he gropes in the trousers he has clung to. Suddenly he produces an open jackknife and waves it.*) Look out! I gotta knife. I'll stab yuh! (GRISWALD *only holds him tighter, trying to capture the knife. A flash of steel!* GRISWALD *groans and clutches his wrist, releasing* TOMMY. TOMMY *and* MILTY *fly up the street.* GRISWALD *stands there stunned, staring at his bleeding wrist.*)

PHILIP. Daddy! Daddy! Daddy! (*He begins to sob at the sight of blood. The* DOORMAN *comes out of the gateway and is immediately excited.*)

DOORMAN. What's the matter?

GRISWALD. (*Jerking his head toward the fleeing boys.*) Catch those boys! (*The* DOORMAN *lumbers up the street in pursuit.* GRISWALD *takes a handkerchief from his breast pocket and presses it to his wrist. Blood seeps through.* GRISWALD, *self-controlled now, tries to quiet the sobbing*

PHILIP.) It's all right, son, it's all right! No, no, no! Now stop crying. Let me have your handkerchief!

GIMPTY. Are you hurt?

GRISWALD. What do you think?

GIMPTY. Can I help?

GRISWALD. It's a little late for that now.

PHILIP. (*Fishes out a crumpled handkerchief and hands it to his father.*) Here.

GRISWALD. Haven't you a clean one?

PHILIP. No.

GIMPTY. You can have mine.

GRISWALD. Never mind. (*To* PHILIP, *who puts his own handkerchief back.*) You should always carry two clean handkerchiefs. Put your hand in my pocket. You'll find one there. No, the other pocket. (PHILIP *finds the handkerchief. The* GOVERNESS *comes down the sidewalk with a* POLICEMAN.)

POLICEMAN. What's the matter?

GRISWALD. Plenty.

GOVERNESS. (*Sees the blood and shrieks.*) Oh! He's bleeding! (*To* PHILIP.) *Qu'est ce qui passe, mon petit?*

PHILIP. That boy stuck him with a knife!

GOVERNESS. (*To* GRISWALD.) *Mon Dieu!* Are you hurt, monsieur? (GRISWALD *ignores her and tightens the bandage.*)

POLICEMAN. Is it deep?

GRISWALD. Deep enough.

POLICEMAN. Better let me make a tourniquet.

GRISWALD. Never mind.

POLICEMAN. Who did it?

GRISWALD. One of these hoodlums around here. I want that boy arrested.

POLICEMAN. Sure. Do you know who he was?

GRISWALD. No.

GOVERNESS. Can I help you, monsieur?

GRISWALD. Yes. Go up and call Dr. Merriam at once. I'm afraid of infection. (*The* DOORMAN *returns, empty-handed, puffing, and mopping his brow.* GRISWALD *frowns.*) Where is he?

DOORMAN. (*Panting.*) Phew . . . I couldn't catch them.

GRISWALD. (*Angry.*) You let them go?

DOORMAN. I tried, sir. They were like little flies . . . in and out . . . Just when I thought I had one of them . . . he ran down the cellar . . . I went after him, but he got away. . . .

GRISWALD. Officer, I want you to find that boy and arrest him. Understand?

POLICEMAN. (*Takes out a notebook and pencil.*) Well, that ain't gonna be so easy, you know.

GRISWALD. Never mind. That's your job! It's pretty serious that a thing like this can happen on your beat in broad daylight.

POLICEMAN. Well, I can't be everywhere at once.

GRISWALD. Before he stabbed me, he and some others beat up my boy and stole his watch. You should have been around some of that time.

POLICEMAN. (*Annoyed at his officiousness. Brusquely.*) Well . . . what's your name?

GRISWALD. My name's Griswald . . . I live here. (*Nods toward the East River Terrace.*)

POLICEMAN. What did the boy look like?

GRISWALD. He was about so high . . . black hair . . . oh, I don't know. I didn't notice. Did you, son?

PHILIP. One of them coughs.

POLICEMAN. Didn't you notice anything else?

PHILIP. No.

GRISWALD. Jeanne?

GOVERNESS. Let me see . . .

POLICEMAN. How was he dressed?

GOVERNESS. They'd been in swimming here. They were practically naked . . . and filthy. And their language was 'orrible.

GRISWALD. (*Irritated.*) He knows that, he knows that! What were they like, though? Didn't you see?

GOVERNESS. It all happened so quickly, I didn't have a chance to, monsieur.

PHILIP. He hit me with a stick.

POLICEMAN. Hm!

GRISWALD. (*Suddenly a bit faint.*) These men can tell you better. They saw it. Jeanne, will you please call Dr. Merriam right away? I'm feeling a little sick.

GOVERNESS. Oui, monsieur! Come, Philippe! (*She goes in, accompanied by* PHILIP.)

GRISWALD. I don't want to make any trouble, officer, but I want that boy caught and arrested. Understand?

POLICEMAN. I'll do the best I can. (*Exit* GRISWALD. *The* POLICEMAN *mutters.*) I wonder who the hell that guy thinks he is . . .

DOORMAN. (*Impressively, rolling the sound on his tongue.*) Mr. Griswald. (CHARLES, *the chauffeur, saunters down the sidewalk.*)

POLICEMAN. What of it?

DOORMAN. Don't you know? He's Judge Griswald's brother.

POLICEMAN. (*His attitude changes.*) Oh!

DOORMAN. (*To the* CHAUFFEUR, *who has reached the gate.*) Oh, I don't think Mr. Griswald'll be using the car now. He was just hurt.

CHARLES. Wha-a-at? What happened?

DOORMAN. He was stabbed. It's a long story. I'll tell you later.

CHARLES. (*Concerned.*) Well, will you call him and see if he wants me?

DOORMAN. (*Starting off.*) Yeah.

POLICEMAN. Hey, wait!

DOORMAN. I'll be right out, officer. Mr. Griswald may need him.

POLICEMAN. Oh, all right. (DOORMAN *and* CHARLES *go in through the gate.*)

CHARLES. What happened?

DOORMAN. These kids around here have been raising an awful rumpus all day, and just now one of them . . . (*Their voices die off.*)

POLICEMAN. (*To* GIMPTY.) Did you see the kids who did this?

GIMPTY. I didn't notice them.

POLICEMAN. You come around here often?

GIMPTY. Yes.

POLICEMAN. Didn't you recognize any of 'em?

GIMPTY. No.

POLICEMAN. Can you describe 'em?

GIMPTY. Not very clearly.

POLICEMAN. (*Annoyed.*) Well, what were they like?

GIMPTY. About so high . . . dirty an' naked. . . .

POLICEMAN. (*Impatiently.*) And they socked that young jalopee in the eye. Yeah. I got that much myself. But that might be any kid in this neighborhood. Anything else?

GIMPTY. No.

POLICEMAN. (*Slaps his book shut.*) Why the hell didn't I learn a trade? (*He starts toward the gate.* DRINA *comes down the street and approaches* GIMPTY. *She looks tired and bedraggled. She has an ugly bruise on her forehead.*)

GIMPTY. (*To* DRINA.) Hey, what's the matter with your head?

DRINA. (*Looking at the* POLICEMAN *and raising her voice.*) We were picketing the store, an' some lousy cop hit me.

POLICEMAN. (*Wheels around, insulted.*) What's that?

DRINA. (*Deliberately.*) One a you lousy cops hit me.

POLICEMAN. You better watch your language or you'll get another clout!

DRINA. Go on and try it!

GIMPTY. (*Urging discretion.*) Sh!

POLICEMAN. Listen! I'm in no mood to be tampered with. I'm in no mood! . . . Not by a lousy Red.

DRINA. (*Quietly.*) I ain't no Red.

POLICEMAN. (*Thick-skulled.*) Well, you talk like one.

DRINA. Aw nuts!

POLICEMAN. You were strikin', weren't you?

DRINA. Sure. Because I want a few bucks more a week so's I can live decent. God knows I earn it!

POLICEMAN. (*Who has had enough.*) Aw, go on home! (*He turns and goes in the gate, addressing someone.*) Hey, Bill, I wanna see you. . . . (*Pause.*)

DRINA. (*To* GIMPTY.) We were only picketing. We got a right to picket. They charged us. They hit us right and left. Three of the girls were hurt bad.

GIMPTY. I'll give you some advice about your brother.

DRINA. I was just lookin' for him. Did you see him?

GIMPTY. Tell him to keep away from here . . . or he's in for a lot of trouble.

DRINA. (*Sits down, exhausted, and sighs.*) What's he done now?

GIMPTY. Plenty.

DRINA. What?

GIMPTY. Just tell him to keep away.

DRINA. Gosh, I don't know what to do with that boy! (*A passing boat hoots twice.* DRINA *ponders her problem a moment.*) There's a feller I know . . . is always askin' me to marry him. . . . Maybe I ought to do that, hm? . . . For Tommy . . . he's rich. . . . What should I do?

GIMPTY (*Disinterested, too absorbed in his own problem.*) That's up to you.

DRINA. Most of the girls at the store are always talkin' about marryin' a rich guy. I used to laugh at 'em. (*She laughs now at herself.*)

GIMPTY. Maybe they're right.

DRINA. (*Looks at him.*) That doesn't sound like you.

GIMPTY. No? How do you know what goes on inside of me?

DRINA. (*Shakes her head and smiles sadly.*) I know.

GIMPTY. (*Curtly.*) Smart girl!

DRINA. (*Very tender and soft. She knows he's suffering.*) What's the matter?

GIMPTY. Nothing.

DRINA. I understand.

GIMPTY. You can't.

DRINA. Why can't I? (*Suddenly exasperated.*) Sometimes, for a boy as bright as you, with your education, you talk like a fool. Don't you think I got a heart too? Don't you think there are nights when I cry myself to sleep? Don't you think I know what it means to be lonely and scared and to want somebody? God, ain't I human? Am I so homely that I ain't got a right to . . .

GIMPTY. No, Drina! I think you're a swell girl. You are.

DRINA. (*Turns away, annoyed at his patronage.*) Oh, don't give me any of that taffy! You don't even know I'm alive!

GIMPTY. Why do you say that?

DRINA. What's the difference? It don't matter. . . . Only I hate to see you butting your head against a stone wall. You're only going to hurt yourself.

GIMPTY. What're you talking about?

DRINA. You know. . . . Oh, I think that lady's beautiful . . . and I think she's nice. . . .

GIMPTY. (*Angry.*) Look! Will you be a good girl and mind your own business?

DRINA. She's not for you!

GIMPTY. Why not? (*The* POLICEMAN *comes out of the East River Terrace, notebook and pencil in hand. He goes to* GIMPTY.)

POLICEMAN. Well, I got something to work on, anyway. . . . Do you know a kid named Tommy something around here? (DRINA *starts, but checks herself.*)

GIMPTY. No.

POLICEMAN. They heard the others call him Tommy. (*Jerks his head toward the gate.*) You know what he's liable to do? With his pull? Have me broke, maybe. The first thing I know, I'll be pounding a lousier post than this! Harlem, maybe. Get a knife in my back. . . . (*Looks up from his notebook, to* DRINA.) Hey, you!

DRINA. What?

POLICEMAN. You live around here?

DRINA. (*Very docile, frightened.*) Yes.

POLICEMAN. Know a kid named Tommy something?

DRINA. No . . . no, I don't.

POLICEMAN. (*Studying his notes.*) I'll catch him. I'll skin him alive!

DRINA. (*Finally ventures.*) What'd he do?

POLICEMAN. Pulled a knife on some high muck-a-muck in there.

DRINA. No!

POLICEMAN. Yeah. Ah, it don't pay to be nice to these kids. It just don't pay.

DRINA. Was the man hurt?

POLICEMAN. Yeah. It looks like a pretty deep cut. Lord, he's fit to be tied! I never seen a guy so boined up! (DRINA *turns and goes up the street, restraining her impulse to run. The* POLICEMAN *jabbers on, complainingly.*) This is a tough enough precinct . . . but Harlem?—There's a lousy precinct! A pal of mine got killed there last year. Left a wife and a couple of kids.

GIMPTY. Is that so?

POLICEMAN. Yeah.

GIMPTY. Too bad! (*As the idea begins to take form.*) Well . . . maybe you can catch Baby-face Martin or one of those fellows, and grab off that forty-two-hundred-dollar reward.

POLICEMAN. Yeah.

GIMPTY. Then you could retire.

POLICEMAN. Yeah, you could do a lot on that.

GIMPTY. Yeah, I guess you could. . . . Say . . . tell me something . . .

POLICEMAN. What?

GIMPTY. Supposin' . . . supposin' a fellow knew where that . . . er . . . Baby-face Martin is located. How would he go about reporting him . . . and making sure of not getting gypped out of the reward?

POLICEMAN. Just phone police headquarters . . . or the Department of Justice direct. They'd be down here in two minutes. (*He looks at* GIMPTY *and asks ironically.*) Why? You don't know where he is, do you?

GIMPTY. (*Smiles wanly back at him.*) Colorado, the newspapers say. . . . No, I was just wonderin'.

POLICEMAN. Well, whoever turns that guy in is taking an awful chance. He's a killer.

GIMPTY. Well . . . you can't live forever. (*A passing tug shrieks its warning signal. And shrieks again.* MARTIN *walks, cat-footed, down the street.*)

POLICEMAN. That's right. (GIMPTY *turns, sees* MARTIN, *and rises.*)

GIMPTY. (*To the* POLICEMAN.) Excuse me.

POLICEMAN. Sure. (GIMPTY *crosses to the other side of the street, and walks away, pretending not to notice* MARTIN.)

MARTIN. Hello, Gimpty! (GIMPTY *accelerates his pace and hobbles off.* MARTIN *sucks his teeth for a second, thinking. Then he adopts an amiable smile and approaches the* POLICEMAN.) Kinda quiet today, ain' it, officer?

POLICEMAN. Not with these kids around.

MARTIN. (*Jerks his head in* GIMPTY'S *direction.*) Dat's a nice feller. Friend of mine. (HUNK *has entered from up the street just after* GIMPTY'S *exit. He is lighting a cigar, when he sees* MARTIN *in friendly conversation with the arch enemy. He stands there, transfixed, match to cigar.*)

POLICEMAN. I had quite a talk with him.

MARTIN. (*Fishing.*) What about?

POLICEMAN. Oh . . . about these kids here.

MARTIN. Zat all?

POLICEMAN. Say, that's plenty! (*He puts his notebook in his pocket.*) You don't happen to know a kid around here named Tommy something, do you?

MARTIN. (*Shakes his head.*) Uh-uh!

POLICEMAN. Well, I'll catch him all right! (*He strides up the sidewalk.* MARTIN *watches him, then laughs. The match burns* HUNK's *fingers. He drops it.*)

HUNK. Jesus!

MARTIN. (*Laughing.*) A pal a mine.

HUNK. Dat's crazy.

MARTIN. Dey don' know me . . . wid dis mug.

HUNK. (*Sighs. This is too much for him. Then he remembers his errand.*) Say, dat dame is heah.

MARTIN. Who?

HUNK. Er . . Francey, or whatevah yuh call huh.

MARTIN. She is?

HUNK. Yeah. I got 'er waitin' on a corner. (*Puzzled.*) I dunno what yuh wanna bodder wid a cheap hustlah like dat fuh.

MARTIN. (*Sharply.*) Wha da yuh mean? Francey ain' no hustlah!

HUNK. (*Skeptical.*) No?

MARTIN. No.

HUNK. (*Smiles weakly.*) O.K. My mistake. We all make mistakes, boss. Dat's what dey got rubbuhs on ee end a pencils faw. (*Laughs feebly.*)

MARTIN. Pretty cute, ain' cha? Maybe yuhr a mistake. Maybe yuhr liable tuh git rubbed out yuhself.

HUNK. (*Frightened.*) I'll git huh now. (*He starts off. A young girl comes down the street, an obvious whore of the lowest class, wearing her timeless profession defiantly. A pert, pretty little face still show-*

ing traces of quality and something once sweet and fine. Skin an unhealthy pallor, lips a smear of rouge. Her mop of dyed red hair is lustreless, strawy, dead from too much alternate bleach and henna. She carries herself loosely. Droop-shouldered. Voluptuous S-shaped posture. There are no clothes under her cheap, faded green silk dress, cut so tight that it reveals the nipples of her full breasts, her navel, the "V" of her crotch, the muscles of her buttocks. She has obviously dressed hastily, carelessly; one stocking streaked with runs dribbles down at the ankle. She accosts HUNK, *impatiently.*)

FRANCEY. Hey, what ta hell's ee idear, keepin' me standin' on a corner all day? I'm busy. I gotta git back tuh da house. Yuh want Ida tuh break my face? (MARTIN *looks at her.*)

MARTIN. Francey! Jesus, what's come over yuh?

FRANCEY. (*Turning sharply to* MARTIN.) How do yew know my name? Who are yew? (*Impatiently.*) Well, who th' hell . . . (*Then she recognizes him, and gasps.*) Fuh th' love a God! Marty!

MARTIN. (*Never taking his eyes off the girl.*) Yeah. Hunk . . . scram! (HUNK *goes up the street, stops at the tenement stoop and lounges there, within ear shot.*)

FRANCEY. (*Eagerly.*) How are yuh, Marty?

MARTIN. Read duh papers!

FRANCEY. Yuh did somethin' to yuh face.

MARTIN. Yeah. Plastic, dey call it.

FRANCEY. They said yuh wuz out aroun' Coloraduh—th' noospapuhs! Gee, I'm glad to see yuh! (MARTIN *slips his arm around her waist and draws her tight to his body. As his lips grope for hers,* FRANCEY *turns her face away.* MARTIN *tries to pull her face around. She cries furiously:* No . . . don' kiss me on a lips!)

MARTIN. (*Releasing her, puzzled.*) What? What's a matter? (*He can't believe this. He frowns.*) I ain't good enough for yuh?

FRANCEY. (*Quickly.*) No. It ain't dat. It ain't yew. It's me. I got a sore on my mouth. Fuh yuhr own good, I don't want yuh to kiss me, dat's why.

MARTIN. I ain't nevuh fuhgot da way yew kiss.

FRANCEY. (*Wistfully.*) I ain't niethuh. (*She laughs.*) Go on! You wit all yer fancy dames. Where do I come off?

MARTIN. Dey don't mean nuttin'.

FRANCEY. Dat chorus goil . . . what's 'er name?

MARTIN. Nuttin'. She ain't got nuttin' . . . no guts, no fire. . . . But yew been boinin' in my blood . . . evuh since . . .

FRANCEY. An' yew been in mine . . . if yuh wanna know.

MARTIN. Remembuh dat foist night . . . on a roof?

FRANCEY. Yeah, I remembuh . . . da sky was full a stars, an' I was full a dreamy ideas. Dat was me foist time. I was fourteen, goin' on fifteen.

MARTIN. Yeah. It wuz mine too. It wuz terrific. Hit me right wheah I live . . . like my back wuz meltin'. An I wuz so sca'd when yuh started laffin' an' cryin', crazy like. . . . (*They both laugh, enjoying the memory, a little embarrassed by it.*)

FRANCEY. Yeah.

MARTIN. Gee, I nevuh wuz so sca'd like 'at time.

FRANCEY. Me too.

MARTIN. (*Draws her to him again, more gently.*) Come eah! Close to me!

FRANCEY. (*Acquiescing.*) Ony don' kiss me on a lips!

MARTIN. Closuh! (*They stand there a moment, bodies close, passionate.* MARTIN *buries his face in her hair.*)

FRANCEY. (*Eyes closed, whispers.*) Marty!

MARTIN. Dose times unduh da stairs. . . .

FRANCEY. A couple a crazy kids we were! We wuz gonna git married. I bought a ring at da five an' dime staw.

MARTIN. Yeah. Ony we didn' have money enough fuh de license. Gee, it seems like yestiddy. We wuz talkin' about it right heah.

FRANCEY. Yestiddy! It seems like a million yeahs!

MARTIN. (*As voices are heard coming from the East River Terrace.*) Wait! (*They separate. He draws his hat over his eyes and turns away as a young couple come out of the gate and walk up the street.*)

GIRL. So many people standing around. What's all the excitement? What's happened?

MAN. The elevator man said someone was stabbed.

GIRL. Really? Who was it, do you know?

MAN. Mr. Griswald, I think he said. Twelfth floor.

GIRL. Oh! Yes? Did he say who did it?

MAN. He said one of the kids around here somewhere. . . . (*When they are well out of sight,* FRANCEY *clutches* MARTIN's *arm.*)

FRANCEY. Marty, listen! Yuh got ta take care a yuhself. Yuh gotta go way an' hide. I don' want 'em to git yuh! I don' wan' 'em to git yuh!

MARTIN. Whatsa diffrince wheah I go? Ey got thuh finger on me everywheah. Ah, frig 'em.

FRANCEY. Dey won't reco'nize yuh. Dey won't. Even I didn't.

MARTIN. Yeah, but yuh can' change ese, Francey. Look! (*He holds up his fingers. The tips are yellow and scarred.*) Tree times I boined 'em wid acid an' t'ings. No good. Dere are some t'ings yuh can't change. But I'll tell yuh what. . . I'll scram out a heah. I'll scram . . . if yew come wit me.

FRANCEY. Ah, what do yuh want me fer? A broken-down hoor.

MARTIN. Shut up!

FRANCEY. I wouldn' be good fuh yuh.

MARTIN. I know what I want.

FRANCEY. (*Laughs crazily.*) Yeah. Dis is

a swell pipe-dream I'm havin'! I'm Minnie de Moocher kickin' a gong aroun'!

MARTIN. Listen! I got de dough now, kid. We kin do it now.

FRANCEY. But I'm sick, Marty! Don't yuh see? I'm sick!

MARTIN. What's a matter wid yuh?

FRANCEY. (*Almost inaudibly.*) What do yuh think? (MARTIN *looks at her for a long time. He sees her. The nostalgic dream is finished. His lips begin to curl in disgust.*)

MARTIN. Why didncha git a job?

FRANCEY. Dey don' grow on trees!

MARTIN. Why didncha starve foist?

FRANCEY. Why didnchou? (MARTIN *makes no effort to conceal his growing disgust. Turns away.*)

FRANCEY. (*Suddenly shouts, fiercely, at the top of her lungs.*) Well, what ta hell did yuh expect?

MARTIN. I don' know. (*A passing tug shrieks hoarsely. The echo floats back.*)

FRANCEY. (*Quietly, clutching at a hope.*) Maybe . . . if yuh got da dough . . . yuh git a doctuh an' he fixes me up . . .

MARTIN. Nah. Once at stuff gits in yuh . . . nah! (*Again the tug shrieks and is answered by its echo. He reaches into his inner breast pocket, extracts a fat roll of bills, peels off several and hands them to her.*) Heah. Buy yerself somethin'.

FRANCEY. (*Her eyes suddenly glued to the money.*) Baby! Dat's some roll yuh got. Yuh cud choke a hoss wid dat.

MARTIN. (*Thrusting it at her.*) Heah!

FRANCEY. (*Takes the money.*) Is it hot?

MARTIN. Yeah. Bettah be careful where yuh spend it.

FRANCEY. Sure.

MARTIN. An' keep yuh lips buttoned up!

FRANCEY. I wouldn' tell on yuh, Marty. Not if dey tied me ta wild hosses, I wouldn't.

MARTIN. Bettuh not.

FRANCEY. (*Folds her money, still fascinated by the huge roll of bills in his hand. Her voice takes on a peculiar whining, wheedling quality.*) Honey!

MARTIN. Yeah?

FRANCEY. Cud yuh spare another twenty bucks? I godda . . .

MARTIN. No!

FRANCEY. Aw, come on, dearie!

MARTIN. No!

FRANCEY. Don' be a tightwad!

MARTIN. (*Reaching the limit of his disgust.*) What ta hell do yuh tink I am? Some guy yuh got up in yuh room? I'll . . . (*He raises his hand, ready to slap her. Again the shriek of a tug, and the echo.*)

FRANCEY. (*Quickly, frightened.*) Nah, fergit it, Marty! I wuz just . . .

MARTIN. Awright! Awright! Now beat it!

FRANCEY. O.K., Marty. (*She starts to go, pauses, turns back.*) Fer old times' sakes, will yuh do me a favor? Please?

MARTIN. (*Shoves the money back into his pocket.*) No!

FRANCEY. Not dat.

MARTIN. What?

FRANCEY. Will yuh kiss me? Heah? Ona cheek? Jus' fuh old times' sakes? Come on. (*He hesitates. She comes close, presses her cheek against his lips. He pecks her cheek, and turns away, scowling. She laughs, a low bitter laugh, at his obvious disrelish.*) Thanks! (*She goes up the street slowly, her purse swinging carelessly, her body swaying invitation, the tired march of her profession. The shriek of the tug is drawn out and distant now. The echo lingers.* MARTIN *spits and wipes the kiss off his lips with a groan of distaste.*)

HUNK. (*Comes down the sidewalk, slowly.*) Well?

MARTIN. Huh?

HUNK. See?

MARTIN. Yeah. Yeah!

HUNK. Twice in one day. Deah yuh ah! I toldja we shouldn' a come back. But yuh wouldn' lissen a me. Yuh nevuh lissen a me.

MARTIN. Yeah.

HUNK. (*Trying to console him.*) I know how yuh feel, Marty. Les go back to St. Louis, huh? Now dat dame yuh had deah—Deedy Cook—Now dat wuz a broad. Regaler. Bet she's waitin fuh yuh . . . wid welcome ona doormat.

MARTIN. Awright! Don talk about dames, Hunk, will yuh? Fuhget 'em. All cats look alike inna dahk. Fuhget 'em. (*A little girl comes out of the gate bouncing a rubber ball.* MARTIN *looks at her, thinks a moment, turns to watch her go up the street. He sucks his teeth a moment, thinking.*)

HUNK. Listen, Marty . . . Let's git outa heah. Too many people know yuh heah. Whaddaya say?

MARTIN. Sh! I'm thinkin'. (*Pause.*)

HUNK. Well, guess I'll go shoot a game a pillpool. (*Starts to go up the street.*)

MARTIN. (*Motions him back, turns to stare at the Terrace Apartments.*) Wait a minute . . . (HUNK *returns.*) Yuh know, Hunk. (*He shakes a thumb at the Apartment.*) Der's a pile a tin in ere.

HUNK. Yeah.

MARTIN. Didja see what dese kids did heah today?

HUNK. No.

MARTIN. Ey got one a dese rich little squoits in a hallway, slapped him around an' robbed his watch.

HUNK. So what? (*A man appears on the terrace, watches them for a second, and then slips away. Two men come down the street talking casually, one of them goes into the tenement, the other, waiting for him, wanders over back of the hopper and is hidden from view.*)

MARTIN. (*Glances at them, lowers his voice.*) Maybe we kin pull a snatch . . . kidnap one a dese babies.

HUNK. We're too hot. Foolin' round wid kids ain' our racket.

MARTIN. Scared?

HUNK. No . . . ony . . . I. : : :

MARTIN. Stop yuh yammerin'! Git a hold a Whitey. See wot he knows about duh mugs in heah! (HUNK *hesitates.*) Come on, Hunk, git goin'!

HUNK. O.K. Yuh duh boss! (*He goes reluctantly. The tap of* GIMPTY'S *cane on the sidewalk is heard approaching, its rhythmic click ominous.* GIMPTY *appears, tight-lipped, pale, grim.* MARTIN *smiles out of one corner of his lips, and throws him a conciliatory greeting.*)

MARTIN. Hello, Gimpty! (GIMPTY *turns away without answering.* MARTIN, *amused, laughs. He is suddenly in a good mood. The man who spied on him from the terrace appears in the gateway and catches* GIMPTY'S *eye.* GIMPTY *points his cane at* MARTIN. *The good mood passes.* MARTIN'S *eyebrows pull together in one puzzled line.*)

MARTIN. What's eatin' yuh, wise guy? (*The man behind the gate draws a revolver, comes quickly up behind* MARTIN *and digs the gun in his back.*)

G MAN. Get em up, Martin! The Department of Justice wants you!

MARTIN. What ta hell . . . ! (*Tries to turn, but the revolver prods him back.*)

G MAN. Come on, get 'em up!

MARTIN. (*Hands up.*) I ain't Martin. My name's Johnson. Wanna see my license? (*He slides his hand into his breast pocket.*)

G MAN. If you're smart, you'll behave yourself!

MARTIN. (*Wheels around, draws his gun, and fires in one motion.*) No, yuh don't . . . (*The* G MAN *drops his gun, crumples onto the sidewalk holding his belly and kicking.* MARTIN *turns to face* GIMPTY, *who has backed away to the hopper.* MARTIN, *his face black and contorted, aims at* GIMPTY.) So yuh ratted, yuh. . . . (*From behind the hopper and the tenement doorway guns explode. Two other* G MEN *appear and descend on* MARTIN, *firing as they come.* MARTIN *groans, wheels, and*

falls, his face in the gutter, his fingers clawing the sidewalk. One of the G MEN *goes to aid his wounded comrade. The other* G MAN *stands over* MARTIN'S *body, pumping bullet after bullet into him, literally nailing him to the ground. The* G MAN *kicks him to make sure he's dead. No twitch!* MARTIN *lies there flat. The* G MAN *takes out a handkerchief, picks up* MARTIN'S *gun gingerly, wraps it in the handkerchief, puts it in his pocket.*)

SECOND G MAN. Where'd he get you, Bob? Come on, sit up here! (*Helps him to sit against the coping.* FIRST G MAN *presses his hand in agony to his wound. From the street there is a rising babble of voices. Tenement windows are thrown up, heads thrust out; the curious crowd to the edge of the terrace, come to the gate, run down the street, collect in small groups, discussing the macabre scene in excited, hushed murmur. A* LADY *comes out of the gate, sees the dead man, screams hysterically, and is helped off by the* DOORMAN. *The* POLICEMAN *comes tearing down the street, revolver drawn. He forces his way through the crowd.*)

POLICEMAN. Out a my way! Look out! (*To the* THIRD G MAN.) What's this?

THIRD G MAN. (*Taking out a badge in a leather case from inside his coat pocket and holding it up.*) It's all right, officer. Department of Justice! (*Replaces the badge.*)

POLICEMAN. What happened? Who's this guy?

THIRD G MAN. Baby-face Martin.

POLICEMAN. Is that him?

THIRD G MAN. Yep.

POLICEMAN. Gese, I was talkin' to him a couple a minutes ago.

SECOND G MAN. Get an ambulance, quick! Will you?

POLICEMAN. (*Crosses to the police box, opens it.*) Box 10 . . . Mulligan. Send ambulance! Make all notifications! Baby-face Martin was just shot by Federal men. He winged one of 'em . . . I don't know . . . yeah . . . here. Gese, I was talking to him myself a few minutes ago . . . Hell, Sarge, I couldn't recognize him. His face is all made over. (*He hangs up. The shrill siren of a radio car mounts to a crescendo, mingles with the screech of brakes, and is suddenly silent. Two more policemen dash on, forcing their path through the crowd. They are followed by* SPIT, *wearing a single roller skate. He edges his way to the front of the crowd.*)

SECOND POLICEMAN. Hi, Mulligan. What have yuh got here?

MULLIGAN. Baby-face Martin!

THIRD POLICEMAN. Did you git him?

MULLIGAN. No such luck. The Federal men got him. He winged one of them. (*Gestures toward the wounded* G MAN.)

SECOND POLICEMAN. Did you notify the house?

MULLIGAN. Yeah. I gave em everything . . . Lend us a hand, will yuh. Git rid of this crowd. (MULLIGAN *stands by* MARTIN's *body, writing in a notebook. The other* POLICEMEN *push back the crowd.* SPIT *slips through, and looks at the dead man with scared curiosity.*)

SECOND POLICEMAN. (*Pushing the crowd.*) Break it up! This is no circus. Come on, break it up!

GIRL IN THE CROWD. Don't push me!

SECOND POLICEMAN. Well, go on home! Go on, break it up!

SECOND G MAN. (*To the wounded agent.*) How you feelin', Bob?

FIRST G MAN. Lousy.

SECOND G MAN. You'll be O.K.

FIRST G MAN. I don't know . . . I don't know! I should've plugged him right away . . . in the back. You don't give a snake like that a break. . . . Anyway, we got him! That's something!

SECOND G MAN. Sure you did, Bob. You'll get cited for this.

FIRST G MAN. That's just dandy! That's just dandy! Give the medal to my old lady for the kids to play with . . . an' remember

they once had an old man who was a . . . hero!

THIRD G MAN. Aw, cut it, Bob. You'll be O.K. Don't talk like that!

DOORMAN. (*Pushing through the crowd.*) Officer! Officer!

MULLIGAN. Get outa here! You with the rest of them. Come on, get back!

DOORMAN. Officer, this is important! That's one of the boys . . . there, that one! He's one of the gang!

MULLIGAN. What boy? What the hell are you talkin' about?

DOORMAN. The one who stabbed Mr. Griswald.

MULLIGAN. What? Oh, where?

DOORMAN. (*Pointing.*) That one there! He's one of the gang.

MULLIGAN. Are you sure?

DOORMAN. Yes . . . yes . . . I'll swear to it!

MULLIGAN. Come here! Hey you! (*Runs over to* SPIT, *grabs his arm. The murmur of the crowd rises.*)

SPIT. Lemme go! I didn' do nuttin. Lemme go!

SECOND POLICEMAN. What is this kid got to do with it?

MULLIGAN. That's somethin' else. (*The clang of an approaching ambulance comes to a sudden halt. Enter, pushing their way down the street, an* INTERNE *carrying a doctor's bag, followed by an* AMBULANCE MAN *carrying a folded stretcher, which encloses a pillow and a rolled blanket. The murmur of the crowd hushes.*)

INTERNE. Hello, Mulligan.

MULLIGAN. Hello, doc. (*To* SECOND POLICEMAN.) Hold this kid a minute. (SECOND POLICEMAN *grabs* SPIT's *arm and drags him back to the crowd on the sidewalk.*)

INTERNE. What's up? (*He comes down to the body.*)

MULLIGAN. Just got Baby-face Martin! (*The murmur rises again as the news is spread.*)

INTERNE. You did? (*He glances at the body.*) He won't need me!

SECOND G MAN. Hey, doc, look at this man! (*The* INTERNE *kneels to the wounded man, examines his wound, sponges it, places a pad over it.*) It's not bad, is it, doc?

INTERNE. (*Cheerfully.*) Not very bad, but we'd better rush him off to the hospital. Here, somebody help get him on the stretcher. (*The* AMBULANCE MAN *opens the stretcher, places the pillow at the head.* SECOND G MAN *and* MULLIGAN *lift the wounded* G MAN *carefully and lay him on the stretcher with words of encouragement. The* AMBULANCE MAN *unrolls the blanket over him.* SECOND G MAN *and the* AMBULANCE DRIVER *carry the wounded man up the sidewalk calling "Gangway." The* THIRD G MAN *accompanies them, holding the wounded man's hand and talking to him. The crowd open a path, and stare, their murmur silenced for a moment.*)

MULLIGAN. (*Pointing to Baby-face.*) Want to look at this guy, doc?

INTERNE. (*Kneels by the body, rips open the coat and vest, cursorily inspects the wounds, rolls back the eyelid, applies a stethoscope to the heart.*) Phew! They certainly did a job on him! Nothing left to look at but chopped meat. God, they didn't leave enough of him for a good P.M.! (*Rises, takes pad and pencil from his pocket, glances at* MULLIGAN's *shield, writes.*) Mulligan . . . 10417 . . . 19th precinct. Have you got his pedigree?

MULLIGAN. (*Reading from his own notebook.*) Joe Martin. 28. White . . . U.S. 5 ft., 9 in. 170 lbs. Unmarried. Occupation . . . (*Shrugs his shoulders.*)

INTERNE. All right. Dr. Flint. Mark him D.O.A.!

MULLIGAN. (*Writing.*) Dead . . . on . . . arrival. . . . (*Enter, pushing their way through the crowd, the* MEDICAL EXAMINER, *followed by the* POLICE PHOTOGRAPHER. *The* PHOTOGRAPHER *opens his camera, adjusts it, and photographs the body from several angles.*)

INTERNE. (*As the* EXAMINER *approaches.*) Hello, doc!

EXAMINER. Hello, Doctor. So they finally got him, did they?

INTERNE. Yes, they sure did.

EXAMINER. It's about time. What have you got on him?

INTERNE. Twelve gunshot wounds. Five belly, four chest, three head. (*Picks up his bag and goes. The* EXAMINER *inspects the body.*)

MULLIGAN. (*To the* DOORMAN.) Hey, find something to cover this up with. (*The* DOORMAN *nods and disappears through the gateway.* MULLIGAN *turns to the* THIRD POLICEMAN, *who is still holding back the crowd.*) Hey, Tom! Stand by while I go through this bum! (*He kneels, and goes through* MARTIN's *pockets, handing his findings to the* THIRD POLICEMAN *who jots them down in his notebook.* MULLIGAN *takes a ring off* MARTIN's *finger.*) Diamond ring. Look at that rock! (*He hands it to the* THIRD POLICEMAN *who pockets it, and makes a note.* MULLIGAN *extracts* MARTIN's *wad of bills.*) And this roll of bills! What a pile! You count it!

EXAMINER. Through with him, boys?

MULLIGAN. (*Rising.*) Yeah.

PHOTOGRAPHER. One second! (*Takes a last photograph.*)

EXAMINER. Well, as soon as the wagon comes, send him down to the morgue. I'll look him over in the morning. Mulligan, you report to me there first thing in the morning, too.

MULLIGAN. Yes, sir. (*The* EXAMINER *goes. The* PHOTOGRAPHER *folds his camera and follows.*)

WOMAN IN THE CROWD. (*To the* SECOND POLICEMAN, *who is holding* SPIT.) Officer! What did this boy have to do with it? Why are you holding him?

SECOND POLICEMAN. Never mind. Stand back!

SPIT. Lemme go! I didn't do nuttin'! Whadda yuh want?

MULLIGAN. (*Goes to* SPIT.) You're one of the gang who beat up a boy here today and stabbed his father, ain't you?

SPIT. No, I yain't. I did'n 'ave nuttn tuh do wid it. It wuz a kid named Tommy McGrath. (*The murmur of the crowd fades as they all listen.*)

MULLIGAN. Tommy McGrath! Where does he live?

SPIT. On Foist Avenoo between Fifty-toid and Fifty-fawt.

MULLIGAN. Sure?

SPIT. Yeah.

MULLIGAN. (*To the* SECOND POLICEMAN.) Take this kid around there, will yuh? Get ahold a Tommy McGrath. He's wanted for stabbin some guy. I got to wait for the morgue wagon.

SECOND POLICEMAN. O.K. (*Drags* SPIT *through the crowd.*) Come on! You show us where he lives and we'll let you go. (*As they go off, the murmur of the crowd rises again. The* THIRD G MAN *crosses to* GIMPTY, *who is leaning against the hopper, white and shaking. The* DOORMAN *comes out with an old discarded coat, the gold braid ravelled and rusty, the cloth dirty and oil-stained.* MULLIGAN *takes it from him.*)

THIRD G MAN. (*To* GIMPTY.) Good work, Mac: Come over to the office and pick up your check. (*He makes his way up the street.* MULLIGAN *throws the coat over* MARTIN'*s body. The murmur of the crowd rises high. A boat horn in the river bellows hoarsely and dies away.*)

CURTAIN

ACT THREE

SCENE: *The same. That night. A very dark night. From the dock the sounds of a gay party, music, babble, laughter.* GIMPTY, *a bent silhouette, sits on the coping leaning against the terrace wall. There's a lamp shining up the street. The lights from the tenement windows are faint and yellow and glum. The lanterns on the gateposts, one red, one green, are lit and look very decorative. There's a blaze of fire crackling out of an old iron ash-can in the center of the street. The* BOYS *hover over it, roasting potatoes skewered on long sticks. Their impish faces gleam red one minute and are wiped by shadows the next as they lean over the flames.*

ANGEL. (*Gesturing wildly.*) All uv a sudden da shots come . . . bing . . . bing . . . bam . . . biff . . :

T.B. (*Superior.*) I hoid da shots foist. I wuz jus walkin' up . . .

ANGEL. (*Angrily.*) Yuh di'not.

T.B. I did so.

ANGEL. Yuh tought it wuz a rivitin' machine, yuh said.

T.B. I di'not.

ANGEL. (*Tops him.*) Yuh did so.

T.B. (*Tops him.*) I di'not.

ANGEL. (*Tops him.*) Yuh did so.

T.B. (*Tops him.*) Ah, yuh mudduh's chooch!

ANGEL. (*Tops him.*) Yeah, yuh fadduh's doop!

T.B. (*Crescendo.*) Fongoola! (DIPPY *runs down the street waving two potatoes.*)

DIPPY. Hey, guys, I swiped two maw mickeys. Look!

ANGEL. Boy, 'at's good!

SPIT. O.K. Put 'em in.

DIPPY. Wheah's Tommy?

SPIT. Put 'em in!

DIPPY. Dis big one's mine, remembuh!

SPIT. Put 'em in, I said!

DIPPY. Don' fugit, dis big one's mine!

SPIT. Shat ap!

DIPPY. Yeah . . . yew . . . yew shat ap!

SPIT. Wha-a-at?

DIPPY (*Cowed, moves away from* SPIT.) Wheah's Tommy?

ANGEL. I dunno. He didn' show up yet.

T.B. (*Reflectively, referring to* MARTIN.) Da papuhs said dey found twenty gran' in 'is pockets.

ANGEL. Twenty G's. Boy 'at's a lot a dough!

SPIT. Boy, he must a bin a putty smaht guy.

T.B. Baby-face? Sure! He wuz a tops. Public enemy numbuh one. Boy, he had guts. He wasn' a scared a nobody. Boy, he could knock 'em all off like dat . . . like anyt'ing! Boy, like nuttn! (DIPPY *takes a stick from the can and holds it against his shoulder, pointed at* ANGEL, *maneuvering it as if it were a machine gun.*)

DIPPY. (*Makes a rapid, staccato bleating sound.*) Ah-ah-ah-ah-ah! Look, I godda machine gun! Ah-ah-ah-ah!

ANGEL. (*Pointing his kazoo at* DIPPY.) Bang Bang!

DIPPY. (*Sore.*) Nah, yuh can't do dat. Yuh'r dead. I shot yuh foist.

ANGEL. (*Ignores that salient point, raises the kazoo again, takes dead aim at* DIPPY.) Bang!

DIPPY. (*Lets loose with his improvised machine gun.*) Ah-ah-ah-ah! Deah. Now I gotcha! Now yuh dead!

ANGEL. Bang!

DIPPY. (*Disgusted.*) Aw-w-w! (*He throws the stick into the fire and turns away.*)

T.B. Gese . . . what I could do wid twenty G's!

ANGEL. What?

SPIT. Snot!

T.B. Yeah, I bet I could buy a boat like dat, huh? (*He points off toward the dock.*)

ANGEL. Look! Dey got lights an' flags an' music!

SPIT. Dey got some hot party on, hey guys?

DIPPY. Look! Look! Dey're dancin'! (*Cavorts about with an imaginary partner, making ribald gestures and singing.*) Yuh're da top, yuh're da coliseum. Hey! I'm

dancin'! Look, felluhs! Look on me! I'm dancin'! Look on me! (*He whirls around and looks at them for approval.*)

T.B. (*Sour-faced.*) Sit down! Yew stink! (DIPPY *stops grinning and dancing simultaneously. He sits down, squelched.*)

ANGEL. Twenty grand! . . .

SPIT. Yeah . . . so what't it got 'im?

ANGEL. Yeah. Yuh see duh pitchuh uv 'is broad inna papuhs? Deedy Cook aw sump'm . . .

T.B. Boy, some nice nooky, huh?

SPIT. Boy, she's got some contrac's now! I heah she's gonna do a bubble dance in a boilesque, I t'ink.

ANGEL. Yeah. My fadduh took one look at huh pitchuh. So 'ee said 'ee'd let 'em shoot 'im too, fuh half an hour wid a fancy floozy like dat. So my mudduh gits mad. So she sez dey wouldn' haf tuh shoot cha. Haf an hour wid at cockamamee yuh'd be dead! (*They all laugh.*) So she spills some boilin' watuh on 'im. So 'ee yells like a bastid an' runs outa da house mad. (MILTY *comes down the sidewalk, breathless with excitement.*)

MILTY. Hey, felluhs, yuh know what?

ANGEL. What?

SPIT. Snot!

MILTY. Balls tuh yew!

SPIT. Ah, I'll mobilize yuh!

MILTY. Yuh know what, guys? Duh cops ah wise tuh Tommy.

ANGEL. Gese!

T.B. No kid! No kid!

SPIT. Aw, bushwah!

MILTY. No bushwah! Deah' lookin' fuh 'im. He tole me hisself. (*To* SPIT.) Fot smelleh! Dey went up tuh his house. Some guy snitched.

T.B. No kid!

SPIT. Did dey git 'im?

MILTY. Nah. Tommy's too wise fuh dem. Dey come in tru de daw. He goes out tru de fire-escape, down a yahd, oveh de fence, trus de celleh, up de stayuhs, out dee udduh street.

SPIT. Wheah's he now?

MILTY. He's hidin' out.

SPIT. Wheah?

MILTY. Wheah duh yuh tink, wheah? Wheah dey don' ketch 'im, dat's wheah.

SPIT. Ah, dey'll ketch 'im.

MILTY. Dey don' ketch Tommy so quick.

SPIT. (*Nervously, looking into the fire.*) How're de mickeys comin'?

T.B. Gese, I bet a dollah dey sen' 'im tuh rifawm school.

SPIT. Sure. Dat's what dey do.

DIPPY. Yeah, dat's what. Ain' it, T.B.?

T.B. Yeah. Dey sent me tuh rifawm school fuh jus' swipin' a bunch a bananas. An' 'ey wuz all rotten too, most a dem.

MILTY. I pity duh guy who snitched. Tommy's layin' fuh him, awright.

DIPPY. Does 'ee know who?

SPIT. (*Trying to change the subject.*) Hey, guys, duh mickeys ah awmost done!

ANGEL. (*Fishing out his potato and poking it with his kazoo.*) Nah, not yet. Look, dis one's hard inside.

DIPPY. (*Reaches to feel* ANGEL's *mickey.*) Yeah. Like a rock . . . Ouch! Dat's hot! (*Licks his fingers.*)

ANGEL. (*Dipping the mickey back into the embers.*) Gese, poor Tommy! If dey ketch 'im, he don' git no maw mickeys like dis fer a long time.

DIPPY. Dey git mickeys in rifawm school, don' dey?

T.B. Slop dey git, slop . . . unless dey git some dough tuh smeah da jailies wid.

SPIT. Aw, shat ap! All a time yuh shoot yuh mout' off about rifawm school . . . like yew wuz 'ee on'y one who evuh went.

DIPPY. Yeah. Yew wuz on'y deah six mont's.

ANGEL. Tom'll git two yeahs.

DIPPY. T'ree, maybe, I bet.

MILTY. Gese, dat's lousy.

SPIT. Ah, shat ap, will yuh?

T.B. Yeah, nevuh mind. Yuh loin a barrel a good tings in rifawm school. (*The* DOORMAN *comes out of the gate, exasperated.*)

DOORMAN. Now I'm not going to tell you again!

SPIT. Ah, go frig! ⎫
T.B. Deah're awmost done. ⎬ *Simultaneously*
ANGEL. Jus' a li'l while. ⎭

DOORMAN. No! Get away from here . . . all of you . . . right now!

GIMPTY. (*Approaches the* DOORMAN *and addresses him in a voice tight and hoarse, hardly recognizable.*) Did you give her my note?

DOORMAN. Yes. She said she'd be out in a moment.

GIMPTY. Thanks. (*He retires to sit again in the shadows.*)

DOORMAN. If you kids don't beat it, I'm going to call a cop! (*Turns to the gate.*)

SPIT. Aw, hold yuh hawses!

DOORMAN. (*Wheels about, threateningly.*) Wha-a-at?

SPIT. (*Scared.*) Nuttn. (*A* LADY *in evening gown and a* MAN *in tuxedo come down the street, talking quietly. The* WOMAN *laughs. As they reach the gate, the* DOORMAN *touches his hat.*)

DOORMAN. Good evening.

MAN AND WOMAN. Good evening. (*The* DOORMAN *follows them through the gateway.*)

SPIT. (*When the* DOORMAN *is well out of earshot.*) Ah, yuh louse, I'll mobilize yuh! (*The boys all roar.*)

ANGEL. Hey, de fire's dyin' down.

T.B. Yeah, we need maw wood.

SPIT. Let's scout aroun' an' soich out some maw wood. I'll stay heah an' guard de mickeys.

T.B. Me too.

SPIT. Yew, too, balls!

T.B. What's a mattuh wid me?

SPIT. What's a mattuh wit yew? Yew stink on ice, 'at's what's a mattuh wit' yew!

T.B. Yeah, well, yew ain' no lily a da valley.

SPIT. Go on now, or yuh git dis mickey . . . red hot . . . up yuh bunny!

T.B. Yeah? (*He begins to cough.*)

SPIT. Yeah! Wanna make sumpm otov it?

T.B. If it wasn't fuh my T.B. . . .

SPIT. Ah, dat's a gag. Anytime yuh put it straight up tuh 'im, he goes . . . (*Imitates the cough.*) My T.B. . . . . Balls!

T.B. Oh, yeah? . . . Look, smart guy! (*He has been holding his hand to his lips. He coughs again, spits, opens his hand, holds it out and displays a bloody clot in the palm. Proudly.*) Blood! (*The boys gasp.*)

ANGEL. Wow!

T.B. Smart guy!

SPIT. Ah, I could do dat. Yuh suck yuh mout'!

DIPPY. (*Sucks his mouth audibly, spits into his hand.*) I can't . . . I can't. How do yuh do it? (DRINA *comes down the street, sees the boys and hurries to them.*)

MILTY. Hello, Drina.

DRINA. Did you see Tommy? (*There is a tired, desperate quality in her tone.*)

MILTY. No.

DRINA. (*To* DIPPY.) Did you?

DIPPY. Nope.

DRINA. Did anybody see him? He hasn't been home at all.

MILTY. No. Nobody saw 'im. Drina.

DRINA. (*Tired, very tired.*) Thanks. Thanks, Milty. (*She notices* GIMPTY *and approaches him.*)

ANGEL. (*In a whisper.*) Whyn't yuh tell huh?

MILTY. (*Also whispering.*) No. Tommy said no.

SPIT. (*Aloud.*) Ah, balonee!

MILTY. (*Whispers.*) Sh! Shat ap!

SPIT. (*Deliberately loud.*) Who fuh! I'll give yuh yuh lumps in a minute.

DRINA. (*To* GIMPTY.) Pete, did you see Tommy?

GIMPTY. What?

DRINA. My brother? Have you seen him at all?

GIMPTY. Oh! No.

DRINA. Gee, he hasn't showed up yet. The cops are looking for him. I'm scared to death.

GIMPTY. I'm sorry.

SPIT. Hey, Drina! Milty knows, but he won't tell!

DRINA. (*Turns quickly.*) Does he?

MILTY. No.

SPIT. He does.

MILTY. (*Quietly to* SPIT.) Ah, yuh louse! (*Aloud to* DRINA.) I do not!

SPIT. (*To* MILTY.) I'll mobilize yuh! (*To* DRINA.) He does so. (DRINA *takes* MILTY *by both shoulders and shakes him.*)

DRINA. Milty, please tell me if you know . . . please! I'm half crazy.

MILTY. Tommy said not tuh tell.

DRINA. (*Pleading.*) But I wouldn't hurt him. You know that. It's for his good. I've got to talk to him. I've got to find out what we're gonna do. (*Pause.*) Milty, you've gotta tell me . . . please!

MILTY. (*Reluctantly.*) Aw right! Come on. . . .

DRINA. (*As they go up the street.*) How is he? Is he all right? Is he hurt or anything?

MILTY. Nah!

DRINA. Why didn't he come home?

MILTY. Don' worry, Drina. Dey won' catch 'im. (*They're out of sight and the voices fade off.*)

SPIT. Hey, Angel. You stay heah wid me. Youse guys git some wood. Go on!

DIPPY. O.K. Watch my mickey.

T.B. Mine too. (DIPPY *and* T.B. *exit up the sidewalk.*)

DIPPY. Me, I'm goin' ovuh on Toid Avenoo.

T.B. I'm goin' ovuh tuh Schultzie's.

DIPPY. Naw, whyn't cha go ovuh on Second Avenoo? (*Their voices fade away.*)

SPIT. Hey, Angel, yew stay heah an' guard dose mickeys.

ANGEL. Wheah yuh goin?

SPIT. I'm gonna trail Milty an' fin' out wheah Tommy is.

ANGEL. What faw?

SPIT. None a yuh beeswax! (*He lopes up the street.* ANGEL *watches him for a while, puzzled, then fishes his kazoo from a pocket, relaxes by the fireside, and hums into the instrument. A shadow detaches itself from the hopper and creeps stealthily toward* ANGEL. *It whispers "Psst! Hey! Angel!"* ANGEL *wheels around, startled.*)

ANGEL. Tommy! Gese!

TOMMY. (*His face glowing red as he leans over the fire toward* ANGEL.) Sh! Shat ap! (*In a hoarse whisper.*) Wheah ah da guys? (*They both talk in whispers.*)

ANGEL. Dey went tuh look fuh wood.

TOMMY. What?

ANGEL. Fuh wood. Maw wood. Milty jus' took yuh sistuh . . .

TOMMY. Is Spit wit de guys?

ANGEL. Yeah.

TOMMY. O.K.

ANGEL. Milty jus' took yuh sistuh tuh yer hideout.

TOMMY. He did? De louse!

ANGEL. Whatcha gonna do, Tommy?

TOMMY. Run away . . . so de bulls don' git me.

ANGEL. (*Impressed.*) Gese!

TOMMY. (*Quietly.*) But foist I'm gonna ketch de guy who snitched. Do yuh know who it wuz?

ANGEL. Me? No.

TOMMY. (*Flaring.*) Don' lie tuh me . . . I'll kill yuh!

ANGEL Yew know me, Tommy.

TOMMY. O.K. I tink I'm wise tuh who done it.

ANGEL. Who?

TOMMY. Spit.

ANGEL. Yuh tink so?

TOMMY. Yeah.

ANGEL. Gese!

TOMMY. Now I'm gonna hide, see? Right back a deah. (*Points up behind the hopper.*) If yuh let on I'm heah . . . (*Ominously.*) I'll put yuh teet' down yuh troat!

ANGEL. Aw, Tommy, yuh know me . . . yuh know me!

TOMMY. O.K. Den do like I tell yuh. When Spit comes back, yew tell 'im like dis . . . Duh guy I stabbed wuz down heah lookin' fuh Spit tuh givvim five bucks fuh snitchin' on who done it. Yuh got dat straight?

ANGEL. Duh guy what he got stabbed . . . wuz down heah lookin' fuh Spit . . . tuh givvim five bucks fuh snitchin' on who done it.

TOMMY. Right.

ANGEL. O.K.

TOMMY. An' rememba . . . yew let on I'm heah, I'll . . .

ANGEL. Aw, Tommy, yew know me.

TOMMY. Aw right. Jus' do like I tole yuh.

ANGEL. Whadda yuh gonna do tuh Spit if 'ee done it? (TOMMY *takes a knife from his pocket, and nips open the blade. The firelight runs along the blade. It looks bright and sharp and hard.* TOMMY *grimly draws it diagonally across his cheek.* ANGEL *grunts.*) Mark a de squealuh?

TOMMY. (*Snaps the blade home and pockets the knife.*) Right.

ANGEL. Gese!

TOMMY. Now, go on playin' yuh kazoo like nuttn happened . . . like I wuzn't heah. (*Footsteps and voices from the gate.* TOMMY *ducks and melts into the shadows of the hopper.* ANGEL *plays his kazoo a bit ostentatiously. The* DOORMAN *opens the gate.* KAY *appears in a shimmering evening gown, lovely and scented.*)

GIMPTY. (*His voice dull and tired.*) Hello, Kay!

KAY. Hello, Pete! (GIMPTY *looks past* KAY *at the* DOORMAN.) Yes?

DOORMAN. Ma'am?

KAY. Anything you want?

DOORMAN. Oh no . . . no, ma'am. Excuse me. (*Exit.*)

GIMPTY. I sent you a note this afternoon. Did you get it?

KAY. Yes, I was out. I didn't get back till late. I'm so sorry, Pete. Forgive me.

GIMPTY. Forget it! (*Two couples in evening clothes come down the street. They are all hectic, gay, and a trifle drunk. They greet* KAY *merrily. She laughs and jests with them, tells them she'll join them shortly, and in the gate they go. Not, however, without one or two backward glances at* GIMPTY. *Their chatter, off, ends in a burst of laughter that fades away.* KAY *turns to* GIMPTY.)

KAY. What a brawl that's turning into!

GIMPTY. Yeah. It seems like quite a party.

KAY. Yes, it is.

GIMPTY. (*After a pause, in a voice so low, it can scarcely be heard.*) Kay . . . did you hear what happened here this afternoon?

KAY. What do you? . . .

GIMPTY. The shooting.

KAY. (*Making talk. Evading.*) Oh, yes. And we just missed it. It must have been exciting. I'm . . .

GIMPTY. I didn't miss it.

KAY. No? . . . Oh, tell me . . . was it very? . . .

GIMPTY. (*Begins to give way to the terror and remorse pent up in him.*) It was pretty horrible.

KAY. Oh . . . of course.

GIMPTY. Horrible!

KAY. (*Realizing by his tone that something dreadful lies in all this, she becomes very tender and soothing.*) Pete, give me your hand. Come here. (*She leads him to the edge of the wharf.*) Sit down. . . . Now, what happened?

GIMPTY. I'd rather not talk about it for a minute.

KAY. If it upsets you, let's not talk about it at all.

GIMPTY. Yes, I've got to . . . but not for a minute. . . .

KAY. All right. (*Underneath them, the River splashes against the bulwark. Off, on the yacht, the band is playing a soft, sentimental melody. The chatter and the laughter from the party float faintly over the water. They sit there for a long time just staring across the river, at its lights, at the factories and signs on the opposite shore, at the bridge with its glittering loops, at the string of ghostly barges silently moving across the river. For a long time. Then she speaks, quietly*)

KAY. I love the river at night. . . . It's beautiful . . . and a bit frightening.

GIMPTY. (*Stares down at the black water swirling under him. He begins to talk, faster and faster, trying to push back into his unconscious the terror that haunts him, to forget that afternoon if only for a few seconds.*) It reminds me of something . . . . What is it? . . . Oh, yeah . . . when I was a kid. In the spring the sudden sun showers used to flood the gutters. The other kids used to race boats down the street. Little boats: straws, matches, lollipop-sticks. I couldn't run after them, so I guarded the sewer and caught the boats to keep them from tumbling in. Near the sewer . . . sometimes, I remember . . . a whirlpool would form. . . . Dirt and oil from the street would break into rainbow colors . . . iridescent. . . . (*For a moment he does escape.*) Beautiful, I think . . . a marvel of color out of dirty water. I can't take my eyes off it. And suddenly a boat in danger. (*The terror in him rises again.*) I try to stop it. . . . Too late! It shoots into the black hole of the sewer. I used to dream about falling into it myself. The river reminds me of that. . . . Death must be like this . . . like the river at night. (*There is no comfort in her big enough for his needs. They sit in brooding silence, which is finally interrupted by the* DOORMAN'*s voice, off.*)

DOORMAN. Miss Mitchell came out here only a moment ago. Yes, there she is now. (*The* DOORMAN *and a* SAILOR *come out of the gate.*)

SAILOR. Miss Mitchell?

KAY. Yes?

SAILOR. Mr. Hilton says we're ready to cast off. We're waiting for you, ma'am.

KAY. Tell him I'll be there in a minute.

SAILOR. Yes'm. (*Exit* SAILOR.)

DOORMAN. (*Turns to* ANGEL, *who is still hovering over the fire.*) Why don't you kids beat it?

ANGEL. Aw-w!

DOORMAN. All right! I'll fix you! (*He strides off up the street.*)

GIMPTY. (*Desperately.*) Kay, there's still time. You don't have to go.

KAY. (*Finality in her quiet voice.*) I'm afraid I do.

GIMPTY. Listen . . . I knew where Martin was. And I told the police.

KAY. You? How did you recognize him?

GIMPTY. I used to know him when I was a kid.

KAY. Oh!

GIMPTY. I know it was a stinkin' thing to do.

KAY. No. It had to be done.

GIMPTY. There was a reward.

KAY. Yes, I know. I read about it. That's a break for you, Pete. You can help your mother now. And you can live decently.

GIMPTY. How about you?

KAY. This isn't the miracle we were looking for.

GIMPTY. (*After a long pause.*) No. I guess you're right.

KAY. How long would it last us? Perhaps a year, then what? I've been through all that. I couldn't go through it again.

GIMPTY. I guess it's asking too much.

KAY. (*Softly, trying to make him see the picture realistically, reasonably.*) It's not all selfishness, Pete. I'm thinking of you too. I could do this. I could go and live with you and be happy—(*And she means it*)—and then when poverty comes . . . and we begin to torture each other, what would happen? I'd leave you and go back to Jack. He needs me too, you see. I'm pretty certain of him. But what would become of you then? That sounds pretty bitchy, I suppose.

GIMPTY. No . . . no, it's quite right. I didn't see things as clearly as you did. It's just that I've been . . . such a dope.

KAY. No! It's just that we can't have everything . . . ever. (*She rises.*)

GIMPTY. Of course.

KAY. Good-bye, darling.

GIMPTY. (*Rises.*) Good-bye, Kay. Have a pleasant trip.

KAY. (*One sob escaping her.*) Oh, Pete, forgive me if I've hurt you. Please forgive me!

GIMPTY. Don't be foolish. You haven't hurt me. It's funny, but you know, I never honestly expected anything. I didn't. It was really just a . . . whimsy I played on myself.

KAY. Pete.

GIMPTY. Yes?

KAY. Will you stay here and wave good-bye to me when the boat goes?

GIMPTY. Naturally. I expected to.

KAY. Thanks. (*She kisses him.*) Take care of yourself! (*She goes quickly.* GIMPTY *follows her to the gate, standing there, peering through the bars, catching a last glimpse of her.* SPIT *trots down the street.*)

SPIT. He wuzn't deah.

ANGEL. No?

SPIT. Nah. Milty's a lot of bushwah. I tole yuh. (*He looks at the fire. Spits into it.* ANGEL *glances backward at the shadows under the hopper.*)

ANGEL. Hey, Spit!

SPIT. What?

ANGEL. Dey wuz a guy heah . . . (T.B. *appears, dragging an egg crate.*)

T.B. Look what I got! Whew! Boy, dat'll go up like wildfire!

SPIT. Babee! Dat's good!

ANGEL. Yeah! Dat's swell! (*They smash up the crate by jumping on it. Then they tear off the slats and break them across the curb. The noise of the crashing and splintering exhilarates them. They laugh and chatter.* DIPPY *enters, puffing and grunting, dragging an old discarded automobile seat by a rope.*)

DIPPY. (*Proud of his contribution.*) Hey, yuh t'ink dis'll boin? I t'ink it'll boin, don' chew? Boy, like a house afire I bet.

ANGEL. Nah, dat'll stink up da place.

DIPPY. (*Disappointed.*) Aw gese, I dragged it a mile. I dragged it fuh five blocks. It wuz way ovuh by Toid Avenoo. (*The* BOYS *throw some of the wood into the fire. It flares up with a great crackling. Tongues of flame shoot up out of the can. The band on the boat plays, "Anchors Aweigh!" There is much laughter and shouting of "Bon Voyage!" "Have a pleasant trip," etc. from the party who have disembarked. The bells and the whistles of the boat blow, the engines throb, and the propellers churn the water.* GIMPTY *stands strained and tense, looking off, through the gate.*)

T.B. Hey, look! Look! Duh boat! She's goin' like sixty. Babee! (*They rush over to the gate.*)

ANGEL. Boy, dat's some boat! Dat's a crackerjack.

DIPPY. Yeah. (*He imitates the sound of the bells, the foghorn, the engine.*) Clang, clang! Oooh! Ch, ch, ch! Poo! Poo! I'm a boat! Look, felluhs! I'm a boat. Ch! Ch! Ch! (*He shuffles around, hands fore and aft.*)

ANGEL. (*Points at the departing boat.*) Lookit duh dame wavin' at us.

DIPPY. (*Waves vigorously.*) Yoo, hoo! Yoo hoo!

T.B. She ain't wavin' at us, yuh dope.

SPIT. At Gimpty.

T.B. How'd yuh like tuh be on 'at boat?

DIPPY. Boy! I bet yew cud cross 'ee ocean in 'at boat. Yuh cud cross 'ee ocean in 'at boat, couldn't yuh, Gimpty?

GIMPTY. What?

DIPPY. Yuh cud cross 'ee ocean in 'at boat, couldn't yuh? (ANGEL *returns to the fire and pokes around in it.*)

GIMPTY. Oh, yeah, I guess you could.

T.B. A cawse yuh could, yuh dope, anybody knows 'at.

SPIT. (*Sees* ANGEL *fishing out a mickey.*) Hey, watcha doin'?

ANGEL. (*Testing his mickey.*) My mickey's done. Dey're done now, felluhs! (*The sounds of the yacht die off in the distance.*)

SPIT. Look out! Look out! Wait a minute! (*They all rush to haul out their mickeys.* SPIT *pushes them aside, and spears the biggest potato with a stick.*)

DIPPY. Hey, Spit, dat big one's mine. Remembuh . . . I swiped it!

SPIT. Shat ap, yuh dope! (*He punches* DIPPY, *who begins to snivel.*)

DIPPY. If Tommy wuz heah, yuh wouldn't do dat.

SPIT. Nuts tuh yew! Who's got da salt?

ANGEL. (*Takes a small packet of newspaper from his shoeshine box.*) Heah, I got it! (*The salt is passed around. They eat their mickeys with much smacking of the lips.*)

DIPPY. (*Who has gotten the smallest mickey.*) Ahl git even witcha!

SPIT. Nuts!

DIPPY. Yew wait till yuh ast me tuh do sumpm fuh yew some day. Jus' wait. See watcha git!

SPIT. (*Spits at* DIPPY.) Right innee eye!

DIPPY. (*Wiping his eye.*) Ah, yuh louse!

ANGEL. (*Remembering the conspiracy. Slowly and deliberately, between munches.*) Hey, Spit.

SPIT. What?

ANGEL. Dey wuz a guy heah . . . yuh know da guy what Tommy stabbed? . . . Well, he wuz heah.

SPIT. What fuh?

ANGEL. He wuz lookin' fuh yew.

SPIT. Fuh me?

ANGEL. Yeah.

SPIT. What faw?

ANGEL. He said he wuz gonna give yuh five bucks fuh snitchin' on who done it.

SPIT. Wheah izee? Wheah'd ee go?

DIPPY. Did yew snitch on Tommy?

SPIT. Sure. Sure I did. (*A chorus of disapproval follows this confession.* SPIT *rises and doubles up his fists. To* DIPPY.) What's it to yuh?

DIPPY. Nuttn'! (SPIT *looks at* ANGEL.)

ANGEL. Nuttn'!

T.B. Yew snitched on Tommy! Gese!

SPIT. Aw, shat ap, 'r I'll give yuh yuhr lumps! (*He turns, looking for the benefactor.*) Wheah'd he go? Which way? I want dat five bucks. (TOMMY *runs from behind the hopper, leaps onto* SPIT's *back, bearing him to the ground.*)

TOMMY. (*Sits astride* SPIT, *his knees pinning* SPIT's *arms down.*) Yuh'll git it, yuh stoo' pigeon! In a pig's kapooch yuh will!

DIPPY. Tommy!

ANGEL. Gese!   } *Simultaneously*

T.B. Wow!

TOMMY. Ahl give yuh sumpm yuh won' fuhgit so easy. Say yuh prayuhs, yuh louse!

SPIT. Lemme go! Lemme go!

TOMMY. Oh, no, yuh don't!

SPIT. Aw, Tommy, I didn' mean tuh. Dey had me! De cops had me! What could I do?

TOMMY. Yuh know watcha gonna git fuh it? (*He takes out his knife.* SPIT *squeals with terror.* TOMMY *jams his hand over* SPIT's *mouth.*) Shat ap!

DIPPY. What's ee gonna do?

ANGEL. Gash his cheek fum heah tuh heah!

T.B. No kid!

ANGEL. Yeah!

DIPPY. Gee whiz! Wow!

SPIT. (*Crying and pleading.*) Tommy, don't, will yuh? I'll give yuh dose bike wheels I swiped. I'll give yuh me stamps. I'll give yuh me immies. I'll give yuh dat five bucks. Ony lemme go, will yuh?

TOMMY. Dis time yuh don' git away wid it so easy, see?

SPIT. Hey, felluhs! Hey, Gimpty! He's got a knife!

GIMPTY. (*Notices for the first time what's happening.*) Stop that, you crazy kid!

TOMMY. No!

GIMPTY. (*Starts toward* TOMMY.) Let him go, Tommy!

TOMMY. Come near me, Gimpty, an' I'll give it tuh yew. Stay back, or I'll give it tuh 'im right now! (*He places the knife point at* SPIT's *throat.* GIMPTY *stops short.*)

GIMPTY. Getting easy, isn't it?

TOMMY. Yeah, it's a cinch.

GIMPTY. Let him up, Tommy!

TOMMY. No!

GIMPTY. Tommy, give me that knife!

TOMMY. No!

GIMPTY. Sell it to me! I'll buy it from you!

TOMMY. No!

GIMPTY. What's a matter? You a yellow-belly, Tommy?

TOMMY. Who's a yeller-belly?

GIMPTY. Only a yellow-belly uses a knife, Tommy. You'll be sorry for this!

TOMMY. Well, he squealed on me! (MILTY *and* DRINA *come down the street.*)

MILTY. I dunno. He wuz heah befaw . . . honest! (*Seeing the fight, he rushes to* TOMMY *and* SPIT.) Wassamattuh, Tommy?

DRINA. (*Rushing to* TOMMY *and* SPIT.) Tommy! Tommy! Where've you been?

SPIT. Drina! Drina, he's godda knife! He wants a stab me!

TOMMY. (*Slaps* SPIT.) Shat ap!

DRINA. Tommy! . . . Give me that knife! . . . What's the matter with you? Aren't you in enough hot water now? Don't you understand what you're doing? (*Screams.*) Give me that knife!

GIMPTY. Go on, Tommy! (*Pause.*)

TOMMY. (*Reluctantly hands the knife to* DRINA.) Heah! (*He rises, releasing* SPIT. *As* SPIT *scrambles to his feet,* TOMMY *kicks him in the rump, yelling.*) Beat it, yuh son uv a . . . (SPIT *runs up the sidewalk.*)

DRINA. (*Sharply.*) Sh, Tommy!

SPIT. (*From a safe distance, turns.*) Tuh hell witcha, yuh bastid! (*Then he redoubles his speed, disappearing around the corner.*)

TOMMY. I'll kill yuh! (*He starts after* SPIT, *but* DRINA *grabs his arm, and pulls him back.*)

DRINA. Tommy, behave yourself!

TOMMY. But 'ee squealed on me, Drina!

DRINA. That's no excuse for this. Now it's knives! (*She snaps the blade shut.*) What'll it be next? What's happening to you, Tommy?

TOMMY. I wuz ony gonna scare 'im.

DRINA. (*Grasps him by the shoulders and shakes him to emphasize what she's saying.*) Listen to me! The cops came up to the house ten minutes ago. They were lookin' for you. You stabbed some man! Why! *Why!* (TOMMY *turns away.*) Don't you see what you're doing? They'll send you to jail, Tommy?

TOMMY. (*All the fight gone.*) No, dey won't. Dey gotta ketch me foist.

DRINA. What do you mean?

TOMMY. I'm gonna run away.

DRINA. Run away? Where to?

TOMMY. I dunno.

DRINA. Where?

TOMMY. Dere a plenty a places I kin hitch tuh. Lots a guys do.

DRINA. And what are you gonna eat? Where you gonna sleep?

TOMMY. I'll git along.

DRINA. How?

TOMMY. I dunno. Some way. I'll snitch stuff. I dunno. (*Belabored and uncertain.*) Aw, lemme alone!

DRINA. I can see what's gonna happen to you. (*Fiercely.*) You'll become a bum!

TOMMY. Aw right! I'll become a bum, den!

DRINA. (*Hurls the knife onto the sidewalk, and screams.*) That's fine! That's what mamma worked her life away for! That's what I've worked since I was a kid for! So you could become a bum! That's great!

TOMMY. (*Shouting back.*) Aw right! It's great! Well, gese, whadda yuh want me tuh do? Let da cops git me an' sen' me up the rivuh, Drina? I don' wanna be locked up till I'm twenty-one. Izzat what yuh want me tuh do?

DRINA. (*Suddenly very soft and tender, maternally.*) No, darling, no. I won't let that happen. I won't let them touch you, Tommy. Don't worry.

TOMMY. Well, what else kin we do?

DRINA. I'll run away with you, Tommy. We'll go away, together, some place.

TOMMY. No, Drina, yuh couldn't do dat. Yer a goil. (*Pause.*) Yuh know what? Maybe, if I give myself up, an' tell em I didn' mean tuh to do it, an if I swear on a Bible I'll nevuh do it again, maybe dey'll let me go.

DRINA. No, Tommy, I'm not gonna let you give yourself up. No!

TOMMY. Yeah, Drina. (*Enter* DOORMAN *with a* POLICEMAN.)

DOORMAN. (*Pointing to the boys.*) There!

POLICEMAN. (*Roars.*) Get ta hell out a here! Go wan home!

T.B. Chickee da cop! (*The* BOYS *scatter.* DIPPY *and* T.B. *duck into the tenement doorway.* ANGEL *and* MILTY *scramble under the hopper. To the* DOORMAN.) Get some water! Put this out. (MULLIGAN, *the policeman, turns to the cringing figures under the hopper.*) Yuh wanna set fire to these houses? Lemme ketch you doin' this

again and I'll beat the b'jesus out a you! (*He slaps the blazing can with his night stick to punctuate the warning. Sparks fly up.*)

TOMMY. (*Slowly.*) Yuh know, Drina, I tink 'at's what I ought tuh do.

DRINA. (*Holding him tight, terrified. In a hoarse whisper.*) No. I won't let you do that.

TOMMY. Yeah. (*He detaches her arm, and goes to* MULLIGAN.) Hey, mister!

MULLIGAN. What do you want? Come on, beat it!

TOMMY. Wait a minute! I'm Tommy McGrath.

MULLIGAN. What of it? (*The other* BOYS *creep back.*)

TOMMY. I'm da kid dat stabbed dat man today.

MULLIGAN. What!!! (*He grabs* TOMMY's *arm. The* DOORMAN *comes running over to verify this.*)

TOMMY. (*His voice shrill and trembly.*) Yeah. He wuz chokin' me an breakin' my ahm . . . so I did it.

MULLIGAN. So, you're the kid. I bin lookin' fuh you.

DOORMAN. (*Who has been staring at* TOMMY, *suddenly elated.*) That's him all right. That's him! Wait, I'll call Mr. Griswald. He'll tell you! (*He rushes off through the gateway.*)

MULLIGAN. All right. I'll keep him here. Don't you worry.

DRINA. (*Goes to* MULLIGAN, *pleading.*) Tommy! No, no, they can't take him, let him go, officer! Please!

MULLIGAN. I can't do that, miss.

DRINA. He didn't know what he was doing. He's only a baby.

MULLIGAN. You tell it to the judge. Tell it to the judge.

DRINA. (*Trying to wrench* TOMMY *free.*) No! Let him go! Let him go!

MULLIGAN. (*Pushes her away roughly.*) Get away. Don't try that! (*To* GIMPTY.) You better take her away or she'll get hurt.

GIMPTY. Drina, come here.

DRINA. No.

MULLIGAN. In a minute I'll take her to the station-house, too.

TOMMY. Aw, Drina, cut it out, will yuh? Dat ain' gonna help.

GIMPTY. He's right, you know.

T.B. (*Sidles over to* TOMMY, *whispering.*) Hey, Tommy if yuh go tuh rifawmatory, look up a guy named . . .

MULLIGAN. (*Shoving* T.B. *away.*) Git outa here! (T.B. *flies across the street.*)

DRINA. Yes, of course he's right. I'm so . . . I just don't know what I'm . . .

DOORMAN (*Enters with* MR. GRISWALD.) Yes, Mr. Griswald, I'm sure it's the boy. (GRISWALD *pushes him aside, and walks briskly to* MULLIGAN.)

GRISWALD. So you've caught him.

MULLIGAN. Yes, sir.

DRINA. He gave himself up!

GRISWALD. Let me look at him. (*He looks searchingly at* TOMMY's *face and nods.*) Yes, this is the boy, all right.

MULLIGAN. Good.

DRINA. He gave himself up.

GRISWALD. (*Turns to her.*) What's that?

DRINA. (*Trying desperately to be calm.*) I'm his sister!

GRISWALD. Oh. Well . . . a fine brother you've got.

MULLIGAN. (*To* ANGEL *and* MILTY, *who have crept to the foreground.*) Come on, get out a here! Beat it! (*They scramble back again under the hopper.*)

DRINA. Listen, mister! Give him another chance. . . . (*She clutches his arm. He winces and draws his breath in pain.*) Please, will you?

GRISWALD. Careful of that arm!

DRINA. Oh! I'm sorry. . . . Give him another chance! Let him go!

GRISWALD. Another chance to what? To kill somebody?

TOMMY. I won' evuh do it again. Yew wuz chokin' me an' I wuz seein' black aready, an' I . . .

DRINA. Have a heart, mister! He's only a kid. He didn't know what he was doing.

GRISWALD. No?

DRINA. No.

GRISWALD. Then you should have taught him better.

DRINA. (*Her impulse is to fight back, but she restrains herself.*) Listen! He's a good boy. And he's got brains. Ask his teacher . . . Miss Judell, P.S. 59. He used to get A,A,A . . . all the time. He's smart.

GRISWALD. Then I can't see any excuse at all for him.

DRINA. (*Flaring.*) All right! He made a mistake! He's sorry! What's so terrible about that?

GIMPTY. Sh! Drina!

GRISWALD. I have a gash half an inch deep in my wrist. The doctor is afraid of infection. What do you say to that?

DRINA. (*With such effort at self-control that she trembles.*) I'm sorry! I'm awfully sorry!

GRISWALD. Sorry! That won't help, will it?

DRINA. Will it help to send him to reform school?

GRISWALD. I don't know. It'll at least keep him from doing it to someone else.

DRINA. But you heard him. He swore he wouldn't ever do it again.

GRISWALD. I'm afraid I can't believe that. He'll be better off where they'll send him. They'll take him out of the gutters and teach him a trade.

DRINA. (*Explodes again.*) What do you know about it?

GRISWALD. I'm sorry. I've no more time. I can't stand here arguing with you. (*To* MULLIGAN.) All right, officer! I'll be down to make the complaint. (*Starts to exit.*)

GIMPTY. (*Stepping in front of* GRISWALD *and blocking his path.*) Wait a minute, mister!

GRISWALD. Yes?

GIMPTY. May I talk to you a moment?

GRISWALD. There's no use, really.

GIMPTY. Just a moment, please?

GRISWALD. Well, what is it?

GIMPTY. You know what happened here today? A man was shot . . . killed.

GRISWALD. You mean that gangster?

GIMPTY. Yes.

GRISWALD. What about it?

GIMPTY. I killed him.

GRISWALD. You what?

MULLIGAN. He's crazy. (*To* GIMPTY.) What are you trying to do?

GIMPTY. It was I who told them where to find him.

GRISWALD. Well, that may be so. Then you were doing your duty. It's simple enough. And I'm doing mine.

DRINA. (*Hysterically.*) No! It ain't the same! Martin was a butcher, he was like a mad dog. He deserved to die. But Tommy's a baby . . .

GIMPTY. Please! That's not the point!

DRINA. It is!

MULLIGAN. (*To* ANGEL *and* MILTY, *who are back again.*) How many times have I gotta tell you! . . . (*They retreat.*)

GIMPTY. Yes, maybe it is. Anyway, I turned him over for my own selfish reasons. And yet the thing I did, Griswald, was nothing compared to what you're doing. . . . Yeah . . . Martin was a killer, he was bad, he deserved to die, true! But I knew him when we were kids. He had a lot of fine stuff. He was strong. He had

courage. He was a born leader. He even had a sense of fair play. But living in the streets kept making him bad. . . . Then he was sent to reform school. Well, they reformed him all right! They taught him the ropes. He came out tough and hard and mean, with all the tricks of the trade.

GRISWALD. But I don't see what you're driving at.

GIMPTY. I'm telling you! That's what you're sending this kid to.

GRISWALD. I'm afraid there's no alternative.

DRINA. Are you so perfect? Didn't you ever do anything you were sorry for later? (*Screams.*) God! Didn't anybody ever forgive you for anything?

GRISWALD. (*Looks at her in silence for a moment. Then, gently, and sympathetically.*) Of course. I'm sorry. I'm very sorry. Believe me, I'm not being vindictive. I'm not punishing him for hurting me. As far as this goes—(*Touches his bandaged wrist.*)—I would forgive him gladly. But you must remember that I'm a father . . . that today he, unprovoked, beat my boy with a stick and stole his watch. There are other boys like mine. They've got to be protected, too. I feel awfully sorry for you, but your brother belongs in a reformatory. (*To* MULLIGAN.) All right, officer! (*He shakes his head and disappears in the gateway.*)

DRINA. (*With a cry of despair.*) What?

MULLIGAN. All right! Let's go! (*To* TOMMY.) Come along.

T.B. (*Edges over to* TOMMY.) Hey, Tommy, wait! Look up a guy named Smokey!

MULLIGAN. Get away from here. I'll bounce one off your head!

TOMMY. (*Looking back to* DRINA.) Don' worry, Drina. I ain' scared.

DRINA. (*Trying to smile for* TOMMY.) Of course not, darling. I'm coming with you. (*Starts up.*)

MULLIGAN. Yeah, I think you better. Come on! (*He calls over his shoulder to the* DOORMAN.) Put out that fire!

DOORMAN. Oh, yes . . . yes, officer! (*Hurries off, through the gate.* MULLIGAN *and* TOMMY *go up the street.* DRINA *starts to follow.* T.B. *catches her arm.*)

T.B. Drina! Drina! Wait!

DRINA. No, I can't, I gotta . . .

T.B. It's important. It's about Tommy!

DRINA. (*Turns.*) What?

T.B. (*Very knowing and very helpful. He's been through this before.*) Look, Drina, dere's a guy at rifawm school named Smokey . . . like dat, Smokey, dey call him Smokey. Yew tell Tommy tuh be nice tuh him and give im t'ings like cigarettes an dat. Cause dis guy Smokey, he knows a lot of swell rackets fuh Tommy when ee gits out . . . cause Tommy's a wise kid an . . .

DRINA. (*Scared, helpless, begins to sob.*) Oh, Mom, why did you leave us? I don't know what to do, Mom. I don't know where to turn. I wish I was dead and buried with you.

T.B. (*Puzzled by this unexpected reaction to his good advice.*) What's a mattuh? What'd I say? I didn' say nuttin'. What'd I say?

GIMPTY. Sh! Shut up! (*He goes to* DRINA, *who is sobbing her heart out, and puts a protective arm around her.*) You poor kid! You poor kid. Stop crying. Stop crying now.

DRINA. I'm all right. I'll be all right in a minute.

GIMPTY. Now you stop crying and listen to me. Tomorrow morning you meet me right here at half past nine. We're going downtown. We're going to get the best lawyer in this city, and we'll get Tommy free.

DRINA. But that'll cost so much!

GIMPTY. Don't worry about that. We'll get him out.

DRINA. Do you really think so?

GIMPTY. I know so.

DRINA. Oh, God bless you . . . you're so . . . (*She breaks into sobs again.*)

GIMPTY. Now, now. You go along now and stick by Tommy.

DRINA. (*Controlling herself.*) You've been so awfully good to us, I . . . I hate to ask for anything else, but . . .

GIMPTY. Sure, what is it?

DRINA. I wish you'd come along with us now. I know if you're there . . . they wouldn't dare touch . . . (*Her voice catches.*) Tommy!

GIMPTY. Me? I'm nobody. I can't . . .

DRINA. I wish you would. Please?

GIMPTY. (*Softly.*) All right. (*They go up the street, his arm still around her, his cane clicking on the sidewalk even after they've disappeared from sight. Awed by the scene, the kids gather about the fire again.*)

ANGEL. Gese, wadda yuh tink'll happen tuh Tommy?

MILTY. Dey'll git 'im off. Dey'll git 'im off. Yuh'll see.

T.B. Even if dey don't, yuh loin a barrel a good tings at rifawm school. Smokey once loined me how tuh open a lock wid a hair pin. Boy! It's easy! It's a cinch! I loined one-two-three, but now I fuhgit . . . (*The* DOORMAN *appears uncoiling a garden hose. He pushes* ANGEL *aside, points the nozzle into the can, and releases the stream. The fire hisses, spits, and dies. A thick pillar of smoke ascends skyward out of the can.*)

ANGEL. (*Looks upward, entranced.*) Holy smokes!

DIPPY. Whee!

ANGEL. Look a dat!

T.B. Boy! Right up tuh duh sky!

ANGEL. Right up tuh duh stahs!

DIPPY. How high ah dey? How high ah duh stahs?

DOORMAN. (*Turning back at the gate.*) And you rats better not start any more trouble, if you know what's good for you! (*He goes in. The boys wait till he is out of ear-shot, then they hurl a chorus of abuse.*)

MILTY. Gay cock of'm yam!

ANGEL. Fongoola!

DIPPY. Nuts ta yew!

T.B. In yuhr hat!

Simultaneously

(ANGEL *plays a mocking tune on his kazoo.* T.B. *sings the lyrics.* To da da da da bushwah. Te da da bushwah.)

ANGEL. Ahl goul him!

DIPPY. (*Laughs.*) Yeah. (*After this outburst, there is a long pause. They watch the smoke curling upward.*)

MILTY. (*Softly.*) Gee! Looka dat smoke!

T.B. Dat reminds me—all a time at ri, fawm school Smokey usta sing a song about Angel—"If I had de wings of a Angel." (*They laugh.*)

MILTY. Angel ain't got no wings.

DIPPY. Real ones got wings. I saw it in a pitcha once. (ANGEL *starts playing "If I had the wings of an angel" on his kazoo.*)

T.B. Dat's right. Dat's it! (*In a quavery voice he accompanies* ANGEL.) If I had de wings of a angel. Ovuh dese prison walls I wud fly . . . (*The others join in, swelling the song.*) Straight tuh dee yahms a my muddah. Ta da da, da da . . . (*A passing tramp steamer hoots mournfully. The smoke continues to roll out of the can, as their cacophony draws out to a funereal end.*) Da . . . da . . . da . . . dum.

CURTAIN

Bury The Dead

BY IRWIN SHAW

*"...what is this world that
you cling to it?"*

To My Mother

CAST OF CHARACTERS

PRIVATE DRISCOLL
PRIVATE MORGAN
PRIVATE LEVY
PRIVATE WEBSTER
PRIVATE SCHELLING
PRIVATE DEAN
JOAN BURKE
BESS SCHELLING
MARTHA WEBSTER

JULIA BLAKE
KATHERINE DRISCOLL
ELIZABETH DEAN
Generals One, Two and Three.
A Captain, a Sergeant, and four infantrymen,
    employed as a burial detail.
A Priest, a Rabbi, a Doctor.
A Reporter and an Editor.
Two Whores.

TIME

The second year of the war that is to begin tomorrow night.

SCENE

The stage is in two planes—in the foreground, the bare stage, in the rear, not too far back, going the entire length of the stage, a platform about seven feet above the level of the stage proper. No properties are used to adorn the stage save for some sandbags, whole and split, lying along the edge of the raised platform and some loose dirt also on the platform. The entire platform is painted dull black. It is lighted by a strong spotlight thrown along it at hip-height from the right wing. It is the only light on the stage. The platform is to represent a torn-over battlefield, now quiet, some miles behind the present lines, where a burial detail, standing in a shallow trench dug in the platform, so that the audience sees them only from the hip up, are digging a common grave to accommodate six bodies, piled on the right of the platform, wrapped in canvas. A sergeant stands on the right, on the edge of the grave, smoking. . . . The soldier nearest him, in the shallow trench, stops his digging . . . .

FIRST SOLDIER. Say, Sergeant, they stink . . . . (*Waving his shovel at the corpses*) Let's bury them in a hurry. . . .

SERGEANT. What the hell do you think you'd smell like, after you'd been lyin' out for two days—a goddamn lily of the valley? They'll be buried soon enough. Keep digging.

SECOND SOLDIER. (*Scratching himself.*) Dig and scratch! Dig and scratch! What a war! When you're not diggin' trenches you're diggin' graves. . . .

THIRD SOLDIER. Who's got a cigarette? I'll take opium if nobody's got a cigarette.

SECOND SOLDIER. When you're not diggin' graves you're scratchin' at fleas. By God, there're more fleas in this army than . . .

FIRST SOLDIER. That's what the war's made for—the fleas. Somebody's got to feed 'em. . . .

FOURTH SOLDIER. I used to take a shower every day. Can you imagine?

SERGEANT. All right, Mr. Lifebuoy, we'll put your picture in the *Saturday Evening Post*—in color!

SECOND SOLDIER. When you're not scratchin' at fleas, you're bein' killed. That's a helluva life for a grown man.

THIRD SOLDIER. Who's got a cigarette? I'll trade my rifle—if I can find it—for a cigarette. For Christ's sake, don't they make cigarettes no more? (*Leaning, melancholy, on his shovel*) This country's goin' to the dogs for real now. . . .

SERGEANT. Lift dirt, soldier. Come on! This ain't no vacation.

THIRD SOLDIER. (*Disregarding him.*) I heard of guys packin' weeds and cowflop into cigarettes in this man's army. They say it has a tang. (*Reflectively*) Got to try it some day. . . .

SERGEANT. Hurry up! (*Blowing on his hands*) I'm freezin' here. I don't want to hang around all night. I can't feel my feet no more. . . .

FOURTH SOLDIER. I aint felt my feet for two weeks. I ain't had my shoes off in two weeks. (*Leaning on his shovel*) I wonder if the toes're still connected. I wear a 8A shoe. Aristocratic foot, the salesman always said. Funny—going around not even knowin' whether you still got toes or not. . . . It's not hygienic really. . . .

SERGEANT. All right, friend, we'll make sure the next war you're in is run hygienic.

FOURTH SOLDIER. In the Spanish-American War more men died of fever than . . .

FIRST SOLDIER. (*Beating viciously at something in the grave*) Get him! Get him! Kill the bastard!

FOURTH SOLDIER. (*Savagely*) He's coming this way! We've got him cornered!

FIRST SOLDIER. Bash his brains out!

SECOND SOLDIER. You got him with that one! (*All the soldiers in the grave beat at it, yelling demoniacally, triumphantly.*)

SEARGEANT. (*Remonstrating*) Come on now, you're wasting time. . . .

FIRST SOLDIER. (*Swinging savagely*) There. That fixed him. The god-damn . . .

FOURTH SOLDIER. (*Sadly*) You'd think the rats'd at least wait until the stiffs were underground.

FIRST SOLDIER. Did you ever see such a fat rat in your whole life? I bet he ate like a horse—this one.

SERGEANT. All right, all right. You're not fightin' the war against rats. Get back to your business.

FIRST SOLDIER. I get a lot more pleasure killin' rats than killin' them. (*Gesture toward the front lines.*)

SERGEANT. Rats got to live, too. They don't know no better.

FIRST SOLDIER. (*Suddenly scooping up rat on his shovel and presenting it to* SERGEANT) Here you are, Sergeant. A little token of our regard from Company A.

SERGEANT. Stop the smart stuff! I don't like it.

FIRST SOLDIER. (*Still with rat upheld on shovel*) Ah, Sergeant, I'm disappointed. This rat's a fine pedigreed animal—fed only on the choicest young men the United State's turned out in the last twenty years.

SERGEANT. Come on, wise guy. (FIRST SOLDIER *goes right on.*)

FIRST SOLDIER. Notice the heavy, powerful shoulders to this rat, notice the well-covered flanks, notice the round belly—bank clerks, mechanics, society-leaders, farmers—good feeding— (*Suddenly he throws the rat away*) Ah—I'm gettin' awful tired of this. I didn't enlist in this bloody war to be no bloody grave-digger!

SERGEANT. Tell that to the President. Keep diggin'.

SECOND SOLDIER. Say, this is deep enough. What're we supposed to do—dig right down to hell and deliver them over first-hand?

SERGEANT. A man's entitled to six feet a' dirt over his face. We gotta show respect to the dead. Keep diggin'. . . .

FOURTH SOLDIER. I hope they don't put me too far under when my turn comes. I want to be able to come up and get a smell of air every once in so often.

SERGEANT. Stow the gab, you guys! Keep diggin'. . . .

FIRST SOLDIER. They stink! Bury them!

SERGEANT. All right, Fanny. From now on we'll perfume 'em before we ask you to put them away. Will that please you?

FIRST SOLDIER. I don't like the way they smell, that's all. I don't have to like the way they smell, do I? That ain't in the regulations, is it? A man's got a right to use his nose, ain't he, even though he's in this god-damn army. . . .

SERGEANT. Talk respectful when you talk about the army, you!

FIRST SOLDIER. Oh, the lovely army . . . (*He heaves up clod of dirt.*)

SECOND SOLDIER. Oh, the dear army . . . (*He heaves up clod of dirt.*)

THIRD SOLDIER. Oh, the sweet army . . . (*He heaves up clod of dirt.*)

FIRST SOLDIER. Oh, the scummy, stinking, god-damn army . . . (*He heaves up three shovelfuls in rapid succession.*)

SERGEANT. That's a fine way to talk in the presence of death. . . .

FIRST SOLDIER. We'd talk in blank verse for you, Sergeant, only we ran out of it our third day in the front line. What do you expect, Sergeant, we're just common soldiers . . .

SECOND SOLDIER. Come on. Let's put 'em away. I'm getting blisters big enough to use for balloons here. What's the difference? They'll just be turned up anyway, the next time the artillery wakes up. . . .

SERGEANT. All right! All right! If you're in such a hurry—put 'em in. . . . (*The soldiers nearest the right-hand edge of the grave jump out and start carrying the bodies over, one at each corner of the canvas. The other soldiers, still in the trench, take the bodies from them and carry them over to the other side of the trench, where they lay them down, out of sight of the audience.*)

SERGEANT. Put 'em in neat, there. . . .

FIRST SOLDIER. File 'em away alphabetically, boys. We may want to refer to them, later. The General might want to look up some past cases.

FOURTH SOLDIER. This one's just a kid. I knew him a little. Nice kid. He used to write dirty poems. Funny as hell. He don't even look dead. . . .

FIRST SOLDIER. Bury him! He stinks!

SERGEANT. If you think *you* smell so sweet, yourself, Baby, you oughta wake up. You ain't exactly a perfume-ad, soldier. (*Laughter.*)

THIRD SOLDIER. Chalk one up for the Sergeant.

FIRST SOLDIER. You ain't a combination of roses and wistaria, either, Sergeant, but I can stand you, especially when you don't talk. At least you're alive. There's something about the smell of dead ones that gives me the willies. . . . Come on, let's pile the dirt in on them. . . . (*The* SOLDIERS *scramble out of the grave.*)

SERGEANT. Hold it.

THIRD SOLDIER. What's the matter now? Do we have to do a dance around them?

SERGEANT. We have to wait for chaplains . . . . They gotta say some prayers over them.

FIRST SOLDIER. Oh, for Christ's sake ain't I ever going to get any sleep tonight?

SERGEANT. Don't begrudge a man his prayers, soldier. You'd want 'em, wouldn't you?

FIRST SOLDIER. God, no. I want to sleep peaceful when I go. . . . Well, where are they? Why dont they come? Do we have to stand here all night waiting for those guys to come and talk to God about these fellers?

THIRD SOLDIER. Who's got a cigarette? (*Plaintively.*)

SERGEANT. Attention! Here they are! (*A Roman-Catholic priest and a rabbi come in.*)

PRIEST. Is everything ready?

SERGEANT. Yes, Father . . .

FIRST SOLDIER. Make it snappy! I'm awful tired.

PRIEST. God must be served slowly, my son. . . .

FIRST SOLDIER. He's gettin' plenty of service these days—and not so slow, either. He can stand a little rushin'. . . .

SERGEANT. Shut up, soldier.

RABBI. Do you want to hold your services first, Father?

SERGEANT. There ain't no Jewish boys in there. (*Gesture to grave*) Reverend, I don't think we'll need you.

RABBI. I understand one of them is named Levy.

SERGEANT. Yes. But he's no Jew.

RABBI. With that name we won't take any chances. Father, will you be first?

PRIEST. Perhaps we had better wait. There is an Episcopal bishop in this sector. He expressed the desire to conduct a burial service here. He's doing that in all sectors he is visiting. I think we had better wait for him. Episcopal bishops are rather sensitive about order. . . .

RABBI. He's not coming. He's having his supper.

FIRST SOLDIER. What does God do while the bishop has his supper?

SERGEANT. If you don't keep quiet, I'll bring you up on charges.

FIRST SOLDIER. I want to get it over with! Bury them! They stink!

PRIEST. Young man, that is not the way to talk about one of God's creatures. . . .

FIRST SOLDIER. If that's (*Gesture to grave*) one of God's creatures, all I can say is, He's slippin' . . .

PRIEST. Ah, my son, you seem so bitter. . . .

FIRST SOLDIER. For God's sake, stop talking and get this over with. I want to throw dirt over them! I can't stand the smell of them! Sergeant, get 'em to do it fast. They ain't got no right to keep us up all night. We got work to do tomorrow. . . . Let 'em say their prayers together! God'll be able to understand. . . .

PRIEST. Yes. There is really no need to prolong it. We must think of the living as well as the dead. As he says, Reverend, God will be able to understand. . . . (*He stands at the head of the grave, chants the Latin prayer for the dead. The* RABBI *goes around to the other end and recites the Hebrew prayer. In the middle of it, a groan is heard, low, but clear. The chants keep on. Another groan is heard.*)

FIRST SOLDIER. (*While the Hebrew and Latin go on*) I heard a groan. (*The* RABBI *and* PRIEST *continue*) I heard a groan!

SERGEANT. Shut up, soldier! (*The Latin and Hebrew go on.*)

FIRST SOLDIER. (*Gets down on one knee by side of grave and listens. Another groan*) Stop it! I heard a groan . . .

SERGEANT. What about it? Can you have war without groans? Keep quiet! (*The prayers go on undisturbed. Another groan. The* FIRST SOLDIER *jumps into the grave.*)

FIRST SOLDIER. It's from here! Hold it! (*Screaming*) Hold it! Stop those goddamned parrots! (*Throws a clod of dirt at end of trench*) Hold it! Somebody down here groaned. . . . (*A head appears slowly above the trench rim at the left end, a man stands up, slowly facing the rear. All the men sigh—the service goes on.*)

SERGEANT. Oh, my God . . .

FIRST SOLDIER. He's alive. . . .

SERGEANT. Why the hell don't they get these things straight? Pull him out!

FIRST SOLDIER. Stop them! (*As the services go on*) Get them out of here! Live men don't need them. . . .

SERGEANT. Please, Father, this has nothing to do with you. . . . There's been some mistake. . . .

PRIEST. I see. All right, Sergeant. (*He and* RABBI *join, hand in hand, and leave. Nobody notices them. All the men are hypnotically watching the man in the trench, arisen from the dead. The* CORPSE *passes his hand over his eyes. The men sigh— horrible, dry sighs. . . . Another groan is heard from the left side of trench.*)

FIRST SOLDIER. (*In trench*) There! (*Pointing*) It came from there! I heard it! (*A head, then shoulders appear over the rim of trench at left side. The* SECOND CORPSE *stands up, passes his hands over eyes in same gesture which drew sighs from the men before. There is absolute silence as the men watch the arisen corpses. Then, silently, a corpse rises in the middle of the trench, next to the* FIRST SOLDIER. *The* FIRST SOLDIER *screams, scrambles out of the trench in rear, and stands, bent over, watching the trench, middle-rear. There is no sound save the very light rumble of the guns. One by one the* CORPSES *arise and stand silently in their places, facing the rear, their backs to the audience. The* SOLDIERS *don't move, scarcely breathe, as, one by one, the* CORPSES *appear. They stand there, a frozen tableau. Suddenly, the* SERGEANT *talks.*)

SERGEANT. What do you want?

FIRST CORPSE. Don't bury us.

THIRD SOLDIER. Let's get the hell out of here!

SERGEANT. (*Drawing pistol*) Stay where you are! I'll shoot the first man that moves.

FIRST CORPSE. Don't bury us. We don't want to be buried.

SERGEANT. Christ! (*To men*) Carry on! (*The men stand still*) Christ! (*The* SERGEANT *rushes off, calling*) Captain! Captain! Where the hell is the Captain? (*His voice fades, terror-stricken. The* SOLDIERS *watch the corpses, then slowly, all together, start to back off.*)

SIXTH CORPSE. Don't go away.

SECOND CORPSE. Stay with us.

THIRD CORPSE. We want to hear the sound of men talking.

SIXTH CORPSE. Don't be afraid of us.

FIRST CORPSE. We're not really different from you. We're dead.

SECOND CORPSE. That's all. . . ?

FOURTH. All—all . . .

FIRST SOLDIER. That's all . . . ?

THIRD CORPSE. Are you afraid of six dead men? You, who've lived with the dead, the so-many dead, and eaten your bread by their side when there was no time to bury them and you were hungry?

SECOND CORPSE. Are we different from you? An ounce or so of lead in our hearts, and none in yours. A small difference between us.

THIRD CORPSE. Tomorrow or the next day, the lead will be yours, too. Talk as our equals.

FOURTH SOLDIER. It's the kid—the one who wrote the dirty poems.

FIRST CORPSE. Say something to us. Forget the grave, as we would forget it. . . .

THIRD SOLDIER. Do you—do you want a cigarette? (SERGEANT re-enters with CAPTAIN.)

SERGEANT. I'm not drunk! I'm not crazy, either! They just—got up, all together— and looked at us. . . . Look—look for yourself, Captain! (*The* CAPTAIN *stands off to one side, looking. The men stand at attention.*)

SERGEANT. See?

CAPTAIN. I see. (*He laughs sadly*) I was expecting it to happen—some day. So many men each day. It's too bad it had to happen in my company. Gentlemen! At ease! (*The men stand at ease. The* CAPTAIN *leaves. The guns roar suddenly. Fadeout.*)

The spotlight is turned on to the lower stage, right, below the platform on which the action, until now, has taken place.

Discovered in its glare are three GENERALS, *around a table. The* CAPTAIN *is standing before them, talking.*

CAPTAIN. I'm only telling the Generals what I saw.

FIRST GENERAL. You're not making this up, Captain?

CAPTAIN. No, General.

SECOND GENERAL. Have you any proof, Captain?

CAPTAIN. The four men in the burial detail and the Sergeant, Sir.

THIRD GENERAL. In time of war, Captain, men see strange things.

CAPTAIN. Yes, General.

SECOND GENERAL. You've been drinking, Captain.

CAPTAIN. Yes, General.

SECOND GENERAL. When a man has been drinking, he is not responsible for what he sees.

CAPTAIN. Yes, General. I am not responsible for what I saw. I am glad of that. I would not like to carry that burden, along with all the others. . . .

FIRST GENERAL. Come, come, Captain, confess now. You were drinking and you walked out into the cold air over a field just lately won and what with the liquor and the air and the flush of victory . . .

CAPTAIN. I told the General what I saw.

SECOND GENERAL. Yes, we heard. We forgive you for it. We don't think any the worse of you for taking a nip. It's only natural. We understand. So take another drink with us now and forget your ghosts. . . .

CAPTAIN. They weren't ghosts. They were men—killed two days, standing in their graves and looking at me.

FIRST GENERAL. Captain, you're becoming trying. . . .

CAPTAIN. I'm sorry, Sir. It was a trying sight. I saw them and what are the Generals going to do about it?

SECOND GENERAL. Forget it! A man is taken for dead and put in a grave. He wakes from his coma and stands up. It happens every day—you've got to expect such things in a war. Take him out and send him to a hospital!

CAPTAIN. Hospitals aren't for dead men. What are the Generals going to do about them?

THIRD GENERAL. Don't stand there croaking, "What are the Generals going to do about them?" Have 'em examined by a doctor. If they're alive send them to a hospital. If they're dead, bury them! It's very simple.

CAPTAIN. But . . .

THIRD GENERAL. No buts, Sir!

CAPTAIN. Yes, Sir.

THIRD GENERAL. Take a doctor down with you, Sir, and a stenographer. Have the doctor dictate official reports. Have them witnessed. And let's hear no more of it.

CAPTAIN. Yes, Sir. Very good, Sir. (*Wheels to go out.*)

SECOND GENERAL. Oh, and Captain . . .

CAPTAIN. (*Stopping*) Yes, Sir.

SECOND GENERAL. Stay away from the bottle.

CAPTAIN. Yes, Sir. Is that all, Sir?

SECOND GENERAL. That's all.

CAPTAIN. Yes, Sir. (*The light fades from the* GENERALS. *It follows the* CAPTAIN *as he walks across the stage. The* CAPTAIN *stops, takes out a bottle. Takes two long swigs. Blackout.*)

The guns rumble, growing louder. They have been almost mute during GENERALS' *scene. The light is thrown on the burial scene again, where the* DOCTOR *is seen examining the* CORPSES *in their graves. The* DOCTOR *is armed with a stethoscope and is followed by a soldier stenographer, two of the* SOLDIERS, *impressed as witnesses, and the* CAPTAIN. *The* DOCTOR *is talking, as he passes from the first man.*

DOCTOR. Number one. Evisceration of the lower intestine. Dead forty-eight hours.

STENOGRAPHER. (*Repeating*) Number one. Evisceration of the lower intestine. Dead forty-eight hours. (*To witnesses*) Sign here. (*They sign.*)

DOCTOR. (*On the next man*) Number two. Bullet penetrated the left ventricle. Dead forty-eight hours.

STENOGRAPHER. Number two. Bullet penetrated the left ventricle. Dead forty-eight hours. (*To witnesses*) Sign here. (*They sign.*)

DOCTOR. (*On the next* CORPSE) Number three. Bullets penetrated both lungs. Severe hemorrhages. Dead forty-eight hours.

STENOGRAPHER. (*Chanting*) Number three. Bullets penetrated both lungs. Severe hemorrhages. Dead forty-eight hours. Sign here. (*The witnesses sign.*)

DOCTOR. (*On next* CORPSE) Number four. Fracture of the skull and avulsion of the cerebellum. Dead forty-eight hours.

STENOGRAPHER. Number four. Fracture of the skull and avulsion of the cerebellum. Dead forty-eight hours. Sign here. (*The witnesses sign.*)

DOCTOR. (*Moving on to next* CORPSE) Number five. Destruction of the genito-urinary system by shell-splinters. Death from hemorrhages. Dead forty-eight hours. Ummn. (*Looks curiously at* CORPSE's *face*) Hum . . . (*Moves on.*)

STENOGRAPHER. Number five. Destruction of the genito-urinary system by shell-splinters. Death from hemorrhages. Dead forty-eight hours. Sign here. (*The witnesses sign.*)

DOCTOR. (*On the next* CORPSE) Number six. Destruction of right side of head from supra-orbital ridges through jaw-bone. Hum. You'd be a pretty sight for your mother, you would. Dead forty-eight hours . . .

STENOGRAPHER. Number six. Destruction of right side of head from supra-orbital ridges through jaw-bone. You'd be a pretty sight for your mother you would. Dead forty-eight hours. Sign here.

DOCTOR. What are you doing there?

STENOGRAPHER. That's what you said, Sir. . . .

DOCTOR. I know. Leave out—"You'd be a pretty sight for your mother you would . . ." The Generals wouldn't be interested in that.

STENOGRAPHER. Yes, Sir. Sign here. (*The witnesses sign.*)

DOCTOR. Six, is that all?

CAPTAIN. Yes, Doctor. They're all dead? (*The* FOURTH CORPSE *offers the* THIRD SOLDIER *a cigarette. The* THIRD SOLDIER *hesitates a second before taking it, then accepts it with a half-grin.*)

THIRD SOLDIER. Thanks, Buddy. I—I'm awful sorry—I—Thanks . . . (*He saves cigarette.*)

DOCTOR. (*Eyes on* FOURTH CORPSE *and* THIRD SOLDIER) All dead.

CAPTAIN. A drink, Doctor?

DOCTOR. Yes, thank you. (*He takes the proffered bottle. Drinks long from it. Holds it, puts stethoscope in pocket with other hand. Stands looking at the* CORPSES, *lined up, facing the rear, nods, then takes another long drink. Silently hands bottle to* CAPTAIN, *who looks around him from one* CORPSE *to another, then takes a long drink. Blackout.*)

Spotlight on the GENERALS, *facing the* CAPTAIN *and the* DOCTOR. *The* FIRST GENERAL *has the* DOCTOR's *reports in his hands.*

FIRST GENERAL. Doctor!

DOCTOR. Yes, Sir.

FIRST GENERAL. In your reports here you say that each of these six men is dead.

DOCTOR. Yes, Sir.

FIRST GENERAL. Then I don't see what all the fuss is about, Captain. They're dead—bury them. . . .

CAPTAIN. I am afraid, Sir, that that can't be done. . . . They are standing in their graves. They refuse to be buried.

THIRD GENERAL. Do we have to go into that again? We have the doctor's report. They're dead. Aren't they, Doctor?

DOCTOR. Yes, Sir.

THIRD GENERAL. Then they aren't standing in their graves, refusing to be buried, are they?

DOCTOR. Yes, Sir.

SECOND GENERAL. Doctor, would you know a dead man if you saw one?

DOCTOR. The symptoms are easily recognized.

FIRST GENERAL. You've been drinking, too. . . .

DOCTOR. Yes, Sir.

FIRST GENERAL. The whole damned army is drunk! I want a regulation announced tomorrow morning in all regiments. No more liquor is to be allowed within twenty miles of the front line upon pain of death. Got it?

SECOND GENERAL. Yes, General. But then how'll we get the men to fight?

FIRST GENERAL. Damn the fighting! We can't have stories like this springing up. It's bad for the morale! Did you hear me, Doctor, it's bad for the morale and you ought to be ashamed of yourself!

DOCTOR. Yes, Sir.

THIRD GENERAL. This has gone far enough. If it goes any farther, the men will get wind of it. We have witnessed certificates from a registered surgeon that these men are dead. Bury them! Waste no more time on it. Do you hear me, Captain?

CAPTAIN. Yes, Sir. I'm afraid, Sir, that I must refuse to bury these men.

THIRD GENERAL. That's insubordination, Sir. . . .

CAPTAIN. I'm sorry, Sir. It is not within the line of my military duties to bury men against their will. If the General will only think for a moment he will see that this is impossible. . . .

FIRST GENERAL. The Captain's right. It might get back to Congress. God only knows what *they'd* make of it!

THIRD GENERAL. What are we going to do then?

FIRST GENERAL. Captain, what do you suggest?

CAPTAIN. Stop the war.

CHORUS OF GENERALS. Captain!

FIRST GENERAL. (*With great dignity*) Captain, we beg of you to remember the gravity of the situation. It admits of no levity. Is that the best suggestion you can make, Captain?

CAPTAIN. Yes. But I have another— If the Generals would come down to the grave themselves and attempt to influence these—ah—corpses—to lie down, perhaps that would prove effective. We're seven miles behind the line now and we could screen the roads to protect your arrival....

FIRST GENERAL. (*Coughing*) Umm—uh— usually, of course, that would be—uh . . . We'll see. In the meantime it must be kept quiet! Remember that! Not a word! Nobody must know! God only knows what would happen if people began to suspect we couldn't even get our dead to lie down and be buried! This is the goddamndest war! They never said anything about this sort of thing at West Point. Remember, not a word, nobody must know, quiet as the grave, *mum! ssssh!* (*All the* GENERALS *repeat the ssssh after him.*)

The light fades—but the hiss of the GENERALS *hushing each other is still heard as the light falls on another part of the stage proper, where two soldiers are on post in the front lines, behind a barricade of sandbags. The sound of guns is very strong. There are flashes of gun-fire.*

BEVINS. (*A soldier past forty, fat, with a pot-belly and graying hair showing under his helmet*) Did you hear about those guys that won't let themselves be buried, Charley?

CHARLEY. I heard. You never know what's gonna happen next in this lousy war.

BEVINS. What do you think about it, Charley?

CHARLEY. What're they gettin' out of it, that's what I'd like to know. They're just makin things harder. I heard all about 'em. They stink! Bury 'em. That's what I say.

BEVINS. I don't know, Charley. I kinda can see what they're aimin' at. Christ, I wouldn't like to be put six foot under now, I wouldn't. What the hell for?

CHARLEY. What's the difference?

BEVINS. There's a difference, all right. It's kinda good, bein' alive. It's kinda nice, bein' on top of the earth and seein' things and hearin' things and smellin' things....

CHARLEY. Yeah, smellin' stiffs that ain't had time to be buried. That sure is sweet.

BEVINS. Yeah, but it's better than havin' the dirt packed onto your face. I guess those guys felt sorta gypped when they started throwin' the dirt in on 'em and just couldn't stand it, dead or no dead.

CHARLEY. They're dead, ain't they? Nobody's puttin' them under while they're alive.

BEVINS. It amounts to the same thing, Charley. They should be alive now. What are they—a parcel of kids? Kids shouldn't be dead, Charley. That's what they musta figured when the dirt started fallin' in on 'em. What the hell are they doin' dead? Did they get anything out of it? Did anybody ask them? Did they want to be standin' there when the lead poured in? They're just kids, or guys with wives and young kids of their own. They wanted to be home readin' a book or teachin' their kid c-a-t spells cat or takin' a woman out into the country in a open car with the wind blowin'. . . . That's the way it musta come to them, when the dirt smacked on their faces, dead or no dead. . . .

CHARLEY. Bury them. That's what I say . . . . (*There is the chatter of a machine gun off in the night.* BEVINS *is hit. He staggers.*)

BEVINS. (*Clutching his throat*) Charley—Charley . . . (*His fingers bring down the top sandbag as he falls. The machine gun chatters again and* CHARLEY *is hit. He staggers.*)

CHARLEY. Oh, my God . . . (*The machine gun chatters again. He falls over* BEVINS. *There is quiet for a moment. Then the eternal artillery again. Blackout.*)

A baby spotlight, white, picks out the FIRST GENERAL, *standing over the prone forms of the two soldiers. He has his fingers to his lips.*

FIRST GENERAL. (*In a hoarse whisper*) Sssh! Keep it quiet! Nobody must know! Not a word! Sssh! (*Blackout.*)

A spotlight picks out another part of the stage—a newspaper office. EDITOR *at his desk,* REPORTER *before him, hat on head.*

REPORTER. That's the story! It's as straight as a rifle-barrel, so help me God.

EDITOR. (*Looking down at manuscript in hand*) This is a freak, all right. I never came across anything like it in all the years I've been putting out a newspaper.

REPORTER. There never was anything like it before. It's somethin' new. Somethin's happening. Somebody's waking up. . . .

EDITOR. It didn't happen.

REPORTER. So help me God, I got it straight. Those guys just stood up in the grave and said, "The hell with it, you can't bury us!" God's honest truth.

EDITOR. (*Picks up telephone*) Get me Macready at the War Department. . . . It's an awfully funny story. . . .

REPORTER. What about it? It's the story of the year— the story of the century—the biggest story of all time—men gettin' up with bullets in their hearts and refusin' to be buried. . . .

EDITOR. Who do they think they are—Jesus Christ?

REPORTER. What's the difference? That's the story! You can't miss it! You goin' to put it in? Lissen—are you goin' to put it in?

EDITOR. Hold it! (*Into telephone*) Macready!

REPORTER. What's he got to do with it?

EDITOR. I'll find out. What are *you* so hot about? . . . Hello? Macready? Hansen from the New York . . . Yeah. . . . Listen, Macready, I got this story about the six guys who refuse to be . . . Yeah. . . .

REPORTER. What does he say?

EDITOR. Okay, Macready. Yeah, if that's the way the Government feels about it. . . . Yeah. . . .

REPORTER. Well?

EDITOR. (*Putting down telephone*) No.

REPORTER. Holy god-damn, you got to. People got a right to know.

EDITOR. In time of war, people have a right to now nothing. If we put it in, it'd be censored anyway.

REPORTER. Ah, this is a lousy business. . . .

EDITOR. Write another human interest story about the boys at the front. That'll keep you busy. You know . . . that one about how the boys in the front-line sing "I Can't Give You Anything but Love," before they go over the top. . . .

REPORTER. But I wrote that last week.

EDITOR. It made a great hit. Write it again.

REPORTER. But these guys in the grave, Boss. Lloyds are giving three to one they won't go down. That's a story!

EDITOR. Save it. You can write a book of memoirs twenty years from now. Make that "I Can't Give You Anything but Love" story a thousand words, and make it snappy. The casualty lists run into two pages today and we got to balance them with something. . . . (*Blackout*)

Rumble of guns. The spotlight illuminates the grave on the platform, where the CORPSES *are still standing, hip-deep, facing the rear. The burial squad is there, and the* CAPTAIN, *and the* GENERALS.

CAPTAIN. There they are. What are the Generals going to do about them?

FIRST GENERAL. (*Pettishly*) I see them. Stop saying "What are the Generals going to do about them?"

SECOND GENERAL. Who do they think they are?

THIRD GENERAL. It's against all regulations.

FIRST GENERAL. Quiet, please, quiet. Let's not have any scenes. . . . This must be handled with authority—but tactfully. I'll talk to them! (*He goes over to brink of grave*) Men! Listen to me! This is a strange situation in which we find ourselves. I have no doubt but that it is giving you as much embarrassment as it is us. . . .

SECOND GENERAL. (*Confidentially to* THIRD GENERAL) The wrong note. He's good on artillery, but when it comes to using his head, he's lost. . . . He's been that way ever since I knew him.

FIRST GENERAL. We're all anxious to get this thing over with just as quickly and quietly as possible. I know that you men are with me on this. There's no reason why we can't get together and settle this in jig time. I grant, my friends, that it's unfortunate that you're dead. I'm sure that you'll all listen to reason. Listen, too, to the voice of duty, the voice that sent you here to die bravely for your country. Gentlemen, your country demands of you that you lie down and allow yourselves to be buried. Must our flag fly at half-mast and droop in the wind while you so far forget your duty to the lovely land that bore and nurtured you? I love America, gentlemen, its hills and valleys. If you loved America as I do, you would not . . . (*He breaks down, overcome*) I find it difficult to go on. (*He pauses*) I have studied this matter and come to the conclusion that the best thing for all concerned would be for you men to lie down peaceably in your graves and allow yourselves to be buried. (*He waits. The* CORPSES *do not move.*)

THIRD GENERAL. It didn't work. He's not firm enough. You've got to be firm from the beginning or you're lost.

FIRST GENERAL. Men, perhaps you don't understand. (*To* CORPSES) I advise you to allow yourselves to be buried. (*They stand, motionless*) You're dead, men, don't you realize that? You can't be dead and stand there like that. Here . . . here . . . I'll prove it to you! (*He gets out* DOCTOR's *reports*) Look! A doctor's reports. Witnessed! Witnessed by Privates McGurk and Butler. (*He reads the names*) This ought to show you! (*He waves the reports. He stands on the brink of the grave, middle-rear, glaring at the* CORPSES. *He shouts at them*) You're dead, officially, all of you! I won't mince words! You heard! We're a civilized race, we bury our dead. Lie down! (*The* CORPSES *stand*) Private Driscoll! Private Schelling! Private Morgan! Private Levy! Private Webster! Private Dean! Lie down! As Commander-in-Chief of the Army as appointed by the President of the United States in accordance with the Constitution of the United States, and as your superior officer, I command you to lie down and allow yourselves to be buried. (*They stand, silent and motionless*) Tell me— What is it going to get you, staying above the earth? (*Not a sound from the* CORPSES) I asked you a question, men. Answer me! What is it going to get you? If I were dead I wouldn't hesitate to be buried.

Answer me . . . what do you want? What is it going to get you . . . (*As they remain silent*) Tell me! Answer me! Why don't you talk? Explain it to me, make me understand . . .

SECOND GENERAL. (*In whisper to* THIRD GENERAL, *as* FIRST GENERAL *glares hopelessly at the* CORPSES.) He's licked. It was a mistake—moving him off the artillery.

THIRD GENERAL. They ought to let me handle them. I'd show 'em. You've got to use force.

FIRST GENERAL. (*Bursting out—after walking along entire row of* CORPSES *and back*) Lie down! (*The* CORPSES *stand, immobile. The* GENERAL *rushes out, moaning*) Oh, God, oh, my God . . . (*Blackout.*)

Spotlight, red, picks out two WHORES, *dressed in the uniform of their trade, on a street corner.*

FIRST WHORE. I'd lay 'em, all right. They oughta call me in. I'd lay em. There wouldn't be any doubt in anybody's mind after I got through with 'em. Why don't they call me in instead of those Generals? What do Generals know about such things? (*Both* WHORES *go off into fits of wild laughter*) Call the War Department, Mabel, tell 'em we'll come to their rescue at the prevailing rates. (*Laughs wildly again*) We're willing to do our part, like the papers say—share the burden! Oh, my Gawd, I ain't laughed so much . . . (*Laugh again. A* MAN *crosses their path. Still laughing, but professional*) Say, Johnny, Johnny, what'cha doin' tonight? How'd ya like . . . ? (*The* MAN *passes on. The women laugh*) Share the burden—Oh, my Gawd . . . (*They laugh and laugh and laugh, clinging to each other. . . . Black-out. But the laughter goes on.*)

The spotlight illuminates the grave— SOLDIERS *of burial detail are sitting around a covered fire.* SECOND SOLDIER *is singing "Swing Low, Sweet Chariot."*

THIRD SOLDIER. This is a funny war. It's rollin' downhill. Everybody's waitin'. Personally, I think it's those guys there that . . . (*He gestures to grave.*)

SERGEANT. Nobody asked you. You're not supposed to talk about it.

FIRST SOLDIER. Regulation 2035a . . .

SERGEANT. Well, I just told ya. (SECOND SOLDIER *starts to sing again.* SERGEANT *breaks in on him*) Say, lissen, think about those guys there. How do you think they feel with you howlin' like this? They got more important things to think about.

SECOND SOLDIER. I won't distract 'em. I got an easy-flowin' voice.

SERGEANT. They don't like it. I can tell.

FIRST SOLDIER. Well, I like to hear him sing. And I'll bet they do, too. I'm gonna ask 'em . . . (*He jumps up.*)

SERGEANT. Now, lissen! (FIRST SOLDIER *slowly approaches the grave. He is embarrassed, a little frightened.*)

FIRST SOLDIER. Say, men, I . . . (CAPTAIN *comes on.* FIRST SOLDIER *stands at attention.*)

CAPTAIN. Sergeant . . .

SERGEANT. Yes, Sir!

CAPTAIN. You know that none of the men is to talk to *them*. . . .

SERGEANT. Yes, Sir. Only, Sir . . .

CAPTAIN. All right. (*To* FIRST SOLDIER) Get back there, please.

FIRST SOLDIER. Yes, Sir! (*He salutes and goes back.*)

SERGEANT. (*Under his breath to* FIRST SOLDIER) I warned ya.

FIRST SOLDIER. Shut up! I wanna lissen to what's goin' on there! (CAPTAIN *has meanwhile seated himself on the edge of the grave and has brought out a pair of eyeglasses with which he plays as he talks.*)

CAPTAIN. Gentlemen, I have been asked by the Generals to talk to you. My work is not this . . . (*He indicates his uniform*) I am a philosopher, a scientist, my uniform is a pair of eye-glasses, my usual weapons test-tubes and books. At a time like this perhaps we need philosophy, need science. First I must say that your General has ordered you to lie down.

FIRST CORPSE. We used to have a General.

THIRD CORPSE. No more.

FOURTH CORPSE. They sold us.

CAPTAIN. What do you mean—sold you!

FIFTH CORPSE. Sold us for twenty-five yards of bloody mud.

SIXTH CORPSE. A life for four yards of bloody mud.

CAPTAIN. We had to take that hill. General's orders. You're soldiers. You understand.

FIRST CORPSE. We understand now. The real estate operations of Generals are always carried on at boom prices.

SIXTH CORPSE. A life for four yards of bloody mud. Gold is cheaper, and rare jewels, pearls and rubies. . . .

THIRD CORPSE. I fell in the first yard. . . .

SECOND CORPSE. I caught on the wire and hung there while the machine gun stitched me through the middle to it. . . .

FOURTH CORPSE. I was there at the end and thought I had life in my hands for another day, but a shell came and my life dripped into the mud.

SIXTH CORPSE. Ask the General how he'd like to be dead at twenty. (*Calling, as though to the* GENERALS) Twenty, General, twenty . . .

CAPTAIN. Other men are dead.

FIRST CORPSE. Too many.

CAPTAIN. Men must die for their country's sake—if not you, then others. This has always been. Men died for Pharaoh and Cæsar and Rome two thousand years ago and more, and went into the earth with their wounds. Why not you . . . ?

FIRST CORPSE. Men, even the men who die for Pharaoh and Cæsar and Rome, must, in the end, before all hope is gone, discover that a man can die happy and be contentedly buried only when he dies for himself or for a cause that is his own and not Pharaoh's or Cæsar's or Rome's. . . .

CAPTAIN. Still—what is this world, that you cling to it? A speck of dust, a flaw in the skies, a thumb-print on the margin of a page printed in an incomprehensible language. . . .

SECOND CORPSE. It is our home.

THIRD CORPSE. We have been dispossessed by force, but we are reclaiming our home. It is time that mankind claimed its home —this earth—its home. . . .

CAPTAIN. We have no home. We are strangers in the universe and cling, desperate and grimy, to the crust of our world, and if there is a God and this His earth, we must be a terrible sight in His eyes.

FOURTH CORPSE. We are not disturbed by the notion of our appearance in the eyes of God. . . .

CAPTAIN. The earth is an unpleasant place and when you are rid of it you are well rid of it. Man cheats man here and the only sure things are death and despair. Of what use, then, to remain on it once you have the permission to leave?

FIFTH CORPSE. It is the one thing we know.

SIXTH CORPSE. We did not ask permission to leave. Nobody asked us whether we wanted it or not. The Generals pushed us out and closed the door on us. Who are the Generals that they are to close the door on us?

CAPTAIN. The earth, I assure you, is a mean place, insignificantly miserable. . . .

FIRST CORPSE. We must find out for ourselves. That is our right.

CAPTAIN. Man has no rights. . . .

FIRST CORPSE. Man can make rights for himself. It requires only determination and the good-will of ordinary men. We have made ourselves the right to walk this earth, seeing it and judging it for ourselves.

CAPTAIN. There is peace in the grave. . . .

THIRD CORPSE. Peace and the worms and the roots of grass. There is a deeper peace than that which comes with feeding the roots of the grass.

CAPTAIN. (*Looks slowly at them, in turn*) Yes, gentlemen . . . (*Turns away and walks off.* FIRST SOLDIER *moves slowly up to the grave.*)

FIRST SOLDIER. (*To the* CORPSES) I . . . I'm glad you . . . you didn't . . . I'm glad. Say, is there anything we can do for you?

SERGEANT. Lissen, soldier!

FIRST SOLDIER. (*Passionately, harshly*) Shut up, Sergeant! (*Then very softly and warmly to* FIRST CORPSE) Is there anything we can do for you, Friend?

FIRST CORPSE. Yeah. You can sing . . . (*There is a pause in which the* FIRST SOLDIER *turns around and looks at the* SECOND SOLDIER, *then back to the* FIRST CORPSE.

Then the silence is broken by the SECOND SOLDIER's *voice, raised in song. It goes on for a few moments, then fades as the light dims.*)

Colored spotlights pick out three BUSINESS MEN *on different parts of the stage.*

FIRST BUSINESS MAN. Ssh! Keep it quiet!

THIRD BUSINESS MAN. Sink 'em with lead. . . .

SECOND BUSINESS MAN. Bury them! Bury them six feet under!

FIRST BUSINESS MAN. What are we going to do?

SECOND BUSINESS MAN. We must keep up the morale.

THIRD BUSINESS MAN. Lead! Lead! A lot of lead!

SECOND BUSINESS MAN. What do we pay our Generals for?

CHORUS OF BUSINESS MEN. Ssssh! (*Blackout*)

Spotlight on the congregation of a church, kneeling, with a PRIEST *praying over them.*

PRIEST. O Jesus, our God and our Christ, Who has redeemed us with Thy blood on the Cross at Calvary, give us Thy blessing on this holy day, and cause it that our soldiers allow themselves to be buried in peace, and bring victory to our arms, enlisted in Thy Cause and the cause of all righteousness on the field of battle . . . Amen . . . (*Blackout*.)

FIRST GENERAL. (*In purple baby spotlight*) Please, God, keep it quiet . . .

(*Spotlight on newspaper office.*)

REPORTER. Well? What are you going to do?

EDITOR. Do I have to do anything?

REPORTER. God damn right you do. . . . They're still standing up. They're going to stand up from now till Doomsday. They're not going to be able to bury soldiers any more. It's in the stars. . . . You got to say something about it. . . .

EDITOR. All right. Put this in. "It is alleged that certain members of an infantry regiment refuse to allow themselves to be buried. . . . "

REPORTER. Well?

EDITOR. That's all.

REPORTER. (*Incredulous*) That's all?

EDITOR. Yes, Christ, isn't that enough? (*Blackout*.)

Spotlight on a radio-loudspeaker. A VOICE, *mellow and beautiful, comes out of it.*

THE VOICE. It has been reported that certain American soldiers, killed on the field of battle, have refused to allow themselves to be buried. Whether this is true or not, the Coast-to-Coast Broadcasting System feels that this must give the American public an idea of the indomitable spirit of the American doughboy in this war. We cannot rest until this war is won—not even our brave dead boys . . . (*Blackout*.)

Guns. Spotlight on FIRST GENERAL *and* CAPTAIN.

FIRST GENERAL. Have you got any suggestions . . . ?

CAPTAIN. I think so. Get their women. . . .

FIRST GENERAL. What good'll their women do?

CAPTAIN. Women are always conservative. It's a conservative notion—this one of lying down and allowing yourself to be buried when you're dead. The women'll fight the General's battle for them—in the best possible way—through their emotions . . . . It's the General's best bet. . . .

FIRST GENERAL. Women— Of course! You've got it there, Captain! Get out their women! Get them in a hurry! We'll have these boys underground in a jiffy. Women! By God, I never thought of it. . . . Send out the call. . . . Women! (*Fadeout*.)

A baby spotlight on the loudspeaker. The VOICE *again, just as mellow, just as persuasive.*

VOICE. We have been asked by the War Department to broadcast an appeal to the women of Privates Driscoll, Schelling, Morgan, Webster, Levy, and Dean, reported dead. The War Department requests that the women of these men present themselves at the War Department Office immediately. It is within their power to do a great service to their country. . . (*Blackout*.)

The spotlight illuminates the FIRST GENERAL, *where he stands, addressing six women.*

FIRST GENERAL. Go to your men . . . talk to them . . . make them see the error of their ways, ladies. You women represent what is dearest in our civilization—the sacred foundations of the home. We are fighting this war to protect the foundations of the homes of America! Those foundations will crumble utterly if these men of yours come back from the dead. I shudder to think of the consequences of such an act. Our entire system will be mortally struck. Our banks will close, our buildings collapse . . . our army will desert the field and leave our fair land open to be overrun by the enemy. Ladies, you are all Gold Star mothers and wives and sweethearts. You want to win this war. I know it. I know the high fire of patriotism that burns in women's breasts. That is why I have called upon you. Ladies, let me make this clear to you. If you do not get your men to lie down and allow themselves to be buried, I fear that our cause is lost. The burden of the war is upon your shoulders now. Wars are not fought with guns and powder alone, ladies. Here is your chance to do your part, a glorious part. . . . You are fighting for your homes, your children, your sisters' lives, your country's honor. You are fighting for religion, for love, for all decent human life. Wars can be fought and won only when the dead are buried and forgotten. How can we forget the dead who refuse to be buried? And we *must* forget them! There is no room in this world for dead men. They will lead only to the bitterest unhappiness—for you, for them, for everybody. Go ladies, do your duty. Your country waits upon you. . . . (*Blackout.*)

Spotlight immediately illuminates the place where PRIVATE SCHELLING, CORPSE TWO, *is talking to his wife.* MRS. SCHELLING *is a spare, taciturn woman, a farmer's wife, who might be twenty or forty or anything in between.*

BESS SCHELLING. Did it hurt much, John?

SCHELLING. How's the kid, Bess?

BESS. He's fine. He talks now. He weighs twenty-eight pounds. He'll be a big boy. Did it hurt much, John?

SCHELLING. How is the farm? Is it going all right, Bess?

BESS. It's going. The rye was heavy this year. Did it hurt much, John?

SCHELLING. Who did the reapin' for you, Bess?

BESS. Schmidt took care of it—and his boys. Schmidt's too old for the war and his boys are too young. Took 'em nearly two weeks. The wheat's not bad this year. Schmidt's oldest boy expects to be called in a month or two. He practises behind the barn with that old shotgun Schmidt uses for duck.

SCHELLING. The Schmidts were always fools. When the kid grows up, Bess, you make sure you pump some sense into his head. What color's his hair?

BESS. Blond. Like you. . . . What are you going to do, John?

SCHELLING. I would like to see the kid—and the farm—and . . .

BESS. They say you're dead, John. . . .

SCHELLING. I'm dead, all right.

BESS. Then how is it . . . ?

SCHELLING. I don't know. Maybe there's too many of us under the ground now. Maybe the earth can't stand it no more. You got to change crops sometime. What are you doing here, Bess?

BESS. They asked me to get you to let yourself be buried.

SCHELLING. What do you think?

BESS. You're dead, John. . . .

SCHELLING. Well . . . ?

BESS. What's the good . . . ?

SCHELLING. I don't know. Only there's something in me, dead or no dead, that won't let me be buried.

BESS. You were a queer man, John. I never did understand what you were about. But what's the good . . . ?

SCHELLING. Bess, I never talked so that I could get you to understand what I wanted while I—while I—before . . . Maybe now . . . There're a couple of things, Bess, that I ain't had enough of. Easy things, the things you see when you look outa your window at night, after supper, or when you wake up in the mornin'. Things you smell when you step outside the door when summer's on and the sun starts to turn the grass brown. Things you hear when you're busy with the horses or pitchin' the hay and you don't really notice them and yet they come back to you. Things like the fuzz of green over a field in spring where you planted wheat and it's started to come out overnight. Things like lookin' at rows of corn scrapin' in the breeze, tall and green, with the silk flying off the ears in the wind. Things like seeing the sweat come out all over your horse's fat flank and seein' it shine like silk in front of you, smelling horsey and strong. Things like seein' the loam turn back all fat and deep brown on both sides as the plough turns it over so that it gets to be awful hard walkin' behind it. Things like taking a cold drink of water outa the well after you've boiled in the sun all afternoon, and feelin' the water go down and down into you coolin' you off all through from the inside out. . . . Things like seein' a blond kid, all busy and serious, playin' with a dog on the shady side of a house. . . . There ain't nothin' like that down here, Bess. . . .

BESS.   Everything has its place, John. Dead men have theirs.

SCHELLING.   My place is on the earth, Bess. My business is with the top of the earth, not the under-side. It was a trap that yanked me down. I'm not smart, Bess, and I'm easy trapped—but I can tell now . . . I got some stories to tell the farmers before I'm through—I'm going to tell 'em. . . .

BESS.   We could bury you home, John, near the creek—it's cool there and quiet and there's always a breeze in the trees. . . .

SCHELLING.   Later, Bess, when I've had my fill of lookin' and smellin' and talkin' . . . . A man should be able to walk into his grave, not be dragged into it. . . .

BESS.   How'll I feel—and the kid—with you walkin' around—like—like that . . . ?

SCHELLING.   I won't bother you. . . . I won't come near you. . . .

BESS.   Even so. Just knowin' . . .

SCHELLING.   I can't help it. This is somethin' bigger'n you—bigger'n me. It's somethin' I ain't had nothin' to do with startin'. . . . It's somethin' that just grew up outa the earth—like—like a weed—a flower. Cut it down now and it'll jump up in a dozen new places. You can't stop it. The earth's ready for it. . . .

BESS.   You were a good husband, John. For the kid—and me—won't you?

SCHELLING.   (*Quietly*) Go home, Bess. *Go home!* (*Blackout.*)
The spotlight picks out CORPSE NUMBER FIVE, PRIVATE LEVY, *where he stands in the grave, with his back to the audience. His woman, a pert, attractive young lady, is sitting next to him, above him, facing him, talking to him.*

JOAN.   You loved me best, didn't you, Henry—of all of them—all those women—you loved me the best, didn't you?

LEVY.   (FIFTH CORPSE) What's the difference, now?

JOAN.   I want to know it.

LEVY.   Its not important.

JOAN.   It's important to me. I knew about the others, about Doris and that shifty-eyed Janet. . . . Henry you're not a live man, are you, Henry?

LEVY.   No, I'm all shot away inside.

JOAN.   Must wars always be fought in the mud like this? I never expected it to look like this. It . . . it looks like a dump heap.

LEVY.   You've gotten your shoes muddy. They're pretty shoes, Joan.

JOAN.   Do you think so, Henry? They're lizard. I like them too. It's so hard to get a good pair of shoes nowadays.

LEVY.   Do you still dance, Joan?

JOAN. Oh, I'm really much better than I used to be. There are so many dances back home nowadays. Dances for orphan relief and convalescent hospitals and Victory Loans. I'm busy seven nights a week. I sold more Victory Loans than any other girl in the League. I got a helmet . . . one of *their* helmets . . . one with a bullet-hole in it, for selling eleven thousand dollars' worth.

LEVY. Out here we get them for nothing, by the million—bullet-holes and all.

JOAN. That sounds bitter. You shouldn't sound bitter.

LEVY. I'm sorry.

JOAN. I heard Colonel Elwell the other day. You know Colonel Elwell, old Anthony Elwell who owns the mill. He made a speech at the monthly Red Cross banquet and he said that that was the nice thing about this war, it wasn't being fought bitterly by our boys. He said it was just patriotism that kept us going. He's a wonderful speaker, Colonel Elwell; I cried and cried. . . .

LEVY. I remember him.

JOAN. Henry, do you think we're going to win the war?

LEVY. What's the difference?

JOAN. Henry! What a way to talk! I don't know what's come over you. Really, I don't. Why, the papers say that if *they* win the war, they'll burn our churches and tear down our museums and . . . and rape our women. (LEVY *laughs*) Why are you laughing, Henry?

LEVY. I'm dead, Joan.

JOAN. Yes. Then why—why don't you let them bury you?

LEVY. There are a lot of reasons. There were a lot of things I loved on this earth. . . .

JOAN. A dead man can't touch a woman.

LEVY. The women, yes—but more than touching them. I got a great joy just from listening to women, hearing them laugh, watching their skirts blow in the wind, noticing the way their breasts bounced up and down inside their dresses when they walked. It had nothing to do with touching them. I liked to hear the sound of their high heels on pavements at night and the tenderness in their voices when they walked past me arm in arm with a young man. You were so lovely, Joan, with your pale hair and long hands.

JOAN. You always liked my hair. (*A pause*) No woman will walk arm in arm with you, Henry Levy, while you cheat the grave.

LEVY. No. But there will be the eyes of women to look at and the bright color of their hair and the soft way they swing their hips when they walk before young men. These are the things that mean life and the earth to me, the joy and the pain. These are the things the earth still owes me, now when I am only thirty. Joy and pain—to each man in his own way, a full seventy years, to be ended by an unhurried fate, not by a colored pin on a General's map. What do I care for the colored pins on a General's map?

JOAN. They are not only pins. They mean more. . . .

LEVY. More? To whom? To the Generals—not to me. To me they are colored pins. It is not a fair bargain—this exchange of my life for a small part of a colored pin. . . .

JOAN. Henry, how can you talk like that? You know why this war is being fought.

LEVY. No. Do you?

JOAN. Of course, everybody knows. We *must* win! We must be prepared to sacrifice our last drop of blood. Anyway, what can you do?

LEVY. Do you remember last summer, Joan? My last leave. We went to Maine. I would like to remember that—the sun and the beach and your soft hands—for a long time.

JOAN. What are you going to do?

LEVY. Walk the world looking at the fine, long-legged girls, seeing in them something deep and true and passionately vital, listening to the sound of their light voices with ears the Generals would have stopped with the grave's solid mud. . . .

JOAN. Henry! Henry! Once you said you loved me. For the love of me, Henry, go into the grave. . . .

LEVY. Poor Joan. (*Stretches out his hand tenderly as if to touch her.*)

JOAN. (*Recoiling*) Don't touch me. (*Pause*) For love of me.

LEVY. Go home, Joan! *Go home!* (*Blackout.*)
The spotlight picks out the THIRD CORPSE,

PRIVATE MORGAN, *and* JULIA BLAKE, *he with his back to the audience, standing in the grave, she above and to the right.* JULIA *sobs.*

MORGAN. Stop crying, Julia. What's the sense in crying?

JULIA. No sense. Only I can't stop crying.

MORGAN. You shouldn't have come.

JULIA. They asked me to come. They said you wouldn't let them bury you—dead and all. . . .

MORGAN. Yes.

JULIA. (*Crying*) Why don't they kill me too? I'd let them bury me. I'd be glad to be buried—to get away from all this . . I—I haven't stopped crying for two weeks now. I used to think I was tough. I never cried. Even when I was a kid. It's a wonder where all the tears can come from. Though I guess there's always room for more tears. I thought I was all cried out when I heard about the way they killed Fred. My kid brother. I used to comb his hair in the morning when he went to school . . . I—I . . . Then they killed you. They did, didn't they?

MORGAN. Yes.

JULIA. It's hard to know like this. I—I know, though. It—it makes it harder, this way, with you like this. I could forget easier if you . . . But I wasn't going to say that. I was going to listen to you. Oh, my darling, it's been so rotten. I get drunk. I hate it and I get drunk. I sing out loud and everybody laughs. I was going through your things the other day—I'm crazy . . . I go through all your things three times a week, touching your clothes and reading your books. . . . You have the nicest clothes . . . . There was that quatrain you wrote to me that time you were in Boston and . . . First I laughed, then I cried, then . . . It's a lovely poem—you would have been a fine writer. I think you would have been the greatest writer that ever . . . I . . . Did they shoot your hands away, darling?

MORGAN. No.

JULIA. That's good. I couldn't bear it if anything happened to your hands. Was it bad, darling?

MORGAN. Bad enough.

JULIA. But they didn't shoot your hands away. That's something. You learn how to be grateful for the craziest things nowadays. People have to be grateful for something and it's so hard, with the war and all. . . . Oh, darling, I never could think of you dead. Somehow you didn't seem to be made to be dead. I would feel better if you were buried in a fine green field and there were funny little flowers jumping up around the stone that said, "Walter Morgan, Born 1913, Died 1937." I could stop getting drunk at night and singing out loud so that people laugh at me. The worst thing is looking at all the books you piled up home that you didn't read. They wait there, waiting for your hands to come and open them and . . . Oh, let them bury you, let them bury you . . . There's nothing left, only crazy people and clothes that'll never be used hanging in the closets . . . Why not?

MORGAN. There are too many books I haven't read, too many places I haven't seen, too many memories I haven't kept long enough. . . . I won't be cheated of them. . . .

JULIA. And me? Darling, me . . . I hate getting drunk. Your name would look so well on a nice simple chunk of marble in a green field. "Walter Morgan, Beloved of Julia Blake . . ." With poppies and daisies and those little purple flowers all around the bottom, and . . . (*She is bent over, almost wailing. There is the flash of a gun in her hand, and she totters, falls*) Now they can put my name on the casualty lists, too. . . . What do they call those purple flowers, darling . . . ? (*Blackout.*)

The spotlight follows KATHERINE DRISCOLL *as she makes her way from* CORPSE *to* CORPSE *in the grave, looking at their faces. She looks first at* CORPSE SIX, *shudders, covers her eyes and moves on. She stops at* CORPSE FIVE.

KATHERINE. I'm Katherine Driscoll. I— I'm looking for my brother. He's dead. Are you my brother?

FIFTH CORPSE. No. (KATHERINE *goes on to* CORPSE FOUR, *stops, looks, moves on to* CORPSE THREE.)

KATHERINE. I'm looking for my brother. My name is Katherine Driscoll. His name—

THIRD CORPSE. No. (KATHERINE *goes on, stands irresolutely before* CORPSE TWO.)

KATHERINE. Are you . . . ? (*Realizing it isn't her brother. Goes on to* CORPSE ONE) I'm looking for my brother. My name is Katherine Driscoll. His name—

DRISCOLL. I'm Tom Driscoll.

KATHERINE. Hel—Hello. I don't know you. After fifteen years— And . . .

DRISCOLL. What do you want, Katherine?

KATHERINE. You don't know me either, do you?

DRISCOLL. No.

KATHERINE. It's funny—my coming here to talk to a dead man—to try to get him to do something because once long ago he was my brother. They talked me into it. I don't know how to begin. . . .

DRISCOLL. You'll be wasting your words, Katherine. . . .

KATHERINE. They should have asked someone nearer to you—someone who loved you—only they couldn't find anybody. I was the nearest, they said. . . .

DRISCOLL. That's so. You were the nearest. . . .

KATHERINE. And I fifteen years away. Poor Tom . . . It couldn't have been a sweet life you led these fifteen years.

DRISCOLL. It wasn't.

KATHERINE. You were poor, too?

DRISCOLL. Sometimes I begged for meals. I wasn't lucky. . . .

KATHERINE. And yet you want to go back. Is there no more sense in the dead, Tom, than in the living?

DRISCOLL. Maybe not. Maybe there's no sense in either living or dying, but we can't believe that. I travelled to a lot of places and I saw a lot of things, always from the black side of them, always workin' hard to keep from starvin' and turnin' my collar up to keep the wind out, and they were mean and rotten and sad, but always I saw that they could be better and some day they were going to be better, and that the guys like me who knew that they were rotten and knew that they could be better had to get out and fight to make it that way.

KATHERINE. You're dead. Your fight's over.

DRISCOLL. The fight's never over. I got things to say to people now—to the people who nurse big machines and the people who swing shovels and the people whose babies die with big bellies and rotten bones. I got things to say to the people who leave their lives behind them and pick up guns to fight in somebody else's war. Important things. Big things. Big enough to lift me out of the grave right back onto the earth into the middle of men just because I got the voice to say them. If God could lift Jesus . . .

KATHERINE. Tom! Have you lost religion, too?

DRISCOLL. I got another religion. I got a religion that wants to take heaven out of the clouds and plant it right here on the earth where most of us can get a slice of it. It isn't as pretty a heaven—there aren't any streets of gold and there aren't any angels, and we'd have to worry about sewerage and railroad schedules in it, and we don't guarantee everybody'd love it, but it'd be right here, stuck in the mud of this earth, and there wouldn't be any entrance requirement, like dying to get into it. . . . Dead or alive, I see that, and it won't let me rest. I was the first one to get up in this black grave of ours, because that idea wouldn't let me rest. I pulled the others with me—that's my job, pulling he others . . . They only know what they want—I know how they can get it. . . .

KATHERINE. There's still the edge of arrogance on you.

DRISCOLL. I got heaven in my two hands to give to men. There's reason for arrogance. . . .

KATHERINE. I came to ask you to lie down and let them bury you. It seems foolish now. But . . .

DRISCOLL. It's foolish, Katherine. I didn't get up from the dead to go back to the dead. I'm going to the living now. . . .

KATHERINE. Fifteen years. It's a good thing your mother isn't alive. How can you say good-bye to a dead brother Tom?

DRISCOLL. Wish him an easy grave, Katherine. . . .

KATHERINE. A green and pleasant grave to you, Tom, when finally . . . finally . . . green and pleasant. (*Blackout.*)

The spotlight illuminates PRIVATE DEAN, *the* SIXTH CORPSE, *where he stands with his back to the audience, listening to his mother, a thin, shabby, red-eyed woman of about forty-five, sitting above and to the right, in the full glare of the spotlight.* DEAN *is in shadow.*

MRS. DEAN. Let me see your face, son . . .

DEAN. You don't want to see it, mom . . .

MRS. DEAN. My baby's face. Once, before you . . .

DEAN. You don't want to see it, mom. I know. Didn't they tell you what happened to me?

MRS. DEAN. I asked the doctor. He said a piece of shell hit the side of your head—but even so. . . .

DEAN. Don't ask to see it, mom.

MRS. DEAN. How are you, son? (DEAN *laughs a little—bitterly*) Oh, I forgot. I asked you that question so many times while you were growing up, Jimmy. Let me see your face, Jimmy—just once. . . .

DEAN. How did Alice take it when she heard . . . ?

MRS. DEAN. She put a gold star in her window. She tells everybody you were going to be married. Is that so?

DEAN. Maybe. I liked Alice.

MRS. DEAN. She came over on your birthday. That was before this—this happened. She brought flowers. Big chrysanthemums. Yellow. A lot of them. We had to put them in two vases. I baked a cake. I don't know why. It's hard to get eggs and fine flour nowadays. My baby, twenty years old . . . Let me see your face, Jimmy, boy. . . .

DEAN. Go home, mom. . . . It's not doing you any good staying here. . . .

MRS. DEAN. I want you to let them bury you, Baby. It's done now and over. It would be better for you that way. . . .

DEAN. There's no better to it, mom—and no worse. It happened that way, that's all.

MRS. DEAN. Let me see your face, Jimmy. You had such a fine face. Like a good baby's. It hurt me when you started to shave. Somehow, I almost forget what you looked like, Baby. I remember what you looked like when you were five, when you were ten—you were chubby and fair and your cheeks felt like little silk cushions when I put my hand on them. But I don't remember how you looked when you went away with that uniform on you and that helmet over your face. . . . Baby, let me see your face, once. . . .

DEAN. Don't ask me . . . You don't want to see. You'll feel worse—forever . . . if you see . . .

MRS. DEAN. I'm not afraid. I can look at my baby's face. Do you think mothers can be frightened by their children's . . .

DEAN. No, mom . . .

MRS. DEAN. Baby, listen to me, I'm your mother. . . . Let them bury you. There's something peaceful and done about a grave. After a while you forget the death and you remember only the life before it. But this way—you never forget. . . . it's a wound walking around forever, without peace. For your sake and mine and your father's . . . Baby . . .

DEAN. I was only twenty, mom. I hadn't done anything. I hadn't seen anything. I never even had a girl. I spent twenty years practising to be a man and then they killed me. Being a kid's no good, mom. You try to get over it as soon as you can. You don't really live while you're a kid. You mark time, waiting. I waited, mom—but then I got cheated. They made a speech and played a trumpet and dressed me in a uniform and then they killed me.

MRS. DEAN. Oh, Baby, Baby, there's no peace this way. Please, let them . . .

DEAN. No, mom . . .

MRS. DEAN. Then once, now, so that I can remember—let me see your face, my baby's face . . .

DEAN. Mom, the shell hit close to me. You don't want to look at a man when a shell hits close to him.

MRS..... DEAN. Let me see your face, Jimmy . . .

DEAN. All right, mom . . . Look! (*He turns his face to her. The audience can't see his face, but immediately a spotlight, white and sharp, shoots down from directly above and hits DEAN's head. MRS. DEAN leans forward, staring. Another spotlight shoots down immediately after from the extreme right, then one from the left, then two more, from above. They hit with the impact of blows and MRS. DEAN shudders a little as they come, as though she were watching her son being beaten. There is absolute silence for a moment. Then MRS. DEAN starts to moan, low, painfully. The lights remain fixed and MRS. DEAN's moans rise to a wail, then to a scream. She leans back, covering her eyes with her hands, screaming. Blackout. The scream persists, fading, like a siren fading in the distance, until it is finally stilled.*)

The spotlight on CORPSE THREE, PRIVATE WEBSTER, *and his wife, a dumpy, sad little woman.*

MARTHA WEBSTER. Say something.

WEBSTER. What do you want me to say?

MARTHA. Something—anything. Only talk. You give me the shivers standing there like that—looking like that. . . .

WEBSTER. Even now—after this—there's nothing that we can talk to each other about.

MARTHA. Don't talk like that. You talked like that enough when you were alive—It's not my fault that you're dead. . . .

WEBSTER. No.

MARTHA. It was bad enough when you were alive—and you didn't talk to me and you looked at me as though I was always in your way.

WEBSTER. Martha, Martha, what's the difference now?

MARTHA. I just wanted to let you know. Now I suppose you're going to come back and sit around and ruin my life altogether?

WEBSTER. No. I'm not going to come back.

MARTHA. Then what . . . ?

WEBSTER. I couldn't explain it to you, Martha. . . .

MARTHA. No! Oh, no—you couldn't explain it to your wife. But you could explain it to that dirty bunch of loafers down at that damned garage of yours and you could explain it to those bums in the saloon on F Street. . . .

WEBSTER. I guess I could. (*Musing*) Things seemed to be clearer when I was talking to the boys while I worked over a job. And I managed to talk so people could get to understand what I meant down at the saloon on F Street. It was nice, standing there of a Saturday night, with a beer in front of you and a man or two that understood your own language next to you, talking—oh, about Babe Ruth or the new oiling system Ford was putting out or the chances of us gettin' into the war. . . .

MARTHA. It's different if you were rich and had a fine beautiful life you wanted to go back to. Then I could understand. But you were poor . . . you always had dirt under your finger nails, you never ate enough, you hated me, your wife, you couldn't stand being in the same room with me. . . . Don't shake your head, I know. Out of your whole life, all you could remember that's good is a beer on Saturday night that you drank in company with a couple of bums. . . .

WEBSTER. That's enough. I didn't think about it then . . . but I guess I was happy those times.

MARTHA. You were happy those times . . . but you weren't happy in your own home! I know, even if you don't say it! Well, I wasn't happy either! Living in three damned rooms that the sun didn't hit five times a year! Watching the roaches make picnics on the walls! Happy!

WEBSTER. I did my best.

MARTHA. Eighteen-fifty a week! Your best! Eighteen-fifty, condensed milk, a two-dollar pair of shoes once a year, five hundred dollars' insurance, chopped meat, God, how I hate chopped meat! Eighteen-fifty, being afraid of everything—of the landlord, the gas company, scared stiff every month that I was goin' to have a baby! Why shouldn't I have a baby? Who says I shouldn't have a baby? Eighteen-fifty, no baby!

WEBSTER. I woulda liked a kid.

MARTHA. Would you? You never said anything.

WEBSTER. It's good to have a kid. A kid's somebody to talk to.

MARTHA. At first . . . In the beginning . . . I thought we'd have a kid some day.

WEBSTER. Yeah, me too. I used to go out on Sundays and watch men wheel their kids through the park.

MARTHA. There were so many things you didn't tell me. Why did you keep quiet?

WEBSTER. I was ashamed to talk to you. I couldn't give you anything.

MARTHA. I'm sorry.

WEBSTER. In the beginning it looked so fine. I used to smile to myself when I walked beside you in the street and other men looked at you.

MARTHA. That was a long time ago.

WEBSTER. A kid would've helped.

MARTHA. No, it wouldn't. Don't fool yourself, Webster. The Clarks downstairs have four and it doesn't help them. Old man Clark comes home drunk every Saturday night and beats 'em with his shaving strap and throws plates at the old lady. Kids don't help the poor. Nothing helps the poor! I'm too smart to have sick, dirty kids on eighteen-fifty. . . .

WEBSTER. That's it. . . .

MARTHA. A house should have a baby. But it should be a clean house with a full icebox. Why shouldn't I have a baby? Other people have babies. Even now, with the war, other people have babies. They don't have to feel their skin curl every time they tear a page off the calendar. They go off to beautiful hospitals in lovely ambulances and have babies between colored sheets! What's there about them that God likes that He makes it so easy for *them* to have babies?

WEBSTER. They're not married to mechanics.

MARTHA. No! It's not eighteen-fifty for them. And now . . . now it's worse. Your twenty dollars a month. You hire yourself out to be killed and I get twenty dollars a month. I wait on line all day to get a loaf of bread. I've forgotten what butter tastes like. I wait on line with the rain soaking through my shoes for a pound of rotten meat once a week. At night I go home. Nobody to talk to, just sitting, watching the bugs, with one little light because the Government's got to save electricity. You had to go off and leave me to that! What's the war to me that I have to sit at night with nobody to talk to? What's the war to you that you had to go off and . . . ?

WEBSTER. That's why I'm standing up now, Martha.

MARTHA. What took you so long, then? Why now? Why not a month ago, a year ago, ten years ago? Why didn't you stand up then? Why wait until you're dead? You live on eighteen-fifty a week, with the roaches, not saying a word, and then when they kill you, you stand up! You fool!

WEBSTER. I didn't see it before.

MARTHA. Just like you! Wait until it's too late! There's plenty for live men to stand up for! All right, stand up! It's about time you talked back. It's about time all you poor miserable eighteen-fifty bastards stood up for themselves and their wives and the children they can't have! Tell 'em *all* to stand up! Tell 'em! *Tell 'em* (*She shrieks. Blackout.*)

A spotlight picks out the FIRST GENERAL. *He has his hands to his lips.*

FIRST GENERAL. It didn't work. But keep it quiet. For God's sake, keep it quiet.... (*Blackout.*)

A spotlight picks out the newspaper office, the REPORTER *and the* EDITOR.

REPORTER. (*In harsh triumph*) It didn't work! Now, you've got to put it in! I knew it wouldn't work! Smear it over the headlines! It didn't work!

EDITOR. Put it in the headlines.... They won't be buried! (*Blackout—Voices call....*)

VOICE. (NEWSBOY *spotted*) It didn't work! Extra! It didn't work!

VOICE. (*In dark. Hoarse whisper*) It didn't work! They're still standing.... Somebody do something....

VOICE. (*Spotted, a clubwoman type*) Somebody do something....

VOICE. (NEWSBOY *spotted*) Extra! They're still standing....

VOICE. (CLUBWOMAN) Don't let them back into the country....

REPORTER. (*Spotted. Triumphantly.*) They're standing. From now on they'll always stand! You can't bury soldiers any more .... (*Spotted, a group, owners of the next four voices.*)

VOICE. They stink. Bury them!

VOICE. What are we going to do about them?

VOICE. What'll happen to our war? We can't let anything happen to our war....

VOICE. (*A* PRIEST, *facing the three men*) Pray! Pray! God must help us! Down on your knees, all of you and pray with your hearts and your guts and the marrow of your bones....

VOICE. (REPORTER *spotted, facing them all*) It will take more than prayers. What are prayers to a dead man? They're standing! Mankind is standing up and climbing out of its grave.... (*Blackout.*)

VOICE. (*In dark*) Have you heard...? It didn't work....

VOICE. (*In dark*) Extra! Extra! It didn't work! They're still standing! (*Spotted,* MRS. DEAN, MRS. SCHELLING, JULIA BLAKE.)

MRS. DEAN. My baby....

MRS. SCHELLING. My husband....

JULIA BLAKE. My lover.... (*Blackout.*)

VOICE. (*In dark*) Bury them! They stink! (*The next set of characters walks through a stationary spotlight.*)

VOICE. (*A* FARMER) Plant a new crop! The old crop has worn out the earth. Plant something besides lives in the old and weary earth....

VOICE. (*A* NEWSBOY, *running*) Extra! It didn't work!

VOICE. (*A* BANKER. *Frantic*) Somebody do something! Dupont's passed a dividend!

VOICE. (*A* PRIEST) The Day of Judgment is at hand....

VOICE. (*The* FIRST WHORE) Where is Christ? (*Blackout.*)

VOICE. (*In dark*) File 'em away in alphabetical order.... (*Spotlight on a man in academic robes, reading aloud from behind a table, after he adjusts his glasses.*)

VOICE. We don't believe it. It is against the dictates of science. (*Blackout—Spot on* SECOND GENERAL.)

SECOND GENERAL. Keep it quiet! (MRS. SCHELLING *walks in front of him. The others follow.)*

BESS SCHELLING. My husband. . . .

JULIA BLAKE. My lover. . . .

MRS. DEAN. My baby. . . . (*Blackout.*)

VOICE. (*A* CHILD) What have they done with my father? (*Spot on* BANKER *at telephone.*)

BANKER. (*Into phone*) Somebody do something. Call up the War Department! Call up Congress! Call up the Roman Catholic Church! Somebody do something!

VOICE. We've got to put them down!

REPORTER. (*Spotted*) Never! Never! Never! You can't put them down. Put one down and ten will spring up like weeds in an old garden. . . . (*Spots at various parts of the stage.*)

VOICE. (*The* THIRD GENERAL) Use lead on them, lead! Lead put 'em down once, lead'll do it again! Lead!

VOICE. Put down the sword and hang the armor on the wall to rust with the years. The killed have arisen.

VOICE. Bury them! Bury the dead!

VOICE. The old demons have come back to possess the earth. We are lost. . . .

VOICE. The dead have arisen, now let the living rise, singing. . . .

VOICE. Do something, for the love of God, do something. . . .

VOICE. Extra! They're still standing.

VOICE. Do something!

VOICE. (*In dark*) We will do something. . . .

VOICE. Who are you?

VOICE. (PRIEST *in spot*) We are the Church and the voice of God. The State has tried its ways, now let the Church use the ways of God. These corpses are possessed by the devil, who plagues the lives of men. The Church will exorcise the devil from these men, according to its ancient rite, and they will lie down in their graves like children to a pleasant sleep, rising no more to trouble the world of living men. The Church which is the Voice of God upon this earth, amen. . . . (*Blackout.*)

CHORUS OF VOICES. Alleluia, alleluia, sing . . . . (*The scream of the bereft mother fades in, reaches its height, then dies off as the holy procession of priests moves solemnly on with bell, book and candle. A* PRIEST *sprinkles the* CORPSES *with holy water, makes the sign of the cross over them and begins in the solemn Latin of the service. At the end he goes into English—his voice rising in ritualistic passion.*)

PRIEST. I exorcise thee, unclean spirit, in the name of Jesus Christ; tremble, O Satan, thou enemy of the faith, thou foe of mankind, who hast brought death into the world, who hast deprived men of life, and hast rebelled against justice, thou seducer of mankind, thou root of evil, thou source of avarice, discord, and envy. (*Silence. Then the* CORPSES *begin to laugh, lightly, horribly. There is a sign from the living men present, and the priestly procession goes off, its bell tinkling. The laughter goes on. Blackout. The* VOICES *again. . . .*)

VOICE. No. . . .

VOICE. NO!

VOICE. It didn't work. . . .

VOICE. We are deserted by God for our evil ways. It is the new flood, without rain. . . .

NEWSBOY. They're licked.

VOICE. This isn't 1918! This is today!

VOICE. See what happens tomorrow!

VOICE. Anything can happen now! Anything!

VOICE. They're coming. We must stop them!

VOICE. We must find ways, find means!

VOICE. (*The* REPORTER, *exulting*) They're coming! There will be no ways, no means!

SEMI-CHORUS. (*Mocking*) What are you going to do?

CHORUS. *What are you going to do?* (*They laugh sardonically.*)

THIRD GENERAL. Let me have a machine gun! Sergeant! A machine gun! (*A bolt of light comes down to a machine gun set to the left of the grave, mid-way between the edge of the grave and the wings. The* GENERALS *are clustered around it.*)

THIRD GENERAL. I'll show them! This is what they've needed!

FIRST GENERAL. All right, all right. Get it over with! Hurry! But keep it quiet!

THIRD GENERAL. I want a crew to man this gun. (*Pointing to* FIRST SOLDIER) You! Come over here! And you! You know what to do. I'll give the command to fire. . . .

FIRST SOLDIER. Not to me, you won't. . . . This is over me. I won't touch that gun. None of us will! We didn't hire out to be no butcher of dead men. Do your own chopping. . . .

THIRD GENERAL. You'll be court-martialed! You'll be dead by tomorrow morning. . . .

FIRST SOLDIER. Be careful, General! I may take a notion to come up like these guys. That's the smartest thing I've seen in this army. I like it. . . . (*To* DRISCOLL) What d'ye say, Buddy?

DRISCOLL. It's about time. . . . (*The* THIRD GENERAL *draws his gun, but the other* GENERALS *hold his arm.*)

FIRST GENERAL. Stop it! It's bad enough as it is! Let him alone! do it yourself! Go ahead, do it!

THIRD GENERAL. (*Whispers*) Oh, my God . . . . (*He looks down at gun, then slowly gets down on one knee behind it. The other* GENERALS *slide out behind him. The* CORPSES *come together in the middle of the grave, all facing the gun.* THIRD GENERAL *fumbles with the gun.* VOICES *call.*)

REPORTER. Never, never, never!

JULIA. Walter Morgan, Beloved of Julia Blake, Born 1913, Died 1937.

MRS. DEAN. Let me see your face, Baby?

MARTHA WEBSTER. All you remember is a glass of beer with a couple of bums on Saturday night.

KATHERINE DRISCOLL. A green and pleasant grave . . .

BESS SCHELLING. Did it hurt much, John? His hair is blond and he weighs twenty-eight pounds.

JOAN. You loved me best, didn't you, Henry? . . . best . . .

VOICE. Four yards of bloody mud . . .

VOICE. I understand how they feel, Charlie. I wouldn't like to be underground . . . now . . .

REPORTER. Never, never!

VOICE. Never!

MARTHA WEBSTER. Tell 'em all to stand up! Tell 'em! *Tell 'em!* (*The* CORPSES *begin to walk toward the left end of the grave, not marching, but walking together, silently. The* THIRD GENERAL *stiffens, then starts to laugh hysterically. As the* CORPSES *reach the edge of the grave and take their first step out, he starts firing, laughing wildly, the gun shaking his shoulders violently. Calmly, in the face of the chattering gun, the* CORPSES *gather on the brink of the grave, then walk soberly, in a little bunch, toward the* THIRD GENERAL. *For a moment they obscure him as they pass him. In that moment the gun stops. There is absolute silence. The* CORPSES *pass on, going off the stage, like men who have leisurely business that must be attended to in the not too pressing future. As they pass the gun, they reveal the* THIRD GENERAL, *slumped forward, still, over the still gun. There is no movement on the stage for a fraction of a second. Then, slowly, the* FOUR SOLDIERS *of the burial detail break ranks. Slowly they walk, exactly as the* CORPSES *have walked, off toward the left, past the* THIRD GENERAL. *The last* SOLDIER, *as he passes the* THIRD GENERAL, *deliberately, but without malice, flicks a cigarette butt at him, then follows the other* SOLDIERS *off the stage. The* THIRD GENERAL *is the last thing we see, huddled over his quiet gun, pointed at the empty grave, as the light dims—in the silence.*)

Curtain

The Fall of The City

A Verse Play for Radio

BY ARCHIBALD MacLEISH

For
A. B. L. and R. A. L.

The first performance over the air occurred Sunday Evening, April 11, 1937, from 7 to 7:30 Eastern Standard Time, over the Columbia Broadcasting System Network.

Production under the direction of Irving Reis, director of the Columbia Workshop.

CAST OF CHARACTERS

VOICE OF STUDIO DIRECTOR ...... House Jameson
VOICE OF ANNOUNCER .... Orson Welles
VOICE OF DEAD WOMAN .... Adelaide Klein
VOICE OF FIRST MESSENGER .... Carleton Young
VOICE OF ORATOR .... Burgess Meredith
VOICE OF SECOND MESSENGER .... Dwight Weist
VOICE OF PRIEST .... Edgar Stehli
VOICE OF GENERAL .... William Pringle

VOICES OF ANTIPHONAL CHORUS.
{
Guy Repp
Brandon Peters
Karl Swenson
Dan Davies
Kenneth Delmar
}

CITIZENS, DANCERS, PRIESTS, SOLDIERS, ETC.

Music composed and directed by Bernard Herman.

Crowd supervision by William N. Robson.

Editorial supervision by Brewster Morgan.

Stage management by Earl McGill.

COPYRIGHT, 1937, BY ARCHIBALD MacLEISH

THE FALL OF THE CITY

VOICE OF THE STUDIO DIRECTOR (*orotund and professional*).

Ladies and gentlemen:
Tis broadcast comes to you from the city
Listeners over the curving air have heard
From furthest-off frontiers of foreign
    hours—
Mountain Time: Ocean Time: of the is-
    lands:
Of waters after the islands—some of them
    waking
Where noon here is the night there: some
Where noon is the first few stars they see or
    the last one.

For three days the world has watched this
    city—
Not for the common occasions of brutal
    crime
Or the usual violence of one sort or another
Or coronations of kings or popular festivals:
No: for stranger and disturbing reasons—
The resurrection from death and the tomb
    of a dead woman.

Each day for three days there has come
To the door of her tomb at noon a woman
    buried!

The terror that stands at the shoulder of our
    time
Touches the cheek with this: the flesh
    winces.
There have been other omens in other cities
But never of this sort and never so credible.

In a time like ours seemings and portents
    signify.
Ours is a generation when dogs howl and
    the
Skin crawls on the skull with its beast's
    foreboding.
All men now alive with us have feared.
We have smelled the wind in the street that
    changes weather.
We have seen the familiar room grow un-
    familiar:
The order of numbers alter: the expectation
Cheat the expectant eye. The appearance de-
    faults with us.

Here in this city the wall of the time cracks.

We take you now to the great square of this
    city. . . .

(*The shuffle and hum of a vast patient
crowd gradually rises: swells: fills the background.*)

VOICE OF THE ANNOUNCER (*matter-of-fact*).

We are here on the central plaza.
We are well off to the eastward edge.
There is a kind of terrace over the crowd
    here.
It is precisely four minutes to twelve.
The crowd is enormous: there might be ten
    thousand:
There might be more: the whole square is
    faces.
Opposite over the roofs are the mountains.
It is quite clear: there are birds circling.
We think they are kites by the look: they
    are very high. . . .

The tomb is off to the right somewhere—
We can't see for the great crowd.
Close to us here are the cabinet ministers:
They stand on a raised platform with awn-
    ings.
The farmers' wives are squatting on the
    stones:
Their children have fallen asleep on their
    shoulders.
The heat is harsh: the light dazzles like
    metal.
It dazes the air as the clang of a gong
    does. . . .

News travels in this nation:
There are people here from away off—
Horse-raisers out of the country with brooks
    in it:
Herders of cattle from up where the snow
    stays—
The kind that cook for themselves mostly:
They look at the girls with their eyes hard
And a hard grin and their teeth show-
    ing. . . .

It is one minute to twelve now:
There is still no sign: they are still waiting:
No one doubts that she will come:
No one doubts that she will speak too:
Three times she has not spoken.

(*The murmur of the crowd changes—
not louder but more intense: higher.*)

THE VOICE OF THE ANNOUNCER (*low but with
increasing excitement*).

Now it is twelve: now they are rising:
Now the whole plaza is rising:

Fathers are lifting their small children:
The plumed fans on the platform are motionless. . . .

There is no sound but the shuffle of shoe leather . . .

Now even the shoes are still. . . .

We can hear the hawks: it is quiet as that now. . . .

It is strange to see such throngs so silent. . . .

Nothing yet: nothing has happened. . . .

Wait! There's a stir here to the right of us:
They're turning their heads: the crowd turns:
The cabinet ministers lean from their balcony:
There's no sound: only the turning. . . .

(*A woman's voice comes over the silence of the crowd: it is a weak voice but penetrating: it speaks slowly and as though with difficulty.*)

THE VOICE OF THE DEAD WOMAN

First the waters rose with no wind. . . .

THE VOICE OF THE ANNOUNCER (*whispering*).

Listen: that is she! She's speaking!

THE VOICE OF THE DEAD WOMAN

Then the stones of the temple kindled
Without flame or tinder of maize-leaves. . . .

THE VOICE OF THE ANNOUNCER (*whispering*).

They see her beyond us: the crowd sees her. . . .

THE VOICE OF THE DEAD WOMAN

Then there were cries in the night haze:
Words in a once-heard tongue: the air
Rustling above us as at dawn with herons.

Now it is I who must bring fear:
I who am four days dead: the tears
Still unshed for me—all of them: I
For whom a child still calls at nightfall.

Death is young in me to fear!
My dress is kept still in the press in my bedchamber:

No one has broken the dish of the dead woman.
Nevertheless I must speak painfully:
I am to stand here in the sun and speak:

(*There is a pause. Then her voice comes again loud, mechanical, speaking as by rote.*)

The city of masterless men
Will take a master.
There will be shouting then:
Blood after!

(*The crowd stirs. Her voice goes on weak and slow as before.*)

Do not ask what it means: I do not know:
Only sorrow and no hope for it.

THE VOICE OF THE ANNOUNCER

She has gone. . . . No, they are still looking.

THE VOICE OF THE DEAD WOMAN

It is hard to return from the time past. I have come
In the dream we must learn to dream where the crumbling of
Time like the ash from a burnt string has
Stopped for me. For you the thread still burns:
You take the feathery ash upon your fingers.
You bring yourselves from the time past as it pleases you.

It is hard to return to the old nearness . . .

Harder to go again. . . .

THE VOICE OF THE ANNOUNCER

    She is gone.
We know because the crowd is closing.
All we can see is the crowd closing.
We hear the releasing of held breath—
The weight shifting: the lifting of shoe leather.
The stillness is broken as surface of water is broken—
The sound circling from in outward.

(*The murmur of the crowd rises.*)

Small wonder they feel fear.
Before the murders of the famous kings—
Before imperial cities burned and fell—

The dead were said to show themselves and
    speak.
When dead men came disaster came. Pres-
    entiments
That let the living on their beds sleep on
Woke dead men out of death and gave them
    voices.
All ancient men in every nation knew this.

A VOICE OVER THE CROWD

Masterless men . . .

A VOICE OVER THE CROWD

When shall it be . . .

A VOICE OVER THE CROWD

Masterless men
Will take a master . . .

A VOICE OVER THE CROWD

What has she said to us . . .

A VOICE OVER THE CROWD

When shall it be . . .

A VOICE OVER THE CROWD

Masterless men
Will take a master.
Blood after . . .

A VOICE OVER THE CROWD

What has she said to us . . .

VOICES TOGETHER

Blood after!

(*The voices run together into the excited
roar of the crowd. The Announcer's voice
is loud over it.*)

THE VOICE OF THE ANNOUNCER

They are milling around us like cattle that
    smell death.
The whole square is whirling and turning
    and shouting.
One of the ministers raises his arms on the
    platform.

No one is listening: now they are sounding
    drums:
Trying to quiet them likely: No! No!
Something is happening: there in the far
    corner:
A runner: a messenger: staggering: people
    are helping him:
People are calling: he comes through the
    crowd: they are quieter.
Only those on the far edge are still shouting:
Listen! He's here by the ministers now!
    He is speaking. . . .

THE VOICE OF THE MESSENGER

There has come the conqueror!
I am to tell you.
I have raced over sea land:
I have run over cane land:
I have climbed over cone land.
It was laid on my shoulders
By shall and by shan't
That standing by day
And staying by night
Were not for my lot
Till I came to the sight of you.
Now I have come.

Be warned of this conqueror!
This one is dangerous!
Word has out-oared him.
East over sea-cross has
All taken—
Every country.
No men are free there.
Ears overhear them.
Their words are their murderers.
Judged before judgment
Tried after trial
They die as do animals:—
Offer their throats
As the goat to her slaughterer.
Terror has taught them this!

Now he is here!

He was violent in his vessel:
He was steering in her stern:
He was watching in her waist:
He was peering in her prow:
And he dragged her up
Nine lengths
Till her keel lodged
On this nation.

Now he is here
Waylaying and night-lying.
If they hide before dark

He comes before sunup.
Where hunger is eaten
There he sits down:
Where fear sleeps
There he arises.

I tell you beware of him!
All doors are dangers.
The warders of wealth
Will admit him by stealth.
The lovers of men
Will invite him as friend.
The drinkers of blood
Will drum him in suddenly.
Hope will unlatch to him:
Hopelessness open.

I say and say truly
To all men in honesty
Such is this conqueror!
Shame is his people.
Lickers of spittle
Their lives are unspeakable:
Their dying indecent.

Be well warned!
He comes to you slightly
Slanting and sprinting
Hinting and shadowing:
Sly is his hiding:—
A hard lot:
A late rider:

Watch! I have said to you!

THE VOICE OF THE ANNOUNCER

They are leading him out: his legs give:
Now he is gone in the crowd: they are
    silent:
No one has spoken since his speaking:

They stand still circling the ministers.
No one has spoken or called out:—
There is no stir at all nor movement:
Even the farthest have stood patiently:
They wait trusting the old men:
They wait faithfully trusting the answer.
Now the huddle on the platform opens:
A minister turns to them raising his two
    arms. . . .

THE VOICE OF THE ORATOR

Freemen of this nation!
The persuasion of your wills against your
    wisdom is not dreamed of.
We offer themes for your consideration.

What is the surest defender of liberty?
Is it not liberty?
A free people resists by freedom:
Not locks! Not blockhouses!

The future is a mirror where the past
Marches to meet itself. Go armed toward
    arms!
Peaceful toward peace! Free and with music
    toward freedom!
Face tomorrow with knives and tomorrow's
    knife-blade.
Murder you foe and your foe will be mur-
    der!—
Even your friends suspected of false-speak-
    ing.
Hands on the door at night and the floor
    boards squeaking.

Those who win by the spear are the spear-
    toters.
And what do they win? Spears! What else
    is there?
If their hands let go they have nothing to
    hold by.
They are no more free than a paralytic prop-
    ped against a tree is.

With the armored man the arm is upheld
    by the weapon:
The man is worn by the knife.

Once depend on iron for your freedom and
    your
Freedom's iron!
Once overcome your resisters with force and
    your
Force will resist you!—
You will never be free of force.
Never of arms unarmed
Will the father return home:
The lover to her loved:
The mature man to his fruit orchard
Walking at peace in that beauty—
The years of his trees to assure him.
Force is a greater enemy than this con-
    queror—
A treacherous weapon.

Nevertheless my friends there is a weapon!
Weakness conquers!

Against chainlessness who breaks?
Against wall-lessness who vaults?
Against forcelessness who forces?

Against the feather of the thistle
Is blunted sharpest metal.
No edge cuts seed-fluff.

This conqueror unresisted
Will conquer no longer: a posturer
Beating his blows upon burdocks—
Shifting his guard against shadows.
Snickers will sound among road-menders:
Titters be stifled by laundresses:
Coarse guffaws among chambermaids.
Reddened with rage he will roar.
He will sweat in his uniform foolishly.
He will disappear: no one hear of him!

There *is* a weapon my friends.
Scorn conquers!

THE VOICE OF THE ANNOUNCER (*the Orator's voice unintelligible under it*).

I wish you could all see this as we do—
The whole plaza full of these people—
Their colorful garments—the harsh sun-
light—
The water-sellers swinging enormous
gourds—
The orator there on the stone platform—
The temple behind him: the high
pyramid—
The hawks overhead in the sky teetering
Slow to the windward: swift to the down-
wind—
The houses blind with the blank sun on
them. . . .

THE VOICE OF THE ORATOR

There is a weapon.
Reason and truth are that weapon.

Let this conqueror come!
Show him no hindrance!
Suffer his flag and his drum!
Words . . . win!

THE VOICE OF THE ANNOUNCER

There's the shout now: he's done:
He's climbing down: a great speech:
They're all smiling and pressing around
him:
The women are squatting in full sunlight:
They're opening packages: bread we'd say
by the look—
Yes: bread: bread wrapped between corn
leaves:
They're squatting to eat: they're quite con-
tented and happy:
Women are calling their men from the
sunny stones:

There are flutes sounding away off:
We can't see for the shifting and moving—
Yes: there are flutes in the cool shadow:
Children are dancing in intricate figures.

(*A drum and flute are heard under the
voice.*)

Even a few old men are dancing.
You'd say they'd never feared to see them
dancing.
A great speech! really great!
Men forget these truths in passion:
They oppose the oppressors with blind
blows:
They make of their towns tombs: of their
roofs burials:
They build memorial ruins to liberty:
But liberty is not built from ruins:
Only in peace is the work excellent. . . .

That's odd! The music has stopped. There's
something—
It's a man there on the far side: he's point-
ing:
He seems to be pointing back through the
farthest street:
The people are twisting and rising: bread
in their fists. . . .
We can't see what it is. . . . Wait! . . . it's
a messenger.
It must be a messenger. Yes. It's a message
—another.
Here he is at the turn of the street trotting:
His neck's back at the nape: he looks tired:
He winds through the crowd with his
mouth open: laboring:
People are offering water: he pushes away
from them:
Now he has come to the stone steps: to the
ministers:
Stand by: we're edging in. . . .

(*There are sounds of people close by:
coughs: murmurs. The Announcer's voice
is lowered.*)

Listen: he's leaning on the stone: he's speaking.

THE VOICE OF THE MESSENGER

There has come . . . the Conqueror. . . .

I am to tell you . . .

I have run over corn land:
I have climbed over cone land:
I have crossed over mountains. . . .

It was laid on my shoulders
By shall and by shan't
That standing by day
And staying by night
Were not for my lot
Till I came to the sight of you. . . .

Now I have come.

I bear word:
Beware of this conqueror!

The fame of his story
Like flame in the winter-grass
Widens before him.
Beached on our shore
With the dawn over shoulder
The lawns were still cold
When he came to the sheep meadows:—
Sun could not keep with him
So was he forward.
Fame is his sword.

No man opposing him
Still grows his glory.
He needs neither foeman nor
Thickset of blows to
Gather his victories—
Nor a foe's match
To earn him his battles.

He brings his own enemy!

He baggages with him
His closet antagonist—
His private opposer.
He's setting him up
At every road corner—
A figure of horror
With blood for his color:
Fist for his hand:
Reek where he stands:
Hate for his heat:
Sneers for his mouth:
Clouts for his clothes:
Oaths if he speak:—
And he's knocking him down
In every town square
Till hair's on his blade
And blood's all about
Like dust in a drouth
And the people are shouting
Flowers him flinging
Music him singing
And bringing him gold
And holding his heels
And feeling his thighs
Till their eyes start

And their hearts swell
And they're telling his praises
Like lays of the heroes
And chiefs of antiquity.

Such are his victories!
So does he come:
So he approaches. . . .

(*A whisper rustles through the crowd*.)

No man to conquer
Yet as a conqueror
Marches he forward. . . .

(*The whisper is louder*.)

Stands in your mountains. . . .

(*A murmur of voices*.)

Soon to descend on you!

(*A swelling roar*.)

THE VOICE OF THE ANNOUNCER

That touched them! That frightened them!
Some of them point to the east hills:
Some of them mock at the ministers: 'Free-
dom!'
'Freedom for what? To die in a rat trap?'
They're frantic with anger and plain fear.
They're sold out they say. You can hear
them.
'Down with the government! Down with
the orators!
'Down with liberal learned minds!
'Down with the mouths and the loose
tongues in them!
'Down with the lazy lot! They've sold us!
'We're sold out! Talking has done for
us!' . . .
They're boiling around us like mullet that
smell shark.
We can't move for the mob: they're crazy
with terror. . . .

A LOUD VOICE (*distant*).

God-lovers!
Think of your gods!

Earth-masters!
Taste your disasters!

Men!
Remember!

THE VOICE OF THE ANNOUNCER

There's a voice over the crowd somewhere.
They hear it: they're quieting down. . . .

It's the priests!
We see them now: it's the priests on the
   pyramid!
There might be ten of them: black with
   their hair tangled.
The smoke of their fire is flat in the quick
   wind:
They stand in the thick of the smoke by
   the stone of the victims:
Their knives catch in the steep sun: they
   are shouting:
Listen!—

VOICES OF THE PRIESTS

Turn to your gods rememberers!

A SINGLE VOICE

Let the world be saved by surrendering the
   world: Not otherwise shall it be saved.

VOICES OF THE PRIESTS

Turn to your gods rememberers!

A SINGLE VOICE

Let evil be overcome by the coming over of
   evil: Your hearts shall be elsewhere.

VOICES OF THE PRIESTS

Turn to your gods rememberers!

VOICES OF THE PRIESTS (*antiphonally*).

Turn to your gods!
      The conqueror cannot take you!
Turn to your gods!
      The narrow dark will keep you!

Turn to your gods!
      In god's house is no breaking!

Turn to your gods!
      In god's silences sleep is!

Lay up your will with the gods!
      Stones cannot still you!

Lay up your will with the gods!
      Blade cannot blind you!

Lay up your will with the gods!
      Danger departs from you!

THE VOICE OF THE ANNOUNCER

It's a wonderful thing to see this crowd
   responding.

Even the simplest citizens feel the emotion.
There's hardly a sound now in the square.
   It's wonderful:
Really impressive: the priests there on the
   pyramid:
The smoke blowing: the bright sun: the
   faces—

A SINGLE VOICE

In the day of confusion of reason when all
   is delusion:
In the day of the tyrants of tongues when
   the truth is for hire:
In the day of deceit when ends meet:
Turn to your gods!

In the day of division of nations when hope
   is derision:
In the day of the supping of hate when the
   soul is corrupted:
In the day of despair when the heart's bare:
Turn to your gods!

(*A slow drum beat.*)

THE VOICE OF THE ANNOUNCER

A kind of dance is beginning: a serpent of
   people:
A current of people coiling and curling
   through people:
A circling of people through people like
   water through water. . . .

CHANTING VOICES (*to the drums*).

Out of the stir of the sun
Out of the shout of the thunder
Out of the hush of the star . . .
Withdraw the heart.

THE VOICE OF THE ANNOUNCER (*the chant
and drums under*).

A very young girl is leading them:
They have torn the shawl from her bare
   breast:
They are giving her flowers: her mouth
   laughs:
Her eyes are not laughing. . . .

CHANTING VOICES

Leave now the lovely air
To the sword and the sword-wearer—
Leave to the marksman the mark—
Withdraw the heart.

THE VOICE OF THE ANNOUNCER (*the chant and drums louder*).

She's coming . . . the drums pound . . . the crowd
Shrieks . . . she's reaching the temple . . . she's climbing it. . .
Others are following: five: ten . . .
Hundreds are following . . . crowding the stairway. . . .
She's almost there . . . her flowers have fallen . . .
She looks back . . . the priests are surrounding her. . . .

(*The drums suddenly stop: there is an instant's silence: then an angry shout from the crowd.*)

THE VOICE OF THE ANNOUNCER

Wait! Wait! Something has happened!
One of the ministers: one of the oldest:
The general: the one in the feathered coat:—
He's driving them down with the staff of a banner:
He's climbed after them driving them down:
There's shouting and yelling enough but they're going:
He's telling them off too: you can hear him—

A DEEP VOICE (*chatter of the crowd under it*).

Men! Old men! Listen!
Twist your necks on your nape bones!
The knife will wait in the fist for you.
There is a time for everything—
Time to be thinking of heaven:
Time of your own skins!

Cock your eyes to the windward!

Do you see smoke on those mountains?
The smoke is the smoke of towns.
And who makes it? The conqueror!
And where will he march now? Onward!
The heel of the future descends on you!

THE VOICE OF THE ANNOUNCER

He has them now: even the priests have seen it:
They're all looking away here to the east.
There's smoke too: filling the valleys: like thunderheads! . . .

THE VOICE OF THE GENERAL

You are foolish old men.

You ought to be flogged for your foolishness.
Your grandfathers died to be free
And you—you juggle with freedom!
Do you think you're free by a law
Like the falling of apples in autumn?

You thought you were safe in your liberties!
You thought you could always quibble!
You can't! You take my word for it.
Freedom's the rarest bird!
You risk your neck to snare it—
It's gone while your eyeballs stare!

Those who'd lodge with a tyrant
Thinking to feed at his fire
And leave him again when they're fed are
Plain fools or were bred to it—
Brood of the servile races
Born with the hang-dog face. . . .

THE VOICE OF THE ANNOUNCER

They're all pointing and pushing together:
The women are shouldering baskets: bread: children. . . .
They smell smoke in the air: they smell terror. . . .

THE VOICE OF THE GENERAL (*louder over the increasing sound*).

There's nothing in this world worse—
Empty belly or purse or the
Pitiful hunger of children—
Than doing the Strong Man's will!

The free will fight for their freedom.
They're free men first. They feed
Meager or fat but as free men.
Everything else comes after—
Food: roof: craft—
Even the sky and the light of it!

(*The voices of the crowd rise to a tumult of sounds—drums: shouts: cries.*)

THE VOICE OF THE ANNOUNCER

The sun is yellow with smoke . . . the town's burning. . . .
The war's at the broken bridge. . . .

THE VOICE OF THE GENERAL (*shouting*).

You! Are you free? Will you fight?

There are still inches for fighting!

There is still a niche in the streets!

You can stand on the stairs and meet him!

You can hold in the dark of a hall!

You can die!

  —or your children will crawl for it!

THE VOICE OF THE ANNOUNCER (*over the tumult*).

They won't listen. They're shouting and screaming and circling.
The square is full of deserters with more coming.
Every street from the bridge is full of deserters.
They're rolling in with the smoke blowing behind them.
The plaza's choked with the smoke and the struggling of stragglers.
They're climbing the platform: driving the ministers: shouting—
One speaks and another:

THE VOICES OF CITIZENS

The city is doomed!
  There's no holding it!

Let the conqueror have it! It's his!

The age is his! It's his century!

Our institutions are obsolete.
He marches a mile while we sit in a meeting.

Opinions and talk!
Deliberative walks beneath the ivy and the creepers!

The age demands a made-up mind.
The conqueror's mind is decided on everything.

His doubt comes after the deed or never.

He knows what he wants for his want's what he knows.
He's gone before they say he's going.
He's come before you've barred your house.

He's one man: we are but thousands!

Who can defend us from one man?

Bury your arms! Break your standards!

Give him the town while the town stands!

THE VOICE OF THE ANNOUNCER

They're throwing their arms away: their bows are in bonfires.
The plaza is littered with torn plumes: spear-handles. . . .

THE VOICES OF CITIZENS

Masterless men! . . .

Masterless men
Must take a master! . . .

Order must master us! . . .

Freedom's for fools:
Force is the certainty!

Freedom has eaten our strength and corrupted our virtues!

Men must be ruled!

Fools must be mastered!

Rigor and fast
Will restore us our dignity!

Chains will be liberty!

THE VOICE OF THE ANNOUNCER

The last defenders are coming: they whirl from the streets like
Wild leaves on a wind: the square scatters them.
Now they are fewer—ten together or five:
They come with their heads turned: their eyes back.

Now there are none. The street's empty— in shadow.
The crowd is retreating—watching the empty street:
The shouts die.

  The voices are silent.

    They're watching. . . .

They stand in the slant of the sunlight silent and watching.
The silence after the drums echoes the drum beat.

Now there's a sound. They see him. They
   must see him!
They're shading their eyes from the sun:
   there's a rustle of whispering:
We can't see for the glare of it. . . . Yes!
   Yes! . . .
He's there in the end of the street in the
   shadow. We see him!
He looks huge—a head taller than anyone:
Broad as a brass door: a hard hero:
Heavy of heel on the brick: clanking with
   metal:
The helm closed on his head: the eyeholes
   hollow.

He's coming! . . .
         He's clear of the shadow! . . .
                  The sun takes him.

They cover their faces with fingers. They
   cower before him.
They fall: they sprawl on the stone. He's
   alone where he's walking.
He marches with rattle of metal. He
   tramples his shadow.
He mounts by the pyramid—stamps on the
   stairway—turns—
His arm rises—his visor is opening. . . .

(*There is an instant's breathless silence:
then the voice of the Announcer low—
almost a whisper.*)

                  There's no one! . . .
There's no one at all! . . .
            No one! . . .
         The helmet is hollow!
The metal is empty! The armor is empty! I
   tell you
There's no one at all there: there's only the
   metal:
The barrel of metal: the bundle of armor.
   It's empty!

The push of a stiff pole at the nipple would
   topple it.

They don't see! They lie on the paving.
   They lie in the
Burnt spears: the ashes of arrows. They lie
   there . . .
They don't see or they won't see. They are
   silent. . . .

The people invent their oppressors: they
   wish to believe in them.
They wish to be free of their freedom: released from their liberty:—
The long labor of liberty ended!
                  They lie there!

(*There is a whisper of sound. The Announcer's voice is louder.*)

Look! It's his arm! It is rising! His arm's
   rising!
They're watching his arm as it rises. They
   stir. They cry.
They cry out. They are shouting. They're
   shouting with happiness.
Listen! They're shouting like troops in a
   victory. Listen—
'The city of masterless men has found a
   master!'
You'd say it was they were the conquerors:
   they that had conquered.

A ROAR OF VOICES

The city of masterless men has found a
   master!
The city has fallen!
The city has fallen!

THE VOICE OF THE ANNOUNCER (*flat*).

The city has fallen. . . .

Golden Boy

BY CLIFFORD ODETS

For Luise

GOLDEN BOY was first presented by the Group Theatre at the Belasco Theatre on the evening of November 4th, 1937, with the following members of the Group Theatre Acting Company:

(In order of speech)

TOM MOODY .... Roman Bohnen
LORNA MOON ...... Frances Farmer
JOE BONAPARTE ... Luther Adler
TOKIO .... Art Smith
MR. CARP .... Lee J. Cobb
SIGGIE .... Jules Garfield
MR. BONAPARTE ... Morris Carnovsky
ANNA .... Phoebe Brand
FRANK BONAPARTE John O'Malley
ROXY GOTTLIEB ... Robert Lewis

EDDIE FUSELI ...... Elia Kazan
PEPPER WHITE ..... Harry Bratsburg
MICKEY .... Michael Gordon
CALL BOY .... Bert Conway
SAM .... Martin Ritt
LEWIS .... Charles Crisp
DRAKE .... Howard Da Silva
DRISCOLL .... Charles Niemeyer
BARKER .... Karl Malden

Direction by HAROLD CLURMAN
Settings by MORDECAI GORELIK

SCENES

ACT ONE

SCENE 1. The office of Tom Moody.
SCENE 2. The Bonaparte home. That night.
SCENE 3. The office. Two months later.
SCENE 4. A park bench. A few nights later.
SCENE 5. The Bonaparte home. Midnight, six weeks later.

ACT TWO

SCENE 1. A gymnasium. Five months later.
SCENE 2. The park bench. A few nights later.
SCENE 3. The office. The following day.
SCENE 4. A dressing room in the Arena. Six weeks later.

ACT THREE

SCENE 1. The office. Six months later.
SCENE 2. The dressing room. The following night.
SCENE 3. The Bonaparte home. Several hours later.

GOLDEN BOY

ACT ONE

SCENE I

The small Broadway office of Tom Moody, *the fight manager.*
The office is scantily furnished, contains desk, chairs, telephone and couch. With Moody *at present is his girl,* Lorna Moon. *There is a certain quiet glitter about this girl, and if she is sometimes hard, it is more from necessity than choice. Her eyes often hold a soft, sad glance. Likewise* Moody's *explosiveness covers a soft, boyish quality, and at the same time he possesses a certain vulnerable quality which women find very attractive.*
The time is eighteen months ago.
As the lights fade in, we catch these two at the height of one of their frequent fights.

MOODY. Pack up your clothes and go! Go! Who the hell's stopping you?

LORNA. You mean it?

MOODY. You brought up the point yourself.

LORNA. No, I didn't!

MOODY. Didn't you say you had a good mind to leave me?

LORNA. No, I said—

MOODY. You said you were going to pack!

LORNA. I said I feel a tramp and I don't like it. I want to get married, I want—

MOODY. Go home, Lorna, go home! I ain't got time to discuss it. Gimme some air. It's enough I got my wife on my neck.

LORNA. What does she say?

MOODY. Who?

LORNA. Your wife—your sweet Goddam Monica!

MOODY. She wants five thousand dollars to give me the divorce. (LORNA *laughs.*) I don't see that it's funny.

LORNA. Look, Tom, this means as much to me as it does to you. If she's out of the way, we can get married. Otherwise I'm a tramp from Newark. I don't like the feeling.

MOODY. Lorna, for pete's sake, use your noodle! When I get rid of Monica, we'll marry. Now, do I have to bang you on the nose to make you understand?

LORNA. Go to hell! . . . But come back to-night. (MOODY's *answer is to look at her, then smile, then walk to her. They kiss.*)

MOODY. If I had the money, I'd buy you something—I don't know what—a big ostrich feather! If Kaplan wins tonight, I'll take you dancing at the Park.

LORNA. He won't win.

MOODY. How do you know? *I* don't know —how do *you* know?

LORNA. Are you crazy? Do you think your Mr. Kaplan can go ten rounds with the Baltimore Chocolate Drop?

MOODY. How do I know?

LORNA. It's the Twentieth Century, Tom— no more miracles. (MOODY's *face turns worried.* LORNA *smiles.*) You know what I like about you—you take everything so serious.

MOODY. Who will if I don't? I've been off the gold standard for eight years. This used to be a gorgeous town. New York was hot with money. Kaplan gets four hundred bucks tonight. In the old days, that was nothing. Those were the days when I had Marty Welch, the heavyweight contender— Cy Webster who got himself killed in a big, red Stutz. In '27 and 8 you couldn't go to sleep—the town was crawling with attractions. . . .

LORNA. My mother died in '28.

MOODY. I haven't had a break in years. "Carry me back to old Virginny"—that's how I feel. There isn't much of a future. (*Suddenly despondent,* MOODY *goes back to his desk.*)

LORNA. I was fooling.

LORNA. Do you think I'd leave you?

MOODY. What about?

MOODY. Why not? I'm an old man. What can I give you?

LORNA. A bang on the nose for a start. But what can I give you?

MOODY. A boy who can fight. Find me a good black boy and I'll show you a mint.

LORNA. Are good boys so hard to find?

MOODY. Honest to God, you make me sick to my stomach! What do you think I took a trip to Philadelphia? What do you think I went to Chicago? Wasn't I up in Boston for a week? You think good boys are laying around like pop-corn? I'd even take a bantamweight, if I found one.

LORNA. How about a nice lady fighter with a beard— (*Preparing to leave.*) Well, I'll see you tonight, Moody.

MOODY (*thoughtfully*). I'd give me right eye for a good black boy.

LORNA. Let me have your right eye for a minute. (*She kisses his eye.* MOODY *begins to embrace her—she eludes his grasp.*) That's to keep you hot. But if the truth were known—"yours till hell freezes over."

MOODY. I need you, I need you, Lorna—I need you all the time. I'd like to give you everything you want. Push your mouth over. . . . (LORNA *holds her face to his; he kisses her. Suddenly a youth is standing at the office door.* LORNA *sees him and breaks away.*)

BOY (*breathing quickly*). Mr. Moody . . .

MOODY (*spinning around*). Don't you knock when you come in an office?

BOY. Sometimes I knock, sometimes I don't.

MOODY. Say your piece and get the hell out!

BOY. I just ran over from the gym . . .

MOODY. What gym?

BOY. Where Kaplan trains. He just broke his hand. . . . (MOODY *stiffens to attention.*) It's a fact.

MOODY (*grasping the phone*). Is Tokio over there? My trainer?

BOY. He's looking after Kaplan. (MOODY *begins to dial the phone but abruptly changes his mind and replaces the phone.*)

MOODY. You can put me in the bug-house right now. Moody is the name, folks—step right up and wipe your shoes! Ah, that Kaplan! That phonus bolonus! (*He sits at his desk in despair.*) Now I have to call up Roxy Gottlieb and cancel the match. His club's in the red as it is.

BOY. I don't think it's necessary to cancel, Tom.

MOODY (*aware of the* BOY *for the first time*). Oh, you don't? Who the hell are you? And who the hell are you to call me Tom? Are we acquainted?

BOY. I wrote you a couple of letters. I can do that stretch.

MOODY. What stretch?

BOY. Why don't you let me take Kaplan's place tonight?

MOODY (*sarcastically*). Go slow and tell me again . . . what?

BOY (*coolly*). I can take Kaplan's place. . . .

MOODY. You mean you want to fight the Baltimore Chocolate Drop? You? (*The* BOY *remains silent.* MOODY *comes out from behind his desk and stands face to face with the* BOY. *With sudden discovery.*) You're cock-eyed too.

BOY (*quietly*). Can't you fix it up with Roxy Gottlieb?

MOODY (*suddenly*). Looka, kid, go home, kid, before I blame Kaplan's glass mitts on *you*. Then you won't like it, and I won't like it, and Miss Moon here, she won't like it.

BOY (*turning to* LORNA). How do you do, Miss Moon. (LORNA *smiles at the* BOY'S *quiet confidence.*) I need a good manager, Mr. Moody. You used to be tops around town— everyone says so. I think you can develop me. I can fight. You don't know it, but I can fight. Kaplan's been through for years. He may be the best fighter in your stable, but he's a stumble-bum for the younger boys growing up. Why don't you give me this chance, Tom?

MOODY. I don't want you calling me Tom! (*He glares at the* BOY *and then returns to the desk and telephone.*)

BOY. I'm waiting for your answer. (MOODY's *answer is an exasperated glance as he begins to dial the phone. The* BOY *half approaches the desk.*) There are forty-three thousand minutes in a month—can't you give me five?

MOODY. I'll give you this phone in the head in a minute! Who are you? What the hell do you want? Where do you fight?

BOY (*with cool persistence*). We ought to get together, Tom.

MOODY. I don't want you calling me Tom. You're brash, you're fresh, you're callow— and you're cock-eyed! In fact, you're an insult to my whole nature! Now get out! (MOODY *turns back to the phone and begins dialing again. The* BOY *stands there, poised on his toes, not sure of his next move. He turns and looks at* LORNA. *She nods her head and gives him a faint smile of encouragement. On phone.*) This is Tom Moody . . . is Tokio there? . . . (*He hangs up the phone and holds the instrument thoughtfully.*) Tokio's on his way over.

BOY. The Baltimore Chocolate Drop is not as good as you think he is. (MOODY *suddenly whirls around and holds the telephone high over his head in a threatening gesture. The* BOY *steps back lightly and continues.*) I've studied his style for months; I've perfected the exact punch to quench his thirst. Did you ever watch closely? (*Acting it out.*) He likes to pull your lead—he hesitates for a second—he pulls your lead—he slips his face away and then he's in. Suppose you catch that second when he hesitates—he's open for the punch!

MOODY (*sarcastically*). And what do you do with his left hook?

BOY (*simply*). Avoid it.

MOODY (*lowering the phone*). Looka, you idiot, did you ever hear of Phil Mateo?

BOY. I heard of him.

MOODY. The Chocolate Drop marked him lousy in twelve minutes and ten seconds. Was Kid Peters within your ken? And did you ever hear of Eddie Newton? The Chocolate gave him the blues in two rounds. And Frisco Samuels and Mike Mason. . . .

BOY. Did you ever hear of me?

MOODY (*sarcastically*). No, who are you? I would honestly like to know—who are you?

BOY (*quietly*). My name is Bonaparte. (MOODY *howls with laughter, and even* LORNA, *sympathetic to the* BOY, *laughs. The* BOY *continues.*) I don't think it's funny. . . .

MOODY. Didn't that name used to get you a little giggle in school? Tell the truth, Bonaparte. Didn't it?

BOY. Call me Joe.

MOODY (*laughing*). And your eyes . . . Didn't they used to get a little giggle too?

JOE. You don't seem as intelligent as I thought you were.

LORNA (*to the laughing* MOODY, *seeing the* BOY's *pain*). Stop it, Tom.

MOODY (*laughing*). You can't blame me, Bonaparte. . . . I haven't laughed for years.

JOE. I don't like it. . . . I don't want you to do it. (*Suddenly* JOE *grabs* MOODY *by the coat lapels.* MOODY, *surprised, shakes him off. At the same time a small, quiet man enters the office. He is* TOKIO, MOODY's *trainer.*)

JOE. I'm sorry I did that, Tom. We ought to be together, Tom—not apart.

MOODY. Tokio, did you send this kid here?

TOKIO. No.

MOODY. Take him out before I brain him! (*He storms back to his desk.*)

TOKIO (*after looking at the* BOY). You hear about Kaplan?

MOODY. This idiot told me. It's the end of everything! I'm off my top with the whole thing! Kaplan was our meal-ticket. I'm up to the throat in scandal, blackmail, perjury, and all points west!

TOKIO (*turning to* JOE). You oughta be ashamed to show your face in this office.

JOE. If Kaplan's mother fed him milk, he wouldn't have those brittle bones.

MOODY. ? ? ? ?

TOKIO (*to* MOODY). This is the boy who did it to Kaplan.

MOODY. ? ? ?

TOKIO. I went down for an apple and I come back and Kaplan's sparring with this kid—picked him up in the gym. The next thing I know, Kaplan's down on the floor with a busted mitt.

JOE (*modestly*). I took it on the elbow.

MOODY. ! ! (*Silence finally.*)

LORNA. Where do you come from, Bonaparte?

JOE. Here.

LORNA. How old are you?

JOE. Twenty-one—tomorrow.

MOODY (*after a look at* LORNA). Fight much?

JOE. Enough.

MOODY. Where?

JOE (*fabricating*). Albany, Syracuse . . .

LORNA. Does Roxy Gottlieb know you?

JOE. I never fought at his club.

MOODY (*harshly*). Does he know you?

JOE. No. (TOKIO *and* MOODY *look at each other. The phone rings.*)

MOODY (*on the phone*). Hello. . . . "What's this you hear?" . . . You hear the truth, Roxy. . . . He bust his mitt again. . . . I can't help it if you got *fifty* judgments on your club. . . . The same to you. . . . Your mother, too! (*Keeping his eyes on* BONAPARTE.) If you tie up your big flabby mouth for a minute, I'll give you some news. I'm in a position to do you a big favor. I got a replacement—*better* than Kaplan . . . Bonaparte. . . . No, Bon-a-parte. (*Holds hand over mouthpiece and asks* BOY.) Is that crap?

JOE. No, that's my name.

MOODY (*back at phone*). That's right, like in Napoleon. . . . (*Looks the* BOY *over appraisingly.*) One hundred and thirty . . .

JOE. Three.

MOODY. Hundred and thirty-three. Your customers'll eat him up. I'll bring him right over . . . you can take my word—the kid's a cock-eyed wonder . . . *your* mother too! (*He hangs up and turns around.* JOE *is the focus of all eyes.*) It's revenge on somebody—maybe God.

JOE (*quietly*). I think you'll be surprised.

MOODY (*sadly*). Do your worst, kid. I've been surprised by experts.

JOE. Don't worry, Tom.

MOODY. Call me Tom again and I'll break your neck!

QUICK FADEOUT

SCENE II

Later that night.
The combination dining and front room of the Bonaparte home. A round dining-room table, littered with newspapers, is lighted from directly above like a billiard table. Plaster busts of Mozart and Beethoven are on the sideboard. A cage of love birds at the other side of the room. Sitting at the table are two men: MR. BONAPARTE, *the father of* JOE, *and a Jewish friend, a* MR. CARP, *who owns the local candy and stationery store.*

As the lights fade in, MR. BONAPARTE *turns his newspaper.* MR. CARP *is slowly pouring beer from a bottle. He begins to sip it as* SIGGIE, MR. BONAPARTE's *son-in-law, enters from the kitchen. He is barefooted, dressed in an undershirt, trousers and hung-down suspenders. He brings his own beer and glass, which he begins to fill with an expert's eye. In the silence,* MR. CARP *takes a long, cool sip of beer combined with a murmur of relish.*

CARP (*finally*). I don't take it easy. That's my trouble—if I could only learn to take it easy. . . .

SIGGIE. What do you call it now, what you're doing?
CARP. Say, it's after business hours.

SIGGIE. That's a business? A man who runs a candy store is an outcast of the world. Don't even sell *nickel* candies—*penny* candies!

CARP. And your taxicab business makes you higher in the social scale?

SIGGIE. So I'm an outcast too. Don't change the subject. Like my father-in-law here—he's always changing the subject when I get a little practical on him. (*Putting his beer on the table and scratching himself under the arms like a monkey.*) You—I'm talking about you, Mr. Bonaparte.

MR. BONAPARTE (*suddenly shooting out two words*). Ha ha! (*He then resumes his reading.*)

SIGGIE. Every time I talk money, he gives me that horse laugh. Suppose you bought me a cab—I could pay it off by the week.

MR. BONAPARTE (*who talks with an Italian accent*). I don't go in taxicab business.

SIGGIE. I am married to your daughter and when you do this little thing, you do it for her and me together. A cab in two shifts is a big source of profit. Joe takes the night shift. I'm a married man so you don't expect me to take the night shift. (ANNA, SIGGIE's *wife, in a night-gown, pokes her head in at the door.*)

ANNA. Come to bed, Siggie. You'll wake up the whole neighborhood. (ANNA *disappears.*)

SIGGIE. See? I'm a married man! You don't expect me to take the night shift.

MR. BONAPARTE (*having heard this talk for months*). No, Siggie . . . no.

SIGGIE. No, what?

MR. BONAPARTE. No taxicab.

SIGGIE. Don't you wanna help your own family, Foolish? After all, Joe's your own son—he's a man, no kid no more—

MR. BONAPARTE. Tomorrow's twenty-one.

SIGGIE. If he don't work he'll turn into a real bum. Look how late he's staying out at night.

MR. BONAPARTE. I don't expects for Joe to drive taxi.

SIGGIE. He's got to do something. He can drive like a fire engine. Why not?

MR. BONAPARTE. He gonna do something.

SIGGIE. What? Play his violinsky in the backyards?

ANNA (*looking in at the door again*). Come to bed, Siggie! Poppa, don't talk to him so he'll come to bed! (ANNA *disappears again.*)

SIGGIE (*annoyed*). Women! Always buzzing around. (MR. BONAPARTE's *only answer is to turn over the newspaper on the table before him.*)

CARP (*reflectively*). Women . . . the less we have to do with women the better. As Schopenhauer says, "Much ado about nothing . . . the comedy of reproduction." (*He wags his head bitterly.*) Women . . . !

SIGGIE. I'm hungry, but I ain't got the heart to go in the kitchen again. It reminds me of how my wife slaves for this family of crazy wops! A fine future for an intelligent woman!

MR. BONAPARTE. She'sa your wife, but also my daughter. She'sa not so intelligent as you say. Also, *you* are not so intelligent!

SIGGIE. You can't insult me, I'm too ignorant! (ANNA *now comes fully into the room. She is buxom, energetic, good-natured and adenoidal.*)

ANNA. Poppa, why don't you let Siggie come to bed? Looka him, walking around barefoooted!

MR. BONAPARTE. I don't stop him. . . .

SIGGIE. Sure he stops me—he stops me every night. I'm worried. I don't sleep. It's my Jewish disposition. He don't wanna help me out, your old man. He wants me to drive a company cab and submit to the brutalities of the foremen all my life. I could be in a healthy little enterprise for myself, but your old man don't wanna help me out.

ANNA. Why don't you buy Siggie a cab, poppa? You got the cash.

SIGGIE. Buy it for Siggie and Joe.

ANNA. For Siggie and Joe—it don't have to be a new one.

SIGGIE (*after giving his wife a stabbing glance*). Sure, even an old one—the way they recondition them now-a-days—

MR. BONAPARTE. Children, gone to bed.

SIGGIE. Don't tell a lie—how much you got in the bank?

MR. BONAPARTE (*with a smile*). Millions.

SIGGIE. Four thousand?

MR. BONAPARTE. No.

SIGGIE. Three? (MR. BONAPARTE *shakes his head.*) Three? . . .

ANNA. What's your business how much he's got?

SIGGIE. Shut up, Duchess! Am I asking for my health? If I wanna take you out of the kitchen, is that the gratitude I get? You and your father, you get my goat! I'm sore!

ANNA. Come to bed, Siggie.

SIGGIE. "Come to bed, come to bed!" What the hell's so special in bed. (ANNA'S *answer is a warm prolonged giggle.*) It's a conspiracy around here to put me to bed. I'm warning one thing: if matters go from worse to worse, don't ever expect me to support this family, I'm warning!

MR. BONAPARTE (*smiling kindly*). We have-a receive the warning. We are in a conspiracy against you—go to bed. (*He turns back to his newspaper.* SIGGIE *sees he has lost again and now turns on his wife.*)

SIGGIE. Who asked you to stick in your two cents about second-hand cabs? As long as I'm not gonna get it, I'll tell you what I want—a first-class job, fresh from the factory. (*He suddenly swats her on the head with a rolled-up newspaper. She hits him back. He returns her blow.*)

ANNA. Don't be so free with your hands! (*He hits her again. She hits him back.*) You got some nerve, Siggie!

SIGGIE (*hitting her again*). The next time I'll break your neck—I'm super-disgusted with you!

MR. BONAPARTE (*standing up*). Stop this . . .

SIGGIE (*turning to him*). And with you, I'm super-finished! (*Turning back to his wife.*) Sit out here with this Unholy Alliance— I'll sleep alone tonight. (*He starts for the door.* MR. BONAPARTE *puts his arm around* ANNA *who begins to sob.*)

MR. BONAPARTE. Hit your wife in private, not in public!

CARP. A man hits his wife and it is the first step to fascism!

SIGGIE (*to* CARP). What are you talking about, my little prince! I love my wife. You don't stop talking how you hate yours. (*Now to* MR. BONAPARTE.) And as for you,

don't make believe you care!—Do I have to fall on my knees to you otherwise? We wanna raise a family—it's a normal instinct. Take your arm off her.

ANNA (*suddenly moving over to* SIGGIE). That's right, poppa. He can hit me any time he likes.

SIGGIE (*his arm around her*). And we don't want you interfering in our affairs unless you do it the right way!

ANNA. That's right, poppa—you mind your g.d. business! (MR. BONAPARTE *repressing a smile, slowly sits.*)

SIGGIE. In the bed, Duchess.

ANNA (*with a giggle*). Good night.

MR. BONAPARTE *and* MR. CARP. Good night. (*She exits. After a belligerent look at the pair at the table,* SIGGIE *follows her.*)

MR. BONAPARTE (*bursting into hushed laughter*). There'sa olda remark—never interfere in the laws of nature and you gonna be happy. Love! Ha ha!

CARP (*gloomily*). Happy? A famous man remarked in the last century, "Pleasure is negative."

MR. BONAPARTE. I feela good. Like-a to have some music! Hey, where'sa my boy, Joe? (*Looks at his watch; is surprised.*) One o'clock . . . don't come home yet. Hey, he make-a me worry!

CARP. You think you got worries? Wait, you're a young man yet. You got a son, Joe. He practised on his fiddle for ten years? He won a gold medal, the best in the city? They gave him a scholarship in the Erickson Institute? Tomorrow he's twenty-one, yeah?

MR. BONAPARTE (*emphatically*). Yeah!

CARP (*leaning forward and dramatically making his point*). Suppose a war comes? Before you know it, he's in the army!

MR. BONAPARTE. Naw, naw! Whata you say! Naw!

CARP (*wagging his head in imitation*). Look in the papers! On every side the clouds of war—

MR. BONAPARTE. My Joe gotta biga talent. Yesterday I buy-a him present! (*With a dramatic flourish he brings a violin case out of the bottom part of the sideboard.*)

CARP (*as the case is opened.*) It looks like a coffin for a baby.

MR. BONAPARTE (*looking down at the violin in its case*). His teacher help me to picka him.

CARP (*the connoisseur*). Fine, fine—beautiful, fine! A cultural thing!

MR. BONAPARTE (*touching it fondly*). The mosta golden present for his birthday which I give him tonight.

CARP. How much, if I'm not getting too personal, did such a violin cost you?

MR. BONAPARTE. Twelve hundred dollars.

CARP (*shocked*). What?

MR. BONAPARTE. You're surprised of me? Well, I waita for this moment many years.

CARP (*sitting*). Ask yourself a pertinent remark: could a boy make a living playing this instrument in our competitive civilization today?

MR. BONAPARTE. Why? Don't expect for Joe to be a millionaire. He don't need it, to be millionaire. A good life'sa possible—

CARP. For men like us, yes. But nowadays is it possible for a young man to give himself to the Muses? Could the Muses put bread and butter on the table?

MR. BONAPARTE. No millionaire is necessary. Joe love music. Music is the great cheer-up in the language of all countries. I learn that from Joe. (CARP *sighs as* MR. BONAPARTE *replaces the violin in the buffet.*)

CARP. But in the end, as Schopenhauer says, what's the use to try something? For every wish we get, ten remains unsatisfied. Death is playing with us as a cat and her mouse!

MR. BONAPARTE. You make-a me laugh, Mr. Carp. You say life'sa bad. No, life'sa good. Siggie and Anna fight—good! They love—good! You say life'sa bad . . . well, is pleasure for you to say so. No? The streets, winter a' summer—trees, cats—I love-a them all. The gooda boys and girls, they who sing and whistle- -(*Bursts into a moment of gay whistling.*)—very good! The eating and sleeping, drinking wine—very good! I gone around on my wagon and talk to

many people—nice! Howa you like the big buildings of the city?

CARP. Buildings? And suppose it falls? A house fell down last week on Staten Island!

MR. BONAPARTE. Ha ha, you make me laugh, ha ha! (*Now enters* FRANK BONAPARTE, *oldest son of the family, simple, intelligent, observant.*)

MR. BONAPARTE. Hello, Frank.

FRANK. Hello, poppa . . . Mr. Carp . . .

CARP (*nodding*). What's new in the world?

FRANK (*dropping newspapers to the table, but keeping one for himself*). Read 'em and weep. March first tomorrow—spring on the way. Flowers soon budding, birds twittering—south wind . . . Cannons, bombs and airplane raids! Where's Joe? Did you give him the fiddle yet?

MR. BONAPARTE. No, not in yet. Siggie and Anna sleep. Hungry?

FRANK (*beginning to undress—putting his coat on the back of a chair*). No, I'm tired. I'll see you in the morning, before I leave.

CARP. Going away again?

FRANK. South. Tex-tiles. There's hell down there in textiles. (*He sits on the other side of the room and looks at a paper.*)

CARP. I don't begin to understand it—textiles! What's it his business if the workers in tex-tiles don't make good wages!

MR. BONAPARTE. Frank, he fighta for eat, for good life. Why not!

CARP. Foolish!

MR. BONAPARTE. What ever you got ina your nature to do isa not foolish!

CARP (*flipping over the newspaper*). For instance—look: playing baseball isn't foolish?

MR. BONAPARTE. No, if you like-a to do.

CARP. Look! Four or five pages—baseball—tennisball—it gives you an idea what a civilization! You ever seen a baseball game?

MR. BONAPARTE. No.

CARP (*wagging his head*). Hit a ball, catch a ball . . . believe me, my friend—nonsense!

FRANK. Poppa, where did you say Joe was?

MR. BONAPARTE. Don't know—

FRANK. Poppa, you better brace yourself in your chair!

MR. BONAPARTE. What? (FRANK *places the paper before* MR. BONAPARTE. *He reads aloud.*)

FRANK. Looka this, Joe's had a fight. "Flash: Chocolate Drop fails to K.O. new cock-eyed wonder." Take a look at the picture.

CARP. What?

MR. BONAPARTE. What?

FRANK. It's my little brother Joie, or I don't know a scab from a picket!

MR. BONAPARTE. Had a fight? That is foolish —not possible.

FRANK (*pointing with his finger*). There's his name—Bonaparte.

MR. BONAPARTE (*puzzled*). Musta be some other boy. (FRANK *suddenly flips over the newspaper. The others immediately see the reason:* JOE *stands in the entrance, in the shadows.*)

JOE (*in the shadows*). Gee, you're up late. . . .

MR. BONAPARTE. We waita for you. (JOE *slowly moves into the light. His face is bruised and over one eye is a piece of adhesive tape.*)

JOE (*seeing their looks*). I had a fight— a boy in the park—

MR. BONAPARTE. He hit you?

JOE. I hit him.

MR. BONAPARTE. You hurt?

JOE. No. (MR. BONAPARTE *casts a furtive look in the direction of the other men.*)

MR. BONAPARTE. Whata you fight him for?

JOE. Didn't like what he said to me.

MR. BONAPARTE. What he said?

JOE (*evasively*). It's a long story and I'm tired.

MR. BONAPARTE (*trying to break a pause of embarrassment*). I was say to Mr. Carp to-morrow is your birthday. How you like to be so old?

JOE. I forgot about that! I mean I forgot for the last few hours. Where do you think I was? Do you want the truth?

FRANK. Truth is cheap. We bought it for two cents. (*He turns over the paper and shows* JOE *his own face.* JOE *looks at the picture, likes it. General silence.*)

JOE (*finally, belligerently*). Well, what are you going to do about it?

MR. BONAPARTE (*still puzzled*). Abouta what?

JOE (*challengingly*). Tomorrow's my birth-day!

FRANK. What's that got to do with being a gladiator?

JOE (*turning to* FRANK, *with sudden vehemence*). Mind your business! You don't know me—I see you once a year; what do you know about me?

FRANK (*smiling*). You're a dumb kid!

MR. BONAPARTE (*starting to his feet*). Hey, waita one-a minute. What'sa for this excite-a-ment?

JOE (*hotly*). I don't want to be criticized! Nobody takes me serious here! I want to do what I want. I proved it tonight I'm good— I went out to earn some money and I earned! I had a professional fight tonight —maybe I'll have some more.

CARP. You honest to God had a fight?

JOE (*glaring at* CARP). Why not?

FRANK (*to* JOE). No one's criticizin'.

MR. BONAPARTE. That's right.

JOE (*half sheepishly*). I don't know why I got so sore. . . .

FRANK. You're expecting opposition all the time—

MR. BONAPARTE. Sit down, Joe—resta you'self.

JOE. Don't want to sit. Every birthday I ever had I sat around. Now'sa time for standing. Poppa, I have to tell you—I don't like myself, past, present and future. Do you know there are men who have wonder-ful things from life? Do you think they're better than me? Do you think I like this feeling of no possessions? Of learning about the world from Carp's encyclopaedia? Frank don't know what it means—he travels around, sees the world! (*Turning to* FRANK.) You don't know what it means to sit around here and watch the months go ticking by! Do you think that's a life for a boy my age? Tomorrow's my birthday! I change my life!

MR. BONAPARTE. Justa like that?

JOE. Just like that!

FRANK. And what do you do with music?

JOE. Who says I'm married to music? I take a vacation—the notes won't run away!

FRANK. You're a mysterious kid. Where did you learn the fighting game?

JOE. These past two years, all over the city —in the gyms—

MR. BONAPARTE. Hey, Joe, you sounda like crazy! You no gotta nature for fight. You're

musician. Whata you say, heh? Whata you do?

JOE. Let's call it a day.

MR. BONAPARTE. Isa no true whata I say?—

JOE. That's all for tonight. (*His lips tightened, he abruptly exits.*)

MR. BONAPARTE. (*calling after him*). Take a gooda sleep, Joe.

FRANK (*smiling*). It looks like the gold bug has visited our house.

CARP (*sadly*). Fortunes! I used to hear it in my youth—the streets of America is paved with gold. Say, you forgot to give him the present.

MR. BONAPARTE (*slowly, puzzled*). I don'ta know . . . he say he gonna fight. . . .

SLOW FADEOUT

SCENE III

Two months later; MOODY's *office as seen before.*

MOODY *is pacing back and forth in one of his fuming moods. Those present include* LORNA, *stretched out on the couch, blowing cigarette smoke into the air;* TOKIO *sitting quietly on the window sill; and* ROXY GOTTLIEB, *comfortably spread out in the desk chair, wearing a big white panama hat which he seldom removes.*

ROXY. They don't like him. They seen him in five fights already. He's a clever boy, that Bonaparte, and speedy—but he's first-class lousy in the shipping department! I bought a piece of him, so I got a right to say it: a mosquito gives out better! Did you read what he wrote in his column, that Drake? He writes he's a regular "brain trust."

LORNA. What's wrong with that?

ROXY. I'll tell you in a capsule: the people who'll pay to watch a "brain trust" you could fit in a telephone booth! Roxy Gottlieb is telling you!

MOODY. Roxy's right. Joe pulls his punches. Two months already and he don't throw his hands right and he don't throw them enough.

LORNA. Tom, what do you want the boy to do? You surely know by now he's not a slugger. His main asset is his science—he's a student.

ROXY (*loftily*). Excuse me, Miss Moon. In the prizefight ring the cash customer don't look for stoodents. Einstein lives in a college—a wonderful man in *his* line! Also, while I think of it, a woman's place is in the hay, not in the office!

MOODY (*indignantly*). Where do you come off to make a remark like that?

LORNA (*standing up*). At the moment a woman's place is in the bar—see you later. (*She looks at the others with a peculiar smile and exits.* MOODY *stares at* ROXY *who realizes he has said the wrong thing.*)

MOODY. I'm worried about that boy!

TOKIO. I'd trust him, Tom. Joe knows his own needs, as he says. Don't ask him to change his style. A style is best when it's individual, when it comes out of the inner personality and the lay of the muscles and the set of the bones. That boy stands a chance to make the best lightweight since Benny Simon.

ROXY. On *your* nose!

TOKIO. He's got one of the best defenses I ever seen. And speedy as the wind.

MOODY. But he won't fight!

ROXY. A momma doll gives out better!

TOKIO. He's a peculiar duck—I want him thinking he's the best thing in shoe leather.

MOODY. He thinks so now.

TOKIO. I don't like to contradict you, Tom, but he don't. It's seventy-five percent front. If you want the goods delivered you have to treat him delicate, gentle—like a girl.

ROXY. Like a girl? Why didn't you say so before?

MOODY. No, Roxy, not you—you just treat him like a human being.

TOKIO. I think we can begin the build-up now.

MOODY. A road tour?

TOKIO. I'd like to take him around the Middle West, about fifteen bouts.

ROXY (*answering a look from* MOODY). I didn't say no. But will he cooperate?

TOKIO. As soon as I find the password.

MOODY. What's the password to make this kid go in and slug—that's the problem. (*There is a knock at the door.* MOODY *calls.*) Yes? (*The door opens and* MR. BONAPARTE *stands there hesitantly.*)

MR. BONAPARTE (*timidly*). My name is Joe Bonaparte's father. I come-a to see my son's new friends.

MOODY (*expansively*). Come in, sit down, Mr. Bonaparte.

ROXY (*sitting comfortably*). Take a seat.

MR. BONAPARTE. Am I interrupt?

MOODY. Not at all.

ROXY. What's the matter with your boy?

TOKIO (*to* MR. BONAPARTE). This is Mr. Moody and Mr. Gottlieb.

MR. BONAPARTE (*sitting*). Good afternoon.

MOODY. We were just discussing your son.

MR. BONAPARTE. I please to hear. I like find out froma you how's this boxer business for Joe. Whata good in it for him.

MOODY. Your Joe's a very clever fighter.

ROXY. Can you take it? We want to make your boy famous—a millionaire, but he won't let us—won't cooperate. How do you like it?

MR. BONAPARTE. Why? Whatta he do?

ROXY (*going over and facing the old man in a lecturing position*). I'll ask *you*. What does he do? What does he do that's right? *Nothing!* We offer him on a gold platter! Wine, women and song, to make a figure of speech. We offer him *magnitudes!* . . .

MR. BONAPARTE (*waiting*). Yes—?

MOODY. But he won't fight.

MR. BONAPARTE (*puzzled*). He'sa fighta for you, no?

ROXY. You're right—no! Your boy's got unexplored possibilities—*unexplored!* But you can't make a purse out of somebody's ear.

MOODY (*trying to counteract* ROXY's *volubility*). My colleague is trying to say that Joe keeps holding back in the ring.

MR. BONAPARTE. Holda back?

TOKIO. He nurses his self—

MOODY. He keeps holding back—

TOKIO. His defense is brilliant—

MOODY. Gorgeous—!

ROXY. But where's the offense? You take but you can't give. Figure it out—where would you be in a traffic jam? You know how to reverse—but to shift in second or high? —nothing!

MR. BONAPARTE (*quietly to* ROXY). Hey, you talka too much—nobody's contradicta you.

ROXY (*after a momentary setback*). "Everybody'sa contradicta me!" Even you, and I never met you before. (*With a reproachful glance he retires to the desk where he sits and sulks.*)

MR. BONAPARTE (*singling out* TOKIO *as a man to whom he can speak*). Who are you?

TOKIO. Your son's trainer. . . .

MR. BONAPARTE. You interest to helpa my boy?

TOKIO (*respectfully*). Very much. . . .

MR. BONAPARTE. Me too. Maybe not so as plan by these-a gentleman here. I don't say price fight-sa no good for Joe. Joe like-a to be fame, not feel ashame. . . .

TOKIO. Is Joe afraid of his hands?

MR. BONAPARTE. I don't know. You tella me what'sa what . . . I don't know price fight. His hand coulda get hurt?

MOODY. Every fighter hurts his hands. Sometimes they break—

TOKIO. They heal up in no time.

ROXY (*flaring out*). What's so special about hands? I suppose your kid plays piano!

MR. BONAPARTE. Coulda get hurt? Coulda break?

ROXY. So what?

MR. BONAPARTE (*up on his feet*). Hey, you! I don't like-a you! You no interest in my boy! (*Proudly.*) My boy'sa besta violin' in New York!

MOODY (*suddenly sickened*). What . . . ?

MR. BONAPARTE. Yes, play the violin!

MOODY. That's it! . . .

ROXY (*anguished by this stupidity*). If I had hair I'd tear it out! Five hundred fiddlers stand on Broadway and 48th Street, on the corner, every day, rain or shine, hot or cold. And your boy dares—! (*Turning to* MOODY.) How do you like it? (*He waves his hands in despair and retires to the desk, where he sits in fuming disgusted silence.*)

MOODY (*repressing a feeling of triumph*). Your boy's afraid of his hands because he fiddles?

MR. BONAPARTE. Yes, musta be!

TOKIO. Why did you come and tell us this?

MR. BONAPARTE. Because I like-a to help my boy. I like-a for him to try himself out. Maybe thisa better business for him. Maybe not. He mus' try to find out, to see whata he want . . . I don't know. Don't help Joe to tell him I come here. Don't say it. (*He slowly walks to the door.*)

MOODY. That means you won't stand in his way?

MR. BONAPARTE. My boy coulda break his hand? Gentleman, I'ma not so happy as you . . . no! (*He slowly exits.*)

MOODY (*joyously*). I'm beginning to see the light! Joe's mind ain't made up that the fist is mightier than the fiddle.

ROXY (*bouncing up and down*). I'll make up his mind. For the money that's involved I'd make Niagara Falls turn around and go back to Canada.

TOKIO. Don't try to bully him into anything.

ROXY. In Roxy Gottlieb he met his match.

MOODY (*explosively*). What the hell's the matter with you, Roxy! Sit down a minute! (ROXY *sits.*)

MOODY. As I see it, the job is to handle him gently, to make him see how much we prize him—to kill his doubts with goodness.

ROXY. I got it: the password is honey! . . .

MOODY. Right! The Middle West tour is on! Tokio goes along to build up a real offensive. I take care of the newspapers here. Chris', I thought it was something serious! I'm getting to feel like 1928 again. Call it intuition: I feel like the Resurrection. (*He gets up and begins to stroll about.*) Once we're out of the tunnel, with thirty bouts behind us—

ROXY. If you hear a noise, it's my mouth watering— (*The telephone rings.* MOODY *answers.*)

MOODY. Hello? . . . Yeah . . . I think he'll win— (*Hangs up.*) Who do you think that was? (*Imitating.*) "Fuseli is speaking." Eddie Fuseli!

ROXY. Fuseli? What's he want?

MOODY. Will Joe win against Vincenti Tuesday. Tokio, from now on it's your job.

TOKIO. I got faith in the boy.

MOODY (*to* ROXY). I have to ask one thing—when Joe comes over from the gym let me do the talking.

TOKIO. And don't mention music! (LORNA *enters.*)

LORNA. Shh! Here's Joe. (JOE BONAPARTE *enters the office. Immediately* MOODY *and* ROXY *put on their softest kid gloves. Their methods of salesmanship will shortly become so apparent that both* JOE *and* LORNA *become suspicious.*)

MOODY (*slowly circling around*). Glad to see you, Joe. Joe, you remember in reference to what we were speaking about yesterday? Well . . . we had several friends on the long distance phone. We're booking fifteen out of town bouts for you. Tough ones, too.

ROXY. Tonight I'm calling my Chicago connections.

MOODY. We talked it over with Tokio and he says—well, tell him what you said, Tokio—tell him the truth.

TOKIO. I think you got a wonderful future.

MOODY (*to* TOKIO). Name the names, Tokio.

TOKIO. Well, I said Benny Simon—as good as Simon, I said.

MOODY. Tokio's gonna work with you—help you develop a right—

ROXY. And a left! What'sa right without a left?

MOODY. Tokio thinks that when he brings you back you'll be a contender for Number One.

JOE (*a little defensively*). Really? . . .

MOODY. But *you* have to help *us* help *you*.

ROXY. Could Webster say it better?

MOODY (*softly singing a siren song, his arms around* JOE's *shoulder*). This job needs gorgeous concentration. All your time and thoughts, Joe. No side lines, no side interests—

JOE (*defensively*). I don't go out with girls.

MOODY. You're in the fighting game. It's like being a priest—your work comes first. What would you rather do than fight?

JOE (*defensively*). I don't know what you mean.

MOODY (*carefully picking his words*). Some boys, for instance, like to save their looks. They'd practically throw the fight to keep their nose intact.

JOE (*smiling wryly*). My looks don't interest me. (LORNA *is listening with rapt attention.*)

MOODY (*still singing the siren song*). Then what's holding you back, Joe? You can tell me, Joe. We've set up housekeeping together, Joe, and I want you to tell me if you can't cook a steak—it don't matter. We're married anyway. . . .

JOE (*uneasily*). Who's being put to bed?

MOODY. What do you mean?

JOE. I don't like this seduction scene. (*To* TOKIO) What are they after?

TOKIO. They think you're afraid of your hands.

MOODY. Are you?

JOE. Half . . .

TOKIO. Why?

ROXY (*bouncing up*). Tell the truth!

JOE. What truth?

MOODY (*holding back* ROXY *with a look*). Are you afraid your hands'll bust, Joe? (JOE *remains silent*). What's a busted hand to a fighter? You can't go in and do your best if you're scared of your mitts . . . can you? You tell me. . . .

JOE. No. . . .

MOODY. Whyn't you give up outside ideas, Joe?

ROXY (*suddenly, in a loud voice to* TOKIO). You shoulda seen that bunch of musicians on 48th Street before. Fiddlers, drummers, cornetists—not a dime in a car-load. Bums in the park! Oh, excuse me, Tom, I was just telling Tokio— (JOE *is now aware that the others know of the violin. Now he is completely closed to them.* MOODY *sees this. He says to* ROXY:)

MOODY (*wrathfully*). What would you like to say, my fine-feathered friend?

ROXY (*simulating bewilderment*). What's the matter? What happened? (*Receiving no answer, he looks around several times and adds, with a shrug:*) I think I'll run across the street and pick up an eight-cylinder lunch.

MOODY. Sprinkle it with arsenic. Do that for me, for me, sweetheart!!

ROXY (hurt). That's a fine remark from a friend. (He haughtily exits.)

JOE. What do you want, Mr. Moody?

MOODY. At the moment, nothing. I'm puffed out. See you tomorrow over the gym.

JOE. Maybe I won't be there. I might give up fighting as a bad job. I'm not over-convinced it's what I want. I can do other things. . . .

TOKIO. I'll see you tomorrow at the gym, Joe. (JOE looks at both the men, says nothing, exits.) That Mr. Gottlieb is a case. See you later.

MOODY (not looking up). Okay. (TOKIO exits. LORNA and MOODY are alone. She blows cigarette smoke to the ceiling. MOODY puts his feet up on the desk and leans back wearily.)

MOODY (snorting through his nostrils). The password is honey!

LORNA. What was that all about? (the telephone rings.)

MOODY (of the ringing bell). If that's for me, tear it up, I ain't in, not even for God.

LORNA (answering). Hello? . . . (Putting her hand on the mouthpiece). It's Mrs. God —your wife. (MOODY makes a grimace of distaste but picks up the phone and puts on a sweet voice.)

MOODY. Yes, Monica, darling. . . . Yeah . . . you and your support. . . . You're gonna fifty-buck me to death! . . . Monica, if I had fifty bucks I'd buy myself a big juicy coffin—what?—so throw me in jail. (He hangs up the phone.) Bitch! That'll be number three. She means it too.

LORNA. What was that scene with Bonaparte?

MOODY. Sweetheart, the jig is up! Believe it or not, Bonaparte's a violinist. Maybe he was on the radio. I don't know what the hell he was. His old man came here and told us. His mitts are on his mind. You can't do a thing with a nut like that.

LORNA. Won't he give up the violin?

MOODY. You heard him stalling. This is the end, Lorna. It's our last chance for a decent life, for getting married—we have to make that kid fight! He's *more* than a meal ticket—he's everything we want and need from life! (LORNA goes over and slaps him on the back.)

LORNA. Pick up your chin, little man.

MOODY. Don't Brisbane me, Lorna. I'm licked. I'm tired. Find me a mouse hole to crawl in. . . .

LORNA. Why don't you ask me when you want something? You got the brains of a flea. Do you want Bonaparte to fight?

MOODY. Do I wanna see tomorrow?

LORNA. I'll make him fight.

MOODY. How?

LORNA. How? . . . I'm "a tramp from New-ark," Tom. . . . I know a dozen ways. . . .

SLOW FADEOUT

SCENE IV

A few nights later.

JOE and LORNA *sit on a bench in the park. It is night. There is carousel music in the distance. Cars ride by in front of the boy and girl in the late spring night. Out of sight a traffic light changes from red to green and back again throughout the scene and casts its colors on the faces of the boy and girl.*

LORNA. Success and fame! Or just a lousy living. You're lucky you won't have to worry about those things. . . .

JOE. Won't I?

LORNA. Unless Tom Moody's a liar.

JOE. You like him, don't you?

LORNA (after a pause). I like him.

JOE. I like how you dress. The girls look nice in the summer time. Did you ever stand at the Fifth Avenue Library and watch those girls go by?

LORNA. No, I never did. *(Switching the subject.)* That's the carousel, that music. Did you ever ride on one of those?

JOE. That's for kids.

LORNA. Weren't you ever a kid, for God's sake?

JOE. Not a happy kid.

LORNA. Why?

JOE. Well, I always felt different. Even my name was special—Bonaparte—and my eyes . . .

LORNA. I wouldn't have taken that too serious. . . . *(There is a silent pause.* JOE *looks straight ahead.)*

JOE. Gee, all those cars . . .

LORNA. Lots of horses trot around here. The rich know how to live. You'll be rich. . . .

JOE. My brother is an organizer for the C.I.O.

LORNA. What's that?

JOE. If you worked in a factory you'd know. Did you ever work?

LORNA *(with a smile).* No, when I came out of the cocoon I was a butterfly and butterflies don't work.

JOE. All those cars . . . whizz, whizz. *(Now turning less casual.)* Where's Mr. Moody tonight?

LORNA. He goes up to see his kid on Tuesday nights. It's a sick kid, a girl. His wife leaves it at her mother's house.

JOE. That leaves you free, don't it?

LORNA. What are you hinting at?

JOE. I'm thinking about you and Mr. Moody.

LORNA. Why think about it? I don't. Why should you?

JOE. If you belonged to me I wouldn't think about it.

LORNA. Haven't you got a girl?

JOE. No.

LORNA. Why not?

JOE *(evasively).* Oh . . .

LORNA. Tokio says you're going far in the fighting game.

JOE. Music means more to me. May I tell you something?

LORNA. Of course.

JOE. If you laugh I'll never speak to you again.

LORNA. I'm not the laughing type.

JOE. With music I'm never alone when I'm alone— Playing music . . . that's like saying, "I am man. I belong here. How do you do, World—good evening!" When I play music nothing is closed to me. I'm not afraid of people and what they say. There's no war in music. It's not like the streets. Does this sound funny?

LORNA. No.

JOE. But when you leave your room . . . down in the street . . . it's war! Music can't help me there. Understand?

LORNA. Yes.

JOE. People have hurt my feelings for years. I never forget. You can't get even with people by playing the fiddle. If music shot bullets I'd like it better—artists and people like that are freaks today. The world moves fast and they sit around like forgotten dopes.

LORNA. You're loaded with fireworks. Why don't you fight?

JOE. You have to be what you are—!

LORNA. Fight! See what happens—

JOE. Or end up in the bughouse!

LORNA. God's teeth! Who says you have to be one thing?

JOE. My nature isn't fighting!

LORNA. Don't Tokio know what he's talking about? Don't Tom? Joe, listen: be a fighter! Show the world! If you made your fame and fortune—and you can—you'd be anything you want. Do it! Bang your way to the lightweight crown. Get a bank account. Hire a great doctor with a beard—get your eyes fixed—

JOE. What's the matter with my eyes?

LORNA. Excuse me, I stand corrected. (*After a pause.*) You get mad all the time.

JOE. That's from thinking about myself.

LORNA. How old are you, Joe?

JOE. Twenty-one and a half, and the months are going fast.

LORNA. You're very smart for twenty-one and a half "and the months are going fast."

JOE. Why not? I read every page of the Encyclopædia Britannica. My father's friend, Mr. Carp, has it. A shrimp with glasses had to do something.

LORNA. I'd like to meet your father. Your mother dead?

JOE. Yes.

LORNA. So is mine.

JOE. Where do you come from? The city is full of girls who look as if they never had parents.

LORNA. I'm a girl from over the river. My father is still alive—shucking oysters and bumming drinks somewhere in the wilds of Jersey. I'll tell you a secret: I don't like you.

JOE (*surprised*). Why?

LORNA. You're too sufficient by yourself . . . too inside yourself.

JOE. You like it or you don't.

LORNA. You're on an island—

JOE. Robinson Crusoe . . .
LORNA. That's right—"me, myself, and I." Why not come out and see the world?

JOE. Does it seem that way?

LORNA. Can't you see yourself?

JOE. No. . . .

LORNA. Take a bird's-eye view; you don't know what's right or wrong. You don't know what to pick, but you won't admit it.

JOE. Do you?

LORNA. Leave me out. This is the anatomy of Joe Bonaparte.

JOE. You're dancing on my nose, huh?

LORNA. Shall I stop?

JOE. No.

LORNA. You're a miserable creature. You want your arm in *gelt* up to the elbow. You'll take fame so people won't laugh or scorn your face. You'd give your soul for those things. But every time you turn your back your little soul kicks you in the teeth. It don't give in so easy.

JOE. And what does your soul do in its perfumed vanity case?

LORNA. Forget about me.

JOE. Don't you want—?

LORNA (*suddenly nasty*). I told you forget it!

JOE (*quietly*). Moody sent you after me—a decoy! You made a mistake, Lorna, for two reasons. I make up my own mind to fight. Point two, he doesn't know you don't love him—

LORNA. You're a fresh kid.

JOE. In fact he doesn't know anything about you at all.

LORNA (*challengingly*). But you do?

JOE. This is the anatomy of Lorna Moon: she's a lost baby. She doesn't know what's right or wrong. She's a miserable creature who never knew what to pick. But she'd never admit it. And I'll tell you why you picked Moody!

LORNA. You don't know what you're talking about.

JOE. Go home, Lorna. If you stay, I'll know something about you. . . .

LORNA. You don't know anything.

JOE. Now's your chance—go home!

LORNA. Tom loves me.

JOE (*after a long silence, looking ahead*). I'm going to buy a car.

LORNA. They make wonderful cars today. Even the lizzies—

JOE. Gary Cooper's got the kind I want. I saw it in the paper, but it costs too much—fourteen thousand. If I found one second-hand—

LORNA. And if you had the cash—

JOE. I'll get it—

LORNA. Sure, if you'd go in and really fight!

JOE (*in a sudden burst*). Tell your Mr. Moody I'll dazzle the eyes out of his head!

LORNA. You mean it?

JOE (*looking out ahead*). Those cars are poison in my blood. When you sit in a car and speed you're looking down at the world. Speed, speed, everything is speed—nobody gets me!

LORNA. You mean in the ring?

JOE. In or out, nobody gets me! Gee, I like to stroke that gas!

LORNA. You sound like Jack the Ripper.

JOE (*standing up suddenly*). I'll walk you back to your house—your hotel, I mean.

(LORNA *stands.* JOE *continues.*) Do you have the same room?

LORNA (*with a sneaking admiration*). You're a fresh kid!

JOE. When you're lying in his arms tonight, tell him, for me, that the next World's Champ is feeding in his stable.

LORNA. Did you really read those Brittannia books?

JOE. From A to Z.

LORNA. And you're only twenty-one?

JOE. And a half.

LORNA. Something's wrong somewhere.

JOE. I know. . . . (*They slowly walk out as*)

FADEOUT

SCENE V

The next week.

It is near midnight in the dining room of the Bonaparte home. An open suitcase rests on the table. SIGGIE *is pouring samples of wine for* LORNA MOON. *He himself drinks appreciatively. To one side sits* MR. BONAPARTE *silently, thoughtfully, watchfully—pretending to read the newspaper.*

SIGGIE. I was fit to be knocked down with a feather when I heard it. I couldn't believe it until I seen him fight over at the Keystone last week. You never know what somebody's got in him—like the man with germs—suddenly he's down in bed with a crisis! (JOE *enters with an armful of clothes which he begins to pack in the suitcase.*)

LORNA. Joe's road tour will do him lots of good. (ANNA *enters and takes off an apron. Silence, in which* SIGGIE *and* LORNA *sip their wine.*)

ANNA. How do you like that wine, Miss Moon? My father makes better wine than any Eyetalian in New York. My father knows everything—don't you, poppa? (*With a faint smile,* MR. BONAPARTE *shrugs his shoulders.*)

SIGGIE. We're thinking of sending the old man to a leper colony. . . .

ANNA. Don't my husband say funny things? Tell her what you told the janitor Tuesday, Siggie.

SIGGIE. Never mind, never mind.

ANNA. You know how I met Siggie? He was a United Cigar Store clerk and I walked in for a pack of Camels and the first thing you know he said something funny. It was raw, so I can't say it. He had me laughing from the first. Seven years and I haven't stopped laughing yet. (*She laughs loudly, pleasurably.*) This will be the first time Joe ever went traveling. Was you ever out of New York, Miss Moon?

LORNA. Oh, many times.

ANNA. That's nice. Far?

LORNA. California, Detroit, Chicago. I was an airplane hostess for two months.

ANNA. That's nice—it's a real adventure. I'd like to fly.

SIGGIE. Stay on the ground! Fly! What for? Who do you know up there? Eagles?

ANNA. It must be a wonderful way to see life.

LORNA (*drinking*). I've seen life in all its aspects. (MR. BONAPARTE *stands up with a smile.* LORNA's *eyes follow him as he exits.*)

LORNA (*to* JOE). I think your father left because he don't like me.

JOE. He likes you.

ANNA. My father likes everybody. He's a very deep man. My father has more friends than any man alive. But best of all he likes his horse, Dolly, who drives the fruit wagon. My father can't sit still on Sunday afternoon—he has to go see what that horse is doing. (*Her eyes catch sight of the suitcase.*) Joe, you don't know how to pack. (*She starts over to assist him.*)

SIGGIE (*querulously*). Rest the feet awhile, Duchess.

ANNA (*explaining her move*). He don't know how to pack. (*Beginning to rearrange the suitcase.* MR. BONAPARTE *returns and hands* JOE *a sweater.*)

MR. BONAPARTE. You forget your good sweater.

JOE. Thanks. (MR. BONAPARTE *sits.* JOE *looks at him sideways.*)

ANNA. When you get out to Chicago, buy yourself some new underwear, Joe. I hear everything's cheaper in Chicago. Is that right, Miss Moon?

LORNA (*after taking another drink*). Chicago? I don't know. I was there only one night—I got news that night my mother died. As a matter of fact, she killed herself.

ANNA. That's very sad.

LORNA. No, my father's an old drunk son-of-a-bitch. Did you ask me about my father?

MR. BONAPARTE (*who has been listening intently*). Yes. . . .

LORNA. Twice a week he kicked my mother's face in. If I let myself go I'd be a drunkard in a year.

ANNA. My father never said one bad word to my mother in her whole lifetime. And she was a big nuisance right up till the day she died. She was more like me, more on the stout side. Take care of your health, Joe, when you're out there. What's better than health?

LORNA (*turning to* MR. BONAPARTE, *with whom she is self-conscious*). The question is, do you like me or do you not?

MR. BONAPARTE (*with a faint smile*). Yes. . . .

LORNA. Your family is very cute— Now do you like me?

MR. BONAPARTE. Yes. . . .

LORNA. Why do you look at me that way?

MR. BONAPARTE. I don't look special. You gonna travel on those train with my son?

LORNA. God's teeth, no! I'm a friend of his manager's, that's all. And a friend of Joe's, too.

MR. BONAPARTE. You are in favor for my son to prizefight? (JOE *looks at his father sideways and exits.*)

LORNA. Certainly. Aren't you?

MR. BONAPARTE. Joe has a dream many year to be superior violin'. Was it boyhood thing? Was it real? Or is this real now? Those are-a my question, Miss Moon. Maybe you are friend to my son. Then I aska you, look out for him. Study him. Help him find what'sa right. Tell me, Miss Moon, when you find out. Help Joe find truthful success. Will you do it for me?

LORNA. I'll be glad to keep my eye on him. (JOE *enters with slippers, which he puts in bag.*)

ANNA (*to* JOE). You could stand some new shirts, too.

SIGGIE. Listen, pop, I'm a natural man and I don't like wise guys. Joe went in the boxing game 'cause he's ashamed to be poor. That's his way to enter a little enterprise. All other remarks are so much alfalfa! (JOE *locks the bag.*)

ANNA (*taking the wine glass from* SIGGIE's *hand*). Drunk as a horse fly!

JOE. It's getting late and the train won't wait.

SIGGIE (*standing up*). My God is success. Need I say more? I'm prouda you, Joe. Come home a champ. Make enough dough to buy your sister's boy friend a new cab. Yes, boys and girls, I'm looking in that old crystal ball and I see strange and wonderful events! Yazoo!

ANNA (*giggling*). Drunk as a horse fly!

JOE (*to* SIGGIE). You can't drive us down to the station in this condition.

SIGGIE. What condition?

ANNA. You're drunk, stupid.

SIGGIE. Shut the face, foolish! Just because I don't hold in my nerves she thinks I'm drunk. If you hold in your nerves you get ulcers. (*To* JOE.) Get your "chapow" and let's go. Or don't you want me to drive you down?

JOE. No.

SIGGIE. I should worry—my cab's in the garage anyway! (*Suddenly he sits.*)

JOE. We'd better start. . . .

LORNA (*to* MR. BONAPARTE). I'd like to have another talk with you some time.

MR. BONAPARTE. Come any time in the evening. You are a very lovely girl. (MR. CARP *stands in the doorway.*) Here is Mr. Carp to say good-bye.

SIGGIE. Come in, my little prince.

CARP (*coming in and shaking hands with* JOE). I wish you good luck in every undertaking.

JOE (*uneasily, because his father is looking at him*). Thanks.

MR. BONAPARTE (*introducing* CARP). Miss Moon, my neighbor, Mr. Carp.

CARP. A pleasure to meet you.

LORNA. Hello. (MR. BONAPARTE *brings the violin case from its hiding place in the buffet.*)

MR. BONAPARTE. Joe, I buy you this some time ago. Don't give cause I don't know whatta you gonna do. Take him with you now. Play for yourself. It gonna remember you your old days of musical life. (JOE *puts down the suitcase and picks up the violin. He plucks the strings, he tightens one of them. In spite of the tension his face turns soft and tender.*)

LORNA (*watching intently*). We better not miss the train—Tokio's waiting.

MR. BONAPARTE (*of violin*). Take him with you, Joe.

JOE. It's beautiful. . . .

MR. BONAPARTE. Practise on the road. (JOE *abruptly turns and with the violin exits.*

The others listen, each standing in his place, as rich violin music comes from the other room. JOE *returns. There is silence as he places the violin on the table in front of his father.*)

JOE (*in a low voice*). Return it, poppa.

ANNA (*hugging* JOE). Have a good trip, Joey.

CARP. Eat in good restaurants. . . . (*There is silence: the* FATHER *and* SON *look at each other. The others in the room sense the drama between the two. Finally:*)

JOE. I have to do this, poppa.

MR. BONAPARTE (*to* JOE). Be careful fora your hands.

JOE. Poppa, give me the word—

MR. BONAPARTE. What word?

JOE. Give me the word to go ahead. You're looking at yesterday—I see tomorrow. Maybe you think I ought to spend my whole life here—you and Carp blowing off steam.

MR. BONAPARTE (*holding himself back*). Oh, Joe, shut your mouth!

JOE. Give me the word to go ahead!

MR. BONAPARTE. Be careful fora your hands!

JOE. I want you to give me the word!

MR. BONAPARTE (*crying out*). *No! No word!* You gonna fight? All right! Okay! But I don't gonna give no word! No!

JOE. That's how you feel?

MR. BONAPARTE. That'sa how I feel! (MR. BONAPARTE's *voice breaks and there is nothing for father and son to do but to clutch each other in a hasty embrace. Finally* MR. BONAPARTE *disentangles himself and turns away.* JOE *abruptly grabs up his suitcase and exits.* LORNA *follows, stopping at the door to look back at* MR. BONAPARTE. *In the ensuing silence* ANNA *looks at her father and shakes her head.* SIGGIE *suddenly lumbers to his feet and sounds off like a chime.*)

SIGGIE. Gong gong gong gong!

ANNA. Gee, poppa . . .

SIGGIE. Come to bed, Anna. . . . Anna-banana . . . (SIGGIE *exits.*)

ANNA. Gee, poppa . . . (*She touches her father sympathetically.*)

MR. BONAPARTE (*without turning*). Gone to bed, Anna. . . . (ANNA *slowly exits.* MR. BONAPAPTE *now slowly comes back to the table and looks down at the violin.*)

CARP (*seating himself slowly*). Come, my friend . . . we will have a nice talk on a cultural topic. (*Looking at the violin.*)

You'll work around a number of years before you make it up, the price of that fiddle. . . . (MR. BONAPARTE *stands looking down at the violin.*)

CARP (*sadly*). Yes, my friend, what is man? As Schopenhauer says, and in the last analysis . . .

SLOW FADEOUT

ACT TWO

SCENE I

Six months later. Present in the corner of a gymnasium are ROXY, MOODY, LORNA *and* TOKIO. *They are looking off right, watching* JOE BONAPARTE *work out with a partner. From off right come the sounds of typical gym activities: the thud of boxing gloves, the rat-a-tat of the punching bag, and from time to time the general bell which is a signal for rest periods. Tacked on the tin walls are an ad for Everlast boxing equipment, boxing "card" placards, a soiled American flag, some faded exit signs.*

The group watches silently for several seconds after the lights fade in. A BOXER, *wiping his perspiring body with a towel, passes from left to right and looks back at* LORNA'S *legs. As* ROXY *watches, his head moves to and fro in the rhythm of* JOE'S *sparring off stage.* ROXY *nods his head in admiration.*

ROXY. Tokio. I gotta give the devil his dues: in the past six months you done a noble job!

TOKIO (*calling off*). With the left! A long left, Joe! . . .

LORNA (*looking off*). Joe's a very good-looking boy. I never quite noticed it before. (*The general bell sounds; the boxing din off stage stops.*)

MOODY (*rubbing his hands enthusiastically*). "Let it rain, let it pour! It ain't gonna rain where we're headed for!"

ROXY. I'm tickled to death to see the canary birds left his gloves.

TOKIO. He's the king of all he surveys.

MOODY. Boy, oh, boy, how he surprised them in the Bronx last night! . . . But one thing I can't explain—that knockout he took in Philly five weeks ago.

TOKIO. That night he was off his feed, Tom. Where do you see speed like that? That's style, real style—you can't tag him. And he's giving it with both hands.

MOODY. You don't have to sell me his virtues—I'm sold. Nevertheless, he got tagged in Philly.

TOKIO. Here's what happened there: we run into some man when we're leaving the hotel. Joe goes pale. I ask him what it is. "Nothing," he says. But I see for myself—a man with long hair and a violin case. When we turn the corner, he says, "He's after me," he says. As if it's cops and robbers! (*The general bell sounds; the fighting din begins again.*)

ROXY. A kidnapper?

LORNA. Don't be a fool. He was reminded . . .

ROXY. Speak when spoken to, Miss Moon!

MOODY (*moodily*). And when he got in the ring that night, he kept his hands in his pockets?

TOKIO. Yeah. I didn't mention this before—it's not important.

MOODY. But it's still a danger—

TOKIO. No. No.

MOODY. But anyway, we better get him away from his home. We can't afford no more possible bad showings at this stage of the game. No more apparitions, like suddenly a fiddle flies across the room on wings! (*The group again intently watches* JOE *off stage.*)

MOODY. Ooh! Did you see that? He's packing a real Sunday punch in that right. (*Calling off.*) Hit 'im, Joe, hit 'im! (*As an indistinct answer comes back.*) Ha ha, looka that, hahaha . . . (*Now turning to* TOKIO.) What's your idea of a match with Lombardo?

TOKIO. Can you get it?

MOODY. Maybe.

TOKIO. Get it.

MOODY. Sure?

TOKIO. It's an easy win, on points at least. (*During the last few lines a thin dark man has entered. His dark hair is grayed at the temples, an inarticulate look in his face. He is* EDDIE FUSELI, *a renowned gambler and gunman.*)

EDDIE FUSELI (*approaching the group*). Hello.

ROXY (*nervously*). Hello, Eddie.

MOODY (*turning*). I haven't seen you for a dog's age, Fuseli.

EDDIE (*pointing off left*). You got this certain boy—Bonaparte. I like his looks. American born?

ROXY. Right from here.

EDDIE (*watching* JOE *off*). Like a cat, never off his position. He appeals to me. (*To* MOODY.) They call you the Brown Fox. What's your opinion of this boy?

MOODY (*coolly, on guard*). Possibilities. . . .

EDDIE (*to* TOKIO). What's your idea?

TOKIO. Tom said it.

EDDIE. Could he get on top?

MOODY (*as above*). I can't see that far ahead. I don't read palms.

EDDIE. Could I buy a piece?

MOODY. No.

EDDIE (*coolly*). Could I?

MOODY. No!

EDDIE (*with a certain tenderness*). I like a good fighter. I like to see you after, Tom. (*Of* LORNA.) This your girl?

LORNA (*pertly*). I'm my mother's girl.

EDDIE (*with a small mirthless laugh*). Ha ha—that's a hot one. (*He coolly drifts out of the scene on his cat's feet. The general bell sounds. The din ceases.*)

LORNA. What exhaust pipe did he crawl out of?

ROXY. I remember this Eddie Fuseli when he came back from the war with a gun. He's still got the gun and he still gives me goose pimples!

MOODY. That Fuseli's a black mark in my book. Every once in a while he shoots across my quiet existence like a roman candle!

LORNA. Sell or don't sell. But better be careful, that guy's tough! (*A* FIGHTER, *robed, hooded with towel, passes across: A* GAMBLING TYPE *passes in the opposite direction. Both look at* LORNA's *legs.*)

MOODY. Give a rat like that a finger and you lose a hand before you know it!

TOKIO. Did you know Joe bought a car this morning?

ROXY. What kinda car?

TOKIO. A Deusenberg.

MOODY. One of those fancy speed wagons?

TOKIO (*agreeing*). It cost him five grand, second-hand.

MOODY (*flaring up*). Am I a step-child around here? I'm glad you tell me now, if only outa courtesy!

ROXY (*indignantly*). Whatta you keep a think like that incognito for?

MOODY. He drives like a maniac! That time we drove to Long Beach? I almost lost my scalp! We can't let him drive around like that! Boy, he's getting a bushel of bad habits! We gotta be careful. (*The general bell sounds again; the fighting din stops.*)

MOODY. Here's the truth: our boy can be the champ in three easy lessons—Lombardo, Fulton, the Chocolate Drop. But we gotta be careful!

LORNA. Here he comes. (JOE *enters in bathrobe, taking off his headgear, which* TOKIO *takes from him.*)

MOODY (*completely changing his tone*). You looked very good in there, Joe. You're going swell and I like it. I'd work more with that long left if I were you.

JOE. Yes, I was speaking to Tokio about that. I feel my form's improving. I like to work. I'm getting somewhere—I feel it better every day.

LORNA. Happy?

JOE (*looking at her intently*). Every day's Saturday!

ROXY (*officiously*). Say, what's this I hear you bought a Deusenberg?

JOE. What's your objection—I might have some fun?

ROXY. I got my wampum on you. I like to know your habits. Ain't I permitted? (JOE *is about to retort hotly when* MOODY *gently takes his arm in an attempt to soothe him.*)

MOODY. Wait a minute, Joe. After all we have your welfare at heart. And after all a Deusenberg can go one fifty per— (EDDIE FUSELI *appears above, unseen by the others. He listens.*)

JOE. Who'd want to drive that fast?

MOODY. And since we're vitally interested in your future—

JOE (*shaking off* MOODY's *arm and saying what is really on his mind*). If you're vitally interested in my future, prove it! Get me some fights—fights with contenders, not with dumb-bunny club fighters. Get me some main bouts in the metropolitan area!—

MOODY (*losing his temper*). For a kid who got kayoed five weeks ago, your mouth is pretty big! (*The general bell sounds; the din begins.*)

JOE. That won't happen again! And how about some mention in the press? Twenty-six bouts—no one knows I'm alive. This isn't a vacation for me—it's a profession! I'm staying more than a week. Match me up against real talent. You can't go too fast for me. Don't worry about autos!

MOODY. We can go too fast! You're not so good!

JOE (*with a boyish grin*). Look at the records! (JOE *abruptly exits.* TOKIO *follows him, first giving the others a glance.*)

MOODY. Boy, oh, boy, that kid's changing!

ROXY. He goes past my head like a cold wind from the river!

LORNA. But you're gettin' what you want—the contender for the crown!

MOODY. I wish I was sure.

ROXY. Frankenstein! (EDDIE FUSELI *saunters down to the others.*)

EDDIE. I thought it over, Tom. I like to get a piece of that boy.

MOODY (*angrily*). I thought it over, too—not for sale. In fact I had a visitation from Jehovah. He came down on the calm waters and He said, "Let there be unity in the ownership."

EDDIE (*with a dead face*). I had a visit, too. He come down in the bar and He ate a pretzel. And He says, "Eddie Fuseli, I like you to buy a piece!"

MOODY (*trying to delay the inevitable*). Why not see me in my office tomorrow?

EDDIE. It's a cheap office. I get depressed in that office.

MOODY (*finally*). I can't make any guarantees about the boy.

EDDIE. How do you mean it, Tom?

MOODY. I don't know what the hell he'll do in the next six months.

ROXY. Eddie, it's like flap-packs—up and down—you don't know which side next!

EDDIE (*with his small mirthless laugh*). Ha ha, that's a good one. You oughta be on the radio.

MOODY. No, it's a fact—

ROXY. We had enough headaches already. He's got a father, but how!

EDDIE. Don't want him to fight?

ROXY. His father sits on the kid's head like a bird's nest! (ROXY *puts his hand on* EDDIE's *arm.*)

EDDIE. Take your hand off. (ROXY *hastily withdraws.*) Let the boy decide. . . .

MOODY. If you buy in?

EDDIE. Let the boy decide.

MOODY. Sure! But if he says no— (*Before* MOODY *can finish* JOE *enters.* EDDIE *whirls around and faces* JOE, *getting his cue from the others. Curiously,* EDDIE *is almost embarrassed before* JOE. *The bell sounds; the din stops.*)

MOODY. Joe, this is Eddie Fuseli. He's a man around town—

EDDIE (*facing* JOE, *his back to the others*). With good connections—

MOODY. He wantsa buy a piece of you—

EDDIE (*whirling around*). I will tell him myself. (*Turning back to* JOE; *with quiet intense dignity*). I'm Eyetalian too—Eyetalian born, but an American citizen. I like to buy a piece of you. I don't care for no profit. I could turn it back to—*you* could take my share. But I like a good fighter; I like a good boy who could win the crown. It's the in-ter-est of my life. It would be a proud thing for me when Bonaparte could win the crown like I think he can.

MOODY (*confidently*). It's up to you, Joe, if he buys in.

EDDIE (*wooingly*). Some managers can't give you what you need—

MOODY. Don't say that!

EDDIE. *Some* managers can't! I'll see you get good bouts . . . also press notices . . . I know how. You're a boy who needs that. You decide . . . (*There is a pause;* JOE'S *eyes flit from* LORNA *to the others and back to* EDDIE.)

JOE. Not my half.

EDDIE. Not your half.

JOE. As long as Mr. Fuseli doesn't mix in my private life . . . cut it up any way you like. Excuse me, I got a date with Miss Deusenberg. (*The others silently watch* JOE *exit.*)

EDDIE. A date with who?

MOODY (*snorting*). Miss Deusenberg!

ROXY. An automobile. It gives you an idea what a boy—"Miss Deusenberg"!

EDDIE. How do you like it, Tom? Big bills or little bills?

MOODY. Don't think you're buying in for an apple and an egg.

EDDIE. Take big bills—they're new, they feel good. See you in that office tomorrow. (*The bell clangs off stage.* EDDIE *starts off, but abruptly turns and faces* ROXY *whom he inwardly terrifies.*)

EDDIE. It's a trick you don't know, Roxy: when a bird sits on your head and interferes with the championship, you shoot him off. All kinds of birds. You be surprised how fast they fall on the ground. Which is my intention in this syndicate. (*He smiles thinly and then moves out of the scene like a cat.*)

MOODY. I don't like that!

ROXY. I'm not so happy myself at the present time. How do you like it with our boy for gratitude? He leaves us here standing in our brevities!

LORNA. What makes you think you're worthy of gratitude?

MOODY (*to* LORNA). For pete's sake, pipe down! Are you with us or against us?

ROXY (*haughtily, to* MOODY). Take my advice, Tom. Marry her and the first year give her a baby. Then she'll sit in the corner and get fat and sleepy, and not have such a big mouth! Uncle Roxy's telling you!

LORNA (*to* ROXY). Couldn't you keep quiet about the father to that gunman? Go home and let your wife give *you* a baby!

ROXY. A woman shouldn't interfere—

MOODY. Peace, for chri' sake, peace! Lorna, we're in a bad spot with Joe. He's getting hard to manage and this is the time when everything's gotta be right. I'm seeing Lombardo's manager tomorrow! Now that gunman's on my tail. You have to help me. You and I wanna do it like the story books, "happy ever after"? Then help me.

LORNA. How?

MOODY. Go after the boy. Keep him away from his folks. Get him away from the buggies—

LORNA. How?

MOODY (*impatiently*). You know how.

ROXY. Now you're talking.

LORNA (*pointing* to ROXY.) You mean the way I see it on his face?

MOODY. For crying out loud! Where do you come off to make a remark like that?

LORNA. You expect me to sleep with that boy?

MOODY. I could tear your ears off for a remark like that!

ROXY (discreetly). I think I'll go grab a corn-beef sandwich. (He exits.)

MOODY (after silence). Are you mad?

LORNA (tight-lipped). No.

MOOD (seductively). I'm not a bad guy. Lorna. I don't mean anything bad. . . . All right, I'm crude—sometimes I'm worried and I'm crude. (The bell clangs; the boxing din stops.)

MOODY. But what the hell, my heart's in the right place. . . . (Coming behind her and putting his arms around her as she looks ahead.) Lorna, don't we both want that sun to come up and shine on us? Don't we? Before you know it the summer'll be here. Then it's the winter again, and it's another year again . . . and we're not married yet. See? . . . See what I mean? . . .

LORNA (quietly). Yes. . . .

MOODY (beaming, but with uncertainty). That sounds like the girl I used to know.

LORNA. I see what you mean. . . .

MOODY (worried underneath). You're not still mad?

LORNA (briefly). I'm not mad. (But she abruptly cuts out of the scene, leaving MOODY standing there.)

MOODY (shaking his head). Boy, I still don't know anything about women! . . .

MEDIUM FADEOUT

SCENE II

A few nights later. LORNA *and* JOE *sit on the same park bench.*

JOE. Some nights I wake up—my heart's beating a mile a minute! Before I open my eyes I know what it is—the feeling that someone's standing at my bed. Then I open my eyes . . . it's gone—ran away!

LORNA. Maybe it's that old fiddle of yours.

JOE. Lorna, maybe it's you. . . .

LORNA. Don't you ever think of it any more —music?

JOE. What're you trying to remind me of? A kid with a Buster Brown collar and a violin case tucked under his arm? Does that sound appetizing to you?

LORNA. Not when you say it that way. You said it different once. . . .

JOE. What's on your mind, Lorna?

LORNA. What's on yours?

JOE (simply). You. . . . You're real for me —the way music was real.

LORNA. You've got your car, your career— what do you want with me?

JOE. I develop the ability to knock down anyone my weight. But what point have I made? Don't you think I know that? I went off to the wars 'cause someone called me a name—because I wanted to be two other guys. Now it's happening. . . . I'm not sure I like it.

LORNA. Moody's against that car of yours.

JOE. I'm against Moody, so we're even.

LORNA. Why don't you like him?

JOE. He's a manager! He treats me like a possession! I'm just a little silver mine for him—he bangs me around with a shovel!

LORNA. He's helped you—

JOE. No, Tokio's helped me. Why don't you give him up? It's terrible to have just a Tuesday-night girl. Why don't you belong to me every night in the week? Why don't you teach me love? . . . Or am I being a fool?

LORNA. You're not a fool, Joe.

JOE. I want you to be my family, my life— Why don't you do it, Lorna, why?

LORNA. He loves me.

JOE. I love you!

LORNA (*treading delicately*). Well . . . Anyway, the early bird got the worm. Anyway, I can't give him anguish. I . . . I know what it's like. You shouldn't kick Moody around. He's poor compared to you. You're alive, you've got yourself—I can't feel sorry for you!

JOE. But you don't love him!

LORNA. I'm not much interested in myself. But the thing I like best about you . . . you still feel like a flop. It's mysterious, Joe. It makes me put my hand out. (*She gives him her hand and he grasps it.*)

JOE. I feel very close to you, Lorna.

LORNA. I know. . . .

JOE. And you feel close to me. But you're afraid—

LORNA. Of what?

JOE. To take a chance! Lorna, darling, you won't let me wake you up! I feel it all the time—you're half dead, and you don't know it!

LORNA (*half smiling*). Maybe I do. . . .

JOE. Don't smile—don't be hard-boiled!

LORNA (*sincerely*). I'm not.

JOE. Don't you trust me?

LORNA (*evasively*). Why start what we can't finish?

JOE (*fiercely*). Oh, Lorna, deep as my voice will reach—*listen!* Why can't you leave him? Why?

LORNA. Don't pull my dress off—I hear you.

JOE. Why?

LORNA. Because he needs me and you don't—

JOE. That's not true!

LORNA. Because he's a desperate guy who always starts out with two strikes against him. Because he's a kid at forty-two and you're a man at twenty-two.

JOE. You're sorry for him?

LORNA. What's wrong with that?

JOE. But what do *you* get?

LORNA. I told you before I don't care.

JOE. I don't believe it!

LORNA. I can't help that!

JOE. What did he ever do for you?

LORNA (*with sudden verve*). Would you like to know? He loved me in a world of enemies, of stags and bulls! . . . and I loved him for that. He picked me up in Friskin's hotel on 39th Street. I was nine weeks behind in rent. I hadn't hit the gutter yet, but I was near. He washed my face and combed my hair. He stiffened the space between my shoulder blades. Misery reached out to misery—

JOE. And now you're dead.

LORNA (*lashing out*). I don't know what the hell you're talking about!

JOE. Yes, you do. . . .

LORNA (*withdrawing*). Ho hum. . . . (*There is silence. The soft park music plays in the distance. The traffic lights change.* LORNA *is trying to appear impassive.* JOE *begins to whistle softly. Finally* LORNA *picks up his last note and continues; he stops. He picks up her note, and after he whistles a few phrases she picks him up again. This whistling duet continues for almost a minute. Then the traffic lights change again.*)

LORNA (*beginning in a low voice*). You make me feel too human, Joe. All I want is peace and quiet, not love. I'm a tired old lady, Joe, and I don't mind being what you call "half dead." In fact it's what I like. (*Her voice mounting higher.*) The twice I was in love I took an awful beating and I don't want it again! (*Now half crying.*) I want you to stop it! Don't devil me, Joe. I beg you, don't devil me . . . let me alone. . . . (*She cries softly.* JOE *reaches out and takes her hand; he gives her a handkerchief which she uses.*)

LORNA (*finally*). That's the third time I cried in my life. . . .

JOE. Now I know you love me.

LORNA (*bitterly*). Well . . .

JOE. I'll tell Moody.

LORNA. Not yet. Maybe he'd kill you if he knew.

JOE. Maybe.

LORNA. Then Fuseli'd kill him. . . . I guess I'd be left to kill myself. I'll tell him. . . .

JOE. When?

LORNA. Not tonight.

JOE. Swiftly, do it swiftly—

LORNA. Not tonight.

JOE. Everything's easy if you do it swiftly.

LORNA. He went up there tonight with six hundred bucks to bribe her into divorce.

JOE. Oh . . .

LORNA (*sadly*). He's a good guy, neat all over—sweet. I'll tell him tomorrow. I'd like a drink.

JOE. Let's drive over the Washington Bridge.

LORNA (*standing*). No, I'd like a drink.

JOE (*standing and facing her*). Lorna, when I talk to you . . . something moves in my heart. Gee, it's the beginning of a wonderful life! A man and his girl! A warm living girl who shares your room. . . .

LORNA. Take me home with you.

JOE. Yes.

LORNA. But how do I know you love me?

JOE. Lorna . . .

LORNA. How do I know it's true? You'll get to be the champ. They'll all want you, all the girls! But I don't care! I've been undersea a long time! When they'd put their hands on me I used to say, "This isn't it! This isn't what I mean!" It's been a mysterious world for me! But, Joe, I think you're it! I don't know why, I think you're it! Take me home with you.

JOE. Lorna!

LORNA. Poor Tom . . .

JOE. Poor Lorna! (*The rest is embrace and kiss and clutching each other.*)

SLOW FADEOUT

SCENE III

The next day: the office. LORNA *and* MOODY *are present. She has a hangover and is restless.*

MOODY. Boy, you certainly double-scotched yourself last night. What's the idea, you making a career of drinking in your old age? Headache?

LORNA. No.

MOODY. I won't let you walk alone in the park any more, if you do that.

LORNA (*nasty in spite of her best intentions*). Well, if you stayed away from your wife for a change . . .

MOODY. It's pretty late to bring that up, isn't it? Tuesday nights—

LORNA. I can't help it—I feel like a tramp. I've felt like a tramp for years.

MOODY. She was pretty friendly last night.

LORNA. Yeah? Did you sleep with her?

MOODY. What the hell's the matter with you, Lorna? (*He goes to her. She shrugs away from him.*)

LORNA. Keep off the grass! (MOODY *gives her a quizzical look, goes back to his desk and from there gives her another quizzical look.*)

MOODY. Why do you drink like that?

LORNA (*pointing to her chest*). Right here—there's a hard lump and I drink to dissolve it. Do you mind?

MOODY. I don't mind—as long as you keep your health.

LORNA. Aw, Christ!—you and your health talks!

MOODY. You're looking for a fight, dolly-girl!

LORNA. And you'll give it?

MOODY (*with a grin*). No, I'm feeling too good.

LORNA (*sitting wearily*). Who left you a fortune?

MOODY. Better. Monica's seen the light. The truth is she's begun to run around with a retired brewer and now *she* wants the divorce.

LORNA. Good, now she can begin paying *you*.

MOODY. She goes to Reno in a few months.

LORNA (*moodily*). I feel like a tramp. . . .

MOODY. That's what I'm telling you— In a few months we'll be married! (*He laughs with pleasure.*)

LORNA. You still want to marry me? Don't I feel like an old shoe to you?

MOODY (*coming to her*). Honest, you're so dumb!

LORNA (*touched by his boyishness*). You're so sweet. . . .

MOODY. And flash!—I signed Lombardo today! They meet six weeks from tonight.

LORNA. Goody. . . .

MOODY (*disappointed by her flippant reaction, but continuing*). I'm still not sure what he'll show with Lombardo. But my present worry is this: help me get that kid straight. Did you speak to him about the driving last night?

LORNA. I didn't see him. . . .

MOODY. It's very important. A Lombardo win clinches everything. In the fall we ride up to the Chocolate's door and dump him in the gutter! After that . . . I don't like to exaggerate—but the kid's primed! And you and I—Lorna baby, we're set. (*Happily.*) What do you think of that?

LORNA (*evasively*). You draw beautiful pictures. (*A knock sounds on the door.*)

MOODY. Come in. (SIGGIE *enters, dressed in cab driver's garb.*)

SIGGIE. Hello, Miss Moon.

LORNA. Hello. You know Mr. Moody.

SIGGIE (*to* MOODY). Hello.

MOODY. What can we do for you?

SIGGIE. For me you can't do nothing. I'm sore. I'm here against my better instinct. (*Taking a roll of money from his pocket and slapping it on the desk.*) He don't want it—no part of it! My father-in-law don't want it. Joe sent it up—two hundred bucks —enough to choke a horse—but he don't want it!

MOODY. Why?

LORNA. That's nice he remembers his folks.

SIGGIE. Listen, I got a father-in-law nothing's nice to him but feeding his horse and giving a laugh and slicing philosophical salami across the table! He's sore because Joe don't come home half the time. As a matter of fact, ain't he suppose to come to sleep no more? The old man's worried.

MOODY. That's not my concern.

SIGGIE. I can't see what it's such a worry. A boy gets in the higher brackets—what's the worry? He's got enough clothes now to leave three suits home in the closet. (*Turning to* LORNA.) It won't hurt if he sends me a few passes—tell him I said so.

LORNA. How's the wife?

SIGGIE. The Duchess? Still laughing.

LORNA. When you getting that cab?

SIGGIE. Do me a favor, Miss Moon—tell him I could use this wad for the first instalment.

LORNA. I'll tell him. Tell Mr. Bonaparte I saw Joe last night. He's fine.

MOODY. I'll see you get some passes.

SIGGIE. Thanks, thanks to both of you. Adios. (*He exits.*)

LORNA. He and his wife are crazy for each other. Married . . . they throw each other around, but they're like love birds. Marriage is something special. . . . I guess you have to deserve it.

MOODY. I thought you didn't see Joe last night.

LORNA. I didn't, but why worry his father?

MOODY. The hell with his father.

LORNA. The hell with you!

MOODY (*after a brooding pause*). I'll tell you something, Lorna. I'm not overjoyed the way Joe looks at you.

LORNA. How's he look?

MOODY. As if he saw the whole island of Manhattan in your face, and I don't like it.

LORNA. You thought of that too late.

MOODY. Too late for what?

LORNA. To bawl me out.

MOODY. Who's bawling you out?

LORNA. You were about to. Or warn me. I don't need warnings. (*Coasting away from the argument.*) If you saw Joe's father you'd like him.

MOODY. I saw him.

LORNA. If you knew him you'd like him.

MOODY. Who wantsa like him? What do I need him for? I don't like him and I don't like his son! It's a business—Joe does his work, I do mine. Like this telephone—I pay the bill and I use it!

LORNA. He's human. . . .

MOODY. What're we fighting about?

LORNA. We're fighting about love. I'm trying to tell you how cynical I am. Tell the truth, love doesn't last—

MOODY (*suddenly quietly serious*). Everything I said about *Joe*—the opposite goes for you. Love lasts . . . if you want it to. . . . I want it to last. I need it to last. What the hell's all this struggle to make a living for if not for a woman and a home? I don't kid myself. I know what I need. I need you, Lorna.

LORNA. It has to end. . . .

MOODY. What has to end?

LORNA. Everything.

MOODY. What're you talking about?

LORNA. I oughta burn. I'm leaving you. . . .

MOODY (*with a sick smile*). That's what you think.

LORNA (*not looking at him*). I mean it.

MOODY (*as above*). I mean it too.

LORNA (*after looking at him for a moment*). You can't take a joke?

MOODY (*not knowing where he stands*). It all depends. . . . I don't like a joke that pushes the blood down in my feet.

LORNA (*coming to him and putting her arms around his neck*). That's true, you're pale.

MOODY. Who's the man?

LORNA (*heartsick, and unable to tell him the truth*). There's no man, Tom . . . even if there was, I couldn't leave you. (*She looks at him, unable to say more.*)

MOODY (*after a pause*). How about some lunch? I'll buy it. . . .

LORNA (*wearily*). Where would I put it, Tom?

MOODY (*impulsively*). In your hat! (*And suddenly he embraces her roughly and kisses her fully and she allows it.* JOE *walks into the office,* EDDIE FUSELI *behind him. They break apart.*)

JOE. The first time I walked in here that was going on. It's one long duet around here.

MOODY. Hello.

EDDIE (*sardonically*). Hello, Partner. . . . (LORNA *is silent and avoids* JOE'S *looks.*)

JOE. How about that fight with Lombardo?

MOODY. Six weeks from tonight.

JOE. He's gonna be surprised.

MOODY (*coolly*). No one doubts it.

JOE (*sharply*). I didn't say it was doubted!

MOODY. Boy, everyone's off his feed today. It started with the elevator boy—next it's Lorna—now it's you! What are *you* sore about?

LORNA (*trying to turn the conversation; to* JOE). Siggie was here looking for you. Your father's worried—

JOE. Not as much as my "manager" worries me.

MOODY. I don't need you to tell me how to run my business. I'll book the matches—

JOE. That doesn't worry me.

MOODY. But you and your speeding worries me! First it's music, then it's motors. Christ, next it'll be girls and booze!

JOE. It's girls already.

LORNA. Joe—

JOE (*bitterly*). Certainly! By the dozens!

EDDIE. Haha—that's a hot one. Don't ask me which is worst—women or spiders.

LORNA. Siggie left this money—your father won't take it. Siggie says buy him a cab— (JOE *takes the money.*)

EDDIE. Your relative? I'll get him a cab. (*To* MOODY.) How about a flock of bouts for Bonaparte over the summer?

MOODY (*bitterly*). All he wants—practice fights—to make him a better "artiste."

EDDIE. That is what we like. (JOE *is looking at* LORNA.)

MOODY. "We?" Where do *I* come in?

EDDIE. You push the buttons, the *right* buttons. I wanna see Bonaparte with the crown.

MOODY (*sarcastically*). Your concern touches me deep in my heart!

EDDIE. What's the matter, Tom? You getting tired?

MOODY (*coolly*). I get tired, don't you?

EDDIE. Don't get tired, Tom . . . not in a crucial time.

MOODY. Get him to give up that Deusenberg.

EDDIE (*after looking at* JOE). That's his fun. . . .

MOODY. His fun might cost your crown.

JOE (*suddenly, to* LORNA). Why did you kiss him?

MOODY (*to* JOE). It's about time you shut your mouth and minded your own goddam business. Also, that you took some orders.

JOE (*suddenly savage*). Who are you, God?

MOODY. Yes! I'm your maker, you cock-eyed gutter rat! Outa sawdust and spit I made you! I own you—without me you're a blank! Your insolence is gorgeous, but this is the end! I'm a son of a gun! What're you so superior about?

EDDIE. Don't talk so quick, Tom. You don't know . . .

MOODY. I wouldn't take the crap of this last six eight months from the President himself! Cut me up in little pieces, baby—but not me!

EDDIE (*quietly*). You could get cut up in little pieces.

MOODY (*retiring in disgust*). Sisst!

EDDIE. You hear me?

MOODY (*from his desk*). You wanna manage this boy? Help yourself—do it! I'll sell my piece for half of what it's worth. You wanna buy?

EDDIE. You are a funny man.

MOODY. Gimme twenty thousand and lemme out. Ten, I'll take ten. I got my girl. I don't need crowns or jewels. I take my girl and we go sit by the river and it's everything.

JOE. What girl?

MOODY. I'm not on speaking terms with you! (*To* EDDIE.) Well?

EDDIE. It would be funny if your arms got broke.

JOE. Wait a minute! Lorna loves me and I love her.

MOODY (*after looking from* JOE *to* LORNA *and back*). Crazy as a bat! (*He laughs.*)

JOE (*frigidly*). Is it so impossible?

MOODY. About as possible as hell freezes over. (*He and* JOE *simultaneously turn to* LORNA.)

JOE. Tell him. . . .

LORNA (*looking* JOE *in the face*). I love Tom. Tell him what? (JOE *looks at her intently. Silence.* JOE *then turns and quietly exits from the office.* MOODY *shakes his head with a grin.*)

MOODY. Eddie, I take everything back. I was a fool to get sore—that boy's a real nutsy-Fagan! (*He offers his hand.* EDDIE *looks at it and then viciously slaps it down.*)

EDDIE (*repressing a trembling voice*). I don't like no one to laugh at that boy. You call a boy like that a rat? An educated boy? What is your idea to call him cock-eyed? When you do it in front of me, I say, "Tom don't like himself" . . . for Bonaparte is a good friend to me . . . . you're a clever manager for him. That's the only reason I take your slop. Do your business, Tom. (*To* LORNA.) And that goes for you, too! No tricks, Miss Moon! (*He slowly exits.* MOODY *stands there thoughtfully.* LORNA *moves to the couch.*)

MOODY. I'm a son of a gun!

LORNA. I feel like I'm shot from a cannon.

MOODY. Why?

LORNA. I'm sorry for him.

MOODY. Why? Because he's a queer?

LORNA. I'm not talking of Fuseli. (*Suddenly* LORNA'S *eyes flood with tears.* MOODY *takes her hand, half sensing the truth.*)

MOODY. What's wrong, Lorna? You can tell me....

LORNA. I feel like the wrath of God.

MOODY. You like that boy, don't you?

LORNA. I love him, Tom.

SLOW FADEOUT

SCENE IV

Six weeks later.

A dressing room before the Lombardo fight. There are a couple of rubbing tables in the room. There are some lockers and a few hooks on which hang pieces of clothing. A door to the left leads to the showers; a door to the right leads to the arena.

As the lights fade in, MR. BONAPARTE *and* SIGGIE *are sitting to one side, on a long wooden bench.* TOKIO *is fussing around in a locker. A fighter,* PEPPER WHITE, *hands already bandaged, is being rubbed down by his trainer-manager,* MICKEY. *Throughout the scene is heard the distant Roar of* THE CROWD *and the clanging of the bell.*

MR. BONAPARTE (*after a silence of intense listening*). What is that noise?

SIGGIE. That's the roar of the crowd.

MR. BONAPARTE. A thousand people?

SIGGIE. Six thousand.

PEPPER WHITE (*turning his head as he lies on his belly*). Nine thousand.

SIGGIE. That's right, nine. You're sitting under nine thousand people. Suppose they fell down on your head? Did you ever think of that? (*The outside door opens;* EDDIE FUSELI *enters. The distant bell clangs.* EDDIE *looks around suspiciously, then asks* TOKIO:)

EDDIE. Where's Bonaparte?

TOKIO. Still with the newspapermen.

EDDIE (*unpleasantly surprised*). He's what?

TOKIO. Tom took him upstairs—some sports writers.

EDDIE. A half hour before a fight? What is Moody trying to do?

TOKIO. Tom's the boss.

EDDIE. Looka, Tokio—in the future you are gonna take your orders from me! (*Pointing to* SIGGIE *and* MR. BONAPARTE.) Who is this?

TOKIO. Joe's relatives.

EDDIE (*going over to them*). Is this his father?

MR. BONAPARTE (*somberly*). Yes, thisa his father.

SIGGIE. And this is his brother-in-law. Joe sent passes up the house. We just got here. I thought it was in Coney Island—it's lucky I looked at the tickets. Believe it or not, the old man never seen a fight in his life! Is it human?

EDDIE (*coldly*). Shut your mouth a minute! This is The Arena—Bonaparte is fighting a good man tonight—

SIGGIE. Ahh, that Lombardo's a bag of oats!

EDDIE. When Bonaparte goes in there I like him to have one thing on his mind—fighting! I hope you understand me. An' I don't like to find you here when I return! I hope you understand that.... (*After a full glance at them* EDDIE *gracefully exits.*)

SIGGIE. That's a positive personality!

TOKIO. That's Eddie Fuseli.

SIGGIE. Momma-mia! No wonder I smelled gun powder! (*Turning to* MR. BONAPARTE.) Pop, that's a paradox in human behavior:

he shoots you for a nickel—then for fifty bucks he sends you flowers!

TOKIO (*referring to the distant bell*). That's the next bout.

SIGGIE (*to* MR. BONAPARTE). Come on, we don't wanna miss the whole show.

MR. BONAPARTE. I waita for Joe.

SIGGIE. You heard what Fuseli said—

MR. BONAPARTE (*with somber stubbornness*). I gonna wait!

SIGGIE. Listen, pop, you—

MR. BONAPARTE (*with sudden force*). *I say I gonna wait!!*

SIGGIE (*handing* MR. BONAPARTE *a ticket*). Ticket. (*Shrugging.*) Good-bye, you're letting flies in! (SIGGIE *exits jauntily.* MR. BONAPARTE *silently watches* TOKIO *work over the fighter's materials. A* SECOND *comes in, puts a pail under the table where* TOKIO *hovers, and exits.* PEPPER WHITE, *his head turned, watches* MR. BONAPARTE *as he hums a song.*)

PEPPER. Oh, Sweet Dardanella, I love your harem eyes,
Oh, Sweet Dardanella, I'm a lucky fellow to get such a prize. . . .
(*To* MR. BONAPARTE.) So you're Bonaparte's little boy, Buddy? Why didn't you say so before? Come over and shake my hand. (MR. BONAPARTE *does so.*)

PEPPER. Tell Bonaparte I like to fight him.

MR. BONAPARTE. Why?

PEPPER. I like to beat him up.

MR. BONAPARTE (*naïvely, not amused*). Why? You don't like him?

PEPPER. Don't kid me, Buddy! (*A* CALL BOY *looks in at the door.*)

CALL BOY. Pepper White! Ready, Pepper White! (CALL BOY *exits.* PEPPER WHITE *slips off the table and begins to change his shoes.*)

PEPPER (*to* MR. BONAARTE). When I get back I'll explain you all the ins and outs. (*A* SECOND *enters, takes a pail from* MICKEY *and exits.* LORNA *enters.*)

PEPPER (*indignantly*). Who told girls to come in here?!

LORNA. Modest? Close your eyes. Is Moody . . . ? (*Suddenly seeing* MR. BONAPARTE.) Hello, Mr. Bonaparte!

MR. BONAPARTE (*glad to see a familiar face*). Hello, hello, Missa Moon! Howa you feel?

LORNA. What brings you to this part of the world?

MR. BONAPARTE (*somberly*). I come-a to see Joe. . . .

LORNA. Why, what's wrong?

MR. BONAPARTE (*with a slow shrug*). He don't come-a to see me. . . .

LORNA. Does he know you're here?

MR. BONAPARTE. No. (LORNA *looks at him sympathetically.*)

LORNA (*finally*). It's a three-ring circus, isn't it?

MR. BONAPARTE. How you mean?

LORNA. Oh, I mean you . . . and him . . . and other people . . .

MR. BONAPARTE. I gonna see how he fight.

LORNA. I owe you a report. I wish I had good news for you, but I haven't.

MR. BONAPARTE. Yes, I know . . . he gotta wild wolf inside—eat him up!

LORNA. You could build a city with his ambition to be somebody.

MR. BONAPARTE (*sadly, shaking his head*). No . . . burn down! (*Now the outside door is thrust open—the distant bell clangs.* JOE *enters, behind him* MOODY *and* ROXY. JOE *stops in his tracks when he sees* LORNA *and his father together—the last two persons in the world he wants to see now. His hands are already bandaged, a bathrobe is thrown around his shoulders.*)

JOE. Hello, poppa. . . .

MR. BONAPARTE. Hello, Joe. . . .

JOE (*turning to* TOKIO). Throw out the girls —this isn't a hotel bedroom!

MOODY. That's no way to talk!

JOE (*coldly*). I talk as I please!

MOODY (*angrily*). The future Mrs. Moody—

JOE. I don't want her here!

LORNA. He's right, Tom. Why fight about it? (*She exits.*)

JOE (*to* MOODY). Also, I don't want to see writers again before a fight; it makes me nervous!

ROXY (*softly, for a wonder*). They're very important, Joe—

JOE. *I'm* important! My mind must be clear before I fight. I have to think before I go in. Don't you know that yet?

ROXY (*suddenly*). Yeah, we know—you're a stoodent—you gotta look in your notes.

JOE. What's funny about that? I do, *I do!!*

ROXY (*retreating*). So I said you do! (PEPPER WHITE *comes forward, about to exit; to* MOODY.)

PEPPER. How 'bout a bout with Napoleon?

MOODY. On your way, louse!

PEPPER (*with a grin*). Pickin' setups? (JOE *suddenly turns and starts for* PEPPER. TOKIO *quickly steps in between the two boys.*)

TOKIO. Save it for the ring! (*The two fighters glare at each other.* JOE *slowly turns and starts back for the table.*)

PEPPER. You think he'll be the champ? Where'd you ever read about a cock-eye champ? (JOE *spins around, speeds across the room—*PEPPER *is on the floor!* MICKEY *now starts for* JOE. TOKIO *starts for* MICKEY. PEPPER *gets up off the floor and finds himself occupied with* MOODY. *For a moment the fight is general.* EDDIE FUSELI *enters. All see him. The fighting magically stops on the second.*)

EDDIE. What'sa matter? Cowboys and Indians? (*To* PEPPER.) Out! (MICKEY *and* PEPPER *sullenly exit.*)

EDDIE (*to* MOODY). I'm lookin' for you! You're a manager and a half! You and your fat friend! (*Meaning* ROXY.) You think this boy is a toy?

JOE. Eddie's the only one here who understands me.

MOODY. Who the hell wantsa understand you! I got one wish—for Lombardo to give you the business! The quicker he taps you off tonight, the better! You gotta be took

down a dozen pegs! I'm versus you! Completely versus!

EDDIE (*quietly, to* MOODY). Moody, your brains is in your feet! This is how you handle a coming champ, to give him the jitters before a bout? Go out and take some air! . . . (*Seeing* EDDIE's *quiet deadliness,* MOODY *swallows his wrath and exits;* ROXY *follows with pursed lips.*)

EDDIE. Lay down, Joe—take it easy. (JOE *sits on a table.*)

EDDIE. Who hurt you, Joe? Someone hurt your feelings?

JOE. Everything's all right.

EDDIE. Tokio, I put fifty bucks on Bonaparte's nose for you. It's my appreciation to you. . . .

TOKIO. Thanks.

EDDIE (*of* MR. BONAPARTE). Whatta you want me to do with him?

JOE. Leave him here.

EDDIE. Tell me if you want something. . . .

JOE. Nothing.

EDDIE. Forget that Miss Moon. Stop lookin' down her dress. Go out there and kill Lombardo! Send him out to Woodlawn! Tear his skull off! . . . as I know Bonaparte can do it! (EDDIE *gives* MR. BONAPARTE *a sharp look and exits. There is silence intensified by the distant clang of the bell and the muted roar of* THE CROWD. TOKIO *looks over at* MR. BONAPARTE *who has been silently seated on the bench all this time.*)

JOE (*not quite knowing what to say*). How is Anna, poppa?

MR. BONAPARTE. Fine.

JOE. Siggie watching the fights?

MR. BONAPARTE. Yes. . . .

JOE. You look fine. . . .

MR. BONAPARTE. Yes, feela good. . . .

JOE. Why did you send that money back? (*There is no answer.*) Why did you come here? . . . You sit there like my conscience. . . .

MR. BONAPARTE. Why you say so?

JOE. Poppa, I have to fight, no matter what you say or think! This is my profession! I'm out for fame and fortune, not to be different or artistic! I don't intend to be ashamed of my life!

MR. BONAPARTE (*standing up*). Yeah, I understanda you. . . .

JOE. Go out and watch the fights.

MR. BONAPARTE (*somberly*). Yeah . . . you fight. Now I know . . . is'a too late for music. The men musta be free an' happy for music . . . not like-a you. Now I see whatta you are . . . I give-a you every word to fight . . . I sorry for you. . . . (*Silence. The distant roar of* THE CROWD *climbs up and falls down; the bell clangs again.*)

TOKIO (*gently*). I'll have to ask you to leave, Mr. Bonaparte. . . .

MR. BONAPARTE (*holding back his tears*). Joe . . . I hope-a you win every fight. (MR. BONAPARTE *slowly exits. As he opens and closes the door the roar of* THE CROWD *swells up for an instant.*)

TOKIO. Lay down, Joe. There's five minutes left to tune you up.

JOE (*in a low voice*). That's right, tune me up. . . . (JOE *stretches out on his stomach and* TOKIO's *busy hands start up the back of his legs.*)

TOKIO (*working with steady briskness*). I never worried less about a boy . . . in my life. You're a real sweetheart. . . . (*Suddenly* JOE *begins to cry in his arms.* TOKIO *looks down, momentarily hesitates in his work—then slowly goes ahead with his massaging hands. The* BOY *continues to shake with silent sobs. Again the bell clangs in the distance.*)

TOKIO (*in a soft caressing voice*). You're getting good, honey. Maybe I never told you that before. I seen it happen before. (*Continuing the massaging.*) It seems to happen sudden—a fighter gets good. He gets easy and graceful. He learns how to save himself—no energy wasted . . . he slips and slides—he travels with the punch. . . . Oh, sure, I like the way you're shaping up. (TOKIO *continues massaging.* JOE *is silent. His sobbing stops. After a moment* TOKIO *continues.*) What was you saying about Lombardo's trick? I understood you to say

he's a bull's-eye for a straight shot from the inside. I think you're right, Joe, but that kind of boy is liable to meet you straight-on in a clinch and give you the back of his head under the chin. Watch out for that.

JOE. He needs a straight punch. . . . (JOE *suddenly sits up on the table, his legs dangling.*)

JOE. Now I'm alone. They're all against me —Moody, the girl . . . you're my family now, Tokio—you and Eddie! I'll show them all —nobody stands in my way! My father's had his hand on me for years. No more. No more for her either—she had her chance! When a bullet sings through the air it has no past—only a future—like me! Nobody, nothing stands in my way! (*In a sudden spurt of feeling* JOE *starts sparring around lightly in a shadow boxing routine.* TOKIO *smiles with satisfaction. Now the roar of* THE CROWD *reaches a frenzied shriek and hangs there. The bell clangs rapidly several times. The roar of* THE CROWD *settles down again.*)

TOKIO. That sounds like the kill. (JOE *draws his bathrobe around him and prances on his toes.*)

JOE. I'm a new boy tonight! I could take two Lombardos! (*Vigorously shaking out his bandaged hands above his head.*) Hallelujah! We're on the Millionaire Express tonight! Nobody gets me! (*The door is thrust open and a* CALL BOY *shouts.*)

CALL BOY. Bonaparte, ready. Bonaparte, ready. (PEPPER WHITE *and* MICKEY *enter as the* CALL BOY *speeds away.* PEPPER *is flushed with victory.*)

PEPPER (*to* JOE). Tell me when you want it; you can have it the way I just give it to Pulaski! (JOE *looks* PEPPER *in the face, flexes his hands several times and suddenly breaks out in laughter, to* PEPPER's *astonishment.* JOE *and* TOKIO *exit.* PEPPER *throws off his robe and displays his body.*)

PEPPER. Look me over—not a mark. How do you like that for class! I'm in a hurry to grab a cab to Flushing.

MICKEY (*impassively*). Keep away from her.

PEPPER. I don't even hear you.

MICKEY. Keep away from her!

PEPPER. I go for her like a bee and the flower.

MICKEY (*in a droning prophetic voice*). The flower is married. Her husband is an excitable Armenian from the Orient. There will be hell to pay! Keep away from her! (*Now in the distance is heard the indistinct high voice of the announcer.*)

PEPPER. You oughta get me a fight with that cock-eye Napoleon—insteada sticking your nose where it don't belong! I could slaughter him in next to nothing.

MICKEY (*impassively*). If you could make his weight and siaughter him, you'd be the next world's champ. But you can't make his weight, you can't slaughter him, and you can't be the champ. Why the hell don't you take a shower? (*The bell clangs—in the arena,* JOE's *fight is on.*)

PEPPER (*plaintively, beginning to dress at his locker*). If my girl don't like me without a shower, I'll tell her a thing or two.

MICKEY. If her husband don't tell you first. (*The roar of* THE CROWD *swells up as the door opens and* MR. BONAPARTE *enters. He is unusually agitated. He looks at* PEPPER *and* MICKEY *and sits on a bench. The roar of* THE CROWD *mounts higher than before, then drops.*)

PEPPER (*to* MR. BONAPARTE). What's the matter with you?

MR. BONAPARTE (*shaking his head*). Don't like to see . . .

PEPPER (*delighted*). Why? Your boy gettin' smeared?

MR. BONAPARTE. They fighta for money, no?

MICKEY. No, they're fighting for a noble cause—

MR. BONAPARTE. If they wasa fight for cause or for woman, woulda not be so bad.

PEPPER (*still dressing behind the locker door*). I fight for money and I like it. I don't fight for under a thousand bucks. Do I, Mickey?

MICKEY. Nope.

PEPPER (*boasting naïvely*). I didn't fight for under a thousand for five years. Did I, Mickey?

MICKEY (*impassively*). Nope.

PEPPER. I get a thousand bucks tonight, don't I?

MICKEY. Nope.

PEPPER (*up like a shot*). How much? How much tonight?

MICKEY. Twelve hundred bucks.

PEPPER. What? Mickey, I oughta bust you in the nose. How many times do I have to say I don't fight for under one thousand bucks! (*To* MR. BONAPARTE.) Now you see what I'm up against with this manager!

MICKEY (*impassively*). Okay, you'll get a thousand.

PEPPER. I better, Buddy! That's all I say—I better! (*To* MR. BONAPARTE.) I tell him I want to fight your kid and he don't lift a finger. (*The roar of* THE CROWD *crescendos and drops down again.*)

MICKEY. You don't rate no fight with Bonaparte. (*To* MR. BONAPARTE, *of* PEPPER.) He's an old man, a fossil!

MR. BONAPARTE. Who?

MICKY. Him—he's twenty-nine.

MR. BONAPARTE. Old?

MICKEY. In this business, twenty-nine is ancient.

PEPPER. My girl don't think so.

MICKEY. Keep away from her. (*The roar of* THE CROWD *mounts up to a devilish shriek.*)

PEPPER. Wow, is your boy getting schlocked!

MR. BONAPARTE. My boy isa win.

PEPPER. Yeah, and that's why you ran away?

MR. BONAPARTE. Whatta the difference who's-a win? Is terrible to see!

PEPPER (*grinning*). If I wasn't in a hurry, I'd wait around to help pick up your little Joie's head off the floor. (*He draws on a sport shirt.*)

MICKEY (*to* PEPPER). What are you wearing a polo shirt on a winter night for?

PEPPER. For crying out loud, I just bought it! . . . So long, Mr. Bonaparte.

MR. BONAPARTE. I aska you please—whatta happen to a boy's hands when he fight a longa time?

PEPPER (*holding up his fists*). Take a look at mine—I got a good pair. See those knuckles? Flat!

MR. BONAPARTE. Broke?

PEPPER. Not broke, flat!—pushed down!

MR. BONAPARTE. Hurt?

PEPPER. You get used to it.

MR. BONAPARTE. Can you use them?

PEPPER. Go down the hall and look at Pulaski.

MR. BONAPARTE. Can you open thees-a hands?

PEPPER. What for?

MR. BONAPARTE (*gently touching the fists*). So strong, so hard . . .

PEPPER. You said it, Buddy. So long, Buddy. (*To* MICKEY.) Take my stuff.

MICKEY. Sam'll take it after. Keep away from her! (PEPPER *looks at* MICKEY *with a sardonic grin and exits followed by* MICKEY.)

MR. BONAPARTE (*to himself*). So strong . . . so useless . . . (*The roar of* THE CROWD *mounts up and calls for a kill.* MR. BONAPARTE *trembles. For a moment he sits quietly on the bench. Then he goes to the door of the shower room and looks around at the boxing paraphernalia. In the distance the bell begins to clang repeatedly.* MR. BONAPARTE *stares in the direction of the arena. He goes to the exit door.* THE CROWD *is cheering and howling.* MR. BONAPARTE *hesitates a moment at the door and then rapidly walks back to the bench, where he sits. Head cocked, he listens for a moment. The roar of* THE CROWD *is heated, demanding and hateful. Suddenly* MR. BONAPARTE *jumps to his feet. He is in a murderous mood. He shakes his clenched fist in the direction of the noise—he roars aloud. The roar of* THE CROWD *dies down. The door opens,* PEPPER'S *second,* SAM, *enters, softly whistling to himself. Deftly he begins to sling together* PEPPER'S *paraphernalia.*)

MR. BONAPARTE. What'sa happen in the fight?

SAM. Knockout.

MR. BONAPARTE. Who?

SAM. Lombardo's stiff. (MR. BONAPARTE *slowly sits. Softly whistling,* SAM *exits with the paraphernalia. The outside door is flung open. In come* JOE, TOKIO, MOODY *and* ROXY, *who is elated beyond sanity.* JOE'S *eyes glitter; his face is hard and flushed. He has won by a knockout.*)

ROXY (*almost dancing*). My boy! My darling boy! My dear darling boy! (*Silently* JOE *sits on the edge of the table, ignoring his father after a glance. His robe drops from his shoulders.* ROXY *turns to* MOODY.)

ROXY. How do you like it, Tom? He knocks him out in two rounds!

MOODY (*stiffly, to* JOE). It's good business to call the sports writers in—

ROXY. That's right, give a statement! (MOODY *gives* JOE *a rapid glance and hurriedly exits.*)

ROXY. I'm collecting a bet on you. All my faith and patience is rewarded. (*As he opens the door he almost knocks over* EDDIE FUSELI.) Haha! How do you like it, Eddie? Haha! (*He exits.* EDDIE FUSELI *closes the door and stands with his back to it.* TOKIO *moves up to* JOE *and begins to remove a glove.*)

TOKIO (*gently*). You're a real sweetheart. . . . (TOKIO *removes the sweaty glove and begins to fumble with the lace of the other one.* JOE *carefully moves this glove out of* TOKIO'S *reach, resting it on his opposite arm.*)

JOE (*almost proudly*). Better cut it off. . . . (MR. BONAPARTE *is watching tensely.* EDDIE *watches from the door.*)

TOKIO. . . . Broke? . . .

JOE (*holding the hand out proudly*). Yes, it's broke. . . . (TOKIO *slowly reaches for a knife. He begins carefully to cut the glove.*)

JOE. Hallelujah! It's the beginning of the world! (MR. BONAPARTE, *lips compressed, slowly turns his head away.* EDDIE *watches with inner excitement and pleasure;* JOE *has become a fighter.* TOKIO *continues with his work.* JOE *begins to laugh loudly, victoriously, exultantly—with a deep thrill of satisfaction.*)

SLOW FADEOUT

ACT THREE

SCENE I

Moody's *office, six months later. Present are* Moody, *acting the persuasive salesman with two sports writers,* Drake *and* Lewis; Roxy Gottlieb *being helpful in his usual manner;* Tokio, *to one side, characteristically quiet . . . and* Joe Bonaparte. Bonaparte *sits on the desk and diffidently swings his legs as he eats a sandwich. His success has added a certain bellicocity to his attitude; it has changed his clothing to silk shirts and custom-made suits.*

MOODY. He's got his own style. He won't rush—

ROXY. Nobody claims our boy's Niagara Falls.

DRAKE (*a newspaperman for twenty years*). Except himself!

MOODY. You newspaper boys are right.

DRAKE. We newspaper boys are always right!

MOODY. He won't take chances tomorrow night if he can help it. He'll study his man, pick out flaws—then shoot at them.

JOE (*casually*). It won't matter a helluva lot if I win late in the bout or near the opening. The main thing with Bonaparte is to win.

DRAKE (*dryly*). Well, what does Bonaparte expect to do tomorrow night?

JOE (*as dryly*). Win.

MOODY. Why shouldn't we have a win from the Chocolate Drop? Look at our record!—

LEWIS (*good-natured and slow*). We just wanna get an impression—

MOODY. Seventeen knockouts? Fulton, Lombardo, Guffey Talbot—?

JOE. Phil Weiner . . .

MOODY. Weiner?

ROXY. That's no powderpuff hitter!

LEWIS. In this fight tomorrow night, can you name the round?

JOE. Which round would you like?

DRAKE. You're either a genius or an idiot!

MOODY. Joe don't mean—

DRAKE (*sharply*). Let him talk for himself.

JOE (*getting off the desk*). Listen, Drake, I'm not the boy I used to be—the honeymoon's over. I don't blush and stammer these days. Bonaparte goes in and slugs with the best. In the bargain his brain is *better* than the best. That's the truth; why deny it?

DRAKE. The last time you met Chocolate you never even touched him!

JOE. It's almost two years since I "never even touched him." Now I know how!

MOODY. What Joe means to say—

DRAKE. He's the genuine and only modest cock-eyed wonder!

JOE. What good is modesty? I'm a fighter! The whole essence of prizefighting is immodesty! "I'm better than you are—I'll prove it by breaking your face in!" What do you expect? A conscience and a meek smile? I don't believe that bull the meek'll inherit the earth!

DRAKE. Oh, so it's the earth you want!

JOE. I know what I want—that's my business! But I don't want your guff!

DRAKE. I have two sons of my own—I like boys. But I'm a son-of-a-bitch if I can stomach your conceit!

MOODY (*trying to save the situation*). They serve a helluva rum Collins across the street—

DRAKE. Bonaparte, I'll watch for Waterloo with more than interest!

MOODY. Why don't we run across for a drink? How 'bout some drinks?

DRAKE. Tom, you can buy me twenty drinks and I still won't change my mind about him. (*He exits.*)

LEWIS (*smiling*). You're all right, Bonaparte.

JOE. Thanks....

LEWIS (*clinching a cigarette at the desk*). How's that big blonde of yours, Tom?

MOODY. Fine.

LEWIS. How does she feel about the wedding bells? Sunday is it? (*This is news to* JOE, *and* MOODY *knows it is.*)

MOODY (*nervously*). Happy, the way I am. Yeah, Sunday.

ROXY. How about the drinks? We'll drink to everybody's health!

LEWIS (*to* JOE). Good luck tomorrow.

JOE. Thanks.... (*They exit,* MOODY *throwing a resentful look at* JOE. JOE *and* TOKIO *are left. In the silence* JOE *goes back to the remains of his lunch.*)

TOKIO. That Drake is a case.

JOE (*pushing the food away*). They don't make cheesecake the way they used to when I was a boy. Or maybe I don't like it any more. When are they getting married?

TOKIO. Moody? Sunday.

JOE. Those writers hate me.

TOKIO. You give them too much lip.

JOE (*looking down at his clenched fists*). I'd rather give than take it. That's one reason I became a fighter. When did Moody get his divorce?

TOKIO. Few weeks ago.... (*Cannily.*) Why don't you forget Lorna?

JOE (*as if not understanding*). What?

TOKIO. I'll say it again . . . why not forget her? (*No answer comes.*) Joe, you're loaded with love. Find something to give it to. Your heart ain't in fighting . . . your *hate* is. But a man with hate and nothing else . . . he's half a man . . . and half a man . . . is no man. Find something to love, or someone. Am I stepping on your toes?

JOE (*coldly*). I won't be unhappy if you mind your business.

TOKIO. Okay. . . . (TOKIO *goes to the door, stops there.*) Watch your dinner tonight. No girls either.

JOE. Excuse me for saying that—

TOKIO (*with a faint smile*). Okay. (TOKIO *opens the door and* LORNA MOON *enters.* TOKIO *smiles at her and exits. She carries a pack of newspapers under her arm.* JOE *and she do not know what to say to each other— they wish they had not met here.* LORNA *crosses and puts the newspapers on the desk. She begins to bang through the desk drawers, looking for the scissors.*)

JOE. I hear you're making the leap tomorrow....

LORNA. Sunday. . . .

JOE. Sunday. (*Intense silence.*)

LORNA (*to say anything*). I'm looking for the scissors....

JOE. Who're you cutting up today?

LORNA (*bringing out the shears*). Items on Bonaparte, for the press book. (*She turns and begins to unfold and clip a sheet of newspaper.* JOE *is at a loss for words.*)

JOE (*finally*). Congratulations....

LORNA (*without turning*). Thanks. . . . (*In a sudden irresistible surge* JOE *tears the papers out of* LORNA's *hands and hurls them behind the desk. The two stand facing each other.*)

JOE. When I speak to you, look at me!

LORNA. What would you like to say? (*They stand face to face, straining. Finally:*)

JOE. Marry anyone you like!

LORNA. Thanks for permission!

JOE. Queen Lorna, the tramp of Newark!

LORNA. You haven't spoken to me for months. Why break your silence?

JOE. You're a historical character for me— dead and buried!

LORNA. Then everything's simple; go about your business.

JOE. Moody's right for you—perfect—the mating of zero and zero!

LORNA. I'm not sorry to marry Tom—

JOE (*scornfully*). That's from the etiquette book—page twelve: "When you marry a man say you like it!"

LORNA. I know I could do worse when I look at you. When did you look in the mirror last? Getting to be a killer! You're getting to be like Fuseli! You're not the boy I cared about, not you. You murdered that boy with the generous face—God knows where you hid the body! I don't know you.

JOE. I suppose I never kissed your mouth—

LORNA. What do you want from me? Revenge? Sorry—we're all out of revenge today!

JOE. I wouldn't look at you twice if they hung you naked from a Christmas tree! (*At this moment* EDDIE FUSELI *enters with a pair of packages. He looks intently at* LORNA, *then crosses and puts the packages on the desk. He and* JOE *are dressed almost identically.* LORNA *exits without a word.* EDDIE *is aware of what has happened but begins to talk casually about the packages.*)

EDDIE. This one's your new headgear. This is shirts from Jacobs Brothers. He says the neck bands are gonna shrink, so I had him make sixteens—they'll fit you after one washing. (*Holding up a shirt.*) You like that color?

JOE. Thanks.

EDDIE. Your brother-in-law drove me over. Picked him up on 49th. Don't you ever see them no more?

JOE (*sharply*). What for?

EDDIE. What'sa matter?

JOE. Why? You see a crowd around here, Eddie?

EDDIE. No.

JOE. That's right, you don't! But I do! I see a crowd of Eddies all around me, suffocating me, burying me in good times and silk shirts!

EDDIE (*dialing the telephone*). You wanna go to the Scandals tonight? I got tickets. (*Into the telephone.*) Charley? Fuseli is speaking. . . . I'm giving four to five on Bonaparte tomorrow. . . . Four G's worth.

. . . Yes. (*Hanging up the phone.*) It's gonna be a good fight tomorrow

JOE (*belligerently*). How do you know?

EDDIE. I know Bonaparte. I got eighteen thousand spread out on him tomorrow night.

JOE. Suppose Bonaparte loses?

EDDIE. I look at the proposition from all sides—I know he'll win.

JOE. What the hell do you think I am? A machine? Maybe I'm lonely, maybe—

EDDIE. You wanna walk in a parade? Everybody's lonely. Get the money and you're not so lonely.

JOE. I want some personal life.

EDDIE. I give Bonaparte a good personal life. I got loyalty to his cause. . . .

JOE. You use me like a gun! Your loyalty's to keep me oiled and polished!

EDDIE. A year ago Bonaparte was a rookie with a two-pants suit. Now he wears the best, eats the best, sleeps the best. He walks down the street respected—the golden boy! They howl their heads off when Bonaparte steps in the ring . . . and I done it for him!

JOE. There are other things. . . .

EDDIE. There's no other things! Don't think so much—it could make you very sick! You're in this up to your neck. You owe me a lot—I don't like you to forget. You better be on your toes when you step in that ring tomorrow night. (EDDIE *turns and begins to dial the telephone.*)

JOE. Your loyalty makes me shiver. (JOE *starts for the door.*)

EDDIE. Take the shirts.

JOE. What do I want them for? I can only wear one at a time. . . . (EDDIE *speaks into the phone.*)

EDDIE. Meyer? . . . Fuseli is speaking. . . . I'm giving four to five on Bonaparte tomorrow. . . . Two? . . . Yeah. . . . (*About to exit,* JOE *stands at the door and watches* EDDIE *as he calmly begins to dial the phone again.*)

MEDIUM FADEOUT

SCENE II

The next night.
The lights fade in on an empty stage. We are in the same dressing room as seen in Act Two. Far in the distance is heard the same roar of THE CROWD. *The distant bell clangs menacingly. The room is shadows and patches of light. The silence here has its own ugly dead quality.*
LORNA MOON *enters. She looks around nervously; she lights a cigarette; this reminds her to rouge her lips; she puffs the cigarette. The distant bell clangs again.* EDDIE FUSELI *enters, pale and tense. He sees* LORNA *and stops short in his tracks. There is an intense silence as they look at each other.*

LORNA. How's the fight?

EDDIE. I like to talk to you.

LORNA. Is Joe still on his feet?

EDDIE. Take a month in the country, Miss Moon.

LORNA. Why?

EDDIE (*repressing a murderous mood*). Give the boy . . . or move away.

LORNA. I get married tomorrow. . . .

EDDIE. You heard my request—give him or go!

LORNA. Don't Moody count?

EDDIE. If not for Bonaparte they'd find you in a barrel long ago—in the river or a bush!

LORNA. I'm not afraid of you. . . . (*The distant bell clangs.*)

EDDIE (*after turning his head and listening*). That's the beginning of the eighth. Bonaparte's unsettled—fighting like a drunken sailor. He can't win no more, unless he knocks the Chocolate out. . . .

LORNA (*at a complete loss*). Don't look at me . . . what'd you . . . I . . .

EDDIE. Get outa town! (THE ROAR of THE CROWD *mounts to a demand for a kill.*)

EDDIE (*listening intently*). He's like a bum tonight . . . and a bum done it! You! (*The roar grows fuller.*) I can't watch him get slaughtered. . . .

LORNA. I couldn't watch it myself. . . . (*The bell clangs loudly several times.* THE ROAR *of* THE CROWD *hangs high in the air.*) What's happening now?

EDDIE. Someone's getting murdered. . . .

LORNA. It's me. . . .

EDDIE (*quietly, intensely*). That's right . . . if he lost . . . the trees are ready for your coffin. (THE ROAR *of* THE CROWD *tones down.*) You can go now. I don't wanna make a scandal around his name. . . . I'll find you when I want you. Don't be here when they carry him in.

LORNA (*at a complete loss*). Where do you want me to go?

EDDIE (*suddenly releasing his wrath*). Get outa my sight! You turned down the sweetest boy who ever walked in shoes! You turned him down, the golden boy, that king among the juven-niles! He gave you his hand—you spit in his face! You led him on like Gertie's whoore! You sold him down the river! And now you got the nerve to stand here, to wait and see him bleeding from the mouth!—

LORNA. Fuseli, for God's sake—

EDDIE. Get outa my sight!

LORNA. Fuseli, please—

EDDIE. Outa my sight, you nickel whoore! (*Completely enraged and out of control,* EDDIE *half brings his gun out from under his left armpit.* JOE *appears in the doorway. Behind him are* ROXY, MOODY *and a* SECOND.)

JOE. Eddie! (EDDIE *whirls around. The others enter the room. In the ensuing silence,* MOODY, *sensing what has happened, crosses to* LORNA.)

LORNA (*quietly*). What happened?

ROXY. What happened? (*He darts forward and picks up* JOE's *arm in the sign of vic-*

tory. The arm drops back limply.) The monarch of the masses!

EDDIE (*to the* SECOND). Keep everybody out. Only the newspaper boys. (*The* SECOND *exits and closes the door.* JOE *sits on a table. Physically he is a very tired boy. There is a high puff under one eye; the other is completely closed. His body is stained with angry splotches.*)

TOKIO (*gently*). I have to hand it to you, Joe....

ROXY (*explaining to the frigid* EDDIE, *elaborately*). The beginning of the eighth: first the bell! Next the Chocolate Drop comes out like a waltz clog, confident. Oh, he was so confident! Haha! The next thing I know the Chocolate's on the floor, the referee lifts our arm, we got on our bathrobe and we're here in the dressing room! How do you like it?

EDDIE (*narrowly*). I like it.

TOKIO (*taking off* JOE'S *gloves*). I'll have you feelin' better in a minute. (*After which he cuts the tapes.*)

JOE. I feel all right.

EDDIE (*to* TOKIO). Gimme his gloves.

MOODY (*wary of* JOE). That's a bad lump under your eye.

JOE. Not as bad as the Chocolate Drop got when he hit the floor!

ROXY. Darling, how you gave it to him! Not to my enemies!

JOE. 'Twas a straight right—with no trimmings or apologies! Aside from fouling me in the second and fifth—

MOODY. I called them on it—

ROXY. I seen the bastard—

JOE. That second time I nearly went through the floor. I gave him the fury of a lifetime in that final punch! (EDDIE *has taken the soggy boxing gloves for his own property.* TOKIO *is daubing the bruise under* JOE'S *eye.*) And did you hear them cheer! (*Bitterly, as if reading a news report.*) Flash! As thousands cheer, that veritable whirlwind Bonaparte—that veritable cock-

eye wonder, Bonaparte—he comes from behind in the eighth stanza to slaughter the Chocolate Drop and clinch a bout with the champ! Well, how do you like me, boys? Am I good or am I good?

ROXY. Believe *me!*

TOKIO (*attempting to settle* JOE). You won the right for a crack at the title. You won it fair and clean. Now lay down....

JOE (*in a vehement outburst*). I'd like to go outside my weight and beat up the whole damn world!

MOODY (*coldly*). Well, the world's your oyster now!

TOKIO (*insistently*). Take it easy. Lemme fix that eye, Joe— (*Now a bustling little Irishman,* DRISCOLL, *hustles into the room.*)

DRISCOLL. Who's got the happy boy's gloves?

EDDIE. Here . . . why? (DRISCOLL *rapidly takes the gloves, "breaks" and examines them.*)

TOKIO. What's the matter, "Drisc"?

JOE. What's wrong?

DRISCOLL (*handing the gloves back to* EDDIE). Chocolate's a sick boy. Your hands are clean. (DRISCOLL *hustles for the door.* JOE *is up and to him.*)

JOE. What happened?

DRISCOLL (*bustling*). It looks like the Pride of Baltimore is out for good. Change your clothes.

JOE. How do you mean?

DRISCOLL. Just like I said—out! (DRISCOLL *pats* JOE'S *shoulder, hustles out, closing the door in* JOE'S *face.* JOE *slowly sits on the nearest bench. Immediately* TOKIO *comes to him, as tender as a mother.*)

TOKIO. You didn't foul him—you're a clean fighter. You're so honest in the ring it's stupid. If something's happened, it's an accident. (*The others stand around stunned, not knowing what to do or say.*)

MOODY (*very worried*). That's right, there's nothing to worry about.

ROXY (*ditto*). That's right. . . .

JOE. Gee. . . . (JOE *stands up, slowly crosses the room and sits on the table, head in his hands, his back to the others. No one knows what to say.*)

EDDIE (*to* MOODY). Go out there and size up the situation. (MOODY, *glad of the opportunity to leave the room, turns to the door which is suddenly violently thrust open.*

BARKER, *the* CHOCOLATE DROP'S *manager, pushes* MOODY *into the room with him, leaving the door open. From outside a small group of curious people look in.* BARKER, *bereft of his senses, grabs* MOODY *by the coat lapel.*)

BARKER. Do you know it? Do you know it?

MOODY. Now wait a minute, Barker— (BARKER *runs over to* JOE *and screams:*)

BARKER. You murdered my boy! He's dead! You killed him!

TOKIO (*getting between* JOE *and* BARKER). Just a minute!

BARKER (*literally wringing his hands*). He's dead! Chocolate's dead!

TOKIO. We're very sorry about it. Now pull yourself together. (EDDIE *crosses the room and slams the door shut as* BARKER *points an accusing finger at* JOE *and screams:*)

BARKER. This dirty little wop killed my boy!

EDDIE (*coming to* BARKER). Go back in your room.

BARKER. Yes he did!! (EDDIE'S *answer is to shove* BARKER *roughly toward the door, weeping.*) Yes, he did!!

EDDIE. Get out before I slug your teeth apart!

JOE (*jumping to his feet*). Eddie, for God sakes, don't hit him! Let him alone! (EDDIE *immediately desists.* BARKER *stands there, a weeping idiot.*)

MOODY. Accidents can happen.

BARKER. I know . . . know . . .

MOODY. Chocolate fouled us twice.

BARKER. I know, I know. . . . (BARKER *stammers, gulps and tries to say something more. Suddenly he dashes out of the room. There is a long silent pause during which* JOE *sits down again.*)

EDDIE. We'll have to wait for an investigation.

TOKIO (*to* JOE). Don't blame yourself for nothing. . . .

JOE. That poor guy . . . with those sleepy little eyes. . . .

ROXY (*solemnly*). It's in the hands of God, a thing like that. (LEWIS, *the sports writer, tries to enter the room.*)

EDDIE (*herding him out*). Stay outside. (*To* MOODY.) See what's happening? (MOODY *immediately leaves.*) Everybody out—leave Bonaparte to calm hisself. I'll watch the door.

TOKIO. Don't worry, Joe. (*He exits, followed by* ROXY. EDDIE *turns and looks at* LORNA.)

EDDIE. You too, Miss Moon—this ain't no cocktail lounge.

LORNA. I'll stay here. (EDDIE *looks at her sharply, shifts his glance from her to* JOE *and back again; he exits.*) Joe. . . .

JOE. Gee, that poor boy. . . .

LORNA (*holding herself off*). But it wasn't your fault.

JOE. That's right—it wasn't my fault!

LORNA. You didn't mean it!

JOE. That's right—I didn't mean it! I wouldn't want to do that, would I? Everybody knows I wouldn't want to kill a man. Lorna, you know it!

LORNA. Of course!

JOE. But I *did* it! That's the thing—I *did* it! What will my father say when he hears I murdered a man? Lorna, I see what I did. I murdered myself, too! I've been running around in circles. Now I'm smashed! That's the truth. Yes, I was a real sparrow, and I wanted to be a fake eagle! But now I'm hung up by my finger tips—I'm no good— my feet are off the earth!

LORNA (*in a sudden burst, going to* JOE). Joe, I love you! We love each other. Need each other!

JOE. Lorna darling, I see what's happened!

LORNA. You wanted to conquer the world—

JOE. Yes—

LORNA. But it's not the kings and dictators who do it—it's that kid in the park—

JOE. Yes, that boy who might have said, "I have myself; I am what I want to be!"

LORNA. And now, tonight, here, this minute —finding yourself again—that's what makes you a champ. Don't you see that?

JOE. Yes, Lorna—yes!

LORNA. It isn't too late to tell the world good evening again!

JOE. With what? These fists?

LORNA. Give up the fighting business!

JOE. Tonight!

LORNA. Yes, and go back to your music—

JOE. But my hands are ruined. I'll never play again! What's left, Lorna? Half a man, nothing, useless. . . .

LORNA. No, *we're* left! Two together! We have each other! Somewhere there must be happy boys and girls who can teach us the way of life! We'll find some city where poverty's no shame—where music is no crime!—where there's no war in the streets —where a man is glad to be himself, to live and make his woman herself!

JOE. No more fighting, but where do we go?

LORNA. Tonight? Joe, we ride in your car. We speed through the night, across the park, over the Triboro Bridge—

JOE (*taking* LORNA'S *arms in his trembling hands*). Ride! That's it, we ride—clear my head. We'll drive through the night. When you mow down the night with headlights, nobody gets you! You're on top of the world then—nobody laughs! That's it— speed! We're off the earth—unconnected! We don't have to think!! That's what speed's for, an easy way to live! Lorna darling, we'll burn up the night! (*He turns and as he begins to throw his street clothes out of his locker.*)

MEDIUM FADEOUT

SCENE III

Late the same night.
In the Bonaparte home sit EDDIE FUSELI, MOODY, ROXY *and* SIGGIE, *drinking homemade wine, already half drunk.* MR. BONAPARTE *stands on the other side of the room, looking out of the window.* FRANK *sits near him, a bandage around his head.*
MOODY is at the telephone as the lights fade in.

MOODY (*impatiently*). . . . 'lo? Hello! . . .

SIGGIE. I'll tell you why we need another drink. . . .

ROXY. No, I'll tell you. . . .

MOODY (*turning*). Quiet! For Pete's sake! I can't hear myself think! (*Turning to the phone.*) Hello? . . . This is Moody. Any calls for me? Messages? . . . No sign of Miss Moon? . . . Thanks. Call me if she comes in—the number I gave you before. (*Hanging up and returning to his wine glass; to* MR. BONAPARTE.) I thought you said Joe was coming up here!

MR. BONAPARTE. I say maybe. . . .

MOODY (*sitting*). I'll wait another fifteen minutes. (*He drinks.*)

SIGGIE. Here's why we need another drink; it's a night of success! Joe's in those lofty brackets from now on! We're gonna move to a better neighborhood, have a buncha kids! (*To* MR. BONAPARTE.) Hey, pop, I wish we had a mortgage so we could pay it off! To the next champ of the world! (SIGGIE *lifts his glass; the others join him.*)

ROXY. Bonaparte.

EDDIE. Don't you drink, Mr. Bonaparte?

SIGGIE. You, too, Frank—it's all in the family. (MR. BONAPARTE *shrugs and comes down, accepting a glass.*)

ROXY. It's in the nature of a celebration!

MR. BONAPARTE. My son'sa kill a man tonight—what'sa celebrate? What'sa gonna be, heh?

SIGGIE. Ahh, don't worry—they can't do him nothing for that! An accident!

EDDIE (*coldly, to* MR. BONAPARTE). Listen, it's old news. It's been out on the front page two-three hours.

MR. BONAPARTE. Poor color' boy . .

MOODY. Nobody's fault. Everybody's sorry— we give the mother a few bucks. But we got the next champ! Bottoms up. (*All drink,* FRANK *included.*)

ROXY (*to* MR. BONAPARTE). You see how a boy can make a success nowadays?

MR. BONAPARTE. Yeah . . . I see.

EDDIE (*resenting* MR. BONAPARTE's *attitude*). Do we bother you? If I didn't think Joe was here I don't come up. I don't like nobody to gimme a boycott!

MR. BONAPARTE (*going back to the window*). Helpa you'self to more wine.

SIGGIE (*to* EDDIE). Leave him alone—he don't feel social tonight.

MOODY. Don't worry, Mr. Bonaparte. Looka me—take a lesson from me—I'm not worried. I'm getting married tomorrow—*this afternoon!*—I don't know where my girl is, but I'm not worried! What for? We're all in clover up to our necks!

SIGGIE. Shh . . . don't wake up my wife. (MOODY *suddenly sits heavily; jealousy begins to gnaw at him despite his optimism.* ROXY *takes another drink.* EDDIE *asks* FRANK, *apropos of his bandaged head:*)

EDDIE. What's that "Spirit of '76" outfit for?

SIGGIE (*grinning to* EDDIE). Didn't you hear what he said before? They gave it to him in a strike—

EDDIE (*to* FRANK). You got a good build— you could be a fighter.

FRANK. I fight. . . .

EDDIE. Yeah? For what?

FRANK. A lotta things I believe in. . . . (EDDIE *looks at* FRANK *and appreciates his quality.*)

EDDIE. Whatta you get for it?

ROXY (*laughing*). Can't you see? A busted head!

FRANK. I'm not fooled by a lotta things Joe's fooled by. I don't get autos and custom made suits. But I get what Joe don't.

EDDIE. What don't he get? (MR. BONAPARTE *comes in and listens intently.*)

FRANK (*modestly*). The pleasure of acting as you think! The satisfaction of staying where you belong, being what you are . . . at harmony with millions of others!

ROXY (*pricking up his ears*). Harmony? That's music! the family's starting up music again!

FRANK (*smiling*). That's right, that's music— (*Now* MOODY *emphatically stamps his glass down on the table and stands.*)

MOODY. What's the use waiting around! They won't be back. (*Bitterly.*) Lorna's got a helluva lotta nerve, riding around in Long Island with him! Without even asking me!

SIGGIE. Long Island's famous for the best eating ducks.

EDDIE (*to* MOODY). You got the champ— you can't have everything.

MOODY. What's that supposed to mean?

EDDIE (*coldly*). That girl belongs to Bonaparte. They're together now, in some roadhouse . . . and they ain't eating duck!

MOODY (*finally, unsteadily*). You don't know what you're talking about!

EDDIE. Moody, what do you figger your interest is worth in Bonaparte?

MOODY. Why?

EDDIE (*without turning*). Roxy . . . are you listening?

ROXY. Yeah. . . .

EDDIE. 'Cause after tonight I'd like to handle Bonaparte myself.

MOODY. . . . Your gall is gorgeous! But I got a contract. . . .

ROXY. Eddie, have a heart—I'm holding a little twenty percent. . . . (*Out of sheer rage* MOODY *drinks more wine;* ROXY *follows his example.*)

FRANK (*to* EDDIE). How much does Joe own of himself?

EDDIE. Thirty percent. After tonight I own the rest.

MOODY. Oh, no! No, sir-ee!!

EDDIE. You're drunk tonight! Tomorrow!

MR. BONAPARTE (*coming forward*). Maybe Joe don't gonna fight no more, after tonight....

EDDIE. Listen, you creep! Why don't you change your tune for a minute!

ROXY (*to* MR. BONAPARTE). What're YOU worried about?

MR. BONAPARTE. My boy usta coulda be great for all men. Whatta he got now, heh? Pardon me fora nota to feel so confident in Joe'sa future! Pardon me fora to be anxious....

EDDIE (*standing up*). I don't like this talk!

SIGGIE. Sit down, pop—you're rocking the boat! Shh! Shh! (*He slips out of the room.*)

ROXY. Does anyone here know what he's talking about?

FRANK. He's trying to say he's worried for Joe.

ROXY. But why? Why? Don't he realize his kid's worth a fortune from tonight on? (*After giving* EDDIE *a quick glance.*) Ain't he got brains enough to see two feet ahead? Tell him in Italian—he don't understand our language—this is a festive occasion! To Bonaparte, the Monarch of the Masses! (*The telephone rings.*)

MOODY (*triumphantly, to* EDDIE). That's my hotel! You see, you were all wrong! That's Lorna! (*Speaking into the telephone.*) Hello? . . . No. . . . (*Turning to* MR. BONAPARTE.) It's for you. (MOODY *extends the telephone in* MR. BONAPARTE*'s direction, but the latter stands in his place, unable to move. After a few seconds,* FRANK *sees this and briskly moves to the telephone, taking it from* MOODY. *In the meantime* MOODY *has begun to address* EDDIE *with drunken eloquence. Wavering on his feet.*) There's a constitution in this country, Eddie Fuseli. Every man here enjoys life, liberty and the pursuit of happiness!

FRANK (*speaking into the telephone*). Yes? . . . No, this is his son. . . . (MR. BONAPARTE *watches* FRANK *mutely as he listens at the telephone.*)

MOODY. There's laws in this country, Fuseli! —*contracts!* We live in a civilized world—!

FRANK (*loudly, to the others*). Keep quiet! (*Resumes listening.*) Yes . . . yes. . . .

ROXY (*to* EDDIE). And there's a God in heaven—don't forget it!

FRANK (*on the telephone*). Say it again. . . . (*He listens.*) Yes. . . .

MOODY (*to* EDDIE). You're a killer! A man tries to do his best—but you're a killer! (FRANK *lowers the telephone and comes down to the others.*)

FRANK. *You're all killers!* (MR. BONAPARTE *advances a step toward* FRANK.)

MR. BONAPARTE. Frank . . . is it . . . ?

FRANK. I don't know how to tell you, poppa. . . .

MR. BONAPARTE (*hopefully*). Yes? . . .

FRANK. We'll have to go there—

EDDIE. Go where?

FRANK. Both of them . . . they were killed in a crash—

EDDIE. Who?! What?!

FRANK. They're waiting for identification—Long Island, Babylon.

EDDIE (*moving to* FRANK). What are you handing me?! (EDDIE, *suddenly knowing the truth, stops in his tracks. The telephone operator signals for the telephone to be replaced. The mechanical clicks call* FRANK *to attention; he slowly replaces the instrument.*)

MOODY. I don't believe that! Do you hear me? I don't believe it—

FRANK. What waste! . . .

MOODY. It's a goddam lie!!

MR. BONAPARTE. What have-a you expect? . . .

MOODY (*suddenly weeping*). Lorna! . . .

MR. BONAPARTE (*standing, his head high*). Joe. . . . Come, we bring-a him home . . . where he belong. . . .

SLOW FADEOUT

Stage Door

BY EDNA FERBER AND GEORGE S. KAUFMAN

STAGE DOOR was produced by Sam H. Harris at the Music Box Theatre, New York, on Thursday night, October 22nd, with the following cast:

OLGA BRANDT	Sylvia Lupas	KENDALL ADAMS	Margot Stevenson
BERNICE NIEMEYER	Janet Fox	FRANK	William Andrews
SUSAN PAIGE	Lili Zehner	TERRY RANDALL	Margaret Sullavan
MATTIE	Dorothea Andrews	SAM HASTINGS	Robert Thomsen
MARY HARPER (Big Mary)	Beatrice Blinn	JIMMY DEVEREAUX	Alex Courtney
MARY McCUNE (Little Mary)	Mary Wickes	FRED POWELL	Walter Davis
MADELEINE VAUCLAIN	Grena Sloan	LOU MILHAUSER	Edmund Dorsay
JUDITH CANFIELD	Lee Patrick	DAVID KINGSLEY	Onslow Stevens
ANN BRADDOCK	Louise Chaffee	KEITH BURGESS	Richard Kendrick
MRS. ORCUTT	Leona Roberts	MRS. SHAW	Helen Ray
KAYE HAMILTON	Frances Fuller	DR. RANDALL	Priestly Morrison
PAT DEVINE	Virginia Rousseau	ELLEN FENWICK	Judith Russell
LINDA SHAW	Jane Buchanan	TONY GILLETTE	Draja Dryden
JEAN MAITLAND	Phyllis Brooks	LARRY WESTCOTT	Tom Ewell
BOBBY MELROSE	Juliet Forbes	BILLY	William Atlee
LOUISE MITCHELL	Catherine Laughlin	ADOLPH GRETZL	Ralph Locke

THE SCENES

ACT I

SCENE 1   Main Room of the Footlights Club. Somewhere in the West Fifties, New York.
SCENE 2   One of the bedrooms. A month later.

ACT II

SCENE 1   Again the main room. A year later.
SCENE 2   The same. Two months later.

ACT III

SCENE 1   The same. The following year. A Sunday morning.
SCENE 2   The same. About two weeks later. Midnight.

STAGE MANAGER—*E. John Kennedy*

STAGE DOOR

ACT ONE

SCENE I

The Footlights Club. A club for girls of the stage.

It occupies an entire brownstone house in the West Fifties, New York. One of those old houses whose former splendor has departed as the neighborhood has changed.

The room we see is the common living room. It is comfortably furnished with unrelated but good pieces, enlivened by a bit of chintz. The effect is that of charm and livability, what with the piano, a desk, a fireplace with a good old marble mantel. Prominently hung is a copy of a portrait of Sarah Bernhardt, at her most dramatic. There is a glimpse of hallway with a flight of stairs. Near the stairway is a hall table that holds mail, messages, papers; an occasional hat is thrown there.

It is an October evening, just before the dinner hour. The girls are coming home, from matinees, from job-hunting, they are up and down the stairs, and presently they will be out again on dinner dates, playing the evening performances, seeing a movie.

Two girls are in the room at the moment, one at the piano, the other at a writing desk. The girl at the piano, OLGA BRANDT, *is dark, intense, sultry-looking.*

BERNICE NIEMEYER, *at the desk, is a young girl definitely not of the ingenue type. This is at once her cross and (in her opinion) her greatest asset as an actress.*

For a moment nothing is heard but the music. The girl at the piano is playing, beautifully and with exquisite technique, Chopin's Opus 9, No. 2.

A girl comes in from the street door, stops for a quick look through the mail, tosses a "Hi!" into the room, and goes on up the stairs. SUSAN PAIGE.

The piano again.

BERNICE (*to* OLGA). What's that you're playing?

OLGA (*her Russian origin evident in her accent*). Chopin.

BERNICE. How did you learn to play like that?

OLGA. Practice. Practice.

BERNICE. How long did it take you?

OLGA (*out of patience*). Oh! (*A little discordant crash of the keys.*)

BERNICE. Well, I was just asking. (*The telephone rings as* MATTIE, *the maid, is descending the stairs, a little pile of towels over her arm.*)

(MATTIE *is colored, about thirty, matter-of-fact, accustomed to the vagaries of a houseful of girls, and tolerant of them.*)

MATTIE. Hello! . . . Yes, this the Footlights Club. . . . (*To the girls in the room.*) Miss Devine come in yet? (*A negative shake of the head from* OLGA, *and a muttered "uh-uh" from* BERNICE.) No, she ain't. (*She hangs up.*)

BERNICE. Was it a man? (*Meanwhile voices are heard as the street door opens. "Oh, no, let's have dinner here and go to a movie." "Well, all right."*)

BERNICE (*pursuing her eternal queries*). Who's that?

OLGA (*a shade of impatience*). Big and Little Mary. (BIG *and* LITTLE MARY—MARY HARPER *and* MARY MCCUNE—*come into view in the doorway. There is a wide gap in stature between the two. One comes about to the other's elbow.*)

BIG MARY. What time is it? Dinner ready yet?

BERNICE. Where've you been? Seeing managers?

LITTLE MARY (*drooping*). Yeh. We're dead.

BIG MARY. We've been in every manager's office on Broadway.

BERNICE. Is anybody casting?

BIG MARY. How do *we* know? We only got in to see *one* of them.

BERNICE. Which one? Who'd you see?

LITTLE MARY. Rosenblatt.

BERNICE. What's he doing?

BIG MARY. Take it easy. It's all cast. (*Her tone implies that this is the stereotyped managerial reply.*)

LITTLE MARY. All except a kid part—ten years old.

BERNICE (*eagerly*). I could look ten years old! (*She becomes a dimpled darling.*)

LITTLE MARY. No. Big Mary had the same idea, and she's littler than you are.

BIG MARY. You're almost as tall as Little Mary. (*The* MARYS *go up the stairs.*)

BERNICE. Listen, why is the little one called Big Mary and the big one Little Mary?

OLGA. Nobody knows. Will you for heaven's sake stop asking questions?

BERNICE. Oh, all right. . . . Where've you been? (*The last remark is addressed to a newcomer who stands in the doorway. She is* MADELEINE VAUCLAIN, *a languid beauty, who runs through a sheaf of letters to discover if there is any mail for her.*)
(*The telephone rings.* BERNICE *picks it up.*)

BERNICE. Footlights Club! . . . (*To* OLGA) Terry Randall come in? (*As she shakes her head*) Not yet. (*Hangs up.*)

MADELEINE. I saw her sitting in Berger's office. I guess she gives up hard.

BERNICE (*alert at once*). Is Berger doing any casting? (*Another girl comes in the street door and dashes upstairs at break-neck speed.* BOBBY MELROSE.)

MDAELEINE. Listen, if you'd make the rounds once in a while, instead of sitting on your bustle and writing letters—

BERNICE (*up the stairs*). I make the rounds, but all you see is the office boys.

MADELEINE. Well, who do you think sees the letters?

BERNICE. Well, if they won't see you and won't read the letters, where do you go from there?

MADELEINE (*calling after her*). If you find out I wish you'd tell me.

MATTIE (*in the dining-room doorway*). Either you girls eating home?

MADELEINE. I'm not.

MATTIE. Anyhow, it's ready. (*Goes.*)

OLGA (*continues playing*). Yes, yes.

MADELEINE. Look, you don't want to go out tonight, do you? I've got an extra man.

OLGA (*a shake of the head*). I am rehearsing.

MADELEINE. Tonight?

OLGA (*with bitterness*). Tonight! I must play the piano for a lot of chorus girls to sing and dance. (*She plays and even sings in a wordless imitation of their infantile tones; a few scornful bars of the music to which the chorus girls are expected to sing and dance. Then she rises, furiously.*) That's what I am doing tonight—and every night! And for that I studied fifteen years with Kolijinsky! (*She storms into the dining room.*)

MADELEINE (*mildly astonished at this outburst*). Well, look, all I did was ask you if you wanted to go out tonight. (*A new figure appears in the doorway. It is* JUDITH CANFIELD, *hard, wise, debunked. She has picked up a letter from the hall table.*)

JUDITH (*with dreadful sweetness*). Oh, goody, goody, goody! I got a letter from home!

MADELEINE. Hello, Judith!

JUDITH (*averting her gaze from the letter as she opens it, she brings herself to look at it with a courageous jerk of the head.*) (*A little laugh of false gayety as the letter meets every expectation.*) Mmmmm! Pa got laid off. (*Turns a page.*) My sister's husband has left her. (*Her eye skims a line or two.*) And one of my brothers slugged a railroad detective. . . . I guess that's all. Yes. Lots of love and can you spare fifty dollars.

MADELEINE. Nothing like a letter from home to pick you up. . . . Look, Judy, what are you doing tonight?

JUDITH (*who has dropped onto a couch, whisked off her pump, and is pulling out the toe of her stocking*). I don't know. Why?

MADELEINE. I've got an extra man.

JUDITH (*brightening*). You mean dinner?

MADELEINE. Yes. Fellow from back home in Seattle. He's in the lumber business. He's here for a convention.

JUDITH. Sounds terrible.

MADELEINE. No, he isn't bad. And he's got this friend with him, so he wanted to know if I could get another girl.

JUDITH. Is the friend also in the lumber business?

MADELEINE. I don't know. What's the difference!

JUDITH. He'll be breezy. "Hello, Beautiful!"

MADELEINE. If we don't like it we can go home early.

JUDITH. Well— (*Weighing it.*) —do we dress?

MADELEINE. Sure!

JUDITH. Okay. I kind of feel like stepping out tonight.

MADELEINE (*going toward the stairs*). Swell. We'd better start. It's getting late.

JUDITH (*tugging at her stocking*). I'll be ready. (MADELEINE *disappears.*)
(JUDITH *wriggles her cramped toes, sighs.*)
(*Still another girl,* ANN BRADDOCK, *has come down the stairs and goes toward the dining room. She is wearing a hat and carrying her coat, which she tosses onto the piano as she passes.*)

ANN. Going in to dinner?

JUDITH. Got a date.

ANN. Well, that's all right for you—you're not working. But I can't go out to dinner, and run around, and still give my best to the theater. After all, you never see Kit Cornell dashing around. (*Righteously, she goes into the dining room.*)

JUDITH (*mutters at first*). Kit Cornell! (*Then raises her voice as the portrait on the wall gives her an idea*). What about Bernhardt! I suppose *she* was a home girl! (*From above stairs and descending the stairway the voice of the House Matron is heard.*)

MRS. ORCUTT. Yes, I'm sure you're going to be most comfortable here. Both of your roommates are lovely girls. Now if you'll just— (*Sees* JUDITH.) Oh— (MRS. ORCUTT *is a woman of about forty-six. In her manner and dress you detect the flavor of a theatrical past. Her dress is likely to have too many ruffles, her coiffure too many curls. She is piloting a fragile and rather wispy girl whose eyes are too big for her face. We presently learn that her name is* KAYE HAMILTON.) Uh—this is Judith Canfield, one of our girls— I'm so sorry, I'm afraid I didn't—

KAYE. Kaye Hamilton.

MRS. ORCUTT. Oh, yes. Miss Hamilton is planning to be with us if everything—uh—she'll room with Jean and Terry, now that Louise is leaving.

JUDITH. That'll be swell. Excuse me. (*Shoe in hand, she limps toward the stairs.*)

MRS. ORCUTT (*a little gracious nod*). Now, that's our dining room. (*A gesture toward it.*) Dinner is served from six to seven, because of course the girls have to get to the theater early if they're working. Now, let me see. You're in the same room with Terry and Jean, so that's only twelve-fifty a week, including the meals. I suppose that will be all right.

KAYE. Yes, thank you.

MRS. ORCUTT. Now, about the reference. (*She looks at a piece of paper she has been holding.*) I'll have that all looked up in the morning.

KAYE. Morning! Can't I come in tonight?

MRS. ORCUTT. I'm afraid not. You see—

KAYE. But I've got to come in tonight. I've got to. (*A girl comes in at the street door, passes through the hallway and goes rapidly up the stairs, humming as she goes.* PAT DEVINE. *Halfway up the stairs we hear her call "Yoo-hoo!"*)

MRS. ORCUTT (*after the interruption*). Well —uh—it's a little irregular. However . . . Did you say your bags were near by?

KAYE. Yes. That is, I can get them

MRS. ORCUTT (*reluctantly*). Well, then, I suppose it's all right. . . . Now, we have certain little rules. As you know, this is a club for stage girls. I assume you are on the stage.

KAYE. Yes. Yes. I'm not working now, but I hope...

MRS. ORCUTT. I understand. . . . Now about callers—men callers, I mean—

KAYE. There won't be any men.

MRS. ORCUTT. Oh, it's quite all right. We like you to bring your friends here. But not after eleven-thirty at night, and—of course—only in this room.

KAYE. I understand.

MRS. ORCUTT. I try very hard to make the girls feel that this is a real home. I was one of them myself not many years back, before I married Mr. Orcutt. Helen Romayne? Possibly you remember?

KAYE. I'm afraid I—

MRS. ORCUTT. That's quite all right. I think that covers everything. If you wish to go and get your bags—Mattie! (*Peering toward the dining room.*) Will you come here a minute?

MATTIE. Yes, ma'am!

MRS. ORCUTT (*she gently pilots* KAYE *toward the doorway*). Now, each girl is given a door key, and there's a little charge of twenty-five cents in case they're lost. Well, good-by, and I'll expect you in a very short time. (*As* MATTIE *has appeared in the dining-room doorway* BERNICE *comes downstairs; crosses the living room.*)

BERNICE. What have we got for dinner, Mattie?

MATTIE. We got a good dinner.

BERNICE (*as she disappears*). Smells like last night. *Is* it? (*The sound of the front door closing.* MRS. ORCUTT, *very businesslike, returns.*)

MRS. ORCUTT. Now, Mattie, there's a new girl coming in as soon as Louise Mitchell leaves. You'll only have a few minutes to get that room straightened up.

MATTIE. Yes, ma'am.

MRS. ORCUTT. Let's see, Terry Randall isn't in yet, is she?

MATTIE. No, ma'am.

MRS. ORCUTT. Well, if I don't see her be sure to tell her there's a new girl moving in with her and Jean. Don't forget fresh paper in the bureau drawers, and— (*Down the stairs like an angry whirlwind comes* LINDA SHAW. *She is clutching a dressing gown about her. Her hair is beautifully done, she is wearing evening slippers; obviously she is dressed for the evening except for her frock.*)

LINDA. Mattie, isn't my dress pressed yet?

MATTIE. Oh! Was you wanting it right away?

LINDA. Right away! When did you *think* I wanted it?

MATTIE. Well, I'll do it right this minute.

LINDA. Oh, don't bother! I'll do it myself! (*Storms out.*)

MATTIE (*following after her*). You never give it to me till pretty near half-past five. (*The telephone rings.* MRS. ORCUTT *answers.*)

MRS. ORCUTT. Footlights Club! . . . Yes, she is. . . . The Globe Picture Company? . . . Mr. Kingsley himself? . . . Just a minute. (*Impressed.*) I'll get her right away. . . . (*Calls toward the stairs.*) Jean! Oh, Jean! (*A voice from above.*)

JEAN. Yes!

MRS. ORCUTT (*in hushed tones*). Mr. Kingsley of the Globe Picture Company wants to talk to you.

JEAN. All right.

MRS. ORCUTT (*back to telephone*). She'll be right down. (*She lays down the receiver with a tenderness that is almost reverence, and takes a few steps away, looking toward the stairway. As* JEAN *appears,* MRS. ORCUTT *affects an elaborate nonchalance and disappears into dining room.*)

(JEAN MAITLAND *is a beautiful girl in her early twenties. She is, perhaps, a shade too vivacious. A better actress off than on. Her hair is blonde, and that toss of her head that shakes back her curls is not quite convincing. An opportunist; good-natured enough when things go her way; she has definite charm and appeal for men.*)
(JEAN *throws her all into her voice as she greets the man at the telephone.*)

JEAN. Hello! Mr. Kingsley! How perfectly— (*Obviously she is met by a secretary's voice. Dashed by this, her tone drops to below normal.*) Yes, this is Miss Maitland. Will you put him on, please? (*Again she gathers all her forces and even tops her first performance.*) Hello! Mr. Kingsley! How wonderful! . . . Well, *I* think it's pretty wonderful. With all the thousands of people at that party I didn't think you'd remember *me.* . . . Yes, I know you said that, but in your business you must meet a million beautiful girls a day. . . . Well, anyhow, half a million. . . . (*Coyly.*) Dinner! You don't mean tonight! Oh! . . . Yes, I did have, but it's nothing I can't break . . . Oh, but I want to. I'd love to. . . . What time? . . . Yes, I'll be ready. I suppose we're dressing? . . . Yes, I'd love to. All right. Good-by. (*As she hangs up the receiver, figures pop out of the vantage points from which they have been listening.* BERNICE *and* ANN *come out of the dining room with* MRS. ORCUTT; *cloppity-clop down the stairs come* BIG *and* LITTLE MARY *and* BOBBY MELROSE. BOBBY *is a soft Southern belle, fluffy, feminine. At the moment she is in a rather grotesque state of metal hair curlers, cold cream and bathrobe.*)

BIG MARY (*a squeal of excitement*). Jean!

BERNICE. I'm dying!

LITTLE MARY. Tell us about it!

BOBBY. What time is he coming?

MRS. ORCUTT. Well, Jeanie, does this mean we're going to lose you to pictures?

BOBBY. Aren't you palpitating?

BERNICE. How soon is he coming? Can I see him?

JEAN. Now listen, you girls, no fair hanging around!

LITTLE MARY. Aw!

JEAN. You've got to promise me—no parading.

BIG MARY. Big-hearted Bertha!

BERNICE. I'll bet you'll let Terry meet him.

JEAN. Well, Terry's different.

ANN. All this fuss about a man! I wouldn't lift my little finger to meet him. (*She stalks into the dining room.*)

LITTLE MARY. She's oversexed!

MRS. ORCUTT (*still among her souvenirs*). David Kingsley! You know, he was Al

Woods' office boy when I played *The Woman in Room* 13.

BERNICE (*not much interested*). Really? (*To* JEAN) What are you going to wear?

JEAN. I wonder if Pat'll let me have her rose taffeta.

BERNICE. Sure she would.

JEAN. And I'll wear Kendall's evening coat.

MRS. ORCUTT (*insistent*). When he became a producer he wanted me for his first play. But by that time I had married Mr. Orcutt— (*From abovestairs comes the sound of half-a-dozen voices haphazardly singing: "Here Comes the Bride!" The group in the room at once knows what this means, and their attention is turned toward the stairs.*)

BIG MARY. Oh, here's Louise!

BERNICE. Louise is going!

BOBBY. Oh, my goodness, I promised to help her pack.

LITTLE MARY. Let's get some rice and throw it!

BIG MARY. Oh, for heaven's sake, that's silly. (FRANK, *the houseman, comes down the stairs laden with bags. He is* MATTIE's *husband—thirty-five or so. Close on* FRANK's *heels comes* LOUISE MITCHELL *in traveling clothes, and wearing a corsage of gardenias. She is accompanied by three girls. One is* SUSAN, *a student at an acting school. The others are* PAT DEVINE, *a night-club dancer, and* KENDALL ADAMS, *of the Boston Adamses.*)
(MATTIE, *broadly grinning and anticipatory, comes to the dining-room doorway.*)
(LOUISE *is ushered into the room on a wave of melody.*)

MRS. ORCUTT. Well, my dear, and so the moment has come. But when you see how saddened we are, you will realize that parting is sweet sorrow, after all. (JUDITH *comes down the stairs, followed by* MADELEINE. *Both in dishabille.*)

JUDITH. Well, Mitchell, you're finally getting the hell out of here, huh?

MRS. ORCUTT. Judith! That seems to me hardly the spirit.

JUDITH. Sorry.

LOUISE. Judy doesn't mean anything.

FRANK (*in the doorway*). Shall I get you a taxi, Miss Louise?

LOUISE. Oh, yes, thank you, Frank. (*The moment of departure has come. She looks about her for a second.*) Well, I guess there's no use in my trying to— Why, where's Terry? I thought she was down here.

KENDALL. Isn't she here?

SUSAN. No.

JEAN. She hasn't come in yet.

LOUISE. Oh, dear, I can't go without seeing Terry.

BERNICE. What's she up to, anyhow? I haven't seen her for days.

JEAN. I don't know. She's gone before I'm awake in the morning.

LOUISE. Well, anyhow, I guess I'd better get out of here before I bust out crying. You've all been just too darling for words, every single one of you— (LINDA, *having retrieved her dress, flashes through the hall and makes for the stairs.*) Who's that? Oh, good-by, Linda. I'm going. (LINDA, *no part of this, tosses a "good-by" over her shoulder as she goes up the stairs.*) And no matter how happy I am, I'll never forget you, and thanks a million times for the perfume, Pat, and you, Susan, for the compact, and all of you that clubbed together and gave me the exquisite nightgown.

BERNICE (*accepting the credit*). Oh, that's all right.

LOUISE. So—I hope I'll make a better wife than I did an actress. I guess I wasn't very good at that—

BIG MARY (*stoutly*). You were so!

LITTLE MARY. You were swell!

LOUISE. I guess I wasn't *very* swell or I wouldn't be getting mar— (*Catches herself.*) —that is, any girl would be glad to give up the stage to marry a wonderful boy like Bob—anyway, I certainly am. Goodness, when I think that for two whole years he's waited back there in Appleton, I guess I'm pretty lucky.

BIG MARY (*obliging, but not meaning it*). Yes. (*The faces about her, while attentive, do not reflect full belief in Louise's good fortune.*)

LOUISE. Well, if any of you ever come out that way with a show, why, it's only a hundred miles from Milwaukee. Don't forget I'll be Mrs. Robert Hendershot by that time, and Wisconsin's perfectly beautiful in the autumn—the whole Fox River Valley—it's beautiful— (*It's no use. She cannot convince even herself, much less the rather embarrassed young people about her. The situation is miraculously saved by the slam of the street door and the electric entrance of a new and buoyant figure.*)

(TERRY RANDALL *has the vivid personality, the mobile face of the born actress. She is not at all conventionally beautiful, but the light in her face gives to her rather irregular features the effect of beauty. High cheekbones, wide mouth, broad brow.*)

TERRY (*breathless*). LOUISE! Dar-ling! I was so afraid you'd be gone. I ran all the way from Forty-sixth Street. Nothing else in the world could have kept me—look— what do you think! I've got a JOB! (*This announcement is greeted with a chorus of excited exclamations. "You haven't! . . Who with? . . . Tell us about it! . . . Terry, how wonderful! . . . Tell us all about it!"*) I will in a minute. . . . Louise, what a darling crazy hat! I just love it on you.

LOUISE. Oh, Terry, have you really got a job! What in?

JEAN. Who is it? Berger?

TERRY. Yes.

BERNICE. I thought he was all cast.

TERRY. He was, all except this one part. It's not big, but it's good. It's got one marvelous scene—you know— (*With three attitudes and a series of wordless sounds—one denunciatory, one tender, one triumphant —she amusingly conveys the range of the part.*)

(*From among the group, "It sounds marvelous! . . . Terry, you'll be wonderful!"*)

FRANK (*in the doorway*). Taxi's waiting, Miss Louise.

LOUISE (*a glance at her wrist watch*). Oh, dear, I can't bear to go. How'll I ever know the rest of it? Why did I ever— I've got to go—Terry, baby! (*Throws her arms about* TERRY, *kisses her. There is general embracing and good-bys.*) Jean! (*She kisses* JEAN, *her other roommate.*) Good-by, good-by! (LOUISE *is hurrying from the room, the others streaming into the hallway to speed her. "Don't forget us! . . . Send us a piece of wedding cake! . . . We want the deadly details. . . ." (From* MRS. ORCUTT) *"I hope you'll be very happy, dear child. Good-by . . . Good-by . . . Good-by!")*

(MATTIE, *giggling, tosses after* LOUISE *a handful of rice that she has brought from the kitchen.* LOUISE *is gone.*)

(*The girls stream back into the room.*)

KENDALL. When do you go into rehearsal, Terry?

OLGA. Yes, when?

TERRY. Right away!

BERNICE. Gosh, Terry, you certainly got a break. Berger wouldn't even talk to me.

LITTLE MARY. Berger's an awful meany. How'd you get to him, anyway?

TERRY. I just stood there outside his door for a week.

PAT. And it did the trick?

BIG MARY. *I* tried that.

BOBBY. It never helped *me* any.

JUDITH. Me neither. I laid there for a whole afternoon once with "Welcome!" on me.

TERRY. I've had a longer run outside his office than I've had with most shows. This was my second week. I was just going to send out for a toothbrush and a camp chair when suddenly he opened the door. He was going to send out for a toothbrush and a camp chair when suddenly he opened the door. He was going. I said, "Mr. Berger!" That's practically all I've said for two weeks —Mr. Berger. (*She gives an assortment of readings of "Mr. Berger," ranging from piteous pleading to imperious command.*)

LITTLE MARY. What did he do?

SUSAN. What happened?

TERRY. He never even stopped. Suddenly I was furious. I grabbed his arm and said, "Listen! You're a producer and I'm an actress. What right have you got to barricade yourself behind closed doors and not see me! And hundreds like me! The greatest actress in the world might be coming up your stairs and you'd never know it."

KENDALL. Terry! What did he say!

TERRY. He said, "Are you the greatest actress in the world?" I said, "Maybe." He said, "You don't look like anything to me. You're not even pretty and you're just a little runt." I said, "Pretty! I suppose Rachel was pretty. And what about Nazimova! She's no higher than this." (*Indicates a level.*) "But on a stage she's any height she wants to be."

JUDITH. P.S. She got the job.

TERRY. Yes. (*A deep sigh that conveys her relief at the outcome.*) And when I walked out on Broadway again it seemed the most glamorous street in the world. Those beautiful Nedick orange stands, and that lovely traffic at Broadway and Forty-fifth, and those darling bums spitting on the sidewalk— (*The doorbell rings. Instantaneously the group is galvanized. The girls realize the lateness of the hour.*)

(BOBBY *takes a peek out the window.*)

BOBBY. Oh, it's my new young man! Mattie, tell him I won't be a minute!

MADELEINE. Wait a minute, Mattie! Give us a chance to get upstairs!

JUDITH (*darting after her, gathering her negligée as she goes*). Yes, Mattie. We don't want to give him the wrong idea of this house. (*A handful of the girls, squealing for time, dash into the dining room.*)

(JEAN *starts up the stairs with* TERRY.)

JEAN. Terry! What do you think's happened to your little girl friend! I'm having dinner with David Kingsley tonight.

TERRY. Jean, how marvelous! Did he say anything about a picture test?

JEAN. Not yet, but it must mean he's interested. Now look, when he gets here I want you to come down and meet him, because you never can tell. (MATTIE, *having waited until the coast was clear, now goes to the front door. There is the sound of a man's voice. "Is Miss Melrose in?" MATTIE's reply, "Yes, she is. Come right in."*)

(*A* YOUNG MAN *stands in the doorway, a trifle ill at ease in these unfamiliar surroundings. He hasn't the look of a New Yorker. There is about him the rather graceful angularity and winning simplicity of the Westerner.*)

MATTIE. You-all can wait in there.

THE YOUNG MAN. Oh, thanks. Just tell her Sam Hastings is calling for her.

MATTIE (*as she goes to the dining-room door*). I think she knows about it— She'll be down directly. (SAM HASTINGS *mutters a thank-you as* MATTIE *passes into the dining room, closing the doors behind her.*)

(*Left alone, and not yet at ease,* SAM HASTINGS *makes a leisurely survey of the room, rather getting in the way of his own big frame as he turns. He decides, unfortunately, on the least substantial chair in the room and sits gingerly on its edge. At once there is a short sharp crack of protesting wood. He is on his feet like a shot. From above-stairs a snatch of popular song. Swift foot-steps are heard descending the stairs. He rises expectantly, but it's not his girl. It is* KENDALL, *who is humming a bit of song as she comes. She pauses on the stairs to fix her stocking. She stops abruptly as she sees a stranger. With a glare at the embarrassed* HASTINGS *she goes into the dining room. Then a peremptory voice shouts from up-stairs; "Judy! You going to stay in the johnny all night?" He clears his throat and looks away, though there's nothing to look away from.*) (*The doorbell rings.*)

(BERNICE *comes out of the dining room. Her eye brightens as she beholds the young man.*)

BERNICE (*summoning all her charm*). Pardon me. You're not Mr. David Kingsley!

SAM. No. My name's Hastings. (*With a syllable of dismissal,* BERNICE *goes on her way, and up the stairs.*)

(*By this time* MATTIE *is opening the front door. A voice inquires, "Miss Paige in?" "Yes, come right in."*)

(*The* BOY *who appears is even younger than* SAM HASTINGS. *Perhaps nineteen. Slight, graceful, dark-haired, rather sensitive look-ing.*)

MATTIE (*calls from the foot of the stairs*). Miss Susan! (SUSAN's *voice from upstairs—* "All right, Mattie!")

(*The two* BOYS *confront each other rather uncertainly. The newcomer in the doorway ventures a mannerly, "How do you do?" "Howdy-do?" There is a little awkward pause.*)

THE NEWCOMER. My name's Devereaux.

SAM. Mine's Hastings.

DEVEREAUX. Yes, I recognized you. I saw you in that Keith Burgess play last month.

SAM. You sure must have looked quick.

DEVEREAUX. I liked that part. You did a lot with it. Too bad the play flopped.

SAM. I don't rightly recall you. Have you done anything lately?

DEVEREAUX. Last month I played Emperor Jones, and I'm cast now for Hamlet.

SAM. Hamlet?

DEVEREAUX. I'm at the New York School of Acting. This is my last year.

SAM. Oh! And then what?

DEVEREAUX. Then I'm going on the stage.

SAM. Did you ever try to get a job on the stage?

DEVEREAUX. Not yet.

SAM. That's more of a career than acting. I've been in New York two years. I'm from Texas. Houston Little Theater. We came up and won a contest, and I stayed. I've had ten weeks' work in two years. Don't ask me how I live. I don't know.

DEVEREAUX. You could go back to Texas, couldn't you?

SAM. Go back! Oh, no! I'm an actor. (SUSAN *runs down the stairs, in street clothes.*)

SUSAN. Hello, Jimmy!

DEVEREAUX. Hello, Sue. Do you know Mr. Hastings?

SUSAN. Howdy-do?

DEVEREAUX. Miss Susan Paige. She's up at the school, too. She's going to do Hedda Gabler.

SAM. Well, you have to start somewhere.

SUSAN (*laughingly*). Yes. (DEVEREAUX *says, "good-by!" There is a word of farewell from* HASTINGS *and* SUSAN *as the doorbell rings.*)

DEVEREAUX (*as he and* SUSAN *go into the hall*). Where do you want to eat?

SUSAN. How much money have you got?

DEVEREAUX. Sixty-five cents.

SUSAN. I've got thirty. That's ninety-five. (*As they open the door they are accosted by a hearty masculine voice, subsequently identified as that of* FRED POWELL. *"This the Footlights Club?"*)

SUSAN. Yes. Won't you just— Mattie! Somebody at the door.

MATTIE (*having appeared in the hallway*). Yes'm, Miss Susan. . . . You gentlemen calling on somebody? (FRED POWELL *and* LOU MILHAUSER *come into view. They are two overhearty Big Business Men out for a holiday. Their derby hats and daytime attire will be a shock to the girls, especially* JUDITH.)

POWELL. Yes, we're calling for Miss Madeleine Vauclain.

MILHAUSER. And her friend.

MATTIE (*at the foot of the stairs*). Miss Madeleine! . . . Couple gentlemen down here say they calling for you and—somebody.

MADELEINE. Coming down!

MATTIE. She's coming down. (*They come into the living room, and finding another man there, offer a tentative greeting; a smile and wave of the hand. Then they look the room over.*)

MILHAUSER. What'd you say this place was? A Home for Girls?

POWELL. Yeah, all actresses. A whole bunch of 'em live here.

MILHAUSER. Kind of a handy place to know about.

POWELL. Yeah.

MILHAUSER (*whisks from his pocket two cellophaned cigars*). Smoke?

POWELL. Thanks. (*As they light up, having tossed the crumpled cellophane jackets to a near-by table,* POWELL *sends a glance of half-inquiry at* SAM. *Hastily, in order to divert any further advances,* SAM *opens his cigarette case and lights a cigarette.*)

MILHAUSER. Certainly is a funny place, New York. Now, you take a layout like this. Wouldn't find it anywhere else in the world.

POWELL. Bet you wouldn't, at that.

MILHAUSER. I—I always thought actresses lived in flats or—uh—hotel rooms.

POWELL. Lot of 'em do.

MILHAUSER (*struck by a new thought*). What about men actors—where do they live?

POWELL. I don't know—Lambs' Club, I guess.

MILHAUSER. Oh, yeah. (SAM HASTINGS *shifts his position a little, throws them a look*). (BOBBY MELROSE, *finally coming down the stairs, saves the situation. She is at her most Southern.*)

BOBBY MELROSE (*from the stairs*). Hello there, Texas!

SAM (*gathering up his coat and hat*). Oh, hello!

BOBBY. Ah hope Ah didn't keep you waitin'.

SAM. No! No!

BOBBY. One thing about me, Ah'm always prompt. (*The outer door closes. They are gone.*)

POWELL. That was a cute little trick.

MILHAUSER. Yeah. . . . Look! What about this one you've got on the fire for me? She any good?

POWELL. Sure, sure. You leave it to Madeleine.

MILHAUSER. Oh, well, as long as she's good-natured. (*There is a rustle of silk on the stairway. "Ah!" exclaims* POWELL, *in anticipation and relief.*)

(MADELEINE *and* JUDITH *descend the stairs in full evening regalia, gathered from the richest recesses of the club—furs, silks, gloves, jewelry.*)

MADELEINE (*furiously, as she catches sight of the men's attire*). Well, is this what you call dressing?

POWELL. Huh?

MADELEINE. Why didn't you come in overalls!

POWELL. Now, now, baby. We got snarled up in a committee meeting, didn't we, Lou?

MILHAUSER. Sure. Sure.

POWELL. This is Ben Dexter, girls. Miss Madeleine Vauclain and—uh—

MADELEINE (*sulkily*). This is Miss Canfield.

MILHAUSER (*coming right up to* JUDITH's *expectations*). Hello, Beautiful! (*Very jovial.*) How about it? Shall we step out and go places?

JUDITH (*sourly*). Yes, let's.

MILHAUSER. Now don't be like that. We're going to have a good time.

POWELL. Sure we are! The works! (*He is piloting* MADELEINE *out to the hallway.*) Come on, boys and girls! Where do you want to eat?

MILHAUSER. I got an idea. How about a little Italian place?

JUDITH. Little Italian *nuts!* I want a decent dinner. (*A slam of the door. They are gone.*)
(KENDALL *comes out of the dining room and busies herself at the mirror.* OLGA *follows, adjusting her hat and cape as she enters.*)

OLGA. Kendall, are you going to your show? I am rehearsing at the Winter Garden, if you want to walk down.

KENDALL. No, it's too early for me. We don't go up till eight-fifty.

OLGA (*with almost too much Slavic bitterness*). The Winter Garden! The star pupil of Kolijinsky, at the Winter Garden! (*She goes.*)

LITTLE MARY (*who, with the inevitable* BIG MARY *at her side, has come into the room just in time to hear this*). Bellyaching, and she's got a job. Look at me. (*She flops into a seat.*) Edwin Booth and I retired from the stage at practically the same time.

KENDALL. I think I'll take a rest before the night show. Matinee days are frightfully tiring. (*She goes up to her room.*)

BIG MARY. Frightfully tiring! Why doesn't she go back to Boston, where she belongs! That'd rest her up.

LITTLE MARY. There ought to be an equity law against society girls going on the stage. "Miss Kendall Adams, daughter of Mr. and Mrs. Roger Winthrop Adams."

BIG MARY. Of Boston and the Lucky Strike ads. (PAT *and* ANN *come out of the dining room. There is the tinkle of china and silver.*)

The doors are shut by MATTIE. *Dinner is over.*)

ANN. What's it like out? It looked rainy when I came in. (*Goes to the hallway for her coat.*)

BIG MARY (*at the window*). No, it's all right. . . . Oh, girls, look! There's the Cadillac again for Linda Shaw.

LITTLE MARY. Is *he* in it?

BIG MARY. No, just the chauffeur, same as always.

PAT. Who's the guy, anyhow? Anybody know?

LITTLE MARY. He doesn't ever come. Just sends the car.

PAT. Well, nice work if you can get it.

ANN (*righteously*). I think it's disgraceful. A nice girl wouldn't want a man to send for her that way. And if you ask me, it gives the club a bad name. (*A warning gesture and a "Pss-s-st!" from* LITTLE MARY *as* LINDA *descends the stairs.*)
(LINDA *is beautifully dressed for the evening. She is wearing the dress whose pressing had annoyed her; her evening cape is handsomely furred. Enormous orchids.*)

BIG MARY. Oo, Linda! How gorgeous!

LINDA (*pausing reluctantly*). Oh, hello.

LITTLE MARY. Come on in. Let's see you.

BIG MARY. What a marvelous coat, Linda!

PAT. Yes, and a very nifty bit of jack rabbit, if I may say so. (*Her finger outlines a collar in the air.*)

LINDA. Oh, that! Mother sent it to me. It used to be on a coat of hers.

LITTLE MARY. It's lovely.

PAT (*mildly*). Oh—Mother has a nice taste in orchids, too.

LINDA (*baring her fangs*). Yes. Don't you wish you had a mother like mine? (*She sweeps out.*)
(*The two* MARYS *dart to the window.*)

PAT. What would you two do without that window? Why don't you pull up a rocking chair!

ANN. Linda Shaw's comings and goings don't interest me. Girls make such fools of themselves about men! (*She goes.*)

BIG MARY. Say! What do you know about Jean? Having dinner with David Kingsley!

LITTLE MARY. Some girls have all the luck. Where'd she meet him, anyhow?

BIG MARY. Oh, some cocktail party.

PAT. I wish *I* could meet him. He can spot picture material just like that. (*She snaps her fingers.*) He's got an eye like a camera.

LITTLE MARY. Yeh, he picked three picture stars last year. Nobody ever heard of 'em before he sent 'em out there.

PAT. Well, *I'll* never meet him. (*She indulges in an elaborate yawn and stretch.*) Oh, what to do till eleven o'clock. Except sleep.

LITTLE MARY. Anyhow, you've got something to *do* at eleven. . . . Look at us!

BIG MARY. Yeh, you're working.

PAT. I hate it. Hoofing in a night club for a lot of tired business men. The trouble is they're *not* tired and there's no business. (*The doorbell rings.*)

BIG MARY (*at the window*). I think it's David Kingsley! It looks like him.

PAT. Kingsley? Are you sure?

LITTLE MARY (*peering*). Yes, that's him. Look, we'd better get out of the way, hadn't we?

BIG MARY. Yes, I guess so. (PAT, *mindful of her pajamas, also gathers herself together.*)
(BERNICE *descends the stairs with rather elaborate unconcern.*)

BERNICE (*too polite*). Oh, pardon me, I just want to speak to—Frank—about—something— (*She dashes into the dining room.*)
(PAT *stands looking after* BERNICE *for a second. Then as* MATTIE *crosses the hallway to answer the door* PAT *makes her own decision and darts up the stairs.*)
(*A man's voice at the door.*)

KINGSLEY (*in the hall*). Miss Maitland, please.

MATTIE. Yessuh. Come right in.

KINGSLEY. Tell her Mr. Kingsley. (DAVID KINGSLEY *enters. Perhaps thirty-six or -seven. A man of decided charm and distinction. He is wearing evening clothes. You see his white muffler above the dark topcoat.*)

MATTIE. If you'll just rest yourself—I'll go right up. (MATTIE *goes up the stairs with a stateliness that indicates her appreciation of the caller's importance.*)
(KINGSLEY *glances about the room a bit. He opens his cigarette case, lights a cigarette.*)
(BERNICE *comes out of the dining room. Her face is turned toward someone in the room she has just left and it is this person she is addressing, apparently all unaware that anyone (certainly not Kingsley) is in the living room. With one quick twist she has altered—or thinks she has altered—the arrangement of her hair so as to make of herself a more arresting type.*)

BERNICE. Yes, Mattie, an actress's life is such an interesting one, if you could only see the different types that I do in the course of a day, Mattie. For example, an English actress came into an office today. (*Goes suddenly very English.*) "My dear Harry, how definitely ripping to see you. Definitely ripping!" And then, Mattie, a little girl from Brooklyn came in. "Listen, I did write for an appurntment! You got a noive!" (*She turns, and to her obvious embarrassment there is* MR. KINGSLEY. *She is a picture of pretty confusion.*) Oh, I am so sorry! I didn't dream anyone was here.

KINGSLEY (*politely amused*). That's quite all right.

BERNICE (*following up her advantage*). I'm —Bernice Niemeyer. (KINGSLEY *bows slightly, murmurs her name.*) Well—I just thought— (*She is dangling at the end of her rope.*)
(*Here she is mercifully interrupted by* PAT's *descent of the stairs. The jacket of* PAT's *pajama suit is missing. Her slim figure is well revealed in the trousers and scant short-sleeved top. Her low-heeled scuffs have been replaced by pert high-heeled mules.*)

PAT. I wonder— (*Makes a slow turn toward* BERNICE—*a turn which by a strange chance serves at the same time to reveal the best points of her figure to the waiting* KINGLEY.) You—you didn't see my book anywhere around here, did you?

BERNICE (*sourly*). What book? (*She goes up the stairs.*)

(PAT *flutters in her quest to a table, goes to the book-shelf, selects a volume, ruffles its pages to make sure that the book meets her mood, then gives a little sigh of delight, clasps the book to her breast and trips up the stairs.*)

(KINGSLEY *barely has time to seat himself again before another aspirant for his approval appears.*)

(*It is* MRS. ORCUTT, *who has shed her workaday dress for something very grand in the way of a silk dinner gown.*)

MRS. ORCUTT (*outstretched hands*). David Kingsley! Little David Kingsley!

KINGSLEY (*a little bewildered, rises to meet the emergency*). Why—how do you do!

MRS. ORCUTT (*coquettishly*). Surely you remember me.

KINGSLEY (*lying bravely*). Of course I do.

MRS. ORCUTT. Who am I? (KINGSLEY *has an instant of panic.*) Now think. Helen who?— Ro—

KINGSLEY (*catches desperately at this straw*). Ro—

MRS. ORCUTT. —mayne! Helen Romayne!

KINGSLEY (*repeating it just the barest flash behind her*). Helen Romayne. Why, of course! Well, what a charming surprise. Imagine your remembering me! A scrubby little kid in the office.

MRS. ORCUTT. But that little office boy became one of the most brilliant producers in the theater. Those beautiful plays! I loved them all.

KINGSLEY. So did I. But something happened to the theater about that time. It was sort of shot from under us.

MRS. ORCUTT. But you've gone right on. You've risen to even greater triumphs in the pictures.

KINGSLEY (*quietly ironic*). Yes, even greater triumphs. (*A step on the stair.* MRS. ORCUTT *turns.*)

MRS. ORCUTT. Well—it was lovely seeing you. I hope you'll be coming again.

KINGSLEY. I hope so, too. (MRS. ORCUTT *makes her escape as* JEAN *appears on the*

stairs, *resplendent in her borrowed finery.* PAT's *rose taffeta, and* KENDALL's *evening wrap.*)

JEAN. So glad to see you, Mr. Kingsley.

KINGSLEY. I'm glad you happened to be free.

JEAN. I guess girls generally manage to be free when you invite them.

KINGSLEY. You don't think my being in the motion-picture business may have something to do with it?

JEAN. Why, Mr. Kingsley, how can you say such a thing!

KINGSLEY. You think it's all sheer charm, huh?

JEAN. Of course. . . . Look, would you mind awfully if I— (*Calls up the stairs.*) Terry! Come *on!*

TERRY (*from above*). I'm coming.

JEAN. That's Terry Randall, my roommate. Did you see *Cyclone*? Or *The Eldest Son*?

KINGSLEY. Oh, yes. In *Cyclone*—she was—

JEAN. It was just a tiny part. She came into the drugstore.

KINGSLEY. Oh, yes. Just a bit, but she was good. . . . Yes, she was excellent! (TERRY *comes down the stairs.*)

(*She is still wearing the plain dark little dress in which we have previously seen her. If it were not for the glowing face she would seem rather drab in comparison to the dazzling* JEAN.)

TERRY (*with great directness*). Well, if you will come calling at a girls' club, Mr. Kingsley, what can you expect?

KINGSLEY. I didn't expect anything as charming as this.

TERRY. Mm! You *are* in the moving-picture business, aren't you?

KINGSLEY. I am, Miss Randall. But my soul belongs to God.

JEAN. Don't you think she'd be good for pictures, Mr. Kingsley? Look. (*Turning* TERRY's *profile to show to the best advantage.*)

TERRY. I think I'd be terrible.

JEAN. Don't talk like that. Of course she's rehearsing now in the new Berger play. That is, she starts tomorrow.

KINGSLEY. Good! I hear it's an interesting play.

TERRY. Do you know the first play I ever saw, Mr. Kingsley?

KINGSLEY. No, what?

TERRY. It was your production of *Amaryllis*.

KINGSLEY. *Amaryllis!* You couldn't have seen that! That was my first production. Ten years ago.

TERRY. I did, though. I was eleven years old, and I saw it at English's Opera House, in Indianapolis. My mother took me. She cried all the way through it, and so did I. We had a lovely time.

KINGSLEY. But *Amaryllis* wasn't a sad play.

TERRY. Oh, we didn't cry because we were sad. Mother cried because it brought back the days when she was an actress, and I cried because I was so happy. You see, we lived seventy-five miles from Indianapolis, and it was the first time I'd ever been in a theater.

JEAN. Now, really, I don't think it's tactful to talk about the theater to a picture man.

TERRY. I'm afraid I'm kind of dumb about pictures. Mother used to say the theater had two offspring—the legitimate stage, and the bastard.

JEAN (*taking* KINGSLEY *by the hand and pulling him from the room*). Come on! And forget I ever introduced her to you. (*He goes, calling, "Good-by, Miss Randall!"*)

TERRY (*calling after him*). Oh, I hope I didn't—

KINGSLEY (*as the door closes on them*). It's all right. I forgive you. (*Left alone,* TERRY *suddenly realizes she has had no dinner. As she goes toward the dining room she calls.*)

TERRY. Mattie! (*She opens the dining-room doors.*) Oh, dear, is dinner over!

MATTIE. Yes. I'm just clearing away.

TERRY. Oh, Mattie darling, could you let me have just anything! Champagne and a little caviar?

MATTIE (*in the dining room*). Well, I'll fix you a plate of something.

TERRY. You're an angel. (KENDALL ADAMS *comes down the stairs, dressed for the street. At sight of* TERRY *she pauses a moment to chat.*)

KENDALL. Isn't it splendid, Terry, about your getting a job!

TERRY. It seems pretty dazzling to me, after six months. I only hope it's as big a hit as yours.

KENDALL. It's queer about being in a hit. You go through everything to get into one, and after a few months you're bored with it. It's like marriage. (*The doorbell rings.*) (*Calls.*) It's all right, Mattie, I'll answer it. . . . Going out, Terry?

TERRY. Not tonight.

KENDALL (*at the street door*). See you later. (*A voice at the door. "Hello there! Who are you!"* KENDALL'S *voice, a film of ice over it. "I beg your pardon!" The man's voice explains, "I'm looking for Jean Maitland."* KENDALL *calls, "Mattie!" and goes on her way. The call is unheard by* MATTIE.)

(KEITH BURGESS *appears in the archway. He is the kind of young man who never wears a hat. Turtle-necked sweater, probably black; unpressed tweed suit; unshaven.*)

KEITH. Where's Jean Maitland?

TERRY. In a taxi with a big moving-picture man.

KEITH. She can't be. She had a date with me.

TERRY. Sorry. It isn't my fault.

KEITH. Who are you?

TERRY. Who wants to know?

KEITH. Are you an actress?

TERRY. Are you dizzy in the morning? Do you have spots before the eyes?

KEITH. My name is Keith Burgess.

TERRY. Is it?

KEITH. Don't you know who I am?

TERRY. Yes. You're a playwright, and you wrote a play called *Blood and Roses* that was produced at the Fourteenth Street

Theater, and it ran a week and it wasn't very good.

KEITH. It was the best goddam play that was ever produced in New York! And the one I'm writing now is even better.

TERRY. Mm! *Two* weeks.

KEITH (*vastly superior*). I don't think in terms of material success. Who cares whether a play makes money! All that matters is its message!

TERRY (*mildly*). But if nobody comes to see it, who gets the message?

KEITH. I write about the worker! The masses! The individual doesn't count in modern society.

TERRY. But aren't the masses made up of individuals?

KEITH. Don't quibble!

TERRY. I'm so sorry.

KEITH. I ask nothing as an individual. My work, my little room—that's all.

TERRY. No furniture?

KEITH. A table, a bed, a chair. My books. My music. And— (*The doorbell has rung, and* FRANK *has crossed the hall to answer it. The voice of* KAYE HAMILTON *is now heard at the door.* KEITH, *accordingly, is forced to suspend for a moment.*)

KAYE. I'm Miss Hamilton. Kaye Hamilton.

FRANK. Oh yes. I think Mrs. Orcutt's expecting you. (MRS. ORCUTT *appears in the hallway just in time to greet the new arrival.*)

MRS. ORCUTT. Glad to see you again, Miss Hamilton. Everything's in readiness for you. Frank, take Miss Hamilton's things right up. Oh! (*As she sees* TERRY *in the living room.*) Terry, this is Kaye Hamilton, who's going to share the room with you and Jean. Terry Randall.

KAYE. I'll try not to be in the way.

TERRY. Oh, don't start that way! Grab your share of the closet hooks.

KAYE. Thank you.

MRS. ORCUTT. Now, if you'll just come with me I'll show you where everything is.

TERRY (*as they start up*). Let me know if I can be of any help.

MRS. ORCUTT (*talking as they ascend*). If you have a trunk check Frank will take care of all that for you.

KAYE. No, no, I haven't got a trunk. (*They are gone.*)
(KEITH, *throughout the above scene, has been observing* TERRY *with an old-fashioned eye of appreciation.*)

KEITH. Hey! Turn around! (*She does so, rather wonderingly.*) You shouldn't wear your hair like that. It hides your face.

TERRY. Oh, do you notice faces? I thought you were above all that.

KEITH. I notice everything. Your head's too big for the rest of you, you've got pretty legs, but you oughtn't to wear red.

TERRY (*surveying him*). I suppose you're known as Beau Burgess! What the Well-Dressed Man Will Wear!

KEITH. Oh, you like snappy dressers, eh? Monograms and cuff links.

TERRY. No, I don't meet very many monograms.

KEITH (*his gaze roaming around the room*). What do you live in this place for? Do you like it?

TERRY. I love it. We live and breathe theater, and that's what I'm crazy about.

KEITH (*eagerly*). Are you? So am I. What do you want to *do* in the theater? What kind of parts do you want to play?

TERRY. I want to play everything I'm not suited for. Old hags of eighty, and Topsy, and Lady Macbeth. And what do I get? Ingenues—and very little of that.

KEITH. Don't take 'em. Wait till you get what you want.

TERRY. Well, it's a nice idea. But did you ever hear of this thing called eating?

KEITH. You mustn't think of that. Why, I've lived on bread and cocoa for days at a time. If you believe in something you've got to be willing to starve for it.

TERRY. I'm willing. But you don't know what it is to be an actress. If you feel something you can write it. But I can't act unless they let me. I can't just walk up and down my room, being an actress.

KEITH. It's just as tough for a writer. Suppose they won't produce his plays? I write about ironworkers and they want grand dukes. I could write potboilers, but I don't. The theater shouldn't be just a place to earn a living in. It should be thunder and lightning, and power and truth.

TERRY. And magic and romance!

KEITH. No, no! Romance is for babies! I write about *today!* I want to tear the heart out of the rotten carcass they call life, and hold it up bleeding for all the world to see!

TERRY. How about putting some heart *into* life, instead of tearing it out?

KEITH. There's no place for sentiment in the world today. We've gone past it.

TERRY. I suppose that's why you never hear of *Romeo and Juliet.*

KEITH (*turning away*). That's a woman's argument.

TERRY. Well, I'm a woman.

KEITH (*once more surveying her*). Why haven't I run into you before? Where've you been all the time?

TERRY. Right here, in and out of every manager's office on Broadway.

KEITH. Me too. But I'm going to keep right on until they listen to me. And you've got to keep right on too!

TERRY. I will! I'm going to! (MATTIE appears in the dining-room doorway.)

MATTIE. You-all want your dinner now, Miss Terry? It's ready.

TERRY. Why, I'd forgotten all about it, Mattie.

KEITH (*taking control*). Never mind, Mattie! . . . How about dinner with me? We'll go to Smitty's and have a couple of hamburgers.

TERRY (*not at all unwilling*). With onions?

KEITH. Sure—onions! . . . Say, what the hell's your name, anyway? (*They start for the door. The two* MARYS *are coming down the stairs again, deep in an argument, as usual.*)

CURTAIN

SCENE II

One of the bedrooms. A pleasant enough but rather cramped room, with three beds, three dressers, three small chairs. There is a bathroom door down left, a window center. A door up left leads to hall.

Each dresser reflects something of the personality and daily life of its owner. Stuck in the sides of the mirrors are snapshots, photographs, newspaper clippings, telegrams, theater programs.

It is night, and through the window we get a glimpse of the city's lights.

At the beginning the room is unoccupied.

KAYE HAMILTON *comes out of the bathroom, closes the door. She is wearing a bathrobe over her nightgown. Goes to her dresser, which is conspicuously bare of ornaments, souvenirs, or photographs. She opens the dresser top drawer, takes out her handbag, removes her money from a small purse and counts it, a process which doesn't take long. Two dollars and sixty cents.*

There is a knock at the door.

KAYE. Yes?

JUDITH (*as she opens the door*). Can I come in? Where's Terry?

KAYE. She isn't back yet. (JUDITH *is wearing sleeping pajamas and she is in the process of doing her face up for the night. A chin strap is tied about her face and ends in a top-knot. A net safeguards her curls.*)

JUDITH. Look, do you think she'd mind if I borrowed some of her frowners? I forgot to get some.

KAYE. I think there's some in her top drawer.

JUDITH (*as she pulls open the drawer*). Thanks. . . . You don't go out much evenings, do you?

KAYE. No.

JUDITH. Any sign of a job yet?

KAYE. No, not yet.

JUDITH. Something'll turn up. It always does. (*She waits a moment for* KAYE's *answer, but there is none.*) You know, you're a funny kid. You've been here a month, and I don't know any more about you than when you came in. The rest of us are always spilling our whole insides, but you never let out a peep. Nobody comes to see you, no phone calls, never go out nights, you haven't even got a picture on your dresser. Haven't you got any folks? Or a beau or something? (*No sound from* KAYE. JUDITH *turns to glance at her.*) Sorry. My mistake. (*The voices of* BIG *and* LITTLE MARY *are heard in the hall.* BIG MARY: "*Mm, somebody's cooking something.*" LITTLE MARY: "*Smells like a rarebit.*")
(*The two* MARYS, *in hats and coats, stick their heads in at the door.*)

LITTLE MARY. Who's cooking? You?

JUDITH. No—Madeleine. Where've you been? Show?

BIG MARY (*dourly*). Yes. We saw the Breadline Players in *Tunnel of Death*.

LITTLE MARY. Come on, let's get some rarebit before it's all gone. (*They disappear down the hallway.*)

JUDITH. Terry's late, isn't she? It's halfpast eleven. And she isn't in the last act?

KAYE. She'll be here in a minute. Have you seen the play?

JUDITH. I haven't had time yet. I'm going tomorrow night.

KAYE. I didn't like it very much, but Terry's awfully good. Just a little part, but you always knew she was on. (PAT *appears in the doorway. She is wearing a tailored suit and hat.*)

PAT (*peering around*). Anybody in here? . . . Well, off to the mines.

JUDITH. Hello, Pat. Going to work?

PAT (*wearily*). Yeh, the night shift. (*She does a rather listless floor-show dance step; disappears.*)

KAYE. I wonder what it'd be like, working in a night club. I wish I'd learned to dance.

JUDITH (*intent on her own reflection in the mirror*). Well, with your looks you'll get along all right. (*She wanders over to* KAYE's *dresser.*) Where's your hand mirror? Why, where's the whole set?

KAYE. I haven't got it any more.

JUDITH (*a little too casually*). It was—gold, wasn't it?

KAYE. Uh-huh.

JUDITH. I see. . . . Got any folks you have to support?

KAYE (*quietly*). No, I haven't any folks.

JUDITH. Well, if you want some, I'm the girlie that can fix you up. Five brothers and four sisters, and you couldn't scare up a dollar eighty among the lot. I've got a little sister named Doris. Fifteen, and as innocent as Mata Hari. She's coming to New York next year to duplicate my success.

KAYE (*somewhat wistfully*). I think it would be rather nice, having a little sister with you.

JUDITH. Yeh, only she won't be with me much. Two weeks, and they'll have her in the Home for Delinquent Girls. (TERRY *enters, a drooping figure. A glance at the two occupants of the room. Her back to the door, she slowly closes it behind her and slumps against it.*)

TERRY. Young lady, willing, talented, not very beautiful, finds herself at liberty. Will double in brass, will polish brass, will *eat* brass before very long. Hi, girls!

KAYE. Terry, what's the matter?

TERRY. We closed. Four performances and we closed.

KAYE. Terry, you didn't!

JUDITH. Tonight! But it's only Thursday!

TERRY. Well, it seems you can close on Thursday just as well as Saturday—in fact, it's even better; it gives you two more days to be sunk in.

JUDITH. But it didn't get bad notices. What happened?

TERRY. We just got to the theater tonight, and there it was on the call board. "To the Members of the *Blue Grotto* Company: You are hereby advised that the engagement of the *Blue Grotto* will terminate after to-night's performance. Signed, Milton H. Schwepper, for Berger Productions, Incorporated."

KAYE. Terry, how ghastly!

JUDITH. Just like that, huh?

TERRY. Just like that. We stood there for a minute and read it. Then we sort of got together in the dressing rooms and talked about it in whispers, the way you do at a funeral. And then we all put on our make-up and gave the best damned performance we'd ever given.

JUDITH. Any other job in the world, if you get canned you can have a good cry in the washroom and go home. But show business! You take it on the chin and then paint up your face and out on the stage as gay as anything. "My dear Lady Barbara, what an enchanting place you have here! And what a quaint idea, giving us pigs' knuckles for tea!"

TERRY. Yes, it was awfully jolly. I wouldn't have minded if Berger or somebody had come backstage and said, "Look, we're sorry to do this to you, and better luck next time." But nobody came around—not Berger, or the author, or the director or anybody. They can all run away at a time like that, but the actors have to stay and face it.

JUDITH. You'll get something else, Terry. You got swell notices in this one.

TERRY. Nobody remembers notices except the actors who get them.

KAYE. The movie scouts remember. What about your screen test?

JUDITH. Yes, how about that? Have you heard from it?

TERRY. Oh, I'm not counting on that. They might take Jean. She's got that camera face. But they'll never burn up the coast wires over me.

JUDITH. Jean can't act. You're ten times the actress that she is.

TERRY. Oh, how do you know who's an actress and who isn't! You're an actress if you're acting. Without a job and those lines to say, an actress is just an ordinary person, trying not to look as scared as she feels. What is there about it, anyhow! Why do we all keep trying? (*The door opens and*

BERNICE *enters—rather solemnly. Her mood fits none too well with the definitely pink pajamas that form the basis of her costume, so you gather that it must have to do with a great filmy bit of black something that she has draped around her head and shoulders, and which trails behind her at enormous length. Obviously, she thinks that Modjeska herself could not have achieved a finer characterization.*)

BERNICE. How do I look?

KAYE. Marvelous.

JUDITH. What *are* you?

BERNICE (*in the voice of a woman anywhere between forty and eighty.*) I'm trying out tomorrow. The Theatre Guild is reviving Madame X. (*She goes—the perfect embodiment of Madame X, or anyhow Little Eva.*) (*Meanwhile* MADELEINE *has come down the hall and now stands lounging in the doorway, a plate of food in one hand, a fork in the other.*)

MADELEINE. Anybody want some chop suey? Terry? Kaye?

TERRY. No, thank you.

KAYE. No, thanks.

JUDITH (*tempted by this*). Chop suey? I thought it was rarebit.

MADELEINE. We didn't have any beer, so I'm calling it chop suey. (*She goes.*)

JUDITH. Certainly sounds terrible. (*Turns, with a hand on the door.*) Look, I guess you want this closed, huh?

TERRY. Yes, please. (*The door closes.* KAYE *and* TERRY *are alone. With a sigh* TERRY *again faces reality. Listlessly she begins to undress.* KAYE *is almost ready for bed. As she turns back the bedclothes she pauses to regard* TERRY.)

KAYE. I know how sunk you feel, Terry. It's that horrible letdown after the shock has worn off.

TERRY. The idiotic part of it is that I didn't feel so terrible after that first minute. I thought, well, Keith's coming around after the show, and we'll go to Smitty's and sit there and talk and it won't seem so bad. But he never showed up.

KAYE. Terry, I shouldn't try to advise you where men are concerned. I haven't been very smart myself—but this isn't the first time he's let you down. Don't get in too deep with a boy like Keith Burgess. It'll only make you unhappy.

TERRY. I don't expect him to be like other people. I wouldn't want him to be. One of the things that makes him so much fun is that he's different. If he forgets an appointment it's because he's working and doesn't notice. Only—I wish he had come tonight. (*She is pulling her dress over her head as she talks and her words are partly muffled until she emerges.*) I needed him so. (*Suddenly her defenses are down.*) Kaye, I'm frightened. For the first time, I'm frightened. It's three years now. The first year it didn't matter so much. I was so young. Nobody was ever as young as I was. I thought, they just don't know. But I'll get a good part and show them. I didn't mind anything in those days. Not having any money, or quite enough food; and a pair of silk stockings always a major investment. I didn't mind because I felt so sure that that wonderful part was going to come along. But it hasn't. And suppose it doesn't next year? Suppose it—never comes?

KAYE. You can always go home. You've got a home to go to, anyhow.

TERRY. And marry some home-town boy— like Louise?

KAYE. I didn't mean that, exactly.

TERRY. I can't just go home and plump myself down on Dad. You know what a country doctor makes! When I was little I never knew how poor we were, because Mother made everything seem so glamorous—so much fun. (*All this time* TERRY *has continued her preparations for bed. At one point in her disrobing she has gone to the clothes closet, hung up her dress, and slipped her nightgown over her head. Unseen there, for a moment, she has gone on talking.*) Even if I was sick it was a lot of fun, because then I was allowed to look at her scrapbook. I even used to pretend to be sick, just to look at it—and that took acting, with a doctor for a father. I adored that scrapbook. All those rep-company actors in wooden attitudes—I remember a wonderful picture of Mother as Esmeralda. It was the last part she ever played, and she never finished the performance.

KAYE. What happened?

TERRY. She fainted, right in the middle of the last act. They rang down and somebody said, "Is there a doctor in the house?" And there was. And he married her.

KAYE. Terry, how romantic!

TERRY. Only first she was sick for weeks and weeks. Of course the company had to leave her behind. They thought she'd catch up with them any week, but she never did.

KAYE. Didn't she ever miss it? I mean afterward.

TERRY. I know now that she missed it every minute of her life. I think if Dad hadn't been such a gentle darling, and not so dependent on her, she might have gone off and taken me with her. I'd have been one of those children brought up in dressing rooms, sleeping in trunk trays, getting my vocabulary from stagehands.

KAYE. That would have been thrilling.

TERRY. But she didn't. She lived out the rest of her life right in that little town, but she was stage-struck to the end. There never was any doubt in her mind—I was going to be an actress. It was almost a spiritual thing, like being dedicated to the church.

KAYE. I never thought of the theater that way. I just used it as a convenience, because I was desperate. And now I'm using it again, because I'm desperate.

TERRY. Oh, now I've made you blue. I didn't mean to be gloomy. We're fine! We're elegant! They have to pay me two weeks' salary for this flop. Eighty dollars. We're fixed for weeks. One of us'll get a job.

KAYE. I can't take any more money from you. You paid my twelve-fifty last week.

TERRY. Oh, don't be stuffy! I happened to be the one who was working.

KAYE. I'll never get a job. I'm—I'm no ta very good actress.

TERRY. Oh, stop that!

KAYE. And there's nothing else I can do and nobody I can go back to. Except somebody I'll never go back to.

TERRY (*facing her*). It's your husband, isn't it?

KAYE (*looks at* TERRY *a moment, silently*). I ran away from him twice before, but I had to go back. I was hungry, and finally I didn't even have a room. Both times, he just waited. He's waiting now.

TERRY. Kaye, tell me what it is! Why are you afraid of him?

KAYE (*she turns her eyes away from* TERRY *as she speaks*). To most people he's a normal, attractive man. But I know better. Nights of terror. "Now, darling, it wouldn't do any good to kill me. They wouldn't let you play polo tomorrow. Now, we'll open the window and you'll throw the revolver at that lamppost. It'll be such fun to hear the glass smash." And then there were the times when he made love to me. I can't even tell you about that. (*She recalls the scene with a shudder.*)

TERRY. Kaye, darling! But if he's as horrible as that, can't you do something legally?

KAYE (*a desperate shake of her head*). They have millions. I'm nobody. I've gone to his family. They treated me as though *I* were the mad one. They're united like a stone wall.

TERRY. But Kaye, isn't there anybody—what about your own folks? Haven't you got any?

KAYE. I have a father. Chicago. I ran away at sixteen and went on the stage. Then I met Dick—and I fell for him. He was good-looking, and gay, and always doing sort of crazy things—smashing automobiles and shooting at bar-room mirrors. . . . I thought it was funny, then.

TERRY (*reaches out wordlessly to extend a comforting hand*). And I've been moaning about my little troubles.

KAYE. You know, I'd sworn to myself I never was going to bother you with this. Now, what made me do it?

TERRY. I'm glad you did. It'll do you good.

KAYE. Yes, I suppose it will.

TERRY (*taking off her robe*). Well, maybe we might as well get those sheep over the fence. Maybe we'll wake up tomorrow morning and there'll be nineteen managers downstairs, all saying, "You, and only you, can play this part."

KAYE (*as she settles herself for sleep*). I suppose Jean'll be out till all hours.

TERRY. There's a girl who hasn't got any troubles. Life rolls right along for her. . . . (*At the window.*) Well, ready to go bye-bye?

KAYE. I suppose I might as well. But I feel so wide awake. (*As* TERRY *opens the window a blast of noise comes up from the street. A cacophony made up of protesting brakes, automobile horns, taxi drivers' shouts, a laugh or two.*)
(KAYE *turns out the top light. From her dresser she takes a black eyeshield and adjusts it over her eyes after she is in bed.* TERRY *does the same, then shouts a "Good night!" loudly enough to be heard above the street din.* KAYE's *good night is equally loud. Simultaneously they turn out their bed lights. For a second—but only a second—the room is in darkness. Then the reason for the eyeshades becomes apparent. A huge electric advertising sign on an adjacent roof flashes on, off, on, off, alternately flooding the room with light and plunging it into darkness.*)

TERRY (*shouting*). Funny if we both *did* get jobs tomorrow!

KAYE. Huh?

TERRY (*louder*). I say, it would be funny if we both got jobs tomorrow!

KAYE. Certainly would! (*A moment of silence in the room.*)
(*The door bursts open.* JEAN *comes in, bringing with her a quiver of excitement. She is in dinner clothes.*)

JEAN (*she turns on the light*). Terry! Wake up!

TERRY. What's the matter?

JEAN (*slams the window down*). We're in the movies!

TERRY. What?

JEAN. Both of us! We're in the movies! They just heard from the Coast!

TERRY. Jean! How do you know? What happened?

JEAN. Mr. Kingsley just got the telegram. They liked the tests, and we're to go to the office tomorrow to sign our contracts. We leave for the Coast next week! Terry! Can you believe it!

KAYE. Oh, girls, how exciting!

TERRY (*bewildered*). Yes. Yes. You mean—right away?

JEAN (*hardly able to contain herself*). Of course we'll only get little parts in the beginning. But there's that beautiful check every week, whether you work or not. And the swimming and the sunshine and those little ermine jackets up to here. No more running around to offices and having them spit in your eye. And a salary raise every six months if they like us. So at the end of three years it begins to get pretty good, and after five years it's wonderful, and at the end of seven years it's more money than you ever heard of.

TERRY. Seven years! What do you mean—seven years!

JEAN. Yes, it's a seven-year contract—that is, if they take up the options.

TERRY. But what about the stage? Suppose I wanted to act?

JEAN. Well, what do you think this is! Juggling? Motion-picture acting is just as much of an art as stage acting, only it's cut up more. You only have to learn about a line at a time, and they just keep on taking it until you get it right.

TERRY (*staring at* JEAN. *A stricken pause. Then she shakes her head slowly. Her decision is made*). Oh, no.

JEAN. What?

TERRY. I couldn't.

JEAN. Couldn't what?

TERRY. That isn't acting; that's piecework. You're not a human being, you're a thing in a vacuum. Noise shut out, human response shut out. But in the theater, when you hear that lovely sound out there, then you know you're right. It's as though they'd turned on an electric current that hit you *here*. And that's how you learn to act.

JEAN. You can learn to act in pictures. You have to do it till it's right.

TERRY. Yes, and then they put it in a tin can—like Campbell's soup. And if you die the next day it doesn't matter a bit. You don't even have to be alive to act in pictures.

JEAN. I suppose you call *this* being alive! Sleeping three in a room in *this* rotten dump! It builds you up, eh?

TERRY. I'm not going to stay here all my life! This is only the beginning!

JEAN. Don't kid yourself! You've been here three years, and then it's three years more, and then another three, and where are you? You can't play ingenues forever. Pretty soon you're a character woman, and then you're running a boardinghouse, like old Orcutt. *That'll* be nice, won't it?

TERRY. I don't know! You make me sound like a fool, but I know I'm not. All I know is I want to stay on the stage. I just don't want to be in pictures. An actress in the theater—that's what I've wanted to be my whole life. It isn't just a career, it's a feeling. The theater is something that's gone on for hundreds and hundreds of years. It's—I don't know—it's part of civilization.

JEAN (*screaming at her*). All right, you stay here with your civilization, eating those stews and tapiocas they shove at us, toeing the mark in this female seminary, buying your clothes at Klein's! That's what you like, eh?

TERRY. *Yes,* I like it!

JEAN. And I suppose you like this insane racket going on all night! (*She throws open the window.*)

TERRY (*yelling above the noise*). Yes, I *do.*

JEAN. And that Cadillac car sign going on and off like a damned lighthouse! (*She turns off the light. Again we see the flash of the electric sign, off, on, off, on.*) I suppose you've got to have *that* to be an actress!

TERRY. Yes! Yes! Yes! Yes! Yes!

JEAN (*not stopping for her*). Well, not for me! I'm going out where there's sunshine and money and fun and—

TERRY (*shouting above her*). And little ermine swimming pools up to here! (*The street noise, the flashing light, and their angry shouts are still going on as the curtain descends.*)

CURTAIN

ACT TWO

SCENE I

The main room of the Footlights Club. It is mid-morning; the sunlight is streaming in.
FRANK, *the houseman, is rather listlessly pushing a carpet sweeper, his attention directed toward an open newspaper lying on a chair. He edges nearer and nearer; his movements with the carpet sweeper become slower and slower, until finally they are barely perceptible.*

ANN BRADDOCK *comes briskly down the stairs with a condescending "Good morning, Frank!" and goes into the dining room,* FRANK's *response having been an absent-minded mumble.*

MATTIE *bustles in from the hall, and her face reflects her irritation as she sees her husband's idling at this busy hour of the day. Lips compressed, she marches straight to him, snatches the carpet sweeper from him and goes off with it.* FRANK *follows meekly after.*

Somewhere in the hall, unseen, a clock strikes eleven.

BOBBY MELROSE, *gaily singing, skips down the stairs and stops for a look through the mail. She finds a letter that gets her full attention, so that she is absorbed in it as she walks more slowly toward the dining room.*

BOBBY. Oh, girls! Here's a letter from Madeleine.

JUDITH (*entering from the dining room*). Where is she this week?

BOBBY. Let's see. This week, Portland and Spokane. Next week, Seattle.

JUDITH. Seattle. That's her home town. (KENDALL ADAMS *dashes down the stairs, struggling into one coat sleeve as she comes. She stops for a quick glance at the mail, shrugging into her coat meanwhile.*) Heh, where're you going?

KENDALL. Rehearsal!

JUDITH. What's the rush?

KENDALL. Late!

JUDITH (*calling after her as she dashes for the door*). You're too conscientious. (*The slam of the door.*) Never gets you anywhere in this business.

TERRY (*coming down the stairs*). Well, what *does* get you anywhere, if I may make so bold?

JUDITH. Clean living, high thinking, and an occasional dinner with the manager.

TERRY (*taking a look through the mail*). What time is it? Shouldn't you be at rehearsal?

JUDITH. No, there's plenty of time. The nuns aren't called until eleven-thirty today.

TERRY (*turning over the envelope in her hand*). Mrs. Robert Hendershot—why, that's Louise! Appleton, Wisconsin. It's a letter from Louise. (*The telephone rings.* TERRY *rips open the envelope and takes a quick look at its pages, which are voluminous.*)

JUDITH (*en route to the telephone*). Maybe it's a Little Stranger. She's been married a year. . . . Hello! . . . She's right here. . . . (*Hands the telephone to* TERRY.)

TERRY. Keith? (*Thrusts the letter into* JUDITH's *hand.*) Here. It's addressed to all of us. (*As* JUDITH *buries herself in the letter* TERRY's *attention goes to the telephone.*) Keith! Isn't this the middle of the night for you! . . . What about? . . . No, I've got to stay free all afternoon on account of Dad. . . . I don't know what time he gets here. He's driving with a friend. . . . Yes, all the way from Elvira. Well, you don't have to like it. He will. . . . No, I can't, because he's only here a day and a half, and this afternoon he wants to see Radio City and the Medical Center and the Battery.

JUDITH (*looking up from her letter*). Has he got a bicycle?

TERRY. And don't forget that you've invited us to dinner. . . . No, not at Smitty's. . . . Well, Dad and Smitty's just don't go together. And look, darling, don't wear a black shirt and don't be one of the Masses tonight. . . . (SUSAN *runs down the stairs and goes to the dining room with a "Good morning!" to the girls.)* What? . . . Well, you can tell me about it at dinner. . . . No, I've got a radio rehearsal.

JUDITH *(still with the letter).* Say, this is a classic.

TERRY. Well, if it's as vital as all that you can come up here. . . . That's my brave boy! *(She hangs up.)*

JUDITH *(her first opportunity to read from the letter).* Get this: "I have gained a little weight, but Bob says I look better not so scrawny. He says maybe I like my own cooking too much, but then he is always joking." *(To* OLGA, *who has come out of the dining room).* It's a letter from Louise.

OLGA. What does she say?

BOBBY *(appearing in the dining-room doorway).* Who said a letter from Louise?

TERRY. Yes, it just came.

JUDITH *(reading, as* ANN *and* SUSAN *come into the dining-room doorway to hear the news.)* "Dear Girlies: I guess you all wonder why I have not written for so long. I honestly don't know where the year has gone to. First there was the house to furnish. We've got the darlingest six-room bungalow on Winnebago Street. And then of course everybody was giving parties for me, and after that I had to return the obligations by giving parties for them. We are all even now. I gave the last one just yesterday—eighteen girls of the young married set, three tables of bridge and one of mah jong, and two people just talked. The luncheon was lovely, if I do say so. Everything pink."

OLGA. You're making it up.

JUDITH. So help me . . . "I am a member of the Ladies' Committee at the Country Club, which gives wonderful Saturday-night dances during the summer." *(She turns to the girls for a moment.)* Japanese lanterns. . . . "But do not think that I have lost track of the theater. We take the Milwaukee *Sentinel* daily, and last week we drove to Milwaukee and saw Walter Hampden in *Cyrano.*"

TERRY *(reaching for the letter).* Let me see! "So now I've told you all my news and you've got to write me just everything about the club. What about you, Terry, have you got a swell part for this season? I thought

I'd die when I saw Jean's picture in *Photoplay,* all dressed up like a real movie star in a little ermine jacket and everything. Jean a movie star! I've been bragging to all my friends. Well, if you girls think about me as much as I do about you, my ears would be about burned off. We have supper here around six o'clock, just as you all do at the club, and when it's over I always think, well, the girls are all beating it down to the show shop and making up to go on and just knocking the audience cold. Only I don't say it out loud any more because Bob says, oh, for God's sake, you and your club! Love to old Orcutt and for goodness' sakes, write, write, WRITE!"

JUDITH *(very low).* Wow.

TERRY. Well, I'll never complain again. This makes my eighteen a week on the radio look pretty wonderful.

OLGA *(as she goes up the stairs).* Everything pink.

BOBBY. We've just been livin' in a bed of roses.

ANN. I could have told her when she left it wouldn't work. *(*BOBBY, ANN *and* SUSAN *go back to the dining room.* TERRY *and* JUDITH *remain in the living room.)*

JUDITH *(getting into her coat).* Well, I might as well get down to the factory.

TERRY. Look, Judith. Think you'll be rehearsing all afternoon?

JUDITH. How do I know! This thing I'm in is a combination of Ringling Brothers and the Passion Play. You never know whether they're going to rehearse us nuns or the elephants.

TERRY. It's just that I'd love you to meet my father, if you have time.

JUDITH. Oh, I want to. He sounds like a cutie.

TERRY. I wonder what's on Keith's mind, getting up so early.

JUDITH. Nothing, is my guess.

TERRY. Judith! Maybe he sold the play!

JUDITH. Maybe. *(Takes the plunge.)* Look, Terry. Where're you heading in with that guy, anyhow?

TERRY. Why, what do you mean?

JUDITH. *You* know. He's been coming around here for a year, taking all your time, talking about himself, never considering you for a minute. Sold his play! Well, if he has he can thank *you* for it. It's as much your play as his.

TERRY. That isn't true.

JUDITH. Don't tell *me*. It was nothing but a stump speech the way he wrote it. You made him put flesh and blood into it.

TERRY (*quietly*). You're talking about some-one you don't understand.

JUDITH. O.K. Forget I ever brought it up. . . . Well—good-by.

TERRY (*rather reserved*). Good-by. (*Takes a couple of typewritten pages out of her handbag.*)

JUDITH. Oh, now you're sore at me. I never can learn to keep my trap shut. But I only said it because I think more of you than anybody else in this whole menagerie. . . . Forgiven?

TERRY. Of course, Judy darling.

JUDITH (*indicating the papers in* TERRY's *hand*). What's that? Your radio?

TERRY. Mmm.

JUDITH. It makes me boil to think of an ac-tress like you reading radio recipes for a living. (*Peers at the script.*) "Two eggs and fold in the beaten whites." The beaten whites! That's us!

TERRY. Anyhow, it's a living for a few weeks. Aunt Miranda's Cooking Class.

JUDITH. Well, you're a hell of an Aunt Mi-randa, that's all I can say. . . . (*Goes.*)
(ANN *and* BOBBY *come out of the dining room.* ANN *is carrying a newspaper.*)

ANN (*seeing* TERRY). Did you read about Jean out in Hollywood? They've given her a new contract with a big raise and she's going to play the lead in *Two for Tonight*.

TERRY. Really! (*Looking over* ANN's *shoul-der.*) How marvelous! (*Takes paper from* ANN *and goes into dining room.*)

BOBBY. It's all a matter of cheek bones. You've got to have a face like this. (*She pushes her round little face into hollow curves.*)

ANN (*getting her coat*). What are you do-ing this morning? Job-hunting?

BOBBY. Uh-huh. Ah thought Ah'd go round to Equity and see what's up on the bulletin board. Maybe there's something new cast-ing.

ANN (*applying her lipstick*). I'm going to try a couple of agents' offices. (*Becomes un-intelligible as she paints the cupid's bow.*) Sometimes they know about new things.

BOBBY. What kind of lipstick's that?

ANN. It's a new one. It's called "I'll Never Tell."

BOBBY. Let me see. (*Tries a daub on the back of her hand.*) Mm. It's too orangey for me. Ah like Tibiscus—good and red— as if you'd been kicked in the mouth by a mule. (*They gather up their handbags and go.*)
(KAYE *comes down the stairs like a little wraith. Near the foot of the stairs she glances over the railing and it is evident that she is relieved to find the living room empty.*)
(*As she is about to go to the street door* MRS. ORCUTT *swoops down on her with a promptness which indicates that she has been waiting for her.*)

MRS. ORCUTT. Oh, Kaye! Could I speak to you just a minute, please?

KAYE. I'm—just on my way to rehearsal.

MRS. ORCUTT (*as she carefully closes the din-ing-room door*). I won't detain you but a second. I just want to— (*The door is closed.*) You must know how reluctant I always am to speak to you on this subject. I try to be as easy as I can with the girls, but, after all, I have my bills to pay, too.

KAYE. But Mrs. Orcutt, I'm rehearsing. You know that. And I'm sure they like me. And just the minute we open I can start pay-ing off.

MRS. ORCUTT. Yes, I know. But plays are not always successful, and the amount has grown rather large. So, taking everything into consideration, I wonder if you'd mind a little suggestion.

KAYE. No. No.

MRS. ORCUTT. Well, it occurred to me that perhaps it might be wise if you were to find some place a little cheaper. By a lucky chance I think I know the ideal place. Of course the girls are a little older, and it's not strictly a theatrical club—more the commercial professions. However, I think you'll find it almost as conveniently situated. Forty-ninth Street, this side of Tenth Avenue. Perhaps, when you have time, you might drop in and look at it. (KAYE *only nods a silent assent.*) Now, now, we mustn't be upset by this. It's just a little talk. (*A rather grim pause which suggests the alternative.*) Now, let's put it out of our minds. Shall we? And let me see a little smile. (*As there is no response from* KAYE, MRS. ORCUTT *smiles for both.*) There! . . . Well, we both have our day's work to do. (MRS. ORCUTT *goes.*)

(PAT, *singing blithely, comes down the stairs. As she passes* KAYE *she chucks her gaily under the chin, says, "H'ya, baby?" by way of morning greeting, and executes a brief and intricate little dance step, all this without pausing on her way to the dining room.*)

(KAYE *stands, a little wooden figure. She turns to go as* TERRY *comes in from the dining room.*)

TERRY. What are you doing—going without your breakfast?

KAYE. I don't want any breakfast. I'm not hungry.

TERRY (*on her way to the stairs*). Well, you're just an old fool, rehearsing on an empty stomach. (*As* KAYE *goes the two* MARYS *come into sight on the stairs, talking as they descend. They pass* TERRY *as she goes up.*)

BIG MARY (*in the throes of trying to memorize a part.* LITTLE MARY, *who is cueing her, follows with the part in her hand*). "Three weeks now since he first came here. What do we know about him—uh—anyhow?" Is there an "anyhow"?

LITTLE MARY. Yeh.

BIG MARY. "What do we know about him anyhow? Only that he spent twelve years in Australia and that he claims to be your second cousin—second cousin—second cousin—"

LITTLE MARY. "I tell you—'" (*The doorbell rings.*)

BIG MARY. "I tell you there is something mysterious going on in this house." Well, that's all, give me the cue.

LITTLE MARY (*scans the part*). Uh—huh—

BIG MARY. Oh, for heaven's sakes! "We must call the police."

LITTLE MARY. Oh, yeh. "We must call the police."

BIG MARY. Now let's go back and do it right. "I tell you there is something mysterious going on in this house."

LITTLE MARY (*as they go into the dining room*). "We must call the police." (*The outer door is opened and we hear a voice subsequently identified as that of* MRS. SHAW, LINDA'S *mother.*)

MRS. SHAW. Good morning.

MATTIE. How-do.

MRS. SHAW. This is the Footlights Club, isn't it?

MATTIE. Yes, ma'am. Won't you come in?

MRS. SHAW. Oh, thank you. (MRS. SHAW *comes into sight. She is a rather cozy little woman of about fifty-five, plainly dressed, sweet-faced and inclined to be voluble.*) (*She speaks rather confidingly now to* MATTIE.) I'm Mrs. Shaw, Linda's mother. She doesn't know I'm coming. I'm surprising her.

MATTIE. Oh—you Miss Linda's mother! For land's sakes!

MRS. SHAW. She doesn't know I'm here. We live in Buffalo. I just got off the train and came right up. Linda hasn't gone out, I hope?

MATTIE (*as she goes toward the stairs*). No, I haven't seen her around yet.

MRS. SHAW. Well, you just tell her there's somebody here to see her, very important. Only don't tell her it's her mother.

MATTIE. Yes'm. (*She disappears.*)

(MRS. SHAW *seats herself and looks about her with bright-eyed interest.*)

(SUSAN *comes out of the dining room, and seeing a middle-aged woman in the room nods politely.*)

MRS. SHAW. Good morning.

SUSAN. Good morning.

MRS. SHAW. Are you a little actress?

SUSAN. Yes, sort of.

MRS. SHAW. I'm Linda's mother. I've come to surprise her.

SUSAN. Oh, what fun!

MRS. SHAW. Which one of the girls are you? Perhaps Linda's written me about you.

SUSAN. I'm Susan Paige.

MRS. SHAW. Are you acting a part on Broadway?

SUSAN. I'm in *Petticoat Lane,* but I'm only an understudy.

MRS. SHAW. Understudy?

SUSAN. That means I play the part in case the leading woman gets sick.

MRS. SHAW. Oh! That's nice. And does she get sick often?

SUSAN. Never! (SUSAN *goes up the stairs as* MATTIE *descends.*)
(MATTIE *appears slightly flustered.*)

MATTIE. I'm awful sorry, I must have made a mistake. I guess Miss Linda must have gone out already.

MRS. SHAW. Oh, dear! Does anybody know where she went?

MATTIE (*edging toward the hall*). Well, I'll see—maybe Mrs. Orcutt knows. (*We have not heard the front door open or close, so silently has* LINDA SHAW *entered the house. She is swiftly tiptoeing up the stairs as* MATTIE *turns and sees her.*) There she is! Miss Linda! Miss Linda! (LINDA *has not heeded the first call, but the second one stops her.*) Your ma's here.

MRS. SHAW. Oh, dear, I was going to surprise you.

LINDA (*frozen on the stairs*). Why—Mother!

MRS. SHAW. I guess I have. Well, aren't you going to come down? (*Holds her arms open wide to embrace her daughter.*)
(LINDA *makes a slow and heavy-footed descent, eyeing first her mother, then* MATTIE. *She is wrapped in a camel's-hair ulster, a little too large for her; on her head is a small beret such as might be worn by a man or woman.*)

LINDA. Mother, how—how wonderful. When did—you—

MRS. SHAW. Why, Linda, child, aren't you glad to see me?

LINDA. Of course I am, Mother. (*Kisses her mother quickly.*)

MRS. SHAW (*as she surveys her daughter's strange attire*). Of all the funny getups!

LINDA. Yes, isn't it silly—I— (*She turns to the gaping* MATTIE.) —Mattie, I'm sure you have your work to do. Why don't you run along?

MATTIE (*reluctant to leave*). Yes—Miss Linda. (*She goes.*)

MRS. SHAW. Where did you get that coat? I never saw that coat before.

LINDA. It belongs to—to one of the girls. . . . I had to go down to the drugstore.

MRS. SHAW. Why—you've got on evening slippers!

LINDA. I just put on the first thing I could find.

MRS. SHAW. Linda Shaw, if you've run out in your pajamas—

LINDA (*backing away from her mother*). No, I haven't. I— (*She realizes she has made a blunder.*) —Yes, I have. Yes.

MRS. SHAW. Linda, what are you wearing under that coat? (LINDA *stands, holding the coat about her.*) Take off that coat! Take off that— (*She jerks it open so that it slides down the girl's arms and drops to the floor, revealing* LINDA *in a black satin evening dress of extreme cut—the narrowest of shoulder straps, bare shoulders, a deep decolletage, the bodice almost backless.*) Linda!

LINDA. I spent the night with a girl friend.

MRS. SHAW. Oh—Linda!

LINDA. Oh, Mother, don't make a scene!

MRS. SHAW (*with repressed emotion*). Linda, go up and pack your things. You're coming home with me.

LINDA. Oh, no, I'm not.

MRS. SHAW. Linda Shaw!

LINDA. We can't talk here, Mother. And there's no use talking, anyhow. I'm never coming home. I'm twenty-two years old, and my life is my own.

MRS. SHAW. Who—who is this man? Are you going to marry him?

LINDA. He *is* married.

MRS. SHAW. I'm going to send for your father. He'll know what to do.

LINDA. Mother, if you make a fuss about this I'll have to leave the club. That girl knows already. And if I leave here I'll go and live with him, and the whole world will know it. Now take your choice. (MRS. ORCUTT *enters, apprehension in her face, steeled for an eventuality. Her quick eye goes from the girl to the mother.*)

MRS. ORCUTT. I'm Mrs. Orcutt, Mrs. Shaw. My maid just told me you were here.

MRS. SHAW. Oh, how do you do, Mrs. Orcutt?

MRS. ORCUTT. I understand you arrived unexpectedly.

MRS. SHAW. Yes, I came down to do a bit of shopping and surprise my little girl, here, and we practically came in together. She spent the night with my niece and her husband—Eighty-sixth Street—they had a rather late party and Linda just decided to— I don't see how these young people stand it. . . . (*A little laugh.*) Doesn't she look silly—this time of day— Linda darling, do run up and change. Why don't you meet me for luncheon at the hotel? Can you do that?

LINDA. Of course, Mother dear.

MRS. SHAW. I'm at the Roosevelt, darling. Shall we say one o'clock?

LINDA (*in quiet triumph*). Yes, Mother darling. (*She goes upstairs.*)

MRS. SHAW. Oh, well, I must run along. I'm only going to be here a day or two and . . . Well, good-by.

MRS. ORCUTT (*accompanying her to the door*). Good-by. It's been so nice. I'm always happy to meet the parents of our girls. And I hope that whenever you are in the city you won't fail to drop in on us. Well, good-by. (*As* MRS. ORCUTT *passes back along the hallway* OLGA *descends the stairs. She is wearing a hat, her coat is over her arm. In one hand she has a few sheets of music, in the other a music portfolio. She tosses her coat over to the piano and props a sheet of music on the rack.*)

(*She sits at the piano, plays a few bars.*)

(BERNICE, *in hat and coat, comes down the stairs. She looks in on* OLGA *and listens to the music.*)

BERNICE. Are you going to play that at your concert?

OLGA (*playing*). Yes.

BERNICE. When's it going to be?

OLGA. In the spring.

BERNICE. Whereabouts, Town Hall?

OLGA. Yes, yes.

BERNICE. Are you going to play under your own name?

OLGA. Certainly.

BERNICE. Well, you've got an interesting name—Olga Brandt. It sounds like a musician. But Bernice Niemeyer! I think that's what's holding me back in the theater. Do you know what? I thought maybe I'd take one of those one-word names, the way some actresses do. I thought, instead of Bernice Niemeyer, I'd just call myself—Zara. (BERNICE *goes.*)

(OLGA *continues with her music. The doorbell rings.* MATTIE *answers.*)

(*As the door opens we hear the voice of* DR. RANDALL, TERRY's *father. His first words are lost under cover of* OLGA's *music.*)

MATTIE. Just go right in and sit down. I'll tell Miss Terry you're here. (*She goes up the stairs.*)

(DR. RANDALL *is a gentle-looking, gray-haired man touching sixty. There is about him a vague quality—a wistful charm—that is not of the modern professional world.*)

(OLGA, *as he enters, is about to launch herself on the finale of the selection she has been playing. It entails terrific chords, dissonances, and actual physical effort. The length of the keyboard seems scarcely adequate.* DR. RANDALL *stands arrested by this. Three times the music pauses as if finished, each time* DR. RANDALL *steps forward to speak and* OLGA *starts again. He gives a little nod of approval as* OLGA *finishes, rises, and gathers up her music and her coat.* OLGA *acknowledges this with a little inclination of her head, and goes.*)

(*The front door slams on her going. Immediately the dining-room doors open and the two* MARYS *come out, still deep in rehearsal.*)

BIG MARY. "I tell you there is something mysterious going on in this house."

LITTLE MARY. "We must call the police."

BIG MARY (*with no particular expression*). "Last night I heard moans and shrieks, and this morning a dead man was found on the doorstep, his head completely severed."

LITTLE MARY. "What about the blood in the library?" (*They disappear up the stairs.*)

(PAT *emerges from the dining room, intent on mastering a fast and intricate dance routine for which she provides her own music. She catches herself at the sight of a stranger, and scampers up the stairs.*)

(DR. RANDALL *has barely had time to react to these somewhat bewildering encounters when a gay high voice from the stairs calls, "Dad!" and* TERRY *comes running down. She hurls herself into her father's arms.*)

TERRY. Dad! Darling! I couldn't be more surprised.

DR. RANDALL. Glad to see me?

TERRY. Glad! I should say so! It's been almost a year.

DR. RANDALL. Too long, my dear. Too long to be separated. . . . Let me look at you.

TERRY. Bursting with health, Doc.

DR. RANDALL. Mmm. (*Pulls down first one eyelid, then the other.*) Look kind of peaked to me. Eat enough greens?

TERRY. Greens! I'm a regular Miss Popeye. Now let me look at you. Say Ah, say Oh, say you love me. (*He laughs as he kisses her.*) Now come on and tell me everything. How's Aunt Lucy? And is she taking good care of you?

DR. RANDALL. Say, you know Lucy! You'd think I was ten years old.

TERRY. I know. Wear your rubbers, have you got a clean handkerchief. Didn't she fuss about your driving all this way?

DR. RANDALL. Carried on like mad.

TERRY. How did you get here so early? You said afternoon. What happened?

DR. RANDALL. Well, when Stacy invited me to come East with him, I didn't know what kind of driver he was. Turned out he's one

of those fellows slows down to eighty going through a town. I dozed off a couple of minutes, once, and missed all of Pennsylvania.

TERRY. He shouldn't have done it, but it does give me more time with you.

DR. RANDALL. Now maybe you've got things to do. You weren't expecting me till three or four.

TERRY. I've got nothing but a silly radio rehearsal. You know—I'm the big butter-and-egg girl. I'll be all through by quarter-past one. Let's have lunch way up on top of something. Shall we?

DR. RANDALL. That's fine. Gives me time to drop in at the Polyclinic a few minutes. Three forty-five West Fiftieth Street. Where's that?

TERRY. It's not five minutes from here. And I'll pick you up at your hotel. Where are you?

DR. RANDALL. New Yorker. Stacy's idea. Full of go-getters.

TERRY. After lunch we'll whirl all over town. We'll see everything. Tonight we're going to the theater, and Keith's taking us to dinner.

DR. RANDALL. Oh, yes. Your young man. I want to meet the boy.

TERRY. Now, Dad, remember, he's not like the boys back in Elvira.

DR. RANDALL. Say, *they're* not like that any more, either.

TERRY. Yes, but Keith's not like anybody you ever met. He's brilliant, and he's written the most marvelous play, and he hates the government and won't wear evening clothes.

DR. RANDALL. Sounds as if he didn't have a nickel.

TERRY. Oh, but he will have! This play will put him over. It's thrilling and beautiful! And oh, Dad, I'm going to play the lead.

DR. RANDALL. Why, Tress, that's wonderful. Your mother would have been very proud.

TERRY. Of course he hasn't sold the play yet. But he will. He's bound to.

DR. RANDALL. Say, I'm going to come back and see you in that if it takes my last nickel.

TERRY (*who has been eyeing him a little anxiously*). Dad.

DR. RANDALL. **Yes, Tress?**

TERRY. You look as though you'd been working too hard. Have you?

DR. RANDALL. I wish I could say I had. But my waiting room looks pretty bleak these days.

TERRY. Isn't anybody sick at all? How about old Mrs. Wainwright?

DR. RANDALL. Yes, folks get sick, all right.

TERRY. Well, then!

DR. RANDALL. Well, it seems just being a medical man isn't enough these days. If you had a cold, we used to just cure the cold. But nowadays, the question is, why did you get the cold? Turns out, it's because, subconsciously, you didn't want to live. And why don't you want to live? Because when you were three years old the cat died, and they buried it in the back yard without telling you, and you were in love with the cat, so, naturally, forty years later you catch cold.

TERRY. But who tells them all this?

DR. RANDALL. Why—uh—young fellow came to town a few months ago; opened up offices.

TERRY. Oh!

DR. RANDALL. Sun lamps, X-ray machines, office fixed up like a power plant. He's the one's looking after Mrs. Wainwright. She's bedridden with sciatica, arthritis and a heart condition, but, fortunately, it's all psychic.

TERRY. Dad, do you mean he's taken your whole practice away from you!

DR. RANDALL. Mm—not as bad as that. The mill folks still come to me.

TERRY. But they haven't any money?

DR. RANDALL. They still have babies.

TERRY. Never you mind. I'm going to buy you the biggest, shiniest, sun-lamp machine ever invented; and fluoroscopes and microscopes and stethoscopes and telescopes. You'll be able to sit in your office and turn a button and look right *through* Mrs. Wainwright, six blocks away.

DR. RANDALL. How about that new doctor? Will it go through him?

TERRY. It'll *dissolve* him. (*The front door slams.* KEITH *strides to the foot of the stairs. The black sweater has given way to a black shirt. Otherwise his costume is about the same. No hat, of course.*)

KEITH (*shouts up the stairs*). Terry!

TERRY. Why—Keith!

KEITH. Oh! I—the door was open. I came right in.

TERRY. Here's Father! He got here this morning.

KEITH (*advancing*). Well! This is indeed a pleasure, sir.

DR. RANDALL. Thank you, young man. I'm glad to know you.

KEITH. Terry has told me so much about you. I've been looking forward to this meeting for a long time, sir.

DR. RANDALL. Oh, that's very good of you.

KEITH (*takes out a crumpled pack of Camels*). May I offer you a cigarette, sir?

DR. RANDALL. Thanks. (*Takes a cigarette.*)

TERRY (*who has been observing all this courtliness with a growing bewilderment*). Keith, Dad doesn't understand that kind of fooling.

KEITH. You never told me, Theresa, that you and your father had such a strong resemblance. The same fine brow, the deep-set, thoughtful eyes. Allow me, sir! (*Lights* DR. RANDALL's *cigarette.*)

TERRY. Keith, will you stop it! What is this act, anyhow?

KEITH (*blandly*). It's no act. What are you talking about?

DR. RANDALL (*pats* KEITH *on the shoulder*). I guess you'll do. . . . Well, children, I've got to be off. You said quarter-past one, Terry?

TERRY. Yes, Father. I'll come to your hotel.

DR. RANDALL (*to* KEITH). Understand we're seeing you later. That right?

KEITH (*absent-mindedly*). What? Oh, yes.

TERRY (*as she accompanies her father into the hallway, their arms about each other's shoulders*). I can't tell you how grand it is to have you here, Dad. . . . Now, don't cross against the lights, and promise to take taxis. Don't try to find places by yourself.

DR. RANDALL. All right, all right.

TERRY. I'll be at the hotel at one-fifteen.

DR. RANDALL. I'll be waiting.

TERRY. Good-by, darling.

DR. RANDALL. Good-by. (TERRY *returns to the living room and* KEITH.)

TERRY. Really, Keith, you can be so maddening. What was all that "Yes, sir," and "How are you, sir?"

KEITH. Can't I be polite?

TERRY. One of the least convincing performances I ever saw.

KEITH. That's right. Hit a fellow when he's down.

TERRY. Keith, what's the matter?

KEITH. I come to you in one of the toughest spots I ever was in in my life, and you jump all over me.

TERRY. I'm so sorry. I didn't know. How could I—what's happened? Is it the play?

KEITH (*unhappily*). Yes.

TERRY. They all turned it down?

KEITH (*reluctantly*). N-no.

TERRY. Keith! Tell me!

KEITH (*unwillingly*). I—I could sign a contract this afternoon.

TERRY. You don't mean it! Who with?

KEITH. Gilman.

TERRY (*almost with awe*). Gilman! Why, he's the best there is!

KEITH. That's what makes it so tough.

TERRY. Keith, for heaven's sake, you're not being unreasonable about this! A Gilman production—why, it's—Keith, no matter what he wants you to do, you've got to do it. What's he want you to change? The second act?

KEITH. No. He likes the play all right. He's nuts about it.

TERRY. Well, then, I don't—understand what—

KEITH (*squirming*). I just can't let him have it, that's all.

TERRY (*something clicks in her mind*). Keith! It's me. He doesn't want me.

KEITH. Well—you see—Gilman's got Natalie Blake under contract, and she *is* a big star, and it just happens to be the kind of part she's been looking for—

TERRY (*crushed*). Did you tell him you thought I would be good in it?

KEITH. Of course. I gave him a hell of an argument. But he just won't do it unless Blake is in it.

TERRY. Well then, that's—that. I wouldn't do anything to— I bow out, Keith.

KEITH. Gosh, Terry! You mean you really would do that for me!

TERRY. The play is the important thing, Keith. I love every line of it. You didn't think, after the way we've worked on it for a whole year, that I'd stand in the way, did you?

KEITH. God, you're wonderful, Terry! You're a great kid! I'm crazy about you! (*He embraces her.*)

TERRY (*evading him*). Please, Keith.

KEITH. There isn't one girl in a million would have taken it like this. And I love you for it. Love you, do you hear!

TERRY. Yes, Keith.

KEITH. Well, look— (*He breaks off as* LINDA *comes down the stairs—*LINDA *in a neat little mink cape, and carrying a costly looking dressing case. There is determination written in her face.*)
(*She gives a swift glance down the hall. Then decides to use* TERRY *as her messenger.*)

LINDA. Terry. Terry, will you do something for me?

TERRY (*absorbed in her own thoughts*). What? . . . Oh, hello, Linda.

LINDA. I don't want to see Orcutt. Will you give her a message for me?

TERRY. Yes, of course.

LINDA. Tell her I'm leaving. I'll send for my things this afternoon. And give her this. (*She thrusts some bills into* TERRY's *hand.*) It's for the whole week.

TERRY. Linda, what's the matter? You're moving? Where?

LINDA. You bet I'm moving. Fast. And nobody'll ever know where. (*She goes.*)

KEITH. What was all that about?

TERRY (*collecting herself*). What? . . . I don't know. She's a strange girl.

KEITH. Well, look, I've got to run. Gilman's waiting in the office for me. He's lining up a hell of a cast. I'm going to meet Natalie Blake this evening. I'm having dinner with her and Gilman.

TERRY. Tonight! Keith, you're having dinner with Father and me.

KEITH. Oh, for God's sake, Terry! I get a chance like this with a top manager and a big star, and you expect me to say (*Lapses into an imitation of a nitwit.*) I can't meet you tonight, I got to have dinner with my girl and her papa. That's what you want me to say, I suppose?

TERRY. No—no.

KEITH (*about to leave*). I'll do the best I can. You know that. This whole thing is for you as much as for me. You know that, don't you?

TERRY. Yes.

KEITH. Well, then! Now look, darling— (TERRY's *gaze, chancing to go toward the stairway, sees a quiet little figure stealing up the steps. She halts* KEITH *with a gesture.*)

TERRY. Why, Kaye, what are you doing back? (KAYE *turns on the stair; looks at* TERRY *for a moment without speaking. Then she starts slowly into the room.*)

KAYE. Terry, they let me out.

TERRY. Oh, Kaye!

KAYE. There was another girl rehearsing when I got there. I'm fired.

TERRY. But they can't do that! How long had you been rehearsing?

KAYE. They still could. This was the seventh day.

TERRY. Darling, don't let it upset you. It happens to all of us. (*A realization of her own recent disappointment comes over her.*) To me. It's a part of this crazy business.

KAYE. Terry, I haven't a cent.

TERRY. Who cares! I've still got my radio job. We'll get along.

KAYE (*dully*). Don't try to fool me. I know about the radio job. You've only got two more weeks. I can't take any more money from you. I owe you more than a hundred dollars.

TERRY. What of it! Now look. Have lunch with Dad and me. Come on down to my radio rehearsal.

KAYE. No, I couldn't, Terry. I just—couldn't. Don't you bother about me. I'm all right.

TERRY (*glances at her wrist watch*). Oh, dear, I hate to leave you like this. Don't be low, darling.

KAYE (*as she goes up the stairs*). I'm all right. Thanks, Terry.

TERRY. Oh, I wish I didn't have to— (*She turns to* KEITH.) It meant everything to her.

KEITH. She'll get something else—the season's just begun. . . . Look, darling, you and your dad have a nice dinner some place and leave my ticket at the box office and I'll be along just as soon as I can. Will you do that, sweet?

TERRY (*dully*). Yes.

KEITH. Okay! That's my girl! (*He gives her a hasty kiss.*) You're the swellest kid that ever lived! (*Dashes off; the slam of the door*).

(TERRY *stands for a moment, trying to pull herself together.* KEITH *and his news;* KAYE's *terrible situation; even the strange behavior of* LINDA—*all these are in her mind. Then* MATTIE *comes into the room, intent on tidying up. With ash receptacle and dust cloth, she makes the rounds.*)

TERRY (*mechanically, as she looks down and finds* LINDA's *money in her hand*). Mattie, where's Mrs. Orcutt?

MATTIE. Back in her room. (TERRY *goes.*)

(MATTIE, *continuing her work, hums a snatch of lively song.*)
(*Then suddenly a piercing scream is heard from upstairs.* SUSAN *hurtles down the steps,*

her face distorted with terror. TERRY *rushes back into the room.*)

TERRY. What is it? What is it?

SUSAN. Up in the hall! She drank something! She's—

TERRY. No! No! (*She rushes up the stairs, followed quickly by* MATTIE. MRS. ORCUTT *and* FRANK *rush breathlessly into the room.*)

MRS. ORCUTT. What's the matter? What happened? (SUSAN, *unable to speak, gestures toward the upper hallway.* MRS. ORCUTT *and* FRANK *run up.*)

(SUSAN, *sobbing, staggers further into the room and drops onto the piano bench, a little huddled figure. Meanwhile we hear frantic voices upstairs:* "Kaye, can you hear me?" "Oh, Lord, look at her!" "Kaye, darling, why did you do it?" "Want me to carry her in her room?" "What'd she swallow? What was it?" "Here's the bottle. Don't say nothing on it." "I'll get a doctor!")

(MRS. ORCUTT *comes quickly down the stairs; goes to the phone, dials. Before she can even finish, however,* TERRY *comes slowly into view on the stairs.* MRS. ORCUTT *looks at her; it is almost unnecessary for* TERRY *to speak.*)

TERRY. It's—no use. (MRS. ORCUTT *hangs up the receiver mechanically.* TERRY *comes slowly down the remaining steps, her eyes fixed straight ahead of her.*)

MRS. ORCUTT (*in a low voice*). It'll be in all the papers. I never should have let her stay here. I felt it from the start. There was something about her. She was—different from the rest of you.

TERRY. Don't say that! It might have been any one of us. She was just a girl without a job, like— (*She is afraid to finish the sentence.*) It might have been—any one of us. (FRANK *and* MATTIE, *huddling together, come into view on the stairs as—*

THE CURTAIN FALLS

SCENE II

Again the living room of the Footlights Club. It is seven o'clock in the evening, about two months later.

Again SAM HASTINGS *is waiting for a tardy* BOBBY. *Obviously it has been a long wait and his patience is frayed. He peers up the stairs, paces the room, crosses to the piano and impatiently fingers a few notes.*

BOBBY *floats down the stairs, as Southern as ever.*

BOBBY. Hello there, honey bun!

SAM. Hello, sugar!

BOBBY (*as she kisses him*). Ah didn't keep you waitin', did Ah?

SAM No. No.

BOBBY (*fussing with his necktie*). Just look at your tie! Ah declare, Ah don't see how Ah can keep on lovin' you, the way you get yourself up.

SAM (*on their way out*). Go on! Everybody knows you're crazy about me.

BOBBY. Ah sure enough am. Ah just can't sleep or eat.

SAM. Honest, honey?

BOBBY. Mhm. Where we going to have dinner? (*They go.*)

(*Two* MARYS *enter from dining room, crossing to stairs deep in an argument.*)

LITTLE MARY. Well, what do you want to do all evening? I'm sick of movies and you don't want to sit around *here*.

BIG MARY. I'll tell you what. Let's go and see Keith Burgess' play.

LITTLE MARY. Keith Burgess' play! We couldn't get into that. The paper says seats eight weeks in advance and fifty standees last night.

BIG MARY. Then two more won't matter. That's all we want to do—stand up.

LITTLE MARY. Yes, but I don't think we ought to ask.

BIG MARY. Good Lord, you don't want to *pay*, do you?

LITTLE MARY. Pay? For theater? You must be out of your mind. (*They go up the stairs.*)

(*Doorbell.* MATTIE *enters from the dining room. Looks back.*)

MATTIE. Did you put a new 'lectric bulb up in Miss Kendall's room?

FRANK (*from dining room*). I will.

MATTIE. Give Miss Terry that telephone message? From Mr. Kingsley.

FRANK. Land sakes, I forgot.

MATTIE. Well, you better tell her—he's important. And you can close up the dining room—everybody's been in that's going to eat. (FRANK *closes the dining-room door.* MATTIE *proceeds to the outer door, and presently we hear her astonished voice.*) Well, I declare! (*The reason for her exclamation becomes apparent as* KEITH BURGESS *comes into the room. He is a figure of splendor in full evening regalia—white tie, top hat, white muffler, beautifully tailored topcoat.*) (MATTIE *goes toward the stairs with her astonished gaze so fixed on this dazzling apparition as to make her ascent a somewhat stumbling one.*)

(KEITH, *waiting, takes out a platinum-and-gold cigarette case, symbol of his seduction; taps a cigarette smartly, lights it.*)

(JUDITH, *the last to finish her dinner, comes out of the dining room eating a large banana. As* KEITH *bursts upon her vision she stops dead, and all progress with the banana is temporarily suspended.*)

KEITH (*removing his hat*). Hello, Judith. (JUDITH *advances slowly to him, grasps the hand that holds the hat, moves it up so that the hat is held at about shoulder height, backs up, lifts her skirts a little, and is about to kick when* KEITH, *outraged, breaks his position and walks away from her.*)

JUDITH. Well, if you don't want to play. (*Takes the final bite of her banana.*)

KEITH. Pixie, eh? (JUDITH *tosses the banana skin on the floor between them; beckons him enticingly.*)

JUDITH. Come to mama!

MATTIE (*descending the stairs*). Miss Terry'll be right down.

JUDITH (*shakes her head dolefully as she picks up the banana skin*). You were more fun in the other costume.

KEITH. You'd better watch your figure, eating those bananas. Starches and show business don't go together.

JUDITH. They do in my show. I got nothing to compete with but elephants.

KEITH. Are there idiots who really *go* to those childish things—pay money?

JUDITH. Say, you can't have *all* the idiots. You're doing pretty good; give us some of the overflow.

KEITH. I suppose you know we broke the house record last week.

JUDITH. Oh, sure. I stayed up all Saturday night to get the returns.

KEITH (*under his breath*). Wisecracker. (TERRY'S *voice is heard as she comes running down the stairs.*)

TERRY. So-o sorry, Mr. Burgess! At the last minute I had a run in my stocking and I had to— (*She stops short as she sees* KEITH'S *magnificent effect. She herself is wearing her everyday clothes.*)

JUDITH (*sensing trouble*). Well, I'll—I'll leave you two young people together. (*She gives the effect of tiptoeing out of the room.*)

TERRY (*dazzled*). Keith! How— (*She curtsies to the floor.*) Did you remember to bring the glass slipper?

KEITH. What's the idea, Terry? I told you on the phone we were dressing.

TERRY. I thought you were joking. You said, "We'll dress, of course," and I said, "Of course!" But I didn't dream you were serious.

KEITH. We're going to an opening night! And our seats are third row center!

TERRY. Downstairs?

KEITH. Down— Where do you think?

TERRY. Darling, we've been to openings before, and we always sat in the gallery.

KEITH. Gallery! We're through with the gallery! I've got a table at the Vingt-et-un for dinner, and after the theater we're invited to a party at Gilman's penthouse. You can't go like that!

TERRY. Give me just ten minutes— I'll go up and change. (*She suddenly recollects.*) Oh, dear!

KEITH. What's the matter?

TERRY. I loaned my evening dress to Susan.

KEITH. Oh, for God's— (*Turns away in disgust.*)

TERRY. It's all right. I'll borrow Judy's pink— Oh, no! Olga's wearing it.

KEITH. This is the god-damnedest dump I was ever in! Sordid kind of life! Wearing each other's clothes! I suppose you use each other's toothbrushes, too!

TERRY (*quietly*). Would you rather I didn't go, Keith?

KEITH. I didn't say that I—

TERRY (*still quietly*). Yes—but would you rather?

KEITH. Now you're playing it for tragedy. What's the matter with you, anyhow!

TERRY. There's nothing the matter with me, Keith. I just can't see us as third-row first-nighters. We always went to see the *play*, Keith. That whole crowd—it makes the audience more important than the show.

KEITH. Listen, I don't like those people any better than you do. They don't mean anything to *me*.

TERRY. Then why do you bother with them?

KEITH. They can't hurt me. I watch them as you'd watch a hill of ants. Insects, that's what they are.

TERRY. Keith, you wrote your last play about people you understood and liked. You lived with them, and you knew them, and they gave you something. You'll starve to death in third-row center.

KEITH. I'm going back to them. I'm no fool. They're keeping my room for me just as it was.

TERRY. Keeping it? How do you mean?

KEITH. Oh, I don't want to talk about it now. Come on, let's get out of here.

TERRY. But I've got to know. Do you mean you've moved without even telling me?

KEITH (*decides to face the music*). Well, I was going to break it to you later. I knew

you'd jump on me. But as long as you've gone this far— I'm going to Hollywood.

TERRY. Hollywood!

KEITH. Yes, to write for pictures.

TERRY. No, no, Keith!

KEITH. Now don't start all over again! If you don't watch yourself you'll turn into one of those nagging— (*He stops as KENDALL comes down the stairs. She throws a glance into the room, in passing, and notices KEITH's unusual attire.*)

KENDALL (*impressed and very friendly*). Hel-lo!

KEITH (*with no cordiality*). H'are you?

KENDALL (*senses she has walked into a hornets' nest*). Good-by. (*Beats a hasty retreat via the front door.*)

KEITH. Let's get out of here.

TERRY. Keith, you can't go to Hollywood! I won't let you! You said you'd never go, no matter how broke you were, and now that your play's a big hit you're going.

KEITH. Well, they didn't want me before it was a hit!

TERRY. Keith, listen—

KEITH. I know what you're going to say. All that junk about its shriveling up my soul. Listen! I'm going to use Hollywood. It's not going to use me. I'm going to stay one year at two thousand a week. That's one hundred thousand dollars. I'll write their garbage in the daytime, but at night I'll write my own plays.

TERRY. But will you? That's what I'm afraid of. *Will* you?

KEITH. You bet I will! And in between I'll keep fit with sunshine, and swimming, and tennis, and—

TERRY. Little ermine jackets, up to here.

KEITH. Huh?

TERRY. It doesn't matter.

KEITH. Believe me, they'll never catch *me* at their Trocaderos or their Brown Derbies.

TERRY (*quietly*). When are you going, Keith?

KEITH. I don't know. Next week.

TERRY. Well—good-by.

KEITH. What!

TERRY. Good-by, Keith, and good luck. It's been swell. (*She turns; runs swiftly up the stairs.*)
(KEITH *goes to the foot of the stairs and calls.*)

KEITH. Terry! What's the— Terry! . . . Terry! (*Only silence from above. He claps his hat on his head and goes. The door slams loudly after him.*)
(*Immediately on the slam of the door* BERNICE *tiptoes down the stairs with a catlike swiftness and soundlessness. Obviously she has been eavesdropping. A quick, comprehensive look around the room, then she scurries to the window, peers out guardedly, so as not to be seen from the street. Turns back from the window just as the two* MARYS *make swift, silent descents of the stairs. The three at once plunge into an elaborate whispered and pantomimic routine revealing their knowledge of the scene which has just taken place between* TERRY *and* KEITH, *and their unbounded interest in its consequences. "Is he gone?" "Yes." "How's Terry?" "Don't know." "Do you think she can hear us!" "Yes." "Wasn't it terrible!" "I thought I'd die." "Poor Terry!" "I never did like him." "Me neither." "We'd better go back up or she'll be suspicious." "Yes, be very quiet."*)
(*With elaborate caution they start to tiptoe up the stairs again. On the stairway one of them turns to the girl behind her. "Shall we ask her if we can do anything?" "No."*)
(*They vanish up the stairs.*)
(*The doorbell rings. From the back of the house we hear* MATTIE's *complaint to* FRANK: "Land sakes, I been runnin' my laigs off. Cain't you pick yourself up go answer that doorbell once!"*)
(FRANK *appears, getting into his housecoat and casting a resentful glance back at the unseen* MATTIE.)
(*As the door is opened by* FRANK *the voice of* DAVID KINGSLEY *is heard: "Does Miss Terry Randall happen to be in?" "Yessuh, I think so. Will you come right in?"* FRANK *comes into sight. "What's the name, suh?"*)

KINGSLEY. Mr. Kingsley.

FRANK. Oh, yeh. You the gentleman telephoned. I clean forgot to tell Miss Terry.

KINGSLEY. Well, as long as she's here . . .

FRANK. Yessuh. (*Pulls himself together and goes up the stairs.*)
(KINGSLEY *comes into the room. He stands a moment, then takes out his cigarette case and lights a cigarette.*)
(FRANK *comes down again.*)

FRANK. I told her you was here.

KINGSLEY. Oh, thank you.

FRANK. And I told her about the phone call, too. (FRANK *goes about his business as* TERRY *comes down the stairs.*)

TERRY. Why, Mr. Kingsley, how dramatic! You're just in the nick of time.

KINGSLEY. I'm glad of that. What's happened?

TERRY. Oh—sort of an emotional crisis. I dashed upstairs to have a good cry, buried my head in the pillow just the way you're supposed to, and guess what?

KINGSLEY. What?

TERRY. The tears wouldn't come. In fact, I felt sort of relieved and light, as though I'd just got over a fever.

KINGSLEY. How disappointing. Like not being able to sneeze.

TERRY. Perhaps I'll be able to manage it later. Tonight.

KINGSLEY. If a shoulder would be of any —help?

TERRY. You're very kind. I'm afraid I have to fight this out alone. . . . Do take your coat off.

KINGSLEY. Thanks. This is rather a strange hour for me to drop in. I did telephone—

TERRY. Oh, Frank doesn't believe in phone messages.

KINGSLEY. They do in Hollywood. They just called me up. Can you take a plane for California tomorrow?

TERRY. Me! (*He murmurs an assent.*)

KINGSLEY. They didn't say what the part was—sort of character-comedy, I believe. Of course they put the picture in production first and then started looking for a cast— the Alice-in-Wonderland method. At any rate, they want a new face in this particular part; they ran off all the screen tests they had on file, and finally came to that one of yours. So there you are. And—oh, yes— they want to know in twenty minutes. Of course it's only four-thirty on the Coast. (*As he glances at his watch.*)

TERRY. You're joking.

KINGSLEY. No, all important things are decided in twenty minutes out there. The more trivial ones take years. Shall I phone them you'll be there?

TERRY. Why—I don't know.

KINGSLEY. You don't mean to say you're hesitating!

TERRY. But it's fantastic! How can I—

KINGSLEY. Dear child, do you mind if I tell you something? (TERRY *looks up at him.*) I've been watching you for several seasons. You've been in the theater for two —three—what is it?

TERRY. Three.

KINGSLEY. Three years. You've appeared in, perhaps, half-a-dozen plays. I wouldn't call any of them exactly hits—would you? (TERRY *merely shakes her head.*) And one or two of them closed before the week was over.

TERRY. You've been doing a lot of detective work, haven't you?

KINGSLEY. No, I didn't need to. I know all about you.

TERRY. You do! That's a little frightening.

KINGSLEY. It's part of my business—watching the good ones. And you are good. You've got fire and variety and a magnetic quality that's felt the minute you walk on a stage.

TERRY (*as he hesitates*). Oh, don't stop!

KINGSLEY. But off stage you're nothing at all. (TERRY *wishes she had left well enough alone.*) When you walk into an office the average manager doesn't see anything there. You might be the little girl who's come to deliver the costumes. They wouldn't see that spark. If Elizabeth Bergner walked in on them unknown—or Helen Hayes—what would they see! Little anæmic wisps that look as if they could do with a sandwich and a glass of milk. But put them on a stage, and it's as if you had lighted a thou-

sand incandescent bulbs behind their eyes. That's talent—that's acting—that's you!

TERRY. Now I—*am* going to cry.

KINGSLEY. But what if they don't see what's hidden in you? Suppose they never discover you. You might go tramping around for twenty years, and never get your chance. That's the stage.

TERRY. Twenty years!

KINGSLEY. But let's say you go to Hollywood. They'll know what to do with you out there. Light you so as to fill those hollows, only take your— (*He is turning her head this way and that to get the best angle.*)— right profile. That's the good one. Shade the nose a trifle. (*Opens her mouth and peers in as though she were a racehorse.*) Perhaps a celluloid cap over those two teeth. They'd make you very pretty. (TERRY *steals a quick look in the mirror. Her morale is somewhat shaken.*) Then you play in this picture. Fifty million people see you. Fan mail. Next time you get a better part. No tramping up and down Broadway, no worries about money. A seven-year contract, your salary every week whether you work or not. And if you make a really big hit, like Jean, they'll tear up your contract and give you a bigger one.

TERRY (*a sudden idea*). Wouldn't they let me do just one or two pictures, instead of this seven-year thing?

KINGSLEY. I'm afraid not. If you make a big hit they don't want another studio to reap the benefit. That's not unreasonable, is it?

TERRY. No, I suppose not. Oh, dear! Everything you say is absolutely sound and true, but you see, Mr. Kingsley, the trouble with me is—I'm stage-struck. The theater beats me and starves me and forsakes me, but I love it. I suppose I'm just that kind of girl —you know—rather live in a garret with her true love than dwell in a palace with old Moneybags.

KINGSLEY. But it looks as though your true love had kicked you out of the garret.

TERRY. Oh, dear, if there was only somebody. Mr. Kingsley, won't *you* help me Won't you tell me what to do?

KINGSLEY. Me?

TERRY. Please!

KINGSLEY. But I work for the picture company.

TERRY. But if you didn't.

KINGSLEY (*quietly*). I'd think you ought to tell them to go to hell.

TERRY. What!

KINGSLEY (*indignantly*). Go out there and let them do all those things to you! (*Again he has a finger under her chin, raising her head as he scans her face.*) That lovely little face! And for what? So that a few years from now they can throw you out on the ash heap! The theater may be slow and heartbreaking, but if you build solidly you've got something at the end of seven years, and seventeen years, and twenty-seven! Lood at Katharine Cornell, and Lynn Fon-

tanne, and Alfred Lunt. They tramped Broadway in their day. They've worked like horses, and trouped the country, and stuck to it. And now they've got something that nothing in the world can take away from them. And what's John Barrymore got? A yacht!

TERRY. You're wonderful!

KINGSLEY. Are you going to Hollywood?

TERRY. NO!

KINGSLEY. Will you go to dinner?

TERRY. YES!

KINGSLEY. That's really all I came to ask you.

CURTAIN

ACT THREE

SCENE I

A Sunday morning at the Footlights Club. The following October.

The girls are scattered about the room in various informal attitudes and various stages of attire. Pajamas, lounging robes, hair nets, cold cream, wave combs. Four or five Sunday papers, opened and distributed among the girls, are in drifts everywhere; girls are lying on the floor reading bits of this and that; lounging in chairs; coffee cups, bits of toast, a banana or an orange show that Sunday-morning breakfast is a late and movable feast. One of the girls is in riding clothes (KENDALL) and bound for a day in the country. All the girls are present except TERRY.

During the year two new girls have joined the club, and now are sprawled at ease with the others.

OLGA, at the piano, is obliging with the latest popular tune. Now and then a girl rather absent-mindedly sings a fragment of the song, leaving a word half-finished as her attention is momentarily held by something she is reading. A foot is waggled in time to the music. PAT, sprawled full-length on top of the grand piano, is giving a rather brilliant performance of dancing with her legs in the air.

LITTLE MARY, on hands and knees, is making a tour of the recumbent figures in search of a certain theatrical news item. In one hand she holds a half-eaten banana.

LITTLE MARY. Where's the list of next week's openings? (*She finds that* BIG MARY *has the page she wants. She settles down to read over her shoulder.*)

BOBBY. Anybody got a muffin they don't want?

TONY GILLETTE (*one of the new girls*). Here!

BOBBY. Toss! (*The muffin is hurled through the air.*)

MADELEINE (*turning a page of the rotogravure section*). Autumn Millinery Modes.

Oh, look at the hats they're going to wear!

SUSAN. Let me see. (*Traverses the distance to* MADELEINE *by two neat revolutions of her entire body, and brings up just behind the outspread papers. Reads:*) "Hats will be worn off the head this winter."

PAT (*a leg suspended in mid-air as her attention is caught by this remark*). Where?

SUSAN. That's what it says. "Hats'll be worn off the head this winter."

BERNICE (*at the desk*). Where're they going to *put* 'em?

LITTLE MARY (*busy with the* American). Did you know that in Ancient Egypt five thousand years ago the women used to dye their hair just like we do?

JUDITH (*furious*). Who's we?

BIG MARY (*to* LITTLE MARY, *who is reading over her shoulder*). Take that banana out of my face, will you!

ELLEN FENWICK (*the other new girl, perusing the department store ads*). "Two-piece Schiaparelli suits—$5.98. You cannot tell the model from the copy."

JUDITH. The hell you can't.

SUSAN (*emerging from the newspaper*). Oh, they're postponing that Lord Byron play because they can't find a leading man.

LITTLE MARY. What are they looking for?

SUSAN. He's got to be young and handsome.

OLGA. There are no handsome men on the stage now any more.

JUDITH. There's a shortage *off* stage, too.

PAT. Looks don't count any more. It's good old sex appeal.

KENDALL. Would you rather go out with a handsome man without sex appeal, or a homely man *with* it?

BERNICE. I'd rather go out with the handsome one.

JUDITH. Sure, and stay *in* with the other one.

ANN (*as* JUDITH's *sally is greeted with a general laugh*). I think you girls are simply disgusting! Men, men, men! It's degrading just to listen to you.

JUDITH. Isn't it though?

BIG MARY. Say, Terry! . . . Where's Terry?

JUDITH. She's still asleep. It's the only chance she gets—Sundays.

BIG MARY. I see that old beau of hers is coming back.

TONY. Who's that?

BIG MARY. Keith Burgess. He used to hang around here all the time.

TONY. Really? What's he like?

JUDITH. He's one of those fellows started out on a soapbox and ended up in a swimming pool.

LITTLE MARY. Terry was crazy about him, all right.

BIG MARY. Yeah.

PAT. And if you ask me, I think she still is.

LITTLE MARY. Really! What makes you think so?

PAT. Somebody just mentioned his name the other day and you ought to've seen her face!

JUDITH. That's not true. She's forgotten he ever lived—that Left-Wing Romeo.

KENDALL. Well, I should think she might, with David Kingsley in the offing. Now, I call *him* attractive!

PAT. Oh, he isn't her type. Anyway, he's just interested in her career.

KENDALL. If it's just her career they eat an awful lot of dinners together.

LITTLE MARY. If it's her art he's got on his mind why doesn't he get her a job? Not much of a career standing behind a sales counter.

BOBBY. Ah think it's perfectly awful the way Terry has to get up at half-past seven every morning. That miserable job of hers.

MADELEINE. It's no worse than what I've got ahead of me.

SUSAN. Well, anyway, you'll be acting.

MADELEINE. Acting! A Number Three Company of *A Horse on You,* playing up and down the West Coast! God! I come to New York to get away from Seattle, and they keep shipping me back there.

BOBBY. You'll be earning some money! Look at Sam and me! We can't make enough to get married. Ah declare Ah'm so bored with livin' in sin.

ANN. Well, really!

LITTLE MARY. Oh, shut up!

JUDITH. Speaking of Seattle, Miss Vauclain, would you be good enough to take that load of lumber off my neck! After all, you put it there.

MADELEINE. It isn't my fault if he fell for you.

PAT. Oh, is Lumber in town again?

JUDITH (*drawing a letter from her pajama pocket*). No; but I've had a warning.

ANN (*impatiently, rising*). Oh, I'm not going to waste my whole Sunday! What time is Jean coming?

MADELEINE. Stick around. What have you got to lose?

ANN. My time's just as valuable as Jean's is.

MADELEINE. Sure. You're in big demand. Sit down.

ANN. Well, if Jean wants to see me I'm upstairs. I don't find this conversation very uplifting. (*Goes upstairs.*)

OLGA. She should be teaching school, that girl.

TONY. Is Jean Maitland as pretty off the screen as she is on? I've never seen her.

ELLEN. Neither have I.

KENDALL. She's much better looking off. They've made her up like all the rest of them on the screen.

OLGA. I hope she will soon be here. I must be at the Winter Garden at one o'clock.

LITTLE MARY. On Sunday!

OLGA (*bitterly*). On Sunday. (*Goes into a few bars of the newest Winter Garden melody. Something very corny.*)

LITTLE MARY (*anticipating her*). We know! Kolijinsky! (*A voice which we later find is that of* LOUISE MITCHELL HENDERSHOT *calls out from the dining room.*)

LOUISE. What's that you're playing, Olga?

OLGA (*not very clearly heard above the music*). "Hillbilly Sam."

LOUISE (*off*). What?

OLGA. Come in here if you want to talk.

PAT. Yes, stop stuffing yourself and come in here. . . . Hey, Louise!

LOUISE (*as she comes out of the dining room*). I was having some pancakes.

PAT. Listen, you've got to cut out those farm-hand breakfasts, now that you're back in New York.

LOUISE (*settles herself in the group*). Imagine getting the *Times* the day it's printed instead of three days later!

JUDITH. You mean you're not lonesome for good old Appleton?

LOUISE. I haven't been so happy in years. (*She turns her attention to the paper.*)

JUDITH. Everything pink.

BIG MARY. Oh, say, Irene Fitzroy has been engaged for the society girl part in *River House*. (*A series of highly interested responses to this announcement. "No!" "Really!" "That's wonderful!" "She'll be good in it!" "Isn't that exciting!"*)

BERNICE. I could have played that Fitzroy part. I dont know why I couldn't be a society girl. (*Assumes a supercilious expression to prove her fitness for the part.*) (*A chorus of: "Sure!" . . . "We know" . . . "You're always the type."*) A real actress can play anything. I may play the French adventuress in *Love and War*. (*A little chorus of astonishment: "Really!" "No kidding!"*)

KENDALL. Do you mean they offered it to you!

BERNICE. Well, not exactly, but I'm writing 'em a letter. (*Another chorus: "Oh, we see" . . . "Letters!" . . . "You and your letters!"*) (*MATTIE comes out of the dining room with a large tray. She is intent on gathering up the coffee cups.*)

MATTIE. You-all knows Mrs. Orcutt don't allow you girls to go laying around downstairs in your pajamas.

JUDITH (*dreamily, as she reads*). Don't give it another thought, Mattie. We'll take 'em right off.

MATTIE. Besides, lookit this here room! (*Takes a banana skin off a small bust of Shakespeare, where it has been draped as a hat.*) Banana skins and newspapers and toast! I should think with Miss Jean coming you'd be getting all slicked up. Big moving-picture star. (*She stoops for a hidden coffee cup.*) And fu'thermore, you ain't supposed to eat breakfast in here. What's the dining room foh! (*She goes back to the dining room with her laden tray.*)

MADELEINE (*to* BERNICE). You still writing that letter about yourself?

BERNICE. Look. How many *l*'s are there in allure?

MADELEINE. Why don't you give up, anyhow?

BIG MARY. Yeh, why don't you take up ballet dancing, or something?

BERNICE (*springs suddenly to her feet, her hands clutching the back of the chair behind her*). Don't you say that to me! I'm never going to give up! I'm as good as— (*She realizes that she is making a spectacle of herself.*) Leave me alone.

KENDALL. Oh, they were just kidding. Can't you take a joke? (TERRY *runs down the stairs, stopping halfway to toss a word of greeting to the girls below.*)

TERRY (*a gesture that embraces them all*). Ah! My public!

JUDITH. Well, Terry, the Beautiful Shopgirl!

PAT. Thought you were never going to get up.

TERRY. I wouldn't, if it weren't for Jean's coming. . . . Heh, Mattie! (*A* "*Yes'm,*" *from* MATTIE *in the dining room.*) Draw one in the dark! . . . Oh, isn't Sunday heavenly! (*Stretches luxuriously.*) I woke up at half-past seven; said, "Nope, I don't have to," and went right back to sleep. Not all day long do I have to say, "This blouse is a copy of a little import that we are selling for $3.95. I am sure you would look simply terrible in it."

JUDITH. I'm going to come down there someday and have you wait on me.

TERRY. If you do I'll have you pinched as a shoplifter.

BOBBY. Honest, Terry, Ah don't see how you tolerate that job of yours. Moochin' down there nine o'clock in the mawnin.' Slaving till six, and after.

TERRY. Oh, it isn't so terrible if you keep thinking that next week that part will turn up. I keep on making the rounds.

ELLEN. But when do you have time for it?

TERRY. Lunch hour.

SUSAN. Then when do you eat lunch?

TERRY. Sundays.

PAT. Just goes to show how cuckoo the stage is. You can act rings around all of us. Well— (*Stretching a bit as she makes for the stairs.*) —I guess I'll go up and put the face together. I look like an old popover.

SUSAN. Me too. Don't say anything good while we're gone.

JUDITH. What are you going to do today, Terry, after Jean goes?

TERRY. I don't know. Who's doing what? Kendall, you're going social for the day, h'm?

KENDALL. Yes, I'm going out to Piping Rock.

TERRY. Piping Rock—isn't that where your ancestors landed?

KENDALL. Thereabouts.

JUDITH. Mine landed in Little Rock.

BIG MARY. Oh, say, Terry! The paper says Keith Burgess gets back from the Coast today. Did you know that? (*A little hush. The eyes of the girls are turned toward* TERRY.)

TERRY. Yes, I know. Why do they call California the Coast instead of New York?

LITTLE MARY. I wonder if that sunshine has mellowed him up any.

BOBBY (*holding up a paper*). Girls, here's Jean stepping out of an airplane!

BERNICE (*jumping up*). Oh, let's see it.

BOBBY (*as three or four girls cluster around her. Reads:*) "Blonde Hollywood Screen Star Alights At Newark Airport."

LITTLE MARY. That's a darling costume!

BIG MARY. I don't like her hat.

BERNICE (*reading*). "Lovely Jean Maitland, Popular Screen Actress, Arrives For Rehearsals Of Broadway Stage Play."

JUDITH. That belle certainly is shot with luck.

BOBBY. That's what she is!

JUDITH. First she goes out and knocks 'em cold in pictures, and now she gets starred on Broadway.

BIG MARY. And she isn't even a good actress. (MATTIE *brings* TERRY's *coffee from the dining room.*)

MATTIE. Here's your coffee, Miss Terry.

TERRY. Thanks, Mattie.

ELLEN. What's she going to do? Quit pictures and stay on the stage?

BIG MARY. No, no. The picture company puts on the play. It's like a personal appearance.

BERNICE (*who has drifted over to the window*). Girls! She's here!

BIG MARY (*darting to the window*). Let's see!

BOBBY. Look at that car, would you!

LOUISE. Isn't it gorgeous!

LITTLE MARY. There she is! She's getting out!

BERNICE. Oohoo! (*Raps on the window.*) Jean! (*With a concerted rush they make for the front door.*)
(*Little Mary:* "She's got on red foxes!"
Bobby: "She looks marvelous, doesn't she!"
Big Mary: "I wonder if she's changed!"
Bernice: "Isn't it exciting!"
Tony: "Don't forget to introduce me!"
Ellen: "Yes. Me, too!"
Louise (Calling up the stairs): "Girls! Yoohoo! She's here!")
(*Meanwhile, on the part of the remaining girls, there is a wild scramble to tidy up the room. Newspapers, cigarette butts, etc.*)

TERRY. Here—pick up the papers! Give them to me! (*With a great bundle of newspapers she dashes into the dining room and out again.*)

MADELEINE. We should have got all dressed up.

JUDITH. Not me. She's seen me worse than this.

OLGA. She will be dressed up enough.

KENDALL. We're acting like a lot of schoolgirls. We'll be asking for her autograph next. (*The squealing in the hallway now mounts to a burst of ecstatic greeting.* "Jean! Jean!" . . . "DAR-ling!" . . . "WON-derful!" . . . "Look grand!" . . . "Jean! Welcome home!")

JEAN (*still in the hallway*). Oh, I'm so excited! How darling of you all to be here! (SUSAN *and* PAT *run downstairs.*)
(*From among the group:* "Are you glad to be back? . . . You haven't changed a bit." (JEAN *comes into view. Her costume is simple and horribly expensive. Her red fox furs are fabulous, her orchids are pure white.*)

JEAN (*embracing girls*). Hello, girls! Madeleine! Olga, how's the music? Kendall! Hello, Judy! This is worth the whole trip—

TERRY. Jean darling!

JEAN. Terry! (*They embrace.*)

MRS. ORCUTT (*looming up in the dining-room doorway*, FRANK *and* MATTIE *just behind her*). Well, well! My little Jean!

JEAN. Hello, Mrs. Orcutt! Mattie! Frank! (*In turn she throws her arms around all three of them. As she embraces* FRANK *a laugh goes up from the group.*) Well, let me get my breath and have a look at all of you.

BERNICE. It's the same old bunch.

TERRY. No, there are two new ones. Ellen Fenwick and Tony Gillette. Miss Jean Maitland.

TONY. Hello.

PAT (*the trumpet sound*). Ta-da-a-ah!

JEAN. Hello, girls. I hope you don't think I'm crazy—all excited like this.

ELLEN. Oh, no!

TONY. We think you're darling. (BERNICE, *before the mirror, is having a private try-on of* JEAN's *red fox and orchids. Enchanting effect.*)

JEAN (*in greeting to* ANN, *who has come rather sedately down the stairs*). Ann! I was just going to ask for you.

ANN. My, you look Hollywood!

JEAN (*recalls the two men who have accompanied her, and who are standing in the hallway. One has a huge camera and tri-*

pod). Oh, boys, I'm so sorry. Girls, this is Mr. Larry Westcott, our New York publicity man—and a wonder. And this is Billy— uh—I'm afraid I never heard your last name.

BILLY. Just Billy.

LARRY. Just want to snap a few pictures. Do you mind?

MRS. ORCUTT (*a hand straightening her coiffure*). Not at all.

LARRY. Human-interest stuff.

BERNICE. You mean with us!

JEAN. Of course!

BOBBY. Oh, I've got to go and fix up. (*A chorus of: "So do I!" ... "I look a fright." ... "Me, too!" ... "We'll just be a minute."*)
(*Up the stairs go* BERNICE, BIG *and* LITTLE MARRY, BOBBY, *and* LOUISE.)
(*MATTIE is doing a little sprucing up, preparatory to being photographed, and* FRANK *buttons his house coat.*)

TERRY. Jean darling, aren't you thrilled at doing a play? When do your rehearsals start?

JEAN. On Wednesday.

BILLY (*speaking to* MRS. ORCUTT *and the two servants. He has his electric apparatus in his hand*). I've got a pretty strong light here. All right if I plug in?

FRANK. Yes, sah. I'll show you. (BILLY *and* FRANK *disappear into the hallway toward the rear of the house.*)

LARRY. Pardon me, Miss Maitland. You were going to ask about our taking some shots upstairs. (*Glancing from* JEAN *to* MRS. ORCUTT.)

JEAN. Oh, yes. Do you mind, Mrs. Orcutt? They want to take some stills of me up in my old room.

MRS. ORCUTT. Of course not.

LARRY. You know—Humble Beginnings in The Footlights Club. They love it.

MRS. ORCUTT. I'd be delighted.

TERRY. Wait a minute! I've got my Sunday wash hanging up there. You can't photograph that!

LARRY. Great! Just what we want!

TERRY. All right. But I never thought my underwear would make *Screenland*.

OLGA. So you are a big actress now, eh, Jean! You are going to be starred in a play.

JEAN. Isn't it silly! I didn't want them to star me in it. I'm scared stiff.

LARRY. She'll be great in it. Look, Miss Maitland, we haven't got a lot of time. Mr. Kingsley is picking you up here at twelve forty-five and then you're meeting Mr. Gretzl.

TERRY. Who?

JEAN. Mr. Gretzl.

JUDITH. What's a Gretzl?

JEAN. He's the Big Boss—Adolph Gretzl.

LARRY. President of the company.

MRS. ORCUTT. Of course! Adolph Gretzl.

OLGA (*dashing to the piano. Improvises and sings*). Of course Adolph Gretzl,
He looks like a pretzl—

JUDITH (*picking it up*). So why should we fretzl—

PAT (*with an accompanying dance step*). And fume. Boom-boom. (*She times this last with a couple of bumps.*)
(*The two* MARYS *come dashing down the stairs.*)

LITTLE MARY. We're ready!

LARRY. Okay! Everybody here now?

BIG MARY. Oh, no. There's more yet. (*At foot of stairs.*) Girls! Hurry! (LOUISE's *voice from upstairs: "Coming!"*)

JEAN. Terry darling, when am I going to see you? I've got loads to tell you and I want to hear all about you. Rehearsals start Wednesday. How about lunch tomorrow?

LARRY. Oh, not tomorrow, Miss Maitland. You're lunching with the press.

JEAN. Oh, dear. Let's see—David Kingsley is taking me to that opening in the evening ... How about tea?

LARRY. Not tea! You've got the magazine people. And you've got photographs all day Tuesday.

JEAN (*turns to* TERRY). But I want to see her. How about Wednesday? I'll get away from rehearsal and we'll have lunch. One o'clock?

TERRY. You won't believe it, but my lunch hour's eleven-thirty to twelve-thirty.

JEAN. Eleven-thirty! What do you mean? (*Down come* BOBBY *and* LOUISE, *refurbished.*)

BOBBY. Ah hope we didn't keep you waitin'.

LARRY (*impatiently glancing at his watch*). All right, Miss Maitland.

JEAN. Oh, fine. Now before we start, everybody, I've got a teentsy-weentsy surprise for you.

BIG MARY. Surprise?

JEAN. Billy, will you bring it in?

BOBBY. Bring what in?

LOUISE. What?

JEAN. It's for all of you, dear Mrs. Orcutt, and the whole dear Footlights Club. (BILLY *enters from the hallway, carrying what is evidently a large picture, framed and covered with a rich red drapery which conceals the subject.*)

BOBBY. Oh, look!

KENDALL. How exciting!

PAT. What is it?

TONY. Looks like a picture.

LITTLE MARY. What of, I wonder?

JUDITH. Papa Gretzl.

JEAN. All right, girls?

BOBBY. We're ready! (JEAN *steps forward, and with a sweeping gesture, throws aside the velvet drape. It is a portrait of* JEAN. *All eyelashes, golden hair and scarlet lips.*) (*A series of delighted and semi-delighted exclamations: "It's Jean!" . . . "Lovely!" . . . "How beautiful!" . . . "Darling!"*)

MRS. ORCUTT (*her dismayed glance sweeping the walls*). It's lovely, Jean, lovely! Now, if we can only find a fitting place to hang it.

LARRY. Well, let's see. (*With a look that alights on the Bernhardt portrait and rests there.*)

(JUDITH *makes a gallant gesture of Hail and Farewell toward the Divine Sarah.*)

JUDITH. So long, Sarah!

LARRY. Now, if you'll all just gather round the picture . . . Okay, Billy?

BILLY (*bringing in his camera*). Ready in a second.

LARRY. Now then, Miss Maitland! You stand right there behind the portrait. And—er— (*He gestures toward* MRS. ORCUTT.)

MRS. ORCUTT (*helpfully*). Me?

LARRY. That's right! Right here beside Miss Maitland. And all you girls fill in this space in front. That's it—right in here, all of you. We want a nice little informal group. A nice little— (*He drops back, surveying the group with the eye of an artist. It becomes immediately apparent that it will be a nice group, all right, but that isn't what* LARRY *wants. His concern is* JEAN MAITLAND.) No, no! You'll all have to crouch down. (*He rushes around, pressing them all down on their knees.*) Everybody down! You too, sister! (*This last is addressed to* MRS. ORCUTT, *who gets down with no little difficulty.*) That's fine! And everybody looking at Miss Maitland!

JEAN (*very sweet*). Frank and Mattie have to be in it. Come on, Frank and Mattie! (*They have been looking a little crestfallen and now take their places at the extreme edge, much elated.*)

LARRY. Sure, sure! It wouldn't be a picture without 'em. We want the whole Twilight Club. Now, then, have we got everybody? (*Looks over his shoulder just as* BILLY *turns on his special light.*)

LITTLE MARY. No, no, where's Bernice?

BIG MARY. Bernice isn't here!

BERNICE (*her voice from the top of the stairs*). I'm ready. Here I am! (BERNICE *has seized on this opportunity to register as undiscovered Hollywood star material. She has made herself up to look like a rather smudged copy of Joan Crawford. Her entrance is undulating and regal.*)

PAT. Heh! That's my new dress!

BERNICE. Well, I had to be right, didn't I?

LARRY. Come on, girlie. Right here. (*Immediately* BERNICE *stares out toward the camera.*) No, no! Look at Miss Maitland. Everybody look at Miss Maitland. . . . Ready, Billy?

BILLY. Okay.

LARRY. Hold still now! And everybody look at Miss Maitland! . . . Right! (*Just as the bulb is pressed* BERNICE *makes a lightning full-face turn toward the camera, all smiles, and back again before they can catch her at it.*) Now then! For the pictures upstairs . . . Miss Maitland?

JEAN. Want to come along, girls? (*The girls certainly* do *want to come along, and they do so. Chattering away, the whole procession streams up the stairs—*MRS. ORCUTT, CAMERAMEN, *and all.* FRANK *brings up the rear with the electrical apparatus.* "You-all using this upstairs too, ain't you?" *An answer from* LARRY: "Yes, bring it right up!") (TERRY *and* JUDITH, *unable to face a second such scene, remain behind, with only the smiling portrait of* JEAN *as company.*) (*Their eyes meet understandingly. There goes* JEAN.)

TERRY (*blandly*). You're not going to be in the—other pictures?

JUDITH. No, if I'm going to work as an extra I want my five dollars a day.

TERRY. I do hope I left my room looking sordid enough.

JUDITH. Say, what about that play they've got her doing? Do you suppose it's really something?

TERRY. Oh, it is. David Kingsley told me about it. He says it's a really fine and moving play.

JUDITH (*a glance at the portrait*). Then why does he let her do it?

TERRY. He couldn't help it. They got it into their heads out on the Coast. It's Gretzl's idea. What do they care about the theater? They think the stage is something to advertise pictures with.

JUDITH. Listen, Jean can't act. If the play's as good as all that, she'll kill it. It doesn't make sense!

TERRY. Now, Judy, haven't you learned not to— (*Of all people,* KEITH BURGESS *suddenly appears in the archway. Though he has been gone a year, he barges right in as though he had left only yesterday. His clothes represent an ingenious blending of the Hollywood style with his own Leftist tendencies. He still wears the sweater, but it is an imported one; the trousers are beautifully tailored, the shirt probably cost eighteen dollars; no necktie, and, of course, no hat.*)

KEITH (*his voice heard in the hallway*). Where's Terry Randall? Oh, there you are!

TERRY. Why, hello, Keith!

JUDITH. Well, if it isn't the fatted calf!

KEITH (*surveying the room*). God, a year hasn't made any difference in *this* dump! (*He casts an appraising eye over* TERRY.) What's the matter with you? You're thin and you've got no color.

TERRY. Well, I haven't been having those hamburgers at Smitty's since you left.

KEITH. That reminds me, I haven't had any breakfast. (*He selects a pear from a bowl of fruit on the table.*) Hope this is ripe. . . . Heh! What's her name out there? (*Shouting toward the dining room.*) Bring me a cup of coffee!

JUDITH (*obsequiousness in her tone*). The deviled kidneys are very nice today.

KEITH (*finding the pear too juicy for him*). God! Give me your handkerchief, Terry.

TERRY. You've got one.

KEITH. That's silk. (*Grabs hers.*)

TERRY. Well, Keith, tell us about yourself. Are you back from Hollywood for good?

KEITH. What do you mean? I'm going back there in three days. I've been working on a plan to put the whole studio on a commonwealth basis, with the electricians right on a footing with the executives, and they won't have it.

TERRY. Who won't have it? The executives?

KEITH. The electricians!

TERRY. Well, I must say you look wonderful. All healthy and sunburned, and I never saw such beautiful trousers.

KEITH (*taking a last bite of the pear*). You're looking terrible. (*The core of the pear in hand, he glances about for some place to deposit it.)*

(Lightning-fast, the perfect servant, JUDITH *is by his side, offering a little ash tray. He drops the pear core on it without a word.)*

JUDITH. Thank you

KEITH *(suddenly he notices* JEAN's *portrait).* What's *this* chromo?

TERRY. It's Cinderella. She's upstairs.

KEITH. Those autograph hounds out there waiting for her?

JUDITH. No, they want another glimpse of *you.*

KEITH. Did it ever occur to you that I didn't come here to see *you?*

JUDITH. You mean there's no—no hope for me at all? *(Crushed, she goes into the dining room.)*

TERRY. Well, Keith! Give me an account of yourself. You've been gone a year—I hardly know what's happened to you.

KEITH. Why—I wrote you, didn't I?

TERRY. Oh, yes. A postcard from Palm Springs, showing the cactus by moonlight, and a telegram of congratulations for my opening in February, which arrived two days after we closed.

KEITH. I got mixed up.

TERRY. But tell me—what do you mean you're only going to be here three days? Your year's up, isn't it?

KEITH. Yeh, but they wouldn't let me go. I had to sign for another year.

TERRY. But, Keith, your plays! Aren't you writing another play?

KEITH. Yes. Sure. I haven't written it yet, but I will this year.

TERRY. I see. I went to see the picture you wrote—what was the name of it? *Loads of Love.*

KEITH. Oh, did you see that? How'd you like it?

TERRY. Very amusing. Of course, the Masses got a little crowded out.

KEITH. Masses! It played to eighty million people. That's masses, isn't it?

TERRY. Yes. Yes, I guess I didn't get the idea.

KEITH. Now, listen, sweet. You know why I'm here, don't you?

TERRY. No, I don't, Keith.

KEITH. Well, look! You can't go stumbling around like this forever. You're not working, are you?

TERRY. Yes.

KEITH. You are? What in?

TERRY. The blouse department of R. H. Macy & Co.

KEITH. What! You're kidding!

TERRY. I have to live, Keith.

KEITH. Good God! Listen, darling. You spend years on Broadway and finish up in Macy's. And look at Jean! Two years in Hollywood and she's a star.

TERRY. They speed up everything in Hollywood. In two years you're a star, in four you're forgotten, and in six you're back in Sweden. *(The doorbell.)*

KEITH. That's the kind of reasoning that's put you where you are! From now on I'm going to take charge of you. You're going to be— *(Breaks off as* MATTIE *crosses the hall.)* There's always somebody coming into this place. It's like Grand Central Station.

KINGSLEY *(heard at the door).* Good morning, Mattie.

MATTIE. Morning, Mr. Kingsley.

KINGSLEY *(appearing in the archway).* Hello, Terry. *(As he sees* KEITH.) Well, hello there!

KEITH. Hello.

TERRY. David! How nice to see you!

KINGSLEY *(a glance at the portrait).* I see I missed the ceremony.

TERRY. They're still shooting up on Stage Six.

KINGSLEY. No, thanks. I'm the official escort, but there are limits. . . . How are you, Burgess? I heard you were coming back?

KEITH *(none too graciously).* How are you?

KINGSLEY. So you've served your year, h'm? Well, you're an exception. You've had the courage to quit when you said you would.

Another year, and you'd have gone the way they all do. Never written a fine play again. (*A moment of embarrassed silence.*)

TERRY (*rather nervously*). Keith is going back to Hollywood for one more year.

KINGSLEY. Oh. I didn't mean to—

KEITH. It amuses me to hear a fellow like you, who makes his living out of pictures, turn on Hollywood, and attack it. If you feel that way about pictures why do you work in them!

TERRY (*hurriedly*). Well, we can't always do what we want to, Keith. After all, you're working in Hollywood, and I'm selling blouses, and David Kingsley is—

KINGSLEY. No, Terry. He's right. I shouldn't talk that way, and I don't very often. But I'm a little worked up this morning. I reread Jean's play last night. (*A gesture toward* JEAN's *portrait.*) And I realized more than ever what a beautiful play it is. That's what's got me a little low. When picture people come into the theater—when they take a really fine play and put a girl like Jean in it—when they use a play like this for camera fodder, that's more than I can stand. The theatre means too much to me.

KEITH. All right! It's a fine play. And you notice it's Hollywood that's doing it.

TERRY. Oh, Keith, let's not get into an argument.

KEITH. It just shows how little you know about Hollywood. You're five years behind the times. They're *crazy* about fine things. Dickens and Shakespeare—they've got a whole staff digging them up.

TERRY. All right! Let's talk about something else.

KEITH. If you go to a dinner in Hollywood what's the conversation! Books, and politics and art! They never even mention pictures.

KINGSLEY. I suppose they put that on the dinner invitation. Instead of R.S.V.P. it says: Don't mention pictures.

TERRY. Oh, what's got into you two! You're a picture man and you're yelling about the stage, and you're a playwright and you're howling about Hollywood!

KINGSLEY. At least I'm honest about it. I work in pictures, but I don't pretend to like it.

KEITH. Who's pretending? I like it and I'm going back there. And what's more, I'm taking Terry with me.

KINGSLEY. What?

TERRY. Keith, don't be absurd!

KEITH. It's time somebody took her in hand, and I'm going to do it. I'm going to marry her.

KINGSLEY. Terry, you can't do that!

TERRY (*hopefully*). Why not, David?

KEITH. Look here, you—

KINGSLEY. I've told you why a hundred times. You belong in the theater.

TERRY. Is that the reason! You certainly *have* told me a hundred times. A thousand! I've sat across a table from you and heard it with the soup and the meat and the coffee. Actress, actress, actress!

KINGSLEY. Of course I've told you. Because you *are* an actress.

TERRY. And I've just realized why. Because you quit the theater yourself, and you've been salving your own conscience by preaching theater to me. That made you feel less guilty, didn't it?

KINGSLEY. Terry, that's not true.

TERRY. Oh, yes, it is. *So* true. Funny I never thought of that before.

KEITH. Look, I've got to get out of here. . . . If I may have just a moment. (*He steps between* TERRY *and* KINGSLEY.) When are we going to get married?

TERRY (*in a deadly tone*). When are we going to get married? We are going to get married, Mr. Burgess, when Hollywood to Dunsinane doth come. That's Shakespeare —you know, the fellow they're digging up out there.

KEITH (*stunned*). Huh?

TERRY. It's too late, Keith. When you walked out on me a year ago, you walked out on yourself, too. That other Keith was cocksure and conceited, but he stood for something. What was it—"thunder and lightning and power and truth?" Wasn't that what you said? And "if you believe in something you've got to be willing to starve for it." Well, I believed in it, Keith. (*She turns* her gaze to KINGSLEY, *then her look includes both of them.*) So—I guess that leaves me just a young lady with a career. Or, shall we say—just a young lady? (*She goes slowly up the stairs.*)

CURTAIN

SCENE II

It is midnight, and the main room of the Footlights Club is in semidarkness. There is a pool of light in the hall and on the stairway from the overhead chandelier.

A little later, when the lights go on, we see that Bernhardt has given way to JEAN MAITLAND.

After a moment of stillness there is the sound of the front door opening, and the two MARYS *are heard coming home.*

LITTLE MARY. Well, I didn't like either the play *or* the cast. And I thought Laura Wilcox was terrible.

BIG MARY. She's always terrible. You know how she got the part, don't you?

LITTLE MARY. Sure. Everybody on Broadway knows. The trouble with us is we've been hanging on to our virtue.

BIG MARY. Maybe *you* have. (*They disappear up the stairs.*)
(*Somewhere in the hallway a clock strikes twelve. Then the door is heard to open again.*)
(*We heard the voice of* JUDITH *at the door.*)

JUDITH. Well, good night. And thank you ever so much.

A MAN'S VOICE. Thank *you.* (JUDITH *comes into sight. Not a very spirited figure. Meanwhile we hear the man still talking.*) I certainly had one swell evening, all right. (*With that he comes into sight. And who is it but good old* LOU MILHAUSER, *the lumber man. He is elaborately decked out in evening clothes, in contrast to the simple little street number that* JUDITH *has on.*)

JUDITH (*with a weak smile*). Yes, so did I. What time is it—about two o'clock?

MILHAUSER. No, it's only twelve.

JUDITH. Oh, really? I guess my watch is fast.

MILHAUSER. Look, I'm going to be here all week. What are you doing tomorrow night?

JUDITH. Tomorrow? That's Tuesday—oh, that's my gymnasium night.

MILHAUSER. Well, how about Wednesday?

JUDITH. Wednesday? Oh, I've got friends coming in from Europe. On the—ah—Mauretania.

MILHAUSER. The Mauretania? I thought they took that off.

JUDITH. Did I say Mauretania? Minnetonka.

MILHAUSER. Well, I've got to see you before I go. Of course I'll be back next month.

JUDITH. Next month? Oh, I spend November in the Catskills. My hay fever.

MILHAUSER. Well, I'll call you anyway tomorrow. On a chance. (*He goes.* JUDITH *waits for the closing of the door*).

JUDITH. Swell chance. (*She goes grimly up the stairs, just as* FRANK *comes into the room—a final round of inspection before going to bed.*)

FRANK. Evening, Miss Judith. You in early, ain't you?

JUDITH (*as she disappears*). It may seem early to you. (FRANK *goes on about his business—locks a window, puts out the desk lamp. Then comes a ring of the doorbell.*)

FRANK (*at the door*). Who's there?

KINGSLEY'S VOICE. Hello, Frank.

FRANK (*a change of tone as he opens the door*). Why, Mr. Kingsley!

KINGSLEY (*in the hall*). I hope we didn't wake you up, Frank. May we come in?

FRANK. Yessah, yessah. Pardon my shirt sleeves. I thought one of the young ladies forgot her key. (KINGSLEY *and another man have come into view. The stranger is a short thickset man who carries himself with great authority in order to make up for his lack of stature. Instinct tells you that this is none other than* ADOLPH GRETZL *himself.*)

KINGSLEY. We wouldn't have bothered you at this hour, but it's terribly important. We want to see Miss Randall.

FRANK. Miss Terry! Why, she goes to sleep early. She got to get up half-past seven.

KINGSLEY (*gently turning* FRANK *around and starting him toward the stairs*). It's all right. Wake her up and ask her to come down.

FRANK. Yessah. You ge'men want to wait in here? (*He turns on the light in the living room, then goes up the stairs.*)

GRETZL (*looking about with disfavor*). I don't like the whole idea. A fine actress don't live in a place like this.

KINGSLEY. But she is a fine actress, Mr. Gretzl.

GRETZL. It don't feel right to me. Something tells me it's no good.

KINGSLEY. Mr. Gretzl, you've had this play in rehearsal for two weeks now. And she can't make the grade. You've got to face it—Jean is a motion-picture actress. And that's all.

GRETZL. She is a beautiful girl. When she comes on the stage they will gasp.

KINGSLEY. You saw that rehearsal tonight. And that's the best she'll ever do.

GRETZL. But she's Jean Maitland! People will come to see Jean Maitland.

KINGSLEY. No, they won't. Theatergoers won't come to see movie stars just because they're movie stars. They've got to act.

FRANK (*coming down the stairs*). Ah woke Miss Terry. She's comin' right down. (*He goes down the hall.*)

KINGLEY. Thank you, Frank. . . . (*Points a stern finger toward the head of the stair.*) Believe me, this girl's an actress.

GRETZL. All right, all right—an actress. Let's see her.

KINGSLEY. She's got presence and authority and distinction! And a beautiful, mobile face. She's exactly right for this play.

GRETZL. If she is such a great beauty and such a wonderful actress, where's she been keeping herself?

KINGSLEY. She's been learning her business.

GRETZL. All right, we'll let her read the part. What else am I here for in the middle of the night? She's got to start tomorrow morning—tonight, even. It's a great big part. Everything depends on it.

KINGSLEY. She can do it. She's young and eager and fresh. Wait till you see her.

GRETZL. That's what I'm— (*He stops as* TERRY RANDALL *comes down the stairs. She is wearing a loose flowing robe over her long white nightgown. Her hair falls over her shoulders; her feet are in low scuffs. She is anything but the dazzling figure described by* KINGLEY.)
(*She comes into the room wordlessly, looking at the two men.*)
(KINGSLEY *advances to her.*)

KINGSLEY. It's sweet of you to come down, Terry. I wasn't sure you would.

TERRY (*looking up at him*). You knew I would, David.

KINGSLEY (*taking her hand and leading her toward* GRETZL.) Terry, this is Mr. Gretzl. This is Terry Randall.

TERRY. How do you do, Mr. Gretzl? (GRETZL *mumbles a greeting. "How do you do?"*)

KINGSLEY. Terry, I suppose I needn't tell you why we're here at this hour. Could you start rehearsing tomorrow morning in this play of Mr. Gretzl's, and open in a week?

GRETZL. Wait a minute, Kingsley. Not so fast, there! Let me look at her. (*He slowly describes a half-circle around her, his eyes intent on her face. As the inspection finishes she turns her head and meets his gaze. But* GRETZL's *inquiring look is now directed at* KINGSLEY.) This is the party you just now described to me!

KINGSLEY (*pulling a typed "part" out of his pocket*). Terry, I know what you can do, but Mr. Gretzl doesn't. Will you read a couple of speeches of this—let him hear you?

TERRY (*a little terrified at the thought*). Now?

GRETZL. Of course *now*. That's what I came for.

KINGSLEY. Would you, Terry?

TERRY. I'll try.

KINGSLEY (*giving her the part*). How about this bit here?

TERRY. May I look at it a second, just to—

KINGSLEY. Of course. (*He turns to* GRETZL.) You know, it's rather difficult to jump right into a character.

GRETZL. What's difficult! We do it every day in pictures. . . . Come on, young lady. Well— (*He turns a chair around, seats himself ostentatiously, and beckons* TERRY *to stand directly in front of him and perform.*)

TERRY (*a deep sigh, and takes the plunge. Reads:*) "Look, boys, I haven't got any right to stand up here and tell you what to do. Only maybe I have got a right, see, because, look—" No, that isn't right. "Because, look—" Do you mind if I start all over?

GRETZL (*annoyed*). All right. Start over.

TERRY (*to* KINGSLEY). What's she want them to do?

KINGSLEY. Strike.

TERRY. Oh. Uh— (*She is off again, less certain of herself than ever.*) —"Look boys—" (*A bad start again, but she quickly recovers herself.*) —"Look, boys, I haven't got any right to stand up here and tell you what to do. Only maybe I have got a right, see, because, look, I'm engaged to be married. We were going to be married tomorrow. You all know who it is. He's right here in this hall." (GRETZL *rises abruptly and begins to pace the floor, his hands behind his back.* TERRY *goes on stumblingly:*) —"In this hall. So if you fellas vote to go on strike, why, I guess it's no wedding bells for me. Don't kid yourself I don't know what I'm talking about. Because I've been through it before. I've been through it with my old man, and

my brothers, so I ought to know." (GRETZL *has picked up a matchbox from the table, and now strikes a match with a sharp rasping sound and lights a long cigar.*) "It means hungry, and maybe cold, and scared every minute somebody'll come home with a busted head. But which would you'd ruther do? Die quick fighting, or starve to death slow? That's why I'm telling you—strike! Strike! Strike!" (GRETZL *has again seated himself in front of her, and as he throws back his head, the better to survey her, a cloud of cigar smoke is blown upward toward her face.*) —"That's why I'm telling you— strike! Strike! S—" (*She has been choking back a cough, but it now becomes too much for her. She stops and throws the part to the floor. Tears and anger struggle for mastery.*) I can't do it! I can't! I won't go on!

KINGSLEY (*angered*). You're a fool if you do.

GRETZL (*rising and buttoning his coat with a gesture of finality*). You must excuse me. I am a plain-speaking man. I don't want to hurt anybody's feelings, but in my opinion this young lady is not anything at all. Not anything.

TERRY. But, Mr. Gretzl, nobody could give a reading under these conditions. It isn't fair. It isn't possible for an actress—you don't understand.

GRETZL. All right. I don't understand. But I understand my business and I know what I see. So I will say good night, and thank you. Come on, Kingsley.

KINGSLEY. I'm sorry, Terry. No one could look a great actress in bathrobe and slippers. And Mr. Gretzl only knows what he sees.

GRETZL. Are you working for me or against me, Kingsley?

KINGSLEY. I'm working *for* you. What are you going to do about your play tomorrow?

GRETZL. I'm going to throw it into the ash can. All I wanted it for was Jean Maitland. So she could make a picture of it. All right. She'll do something else. I can get plenty of material.

KINGSLEY. It's incredible that anyone should be so stupid.

GRETZL (*rising to his full height*). Mr. Kingsley, you are *out!* You will hear from our lawyers in the morning.

TERRY. Oh, David!

KINGSLEY. It's all right, Terry. Gretzl, if you've lost your interest in the play, how about selling it to me?

GRETZL. I see. You're going back into the theater, eh?

KINGSLEY. I might. Will you sell it to me?

GRETZL. How much?

KINGSLEY. Just what it cost you.

GRETZL. All right. See Becker in the morning. He'll fix it up. Good night.

KINGSLEY. Good night.

GRETZL (*as he goes*). And *I* am the stupid one? Huh!

TERRY. David! David, oh, my dear, you mustn't do this just for me.

KINGSLEY. No, I'm not one of those boys who puts on a play just so that his girl can act in it. . . . By the way, you *are* my girl, aren't you?

TERRY (*brightly*). Oh, yes sir.

KINGSLEY. I just thought I'd ask. (*He takes her in his arms and kisses her.*) You know, I had a couple of nasty weeks, Terry, after you drove me out into the cold.

TERRY. Weeks? It seemed like years. (*Again he embraces her—just as* MRS. ORCUTT *enters, in bathrobe and slippers.*)

MRS. ORCUTT. I'm sorry, Mr. Kingsley, but this is against the rules.

TERRY. Mrs. Orcutt, it's the play!

KINGSLEY. My apologies, Mrs. Orcutt. This may look a little strange. But I came up on business.

MRS. ORCUTT. Frank said there was another gentleman.

TERRY (*gaily*). But he's gone! And, oh, Mrs. Orcutt! I'm going to do the play! (*At the end of this announcement, as she says "play," her hand goes to her mouth, like a little girl's; she is surprised to find herself crying.*)

MRS. ORCUTT. Terry, my child!

KINGSLEY. Darling, you're tired. You must get your sleep. (*There is a farewell kiss, with the full approval of* MRS. ORCUTT.) Good night.

TERRY. Good night.

KINGSLEY. Eleven in the morning, at the Lyceum.

TERRY (*in a low voice*). I'll be there. (KINGSLEY *is gone.*)

MRS. ORCUTT. Terry, dear, I'm so happy for you. Aren't you thrilled?

TERRY (*her eyes glowing*). It was like Victoria. When they came to tell her she was Queen.

MRS. ORCUTT. Dear child! But now you must run along to bed and get your sleep.

TERRY. No, no. I must learn my part. And I must be alone. I want a room by myself tonight. Please, Mrs. Orcutt.

MRS. ORCUTT. I'll see what I can do. (*She goes, first switching off the main light.*) (TERRY *stands alone in the semi-darkened room. A light from a street lamp shines through the window and strikes her face. For a moment she stands perfectly still. Then the realization of her new position comes over her. She seems to take on height and dignity.*)

TERRY. Now that I am Queen, I wish in future to have a bed, and a room, of my own. (*She stands transfixed as the curtain falls.*)

CURTAIN

AUTHORS REPRESENTED

MAXWELL ANDERSON (b. 1888).

White Desert, 1923.

What Price Glory? (with Laurence Stallings), 1924.

First Flight (with Laurence Stallings), 1925.

Outside Looking In, 1925.

The Buccaneer (with Laurence Stallings), 1925.

Saturday's Children, 1927.

Gods of the Lightning (with Harold Hickerson), 1928.

Gypsy, 1929.

Elizabeth, the Queen, 1930.

Night Over Taos, 1932.

Both Your Houses, 1933.

Mary of Scotland, 1933.

Valley Forge, 1934.

Winterset, 1935.

The Wingless Victory, 1936.

High Tor, 1937.

The Masque of Kings, 1937.

The Star Wagon, 1937.

Knickerbocker Holiday, 1938.

PHILIP BARRY (b. 1896).

A Punch for Judy, 1921.

You and I, 1923.

The Youngest, 1924.

In a Garden, 1925.

White Wings, 1926.

John, 1927.

Paris Bound, 1927.

Cock Robin (with Elmer Rice), 1928.

Holiday, 1928.

Hotel Universe, 1930.

Tomorrow and Tomorrow, 1931.

The Animal Kingdom, 1932.

The Joyous Season, 1934.

Bright Star, 1935.

Spring Dance (adapted from play by Eleanor Golden and Eloise Barrangon), 1936.

The Philadelphia Story, 1939.

S. N. BEHRMAN (b. 1893).

The Second Man, 1927.

Love Is Like That, 1927.

Serena Blandish, 1929.

Meteor, 1929.

Brief Moment, 1931.

Biography, 1932.

Rain from Heaven, 1934.

End of Summer, 1936.

Amphitryon 38 (adapted from comedy by Jean Giraudoux), 1937.

Wine of Choice, 1938.

No Time for Comedy, 1939.

CLARE BOOTHE (b. 1903).

Abide With Me, 1935.

The Women, 1936.

Kiss the Boys Goodbye, 1938.

MARC CONNELLY (b. 1891).

Wisdom Tooth, 1926.

The Wild Man of Borneo (with Herman J. Mankiewicz), 1927.

The Green Pastures, 1930.

The Farmer Takes a Wife (with Frank B. Elser), 1934.

PAUL GREEN (b. 1894).

The No 'Count Boy, 1925; numerous one-act plays produced.

In Abraham's Bosom, 1926.

The Field God, 1927.

The House of Connelly, 1931.

Roll, Sweet Chariot, 1934 (also Tread the Green Grass, produced by "little theatres").

Hymn to the Rising Sun, Unto Such Glory, one-act plays, 1936.

Johnny Johnson, 1936.

LILLIAN HELLMAN (b. 1905).

The Children's Hour, 1934.

Days to Come, 1936.

The Little Foxes, 1939.

JOHN CECIL HOLM (b. 1906).

Three Men on a Horse (with George Abbott), 1935.

GEORGE S. KAUFMAN (b. 1889).

Dulcy (with Connelly), 1921.

To the Ladies (with Connelly), 1922.

Merton of the Movies (with Connelly), 1922.

Helen of Troy N. Y. (book by Kaufman and Connelly), 1923.

The Deep Tangled Wildwood (with Connelly), 1923.

Beggar on Horseback (with Connelly), 1924.

Be Yourself (book by Kaufman and Connelly), 1924.

Minick (with Edna Ferber), 1924.

The Butter and Egg Man, 1925.

The Cocoanuts (book by George S. Kaufman), 1925.

The Good Fellow (with Mankiewicz), 1926.

The Royal Family (with Ferber), 1928.

Animal Crackers (with Morrie Ryskind), 1928.

June Moon (with Ring Lardner), 1929.

The Channel Road (with Alexander Woollcott), 1929.

Strike Up the Band (musical comedy by Morrie Ryskind), 1930.

Once in a Lifetime (with Moss Hart), 1930.

The Band Wagon (with Howard Dietz), 1931.

Of Thee I Sing (with Morris Ryskind), 1931.

Dinner at Eight (with Edna Ferber), 1932.

Let 'Em Eat Cake (with Morris Ryskind), 1933.

The Dark Tower (with Alexander Woollcott), 1933.

Merrily We Roll Along (with Moss Hart), 1934.

First Lady (with Katherine Dayton), 1935.

Stage Door (with Edna Ferber), 1936.

You Can't Take It With You (with Moss Hart), 1936.

I'd Rather Be Right (with Moss Hart), 1937.

The American Way (with Moss Hart), 1939.

SIDNEY KINGSLEY (b. 1906).

Men in White, 1933.

Dead End, 1935.

Ten Million Ghosts, 1936.

JACK KIRKLAND (b. 1904).

Tobacco Road (dramatization of Erskine Caldwell's book), 1933.

Tortilla Flat (from the novel by John Steinbeck), 1937.

I Must Love Someone, 1939.

ARCHIBALD MacLEISH (b. 1892).

Panic, 1935.

The Fall of the City, 1937.

Macbeth, 1937 (radio version).

Air Raid, 1938.

CLIFFORD ODETS (b. 1906).

Awake and Sing, 1935.

Waiting for Lefty, 1935.

Till the Day I Die, 1935.

Paradise Lost, 1935.

Golden Boy, 1937.

Rocket to the Moon, 1938.

MARK REED

She Would and She Did, 1919.

Skyrocket, 1929.

Petticoat Fever, 1935.

Yes, My Darling Daughter, 1937.

IRWIN SHAW (b. 1912).

Bury the Dead, 1936.

Siege, 1937.

The Gentle People, 1939.

ROBERT E. SHERWOOD (b. 1896).

The Road to Rome, 1927.

The Love Nest, 1927.

The Queen's Husband, 1928.

Waterloo Bridge, 1930.

This Is New York, 1930.

Reunion in Vienna, 1931.

The Petrified Forest, 1935.

Idiot's Delight, 1936.

Tovarich (adapted from comedy by Jacques Deval), 1936.

Abe Lincoln in Illinois, 1938.

JOHN STEINBECK (b. 1902).

Of Mice and Men, 1937.

SPEWACKS (BELLA, b. 1900, and SAMUEL, b. 1900).

The Solitaire Man, 1926.

Poppa, 1928.

The War Song, 1928.

Clear All Wires, 1932.

Spring Song, 1934.

Boy Meets Girl, 1935.

Leave It to Me, 1938.

Miss Swan Expects, 1939.

EDNA FERBER (b. 1887).

Our Mrs. McChesney (with G. V. Hobart), 1915.

The Eldest, 1920.

$1200 a Year (with Newman Levy), 1920.

Minick (with George S. Kaufman), 1924.

The Royal Family (with George S. Kaufman), 1927.

Dinner at Eight (with George S. Kaufman), 1933.

Stage Door (with George S. Kaufman), 1936.

GEORGE ABBOTT (b. 1887).

The Fall Guy (with James Gleason), 1925.

A Holy Terror (with Winchell Smith), 1925.

Love 'Em and Leave 'Em (with John V. A. Weaver), 1926.

Broadway (with Philip Dunning), 1926.

Four Walls (with Dana Burnett), 1927.

Coquette (with Ann Bridgers), 1927.

Ringside (with E. E. Paramore and H. Daab), 1928.

Those We Love (adapted with S. K. Lauren), 1930.

Lilly Turner (adapted with Philip Dunning), 1932.

Heat Lightning (with Leon Abrams), 1933. 1933.

Ladies' Money (adapted with L. Hazard and R. Flournoy), 1934.

Three Men on a Horse (with J. C. Holm), 1935.

On Your Toes (with Rodgers and Hart), 1936.

Sweet River (from *Uncle Tom's Cabin*), 1936.

MOSS HART (b. 1904).

Jonica (with Dorothy Heyward), 1930.

Once in a Lifetime (with George S. Kaufman), 1930.

Face the Music (with Irving Berlin), 1932.

As Thousands Cheer (with Irving Berlin), 1933.

The Great Waltz (adaptation), 1934.

Merrily We Roll Along (with George S. Kaufman), 1934.

Jubilee (with Cole Porter), 1935.

You Can't Take It With You (with George S. Kaufman), 1936.

The Show Is On, 1936.

I'd Rather Be Right (with George S. Kaufman), 1937.

The American Way (with George S. Kaufman), 1939.

A SELECT LIST OF PRODUCED PLAYS [1930-1940]
BY OTHER AUTHORS

EUGENE O'NEILL

Mourning Becomes Electra, 1931.

SIDNEY HOWARD

The Late Christopher Bean (adaptation of French comedy by René Fauchois), 1932.

Dodsworth (adaptation of novel by Sinclair Lewis), 1934.

Yellow Jack, 1934.

ELMER RICE

The Left Bank, 1932.

Counsellor-at-Law, 1931.

JOHN HOWARD LAWSON

Success Story, 1932.

Marching Song, 1937.

RACHEL CROTHERS

Susan and God, 1937.

THORNTON WILDER

Our Town, 1938.

OWEN DAVIS (with DONALD DAVIS)

Ethan Frome (adaptation of Edith Wharton's short novel), 1936.

ZOE AKINS

The Old Maid (adaptation of story by Edith Wharton), 1935.

SAMSON RAPHAELSON

Accent on Youth, 1936.

JOHN WEXLEY

The Last Mile, 1930.

They Shall Not Die, 1934.

LYNN RIGGS

Green Grow the Lilacs, 1931.

Russet Mantle, 1936.

DU BOSE and DOROTHY HEYWARD

Mamba's Daughters, 1938.

BEN HECHT and CHARLES MacARTHUR

20th Century, 1932.

LAWRENCE LANGNER and ARMINA MARSHALL

The Pursuit of Happiness, 1933.

PAUL OSBORN

The Vinegar Tree, 1930.

On Borrowed Time (adapted from novel by Lawrence Edward Watkin), 1938.

SUSAN GLASPELL

Alison's House, 1930.

VIRGIL GEDDES

Native Ground (published version), Mangled Production, 1932.

From the Life of George Emery Blum (published version), 1934.

LEOPOLD ATLAS

Wednesday's Child, 1934.

ROBERT ARDREY
How to Get Tough About It, 1938.

E. P. CONKLE
200 Were Chosen, 1936.
Prologue to Glory, 1937.

ROBERT TURNEY
Daughters of Atreus, 1936.

GEORGE O'NEIL
American Dream, 1933.

T. S. ELIOT
Murder in the Cathedral, 1935.

EMMET LAVERY
The First Legion, 1934.

WILLIAM SAROYAN
My Heart's in the Highlands, 1939.

STEPHEN VINCENT BENET
The Devil and Daniel Webster, 1939.

HARDIE ALBRIGHT
All the Living (adapted from "I Knew 3000
Lunatics," by Dr. Victor Small), 1938.

SINCLAIR LEWIS and JOHN C. MOFFITT
It Can't Happen Here (adapted from the
novel), 1936.

VICTOR WOLFSON
Excursion, 1937.

MARC BLITZSTEIN
The Cradle Will Rock, 1937.
ALBERT MALTZ
Black Pit, 1935.

PAUL PETERS
Stevedore (with George Sklar), 1934.

ALBERT BEIN
Little Ol' Boy, 1933.
Let Freedom Ring (adapted from a novel by
Grace Lumpkin), 1935.

ARTHUR ARENT (and staff of Federal Thea-
tre's "Living Newspaper")
Power, 1937.
One-third of a Nation, 1938.

LENORE COFFEE and WILLIAM JOYCE
COWEN
Family Portrait, 1937.

ROBERT L. BUCKNER and WALTER HART
Primrose Path (adapted from Victoria Lincoln's novel, "February Hill"), 1939.

ARTHUR KOBER
Having Wonderful Time, 1937.

ROSE FRANKEN
Another Language, 1932.

JAMES HAGAN
One Sunday Afternoon, 1933.

LAWRENCE RILEY
Personal Appearance, 1934.

JOHN MURRAY and ALLEN BORETZ
Room Service, 1937.

JULIAN THOMPSON
The Warrior's Husband, 1932.

GILBERT SELDES
Lysistrata (adapted from Aristophanes' comedy), 1930.

BIBLIOGRAPHY

Selected List of Books on the Contemporary American Theatre, 1930-40

ANDERSON, JOHN: *The American Theatre.* New York: The Dial Press, 1938.

> An admirable brief introduction to the history of the American theatre with a concluding survey of recent trends.

ARCHITECTURE FOR THE NEW THEATRE. Essays by Bel Geddes, Simonson, and others. New York: Theatre Arts, 1935.

BLAKE, BEN: *The Awakening of the American Theatre.* New York: Tomorrow Publishers, 1935.

> A highly informative pamphlet, dealing with the rise and development of the social or "left" theatre of the 'thirties.

BLOCK, ANITA: *The Changing World in Plays and Theatre.* Boston: Little, Brown & Company, 1939.

> This study of important social ideas and trends in the modern drama contains detailed studies of a number of contemporary American plays.

BRICKER, HERSCHEL L. (Editor) : *Our Theatre Today.* New York: Samuel French, 1936.

> A collection of essays on various phases of the theatre.

BROWN, JOHN MASON: *Two on the Aisle: Ten Years of the American in Performance.* New York: W. W. Norton & Co., 1938.

> A collection of incisive and excellently written reviews by the brilliant lecturer and critic of The New York Post.

EUSTIS, MORTON: *Broadway, Inc.: The Theater as Business.* New York: Dodd, Mead & Co., 1934.

Players at Work. New York: Theatre Arts, 1937.

> Nine prominent actors and actresses discuss their methods.

FLEXNER, ELEANORE: *American Playwrights 1918-1938.* With a Preface by John Gassner. New York: Simon and Schuster, 1939.

> An analytical and provocative examination of the important playwrights by a critic who stresses their relation to current social problems and trends.

KOZLENKO, WILLIAM (editor) : *The One-Act Play Today.* New York: Harcourt, Brace & Co., 1938.

> A symposium by Percival Wilde, Walter Prichard Eaton, Michael Blankfort, Gilbert Seldes, Alfred Kreymborg, Barrett H. Clark, Glenn Hughes, and John Gassner.

LAWSON, JOHN HOWARD: *Theory and Technique of Playwriting.* New York: G. P. Putnam's Sons, 1936.

> Valuable as a contemporary playwright's analysis of dramatic technique.

MANTLE, BURNS: *The Best Plays* of 1930, 1931, 1932, 1933, 1934, 1935, 1936, 1937, 1938. (A volume for each year.) New York: Dodd, Mead & Company.

> Invaluable records of performances of each season, condensations of selected plays, and notes on their authors.

Contemporary American Playwrights. New York: Dodd Mead & Co., 1938.

A biographical dictionary of American playwrights; a useful source-book.

McCANDLESS, STANLEY R.: *A Method of Lighting the Stage*. Revised edition. New York: Theatre Arts, 1939.

Modern Stage Design. New York: Theatre Arts, 1935.

MOSES, MONTROSE J. and BROWN, JOHN MASON (editors) : *The American Theatre as Seen by Its Critics*. New York: W. W. Norton & Co., 1934.

A compilation of American criticism, including reviews of the drama between 1920 and 1934 by John Anderson, Brooks Atkinson, Robert Benchley, John Mason Brown, Gilbert Gabriel, Percy Hammond, Joseph Wood Krutch, Rich- ard Lockridge, Burns Mantle, George Jean Nathan, Walter Winchell, Stark Young, and others.

NATHAN, GEORGE JEAN: *The Morning After the First Night*. New York: Alfred A. Knopf, 1938.

Another collection of scintillating criticism by Mr. Nathan.

QUINN, ARTHUR HOBSON: *A History of the American Drama from the Civil War to the Present Day*. New York: F. S. Crofts, 1936.

An authoritative history which examines the contemporary drama in some detail.

SIMONSON, LEE: *The Stage Is Set*. New York: Harcourt, Brace & Co., 1932.

A notable study of scenic design through the ages, containing illuminating comments on current stage-craft and a deeply reasoned analysis of style in contemporary American playwriting.

SKINNER, RICHARD DANA: *Eugene O'Neill: A Poet's Quest*. New York: Longmans, Green & Co., 1935.

A comprehensive, if somewhat mystical, study of our major playwright.

TRAUBE, SHEPARD: *So You Want To Go Into the Theatre*. Boston: Little, Brown & Co., 1936.

A handbook of facts about the contemporary theatre.

WHITMAN, WILLSON: *Bread and Circuses*. New York: Oxford University Press, 1937.

A history of the rise and development of the Federal Theatre.

WINTER, SOPHUS KEITH: *Eugene O'Neill. A Critical Study*. New York: Random House, 1934.

Also consult the following periodicals:

Theatre Arts

Theatre Guild Magazine

New Theatre; New Theatre and Film.

Stage

Theatre Workshop

One Act Play Magazine

"Tac"